MW01515769

JAMES THE BROTHER OF JESUS AND THE DEAD SEA SCROLLS II

The Damascus Code, the Tent of David,
the New Covenant, and the Blood of Christ

Robert Eisenman

Grave Distractions Publications
Nashville

James the Brother of Jesus and the Dead Sea Scrolls II

The Damascus Code, the Tent of David, the New Covenant, and the Blood of Christ

Grave Distractions Publications
Nashville, Tennessee
www.gravedistractions.com

Cataloging-In-Publication Data
Eisenman, Robert
ISBN: 978-0-9855991-6-4

Redaction work by Dennis Walker
Cover Design by Brian Kannard and Robert Eisenman

James the Brother of Jesus and the Dead Sea Scrolls II:
The Damascus Code, the Tent of David, the New Covenant, and the Blood of Christ

1.James, Brother of the Lord, Saint. 2. Christianity-Origins. 3. Paul, Apostle, Saint. 4. Dead Sea Scrolls - Criticism, Interpretation

Printed in the USA

Electronic versions of this text are available.
For more information visit:
http://www.gravedistractions.com

"It is related that the children of Zadok the Priest, one a boy and the other a girl, were taken captive to Rome, each falling to the lot of a different officer. One officer resorted to a prostitute and gave her the boy. The other went into the store of a shopkeeper and gave him the girl in exchange for some wine (this to fulfill Joel 4:3: 'And they have given a boy for a harlot and sold a girl for wine'). After awhile, the prostitute brought the boy to the shopkeeper and said to him, 'Since I have a boy, who is suitable for the girl you have, will you agree they should cohabit and whatever issues be divided between us?' He accepted the offer. They immediately took them and placed them in a room. The girl began to weep and the boy asked her why she was crying? She answered, 'Should I not weep, when the daughter of a High Priest is given in marriage to one (like you), a slave?'

He inquired of her whose daughter she was and she replied, 'I am the daughter of Zadok the High Priest.' He then asked her where she used to live and she answered, 'In the upper marketplace.' He next inquired, 'What was the sign above the house?' and she told him. He said, 'Have you a brother or a sister?' She answered, 'I had a brother and there was a mole on his shoulder and whenever he came home from school, I used to uncover it and kiss it.' He asked, 'If you were to see it now, would you know it?' She answered, 'I would.' He bared his shoulder and they recognized each other. They then embraced and kissed till they expired. Then the Holy Spirit cried out, '*For these things I weep*'!"

(Lamentations *Rabbah* 1:16.46 and *Gittin* 58a)

"You will deliver the Enemies of all the Countries into the hand of the Poor (the *Ebionim*) to cast down the Mighty Ones of the Peoples, to pay (them) the Reward on Evil Ones...and to justify the Judgments of Your Truth...You will fight against them from Heaven..., for You commanded the Hosts of Your Elect in their thousands and their Myriads, together with the Heavenly Host of all Your Holy Ones...to strike the Rebellious of Earth with Your awe-inspiring Judgments...For the King of Glory is with us...and the Angelic Host is under His command...(They are) like clouds, moisture-laden clouds covering the Earth – a torrent of rain shedding Judgment on all that grows."

(The War Scroll from Qumran, XI.17–XII.10 and XIX.1–2)

"'*Of what use are graven images, whose makers formed a casting and images of Lying...?*' The interpretation of this passage concerns all the idols of the Nations, which they create in order to serve...These will not save them on the Day of Judgment...'*But the Lord is in His Holy Temple. Be silent before Him all the World*'! Its interpretation concerns all the Nations who but serve stone and wood. But on the Day of Judgment, God will destroy all the Servants of Idols and Evil Ones off the Earth."

(1QpHab XII.10–XIII.4 on Habakkuk 2:18–19)

Contents

Chronological and Genealogical Charts

MACCABEAN PRIEST KINGS

Mattathias, 167–166 BC
Judas Maccabee, 166–160
Jonathan, 160–142
Simon, 142–134
John Hyrcanus, 134–104
Alexander Jannaeus, 103–76
Salome Alexandra, 76–67
Aristobulus II, 67–63
Hyrcanus II, 76–67 and 63–40
Antigonus, 40–37

HERODIAN KINGS, ETHNARCHS, OR TETRARCHS

Herod, Roman–supported King, 37–4 BC
Archelaus, Ethnarch of Judea, 4 BC – 7 CE
Herod Antipas, Tetrarch of Galilee and Perea, 4 BC – 39 CE
Philip, Tetrarch of Trachonitis, 4 BC – 34 CE
Agrippa I, Tetrarch and King, 37–44
Herod of Chalcis, 44–49
Agrippa II, 49–93

ROMAN EMPERORS FROM 60 BC TO 138 CE

Caesar, 60–44 BC
Mark Anthony and Octavius, 43–31 BCE
Octavius (Augustus), 27 BCE – 14 CE
Tiberius, 14–37
Caligula, 37–41
Claudius, 41–54
Nero, 54–68
Galba, 68–69
Otho, 69
Vitellius, 69
Vespasian, 69–79
Titus, 79–81
Domitian, 81–96
Nerva, 96–98
Trajan, 98–117
Hadrian, 117–138

ROMAN GOVERNORS

Antipater (Herod's father).Procurator, 55–43 BC
Coponius, 6–9 CE
Ambivulus, 9–12
Rufus, 12–15
Valerius Gratus, 15–26 (perhaps 15–18)
Pontius Pilate, 26–37 (perhaps 18–37)
Fadus, 44–46
Tiberius Alexander, 46–48
Cumanus, 48–52
Felix, 51–60
Festus, 60–62
Albinus, 62–64
Florus, 64–66

EARLY CHURCH AND OTHER SOURCES

Philo of Alexandria, *c.* 30 BC –45 CE
Clement of Rome, *c.* 30–97 CE
Josephus, 37–96
Ignatius, *c.* 50–115
Papias, *c.* 60–135
Pliny, 61–113
Polycarp, 69–156
Justin Martyr, *c.* 100–165
Hegesippus, *c.* 90–180
Tatian, *c.* 115–185
Lucian of Samosata, *c.* 125–180
Irenaeus, *c.* 130–200
Clement of Alexandria, *c.* 150–215
Tertullian, *c.* 160–221
Hippolytus, *c.* 160–235
Julius Africanus, *c.* 170—245
Origen, *c.* 185–254
Eusebius of Caesarea, *c.* 260–340
Epiphanius, 367–404
Jerome, 348–420
Rufinus of Aquileia, *c.* 350–410
Augustine, 354–430
St Cyril of Jerusalem, 375–444

The Herodians

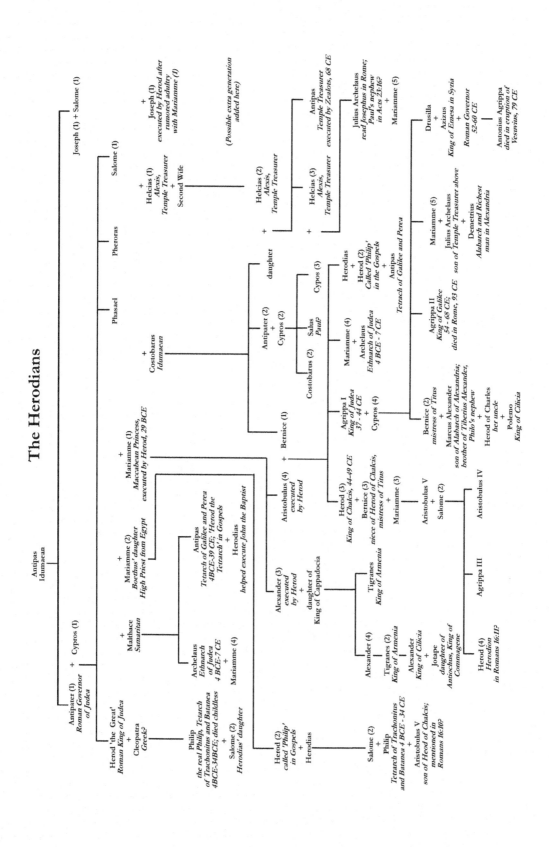

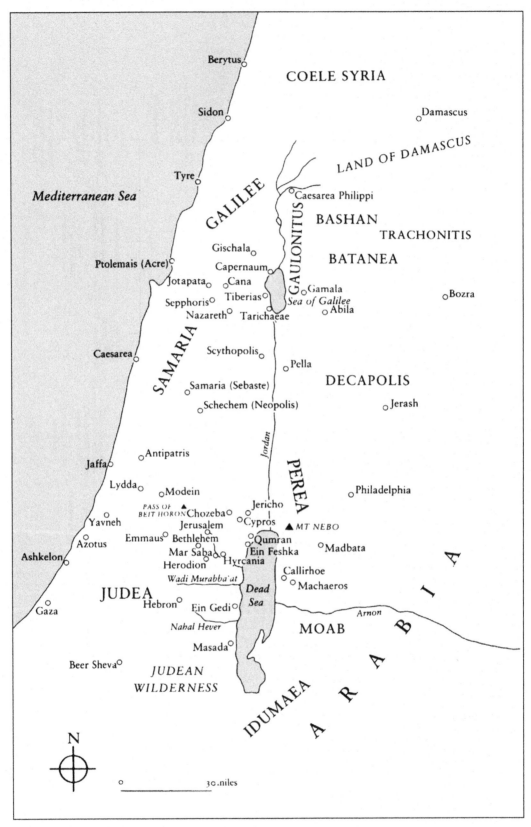

Map of Judea showing Galilee, Perea, the Decapolis, Idumaea, Coele Syria, the Land of Damascus, and Arabia (vast, with a big 'A' - how the Romans saw it!)

Introduction

Christianity and Essenism

In a book aimed at demonstrating the relationship of the Dead Sea Scrolls to Early Christianity, one should perhaps begin with the proposition that there were not two Messianisms at the end of the First Century/beginning of the Second Century in Palestine – only one. Nor was there really any such thing at this time as 'Christianity' *per se*, Christians having first been called 'Christians', according to Acts 11:26, in the early to mid-Fifties of the Common Era in a place called 'Antioch' in Northern Syria (a denotation we shall have cause to question below).

So why use the term 'Christian' at all? Because one must communicate and, in order to do so, one must use words however misleading or inadequate these may be. At the outset it should be appreciated that the use of questionable or imprecise terminologies of this kind often produces all the confusion surrounding these matters. The author takes the proposition that there was no such thing as 'Christianity' in the First Century in Palestine, along with the one about there being only one Messianism in Palestine or the Land of Israel in the First Century (in his view, the one found in the Dead Sea Scrolls[1]), as truisms. The two points are more or less equivalent anyhow. At the very least one entails the other, though the first-time reader might not appreciate them as such at this point.

One needs only one final proposition to complete the structure of these mutually interconnected terminologies and that is, 'Essenism' was what 'Christianity' was in First-Century Palestine, certainly before the fall of Masada in 73 CE – whatever meaning one might wish to give to the 'Christianity' we are talking about at this point. This is not to say precisely what one might mean by 'Essenism' either, only that if one is calling documents like the Dead Sea Scrolls *Essene*, then one must define Essenism – whether inclusive of Jesus or without him – by what the Scrolls themselves say it is and not by what the often tendentious or inaccurate descriptions of the various commentators such as Josephus, Philo, or early Christian writers might say it is.[1]

'Essenism' flourished sometime before the fall of the Temple in 70 CE, after which it seems to have become absorbed into one or more of the several movements known to early Church writers as Ebionites, Elchasaites, Masbuthaeans (known in Southern Iraq and in the Koran as the *Subba‘* or 'Sabaeans' – that is, 'Immersers' or 'Daily Bathers'), Manichaeans, and even 'Christians' themselves. All of these are not necessarily separate or mutually exclusive terminologies. In fact, they may be designating the same phenomenon from the standpoint or native tongue of a different observer whether writing in Greek, Aramaic, Syriac, or some other language. This brings us back to our original proposition, namely that there was no such thing as 'Christianity' in Palestine in the First Century, that is, no belief in Jesus as 'the Christ' *per se*, and this probably not until well into the Second Century sometime before the Bar Kochba Uprising.[2]

Antioch, Ananias, and Jude the Brother of James

Though the Antioch in Acts (and Galatians) is generally considered to be Antioch-on-the-Orontes in Syria (the 'Antioch' that is closest to the Mediterranean), there were at least *four* Antiochs in Asia at this time – the founder of the Seleucid Dynasty in Syria after Alexander the Great's death having apparently harbored an inordinate affection for his father Antiochus.

These included Antioch-in-Pisidia, now part of Turkey, described in Acts 13:14–50. There was Antiochia Charax, 'Charax Spasini' or present-day Basrah at the mouth of the

Tigris River on the Persian Gulf. In Josephus, Charax Spasini was the place where Izates, the favorite son of Queen Helen of Adiabene, first met the itinerant merchant *cum* missionary Ananias, an individual also apparently appearing in both Eusebius and Acts. Adiabene was the area around the source of the Tigris in Northern Iraq, roughly equivalent to modern-day Kurdistan and not very distinct from what Eusebius calls 'the Land of the Edessenes' or 'Osrhoeans' (Assyrians) 'beyond the Euphrates'.[3] Finally, there was Antioch-by-Callirhoe or Carrhae on the Upper Euphrates in the region of Abraham's place-of-origin Haran in Northern Syria – also now Southern Turkey – what Eusebius will denote as 'the Land of the Edessenes', a city which eventually became known as Edessa. This city – famous ever after not only in the history of the Crusades, but also in 'Holy Shroud' historiography and hagiography – is my choice, historically speaking, for the real Antioch in Paul's Letters and in Acts.

Not only does the Ananias involved in the conversion of Izates play a role in Acts 9:9– 19's picture of Paul's encounter in Damascus on 'a street called the Straight' at the house of one 'Judas', but a similar Ananias plays a prominent role in Eusebius' narrative of another conversion – that of 'King Agbarus' or 'King Abgarus' of the Osrhoeans (and characterized by him as 'the Great King of the Peoples beyond the Euphrates'), a narrative Eusebius claimed to have found in 'the Royal Archives of Edessa' – Antioch-by-Callirhoe – and to have personally translated into the Greek from Syriac or Aramaic.

In these parallel conversion narratives, a namesake of the Judas at whose house Paul is supposed to have stayed in Damascus also appears in the story Eusebius conserves. In this version, Ananias is the courier between Jesus and King Agbarus. In Josephus' picture of Izates' conversion (also a King-to-be at another such Antioch), he is associated with another unnamed teacher (Paul?). Together they get in among the women in Izates' father 'Bazeus'' (Agbarus?) harem and teach that circumcision is unnecessary for conversion.[4]

The Judas in the account Eusebius claims to have found in the Royal Archives at Edessa is Judas Thomas, that is, 'Judas the Twin' – in John, the patently redundant 'Didymus Thomas' or Twin Twin, both *Didymus* in Greek and *Thoma* in Aramaic meaning 'twin'; in the Gospel of Thomas, 'Didymus Judas Thomas', most probably Jesus' third brother Judas or 'Jude the brother of James' in the Letter by that name in the New Testament; and in the Koran, even 'Hudhud' a bird![5] In Eusebius' discussion of these events this 'Judas' has something to do with a disciple named 'Thaddaeus' – in the Gospels, an 'Apostle' as well.[6]

To bring this particular cluster of appellatives full circle, the latter is rather referred to in Matthew 10:3 as 'Lebbaeus who was surnamed Thaddaeus'. In Mark 3:18 this is simply 'Thaddaeus', but in Luke 6:16 and Acts 1:13 he is replaced by someone called 'Judas (the brother) of James' – again probably the third brother of Jesus named 'Judas' or 'Jude'.[7]

Stephen and the Hellenists

Notwithstanding this plethora of confusing overlaps, the Community Acts 11:26 appears to be describing as 'Christian' in its picture of early events at Antioch is certainly a Hellenistic or 'Greco-Judaic' one – if it can really be said to be 'Judaic' at all. Six lines earlier, Acts 11:20 refers to it or the Community preceding it as 'Hellenist'. As just remarked, one must be careful of such denotations as they may represent a circumlocution or euphemism for something entirely different – sometimes, in fact, something just the opposite. This would be true, for example, in the dispute between 'Hellenists' (*Hellenistai*) and 'Hebrews' in Acts 6:1–5 over 'the daily ministration for widows' (*diakonia*) and 'waiting on tables' (*diakonein*) which serves to introduce the highly-polemicized and largely fictional story about someone Acts ultimately ends up calling 'Stephen'.[8]

In this story, 'the *Hellenistai*' (6:1) are probably not 'Hellenes' or 'Hellenists' at all nor are 'Hebrews' probably Hebrews. In it 'Hebrews' most likely refers to principal Apostles as per Paul's use of the term in 2 Corinthians 11:22 to depict those he is contemptuously dismissing as 'Super Apostles' or 'Apostles of the Highest Degree'. Nor is the 'dispute' between so-called 'Hellenists' and 'Hebrews', pictured in Acts 6:1–6's run-up to its introduction of this 'Stephen', probably about 'serving tables' or 'ministering to widows', however picturesque or charming the circumstances of this episode appear to be.

Nor can it be said that 'Stephen' – probably not even an historical personage (at least not in the context and circumstances presented by Acts[9]) – is one of 'the Hebrews' as the episode impenetrable, implies. Neither in this presentation is he one of 'the Hellenists', though in the final analysis he probably is and, archetypically speaking at least, typifies what a 'Hellenist' might have been if one existed at this time – basically one of Paul's newly-converted Gentile followers.

So do the other six members of 'the Seven' enumerated here in Acts 6:5, all with patently Grecian names – two seemingly right out of Plato ('Timon' and 'Parmenas'). A third, the never-heard-of-before-or-since 'Nicolaus, a proselyte from Antioch' (thus!), probably reflects one of Josephus' sources, the wily Herodian diplomat *cum* historian 'Nicolaus of Damascus'.[10] Notwithstanding, it should be observed that in the Damascus Document there are certainly a species of Gentile proselytes or converts delineated who are far more exacting, scrupulous, and demanding, Judaically-speaking, than any of these 'deaconizing Seven' in Acts.[11] In actuality, Stephen like Ananias and Judas Thomas above represents another of these *doppelganger* characters as well.

In the parallel source represented by 1 Corinthians 16:15, another Stephen, that is, he or a namesake of his, is referred to by Paul as 'the first-fruit in Achaia' – meaning presumably Paul's first convert on the Greek mainland, probably in Corinth – 'the members of whose house appointed themselves to the service (*diakonia*) of the Saints'. Of course, to the perspicacious reader, the telltale employment of the usages *diakonia*/*diakonein*, upon which the modern English word 'deacon' is based, seals the philological overlap. Not only does Paul allude to the excellence of this 'service' including, one would assume, 'table service' (*diakonian* – 16:17–18); but I think it can safely be said that this passage is the basis for Acts 6's multiple references to ministering (*diakonia* – 6:1), service (*diakonein* – 6:2), or Ministry (*diakonia* – 6:4) above which form the backbone of its introduction to Stephen – *diakonia* or its variants being repeated three times in four lines in case we missed the point!

Of course, all this sometimes playful and always purposeful obfuscation typifies Acts' bizarre and often malevolent sense of humor or word-play. In Josephus – if one acknowledges the parallel of identical names cropping up in chronologically-parallel narratives however dissimilar or unfamiliar the context or circumstances may superficially appear – Stephen is 'the Emperor's servant' with dispatches and monetary tender from abroad (presumably from Corinth too), who is beaten and robbed by rampaging Jewish Revolutionaries almost within eyeshot of the walls of Jerusalem in the aftermath of the Passover stampede in the Temple of 49 CE.[12]

This stampede, in which Josephus estimates – depending on which source one is following, the *War* or the *Antiquities* – some 300 or 3000 people were trampled to death (extra zeroes not being terribly germane in ancient numeration), was occasioned by a Roman Centurion on guard on the roof of the Temple arcade who lifted up his tunic and derisively exposed himself to the crowd, presumably to show at one and the same time both his uncircumcision and his contempt.

From this perspective, the 'Stephen' in Josephus and the 'Stephen' Paul refers to as his 'first fruit of Achaia' are not two separate individuals. Nor is the character whose demise Acts refurbishes into a vicious attack by horrid Jewish agitators to replace the attack by Paul on the fabled Leader of 'the Jerusalem Church' James the Just 'the brother of the Lord'. All the elements are there as conserved in that important counterweight to the presentation in the Book of Acts, the Pseudoclementine *Recognitions*.[13]

There is one last 'Stephen' of note in this circle of relevant 'Stephen's at this time and that is the 'Stephen' responsible for the assassination of Domitian (81–96 CE). Domitian had wreaked singular destruction on the circle of influential early Christians in Rome, beginning with Epaphroditus (seemingly Paul's colleague in Philippians 2:25 and 4:18 and, in a previous embodiment, Nero's secretary for Greek letters – not to mention the influential person Josephus pays homage to in his *Vita* as encouraging all his works[14]) and ending with Flavius Clemens, probably the very 'Clement' featured in Pseudoclementine narrative just mentioned above. Nor, seemingly, was Josephus exempt from Domitian's wrath, not surprisingly in view of Josephus' own connection probably with this same Epaphroditus, towards whom Domitian seems to have had a more than ordinate animus since he ultimately had him executed as well – probably along with Flavius Clemens and possibly even Josephus in the events leading up to Domitian's own assassination in 96 CE.[15]

This Stephen is the servant or slave of Flavia Domitilla, for whom one of the earliest and largest Christian catacombs in Rome – the Domitilla Catacomb – is named. She was a relative of the Emperor and either the wife or niece of this very dame Flavius Clemens.[16] In regard to this name 'Flavia', one should remember Josephus' own adopted patronym, 'Flavius Josephus'. There can be little doubt that Stephen's assassination of Domitian was revenge for the execution of Flavius Clemens and probably encouraged by Flavia Domitilla herself.

If the character Josephus presents us with in the late Forties was identical to Acts' and Paul's 'deaconizing' and 'table-waiting' Stephen above, how much fun it would have been for the author of Acts to transform an attack on James in the Temple at Passover in the hated Pseudoclementine *Recognitions* by Acts' own narrative hero Paul (clearly dubbed in the *Recognitions* as 'the Man who is our Enemy'[17]) into an episode delineating an attack 'by the Jews' – and invested with the substance and circumstances of the two attacks on James as reported in all early Church sources and Josephus – on the archetypical Gentile believer 'Stephen'. The Czar's minions in *The Protocols of the Elders of Zion* could not have imagined a better scenario. Unfortunately it just did not happen.

Paul's attack on James, Hellenists at Antioch, and Elymas Magus on Cyprus

Not only does Acts randomly mix into its account materials from James' fall from the Pinnacle of the Temple as set forth by Hegesippus – material delightfully parodied in the Synoptics' picture of the 'temptation of Christ by the Devil' on the Pinnacle of the Temple[18] or James' 'headlong' fall from the Temple steps in the Pseudoclementine *Recognitions*, but in all these accounts, the several descriptions of how Stephen/James 'cries out with a loud voice' (Acts 7:60) or the Jewish crowd 'cried out' (Acts 7:57) are exactly the same. So basically are the final words attributed to Stephen who, 'seeing the Heavens open, falls to his knees' and, Christlike, both utter the words, 'Lord, do not lay this Sin to them' (Acts 7:60).

This is to say nothing of the long speech Stephen is portrayed as making to the High Priest and Sanhedrin prior to his stoning, telling them their whole history up to the building of the Temple by Solomon (Acts 7:2–53) – as if a Jewish Sanhedrin would need such a review! – but which rather ends with the 'killing all the Prophets' accusation (or rather 'libel') and contains elements from the Letter of James about 'keeping the Law' and an actual phrase based on Ezekiel 44:7 used in the Habakkuk *Pesher* from the Dead Sea Scrolls, the 'uncircumcised heart'.[19]

Not only is this speech clearly lifted from Joshua's 'Farewell Address' to the assembled Tribes on Mounts Ebal and Gerizim in Joshua 24:2–15, but Joshua 24:32 actually points the way to the source of the glaring error Stephen makes in Acts 7:16, where he identifies Abraham's burial site as 'the tomb which Abraham bought for a certain sum of money from the Sons of Hamor in Schechem' and not the one a hundred miles or so further South which Abraham bought from Ephron the Hittite at Mamre in Hebron. This mistake would have caused eruptions of laughter. Moreover, the mistake is easily comprehensible as a too-hasty reading of Joshua 24:32 where the burial place of Joshua's ancestor Joseph, 'the plot of ground Jacob bought for a hundred pieces of silver from the sons of Hamor the father of Shechem' is specifically evoked.

To further point up the artificiality of this episode, Acts has Stephen (in whose face one could 'see the face of an Angel') now predicting – like Jesus in the Gospels – that 'Jesus the Nazoraean would destroy this Place' (the Temple) and 'change the customs delivered by Moses' (6:14–15). This is certainly written after the fall of the Temple in 70 CE, only here it is not God or the Romans who will be coming to 'destroy this place' but now 'Jesus the Nazoraean' and the metamorphosis is complete. Of course, not only does Stephen (in place, one must suppose, of the Leader of 'the Party of the Circumcision', James) almost become a 'Jesus' himself; his suffering and torment at the hands (importantly, of 'the Jews') almost replicates that of his Biblical prototype Jesus as well.

Figuratively, the name 'Stephen' means 'Crown' in Greek, an image, for instance, which Eusebius makes much of two centuries later in characterizing him as 'the first after our Lord … to receive the Crown answering to his Name of the Victorious Martyrs of Christ'.[20] But, as both H.-J. Schoeps and myself have shown, the execution by stoning carried out by Eusebius' 'murderers of the Lord' and Stephen's reaction to it (to say nothing of the crowd's) have as much or more to do with James' fate and martyrdom than any archetypical Gentile convert by the name of 'Stephen' at this moment in early Church history in Palestine. In fact, the very Crown we are speaking about here was also often used to describe the hair of unshorn *Nazirites* like James.[21]

'Hellenists' may be Gentiles or 'Hellenizers' but, in the writer's view, sometimes they may even represent 'Zealots'. If the parallels with contemporary episodes in Josephus delineating the attack on 'the Emperor's Servant Stephen' not very far from the walls of Jerusalem itself by crazed Revolutionaries, as well as those with the disputes running through Books XIX–XX of the *Antiquities* between Greeks and Jews in Caesarea (Hellenists and Hebrews in Acts) or 'Zealots' and toadying Jewish turncoats, are recognized as the real historical templates underlying these chapters in Acts – transmogrified here via the magic of art in the interests of retrospective theology – then this is certainly the case.[22] There is a precedent for this, namely the use of 'Canaanites' or 'Cananaeans' in Mark and Matthew based on the Hebrew word *Kanna'im* or 'Zealots'.[23] This is easily recognized in the shift from 'Simon the Cananaean' or 'Canaanite' in Apostle lists in Matthew 10:4 and Mark 3:18 to 'Simon *Zelotes*' in Luke 6:15 and Acts 1:13. This, in turn, parallels the shift already called attention to above from 'Thaddaeus' to 'Lebbaeus surnamed Thaddaeus' in Mark and Matthew to 'Judas (the brother) of James' in Luke (no doubt, too, 'Jude the brother of James' in the Letter ascribed to his name[24]).

There are also problems with designations such as 'Cypriots' or 'Cyrenians' which do not always represent what they seem. Take for example the case of Simon Magus' double in Paphos on 'Cyprus' in Acts 13:4–12, the supposedly Jewish magician and 'false prophet whose name was Bar-Jesus'; this name is further alluded to as 'Elymas Magus' in the Greek of Acts 13:8. Nor is this to mention the virtual repeat of this episode in 'the Seven Sons of Sceva' episode in Acts 19:10–20 – supposedly the sons of a 'Jewish High Priest', who were also going around Asia casting out Evil spirits or 'practicing magical arts' – the very name of whom, *Sceva,* in Hebrew means 'Seven'. It is in this episode on Cyprus, too, right at the beginning of Paul's first missionary journey, as Acts depicts it, that Paul meets his namesake, one 'Sergius Paulus', the former never seemingly called '*Saulos*' ever again. Nor is the latter ever heard from again. Neither is this to mention that Simon Magus' place of origin and principal theater of operations, according to both early Church accounts and the Pseudoclementines (but not Acts), seems originally to have been 'Samaria', the town of *'Gitta'* there being his birthplace.[25]

What am I saying? Actually, sometimes 'Cyprus' may mean 'Samaria' because the earlier confrontation between Simon Magus and Peter in the aftermath of the 'Stephen' episode in Acts 8:14–24 – being parodied here in Acts 13:6–12's 'Elymas Magus' episode – almost certainly took place either in 'Samaria' or 'Caesarea', the closest major coastal city to Samaria, as it does, for instance, also in the Pseudoclementines. Caesarea is also the locale in which Josephus places the character he calls in the Antiquities 'a Magician called Simon'.[26] In some manuscripts this is *'Atomus'*, an almost certainly garbled allusion to the characteristic doctrine assigned to Simon Magus according to the Pseudoclementines and early Church reports, the incarnated or Primal Adam ideology of which, for Paul in 1 Corinthians 15:22 and 45–48, Jesus is 'the Second' or 'Last' – 'the Lord out of Heaven'.[27]

The reason for this particular geographical confusion – above and beyond the purposeful obfuscation involved – is probably because Jews in this period (including Josephus) often referred to Samaritans as 'Cuthaeans'.[28] This seems, in some convoluted manner to have become confused in translation with *Kittim*, an important usage also in the Dead Sea Scrolls which, despite the fact that its earliest signification must surely have been 'Crete', even in the Bible represents *Cyprus*, the closest island of any size in the direction of Crete off the Judean coast.[29] This is to say nothing of the additional possible confusion between *'Cuth'*, *'Kitte'*, and *'Gitta'* in the above-mentioned allusion to Simon Magus' birthplace.

Herodians at Antioch

Notwithstanding all these points, among these founding members or 'Hellenists' in the Christian Community of Antioch (where 'the Disciples were first called Christians' – 11:26), as Acts presents them, were even individuals of the Herodian genus. Though not himself expressly listed as a founding member of the Community in Acts, a good example of this kind of individual would be 'Titus' (in other presentations, also possibly 'Timothy' – not always distinguishable from one another[30]), 'the son of a certain Jewish believing woman whose father was a Greek' (Acts 16:3). The situation described by this last would be typical of descendants of either of Herod's two Jewish wives both named 'Mariamme' ('Mary').[31]

Another individual of this genus – who along with 'Judas Barsabas' (to say nothing of Barnabas and Paul) is described as bringing the letter containing James' directives to overseas communities 'down to Antioch' in Acts 15:27 – is 'Silas' (elsewhere possibly 'Silvanus', its equivalent in Latin, and, like 'Titus' and 'Timothy', not always distinguishable one from the other). In coeval materials in Josephus from the Forties to the Sixties CE, an individual called Silas is the Commander of King Agrippa's bodyguard in Caesarea.[32] This, like many of the parallels noted above, may simply be coincidental, but if these other equivalences hold – and their number does begin to mount up – there is no reason to think it is. Both Silas and Judas, interestingly enough, are referred to in Acts 15:32 as 'Prophets', 'strengthening and exhorting the brothers by much discourse'. Not only is this Prophet designation – or usually rather 'pseudo-prophets' – being widely used in Josephus in this period; but in this imagery of 'Strengthening' we again have language paralleling what we shall encounter in both the Damascus Document from Qumran and early Church accounts of James.[33]

Another of these match-ups, officially listed among these five founding 'certain ones' or 'some' – almost always an expression, whether in Acts or Paul's Letters, involving either disparagement or an unwillingness to be straightforward or forthcoming[34] – and 'the prophets and teachers of the Assembly at Antioch' in Acts 13:1, is 'Niger'. A parallel 'Niger' in Josephus – possibly another coincidence but also possibly not – is a pro-Revolutionary turncoat Herodian 'Man-of-War' who participated in the first battles of the War. Later he is military chieftain of the unruly Idumaeans on the other side of the Jordan in Perea (whoever these might be considered as being – as we shall see as we progress, possibly 'the Violent Ones of the Gentiles' mentioned in the Habakkuk and Psalm 37 *Peshers* as responsible for the destruction of the Wicked Priest, 'paying him the Reward with which he rewarded' the Teacher of Righteousness and his followers among 'the Poor', that is, 'destroying them', and in the second-named as 'taking vengeance upon him for what he had done to the Righteous Teacher'[35]).

It should be appreciated, too, that the national affiliation 'Idumaeans' (Biblically-speaking, the Edomites, a euphemism as well in the *Talmud* for both Romans and Herodians) further solidifies an Herodian connection for these 'Violent Ones of the Gentiles' (as they are called in the Dead Sea Scrolls) or 'Men-of-War', despite their pro-Revolutionary orientation – Herod's mother having been of either Idumaean or Arab extraction and Herodians generally, therefore, being popularly known as Idumaeans.[36] In Josephus, Niger suffers a terrible fate at the hands of his erstwhile comrades, who do not seem to have considered him either loyal or revolutionary enough; and the agonizing portrait of his death carrying his own cross out of the city is, in the author's view, seemingly the template for the picture of Jesus' last moments in the Gospels – itself possibly even penned by one of this 'Niger''s disillusioned followers.[37]

Another of these 'certain ones' at Antioch is a sometime traveling companion of Paul, called in Paul's Letters and here in Acts, 'Barnabas'. However, in Acts 4:36 he was called a 'Cypriot Levite named Joses'. Not only is there once again the issue here of what actually is intended by the designation 'Cypriot', but also the interesting coincidence that 'Joses' is the name in the Synoptic Gospels of Jesus' fourth brother. Nor is this to say anything about the basic overlap or resemblance of names like 'Barnabas', 'Barsabas', and 'Barabbas', their signification, or the connection of, at least, some, such as 'Joseph Barsabas' and 'Jesus Barabbas', with similar sounding names among the members of Jesus' family generally.[38] Further penetration of these tantalizing connections, however, is perhaps not possible.

Be these things as they may, a third of these so-called 'prophets and teachers' of 'the Church at Antioch' in Acts 13:1 (equivalent to 'the Hellenists' above in Acts 11:20'?) is '*Saulos*' or Paul himself.[39] It should be appreciated that *Ecclesia* in Greek ('Church' in English) is '*Edah*' in Hebrew, itself an extremely important usage across the board in Qumran documents usually translated in English as 'Congregation.' (We use the word *Qumran*, the Arabic denotation for the location where the Scrolls were found, interchangeably with the Scrolls themselves and their content, a practice in wide use in the field.) 'Assembly' – called 'the Jerusalem Assembly' by some; 'the Jerusalem Church' by others – is also an important usage for all descriptions of James and the Council of Elders ('Presbyters' in Acts 15:2–4, 22, 21:18, etc.), he headed, not only in Acts but in the Pseudoclementines as well.[40]

The fourth of these five 'prophets and teachers' in Acts 13:1 is '*Loukios* the Cyrenian', most probably an approximation for the alleged author of Acts and the Gospel under his name, and, like Barnabas, a seeming traveling companion of Paul. Here 'Cyrenian' probably does represent the area of Cyrenaica (present-day Libya) next to Hellenistic Egypt, from where '*Lukas*' presumably came, and a wide area of revolutionary '*Sicarii*' activity even after the Temple fell in 70 CE,[41] though this is probably not the case for someone like 'Simon the Cyrenean' in the Gospels, portrayed as *carrying the cross for Jesus* in Mark 15:21 and Luke 23:26 and who apparently resides in Jerusalem.

Together with appellatives like 'Barnabas', 'Lebbaeus', and 'Barsabas', it is a cognomen of some kind, but so in reality too is 'Niger', the reference to whom actually reads, 'Simeon who was called Niger'. In Greek 'Niger' means 'Black', in which case it could have overtones with another interesting character in the contemporary 'Antioch- by-Callirhoe': 'Abgar the Black' or 'Agbar *Uchama*' in Eusebius' fabulous correspondence.[42] In Semitic languages generally it can, it would appear, also carry the connotation, 'shoemaker', whatever one wishes to make of that in the context we are discussing above – if anything.

The 'Simeon' aspect of the appellation is curious as well since it is a name most often associated with 'Simeon bar Cleophas', the successor to James and second successor to Jesus in the Leadership of 'the Jerusalem Church', considered by most to be the cousin germane of both.[43] But if 'Cleophas', who is normally represented in early Church tradition as the brother of Jesus' father Joseph and the husband of 'Mary the mother of James, Joses, Simon, and Judas',[44] is the same as 'Clopas' in John 19:25, 'Cleopas' in Luke 24:18, and most likely 'Alphaeus' in Synoptic Apostle lists; then 'Simeon bar Cleophas' is probably hardly distinguishable from Jesus' second brother 'Simon' and not his 'cousin germane' as early Church sources would have it, in which case, he is also probably to be identified with 'Simon the Cananaean'/'Simon the Zealot' in Gospel Apostle lists and possibly even another Simon, 'Simon (the father or brother) of Judas Iscariot' in John 6:71.[45]

It should be noted, too, that Peter or 'Cephas' (n.b., the homophonic relation of 'Cephas' to 'Cleophas' and, for that matter, 'Caiaphas') – another of these 'Twin Twin' repetitions, Peter in Greek and 'Cephas' in Aramaic both meaning 'Rock' – normally considered to be 'Simon Peter' the successor to Jesus in orthodox Christian tradition, is at one point anyhow referred to as 'Simeon'. This comes, yet again, during the crucial succession of speeches in Acts 15's portrayal of the fabulous 'Jerusalem Council' (15:14), speeches which have much in common with earlier ones at the beginning of Acts (2:14–3:26) and a parallel set of speeches in the Pseudoclementine *Recognitions* just prior to the portrayal there of Paul's physical assault on James.

We say 'fabulous' and 'portrayal' because Acts' narrative is just this, an artistic and retrospective recreation. The points it makes have almost nothing in common with the picture Paul provides in Galatians 1–2 and, as well, very little in common with what we know of what Leaders like James or Simeon bar Cleophas actually would have said from other sources. On the other hand, they will have important terminological connections with well-known allusions in, for instance, the Damascus Document.[46] This would make the 'Simeon' in question in Acts 15's portrait of the 'Jerusalem Council' (not to mention the Simon who suddenly appears in Luke 24:34's presentation of the aftermath of Jesus' first post-resurrection appearance on 'the road to Emmaus' to 'Cleopas' and an unnamed other[47]) to have more in common with James' successor in 'Ebionite' or 'Jewish Christian' tradition, 'Simeon bar Cleophas', than with Jesus' successor in more Western orthodox sources and tradition, 'Simon Cephas' or 'Peter'.

Mix-ups of this kind surround the pivotal character known variously as 'Simon', 'Peter', 'Cephas', and/or 'Simeon', whom we have much cause in Palestine anyhow at this time to identify with 'Simeon bar Cleophas', James' successor in the Leadership of 'the Jerusalem Church' and the so-called 'cousin germane of our Lord' – Jerome's ploy of identifying the brothers of Jesus as 'cousins' already having taken hold in the literature by this point.[48] This is to say nothing about the fact that, according to the historiography of Acts, at the time of the date of the supposed 'Jerusalem Council', the character it is calling Peter had already fled with a death sentence on his head for having escaped from prison after having been arrested (12:4–19).[49] This anyhow is Acts' testimony if it can be trusted. But it is difficult to imagine that the orthodox Peter could, somehow, suddenly have returned to peacefully participate in this Council in Acts 15:6–30 whatever its proceedings.

Two coins from 134-35 CE: **Left**, the Emperor Hadrian who renamed Jerusalem after himself; **Right**, the Palm Tree of Bar Kochba (*Shim'on* on coin), whom Hadrian destroyed.

'Manaen the Foster Brother of Herod the Tetrarch'

This brings us to the fourth person mentioned in Acts 13:1 – just before *Saulos* is renamed *Paulos* in Acts 13:9 – the fifth among these 'Prophets and teachers' of 'the Antioch Assembly', 'Manaen the foster brother of Herod the Tetrarch'. This is one of the most revealing testimonies in New Testament Scripture because it unequivocally – and, one might say, even unashamedly – reveals that there were *Herodians* involved in the foundation of the Church at Antioch where 'Disciples were first called Christians' around 55 CE. This is no insignificant datum.

In *James the Brother of Jesus*, I expressed the opinion that what one has in such instances is a species of shell-game.[50] We identified this sort of shell-game with regard to the Central Triad of the 'Jerusalem Church' depending on which source and which and whose brother one is talking about – Peter, James, and 'John his brother' in the Gospels and 'James, Cephas, and John' in Galatians. In the manner in which these 'Central Three' are presented in the Gospels, the most famous James appears to be 'the brother of John' and, therefore, one ends up with the well-known 'John and James the two sons of Zebedee' or 'the Sons of Thunder' however one wishes to express it, none of which formulations appears historically very realistic.

It only takes a little reconstruction to arrive at the 'Cephas, John, and James his brother' – meaning 'James the brother of the Lord' – as 'the Central Three' according to Paul's testimony in Galatians 1:19 and 2:9. The epithet 'his brother' would then no longer apply to 'James the brother of John', a character nowhere mentioned by Paul; but rather – and this probably more accurately – 'James the brother of Jesus'. This was obviously how Paul saw it and, because of this, made no mention of any James other than 'the brother of the Lord' and seems to know no other. This would appear to be the thrust of most traditional extra-Biblical literature too, where more is known about 'James the Just' or 'James the brother of Jesus' (to be fair, in Galatians 1:19 he is only referred to as 'James the brother of the Lord') than someone called 'James the brother of John' as in Mark 3:17 and 5:37, unless 'John' and 'the Lord' can be considered to mean the same thing – a dubious proposition.

In any event, this other 'James the brother of John', historical or otherwise, conveniently disappears from Scripture in Acts 12:2 just prior to Acts' introduction of this other James in 12:17. This disappearance of James the brother of John consonant with the sudden appearance of the really significant James just a few lines later, off-hand or otherwise is, from the standpoint of early Church history in Palestine, the really significant information as well. *This* James appears, as it were, unheralded and unintroduced though the text appears to think we already know or should know who he is.[51]

The same is true of the reference to one 'Manaen the foster brother of Herod the Tetrarch' as one of the principal members of the founding Community at Antioch in Acts 13:1. We shall have more to say about which Antioch is intended here in due course, but 'Manaen' is probably defective as there is no other known personality with such a name in any source one can point to. Rather the appellation, as it stands in Acts, probably represents a corruption of the Ananias we have already met above, who forms a set piece of the presentation of Paul's conversion in Damascus in Acts 9:12–17. In this sense 'Damascus' in Acts can simply be seen as a parallel to or write-in for Edessa and what is going on there at about this time or, even possibly, Adiabene in Josephus – all fairly contiguous areas.[52]

Properly speaking, the character being referred to in multiple contexts as 'Ananias' probably should have been mentioned among 'the Prophets and teachers of the Antioch Assembly' anyhow.[53] Though Acts places him in Damascus, he or a namesake of his is clearly functioning, according to Eusebius' source, in Edessa where he is associated with the conversion of the King there, Abgarus or Agbarus, 'the Great King of the Peoples beyond the Euphrates'.

Also in Josephus' account of the conversion of Queen Helen (possibly one of 'Agbarus'' wives as we shall see below – and perhaps even his principal one) and her favorite son Izates at the beginning of the all-important Book Twenty of The *Antiquities* ending with the death of James, yet another character called Ananias is to be met in two locales, once in the South at the mouth of the Tigris at Charax Spasini (modern-day Basrah – also Antiochia Charax) and, following this, on the Upper Euphrates closer to Edessa or 'the Land of the Edessenes' – possibly including Adiabene adjoining it. Nor do we consider all of these to be separate renderings or episodes.

The women, such as Helen of Adiabene in this Great King's harem – also possibly his sister or half-sister – whom Ananias and another companion Josephus mysteriously declines to mention (Paul?) get in among and convert, 'have a horror of circumcision'. This last, in turn, is perhaps the principal issue behind Paul's polemics in Galatians, a letter being addressed seemingly to those in either a Northern Syrian or an 'Asian' context. This is perhaps why Abraham plays such an important role in its polemics, not those only directed against erstwhile companions but also those in the Letter of James, in some respects its ostensible answer – Abraham himself being celebrated as having originated in this area.

To go back to Herod the Tetrarch, to whom this Manaen is supposed to have stood in a quasi-fraternal relationship: not only is this Herod well known as the eventual husband of the sister of King Agrippa I, Herodias, but he or she would seem to bear much of the responsibility for the death of John the Baptist, whichever presentation of these events one chooses to follow – either that of the Gospels or of Josephus.[54] It is hardly credible that an individual with such a background and called, therefore, 'the foster brother of Herod the Tetrarch' could have been reckoned among the founding 'Prophets and teachers of the Church at Antioch', as Acts would have it, unless the apposition were accidentally or purposefully displaced – which is what we meant by a 'shell-game' in the first place – and it rather applied, not to an insignificant unknown such as 'Manaen', but rather to Paul himself.

I have expressed the position that Paul was an Herodian, one of the proofs of which were his greetings to his 'kinsman Herodion' ('the Littlest Herod') at the end of Romans 16:11 – presumably Herod the Sixth, the son of Aristobulus and Salome, to whose household he appears already to have sent greetings in the previous line (16:10).[55] The Salome in question is the very person whose dance is pictured in the Synoptic Gospels as being the cause of John's demise, a dance never mentioned in Josephus though her marriage to another of her mother's uncles, Philip, is. In the Synoptics, this Philip evolves into her mother's first husband, an individual Josephus rather identifies as actually having been named Herod not Philip. In Josephus, it is rather Salome's husband who is named Philip, 'who died childless'.[56]

As it turns out, just such a relative of Herod the Tetrarch (elsewhere, 'Herod Antipas') named 'Saulos' does exist in the Herodian family at this time. Furthermore, as described by Josephus, he is involved in activities not unsimilar, as we shall see, to Paul's – namely, leading a riot in Jerusalem after the death of James similar to the riot led by Paul described in Acts 8:1–3 directly following the stoning of Stephen or the riot which Paul – described as 'the Enemy' – is pictured as leading in the Pseudoclementine *Recognitions* that ends up in James being thrown 'head-long down the Temple steps'.[57] He is also involved, like his namesake Paul, in an appeal to Caesar – in both, Nero Caesar – but more about all these things in due course.[58]

If Paul and not Manaen was 'the foster brother of Herod the Tetrarch', identical with the individual called 'Saulos' in Josephus, it would not be at all surprising if he were also involved earlier in his career in the death of John the Baptist and his flight from Damascus at this time (as per the picture in 2 Corinthians 11:32–33 – not the sanitized and refurbished one in Acts

9:23) in order to escape the soldiers of King Aretas related to these circumstances. The circumstances were that this Paul or 'Saulos' was in Damascus – the real Damascus and not the more complex one in the Scrolls or the one revised in Acts 9:2–25 – on a mission of some sort in support of his kinsman or foster brother Herod the Tetrarch, the recently-acquired husband of the despised Herodias, the marriage of whom triggered the death of John. Actually Aretas, the Arab King of Petra further South, had just taken military control of Damascus at this time.[59]

To put this more succinctly: if we sometimes consider constructs like 'the foster brother of Herod the Tetrarch' to be laterally displaced, we can arrive with far more sense at the insight that, in the early Christian Community at Antioch (whichever 'Antioch' one might ultimately think this to be) 'where Christians were first called Christians', the individual brought up with Herod the Tetrarch was Paul not 'Manaen' (the likely original of which was 'Ananias') – precisely that 'Saulos' who eight lines further along in Acts 13:7 receives his Greco-Latin name after a far too felicitous exchange with 'Sergius Paulos' (pictured as the Roman proconsul of Cyprus at this time).

Elsewhere Paul is pictured as having made the assertion of having persecuted the followers of 'the Way unto death' (Acts 22:4 and Galatians 1:13 and 23). This is just the conclusion we would arrive at in our interpretation of the curious double version of Paul's descent down the walls of Damascus 'in a basket' to escape the representatives of King Aretas trying to arrest him in 2 Corinthians 11:32–33. Via the miracle of art, Acts 9:23 refurbishes this – while at the same time injecting another fairly virulent dose of anti-Semitism – into a descent by Paul down the walls of Damascus in a basket *to escape the Jews*. It is now 'the Jews' who are presented as the ones who 'want to kill him' and not 'the Ethnarch of Aretas' as in 2 Corinthians 11:32.

In fact, a Monarch by the name of Aretas did play a role in the circumstances surrounding John the Baptist's death, but he was on the same side as John because Herod the Tetrarch had divorced his original wife (Aretas' daughter) to prepare the way for his marriage to Agrippa I's sister and Salome's mother, Herodias. As Josephus puts it in the *Antiquities*, the people were glad at Herod's discomfiture in the subsequent mini-war he fought with Aretas over this affair and took it as a sign of God's vengeance or displeasure 'at what he (Herod) had done to John'.[60] In addition, it is apparent that 'the Jews' in Josephus' diverging account were on the same side as John and *not against him* as the Gospels often portray – John being a popular religio-political reformer for the mass of Jews who, according to Josephus, seemed willing to do 'anything he should suggest' including Revolution; while, on the other hand, the Herodians were a Greco-Arab alien Dynasty *imposed on them by the Romans* from outside, most of whom not even considered as Jews![61]

This is backed up as well by later Syriac/Armenian sources which claim – reliably or not – that their ruler 'Abgar' (Abgar the Black?) helped Aretas in his campaign against Herod Antipas or Herod the Tetrarch,[62] the individual we are supposed to think had a 'foster-brother' among the earliest 'Prophets and teachers' of the 'Christian' Assembly at Antioch. Once again, our suggestion is that the actual foster brother of Herod the Tetrarch was not Manaen but Paul himself, which makes perfectly good sense in the context. This is particularly true when one considers Paul's Roman Citizenship (which all Herodians possessed[63]), his consistently pro-Roman orientation both as pictured in Acts and in his letters, his easy entrée as a young man into Jerusalem upper-class circles, including the letters he gets from the High Priest to arrest those 'of the Way' in 'Damascus' (Acts 9:2) – to say nothing of the ease with which his nephew later (whoever he may have been) is able to communicate with the Chief Captain of the Roman Guard in the Temple who is holding Paul in protective custody (Acts 23:19) and, finally, his incarceration in Agrippa II's Palace in

Caesarea in what appears rather a loose form of house arrest than an actual incarceration in Acts 23:35.

Therefore we have alluded to him as the *Herodian* Paul and, therefore too, it is possible to assert that Paul not 'Manaen' (whoever he might have been) would have more likely been the one brought up with Herod the Tetrarch, a fact Acts' Lukan artificer would have been at pains to obscure. With only a slight lateral displacement – just as with 'James his brother' meaning 'James the brother of John' (not 'James the brother of Jesus') above – this is exactly what one ends up with and this embarrassing fact is easily over-written and erased. These things as they may be, these are the kinds of analyses and insights one is able to achieve and will achieve further below if one pursues this kind of information without preconceptions or prior commitment and with a modicum of common sense and intelligence.

The Anti-Semitic Peter

Another rewarding avenue of analysis are the speeches attributed to Peter in Acts and the contrast of these with the portrait of Peter in the Pseudoclementines. In Acts, Peter is presented as a mouthpiece for anti-Semitic invective, but this kind of Peter is hardly, if ever, in evidence in the Pseudoclementines, whichever version one consults, the *Homilies* or the *Recognitions*. In our view, the Pseudoclementines do not simply parallel Acts; rather, they are *based on the same source* as Acts, to which they are the more faithful. This is certainly the case with the *Recognitions*, the First Book of which links up with Acts in an almost point-for-point manner – albeit approaching most issues from a *completely opposite ideological orientation*. In addition there is the common vocabulary not only with Acts, but also documents at Qumran like the Damascus Document.

There are some five or six speeches attributed to Peter in Acts. In almost every one, he is presented as making the same telltale 'Blood libel' accusation which is never even alluded to in the Pseudoclementine narratives. Rather, in the latter, Peter emerges as a gentle soul, never quick to anger – the archetypical *Essene* as it were – who, like those described in Josephus, 'wears threadbare clothes' and arises at dawn to greet the sun in prayer, following which he always immerses himself – that is, in the Pseudoclementines Peter is a Daily Bather.[64] Finally in the Pseudoclementines, he is the inveterate *Jamesian*, preaching absolute adherence to a more faithful rendition of James' directives to overseas communities even than those depicted in Acts.[65]

It is obviously this sort of portrait that is being deliberately gainsaid in Acts. Not only does Peter receive a 'Paulinizing' vision in Jaffa where he learns not to make distinctions between 'Holy and profane', nor 'to call any man profane' (Acts 10:14–15 and 28) just in time to greet the representative of the Roman Centurion Cornelius (10:19–22); this vision, of course, makes it possible for him to come and visit Cornelius' house and keep 'table fellowship' with him – the prototype for the whole Gentile Mission of Paul and the opposite of the outcome of the confrontations in Antioch in Galatians 2:11–14 after the representatives from James come down from Jerusalem. In this last Peter parts company with Paul and together with Barnabas chooses no longer to keep company with him in either 'work or purse' (the language of Qumran – cf. Acts 15:39 above[66]), in return for which Paul accuses both of them of 'hypocrisy' (Galatians 2:13).

But, of course, the position of the real Peter comes across even here in his exclamation in response to the Heavenly Voice accompanying this storybook vision of a tablecloth descending from Heaven, commanding him 'three times' to eat unclean foods and 'not separate Holy from profane': 'no Lord no, I have never eaten any profane or unclean thing' (Acts 10:14). Indeed, Peter becomes the swing figure exploited in Acts at every opportunity to make the point of its anti-Semitic invective. How completely unhistorical, if we are to judge by the Pseudoclementines, and how sad.

The first of these speeches occurs in Acts 2:14–36 when Peter speaks on Pentecost to the 'Jews and Pious persons from every Nation of those under Heaven who were dwelling in Jerusalem' (2:5), addressing them: 'You took him with your lawless hands and, having crucified him, put him to death', meaning 'Jesus the Nazoraean, the man set up by God with mighty works and wonders, and signs which God worked through him' and 'given up' with 'the foreknowledge of God' (Acts 2:22–23). Now quoting Scripture, Peter continues making the second of these 'Blood libel' accusations: 'He was a Prophet and knowing that God had sworn to him with an oath ... to sit upon His Throne, the Lord said to my Lord, "Sit at My right hand until I place your Enemies as a footstool beneath your feet." So therefore, let all the House of Israel know that God made him both Lord and Christ – this same Jesus whom you crucified.' (Acts 2:30–36)

This in its totality is his first speech, to the Assembled Multitudes on Pentecost, and the doctrinal invective it contains is patent. The Peter pictured here was surely not going to win many friends or influence many people in Jerusalem with this kind of language, but the speech obviously was not intended for the ears of those living in Jerusalem despite its context and the ostensible greeting of the opening line to 'all you who inhabit Jerusalem'; but rather to the wider cosmopolitan audience to which it has always been found more meaningful.

The next speech follows almost immediately in the next chapter when 'Peter and John go up to the Temple at the ninth hour' (3:1). Acts is always interested in this type of detail (James for some reason is now absent and it should be obvious to the reader by now why). After straightening out a cripple's crooked bones (thus), Peter again launches into a like-minded speech, clearly paralleling ones in the debates on the Temple steps recorded in the First Book of the Pseudoclementine *Recognitions*. In that version of quasi-parallel proceedings which pictures one Apostle speaking after another, Peter finally precedes James in a speech to the Assembled Multitudes, but the message is completely different from the one here in Acts.[67]

The issue under discussion in the *Recognitions* is the nature of the Messiah and the 'Primal Adam' ideology; but in Acts at this juncture, Peter rather berates the crowd over the fact of his miracle-working:

"Men, Israelites, why do you wonder at this ... as if we made him walk by our own Power.... The God of Abraham and Isaac and Jacob, the God of our Fathers, glorified His Servant Jesus, whom you delivered up (here the third instance of the 'Blood libel' accusation being attributed to Peter), denying him in the presence of Pilate after he had decided to release him. But you denied the Holy and Righteous One and demanded that a man who was a murderer be given to you instead."(3:12–14)

This is the approach of the Gospels, but neither here nor in them is it explained why Pilate as Roman Governor should have offered the Jewish crowd this kind of choice between 'Barabbas', as the Gospels flesh this out, and Jesus.

Still, to drive the point home and, as in the preceding chapter, making the 'Blood libel' accusation two times in the same speech, Peter is made to add: 'And you killed the author of life whom God raised up from the dead (this is the fourth such accusation – not a very good proselytizing technique), of which we are the witnesses' (3:15). Here Acts gives the number of those who heard and, therefore, believed as 'five thousand' (4:4), but this is the number Josephus originally gives for the number of 'the Essenes', as we shall see, as well as the number of the original followers of the Maccabees.[68] It is also the number of James' followers in the Pseudoclementine *Recognitions* who flee down to the Jericho area after James has been thrown down and left for dead in the riot allegedly instigated by Paul in the Temple and, of course, the number of people before whom Jesus performs his signs or miracles in the Gospels (though sometimes this alternates with 'four thousand').[69]

The next occurrence of this sort of accusation again follows almost immediately. It takes place before the High Priest, the Prefect Alexander (Philo's nephew Tiberius Alexander, which would put the timeframe, given the scenario of the Gospels, in the mid-Forties, not a very likely chronology[70]), the Rulers, Elders, other High Priests, and Scribes representing, as stated further along, 'the Sanhedrin'. Here Peter is presented as saying: 'Rulers of the People and Elders of Israel, if we are tried today for a good work to a lame man who has been cured, let it be known to you all and all the People of Israel that it is in the name of Jesus Christ the Nazoraean, whom you crucified (the fifth such accusation in three chapters), whom God raised from the dead. It is by him that he standing before you has been made whole.' (4:8–10)

The fourth speech of this genre Peter makes again occurs in the next chapter, this time directly paralleling the picture in the Pseudoclementine *Recognitions* because he and all the Apostles have been 'standing' (the 'Standing' notation is of extreme importance in the Pseudoclementines and it relates to that of 'the Great Power' – we have already encountered a hint of it in 2:11 and now in 4:10 above[71]) and preaching in the Temple (5:12). The standard arrest then takes place, though the prisons must have been exceptionally large since now one has to do with 'all the Apostles' not just Peter and John; and after a miraculous escape, once again, they (Peter and all the Apostles not just Peter and John) are 'standing in the Temple and teaching the People'. In addition, like the Essenes and the picture of Peter's 'daily-bathing' in the Pseudoclementine *Homilies*, the time now is 'at dawn' (5:21).

Yet again they ('Peter and the Apostles') are arrested and placed before what is now called 'the Sanhedrin', a body that must have found it unusual, if not more than a little inconvenient, to have so many meetings in so short a span of time. Responding to the High Priest's admonishment 'not to teach in this Name', 'filling Jerusalem with' and 'bringing upon us the Blood of this Man' (this last, 'filling Jerusalem with Blood', etc., being specifically alluded to in the Habakkuk *Pesher* as we shall see[72]); Peter insists, 'It is right to obey God rather than men.'

Peter then completes his defense (5:30–31) with the sixth allusion to the 'Blood libel' accusation in just four chapters (not a very politic defense in the circumstances but then the formula is not meant for these circumstances): 'The God of our Fathers raised up Jesus, whom you killed by crucifixion, a Prince and a Savior whom God has exalted by His right hand.' These words, 'by His right hand', are the ones Jesus uses in last appearances in the Gospels and the proclamation attributed to James in the speech he makes on the Pinnacle of the Temple before being stoned in early Church texts and the Second Apocalypse of James from Nag Hammadi. It will also be part of the climactic *Pesher* on Habakkuk 2:16's 'Cup of the right hand of the Lord' which will be exploited to describe how 'the Cup of the Wrath of God would swallow him' (the Wicked Priest) as a 'Reward' for what he did to the Righteous Teacher and his followers among 'the Poor' (i.e., the *Ebionites*).[73]

This is the last in this series of speeches attributed to Peter making this accusation but, should the reader have missed the previous ones, the message is pretty obvious. It is followed by yet another in the next chapter, but this time attributed to 'Stephen' (Acts 7:48–56), the historicity of whom we have already called into question. As Stephen reformulates this libel he again refers, as Peter, to 'Heaven is My Throne and Earth a footstool for My feet' from Isaiah 66:1–2 and Psalm 110:1. He also adds a reference to circumcision – in this case, the 'uncircumcised heart' from Jeremiah 9:26, Ezekiel 44:7–9 and Romans 2:29, a usage specifically applied in the Habakkuk *Pesher* to the destroyer of the Righteous Teacher, known now rather famously as 'the Wicked Priest'.

'Stephen''s presentation, which is no more accurate than Peter's, is as follows: 'O you stiff-necked and uncircumcised in heart and ears, always resisting the Holy Spirit, as your

Fathers were, so are you. Which one of the Prophets did your Fathers not persecute? And they killed the ones who prophesied the coming of the Just One, of whom you now have become the Betrayers and murderers' (7:51–52). Here the characterization of 'Judas Iscariot' in the Gospels has now been turned against the Jewish People as a whole, not only illustrating the true intent of such characterizations – but, sadly, as he has always subconsciously been taken to represent these last nineteen hundred years. It is probably also useful to remark that allusion to such 'Betrayers' or 'Traitors' is again known in the literature at Qumran, in particular and as usual, in both the Habakkuk *Pesher* and Damascus Document.[74]

Sadly as well, this accusation has been picked up and repeated *ad nauseam* in the Koran even to this day as almost a set piece of anti-Semitic vilification notwithstanding the fact that, as just observed, there is hardly a single prophet in the Old Testament 'the Jews' can actually be accused of having killed – not Moses, not Nathan, not Elijah, not Elisha, not Amos, Micah, or Hosea, not Isaiah, not Jeremiah, not Ezekiel, etc. (unless it be perhaps Zechariah though the circumstances surrounding his death are far from certain[75]).

The charge is actually anticipated in Paul, who makes the same accusation in a probably uninterpolated section of 1 Thessalonians 2:14–16: 'For brothers, you become the imitators of the Assemblies of God in Judea ... because you also suffered the same thing from your own Countrymen as they did from the Jews, who both killed Jesus and their own Prophets and expelled you, displeasing God and being the Enemies of the whole Human Race (here is the final Diabolical piece in this terrifying polemic).' It should be clear to even new readers that what one has here is an extremely telling reversal of 'the Enemy' accusations in both the Pseudoclementine *Recognitions* and James 4:4, to say nothing of Matthew 13:13–44's Parable of the Tares and not to mention Paul's awareness of these accusations in Galatians 1:20, 4:16, and elsewhere.[76] Historically, despite its patent untruth, this accusation has proved to be of the utmost durability and probably formed, as just suggested, the basis of most of the invective so far excerpted – not to mention the intractability of the 'Devil People' accusation worldwide.

Of course, Stephen then goes on to have the vision reported of *James* when he is stoned in all early Church sources, punctuated as in these by the actual vocabulary of 'crying out', 'crying out with a loud voice', etc. – expressions forming the backbone of Hegesippus' tradition. There is also the allusion to 'falling asleep' so conspicuous in the parallel scenario in the *Recognitions* and in Paul.[77] This vision actually uses the language of 'seeing Heaven open and the Son of Man standing at the right hand of God' (Acts 7:56) of Peter's last speech and the final last-breath words of both James in Early Church accounts and Jesus in the Synoptics.[78]

One last speech is recorded of Peter before his arrest, escape, and final unlikely return and appearance before the so-called 'Jerusalem Council'. It follows his vision of the Heavenly tablecloth, in which he learns 'not to call any man profane or unclean' (Acts 10:11, 15, and 28 above). We have already stressed the 'Paulinization' going on here. Contrary to the clear portrait of Peter and/or 'Cephas' by Paul in Galatians, not to mention Peter as the thoroughgoing 'Jamesian' in the Pseudoclementine *Homilies* and *Recognitions*[79]; this apocryphal episode turns Peter into a rank-and-file 'Paulinist'. Yet, even here, the real Peter shines through. For instance, in his first response to the Heavenly Voice instructing him to 'kill and eat', to which Peter answers, as already signaled, 'No Lord, for I have never eaten anything profane or unclean' (10:14). This is so unequivocal that it contradicts even the portrait later on in Galatians where Peter is presented as following a more middle-of-the-road approach and Paul has the temerity to accuse both him and Barnabas of 'hypocrisy' (2:13).

But this passage in Acts is clearly written by a Gentile as well – probably in either Alexandria or Rome. This is because it has Peter stating in his first conversation with the Roman Centurion Cornelius – raising him up after the latter 'fell at his feet' – having already just learned on a rooftop in Jaffa that 'table fellowship' with and visiting Gentile homes was permitted: 'You know that it is not lawful for a Jewish man to join himself with (in the language of the Damascus Document, become 'Joiners' or *Nilvim*[80]) or come near one of another Race (Acts 10:28).' Not only is this patently inaccurate, but no Jew could have ever written or said it – even a Backslider or turncoat like Josephus – as the issue was far more complex than this. It had to do with purity regulations and/or contracting impurity or defilement and would even have applied to contact with – to use the vocabulary of the Habakkuk *Pesher* – non-'*Torah*-Doers in the House of Judah', meaning 'Jews'[81]). Rather, this is how Jews would have been perceived by uncomprehending outsiders – since it is not that Jews could not go near foreigners; it is only that one would find it difficult to keep 'table fellowship' (as the issue is referred to in contemporary scholarship) with them or be in touch with people not keeping the Law, whether Backsliding Jews or Gentiles.

To repeat, this could not have been written by someone who was Jewish. Rather it is how Jewish behavior might have appeared to non-Jewish and certainly jaundiced and even hostile eyes. In particular, this is how an anti-Semitic individual (possibly even one of the ubiquitous 'Hellenists' mentioned above) would have framed such an observation – not patently the historical Peter, at least not as he is depicted in documents like the Pseudoclementines unless, of course, one views Peter as a man hobbled by anti-Semitic stereotypes, which the present writer does not.

The character 'Cornelius' is also an impossibility, for it would not have been possible to find at this time a 'Righteous and God-fearing Centurion' of the Caesarean contingent of Roman Soldiers, 'highly spoken of by the whole Nation of the Jews' (Acts 10:22 – 'Pious' and 'doing many good works on behalf of the People and praying to God continually' as Acts 10:2 puts it preceding this). Not only is it hard to refrain from outright guffawing here, this is an obvious inversion and clear overwrite because, as even Josephus has attested, the Caesarean regiment of Roman Soldiery was among the *most brutal in Palestine*. It was they more than any other Roman troops that goaded the Jews into revolt, so much so that when Titus – not someone particularly known for his liberality or largesse and certainly not his concern for the Jews – had finally pacified the country in 70 CE, the Caesarean regiment was the first to be banished from it because of its previous record of unmitigated cruelty.[82]

In fact, like so many of these epithets, the descriptions 'the Righteous One', 'Pious', 'highly spoken of by the whole Nation of the Jews', and 'supplicating God continually', apply more appropriately to someone like James than anyone else one can specify in this Period. Notwithstanding, even here I have already expressed the opinion that what one really has to do with is a refurbishment of the visit of 'a certain Simon' who called the people into an Assembly in Jerusalem, as described by Josephus, to Agrippa I (37–44 CE) in Caesarea 'to see what was done there contrary to Law' – the reason of course being, that Agrippa I was perhaps the only Herodian highly spoken of by a goodly portion of the Jews not only because of the Maccabean blood on his father's side (via Herod's original Maccabean wife Mariamme), but also, contrary to the behavior of other Herodians, his self-evident attempts at conciliating his fellow Countrymen.[83] Even the *Talmud* portrays this Agrippa's concern to ingratiate himself over such matters.[84]

In other words, the 'Simon' at this time in Josephus was a 'Zealot' who wanted to bar mixed-blood persons or foreigners from the Temple, not admit them, as Acts portrays its 'Simon', his contemporary. But, as we shall see in the end, even the name 'Cornelius' will have particular relevance towards some of the issues circulating in this Period and beyond – especially the *Lex Cornelia de Sicarius et Veneficis*, attributed to the legendary Roman General, Publius Cornelia Scipio, but probably not put into real effect until after the First Jewish Revolt by Nerva (96–98 CE) and repressively applied by Hadrian (117–38 CE) to discourage both Revolution and 'circumcision' across the board.[85]

Again Peter repeats in the speech he now makes to this Cornelius on going into his house – for perhaps the seventh or eighth time (depending on whether one includes the one attributed to Stephen) – the usual 'Blood libel'. If we had not got the point by now, we would perhaps have gotten it after this. After describing how 'God anointed Jesus, who was from Nazareth, with the Holy Spirit and with Power' (the 'Great Power' ideology again) and how Jesus then went around 'doing good (as in 10:2 earlier, note the 'Jamesian' language of 'doing' here, now attached to Hellenistic curings and other miracles) and 'healing all who were being oppressed' – significantly not by Rome, but 'by the Devil' (*Diabolou*)! – Peter now adds, 'which he did both in the Country of the Jews and in Jerusalem' (this clearly an exposition aimed and directed at non-Jews), but 'whom they (the Jews) put to death by hanging on a tree' (Acts 10:39 – the typical description of crucifixion Acts has already had Peter use in 5:30 and used by Paul in Galatians 3:13).

By way of introduction to these matters, Peter alludes to two points important in many descriptions of James: 1) 'God is not a respecter of persons' (10:34), which is a fundamental set piece of all early Church descriptions of James – already highlighted above and parodied by Paul at the beginning of Galatians, 'do I persuade men or God or do I seek to please men' (1:10).[86] 2) 'In every Nation, he who fears Him (God) and works Righteousness is acceptable to Him' (10:35), which is basically the approach of the Damascus Document with its emphasis on 'works Righteousness' and, in particular, at the end of the exhortative section of the Cairo recension, where 'fearing God' and 'God-Fearers' are several times evoked – to whom its 'New Covenant in the Land of Damascus' is also clearly addressed – but 'God-Fearers' who obey the Law not those who disobey it.[87]

Like Stephen's speech above, the very introduction to these points – supposedly spoken by 'an Angel of God' ('a man in bright clothing at the ninth hour of the day') to another of these ubiquitous 'certain ones' Acts is always referring to (this time the Roman Centurion Cornelius – 10:1–4 and 30–33) – is reminiscent of the opening appeals of the Damascus Document, which we shall further elucidate as we proceed. As Acts puts this, 'Now therefore … hear all the things which God has commanded you, and … opening his mouth, etc.' – here again, the telltale plays on 'uncircumcising' one's ears, eyes, and ultimately one's heart, we have already encountered in the speech attributed to Stephen above.

In the Damascus Document the parallel position runs as follows: 'Hear now all you who know Righteousness and consider the works of God…. Hear now, all you who enter the Covenant and I will unstop your ears …' etc.[88]

And later: 'And God shall heed their words and will hear and a Book of Remembrance shall be written out before Him for God-Fearers and those considering His Name, until God shall reveal Salvation (*Yesha'*) and Righteousness to those fearing His Name.'[89] In the last line, as we shall have cause to repeatedly point out as we progress too, the reference will actually be to 'seeing *Jesus*' (*Yeshu'a*) or 'seeing His Salvation': 'And their hearts will be strengthened and they shall be victorious … and they shall see His Salvation (*Yeshu'ato*), because they took refuge in His Holy Name'.[90]

The Attack by Paul on James on the Temple Steps

Perhaps the most astonishing notice in all extra-Biblical literature is the one found in the Pseudoclementine *Recognitions* describing an actual physical assault by Paul on James on the Temple steps in Jerusalem. Nor should one fail to remark the absence of this attack from the parallel account known as the Pseudoclementine *Homilies*, which appears to refashion its narrative of early Christian history to expressly avoid mentioning it.[91] The same is true, of course, of Acts where the assault on the archetypical Gentile Christian believer 'Stephen', which introduces Paul and which Paul 'entirely approved of' (8:1), replaces it.

As Acts 8:3 describes these things, Saul (or 'Paul') then proceeds to 'ravage the Assembly in Jerusalem, entering their houses one by one, dragging out men and women to be delivered up into prison'. This mayhem continues into the next chapter with the picture of Paul 'breathing threats and murder (even in Acts, Paul is extremely violent) against the Disciples of the Lord', obtaining letters from the High Priest 'to Damascus, to the synagogues', advising that, 'if he found any who were of the Way, whether man or woman, he should bring them bound to Jerusalem' (Acts 9:1–2).

For its part the *Recognitions* starts off with the parallel picture of debates on the Temple steps, the most important speakers in which are Peter and James. In Acts' picture, of course, James is totally missing or deleted from such activities while in the *Recognitions* it is John who plays almost no role. In the midst of these debates, a man identified only as the 'Enemy' (in margin notes, he is identified as Paul) bursts upon the scene and leads a riot of killing and mayhem on the Temple Mount, paralleling that in Acts above, in the course of which he actually takes a club from the pile of faggots next to the altar and assaults James, 'casting him headlong' down the Temple steps where he leaves him for dead. No wonder this assault is nowhere to be found in more orthodox accounts; nor, for that matter, in the *Homilies*.

The 'headlong' phraseology in *Recognitions* is important as it links up with testimony in Jerome about James' death and what seems to be yet another variant – Acts 1:18's obscure picture of the 'headlong' fall Judas Iscariot takes 'as a Reward for Unrighteousness' in a Field 'of Blood'. Since the 'Enemy' then obtains letters from the High Priest and pursues the early Christian Community down to Jericho on his way to Damascus, the relationship of said events with the activities of Paul in Acts 9:1–25 is for all intents and purposes confirmed. In the author's view, this is real 'Essene' history not that of what we call 'Christianity'.

'Christianity' is to be found in the refurbished portraits one finds in the Gospels and Acts. We have to see the Pseudoclementines – romantic history or literary romance perhaps, but so is Acts – as history *from the inside*, from the perspective of persons or personages in 'the Essene Movement' as it were. Identities which are only hinted at through circumlocutions and tantalizing nom-de-guerres in the Dead Sea Scrolls, in the Pseudoclementines are spoken of overtly and by name. Through them we get, perhaps, a clearer picture of the divisions of 'Early Christianity' in Palestine in the First Century and a handle on persons only vaguely hinted at in the Scrolls or totally obliterated in Acts.

As in Hegesippus, Jerome, the *Recognitions*, and Acts, we must carefully consider all these episodes involving the usages 'throwing down', 'casting down', 'headlong', or 'causing to stumble'.[92] In the Habakkuk *Pesher*, for example, this last is exactly what is said to happen to the followers of the Righteous Teacher – there called, as already alluded to, 'the Poor' or 'the Perfect of the Way' (compare this with 'those of the Way' in Acts 9:22 whom Paul 'confounds') – when the Wicked Priest 'appeared to them at the completion of the Festival of their Rest' (thus – *Yom Kippur*).[93] Not only is the Wicked Priest in this episode described as 'not circumcising the foreskin of his heart' and 'swallowing them', but also 'causing them to stumble' or, quite literally, 'casting them down'. According to the Habakkuk *Pesher*, he does this in the process of 'conspiring to destroy the Poor', the last being coeval with those '*Torah*-Doers' referred to as 'the Simple of Judah doing *Torah*' in both Habakkuk and Psalm 37 *Peshers* and to whom, Habakkuk 2:4's 'the Righteous shall live by his Faith' is rightfully considered to apply.[94]

Unlike Peter in Acts 10:15, these 'Simple' *Torah*-Doers have not yet learned 'not to call any thing' or 'any man profane or unclean'; but rather, in the manner of Josephus' 'Zealots' and/ or 'Essenes', they refuse 'to call any man Lord' or 'eat forbidden things'. In the version of this testimony preserved in the Third-Century heresiology attributed in Rome to Hippolytus, this last becomes more specifically – and probably more accurately – 'things sacrificed to idols', a prohibition intrinsic not only to James' directives to overseas communities in Acts but the document scholars call *MMT*.[95]

For Hippolytus, said 'Essenes' (actually he calls them 'Zealot Essenes' or '*Sicarii* Essenes') are prepared to undergo any sort of bodily torture, even death, rather than 'eat things sacrificed to idols' or 'blaspheme the Law-giver' (meaning Moses).[96] They are also, as the Scrolls make plain, 'the Ebionites' or *Ebionim* (the Poor), in all early Church heresiologies the direct successors of 'the Essenes' and virtually indistinguishable from what these same heresiologists are calling Elchasaites, Masbuthaeans, Sampsaeans, or Sabaeans – the last-mentioned, in later Islamic lore, doubtlessly indicating 'Daily Bathers'. We shall have more to say about all these terminologies presently when discussing the 'Nazoraean' or life-long 'Nazirite' language of 'abstention' or 'keeping away from (*lehinnazer*) things sacrificed to idols' or 'the pollutions of the idols' one finds both in the Scrolls and in Acts. These 'Ebionites' are also the followers of James *par excellence*, himself considered (even in early Christian accounts) to be the Leader of 'the Poor' or these selfsame 'Ebionites'.[97]

To go back to the attack by Paul on James: as already signaled, James did not die in this attack. He was only left for dead, breaking, as the Pseudoclementines and later Jerome make clear, one or both his legs.[98] James does not die for another twenty years, the two episodes being neatly telescoped or conflated into one in both the description of Stephen's stoning in Acts and early Church accounts of James' death. James, rather, is carried out of the Temple to a house – not the house of 'the Disciple Jesus loved' as in the Gospel of John (19:26) but, rather, a house James possesses in Jerusalem. This is also the gist of Acts 12:12 when Peter, after his escape from prison, goes to the house of 'Mary the mother of John Mark' – another character never heard of before or since (more Gentile Christian dissimulation?). No, Mary the mother of James! There he, quite properly, leaves a message for 'James and the brothers' that he is going abroad. This constitutes the introduction of the real James in Acts, the other James having conveniently been removed just ten lines earlier in Acts 12:2.

The next morning, the Disciples numbering some *five thousand*, carry James' inert body down to Jericho. In the meantime the 'Enemy' (Paul) gets letters from the High Priest – in passing, it should be remarked that these 'letters' are the only ones Paul ever receives. They are not from James, the proper appointment procedure as set forth in the Pseudoclementine *Homilies* and endlessly and sarcastically belittled, as we shall delineate, in 2 Corinthians 3:1–16, 5:12, 9:1–3, 10:8–18, etc.[99]

Paul pursues the members of the Early Christian Community (should we rather at this point be saying 'Essenes'?) through Jericho on the way to Damascus where he misses them because, in the meantime, James together with all his followers have gone *outside of Jericho* (Qumran?) to visit the tomb of two of the brothers 'who had fallen asleep' (n.b., the parallel language in Acts 7:60 above). The detail and geographical precision here, as in the matter of the assault in the Temple preceding it, is impressively convincing. The tombs of these brothers miraculously 'whitened of themselves every year because of which miracle the fury of the Many against us was restrained, because they perceived that our brothers were held in *Remembrance before God*'.

This is the kind of startling originality one encounters in this first section of the *Recognitions*. Not only do we have the notice of an attack on James by the 'Enemy' Paul, from which James will still be limping a month later when it came to sending out Peter on his first missionary journey – from somewhere outside of Jericho – to Caesarea (and not to Samaria) where he does however, encounter Simon Magus; but who would have thought to place the entire Early Christian Community to the number of some five thousand in these environs, that is, before the discovery of the Dead Sea Scrolls some nineteen hundred years later just a few miles south of Jericho at Qumran?

Yet here we have just such a testimony in these incomparable notices in the Pseudoclementines which do not simply, in the writer's view, parallel but are rather based on the same source as Acts – to which they are the more faithful. This is certainly the case concerning the *Recognitions*, the First Book of which, as already observed, links up with Acts in a point-for-point manner, albeit from a completely opposite ideological orientation. Then, of course, there is the common vocabulary, not only with Acts but also the Damascus Document from Qumran – as, for instance, the phraseology, 'remembered before God', in the *Recognitions* at the end of the last part of the historical exposition of the Damascus Document where, as with the Angel's words to Cornelius in Acts, the thrust is primarily directed at 'those who fear God' or 'who are God-Fearers'.

Dating the Scrolls: Internal vs. External Data

It has been my position from the beginning that there are two kinds of data at Qumran, *external* and *internal*. 'External' are things like archaeology, palaeography, and carbon dating, but these rather turn out to often be either imprecise or unreliable. In a situation of the kind represented by the materials and discoveries at Qumran, when there is a contradiction between the results of such disciplines and the *internal* data – meaning, what the documents themselves say, to which the rest of this book will be dedicated – then the internal data must take precedence, given the quality and kind of external data that exists for Qumran.

What, for instance, might be considered 'internal data'? Primarily the most important allusions at Qumran. These include references such as 'making a Straight Way in the wilderness', alluded to twice in the Community Rule and, as is well known, associated with the teaching and coming of John the Baptist *in the wilderness* in the Synoptic Gospels.[100] A related terminology is 'the New Covenant', a phrase originally based on Jeremiah 31:31 and a central theme of the Damascus Document, known of course as the basis of the phrase the 'New Testament' (i.e., the 'New Covenant').[101] Equally important is the allusion to and exposition of Habakkuk 2:4, perhaps the climax of the Habakkuk *Pesher* and perhaps the central Scriptural building block of early Christian theology as set forth by Paul in Romans, Galatians, and Hebrews and, of course, in James.[102]

Related to these and, in particular, this last are the repeated reference to the two 'Love Commandments' of Piety and Righteousness (I will capitalize important concepts throughout this book) – in Josephus defined as, 'loving God' and 'loving your neighbor as yourself' – and Justification theology generally. Not only are these the essence, allegedly, of Jesus' teaching in the Gospels and James' in the Letter ascribed to his name in the New Testament and in early Church literature generally,[103] but they are also the basis in the picture provided by Josephus of John the Baptist's teaching and a central category of 'Essene' doctrine as well.[104]

Then there is the wide use of 'Zealot' and 'Nazirite' terminology (in the sense of *Nazoraean* or *Nazrene*), designations known to the First Century but not clearly attested to in any consistent manner earlier.[105] Related to these is 'the Poor' (in early Church literature, 'the Ebionites'), the only really clearly identifiable term of self-designation in the Dead Sea Scrolls, a nomenclature also designating the followers of James *par excellence* and the group succeeding or basically coeval with 'the Essenes'. In a controversial reference in the Habakkuk *Pesher* – a document which, together with the Psalm 37 *Pesher*, definitively denotes the followers of the Righteous Teacher as 'the Poor', that is, we are definitely in the realm both of the Ebionites and of Ebionite literature. Not only would both of these be 'destroyed' or 'swallowed' by the Wicked Priest but he would be made to 'drink the Cup of the Wrath of God' and 'paid the Reward which he paid the Poor' (i.e., the *Ebionim*)![106]

Here 'the Cup of the Lord' relates to Divine Vengeance which is also the sense of parallel allusions in the New Testament Book of Revelation. Again there is an allusion to the same theme in the Psalm 37 *Pesher* and, as opposed to the superficial analyses early on in Qumran Studies, the allusion – as we shall see more fully – has nothing whatever to do with the 'drunkenness' of the Wicked Priest or consonantly any 'banquet' or 'dinner party' he might have been attending,[107] except *metaphorically* in that, as in Revelation 14:8–10 and 16:19, 'drinking his fill' of such a Cup has to do with 'drinking his fill of the *Cup of the Wrath of God*' or the *Divine Vengeance* which would be visited upon or 'paid' the murderer of the Righteous Teacher for what he (the Wicked Priest) did to him and his followers among 'the Poor'.[108] The attestation of this usage in Revelation, not to mention the allusion to 'the Poor' connected in some manner with James in Galatians 2:10, again, should be seen as chronologically definitive *internal* data no matter what the external.

To name a few other such First-Century dating parameters: there is the insistence on 'fornication' as descriptive of the behavior of the Ruling Establishment in the 'Three Nets of *Belial*' section of the Damascus Document. In it, regardless of its meaning in any other context, 'fornication' is specifically defined in terms of polygamy, divorce, marrying nieces and, curiously enough, sleeping with women during their periods, all things that, taken as a whole, can be said to be descriptive of Herodians and not Maccabeans. Among Herodians, in particular *niece marriage was rampant* and an aspect of purposeful family policy.[109]

Another of these 'Nets' had to do with 'pollution of the Temple'. Not only was this a matter not unrelated to 'things sacrificed to idols', and in relation to Hippolytus' *Sicarii* Essenes and in the Qumran document known as *MMT*, it is likewise a matter connected to *James' directives to overseas communities*, where it is also expressed in Acts 15:20 in terms of the variation 'pollutions of the idols'. Interestingly enough, too, this condemnation of 'eating things sacrificed to idols' is even found and grouped together with both 'fornication' and the language of 'being led astray' in Revelation 2:20.[110] These are additional *First-Century* dating parameters.

Much debate, too, has crystallized about the term 'the *Kittim*', so important to the literature and outlook of Qumran especially in the Commentaries (*Pesharim*), the War Scroll, and those documents related to it.[91] Several references are absolutely critical for the correct elucidation of this seemingly purposefully obscure allusion and archaism. The first is in the Nahum *Pesher* where 'the *Kittim*' are specifically identified as 'coming after the Greeks'.[111] Several others come in the Habakkuk and Psalm 37 *Peshers* where, in the former anyhow, they are specifically described as 'pillaging the Temple'.[112] Josephus is very specific about this point and makes it quite plain that there was no 'pillaging of the Temple' by the Romans either in 63 BCE under Pompey because they wished to ingratiate themselves with the People; nor by Herod in 37 BCE who, Josephus tells us, actually had the soldiers paid out of his own pocket expressly to avoid such a happenstance.[113]

That leaves only Vespasian and his son Titus who *did, in fact, plunder the Temple* in 70 CE, and used the proceeds afterwards to pay for the abomination now famously referred to worldwide as 'the Colosseum'.[114] There can be a no more definitive chronological placement of the Habakkuk *Pesher* than this extremely telling allusion and this is what is meant by a proper appreciation of the internal data being frustrated or rendered meaningless by inept and over-inflated interpretation of and reliance upon the external. Of course, in this context there is also the decisive reference to the *Kittim* 'sacrificing to their standards and worshipping their weapons of war', which we shall further discuss in due course as well.[115] It has been pointed out by numerous commentators, but seemingly to little avail, that this is *Roman military practice* not Hellenistic or Greek – and, specifically, *Imperial Roman from Augustus' time forward*, since the Emperor whose bust was on the standards had, commencing in that period, been deified and worshipped as a God.[116]

Just as telling is the reference, immediately following this in the same document, to how these same violent and brutal *Kittim*, who conquered 'Nation after Nation', had 'no pity even on the fruit of the womb' – Josephus describes just such carnage by the Sea of Galilee in 67 CE in the run-up to the siege of Jerusalem two years later, where the Romans did actually kill just such infants – and 'whose eating was plenteous', 'parceled out' their taxes like *fishermen catching fish in their nets*.[117] Here, to be sure, one has a combination of motifs familiar in the 'fishermen' and 'nets' themes in the Gospels – of course, as always, with reverse or trivializing signification. Matthew 17:25–27 even goes so far in response to matters concerning the paying of tribute (in this case, delineated in terms of paying the Temple tax) to actually portray Jesus as sending Peter (also a Galilean 'fisherman') to the Sea of Galilee to retrieve the required coinage out of the mouth of a fish!

In addition, however, it is clear that what is being described in this pivotal section of the Habakkuk *Pesher* is the well-known Roman administrative practice of *tax-farming*, particularly among the petty Kings in the East (like the Herodians who functioned as Roman juridical and tax-gathering officials – in the Gospels, that is, *Publicans*!), and which the Romans practised so assiduously in the Eastern part of the Empire (therefore, the Census referred to in Luke).[118] Once again, these petty or Eastern Kings were specifically referred to in Roman juridical language as 'Kings of the Peoples' – of which such Herodians were prototypical. Here, too, the exact phraseology actually appears in the Damascus Document in describing just such kinds of 'pollution', which included even 'polluting the Temple Treasury', 'robbing of Riches', and 'approaching near kin for fornication' – meaning *marriage with nieces and close family cousins*.

Of course, once one has accepted such evidence, it must be accepted, as we have been trying to point out, that all sectarian texts have to have been written at more or less the same time since they all use the same vocabulary, refer to the same *dramatis personae*, and express basically the same concerns and orientation. As hard as this may be to appreciate for those making superficial analyses on the basis of pseudo- or quasi-scientific external data, this is true and defeats both palaeographic theorizing and archaeological reconstructions, such as they are, not to mention the *wishful thinking* embedded in the unrealistic expectation or inflation of the 'results' of radiocarbon test data interpretation. To be sure, there may be copies made of copies, but all of the key extra-Biblical or sectarian texts – except some very early apocryphal and pseudepigraphic texts – particularly those including real historical indications or dating parameters, had to have been written in more or less the same period of time.

One could go on perhaps endlessly to give examples of allusions or expressions from the Scrolls demonstrating a First-Century CE provenance but not a particularly earlier one. Two of the most telling of these are 'the House of his Exile' or 'his Exiled House', used in the Habakkuk *Pesher* to describe a final confrontation of some kind between the Wicked Priest – clearly the Establishment High Priest – and the Righteous Teacher, which seems to have ended up in the destruction of the latter along with a number of his followers referred to, as just noted, as 'the Poor' (*Ebionim*).[119] No sense whatever has ever been made of this 'House of Exile' by any commentator, but, as we shall demonstrate, it clearly relates to the 'Exile' of the Sanhedrin around the Thirties to the Sixties of the Common Era, frequently attested to in the Talmud,[120] from its place of sitting in the Great Stone Chamber on the Temple Mount to a 'House' outside its precincts (not unlike the trial at 'the House of the High Priest' in the Luke 22:54/Matthew 26:57) – the implication being that, because of this, all capital sentences imposed in this Period under such jurisdiction were to be considered unlawful or invalid.

Finally there is the reference in the Damascus Document to 'raising' or 're-erecting the fallen Tabernacle of David' in a Land North of 'Damascus'.[121] But this usage is also one expressly attributed to James in his speech at the famous 'Jerusalem Council' in Acts 15:16, which we shall consider in detail in the second part of this book. Another such allusion, expressly attributed to James in early Church accounts of the circumstances leading up to his death (to say nothing of Jesus'[122]), is the proclamation of 'the coming of the Heavenly Host upon the clouds of Heaven' which will, as we shall also see, form the backbone of two extensive apocalyptic sections of the War Scroll.[123]

There, of course, it is 'the Star Prophecy' of Numbers 24:17 which is being both evoked and expounded and, once again, we have come full circle, because according to Josephus this was the 'ambiguous Prophecy' – 'ambiguous' because it was capable of multiple interpretations – that *most moved the Jews to revolt against Rome.*[124] To put this in another way: this Prophecy, referred to *upwards of three times* in the extant corpus at Qumran, together with Isaiah 10:34–11:5, also extant in *Pesher*-form in at least two contexts at Qumran, was the *driving force behind the Revolt against Rome* – again, yet another unambiguous dating parameter. One need not mention, of course, the fact of the emergence of the whole Christian tradition, itself another response to this 'ambiguous' Prophecy. Then, of course, there is the very term 'Damascus' itself, the esoteric meaning of which we shall attempt to delineate at the end of this book. Though one could go on, this is the kind of powerful *internal* evidence that exists for a First-Century provenance of many crucial and interrelated sectarian texts among the Scrolls.

View of the steps of the Temple where Paul attacked and threw James down leaving him for dead with Pinnacle and Mount of Olives Cemetery in the background.

Right: The City of Edessa (*'Antioch Orrhoe'*), from which both King Agbar of the Edessenes (*'the King of the Peoples beyond the Euphrates'*) and his wife and half sister, the fabulous Queen Helen of Adiabene came with the Pool of Abraham and the Plain of Haran - Abraham's childhood home - to the South in the background.

PART I

THE NEW COVENANT IN THE LAND OF DAMASCUS

Chapter 1
Essene Bathers in the East and Abraham's Homeland

Life-long Naziritism and the 'Perfect Holiness' Lifestyle

The traditions about James' 'Holiness from his mother's womb' or life-long Naziritism, vegetarianism, and abstention from sexual relations are to be found in the early Church fathers Hegesippus, Origen, Eusebius, Jerome, and Epiphanius.[1] Though many of these notices go beyond what is normally associated with a Nazirite or 'Perfect Holiness' lifestyle,[2] they persist in all sources relating to James and among all groups seemingly descended or claiming descent from him. They also appear, not surprisingly, to relate to what numerous persons in different contexts are calling 'Essenes'.

Where James' sexual continency – his 'life-long virginity' as Epiphanius graphically describes it[3] – is concerned, this may have been a concomitant of his 'life-long Naziritism,' as it was of people contemporary with and not too different from him, such as the individual Josephus' calls *Banus* and those he denotes as 'Essenes'.[4]

Obliquely too, it provides a clue as to how this claim came to be reflected – or retrospectively absorbed as the case may be – into the more familiar one of Mary's life-long virginity or, as this was first seemingly enunciated in the early Second Century, her *perpetual* virginity.[5] The 'perpetual' aspect of this claim can certainly with more justification, be applied to James since, even according to orthodox theology, Mary had at least one son and perhaps more, not to mention at least one daughter.[7]

The claim of Mary's perpetual virginity, in any event, had an anti-James undercurrent to it meant to deny the credibility of there actually *being* any 'brothers' as such or, as the polemic shook out, half-brothers, cousins, or 'milk brothers'.[8] Incredibly enough, the claim for Mary's perpetual virginity is first made in a text: *The Protevangelium of James*, attributed to James and actually put into his mouth, the implication being, of course, that he, the closest living relative, heir, and even successor, would have known about these kinds of things better than anyone else – and no doubt he did.[9]

The motifs of sexual continency and abstention from meat or vegetarianism, whether part of a 'Nazirite' oath procedure of some kind – temporary or life-long – are also to be seen in the notices from Rabbinic literature and Acts about exactly such kinds of Nazirite oaths on the part of extreme irredentists or revanchists.[10] In Acts 23:12–21, such persons vow 'not to eat or drink' until they have killed Paul, the implication being that they will not eat meat or drink wine. In Rabbinic sources, the implication shifts to waiting until the Temple should be reborn or rebuilt, and the interconnectedness of these imageries to Paul's and the Gospels' presentations of *Jesus' body as Temple* should be clear.[11] From 1 Corinthians chapters 8–12, where he is actually discussing James' directives to overseas communities, Paul himself speaks about 'eating and drinking', to wit, 'have we not every right to eat and drink?' (9:4). Such challenges not only lead up to his ultimate allowing of 'eating' or 'partaking of things sacrificed to idols' – in fact, 'all things sold in the marketplace' (10:25) – and his 'for me all things are lawful' assertions (10:23 repeating 6:12), but also his climactic final formulation of 'Communion with' the body and blood of Christ Jesus (10:16).

The Gospels also emphasize this kind of Naziritism when they describe John the Baptist as 'coming *neither eating nor drinking*' – this, as opposed to the more Paulinized description of Jesus 'coming eating and drinking' in Matthew 11:18–19 and Luke 7:33–34. Such ideologies are immediately reinforced by the portraits of Jesus as a 'glutton' and 'wine-bibber', and the portrait of Jesus 'eating and drinking with publicans and Sinners' generally throughout the Gospels.[12]

As Paul develops this ideology and these esotericisms in his final enunciation of the true meaning of 'the Cup of the Lord' and 'drinking' it as 'the New Covenant in (the) Blood' of Christ, he totally *reverses* the lifelong or temporary Nazirite notion of 'not eating or drinking' and rather aims at those who would 'eat this bread and drink' this Cup 'unworthily' (1 Corinthians 11:27). In a final crowning, and what might be construed as a cynical reversal of this ideology, such persons now become 'guilty of the body and blood of the Lord', a frightening accusation in any context, as the history of the Western World has demonstrated. Using this imagery, which we already have found present in the Habakkuk *Pesher*, such persons will now actually 'drink vengeance to themselves, not seeing through to the Blood of Christ' (11:29), an equally terrifying imprecation.[13] As we shall see towards the end of this book, one understanding of this phraseology will be that such persons do not understand the word 'Damascus' according to its proper or esoteric sense – such things, as he would have it in Galatians 4:24 (when speaking about 'casting out the slave woman' and 'Agar which is Mount Sinai in Arabia') 'being allegory'.

By contrast, as noted, in Rabbinic sources such temporary or life-long Nazirite oaths shift and take on a wholly different, more nationalistic – even 'Zionistic' – sense of 'not eating or drinking' until one should see the Temple rebuilt.[15] For these sources and Karaism to follow, including later witnesses like the Eleventh-Century Spanish-Jewish traveler Benjamin of Tudela, such oaths are a consequence of mourning for the destruction of the Temple and waiting for it to be rebuilt which, in turn, blossom into a full-blown Movement, 'the Mourners for Zion', the origins of which, though clouded in obscurity, have to be understood in terms of the events of this period.[16]

Such a period of 'waiting' relating to the rebuilding of the Temple resembles nothing so much as the well-known one associated with 'the Disciple Jesus loved' at the end of the Gospel of John or that 'delay' in the Habakkuk *Pesher*, which goes in Christianity later by the name of 'the Delay of the *Parousia*', based in the *Pesher* on Habakkuk 2:3: 'If it tarries, wait for it, for it will surely come and not delay'.

The notion of such 'Mourners for Zion' is highly underestimated in the history of this period and deserves a good deal more attention than it usually gets. There can be little doubt that one can still discern its influence, however metamorphosized, in the black garments worn by Jewish Hassidic groups to this day – to say nothing of Christian ones. It also paves the way for the development of Karaism in Judaism which, with the appearance of Dead Sea Scrolls material in Jerusalem at the beginning of the Ninth Century, reached what some might consider a final fruition.[17]

Karaism itself certainly grew out of movements such as these 'Mourners for Zion' forming part of its own ideology. 'The Mourners for Zion' themselves had already been functioning in Palestine and places further East prior to the emergence of Karaism in the Seven Hundreds CE. In fact, such 'Mourners' were already influencing a series of Messianic Uprisings in the East in areas being treated in this book, namely Kurdistan, Northern Iraq, and Persia, a happenstance that may not be coincidental.[18]

Nor is it too much of a stretch to put the Crusaders in a similar category as these 'Mourners' and undoubtedly a case can be made that these 'Mourners for Zion' had a tenuous, even if underground, influence on groups like 'the Templars' and, if real, possibly the now infamous inner coterie known to some as 'the *Priory de Sion*',[19] both of which preserving some semblance of their name. This may even extend to 'the Cathars'/'the Pure' whose Priests, carrying on this theme of 'mourning', however bizarre, actually wore black rather than the more typical white. In Jerusalem, unfortunately, all such Jewish groups were probably liquidated in the general blood-letting that occurred in 1099 after it fell at the end of the First Crusade – a possible consequence of their own success – though perhaps not before many of their ideas were communicated to groups such as the Templars (and 'the *Priory*,' if it ever really existed – a doubtful proposition).

Notices such as 'life-long Naziritism' and 'Perfect Holiness' – 'Holiness from his mother's womb', as all our descriptions of James put it – are also to be found in Gospel descriptions of John the Baptist and in the way Paul describes himself in Galatians 1:15–16 – seemingly in competition with James – as 'separated' or 'chosen' by God from his 'mother's womb' to 'reveal His Son in' him. They are also found in the Dead Sea Scrolls, particularly in the Hymns.[20]

We have just seen how the Gospels of Matthew and Luke insist that John 'came neither eating nor drinking', seemingly implying that like James thereafter John too was a vegetarian. As Luke also puts this earlier in the form of a prophecy by 'an Angel of the Lord': 'He shall be great before the Lord and *never drink wine or strong drink* and he shall be filled with the Holy Spirit even *from his mother's womb*.' (1:15) This clearly implies that, for Luke anyhow, John like James was 'a lifelong Nazirite', a condition that apparently entailed for Matthew and Luke – as in early Church descriptions of the details of James' life – in addition to abstaining from wine and strong drink, abstention from meat.[21]

Extreme Nazirites may have insisted, in the manner of James, on going as far as vegetarianism as Judas Maccabee in a previous epoch seems to have done when, according to 2 Maccabees 5:27, he 'withdrew into the wilderness along with about nine other companions' – 'the Ten Just Men' of Jewish mystical lore, upon whose existence the continued existence of the universe was predicated[22] – Rechabite-style, *'eating nothing but wild plants to avoid contracting defilement'*. The situation 2 Maccabees is describing here at the beginning of Judas' Revolt against the Hellenizing Seleucids in Syria would appear to have been particularly applicable when 1) the Temple had been defiled; 2) was no longer functioning; or 3) the charge of 'pollution of the Temple' or the corruption of its sacrifice practices was in the air or perceived as valid.

This charge in particular is fundamental to almost all Qumran documents, as it is in so-called 'Jewish Christian' or 'Ebionite' ones.[23] The rationale here would be that, with the corruption or 'pollution of the Temple', the permission to eat meat – which in biblical terms was dependent upon Noah's atoning sacrifice after the flood in Genesis 8:20–9:17 – was no longer viable or had been withdrawn. At Qumran too, as among Essene groups generally (not to mention those following John the Baptist, if they can be differentiated in any real way from the previous two), the practice of 'bathing' was fundamental – in large part 'daily bathing'.[24]

Extreme purity regulations, however, to the extent of abstaining from meat or wine, are not clearly articulated either at Qumran or in the various descriptions of Essenes that have come down to us. In the Scrolls, the latter may have rested on the distinction between 'new wine' and older more alcoholic kinds, since 'wine' is generally referred to quite freely in them but not what kind of wine, a distinction that does not go unnoticed in Gospel commentary.[25] On the other hand, 'pure food' – whatever might have been meant by this either in Qumran documents or among Essenes – was insisted upon for all full-fledged participants in such groups, meaning those in the higher stages of Community membership,[26] and this may have involved a certain amount of vegetarianism not very different from that reflected in these descriptions of James and implied in the ones about John.[27] Certainly Paul's remonstrations *against* precisely such kinds of persons, whom in Romans 14:1–15:2 and 1 Corinthians 8:7–15 he refers to in the most intemperate manner conceivable, basically calling vegetarians like James 'weak' (certainly 'weak in Faith' or 'having weak consciences' – 'conscience,' as we shall repeatedly see, being one of his favorite euphemisms for 'keeping the Law'[28]), make one suspect that special dietary observance of this kind did include what others perceived of as vegetarianism.

Nazirite Bathing Groups in the East

Nazirite or 'bathing' groups such as at Qumran or in Northern Syria are variously referred to by early Church fathers and others as Nazoraeans, Ebionites, Elchasaites, Sampsaeans, Masbuthaeans, Sabaeans, Naassenes, Jessaeans, and Essenes.[29] In fact, whatever the term 'Essene' might have meant, there is every likelihood that it was generically applied, at least by Palestinian and Egyptian commentators of the First Century (namely Josephus and Philo) and the Second-Century Christian heresiologist Hippolytus, to all bathing groups of this kind. In other words, however one chooses to define the term – and there is even now no agreement on this definition[30] – 'bathing' is an integral aspect of it – in particular 'daily bathing' ('Hemerobaptists' in early Church sources; Masbuthaeans, *Sobiai* or Sabaeans in Syriac, Aramaic, and Arabic ones).

Writers from these times – 'heresiologists' in some vocabularies, that is catalguers of 'heresies' (the designation is significant in illustrating their outlook) – were fond of multiplying these groups into an endless panoply of schisms and sects depending on whose writings they had seen, whether they understood the terminologies they were seeing or not, or were themselves able to pronounce or transliterate the terms in an accurate manner.[31] Though the term 'Essene' may have been popular in Palestine or Egypt, in a different tradition, the very same group may have been known by a different appellative based on a somewhat different linguistic root or phraseology.

'Sabaeans', for instance, a term that has come down to us through the Koran and Islamic usage, is probably the same as what goes in Aramaic and Syriac sources as either Masbuthaeans or *Sobiai*, that is, Bathers or Immersers. It is also probably interchangeable with what the Fifth-Century heresiologist Epiphanius, somewhat mysteriously, calls 'Sampsaeans', which he thinks, because of a homophonic root in Hebrew meaning 'sun', has something to do with their worship of the sun.[32] Perhaps he is right, as many of these groups do seem to have prayed at dawn to greet the rising sun, but the term probably has more to do with consonantal confusions as expressions were transliterated from one language to another.

Though many of these writers think they are eponymous designations referring to a person – as Christianity does 'the Christ' – usually the founder, often they are conceptual describing some aspect of the tradition that seemed particularly significant to the commentator – as, for instance, the Elchasaites and their eponymous founder 'Elchasai'.[33] Notwithstanding, almost all really are but an adumbration probably of the same basic ideological orientation regardless of chronology or place. Therefore in these catalogues, the same group may at times be called Essene or at other times, Ebionite, Elchasaite, Sampsaean (basically the same as Elchasaite anyhow), Jewish Christian, Sabaean, or some other such appellation. What all the foregoing, anyhow, would have in common is an emphasis on *bathing*.

According to most of these early Church heresiologists, these groups mostly inhabited the area around the Dead Sea, particularly the Eastern side of the Jordan in what was called Perea or the area around Damascus and north from it – referred to in the Damascus Document as 'the Land of Damascus' and, even possibly, in Matthew 4:15 as 'Galilee of the Gentiles' – on up to Northern Syria and beyond across the Euphrates to the Tigris (what more latterly is often referred to as 'the Fertile Crescent'). 'Perea', it should be observed, was the area on the other side of the Jordan where John the Baptist, particularly important in most of these traditions, is pictured as originally operating. Not only is this an area in which there are extremely attractive warm water springs, in fact it is well known that John was even executed there at the Maccabean/Herodian Fortress of Machaeros.[34]

Matthew 4:15's 'Galilee of the Gentiles' makes it clear it is based on Isaiah 8:23–9:1, where the *Galil* or 'Circle' being referred to as 'seeing a great light' (*Galil* meaning 'Circle' in

Hebrew) is quite explicitly designated as being 'beyond Jordan'. In this sense, the term really means 'the Region' or 'Circle of the Gentiles' beyond the Jordan River – normally referred to as 'the Fertile Crescent' – not the Galilee in Northern Israel as the Gospels take it to be. These are the same areas in which one encounters a bewildering plethora of petty kings – 'the Kings of the Peoples' as Roman sources designate them.[35]

We have already seen that this expression, 'the Kings of the Peoples', is also used in a key portion of the Damascus Document where 'the Kings' of the Ruling Establishment referred to are also alluded to as 'the Princes of Judah' and their offences, such as fornication, incest, pollution of the Temple, and illegally amassing Riches, are vividly delineated.[36] This also provides a good dating tool if such were needed and a further indication that the *Sitz-im-Leben* of documents making references such as this was Roman – in particular Imperial Roman – and not Seleucid or Hellenistic. In fact, all such petty, Greek-speaking, tax-farming Kings in the Eastern areas of the Empire should probably be included in this category as this was how they were referred to in Roman jurisprudence – 'the Peoples' being the subject Peoples in Asia Minor, Northern Syria and Mesopotamia, and even Palestine.

In this regard, the allusion to tax-farming is particularly appropriate since this is an issue having singular resonance with Gospel portrayals of people involved in such activities, especially in the picture of those called 'publicans' or 'tax-collectors' interacting with or 'keeping table fellowship' with Jesus or 'the Messiah'. It should be appreciated that a picture such as this also had political or theological implications as, of course, did the charged reference to 'prostitutes' usually accompanying it – the point being that one should not object to or disapprove of such persons, but rather conciliate them or accommodate them.

The Descendants of Queen Helen of Adiabene

The same Rulers can also sometimes be found referred to in Roman sources as 'Arabs'.[37] Not only must the Herodian family in Palestine, which also gained footholds as model Roman bureaucrats in Lebanon, Syria, and Asia Minor in this period, be reckoned among such 'Arabs', but so should Kings like the First-Century Northern Syrian Monarch Eusebius calls 'Agbarus' or 'Abgarus' – in variant manuscripts even 'Albarus' or 'Augurus' – 'the Great King of the Peoples beyond the Euphrates'.[38] It is to Constantine's Bishop Eusebius, formerly Bishop of Caesarea in Palestine and responsible for some of the most far-reaching innovations concerning the Christianity ultimately adopted into the Roman Empire, that we owe this latter title – the use of the term 'Peoples' in it being both revealing and giving it an aura of credibility.[39]

Terminologies such as 'Kings of the Peoples' and 'Arab' should also probably extend to families like the one Josephus, the Talmud, and Eusebius himself refer to as 'the Royal House of Adiabene' on the borders of this 'Abgar' or 'Agbar''s Kingdom 'beyond the Euphrates' – basically today's Kurdistan. Neighboring the Parthian or Persian Empire further East, it is an area which would include the now familiar cities of Mosul, Arbil, and Kirkuk. Nor is it really clear whether these two dynasties, the Edessene and that of Adiabene, contiguous as they were can be distinguished in any real way from one another. Some Armenian and Syriac sources suggest they cannot.[40] Whether they can or not, all had strong political and marital connections with each other.

Eusebius claims to have personally found and translated the account of Agbarus' conversion to what he considers to be 'Christianity' from a document in the Royal Archive at Edessa. For Strabo and Pliny this is originally 'Antioch Orrhoe' (meaning 'Assyrian Antioch') or 'Antioch-by-Callirhoe' (a tributary of the Euphrates) as opposed to 'Antioch-on-the-Orontes' further West (the former capital of the Seleucid Kingdom and the Antioch everyone thinks they are talking about when speaking of Antioch) or 'Antioch in Pisidia' in Asia Minor

(Acts 13:14). Eusebius dates Agbarus' conversion to 29 CE, extremely early by any reckoning and about the same time, not incuriously, that Josephus provides the parallel story of the conversion of Queen Helen of Adiabene and her family (presumably including her husband).[41] The story is to be found at the beginning of the all-important Book Twenty of the *Antiquities*, climaxing with the account of the death of James in 62 CE and ending with an enumeration of all the High Priests in the Temple up to the time of its destruction.

The "Ad'/'*Ed*' in 'Adiabene' and 'Edessa' links up with the eponymous teacher in these areas variously referred to in Apocryphal, Syriac, and Arabic sources as "Ad', "Adi', 'Addai', and even 'Thaddaeus', not to mention another name having a certain phonetic equivalence to this last, 'Judas Thomas'.[42] Some Armenian sources, based probably on earlier Syriac ones, actually consider Queen Helen both King Agbar's wife and half-sister.[43] All these monarchs had multiple wives and large numbers of concubines and sister and half-sister marriage was, seemingly, one of the characteristic practices of the area, just as it appears to have been in the biblical story of Abraham and Sarah – also pictured as originating in Northern Syria/Iraq.

In fact, if one takes the chapter headings in Eusebius' narrative seriously, whether late additions or otherwise, the implication is that 'Agbarus' or 'Abgarus, the King of the Osrhoeans' ('the Assyrians') and 'the Great King of the Peoples beyond the Euphrates' (Adiabene being precisely one of those areas 'beyond the Euphrates') and Helen, designated in such headings as 'the Queen of the Osrhoeans', are linked by marriage as well. In addition, Eusebius identifies Agbar as 'Abgar *Uchama*' or 'Abgar the Black' – in Syriac sources seemingly Abgar III who died around 45–50 CE.[44]

Even this designation, however recondite, has real bearing on the parallels – even, in fact, the parodies – of these 29–30 CE timeframe conversions in the peculiar stories Acts provides: the first of these, as already signaled, being Paul's conversion in Acts 9:9–20 at Damascus 'on a Street called the Straight' – tellingly, 'neither eating or drinking' – at 'the house of one Judas'. It is here Paul is pictured as meeting 'a certain Disciple by the name of *Ananias*', as we saw, also prominent in Eusebius' story of the conversion of King Abgar as well as Josephus' description of the conversion of Queen Helen and her sons.[45]

The second of these stories is the one Acts 8:26–40 provides of the conversion of the 'Ethiopian Queen's eunuch' on the road to Gaza. As I have already argued, there was no 'Ethiopian Queen' at this time except in the annals of Strabo's *Geography* some seventy-five years before. There she is designated rather as the Nubian 'Queen of Meroe' up the Nile in today's Sudan or Nubia. This is a notice, not only picked up by Pliny in his *Natural History* in the 70s of the Common Era, but undoubtedly also the source of Acts' somewhat misleading co-option of the appellative 'Kandakes' to describe her.[46] Nor would or did such a 'Queen' send her 'Treasury Agents' some thousand miles north up to Jerusalem laden with coin, as Acts 8:27 would have it, and certainly not in approximately 25 BCE.

Not only would such a trip have been impossible for anyone from Nubia carrying such 'treasure' – to say nothing of Ethiopia – but there is no record that the principal court officials of such Queens (or for that matter Kings) were eunuchs, there being no harems there to protect. This was rather a custom of states dominated culturally by and on the border of Persia, such as Helen's or her husband's where there *actually were eunuchs*. In fact, it was Queen Helen, probably part of a huge harem of her putative brother and greater King who did, in fact, send her treasury agents to Jerusalem.

This is the picture one gets in Josephus, the Talmud, and Eusebius dependent upon them, all of whom make it clear that from there (either Palestine or Jerusalem), she and her sons Izates and Monobazus – both of whom circumcised themselves![47] – sent these agents down to Egypt and out to Cyprus to buy grain to relieve 'the Great Famine' that, as Acts paraphrasing Josephus puts it, 'was then over the whole world' (11:28). It is because of these famine relief efforts that in all these sources (including later Armenian ones) Helen and/or her sons win undying fame. It is also possible to conclude that it is for this reason Acts 8:26–27 refers to this Queen's agent as being 'on the road to Gaza', the traditional gateway to Egypt.[48]

Acts 11:27–30, of course, puts Paul among those who brought famine relief up from Antioch to Jerusalem. Philip, too, in 8:26 received his command to 'go down from Jerusalem to Gaza' from a mysterious Angel of some kind – upon which way he then encounters this curious eunuch of the Ethiopian Queen – in response to a mysterious oracle by an unknown prophet pointedly named 'Agabus' – an obvious garbling, as we shall argue below, of Agbarus/Abgarus, clearly indicating the source from which Acts lifted the narrative. For his part, Paul never mentions such a visit in his version of these events in Galatians 1:17–20 and denies, on pain of an oath that he was 'not lying', that he had ever been to Jerusalem in the 'fourteen years' since the visit when he saw 'none save Peter' and 'James the brother of the Lord' and his return – again 'as a result of a revelation' – taking Barnabas and Titus with him, to lay before 'those considered something' the gospel as he proclaimed it 'among the Peoples' (2:1–2 – as usual, the pivotal reference to 'Peoples').[49]

Acts 12:1–24 not only conspicuously fails to delineate this 'famine relief' mission 'to the brothers dwelling in Judea' except, curiously, to announce its conclusion in 12:25 and somewhat backhandedly allude to James in 12:17, but it is doubled by another trip Paul and Barnabas make 'up to Jerusalem' which Acts describes in some detail, starting in 15:1–2 when introducing the storied 'Jerusalem Council'. Of course, if Paul and Barnabas did actually make such a trip, as Acts seems to think they did, with 'famine relief funds' from 'the Disciples' in Antioch up to the 'the Elders' in Jerusalem, this would probably, in effect, put both him and Barnabas among the representatives of either Queen Helen, her husband, and/or her sons Izates and Monobazus, at the conversion of whom Josephus has already placed (along, curiously, with *an unnamed other*) a namesake of Paul's companion in Damascus, 'Ananias'.[50]

It should also be appreciated that, first of all, the trip by Paul and Barnabas up 'to the Elders in Jerusalem' described in Acts 15:2 is begun, not as in Acts 11:27 by Agabus 'coming down from Jerusalem to Antioch' but by '*some* coming down from Judea' and 'teaching the brothers that unless you were circumcised according to the tradition of Moses, you could not be saved' (15:1). Second of all, it is in fact rather the conversion of Helen's favorite son Izates – according to later Syriac sources, 'King Ezad'[51] – and his brother Monobazus who, after reading the passage about Abraham circumcising all his household in Genesis 17:9–14, insist on *being circumcised* as opposed to Ananias and his unnamed companion's teaching.

This would also appear to be the butt of Acts' somewhat disingenuous and even rather malicious description of its Queen's 'treasury agent' as a *eunuch*. Nor is this to mention the perceived relative 'blackness' of these Northern Syrian, Mesopotamian Kings or Queens – possibly reflected in Agbarus' cognomen in Eusebius as *Uchama* – meaning Black – and the perception, in Roman texts of all of them anyhow as 'Arabs'!

Elchasaite Bathing Groups and the *Subba‘* of the Marshes

One of the groups which seems to have flourished in both Palestine, and across Jordan, and further East in these times were the 'Elchasaites'. Though the sources regarding them are unclear, they first come to the fore about 100 CE, and are considered to have taken their name from their leader, one *Elchasai*. The precise meaning of this term, probably a title, is debated. Some, preferring to consider its Aramaic root, define it as 'Hidden Power'; others, 'the Righteous' or 'Perfect One'.[52] If the latter, then the connection in this period with James-type leaders or other *Zaddikim* ('Righteous Ones') is patent.

If *Elchasai* is a title, it is not very different from the usage 'Righteous Teacher' at Qumran or one of his ideological descendants. This is the problem with many such denotations.

Names like either '*Bazeus*' or '*Monobazus*' – the most prominent name among Helen's relatives and descendants – could well have been equivalent to what goes in more Semitic renderings as '*Agbarus*' or '*Abgarus*'.

However this may be, the leader of these Elchasaites in Palestine – if they existed in any separate way and were not simply local variations of groups like the Essenes or Ebionites – would certainly have been a contemporary of James' 'cousin' – as already suggested, possibly his putative brother – Simeon Bar Cleophas, who reigned over what was left of James' Jerusalem Assembly and, according to reports in early Church literature (themselves difficult to credit where chronology is concerned), survived into and was crucified under Trajan's reign![53]

Nor is this to say anything about another putative contemporary of this Elchasai and Simeon, 'Simeon bar Yohai', the eponymous founder of *Zohar* tradition.[54] Epiphanius together with Hippolytus, our main sources for this bewildering plethora of sectarian and bathing groups, relates 'the Elchasaites' to both 'Nasaraeans' (or 'Nazoraeans') and 'Ebionites'.[55] Nor does Epiphanius distinguish to any extent between these last, that is, 'Nazoraeans' and 'Ebionites'. For him Elchasai was originally an *Ossaean* (clearly he means 'Essene' here) with followers on both sides of the Dead Sea and further north in Syria and Northern Iraq. These latter areas, in turn, are where the conversions of King Abgar/Agbar and Queen Helen's family occurred – whether to Christianity or Judaism, or something in between.[56]

These Elchasaites also seem to have spread down into Southern Iraq. In the Koran and later Arab sources they are referred to as 'Sabaeans', a term itself going back to Greco-Aramaic and Syriac usages like *Sobiai* and 'Masbuthaeans', that is, Immersers or Daily Bathers. Again, this was the same area where Queen Helen's favorite son Izates was living at Charax Spasini (today's Basrah). Curiously this town, which was a trading center at the mouth of the Tigris, was another of those cities known as *Antioch* – this time, 'Antiochia Charax', the fourth we have so noted.

It is here this highly favored son of Queen Helen (strikingly, Josephus uses the term 'only begotten' that the Synoptic Gospels use to describe Jesus[57]) was living when he was converted in the Twenties of the Common Era to something Josephus presents as approximating 'Judaism'. In his version of this episode, Izates was converted by the Jewish teacher Ananias.[58] We say 'approximating' here, because what Ananias and his unnamed companion taught (whom, given the circumstances and teaching involved, we take to be Paul) did not require circumcision – a strange sort of Judaism!

Ananias, whom Josephus refers to as a merchant, also appears in parallel texts like the one Eusebius claims he found in the Royal Archive of the Edessa describing Agbarus' conversion to what Eusebius thinks is Christianity, though the date is only 29–30 CE or thereabouts. And as already remarked, he also appears in Acts' presentation of the aftermath of Paul's conversion at a house of one 'Judas' on 'a street called the Straight' in Damascus.[59]

Just as in Scroll delineations of its 'New Covenant in the Land of Damascus', Acts also considers the conversion of the character it most cares about to have taken place 'on the road to (or 'in the Land of ') Damascus', which might have wider implications, as we shall eventually see, than the first-time reader might initially imagine.[60] One consequence of this correspondence is that the 'Covenant' in the first might simply be reversing the other, that is, unlike the more 'Paulinizing' one in Acts, Qumran's 'New Covenant in the Land of Damascus' rather insisted on 'separating Holy from profane' as well as 'setting up the Holy Things according to their precise specifications'.[61]

Not only did Mani (216–277 CE), the founder of Manichaeism, reportedly come from an Elchasaite family living in the same general locale in Southern Iraq as Izates when he was converted – a place the sources refer to as 'Mesene',[62] but the Mandaeans, who represent themselves as the followers of John the Baptist and are in all things absolutely indistinguishable from these same Elchasaites, inhabit Southern Iraq down to this very day.[63] They have been referred to in Arab texts for over a thousand years as 'Sabaeans' – again, Arabic for 'Baptizers' or 'Daily Immersers' (not persons from Southern Arabia as normative Islam usually considers the term to mean) and, in popular parlance, used by Arabs then and still today, 'the *Subba*' of the Marshes'. These Mandaeans also refer to their priest class as '*Nasuraiya*', that is, 'Nazoraeans' (compare this with the town of *Naziriyya* fought over by US forces in the war in Iraq).

This is the area that in later times ultimately becomes a hotbed of Shi'ite Islam as it clearly still is today. The key seems to have been 'the Primal Adam' ideology associated, according to all commentators, with groups like the Ebionites and Elchasaites. It, in turn, was transformed into what became the *Imam* or Hidden *Imam* idea so integral to Shi'ite though not Sunni Islam.[64] The Hidden *Imam* idea is basically a variation of this 'Primal Adam' or 'Standing One' notation fundamental, according to the Pseudoclementines, Hippolytus, and Epiphanius, to groups like the Ebionites, Elchasaites, Jewish Christians, and, even before these, Simon Magus.[65]

The idea would also appear to be present in one form or another in Qumran documents and echoes of it are identifiable across the breadth of New Testament literature – though not perhaps to the uninitiated reader – in the never-ending allusions to 'standing' one encounters in it.[66] Like the Elchasaites preceding them, the Manichaeans were precursors of Islam and, for the most part – in this part of the world anyhow, probably absorbed into it. Indeed, Muhammad has many doctrines in common with the traditions represented by both groups, in particular, the idea of the 'True Prophet' or the 'Seal of the Prophets' and the importance of Abraham in the salvationary scheme he is delineating.[67]

The Land of Noah and Abraham's Religion

The connection to Abraham of traditions relating to religious ideas arising in these areas should not be underestimated. It is important to realize that Edessa, the capital of Eusebius' 'Great King of the Peoples beyond the Euphrates', is basically the sister city of Haran some thirty miles south. Haran is well known in the Bible as Abraham's place of origin before he received the call to depart for the Land of Israel (Genesis 11:28–32), a fact its inhabitants are not slow to advertise to this day. Nor were they in ancient times as Abraham's fame grew more and more legendary.

Not only do shrines and legends connecting Abraham with sites in this area persist to this day, Paul and Muhammad – whose respective salvationary schemes, while not always distinguishable from one another, pivot on the spiritual status of Abraham – both emphasize their common connection to 'the Faith' or 'Religion of Abraham'.[68] So does the ideologically opposite and, in this sense, parallel salvationary scheme set forth in the Letter of James and, if one looks carefully, one can detect the same ideological focus on Abraham across the breadth of the Qumran corpus.[69]

Paul makes his allusion to Christianity being 'Abraham's Religion' in Galatians 3:6–4:31 and Romans 4:1–22 and 9:7–9, even going so far as to claim that Christians were the true 'Heirs to' or 'Children of the Promise' and 'were justified' in the way 'Abraham was justified' – his famous 'Justification by Faith' polemic.[70]

In James however, Abraham 'is justified by works', his 'Faith' rather 'Perfected' or 'made Perfect' – according to some translations 'completed' – by 'works'. This then fulfills the biblical passage about Abraham's 'Belief', that he 'believed God and it was counted' or 'reckoned to him as Righteousness'. It is as a result of this that, according to James 2:22–23, 'he was called Friend of God', all terminologies well-known to the Dead Sea Scrolls.[71] This position, of course, is the opposite of that of the stated opponent of James – 'the Empty' or 'Foolish Man' (2:20) – that Abraham was saved 'by Faith only' and thought by most to reflect the position that can be identified with Paul in Galatians 2:16–3:7 above.[72]

For Muhammad, Islam is 'Abraham's Religion' (for Paul, the term is 'Abraham's Faith'). But as in the Dead Sea Scrolls and the Letter of James, Muhammad goes even further designating Abraham as 'the Friend of God' – the epithet for him ever after in Islam to this day to the extent that *al-Khalil* ('the Friend') is used in place of Abraham's very name itself.[73] The difference between Muhammad's arguments, as they develop in the Koran, and Paul's, however, is that for Paul, Abraham's 'Faith' (using the language of Genesis 15:6) 'was reckoned to him as Righteousness' before the revelation of the *Torah* to Moses and, therefore, Abraham – as he puts it so inimitably – could not have been 'justified by the Law'. For Muhammad, following Paul's ploy, it was rather 'Abraham's Religion' that came before both Judaism and Christianity or, as he so inimitably puts it in the Koran, before either Judaism or Christianity could corrupt 'the Religion of Abraham' with their 'lies' (2:145–56).

If these arguments were directed to the inhabitants of Northern Syria (as to some extent, in the writer's view, they are in the Dead Sea Scrolls as well), then the evocation of Abraham's salvationary status is perhaps neither accidental nor very surprising, particularly where those seeing themselves as inhabiting 'Abraham's homeland' were concerned.

MMT actually uses the language of 'works reckoned as Righteousness' (only really to be found elsewhere in the Letter of James) in addressing the King it compares to David, who would appear to be its respondent; and 'his People', that is, as we shall see, seemingly a foreign People.[74] By implication, this compares the salvationary state of this King with Abraham's salvationary state, providing further evidence that this King is probably a foreigner and linking him to the individual Eusebius is calling 'the Great King of the Peoples beyond the Euphrates' and, even perhaps, Queen Helen's son Izates – if the two, in fact, can be differentiated in any real way.[75]

In the same vein, Muhammad's subsequent ideological reliance on Abraham – prefigured, as it were, by Paul – is not so surprising either. Certainly Paul visited this area. But, in our view, so did Muhammad. Plainly he was heir to the traditions, however garbled, stemming from these lands as suggested by the striking references he provides to them in the Koran.[76] If Muhammad participated in the caravan trade, as the *Biographies of the Prophet* insist, then surely he visited the trading center Charax Spasini (modern Basrah) at the Southern end of the Tigris. It is here, in our view, he would have become familiar with the kinds of ideologies and new salvationary schemes we have been delineating above.

Nor are such foci surprising in a text like the Damascus Document which, as its name implies, focuses on 'the New Covenant in the Land of Damascus', in particular, the region 'north of Damascus' where for it, at some point, 'the fallen tent of David' was going to be re-erected.[77] As we shall see, Acts 15:16 puts the same words about 're-erecting the fallen tent of David' into James' mouth in its portrait of his speech at the Jerusalem Council, another incontrovertible parallel between Acts' portrait of events it considers central to the development of the early Church and Qumran's picture of its own history.[78] The position of this book will be that, not only are all these allusions parallel, but they argue for a parallel chronological provenance for documents in which they are to be found. In addition, they are directed towards conversion activities in areas where Abraham's name and his salvationary state were looked upon with more than a passing reverence.

Not surprisingly, too, when James does send his messengers Silas and Judas Barsabas 'down from Jerusalem' to this region in Acts 15:22–35, it is to *Antioch* they direct their steps – the only question being, as we have suggested, *which Antioch was intended*. Was it the one assumed in normative Christian tradition and by all commentators (though never proven) Antioch-on-the-Orontes, where nothing of consequence appears to have been happening in this period, or the more historically significant 'Antioch-by-Callirhoe' or 'Antiochia Orrhoe', also known as Edessa and all but indistinguishable from Abraham's city Haran, where all these incredible conversions were going on and Abraham's name was held in such regard? As far as I can see, the answer should be obvious – the second.

Izates' Conversion and Circumcision

The connection of so many of these traditions and ideologies with Abraham is not simply fanciful as the theme, whether in the Koran, earlier Christian writings, Josephus, the Talmud, and even in the Dead Sea Scrolls, is too persistent to be ignored. Not only do the people of Urfa connect the spring at Callirhoe (from which 'Antiochia-by-Callirhoe' or 'Edessa Orrhoe' derives its name) to Abraham to this day, but he was said to have been born in one of the caves in its environs as well.[79] Like the legends connected to both the births of John the Baptist and Jesus in Luke's Infancy Narrative and the *Protevangelium of James*, Abraham too, according to these 'apocryphal' traditions, was said to have been 'hidden' by his mother there.[80]

For Josephus, this is the Kingdom near Haran which was originally given to Helen's favorite son Izates by his father (whom Josephus calls '*Bazeus*' – whatever or whomever is intended by this).[81] Josephus calls this area, which *Bazeus* (evidently defective) gave Izates, 'Carrae', thus tightening even further the connection between Eusebius' 'Great King of the Peoples beyond the Euphrates' and the Royal House of Adiabene. If this was Carrhae just south of Edessa – namely, the place of Abraham's origin Haran – then, of course, we are once again in the framework of Abraham's homeland and heritage – all the more reason why Izates should take Abraham for his role model.

The etymological development from Haran to present day Urfa, the name by which Edessa goes in Turkey to this day, is also not completely irrelevant, going from *Haran* to *Hirru* to *Orhai* to *Orrhoe* to *Osrhoe* – the Kingdom over which 'Agbarus' reigned according to Eusebius – and finally to *Ruha* in Arabic, from which the present day Turkish *Urfa* is derived.

In the story of Izates' conversion, the portrayal of Abraham as the role model for Izates' ultimate decision to have himself circumcised, as opposed to Paul's position on this issue and the position of Izates' original teacher Ananias, is pivotal as well. As we saw, Ananias is also a principal player in Acts' picture of parallel events – 'Damascus' there corresponding to the picture in the Scrolls, taking the place of wherever it was in Northern Syria or Iraq that Helen's family was living at the time of her conversion. The story, as already remarked, is also to be found in the Talmud's presentation of these events and, in my view, by refraction in the New Testament's picture of the conversion of the Ethiopian Queen's eunuch as well.[82]

In the Talmud and Josephus, which both focus on the same event, Izates is reading the passage about Abraham circumcising his whole household – in Genesis 17:12 supposed to include even the 'stranger dwelling among them' (conversely, in Acts 8:32–33 the Ethiopian Queen's eunuch is reading 'the Suffering Servant' passage from Isaiah 53:7–8) when the more 'Zealot' teacher from Galilee, whom Josephus is referring to as 'Eleazar' ('Lazarus'? – in the parallel represented by Acts 8:30 this character becomes 'Philip'), convinces Izates and Monobazus his brother that they should circumcise themselves too. Whereupon, they immediately do so.[83]

For his part, the Queen's eunuch – 'on his chariot' – who is reading the Suffering Servant passage from Isaiah when a teacher named 'Philip' calls him to be baptized, immediately orders his chariot to stop, whereupon both Philip and the eunuch went down into the water, and Philip baptized him. In our view, what we essentially have here is a Gentile Christian *parody* of Izates' conversion replete with a sarcastic characterization of circumcision as castration which would have had particular meaning for Roman audiences especially after Nerva's time (96–98 CE), and all the more so, after Hadrian's (117–138 CE).[84]

Per contra, using Abraham as their prototype, both Josephus and the Talmud emphasize the 'circumcision' aspect of the conversion process despite the fact that at least Josephus portrays Queen Helen, the mother of Izates and Monobazus, as 'having horror of circumcision' because it would put her in ill repute with her people. Despite her conversion, allegedly to Judaism, circumcision as such was evidently not part of the religion she was taught by Ananias and his unnamed companion.[85] Consequently, not only is this the pivotal point in the controversy between Ananias and Eleazar over Izates' conversion, but it is also the background against which Paul develops his whole polemic in Galatians, in particular, the dispute at Antioch in Galatians 2:7–12 where Paul calls the 'some from James', of whom Peter 'was afraid' and, after whose coming, 'separated himself and withdrew' from 'eating with the Gentiles' (*Ethnon*), 'of the Circumcision' or 'the Party of the Circumcision'.

Therefore, just as the Philip/Ethiopian Queen's eunuch conversion episode is a Gentile Christian parody of the Izates/Monobazus one, this whole tangle of data is echoed in Acts 15:1–3's seemingly parallel portrayal of basically the same situation in its run-up to the so-called 'Jerusalem Council', when these ubiquitous 'some' – already referred to several times earlier in Acts (these same 'some' even appear in the Gospels) – 'come down from Judea' to Antioch and 'teach the brothers that *unless you were circumcised*, you could not be saved'.

Nor is it inconsequential that Abraham's paradigmatic support for circumcision is also cited by the Damascus Document at Qumran.[86] This occurs in the Damascus Document after evoking Deuteronomy 23:24 and 27:26, emphasizing the necessity of 'keeping the Commandments of the *Torah*' and 'not to depart from the Law' even at 'the price of death'[87] and is put as follows: 'And on the day upon which the man swears upon his soul (or 'on pain of death') to return to the *Torah* of Moses, the Angel of *Mastema* (meaning here 'Divine Vengeance')[88] will turn aside from pursuing him provided that he fulfills his word. It is for this reason Abraham circumcised himself on the very day of his being informed (of these things).'[89] Just as in the case with Izates' and Monobazus' conversion, the reference is to Genesis 17:9–27 and Abraham's obligation therein set forth, to 'circumcise the flesh of his foreskin' and that of all those in his household – this last being an important addendum – which, the biblical passage adds, he accomplished 'on *that very day*' although he was ninety-nine years old.

But, of course, not only is this exactly what Column Sixteen of the Damascus Document above specifies, but it is exactly what Izates and Monobazus do when 'Eleazar from Galilee' points this out in the text they are reading. Just as in Acts 8:38's depiction of the Ethiopian Queen's eunuch immediately jumping down from his chariot, the emphasis is on the instantaneousness of the response.

Not only does the Damascus Document – like the Letter of James and the Koran following it – designate Abraham as 'a Friend of God', it does so in the same breath that it describes Abraham as 'a Keeper of the Commandments of God'. This last is also, as we shall see, basically the esoteric definition of 'the Sons of Zadok' (possibly too 'the Sons of Righteousness' or 'of the Righteous One') in the Community Rule at Qumran.[90] In fact, in the Koran, just as in James 2:21–23, the parallel is to the new terminology in Arabic '*Muslim*' or 'one who has surrendered' to God's will. Of course, being 'a Keeper not a Breaker' is repeatedly emphasized throughout the Dead Sea Scrolls and is a fundamental ideology of James 2:8–12 as well, particularly in the background to its statement of both 'the Royal Law according to the Scripture' to 'love your neighbor as yourself' and 'keeping the whole Law, but stumbling on one small point' bringing upon one the 'guilt of (breaking) it all'.

To bring us full circle: one could conclude, therefore, that being 'a Keeper', 'a Friend of God', and even 'a *Muslim*' are basically all parallel denotations and that, in all contexts,

Abraham is so designated because he responds positively to God's 'testing' and is prepared to carry out God's Commandments. In James 2:21 and in Hebrews 11:17, in particular, this 'surrendering to God's will', as it is put in the Koran, is deemed a kind of 'test'. It is also worth remarking and certainly not insignificant that in Hebrews the term 'only begotten' is applied to Isaac just as in Josephus it is to 'Izates' and in the Synoptic Gospels to Jesus.[91]

View of the Qumran marl, mainly consisting of Cave 4 - where the lion's share of the Scrolls were found - but also 5-6, with the settlement across the Wadi and Dead Sea in the background - the attempts by the surveyors to find 'hidden pockets' in the rock-solid marls also clearly visible.

The Burial Monument or Enclosure (referred by some as '*the Mausoleum of the Righteous Teacher*') at the Head of the Cemetery at Quman, with the Dead Sea and Jordan in the background - in the author's view, possibly referred to in the Pseudoclementine *Recognitions*.

The excavated view of 'the Mausoleum', discovered by two CSULB students in 2002 — not only showing its splendid location overlooking the Dead Sea and Jordan to the East, but being at the 'top' or 'head' of the whole graveyard to the West (where the burials were all north to south), while its one or two special burials were, as shown, east to west.

Chapter 2
Peter as a Daily Bather and the 'Secret Adam' Tradition

Sabaeans, Masbuthaeans, and the *Subba'* of the Marshes

To go back to Elchasai, Hippolytus tells us that he was supposed to have 'preached unto men a new remission of sins in the second year of Hadrian's reign' (119 CE). In addition he calls him 'a certain Just Man', meaning Elchasai too was a *Righteous One* – again, the manner of how all early Church sources refer to James and the Dead Sea Scrolls refer to the Teacher of Righteousness/Righteous Teacher.[1] Hippolytus reports as well that Elchasai insisted (like the 'some from James' above) that 'believers ought to be circumcised and live according to the Law'.[2]

Importantly, in Arabic 'Elchasai' can mean 'Hidden'. We have already touched upon how the 'Hidden' terminology can relate to stories about the birth of John the Baptist and Jesus in the Infancy Narrative of Luke and the *Protevangelium of James*, to say nothing about Edessan stories about Abraham. Nor is this to mention the whole tradition of 'the Hidden *Imam*' in Shi'ite Islam. In Jewish mystical traditions as incorporated in the *Zohar*, a parallel allusion occurs in the description of how Noah 'was hidden in the ark' to escape 'the Enemy' who wanted to kill him.[3] Though an odd story, to say the least, to be found in an allegedly 'medieval' document like the *Zohar*, it does bring us back, however circuitously, to how the ark was related by Hippolytus and Josephus to Queen Helen's and Izates' homeland and, not surprisingly, in the Koran to the story of the destruction of the Tribe of 'Ad and the messenger sent to it, Hud (that is 'Judas' – in Hebrew, *Yehudah*; in Arabic, *Yehud*).[4]

In Arabic too, the root of *Subba'*, a term related to those Hippolytus calls *Sobiai* whom he identifies with the Elchasaites,[5] is 'to plunge' or 'immerse', which is the same for Aramaic and Syriac. In fact, John the Baptist is actually known in Arabic as – and this not just by Mandaeans who take him as their paradigmatic teacher – *as-Sabi'*, meaning 'the Baptizer' or 'Immerser'.[6] This leads directly into the issue of what can be understood by those called 'Sabaeans' in the Koran,[7] who must be seen as basically the same group as the *Subba'* or Hippolytus' *Sobiai* (and, as we shall see, Epiphanius' 'Masbuthaeans') despite slight variations in spelling and later Islamic ideological attempts to obscure it.

As Muhammad uses the term in the Koran–often within the context of discussions about Abraham[8] – he does so to designate a group intermediate between Jews and Christians, about whom he appears to have personal knowledge. All three he describes as 'believing in *Allah* and the Last Day and doing good works' (2:62). The perspicacious reader will immediately recognize these as the exact parameters of the debate between Paul and James, particularly as set forth in the Letter of James with its insistence on 'Faith (that is, 'Belief') and works working together', while at the same time citing Abraham's willingness to sacrifice Isaac.[9]

Muhammad uses almost the precise words to describe one particular community among those he labels 'Peoples of the Book', with whom he seems particularly familiar and of whom, unusually fond. The people of this community, as he puts it, 'recite the revelations of *Allah* in the night season' – which is certainly paralleled by those Josephus is calling 'Essenes' and in the literature found at Qumran[10] – and: 'believe in *Allah* and the Last Day and enjoin Right conduct and forbid indecency, and vie with each other in good works, for they are of the Righteous (*Salihin*).[11] *Salihin* in Arabic is the same root as and the plural of that 'Salih', who with 'Hud' (a contraction of *Yehudah* – Judas as we have seen), is a messenger to 'Ad and a 'brother' to the Tribe Muhammad calls 'Thamud' – a corruption, in our view, of 'Thomas' or, if one prefers, 'Judas Thomas', the same 'Judas Thomas who taught the truth to the Edessenes' in early Christian literature previously.[12]

Essenes, Ebionites, and Peter as a Daily Bather

Epiphanius refers to Essenes not only as 'Ossaeans', but also 'Esseneans' or 'Jessaeans' – the last, he claims, after David's father and Jesus' forbear 'Jesse' or, for that matter, Jesus' very name itself.[13] However, he also seems to appreciate that 'Essene' can derive from the Hebrew root, 'to do', that is, 'Doers' (Hebrew, *Osim*) or the Doers/Doers of the *Torah* we shall meet in due course in the Dead Sea Scrolls and the thrust of the language of 'doing' or 'works' in all doctrines associated with James or ascribed to him. The Letter of James also actually uses 'Doers', meaning 'to do the Law', three different times.[14] In another important overlap, the same usage appears in the Habakkuk *Pesher*, surrounding the exposition of 'the Righteous shall live by his Faith' so dear to Pauline exposition.[15]

Whatever one might think of the validity of Epiphanius' derivations and though his 'Essenes' are hardly distinguishable from those he is also calling 'Ebionites'; as he sees it, before Christians were called 'Christians' in Antioch in Acts – that is, around the time of Paul's and Helen's Famine relief efforts in the mid-Forties – in Palestine they were known as 'Essenes' and, after that, 'Nazoraeans'.[16] From our perspective, this is about right with the reservation that Epiphanius and other early Christian writers have little or no idea what these denotations actually signified.

In fact, for the group called 'Galileans' among 'the Seven Sects of the Circumcision' comprising Judaism of this period according to Hegesippus (c. 150 CE) as conserved in Eusebius (c. 320 CE) – including 'Pharisees', 'Sadducees', 'Essenes', 'Samaritans', 'Baptists', etc. – Epiphanius substitutes the term 'Nazoraeans'.[17] In doing so, he provides testimony, however indirect, that the group most instinctively refer to as 'Zealots' were from their perspective all but indistinguishable from 'Nazoraeans', the same group most consider coextensive with 'Christians'. Once again, this brings home the point that the literature concerning these matters in this period is, depending on the perspective of the writer, filled with and confused by *many names for the same basic movement.*

Though these 'sects', as Eusebius and Epiphanius like to call them, also include another group both refer to as 'Hemerobaptists' or 'Daily Bathers', Eusebius – again dependent on Hegesippus – in effect, repeats himself by including in the same list yet another group he calls 'Masbuthaeans'. Once again, this terminology represents a Greek attempt to transliterate groups like Hippolytus' *Sobiai* and the Aramaic/Syriac term for 'wash'/'immersed', that is, 'Baptizers'. This not only moves into the Arabic *Subba'*, but also the same Arabic/Islamic 'Sabaeans', some incarnations of whom seem certainly to have been based in the neighborhood of Abraham's Haran in Northern Syria.

Epiphanius for his part multiplies these basically parallel or synonymous groups by introducing others in the course of his narrative like 'the Sampsaeans', yet another attempt to approximate the Arabic/Syriac 'Sabaeans' in Greek. In this context, one should appreciate the epigraphical mix-ups between 'P' and 'B' in Arabic (there being no 'P' as such in Arabic) and juxtapositions of letters that occur when names move from one language to another, as for example 'Abgarus' to 'Agbarus' from Semitic to Western languages. Once more we have come full circle, because Epiphanius not only locates these 'Sampsaeans' around the Dead Sea and further east across the Jordan and in Northern Iraq, but proceeds to observe that they are not to be distinguished from 'the Elchasaites', which should have been obvious in the first place.[18]

What Epiphanius, who actually was someone of Jewish Christian or 'Ebionite' background from Palestine – though he later removed to mainland Greece – has apparently done is confuse the terms 'Sabaeans', *'Sobiai'*, or 'Masbuthaeans' reflecting more Semitic usage, with the linguistic approximation in Greek 'Sampsaean'. Nor does he, yet again, distinguish their doctrines to any extent from the 'Nasarenes' or 'Nazoraeans', whom he definitely identifies as doctrinally following James, and chronologically, following 'the Ebionites' whom we know followed James.[19]

Since all such 'Essene' or 'Sabaean' groups were 'Daily Bathers' of one kind or another, it would appear that James was one as well.[20] This is also the way Peter is portrayed both in the Pseudoclementines and by Epiphanius, the one probably dependent on the other.[21] So was James' contemporary, the teacher Josephus cryptically denotes as '*Banus*', the transliteration of whose name has not yet been solved (though via the Latin, it probably points to his 'bathing' activities), and with whom Josephus seems to have spent a quasi-Essene-style novitiate 'in the wilderness' – the reason probably he knows so much about Essenes. Nor is it without relevance, when considering these things, that in the Pseudoclementines as well, Peter is also portrayed as a definitive 'Jamesian'.[22]

For the *Subba* of Southern Iraq, just as with so-called 'Essenes', these rituals included daily ablution and purification in addition to a more all-encompassing immersion. This immersion was known to them even then as '*Masbuta*' – from which clearly Eusebius via Hegesippus gets his 'Masbuthaeans' – and it included both the notion of washing away of sins and even a 'laying on of hands', the Priest interestingly enough laying one hand on his own head,[23] all notions except the last known to Christianity.[24]

Epiphanius includes the note about Peter being a Daily Bather in the context of his discussion of those he is calling 'Ebionites'—an honored term of self-designation in widespread use at Qumran.[25] Not only does he think that the terminology 'Ebionites', like that of the 'Elchasaites' above, relates to a teacher called '*Ebion*'—meaning that, as he sees it, 'Ebion' is a person not a concept; he also seems to think that, as the 'Elchasaite' teacher in Hippolytus, this 'Ebion' went to Rome.[26] He observes: 'They say that Peter was a Daily Bather even before he partook of the bread.'[27] That is, Peter is a complete 'Essene'.

Epiphanius combats this description in the most vituperative manner imaginable, insisting that it was because 'the Ebionites' were so 'lewd and filthy that they bathed so often'![28] His approach is reminiscent of how Eusebius characterizes the Ebionites. Coming from Caesarea in Palestine, Eusebius like Epiphanius also knew Hebrew. In an ideological reversal that should by this time be all too familiar, he insists in a derisive play on the Hebrew meaning of their name that they were called 'the Poor' because of 'their mean and poverty-stricken notions about the Christ', meaning that what today we would call their 'Christology' was 'poverty-stricken'! – an exposition even the beginning reader will recognize as both dissimulating and malevolent.

However, by contemptuously and sarcastically depicting Ebionites as seeing 'Christ' as merely a man, generated by natural not supernatural means, advanced above other men in the *practice of Righteousness* or virtue, and only 'a prophet', Eusebius inadvertently gives us insight into their *actual* doctrines. Where the matter of 'a Prophet' is concerned, one will be able to immediately discern the outlines of the 'True Prophet' ideology of the Ebionites, which is such a set-piece of the Pseudoclementine literature and reflections of which are also discernible in the Dead Sea Scrolls, in particular, the Community Rule, proceeding down through Elchasaism, Manichaeism, and ultimately into Islam.[29]

For the writer, the aspects of their conduct Epiphanius records, for the most part probably drawing on the Pseudoclementines, are rather the true parameters of Peter's existence – these, as opposed to childish episodes incorporating ideological reversal as, for instance, the descent of 'the table cloth' from Heaven 'by its four corners' in Acts 10:11, in which Peter learns not to make distinctions between Holy and profane and to call no food unclean (10:12–16 repeated in 11:8), the very opposite of communities such as at Qumran and groups like those following James like 'the Ebionites'.

Aside perhaps from the material in Galatians, which relates Peter to these same areas of Northern Syria where groups such as the Ebionites, Elchasaites, and Masbuthaeans appear to have been prevalent at this time (as to some extent they still are today), materials delineating Peter's pious Essene-like behavior – for instance, that he wore 'threadbare clothes' and, as among Essenes and at Qumran, he prayed every morning at dawn and bathed every day (this 'before partaking of bread' as Epiphanius conserves it above) – are perhaps the only properly historical materials about Peter we have. As an aside, it should perhaps also not go unremarked that, like Epiphanius' mysterious teacher 'Ebion' and Hippolytus' 'Elchasaite' teacher he thinks is called 'Sobiai', Peter too reportedly ended up going to Rome. Whether accurate in Peter's case – for which Acts provides no verification – it would certainly appear to be accurate in the case of Hippolytus' 'Elchasaite' teacher named 'Sobiai'.

One of the reasons for the kind of daily purification activity Epiphanius so derogatorily dismisses, known not only to the Pseudoclementines but also so characteristic of the 'sectaries' at Qumran – at least among those extreme Essenes Hippolytus insists on also calling either 'Zealot' or 'Sicarii'[30] – is that even casual contact with Gentiles was thought to be polluting in some manner. This, of course, immediately gives rise to issues like the 'table fellowship' one between the 'some from James' who 'came down to Antioch' and Paul in Galatians 2:11–14. In the 'Heavenly tablecloth' episode, even Peter is pictured as citing this excuse in Acts 10:14 when he is at the point of learning he 'should not call any man unclean nor any thing profane' and could eat forbidden foods.

Notwithstanding, it is just the opposition to allowing persons who either were not circumcised and did not keep the Law to discuss matters relating to it that were the key issues for those extreme Essenes whom Hippolytus insists were called either 'Zealots' or 'Sicarii', a picture in some ways more accurate and more incisive than the received Josephus.[31]

Not only did normative Essenes, according to the received portrait in Josephus, refuse to eat on pain of death 'forbidden things', but as Hippolytus refines this picture, what those he refers to as 'Zealot' or 'Sicarii Essenes' refused to eat were the Jamesian category of 'things sacrificed to idols' (Acts 15:29 and 21:25). No wonder Epiphanius is so enraged at the picture of Peter he finds in allegedly 'Ebionite' literature – but more about these things later. To repeat – his materials bring us back to the location of these groups in Northern Syria and Southern Iraq, the two areas Josephus focuses upon in his story of the conversion of Queen Helen, her two sons Monobazus and Izates, and possibly also her husband 'Bazeus' – if his identity could be precisified in any final way.

The Son of Joseph and 'the Taheb', 'Tabitha', and 'Tirathaba'

For the Mandaeans of Southern Iraq, John the Baptist was their teacher and one of their titles for him was 'as-Sabi' ibn Yusufus', 'the Baptizer the Son of Joseph'. Not only does the second part of this title echo similar ascriptions related to Jesus' parentage in Christian tradition, but a second 'Messiah', called 'the Messiah ben Joseph' – this as opposed to the Davidic Messiah/'the Messiah ben Judah' – was also considered to have been executed in Rabbinic tradition in the region of Lydda possibly even by crucifixion.[32]

Not only does this title – which the Gospels take as definitively genealogical even though Jesus was not supposed to have been Joseph's son – possibly imply an overlap with Samaritan Messianic pretensions, but the title, 'Son of Joseph', dovetails perfectly with Samaritan tradition, since the Samaritans generally considered themselves Sons of Joseph, that is, descendants of the Biblical Joseph. In the Dead Sea Scrolls, too, the curious additional parallel represented by the terminology 'Ephraim'/'the Simple of Ephraim' (in the Nahum *Pesher* grouped alongside 'the Simple of Judah doing *Torah*') should not be overlooked – 'Ephraim' being another biblical euphemism for 'Samaria'.[33]

The issue of what to make of this 'Son of Joseph' in Messianic tradition is fraught with difficulties. In the Talmud, as tenuous as its traditions sometimes are, there certainly is indication of a Messianic individual crucified in the Lydda region – an area contiguous to and on the periphery of Samaria.[34] There would appear to be some substance to the story as there certainly was a Messianic 'Restorer' or 'Redeemer' tradition in the adjacent area of Samaria at this time, alluded to in Josephus and denoted in Samaritan tradition, 'the *Taheb*'.[35]

This individual may or may not have been equivalent to the famous 'Simon Magus', known in the Pseudoclementine *Recognitions* and other early Church writings to have come from the Samaritan village of Gitta, whom we know was often supposed to be imitating Jesus.[36] In fact, according to these same *Recognitions* and/or *Homilies*, he and a colleague of his, Dositheus – both Disciples of John the Baptist – were principal originators of 'the Secret Adam'/'Primal Adam' ideology. Therefore, too, in some versions of Josephus, his alter ego and double in Caesarea – another Rasputin-like 'magician called Simon' in the employ of the Roman Governor Felix and the Herodian family[37] – is even referred to as 'Atomus', probably a Greco-Latin corruption of 'Adam' reflecting the principal doctrine associated with his person, 'the Primal Adam'.[38]

It should be remarked that Caesarea, the Roman administrative center in Palestine and the closest large seaport to Samaria, was also the locale of the initial confrontation between Peter and the 'Simon Magus' in the Pseudoclementine literature as well. Nor can there be any doubt that something of these matters is being reflected in Acts 8:4–25's portrayal of the confrontations between both 'Philip' and Peter with Simon Magus over Simon's Messianic ('Primal Adam'?) posturing 'in many villages of the Samaritans'. But in Acts, these confrontations occur in *Samaria*, not Caesarea – seemingly reflecting Simon Magus' place of origin – and 'Philip' only goes to Caesarea later, after his encounter with the Ethiopian Queen's eunuch. Furthermore, Acts 8:17–24 portrays the Simon Magus affair somewhat disingenuously, as having basically to do with buying the 'Power' imparted by 'laying on hands' for money. While the vocabulary is probably accurate, the import is misleading – probably purposefully. In addition, it is employing both the 'Great Power' vocabulary attributed to Simon Magus in the Pseudoclementines and of the Elchasaites *cum* Mandaeans and the 'laying on of hands', which becomes such an integral fixture of the practices of these same Mandaeans.[39]

In any event, the episode ends inconclusively enough with: 'and they (seemingly inclusive of Simon Magus) preached the Gospel in many villages of the Samaritans' (8:25). However this may be, 'Philip' then turns into the protagonist of the conversion of the Queen's eunuch before suddenly dematerializing – 'the Spirit of the Lord took Philip away so that the eunuch never saw him again' (8:39). 'Having been found at Azotus' – modern-day Tel Aviv – once again, he 'preached the Gospel in all the cities (inclusive probably of Lydda) until he came to Caesarea' (8:40), where he seems to have been going in the first place since he had there 'four virgin daughters who were prophetesses' (21:9)!

For his part Peter follows 'Philip' and he, too 'passes through all' (9:32 – whatever this means). Nevertheless he actually does 'go down to the Saints that lived at Lydda'. While there, however, what he is doing – in place presumably of the crucifixions occurring there in both Josephus and the Talmud – is rather curing 'a certain' paralytic with the name of Virgil's hero in *The Aeneid*, 'Aeneas', 'who had been lying in bed for eight years' (9:33; sometimes it really is hard to refrain from laughing). Because 'Lydda was nearby Jaffa', the Disciples, having heard Peter was there, invite him to come to Jaffa to raise 'a certain Disciple named *Tabitha*' – female because the form in Aramaic is feminine – 'which being interpreted means *Dorcas*' (now 'gazelle' in Greek!), who had 'become ill and died' (9:36–38). This is all supposed to be taken seriously.

But to go back to Simon's Samaritan origins, which Acts seems unaware of or, at least, never makes clear – we must rather wait for the Pseudoclementines and Churchmen like Clement of Alexandria, Irenaeus, and Eusebius to clarify these.[40] In the Pseudoclementines,

Peter becomes the hero of a whole string of confrontations with Simon Magus north to Lebanon and Syria, but beginning with this one in Caesarea.[41] For its part, Acts 8:10 in the midst of what for it is a first confrontation in Samaria even describes Simon – like 'Elchasai' – as 'the Power of God which is Great'. However this may be, its emphasis throughout this whole fantastic and certainly unhistorical episode (if it is historical, it has been tampered with) on 'Power' and 'laying on of hands' – both cornerstones of 'Mandaean' tradition – is nothing less than startling.[42]

Nor can there be any doubt as well that the New Testament is inordinately sympathetic to individuals of a 'Samaritan' background as opposed to a 'Judean' or 'Jewish' one. Over and over again in the works of early Church heresiologists we hear about individuals from a Samaritan cultural milieu being the recipients of John the Baptist's teaching and its offshoots – the implication of the curious Mandaean notation for John the Baptist of 'as-Sabi' ibn Yusufus' in the first place.[43] In the Pseudoclementine *Recognitions*, for instance, both Simon Magus and an individual named 'Dositheus' – both also later portrayed as heads of 'sects' of their own just as 'Ebion', the Ebionites, and 'Elchasai', the Elchasaites – are portrayed, as we saw, as Samaritan Disciples of John the Baptist.[44]

Dositheus, also seemingly referred to in Josephus as 'Doetus' or 'Dortus' (and the head supposedly – according to the heresiologists – of his own sect 'the Dositheans'[45]) is evidently one of those crucified in the disturbances between Samaritans and Jews at Lydda.[46] He also seems to reappear in the 'Dortus'/'Dorcas' story in Acts 9:36–43 above where Peter resurrects someone in Jaffa he calls 'Dorcas' – 'Tabitha' a 'Doe'! As Acts 9:43 expresses this in its own inimitable way – again using the language of 'a certain': 'and he (Peter) stayed many days in Jaffa with a certain Simon', but now the 'Simon' the text is talking about is not Simon Magus but allegedly 'Simon a tanner'! This occurs in Acts, right before the orthodox Simon's 'tablecloth' vision where, it will be recalled, Peter gets Paulinized, learning to call 'no man profane', and just following Peter's brief sojourn in the same Lydda – a town we just heard about in the Talmud in connection with the crucifixion of 'the Messiah ben Joseph' and in Acts, the scene of Peter's curing of another 'certain' paralytic, so curiously named 'Aeneas', by invoking the name of the Messiah Jesus.

The magical words Peter is depicted as uttering here, are illustrative: 'Aeneas, rise up, Jesus the Christ has healed you' (9:34), as they may point the way to a solution of many of the historical problems raised in this book. What we are trying to say here is that 'Jesus (i.e. 'the Savior') the Christ' may originally have been *part of a magical formula*, invoked in such healing attempts in a Hellenistic milieu and around which many of these miracle tales then came to be fashioned. It also, of course, takes the place of the crucifixion of 'the Messiah ben Joseph' – whose counterpart this 'Joshua' most certainly was – here at Lydda according to the Talmud.

Certainly the *Taheb* traditions among the Samaritans have something to do with all these relationships but, in the writer's view, they also have something to do with the Gospel presentations of stories about Pontius Pilate and Jesus. The name 'Jesus' itself has to be seen as related to the '*Taheb*' who was, in fact, just such a 'Joshua' or 'Jesus *redivivus*' (Joshua being the scion of the principal Northern Tribe of Ephraim). So does the title 'Son of Joseph', from which the Talmudic 'the Messiah ben Joseph' is derived – 'Joseph' being the patronymic hero of the North. In particular, this is true of Joshua's tribe, Ephraim (the preferred son of Joseph according to the blessing of his father Jacob in Genesis 48:13–20), all of whom were seen as 'Sons of Joseph' *par excellence*.

Though surviving Samaritan tradition is difficult in the extreme to penetrate, what does emerge is that there is a 'Redeemer' figure referred to there as 'the *Taheb*' – from this, possibly, the curious 'Disciple named *Tabitha*', whom Peter is pictured as resurrecting after she had already 'been washed' in Acts 9:37–41. If true, this is an incredible transformation, once again, pointing up the *modus operandi* and mischievous dissimulation embodied in New Testament narrative of this kind.

We have already seen that the term 'the *Taheb*' actually would appear to mean 'the Restorer' and what this Joshua *redivivus* or 'Restorer' was supposed to restore was the Mosaic legacy as represented by the figure of Joshua – 'Jesus'.[47] In fact, this is something of what Josephus portrays when he presents 'the tumult' in Samaria that was so serious that it really did end up in Pontius Pilate's recall from Palestine.[48] This is highly underestimated and a rare occurrence even in view of the brutality shown by other Roman governors. In this episode, an individual, obviously supposed to be 'the *Taheb*' (though Josephus never actually calls him this), is clearly trying to present himself as a 'Joshua' or 'Jesus *redivivus*', since he wishes to lead a massed multitude up to Samaria's 'Holy Mountain, Mt. Gerizim' where Joshua had originally read the Mosaic Law to the assembled tribes (Joshua 8:33–35).

The way John the Baptist is presented in Josephus, whose effect on the crowd (which 'seemed prepared to do anything he would suggest') at *almost precisely the same time* is comparable in almost every way.[49] What the Samaritan 'Impostor' prevails on the crowd to do is to restore 'the sacred vessels', presumably of the Temple, that had allegedly been 'deposited in that place by Moses'.[50] But, as Josephus portrays it, these crowds, which had congregated 'at a certain village called Tirathaba' were now set upon and slaughtered by 'a great troop of horse and men' commanded by Pontius Pilate.

Others were taken alive, 'the principal and most powerful of whom' Pilate ordered to be crucified just as Christian tradition considers its 'Jesus' to have been.[51] These must have included the individual claiming to be 'the *Taheb*' unless he managed to escape. There is no comparable story in the received Josephus about Pilate's interaction with Jewish or Samaritan crowds and a Messianic 'Restorer' or 'Redeemer' figure, whom he cruelly and brutally crucified and for which he was ultimately actually recalled, unless it be this.[52]

Nor can there be much doubt that we have in these activities the kernel of events being transformed in Acts' picture of Peter's encounter with 'a certain *Tabitha* which interpreted is *Dorcas*' and, in Josephus, probably '*Dortus*' or '*Doetus*'. Such overlaps of 'the Taheb' story – including the common denotation 'Son of Joseph' – with that of the 'Jesus' or the 'Christ' make it seem pretty certain that there was some original or underlying version of materials about this 'Son of Joseph'/'*Taheb*' personality, owing its origins to and based upon Samaritan originals, that went into the Gospels. But further than this it is impossible to go.

This amazing transformation of 'the *Taheb*' and/or 'Tirathaba' into '*Tabitha*' – most likely we have a progression here and all three are related – is perhaps a more vivid indication of the New Testament's working method than even the transformation of the circumcised convert Izates, reading Genesis 17 on God's instructions to Abraham, into the Ethiopian Queen's eunuch reading Isaiah 53:7 – interpreted for him by Philip as 'the Gospel of Jesus'[53] – immediately going down into the water and being baptized.

But unfortunately one must go further – just as Josephus characterizes the Samaritan Messiah as 'considering Lying of little import', there are historical lies here, lies – however benignly-intentioned – meant to undermine, belittle, and deceive, which unhappily have done their work all too well over the last two thousand years and are still, sad to have to say, so doing.

Joseph Barsabas Justus and the Sabaeans

In Mandaean tradition, John's father is called '*Abba Saba Zachariah*'. The Mandaean tradition too, dating the exodus of John the Baptist's followers from across Jordan to the year 37–38 CE (around the time, as well, of Pontius Pilate's destruction of the Samaritan 'Restorer' and his followers), more or less agrees with the date Josephus gives for John the

Baptist's execution across Jordan in Perea. Josephus puts this, as we have seen, at the end of both Pontius Pilate's Governorship and Herod Antipas' Tetrarchy, well past the normal date for Jesus' execution given in the Gospels of between 30–33 CE.[54]

It is interesting that for Josephus, John the Baptist taught 'Piety towards God and Righteousness towards one's fellow man' – the Righteousness/Piety dichotomy clearly recognizable throughout the Dead Sea Scrolls, the Letter of James, and considered the essence of Jesus' teaching in both the Gospels and by the early Church polemicist Justin Martyr.[55] For Josephus, John the Baptist was executed by Herod the Tetrarch because he feared that John was so popular that the people would do anything he might suggest. In other words, the execution of John was a preventative one, because Herod feared John might lead an Uprising.[56]

In fact, Josephus portrays John as being so popular that he says the people considered Herod's defeat by King Aretas as punishment for what he had done to John. This is to say that John the Baptist *was a popular leader* and his death resulted from this, and not from some 'seductive dance' performed by Herodias' daughter (unnamed in the Gospels, but Josephus tells us she was 'Salome'), the subject of popular imagination every since.[57] But this mini-war between King Aretas and Herod does not seem to have occurred until approximately 37 CE.[58] Therefore, John could not have been executed much before that time since the divorce by Herod of Aretas' daughter was ostensibly driving the hostilities.[59]

Christian sources are extremely insistent (particularly Hippolytus, but also Epiphanius two centuries later) that Elchasai had 'a book', that is, the one Hippolytus says was given to *Sobiai* ('*Sobiai*' of course, apparently relating to 'Masbuthaeans' or 'Sabaeans'). Hippolytus actually gives the name of the 'Syrian' follower who brought this book to Rome as 'Alcibiades' – another of these seeming corruptions as expressions moved from Aramaic or other Semitic languages into Greek, this time, patently, of the name 'Elchasai' as it was transliterated from Aramaic or Syriac. Hippolytus' younger contemporary, Origen, also claims to have seen this 'book' while residing in Caesarea on the Palestine coast.[60]

Modern scholars have been attempting to reconstruct this 'book' attributed to Elchasai. All acknowledge it to have been 'Jewish Christian' or Ebionite and related to a book that also has only recently come to light, *The Mani Codex*.[61] Among the previously inaccessible manuscripts from the Dead Sea Scrolls, another book, *The Book of Giants*, which has recently come to light, was also known to Manichaean sources.[62] That Muhammad seems to know about this 'book' or 'books' seems clear from his insistent designation of the group he is calling 'Sabaeans', together with Jews and Christians as one of the three 'Peoples of the Book' or 'Protected Persons'/'*Dhimmis*'.[63] Curiously enough, he is not perceived as having included Mani's followers in this category and, therefore, they were later persecuted by Muslims. Nevertheless, in so far as they were not distinguishable from 'Elchasaites', they too were probably also originally subsumed under this notation 'Peoples of the Book'.

Nor does Muhammad mention Mani any more than he does Paul. Neither do any of these other groups, presumably because Paul and Mani were, ideologically speaking, so close, and because all, including 'the Ebionites' or so-called 'Jewish Christians' – the Mandaeans do not mention Paul either except to speak mysteriously about an 'Enemy'[64] – were so violently opposed to Paul. It is, however, not without interest as we have seen that, even in the Book of Acts, Paul has a companion with the Mani-like name, 'a certain Mnason' (21:16 – if this is not just another garbling of someone like 'Ananias' again), called there 'an early Disciple' and 'a Cypriot' – this last, as already underscored, often a stand-in for Samaritan.[65]

As we saw, Josephus calls the stand-in he knows for Simon Magus in Caesarea – the 'Magician' also designated in some manuscripts as 'Atomus' – as coming from 'Cyprus'. On the hand, Acts 13:6 calls the 'certain magician and Jewish false Prophet' – again the inversion of the 'True Prophet' ideology – it pictures Paul as encountering on 'Cyprus', 'Bar Jesus', a name it admits is equivalent to '*Elymas* Magus'. Not only does Acts depict this 'magician' standing side-by-side with Paul's namesake, 'the Proconsul Sergius Paulus', just as Josephus does the 'Magician' he knows as 'Simon' with the Roman Prefect Felix; but it also pictures Paul as addressing him as follows: 'O Son of the Devil, full of guile and all cunning, the *Enemy* of all Righteousness, will you stop perverting the *Straight Ways* of the Lord?' (13:10).[66]

Then, too, in the Book of Acts, Paul has another colleague called 'Manaen' described as one of the original founders of the 'Church at Antioch' (whichever Antioch may be intended by this) and 'a foster brother of Herod the Tetrarch' (13:1). This is the same Herod involved with matters relating to John the Baptist's death, in connection with which Paul's curious escape 'down the walls of Damascus in a basket' from the representative of King Aretas in 2 Corinthians 11:32–33 may have occurred.

But, as we have already suggested, this denotation 'Manaen' for a founding member of 'the Church at Antioch' probably points to a garbling of the name of Paul's other, more well-known, companion, 'Ananias', missing from this enumeration. As for the 'foster brother' part of the designation or 'the man brought up with' this same Herod responsible for the death of John the Baptist, this most probably (via a deft bit of editorial displacement) represents Paul himself not Ananias.

Except for a few historians like al-Biruni and *The Fihrist*, Muslims generally think that the Sabaeans, about whom the Prophet speaks so familiarly and approvingly in the Koran,[67] were from Southern Arabia and an area called 'Saba' (today's Yemen) from which they probably disappeared as an identifiable group almost a thousand years previously – that is, in the era not long after Solomon's time. Like the Christians before them, they 'forget' or, simply, just do not know that there were 'Sabaeans' of the kind we have delineated above (namely 'Elchasaites' or 'Masbuthaean Baptizers'), making the same anachronistic genre of mistake Acts makes in its evocation of 'the eunuch of the Ethiopian Queen' it calls '*Kandakes*'.

If Acts is genuinely simply confused in styling the monarch the Greeks and Romans at this time knew as 'Queen Helen of Adiabene' as 'Queen of the Ethiopians' – mistaking 'Sabaean' for 'Shebaean' (as in 'Queen of Sheba') – then it is also providing just the slightest hint that this Helen may have espoused the kind of Judaism represented by such '*Sobiai*' or 'Masbuthaeans' in Northern Syria or Mesopotamia, Talmudic claims of her adoption of mainstream Judaism notwithstanding.[68] The reader should remember that the Medieval Jewish traveler, Benjamin of Tudela, was still listing the 'Elchasaite Synagogue' he encountered in this area as 'Jewish' as late as the Eleventh Century.[69] If Acts likewise is mistaking 'Shebaean' for 'Sabaean', then it would provide proof that the appellation 'Sabaean' was already in use among 'bathing' groups in Northern Mesopotamia and Syria at the time Acts was being put into its final form.

This is possibly the implication behind names like 'Judas Barsabas' and 'Joseph Barsabas Justus', also to be found in Acts but nowhere else and themselves both confusing and hard to distinguish from each other. 'Judas Barsabas' (whom, as should be clear by now, we do not distinguish from 'Judas the brother of James', 'Judas Thomas', 'Judas *Zelotes*', 'Lebbaeus who was surnamed Thaddaeus', and even, perhaps 'Judas Iscariot'), like 'Agabus' before him in Acts 11:27, 'goes down from Jerusalem to Antioch' with Barnabas, Paul, and Silas, not to predict the Famine but to deliver James' letter. With Silas and also like 'Agabus', he is also called a Prophet in Acts 15:32 – so too, according to Josephus, was 'Theudas!'[70]

'Joseph Barsabas Justus', it will be recalled, is the defeated candidate in the election to fill the 'Office' (*Episkopon*) of another 'Judas' – Judas Iscariot, even though this Iscariot was never presented as holding such an 'Office'/'Bishopric' or title in the first place. Not only are these 'Barsabas' names (to say nothing of quasi-related 'Barabbas' ones) tied to the known names associated with Jesus' family members, but we would say that this 'Joseph Barsabas Justus' (the 'Justus' part of which in Acts 1:23 is actually retained in the Latin and not in its

Greek equivalent – the 'Joseph' part of which once again being, in our view, the alleged patrimony) relates to the missing introduction and election of James in Acts to succeed Jesus in the 'Office' of *'Bishop of the Jerusalem Assembly'*.[71]

So one can conclude that we have clear evidence that this group of Sabaean Daily Bathers, closely associated with what early Christian heresiologists like Hippolytus or Epiphanius are calling either 'Nasarenes'/'Nazoraeans', 'Essenes'/'Ossaeans', 'Ebionites', or 'Elchasaites', existed at least as early as Acts' transmutation of materials about Queen Helen of Adiabene into the 'Queen of Sheba', 'Meroe', 'Ethiopia', or what have you. In addition, they are also to be connected – at least where Northern Mesopotamia and Syria were concerned – with the missionary activities of someone called 'Judas' (*'Hudhud'*, a bird, in the story about the Queen of Sheba in the Koran!) or 'Addai' (that is, 'Thaddaeus' – in some manuscripts called 'Judas the Zealot'; in other contexts', as we have seen, 'Judas of James'/'Judas the brother of James' and in the *Second Apocalypse of James* from Nag Hammadi, even 'Theudas the brother of the Just One'[72]).

It should, also, be emphasized that, aside from the still extant Mandaean *Nasoraia* in Southern Iraq, these *Nasrani* – 'Christians' in Islam; *Notzrim*/'Keepers' in Judaism – give way in Northern Syria to a secretive group even today known by insiders as *'Nusayri'* (an obvious allusion to their Judeo-Christian/*Nasrani* origins) and by outsiders, as *"Alawwis"* (the plural of 'Ali) – this last though also secret alluding to the series of 'Hidden *Imam*s' or 'Secret Adams' succeeding 'Ali (and possibly another, even earlier, teacher 'Adi).[73]

Nor should it go unremarked that these *Nusayri*, to which the Assad family of Syria belongs, were also said to follow another native Northern Syrian prophet that even today they call by the telltale name of *"Adi"*![74] Although primarily a Shi'ite group, as the name *Alawwi* suggests, there are in this *"Alid"* notation the traces of the Islamic *Imam* doctrine – *"Ali"* being 'the Hidden *Imam' par excellence* for Shi'ite Muslim groups of no matter what derivation. The secretive nature of these groups, including related ones such as 'the Druze' in Southern Lebanon, Syria, and Israel/Palestine (named after a Twelfth-Century Isma'ili Shi'ite agitator al-Darazzi), is not unrelated also to 'the Secret Adam' idea so prized by Gnostic-style groups preceding them in these same areas.

Though a little more straightforward than these later, perhaps more Gnosticizing doctrines of 'Sabaean' or 'Daily Bathing' groups, first reported in Irenaeus' description of 'the Ebionites' or Hippolytus' description of 'the Elchasaites',[75] the hint of the same or a similar conceptuality is already present across a wide range of key documents pertaining to groups such as those at Qumran, including the Damascus Document, the Community Rule, the War Scroll, Hymns, etc.[76] The same conceptuality is to be found in Paul in 1 Corinthians 15:20–58 which includes not only the language of 'the First Adam', but the 'Heavenly Secret' as well.

Though originally based on an Arabic root meaning 'being' or 'standing before' – in normative Sunni Islam meaning only in prayer (i.e., 'the Prayer Leader') – in Shi'ite Islam, 'the *Imam*' becomes something far more exalted, even bordering on the supernatural, as 'the Christ' in Christianity. What the *Imam*-doctrine became in Shi'ite Islam was an incarnationist notion of the Divine specifically coming to rest in or on 'Ali and the members of his family and/or their descendants.

Nevertheless, this Shi'ite Islamic doctrine of the *Imam* is nothing other than the Ebionite/Elchasaite 'Hidden' or 'Secret Adam' ideology, 'the *Adam Kasia*' of the Mandaeans or 'the Christ' (whatever this was supposed to mean) as theologians such as Paul proceed to translate it into Greek. This last – now referred to as 'the Holy Spirit' – is pictured in the Gospels as coming to rest on Jesus' head in the form of a dove when he emerges from the baptismal waters (the probable origin of Muhammad's *'Hudhud'*/'a bird').

The transfer of this doctrine of multiple Christs, *Imam*s, or 'Alis that could be seen as incarnated in any given individual or at any given time and place became extremely useful for

Shi'ite Islam, 'Ali being Muhammad's closest living relative and, according to some – like James and Jesus' other relatives in Christianity – his rightful and only authentic heir. Of course in this kind of derivative or later thinking, 'Ali or 'the *Imam*' is the heir of 'the Prophet' not of a supernatural being as Christianity would have us believe Jesus is. But even in Ebionite tradition – reflected seemingly in John 6:14 and 7:40 – it should be appreciated that Jesus was considered to be *the True Prophet* referred to in Deuteronomy 18:15–19, a fundamental conceptuality of the Pseudoclementines and a biblical proof-text also extant and subjected to exegesis at Qumran.[77] So was Mani and, following this of course, Muhammad in Islam.

The framework for all these ideas already present in the Qumran documents earlier, including the widespread idea of 'standing' (at the root of both the Elchasaite/Ebionite ideology of 'the Standing One' and 'the *Imam*' doctrine in Islam – to say nothing of 'the Christ' in Christianity[78]). In addition to relating to the doctrine of 'the Standing One' – itself indistinguishable from the notions of 'the Primal' or 'Secret Adam', traces of it run through all the Gospels and Jesus and/or his Apostles are repeatedly placed in a varying set of circumstances and descriptions in which they are alluded to – often for no apparent contextual reason – as 'standing'.[79] Along with the ideology of 'the True Prophet', it is a basic conceptuality of the Pseudoclementines, which give detailed descriptions of it in several places and where it is also depicted, surprising as this may seem, as the basic component of the ideology of the Samaritan 'pseudo-Messiah' or 'Magician' Simon Magus, along with Dositheus, both Disciples of John the Baptist.[80]

The Relationship of Theudas, Barsabas, and Paul

Finally, early Christian tradition – namely in the hands of the Second-Century theologian Clement of Alexandria – is aware that Paul and the individual most call 'Theudas' (a variation obviously of the name 'Thaddaeus') knew each other and the one was a disciple of the other or vice versa.

In fact in some Syriac sources, the replacement for 'Thaddaeus' in Lukan Apostle lists, 'Judas of James', is again replaced, by another variation, 'Judas the Zealot'.[81] This inevitably brings us back to that other 'Judas', surnamed 'the Iscariot'. In turn, this last in the Gospel of John – itself having no Apostle lists – is rather characterized as either 'Judas (the son)' or '(brother) of Simon Iscariot'.[82] For his part Simon Iscariot starts this circle all over again and, just as Judas Iscariot is to 'Judas *Zelotes*', is itself patently not unconnected to the name found in the Apostle lists of Luke/Acts, 'Simon *Zelotes*'/'Simon the Zealot'.[83]

Not only is it possible to look upon this 'Theudas' as a double for 'Thaddaeus'/'Judas Thomas'/'Judas (the brother) of James'/and now 'Judas the Zealot', but in the *Second Apocalypse of James* from Nag Hammadi, he is described, as either the 'father' or 'brother of the Just One' – the latter being James' cognomen. It is the sobriquet which Acts 1:23 attaches to that 'Joseph Barsabas *Justus*' it portrayed as the defeated candidate in the election to fill 'the Office' of 'Judas Iscariot' – a sobriquet which for some reason Acts finally felt unwilling to discard!

The *Second Apocalypse of James* from Nag Hammadi also makes it clear that this 'Theudas' was the one to whom James transmitted his teachings.[84] Just as interesting, where both Apocalypses of James are concerned, the role of Theudas in the *Second Apocalypse* is doubled by that of Addai in the First – both clearly being variations of 'Thaddaeus'. In addition, both are placed in some relationship to James, whether familial or doctrinal.[85] These are very curious notices and add to the sense that something very mysterious is being concealed behind the name 'Theudas'.

For Josephus, as we saw, Theudas is a Messianic contender and another of these Jesus/ Joshua *redivivus*-types. Though Josephus labels him a 'Deceiver' or an 'Impostor', nevertheless, he cannot hide the fact that 'the multitudes' thought of him 'as a Prophet'.[86] According to him, what Theudas attempted to do – in the manner of Jesus in the Gospels[87] – was to lead a reverse exodus back out into the wilderness and, 'Joshua' or 'Jesus'-like, part the River Jordan to let the multitudes go out 'with all their belongings' rather than come in. Presumably the reason behind this was because the land was so corrupted and polluted by a combination of both Herodian and Roman servitors – why else?

This is exactly the kind of reverse exodus 'out from the Land of Judah to dwell in the Land of Damascus' that forms the central set piece of the Damascus Document, providing it with its name. Not only was the aim of this 'to dig the Well of Living Waters', there 'to re-erect the Tent of David which is fallen',[88] but this is the context of the evocation of 'the New Covenant in the Land of Damascus', the principal legal requirements of which were, as we shall see, 'to love, each man, his neighbor as himself' ('the Royal Law according to the Scripture' of the Letter of James) and 'to set the Holy Things up according to their precise specifications' – that is, 'to separate Holy from profane' and not to mingle them or abolish such distinctions.[89]

It is also, of course, exactly the kind of activity that Josephus rails against in both the *War* and the *Antiquities*, in particular as he puts it, 'leading the People out into the wilderness, there to show them the signs of their impending freedom' or 'redemption' – the word changes from the *War* to the *Antiquities*.[90] Josephus calls such leaders 'Impostors', 'Magicians', 'Deceivers', 'religious frauds', or 'pseudo-Prophets' – 'in intent more dangerous even than the bandits' or 'Innovators' (meaning, 'Revolutionaries', but with the secondary meaning too, of course, of religious 'innovation'), with whom they made common cause.[91]

This is exactly the kind of activity 'in the wilderness' on the other side of the Jordan or Lake Gennesaret that the Gospels portray Jesus as engaging in when they picture him as 'multiplying the loaves', 'the fishes', and 'the baskets' of grain to feed 'the multitudes' (at Qumran, 'the *Rabbim*'), who went out with him to these locations, and there performing other such magical 'signs and wonders'.[92] It is also the kind of activity Josephus depicts the unknown Deceiver as engaging in at '*Tirathaba*' and on 'Mount Gerizim' – in his case, to show 'the multitudes' the sacred vessels that Moses had supposedly caused to be buried there – and, in addition, explains why the Gospels are so insistent on repeatedly delineating all these so much more Hellenized 'mighty works and wonders', like raisings, curings, and exorcisms, on the part of their Messianic leader Jesus.

First of all, 'Theudas' is another of those characters like James, John the Baptist, 'James and Simon the two sons of Judas the Galilean', '*Sadduk* a Pharisee', 'Onias the Righteous' ('Honi the Circle-Drawer'), the Samaritan 'Restorer', and others whom, for one reason or another, Josephus left out of the *Jewish War* but included in the *Antiquities* twenty years later – at that point, evidently feeling secure enough to mention them.[93] Secondly and perhaps more important, the note about Theudas he does provide comes right after his long excursus on the Queen Helen story at the beginning of Book Twenty, the book basically reaching a climax with the death of James. Strikingly too, it both introduces his description of 'the Great Famine that was then over Judea' and Queen Helen's famine-relief activities relating to it and is itself immediately followed by his notice about the crucifixion of 'the two sons of Judas the Galilean' in 48 CE, which will produce the well-known anachronism in Acts 5:36–37 concerning both Theudas and this Judas.[94]

Nor is Acts unaware of Theudas' importance and it is certainly not incurious that the beheading of Theudas in the mid-Forties CE parallels the execution 'with a sword' in Acts 12:1–29 by 'Herod the King' of 'James the brother of John'.[95] This chapter, which is sandwiched between both the notice about 'a Prophet called Agabus' predicting the Famine and Paul and Barnabas' famine relief mission to Judea on behalf of the Antioch Community and their 'return' (Acts 11:29–30 and 12:25), while studiously avoiding providing any details concerning this mission, actually goes on to introduce James and another character called 'Mary the mother of John Mark' – whoever she might have been – to whom Peter goes to leave a message for 'James and the brothers' (12:12–17).[96]

Since Josephus loves detailing the executions of troublesome agitators of any kind, that the beheading of 'James the brother of John' – a character never alluded to in any of Paul's works either – is missing from the *Antiquities* is astonishing. In our view, however, it is not missing. Rather the concomitant beheading of 'Theudas' at this juncture in the *Antiquities* has simply been replaced in Acts by the execution of this James 'with the sword' and it is the 'brother' aspect of the whole tangle of notices that provides the clue to the overwrite.[97]

Notwithstanding these things, Acts 5:36–37's anachronism regarding 'Theudas', 'Judas the Galilean', and 'the Census of Cyrenius' comes in a speech attributed to 'a certain Pharisee named Gamaliel' we shall also have cause to discuss further below. This anachronism has to do with a too hasty reading of the notice about 'Theudas' in the *Antiquities* as well. The problem is that Acts via Gamaliel pictures 'Judas the Galilean' as both 'arising in the days of the Census' (that is, 7 CE), but coming *after* 'Theudas', whom it depicts as 'rising up' before him and 'claiming to be somebody' (in Josephus, of course, what he claimed to be was 'a Prophet' – the 'True Prophet'?).

In fact, it is the unraveling of this anachronism that definitively dates Acts as having been written *sometime after the publication of the Antiquities in* 93 CE. The reason is quite simple: the notice about Theudas' beheading in the *Antiquities* is immediately followed by both the panegyric to Queen Helen's own famine relief activities and the notice about the crucifixion of Judas the Galilean's 'two sons' c. 47 CE, as in Acts 5:37, the destruction of Judas and his followers. It is at this point that Josephus adds the statement describing Judas which Acts then carelessly reproduces, oblivious of the anachronism. In the *Antiquities*, this reads: 'that same Judas who caused the people to revolt from the Romans at the time Cyrenius came to take a Census of their belongings'. This represents the source both of the presentation of the birth of Jesus in Luke and the anachronism represented by the faulty chronological sequencing in Acts at this point.[98]

Early Christian tradition too – as also reproduced by Clement (full name Titus Flavius Clemens) – in some manner associates Theudas' teaching with another individual descended from 'Essene'/'Ebionite' tradition. This is Valentinus, also an Alexandrian flourishing in the early to mid-100s, one of the first definitively-identifiable 'Gnostics'.[99] Not only is this forebear of Clement – possibly even his grandfather – all but indistinguishable, in our view, from the first 'Clement', who was the second or third 'Bishop' or 'Pope' in Rome (in succession to Peter) depending on who is doing the reckoning; he is also, in our view, the eponymous hero of the Pseudoclementines, a proposition that in view of his importance makes a good deal of sense.[100]

The Domitian (81–96 CE) who executed Flavius Clemens was also responsible for the execution of Josephus' patron Epaphroditus – possibly Paul's 'brother, co-worker, and comrade-in-arms' in Philippians 2:25 and 4:18 – and also possibly Josephus' own mysterious disappearance from the scene at around this time as well.[101] Domitian's execution of Flavius Clemens was apparently accompanied by the execution or exile of his niece (or wife), Flavia Domitilla, after whom one of the biggest Christian catacombs in Rome, the 'Domitilla Catacomb' is named.[102] Both, as their prénoms probably imply, were members of Vespasian's family circle originally intended at some point to succeed him. It is also worth noting that this execution(s) triggered Domitian's own assassination – this time by Domitilla's own 'servant', another of these curious 'Stephen's.[103]

Origen (185–254 CE), who succeeded Clement in Alexandria, also shows some awareness of Theudas as a Messianic individual of sorts or part of the Messianic tradition.[104] These are peculiar notices, indeed, and hint at something very important lying behind the name 'Theudas'. This is particularly the case when they are ranged alongside Paul's own testimony both about 'traveling' around with women and knowing 'the brothers of the Lord'. His self-justifying protestations these details comprise come in response to accusations in 1 Corinthians 9:1–4, obviously complaining about his 'eating and drinking' – a theme we have already explicated to some extent above.

The whole theme is particularly instructive when ranged beside those quasi-'Nazirites' in Acts 23:12–14 who take precisely the opposite kind of oath, namely, '*not to eat or drink*' and this, in particular, 'not until they have killed Paul'. As we saw as well, the theme also provides insight when ranged against those 'Mourners for Zion' who, in Talmudic literature, take an oath '*not to eat or drink until they see the Temple restored*'.[105]

Of equal importance, in the lines leading up to this testimony to his acquaintance with 'the brothers of the Lord', are the questions Paul himself confirms were being raised both as to the legitimacy of his 'Apostleship in the Lord' and his claim of 'having seen Jesus Christ our Lord' (1 Corinthians 9:1–3), not to mention what he refers to in Galatians 2:4 as 'the freedom' he enjoys – by which he clearly means 'freedom from the Law' and 'freedom from circumcision' – 'in Christ Jesus'. It is because of his pique over being asked such questions that he then asserts his 'authority', as he puts it, not only 'to eat and drink' (by which he again means, *inter alia*, not to have to keep in any scrupulous manner Mosaic purity and/or dietary laws), but also to travel with women, another accusation which by induction one can tell was clearly being lodged against him.

His response to this last is itself followed by a whole litany of famous self-serving retorts, such as 'is it only Barnabas and I who do not have the authority to quit work', 'who ever serves as a soldier at his own expense', or the equally famous evocation of Deuteronomy 25:4, 'You shall not muzzle an ox treading out corn', while at the same time making it crystal clear that what was on his mind was 'the Law of Moses' (1 Corinthians 9:8–9): 'Do we not have the authority to take around a sister, a wife, as the other Apostles do and (as do) the brothers of the Lord and Cephas (1 Corinthians 9:5)?' Not only is the allusion to 'the brothers of the Lord and Cephas' separate and distinct from 'the other Apostles', but, for our purposes, this last clearly demonstrates that Paul knew 'the brothers of the Lord' or, if one prefers, 'of Jesus', in particular, the third brother known in the various sources, as we have been developing them, as 'Judas (the brother) of James'/'Judas the Zealot' or 'Thaddaeus'/'Theudas'/'Judas Thomas' ('Judas the Twin') and that they – or at least 'Judas' – did have families.

This, in turn, concurs with materials from Hegesippus claiming that the descendants of Jesus' third brother, 'Judas' (or 'Jude' if one prefers), were questioned in either Vespasian's or Domitian's time – or both – and executed in Trajan's.[106] In fact, the variant source we have already referred to above which designates 'Lebbaeus who was surnamed Thaddaeus' or 'Judas of James' as 'Judas the Zealot' confirms this too and even knows where this 'Judas the Zealot' was buried – '*Berytus*' or 'Beirut'. Therefore, unlike James and the individual 'Simeon bar Cleophas', who succeeded James – normally seen as James' first cousin, but whom we consider to be the putative second brother of Jesus (his parallel in Apostle lists being 'Simon the Zealot' or possibly even, in our view, 'Simon Iscariot'), *these notices imply that Judas at least was married and had children – even grandchildren.*

Coin from '*Year 2*' of the Uprising against Rome depicting a ceremonial amphora on obverse and grape leaf with the logo '*the Freedom of Zion*' on the reverse.

Chapter 3
James as Rainmaker and 'Friend of God'

James in the Temple as Opposition High Priest

It is primarily to Eusebius, Epiphanius, and Jerome (mostly via Hegesippus in the Second Century) that one must also turn to get a picture of James' person – in particular, what he was doing on the Temple Mount and the nature of the clothing he wore there.[1] All present James, whether a product of their imagination or otherwise, as functioning as an 'Opposition' High Priest of some kind and doing the sort of things in the early Sixties CE, if not before, that a High Priest normally did – what kind of High Priest, we shall attempt to delineate as we proceed.[2]

Not only does Epiphanius present these things even more forcefully than Eusebius – in this he is supported by Jerome – actually citing Clement of Alexandria and Eusebius as his sources, insisting that James actually wore the diadem or head-plate of the High Priest with the inscription 'Holy to God' on it, but also that he went into the Holy of Holies or Inner Sanctum of the Temple, if not regularly, at least once – there to render a *Yom Kippur*-style atonement on behalf of the whole People.[3]

In the received Eusebius, again obviously relying on Hegesippus, this is reduced somewhat or, as the case may be, garbled. There Eusebius claims, rather obscurely, that James 'used to go into the Temple ('Sanctuary') regularly alone'. Moreover he provides the description of 'his supplication on behalf of the People on his knees before God' until they 'turned as hard as camel's hide' – the more general 'Sanctuary' or 'Temple' being substituted for Epiphanius' and Jerome's more specific 'Holy Place' or 'Holy of Holies'/'Inner Sanctum'.[4]

Furthermore Eusebius reports that James was called 'the Righteous' or 'Just One' and '*Oblias*' (which Hegesippus appears to define as 'Protection of the People') on account of 'his exceeding great Piety', and that these titles were to be found by searching Scripture – or, as he so inimitably puts it, 'as the Scripture declares concerning him' – him and, one might add, Jesus.[5] Nevertheless, his presentation of James 'kneeling before God' in 'the Temple alone' is patently impossible unless he means by this, as Epiphanius and Jerome do, 'the Holy of Holies' or 'Inner Sanctum of the Temple', since the Temple as a total entity was a public building and no one ever went into it 'alone' as he puts it – there 'to intercede on his knees for the forgiveness of the People' – at least not in its public parts or outer precincts.

So, if we are to credit Eusebius' redaction or transcription of Hegesippus, a solitary atonement of this nature – just as Epiphanius and Jerome declare – would have had to have taken place in the 'Inner Precincts' (the Inner Sanctum or the Holy of Holies itself), and this by the High Priest only once a year, on *Yom Kippur*. So if James ever really did go into the Temple 'by himself' in the manner all three describe, then the version conserved by Epiphanius and Jerome – if not more detailed – is certainly the more comprehensible.

All three also make much of the 'linen clothes' James was supposed to have worn – just as Josephus predicates of Essenes and that *Banus* with whom he (Josephus) spent a two-year novitiate in the Fifties CE.[6] *Banus*, he tells us, took only cold baths and wore only 'clothes that grew on trees' – a charming way to translate the idea of wearing only linen.[7] Epiphanius adds the detail (perhaps real – perhaps imagined) that he wore no footwear.[8] This last, of course, was true of all Priests and persons generally when entering the Temple, just as it is in all mosques to this day.[9]

While this is found in no other source other than in Epiphanius, for his part he is missing another tradition about James mentioned in all the other sources – namely the practice definitive also of Josephus' Essenes of *not anointing himself with oil*.[10] Eusebius adds to this last, again doubtlessly relying on Hegesippus, he did not 'go to the baths', but this too is probably garbled. For his part, Epiphanius reproduces this as 'he did not wash in a bath'.[11] Both are probably wrong or perhaps it would be more appropriate to say their true intent or meaning has been lost in transmission or translation.

The reason for this is once again simple: if James did go on the Temple Mount in the manner they describe, then he would have had to have taken a cold-water, ritual immersion-style bath, as all persons entering its hallowed precincts did. There would have been no exceptions to this – and this is probably the root of the conundrum. In fact, the mistake is similar to the one made in reading Josephus' descriptions of Essenes, namely, that 'they preferred being unwashed' or, more accurately probably, 'they preferred having dry skin' – once again meaning, that when they did take 'baths' or, more properly, 'immerse themselves' they did not 'anoint themselves' or *use oil in the Greco-Roman manner*. It patently did not mean they did not bathe.

This, at once, both illumines the problem and provides the solution. What these 'Daily Bathing' Essenes did was *not* go to Roman baths, for certainly Josephus' 'Essenes' were 'Daily Bathers'. So was Josephus' *Banus* (a name presumably via the Latin implying 'bathing'), as certainly was James despite these testimonies to the contrary. What such testimonies must be understood as saying is that they did not take hot baths, but rather cold ones, just as Josephus relates *Banus* did. Nor did they, as was common in such bathing establishments, 'anoint the skin with oil' – both being, as it were, two sides of the same coin.

The special characteristics of James' person and behavior described in the reports about him, preserved by Eusebius and supported by Epiphanius and a little more cursorily in Jerome, are for the most part associated with those Josephus and others are calling 'Essenes' as well. In addition to common characteristics such as these, however, the reports about James go even further and, to a certain degree reflect what is also to be found in Ezekiel's description of the 'Sons of Zadok' 'serving' in the newly reconstructed Temple, including 'wearing only linen and no wool', 'no razor coming near his head' (a variation of what Ezekiel 44:20 is describing as 'not shaving' or 'cutting their hair' but rather 'polling it'), and the Nazirite-like requirement of 'drinking no wine'.

As Ezekiel 44:17 puts the first of these: 'And it will be, when they ('the Priests, the Levites who are Sons of Zadok') enter into the gates of the Inner Court, they shall wear only linen garments and no wool shall touch their flesh.' It is at this point, too, that they are enjoined, not to 'shave their heads' (44:20 – as Hegesippus puts it with regard to James, 'no razor came upon his head'), but rather 'only to poll their hair' and, while they are 'in the Inner Court' of the Temple, 'to drink no wine' (44:21).

The twin requirements about 'wearing only linen' and 'no wool touching their flesh' are particularly interesting, especially when trying to link James up with other notices at Qumran.[12] Even the ban on carrion associated with James' directives to overseas communities in Acts 15:20–29 and 21:25 (not incuriously, preceded in 21:24 by James' 'temporary Nazirite' oath-procedure injunction to 'shave their heads') and, even more specifically, in the Pseudoclementines, is also to be found in Ezekiel 44:31's description of these 'Sons of Zadok' in the New Temple who 'were to eat no flesh of anything dying naturally or that has been savaged, either a bird or any other living creature'. A more perfect description of the ban on carrion in James' instructions to overseas communities is not to be found.[13]

4Q285 identifying '*the Root of Jesse*' from Isaiah 11:1-5 with '*the Branch of David*' and, in turn '*the Nasi of the Assembly*'('*the Nasi of Israel*' found on Bar Kochba coins.)

James as Rainmaker, Noah the First *Zaddik*, and the Eschatological Rain and Flood Tradition.

Strikingly, Epiphanius provides yet another curious detail about James, missing from the descriptions provided by these various other sources: that once during a famine he brought rain, that is, James was a 'Rainmaker'.[14] In this regard, it is useful to recall that whatever else Epiphanius might have been, he was a Palestinian and, originally probably, 'an Ebionite' or 'Jewish Christian'. Whether this activity attributed to James took place during the Famine introducing Josephus' 'Theudas' episode and so important to Paul's and Queen Helen's famine-relief activities is impossible to say. However, if it did occur 'at the time of the Famine', then it would make this notice in Epiphanius all the more meaningful.[15]

Alluding to this event in between his description of James wearing the diadem of the High Priest and entering the Holy of Holies and the general drift of the information he provides about James being called 'the Righteous' or 'Just One', Epiphanius describes the rainmaking on his part as follows: 'Once during a famine, he lifted his hands to Heaven and prayed, and at once Heaven sent rain.'[16] This rainmaking ascribed to James is no ordinary matter. If authentic, the notice has to be considered connected to James' '*Noahic*' status as 'the Just One', like Noah, 'Perfect and Righteous in his generation' (Genesis 6:9).

Here we come to some uniquely Palestinian concepts common to early Church traditions about James and ideologies permeating the Dead Sea Scrolls. Not only does James' status of *Zaddik* – to say nothing of his rainmaking – remount to his relationship to the first biblical *Zaddik*, Noah, and his salvationary activity at the time of the first apocalyptic Flood, but it bears on James' participation, like 'the Sons of Zadok' and 'the Elect of Israel' at Qumran generally, in the final apocalyptic Judgment on mankind or, at least, *his calling down this Judgment in the Temple* in terms of images first evoked by the apocalyptic visionary Daniel – images also attributed to Jesus in the Gospels and later to be found in climactic passages in the Dead Sea Scrolls.[17]

This idea of participation in final apocalyptic Judgment is outlined in the Habakkuk *Pesher* from Qumran with regard to 'the Elect of Israel' and dominates climactic portions of the presentation in the War Scroll.[18] In fact, in this document, one can actually find a description of the coming of the Messiah with the Heavenly Host in final apocalyptic Judgment. But this is also the case in the Damascus Document's crucial exegesis of Ezekiel 44:15, where the all-important 'Sons of Zadok' are identified as 'the Elect of Israel called by name who will stand in the Last Days' ('stand up', if the sense is that of resurrection), and 'justify the Righteous and condemn the Wicked' – all allusions which must be considered eschatological.[19]

In Hegesippus' portrait, James is pictured as calling down this Judgment in the Temple in terms of the imagery of the Messiah coming on the clouds of Heaven (described in terms of the coming of 'the Myriads of Angels and Spirits' or 'the Heavenly Host' in the War Scroll from Qumran[20]), first evoked, as just noted, in apocalyptic visions of Daniel 7:13–14. The same proclamation is attributed to Jesus, albeit perhaps retrospectively, in several key places in the Gospels.[21] There Jesus is described in two separate contexts – first in 'the Little Apocalypses' – as proclaiming that 'they shall see the Son of Man coming on the clouds of Heaven with Great Power and Glory' (Luke 21:27). Both Mark 13:27 and Matthew 24:31 add the 'sending of His Angels' and 'Elect from the four winds' to this array. Not only should one note the overlap in general with the 'Elect' language in various contexts in the Scrolls in which 'the Holy Angels' also appear, but the Elchasaite/Simon Magus/Pseudoclementine-like language of the Power/Great Power.[22]

The same proclamation is repeated at 'the *High Priest's house*' in response to the question, 'are you the Christ, the Son of God': 'and you shall see the Son of Man sitting at the right hand of Power and coming on the clouds of Heaven' (Matthew 26:63–64/Mark 14:61–62).

Not only is this the exact proclamation attributed to James in the Temple in 62 CE, three and a half years before the outbreak of the War against Rome, in response to basically the same question (here attributed to 'the Scribes and the Pharisees'; cf. too its reflection, not surprisingly, in the speech attributed to James' stand-in 'Stephen' in Acts 7:55–56), but it will also be the kind of visionary proclamation that will be set forth in climactic portions of the War Scroll from Qumran, both in terms of 'cloud' imagery and the *coming of rain*. This is the same 'coming' and 'sending of rain' which as 'the Sermon on the Mount' in Matthew 5:45 too will aver – in describing how to be 'Sons of Your Father who is in the Heavens' (plural 'Divine Sonship' as at Qumran[23]) and 'Perfect as Your Father who is in the Heavens is Perfect' (plural, too, as in the Hebrew '*Shamaim*' – 'Heavens' is plural) will 'fall on the Just and Unjust alike'.[24]

The Rabbinical catalogue of traditions called *The Abbot de Rabbi Nathan* (*The Fathers according to Rabbi Nathan*) associates rainmaking or rains coming in their proper season with *proper Temple service*.[25] This theme of proper Temple service, performed by unpolluted Priests and expressed in terms of 'choosing a High Priest of higher purity', is a favorite one in this period.[26] In these important passages in the *Abbot de Rabbi Nathan*, there is just the slightest hint of a link to the kinds of sacrifice and offering of thanks Noah made to God after the Flood in Genesis 8:15–9:17. At the very least, Noah's salvationary activities in this episode are connected to the coming of rain, and, in the 'rainbow sign' material at its close, its cessation. In some sense, therefore, where these very obscure concepts of 'eschatological rain' or 'flood' are concerned, Noah can be viewed as the first atoning Rainmaker and his salvationary activities associated with the coming of rain and its cessation.

The repetition of both of these themes, that is, the coming of rain and its cessation, will also be ascribed to the prototypical prophet Elijah, as they will to the odd person we shall discuss more fully below, 'Nakdimon ben Gurion' – James' contemporary, who at a time of drought is also pictured as 'making rain' like James.[27] Both themes, that is, the bringing of rain and its cessation, will be evoked too in apocalyptic portions of the Letter attributed to James where, to come full circle, the whole ideology of bringing and halting rain is connected to 'the *efficacious prayer of the Just One*' (5:17–18).[28]

Not only was Noah the first 'Righteous One' or '*Zaddik*' ('Righteous and Perfect in his generation'), a fact that our literature is not slow to remark, but, for the Rabbinic sages, so 'Perfect' was he that he was *born circumcised*[29] However bizarre this claim might seem to us today – the Rabbis still contend such persons, while rare, do exist – it connects the 'circumcision' ideal to the 'Perfection' one and, by implication, that of the atoning, rainmaking *Zaddik* – all themes in one way or another related to the extant picture of James. In another sense, the Primordial Flood that wiped all life from the earth except 'Noah the Righteous'[30] and his family can be seen as an eschatological one and there is certainly a note of this in Genesis 9:8–9:17's account of the promise God makes to Noah after his 'Righteous' sacrifice when He displayed for him the Rainbow Sign.

Canny as ever, the Gospels pick this eschatological sense up as well, in apocalyptic statements attributed to Jesus in the 'Little Apocalypses' again though the 'sign' for Matthew 24:17/Mark 13:14 is Daniel's 'Abomination of the Desolation standing where it ought not to stand'; while for Luke 21:20, prescient as ever too, it is 'Jerusalem surrounded by armies' – fairly convincing evidence that all three were written after the fall of the Temple. This is how Kabbalistic Jewish documents like the Medieval *Zohar* – that itself may go back to Second Temple sources – see the Flood as well, asserting that Noah 'who sought Righteousness', 'withdrew' or 'hid himself in the ark'.

In other notices in the *Zohar*, this is expressed as: 'Noah was *hidden* in the ark on the Day of the Lord's Anger and was placed beyond the reach of the *Adversary*.' In this passage, not only do we have hints of the 'Hidden' terminology that will so permeate the New Testament and apocryphal texts associated with John the Baptist, but also 'the Enemy' sobriquet so strikingly applied to the assailant who attacked James on the Temple Mount in the Pseudoclementine *Recognitions*. Not only is this 'Enemy' fundamental to 'Jewish Christian' or 'Ebionite' theology about Paul, but it is also to be found in Matthew's 'Parable of the Tares' – probably the single instance of a pro-'Jewish Christian' or Ebionite parable in the Gospels (13:25–40). It is applied, too, to the opponent of the author of the Letter of James 4:4[31] ('by making yourself a friend of man, you turn yourself into an *Enemy* of God') and known to Paul in Galatians 4:16 ('your *Enemy* have I then become by speaking Truth to you'), most likely in debate with or response to James where, by implication, it is reversed.

All lead into a new, albeit ephemeral, ideology from this period – also reflected in the War Scroll from Qumran as just signaled – 'eschatological rain'. Not surprisingly – aside from James' related proclamation in the Temple in early Church witnesses to the circumstances surrounding his death – 'rainmaking and the theme of 'coming eschatological Judgment' are also intrinsic to James' Letter, not to mention the one ascribed to 'Jude the brother of James' – his putative brother.[32] As we shall see in more detail as we proceed, in some of the most splendid eschatological imagery of any biblical document, James 5:8–11, – following its condemning 'the Rich' for 'killing the Righteous One' (5:6) and just before evoking Elijah's saving activity of both bringing and stopping the rain – evokes the theme of the imminent 'coming of the Lord' or 'the Lord of Hosts', that is, of coming eschatological Judgment.

Here not only does one find an extremely aggressive apocalypticism, asserting that 'the cries of the reapers have reached the ears of the Lord of Hosts', but also a double entendre playing off the parallel theme of 'the Last Judgment', 'the Rich have amassed for themselves treasure in the Last Days' (5:3). It ends amid the splendid imagery of 'spring' and 'late rain' (5:7) – imagery known, as we shall see, in similar contexts to the Talmud[33] – by evoking final eschatological Judgment on all mankind and, along with it, the just-mentioned efficacious *Power* of the 'prayer of the Just One' (James 5:9–16). This last theme is connected in James to the 'Zealot' priestly forerunner Elijah – 'Zealot' because of the repeated description of him in Kings and derivative notices as having 'a *burning zeal* for God' (1 Kings 19:10).[34] As James 5:17–18 puts this – he both 'prays for it not to rain' and then, after 'three years and six months', to rain again.[35]

In other words, James' activity is being compared to that of Elijah, who, in 1 Kings 18:1–45, brings on a whirlwind – imagery duplicated in introductory portions of the Nahum *Pesher* from Qumran not originally available in earlier translations of Qumran documents, not to mention in Ezekiel (aside from Isaiah, perhaps Qumran's favorite prophet).[36] In such a context, therefore, James too can be viewed as a 'Zealot' and, indeed, he is indisputably presented as such – or at least the majority of those who follow him are – in the last notice about him in Acts 21:21. There James is presented as explaining to Paul that the majority of his followers in the so-called 'Jerusalem Assembly' or 'Church' are 'Zealots for the Law'.

This is also the implication behind Paul's defensiveness over the 'Enemy' epithet in Galatians 4:15–19, an allusion which flows directly into just such an evocation and three times in the next two lines plays off and clearly displays Paul's obsession with the idea that those opposing him are consumed by 'zeal', that is, they were 'zealous to exclude', (as of course those called 'Zealot' or '*Sicarii* Essenes' in Hippolytus would have been[37]), not – as he then puts it so disingenuously[38] – 'zealous for the right thing'. Not only were they, therefore, 'Zealots for the Law'; they were certainly 'zealous for circumcision'.

Also in the allusion to Elijah in the Letter of James above, there is just the slightest hint of the kind of prefiguration, in the 'zeal' being referred to in 'the efficacious prayer of the Just One', of James' own 'efficacious prayer' and 'zeal'. In the same way that Synoptic tradition represents Elijah as prefiguring John the Baptist – both, as it were, fulfilling the same kind of incarnationist function – the implication of this evocation of Elijah's powerfully 'zealous' rainmaking in this Letter is that James, too, is one of these pre-existent 'Priestly' Rainmakers, 'consumed by a burning zeal' and an 'Elijah *redivivus*'. Nor should it be forgotten that the evocation in it of both 'early and late rain' (5:7), once again, has to do with coming eschatological Judgment.

Numerology, 'Eating and Drinking', and the Pre-Existent *Zaddik*

In the subject matter of the Letter of James, therefore, there are hints of both the kind of atonement James ('the Just One') is depicted as making in all early Church sources in the Holy of Holies on at least one particular Day of Atonement – if not many – and the proclamation 'on the Pinnacle of the Temple' he is pictured in these same sources as having made just before he was killed.[39] This last, as we just saw, is that of 'the Son of Man sitting on the right hand of the Great Power' – one of the actual definitions in Aramaic, it will be recalled, that Epiphanius gives of the term '*Elchasai*', namely 'Great Power' – and 'about to come (in the manner of Daniel 7:13) on the clouds of Heaven'.

While the timeframe spoken of in James 5:17 of 'three years and six months' is not precisely the more general one 1 Kings associates with Elijah's rainmaking when it speaks of how 'after three years' Elijah commanded that the drought be ended (18:1), still the two are basically the same and this is clearly the point the writer of James is intent on conveying. For its part, Luke 4:24–25, which now has Jesus compare his own miracles to Elijah's, also evokes 'three and a half years' to describe the period when 'Heaven was shut up and there was a great famine throughout the land'.

Even more significantly, whether coincidentally or otherwise, this timeframe is also that of Daniel 12:7's chronology of 'a time, two times, and a half' or, as this is more or less repeated in Daniel 8:14 earlier, 'two thousand three hundred evenings and mornings'. In Daniel, this timeframe is usually thought of as relating to the interruption of the perpetual sacrifice at the time of the Maccabean Uprising, when Antiochus Epiphanes erected 'the Abomination of the Desolation' in the Temple – thought to have been a statue of the Olympian Zeus[40] – alluded to as well in Daniel 8:13 and 12:11 together with allusions to 'the End Time' (1 Maccabees 1:55).

But an alternative scheme of reckoning could just as easily have seen this chronology as applying to the time between the death of James in 62 CE and the stopping of sacrifice in the Temple on behalf of Romans and other foreigners and the rejection of their gifts by the 'zealous' lower priesthood *approximately three and a half years* later, an event which started the Uprising against Rome and the cataclysmic events unleashed thereby.[41]

If one accepts the relationship of this with Daniel, then this whole cluster of notices can throw light on how the timeframe in Daniel was seen in the Second Temple Period. The presence of this reference to 'three and a half years' at this juncture in the Letter of James – an important yardstick in Daniel's eschatology – might be an indication both of *how James' death was seen by his followers and how the coming of this final apocalyptic Holy War, represented by the Uprising against Rome, must have been seen by its participants.*[42]

Even early Church sources like those collected by Eusebius take a similar view of the relationship of James' death to the cataclysmic events that, as far as they were concerned, immediately followed his death and were not unrelated to it.[43] It should be appreciated that even earlier than Eusebius, Origen claims to have seen – in the copy of Josephus' works he too evidently found in the library of Caesarea – a statement connecting James' death and not Jesus' directly to the fall of Jerusalem that followed it, to which he, like Eusebius thereafter, took great umbrage – the reason perhaps why the notice has disappeared from all normative copies of Josephus ever since.[44]

However these things may be, the Talmud devotes a whole section of one of its oldest and most accurate books, Tractate *Ta'anith*, to the subject of 'rainmaking'. In doing so, it evokes Isaiah 45:8 about 'the Heavens pouring down Righteousness (*Zedek*) and the Earth opening and bringing forth Salvation (*Yesha'*), and Justification (*Zedakah*) growing up together (with them)'. This is clearly one of the most triumphant 'Messianic' passages in Scripture, culminating in the assertion in Isaiah 45:17 of Israel's redemption or, as the text expresses it, 'Israel will be *saved* in the Lord with an everlasting *Salvation*' (*Yeshu'a*). A number of Qumran texts emphasizing precisely this kind of 'saved'/'saving'/'Salvation' (*Yesha'*/*Yeshu'a*/*yizzil*) have come to light – these in addition to the several known notices of this kind in the Damascus Document, the Community Rule, and the Habakkuk *Pesher*.[45] The rich vocabulary of the passage quoted above – in fact, the whole section of Isaiah in which it is found – is important regarding the subject of such 'Messianism' as well.

Talmud *Ta'anith* specifically interprets this passage from Isaiah to mean that 'rain will not fall unless Israel's sins are forgiven' which, by implication, associates these matters somewhat with *Yom Kippur* or, at least, the central activity of that commemoration, *atonement*. Here we are beginning to encounter not one but several of the themes connected to James' activities in our sources, including one that we have already highlighted above, his *praying for the forgiveness of the People in the Temple*, and the other, of course, his rainmaking.

In the same passages, *Ta'anith* compares 'the day on which rain falls to the day on which Heaven and Earth were created', evoking the same imagery of 'spring rain' which we encountered in the Letter of James regarding the imminent 'coming of the Lord'.[46] This not only ends by alluding to Elijah's efficacious rainmaking, but also evokes another allusion related to Isaiah 45:8, that of 'the farmer waiting for the precious fruit of the Earth' (James 5:7).

The word *Ta'anith* uses in connection with the coming of such 'spring rain' is *yoreh*, the primary meaning of which is 'pouring down'. '*Yoreh*' is, of course, homophonic for the designation *moreh* or 'teacher' in Hebrew; and exactly the same usage appears on at least one occasion in the Damascus Document as a variation on the Teacher of Righteousness, that is, instead of his being a '*Moreh ha-Zedek*', he is a '*Yoreh ha-Zedek*' – meaning, 'he *pours down Righteousness*' just as, presumably, these 'spring rains' do.[47]

These are admittedly complex imageries but the reader will, at least, appreciate the fertility of the ancient artificer's mind and that they are certainly present in the documents before us where they are being formulated with great precision. Jerome, in his work, also interprets this passage in Isaiah in terms of coming eschatological Judgment. In his translation, however, it does not simply involve 'letting the clouds pour down Righteousness', but 'let the clouds *pour down the Just One*', an important variation where James is concerned – to say nothing of the Teacher of Righteousness! In the War Scroll too, as we shall delineate further below, these clouds '*pour down Judgment*' (*Mishpat*).[48]

In connection with these themes of 'Heaven and Earth' and James' rainmaking, not only do these words have to do with James' pre-existent *Zaddik*-status but the 'Pillar' imagery Paul employs to designate the Leadership of 'the Jerusalem Assembly' in Galatians 2:9, itself probably based on 'the *Zaddik* the Pillar' or 'the *Zaddik* the Foundation of the world' phraseology found in Proverbs 10:25 – again, as Paul uses the term, therefore alluding to James' *Zaddik*-status.

The same kinds of references to 'Heaven and Earth' also appear in the Synoptic Gospels. In a variation in 'the Little Apocalypses' above, all three Gospels – in the context, it should be emphasized, of alluding to 'seeing the Son of Man coming on the clouds of Heaven with Power' – speak of 'Heaven and Earth passing away' but not Jesus' words.[49] The version in Matthew 24:30–34 goes, however, even further because it actually compares – not insignificantly – 'the coming of the Son of Man' to 'the days of Noah', then evoking obscure imagery about how 'they were eating and drinking, marrying and giving in marriage, until the day when Noah entered into the ark' (24:37–38).

Not only do assertions such as these further reinforce the connection of these kinds of eschatological allusions to 'the first *Zaddik*' Noah's paradigmatic 'rainmaking' and soteriological activity, but these seemingly tendentious references to 'eating and drinking' (to say nothing of 'marrying and giving in marriage') also connect to the 'eating and drinking' theme we have called attention to above – particularly as reflected in Paul's polemical discussions in 1 Corinthians 8:1–11:34 – as the bone of contention between Paul and James and, by extension, the several prohibitions relating to these in James' directives to overseas communities. Not only do these relate – where one of these, 'fornication', was concerned – to the 'marrying and giving in marriage' theme above, but also of the kind of temporary Nazirite oath procedures so inimically opposed to Paul's positions.

In turn, this last complex of issues has a direct link to what the Rabbis (and perhaps others) were subsuming under the phraseology 'the Noahic Covenant' – itself classically associated with similar prohibitions (in particular, 'manslaughter', 'idolatry', and 'fornication') – and to Noah's paradigmatic salvationary personality.[50] This 'Covenant' has relevance not only to James functioning as the 'Bulwark' or 'Protector of the People' and his '*Oblias*' status as reported in early Church testimony (itself possibly even relating to the puzzling 'Lebbaeus' denotation)[51], but also the actual terms of his directives to overseas communities as recorded in Acts and refracted in Paul's polemics in 1 Corinthians and in the Pseudoclementine *Homilies*. Most noteworthy among these, of course, is the fundamental requirement to 'abstain from blood', a prohibition Noah also received in the context of the atoning sacrifice he is pictured as making in Genesis 9:5 at the end of the Flood episode.[52]

These Noahic prohibitions, because of the theory behind them that they were imposed upon Noah in the aftermath of the Flood, were seen at least by the Rabbis (and probably by others as well) as being *applicable to all mankind* and not specifically to Israel alone. They also included the categories of 'pollutions of the idols', as Acts 15:20 at one point puts it (elsewhere, this category is expressed as 'things sacrificed to idols' and 'fornication' – two of the other categories of James' prohibitions reflected in 1 Corinthians by Paul, the Pseudoclementines, and now in the curious 'Letter' or 'Letters' Qumran scholars refer to as *MMT*.

One can well imagine that Noah was seen as a vegetarian too (as James was, John the Baptist appears to have been, and Peter is portrayed as being in the Pseudoclementines[53]), at least during the actual period of the Flood itself – this before his sacrifice at its end when the permission to eat meat was restored and connected, importantly, to blood vengeance (Genesis 9:5). This last, too, of course, inevitably entailed both the prohibition on blood as well as the one of 'manslaughter'. As Genesis 9:4 puts this in its own inimitable way: because 'the life (of the living being) was in the blood', Noah learns not to consume flesh with blood in it.

Not only is this prohibition on blood also a cornerstone of James' directives, if one looks closely at it, one can see how Paul has allegorically turned it around in his 'communion with the Blood of Christ' polemic arising out of his discussions of James' directive on 'things sacrificed to idols', his own insistence on 'all things are lawful to' him, and 'drinking the Cup of the Lord' but not 'the Cup of Demons' in 1 Corinthians 8:4–13 and 10:17–32.

Though 'strangled things', the last category in James' prohibitions to overseas communities, are not specifically evoked in the picture of Noah's sacrifice in Genesis, 'killing' – which may be seen as related – in the sense that carrion has been killed by other beasts – is, since the 'blood vengeance' that then follows is connected to both 'man and beast'.

Jewish Revolutionary coin from 'Year 4' reading '*Freedom of Zion*.'

The *Zaddik*-the-Pillar-of-the-World and the 'Zealot' Priesthood

We have already delineated the applicability of the *Zaddik*-notion to the persons of both James and Noah by calling attention to the Medieval *Zohar*'s references to Noah. One of these passages also explains the 'Pillar'-notation as applied by Paul to James, Cephas and John and connected to his understanding of 'the Central Three' in Galatians 2:9.[54] It reads in part: 'Noah was a Righteous One … after the Heavenly ideal. Scripture says, 'the Righteous One is the Pillar of the world' (Proverbs 10:25)…. So Noah was called 'Righteous' (*Zaddik*) below … a true copy of the Heavenly ideal, and … an incarnation of the world's Covenant of Peace (i.59b on 'Noah').[55] It is interesting that this foundational, allegedly Medieval, work of '*Kabbalah*' tradition also seems to understand the 'Oblias' or 'Protection-of-the-People' notation as it was applied to James in early Church literature.

One encounters an excellent approximation of this, most notably in the section entitled 'Phineas', the paradigmatic 'Zealot' High Priest and progenitor of the line of Zadok. One should add that, as such, he was also the ancestor of Elijah, Jesus ben Yehozedek, the High Priest of the return from Exile, and Joiarib, the first and principal Priestly course in the Temple from which the Maccabees claimed descent.[56] It reads as follows: 'When God desires to give healing to the Earth, He smites one Righteous One … with suffering … to make atonement … and sometimes all his days are passed in suffering to Protect the People' (iv.218a-b on Phineas). The connection of this with Christian materials relating to the presentation of the scriptural 'Jesus' should be obvious and one could not have a better picture of 'the Suffering Righteous One' than this. But it is also hard to believe that its relevance to materials related to James and, by extension, his *Zaddik*-status among persons of the 'Zealot'/*Sicarii* mindset – for whom 'Phineas' was such an important paradigmatic archetype – could be simply accidental or fanciful.[57]

'The Covenant of Peace', referred to as being 'sealed with Noah' in this '*Zaddik*-the-Pillar -of-the-world' passage, can be seen as just another adumbration of 'the Zadokite Covenant' detailed in Ezekiel's vision of the reconstructed Temple – in turn forming the basis of the exposition of 'the Sons of Zadok' in the Damascus Document from Qumran.[58] But it should also be observed that, aside from being evoked by Ezekiel (34:25 and 37:26) regarding the eternal promises of the Davidic Kingship, this 'Covenant' is evoked, too, at the end of Ecclesiasticus (called by academics after its putative author 'Ben Sira') in relation to Phineas – again the prototypical archetype of the 'Zealot' orientation.

In another, not incurious parallel, this same 'Covenant of Peace' is evoked in the climax of the War Scroll's exposition of 'the Star Prophecy' in the context of which the coming of the Heavenly Host upon the clouds 'to shed Judgment like rain upon all that grows' is evoked.[59] Ben Sira or Ecclesiasticus calls 'Phineas son of Eleazar, third in Glory' after Moses and Aaron. It then affirms, that 'because of his *zeal*' and 'because he stood firm', '(he) *atoned for Israel*. Hence a Covenant of Peace was sealed with him, making him Ruler of both Temple and People and securing to him and his descendants the High Priestly dignity for ever' (45:23ff.). The whole stems from the original use of these terms to picture Phineas in Numbers 25:6–15. There, because of his 'zeal' ('like that of the Lord's') in turning away pollution from the wilderness camp of Israel and the Divine 'Wrath' that would have ensued over the twin issues of mixing with foreigners and intermarriage, he was vouchsafed this eternal 'Covenant of Peace' and 'the right to perform the atonement over the Sons of Israel' in perpetuity. This puts things about as succinctly as one can put them and explains the basis of all these allusions. Phineas is therefore like Noah is therefore like Elijah is therefore like James – or, in orthodox Scripture, if one prefers, James' reflection Jesus. Perhaps even more germane, in Rabbinic tradition, Phineas is also a Rainmaker, meaning that, like Elijah, he is one of these Heavenly incarnated forerunners.[60]

For 1 Maccabees 2:23–27, this is the same Covenant that is extended to the progenitor of the Maccabean family and, by implication, his sons after him in perpetuity because he killed backsliders who were cooperating with foreign power or foreign edicts abolishing both Covenant and Law. In doing so, to use the words 1 Maccabees uses, 'he *acted as Phineas did* against Zimri son of Salu', crying out, 'Let everyone who has *zeal for the Law* and takes his stand on the Covenant, come out and follow me.' The 'Zealot' nature of this Covenant, therefore – in spite of the fact of its being characterized 'a Covenant of Peace' – should be clear.

Ben Sira, echoing 1 Kings 19:10–14, also sees Elijah as having this same 'burning zeal for the Law', for which reason 'he was taken up to Heaven itself'. Aside from the allusion to Enoch in Genesis 5:21–24 (which produced an inordinate interest in this character in the Second Temple Period) and the one it alludes to about Elijah in 2 Kings 2:1, this is one of the earliest 'Heavenly ascent' motifs. Again the subject is also reflected by Paul in 2 Corinthians – this time in the important description in 12:2–5: 'I knew a man fourteen years ago who was caught up to the Third Heaven where he heard unspeakable sayings that it is not permitted a man to speak'. It is also perhaps reflected in the document associated by tradition with James, the *Ascents of James*.[61]

The Hebrew version of Ben Sira was found for the first time in 1897 in the repository of Medieval Hebrew manuscripts known as the Cairo *Genizah*, where the most complete exemplar of the Damascus Document, which we still use today, was also originally found. In 1964 it was discovered again in, of all places, the ruins of the *Sicarii* stronghold of Masada, where the 'Zealot' hold-outs from the Jewish War committed suicide in 73 CE. Previously it had only been known through Greek and other languages. Not only does it give the original of the notation in English, 'Famous' or 'Illustrious Men', as *Anshei-Hesed*/'Men of Piety' (*Hesed* being in Hebrew a word which in some contexts is also translated as 'Grace'); it associates this 'perpetual Covenant' – 'the Covenant of Peace' which was sealed with Phineas and his descendants in Numbers and with those for whom God's 'Servant David' was to be 'a Prince forever' in Ezekiel – with those it refers to, as well, as 'the Sons of Zadok'.

As already explained, this term was first coined by Ezekiel in his vision of the new or reconstructed Temple.[62] In his vision, such 'Sons of Zadok' were described as 'keeping charge of My Sanctuary' and preserving it from pollution, material fundamental to the Damascus Document.[63] Not only were they to clothe themselves like James and the Essenes only 'in linen garments', but like James 'no wool was to come upon their flesh' and 'no razor was to come upon their heads' (Ezekiel 44:17). Rather, as already underscored, 'they were to poll their hair' – missing from descriptions of James, but probably to be inferred.

In emulation of Phineas' zeal presumably too, they were instructed in 44:7 to *bar uncircumcised persons and foreigners generally from the Temple*,[64] no doubt, the epitome of what was meant by proper Temple service. No doubt, too, this was the way James was seen by his supporters, the majority of whom even Acts acknowledges were 'Zealots for the Law'. Here, then, all our key terminologies converge: 'the Zealot', 'the Zadokite' (or, if one prefers, 'the Zaddikite'), and what one might call 'the Jewish Christian'.

In the light of these materials in Ezekiel and, no doubt, those in the Scrolls, it is a not incurious bit of disingenuousness that Josephus in the *Jewish War* rather characterizes the 'Zealot' decision in 66 CE on the part of the probably 'Jamesian' Lower Priesthood to stop sacrifice on behalf of Romans and other foreigners and reject their gifts in the Temple that triggered the Uprising against Rome, as 'an Innovation with which our Forefathers were unacquainted'.[65]

Gen 49:14 *Pesher,* identifying '*Sceptre*' as '*Messiah of Righteousness*' and '*Branch of David*' (both singular).

Chapter 4
Other Rainmaking *Zaddiks* in the 'Primal Adam' Tradition

Honi the Circle-Drawer or Onias the Just, 'the Friend' or 'Beloved of God'

For the Talmud, several other individuals are associated with rainmaking. The first, Honi the Circle-Drawer – 'Onias the Just' in Josephus[1] – is a Rainmaker in both Jerusalem and Babylonian Talmuds (that is, the traditions as they were transmitted in both Palestine and Mesopotamia). 'Circle-drawing' itself perhaps relates to the Essene Sabbath observance practice – also reflected at Qumran – of drawing a perimeter, outside of which a given individual would not move even to defecate.[2] In Honi's case, the circles are the ones to which he confines himself in order to *cause rain to fall*.

He is a Rainmaker in Josephus as well, where he also bears the telltale cognomen, as we just saw, 'the Just' or 'Righteous One'.[3] This manifestly prefigures the epithet early Church texts always ascribe to James, who – if John the Baptist's family and Jesus' family were indeed related as the Gospel of Luke depicts – may also have been Honi's putative descendant as well.

As Josephus describes it – with a good deal more precision, as usual, than Talmudic texts – Onias put an 'end to a certain famine … praying to God', thereby echoing the Letter of James and prefiguring 'the Famine' all sources refer to in the 46–48 CE period.[4] As in James' final triumphant evocation of Elijah praying for it both to rain and not to rain and the efficacious 'prayer of the Just' or 'Righteous One much prevailing', Honi also prays for it both to rain and not to rain.[5] This is the focus of Talmudic accounts as well. The Jerusalem Talmud will actually compare his situation to Elijah's in the manner in which he importuned God like 'a Son to a Father'. Therefore, Honi too, again like one of his putative descendants John the Baptist (possibly 'Hanin' or 'Hanan the Hidden', as we shall see, in Talmudic sources below), is an 'Elijah *redivivus*'.[6] But for the Talmud, this 'sonship' relation of Honi to God will also present something of a problem.

In his description of what has to be seen as a parallel situation, Josephus will describe this Honi ('Onias the Righteous') – as the 'Beloved' or 'Friend of God whose prayers God heard'. In this context it is important to remark that 'Friend of God' and 'Son of God' are, for all intents and purposes, synonyms. As explained above, since 'Friend of God' – applied in James 2:21–24 to Abraham in the context of describing how he was 'made Righteous' or 'justified by works', not just 'by Faith' because of the willingness he displayed to sacrifice his son Isaac – is equivalent to how Muhammad designates Abraham attaching the new term '*Muslim*' to him; '*Muslim*', too, can be considered yet another synonym of these other two.

Just as James applies the 'Friend of God' terminology to Abraham because, when he was 'tested' he 'put his Faith in God' and 'offered his son Isaac on the altar', James also reflects the kind of prayer Honi is pictured as making in Rabbinic literature – namely, 'of talking to God *like a Son*' (here, the 'sonship' motif really is being brought into the equation). It does so three chapters later in 5:13–18 when it climactically evokes 'the fervent working prayer of the Just One much prevails', citing Elijah as its paradigm (who in its language, both 'prayed for it not to rain' and 'three years and six months' later for it to rain). But the 'Friend' – or 'Son' – notation would obviously apply to other like-minded and fervently praying suppliants as well.

To close another of these fundamental language circles, the Damascus Document, now specifically developing its sacred history in terms of those 'who kept the Commandments' or were 'Keepers', uses the same kind of terminology to describe the first person it denotes as 'a Friend of God' – Abraham. 'He (Abraham) was made a Friend of God because he *kept the Commandments* and did not choose the will of his own spirit'.[7]

To be precise, in place of 'Friend' the Damascus Document (CD) is using another basic synonym to refer to Abraham and his descendants, Isaac and Jacob, 'Beloved of God'. CD also applies yet another fundamental terminology to them: 'Heirs of the Covenant forever'. This is a usage Paul appears to know as well, only he changes it into 'Heirs according to the Promise' (Galatians 3:29, Hebrews 6:17, etc. – in James 2:5, 'Heirs to the Kingdom').

This 'Beloved of God' language is also possibly reflected in that of 'the Disciple Jesus loved' or 'the Beloved Apostle' in the Gospel of John.[8] It is this language of 'making oneself a friend of men and thereby turning oneself into an Enemy of God' of James 4:4 too, which Paul is so anxious to counter, particularly in the introduction to Galatians regarding the accusation that was obviously circulating at the time concerning him of 'seeking to please men' (1:10). It is also in 4:16: 'so by speaking Truth to you, your Enemy have I become', itself obviously both responding to and incorporating the parallel Jamesian aspersion.

Paul also uses these kinds of allusions as a springboard to parody another description applied to James in early Church literature, again dependent upon Hegesippus, of 'not deferring to persons'.[9] Oblivious of its original meaning here and in the Letter of James and, showing his usual mastery of repartee and rhetorical inversion, Paul reverses this in Galatians 2:6, attacking the very 'importance' of the Jerusalem 'Pillars' whose 'repute conferred nothing' nor 'made any difference' to him – for 'God does not accept the person of men'. So in this sort of nimble verbal exchange, Paul actually uses the phraseologies of his interlocutors to attack the very Leadership of 'those of repute' or 'reckoned to be something' of the Jerusalem Assembly itself, presumably including James.

Elsewhere he varies this phraseology with 'God has no favorites', but by implication he is using these allusions to attack those he refers to in 2 Corinthians 11:5 and 12:11 as the 'Highest' or 'Super Apostles', who certainly comprise this Leadership and whom he also contemptuously dismisses as 'Hebrews' (11:22). Another thing these 'Super Apostles' or those he calls 'dishonest workmen' in 2 Corinthians 11:13 do, playing off their attachment to 'written letters' and/or 'letters written in stone' (his double entendres are always cruelly dismissive as well), is 'recommend themselves' or 'write their own letters of recommendations' (3:1–7 and 10:12–18).[10]

Not only are these Apostles (Paul calls them 'Pseudo-Apostles' in 2 Corinthians 11:13) manifestly indistinguishable from the Leadership of the Jerusalem Assembly who, throughout Galatians, appear to be insisting on circumcision, but the attack would also be on Jewish claims to 'chosenness' generally, as it is on the 'written words' incorporating it. Correlatively the attack supports 'the Gospel as (he – Paul) taught it among the Peoples' (Ethnesin – Galatians 2:2) opposed, or so it would appear, to James' 'circumcision' one. Such are his rhetorical and polemical skills.

For James 2:5, of course, it is 'the Poor of this world whom God chose as Heirs to the Kingdom He promised to those that love Him'. This last, it will be recalled, is the second part of the 'Righteousness'/'Piety' dichotomy or the first of the two 'love' Commandments. For Muhammad in the Koran 2:130–36, the Damascus Document's 'Beloved of God' – Abraham, Isaac, and Jacob (Muhammad adds 'Ishmael' to these) – are now rather 'Muslims', that is, those who have 'surrendered to God', an alternative, as explained, to the use of 'Friend' in James – 'Beloved' at Qumran.

For Muhammad, therefore, 'Abraham's Religion' is simply Islam, just as for Paul, prefiguring him, it was 'Christianity'. Muhammad even refers to Abraham and, for instance, those Sabaean-like 'People of the Book', who follow him, as being 'of the Salihin' – or 'of the Righteous' (Koran 3:113). These last 'believe in Allah and the Last Day, enjoin Righteousness, forbid fornication' and 'vie with each other in good works'. For James, too, and Josephus, 'the Zaddik', the true 'Friend' or 'Beloved of God', can actually intercede with God through 'his prayer' to bring rain in times of extreme drought or famine. Therefore these ascriptions,

Chapter 4: Other Rainmaking *Zaddiks* in the 'Primal Adam' Tradition •40 such as 'the Beloved of God' and 'Righteous One' attached to Honi's name and echoed in Talmudic accounts as well, have more than routine significance.

The Stoning of Honi the Circle-Drawer as Prefiguring James

Josephus' description of the death of Honi is, not surprisingly, missing from Talmudic accounts which – while continuing the theme of his praying for rain – also have Honi waking from a long sleep in his grandson's time and praying rather for his own death! One will have to acknowledge, as we proceed, the odd sense of humor of some of these Talmudic hagiographers though, unlike that of Acts, at least it is not overtly malevolent.

In Josephus' account, not only did Honi once pray for rain in the midst of a famine, but God also 'took vengeance upon them' (the Pharisees who stone him) by sending the most violent hurricane or cyclone. This is the same 'whirlwind' symbolism from the story of Elijah, 'a whirlwind' also signaled in Ezekiel's prophecies and evoked in detail in the First Column of the Nahum *Pesher* from Qumran. In Ezekiel 13:12–14, this will be directed against 'the wall upon which the daubers slapped plaster', a crucial image in the Damascus Document too, for those it calls 'the Seekers after Smooth Things' (the Pharisees) as well[11] – in Ezekiel 13:10 'those who lead (the) People astray, crying "Peace" when there is not peace!' It should be appreciated that Honi's death is clearly the work of the Pharisees (those who backed Salome Alexandra's older, more Pharisee-minded son, Hyrcanus II – c. 76–40 BCE) – therefore doubtlessly too, the Talmud's reticence as heir to Pharisaic tradition in speaking of it. Both Talmuds hint at the reasons for Honi's stoning, but do not in fact mention that he was stoned. It is left to Josephus to apprise us of this.[12]

The circumstances behind this stoning in Josephus are important both in that they exactly prefigure the death of James and in the insight they provide into the political configurations of the time.[13] According to Josephus, Honi is stoned by these Pharisaic supporters of both Salome Alexandra and her son Hyrcanus II. The disapproval of Honi by Pharisaic leaders, in particular Salome Alexandra's 'kinsman' Simeon ben Shetach, will also emerge in these same Rabbinic sources and, by implication too, the reason for his stoning.[14] Ostensibly, this was his refusal to condemn Hyrcanus' younger and more nationalist brother Aristobulus II (c. 67–49 BCE), the Priestly supporters of whom had taken refuge in the Temple after Aristobulus' untimely capture by deceit by the Romans and were refusing to surrender. This is the background to Honi's stoning.[15]

The time is Passover, 65 BCE, two years before the Romans under Julius Caesar's associate-to-be Pompey stormed the Temple with the help of these more collaborationist Pharisees, thereby putting an end to an independent Jewish State.[16] The attitude of Aristobulus' Priestly supporters in the Temple must be seen as 'proto-Zealot' or, what should perhaps be called, 'Purist Sadducee', and even later – as, for instance, like those at Qumran – 'Messianic Sadducees'[17] ('Sadducee' being a transliteration into Greek of the Hebrew, *Zadduki* or *Zaddoki*, the Z-D-K root of which also carrying the secondary meaning of 'Righteousness' or 'being Righteous'). This is, also, the sense clearly of 'the Sons of Zadok'/'of the *Zaddik*' at Qumran.[18]

Ranged against these Purist Sadducees is a newer more accommodating or compromising group, familiar from portraits in the New Testament and Josephus purporting to depict the First Century CE, that should be called 'Herodian Sadducees' or even 'Boethusian Sadducees' after the High Priest of that name (Boethus) whom Herod brought in from Egypt after doing away with most, if not all, of the Maccabees. Those he did not murder he married![19]

Aristobulus' supporters patently have an attachment to national independence and oppose any accommodation to foreign rule in Palestine while the proto-Pharisees who oppose him – even at this time – just as patently do not. The same can be said of Aristobulus' father, Alexander Jannaeus (c. 104–76 BCE), who was opposed as well by the same kind of Pharisees and must be seen as one of these original Purist or more nationalistic Sadducees.[20]

Nor was Alexander a collaborationist or accommodating Sadducee of the stripe of the later ones in the Herodian Period we have just highlighted above. Nor, certainly, was his father John Hyrcanus (c. 134–104 BCE).[21]

On the other hand, Alexander Jannaeus' wife, Salome Alexandra (d. 67 BCE), the kinswoman of the 'Simeon ben Shetach' who was one of the original foundational 'Pairs' and transmitters of Pharisee tradition according to the *Abbot* literature (*The Pirke Abbot* and *The Abbot de Rabbi Nathan* we shall have cause to refer to further below), is manifestly pro-Pharisaic. Josephus makes it very plain that even her husband Alexander Jannaeus knows this.[22] Moreover he is very straightforward in identifying as 'Pharisees', the people who were responsible for the stoning of Honi the Circle-Drawer and the collaborators who cooperated with the Romans the first time they stormed the Temple in 63 BCE. So is Salome's oldest son Hyrcanus II, executed by Herod in 29 BCE, meaning 'a Pharisee'. He allies himself with Herodian family interests and together with such Herodians must be seen as primarily responsible for bringing the Romans into the country and paving the way for the Roman/ Herodian takeover and an end of Jewish independence.[23]

For his part Aristobulus – later poisoned by Pompey's supporters on his way back to Palestine with two legions after Caesar had freed him in 49 BCE – had earlier been *unable to debase himself before Pompey* in the 65–63 events. As Josephus – no friend of resistance-minded Maccabeans, though proud of his own well-advertised Maccabean blood[24] – describes the episode at that time (in fact, a fateful one and perhaps a turning point in Jewish history[25]): Aristobulus 'turned sick of servility', returned to Jerusalem to take refuge with his 'purist Priestly' supporters in the Temple before his duplicitous capture by the Romans. Aristobulus, therefore, is patently not a 'Pharisee', nor an accommodating or collaborationist Saducean of the Herodian Period thereafter – the one most are familiar with through the rather distorted historical lens of the Gospels and the Book of Acts. This later breed of Saducees, as Josephus makes clear, were 'dominated by the Pharisees in all things' and supported and were supported by the Herodian Dynasty, even paying bribes to Roman Governors for the privilege of serving as High Priests.[26] This is clearly not the behavior of any truly credible Maccabean High Priest.

These matters are very complex. Plus they have been highly polemicized over the last two millennia. Nevertheless in this context Honi the Circle-Drawer or Onias the Just emerges as supporting, not opposing Aristobulus' 'Purist Saducean' Priestly followers who had taken refuge in the Temple. One should keep this in mind when it comes to considering the deaths of James and other like-minded Messianists in the next century. Just as Honi's James-like cognomen 'the Just' implies – so admired was Honi by the general population because of his Righteousness and Piety that, when the Pharisees outside the Temple attempted to force him to condemn the supporters of Aristobulus within, he refuses to do so. Whereupon they (the Pharisees) immediately stone him.[27] As already suggested, this refusal is the ostensible reason for his stoning, but the legal justifications at this point for this are hazy. The real reasons however, which are similar to those behind the stoning of James (his putative descendant and heir) one hundred and twenty-seven years later, will emerge in the Talmudic sources we shall note below.[28]

In the picture provided by Josephus (certainly based on a source like Nicolaus of Damascus – an Herodian diplomat in Rome – and not his own view), Aristobulus' 'Purist Saducean' supporters are the *lower priests* in the Temple responsible for the daily sacrifices. As Josephus describes it, they have paid the Pharisees outside the city besieging them in the Temple (with help from the 'Arab' King of Petra in support of Hyrcanus II, itself arranged by Herod's father Antipater[29]) in good faith for animals to make the necessary sacrifices prescribed for Passover.[30] As usual, in these pivotal situations, the time is Passover and, once again – if such were needed – we have a good example of the scrupulousness of such 'nationalist' or 'Purist Sadducees' even under extreme duress, their unwillingness to resort to bribery, and their *Piety*, putting proper Temple service even above their own safety.

Even in the picture provided by Josephus – not someone who would normally be very sympathetic to their cause (as already noted, certainly based on a source and probably not his own perspective) – the Pharisees cheat them and refuse to hand over the animals Aristobulus II's supporters besieged inside the Temple had already paid for.[31] These are key moments and turning-points in the history of the period and even perhaps Jewish history as a whole. Not only does Josephus (or his source) literally describe the behavior of these presumable 'Pharisees' who betray their trust – even if to their opponents – as 'Impiety towards God' (the opposite of the 'Piety towards God' so highly sought after by such opposition groups as '*Sicarii* Essenes' or 'Proto-Christians'),[32] but these points are, not surprisingly, missing from Talmudic accounts.

It should also be borne in mind that these Priestly supporters of Aristobulus in the Temple are the same hold-outs who, one or two years later, are ultimately cut down while faithfully proceeding with the sacrifices in the midst of the Roman assault on the Temple – another example of their extreme Piety and what, once again, has to be considered 'proper Temple service' according to a Righteousness-oriented 'Purist Sadducean' or 'Zealot' mentality in this period. In fact, so 'zealous' were they in this regard, *even at the expense of their very lives*, that, as Josephus himself avers, the Romans were themselves amazed.[33]

For his part, Josephus also notes, rather laconically and almost as an afterthought, that most of the killing in the assault as it was finally conducted by Pompey on the Temple Mount was carried out by the opponents of these '*Torah*-doing', 'Covenant-keeping', Priestly partisans of Aristobulus (and, by extension, Honi), who have to be seen as Pharisees. It is they who actually cooperated with the Romans in storming the Temple.[34] These Pharisees, Talmudic attempts at heroicization or idealization notwithstanding, have to be seen as characterized over the next hundred and thirty years – even in the picture Josephus, a self-professed Pharisee, himself provides – by unstinting support for Herod, his heirs, and Roman rule in Palestine generally.

Because of said 'Impiety', Aristobulus' 'Zealot'-minded Priestly supporters pray to be avenged on their own countrymen of the opposite persuasion, in response to which God now 'sends', as Josephus describes it, 'a violent windstorm' – or '*whirlwind*' – which 'destroyed the fruits of the whole country'.[35] This is an obvious case of 'pietistic' intercession or, as Tractate *Ta'anith* would have it in describing Honi, 'importuning God like a Son to the Father'. At the same time, it is the inverse of the situation, pictured in Isaiah 45:8 and evoked in the same Tractate, of 'the Heavens raining down Righteousness' and the Earth 'causing Salvation to spring up and Justification to grow'.[36] Rather the event Josephus describes in his *Antiquities* (as usual it is missing from the *War*) is more like that delineated in the War Scroll and the passage from Ezekiel 13, remarked above, on 'the Daubers on the Wall' in the Damascus Document – who 'cry "Peace" when there was no peace' – as it is that in Matthew's 'Little Apocalypse' of the Heavens 'raining down' Judgment 'on the Just and Unjust alike'.[37]

Not only should this be viewed as punishment for the 'Impiety' of the Pharisee besiegers of Aristobulus' supporters' in cheating them (n.b., how this theme of 'cheating' is clearly also present in James 4:3–4:9 on 'the Rich' cheating the mowers in the field and a similar Judgment is being patiently awaited), and an answer to the prayers of Pious 'Zadokite' or 'Righteous' Priests attempting to do proper Temple service in the midst of all the carnage; but it is also *Vengeance for the stoning of Honi*, 'the Righteous' and 'Beloved of God', by these same persons that preceded it. Though, strictly speaking, Josephus does not specify that this Vengeance is for Honi's death, nevertheless, at the same time, he does not distinguish between the two succeeding events to any extent, nor for that matter the punishment for them. But the cause of the punishment – the 'Impiety' of the besiegers on both counts – should be clear and it is echoed one hundred and twenty-five years later in the events surrounding the stoning of James and the punishment inflicted, according to the view of his supporters – conserved, it would seem, in at least one version of Josephus and in Hegesippus – *for this*.

Both Talmuds recount the complex of views surrounding Honi's behavior, but particularly the Palestinian one has Honi debating Simeon ben Shetach, the most famous Pharisee Leader of the time and the kinsman of Alexander Jannaeus' wife, Salome Alexandra.[38] In this account, the issue is whether, in originally 'importuning God as a Son to a Father' to bring the rain and fill the cisterns and, thereafter, praying for the rain to cease, Honi was not guilty of 'blasphemy' or, as the Jerusalem Talmud puts this, 'profanation of the Name'; and here, significantly enough, the comparison with Elijah is cited![39] Though not expressed in so many words, this is obviously Simeon ben Shetach's position, in pronouncing the ban on Honi – 'profanation of the Name' being a way of expressing the infraction of 'blasphemy', in turn, a pivotal motif in all early Church accounts of James' stoning too.[40]

Honi's response, as conserved in the Talmud, alludes to his exalted status 'among the People' and their recognition of him as the 'Friend of God' and '*Zaddik*'.[41] Though arcane, the gist of this response is that, for the sake of 'the contrary decision' or 'adjudication by a *Zaddik*/Just One', God would annul a punitive decree or banning, even one as extreme as this one on 'profanation of the Name' or 'blasphemy' clearly being pronounced upon him, according to this account in Tractate *Ta'anith*, by the Pharisee Establishment in the person of its most prominent representative, Salome Alexandra's kinsman, Simeon ben Shetach.[42]

If this Talmudic account is to be credited, not only do we have in it the confirmation of Honi's status – reported as well in Josephus and anticipating that of James – as 'the Just', 'Righteous One', or '*Zaddik*' of his generation, but a reflection of the background issue that eventually led to his stoning. As in the stoning of James the Just one hundred and twenty five years later, against a similar backdrop and for similar reasons; this can be seen as having been occasioned by accusations on the part of the Pharisaic Establishment of 'Profanation of the Name', or, to put this in another way, pronouncing the forbidden Name of God as James must have done at least once, probably in the year 62 CE, if the account of his *Yom Kippur*-style atonement in the Inner Sanctum of the Temple as an 'Opposition' High Priest of some kind, as reported in all sources, is to be credited.[43]

Other Rainmaking *Zaddik*s in the 'Hidden' or 'Secret Adam' Tradition

Not only does Josephus designate Honi, who 'prayed to God to end the drought' and 'whose prayers God heard and sent them rain', *Zaddik* and 'Beloved of God', but he also describes how in the midst of all these troubles Honi 'hid himself', obviously for protection but also yet again suggesting the 'Hidden' ideology we have been highlighting above.[44] This 'Hidden' notation is picked up in the Talmud in terms of a 'Rip van Winkle'-style extended-sleep narrative connected to Honi's person, and it also applies this to another of Honi's putative descendants, another 'Rainmaker', Hanan or Hanin *ha-Nehba*, that is, 'Hanan the Hidden'.[45] This Hanin or Hanan (in English 'John') is portrayed as the son of one of Honi's daughters, making him a grandson of Honi on the female side. Moreover, not only is the individual called 'John the Baptist' in the Gospels and in Josephus often identified with Hanan the Hidden, but some texts have Elizabeth, John the Baptist's mother, as the daughter of one '*Anon*', that is, 'Onias' or 'Honi'.[46]

It should be recalled that according to the Infancy Narrative of Luke, John's mother and Jesus' mother were kinswomen (1:36) both, therefore, presumably carrying priestly blood at least on their mothers' side.[47] We have already seen how in the Second-Century 'Infancy

Gospel' ascribed to James and called therefore, *The Protevangelium of James*, John's mother Elizabeth tried to 'hide' her son in a cave (22:3). But in the same narrative, Mary too is described as 'hiding' the infant Jesus in a cave (18:1) whereas in the semi-parallel materials in Luke, Elizabeth is alternatively described as, rather, 'hiding herself for five months' (1:24).

Muhammad, in *Surah*s 3 and 19 of the Koran, also knows something of this 'Hidden' ideology as applied to both John and Jesus and there, too, events surrounding their respective mothers are likewise conflated.[48] He also shows some familiarity with the 'Primal Adam' doctrine, pronouncing, for instance, in *Surah* 3:19 that 'the likeness of Jesus with *Allah* is as the likeness of Adam' – a perfect statement of the doctrine; or in 19:17, in describing how God's 'Spirit' was sent to Mary, that 'it assumed for her the likeness of a Perfect Man', again betraying more than a little contact with groups conserving this kind of doctrine in Syria and Iraq.[49] Just like those 'People of the Book' in 3:113–14 above, 'who recite the revelations of *Allah* in the night season' and 'believe in *Allah*, the Last Day, enjoin Righteousness, and forbid fornication' – a perfect Jamesian combination – he also knows that John, Jesus, and Elijah (the grouping of these three together is in itself telling) 'are of *the Righteous*' (6:85).

Since we have already encountered this same 'Hidden' and '*Zaddik*' language in the Medieval *Zohar* above – there used to describe the prototypical, rainmaking *Zaddik* Noah 'the Righteous', who '*hid himself* in the ark … on the Day of the Lord's *Anger* to escape from the *Enemy*' – it is difficult to escape the impression that these allusions are not simply accidental and that the ideology behind them is connected in some way with the rainmaking *Zaddik* or 'Friend of God'.

It has also gone into Shi'ite Islam, attaching itself to the '*Imam*' concept and producing in all functioning Shi'ite ideologies of whatever kind the notion of 'the *Hidden Imam*'. This in turn is but a variation of the Ebionite/Naassene/Elchasaite 'Secret Adam' or 'Hidden Power' doctrine or 'the Christ' that descends – in Christian scripture, in the form of a dove – to be incarnated in any time or place in a variety of recipients usually connected in a familial manner to one another.

As this is expressed in the Pseudoclementine *Recognitions*: 'Know then that Christ, who was from the beginning and always, was ever present with the Pious, though secretly, through all their generations – especially with those who waited for him, to whom he frequently appeared (1.52).'[50] In earlier, more Palestinian, terms this same doctrine might be described as the 'pre-existent *Zaddik*'. John the Baptist – himself possibly identical with Hanan or Hanin *ha-Nehba* – is referred to in Mark 6:20 as 'a Just Man and Holy' and considered, in the Synoptics anyhow, an Elijah *redivivus* (Matthew 11:14 and pars.), meaning, an Elijah come-back-to-life or an incarnation of Elijah. This is not true for the Gospel of John which is intent on denying this point (1:21–25).

For his part, Josephus calls John 'a good Man', and both he and Mark apply the same word in Greek to him, 'Man'/*Andros*, a term that fairly permeates the sections of the Koran and other like-minded documents where John and Jesus are being referred to.[51] John is also referred to as 'Enosh' – '*Enosh*' meaning 'Man' in Aramaic – in Mandaean Scripture, which is probably the origin of Muhammad's several references to him using a similar vocabulary. 'Man', of course, in Hebrew is '*Adam*', so once again, whether coincidentally or not, we are in the framework of the 'Primal' or 'Secret Adam' tradition.[52] Of course Jesus is portrayed in Gospel tradition, figuratively or literally, as 'the *Son of Man*'. This characterization may be at the root of the confusion between 'the Son of Man' as it has come down to us in Christian Scripture and Daniel 7:13's original allusion to seeing 'one like a son of man coming on the clouds of Heaven', on which it is supposed to be based, meaning literally, someone who *looked like* a 'man' but who – since he was riding on the clouds of Heaven – was *not really a man but something more*.[53]

This ideology of 'the Last' or 'Secret *Adam*', in turn, bears an eschatological dimension of 'the Lord out of Heaven' *shedding Judgment* that brings us back both to James' proclamation in the Temple of 'the coming of the Son of Man with the Heavenly Host in Glory' and the scenario of final apocalyptic War led by the Messiah – also expressed in terms of 'the clouds shedding Judgment like rain' as we saw – in the War Scroll.

Peculiar as it may seem, this kind of phraseology is also reflected in the Qumran Hymns, which asserts that God appeared to its author in His 'Power as Perfect Light'.[54] It is in this context that it refers to both 'Man' (*Enosh*) and 'the Son of Man' (*Ben-Adam*), while at the same time alluding to 'Perfection of the Way' and 'Justification', concluding: 'The Way of *Enosh* (Man) is not established, except by the Spirit God created for him to make Perfect a Way for the Sons of Man (*Adam*) in order that they will know all His works with His Mighty Power (here, the Elchasaite 'Hidden' or 'Great Power' language yet again) and the abundance of His Mercies on all the Sons of His Choice.'[55]

In Mark, it is rather Herod the Tetrarch who calls John 'a Just Man and Holy' (that is, in Hebrew, '*Zaddik* and *Kedosh*') – however incredible this may seem – and it is he who, 'hearing him gladly', supposedly wished to 'keep him safe' ('hide' him?)! It would be hard to refrain from guffawing were it not for concern over what some might call their 'Faith'. It should be appreciated that the words 'a Just Man and Holy' are almost precisely those used in Early Christian tradition to describe James who was not only referred to as a 'Just One', but also as wearing the High-Priestly diadem with the words 'Holy to God' inscribed upon it. Moreover the texts go even further than this in the contention that he was 'considered Holy from his mother's womb'. But so too, probably, was John the Baptist, particularly in Mark 6:20 above, but even more so in Luke.

Though Luke 1:15 does not use precisely this terminology, it is almost the same: 'For he shall be *great* before the Lord and shall *never drink wine or strong drink* and he shall be *filled* with the Holy Spirit even from his mother's womb'. That is, not only did John like James 'not drink wine or strong drink' but, like James too, he was 'a Nazirite' or 'Holy from his mother's womb'.

This allusion to 'being Holy from (one's) mother's womb' is actually replicated with even more pertinence in sections of the Hymns. These not only include the sobriquet '*Oblias*' or 'Protection of the People', but an allusion also to providing Jerusalem with 'a Bulwark' – both undoubtedly connected to characterizations such as the one above.[56] In fact, the language of this 'extreme Holiness' regime permeates the Damascus Document which even goes so far as to employ the nuance and metaphor of Naziritism or, what we shall call as we proceed, the language of '*N-Z-R*' – the root, that is, of 'the *Nazir*'.[57]

These, then, are the categories of the 'Opposition', rainmaking *Zaddik* or '*redivivus*' tradition. So Righteous, for instance, is Elijah and so 'consumingly zealous', as 1 Kings 19:10 –14 would put it, that he does not die but is taken up to Heaven alive (2 Kings 2:1–11) – 'in a whirlwind' no less. It is perhaps for this reason that, prefiguring Jesus, he was seen as being able to come back to earth and alive again or, as it were, become incarnated. We have already seen how the Jerusalem Talmud actually compares Honi to Elijah, even to the extent – incomprehensibly in our view – of applying the same 'ban' or 'blasphemy' charge Simeon ben Shetach leveled against Honi to Elijah! Notwithstanding, in the style of Noah, Elijah is perhaps the paradigmatic primordial Rainmaker and *Zaddik*. It is perhaps for this reason that James 5:16–18 in conclusion refers to him as a 'Man, who in a prayer, prayed for it' both to rain and 'not to rain' and, perhaps even more to the point, as an example of the saving Power 'of the prayer of the Just One'.

The fact of Elijah's 'consuming zeal for the Lord of Hosts' is twice referred to in 1 Kings 19. Here the reference is specifically to 'the Lord God of Hosts'. Again, this is almost exactly the language of the proclamation of James 5:1–8, following its allusion to how the workers, being cheated in the fields by 'the Rich', were advised to wait 'patiently until the coming of the Lord' (the 'of Hosts' part already specifically evoked in 5:4). This is varied slightly, but significantly in the light of new concerns over martyrdom in time of Holy War, in Mattathias' final testament to his sons in 1 Maccabees 2:49–94, which rather asserts: 'This is the time to have a *consuming zeal for the Law* and to give your lives for the Covenant of our Forefathers'.[58] To this, 2:58 added the pivotal, that '*for his consuming zeal for the Law, Elijah was caught up into Heaven itself*'.

Curiously, it was in 1 Kings 19:4–15 that Elijah was not only described as taking *refuge in a cave* – 'hiding himself' once again? – to escape from Jezebel and King Ahab after having just made rain and slaughtering all their prophets of '*Baal*', but also as 'going *into the wilderness*'. There, he 'sat under a carob tree' and 'wished to die' (a feature of the tradition complex that will also reappear in 'Honi' stories in Rabbinic literature) before significantly, as this is put in 1 Kings 19:15, making his way to 'the *wilderness of Damascus*'. This motif of 'sitting under a tree' will also resurface in these *redivivus*-type stories about Honi, as it will in their mutation in the one about 'Nathanael' – a stand-in, in our view, for James in the New Testament in the Gospel of John 1:49–51. Notices such as these show Honi, just like John, to be another of these Elijah *redivivus*es, not only in the matters of being placed under ban and being a Rainmaker, but also as to his basic persona.

In an additional tradition stemming from this period Elijah, in turn, is considered to have been the incarnation of another of these High-Priestly primordial Rainmakers, the archetypical 'Zealot' High Priest Phineas.[74] It is possible, therefore, to conclude that this '*redivivus*' or incarnationist rainmaking tradition is in some manner connected to the parallel one about High-Priestly 'zeal' and/or Perfect Holiness and Righteousness as *determining one's qualifications to serve* at the altar of God in the Temple.

In Numbers, it was this Phineas who killed backsliders and persons intermarrying with foreigners to prevent 'pollution' in the archetypical desert camp.[59] But just as Elijah's 'consuming zeal for the Law' is referred to in the speech attributed to Mattathias in 1 Maccabees 1:58 above, Mattathias himself – whose own Phineas-like 'zeal' in killing collaborating backsliders was already depicted earlier in 1 Maccabees 1:24 – likewise, invokes Phineas' paradigmatic 'zeal for the Law' in this farewell Testament to his sons (1:54). This he puts as follows – in the process tacitly declaring his own legitimate 'Zadokite' ancestry and, consequently, that of his family descending from Phineas: 'Phineas our father, in return for his *burning zeal*, received a Covenant of Everlasting Priesthood (the incongruously-designated 'Covenant of Peace' again)'.[60]

Abba Hilkiah Makes Rain

The Babylonian Talmud also refers to another mysterious, rainmaking grandson of Honi the Circle-Drawer contemporary with James, 'Abba Hilkiah'.[61] These 'Abba'-names, which signify 'Father', are very curious. It has been suggested that 'Abba'-names such as these may in some manner denote 'Essenes' which, in the more general way the term seems to be used, probably has an element of truth to it.

To give an additional example from the Talmud, Rabbinic literature ascribes the catalogue of what are usually referred to as 'the Zealot woes', to one 'Abba Joseph bar Hanin' – identity otherwise unknown – that is, 'the Son of Hanin the Father of Joseph', a very curious designation indeed. This catalogue of 'woes' attacks the various High-Priestly families in the Herodian Period in the most extreme manner conceivable and is expressed as follows: 'Woe unto me for the Boethusians. Woe unto me for their curses. Woe unto me from the Sons of Ananus (the family pictured in both Scripture and Josephus as being involved in the execution of Jesus and the judicial murder of James). Woe unto me for their slanders.... For they are the High Priests, their sons are Treasurers, their sons-in-law are Captains of the Temple, and their servants smite the People with clubs.'[62] Not only is this a completely surprising passage utterly atypical of the Talmud – therefore the reference to it as 'the Zealot woes' – but one should note the references to both 'Boethusians' and 'Sons of Ananus', the condemnatory attitude towards both, and the references to Treasurers, Captains of the Temple, and how *their servants beat the People with sticks*, all subjects conspicuous in Josephus' picture of the progression of events leading up to the War against Rome in the Sixties CE.

The note in these 'Zealot woes' about the High Priests sending 'their servants to beat the People with sticks' actually echoes two notices in Josephus' *Antiquities*, one just preceding the stoning of James and the other right after it. In both notices, the High Priests are described as 'sending their servants to the threshing floors', beating the People 'with sticks', and stealing the tithes of the 'Priests of the Poorer sort'.[63]

Not only does the repetition of this notice indicate some confusion on Josephus' part about events surrounding the death of James (or at the very least some overlap), but in the Pseudoclementine *Recognitions* and in events surrounding 'the stoning of Stephen' – the reflection of the stoning of James in Acts – Paul is implicated in similar kinds of attacks. Once again, there is the problem here of a chronological disconnect. Of course, whatever else might be meant by the allusion to 'Priests of the Poorer sort', it certainly reflects the manner in which all accounts refer to the followers of James.

For his part, though 'Abba Hilkiah' is never heard from again in any Talmudic legend, the name 'Hilkiah' is certainly Priestly and surfaces at various critical junctures in pre- and post-Exilic history. He plainly appears to have been a member of the original High Priest line, meaning he was a 'Zadokite' and, as such, a direct lineal descendant of the Zadok who functioned as High Priest in David's time (1 Chronicles 6:13 and 6:45). Not only was one of his forebears seemingly involved with the Prophet Isaiah (Isaiah 36:3–22), but Ezra himself is pictured – in what is probably an artificial genealogy anyhow, borrowed from Jesus Ben Yehozedek, the son of the last High Priest of the First Temple and, therefore, a 'Zadokite' as well[64] – as one of his descendants (Ezra 7:1–5). The latter takes Ezra back through 'Hilkiah' to 'Zadok' and thence to Phineas – that is, Ezra himself, according to the overt implications of this genealogy, is at the same time both a 'Zadokite' and a 'Zealot High Priest'. The only problem is that the genealogy is, as just underscored, basically the same one accorded Jesus ben Yehozedek – the first High Priest of the Return.[65]

The circumstances surrounding Abba Hilkiah's rainmaking, described in Rabbinic tradition as at 'a time of drought', certainly are striking and parallel the traditions about James in Hegesippus, the Pseudoclementines, and the notice in Epiphanius about James' rainmaking.[66] In the Babylonian Talmud, for example, so frightened are the Rabbis of Abba Hilkiah that they will not approach him. Rather, they send little children to him, while he is 'working in the fields', to ask him to make rain.[67] The same motifs reappear in a tradition preserved by Jerome relative to James' pre-eminent 'Holiness', that James was held in such reverence among the people of Jerusalem and considered 'so Holy' that the little children used to try 'to touch the fringes of his garments as he passed by'.[68] Not only are both James and 'Abba Hilkiah', therefore, more or less contemporary, *making rain in a time of drought*, but both individuals are treated by all who approach them – friend and enemy alike – with a kind of reverential awe bordering on fear.[69]

A similar, albeit less convincing, portrait of 'Jesus' in the Synoptic Gospels has come down to us as orthodox tradition – another probable instance of real traditions relating to James' person being retrospectively absorbed into the portraits of Jesus. The individuals involved in the 'touching' activity relative to Jesus' person or garment run the gamut from women with an unstoppable discharge of menstrual blood (*sic!*) to these same 'little children', as well as the blind, paralytics and, as a prelude to one curing or raising incident, *even a Roman centurion!*[70] The comedy of these episodes, sacred or profane, should not be ignored and all must be strenuously doubted or taken to a certain extent as a parody – often malevolent parody – of cherished Jewish beliefs, customs, and taboos.

The note in the Babylonian Talmud's version of the Rabbis sending 'little children' to ask Abba Hilkiah to make rain of his being 'in the fields' not only dominates the story, but to some extent parallels the allusion in the Letter of James to the workers 'in the fields' being cheated of their wages. In James 5, this acts as a prelude to apocalyptic evocation of the imminent 'coming of the Lord of Hosts' and final eschatological Judgment ultimately expressed in terms of 'waiting patiently' for 'the coming of spring rain'. Again, we have come full circle and have the note of 'the coming of rain' – to say nothing of that of 'waiting patiently' which links up with similar expressions in both the Habakkuk *Pesher* and the Gospel of John.[71]

Jacob of Kfar Sechania's Curious Tradition about 'Jesus the Nazoraean' and Judas Iscariot's 'Bloody' Suicide

We have already touched upon how, in regard to a previous *Zaddik* Honi, the Pharisee opponents who ultimately stone him cheat the resistance-minded Priests in the Temple, who are intent on carrying out the Passover sacrifices according to their precise specifications. Moreover these hold-outs are the same individuals whom Honi refuses to condemn. To further extend the reverse parallel with the Letter of James, in the Rabbinic legend, Abba Hilkiah doesn't wish to *cheat* his employees. As in the case of another character in the Talmud paralleling James, 'Jacob of Kfar Sechaniah' or 'Jacob of Sihnin', the locale is probably Galilee.[72]

In the quasi-parallel pictures of both Hegesippus via Eusebius and the Pseudoclementine *Recognitions*, the requests become those made to James (either by 'the High Priests' or 'the Scribes and the Pharisees') to come to the Temple either to debate or to quiet the crowds 'hungering after the Messiah' at Passover and, in both, the motif of hesitant reverence is strong.[73] In Hegesippus and early Church accounts dependent on him, James then rather proclaims the imminent coming of the Messiah 'on the clouds of Heaven'. In all sets of traditions however, Hegesippus, the Pseudoclementine *Recognitions*, and the Talmudic Tractate *Ta'anith*, James or Abba Hilkiah, or both, are almost always presented as *hostile* to the Herodian Pharisaic/Saducean Establishment and treat its emissaries with contempt.

'Jacob of Kfar Sechaniah' or 'Sihnin' is another individual with the same name as James in Rabbinic tradition. In the Talmud, he is the bearer of a curious tradition about 'Jesus the Nazoraean', the only one Talmudic literature conserves or was allowed to conserve in this name![74] The tradition is attributed to the allegedly 'heretical' and obstreperous 'Rabbi Eliezer ben Hyrcanus' – 'obstreperous' because of run-ins (interestingly enough, along with another colleague, 'Rabbi Joshua')[75] with Rabban Gamaliel, the grandson of Paul's professed teacher by that name.[76] In this tradition, as he reports it, Eliezer meets this 'Jacob' or James in Kfar Sechaniah or Sihnin, presumably in Galilee. In response to a question Eliezer poses him about 'a prostitute's hire' or 'wages' given or dedicated to the Temple – an odd question to begin with – Jacob replies with one of his own about what 'Jesus the Nazoraean' said on the subject.

Not only do we have the 'wages' motif here that we just saw in the material from James about 'the Rich' *cheating the workers in the field of 'their wages'* and its inverse parallel in Talmud *Ta'anith*'s portrait of Abba Hilkiah *not cheating the workers in his fields*, but this is clearly a special case of 'gifts to the Temple' in general, whether on the part of foreigners or other types of persons deemed impure for one reason or another (as, for example, the well-known 'harlots' or 'prostitutes' who share Jesus' table according to Gospel portraiture – again, surely relevant here) – the rejection of which was so important for this period particularly in the run-up to the War against Rome as Josephus presents it.[77]

Crucially, this Talmudic tradition attributed to 'Eliezer ben Hyrcanus' about 'Jacob of Kfar Sechania' or 'Sihnin' in the name of 'Jesus the Nazoraean' parallels and, in the writer's view, is the actual basis for Matthew 27:3–10's depiction of Judas Iscariot's 'thirty pieces of silver' as 'the price' of 'innocent Blood' – a portrait which embodies the three motifs of 'wages', 'gifts to the Temple', and 'Blood', and, by implication, a fourth, the Damascus Document's 'pollution of the Temple'.

Though not paralleled in any of the other Gospels, the version in Matthew is extensively revised in Acts 1:18–20. In Acts, Judas doesn't 'hang himself', but rather dies somewhat mysteriously and, something like James in early Church accounts, after 'a headlong fall' – from where is unclear, but into a 'Bloody Field' they called 'the *Akeldama*',[78] – 'his guts (like James' head, previously) all bursting open and blood gushing out' (*thus* – Acts 1:18). Matthew 27:6's 'wages' or 'price of Blood' now metamorphose into Acts 1:19's 'the Field of Blood' ('called in their language *Akeldama*') and, instead of a proof-text allegedly from 'the Prophet Jeremiah', which Matthew 27:9 quotes as: 'I took the thirty pieces of silver, the price of him on whom they priced, on whom they of the Sons of Israel priced' (*sic*); Acts 1:20 rather applies passages from Psalms 69:25 and 109:8 – the second, in our view, leading into the palimpsest of the missing election of James as 'Bishop' of the early Church.[79]

However this may be, the problem is that Matthew 27:9–10 is *not quoting from 'the Prophet Jeremiah'*, as it mistakenly thinks or claims, but rather from 'the Prophet *Zechariah*' – and this not a little disingenuously – a matter which will, however tangentially, also have to do with the not-unconnected issue of the missing introduction of James in Acts. The extant passage in Matthew – which is a loose quotation of Zechariah 11:12–13 – was, in its original context, actually an extremely angry one. Invoking the language of 'breaking My Covenant' in Zechariah 11:10, this had to do with God instructing the Prophet to contemptuously '*cast*' the paltry '*wages*' owed him for services rendered in shepherding His flock '*into the Temple Treasury*'.

Not only is this the proof-text which somehow Matthew 27:3–6 manages to apply to Judas Iscariot's 'betrayal of innocent Blood' and suicide (always an appropriate theme, however distorted, where '*Sicarii*' are concerned, and quite a feat by any literary measure), but it is from this, too, that Matthew gets its proverbial 'thirty pieces of silver', which becomes such a useful quantitative element in its narrative but, once again, not paralleled in any of the other Gospels – though it will be pivotal for materials connected with Judas' criticism of Jesus in the 'Mary'/'Martha' affair and interlocked with Rabbinic tradition we shall delineate further below. Furthermore, it is as a result of the evocation of this citation in Matthew that the High Priests respond and are able to explain that: 'It is not lawful to place them ('the pieces of silver') into the Treasury for it is the price of Blood' (27:8).

For their part, the two passages Acts 1:20 quotes from Psalms will immediately give way to the election to replace 'Judas', in which the individual with the curious name of 'Joseph Barsabas Justus' was the defeated candidate. Psalm 69, the source of the first citation, is also a source of many familiar proof-texts including: 'zeal for Your House consumes me' (69:9 – 'My Father's House' in John 2:16) and 'when I was thirsty, they gave me vinegar to drink' (69:21 – Matthew 27:34, 48 and pars.) – this, despite the fact that the Psalm is a completely 'Zionistic' one, which ends with the assertion that 'God will save Zion and rebuild the towns of Judah', which will be 'handed down to His Servants' descendants and lived in by those who love His Name' (69:35–36). This last, of course, is exploited in James 2:5 above in 'the Kingdom prepared for those who love him' and throughout the Damascus Document.[80]

The original passage, as it appears in Psalms, calls out for the Lord's even more terrible 'vengeful fury' and 'hot anger' on the narrator's persecutors in the plural, so that 'their camp would be reduced to ruin and none would inhabit their tents'. This passage which in its original context is at all times plural is pointedly changed to singular in the citation in Acts 1:18–20 where it is applied, as we saw, to the 'headlong fall' Judas Iscariot takes in the 'Field of Blood called Akeldama'.

The second, from Psalm 109:8, reads: 'Let another take his Office' (Episcopate) which, as we have already seen as well, has more to do with the position occupied by James in the progression of these events than any position ever held by the ephemeral individual the Gospels denote as 'Judas' – whomever he may have been. What is, however, equally interesting is that the Psalm in question not only refers to 'Lying'/'a Lying Tongue' (109:2), a favorite usage both at Qumran and in the Letter of James,[81] but it is completely 'Ebionite' – meaning, like the Qumran Hymns, it repeatedly refers to 'the Poor' (*Ebion*) as well as 'the Meek' ('*Ani*) – but even more to the point, to 'the soul of the Poor One' (once again, '*Ebion*' – 109:16 and 22).[82]

In fact, the last two lines are classic in this regard and therefore, worth citing in full: 'I shall praise Him among the *Many*, for He shall *stand* at the right hand of the *Poor*, to *save* him from the Judgments of his soul (109:30–31).' One can imagine what the exegetes at Qumran would have made of this Psalm which, in substance, so much parallels Psalm 37 expounded there.[83] In the writer's view, Psalm 109 probably was too, that is, expounded at Qumran. Therefore it was on the basis of such vocabulary – namely *Zaddik* (Righteous One), *Rasha'* (Evil), *Ebion* (Poor One), *Belial/Ba-La-'a*, *Shamar* (Keep), *Sheker/Chazav* (Lying), *Rabbim* (Many), etc. – that they appear to have selected the texts they chose to expound, the commentary on it either not having been written down, not preserved, or not so far been found.

Nor is it insignificant that a Psalm – the Greek rendering in which, of the Hebrew *Pekudato* (His Command) or 'Office', is 'Episcopate' (109:8) – which makes so many references to both 'Lying' and the 'Salvation of the Poor' (this last, the name of James' Community in whatever the source), is evoked in Acts just at the point where the introduction and/or election of James as successor to his 'brother' should or would have occurred in a more 'Ebionite' text. One should note that in 109:6–7 introducing this, the Judgment upon those 'returning Evil for Good, hatred for Love' is to be executed – just as in the Damascus Document which invokes 'the Angel of *Mastema*' upon those neglecting circumcision – by 'Satan standing at his (the Evil Person's) right hand' to assure he will 'be condemned'.

Matthew 27:10 also adds the curious phrase, 'as the Lord commanded me' – nowhere to be found in the original of the received Zechariah 11:12 either in the Masoretic or the Septuagint – deformed, as this passage from Zechariah may be to suit the exegesis the Matthean artificer desired. Not only does Matthew 27:9 render this, 'the price of him who was priced, on whom they of the Sons of Israel set a price', again nowhere to be found in the original in Zechariah (in particular, 'the Sons of Israel' has been purposefully introduced – curiously in place of 'the Meek' or 'the Poor' in Zechariah 11:11 – to serve the ignoble aims of the artificer. In fact, 'the Sons of Israel' is nowhere to be found in the received version of Zechariah at all), but Matthew 27:10 does add – obviously attempting some conformation with Acts picture of 'the Akeldama' – 'and gave them ('the thirty pieces of silver') for a Potter's Field'. Once again, however, 'Potter's Field' as well nowhere appears in the original of Zechariah 11:13, upon which it is ostensibly claiming to be based, which only conserves: 'and cast them to the Potter in the House of the Lord' – in the context, as is generally agreed, carrying the meaning of 'Temple Treasurer' or 'Treasury'). Nor can this be in any way reconciled with what appears in Matthew 27:10 however one chooses to rework it!

Nevertheless, at this point Matthew 27:10 does conclude laconically with the addition of the single phrase, 'as the Lord commanded me', again nowhere appearing in the original Zechariah but, in our view, pointing the way towards resolving the complex of issues surrounding these proof-texts. In order to understand this, one must appreciate that what was originally being described *in the document underlying Acts* was the election to succeed Jesus not the one 'to succeed Judas'. It is Jesus who is really 'missing' at this point and in need of succession, not the ephemeral 'Judas'. The latter's disappearance or demise is rather made up on the basis of the absurd use of this Biblical passage, bowdlerized and mistaken-attributed as it may be. Nor is the use of this emblematic name 'Judas' – the name of a series of revered Jewish leaders including Judas Maccabeus, Judas the Galilean, and evocative of the very nation itself – to say nothing of the secondary title '*Sicarios*' either accidental or incidental, but rather *insightfully calculated to incite intense anti-Jewish feeling*, which it has not failed to do over the millennia, its originators having doubtlessly succeeded beyond even their wildest dreams! It is this, perhaps, that the Gospel of Judas may help alleviate – since, while nevertheless still antinomian, it tries to portray Judas as Jesus' favorite Disciple – but, of course, probably never to the extent necessary.

A Prostitute's Hire, the 'Rechabite' Introduction of James, and the Construction of a Latrine for the High Priests

The description that would have been used at this point to introduce the person of James in a proper historical narrative and explain how he came to occupy the Office he did, namely that of 'Bishop' or '*Mebakker*'[126] of the Jerusalem Church, could easily have incorporated the proof-text about 'the Poor' from Psalm 109, which Acts applies to the 'election' of the almost unknown and never-heard-from-again Apostle by the name of 'Matthias' – a name already present for all intents and purposes in Apostle lists (such as they are).[84]

To provide a more intimate description of who and what James, in fact, actually was and how 'life-long Nazirites' like him might have been perceived at the time, it would have been even more striking to include the Prophet Jeremiah's unique delineation of the clan of Rechabites to whom James, as a life-long Nazirite and possibly even an 'Essene', would have been thought either to resemble or relate. Not only were such Rechabites important as actual prototypes of what 'Zealots' ('Jonadab son of Rechab' actually being so characterized in 2 Kings 10:16 and, as such, another of these paradigmatic 'Zealot' forerunners) and, to some extent, 'Essenes' – to say nothing of 'Nazoraeans' – were actually seen to be, but Jeremiah 35:3–19 really does provide a good description of James as he has come down to us.

Principal among 'the commandments which Jonadab son of Rechab' gave to his descendants was the one '*to drink no wine*' (35:14), which such 'Rechabites' held in common with 'Nazirites' and which we would claim basically to be at the core of this missing proof-text regarding James. Regarding this ban on 'drinking wine', it is certainly not incurious that in the Synoptics, the picture of Judas Iscariot's 'treachery' actually occurs in the context of the Last Supper where Jesus is pictured as announcing, following Paul in 1 Corinthians 11:25, 'This Cup is the New Covenant in my Blood' (Luke 22:20 and pars.). But in the Synoptics, this is accompanied by the additional peculiar phraseology bearing on our subject and reflecting these singular Rechabite/Nazirite/Jamesian restraints, 'I will not drink henceforth of the fruit of the vine until the Kingdom of God shall come' (Luke 22:18 and pars.). So here, of course, is the very ban on wine right in the context of the Last Supper and Judas' imminent 'betrayal'.

Furthermore, as Jeremiah reports, such 'Sons of Rechab' were instructed, again not unlike 'Essenes' and Josephus' mysterious teacher '*Banus*', 'to build no houses', 'but to dwell in tents so that you may live many days upon the land which you inhabit' (35:7). The 'tent' theme is particularly important where Essenes were concerned and it is already to be encountered in the original of Psalm 69:25 underlying Acts 1:20 and, like Essenes too, they were 'long-lived'.[85] Interestingly enough, 35:8 adds that, like 'the Sons of Zadok' at Qumran as well and, in our view, 'the Nazoraean', Jacob of Kfar Sechania will now refer to in the tradition he will report about 'Jesus' below, 'they *kept* them' or, as Matthew 27:10 would have it, they did what they were 'commanded' to do. One could say the same about groups like 'the Mandaeans' in Southern Iraq, who still conform to teachings of this kind to this day. Nor should it go unremarked that 'drinking no wine' is a fixture of Islamic practice even today.[86]

Where the 'command to drink no wine' – which the Rechabites hold in common with the Nazirites and, of course, James – is concerned, it appears over and over in Jeremiah 35, setting down Jonadab's 'commandments' to his sons on this subject and the wilderness lifestyle generally.[87] E.g., 'we will drink no wine' as 'our father commanded us' (35:6), 'we have *dwelt in tents* and obeyed and done according that Jonadab our father commanded us' (35:8–10), 'the words that Jonadab son of Rechab commanded his sons' and 'they observed their father's commandment' (35:14) and, finally the active as opposed to the passive: 'the sons of Jonadab the son of Rechab have *set up the commandment* of their father which he commanded them' (35:16).

In fact, this allusion to 'setting up' (*hekimu*) here is actually the pivotal usage employed in the Damascus Document to describe how 'those entering the New Covenant in the Land of Damascus were *commanded to set up* the Holy Things according to their precise specifications'.[88] It is also the basis in that document for both the 're-erecting' (or '*setting up*') the fallen tent of David' and 'raising the Covenant' and 'the Compact (that is, 'the New Covenant') in the Land of Damascus' itself[89] – the counterpart to 'the New Covenant in the Blood of Christ' in Paul and the Gospels.[90] Nor can it be overlooked that this 'Covenant' is the very opposite, of course, of 'the New Covenant' that Peter is taught and, through him, that which was taught to the 'household of the Roman Centurion in Caesarea' with the telltale name of 'Cornelius' (the name of the Roman law in this period aimed at '*Sicarii*' and forbidding 'circumcision' as a kind of bodily mutilation on pain of death – 'the *Lex Cornelia de Sicarius et veneficis*'[91]).

Jeremiah 35:18–19 concludes as follows: 'Therefore, thus saith the Lord God of Hosts, the God of Israel, because you have obeyed the commandment of your father and kept all of his commandments and done all that He commanded you, thus says the Lord of Hosts, the God of Israel, Jonadab son of Rechab shall not lack a man to stand before Me forever.' This is the proof-text we consider to have actually been present in the original – probably 'Ebionite' – source being drawn upon and so egregiously and disingenuously *overwritten* at this point in Acts 1:20. Its traces, as incredible as it may seem, are probably actually to be detected as well in the curious and patently implausible, related description of Judas Iscariot's *Sicarii*-like suicide in Matthew 27:3–10, itself incorporating a proof-text seemingly having, despite its parallel refurbishment, nothing whatever really to do with the events in question either.

The point is ostensibly being presented as having to do with the rejection by 'the Chief Priests and the Elders' of 'the price of Blood' as 'unlawful' for inclusion 'in the Temple Treasury' (27:6). Then, through the tendentious citation of Zechariah 11:11–12 and the mischievous inclusion of 'the Sons of Israel' there, one so-called 'traitor''s defection is being blamed upon a whole People, but hardly to be considered as a serious accusation, despite the fact that it has been taken up historically as such by the mindless multitude obsessed, somehow, with 'Blood' lust ever since!

Granted, this is a rather tortuous and round-about task for the novice reader to follow where this particular bit of dissimulation is concerned but, unfortunately, these are the kinds of twists and turns the serious scholar of New Testament history will have to follow if he or she really wishes to unravel the almost serpentine deformations incorporated in many of these traditions.

Aside from the 'Bloody-mindedness' of all these kinds of New Testament passages – itself not without consequences where the new directive of 'drinking the Blood of Christ' is concerned – the issue of 'sleeping' or 'not sleeping with women during their menstrual flow' is parodied, too, in the 'touching Jesus' episode regarding the woman with an over-abundant menstrual flow.[92] The issue of 'sleeping with women during their periods' will, of course, also be pivotal in the 'Three Nets of *Belial*' accusations in the Damascus Document where it is the key point bridging the 'fornication' and 'pollution of the Temple' charges there. Not only is it related to that of 'a prostitute's hire', but the whole issue of barring Herodians and gifts from or on their behalf in the Temple, since Herodian Princesses, in particular, were seen by their 'Zealot'-style opponents as no better than prostitutes. Therefore, too, the more cosmopolitan scenes of Jesus eating with prostitutes, tax-collectors, and other Sinners in the Gospels are included, in our view, expressly to counteract this.[93]

As this is explained in Columns Four to Five of the Damascus Document relating to those 'sleeping with women during their periods' – itself a clear indication of how Herodians were perceived, to say nothing of their easy intercourse with their Roman overlords who were obviously also perceived in the same way – the identifying, laconic modifier is added, 'and *every one of them marry their nieces*' or 'close family cousins', thereby further strengthening the identification of the group involved in such activity with Herodians and not Maccabeans. Not only could this characterization *not* have applied to any Jewish Priesthood, regardless of its orientation, but it certainly could not have applied to Maccabeans, about whom there is no evidence of such policy.[94] Furthermore, as the Damascus Document makes plain, the charge is but a special case of the ban on 'fornication' in general and, because of the historical circumstance just alluded to, the one of 'pollution of the Temple' connected to it in the 'Three Nets of *Belial*' accusations, already signaled above.[95]

The explanation for this is simple. Those coming in contact with persons behaving in such a manner, that is, 'sleeping with women in their periods' (namely, Herodians and their Roman overlords) – meaning in this period clearly the High Priests whom the Herodians and their Roman overlords appointed – thereby incur their 'pollution', a point also specifically made in the Damascus Document following these same accusations, namely, '*no one who approaches them* can be cleansed. Like someone cursed, his house is guilty – unless he was forced.'[96] Nor are they observing proper 'separation' in the Temple, 'clean from unclean', 'Holy from profane', the concomitant part of the description of such persons in the Damascus Document.[97] This last, finally, also carries over to accepting gifts from and sacrifices on behalf of such persons (even the Emperor of Rome) in the Temple – the issue, as already explained, *which was the immediate cause or and that triggered the War against Rome*.[98]

It is now possible to return to Rabbi Eliezer ben Hyrcanus' encounter in Galilee with 'Jacob of Kfar Sechaniah' in the Talmud and the opinion Jacob heard 'Jesus the Nazoraean' express concerning what to do with 'the wages of a prostitute' or 'a prostitute's hire' (in this case, not the field laborer's 'hire' or Judas Iscariot's 'hire' according to Matthew's tendentious portrayal) given as a gift to the Temple. It should now be clear how much this issue relates to the points we have just been making – the idea of its being 'the price of Blood' having a direct bearing on precisely the perception of this kind of activity, namely gifts from persons 'sleeping with women in their periods' or those incurring 'pollution' from such persons doing service in the Temple and the manner in which the Herodian family was conducting itself in familial relations.

Not only is Jesus' response, as pictured in the Talmud, a good example of his sense of humor – refreshing for a change, to say the least – not normally considered present in most Gospel narratives (except by the writer), but, more germane, it completely *gainsays* New Testament traditions of a similar genre depicting Jesus as 'keeping table fellowship' with prostitutes, tax-collectors, 'gluttons' (a euphemism for persons not keeping dietary regulations), and other such individuals. Moreover, the sardonic sense-of-humor displayed by this 'Jesus the Nazoraean' in his response makes the whole Talmudic tradition, in the present writer's view, even more credible.

As Jacob transmits this, Jesus the Nazoraean's answer is that it was appropriate to use gifts given to the Temple of this kind – that is, from 'a prostitute's hire' – to construct a *latrine for the High Priests*! Anyone who cannot see how this tradition, as it appears in the Talmud, has been transformed in the highly tendentious 'Judas Iscariot' materials, also involving gifts to 'the Temple Treasury' and so steeped in allusions to Blood, is just unaware of and exhibiting no appreciation of the process of tradition manufacture and/or elaboration in this period.

We shall see how this elaboration continues, reverberating back and forth between Talmud, Gospels, and Acts, particularly as concerns the 'thirty pieces of silver' which have become so proverbial and comparable allusions to fabulous 'Riches' and precious ointments, at times also involving Judas Iscariot, but also others, when it comes to considering the last and final Rainmaker in Talmudic tradition 'Nakdimon ben Gurion'. Of course, just as some of the other characters we have been considering – such as Ananias, Agbarus, Theudas, and the Adiabenean Queen – the double or alter ego of this 'Nakdimon' in the Talmud reappears in the Gospel of John as 'Nicodemus' described, as we shall see in due course, as 'a man of the Pharisees' and 'a Ruler of the Jews' (*thus!*) and pictured in John 19:39 (along with 'Joseph of Arimathaea') as 'bearing a hundred weight' of expensive 'ointments' or 'perfumes' with which he helped prepare the body of Jesus for burial.

Above left: CSULB Walking Survey of the Dead Sea shores in 1989-92; **Right:** Hot volcanic river flowing down on the East Side of the Dead Sea beneath Machaeros where Herod bathed during his fatal illness and John the Baptist was beheaded.

Chapter 5
Revolutionary Messianism and
the Elijah *Redivivus* Tradition

Elijah's Cave-Dwelling, Honi's Extended Sleep, and Revolutionary Messianism

Both the Palestinian and the Babylonian Talmuds now go on to relate a story about how Honi went to sleep for seventy years under a carob tree – not unlike Buddha 'under the Bodhi tree' or, in the case of the Nathanael-type stand-in for James in the Gospel of John, 'under a fig tree'.[1] When Honi awakes in his grandson's generation nobody knew or recognized him, whereupon he immediately prayed for death and died – another example of the Talmud's sense of humor.[2] This is a very curious, even sardonic, story. Not only are the number 'seventy' and the element of 'carob tree' significant for our period, but so too are Honi's going to sleep and praying for death.

The Palestinian Talmud even preserves a puzzling further variation of this story, which has Honi the grandfather of yet another individual, once again called 'Honi the Circle-Drawer'.[3] Whether this individual is supposed to be the same as the one the Babylonian Talmud is calling 'Abba Hilkiah', with whom he would be contemporary – he probably is – or just another individual in the *redivivus* tradition, confused in the Palestinian Talmud with Honi, is impossible to say. Not only this, the Palestinian Talmud puts these events at the time of the destruction of the First Temple when they clearly must be seen in relation to or in the context of the destruction of the Second. What appears to be confusing these traditions is the *redivivus*-ideology they all seem to be wrestling with or trying to present, however imperfectly.

As with the descendants of the Hilkiah involved in Josiah's Reform and Jeremiah's forebear previously, we seem to be involved with a line or even a clan of such individuals much like the Rechabites – or should we rather call them 'proto-Essenes' or 'Ebionites'? – highlighted above as having to do with either James or his 'cousin' (even his putative brother), Simeon Bar Cleophas. At least this is the information one can garner by superimposing Epiphanius' version of events on Eusebius'. Certainly we have confusions of traditions, overlapping individuals and probably – since they all seem to involve rainmaking and 'falling asleep and waking up later' – a variation on the *redivivus* 'Zealot' (and, as it will turn out, 'Zadokite') Priestly line coming down from Phineas through Zadok to Elijah to Honi to either James or John the Baptist, or both.

This is exactly the theme we now encounter in the Palestinian Talmud with regard to this second 'Honi the Circle-Drawer', for he too goes to sleep and wakes up again seventy years later – this time, supposedly in the time of Zerubbabel after the Temple has already been destroyed and rebuilt again.[4] The 'seventy years' involved here is certainly based upon Jeremiah 29:10's numerology for the length of the Exile, a characterization which also includes the notions of a 'Visitation' and the vocabulary of 'the Wrath', all of the utmost importance for the eschatological scheme of both the War Scroll and Damascus Document as well.[5] In Daniel 9:2–27, this number 'seventy' is actually referred to with reference to Jeremiah and reinterpreted, not only in terms of 'the Period of Wrath', but also successive devastations of Jerusalem concluding importantly with the setting up of 'the Abomination of the Desolation' in the Temple. Of course, according to the chronology of the story of the 'second' Honi in the Palestinian Talmud, which puts him at the time of the destruction of the First Temple, none of this makes any sense whatsoever.

Such is often the case with the Talmud based, as its traditions sometimes are, on garbled oral tradition and/or possible copyists' error. Still, it is interesting that this second Honi goes to sleep *in a mountain cave* rather than – as the first Honi – 'under a carob tree'. This brings us to a possible solution to our problem – if there is one. As we have already underscored above, Honi like John the Baptist is an Elijah *redivivus* or an Elijah come-back-to-life. In fact, it is very probable that he, not John (since John is most likely his descendant and one of these 'Hanin's or 'Honi's) is the original behind the Elijah *redivivus* ideology as reported in the New Testament.

What we are witnessing in later Gospel rewrites of this conceptuality – the Gospel of John, as we have seen, specifically denying the ideology where John was concerned – are themes from other narrative sources being absorbed into their 'Jesus' story. We have already remarked this happening with regards to elements from James' biography. It also happens regarding themes surrounding the series of other charismatic agitators, 'Innovators', 'Impostors', or 'Pseudo-prophets' described in Josephus – the derogations are his not the author's – for instance, Theudas leading the People across Jordan in a reverse exodus, the Samaritan Messiah apparently brutally crucified along with a number of his followers by Pontius Pilate, or 'the Egyptian' on the Mount of Olives for whom Paul is supposedly mistaken in Acts 21:38 (here, for instance, the terminology '*Sicarii*', as we saw, was actually used to describe his followers), and others. In Acts this kind of absorption of materials from other sources is raised to the level of art.

That this is the implication of the 'second' Honi story (to say nothing of the first) is strengthened by its relation to the 1 Kings 19:10 story citing Elijah's 'burning zeal for the Lord of Hosts'. Not only is Elijah '*filled with*' or 'consumed' by such 'zeal' but, in this episode, before going into the cave and thence 'into the wilderness' of Sinai 'to stand upon the mountain before the Lord' and witness the miracles or 'earthquake', 'fire', and 'whirlwind' (19:9–12), he also 'sits down under a carob tree' and this, too, actually 'in the wilderness' (1 Kings 19:4). Here Elijah prays – as in the Honi stories – that 'he might die' and *he too then falls asleep!*

In the 'Honi' stories the order is just reversed. In John 1:45–51's variation involving 'Nathanael' – where Jesus is now pictured as uttering the typically Greco-Roman anti-Semitic gibe, 'Behold an Israelite in whom there is no guile' (*sic*), and in line with John's distinct denial that John the Baptist was 'the Elijah-come-back-to-life' – it is now Nathanael not John who is 'the Honi' or 'Elijah *redivivus*'. The vision Jesus predicts Nathanael will see in return for having recognized him as 'the Son of God' is, yet again, just another variation on the one accorded James in the Temple in early Church literature and Stephen in Acts 7:53–58 (before he, too, was 'cast out of the city' – *ekbalontes* – and stoned). Even 'the mountain cave' element of the Palestinian Talmud's 'second' Honi story is prefigured in 1 Kings 19:8 above as 'the Mountain of the Lord in Horeb' where Elijah – and Jesus, thereafter, according to additional Synoptic Gospel portraiture – is also now to spend 'forty days and forty nights'.

But Elijah does not sleep for seventy years, as the Honi stories revamp this aspect of the story in the light of the new eschatology of the coming Wrath and the *redivivus*-tradition attaching itself to Honi's family line and that of rainmaking *Zaddiks* generally. Rather in 1 Kings, Elijah is twice awoken by 'the Angel of the Lord' and told to 'eat and drink' – another important motif retrospectively incorporated into Gospel portraiture. This is because, during 'the forty days and nights' he is about to spend – like Moses on the Mountain in Sinai – there presumably will be no food.

So now we have the twin themes of a Moses-like 'wilderness' experience tied to 'a burning zeal for the Lord of Hosts'. This ideological combination can, in turn, be read into the temporary Nazirite procedure of 'not eating and drinking', revised into the kind of vegetarianism and abstinence followed by even 'life-long Nazirites' and later 'Mourners for Zion' – positions which Paul consistently reverses to the extent even, as already signaled above, of 'drinking the blood' of the Messiah (to say nothing of 'eating' his flesh), as do the

Gospels along with him even to the extent of portraying 'the Son of Man' as 'coming eating and drinking'.[6]

A good example of the opposite sort of behavior are the temporary Nazirite-type oaths which the *Sicarii*-style assassins vow in Acts 23:21 'not to eat or drink until they have killed Paul' (for 'the Mourners for Zion', it will be recalled, it was 'not to eat or drink until they had seen the Temple rebuilt' – in 1 Corinthians 3:9–17, Ephesians 2:21, and the Synoptics, of course, identical with Jesus[7]). Typically, Acts laconically describes such persons simply as 'Jews'.

These 'Honi the Circle-Drawer' stories in the two Talmuds, despite their confusion over which Honi is actually being referred to and when he lived, together with their expansion of Elijah's paradigmatic activity – whether falling asleep under a carob tree or in a mountain cave – must be seen as part and parcel of an incarnationist *Zaddik* or 'Primal Adam' tradition which includes the elements of 'consuming zeal for the Lord', 'rainmaking' (probably to be taken more in its eschatological sense than a natural one), and 'the Friend of God' ideology. Similar stories will be told in later Talmudic tradition about Simeon Bar Yohai, the progenitor of *Zohar* tradition, who together with his son hides 'in a cave' for years in the Trajan/Bar Kochba Period.[8]

The only difference between the Hebrew version of this conception, as we encounter it in Palestine from the person of Honi onwards, and others – including that of 'the Christ' and the later Shi'ite Islamic *Imam* further afield – is that in Palestine, the *Zaddik*-ideal becomes associated with the ongoing Revolutionary strife against all vestiges of foreign rule and concomitant 'consuming zeal for the Lord of Hosts' directed against Jewish Law-breakers and backsliders too.[9] This, in turn, becomes entwined in the First Century CE in Palestine with the struggle against the Herodian Royal Family and their hangers-on or collaborators. This would include the High Priesthood appointed by this family and the Roman Procurators in succession (or allied) to it – which, therefore, should be called, as we have already pointed out, the 'Herodian' High Priesthood, by this time already being called 'Sadducees' as well – and teachers like Paul.

This 'Zealot', rainmaking *Zaddik*-tradition attaches itself to putative second or third-generation descendants of Honi such as John the Baptist and James and, through them, the Messianic ideal, no matter what definition of it one finally chooses to use. By contrast, the Elijah *redivivus* tradition in its initial manifestation only attached itself to Honi. Where Paul is concerned, so practised was he in polemical dialectic and rhetorical debate that in Romans 13:2–3 he is even able to invert the issue of 'Law-breaking' to encompass rather, those who break *Roman* Law (as he puts it so cannily, 'the Authorities God appoints' and their 'Ordinances') not Jewish Law and it is now patently Roman Law that is being referred to as 'the Ordinances of God' not Mosaic.

Furthermore, in Romans 13:4–10, he even goes so far as to use the all-Righteousness Commandment, 'love your neighbor as yourself' (in James 2:8 'the Royal Law according to the Scripture'), to *support paying taxes* to Rome, which every Government official – who in Paul's agile dialectic have now suddenly been turned into 'the Servants of God' has a right to expect. In 2 Corinthians 11:13–15, as already remarked, he even turns this designation as it relates to the actual Leadership of the Movement around as well. Now this Leadership, whom he claims – like 'the Sons of Zadok' at Qumran[10] – are being designated by some as 'Servants of Righteousness' (which would clearly have to include James, Peter – 'Cephas' in Galatians 2:9 – and John 'whose End shall be according to their works', vocabulary very close to what one also finds at Qumran[11]), are rather merely *'disguising themselves as Apostles of Christ'* and are, as we have seen as well, in reality only 'deceitful workmen' and Satan-like 'Pseudo-Apostles' (2 Corinthians 13:13)!

In 1 Corinthians 8:1–13, where he actually uses the 'Piety' language of 'loving God' and builds towards rejecting James' ban on 'things sacrificed to idols', Paul dismisses such 'scruples' as the 'weak consciences' of the ubiquitous 'some'. In doing so, he actually uses the 'puffed up' language we shall encounter, as we proceed, in the Habakkuk *Pesher*, based on Habakkuk 2:4 where it introduces the all-important biblical proof-text, 'the Righteous shall live by his Faith'. But as Paul uses the expression, he applies it to what is clearly the Leadership of the Jerusalem Church, 'puffed up' by its own 'Knowledge' when it should be 'built up' by 'love'; or, as he so cannily puts it in 8:1 – using what we shall see to be the pivotal language of 'building' – 'love builds up'. For its part, the Habakkuk *Pesher*, introducing its key exegesis of this same 'the Righteous shall live by his Faith', actually interprets it in terms of the punishment the Guilty 'will multiply upon themselves when they are judged' – presumably at the Last Judgment, the *Pesher* always being very consistent on allusions of this kind to 'the Last Judgement'.[12]

The Days of Noah and the Coming Eschatological Flood

Of course the biblical story about Elijah, in imitation of Moses, to say nothing of Noah, spending 'forty days and nights on the Mountain of God in Horeb' prefigures Jesus' Temptation for forty days and forty nights 'in the wilderness' as retold in Gospel narratives – with, to be sure as is usually the case, precisely the opposite effect since, as the Gospels retell it, the whole episode is viewed as the result of 'Devilish' or 'Satanic' manipulation.[13] The Pseudoclementine *Homilies* also alludes to this confrontation 'in the wilderness' with the Devil but according to it the victors are those following James – 'Satan's servants' being, in fact, Apostles such as Paul, who have no written credentials from James and do not teach his position on 'abstaining from blood, fornication, things sacrificed to idols, and carrion', but are rather sent to 'deceive' – that is, it is *they* who are 'Satan's Servants' or 'Deceivers' not vice versa![14]

For their part, as the Synoptics present this episode, the focus is shifted and it is rather aimed at just those kinds of charismatic Revolutionaries, to whom Jesus (if he existed as such) must have belonged and who, together with extreme purity-minded '*Zaddik*' or 'Zadokite' Leaders (who in other contexts go by the name of 'Nazirites' or 'Nazoraeans'), were indulging in the same sort of '*redivivus*' posturing that commentators like Josephus considered so fraudulent.[15] Josephus also basically evokes the same two themes of a 'wilderness' sojourn and Satanic manipulation and, in his accounts, what these 'Impostors' and 'Religious Frauds' – 'who were in intent more dangerous even than the Bandit Leaders or Revolutionaries' – were doing was 'leading the People out into the wilderness there to show them the signs of their impending Freedom' or 'Redemption' – 'signs', the Gospel narratives seem to imply, that were no better than 'Temptation by the Devil'.

Actually, scriptural stories about Elijah generally prefigure those about Jesus, including raising the dead, curing, etc., the only difference being that the more xenophobic portrayal of Elijah's attitude of apocalyptic 'zeal' is, in almost every instance, jettisoned. On the contrary, guided by the anti-nationalist antinomianism of teachers like Paul, it has been totally reversed into the mirror opposite comprising an amorphous form of cosmopolitanism reflecting the ideals of the Roman '*Pax Romana*' wholly at odds with the normative ethos of Palestinian 'Messianism' as reflected in the Dead Sea Scrolls and the general 'Elijah *redivivus*' tradition resting on 'a consuming zeal' for either God or the *Torah* of Moses, or both.

In fact, if one looks closely at the above episode, where Elijah encounters 'the Angel of the Lord' in a cave, one will even be able to detect the prefiguration of the earliest *surah*s of the Koran depicting, as they do, Muhammad's opening visionary experiences 'in a cave'.[16] These include the theme of all-night vigils in caves such as this, coming out and wrapping himself in his 'cloak' or 'raiment', and being told by the Angel – in this case, purportedly Gabriel – 'Arise and warn' (*Surah* 84:1–2 – 'The Cloaked One').[17] In Elijah's case, it will be recalled, it was, rather, 'Arise and eat' – presumably to prepare himself for the journey to the Mountain of the Lord in Sinai![18]

For its part, the Palestinian Talmud also compares Honi's 'rainmaking' to Isaiah 54:9's 'this is like the days of Noah', which itself echoes or is echoed in the Synoptics' 'Little Apocalypses' and, according to Gospel portraiture, words attributed to Jesus. This reads in Matthew 24:37, 'But as the days of Noah, so shall be also the coming of the Son of Man'. In it, such 'days' are compared to final eschatological Judgment, just as they are in the Talmud. As Matthew 24:30 puts this: 'Then shall appear the sign of the Son of Man in the sky ... and they shall see the Son of Man coming on the clouds of Heaven with *Power* and Great Glory'. As the Damascus Document puts a similar idea in the summation at the end of its historical and exhortative section: 'And they shall see *Yeshu'ato*' ('His Salvation').[19] One should also note, by implication, that the Noahic 'Flood' is being equated with 'the coming of the Son of Man on the clouds' – once again, apocalyptic rain and storm cloud-imagery. This in turn is the key eschatological proclamation attributed to James in early Church accounts of the prelude to his death in the Temple on Passover – perhaps, even more likely, *Yom Kippur* since James is depicted in these accounts as being in the Inner Sanctum of the Temple doing an atonement on behalf of the whole People, an activity normally associated with *Yom Kippur*.

Not only does the Jerusalem Talmud consider that *rain is withheld* for the sins of idolatry, fornication, and murder – or, as it puts it, 'polluting the ground with Blood because Blood pollutes the Land'[20] – again the basic categories of James' directives to overseas communities and 'the Noahic Covenant' generally; it also connects the story of Honi 'filling up cisterns, pits, and caverns', the implications of which we shall explore more fully below, with repeated reference to a 'Stone' in the Temple (in this instance, 'the Stone of Lost Property'). But this, too, contains just the slightest echo of the 'Hilkiah' material, delineated in 2 Kings 23:4, in which Josiah is depicted as 'standing by the Pillar' when he swears 'to keep the Covenant'. This kind of 'Pillar' or 'Stone' also mysteriously reappears in the story of James' death in the *Second Apocalypse of James* from Nag Hammadi. Nor is this to mention 'Stone' and 'Cornerstone' symbolism generally at Qumran, particularly in the Community Rule, where the 'Wall that will not shake on its Foundations' and 'Fortress' imagery abounds – to say nothing of in the New Testament.[21] In this *Second Apocalypse*, James is pictured as 'standing beside the *Pillar of the Temple* beside the *Mighty Cornerstone*' when his opponents decide 'to *cast him down*' – the language of almost all these early Church accounts of his death.[22]

Curiously in this account – which is obviously drawn from the same material as the one Eusebius conserves from Hegesippus – after forcing him to 'stand in a pit', James' executioners place 'a stone on his abdomen' oddly echoing the 'stoning' aspect of the affair in more familiar contexts. But even here there is either an echo or prefiguration of execution scenarios for 'blasphemy' in the Talmud's *Mishnah Sanhedrin* where, in one description anyhow, a heavy stone is placed on the malefactor's abdomen and considered to be the equivalent of stoning![23]

We shall also presently see how the last of these legendary Talmudic Rainmakers Nakdimon ben Gurion will be pictured as basically repeating Honi's miracle-working of 'filling up the cisterns, pits, and caverns', only in Nakdimon's case he will 'refill twelve Temple cisterns' to 'overflowing'.[24] This language of 'filling' will then reverberate back and forth through a multitude of Talmudic and New Testament episodes we shall examine in detail presently, until one's head will fairly spin from all the interconnections, rhetorical flourish, and word-play – word-play not so different from that we have already seen Paul use to such devastating effect in his method of allegorical and rhetorical repartee.

Curiously too, the Talmud seems to think that in some manner the prophet Habakkuk prefigured Honi's 'circle-drawing' and 'praying for rain'.[25] One can, again, take this in an eschatological sense since Habakkuk will be seen as a key eschatological prophet for the sectaries at Qumran and, to be sure, early Christianity as well.[26] This parallel, however, is not simply fanciful for, in these sections on the prototypical Rainmakers in the Talmud, the prophecy in Habakkuk 2:1–2 of 'standing upon his Watchtower and fortifying himself firmly on his Bulwark' – language strongly reminiscent, as well, of the imagery of early Church descriptions of James – is applied to the actual process of Honi drawing his circle and 'taking his stand' within it.[27]

This prophecy also reappears in the Habakkuk *Pesher*, where it is expounded in terms of the Righteous Teacher's ability to understand scriptural prophecy and foresee 'the appointed End'.[28] The crucial exegeses of Habakkuk 2:3 and 2:4 on 'waiting for' the final vision and 'the Righteous living by his Faith' that then directly follow are interpreted in terms of what in Early Christian theology becomes known as 'the Delay of the *Parousia*' and how those Jews 'who *do* the *Torah*' will 'be saved' at the time of the Last Judgment at the End of Time, while those following the more backsliding approach of a teacher very much resembling Paul – playing off the usage 'puffed up' in the first part of Habakkuk 2:4 – will have 'their guilt multiplied upon them when they are judged'.[29]

In fact, the text of the Habakkuk *Pesher*, while somewhat damaged at this point, actually can be used to clarify a questionable recension in the Cairo Genizah version of the Damascus Document – itself leading up to the all-important definition of 'the Sons of Zadok' of Ezekiel 44:15. The text which reads taking one's 'stand upon one's *net*' (*metzudo*), a somewhat opaque allusion, probably should read – in view of the keen interest shown in this metaphor just detailed in the Habakkuk *Pesher* above – 'upon one's Watchtower' (*mishmarti*).[30] In the Habakkuk *Pesher*, the exposition of this term 'Watchtower' is eschatological and it is interpreted in terms of 'the Last Days', their 'delay' or 'extension', and how 'God made known the Mysteries of the words of the Prophets' – uniquely as it were – to the Righteous Teacher.[31]

Nor can there be any doubt that the interpretation of the all-important Habakkuk 2:4 that follows in the Habakkuk *Pesher*, 'the Righteous shall live by his Faith', expounded here at Qumran and in Galatians, Romans, and James, is, as we shall also see more fully as we proceed, eschatological as well, that is, its exposition will relate to 'the Last Days' or 'the Day of Judgment' too.[32] As in the War Scroll, once again demonstrating the basic circularity of all these materials and their inter-relationships, the enemies in the Habakkuk *Pesher* at this juncture are 'the *Kittim*' too – meaning, according to our interpretation, the Romans.

Simeon Bar Yohai, the Karaites, *Elchasai*, and Paul

A similar 'Hidden' or 'disappearing'/'re-appearing' tradition is associated in the Talmud, with the eponymous transmitter of *Zohar*-tradition in early Second-Century Palestine and a contemporary of Elchasai, Simeon bar Yohai. Simeon was another Rabbi with distinctly 'Zealot' attitudes, harboring an extreme antagonism towards Rome and all vestiges of Roman rule in Palestine. A Disciple of the equally 'Zealot' Rabbi Akiba, Simeon was supposed to have 'hidden himself in a cave' together with his son after the death of his mentor, *eating nothing but carobs for some twelve years* (this number 'twelve' will grow in importance when it comes to telling of the story of Nakdimon's 'twelve cisterns' below) to escape Roman retribution (and even perhaps 'the *Sicaricon*'![33]).

This note about his 'cave-dwelling' is interesting relative to the Dead Sea Scrolls and other activity we have been observing including Koranic revelations in Islam thereafter. But it also tallies with traditions preserved by the Jewish Karaites, the sect opposed to Rabbinic

Judaism in the Middle Ages. They asserted, not only that Jesus' teaching was 'the same as' someone they called 'Zadok', but that the ban on 'niece marriage', we know from writings, such as the Damascus Document and the Temple Scroll at Qumran, was one of his (Jesus') fundamental teachings.[34] Needless to say, this information is not conserved by any other source.

Not only do the Karaites folloe this 'ban on niece marriage' themselves – whereas Rabbinic Judaism followed by Christianity and Islam do not – they also attribute it, not surprisingly, to 'Zadok'. Even more to the point, where 'cave-dwelling' is concerned, a group they refer to simply as 'the *Magbrarians*' or 'Cave-Dwellers' is placed chronologically between the group led by the Teacher they refer to as 'Zadok' and Jesus. Of course, this would make it similar to a group Hippolytus in the Third Century is calling '*Sebuaeans*' (that is, 'Sabaeans') or 'Naassenes'. That is, according to Karaite heresiology, first came 'Zadok', then 'the Cave-Dwellers', and then came Jesus, all linked in an unbroken progression of some kind.

These matters will probably never be sorted out completely but that they relate in some manner to a 'Hidden' tradition associated with a line of *Zaddiks* connected to Honi's family and taking Elijah as their prototype should be clear. That this line is also connected with rainmaking – whether actual or eschatological – should also be clear. Regardless of the truth of Epiphanius' notice about James' rainmaking, that such a procedure or ideology is connected to his person, even if only symbolically through his *Zaddik*-nature, is not insignificant. In this connection, the reappearance of all these Honi look-alikes just prior to the fall of the Temple in 70 CE should not go unremarked, nor should James' death in almost precisely the manner of Honi and for probably very similar reasons – in James' case (if not Honi's), at the hands of a more accommodating Priestly Establishment.

That this line is also linked to the '*redivivus*' ones, whether the 'Zealot'-Priestly one stemming from Phineas and Elijah or the one the Synoptics suppose they are dealing with in portraying Elijah as reborn in John the Baptist, should also be clear. In turn, these lines are paralleled by the 'Jewish Christian'/Ebionite/Elchasaite 'Primal Adam' or 'Man' – one in Pseudoclementine and Sabaean tradition described above. As Muhammad, another heir to this tradition – probably via 'the Sabaeans' (that is, 'the Elchasaites') either in Northern Syria or Southern Iraq or the Manichaeans descended from them – puts this in the Koran: 'Behold, the likeness of Jesus with *Allah* is the likeness of *Adam*. He created him of the dust. Then He said unto him: "Be!" And he was' (3:59). Paul himself shows great familiarity with this doctrine in 1 Corinthians, referring to it as 'the Primal' or 'First Man Adam' or 'the Second Man'/'the Last Adam' (15:21 and 45–48) and his whole discussion of these matters precedes his delineation of the state man will enjoy after the Resurrection.

For his part, Epiphanius sets forth one of the best descriptions of this 'Secret' or 'Second Adam' doctrine imaginable in a passage in which he describes how 'the False Prophet Elchasai joined … those called Sampsaeans (Sabaeans), Osseneans (Essenes), and Elchasaites' (here the basic coextensiveness of these three groups again). This he puts as follows: 'Some of them say that Christ is Adam and the first to be made and given life by the Spirit of God. Others of them say that he is from above, having been created before everything, being Spirit and above the Angels and Lord of all, and is called 'Christ' … but He comes here when he wants, as when he came in Adam.... He came also in the Last Days and clothed himself in Adam's body....'[35]

Two hundred years before, Irenaeus in Western Europe, in discussing 'the Ebionites' whom he already knew were hostile to and had rejected Paul, puts the same proposition in similar terms:

"Therefore do these men reject the commixture of the Heavenly wine and wish it to be the water of the world only, not receiving God so as to have union with Him, but they *remain in that Adam* who … was expelled from Paradise not considering that, as at the beginning of our formation in Adam, that breath of life proceeded from God ... so also in the *Last Days* the Word of the Father and the Spirit of God, having become united with the ancient substance of Adam's formation, rendered Man living and Perfect, receptive of the Perfect Father."[36]

Though Irenaeaus, living in Lyons in Transalpine Gaul, never mentions groups like Epiphanius' 'Elchasaites' or 'Sabaeans' – denotations which were mainly only known in the East and probably had not traveled that far West (for instance, western authors like him, Hippolytus, and Tertullian, do not seem to even know Hegesippus); still it should be clear that this kind of theorizing about 'Adam' was alive and well even in the Western Empire.

For the Koran (2:34 and variously) and Islam thereafter, as with Epiphanius' 'Ebionites' and 'Elchasaites', Adam is above the Angels who prostrate themselves to him, 'all save *Iblis*' – the '*Belial*' we shall encounter throughout the Dead Sea Scrolls. In other words, this 'Primal' or 'Supernatural Adam' is 'the Son of Man' ('Man' and 'Adam', as we have seen, being for all intents and purposes indistinguishable in Hebrew) or, as the newer Greek usage now developing in the West would put it, 'the Christ' who 'in the Last Days' was going to 'come upon the clouds of Heaven' leading the Heavenly Host. It is extraordinary that we should have to go as far afield as Irenaeus in France to explain this tantalizing allusion to 'Christ' as 'Perfect Man' in the Koran!

As Paul puts it in line with his teaching 'spiritual things spiritually' in 1 Corinthians 2:13–15 and his Philo-like poetic allegorizing: 'So also it has been written, "The First Man Adam became a living soul; the Last (or 'Second') Adam became a life-giving Spirit"' concluding, as we saw above: 'The First Man is out of the earth, made of dust. The Second Man (meaning Jesus), the Lord out of Heaven (1 Corinthians 15:45–47).' Again, this is a perfect rendition of the 'Man' or 'Adam' ideology we have been encountering, the First Adam 'made of dust' (which Paul repeats twice more in 1 Corinthians 15:48) prefiguring Muhammad on 'the likeness of Jesus with God being the likeness of Adam'. This gave rise to the idea of Jesus as 'Second Adam', the bringer of Heavenly Judgment and Paul's 'Lord out of Heaven'.

One immediately sees that this is a *redivivus* tradition paralleling the one involving rainmaking and Priestly 'zeal' attaching itself to Phineas, Elijah, and Honi or, if one prefers, Elijah's incarnation in John. Likewise, 'the Son of Man' (that is, 'the Son of Adam'), based on the notice in Daniel 7:13 about 'one like a Son of Man coming with the clouds of Heaven' is but a variation of 'the Lord out of Heaven' or 'Second Adam' notation. However this time, in addition to the supernatural dimension as in Christianity-to-come, it also carries an *eschatological* one, that is, 'the Son of Man' is now combined in the new Hebrew 'Messianic' ideology with the additional imagery of 'the Messiah coming on the clouds of Heaven' to *render final apocalyptic Judgment on all mankind*.

This in turn is expressed in terms of 'rain' – now eschatological rain – in turn, carrying with it the connotation of a 'Last Judgment' that in the words of the War Scroll and Matthew 5:45 will fall on 'the Just and Unjust alike' or 'upon everything that grows'.[37] The same ideology is also to some extent announced in the Letter of Jude, in which Jude uses a passage freely quoted from Enoch 1:9: 'The Lord will come with myriads of his Holy Ones to execute Judgment against all and condemn all the ones who were ungodly among them regarding all their works of ungodliness which they did in an ungodly way.'[38]

Enoch is an extra-biblical text using apocalyptic imagery, inspired seemingly by the same visionary impetus as Daniel, which, though widely copied and expanded in post-biblical times, never penetrated either Jewish or Christian canons despite being highly prized in sectarian environments such as at Qumran.[39] Not only is this passage from Enoch, which is quoted in Jude 1:14, extant in fragments found at Qumran, but Jude 1:11 preceding it and allusion to 'Adam' in 1:14 as well, instead of using the language of the Damascus Document's 'Belial', employs like Revelation 2:14 the linguistically-related usage 'Balaam'.[40]

In fact Revelation 2:14 conflates James' directives to overseas communities with the Damascus Document's 'Three Nets of *Belial*'. This is expressed in the latter in terms of the 'nets' with which 'Belial' attempted 'to ensnare Israel', presenting them 'as three kinds of Righteousness' – nothing of course could better express Herodian family policy than this. On the other hand, Revelation rather expresses this as: 'Balaam taught Balak (again the variations on 'Belial') to cast (*balein*) a snare before the Sons of Israel to eat things sacrificed to idols and commit fornication.' All the key usages for both the Scrolls and the Paul/James polemic are here.

Replete with other language such as 'grumbling', 'boasting', and 'Light and Dark' imagery so familiar both in a Jamesian context and in the Dead Sea Scrolls, Jude (which is actually ascribed to '*the brother of James*') uses the Messianic-style imagery of 'Salvation', 'stars', and even 'clouds' ('clouds without water' in 1:12). It puts this scenario for apocalyptic Messianic 'Judgment upon the clouds' – intending doubtlessly by 'Lord' here, 'the Messiah', or, as it appears at this point and elsewhere in Paul, 'the Lord Jesus Christ' (1:12–17, 21, and 25).[41] This could not be more parallel to the exegesis of 'the Star Prophecy' in the War Scroll from Qumran as we shall see in due course below.

For Paul, in discussing his ideas about 'the First Man Adam' and Jesus as 'Second Adam' being 'the Lord out of Heaven', this 'coming of the Son of Man on the clouds of Heaven' is transformed into a discussion simply about the difference between earthly and Heavenly existence. But in his masterful use of rhetorical allegory, Paul also appears to be playing on language familiar as well from the Messianic portions of the War Scroll and the exposition of the Star Prophecy from Numbers 24:17 it contains in Columns Eleven to Twelve.[42] In referring to Adam as being 'formed out of the dust' (1 Corinthians 15:48), the War Scroll's triumph of 'those bent in the dust over the Mighty of the Peoples' now appears to be transformed in Paul into 'the First Man' ('the Primal Adam') or the earthly man 'formed out of the dust'.[43]

Likewise, the War Scroll's idea of the 'Victory' by 'the Star' Messiah together with 'the Poor' (*Ebionim*), 'the Downcast of Spirit' (compare this to 'the Poor in Spirit' in Matthew 5:3's Sermon on the Mount) or 'those bent in the dust', and the Heavenly Host upon the 'clouds'; Paul now likens to 'a Mystery', in the sense of a Hellenistic 'Mystery'. This 'Mystery' in 1 Corinthians 15:51 – in other words, this 'Victory' – is now the one that God 'gives us by our Lord Jesus Christ' and, in the typical Hellenizing allegorizing style – which he characterizes as 'teaching spiritual things spiritually' in 1 Corinthians 2:13 – it is now 'Victory' over *death*, not 'Victory' over *Rome* or, as the War Scroll so exuberantly expresses this concept, Victory 'over the Mighty of the Peoples' or 'the *Kittim*'. As Paul so deftly transposes this 'Victory' in 1 Corinthians 15:55, it becomes, 'Death where is your sting? O Hades (note now, the complete Hellenization of the vocabulary here), where is your Victory?'

The Cave IV-VI marl, overlooking Wadi Qumran, from where the lion's share of the manuscripts came and showing the incredibly beautiful empty spaces where archaeologists and others have broken into the inner areas and the possibility of even more inner-area chambers still left to be explored

PART II

THE NEW TESTAMENT CODE: NAKDIMON AND NICODEMUS

Chapter 6
'Do Not Throw Holy Things to Dogs'

Nakdimon Ben Gurion's Rainmaking and his Twenty-one Years of Grain Storage

The Babylonian Talmud presents one 'Nakdimon ben Gurion', a contemporary of James who prayed for rain just before the fall of the Temple in 70 CE.[1] Josephus, reversing the name of the same or similar character into 'Gurion the son of Nakdimon', actually calls him 'Nicodemus', corresponding to the Nicodemus in the Gospel of John who brought an expensive mixture of myrrh and aloes to prepare Jesus' body for burial (19:40). The *Midrash Rabbah* on *Genesis* calls him – even in the Hebrew – *Nicodemon* (i.e., Nicodemus).[2] Rabbinic sources generally portray him, like James, going into the Temple and making rain at the time of a famine, this one apparently during the siege of the Temple by the Romans in 68-70 CE.[3] Like Elijah and Honi before him, Nakdimon is able to bring sunshine as well.[4]

Two sources, *Ta'anith* explicitly and *Abbot de Rabbi Nathan* (*ARN*) implicitly, play on the Hebrew root of his name, *Na-Ka-Da*, meaning 'to pierce or break through', as the sun 'breaks through the clouds', and portray him miraculously bringing the sun back after it had already set. Thus for *ARN* 'the sun broke through again' and 'continued shining for his sake'. *Ta'anith* compares him even more flamboyantly to Joshua and Moses, declaring that 'for the sake of three, the sun broke through'. At this point *ARN* (quoting Joshua 10:13-14) even asserts that Nakdimon was so favored by God that he could even make the sun stand still – another Joshua or Jesus-like sign or miracle.

These curious, even bizarre, traditions about Nakdimon give the impression that more underlies these events than might be supposed, especially when other rainmakers and quasi-contemporaries such as James, Abba Hilkiah, and Hanin the Hidden are taken into account. Clearly we have a combination of themes based on the portraits of Elijah and/or Honi the Circle-Drawer (Josephus' 'Onias the Righteous') in biblical and Rabbinic narrative and in Josephus. The *ARN* ascribes to Moses the circles Honi drew and in which he stood to pray to bring rain, perhaps due to Moses' ability 'to make the sun shine through'. In Moses' case this is the prayer he made to cure Miriam's leprosy.[5]

Yet someone as Rich as the Nakdimon of rabbinic legend could not be thought of as having accomplished anything remotely resembling rainmaking and other such miraculous feats. Nor would such a Rich individual be described in terms of his piety, *Zaddik*-status, and Friendship with God. No doubt the same kind of subversion of native Palestinian materials is going on in Rabbinic tradition that we have already encountered in the Gospels and in the Book of Acts.

Ben Kalba Sabu'a and Nakdimon ben Gurion Supply Jerusalem with Enough Grain to Last for Twenty-one Years

In Rabbinic sources, Nakdimon is an individual the Scrolls and the Gospels would classify as *Rich*.[6] One of these fabulously wealthy types with whom Nakdimon is often associated has a tantalizing pseudonym, 'Ben Kalba Sabu'a' (*Ben Kalba* meaning 'Son of the Dog' in Aramaic – female 'dog' in homophonic Hebrew). As with Nakdimon, his name is explained in terms of things he has done or the meaning of his name, thus the description: 'no Poor were ever turned away from his door' and, when 'they came to his house hungry as a *dog*, they went away *filled*' (*Sabu'a* in Aramaic carrying the sense of 'being filled').[7]

Not only are some of these allusions related to subjects we have been discussing above, but the dog/female dog aspect (*kalba*) of the exposition echoes, ever so slightly, the episode in the Gospels about Jesus' encounter with the 'Cananaean' or 'Greek Syrophoenician woman', where Jesus complains about 'taking the children's bread and casting it to the dogs' (Mt 15:26 and Mk 7:28 – *balein* once again and actually *kunariois*/little dogs).[8] No less important, the second part of *Ben Kalba Sabu'a*'s name, *Sabu'a* or 'filled', can also have the sense in both Syriac and/or Aramaic of being 'immersed' or 'to bathe'. With a little imagination Ben Kalba Sabu'a would be the 'Son of the Sabaean Dog' or 'of the Sabaean Bitch'.

As we shall see, both Nakdimon and Ben Kalba Sabu'a will be tied to the number *twenty-one*, Nakdimon in the number of cisterns he will be able *to fill* in his miraculous activities at a time of drought, and Ben Kalba Sabu'a in the number of years that either he or Nakdimon could have fed the entire population of Jerusalem had not the Zealots in their monstrousness burned his or Nakdimon's immense granary reserves and mixed mud with them![9] According to Talmudic tradition, *twenty-one* is the number of years of Queen Helen of Adiabene's three successive Nazirite oath periods. These had been laid upon her by the Rabbis for perceived infractions of the biblical law of adultery; Helen erected a gold plaque in the Temple courtyard on which was engraved the 'suspected adulteress' passage from Numbers 5:11-31,[10] which immediately precedes the rules appertaining to *vows of the Nazirites and their oaths* in 6:1–21. Ben Kalba Sabu'a is also associated in some manner with the fabulous tomb which Queen Helen and her son built in Jerusalem.[11] This well-built family mausoleum still exists today and can be easily visited.[12] Furthermore, not only did the Second Revolt-era 'Zealot' Rabbi Akiba marry Rachel, Ben Kalba Sabu'a's daughter, but one of Akiba's more well-known students was one 'Monobaz', a descendant obviously in the next generation of this same Helen or Ben Kalba Sabu'a, or both, and probably Rachel's brother.

Both Nakdimon and Ben Kalba Sabu'a are linked with two other wealthy individuals. The first is the cryptically named '*Ben Zizzit Ha-Kesef*'.[13] The other, one 'Boethus', will be grouped with these Rich men more because of his daughter Martha's Riches and extravagant behavior than his own. The name 'Boethus' apparently evokes the reigning representative of that family Herod brought in from Egypt to take over the High Priesthood after he had disposed of his Hasmonaean wife Mariamme; in one tradition Martha is referred to as Miriam/Mary.[14]

We can now ascribe cistern-filling, water-supply, and famine-relief efforts to six different persons: Queen Helen, her son Izates, Paul and Barnabas, Ben Kalba Sabu'a, and Nakdimon. The latter not only promises (in *Tractate Gittin*) to supply Jerusalem with enough grain for *twenty-one years* (the implication being during the final Roman siege; in *ARN* Ben Kalba Sabu'a promised enough grain for twenty-two years not twenty-one[15]), but he also gives twelve talents of silver as surety to an unidentified Rich foreign lord or grandee to advance him 'twelve cisterns of water' so that he could fulfill his promise to fill the Temple cisterns by that amount.[16] One should note the numbers twelve and twenty-four in these traditions, as well as all allusions to *full, fill, filling, sated,* or *satiated*.

In both *Ta'anith* and *ARN* this recondite story takes place inside the Temple. While fulfilling these promises, Nakdimon – like James – is pictured *making rain*. In fact, so much rain does he make for the benefit of pilgrims coming to Jerusalem to celebrate the Passover that he *fills* the Temple water cisterns to *overflowing*.[17] The characterization of this process as 'overflowing' will be another motif to watch in these intertwining stories as we proceed.

The efforts of Nakdimon and his colleague Ben Kalba Sabu'a to relieve the famine and supply Jerusalem with grain reflect the famine relief efforts in the 40s of Queen Helen and her son Izates, not to mention those of Paul and his nascent Antioch Community in Acts. Helen, her husband, and/or her sons were also involved in giving the golden candelabra to the Temple which stood in front of its entrance, before Titus took it as booty to Rome using it in his victory celebrations as famously pictured on the Arch dedicated to his name. Helen and/or her husband (*Bazeus* in Josephus; 'King Monobaz' in the *Talmud*) are also credited with donating the golden handles for vessels used on *Yom Kippur* in the Temple and, of course, the gold plaque noted above.

Perhaps even more germane, Helen, whom we have elsewhere referred to as the 'Sabaean Queen', *actually did* send her Treasury agents to Jerusalem to supply it with grain during the famine. We have related this to Acts 8:26–40's story of the conversion of the Ethiopian Queen's eunuch. In addition, the *twenty-one* years of her three successive Nazirite oaths can be seen as roughly the amount of time between this first famine and the stopping of sacrifice on behalf of foreigners and the rejection of their gifts in the Temple that began the Uprising against Rome in 66 CE.

Regarding the twelve talents of silver Nakdimon had promised to pay if he were late in fulfilling the surety he had pledged, his Rich creditor finally asks him either to refill the cisterns by the stipulated date or pay an additional twelve talents, for a total of twenty-four.[18] It is at this point in this oddly-labored story that Nakdimon's/Nicodemus' rainmaking occurs and he actually goes into the Temple and, like James, prays for rain.

As this is described in Talmudic tradition: 'He wrapped himself in his cloak and stood up to pray.' The Jerusalem Talmud even knows the words of Nakdimon's prayer. Of course, we have already encountered this theme of 'wrapping himself in a cloak' (again, a prayer shawl evidently being intended); that was when Elijah's 'consuming zeal for the Lord of Hosts' in a cave on Mount Sinai was evoked in 1 Kings 19:9–14. Nakdimon, in this prayer, claims that it was not for his 'own Glory' nor that of his own 'house' but rather for God's 'Glory' that he would perform the sign or miracle, namely, *filling the cisterns* in order that there should be enough water in the Temple to accommodate even those on pilgrimage.[19] In the process, Nakdimon alludes to his 'father's house', the very cry that John 2:17 (evoking Psalm 69:9) puts into Jesus' mouth when depicting his 'consuming zeal' and 'purification of the Temple'. When Honi used similar language, the Pharisee leader Simeon ben Shetach considered pressing blasphemy charges against him for 'speaking to God like a son'.[20] According to *Ta'anith*, this was because in his prayer – much like Nakdimon's prayer in *Ta'anith* here as well – Honi had added the words about being 'looked upon as one of (God's) household'. Simeon relents, saying: 'If he were not Honi, I would have excommunicated him'![21]

All this is rife with meaning for future events. Honi's 'blasphemy', presaged in these Friendship/Sonship claims by these rain-making *Zaddiks*/Adam *redivivuses*, is echoed in the Gospels as similar charges are leveled against Jesus. For the Gospels, the blasphemy charge concerns a perceived claim of divine Sonship made by Jesus (or made retrospectively on his behalf by his Hellenizing enthusiasts or partisans).[22] When evaluating the New Testament's focus on the Son of God motif amid accusations of blasphemy, it is well to recall the controversy over these rainmaking *Zaddiks* and Elijah *redivivuses* like Honi as prefiguring the accusations against the person in the Gospels called 'Jesus' or '*Savior*'.

Nakdimon Fills the Cisterns and Hanan the Hidden Locks Himself in the Toilet

So Nakdimon prayed, as the story goes, and 'immediately the sky was covered by clouds until the *twelve wells* were *filled* with water' in a torrent so strong that they '*filled* beyond *overflowing*'. Then much wrangling ensues over 'the wages which were held back' from Nakdimon by the foreign lord or those Nakdimon held back from him, whereupon Nakdimon again enters the Temple, wraps himself in his cloak a second time, and prays for it *not to rain*! This time he even evokes 'the Beloved' or 'Friend of God' language we have been describing above with regard to James, Honi, and Abraham in writings like the Damascus Document, Tractate *Ta'anith* and the New Testament.

This wrangling over payment due and not performed reflects to some degree Josephus' account of the stoning of Honi as well, when the Pharisees besieging the Temple refuse to provide the Priests inside with the animals they have already paid for. It was at this point that the Maccabean Aristobulus' and Honi's supporters inside the Temple pray to God, who then sends a whirlwind or an intense rainstorm to 'repay them for their impiety' and, presumably, their prior 'impiety' in having stoned Honi.[23]

In fact, *Ta'anith* connects Nakdimon and Honi in almost the very next line, when it adds the curious statement that *'his name was not Nakdimon but Boni'*. It then explains that he had only been called 'Nakdimon' 'because the sun broke through (*nikdera*) on his behalf'![24] But this is what we have been trying to point out from the beginning: when the *Talmud* is talking about Nakdimon, it really is talking about Honi or, more comprehensibly, a Honi *redivivus*, as little else can be made out of this ludicrous alias. Nor is this to say anything about the real reason for Honi's stoning – and, consequently, about the rainmaking and stoning of James – namely, *refusing to cooperate with the dictates of foreign power*.

In another startling variation on traditions regarding Hanan/Hanin's cognomen, *Ha-Nehba* (the Hidden), the Talmudic tradition sarcastically observes that he was given this cognomen *'because he used to hide himself in the toilet'*.[25] Again, this story is typical of Talmudic narrative which, like the Gospels, is often so absurd and malicious that it fairly jolts one and makes one laugh outright. But this is the way these writers often treated their ideological opponents. This tradition carries overtones of the scurrilously humorous Jacob of Kfar Sechania story about Jesus the Nazoraean's position on gifts from prostitutes' earnings given to the Temple: they should be used to build an *outhouse* for the High Priests. Surely Jesus' purported response to this question is important, not only *vis-a-vis* persons perceived as being no better than prostitutes (perhaps including Bernice, her sister Drusilla, and even possibly Queen Helen herself), but also the picture of Jesus in the Gospels keeping table fellowship with prostitutes and tax-collectors.

Moreover, Nakdimon in these odd Talmudic miracle tales now asks the foreign lord to pay him for the excess wells of water produced out of the *overflow* his efforts had produced. Thus he gives his creditor a chance to object that the day was already done and the sun already gone, so he (the creditor) owed Nakdimon nothing, setting the stage for Nakdimon's even more celebrated miracle, from which he supposedly derived his name, namely, making the sun 'shine through', 'pierce through the clouds' or, in the manner of the Lord's special dispensation to Joshua, 'making the sun stand still'.

What does finally shine through in these convoluted stories is the connection of the twenty-four cisterns that are being *filled* with the twenty-four priestly courses in the Temple. One can draw an even more impressive connection to Epiphanius' description of the 'Standing One' or 'the High Power which is above God the Creator' and thought of, as well, in terms of being 'the Christ and the Great Power of the High God which is superior to the Creator of the world',[26] the dimensions of which are: *'Twenty-four schoeni or ninety-six miles in height and six schoeni or twenty-four miles in width'*.[27]

Rabbi Akiba's Disciples

An even more germane parallel relates to the Royal House of Adiabene and involves the 'Zealot' Rabbi Akiba, who supported the Bar Kochba Uprising in 132–36 CE, one of the important students of whom was also called *'Monobaz'*. The two times either 'twelve talents of silver' or 'twelve cisterns of water' in the Nakdimon stories likely echoes the double period of twelve years 'the Poor shepherd', Rabbi Akiba, reportedly worked to earn the right to marry the daughter of Nakdimon's 'Rich' colleague Ben Kalba Sabu'a.[28] Rachel, as she is called in the *ARN*, in her model faithfulness encourages this 'Poor' country boy in his studies and, rather than marry him immediately, pays for the two consecutive 'twelve-year' study periods he seems to have spent with the famous quasi-heretical Rabbi Eliezer ben Hyrcanus.[29]

In Talmudic tradition, Rabbi Akiba was not only one of the most nationalist rabbis, he was also the rabbi who proclaimed Bar Kochba *the Messiah* at the time of this Uprising from 132–36 – much to the reported derision of his peers and confrères. Akiba applied to Bar Kochba the famous 'Star Prophecy' from Numbers 24:17, a prophecy we have seen reflected in the New Testament, the Scrolls and Josephus as well. Called 'Ben Kalba Sabu'a's shepherd', Rabbi Akiba was also pictured as twice returning to his wife Rachel with 'twelve thousand Disciples' (no doubt evocative of the number of adepts ready to participate with Bar Kochba in the Second Jewish Revolt against Rome[30]). Ultimately he too was martyred in the cruelest of ways.[31]

Rabbi Akiba's teacher, R. Eliezer ben Hyrcanus, was considered a Christian sympathizer of sorts and was perceived of as knowing a tradition from 'Jesus the Nazoraean' via 'Jacob of Kfar Sechania' about the aforementioned 'prostitutes' wages' and the High Priest's 'outhouse'. Eliezer's testimony to 'Jesus the Nazoraean' in the Talmud is one of the most convincing concerning this personage on record, though its wry humor and intense anti-Establishmentism is quite different from Gospel portrayal. Ultimately excommunicated by the Rabbis for being a little too self-assertive and opposing Rabban Gamaliel II, Lamentations *Rabbah* significantly calls Eliezer, '*Liezer*'.[32] Chronological difficulties aside, he (or a prototype of his) is still one of the best candidates for the mysterious 'Galilean' Rabbi Josephus calls 'Eliezer', who countermands Ananias' and his companion's teaching that circumcision was not required for the conversion of the males in Queen Helen's household.[33]

More to the point, the Talmud tells us one of Rabbi Akiba's students is one 'Monobaz', as we have seen, who must have been a descendant of this family. 'Monobazus' is the name of Queen Helen's second son and probably the name of her husband 'Bazeus'. It is the name as well of one of Helen's two descendants who both distinguish and martyr themselves in the opening engagement of the Jewish War against Rome in 66 CE at the Pass at Beit Horon.[34] Thus for the Talmud, Rabbi Akiba was involved with the family of Queen Helen of Adiabene in two ways. Firstly, one of them was clearly his disciple. Secondly, he probably married into this Royal family; this daughter ('Rachel' in ARN) of Ben Kalba Sabu'a paid for the twenty-four years of study he pursued that seem to have matured into extreme revolutionary sympathies as well as the materialization eventually of twenty-four thousand Disciples. Obviously, Ben Kalba Sabu'a is a *nom à clef* for the scion of that family.

Ben Kalba Sabu'a's Doorstep and 'Casting Holy Things to Dogs'

One possible reading of Ben Kalba Sabu'a's name is as a derogatory reference to one of the descendants of the convert to Judaism Queen Helen, *Kalba* signifying 'dog' or 'bitch' in Hebrew. Even if this doubly derogatory sense of 'the Son of the Sabaean Bitch', which we are imputing to it on ideological grounds, turns out not to be present, there can be no doubt of the significance of a veiled reference to someone ('Nakdimon') having a connection to someone else ('Ben Kalba Sabu'a') whose name in the Syriac or Aramaic carries the sense of *bathing* or *bathers*. These last in Arabic are referred to as 'Sabaeans' and, in all three, the use of the letter '*ayin* as opposed to *alef* is determinant.

Aside from the repetitious evocations of 'dog' or 'dogs' to expound Ben Kalba Sabu'a's name is a theme prominent in New Testament as well: that of being *sated, satiated, full,* or *filled*. We encountered this theme in the matter of '*filling*' Nakdimon's or his Rich patron's cisterns, but it will feature in Gospel narratives as it will, to some extent, in the Dead Sea Scrolls.

Tractate *Gittin*, supported by *ARN*, grapples in a most humorous way with Ben Kalba Sabu'a's name. He was called this because one '*came to his door hungry as a dog and went away filled*.[35] Not only is this last usage, '*Sabu'a*' or '*filled*', related in both Syriac and Aramaic to *immersion*, it carries with it in Hebrew the additional sense of 'sated' or 'satiation', which is the whole point of the Talmudic exposition. Here one should also pay especial attention to the verb 'come' or 'came,' which will reappear in a dizzying number of New Testament contexts as well – more than would normally be expected. The same will be true to a somewhat lesser degree of the expression *his door, doorway, stoop*, or *porch*, instances of the use of which we have already started to encounter in the case of Abba Hilkiah's wife.

This is particularly true of Luke 16:22's further variant on the motif of these 'dogs' having to do with 'a certain Poor man named Lazarus' with a 'body *full* of sores who was laid at the *doorstep*' of 'a certain Rich man clothed in purple and fine linen' – this 'Poor man Lazarus' himself being characterized, in turn, as 'wanting to be *satisfied* from the crumbs that fell from the Rich man's table', while 'the dogs *came* and licked his sores'! The laid at/laid down motif will reappear in the additional Nakdimon story we shall highlight below in 'the woolen clothes laid down for him by the Poor, so his feet would not touch the ground'; note here, too, 'the Poor' allusion we just saw with regard to 'Ben Kalba Sabu'a's doorstep', Abba Hilkiah's house, and Luke's characterization of 'Lazarus'.

Here we already have many of the motifs we have been calling attention to, including 'the Poor' and 'the Rich man', 'the doorstep', the pivotal allusion to 'being satisfied', to say nothing of his body being 'full of sores', and of course 'the dogs', which we shall be analyzing more thoroughly as we proceed. Furthermore, this whole thematic complex will move into other material in John about this 'Lazarus' ('Liezer' above?) – the body of whom was resurrected after it 'had already begun to stink' (11:39–44) – who will have two sisters, Mary and Martha, names we shall also encounter in those of the daughters in these Talmudic 'Rich Men' stories, who will themselves be involved in what we shall in turn see to be tell-tale 'perfume' and 'expensive spikenard ointment' ministrations (John 11:1–3 and 12:1–6).

In Matthew 15:21–28 and Mark 7:24–30 the references to 'dogs' will also occur, but there they will relate to what Jesus did with a Canaanite/Cananaean/Greek Syrophoenician woman out of whose daughter he 'casts a demon' or 'an unclean spirit'. In this context, Mark 7:26 will actually use the term '*ekballe*' so important in other milieux, as we have already seen and shall see further to express how 'the children should first be satiated' or 'filled'. In Mark 16:9 *a propos* of Mary Magdalene, a variation of the same term '*ekbeblekai*' will be used; whereas Matthew 15:17, which does not conserve any description of this kind concerning 'Mary Magdalene', rather reserves this usage for the food Jesus says 'goes into the belly and is *cast – ekballetai* – into the toilet bowl*' preceding his 'withdrawal into the parts of Tyre and Sidon'. Of course, both Matthew 15:26/Mark 7:27 conclude with the famous saying of Jesus: 'it is not good to take the children's bread and cast it (*balein*) to the *dogs*'. An earlier version of this same 'casting Holy Things to dogs' phrase (here '*balete*') is to be found in Matthew's Sermon on the Mount. As that iteration has it, don't give anything to 'dogs' – intending no doubt Gentiles and/or backsliding Jews (the 'casting down' will reappear in the second part of the injunction, to 'cast no pearls before swine'). It combines this same language of 'casting down' with 'dogs', but this time Jesus is speaking to his Disciples who '*came* to him', not to the Canaanite/Greek Syrophoenician woman and reads in the more native Palestinian or normative Hebrew manner, 'Do not give Holy Things to dogs, nor cast down your pearls before the swine, lest they should trample upon them with their feet and, turning around, rend you' (Matthew 7:6).

Once again one should note here the expression we have been calling attention to as endlessly repetitive, the casting out/casting down language derived from Greek *ballein*, not only relating to what happens to Stephen in Acts 7:58 (they 'cast him out of the city') and early Church literature to James ('cast down' either from the steps of the Temple by 'the Enemy' Paul in the Pseudoclementine *Recognitions* or, in early Church literature, from 'the

Pinnacle of the Temple' by the allegedly angry Jewish mob before, like Stephen, he too is stoned), but in Josephus to what his prototypical 'Essenes' do to backsliders – namely, '*cast them out*'.[36]

It is also related – at least homophonically – to the *Ba-La-'a* or 'swallowing' language (the root is a homophone) one encounters in Hebrew in the Dead Sea Scrolls relative to what the Wicked Priest does to the Righteous Teacher and his followers – called there 'the Poor'/the *Ebionim* – that is, 'swallows them'.[37] This, in turn, points to the characteristic activity of the Romans and/or their Herodian agents (the '*Amim* and the *Yeter ha-'Amim* of the Habakkuk *Pesher*[38]), 'swallowing', itself related to another seeming variation, '*Balaam*' – whose name in the Talmud, anyhow, is phonetically interpreted to mean 'swallowing the People', which the Herodians did so conspicuously.[39]

To complete this circle, a term like 'Balaam' cannot really be distinguished in any way from 'Belial' in the Scrolls, a name based on the same root. In the New Testament, this moves into allusions like *Beliar* and *Diabolos*, also based on parallel roots. Not insignificantly, in Revelation it goes back to the original 'Balaam' (and 'Balak,' too, a further variation – to say nothing of 'Beelzebub' or, for that matter even, 'Babylon') and his 'net' or 'nets', terminology that will be so pivotal to the Damascus Document's delineation of the conduct of the then-reigning Establishment, the Herodians.[40]

In Matthew 7:6 too we see one of the first of many adumbrations of the language of 'feet'. Here, also, the 'dogs' are 'dogs' (*kunes*), not 'little dogs' (*kunaria*) as in Mark/Matthew's Greek Syrophoenician/Canaanite woman's retort (who is also portrayed in Mark 7:25 as 'falling at Jesus' *feet*'), but the effect is the same. In fact, if one takes these several motifs (in particular, that of 'casting down Holy Things to dogs' or 'swine' or 'casting down crumbs to dogs under the table') as a single cluster, Jesus' caution here in Matthew 7:6 can actually be seen as a reply in advance to the later complaint by this Canaanite woman which finally does lead to his curing her daughter.

That these Gospel allusions to 'dogs' do, in fact, have to do with Gentiles is made clear in the version of this encounter conserved in, of all places, the Pseudoclementine *Recognitions*. There the 'dogs' are overtly identified as a Hebrew way of referring to Gentiles and the woman in question actually gets a name, '*Justes*' – the feminine equivalent of '*Justus*'.[41] Whether this is an earlier or derivative version of the encounter in Mark and Matthew above has to be decided, but in the writer's view the version in the *Recognitions* is more complete and also probably earlier.

To show the link between all three sets of material as the Gospels preserve them, that is, Matthew and Mark's Syrophoenician woman's 'crumbs falling from the master's table'; 'the little dogs under the table eating the children's crumbs'; and the earlier 'not throwing Holy Things to dogs', it would be well to set out more fully the description of the man Luke alluded to as 'a certain Poor One': 'Now there was a certain Rich Man and he was clothed in purple and fine linen, enjoying himself in luxury daily. And there was a certain Poor Man named Lazarus, who was laid out on his doorstep, whose body was full of sores and he was desiring to be filled from the crumbs which fell from the Rich Man's table, so that even the dogs came to lick his sores' (16:19–21).

One could not get much closer to the Talmudic notice purporting to decipher Ben Kalba Sabu'a's name just cited ('no Poor were ever turned away from his door') than this, always making allowances, of course, for the disparagement inherent in the parody. The linguistic coincidences, which cannot be accidental, include the 'desiring to be filled' or 'satiated'; the 'came', or 'coming' language; 'being laid at' 'the Rich Man's doorstep'; the allusion to 'daily', which we shall repeatedly encounter below; and, of course, the 'Poor'. These go a long way towards establishing the linguistic connection to the Talmudic depiction of its 'Ben Kalba

Sabu'a'. The person or persons who created this description certainly knew what he or they were doing.

In a climactic section of the Habakkuk *Pesher* we shall see a similar allusion to 'being filled', this time applied to the Wicked Priest who destroys the Righteous Teacher and his followers among 'the Poor', i.e. the *Ebionim*.[42] This 'Priest' (meaning the High Priest), as a result of his 'walking in the ways of *satiety*' would 'drink his fill' of 'the Cup of the Wrath of God', meaning the *Divine Vengeance* which would be taken on him for what he did to the Righteous Teacher.[43] This is reinforced in the next lines: 'and he (the Wicked Priest) will be paid the reward he paid the Poor' – namely destruction.[44]

Nakdimon's Daughter Miriam, Boethus' Daughter Martha, and Lazarus' Two Sisters

The notices about these fabulously wealthy individuals in the Talmud also usually involve their daughters or even daughters-in-law, just as in the case of the Greek Syrophoenician/Canaanite woman. For instance, in the case of 'Nakdimon's daughter Miriam', *ARN* also describes 'her couch' as 'overlaid with a spread worth twelve thousand dinars'. Here we have 'twelve thousand' again, encountered above in the number of Rabbi Akiba's Disciples, to say nothing of the amount of Nakdimon's surety or the number of cisterns he filled and the variation of the language of 'laying out' which 'overlaid' contains; but the allusion 'couch' also forms part of the Talmudic exposition of the name of Nakdimon's other Rich colleague, variously called '*Ben Zizzit Hakeseth*' or '*Siset Hakkeset*'. The *ARN* expounds this name in terms of the 'silver couch upon which he reclined before the Great Ones of Israel'.[45]

A similar allusion to 'couch' will comprise part of the tradition *ARN* conserves about the great wealth of its hero Rabbi Akiba, who started in poverty so extreme as to be virtually inexpressible. Rabbinic hyperbole aside, in later life after he had obviously inherited his father-in-law Ben Kalba Sabu'a's wealth, Rabbi Akiba supposedly 'mounted his couch with a ladder of gold', while 'his wife (Rachel) wore golden sandals' (allusions to 'footwear' or the lack thereof will also be a set piece of our traditions) and 'a golden tiara' reportedly shaped like the City of Jerusalem. This tradition remounts to his father-in-law Ben Kalba Sabu'a's Riches, to say nothing of Queen Helen's family's – Ben Kalba Sabu'a's putative forebears – own expensive gifts to the Temple (which included both the seven-branched candelabra at its entrance, taken to Rome for his 'Triumph' by Titus, and the plaque with the passage from Numbers dealing with 'the suspected adulteress', both also of gold); but also a youthful promise Akiba had made to his wife in the winter after their marriage when they had nothing but straw upon which to sleep (a prototype of the 'Jesus in the manger' story?).[46]

For her part, Nakdimon's daughter is characterized in the Tractate *Kethuboth* needing 'an allowance of four hundred dinars daily just for her perfume basket'. Even this she is contemptuous of, saying to the Rabbis who administered it (presumably because by this time she was apparently a widow), 'May you grant such a pittance to your own daughters!'[47] This speech seemingly mixes with one attributed in Lamentations *Rabbah* to 'Boethus' daughter Miriam' (actually meaning 'Martha' but, as we said, these mix-ups are common and they will become quite blatant in the Gospel of John), unless we have two widows here both awaiting the levirate decision to remarry (another important theme in the Synoptics) – a doubtful proposition.

Motifs such as these, in particular the costliness of the 'perfumes' or 'ointments', and the allusion to 'daily', as noted in Luke's description of his 'a certain Rich Man' (the one with the 'certain Poor man named Lazarus lying on his doorstep'), will be mainstays in Gospel accounts of events leading up to Jesus' death and burial. For example, one of these 'expensive perfume' or 'ointment' episodes rather occurs at Lazarus' own house 'in Bethany' in the

Gospel of John 11:1–3 (repeated in 12:1–11) and relates notably to Lazarus' two sisters, Mary ('Miriam') and the other, Martha (Boethus' daughter's name).

A small piece of this tradition will also appear earlier in Luke 10:38–42, this time 'in a certain village' at the house of 'a certain woman named Martha', not at Lazarus' house – Lazarus (who will appear later in Luke 16:20) having been excised. Nevertheless, even in this episode, Mary will be 'sitting at (Jesus') feet' and the argument, pregnant with significance, breaks out over 'serving' (*diakonian* – the same 'serving' we have already seen relative to the complaints of 'the Seven' against 'the Twelve' over '*serving* tables' in Acts and Paul's allusion to the good '*service* the Saints received' at 'the house of Stephen, the first-fruit of Achaia' – thus! – in 1 Corinthians 16:15).

In the other Synoptics, Matthew and Mark, a different piece of this tradition will take place 'at Simon the Leper's house' but now the woman who 'comes' is unnamed (Matt. 26:6–13/Mark 14:3–10). She is also unnamed in Luke 7:37 where she is called, conspicuously, 'a woman of the city who was a Sinner'.

Not only does this episode include, as in John, 'kissing (Jesus') feet', 'wiping them with the hairs of her head', and 'anointing his feet with ointment' but now, rather, a parable Jesus tells to an unidentified 'Simon', comparing this 'woman who was a Sinner' and 'the Pharisee' to 'two debtors who owed a certain creditor', one 'five hundred pieces of silver and the other fifty' (clearly another anti-Jerusalem Church parable because it is about 'great Sinning' rather than 'great Righteousness').[48] Compare this, too, with Acts 15:5 about 'certain of those of the sect of the Pharisees' whose insistence on circumcision triggers 'the Jerusalem Conference', to say nothing of the parallel with the debt of 'twelve talents of silver' Nakdimon owes his creditor.

In John 11–12, Mary and Martha in two successive episodes 'anoint (Jesus') feet' (as does Luke 7:37–50's unidentified female 'Sinner') – at least 'Mary' does (12:2–3, prefigured not a little anachronistically in 11:2). Martha, it seems, is only doing the 'serving' (12:2), a matter about which she is pictured as complaining bitterly. Also note the allusion to 'feet' which Mary will anoint with 'a hundred-weight of ointment of pure spikenard of great price' in John 12:3 and which the unidentified 'Sinning Woman' just did as well in Luke 7:38. Prior to this, when Jesus is about to resurrect her brother Lazarus (John 11:32), like Ben Kalba Sabu'a's daughter greeting Rabbi Akiba, 'seeing Jesus, Mary fell at his feet'.

Jesus' 'feet' – whether Mary or her stand-in is 'sitting' at them, 'wiping them with her hair', 'kissing them', or 'anointing them with expensive ointment of pure spikenard' – will appear repeatedly in tradition after tradition. Also the locale, specifically noted in John 11:18 and 12:1 as being 'in Bethany', will be the connecting link between the several traditions, since Mark 14:3 and Matthew 26:7 will picture the same basic incident as taking place at 'Simon the Leper's house in Bethany', when the 'woman comes' with 'the alabaster flask of pure spikenard ointment of great worth' to anoint him (Matthew actually reads, dropping the 'spikenard', 'with an alabaster cask of very precious ointment').

The Woman at Simon the Leper's House, Jesus' Feet, and Rabbi Eliezer's Bad Breath

To drive home the motif of 'feet' and several others in John, Mary is not only pictured twice wiping Jesus' 'feet with her hair' (twice as well in Luke), but also 'falling down at' Jesus' 'feet' (11:32). We shall see this motif of 'falling down at his feet' repeated, interestingly, twice too in Rabbinic tradition in *Kethuboth*'s story about how Ben Kalba Sabu'a's daughter Rachel 'falls down at' Rabbi Akiba's feet after his several returns from study with his several times 'twelve thousand Disciples'. In this tradition, Rachel is also pictured, not as 'wiping (his feet) with her hair' as here in John, but as simply rather 'falling at his feet and kissing them'.[49]

We saw this motif in Luke 7:38's 'woman of the city who was a Sinner'. In fact, this 'kiss', portrayed as very 'ardent' or 'loving', becomes the source of Jesus' complaint against Simon above, whom he seems to feel did not 'love him' enough and did not show him enough adoration or obeisance – typical of the Gospel's Gentilizing approach.

We have the 'serving' theme as well in John 12:3's picture of Martha doing the 'serving' (*diakonei*) while Mary goes about her 'anointing his feet' and 'hair wiping' ministrations – an activity that in Luke 10:40's version causes all the trouble. This allusion relates to the issue of 'daily serving' (*diakonia*) in Acts 6's 'deacon'-appointment introduction of its 'Stephen' episode, in which the 'Seven Men' and 'Stephen' are described as *full* of the Holy Spirit'. Note the curious parallel with Luke 16:20's 'Poor Man' Lazarus, whose body was rather described as *full* of sores' – 'full of sores' replacing 'full of the Holy Spirit' in Acts 7:55.

After 'Martha does the serving' in John 12:2, then, it is rather 'the house' which is next described, pointedly and strikingly, as *filled* with the smell of the *ointment*' or 'the perfume' – here, not only our filled/full allusion but also that of 'the ointment' or 'perfume', now combined with the new one of 'the smell' or 'the odor'. This theme of Martha's 'serving' rather than Mary's expensive anointment and hair-wiping ministrations will form the basis of Luke 10:38-42's more compressed and obviously derivative version of these events, specifically now at 'Martha's house' (10:38). This episode is the second of these basically interchangeable encounters in the same Gospel. The first was at 'the house of the Pharisee' (a write-in clearly for what is being represented as the 'James Party' in both Acts and Galatians) who, in the guise of 'Simon', will bear the brunt of the creditor/wages-parable rebuke.

As already intimated, this 'smell' or 'odor' motif will reappear with surprising ramifications in the more colorful Talmudic tradition having to do with 'dung', specifically, the dung Rabbi Eliezer (Lazarus' namesake) puts into his mouth because he was hungry on the Sabbath but which gave him bad breath. Nor is this to mention the 'dung' which we shall encounter in other scenarios and traditions relative to these spoiled daughters or daughters-in-law of these proverbial Rich parvenus and relative to Rabbi Yohanan ben Zacchai himself, whose two Disciples putting dung into his coffin to convince both 'the Zealots' and the Romans not to stab (or 'pierce') him with their swords because he was already dead.[50]

Where Eliezer ben Hyrcanus himself is concerned, the 'dung' in question allows his mentor, this same Yohanan b. Zacchai, to observe and turn what was essentially the negative impression the young Eliezer was making into a positive: 'Just as an offensive smell came forth from your mouth, so shall a great name go forth from you in (teaching) *Torah*.'[51]

The relation of this to Jesus' calling 'the Pharisees' 'Blind Guides' (the 'Jamesian Party' again and evoking the *Maschil* at Qumran[52]) concerning 'that which enters the mouth going down into the belly and being cast out (*ekballetai*) the toilet bowl' in Matthew 15:17 should be obvious. As this reads in Matthew 15:11, purporting to respond to disputes concerning 'the Pharisees'' insistence on 'eating with clean hands' and purity regulations generally: 'Not that which enters into the mouth defiles the man but that which goes forth from the mouth, this defiles the man.' In fact, Matthew 15:18 adds: 'but the things going forth out of the mouth come forth out of the heart and they defile the man'. Again, the negative parallel with the 'great odor' of the *Torah* 'going forth out of the mouth of Rabbi Eliezer should be clear.

Furthermore, this allusion to both the 'stench' of Rabbi Eliezer's breath in the *ARN* and the lovely 'smell of the ointment' of pure spikenard 'filling' Lazarus' house in John 12:3 is presaged even earlier in John 11:39 in the context of Lazarus' startling resurrection. There the 'stink' of Lazarus' body – not unlike Rabbi Yohanan's body above with the 'dung' in his coffin – dead 'for four days', becomes a key component of more of Martha's complaining in 11:21–22,[53] duplicated in 11:32 when Mary complains that if Jesus had been there her 'brother would not have died'. These *complaints* metamorphose back into the issue of 'table service' (*diakonian*) again, Martha (as in John 12:2) doing all the 'serving' (*diakonein*), while her sister 'Mary', now 'sitting at Jesus' feet' no less, enjoys all the attention!

Jesus' response is classic and suitably arcane: 'Mary has chosen the good part,' which directly echoes a phrase at the end of the First Column of CD referring to 'those who sought Smooth Things and chose illusions' – normally considered Pharisees but, in the writer's view, also intended to include Pauline Christians – 'they chose the fair neck', a passage generally based on Isaiah 30:10–13, meaning, seemingly, 'they chose the easiest way'.

Another variation of the 'anointment' theme is found in Matthew and Mark where Jesus encounters the unnamed woman carrying the alabaster flask at 'Simon the Leper's house'. This is still 'at Bethany' as in John, but not 'Martha's house' or even 'Lazarus'' (though, in reality, it is). 'Simon the Leper' now stands in for 'Simon the Pharisee' and in John 12:4 even 'Simon Iscariot'. Paralleling Lazarus' 'sister Mary' in John, this unnamed woman 'comes' in with 'an alabaster cask of very precious ointment' to anoint Jesus' 'head' and not 'his feet', as 'Mary' does in John 12:3. Literally in Mark 14:3/Matt. 26:7, she 'poured it on his head while he reclined', meaning he was 'eating at the table' or 'dining'. The locale, Bethany, is the key detail connecting Matthew and Mark's episodes to John's.

Both Mark and Matthew repeat John 12:3's allusion to 'pure spikenard ointment of great price' – Mark verbatim, though Matthew discards the 'pure spikenard' and 'great price' in favor of 'precious ointment' – again demonstrating the two sets of material to be integrally related. Luke even discards Matthew's 'precious' keeping only the 'alabaster flask of ointment'. John rather discards the 'alabaster flask' part of the phrase – though conserving all the rest – substituting an entirely new expression: 'a hundred weight' or 'litra' to be encountered again in his later picture of 'Nicodemus having come', 'bearing about a hundred weight of mixture of myrrh and aloes' (19:39). This in itself, even if only indirectly, again demonstrates the basic interconnectedness of the Nicodemus and the Mary/Miriam scenarios at least as far as the Gospel of John is concerned.

Once more, the 'precious ointment', 'perfume', and/or 'spikenard' is the point of the various presentations, as it will be in the Talmudic ones involving 'Nakdimon's daughter Miriam', 'Boethus' daughter Martha', and others. Of particular note is its value, whether the 'four hundred dinars' of the 'Nakdimon's daughter Miriam' episode and its variations or the 'hundred weight of ointment of pure spikenard of great value' and its variations, to which Matthew, Mark, and ultimately Luke add the additional note of the 'alabaster flask'.

Though the unnamed woman – who becomes Mary (*Miriam*) in John – is pictured as 'anointing his head' rather than 'his feet', nevertheless both the locale 'at Bethany' in Matthew and Mark is the same as in John, and the note of 'precious ointments' or 'pure spikenard' is absolutely the same. In Lamentations *Rabbah*, 'Miriam' is misidentified as Boethus' daughter not Nakdimon's or Nicodemus' and the amount is augmented to 'five hundred dinars'. Elsewhere in Talmudic tradition, 'Boethus' daughter' (returning to her correct identification as 'Martha'), to show her arrogant extravagance, requires 'a Tyrian gold dinar every Sabbath eve just for her sweetmeats' ('spice puddings' according to some translations). Here, the 'weekly' motif takes the place of the 'daily' one, but the effect is the same. Of course, there is the usual ever-recurring allusion in all these episodes – in the Gospels as well as in the notice about the Poor 'coming' to Ben Kalba Sabu'a's door 'hungry as a dog and going away filled' – of 'coming'/'came'.

One might remark, too, the somewhat less common one of 'pouring out' – as in the case of the woman with the 'alabaster flask' in Matthew and Mark, who 'pours out' the precious ointment on Jesus' head. The use of this expression will become ever more pivotal as we proceed, especially when one considers both 'the Man of Lying' at Qumran (in some descriptions, 'the Pourer out of' or 'Spouter of Lying',[54] characterized in the Damascus Document as 'pouring out over Israel the waters of Lying'[55]) and Jesus' 'blood' in New

Testament/New Covenant Communion scenarios in the Synoptics (Matt. 26:28 and pars.) – generally characterized as 'poured out for (the) Many' too. In Luke 10:38–42, to bring us back full circle, the same encounter takes place at 'Martha's house' – no relation to Lazarus indicated and no suggestion of 'in Bethany' whatsoever but, rather, the far vaguer 'a certain village'. Still Martha is 'complaining' (cf. both the complaints of Nakdimon's daughter above and Boethus' daughter below about the paltriness of the allowance the Rabbis were willing to provide them). About what? Not about the parsimony of the Rabbis, but rather, as we just saw, her sister Mary anointing Jesus' 'feet' while she had to do all the 'service'!

Above left: The artificially hollowed-out interior of Cave 4 where most mss. stored. **Above right:** The also artificially hollowed-out water channel and *raison d'être* of the Community. **Below:** Wharf on Dead Sea near Qumran.

Chapter 7
Mary Anoints, Martha Serves, Judas Iscariot Complains

Judas Iscariot not Martha Complains about not Giving to the Poor

As John will now present this scenario, these 'complaints' will rather migrate into the mouth of Judas Iscariot over Mary's waste of such expensive ointment or perfume (the Rabbis, it will be recalled, were trying to stop this sort of wastefulness in the matter of Nakdimon's daughter *Miriam*'s profligate use of her widow's allowance) and, in a further charged addition, her lack of concern for 'the Poor' (12:4–8). Not only is the playfulness of these Gospel craftsmen really quite humorous but it is not completely unconnected with the Talmudic theme of the Rabbis' stinginess, on the one hand and Ben Kalba's Sabu'a's contrasting concern for 'the Poor' on the other.

Of course, the same '*diakonian*' used here in Luke 10:40 to express Martha's concern at having to do 'so much *serving*' will go on to occur three times in four lines in the picture Luke draws as well in Acts 6:1–4 and there it is not only coupled with the word 'daily' but also the theme of 'widows'. In this presentation, the 'complaints' ('murmuring', it is called[1]) were those of supposed 'Hellenists' against 'the Hebrews' in the matter of 'their widows being overlooked in the *daily serving*' (whatever was meant by this and however far-fetched it may seem).

But even here, the various notes about the 'widows', 'the daily service', and the issue of 'waiting on tables' reverberate with our other sources in the manufacture of these traditions, the one about Nakdimon's and/or Boethus' daughters being 'widows' and either their 'daily' or 'weekly' allotment of 'perfumes', 'sweetmeats', or 'pension', and the other, Martha's problem with Mary as Luke 10:40 portrays it. Whereas in Acts 6:2 the complaints these 'Hellenists' make are detailed in terms of having to 'serve tables' (*diakonein*), not just while 'the widows were overlooked' (meaning obscure), but while 'the Twelve were drawn away from service (*diakonia*) of the word' (6:4 – in 6:2 'the word of God'); 'at Martha's house' here in Luke, it is rather Martha having to do 'so much service' – much like the alleged 'Hebrews' in Acts 6:2 (clearly meant to be 'the Jerusalem Apostles') – while her sister Mary does nothing but 'sit at Jesus' feet and listen to his words'.

In Mark 14:10–11 and Matthew 26:14–16, the corresponding encounter at 'Simon the Leper's house' at 'Bethany' is immediately followed by evocation of Judas Iscariot's departure to betray Jesus 'to the Chief Priests' for thirty pieces of silver, though now the 'complaints' will be by Jesus' Disciples in Matthew 26:8 or the ever-ubiquitous 'some' in Mark 14:4. With regard to the 'silver' motif in these last, it will be important to have regard to the same motif in the exposition of '*Ben Zizzit Ha-Kessef*'s name, to say nothing of the 'twelve talents of silver' in the surety required in the story of Nakdimon's miraculous rainmaking – but more about both of these things later.

The parallel episode 'at Bethany' to that in Mark and Matthew in John's account rather takes place, as has now become clear, at Lazarus' house – the same 'Lazarus' who is described in Luke 16:19–22 as 'a certain *Poor Man* laid at the *doorway* of a certain Rich Man', 'whose sores the *dogs came* and licked'. In the parallel Rabbinic material about Nakdimon it was 'the Poor' who came to Nakdimon's 'door', though both are manifestly the same. Nor should one forget the parallel to the predicate 'laid at' in the description of Nakdimon's daughter Miriam's bed as 'being overlaid with a spread worth twelve thousand silver dinars'. There will be more. Notwithstanding in Luke 10:38, this is not the house of 'a certain Poor one named Lazarus' but, rather, of 'a *certain* woman named Martha' – location unspecified and expressed only as 'a certain village', but never mind. To go back to the dispute between Judas Iscariot and Jesus in John 12:5-8 and the 'three hundred dinars' that 'Judas' felt 'should have been given to the Poor': as with the motif of 'serving tables' in Acts 6:2-4 above, the allusion to 'the Poor' is also repeated three times in four lines, just in case we missed the point. Hopefully, we didn't – we got it. Still, if the reader's head begins to reel by this time, it would not be surprising since the multiplicity of these repeating references does become dizzying.

Nevertheless one would be well-advised to keep going, preferably with a Greek-English Interlinear translation of the Gospels at one's side in order to catch these linguistic nuances and overlaps. Instead of being used to characterize the 'Lazarus' in Luke 'whose body was full of sores' (the 'filled' allusion) and 'licked by dogs', John 12:5 now puts this same allusion to 'the Poor' into the mouth of the archvillain in Christian tradition, 'Judas the son' or 'brother of Simon Iscariot'– this last, as also already underscored, replaced in Mark and Matthew by the encounter with 'Simon *the Leper*', another bit of not-so-subtle disinformation perhaps even more malevolent than the original 'Judas Iscariot' libels. It should be recalled that following the anointment of Jesus' head 'with precious ointment of pure spikenard' by the unnamed woman at 'Simon the Leper's house at Bethany', we had already encountered 'Judas'– tantalizingly referred to in Mark 14:10 as 'Judas the Iscariot' as opposed to the more normative 'Judas Iscariot' in Matthew 26:14 (in John 12:4 and 13:26 at this juncture, 'the son' or 'brother of Simon Iscariot') – 'going out to betray him to the Chief Priests'.

In Matthew and Mark, the whole sequence then leads directly into Jesus announcing – to use the 1 Corinthians 11:25 phraseology of Paul – 'This is the Cup of the New Covenant in my blood' and, as Matthew 26:28 and Mark 14:24 now add, 'which is poured out for the Many'. Here Paul's 'drink it in remembrance of me', has been transformed in Mark 14:9 and Matthew 26:13 into Jesus' rebuke to his Disciples (in Mark 14:4 above, the 'some') over their parallel 'complaints' about the unnamed woman's wastefulness at Simon the Leper's house and the Gospel being preached throughout the world 'in remembrance of' or 'as a memorial to her', namely, the unnamed woman (with her obvious 'Gentile Christian' overtones), who had just 'anointed him', '*pouring out*' the expensive ointment of pure spikenard upon his head.

Of course, the whole phraseology is reprised in the last section of the exhortation of the Damascus Document where it is stated (to repeat): 'A Book of Remembrance will be written before Him for God-Fearers (that is, Gentiles) and for those reckoning His Name until God shall *reveal Salvation* ('*Yesha*' – in Greek, 'Jesus') and Justification (*Zedakah*) to those fearing His Name.'[2] It should be appreciated that in Matthew 26:8–16/Mark 14:3–9's version of this cluster of complaints about the costliness of the perfume that the unnamed woman (Martha's sister 'Mary' in John) had wasted, the above allusion to 'the Poor' is put into the mouth of 'his Disciples' taken as a whole (26:8 – in Mark 14:4, the 'some' as we saw), not Judas alone as in John 12:4. The addition, however, in John 12:7 – following Mary's anointing Jesus' feet, then 'washing them with her hair' – 'she has kept it for the day of my burial', is common to all three!

In Matthew 26:12 this reads: 'in pouring this ointment upon my body this woman did it for my burial' while, in Mark 14:8, it changes slightly to: 'she came beforehand to anoint my body for burial' (again, note here the addition – pertinent or otherwise – of the verb 'come'/'came'). Of course, not only does Mark 14:3 add 'of pure spikenard' from John 12:3 to Matthew's less precise 'alabaster flask of very precious ointment', but even more to the point in Mark 14:4, the very next line, those making the complaints now become the even more general, yet ubiquitous, 'some'.

It should perhaps be reiterated at this point that the use of the basically interchangeable 'some'/'a certain' and/or 'certain ones' generally in Gospel and Acts portraiture (all really the same word in Greek) is particularly important where individuals having a connection with James' Jerusalem Assembly are concerned – called, not irrelevantly, in early Church accounts, the *Ebionim* or 'the Poor', as, for instance, Paul's Galatians 2:12's '*some* came from James' following James' admonition 'to remember the Poor' in 2:10; or, provoking the so-called 'Jerusalem Council' above, Acts 15:1's '*some* came down from Judea, teaching the brothers, according to the Law of Moses, that unless you were circumcised you cannot be saved'.

Also note the perhaps not completely unconnected usage in both cases again of the verb 'to come' and the 'Salvation' motif of the Damascus Document connected with the theme of circumcision. In Rabbinic tradition, it is important to observe that the description of Nakdimon's wealth comes amid debate over the sincerity or lack thereof of his charity and notices questioning the reality of his concern for 'the Poor' which, in the writers' view, are laterally transferred and only slightly refurbished in these striking polemics of John's 'Judas the son' or 'brother of Simon Iscariot' or Mark's telltale 'some' and Matthew's 'his Disciples' with Jesus over the wastefulness of these various women either anointing 'his head' or 'his feet' with 'precious ointment' or 'pure spikenard', to say nothing of 'wiping them with (their) hair'!

The notice in Tractate *Ketuboth* which triggers this debate, Rabbinic hyperbole aside, literally reads: 'When he (Nakdimon) walked from his house to the house of study, woolen clothes were laid out beneath his feet and the Poor followed behind him gathering them up.'[3] Here we have the typical motifs of 'being laid out', 'the Poor', and 'his feet', with which we began our discussion. In addition, there is also the one of 'woolen clothes', an allusion which will recur in other sources. Not only does it echo Ezekiel 44:17's requirement for Zadokite Levites or Priests serving at the altar of the Temple above; but, in particular, also Epiphanius' description of James in the context of his depiction of the atonement he made in the Inner Sanctum of the Temple on behalf of the whole People, that is, that he 'wore no woolen clothes'.[4] In this description, Epiphanius also includes the note about James' footwear or lack thereof, again probably echoing the strictures of Ezekiel's 'Zadokite Covenant' as we saw. Furthermore, we also shall encounter some of the same motifs in descriptions of '*Ben Zizzit Ha-kesef*' below.

In addition to these, however, Jerome preserves a tradition (as we saw above) about how James was held in such awe among the People and considered 'so Holy' that the little children used to try 'to touch the fringes of his garments' as he passed by – here, a variation of the 'clothing' motif we shall encounter so insistently as we proceed.[5] A similar portrait – albeit perhaps somewhat less convincing – of the crowd's response to Jesus has come down to us in the Synoptic Gospels, another probable instance of a real tradition relating to James being retrospectively absorbed and attached to Jesus instead. The individuals involved in this 'touching' activity of Jesus' person or 'garments' in these accounts run the gamut from women with an overflow of menstrual blood to these same 'little children', 'the blind', paralytics, and, in the prelude to one curing or raising, even a Roman Centurion![6] The humor of these sketches should not be overlooked and, no matter how amusing many of them may be, all should be looked upon as parody – in some cases, malevolent parody – of cherished Jewish beliefs or taboos.

However, what should be appreciated is that not only do we have in these legendary portraits of 'Nakdimon' the theme of 'the Poor' – the name of the Community James is said to have headed in Jerusalem – but also the *inversion* of the 'touching his clothes' theme, in that now it was Nakdimon who was held in such reverence by 'the Poor' that they even followed after him making it possible for his *feet* not to have to touch the dirt of the ground; or, vice versa perhaps, his wealth was so great that he could afford to abandon such 'clothes' in a display of false charity on behalf of these same 'Poor'. In either case, the point is the same and, as we shall see further below, integrally connected to Judas Iscariot's complaints.

In a further adumbration of this Nakdimon's 'feet' and 'clothes' story, we shall also see that it will be 'Miriam the daughter of Boethus' (actually, the tradition, as will become ever clearer as we proceed, should have read 'Martha the daughter of Boethus'), for whom on *Yom*

Kippur not 'woolen clothes' or 'garments' but rather 'cushions' or 'carpets' were laid from the door of her house to the Temple (the 'laid out' and 'doorstep' motifs from both the 'Nakdimon' and Luke's 'Poor man Lazarus licked by dogs' stories), so that 'her feet might not be exposed'.[7] Here, once again too, the telltale motif of 'feet' – now 'her feet'! We shall encounter such details again not only in the details about Boethus' daughter's 'feet' but the 'feet' of many of these other legendary characters so intrinsic to our discussion and how they, too, were 'exposed'.[8]

'The Poor You have with You Always but You do not Always have Me'

But to go back to Nakdimon – in relation to the 'woolen garments' which were 'laid out for his feet' which 'the Poor' then 'gathered up', the Rabbis debate whether he really cared about the Poor and practiced real charity, rather concluding, he did this 'for his own glorification'.[9] This leads them into discussions of an aphorism, seemingly well known at the time, 'in accordance with the camel is the burden', which they interpret as meaning, the Richer the man the more he should bear. It will not escape the reader that the elements of this saying are very familiar and will lead, in turn, to interesting ramifications relative to comparable (or derivative) sayings attributed to Jesus in Scripture, also comparing camels to Rich men, to say nothing of other formulations we shall encounter, not only in the Gospels, but also in the Scrolls, about 'Glory' or 'glorying'.

In fact, from a certain perspective, one might perhaps say the same thing the Rabbis are saying about Nakdimon about Jesus' words above, to wit, 'the Poor you have with you always, but you do not always have me' (John 12:8 and pars.) – a kind of 'glorying' or, if one prefers, 'vainglory'. We have seen other examples of this somewhat unseemly portrait of Jesus – which the writer does not consider at all historical but which, rather, resembles what Greco-Hellenistic 'gods' required in the service due them.[10] For example, in Jesus' rebuke of Simon in Luke 7:44–46 – directed too at the Pharisee at whose house he was dining – in the matter of not welcoming him sufficiently, by which he means their 'not bathing (his) feet with her tears', nor 'wiping them with the hair of her head', nor 'anointing (them) with ointment', nor lovingly 'kissing (them)'; and of course, the response here is precisely the impact of the Talmudic aphorism cited with regard to Nakdimon above – to quote freely: 'whoso loved much, much is forgiven' (meaning the woman who had 'many Sins'). *Per contra*: 'whoso loved little, little is forgiven' – one couldn't get much more 'Pauline' than this.

But in John, Judas' statement about 'selling (the perfume) for three hundred dinars' and giving the proceeds 'to the Poor' (12:5) is followed by the narrational aside: 'He (Judas) did not say this because he cared about the Poor, but because he was a thief and held the purse' (12:6)! Not only is 'being a thief and holding the purse' being substituted for the phrase, 'his own self-glorification' in Talmudic literature, which would not exactly have fit the context, but for the first time, we hear that Judas was 'the Purser' of 'the Twelve', a position familiar in 'Essene' practice.[11] It is also the first time we have heard about this wretched knavery! In Matthew 26:9–15 and Mark 14:3–10, it also comes directly after Jesus is pictured as saying: 'The Poor you have with you always, but you do not always have me', that Judas Iscariot is depicted as 'going out to the High Priests' in order 'to betray him' (literally, 'deliver him up').

This being said, in Acts 5:1–13 we are confronted with an odd little episode as well about 'a certain *Ananias*' (familiar phraseology) and 'his wife Sapphira'. In the manner of Essenes too, they are pictured as required to give the proceeds of the sale of 'a possession' of theirs and '*lay it* at the *feet* of the Apostles' and, when they 'kept back part of the price', both die in a horrendous manner (at Peter's direction!). This is followed by the laconic comment, 'And many signs and wonders among the People came to pass by the hands of the Apostles', and

Acts' narrational 'glue': 'more believers were added to the Lord, multitudes both of men and women' (5:12–14).

But, even more importantly, it is preceded by the words: 'A great fear came upon the whole Assembly (*Ecclesian*) and on all who heard these things' (5:11). These resemble nothing so much as the words with which the first prefatory letter to the Pseudoclementine *Homilies* – called 'The Epistle of Peter to James' – ends, where the assembled Elders, after hearing James speak, are described as 'being in an agony of terror'.[12] The whole scene transpires in the wake of James reading the attack in the letter on the '*lawless and trifling preaching of the man who is my Enemy*' (considered almost unanimously by all commentators as an attack upon Paul), because of which 'some from among the Gentiles have rejected my preaching about the Law'.

This is followed both by Peter's and then James' injunction endorsing it, 'not to communicate the books of my preaching' to anyone who has not 'been tested and found worthy according to the initiation of Moses' which, James immediately makes clear, meant 'a probation of six years' before being 'brought to a river or a fountain which is living water, where the regeneration of the Righteous takes place' (the language here, of course, is completely that of the Community Rule of the Dead Sea Scrolls[13]). Moreover, James adds at this point, 'which we ourselves, when we were regenerated, were made to do for the sake of not sinning' – featuring the same concentration on 'forgiveness for sin' which was the original issue in the parable Jesus tells in Luke 7:47 about the alien woman, who having 'loved much', 'had her many sins forgiven' with which we began this whole circle of notices.

It is at this point that 'the Elders', who have been listening to both James read Peter's letter and James' own admonitions thereafter, now take the oaths to 'keep this Covenant', thereby having 'a part with the Holy Ones' – language, once again, that is almost a facsimile of that found in Qumran documents[14] – in particular, emphasizing that they 'will not lie' (cf. Paul's protestations to this effect in the letters attributed to him[15]).

This is, of course, the basic gist of the episode in Acts with which we began, which described how 'Satan filled' the hearts of Ananias and Sapphira, causing them, in 'keeping back part of the value of the land', to *lie* to the Holy Spirit' and 'lie' not just to men but 'to God' (5:3–4). It is at this point that the 'great fear (that) came upon all who heard these things' is depicted in Acts 5:5 that so much parallels and reverberates with the 'agony of terror' in this prelude to the Pseudoclementine *Homilies*, characterizing the frightened reaction of all those present when they heard James allude to how they would be accursed, both living and dying, and be punished with everlasting punishment' if they should 'lie'.[16] In the author's view, the implied parallel between the two accounts could not be more exact.

That having been said – to go back to Jesus' comment to 'Simon the Pharisee' concerning the woman 'who washed his feet with her tears', 'ardently kissing them', and 'dried them with the hair of her head' in Luke 7:44–47, to the effect that to 'who so loves much, much is forgiven' – one could not get much closer to the Rabbis' reaction to Nakdimon's treatment of 'the Poor' – '*in accordance with the camel is the burden*' – than this either! Whereas in Nakdimon's case, the use of the expression 'the Poor' served to introduce the fact that they were contemptuously allowed to 'gather up the woolen clothes that had been laid', so his feet would not have to touch the ground; in John 12:5–6 (rephrased in Matthew 26:8 and Mark 14:3 and attributed to either 'the Disciples' as a whole or the 'Some'), it forms the crux of the ideological exchange between Jesus and Judas (the son or brother) of Simon Iscariot' (in Matthew and Mark, anyhow, 'about to deliver him up' or 'betray him'[17]) concerning these same 'Poor' – the latter character, as already suggested, capable of being seen or actually having been seen as representative of all Jews or at the very least, anyhow, those of the 'Ebionite'/'Zealot' strain of thinking – namely Epiphanius' '*Sicarii* Essenes' already called attention to above.

Martha's Complaints, Mary's Wastefulness, and Nakdimon's Daughter's Arrogance

Let us go over all these points again, repetitive or dizzying as this may be. John does so on several occasions, so why shouldn't we? As already remarked, in John 11:2 earlier, Mary 'the sister of the sick man Lazarus' had been described as 'anointing the Lord with ointment and wiping his feet with her hair'. In Luke 7:38 and 44, where Jesus is pictured as telling a parable to another 'Simon', 'at 'the house of the Pharisee', it is yet another unnamed 'woman of the city who was a Sinner', who was 'kissing his feet', 'anointing them with ointment', and 'wiping his feet with the hairs of her head'! By contrast, in John 12:2-3, while 'Martha served', it was Mary who was rather described – just as in Mark's variation at 'Simon the Leper's house' – as 'bringing in a hundred weight of expensive ointment of pure spikenard' and, more specifically at least in John, anointing Jesus' feet with it 'and wiping them with her hair'. Nor should the aside about 'the house being *full of the smell of the perfume*' be ignored. At this point the complaining is not being done by Martha over the issue of 'table service', as in Luke's version of the events at 'Martha's house', but rather by Judas', who (though also alluded to earlier in John 6:71 as 'about to deliver him up being one of the Twelve' is now presented in a really substantive manner.

In Matthew and Mark's 'Simon the Leper' scenarios, of course, it was 'the Disciples' or the mysterious 'some' who did the 'complaining' over the value of the precious ointment the unnamed woman had poured over Jesus' head – in Mark 14:5, again reckoned as 'three hundred dinars' as in John 12:5; in Matthew 26:9, it was worth 'much'. It is at this point that 'Judas the Iscariot' is introduced into the narrative, not 'complaining' as in John, but as immediately going out 'to deliver him up' (Mark 14:10). Here Matthew 26:15 too, now finally gives its quantification to the amount, 'thirty pieces of silver', to be picked up in 27:3 and 27:9 that follow in Matthew's (but not the other Gospels') 'casting the pieces of silver into the Temple' scenario in the next chapter – a figure not to be considered independent, clearly, of the 'three hundred dinars' in Mark 14:5 and John 12:5, the one simply being a decimal multiple of the other.

Actually in John 11:21 earlier, Martha had already been complaining to some extent to Jesus that, if he had come sooner her 'brother would not have died', and following this, in 11:39, about the 'stink' or 'smell' of Lazarus' rotting corpse already dead 'for four days'. It is then directly after this in more or less a repeat of all these things in the next chapter too, that John 12:5 has 'Judas of Simon Iscariot, one of his Disciples' and 'the man who was going to deliver him up', say: 'Why wasn't this ointment sold for three hundred dinars and the money given to the Poor?'

Not only has the 'Simon' of the 'Simon the Leper' encounter in Matthew/Mark above now plainly floated into the material about Judas here in John (or vice versa); but the valuation of 'three hundred dinars' of 'the precious ointment of pure spikenard' in John and Mark, as just underscored, is nothing but a reformulation of the 'thirty pieces of silver' Judas Iscariot then receives for the price of his 'betrayal' or 'delivering him up' in Matthew 26:15 (unparalleled in either John, Mark, or Luke). It should also be observed that in the curious material that follows in Matthew 27:3–10 about 'the price of blood', in which Matthew thinks it is citing Jeremiah, but which is actually rather a free translation of Zechariah 11:12–13 about throwing 'the wages of thirty pieces of silver into the Temple Treasury', Matthew quotes 'the Chief Priests' as saying 'it is not lawful to put them (the 'thirty pieces of silver') into the Treasury, for it is the price of blood'.

Aside, however, from attributing this proof-text to the wrong prophet – a comparatively minor error – this again echoes the response Eliezer ben Hyrcanus reported hearing from Jacob of Kfar Sechania about what 'Jesus the Nazoraean' taught concerning whether it was lawful or not to give 'the wages' earned from 'a prostitute's hire' to the Temple. As already to some extent suggested, this is an extremely charged statement in view of the perceived behavior of Herodian princesses such as Herodias, Bernice, and Drusilla – and possibly even that of Helen of Adiabene herself. Jesus' response, that it was permissible to 'use them to build an outhouse for the High Priest', is also probably, as we said, the only real historical notice about him remaining in the whole of the Talmud, the rest having long ago fallen victim to years of censorship.[18]

Nevertheless, even the reference to 'High Priest' here plays back into the notices in the Gospels about 'Judas Iscariot going to the High Priests in order to betray him' – further amplified in the picture of these same High Priests refusing to put Judas' 'pieces of silver' into 'the Treasury because it was the price of blood' in Matthew 27:6. Moreover, the connection of this Talmudic tradition – possibly even going back to James – to this material uniquely developed in Matthew out of the price for 'the precious ointment of pure spikenard' which 'should have been given to the Poor', quoted in John 12:5 in a speech attributed to 'Judas Iscariot' as well, should be patent.

Not only do we have here the matter of the poorly-explained issue of why Judas' 'wages' or 'hire' would not be acceptable in the Temple, but also the issue of the 'price of blood', in this instance carrying the additional meaning of 'menstrual blood' which was so abhorrent to the priest class – to say nothing of the people generally – and, once again, a key concern of the Damascus Document from Qumran.[19] Just as important is the additional play in the amount of 'three hundred dinars' for 'the measure of ointment of pure spikenard of great value' of John 12:5 (in Mark 14:3, 'alabaster flask of ointment of pure spikenard of great value') on the Talmudic tradition citing 'four hundred dinars' as the allowance provided by the Rabbis for Nakdimon's daughter Miriam's/Mary's 'daily perfume basket'. In Lamentations *Rabbah*, even this is augmented by another hundred dinars, as we saw, to 'five hundred dinars' which, in turn, suggests the 'four' to 'five thousand' augmentations in the number of followers Jesus is pictured as feeding – in Matthew 15–16/Mark 6–8 as well – in the several 'multiplication of loaves'/'wilderness exodus' episodes which we shall presently examine in more detail below.[20]

This 'dinar' theme will reappear over and over again in these Talmudic narratives about these various Rich daughters. So will the one related to it about 'levirate marriage', implied in the Rabbis having to provide 'maintenance' or an 'allowance' to support these 'widows'. As we shall see further below, this will have to do not only with Nakdimon's daughter 'Miriam', but Boethus' daughter 'Martha' – the issue of 'the *levir*' being of particular importance where the remarriages of both were concerned. Nor do a 'hundred dinars' matter very much as the valuations of these precious 'perfumes', 'spikenards', or 'ointments' move from one tradition to the other. In these overlaps and interdependencies it is always useful to remark the Talmud's this-worldly earthiness – or what some would call its vulgarity or crassness; others, reality (particularly noticeable in the above story about Jesus' opinion of 'the High Priest's privy', which is actually quite funny) – as opposed to the New Testament's more idealized and Hellenized other-worldliness which, no doubt, accounts for its enduring appeal despite the obviously secondary nature of many of its traditions.

The points concerning this cluster of usages stemming from Nakdimon's rainmaking, his and his colleague Ben Kalba Sabu'a's extravagant Riches, and their daughters' or daughters-in-law's expensive perfumes are so important that it would also be well to look at them again with more precision. It is important to do so, not only because they are so complex, but because they bear to some extent both on how the Gospel narratives themselves were put together, but also, as it will turn out, the details of the preparation of Jesus' body, his tomb and, as we shall finally suggest, even perhaps the legendary 'Tomb of St James'.

In these Rabbinic traditions paralleling Luke's 'a certain Rich Man clothed in purple and fine linen who used to feast every day in splendor', the third of this trio or quartet of fabulously 'Rich' individuals in Jerusalem's last days, '*Ben Zizzit*' was supposedly so characterized because he used to lie at the head of the Great Ones of Israel on a silver couch.[21] Not only does this incorporate a pun on his cognomen '*Hakkeset*' which, depending on how it is transcribed, can either mean 'cushions'/'couch' (*keset*) or 'seat' (*kise*), but it can also be seen as involving a play on the 'silver' (*kesef*) or 'silversmith' motifs. Elsewhere, it was rather Nakdimon's daughter who supposedly 'needed an allowance of four' or 'five hundred dinars daily just for her perfume basket', whose 'couch was overlaid with a spread worth twelve thousand dinars'.[22]

In the *ARN* '*Ben Zizzit*' is rather called '*Sisit Hakkeset*', but the play is still clearly on the word *keset* which can mean either 'cushions' or 'couch' as we just saw. In *Gittin* (the Talmudic Tractate on 'Divorce') however, where he is called '*Ben Zizzit Hakeseth*', the interpretation is provided, as previously signaled, that this was because 'his fringes (*zizzit*) used to trail on cushions', so the play is on both the fact of 'his fringes' and their 'trailing on cushions'. But there the important addition appended: 'Others say he derived the name from the fact that his seat (*kise*) was among the Nobility (or 'Great Ones') of Rome',[23] which varies the one on 'lying at the head of the Great Ones of Israel on a silver couch' just noted with regard to him. Whoever he was, however, he was clearly an Establishment person of some kind.

Nevertheless in this cluster of traditions, whether evoking Nakdimon, his colleagues Ben Zizzit and Ben Kalba Sabu'a, or the Rich Herodian High Priest Boethus, it cannot be emphasized too often that their daughters or daughters-in-law are almost always named 'Miriam' (Mary) or 'Marta' (Martha). Boethus, whose daughter Martha is actually described in these traditions as 'one of the Richest women in Jerusalem', seems to have had his grandiose family tomb in the Kedron Valley beneath the Pinnacle of the Temple from which James, according to early Church tradition, 'was cast down'.[24] It is perhaps not unrelated that this same tomb, as already remarked, has always been referred to, for some reason, in early Christian pilgrimage tradition as well as 'the Tomb of St James'.[25] This clan (called 'the Boethusians'), which Herod imported from Egypt in the previous century after executing his Maccabean wife, the first Mariamme/Miriam/or Mary, and marrying the second, the next Mariamme or Mary of that generation, was therefore always absolutely beholden to the Herodian family and the Establishment Herod had created.

Mary's Perfume Allowance and Martha's Spice Puddings

In further traditions about this Nakdimon's daughter or his daughter-in-law (we will see an additional parallel to these *daughters* in the case of the Syrophoenician woman's daughter out of whom Jesus *casts* an evil spirit or demon below), *ARN* specifies the actual reason the Rabbis were supervising her allowance, namely, 'she was awaiting a decision by the *levir*' – meaning the decision by her deceased husband's brother to allow her as a widow to remarry (the concomitant being, of course, that she was obviously without children at this point otherwise the procedure would have been unnecessary).

This is patently another theme that will reappear in New Testament tradition, most famously in John the Baptist's protests over Herodias' marriage to Herod Antipas, to which picture we would most strenuously object. It was also probably the reason for all these 'widow'/'in-law' confusions in the first place. In the case of Herodias' remarriage, for starters, this is presented as having taken place after a divorce – which was probably true, because her various uncles, as it were, were vying with each other for this connection since Herodias' brother, Agrippa I, was on his way towards becoming the first Herodian King since their grandfather's demise forty years before, and theirs was the preferred line within the family carrying Maccabean blood through their grandmother Mariamme (the first of these 'Mary's just mentioned above) – so it is not clear if the issue of 'levirate marriage' ever applied.

In the second place, already explained too, Herodias had not previously been married to anyone called 'Philip' at all. In fact, she seems to have been married to another son of Herod, also called 'Herod' (the son of Herod's second or 'Boethusian' wife, also named Mariamme) and another of her uncles. The Philip involved in the story actually did – according to Josephus who makes a special point of it, the only point he does make concerning him – die childless and in any event, actually was rather married to Herodias' daughter Salome![26] In Salome's case, her remarriage to another close cousin, the son of Agrippa I's brother – also called Herod as we have seen, this one 'Herod of Chalcis' – and possibly that 'Aristobulus' Paul refers to so congenially in Romans 16:10 before mentioning Herodion ('the Youngest Herod' – probably Herod VI, their son) – probably did involve the issue of levirate marriage!

But the parameters surrounding John's objections to Herodias' divorce and remarriage to another of her uncles, Herod Antipas probably should have been the proscriptions detailed in principal Dead Sea Scrolls over the more integrally-connected issues of marriage with nieces, polygamy, and – particularly where such Princes or Princesses were concerned – divorce, marriage with non-Jews, close family cousins, and the like.[27]

In the Talmud, the traditions about this much-derided daughter of Nakdimon become even more absurd. Instead of the 'four hundred' or 'five hundred dinars' she needs 'for her perfume basket daily', in *Kethuboth* – in the same context of 'waiting for the *levir*' – she or Boethus' daughter Martha are now said to need 'a Tyrian gold dinar every Sabbath evening (here our 'dinar' theme again as well as the 'weekly'/'daily' one, together with a new one – that of 'Tyre') just for sweetmeats' or 'spice puddings' as we saw.[28] Even the reference to 'Tyrian' or 'Tyre' here will have its ramifications for allusions in Matthew and Mark to the same locale in their account of Jesus' encounter with the Canaanite/Greek Syrophoenician woman and her daughter, to say nothing of 'Sidon and Tyre' elsewhere in Synoptic allusion. It can also possibly be connected in Christian tradition to the story about Simon Magus and the consort with the curious name of 'Helen' he was reported to have found 'in a brothel of Tyre', itself, in turn, possibly bearing elements of the story of 'Queen Helen of Adiabene', not to mention the issue of her 'suspected' alleged adultery.

This notice in the *ARN* that she was awaiting a levirate marriage (that is, the permission of her brother-in-law for her to remarry) fleshes out many of the allusions we have already been encountering. Such bizarre and fanciful detail as 'her sweetmeats' or 'spice puddings' aside, so many coincidences in detail with the Judas Iscariot, Mary, Martha, precious Spikenard, dinars complex of materials can hardly be considered purely accidental. The 'dinars' theme – both as actual dinars and as 'pieces of silver'[29] – will reappear in another famous variation, whether related or not, the portrayal of Judas Iscariot/the Iscariot's 'betrayal'/'delivering up' of Jesus or his objection to Mary/Miriam's extravagant waste of 'precious perfume' (her 'perfume box'?). Of course Judas' cognomen in this regard, in the light of the many *Sicarii* connections to these episodes, is not insignificant; while the 'every single Sabbath eve' and 'spice puddings' motifs patently represent more Rabbinic hyperbole.

In fact, as *Kethuboth* – in the context of 'awaiting the decision of the *levir*' – had already put the matter earlier, it is rather 'the daughter-in-law of Nakdimon ben Gurion' to whom the Rabbis grant such an allowance and now this is expressed in terms of 'two *secah*s of wine for her sweetmeats' or 'spice puddings every week'.[30] Again we have the repetition of the motif of chronological regularity expressed in 'weekly' terms not 'daily' ones.

This being said, in Lamentations *Rabbah* – typical of this kind of tradition confusion or migration – the Rabbis go back to the 'daily' not the 'weekly' framework for these activities and grant this allowance of 'two *secah*s of wine' with respect only to the widowhood and not the remarriage of 'Miriam the daughter of Boethus' (*sic*) after the death of her husband Jesus ben Gamala. This 'Jesus' was murdered, it will be recalled, along with Ananus ben Ananus and other collaborating High Priests 'appointed by Herodians' by those Josephus calls

'Idumaeans' and their confederates, whom he is at this point finally willing to identify as 'Zealots' – in our view, probably taking vengeance, if not for 'the Righteous Teacher' at Qumran, then certainly for the death of James.

Never mind that it is 'Martha the daughter of Boethus' that is really meant here – this is the third interlocking tradition about such 'daily' or 'weekly' allowances granted by the Rabbis to these improvident daughters. Showing that we are not dealing with separate traditions – for her part in *Kethuboth*, Nakdimon's 'daughter-in-law' (name not provided) is pictured as being contemptuous even of this, standing up and declaring once more, 'make such a grant for your own daughters'! To be sure, this is precisely what 'Nakdimon's daughter Miriam' (the real 'Mary' or 'Miriam' in these traditions) was pictured as saying in respect of her daily allowance of 'four' to 'five hundred dinars' thereafter in both *Kethuboth* and Lamentations *Rabbah*.[31] That we have here, too, but a slight variation of the tradition about Nakdimon's daughter is made clear when one Rabbi, probably sarcastically, defers even to this – noting by way of explanation in his response that 'she was a woman awaiting the decision of the *levir*'.

Here of course, we have what appears to be a further confusion, this time between 'Nakdimon's daughter-in-law' and 'Martha the daughter of Boethus' – herself awaiting a second marriage to Josephus' friend, the highly-regarded, though unfortunate, High Priest Jesus ben Gamala. In fact, this is made clear in Lamentations *Rabbah* as well, which, in talking about this 'Miriam the daughter of Boethus' (what is meant here is, of course, '*Martha* the daughter of Boethus') provides the description of how, in order for her to see her husband Joshua (Jesus) ben Gamala 'read in the Temple on *Yom Kippur*, carpets (or 'cushions') were laid from the doorway of her house to the entrance of the Temple so that her feet would not be exposed. Nevertheless they were exposed.' It is at this point Lamentations *Rabbah* makes the addition that when her husband Joshua (ben Gamala) died, the Rabbis allowed her two *secah*s of wine daily.[32]

Once again we have the 'daily', 'allowance', and telltale 'feet'/'foot exposure' themes we have already encountered regarding Nakdimon's daughter Miriam above. Moreover, this is obviously just a variation of another tradition about Nakdimon, the one about 'when he walked from the door of his house to the house of study, the Poor gathered up the woolen clothes laid down under his feet'. Of course, aside from the additional laconic remark, 'nevertheless they were exposed', which really is very striking, there is also the repetition of the 'doorway', 'cushions'/'carpets', something 'being laid down' (in Luke's episode about 'the dogs' at the 'Rich Man's door', 'someone' or 'a certain Poor One named Lazarus') and, as ever, 'her (if not 'his') feet' themes.

The Rabbi Eleazar ben Zadok Traditions and 'In Accordance with Camel is the Burden'

Another Rabbi – interestingly enough one 'Eleazar ben *Zadok*' with whom many of these traditions are connected ('Zadok', possibly his father, was another Rabbi widely associated in Talmudic tradition with 'mourning for the Temple', praying and fasting 'for forty years' before the fall of Jerusalem and, as we have signaled, a name paradigmatic in the Dead Sea Scrolls as well[33]) – on the subject of Nakdimon's daughter Miriam's overweening pride quotes a verse from Song of Songs 1:8, 'go your way forth by the footsteps of the flock and feed your offspring', adding seemingly by way of exposition, 'May I not live to behold the consolation (of Zion) if I do not see her gathering barley corns from beneath the feet of horses in Acco'. Here, of course, we have the 'feet'/'footsteps' theme again, and a new one, 'barley corns' or 'grain'.[34]

This same Rabbi Eleazar ben Zadok quotes the aphorism in Lamentations *Rabbah* and elsewhere, 'May I not live to behold the consolation' – meaning, 'of Zion' – concerning similar suffering and the 'feet' of another Mary, not Nakdimon's daughter Miriam but, once again, 'Miriam the daughter of Boethus'.[35] Again he obviously means Martha, but this is the same genre of confusion between 'Mary' and 'Martha' that found its way into the Gospels – particularly John. Even in this last, Martha, as we saw, is quoted as saying to Jesus, 'If you had been here, my brother (Lazarus) would not have died' (11:21). Eleven verses later in John 11:32, Mary – now also portrayed as 'falling down at his *feet*' – is depicted as saying precisely the same thing: 'If you had been here, my brother would not have died.' This is the sort of tradition overlap we have been speaking about. It is eerie and probably not accidental.

The same basic tradition about Nakdimon's daughter will again be told in *Kethuboth*, this time in the name not of Rabbi Eleazar ben Zadok but of Rabbi Yohanan ben Zacchai, pictured – to some extent like 'Jesus' is in the Gospels (Matthew 21:7 and pars.) – as 'outside Jerusalem riding a donkey while his Disciples followed after him'.[36] But what Rabbi Yohanan now sees, unlike Eleazar ben Zadok above, is this 'girl picking barley corns' or 'grain from among the dung of Arab cattle' – here again the 'barley corns' or 'grain' theme, but now connected with the one about 'dung' we have already remarked previously and shall have cause to remark further. One should also not ignore how in the Gospel version of this tradition, in Luke 19:36 'his Disciples', after 'having thrown their garments on the ass of a colt' (in Mark 11:7, '*epebalon*'/'cast their clothing'), 'laid out their garments in the way'. Though in Matthew 21:8/Mark 11:8/John 12:18, this second part is specifically attributed rather to 'the Many' or 'the multitudes' (*sic*) but, whatever the sense here 'the garments' are being pictured as 'laid out' or 'spread' much as in the Nakdimon ben Gurion or Mary the daughter of Boethus tradition.

It is interesting that in the context of this same cycle of traditions which started with those about the Talmudic Rich Men – in particular, the ones about 'the Poor' who '*came* to Ben Kalba Sabu'a's *door hungry as a dog* and went away *filled*' and the promise both he and Nakdimon ben Gurion made to supply everyone in Jerusalem with *grain* for twenty-one or twenty-two years – *ARN* provides the following tradition that: 'When Vespasian came to destroy Jerusalem … (and) looked at their excrement ('dung') and saw there was no sign of corn (that is, 'barleycorns') in it (meaning 'only straw'), he said to his troops, 'If these who eat nothing but straw kill so many of you in this fashion, how many of you they would kill if they ate everything you *eat and drink*.'[37]

Clearly, not only are these several episodes about Nakdimon's and Boethus' daughters not two separate traditions – 'the feet of horses in Acco' in the *ARN* having now been interchanged with 'the dung of Arab cattle' in *Kethuboth*, but they also incorporate the resultant 'famine', 'grain', and 'dung' motifs. This is to say nothing about the various 'grain' and 'loaves' traditions both in these sources and, in particular, those related to Jesus' miracles we shall presently encounter in all four Gospels below.

However these things may be, the tradition about Nakdimon's daughter Miriam, in the name of Rabbi Yohanan ben Zacchai, now contrasts the condition he finds her in after the fall of the Temple with the prodigiousness of her dowry, 'a million *dinar*s besides what was added from her father-in-law's house' (again the confusions over 'in-law's – once again, in our view, intending Nakdimon). This is followed up in *Kethuboth*, as well, by another description of Nakdimon's incredible wealth, the one depicting 'the *Poor*' 'gathering up the *woolen clothes* that had been *laid* for his *feet*', in turn, followed by the Rabbinic discussion of the issue of the sincerity of his proverbial charity, the apparent meaning of which was that this was not real charity to treat 'the Poor' in this way, even though they probably 'gathered up' and kept 'the woolen clothes'.[38]

It is at this point in *Kethuboth* that the important aphorism is added evoking the pivotal motif of 'the camel' relating to 'his Riches' and his 'charity', that is, 'in accordance with the camel is the burden' – meaning that extraordinary charity was only to be expected on the part of one so Rich. However, the same aphorism is quoted later in this same Tractate with perhaps even more justice in relation to recovering the dowry of 'Martha the daughter of Boethus', already characterized above as awaiting permission of 'the *levir*' to marry Josephus' friend, Jesus ben Gamala.[39] He was High Priest from 63 CE directly following James' death until 65 CE, when he was brutally dispatched along with the individual actually responsible for James' judicial murder, Ananus ben Ananus, by 'the Zealots' and their 'Idumaean' allies as the Uprising against Rome moved into what can best perhaps be termed its 'Jacobite' phase in 68 CE.[40]

The reason one says 'with more justice' here is because the allusion to '*gamal*' or 'camel' would more appropriately play on the name of this 'Boethusian' High Priest, of which it actually constitutes a part, meaning, it would seem, the town of Gamala from where he – and, interesting enough, Judas the Galilean – seems to have come (curiously enough, the same place for which Josephus was supposed to have prepared defences).[41] This 'Gamala' was so named because of its situation on an inland mesa overlooking the Sea of Galilee that had the shape of the hump of a camel. Nor is this to say anything about the curious 'eye of the camel' aphorisms connected to these Poor Man/Rich Man allusions in famous discourses attributed to Jesus we shall discuss further below.

Notwithstanding, the Boethus then, to whom this Jesus b. Gamala became connected through his Rich daughter Martha, was one of the more accommodating High-Priestly clans, willing to live both with Roman power in Palestine and its Herodian representatives – a fact that may have explained this Jesus' rather violent death, as it did that of his even perhaps more accommodating colleague, Ananus ben Ananus, responsible for the death of James.

Judas' Concern for 'the Poor' Revisited and James' Charge to Paul to 'Remember the Poor'

To go back to John and to make the connection with these stories about Nakdimon's or Boethus' daughter even more plain, the narrator in John 12:6 in an aside reflecting the Talmudic debates on Nakdimon's real or alleged charity, adds, 'he said this not because he cared about the Poor, but because he was a thief' – but now, of course, the reference is not to Nakdimon's false charity but Judas Iscariot's. Clearly this statement, made by the narrator, makes no sense without presupposing knowledge of the previous Rabbinical debates about the legitimacy of Nakdimon's charity – one can probably assume, therefore, that the author of John knew this tradition.

Since this issue of 'being a thief' is a new theme we haven't heard before – at least not in the Gospels – the narrator, fairly running away with himself, proceeds then to impart the interesting new fact that since Judas had charge of the common purse, 'he used to help himself to what was put therein' (12:6). Given the symbolic nature of the character represented by Judas, as we have been delineating it, this is perhaps more of the covert anti-Semitism one finds, for instance, in Acts' portrayal of its basically non-existent Stephen.

In the parallel Synoptic material in Matthew and Mark 'at Simon the Leper's house' where it is 'the Disciples' or '*some*', not Judas, who are indignant and are the ones who do the complaining about the wastefulness of the woman with 'the alabaster flask' who poured the 'precious ointment of pure spikenard' on Jesus' head rather than 'his feet'. Nevertheless it is, as always, 'the Poor' who form the crux of the complaints, as they do in the Nakdimon, Lazarus, and now these Judas Iscariot materials. We shall see below how these allusions play off Rabbi Akiba's response to those who would contend they 'were too Poor to study *Torah*', namely, 'Was not Rabbi Akiba very Poor and in straitened circumstances?'[42]

In both sets of tradition, John and the Synoptics, Jesus is pictured as saying something clever about his own coming death, specifically: 'The Poor you have with you always, but you will not always have me.' Of course, none of this can be taken as the least bit historical but rather as we have been showing, simply more rhetorical repartee playing off the matter of 'the precious ointments' and/or 'perfumes' and Jesus' coming burial scenario, either meant for the anointment of his body or simply the antidote to noxious odors – to say nothing of the picture of the 'perfume box' of Nakdimon's pampered daughter Miriam in the Talmud.

As John 12:7 sees these things, the exchange sets the stage for Jesus' death, not only because of the comment he is portrayed as making (echoed as well in Matthew 26:12/Mark 14:8): 'to leave her alone because she has kept it for the day of my burial'; but also in John 12:10 because 'the Chief Priests' then 'plot together so they might also put Lazarus to death' because many of the common Jews – when 'seeing Lazarus' 'raised from the dead' – would 'believe on Jesus on account of him' (*thus* –12:9–11).

Not only do we have here the usual Pauline theological note, but this side comment appears so totally confused that, at first, it is impossible to decipher it. Not only does it draw on the Judas Iscariot materials in the Synoptics (note, for instance too, how in Matthew 26:4, introducing these materials – like John 12:10 above on its 'Lazarus' – it is 'the Chief Priests' and 'Elders of the People', who 'plot together in order that they might seize Jesus' and 'kill him'!), but in normative theology it is because of Jesus' resurrection not Lazarus' that one is supposed to believe.

For Matthew 26:10–13 and Mark 14:7–10, anyhow, the whole presentation is framed – unlike in John, where the framework is rather that of Judas Iscariot's complaints about 'the Poor' – within the context of the worldwide Gentile Mission or, as both express this through the picture of their Jesus' rejoinder to his Disciples on the 'good work' of the woman who anointed his head with 'the very precious ointment' while 'he reclined': 'Wherever this Gospel is preached throughout the whole world that which this woman did will also be spoken of as a memorial for her.' One should note here the Jamesian/Dead Sea Scroll emphasis on what 'this woman *did*' or '*doing*' – even the expressed allusion in Matthew 26:10/Mark 14:6 that 'she has done a good *work* towards me' – in three lines out of four in both these passages. This is to say nothing of the allusion to 'memorial' or 'remembrance' in Matthew 26:13/Mark 14:9, which we have already called attention to in the Damascus Document above. Nor is this to say anything about James' words as reported by Paul in Galatians 2:10 to 'remember the Poor' which he says he 'was indeed most anxious to do' and which we shall have cause to elaborate more fully below – but now with quite another signification. Moreover the 'good work', referred to now in both Matthew and Mark, is 'breaking the alabaster flask' and 'pouring' the 'very precious pure spikenard ointment', it contained, 'on his ('Jesus'') head' – not a 'work' of the Law.

John's account, of course, like Acts' entire 'Stephen' episode – not to mention the Synoptic 'Lazarus'/'Canaanite woman' episodes – is replete with anti-Semitism; and this episode, in particular, where 'the Chief Priests' are represented as not only wishing to kill Jesus (cf. Matthew 26:4) but Lazarus as well – on account of (the) 'many of the Jews (seeing what Jesus had done) were believing on Jesus because of him' (John 12:10-11) – is a particularly noteworthy example, the reference to 'the Jews' portraying them as a completely 'alien' People. Notwithstanding, the retrospective and mythological nature of the whole scenario in both sets of materials should be patent.

Of course, whereas Matthew and Mark have no 'dogs licking Lazarus under the table' episode, Luke has no 'Canaanite'/'Syrophoenician woman' encounter. Nevertheless, just as the thrust of Matthew and Mark's 'Canaanite'/'Greek Syrophoenician woman''s retort to Jesus implies that she has something to teach even Jesus; or, to put this in another way, the Jewish Messiah Jesus has something to learn even from a lowly Gentile believer. In particular, the 'Tyre' allusion in Matthew 15:21 and Mark 7:24 – interestingly, in Luke 6:17 the 'parts'/'coasts of Tyre and Sidon' allusion is tied rather to one about the People 'trying to touch' Jesus, when 'the power went out of him' – will have, as already suggested, real importance in traditions about some of these women, such as, for instance, Simon Magus' companion Helen, whom Christian tradition says he found 'in the brothels of Tyre', to say nothing of the 'Tyrian gold *dinar*' Boethus' daughter Martha or Nakdimon's daughter Miriam is said 'to need every Sabbath evening just for her sweetmeats' or 'spice puddings'!

'The Crumbs that Fall from the Rich Man's Table'

The polemic in the Lukan counterpart of these two presentations – where 'the dogs' rather lick Lazarus' sores and do not just 'eat the crumbs under the table' and where Lazarus is presented as 'a certain Poor Man desiring to be filled from the crumbs' under 'a certain Rich Man's table', himself described as 'clothed in purple and fine linen' (how believable is this?) – ends in a fulsome attack on Judaism, the Law, and Jewish 'blindness' generally in the face of such seemingly overwhelmingly convincing miracles as Jesus' (not Lazarus') coming resurrection from the dead.

In Luke 16:22–31, this is expressed in the manifestly mythological picture of the afterlife that follows – this in place of the picture of Jesus' resurrection of Lazarus 'from among the dead' in John. As Luke 16:22 laconically depicts this, 'the Poor Man (Lazarus) died and he was carried away by the Angels into the bosom of Abraham' (the counterpart of Lazarus' resurrection in John – now abstracted into a parable or an allegory). At this point, then, 'the Rich Man also died' and, 'being in the torment of Hades' (one could hardly get a more Hellenized version of the afterlife than this), 'cried out for mercy' to 'Abraham afar off' – presumably meaning 'in Heaven', 'Lazarus on his bosom' (16:23).

Though there is no hint here of Lazarus' resurrection into the present world but rather this 'far-off' one or 'Heaven', still Abraham's rebuke in the doctrinal discussion that follows of 'the Rich Man' as one of the followers of 'Moses and the Prophets' (note the Pauline theological implications) does turn on the theme that, even if 'one came to them (i.e., Jews) from the dead, they would not be repent' (16:30).

Not only do these passages from Luke anticipate the next step in John 11:17–45, that is, Jesus' resurrection of Lazarus, 'four days in the tomb' and already 'stinking' (to whom in 11:34 even the predicate, 'having been laid', is applied), but the very next line in Luke 16:31 reiterates, with even clearer bearing on John's narrative, again with the signification of a final conclusion by Abraham presented as answering Lazarus' query: 'even if someone were to rise from the dead, they (again meaning, 'the Jews'), would not be persuaded'. Moreover, as if to add insult to injury, the words Luke puts into Abraham's mouth here seem to carry an echo of the language used in the opening exhortative of the Damascus Document, to wit, 'hear, all you who know Righteousness' and 'hear me, all who enter the Covenant',[43] but as always with reverse dialectical effect, that is, how could 'they be persuaded' (meaning 'the Jews' again), since they don't even 'hear Moses and the Prophets' (*thus*)!

The themes here in Luke parallel the Lazarus episode in John, including even the precise antithesis of this, 'Then *many* of the Jews, who *came* to Mary and saw what Jesus *did*, believed on him' (11:45). While others, it seems (the ubiquitous 'some' again), 'went to the Pharisees and told them what Jesus had *done*' (11:46 – again, the repetition of the 'doing' theme). This then provokes the next step in John's plot-line (no pun intended), namely, the picture of 'the Chief Priests (as in Matthew 26:4 above) plotting together how they might kill' Jesus as well as Lazarus (11:47-53 – n.b., in this scene how even Caiaphas is pictured as 'prophesying'!) just as in 12:10–11, immediately following, they will then do regarding Lazarus.

To leave Lazarus for the moment – in Mark 7:25–27, Jesus is pictured as 'casting out (*ekbale*) unclean spirits' or 'demons' from 'the Greek Syrophoenician woman's daughter' (note that here too, she is depicted as 'falling at his feet' and 'the children' are characterized as about 'to be filled' or 'satisfied') and in 7:24, the implication seems simply to be of his 'hiding' (the 'hidden' language) in a non-Jewish household – the allusion to 'unclean spirits' carrying with it its own additional polemic in terms of Jewish 'cleanliness' requirements we shall highlight further as we proceed.

On the other hand, in Matthew 15:21–28 – where the 'casting' allusion is not used in relation to 'casting unclean spirits' out of the 'Canaanite woman's daughter' as in Mark 7:26, but rather in relation to 'the crumbs falling from the tables of their masters', now expressed in terms of 'taking the childrens' bread and *casting it* (*balein*) to the little dogs' – the anti-Jewish and pro-Gentile Mission slant, as in 'Lazarus being carried away by the Angels into Abraham's bosom' in Luke 16:22, is plain. This is achieved in Matthew 15:24 by having the episode clearly prefaced by Jesus' assertion, 'I was not sent except to the lost sheep of the House of Israel', just as the counterpart in Luke 16:21's 'Poor Lazarus wanting to be *filled* from the crumbs which fell from the Rich Man's table' – note the parallel with Mark 7:27's 'let the children first be filled' – is prefaced by its compressed version of Matthew 5:18's Sermon on the Mount, starting with 'not serving two masters' in 16:13 and ending with the 'not a jot or tittle shall pass from the Law' assertion in 16:17.

This is also true of Luke 6:17's earlier evocation of Matthew/Mark's 'coasts of Tyre and Sidon' (in Matthew 15:21 and Mark 7:31, this is 'parts' or 'borders of Tyre and Sidon'), which is immediately followed in 6:18–19 by 'those troubled by unclean spirits also coming', 'the whole crowd seeking to touch him (Jesus)', 'the Power going out of him and healing them'!, and reprising another part of Matthew's 'Sermon on the Mount', starting with 'Blessed are the Poor' in 6:20 and ending with the 'house built without a foundation' in 6:49. One should also not fail to observe that the 'coming' and 'falling' in Mark 7:25 above is rather that of the 'Greek Syrophoenician woman falling at Jesus' feet', whereas in Matthew 15:27 and Luke 16:21, the 'falling' remains that of 'the crumbs from the table'. But now, unlike in Luke, in Matthew 'the crumbs fall to the little dogs' while 'their masters' take the place of the 'Rich Man' in Luke!

In all these traditions we are, once more, face to face with the kinds of inversions or polemical reversals we shall see in Paul's reversal of James' position on 'things sacrificed to idols' and eating 'unclean foods' in 1 Corinthians 6-12 both, as we have alluded to it above and will treat further below. In the first place, there is the play on the allusion to 'dog' or 'dogs' (singular or plural, masculine or feminine is beside the point) – already signaled in relation to the Talmud's rather droll exposition of Ben Kalba Sabu'a's pseudonym; but now, in addition to the allusion to them in Luke's 'Poor Lazarus' episode, there is the evocation of them in Matthew/Mark's depiction of Jesus' 'exorcism'/'curing' of the 'Greek Syrophoenician'/'Canaanite woman's daughter' in the explanation that 'even the dogs under the table eat the children's crumbs'/'eat the crumbs that fell from their masters' table'.[44]

As these expand in other directions to encompass Luke's the 'Poor man Lazarus longing to be filled from the crumbs that fell from the Rich Man's table', the issue turns – as it did in John – into one involving Resurrection. In fact, Luke 16:19–31's version of the scenario of the 'certain Poor Man Lazarus' under 'a certain Rich Man''s table', 'his sores licked by dogs', does not quite end up in a discussion of whether this was 'true charity', as in the case of 'Nakdimon' in Talmudic tradition above; but rather it does go on to picture the Rich Man's torment in 'Hades', 'suffering in this flame', moving on into the anti-Semitic attack on the stiff-neckedness of the Jews and the presentiment of Jesus' coming resurrection and 'return from the dead', to which the pointed comment is attached: 'even then they would not be persuaded' (16:31).

For its part, in John's picture of these all-important goings-on at Lazarus' house, paralleled by what takes place in Luke at 'Martha's house' (in Matthew/Mark, at 'Simon the Leper's house'), the Synoptic presentation of 'Judas Iscariot going to the Chief Priests' to 'deliver him up' (Matthew 26:14–15 and pars.) is included; but now rather in the characterization of Judas as 'the son' or 'brother of *Simon Iscariot*' (John 12:4 and 13:29–31 – the second, pivotally, at 'the Last Supper') – in other words, the 'Simon' characterized as 'the Leper' in both Matthew and Mark (or even 'Simon the Pharisee' earlier in Luke), only now with completely different signification. Put in another way, in place of 'Simon the Leper' or 'Simon the Pharisee' in these Gospels, as already remarked, we should now have to probably read Simon the Cananaean, Simon *Zelotes*, or even Simon Iscariot.

Though the complaints about 'the Poor' that Judas is pictured as making against Jesus in John 12:4–8 are folded into those 'the Disciples' and the 'some' make against the woman who anoints Jesus' head at 'Simon the Leper's house' in Matthew and Mark – only in John they are far more theoretical or theological – they also mirror Nakdimon's daughter Miriam's (or his unnamed daughter-in-law's) complaints, albeit reversed. Now the amounts are not too little as in Talmudic tradition, but too costly as in the Gospels. It is worth observing, yet again, that this is often the way this kind of data moves from one tradition to the other – much in the way the whole ethos of the Dead Sea Scrolls is largely reversed in New Testament reformulation.

Of course, in Luke's abbreviated and clearly secondary version of these encounters, Martha is pictured as complaining about Mary 'sitting at Jesus' feet' while she has to do all the 'serving'; whereas her Talmudic counterpart rather complains either about the paltriness of her 'daily perfume allowance' or the stinginess of the weekly 'widow' allocation the Rabbis are prepared to allot her. On the other hand in John, 'Judas of Simon Iscariot' is rather complaining about Mary's profligacy in wasting such 'expensive perfume' or 'pure spikenard ointment' and not 'giving it to the Poor'. In John as well, it should be recalled that the famous 'thirty pieces of silver' of Matthew 26:15/27:3's Judas Iscariot's 'price of blood'/'suicide' scenario (itself significant) – in Mark 14:11, this was only the more indeterminate 'silver' or 'money' and no numerical amount was attached, all the rest being the same – is now augmented some tenfold. Thereupon Judas is depicted as crying out, 'Why was this ointment not sold for three hundred dinars and given to the Poor?' – a noble sentiment, but the amount in the one is basically reconfiguring the amount of the other.

Notwithstanding, in Mark 14:5's 'Simon the Leper's house' scenario, we now rather get John 12:5's more precise formulation for the value of the 'precious spikenard ointment' of 'three hundred *dinar*s' (the 'some' now 'complaining' or 'murmuring' – not either the Disciples in Matthew or Judas in John) as opposed to the vaguer 'much' in Matthew 26:9 or the 'money', Mark 14:11 then goes on to designate as Judas Iscariot's betrayal 'price'. This is not surprising as only Matthew had the precise amount of this last (supposedly taken, it will be recalled, from 'the Prophet Jeremiah' when it was, in fact, Zechariah!). Accordingly and unlike in John and Mark, therefore, in Matthew 26:9 the price of 'the precious ointment' now becomes somewhat less precise: 'For what, this waste? This ointment could have been sold for much and given to the Poor.' Were one to ask which of these multiple variations and spin-offs came first, it would be perhaps impossible to say. Still, it should be observed, that the relationships are far more complex than is generally thought, since Mark here is clearly dependent on John and not Matthew. But in the writer's view, it doesn't really matter, since almost all are secondary anyhow – most probably actually going back to these hyperbolic amounts conserved in Talmudic tradition about these ostentatiously Rich Men's daughters or daughters-in-law.

'Remember the Poor' and 'the Camel and the Eye of the Needle'

We may see this ideological exchange in John on the subject of 'the Poor' as symbolic of the whole period, while Judas 'the Iscariot' in John 14:22 represents the more historical 'Judas the Galilean', the founder of both 'Zealot' and *Sicarii* Movements as far as Josephus is concerned[45] – and, in our view, the entire 'Messianic' Movement contemporary with them. One can see in John's concern to counter-indicate Judas' rebuke of Jesus over Mary's 'wastefulness' that taking the wealth of the Rich and giving it to the Poor was a cornerstone of the ideology of these 'Movements' – therefore the designation 'the Poor'. Furthermore, this same ideology was, in Jesus' retort to this same Judas (in John later, 'the Iscariot' – in Matthew, 'his Disciples'; in Mark, the ubiquitous 'some'), at the same time now being aggressively undermined, Hellenized – the kind of obeisance being demanded by Jesus here being typical of that paid to any number of Hellenistic Deities[46] – and, in the interests of the *Pax Romana*, pacified.

Though this historical point just barely shines through the patent attempt at dissimulation on the part of these New Testament narratives, so layered and artfully constructed are they, still, it is exactly what one would expect since even Josephus makes it clear that 'the Innovators' (Revolutionaries) responsible for the War against Rome – aside from burning the palaces of the 'Rich' Herodians and High Priests and burning all the debt records – 'wished to turn the Poor against the Rich',[47] meaning, one has in his account one of the first clearly-documented class struggles in written history.

One should also appreciate in these ideological exchanges between Judas and Jesus on the subject of 'the Poor' the echo of James' admonition relative to the continuance of Paul's Gentile Mission in Galatians 2:10 that he (Paul) should only 'remember the Poor', which he says he 'was most anxious to do'.

Not surprisingly, this occurs right after the allusion in Galatians 2:6–9 to 'James, Cephas, and John' – 'these reputed Pillars', not that 'their importance' or 'repute meant anything to' him. Echoing Jesus' declaration to the Canaanite/Cananaean woman in Matthew 15:24: 'I was not sent except to the lost sheep of the House of Israel', these 'Pillars', according to him, were to be 'the Apostleship of' and supposed only to go 'to the circumcision', while he and Barnabas were 'to go to the uncircumcision' or 'the Gentiles'.

Also, not surprisingly, it is followed two lines later by the note about the '*some* from James' who came down from Jerusalem (2:12) and how Peter, whose habit before had been to 'eat with the Gentiles', then immediately 'separated himself (that is, from Paul and from 'table fellowship with Gentiles' generally) for fear of those of the circumcision'.

In this context too, then, one sees both Judas Iscariot and Simon *Zelotes* as representing the more 'Zealot'/*Sicarii* orientation of the Essenes/Judeo-Christians, particularly if '*Sicarii*' also carries with it the sense of 'forcible circumcisers' in the sense of the Roman ban on such 'bodily mutilations' generally, 'the *Lex Cornelia de Sicarius et Veneficis*', while Jesus embraces the more overseas Hellenizing and Paulinizing line – including displaying not a little derisive contempt – 'the Poor' being unimportant as compared to him, that is, to put it in the manner of the three above-mentioned Gospels, 'the Poor you have with you always, but you do not always have me'.

Regarding Nakdimon's 'charity', Rabbinic tradition picks up this theme as well, concluding that his allowing 'the Poor' to gather up 'the woolen clothes that had been laid', so that 'his feet' would not have to touch the dirt of the ground, was *not real charity*. Their conclusion was rather, that it was for 'self-glorification' only. It was at that point, it will be recalled, that they went on to cite the aphorism, 'in accordance with the camel is the burden' which, in the context, obviously meant, the richer he was the more he owed.[48]

Though we showed this to have an equally obvious corollary in the matter of the wealth acquired by Josephus' friend 'Joshua ben Gamala' – whose patronym meant 'camel' – when he married Boethus' daughter Martha, this too, with just the barest amount of reshuffling, had an easily-recognizable parallel in the favorite Synoptic aphorism about 'a Rich Man', 'a camel', and 'the eye of a needle' – whatever one might ultimately take this to mean – actually *comparing the 'Rich Man' to the 'camel'*: 'Easier would it be for a camel to go through the eye of a needle than for a Rich Man to enter the Kingdom of God' (Matthew 19:24 and pars.).[49] The relationship of this curious saying – the meaning of which is, admittedly, obscure and has been debated – to these 'Rich Man' and 'camel' aphorisms in the Talmud should be patent.

In all three Synoptics, the series of commandments preceding this 'camel'/'eye of a needle' pronouncement finally ends with the emphatic directive to *'sell all that you have and give to the Poor'*. Not only is the demand delivered this time with positive, not negative effect – meaning, now 'the Poor' are of *primary* importance and not of secondary significance behind the 'God-Man Jesus' – but in Matthew 19:19 anyhow, it is delivered in the context of yet another enunciation of the 'all-Righteousness' Commandment 'you shall love your neighbor as yourself' – the first part of the Righteousness/Piety dichotomy, a fixture of the salvationary scheme set forth in the Damascus Document of 'the New Covenant in the Land of Damascus'.

It will be recalled that in Paul's dialectic in Romans 13, 'loving your neighbor as yourself', was to some degree being used to countenance the payment of 'taxes' to 'the Servants of God' – implying that it was the Roman Authorities, not the Jerusalem Assembly leaders who were 'the Servants of God' and to whom such 'love' in the form of 'tribute was due', the very opposite of what the Revolutionary Movement begun by 'Judas the Galilean' had demanded.[50] The reason for this, according to Paul's initial, somewhat self-serving polemic in 13:1, was that since 'there was no Authority except from God', those considered 'the Authorities had been appointed by God'!

It was this commandment too – 'the Royal Law according to the Scripture' in James 2:8, which Josephus pictures as the fundamental principle by which Essenes conducted themselves towards their fellow man, as opposed to their duties towards God – 'loving God', which was the first.[51] It was this that dictated the 'poverty' regime of groups such as these Essenes and their counterparts, 'the Ebionites' or 'the Poor'. The implied rationale was that you could not demonstrate 'love for your neighbor' or 'Righteousness towards your fellow man' if you made economic distinctions between such a one and yourself[52] – therefore, Jesus' directive here in the Synoptics: *'If you would be perfect, sell what you have and give to the Poor'*.

Map of Eastern Mediterranean, what was then called *'Arabia'* by both the Romans and the Jews, *'Asia'* including Galatia, Cilicia, and Cappadocia, Upper and Lower Armenia, Edessa and *'the Land of the Edessenes'*, and Helen's Adiabene.

Chapter 8
'Every Plant which My Heavenly Father has not Planted Shall be Uprooted'

'Even the Dogs Eat the Crumbs under the Table'

Let us try to summarize a few of these things. As we have seen, Luke's variation on these 'Rich', 'dogs', 'crumbs', and 'filling' motifs combine Talmudic 'sated as a dog', 'Rich', 'coming', and 'Poor' allusions with Mark and Matthew's Canaanite/Greek Syrophoenician woman's retort to Jesus: 'even the dogs eat of the crumbs which fall from the table of their masters'. This is Matthew 15:27. Mark 7:28 has: 'even the dogs under the table eat of the children's crumbs'. Not only are all these textual variations noteworthy, one should not forget Jesus' apparent prior rejoinder in Matthew 7:6's Sermon on the Mount: 'Do not give what is holy to dogs, nor cast (*balete*) your pearls before swine (here, it is important to note, the 'casting' is associated with the 'swine' not the 'dogs')'.

Notwithstanding, it is difficult to miss the connection of this with Jesus' pronouncement in Matthew 15:25 seemingly obviating it: 'It is not good to take the children's bread and to cast it (*balein*) to the dogs, lest they should trample them with their feet.' Here the 'feet' motif in what has to be considered an odd milieu indeed, but it will have overtones with Talmudic materials about the fate of these same 'Rich Men's daughters' and various references to their own 'feet' and those of animals.

This curious depiction of what transpired at this Rich Man's house – all 'clothed in purple and fine linen' – in Luke is also a bridge to John's picture of what went on at 'Lazarus' house' and the issues debated there, again against the background of multiple evocation of Jesus' 'feet', 'the Poor', and Lazarus' two sisters' 'precious spikenard ointment' or 'perfume' ministrations.

Just as Matthew and Mark's encounter on the parts/borders of Tyre and Sidon with the Greek Syrophoenician/Canaanite woman is absent from Luke and John, the Lazarus episodes in John and Luke, incongruous as they may be, are missing from Matthew and Mark. There is however a caveat here – the particulars of John's Lazarus encounter partly turn up in Matthew and Mark's 'Simon the Leper' episode and partly in Luke's picture of the goings-on at 'Martha's house' – the connecting links being the Bethany locale, the repetitive use of the verb 'to come', the ever-present evocation of 'the Poor', the recurrent use of the telltale 'some'/'certain ones', and the whole activity of 'anointing' Jesus' 'head' or 'feet'. Nor does John have any 'dogs under the table' episode. Rather it evolves into something entirely different – an albeit recognizable scenario.

Still like Luke's 'a certain Poor man named Lazarus' and the complaints of the Disciples or the 'some' in Matthew and Mark about 'giving to the Poor', the adumbration of these themes in John both alludes to 'the Poor' and moves into a number of other usages of the utmost importance for this tradition-cluster centering around this set of Rich Men and women in Palestine. In particular, it moves from the way John transforms Luke's resurrection scenario ('carried away by the Angels' after his death 'to the bosom of Abraham') to allusions to Jesus' coming burial scenario (in our view, ultimately having to do with members of the Royal Family of Adiabene) to these constant evocations of 'costly perfumes', 'precious ointments', and 'his' or someone's/something else's 'feet'. In turn, these bring us full circle back to the original Talmudic allusions regarding these fabulously Rich Men, their daughters, and, of course, 'the Poor' coupled with evocations of these Rich Men or women's 'feet'. Admittedly, all these overlaps and variations are hard to follow without following the actual texts directly, but the reader should do his or her best.

Not only does this idea of being ostentatiously 'Rich' find expression in Luke's version of the Lazarus material – to wit, 'a certain Poor man Lazarus ('laid at his doorstep') longing to be filled from the crumbs falling from the Rich Man's table', but it also constitutes a part of the picture in the Synoptics of 'Joseph of Arimathaea's coming' to claim and prepare Jesus' body for burial in 'his' (Joseph's) tomb in Matthew 27:57 and pars. Despite the widespread familiarity with the name 'Nicodemus', this picture in the Synoptics involves no Nicodemus and it is, rather, only in John that 'Joseph of Arimathaea' is associated with this other character called Nicodemus ('Nakdimon') who also 'came' – 'the one who first *came* to Jesus by night bearing a mixture of myrrh and aloes about a hundred weight' (19:39 – 'litras', the same 'litra' we encountered in John 12:3's picture earlier of the amount of 'ointment of pure spikenard of great worth' with which Mary anointed Jesus' 'feet' – in the Synoptics, it will be recalled, the measure was only expressed in terms of 'an alabaster flask'/'cask' and not 'litras').

As we also saw above, in his original introduction of this 'Nicodemus' or 'Nakdimon', John called him 'a man of the Pharisees, a Ruler of the Jews' – a bit of an exaggeration obviously – 'Pharisees' often being substituted in New Testament parlance (as, for instance, in Acts 15:5 provoking the Jerusalem Council) for 'the Party' or the 'some insisting on circumcision' of James.

Not only do all the various tomb and burial scenarios include motifs of 'linen', 'cloth', or 'clothes', there is often the mention, as just underscored, of the verb 'to come' as, for example, in John 12:1's Jesus 'coming to Bethany where was Lazarus who had died and whom he raised from the dead'. In Luke's further variation on these themes, the dogs 'come' as well – as they do in Matthew 15:27's 'Canaanite woman''s rejoinder to Jesus, that 'even the dogs eat of the crumbs that fall from their master's table' – though only 'to lick' Poor Lazarus' sores. Here, however, it is rather 'Poor Lazarus' who is going to eat 'the crumbs'. No doubt, Luke should have included the 'dogs under the table' portion of the 'Canaanite'/'Greek Syrophoenician woman''s retort to Jesus which, of course, is implied, since that is where 'the crumbs' (in Mark 7:28, 'the children's crumbs') would have 'fallen' if there had been any!

John's 'Cana in Galilee' and God's 'Glory'

Aside from these 'Rich', 'Poor', 'fall', 'filled', 'doorstep', 'dog', and 'came' motifs, one should also not ignore, in Matthew 15:22's version of 'a woman, a Cananaean came out' to him, the possible play on the Cananaean/'Zealots'- theme generally. This must of necessity be seen as including the phrase 'Cana of Galilee' in John 2:1–11, 4:46 and 21:2. One must also see in the second part of this expression, 'Galilee', another possible play on Eusebius' version (seemingly based on Hegesippus), in delineating the number of Jewish 'sects' at the time of Jesus, of 'Galileans' as an alternate nomenclature for 'Zealots'.[1] In this passage, it was 'in Cana of Galilee' that Jesus 'fills' – in the manner of Nakdimon's 'twelve cisterns' above (for Ben Kalba Sabu'a, Luke, and further along in John, it will be recalled, it was 'Poor Lazarus' and 'the room' that were 'filled') – 'six stone water vessels to the brim', then turning them into 'wine' (John 2:9). It is this 'filling to the brim' aspect of the tradition which sharpens the relationship with Nakdimon's 'filling' the Rich Lord's water cisterns 'to overflowing' above. In 2:6 it was 'the master of the feast's 'six stone water vessels standing (note the 'standing' usage) according to the 'purification'/'cleansing (practices) of the Jews' (this last phrase in itself confirms this as having been written by Gentiles for Gentiles).

This is one of the notorious 'signs' or 'miracles' Josephus refers to so scathingly in his several descriptions about how these 'wonder-workers' or 'Impostors' led the people out into the wilderness, there 'to show them the signs of their impending freedom' or 'Redemption'. It was such 'Impostors' and 'religious frauds', it will be recalled, that he (Josephus) considered more dangerous even than 'the Revolutionaries' or 'Innovators' (the actual term he uses for these last[2]). For John 2:11, the theme recurs with the words: 'These were the beginning of the *signs Jesus did in Cana of Galilee*'.

Not only does the description of this first miracle in John include a possible esoteric play on James' 'drinking no wine' and cold water 'bathing' habits, but it is in this context and following that John 2:1 and 2:12, too, actually evokes 'his (Jesus') mother and his brothers'. It is also as a consequence of these 'signs' or 'miracles' that John, unlike the Synoptics, portrays 'his Disciples as believing on him' because 'he revealed his Glory' (2:11).

Furthermore, it is directly after this episode that John 2:13–17 – perhaps not insignificantly – positions its version of the expulsion of the money-changers from the Temple. To this, it is – once again – 'his Disciples' who apply the famous line from Psalm 69:9, 'zeal for Your House consumes me'. We have already seen a variation of this line applied in Tractate *Ta'anith* and *ARN* in the prayer Nakdimon makes to God regarding his own 'miracle' of 'filling' the water cisterns of the Temple. Probably not coincidentally, it is at this point that John 3:1 first introduces the character it calls 'Nicodemus, a Ruler of the Jews', a character missing from the other Gospels with whom John 3:3–22 pictures Jesus as carrying on a sophisticated discussion about 'Christology', 'Light and Darkness', and 'born-again' theology.

Again this discussion begins with Nicodemus, who '*comes* to Jesus by night', saying to him (in quasi-parallel to the words the Talmud uses to describe Nakdimon, 'for whose sake the sun delayed its setting'): 'no one is able to do the miracles that you are doing unless God is with him' (John 3:2).[3] It also contains an allusion like the one Paul uses in 2 Corinthians 12:2–4 in speaking about 'knowing a Man in Christ fourteen years ago' (the same timeframe as in Galatians 1:19 and 2:1 between the two meetings he has with James), who 'was caught away to the Third Heaven' or 'Paradise', where 'he heard unutterable things'. In John 3:12–13 this is: 'Will you believe if I say to you Heavenly things? No one has gone up into Heaven' except 'the Son of Man who is in Heaven'.

But more arresting than any of these and, in our view, further indicative of dependence on Rabbinic tradition – if one actually examines the prayer Nakdimon is pictured as making in both *Ta'anith* and *ARN* (and, one might add, the one Honi is pictured as making prior to this too in *Ta'anith*), the words Nakdimon is portrayed as using to *fill* the Temple water cisterns and *bring the rain* are as follows: 'Master of the Universe, it is revealed and known to You that not for my own glory did I do this, nor for the Glory of my Father's House did I do this, but only for Your Glory I did it, so that there might be water for the pilgrims.'[4] In the Honi episode in *Ta'anith* that precedes this, it will be recalled, it was because Honi added the words 'because I am looked upon as one of Your Household', meaning God's 'Household' (it is this which is almost exactly the gist of Nicodemus' introductory declaration to Jesus above: 'no one is able to do these miracles unless God is with him'), that the Pharisee 'Father', Simeon ben Shetah, is said to have declared: 'If he were not Honi, I would have excommunicated him.'

But here in *ARN/Ta'anith*, the matter of 'Glory', whether God's or Nakdimon's, forms the backbone and basis of the prayer. It cannot be accidental that in the sequence in John 2:2-2:11 above, after '*filling* six stone water-vessels with water' in 2:6–7 at the marriage 'in Cana of Galilee', which Jesus then promptly turns into wine, the following words are added by the narrator: 'This was the beginning of the miracles Jesus did at Cana in Galilee, revealing his Glory, and his Disciples believed on him' (2:11). What should be immediately clear is that the 'Glory' Jesus 'reveals' here goes right back to the 'Glory' that was 'revealed' and 'known to' God in the matter of Nakdimon's rainmaking – in his case, so that 'the pilgrims would have enough water for the Festival', if not 'wine' for the 'Cananaean' marriage celebration.

The resemblance is uncanny; the sequencing precise; and, in the writer's view, this unexpected result of comparing the 'Glory' evoked in both episodes is proof on the order of that achieved concerning the dependence of Luke's presentation in Acts of the conversion of 'the Ethiopian Queen's eunuch' (who was reading Isaiah 53:11 when 'Philip' jumped up on the back of his chariot and asked him whether he knew the significance of what he was reading) on the Talmudic presentation of the conversion of Queen Helen's two sons, who were reading Genesis 17:10–14 on how Abraham circumcised his whole household 'including the foreigner not born within it' which formed the climax of *James the Brother of Jesus* (Penguin, 1998).

The Unfaithful Servant and the Twelve Water Cisterns

In Luke, 'the dogs under the table who lick Poor Lazarus' sores' in 16:19–31 – the Synoptic counterpart to 'casting the children's crumbs to the dogs under the table' in Matthew and Mark – follows directly upon the abbreviated version in 16:15–18 of Matthew 5:17–18's 'not one jot or tittle' allusion.

The idea in Luke 16:16–17 of 'one tittle of the Law not failing' is not only preceded by its version of Matthew 6:24's 'a servant not serving two lords' (Luke 16:13), but the whole sequence, leading up to this 'Poor Lazarus on the Rich Man's doorstep' episode, follows another tortuous parable in 16:1–15, 'the Parable of the Unfaithful Servant', which actually begins with the introduction of the whole theme of the rest of the Chapter 16 to follow – namely, 'a certain Rich Man'. Not only is this Rich Man, as in the Nakdimon episodes, once again alluded to as 'lord' or 'master' in 16:5, but the Parable includes for our purposes the key motifs of haggling over the numbers of his bath-storage facilities just alluded to in the Nakdimon parallels, but also of 'grain' or 'wheat'-provision amounts (16:6–8, which are, of course, part and parcel of all these 'Rich Men' supplying Jerusalem with enough 'grain' or 'barley corns' for 'twenty-one or twenty-two years' in the Talmud and Josephus above[5]).

This convoluted 'Unfaithful Servant Parable' must ultimately be seen as another variant or spin-off of these 'Nakdimon'-miracle tales from Rabbinic tradition, themselves turning on the theme of haggling with the Rich lord over 'twelve talents of silver' and 'filling the twelve water cisterns' – the same amounts, of course, as the 'twelve hand baskets of wheat and barley' encountered in John. Not only does this seemingly purposefully obscure parable include the same genre of personage again referred to by the 'master' or 'lord' denotation (in 16:5 and 8, *kurios/kurion*), but from the outset in 16:1 it raises the same telltale concern over their 'wastefulness' – here that the manager or representative was 'wasting his (the 'master'')s goods'. In these abstruse exchanges we already saw that another important Qumranism, 'the Sons of Light' (16:8), was incorporated – but there are also additional allusions to 'digging' in 16:3 and 'scoffing' in 16:14.

No less telling, the whole discussion from 16:8–14, supposedly between 'the master' and his 'unjust servant' and dealing with 'false Riches', 'the Unrighteous', 'the Pharisees', 'making yourselves friends of this world' (compare with James 4:4), and 'servants', reflects not a little Paul's own barely concealed attack on the Jerusalem Apostles in 2 Corinthians, called by him in 11:22 'Hebrews' and 'Super Apostles' or 'Apostles of the Highest Degree' in 12:11.

In making this attack Paul uses the quasi-Qumranism, 'Satan transforming himself into an Angel of Light', and compares this to how 'pseudo-Apostles (clearly meaning the 'Super Apostles') turn themselves into Servants of Righteousness'. This last, too, is almost a total Qumranism. It is co-extensive as well with what Paul is also referring to in 2 Corinthians 11:13 as 'Apostles of Christ'. Furthermore, this in turn is preceded in 11:12, one should note, by the additional important Qumranism 'cutting off', which we shall see to be of such consequence in the Damascus Document's historiography – to say nothing of its parody as well by Paul in Galatians 5:12, who uses it somewhat crudely to attack those who 'are troubling' his communities with 'circumcision'!

It is, therefore, during the course of this rather tortured Parable in Luke 16:1–16, ending with 'not serving two masters' and 'forcing the Kingdom of Heaven', that the twin motifs of 'baths' and 'grain'/'wheat' are raised and over which 'the unjust servant' bargains with 'his master's debtors'. It is these motifs which so parallel those in the Nakdimon 'rainmaking' tradition of bargaining over 'the lord's' water cisterns (in our view, Luke 16:6 transforms this into 'a hundred baths of oil') or his 'supplying Jerusalem with enough grain for twenty-one years' – e.g., the 'hundred cores of wheat' that Luke 16:7 here considers owing 'the master's servant'. Both amounts actually incorporate the 'hundred' numeration, multiples of which form so much a part of the 'perfume'/'precious ointment' traditions and their further adumbration in the various Gospel *dinar* descriptions.

The interchanges between 'the lord's servant' and 'his master's debtors' in Luke 16:5–6 also include the *pro forma* element of haggling over numbers – now 'fifty', 'eighty', and 'a hundred'. In the Nakdimon stories, it is the haggling over the number of wells and who owes whom and what amount. It is this 'haggling' that Luke uses as a springboard to produce his version of the famous aphorism, 'no one can serve two lords' ('God and Mammon'), better known in Matthew's Sermon on the Mount. In Luke 16:13, in keeping with the business nature of the parable and playing on the 'lord' theme, this reads: 'No servant can serve two lords, for either he will hate the one and love the other or he will hold to the one and despise the other. You cannot serve God and Mammon.' It is at this point that these preliminaries give way in Luke to its version of Matthew 5:18 – taking off from the allusion to 'not coming to abolish the Law and the Prophets but to fulfill them' in 5:17: 'Verily I say unto you, that until Heaven and Earth pass away, not one jot or tittle shall pass away from the Law until all these things are accomplished.' Or as Luke 16:17 puts it: 'Easier would it be for Heaven and Earth to pass away than for one tittle of the Law to fail.'

In 16:18 this is immediately followed by the ban on 'divorce' which, as in the Damascus Document and in Matthew 5:32 and 19:9, is linked to the issue of 'fornication'.[6] Here too Jesus' attack on 'the Pharisees' must be seen as equivalent to similar ones on the ever-present 'some'. It is also reflected in Jesus' like-minded attack on the Pharisees as 'Blind Guides' in Matthew 15:1–20 and Mark 7:1–23, in the context of declaring 'all foods clean' and 'eating with unwashed hands does not defile the man' leading up in both to the 'not taking the children's bread and casting it to the dogs' episodes in 15:21–28 and 7:24–30, which we shall analyze further below.

We have already seen too how the 'Poor' motif is echoed in the complaints at 'Simon the Leper's house' in Matthew and Mark and those of 'Judas of Simon Iscariot' at Lazarus' house in John and Jesus' rather vainglorious response in all three, 'the Poor you have with you always, but you do not always have me'. However, this exchange cannot be completely differentiated from the one in Rabbinic literature concerning the extreme 'poverty' of the key Rabbinic hero, Rabbi Akiba, when he was young. In fact at one point, to illustrate Rabbi Akiba's 'poverty', at the time he married Ben Kalba Sabu'a's daughter before her father became reconciled to their marriage, his wife Rachel is portrayed as having to 'sleep on straw' and picking it 'from his (Rabbi Akiba's) hair'.

One should pay particular attention here to the 'hair' motif once more, but this time it is now Rabbi Akiba's hair and not either Lazarus' sister Mary's hair nor that of the unidentified female 'Sinner' in Luke, anointing Jesus' feet and 'wiping them with her hair'![7] One should also note here the theme of 'straw', so important in the picture in both Josephus and the Talmud – should one again choose to regard it – of 'the Zealots' ('the *Barjonim*'/'*Biryonim*' in the Talmud) burning Ben Kalba Sabu'a's/Nakdimon's and/or Ben Zizzit's 'grain' stores or mixing, in their desperation, such 'grain' or 'straw' with the bricks they used to shore up

Jerusalem's defences.[8] Nor is this to say anything about the portraits of the 'feet' of these various Rich Men's daughters we have been highlighting and will highlight further below, both during and after the War against Rome, amid 'the straw' and 'mud' of various Palestinian cities as, for instance, Jerusalem, Lydda, or Acre.[9]

It is at this point that Tractate *Nedarim* (on the bride's dowry) depicts Rabbi Akiba as promising his wife 'a golden Jerusalem' – apparently the tiara in vogue among the ladies of the day depicting the city of Jerusalem and manifestly an 'irredentist' statement of some kind. But it also depicts the Prophet Elijah as coming to Akiba in the guise of a mortal (the 'Elijah *redivivus*' theme and an essential element of Gospel portraiture at least in the Synoptics) and crying out at the door, 'Give me some straw for my wife is in confinement and I have nothing for her to lie on' (the root perhaps of the 'no room at the inn' scenario in Luke 2:5–17). Not only is this 'crying at the door' a theme both present in the Letter of James 5:9 and the proclamation in the Temple at Passover attributed to James in all early Church literature,[10] but the tradition as a whole is, in some manner and in the characteristically 'earthy' Talmudic style, both comparing and connecting Rabbi Akiba with the Prophet Elijah. At this point, in typical Rabbinic style, Rabbi Akiba is pictured as wryly observing to his wife, 'You see there is a man who lacks even straw'!

These things as they may be, following allusion to Rabbi Akiba's teacher, 'Rabbi Eliezer b. Hyrcanus' (Lazarus?), and pivotal usages such as 'uprooting', 'casting', and 'hidden' – all of which we shall encounter again, as we proceed, in the run-up in Matthew 15 and Mark 7 to the exorcism of the 'Canaanite'/'Greek Syrophoenician woman's daughter' – *ARN* notes how Rabbi Akiba's example will condemn all the Poor for, when they will be accused (Judas Iscariot's or the Disciples' accusation against either Lazarus' sister Mary or 'the woman with the alabaster flask' about anointing Jesus' head or his feet?), 'Why did you not study *Torah*?' (the content of these stories or traditions are, as should by now be fully appreciated, almost always one hundred and eighty degrees inverted) and they plead, 'Because we were *too Poor*' ('the Poor you have with you always' paradigm in the above episodes?); the response will be, 'Was not Rabbi Akiba very Poor and in straitened circumstances?'[11]

However dramatic this may be, the allusion to 'uprooting' connected to this notice in the *ARN*, which – at least in Matthew – precedes Jesus' exchange over 'not taking the children's bread and casting it to the little dogs', will be a particularly important one. Here in Matthew it will be found in another rebuke Jesus makes in a polemical exchange about 'the Pharisees' as 'Blind Guides' – in this instance, not to the Canaanite woman, but to his own Disciples again: 'Every plant which my Heavenly Father has not planted shall be rooted up' (Matthew 15:13). The inverted parallel to this – which, as at Qumran and as we shall show further below, will also involve a 'Guide' or '*Maschil*'[12] – will be present in the Damascus Document's dramatic opening imprecation about how God caused 'a Root of Planting to grow (the parallel is here!) from Israel and from Aaron to inherit His land and to prosper on the good things of His Earth'.[13] The linguistic interdependence of this and much else in the depiction of Jesus' arguments in Matthew 15:1–20 and Mark 7:1–23 with the 'scribes and Pharisees from Jerusalem' should be clear to all but the most stubbornly obdurate reader. This is Matthew 15:1, but in Mark 7:1 this changes into the even more pregnant 'the Pharisees' and the telltale '*some* of the scribes who had come from Jerusalem', a euphemism evocative of Paul's interlocutors from James' Jerusalem Assembly.

'Suffer the Little Children to Come unto me and Do not Hinder them'

In *ARN*, this exchange concerning Rabbi Akiba's incredible application to 'studying *Torah*', as opposed to those claiming to be 'too Poor' to do so, is directly followed by yet another, equally striking allusion – this time to 'little children' and/or Rabbi Akiba's own 'little children'. It reads: 'If they plead, "we could not study *Torah*" because of our little children (that is, instead of 'because we were too Poor'), the response should be, "Did not Rabbi Akiba have little children too?"' Not only should it be clear that this bears on Jesus' admonition to 'Let the children first be filled' and 'it is not good to take the children's bread and cast it to the little dogs' in both Matthew and Mark (all allusions for the moment to 'being filled' aside) – but also to the several references to 'little children' throughout the Gospels.[14] Perhaps the most striking and well-known example of these is the one that comes just following the imaginative presentation concerning fornication and adultery in Matthew 19:12 (itself clearly playing off Column Four of the Damascus Document on the same subject[15]) about 'eunuchs from the mother's womb' and 'those making themselves eunuchs for the sake of the Kingdom of Heaven', just preceding allusions, too, to 'keeping the Commandments' in 19:17 and 'a Rich Man not entering into the Kingdom of Heaven' in 19:24.

Just as the rebuke to the woman who came to him with an alabaster cask of very precious ointment at 'Simon the Leper's house' in Matthew 26:7 later and that to 'his Disciples' about 'planting', 'uprooting', and 'Blind Guides' in Matthew 15:12 earlier, this is once again aimed at the Disciples, now pictured as objecting to Jesus' having 'laid hands' on 'little children' (Matthew 19:13-15 and pars.). In response, in what is now becoming something of a pattern, Jesus immediately rebukes these same Disciples, making the now celebrated remark: 'Suffer the little children to come unto me.' Similarly, preceding this there is yet another, equally proverbial rebuke – again directed against the Disciples – insisting that, 'unless you become as the little children, you shall in no wise enter the Kingdom of the Heavens' (Matthew 18:1-4 and pars.)

Not only should the interconnectedness of all these 'Kingdom of Heaven' allusions be obvious, but that all have to do with castigating those – as, for example, the unnamed circumcisers 'confusing' or 'troubling' Paul's new Gentile Christian communities in Galatians 5:12 – throwing up inconsequential legal barriers (such as 'circumcision') should be obvious as well. We mean 'inconsequential' *as deemed by Paul* since, as he also puts this in Galatians 5:14 – again clearly both alluding to and pre-empting the sentiment expressed in James 2:8-2:10: 'For the whole of the Law is fulfilled in one sentence, you shall love your neighbor as yourself.' Here too, strikingly, he evokes his 'freedom' ideology, by which he always means 'freedom from the Law' and not 'freedom from Rome', and pointedly characterizes his opponents as 'biting and devouring one another'.[16]

It should be obvious that these are all anti-Jerusalem Church aspersions, since they are usually followed up by and tied to equally proverbial statements like 'the First shall be Last and the Last shall be First' (Matthew 19:30, 20:16 and pars.) – again patently having to do with Paul's new Gentile communities and those, like him, making no such insistences on seemingly picayune legal requirements for 'Salvation'. Why 'patently', because Paul first made the allusion to being 'last' in his 1 Corinthians 15:8 Jesus sighting-order determinations – also, importantly enough, citing James even if albeit defectively – 'And last of all he appeared, as if to one born out of term (or 'to an abortion'), also to me'.

But 'the First' is an extremely important expression at Qumran, carrying with it the signification of 'the Forefathers' or 'the Ancestors' and the sense is always those who observed or gave the *Torah*, while 'the Last' – aside from Paul's evocation of it regarding his own post-resurrection appearance role – usually has to do with 'the Last Times' or 'the Last Days', denoting the 'present' or 'Last Generation' as opposed to 'the First'.[17] In the Gospels, once again turning Qumran ideology on its head, 'the Last' are these 'simple' or 'little children' – representative of Paul's new Gentile Christians, knowing or required to know little or nothing about such onerous legal requirements, yet still in a state of 'Salvation', or, as it were, 'in Jesus'. The 'simile', 'symbolism', 'parable', or 'allegory' – as the case may be – in all these allusions is not hard to figure out, despite endless scholarly attempts at evasion or posturing to the contrary.

Mark 10:13–14, followed by Luke 18:16–17, is even more severe, rather expressing Matthew's 'little children' incident as follows: 'And they brought little children to him that he might touch them, but the Disciples rebuked those who brought them. But when Jesus observed this, he was very displeased and he said unto them, "Suffer the little children to come to me and do not hinder them".' Not only is this a good deal stronger than Matthew and one would have to be completely simplistic not to realize it was directed both against Jews and the Jerusalem Apostles and for the new Gentile Mission of Paul, but we have the 'touching' motif too that we have already encountered in several miraculous 'curing' episodes above (when 'the Power' often 'goes out of him' – and, even more importantly, in Jerome's testimony regarding James concerning how 'the little children' or 'the People used to run after him and try to touch the fringes of his garment as he passed by'.[18]

Nor is this to say anything about the statement, following the rebuke comparing Rabbi Akiba's dedication to '*Torah* study' to that of those claiming to be 'too Poor' or making the excuse of having 'little children' above, 'that Rabbi Akiba started studying *Torah* and by the end of thirteen years he taught *Torah* in public'. For whatever it's worth, like the picture of Rabbi Akiba's wife about to give birth to a child in a quasi-manger and being visited by 'the Prophet Elijah' having points in common with Luke 2:7, this is not completely unrelated to the picture in Luke 2:46 of Jesus teaching in the Temple – though the age cited in the Lukan tradition is 'twelve years old' and that in the Rabbi Akiba one, 'thirteen' – close enough. Of course in Luke, the number is always 'twelve', as it is for the age of Jairus' 'little daughter', the number of years the 'certain woman' had been sick 'with a flow of blood' and, as it will be, for 'the twelve baskets full of broken pieces' below.

We have also already encountered several usages in John not dissimilar to ones found in the Rabbi Akiba tradition, particularly concerning his wife. This is most in evidence in the picture both of how she and ultimately her father – Rabbi Akiba's father-in-law Ben Kalba Sabu'a – 'falls on his (or 'her') face and kisses his (Rabbi Akiba's) feet'.[19] The parallel this represents, however far-fetched, with John's portrayal of Lazarus' sister Mary 'falling down at his feet' in John 11:32 and similar portrayals of the unknown female 'Sinner' with the 'alabaster flask of ointment' at 'the Pharisee's house' in Luke 7:37, 'falling at his feet', 'wiping them with the hairs of her head', and 'kissing them lovingly' should not be overlooked.

In John too, as should by now be indelibly fixed, it is 'Judas (the son or brother) of Simon Iscariot' who makes the complaint about not giving the price of the precious ointment 'to the Poor', whereas the 'plotting' normally associated with his name and evoked in 12:10, interestingly enough is not between Judas and the High Priests, as in the Synoptics (Matthew 26:15 and pars.).[20] Rather, the 'plotting' takes place only between the High Priests themselves since, in John, the Synoptic 'thirty pieces of silver' or '*dinars*' motif is entirely missing in favor of the 'three hundred *dinars*' for the value of the 'precious spikenard ointment'.

In John 11:50, too, the motive of the High Priests – since 'many of the Jews were coming to Mary and seeing what Jesus did (to Lazarus)' – is rather that, it was better that one man should die for the People than that the whole Nation should perish. Nor is the 'plotting' or 'betrayal' at this point in John 12:10–11, as we have seen, about identifying or betraying Jesus *per se* as in the Synoptics; but rather the 'plotting' is about putting Lazarus back to death, since it was on his account that 'many of the Jews were leaving and believing on Jesus'! This 'plotting' theme will also be conspicuous in the Scrolls, most notably in the Habakkuk *Pesher* and the 'plotting' evoked there on the part of 'the Wicked Priest' is rather to 'consume', 'eat', or 'destroy the Righteous Teacher'.[21] Once again, it should be clear that what we are witnessing here are numerous rewrites of the same or similar material as one tradition reworks, absorbs, or transforms another.

Feeding Five Thousand with 'Five Loaves and Two Fishes', 'Filling Twelve Baskets', and 'the Children First being Filled'

To go back to the presentation of Jesus' encounter with the Cananaean/Greek Syrophoenician woman in Mark and Matthew: the exchange between the two of them has to do with another of these 'daughter's who, like her mother – though she comes from 'the border areas'/'parts of Sidon and Tyre' (in other words, she is supposed to be a Gentile, which Mark 7:26 makes clear) – goes unnamed. Notwithstanding, what she wants Jesus to do in Mark 7:25 is 'to cast' (*ekballē*) 'an unclean spirit' – 'a demon' in both Mark 7:26 and Matthew 15:22 – 'out of her daughter'.

Jesus' response – seemingly playing on the non-Jewish origins of this mother and her daughter – turns on the following statement: 'First to be *filled* (or 'sated'/'satisfied') should be the *children*. It is not good to take the children's bread and cast it (*balein*) to the little dogs (paralleling 'the little children' above, increasing the 'Gentile Christian' overtones of this episode).' This is from Mark 7:27, the fuller exposition. Matthew 15:26, for its part, omits the allusion to 'filled' and, therefore, the first reference to 'children', but it does pick up the second, that is, 'it is not good to take the children's bread and cast it to the little dogs', as well as the reference to '*balein*'. Moreover, in Mark 7:25, the 'daughter' is actually even her '*little* daughter' and 7:24–25 also includes the usual telltale introductory usage 'a certain woman', the fact that Jesus 'could not be hidden', and the mother, once again, both 'coming' and 'falling at his feet'.

Not only does the omnipresent 'casting' language permeate the episode but Mark's use of the 'satiated' or 'filled' vocabulary mirrors or, at least, evokes that in Luke's account of the 'Poor Man Lazarus longing to be filled' – to say nothing of his 'dogs' – again showing the basic interconnectedness of these three encounters, not to mention the Talmud's Ben Kalba Sabu'a, the cognomen of whom in Aramaic, as we saw, actually means 'filled' and to whose '*door one came hungry as a dog and went away filled*'!

We shall ultimately also actually encounter this same language of 'being filled', 'sated', or 'satiated', in the Habakkuk *Pesher*'s description of the final destruction of the Wicked Priest, in which the latter is depicted – as in Revelation – as 'drinking the Cup of the Wrath of God to *filling*' or 'to satiation'.[22] This last means 'to the dregs' or – paralleling similar significations in Revelation 14:10 and 16:19[23] – that 'he would drink his fill' of the Divine Vengeance which 'would come around to him' for what he had done to 'the Righteous Teacher' and those of his followers (called 'the Poor' or *Ebionim* – in our view, James and his Community, pointedly referred to in early Church literature, as will by now have become crystal clear, as 'the Ebionites' or 'the Poor').

There is a slight hint here, should one choose to remark it, of Nakdimon 'filling' his own 'baths' or 'water cisterns' or those of the master or lord with whom he is negotiating. Nor is this to mention 'the six stone water-vessels' at the wedding 'in Cana of Galilee', which Jesus '*filled*, revealing his Glory' in John 2:6 or 'the twelve hand baskets of fragments from the five barley loaves' which 'the Disciples' will 'fill' from the 'overflow' or 'remains' in the 'feeding the five thousand' (on the other side 'of the Sea of Galilee') in John 6:13 and other various spin-offs.

In fact, this decisive encounter with the daughter of the Canaanite/Greek Syrophoenician woman in Mark and Matthew is sandwiched between two others, the first in both Matthew 14:13–23 and Mark 6:30–46: the feeding of the 'five thousand in a place in the desert' involving this same overflow in John 6:9–13 of 'twelve baskets full of fragments', meaning, of course, as in John, of 'barley loaves' or 'grain'. So important was this episode evidently thought to be that now one even finds it in Luke (9:10–17). In fact in Matthew 14:20 and Luke 9:17, it is the 'multitudes' or the telltale 'Many' who are again characterized as being 'satisfied' or 'sated', while in John 6:12 this comes across as 'when' or 'after they were filled'.

Each now also includes the additional motif of 'five loaves and two fishes', adding up to the number 'seven', a numeration that will grow in importance as we proceed, and, of course, all have the characteristic allusion to 'and they did all eat and they were satiated' or 'filled' (Matthew 14:20 and pars. – in John 6:12, as just alluded to, 'when they were filled'). To these Mark 6:37 and John 6:7, in line with their respectively more extensive storylines, add the additional *pro forma* important allusion to 'two hundred *dinars* of bread' – again, the 'bread' of 'the children' above – or 'loaves' (in John 6:13, 'loaves' – more intelligibly, no doubt, of 'barley' or 'wheat'). Once again then here, not only do we have another indication of intertextuality between John and Mark as against the other Synoptics, but also, an additional variation on both the 'hundreds' and the '*dinars*'.

Interestingly enough, in John 6:1-5's account of these 'twelve hand baskets' and 'two hundred *dinars*' – where, as in all four (at this point), it is the same 'five thousand' who are being fed – the time is specifically denoted as being 'near Passover, the Feast of the Jews' (6:4). Once again this is clearly being aimed at non-Jews, and for the same reasons, the whole episode in John 6:3 being equated with Moses' Exodus sojourn in the desert – Jesus being portrayed as 'going up into the mountain' 'with his Disciples' (repeated in Matthew 14:23 and Mark 6:46, but with different sequencing). This time in John, however, it is 'Philip' rather than 'the Disciples' (as in the Synoptics) who – in response to Jesus' question, on 'seeing a great crowd', 'whence shall we buy loaves that these may eat?' – replies in terms of the 'two hundred *dinars*' (6:5-7). In the Synoptics this is turned around and it is 'the Disciples' who raise this question not Jesus (Mark 6:36 and pars.). Notwithstanding, in Luke 9:12 it is the Twelve who recommend sending 'the Many' away.

Be these things as they may, it is here Philip responds that even 'two hundred *dinars*' (worth) of loaves are insufficient for them. In Mark 6:37 it is 'his Disciples' who again make this response, but note, in particular, the '*dinars*'/'pieces of silver' motif – this time in a factor of 'two hundred's not 'three', 'four', or 'five'. Here, too, 'Andrew the brother of Simon Peter', 'one of his Disciples', suddenly also appears. One wonders what would be the effect of switching one or another of the other 'Simon's in here, e.g., 'Simon the Cananaean', 'Simon the Leper', or even 'Simon Iscariot' – 'Andrew' basically being a derivative of the Greek '*Andros*'/'Man' (*Enosh/Bar-Adam* in Aramaic and *Ben-Adam* in Hebrew)?[24] He brings forward 'a little boy', not the 'little daughter' of Mark 7:25 above (here too, the variation on the 'little children' theme, we just saw above, in Jesus' request to 'his Disciples', 'to let the little children to come unto' him in order that he should 'lay hands on' or 'touch them' in the run-up to the 'Rich man', 'camel', and 'eye of the needle' scenario in all three Synoptics, now reduced to just one small boy and accompanied, this time, by the 'wheat' or 'barley' motif). It is he, the 'little boy' as opposed to the Disciples or the Twelve in the Synoptics, who now has the 'five barley loaves and two small fishes', out of which Jesus will perform another of his great 'signs' (John 6:9–14).

It is interesting that these portraits of Jesus feeding the five thousand in Mark 6:30–46 and Matthew 14:13–23 come directly after the description of John the Baptist's execution by 'Herod' (Mark 6:14–29/Matthew 14:1–12), in particular, their depiction of John's 'head' being brought to Herodias' 'daughter' (unnamed) 'upon a platter'. Not only is this a completely inaccurate portrait, but it is probably based on the picture in Josephus of how Nero's Jewish-leaning wife Poppea – who, according to him, in the period just prior to the Revolt against Rome, 'was interested in religious causes' – prevailed upon Nero to behead his former wife, whom he had previously only exiled, and, thereafter, have her head brought to her 'on a platter'![25] If this is so, then we have in this Gospel rewrite, yet another marvelous example of pro-Roman and Hellenizing, anti-Jewish disinformation.

In any event, Jesus then takes 'the loaves' and 'the little fishes' (*sic*) and gives them to his Disciples and 'when they were *full*', 'they gathered up the fragments' or 'broken pieces', 'filling up twelve hand baskets with broken pieces' from 'the overflow' (John 6:11–13 – here of course the 'overflow' theme, together with yet another allusion to 'filling', as in the Nakdimon story and his 'filling up' the lord's 'twelve cisterns to overflowing', which is to say nothing of 'the twelve hand baskets', that is, Nakdimon's 'twelve water cisterns', etc., etc.).

It is at this point, showing just how important the implications of all these various numbers were to the authors of these traditions, that John 6:14 actually has 'the men' – seemingly meaning his Disciples – overtly identify Jesus, once again 'seeing the sign that he had done' (certainly not meant as 'works of the *Torah*', but rather more magical, Greco-Roman, god-like 'miracles'), as the Ebionite 'True Prophet who is coming into the world'. Here, in the enigmatic wording of this obscure prophecy, perhaps the real sense and basis of all these ideological allusions to 'coming' we have been repeatedly encountering throughout these traditions.

Now only Seven Loaves and a Few Small Fishes to Feed Four Thousand, and Queen Helen's Famine-Relief Activities

More interesting even than this, the whole episode from Mark 6:32–44 and Matthew 14:15–21 is repeated a chapter or two later in Mark 8:4–9 and Matthew 15:33–38, where the number 'seven' will begin to take on its definitive signification (in fact, a third version, as we shall see, will occur in Mark 8:16–21 and Matthew 16:7–12 that will try to explain the discrepancies between the first and the second), in a direct follow-up to the curing of the Canaanite/Greek Syrophoenician woman's daughter.

Not surprisingly, this repetition is not to be found in either John or Luke. In other words, the healing of this 'daughter' in Mark and Matthew – also not to be found in John or Luke, at least not in the form of Mark and Matthew – is couched between two episodes basically saying or repeating the same thing only, as we shall now see, the figures are different. It is here that the curious mix-ups or overlaps between 'five' and 'four thousand' occur (the number of 'the Essenes' in Josephus, the followers who flee with James after Paul's attack in the Pseudoclementines, and 'the number of the men who believed' after 'Peter and John' were first arrested in Acts 4:4 – in Acts 2:41, after 'Peter''s earlier speech referring to 'the True Prophet', it was 'three thousand'), which we have already identified as of the same genre as those in Rabbinic accounts of the 'daily' amounts of four–five hundred *dinar*s required 'to fill' Nakdimon's daughter Miriam's (or his daughter-in-law's) 'perfume basket'. Again, the figures are different, but only by a factor of ten, and the point is more or less the same.

It is immediately made clear in this second version of this picture of those 'fainting away' from hunger and 'needing to be fed in the wilderness' in Mark 8:2 and Matthew 15:33 – yet a third in Mark 8:16–21 and Matthew 16:7–12, as just remarked, will by way of explanation directly follow this second – that we are dealing with the same Messianic 'signs in the wilderness', also just underscored in John 2:18, 4:48, and 6:30 and which Jesus discusses in detail in the intervening material in Mark 8:11–15 and Matthew 15:12–14 and 16:1–12. In the same manner as Jesus' attack on the Pharisees as 'Blind Guides' and dietary regulations in Matthew 15:12–20 (both of which we shall directly analyze below) in the prelude to his encounter in Matthew 15:21–28 and Mark 7:24–37 with the 'Greek Syrophoenician'/'Canaanite woman's daughter'; these second and third 'signs from Heaven'/'feeding'/'filling' episodes occur in the context of an attack in Matthew 16:6 (reprised in Matthew 16:11–12) on what Jesus now refers to as 'the *leaven* of the Pharisees and Sadducees' – in Mark 8:15, 'the leaven of the Pharisees and the leaven of Herod'!

It is these same 'signs and wonders' about which Josephus becomes so agitated in his condemnations of those he calls 'Impostors' and 'miracle-workers' who were 'showing the People the signs of their impending freedom' or – depending on which of his two works one is quoting – 'the signs of their Redemption' and whom he considered 'more dangerous even than the Revolutionaries'. As we have seen as well – even this 'freedom', Paul much abuses and allegorizes into something anti-Mosaic, turning it against those he refers to in 1 Corinthians 8:7–13 as 'having scruples' or 'with conscience' – his code, it will be recalled, for 'observing the Law'.

It should also be appreciated that all these 'feeding' episodes and any other ones evoking 'barley', 'wheat', or 'grain' usually reflect to some degree the celebrated 'famine relief' efforts of Queen Helen of Adiabene (in Josephus, for instance, grouped together – as we have seen above – with the performance of just such a miraculous 'sign' or 'wonder', that is, 'parting the Jordan River in reverse' – by the curious character he denotes only as 'Theudas'[26]), who sent her 'treasury agents' to buy grain for Jerusalem to places as far away as 'Egypt and Cyprus'.[27] Activities such as these are, in turn, reflected in Paul and Barnabas' Antioch activities in Acts 11:28–30 and 12:25, where 'Christians' were 'first called Christians' (11:26).[28]

Of course, Acts promises to tell us this story of Paul and Barnabas' 'famine relief' mission but, in the space between these two notices, does nothing of the kind. However this may be, the interesting thing is that Acts follows up its original notice about 'all the Disciples deciding to send relief to the brothers dwelling in Judea' (also referred to as 'the Elders'/ *Presbyterous* – note the parallel, too, here with those 'dwelling' in 'the Land of Judah' in the Damascus Document above[29]) 'by the hand of Barnabas and Saul' in 11:29–30 with the note about 'Herod the King' beheading 'James the brother of John' in 12:1–2 (i.e., executed him 'with the sword').

Of course, if we follow Josephus' sequencing, what the author of Acts probably originally overwrote here was 'Judas the brother of James', not 'James the brother of John' – or rather even, 'Theudas' (elsewhere, as we have already also suggested, 'Thaddaeus'), the delineation of whose 'signs' in leading the People out in the wilderness comes in Josephus in between his two notices about 'the Famine' and the undying fame of Queen Helen of Adiabene's 'famine relief' activities.

In Mark 8:5–6 and Matthew 15:34–35, however, the picture of 'five loaves and two fishes' of the first 'feeding' episode (of course, childishly mythologized so as to appeal to the reader's grossest credulity) disappear in favor of their sum, that is, 'seven loaves and a few little fishes' (in Mark 8:5–6, only 'seven loaves', Matthew 15:34–36's 'and a few little fishes' – note the incidence of the adjective 'little' – having already dropped away!). Of course, in Matthew 15:37/Mark 8:8, after 'the Multitude' or 'the Many' had eaten 'and were *filled*', there is the matter again of 'the overflow' of all the 'broken pieces' which – instead of the 'twelve hand baskets full' of the earlier delineation (Matthew 14:20/Mark 6:43) – are now reckoned as 'seven hand baskets *full*' (Matthew 15:37/Mark 8:8), evidently absorbing by a kind of refraction the number 'seven' from the quantification 'seven loaves' just preceding it.

This last, as we have already explained, patently corresponds to the 'overflow' in the Nakdimon story of his 'twelve cisterns filled to overflowing', which, in a twist that only a Talmudic mind would appreciate, Nakdimon then tries to resell back to the 'lord' or 'master'. To be sure, in all four Gospels previously, this was 'twelve baskets filled with broken pieces' (Matthew 14:20/Mark 6:43/Luke 9:17/and John 6:13, the latter adding 'from the five barley loaves') and it will be 'twelve' again when the third version in Mark 8:19 makes the final reconciliation and recapitulation of all these materials!

In the Nakdimon story, it will be recalled, it was when the 'lord' hesitated to repay the surety of 'twelve talents of silver' that Nakdimon (like Joshua) made the sun reappear after it had already set, because of which he allegedly received his *nom à clef* 'Nakdimon', meaning

'Shining Through'. But more significant even than this – just like 'those who went to Ben Kalba Sabu'a's door hungry as a dog and went away filled', the 'Poor man Lazarus wanting to be filled from the scraps that fell from the Rich man's table' and, still more germane at this point perhaps, 'the children who should first be filled' before 'the dogs under the table' in the Syrophoenician woman's daughter episode – Jesus is asked in the matter now of the 'seven hand baskets full', could all these 'be filled' or 'satisfied' (Mark 8:4/Matthew 15:33)? In both Gospels, as we saw, the right answer is given – this time by the narrator – 'and they did eat and were *satiated*' or '*filled*' (Mark 8:8/Matthew 15:37).

For good measure both episodes are then, as just remarked, recapitulated *yet a third time* – though here the ostensible venue of the action is 'on a boat' going across the Sea of Galilee from 'Dalmanutha' to 'Bethsaida' in Mark; in Matthew, only somewhere called 'the borders of Magdala' – because 'they had forgotten to take the bread'! (Matthew 16:5–11/Mark 8:17–21). But the whole point is obviously to reconcile the two earlier versions in some way, so one has the clear indication in both Gospels that the narrator is not only well aware of the contradictions, but views all three episodes as part of a single whole.

Now both quantities for the number of those fed are cited, 'five thousand' and 'four thousand' (Matthew 16:9–10 and Mark 8:19–20), but after some complicated number crunching – calisthenics might be more accurate – Mark finally comes up with 'the twelve hand baskets full of broken pieces' for the number 'taken up' or 'filled', which was the original of all four Gospels in the first place – corresponding, of course, to Nakdimon's 'twelve cisterns' or 'water pools', with which we began the whole excursus. Nor is the whole complex unrelated, as we shall see, to both Helen of Adiabene's and Paul and Barnabas' 'famine-relief' efforts.

For its part, Matthew 16:11–12 satisfies itself – since its main interest is the continuation of the attack on 'the *leaven* of the Pharisees and Sadducees' – to speak portentously only about the more general 'bread' and its 'leaven'. Here Jesus speaks to his followers like some divine Dionysus, Asclepius, or Apollo come down to sort out their problems. After warning about 'the leaven of the Pharisees and the leaven of the Herodians' above (Mark 8:15 – in Matthew, just alluded to, this changes to 'the leaven of the Pharisees and Sadducees'), both have Jesus questioning his Disciples, 'Do you yet not perceive' or 'understand' (Matthew 16:9/Mark 8:17 and 21 – I hope we do) – Matthew 16:10 then having Jesus manfully trying to summarize the whole convoluted issue of the numbers as follows: 'Do you not yet perceive, nor remember the five loaves and the five thousand and how many hand baskets you took and the seven loaves and the four thousand and how many hand baskets you took?' In the end, as just remarked, it is left to Mark 8:19 to come up with the right answer: 'They said to him, "Twelve"'!

If we now add to this the 'two hundred *dinars*' given by Mark 6:37, we basically have all the numbers and their multiples or variations from the Talmudic Nakdimon/Boethus/and their daughters/daughters-in-law traditions – the 'seven's, for instance, having to do with the three 'seven'- year, temporary Nazirite-style penances put upon Queen Helen of Adiabene by the Rabbis. It is, also, always useful to again remark that the variation of the 'loaves' (whatever the final number), as opposed to 'the twelve baskets full of fragments' simply corresponds to the addition of the element of the 'twelve talents of silver' over and above the 'twelve water cisterns' in the Nakdimon miracle stories.

Nor is any of this, finally, to say anything of Nakdimon and his colleagues' 'twenty-one' or 'twenty-two years' of grain-storage activity to relieve the famine in Jerusalem – though actually it does. We have already explained that this 'twenty-one years' in Rabbinic tradition reflects, in turn, the three successive seven-year Nazirite oath-style penances – just remarked above – supposedly (and curiously) placed upon Queen Helen of Adiabene by the Rabbis for reasons which were unclear, but very likely having to do with adultery or some such similar issue (therefore her interest in having the passage on the 'adulterous woman' from Numbers 5:13–31 – itself followed by the one on 'Nazirite oaths' in Numbers 6:1-21 – placed in an expensive plaque of gold leaf on a wall of the Temple courtyard[30]).

But we have just seen in these various 'fainting of hunger in the wilderness' and 'longing to be filled'/'needing to be fed' descriptions in the Gospels (poeticized allusions, obviously, to a situation requiring 'famine relief') the constant reiteration of the number 'seven' in the 'seven baskets full of fragments' and 'the seven loaves' valuations, to say nothing of the 'five loaves and two fishes' from which 'they all ate and were satisfied' in Mark 8:4-8 and pars. Compare this with the Rabbinic 'Ben Kalba Sabu'a' tradition, a name in itself having either to do with 'dogs', 'immersion', or 'being satiated' or 'filled', and how they 'came to his door hungry as a dog and went away filled'.

Can anyone really doubt that those initially responsible for these traditions in the Gospels, such as they are – and I use the expression 'tradition' charitably – knew the truth about what was going on in Palestine in this period and the real issues actually being debated there, but rather substituted these often nonsensical and sometimes even ridiculous miracle tales that so much appeal to the naive and credulous, not only at that time but, it would seem, at all times and in all places since? 'The Truth', as one might refer to it, really 'will – to use the words of John 8:32 – set you free' and, in a very real sense, it has to do with these more Revolutionary, Messianic heroes and Movements, themselves probably connected in some manner to the activities of Queen Helen of Adiabene and her descendants – new converts to Judaism far more 'zealous' (as we have been seeing) than any Herodian ones.

'Eating with Unwashed Hands do not Defile the Man' and 'Making all Foods Clean'

One last point that should at this juncture perhaps be made. The encounter with the unnamed Cananaean/Syrophoenician woman out of whose daughter Jesus 'casts an unclean spirit' or 'demon' is also preceded in Mark 7:1–23 and somewhat less so in Matthew 15:1–20 by the pro-Pauline polemics – in Mark 7:6–7 and Matthew 15:9 quoting Isaiah 29:13 – having to do with 'teaching as doctrines the commandments of men'. This is a very important allusion and plays off the critique of 'the Enemy' Paul, mirrored in Galatians 1:10–11's 'seeking to please men' – and even before this in 1:1, where Paul makes the claim of being 'an Apostle not through men or of man'.

Furthermore and even perhaps more germane, these polemics in Mark 7:1–23 and Matthew 15:1–20 actually evoke the famous Talmudic Tractate *Pirke Abbot* (*The Traditions of the Fathers* which, as we have already seen, has as its variation the *ARN* or *The Fathers According to Rabbi Nathan*) – here in Mark 7:3–5 and Matthew 15:2, '*The Traditions of the Elders*'. This designation 'Elders' or '*Presbyteron*' is used, as we have seen, at various junctures in the Gospels and the Book of Acts and is the actual designation for James' Jerusalem Community in both Acts 21:18 and the Pseudoclementine *Homilies* above.[31] In perhaps the most convoluted reasoning we have yet encountered in our discussion, these polemics also invoke the Mosaic Commandment, 'Honor your father and your mother' (Mark 7:10/Matthew 15:4) and, in doing so, leave no doubt that we are in fact dealing with 'the Fathers'. Just as importantly, in Mark 7:1–5 'the Pharisees' are invoked as well – three times in five lines! As we have several times had cause to remark, this is an expression that often acts as a 'blind' for those of the 'Jamesian' persuasion within the early Church – as, for example, in Acts 15:5 at the renowned 'Jerusalem Council', the elusive '*some* who believed' of 'the sect of the Pharisees', who provoked the 'Council' by their insistence on 'circumcision' and 'keeping the law of Moses'!

Not only have we just encountered these same 'Pharisees' in the two 'filling those fainting from hunger' episodes in both Mark 8:11–14 and Matthew 16:1–12, but in this run-up to the 'dogs eating of the crumbs falling from their master's table' episode (in the variation in Luke 16:21, 'the Rich Man's table'), the evocation of these same 'Pharisees' is being used to attack those of the James school over the issue of table fellowship with Gentiles (an issue clearly being raised by Paul in Galatians 2:11–14). Moreover, there is the additional derivative attack, which now seems to us, if not bizarre, at least primitive, on the Jewish People as a whole – in this case, plainly, meant to include the Jerusalem Community of James, and others of this mindset – that 'eating with unwashed hands does not defile the man' (Matthew 15:20/ Mark 7:2–3).

Not only is this attack framed in terms of the charged words, 'keeping', 'breaking', and 'holding fast to', familiar in various Dead Sea Scrolls' texts, but it derogates 'washing one's hands before eating' only to the level of a 'tradition of men breaking the (obviously 'Higher') Commandment of God'. In the odd logic being displayed in this clearly pro-Pauline exposition, the meaning of this last would appear to be the Mosaic Commandment and that of humanity generally, to 'honor your father and your mother' (Mark 7:8–9/Matthew 15:3 and 15:19).

The argument, which is childish and self-serving in the extreme, seems to turn on the point that since one's parents might have 'eaten with unwashed hands', the Commandment not to do so – which the Gospel Jesus is pictured as dismissing here merely as 'a Tradition of the Elders' – would be contradicting the Higher Commandment (the one he is terming a 'Commandment of God') not to dishonor them! This appears to be the gist of what seems a very tortured and largely unintelligible argument but, to judge by the time spent on it in Mark as well as Matthew, clearly a pivotal one as well. Still, should the reader feel it represents the true words of the Jesus he or she holds sacred or admires, then that person is welcome to do so. But the conclusion is ridiculous, namely 'don't wash your hands before eating'. As stated, the writer sees it as a striking example of retrospective pro-Pauline polemics and, consequently, feels it to be a service historically-speaking to rescue Jesus from this particular bit of prejudiced sophistry.

Furthermore, these polemics clearly evoke Paul's attack on Peter in Galatians 2:13, in which Paul accuses him of 'hypocrisy'. It is actually this charge that Mark 7:6 portrays Jesus as making in commencing his attack on 'the Pharisees and some of the Scribes' (note the telltale allusion to 'some' here and in Matthew 15:1's 'Scribes and Pharisees from Jerusalem'): 'Well did Isaiah prophesy concerning you Hypocrites as it is written (in Isaiah 29:13), "this People honor Me with the lips but the heart is far away from Me"'.

Moreover, vocabulary such as 'lips', 'heart', and 'vain'/'vanity' is absolutely fundamental to the Qumran lexicon, as it is some extent the Letter attributed to James.[32] In fact, as we have been trying to illustrate, to unravel these things takes quite a good deal of sophistication – which is why history before the discovery of the Dead Sea Scrolls has been so slow to do so (the key or 'Rosetta Stone', as it were, just not being available) – because the people who put them together were extremely clever and, if the truth were told, artful. Nor did we have the rudimentary data to deconstruct them. Now we do. Here, once again, the last word belongs to Plato who wished to bar just such persons from his ideal 'Republic', that is, the people who spun these kinds of 'mystery'-oriented miracle tales about the 'gods' by which the average people lived, and in so doing, misled them.[33]

Both Mark 7:6–7 and Matthew 15:7–9 picture Jesus as using this passage to attack the 'vanity' of those who 'teach as their doctrines the commandments of *men*', meaning, 'the Traditions of the Elders' just mentioned in Mark 7:5 and Matthew 15:2 above. Not only is this clearly an attack on what in Rabbinic parlance would be called 'oral tradition', but it turns around the parameters of Paul's debates with those of the 'Jamesian' school or, if one prefers, inverts their arguments turning them back against themselves. Again, the meaning both Mark and Matthew are clearly ascribing to their Jesus from the start here is that 'Hypocrites' of this kind, following 'the Tradition of the Elders', are 'forcing people to wash their hands before eating', something which most people nowadays would consider as not only normal, but hygienic; however in Paul's inverted invective something Paul (to say nothing about Jesus) would obviously consider quite reprehensible.

In Galatians 2:13, as we just pointed out, Paul uses the word 'hypocrisy' to attack 'Cephas' in the context of referring to the proverbial 'some from James' who 'came down' from Jerusalem to Antioch. He even accuses him 'and the rest of the Jews' with him (*sic*) – including his erstwhile traveling companion 'Barnabas' (whoever he may have been) – in 2:13 of, not just propagating 'their hypocrisy' but 'not walking Upright' and 'jointly dissembling' as well. The reason for this last, it will be recalled, is that prior to the 'coming' of these 'some from James' down to 'Antioch', 'He ('Cephas') was eating with the Peoples; but when they came, he drew back and *separated himself* for fear of those of the circumcision' (Galatians 2:12).

This allusion to 'those of the circumcision' is also intrinsic to Acts 11:2–3's description of how these same 'those of the circumcision' complained that Peter 'ate with uncircumcised men' (the 'table fellowship' theme again coupled with the 'circumcision' one). This came after Peter's 'heavenly tablecloth' vision, in which he learned to call 'no man' or 'no thing' either 'profane or unclean' (10:15 and 28), after which he promptly went to visit the house of the Roman Centurion Cornelius – described in Acts' own inimitable way as a 'Pious One and Righteous', 'fearing' and 'supplicating God continually' (that is, 'a God-Fearer'), and 'esteemed by the whole Nation of the Jews' (*sic*), whose 'works were remembered before God' (11:2 and 11:30)!

This whole episode in Mark 7:1 and Matthew 15:1, as already alluded to, also begins with this same idea of 'the Pharisees and some of the Scribes *coming down from Jerusalem*' (in Mark 8:15 and Matthew 16:6, it will be recalled, this allusion morphs into the polemical derogation of 'the leaven of the Pharisees and the leaven of Herod' or 'the leaven of the Pharisees and Sadducees'). Here the 'some of the scribes' clearly corresponds to the 'some from James' and 'those of the circumcision' in Galatians 2:12 and Acts 11:2 above. Their complaint is now portrayed as being about 'seeing *some* of his *Disciples* eating with unwashed' or 'polluted hands' (Mark 7:2; in Matthew 15:1, this becomes 'not washing their hands when they eat bread').

But of course we have already seen that these same allusions to 'coming down from Jerusalem' and 'circumcision' recur in Acts 15:1's picture of events triggering the celebrated 'Jerusalem Council' above. Not only do they basically recapitulate the scenarios just highlighted in Acts 11:2 and Galatians 2:12 about the objections of the 'some' or 'those of the circumcision' to the Gospel Paul was 'proclaiming among the Gentiles' (compare with Paul's own words to this effect in Galatians 2:2), but once again they are followed up by allusion in Acts 15:2 – as in Mark 7:1 and Matthew 15:1 – to 'the Elders in Jerusalem' (*Presbyterous*) and in 15:5, 'the Heresy/Sect of the Pharisees', to say nothing of Peter's being, as usual, the first to speak, though here somewhat more conciliatorily than in previous speeches attributed to him and even though he had according to Acts 12:17–19 already fled the country with a presumable death sentence on his head.

Acts 15:1 reads – it will be recalled though it bears repeating – 'And some, having come from Judea, were teaching the brothers that, unless you are circumcised, you cannot be saved.' Here the usage 'Judea' is substituted for 'Jerusalem' in Mark and Matthew above (in Acts 11:2 this is rather turned around and Peter goes '*up* to Jerusalem'), but this is made good by the mention of 'the Elders in Jerusalem' in the very next line 15:2 and then again in 15:4. Even more importantly, the same allusion to 'teaching' being employed here is repeated twice each in Mark 7:7 and Matthew 15:9 – presumably, just so we would not miss the point and forms the basis of the whole polemic there. Therefore and in this manner, the whole circle of all these interconnected allusions is complete.

'Spitting on the Tongue', 'Unstopping Ears', and 'Declaring all Things Clean'

As in all of the previous episodes above, the denouement of this abolishing purity requirements/table fellowship episode in Mark 7 and Matthew 15, which sets the stage for the Canaanite/Greek Syrophoenician woman/dogs under the table encounter that follows in the same chapters and further legitimizes the Pauline Gentile Mission, once more has Jesus in 7:17 entering a 'house' (as he does yet again in Mark 7:24). In Mark 7:17, this is typically 'away from the multitude' to rebuke the Disciples. In Matthew 15:15 there is no house[34] and the rebuke is – because of Galatians 2:11–14 – only to Peter. Still, 'the *multitude*' from Mark 7:17 are the ones already portrayed earlier in Mark 7:14 and Matthew 15:10 as the ones being addressed by Jesus on the subject of 'pure foods', 'unwashed hands', 'Blind Guides', and 'Uprooted Plants'.

In both Gospels, Jesus' discourse begins with the words, 'hear and understand', again seemingly playing off the opening exhortations of the Damascus Document which read, 'hear, all you who know Righteousness, and understand' (1.1) – 'and now listen to me all who enter the Covenant and I will unstop your ears' (2.2). But in Mark 7:16 in the midst of Jesus' attack on 'the Tradition of the Elders' and 'purifying all food' preceding this, the same 'ears' metaphor from Column Two of the Damascus Document, just reproduced above, actually appears, to wit, 'If anyone has ears, let him hear'.

This is not the only place it appears in this episode. Mark's Jesus repeats this in 8:18, in the midst of the third and harmonized version of 'the feeding of the four thousand' episode: 'Having eyes, do you not see? Having ears, do you not hear?' But Mark even goes further than this. It also appears in the nonsense material that intervenes in 7:32–37, following his version of 'the dogs under the table' episode in 7:24–30, in the miracle that Jesus is then pictured in 7:33–35 as doing in 'laying hands' on a deaf and dumb person, curing him. For its part, Matthew 15:29–31 omits this and, at this point in 15:31, only depicts 'the *Rabbim*' as, once again, 'glorifying the God of Israel' after having 'thrown down at his feet' the 'dumb', 'maimed', 'blind', and 'lame', they 'had with them', for him to cure.

These things also involve the process of 'unstopping someone's ears', but Mark now rather proceeds to dramatize it in the form of a deaf and dumb person whose 'ears' will literally now be 'unstopped' (7:32). This miracle – not specifically depicted in Matthew except by the more general allusion to their 'seeing the dumb speaking' in 15:31 – takes place after Jesus left 'the borders of Tyre and Sidon' and, the unnamed Greek Syrophoenician woman's daughter, 'lying on the bed', 'the demon having departed' (7:30–31). Jesus then somehow 'came to the sea of Galilee' from 'the borders of Tyre and Sidon' (in the manner in which Philip, somewhat disembodiedly, in Acts 8:26-40 gets to Caesarea after having taken the road from Jerusalem to Gaza) – this, after going 'through the midst of the borders of the Decapolis', that is, on the other side of the Sea of Galilee and known to Gospel writers, as well as to the readers of Josephus, as another predominantly Gentile area!

In Mark, Jesus' activity comes right before 8:1–9 and 14–21's second and third versions of Jesus' 'multiplication of the loaves' miracle. So, not only is the performance of miracles on behalf of Gentiles continued, but so obsessed is Mark with this metaphor from the Damascus Document of 'unstopped ears' and, in the process, trivializing it and reducing it to the level of banality, that he is now prepared to depict Jesus as performing yet another miracle in a predominantly Gentile area – and this, despite the fact that in both 8:10–13 and Matthew 16:1–4 to follow, in response yet again to more 'Pharisee' prodding he impatiently asserts: 'Why does this generation seek a sign? Verily I say unto you, there shall be no sign given unto this generation.' What is this miracle? Mark 7:33–34 now depicts Jesus as 'unstopping the ears' of 'a deaf man' in the following manner: 'Putting his fingers into his ears and having spit, (he) touched his tongue (thus) and, looking up to Heaven, he groaned and said

'*Ephphatha*', that is, 'be opened' (this is real Hellenistic magic, the language being Aramaic, but even explained and translated for the benefit of the Greek audience), and immediately his ears were unstopped! Need one say more?

However the reader might respond to the imbecility of the picture of this 'miracle' – based, as we contend it is, on reducing serious allusions in the Damascus Document to the level of idiocy – to go back to Matthew 15:16: there the rebuke about 'being yet without understanding' is directed at Peter alone. Notwithstanding, prior to this, after 'calling the Multitude' or 'the Many to him' (15:10, reprised in Mark 7:14), Jesus does actually address 'the Disciples' in Matthew in 15:12 as well. There the reproof he gives 'the Disciples' concerning staying away from 'the Pharisees' and 'leaving them alone' – which includes the 'Blind Guides', 'planting', and 'uprooting' allusions – comes in the wake of his enunciation of the following famous doctrine: 'Not that which enters the mouth defiles the man, but that which proceeds out of the mouth, this defiles the man' (15:11).

This allusion to 'the Pharisees', the evocation of whom initiated the whole series of encounters right from the beginning of Mark 7:1 and Matthew 15:1, comes – as Matthew 15:12 now phrases it – because 'the Disciples' reported to Jesus that 'the Pharisees were offended by what they heard him saying' (the reader should appreciate, it would be so easy to read here, 'what they heard Paul saying'). It must be reiterated that expressions like 'the Pharisees', regardless of their overt meaning in any other context, have a covert meaning as well and this is the key to understanding 'The New Testament Code' such as it is. They – like 'the Scribes'/'some of the Scribes who came down from Jerusalem' coupled with them in Matthew 15:1 and Mark 7:1 above – are, in this context in the Gospels, a stand-in for 'the James Community' in Jerusalem. Not only did this Community insist on circumcision, but also its legal consequences, such as purity regulations that included measures of bodily hygiene like 'washing their hands' that seem, in the picture Mark and Matthew are presenting, to so upset their 'Jesus' here.

It is also perhaps not without relevance that an expression like 'Pharisees'– *Perushim* in Hebrew – carries with it the meaning of 'splitting away' or 'separating themselves from', the implication being that, in some contexts, it can even be understood as 'heretics' which, in fact, is one of the appositions Acts applies to it in 15:5. Nor should the reader overlook the fact that Matthew's picture of Jesus reproving the Pharisees follows his exhortation to 'the Many'/'the *Rabbim*' in 15:10 to 'hear and understand' (in Mark 7:14, 'hear me all of you and understand') – a phrase, as we just saw, that has to be seen as comparable to CD I.1's: 'Now hear, all you who know Righteousness and understand the works of God'. Matthew 15:14 also pictures Jesus as calling these Pharisees 'Blind Guides' (an allusion we shall presently show to be charged with significance) because of their complaints against his teaching that 'eating with unclean hands does not defile the man' (15:20), as well as related matters concerning purity and dietary regulations, themselves having a bearing on the key issue in Galatians 2:11–14 of table fellowship with Gentiles.

It is at this point that Jesus in Matthew 15:14 then cautions his Disciples (none of this paralleled now in Mark) to 'leave them alone' – the sense of which allusion will be of particular importance when it comes to discussing the exegesis of 'the Way in the wilderness' of Isaiah 40:3 in the Community Rule below. Before doing so, however, it would be well to point out that even the line in Matthew 15:19, preceding 15:20 on 'eating with unclean hands not defiling the man', enumerates 'the things which proceed out of the mouth' (thereby, according to the discourse being attributed here to Jesus, 'coming forth out of the heart' and, most famously, therefore 'defiling the man') as: 'Evil thoughts, murders, adulteries, fornications, thefts, lies, blasphemies – these are the things that defile the man' (Mark 7:22 adds 'greedy desires, Wickednesses, deceit, lustful desires, an Evil eye, pride, and foolishness').

But this catalogue of 'Evil' inclinations almost precisely reprises one of the most famous passages in the Community Rule – 'the Two Ways': 'the Ways of Darkness' and 'the Ways of Light'. In this document, 'the Spirit of Evil'/'Ungodliness' or 'of Darkness' is depicted even more lengthily as: 'greediness of soul, stumbling hands in the Service of Righteousness (cf. 2 Corinthians 11:15), Wickedness and Lying, pride and proudness of heart, duplicitousness and deceitfulness, cruelty, Evil temper, impatience, foolishness, and zeal for lustfulness, works of Abomination in a spirit of fornication, and ways of uncleanness in the Service of pollution (as opposed to the proper 'Service of Righteousness' of 'true' Apostles), a *Tongue* full of blasphemies, blindness of eye and dullness of ear, stiffness of neck and hardness of heart in order to walk in all the Ways of Darkness and Evil inclination'.[35]

Blind Guides, the *Maschil*, and Walking in the Way of Perfection

This is quite a catalogue, but the parallels with Matthew and Mark do not stop here. Even the allusion to 'Blind Guides', to say nothing of 'leave them alone', which Matthew depicts Jesus as applying to the Pharisees, actually seems to parody the pivotal character evoked at Qumran (in particular, in the Community Rule again, but also in the Hymns), 'the *Maschil*' or 'the Guide'. He is defined, just like 'the Teacher of Righteousness'), as instructing 'the Many' in the Ways of Righteousness.[36]

In the Community Rule this *Maschil* or Guide is pictured, *inter alia*, as 'doing the will of God' (that is, being 'a Doer' not 'a Breaker' in the manner of the recommendations in James 1:22–25) and 'studying all the Wisdom that has been discovered from age to age', to *separate* and evaluate the Sons of the Righteous One according to their spirit and fortify the Elect of the Age according to His will as He commanded and, thereby, to do His Judgment on every man according to His spirit'.[37] This does begin to become New Testament-like. Not only does it hark back to the 'Two Spirits', with which we began this discussion, and Paul's 'knowing the things of man according to the spirit of man which is in him' of 1 Corinthians 2:11–15, but this description of 'the Guide' in the Community Rule then goes on to actually evoke two allusions, 'clean hands' and 'not arguing with the Sons of the Pit' – in other words, the '*leave them alone*' just encountered in passages from Matthew 15:14 and, perhaps even more strikingly, yet another – the third, 'the Pit', an allusion known throughout the Dead Sea Scrolls and which we shall presently encounter in Jesus' further disparagement of these 'Blind Guides' as we proceed: '(The *Maschil* shall allow) each man to draw near according to the *cleanness of his hands* and his wisdom and, thus, shall be his love together with his hate. Nor should he admonish or argue with the Sons of the Pit.'

Furthermore, the Guide or *Maschil* is commanded in this telling concluding exhortation of the Community Rule to rather: 'conceal the counsel of the *Torah* (that is, 'the Law') from the Men of Evil, confirming the Knowledge of the Truth and Righteous Judgment to the *Elect of the Way* … comforting them with Knowledge, thereby guiding them in the Mysteries of the Marvelous Truth…, that is, to walk in Perfection each with his neighbor'.[38] We shall hear more about all these concepts presently.

This leads directly into the second citation of Isaiah 40:3's 'preparing a Straight Way in the wilderness' passage: 'For this is the time of the preparation of the Way in the wilderness. Therefore he ('the *Maschil*' – in Matthew above, Jesus' 'Blind Guide') should guide them in all that has been revealed that they should do in this Time to *separate* from any man who has not turned aside his Way from all Evil.'

To further demonstrate the interconnectedness of these kind of usages, the denotation 'the Sons of the Pit' is immediately reprised in these climactic passages from the Community Rule: 'These are the rules of the Way for the Guide in these Times: Everlasting hatred for the Sons of the Pit in a spirit of secrecy, to leave them to their Riches and the suffering ('*amal*) of their hands, like the slave to his Ruler and the Meek before his Lord.' Not only do we have the 'master' and 'lord' vocabulary here, but also again that of 'hands' – this time in the sense of 'that which their own hands have wrought' – the same 'hands' presumably that were to remain 'unwashed' when eating in Jesus' crucial 'toilet bowl' homily in both Matthew and Mark above. Furthermore, the implication of the whole simile embodied in this passage would appear to involve 'the Judgment Day', since the Hebrew '*amal* – as in the all-important Isaiah 53:11 proof-text and the Habakkuk *Pesher*, seemingly like the Gospels dependent upon it – is eschatological and also part of the vocabulary here. The conclusion of all this is quite extraordinary: 'And he (both 'the *Maschil*' and the rank and file) shall be as a man *zealous for the Law*, whose Time will be the Day of Vengeance, to *do* all His will in all the work of his *hands* ... delighting in all the words of His *mouth* and in all His Kingdom as He commanded.' The reader should pay particular attention to all these usages, but especially: 'doing the will of God'; 'separating the Sons of the Righteous One' and 'not disputing with the Sons of the Pit', but 'leaving them to their Riches' and 'the works of their hands'; and finally 'doing all His will in all the work of his (the *Maschil*'s or the adept's) hands' and 'delighting in all the words of His mouth'.

'Every Plant shall be Uprooted' and the Messianic 'Root of Planting' Imagery

In conclusion, one should also remark that leading into this allusion to the Pharisees as 'Blind Guides' in Matthew 15:14, Jesus is pictured as evoking the 'plant' or 'planting' vocabulary that Paul also uses with regard to 'God's plantation' or 'growing place' and 'God's building' in 1 Corinthians 3:6's: 'I planted, Apollos watered, but God caused to grow'. In the writer's view this, too, plays off the Messianic 'plant' and 'planting' imagery at Qumran in general, in particular, 'the Root of Planting' with which the Damascus Document follows up its opening imprecation to 'hear and understand'. This reads, as we have already partially seen, as follows: 'And in the Age of Wrath ... He (God) visited them and caused a *Root of Planting to grow* (these are some of the same words Paul uses in 1 Corinthians 3:6–8 above) from Israel and Aaron to inherit His Land (Paul's 'field' or 'growing place' imagery, just cited in 1 Corinthians 3:9 above) and to prosper on the good things of His Earth.'[39]

In Matthew 15:13–14 the preliminary characterization introducing Jesus' 'Leave them alone, they are Blind Guides' reproof about the Pharisees reads: 'But he answered, saying, "Every plant which My Heavenly Father has not planted shall be uprooted"'! Of course the 'uprooting' or 'rooting up' language here is exactly the same as 'the Root of Planting' just encountered in the opening exhortation of the Damascus Document – the 'uprooting' playing off the 'Root of Planting' that God 'caused to grow', and the 'Planting', the 'Planting' part of the 'Root' imagery. Likewise, Paul's parallel 'Apollos planted, I watered, and God caused to grow' from 1 Corinthians 3:6 not only plays off, but is an actual verbatim quotation of the remainder of this all-important preliminary metaphor in the Damascus Document.

But in addition in these pivotal allusions in 1 Corinthians 3:6–11 to 'God's Plantation' and 'God's Building' – of which Paul himself is 'the architect' or 'builder' just as he was 'the gardener' or 'husbandman' in the previous few lines, Paul also uses the further imagery of 'laying the foundations', widespread at Qumran – in particular, in both the Damascus Document and the Community Rule, but also in Hymns.[40]

In fact, these imageries are preceded in 1 Corinthians 2:4–6 by material in which Paul attacks 'the wisdom of men' and 'the wisdom of the age'. One should compare allusions such as these to the Community Rule (1QS 9.12–13)'s instructions to 'the *Maschil*' to: '*Do* the will of God in accord with everything that has been revealed from age to age and study all the wisdom that has been discovered according to the law of that age'. One can't get a much closer fit than this or, for that matter, the Damascus Document's 'the Root of Planting' to Matthew's 'every plant which my Heavenly Father has not planted shall be uprooted'.

Here too Paul evokes 'the perfect' and 'their wisdom' and speaks of 'the Rulers of this Age', another usage not so different from the allusion in the Community Rule to 'the Wisdom of God' above (as opposed to 'human wisdom') revealed as if 'in a Mystery'[41] – 'Mysteries' in the Community Rule having to do with 'walking Perfectly', 'the Rulers of the Age', and 'making a straight Way in the wilderness' already cited above.[42]

Later, speaking of 'the reward each shall receive according to his own labor' and attacking 'the words which human wisdom teaches', Paul rather evokes in 1 Corinthians 2:13 –14 'the words the Holy Spirit teaches' and 'communicating spiritual things spiritually'. The perspicacious reader will be able to discern counterparts to all these usages in just the material from column Nine of the Community Rule defining the character and the function of 'the Guide'. This could partially, but not exhaustively, include 'doing Judgment on each man according to his spirit', 'leaving the Men of the Pit to their Riches and the work of their hands' (meant eschatologically), 'being as a man *zealous for the Law* whose Time is the Day of Vengeance to *do* (God's) will in all work of his hands', and 'delighting in all that has been said by his *mouth*'.

Even more telling, all these imageries that Paul uses in 1 Corinthians 3:9–14 evoking 'building', in particular, himself as the 'wise architect', his Community as 'God's Building', and the 'laying the foundations' and 'building up' language would appear to be very familiar to the author of the Habakkuk *Pesher* who uses the very same imagery of 'the architect' and/ or 'building up' to attack its omnipresent adversary, 'the Man of Lies' or 'Spouter of Lying' as 'building a worthless city upon blood and erecting an Assembly upon Lying for the sake of his Glory'.[43] Here, once again, we have the language of 'Glory' or 'glorying' we have been underscoring above and, in our view, an allusion to a Community like Paul's, 'built upon' the idea of 'Communion with the blood of Christ'.

In addition to this, one should appreciate that in 1 Corinthians 2:7, preceding the above, Paul has just used the same language of 'the wisdom of God', 'Mystery', and of 'Glory' when he asserts: 'But we speak the Wisdom of God in a Mystery which God has hidden and preordained for our Glory before the Ages'. Here not only the same 'Glory' alluded to in Column Ten of the Habakkuk *Pesher*, but also 'the Ages' encountered in 1QS 9.13, which is to say nothing of the language of 'Hidden' and 'Mystery' already underscored above as well.

Furthermore, the idea of 'God's Building', 'God's House', or 'God's Temple' – all more or less synonymous in Hebrew – which Paul goes on to apply in 1 Corinthians 3:9–17 to his new Gentile Christian Community is nothing less than the imagery of 'House of the *Torah*', used throughout the Damascus Document to describe 'the Community' it is addressing in its final exhortative above – not to mention 'the House of Faith God built' earlier 'for them' in Column Three of the Damascus Document, 'the likes of which never stood from ancient times until now'.[44]

Neither is this to say anything about the allusions to 'the Men of Perfect Holiness' or 'the Perfection of Holiness' leading into the two evocations of 'the House of the *Torah*' in the last Column of this exhortative (Column Twenty of the Cairo Genizah version) or 'those fearing God' ('the God-Fearers') or the '*Hesed*' ('Grace' or 'Piety') God would show 'to the thousands of them that love Him', following it.[45] Not only is this last easily recognizable as the first part of the *Hesed/Zedek* dichotomy, the two 'Love' Commandments we have alluded to above, but it is once more exactly equivalent to what Paul enunciated in 1 Corinthians 2:9 – phrasing this as 'the things which God has prepared for those that love Him' – and the variation of both one finds in James 2:5 concerning how 'God chose the Poor' to be 'Heirs to the Kingdom which He promised to those who love Him'.

The very next line in Matthew 15:14 continues the borrowing: 'They are Blind Guides leading the Blind and, if the Blind lead the Blind, both will fall into the Pit.' Here one has in both subject and predicate, the image of the *Maschil* just as in several of the passages quoted from the Community Rule above. Nor is this to say anything of yet another adumbration of the language of 'falling' we have already encountered throughout the numerous Gospel passages we have analyzed above.

But more importantly and combined with this is the language and imagery of 'the Pit', in particular, that of 'the Sons of the Pit' used to attack all the enemies of the Community including, presumably, persons of the mindset of Paul. Even more to the point, we are again in the process of *one reversing the other*, that is, someone using the very language of another person and turning it back on that other person to undermine him. Here, note that in Matthew 15:14 it is both 'the Blind Guides' and 'the Blind' they lead who, metaphorically, will fall into 'the Pit'!

Can anything be more cynical and derisive than this and can any of it be accidental? The author seriously doubts it. This is the reason for the extensive detail employed in trying to elucidate all these usages. Indeed, this whole allusion at this point in Matthew, which seems innocuous enough, actually plays on yet another seemingly completely unrelated passage. This concerns regulations governing the Sabbath in the Damascus Document as well, most of which are generally counter-indicated in the Gospels. In the process, Matthew 15:12-14 makes fun of and shows Jesus' contempt for it too, namely, if a man's 'beast *falls into a pit* on the Sabbath, he shall not lift it out'.[46]

But even here, the borrowing does not stop. In the very next lines from this First Column of the Damascus Document, one comes upon the final linchpin of all this borrowing. This comes in the very introduction of the renowned 'Righteous Teacher' himself – 'the Guide of all Guides', as it were. It reads: 'And they were like blind men groping for the Way for twenty years. And God considered their works, because they sought him with a whole heart and He raised up for them a Teacher of Righteousness to guide them in the Way of His heart.'[47] Of course, nothing could show the interconnectedness of all these imageries better than the appearance of this allusion to 'being like blind men' and how they were to be 'guided by the Teacher of Righteousness' in 'the Way' of God's 'heart', following directly upon the one to 'planting' the all-important Messianic 'Root', which God then 'caused to grow' and preceding the equally pivotal introduction of the proverbial 'Teacher of Righteousness' here in the Damascus Document as well.

The reason for all this borrowing, parody, and derogation has to have been that so original and impressive were these new ideas and usages we now know from the discovery of the Dead Sea Scrolls, and so well versed were some of the original creators of much of the above-material from the Gospels, to say nothing of the material in Paul, that they were unable to resist repeatedly playing off them and, as I have been at pains to point out, *reversing* or *inverting* the actual original sense or meaning. This was not only intentional and, in my view, political – but it also resulted from a kind of playful malevolence; that is, it gave the people who were originally responsible for creating the traditions upon which many of these documents are based – people, mostly probably in Rome, who had lost everything because of many of the ideas excerpted from the Scrolls above – a good deal of pleasure and they had a lot of fun doing so. That is to say, they really derived a lot of pleasure from shoving this version of 'the Messiah' or 'the Savior' down the throats of the People who had originally created him.

Coin honoring Empress Poppea, who received Josephus warmly when he went to Rome, but whom Nero kicked to death in 65 CE shortly before Jewish War.

117 • Part II: The New Testament Code: Nakdimon and Nicodemus

Chapter 9
The Dogs who Licked Poor Lazarus' Sores

'Casting Unclean Spirits out' of Daughters and 'Toilet Bowl' Issues again: the Themes Migrate

At this point, it would be well to review the sequencing of these important passages from Matthew 14–16 and Mark 6–8 dealing with 'making all foods clean', the permissibility of activities in predominantly Gentile areas, and the several 'signs'-miracle performances, in particular ones bearing on famine relief, evidently a major historical event in the period from the 40s to the 60s CE which left, judging by reports about it in Josephus, Acts, and Talmudic literature – and their reflection in early Church accounts – a deep impression upon all considering it.

There are also, in the portrayal of these things, the reverberations of the 'casting' vocabulary sometimes used with regard to 'casting out (ekballe) unclean spirits' or 'evil demons', and sometimes in the polemics surrounding Paul's contention in 1 Corinthians 6:13 of 'food being for the belly and the belly for food', or, as Matthew 15:17 will ultimately portray Jesus as so graphically expressing this: 'Everything that enters the mouth, goes into the belly, and is cast out (ekballetai) down the toilet bowl.'

As these episodes progress, starting in Matthew 14:13–23 and Mark 6:30–46 with Jesus' first multiplication of the loaves/feeding the five thousand, they move from 'the Pharisees and some of the scribes from Jerusalem' holding to 'the Tradition of the Elders' and objecting to 'his Disciples eating with unwashed hands' (a euphemism for complaints against Paul's Gentile Mission) into the arguments over 'teaching the doctrines of men' as opposed to 'the Commandments of God' (Matthew 15:1–9 and Mark 7:1–14).

In Matthew 15:10, these give way to the attacks on 'the Pharisees' as 'Blind Guides' (i.e., the Leadership of 'the Jerusalem Church' of James and/or the Leadership of the Community at Qumran, should one choose to regard it) and the contention that 'the Plant' which they made claims – in the Damascus Document – to have 'planted', would 'be uprooted'. The characterization of this 'Plant' included the immediate further assertion that both the followers whom they 'led' ('the Blind') and themselves, 'the Blind Guides' or 'the Leaders', would then 'fall into' the same 'Pit' to which they so graphically consigned others (again in the Damascus Document). This is about as near to a definitive proof that the authors of these passages in the Gospel of Matthew knew the Damascus Document as one could provide.

These attacks culminate in both Matthew and Mark in attacks on Peter or the Disciples, or both – attacks continuing the 'toilet bowl' analogy but adding a new one, as per Paul's 'all things to me are lawful' and 'I personally am free' protestations in 1 Corinthians 6:12 and 9:1 and the point ultimately of the whole exercise – these things Jesus said 'making all foods clean' (Mark 7:19, of course, gets the point. Matthew, atypically here, is a little more reticent) which all the Disciples and Peter are unable 'to perceive' being 'yet' or 'also without understanding' (7:17/15:16).

To reinforce the matter of 'making all foods clean' and the permissibility of activities in predominantly non-Jewish areas, these episodes then move on to the curing of the Canaanite/Syrophoenician woman's daughter in the 'border areas of Tyre and Phoenicia' and ultimately Jesus' multiplication of the loaves/famine relief miracles, all basically utilizing the parameters of Nakdimon's famine relief efforts and his own great miracle of 'filling' the lord's 'twelve cisterns to overflowing'. In Matthew and Mark, this curing of the 'Syrophoenician woman's daughter' in the 'Tyre and Sidon borderlands' is itself sandwiched between their respective versions of either the 'feeding the four' to 'five thousand' scenario (according to Mark 7:37, 'in the border areas of the Decapolis') and their presentation of Jesus' polemics on 'unwashed hands', 'bodily purity', and the ritually neutral character of 'food going down the toilet bowl'.

At the risk of some repetition, it would be well to go over this episode one final time, just to get it absolutely clear, since only then can one complete the picture of the strange dislocations and vocabulary transferences taking place from Gospel to Gospel and from Rabbinic tradition to New Testament. Once again, Mark 7:24 begins his version of 'casting out' of 'the unclean spirit' with the *pro forma* notice about how Jesus entered 'a house' – owner's name unspecified. A few lines earlier in Mark 7:17 it was Jesus entering 'into the house' of another unnamed person, this time, 'away from the multitude'/'the Many', both of which entrances are missing from Matthew 15:15 and 15:22's version of the same events.

In this 'house', the Disciples prod him (Jesus) – paralleling Peter's similar prodding in Matthew 15:15 – to expound the Parable, but which 'parable' is intended is difficult to comprehend, since what follows is more in the nature of a simile or homily and not a parable. Be this as it may, Jesus now provides the afore-referenced Parable, to wit, 'whatever goes into the man goes out into the toilet drain', the point of which according to Mark 7:19 was, as just underscored, 'making all foods clean'. In 7:24, however, taking advantage of the issue of whose house Jesus was staying in when the 'Greek woman, a Syrophoenician by Race came and fell down at this feet', Mark once again alludes to the 'Hidden' ideology already called attention to above. He does so with the words – 'whose house, Jesus wanted no one to know, but he could not be hidden'.

It is worth noting the evocation of another such 'parable' in *ARN* tradition, alluded to above as well, which couples an allusion to being 'hidden' with a parable centering on Rabbi Akiba's Poverty being a reproach to those 'claiming to be too Poor to study *Torah*'. This 'Parable' as well was surrounded by allusions to 'casting down', 'uprooting', the 'hidden being brought to light', and the additional motif of those pleading they 'could not study *Torah* on account of (their) little children', allusions not unsimilar to many we shall continue to encounter in this picture of Jesus 'casting the unclean spirit out of' the Syrophoenician woman's daughter.[1]

Mark 7:25's description of this 'certain woman', as he terms her, 'whose little daughter had an unclean spirit' is, once again, instructive too in view of the subject of 'cleanliness' or 'uncleanliness' – in the Parable that just preceded it – of what was or was not just 'cast' or 'gone down into the toilet bowl'. So is the language of 'casting out' with which Mark 7:26 begins its version of how the woman approached Jesus, i.e., 'she besought him to cast (*ekballe*) the demon out of her daughter'.

Though we have already gone over most of this before, it is not without profit to repeat these transferrals to show how such slight differences in vocabulary move from and are re-absorbed in one redaction or occurrence to another. In fact, the reason repetition of these motifs is helpful is that they show, curiously, that it is not so much the event itself that is so important to the various narrators, redactors, or artificers, but rather the use of a given expression, wording, or phraseology and finding a convenient context in which to employ it. To the modern mind this is – as it was, most probably, earlier as well – a rather incomprehensible way to proceed, which is why so few over the years have either grasped or bothered making an issue of it.

Of course, to make the circle of all these usages complete, Mark's 'let the children first be filled' and the Talmud's 'going away full' are likewise now making their appearances in Luke's 'a certain Rich man clothed in purple and fine linen' variation, but the connecting link between all of them should always be seen as the allusion to 'dogs'. We have already pointed out the reason why Mark 7:26's 'casting out' allusion is missing from Matthew 15:22's initial version of the Cananaean woman's request to Jesus – despite the fact that its variation does finally come into play in both versions of Jesus' proverbial response ultimately to both unnamed women's requests: 'It is not good to take the children's bread and cast (*balein*) it to the dogs' – and this should by now be clear. The reason is that Matthew 15:17 used the word '*ekballetai*' to characterize what Jesus had said a few lines earlier concerning what was '*cast out* down the toilet bowl' – and, therefore, of no legally-efficacious import – whereas Mark 7:19 had not, only noting a little more prosaically that it had 'gone out into the toilet drain'!

Of course Mark 7:27's otherwise fuller version of this all-important exchange with the Syrophoenician woman uses the more ideologically charged expression 'sated' or 'filled' to introduce its version of 'not casting the children's bread to the dogs' – namely, 'Let the children first be filled'. On the other hand, both Gospels use the omnipresent 'came' or 'come' (Matthew three times), that is, in Matthew 15:22, for instance, the unnamed woman, 'having *come* out of the border areas of Tyre and Sidon, cried out to him'; whereas in Mark 7:25 she simply '*came and fell at his feet*' which, even more importantly, evokes once again yet another favorite allusion, 'his feet'! Of course, in Luke 16:21's version of these materials this metamorphoses into 'even the dogs came and licked his feet' – meaning Lazarus', not Jesus'! – and the circle of these allusions spreads ever wider.

The rest of this encounter we have already largely analyzed. In Matthew 15:27 the woman, in uttering the celebrated 'even the little dogs eat of the crumbs which fall from their masters' table', incorporates the 'falling' usage just employed in 'she fell at his feet' – which is to say nothing of its evocation of the omnipresent 'lord' or 'master' motif from Column Nine of the Community Rule, Gospel parables probably not unrelated to it, and the Talmudic story about Nakdimon's 'master's water cisterns' – perhaps coincidental, perhaps not. For its part, Mark 7:28's version of the unnamed woman's proverbial retort to Jesus is then framed – somewhat differently from Matthew 15:27's above, no doubt because, in the odd mindset of its authors or redactors, the falling/fell usage had already been employed two lines previously in her 'falling at his feet' – in terms of the equally celebrated: 'and she answered, saying to him, "Yea Lord, but even the little dogs under the table eat of the children's crumbs"'.

Not only is there no 'falling' allusion here at all (because Mark had just used it in the previous sentence), but 'the crumbs' now migrate from the 'masters' table' to 'the little dogs eating under the table' and now they are 'the children's'. Again there is 'the dogs' allusion here, but the 'little' from the 'little children' of Gospel narrative generally and those in the Rabbinic Parable about Rabbi Akiba's '*Torah* study' (to say nothing of the Syrophoenician woman's 'little daughter' earlier) has migrated to the 'little dogs'!

Of course, the 'under the table' theme too, just as the 'coming' one, will now migrate to Luke's version of the 'dogs' (now normal size and not 'little') 'coming', not to 'eat the crumbs', but to lick the 'Poor Man Lazarus' sores' – 'under the table'. Again, it is worth keeping in mind that, just as Luke has no Canaanite/Greek Syrophoenician woman 'dogs' episode, Mark and Matthew have no 'dogs licking Lazarus' sores' episode – and John has no 'dogs' episode at all!

Casting out Mary Magdalene's Seven Demons and Casting Down the Toilet Bowl Again

Moreover, these circuitous machinations do not end here. In other accounts, the woman out of whose daughter Jesus casts 'an unclean spirit' or 'demon', as we have already suggested to some degree, will transmogrify into 'Mary Magdalene out of whom he (Jesus) cast seven demons' (Luke 8:2 and Mark 16:9). Regarding this last and taking into account the persistent 'Tyre' allusions in Mark and Matthew, it is not completely unwarranted to identify yet another mutation in this circle of materials in the parallel represented by the portrait of Simon Magus'

'Queen', called – like the Queen of Adiabene – 'Helen' in all early Church sources who is perhaps not totally unrelated to this Northern Syrian or Arabian Queen who is depicted in clearly hostile early Church sources as having, significantly, been picked up by Simon in a brothel in Tyre. Perhaps we can dismiss a certain amount of hyperbole here too.

The perspicacious reader will quickly recognize as well that the 'crumbs that fall from their masters' table' of Matthew 15:27 now also migrate over to Luke 16:20. It is instructive too to recall that, in Luke 16:20–21's version of these events, 'the crumbs' are rather those that now 'fall from the Rich man's table' to 'a certain Poor Man named Lazarus' – 'the Rich Man' replacing Matthew 15:27's 'their masters', as we saw, though the 'falling' in Matthew has nothing to do with anyone 'kissing' or 'licking' Jesus' 'feet'. However, now it is Lazarus, as noted, who 'wants to be *satisfied*' or '*filled* from the crumbs which fell from the Rich Man's table' and whose sores 'even the dogs came and licked', not the 'children should first be filled' of Mark 7:27's further variation of it.

To go back to Matthew and Mark, so convinced is Jesus by the unnamed 'Canaanite woman''s clever riposte – as if disagreements over purity issues of this kind could simply be solved by lighthearted and casual rhetorical give-and-take or one-upmanship – that he proceeds 'to cast unclean spirits' out of Gentiles too in areas outside of Palestine proper (that is, in 'Tyre and Sidon' and later even 'the Decapolis'). The Pauline Gentile Mission implicit in this depiction is well served as is ideologically-speaking, where legal requirements are concerned, the child-like simplicity of these 'little' people, since that is really what is at stake in these episodes and this debate. Nor is this to say anything about the debate and resolution of the unclean foods issue that precedes and introduces it in both Gospels, now transformed into the patently trivializing and dissimulating one of 'possession by unclean spirits' or 'demons'. This is continually true of the modus operandi of the Gospels and probably just about every reference to 'unclean spirits' or 'demons' should be seen in this context.

In this connection, too, one should pay particular attention to Paul's reference to 'the table' in the Temple in the same breath as 'the table of demons' in 1 Corinthians 10:21, implying an interconnection of sorts if one could actually understand, through all the dissimulation here, what was actually being said. Not only does this come in continuation of his wrestling in 10:18–20 with the question of 'things sacrificed to idols' ('what then do I say, that an idol is anything or that which is sacrificed to an idol is anything?'), it precedes his second evocation of his 'all things lawful being lawful for me' pronouncement in 10:23, concluding in 10:25 with: 'Eat everything that is sold in the marketplace, in no way making inquiry on account of conscience'.

For its part Luke 8:2, lacking the Syrophoenician woman's daughter episode, attaches these 'unclean' or 'Evil spirits', as we just mentioned, to its introduction of Mary Magdalene, 'out of whom seven demons had gone', and here we have the same conundrum – as in the case of the 'toilet bowl' situation – only in Mark, anyhow, now reversed. As should be readily apparent, this last in Luke now combines Mark 7:19's 'going out', as in his 'going out down the toilet bowl', with Matthew 15:22's 'my daughter is miserably possessed by a demon'.

There is also just a suggestion in both of these descriptions – for whatever it's worth – of the language of Luke's 'Seven sons of Sceva' episode in Acts 19:13–18, portrayed as going around (the Diaspora presumably) exorcizing 'Evil spirits'. Not only are they themselves referred to by the ubiquitous 'some', but so is the sub-class in Acts 19:13 to which they seem to have appertained, namely, 'some of the Jews wandering around exorcizing Evil spirits'! It too, though, is clearly another nonsense episode paralleling Paul's encounter with 'Elymas Magus' (Simon Magus?) in Acts 13:8 in Cyprus earlier.

In the encounter with the clearly pseudonymous 'Seven sons of Sceva' (himself characterized in 19:14 as 'a Jew' and 'a High Priest'!), though the locale is uncertain, it would appear to be Asia once again – the ubiquitous 'Jews from Asia' who make trouble for Paul in the Temple, 'stirring up the multitude' who 'laid hands on' Paul in Acts 21:27 thereafter? Nevertheless, it does appear to have just an element of truth underlying it, that is (aside from the telltale 'some' attached to yet another use of 'doing' in the phraseology, 'who were doing this', viz., 'Jews wandering around exorcizing Evil spirits in the Name of the Lord Jesus', i.e., 'the Lord Savior'), if one could substitute the words 'going around teaching the James position on table fellowship', 'bodily purity', or 'dietary regulations' for the words, 'exorcizing Evil spirits'. Furthermore, it does draw on the overlap to the unsophisticated mind between the number 'Seven' – *Sheva'* (also meaning 'oath' in Hebrew) – and '*Sceva*' in Greek transliteration, as certainly no 'High Priest' was ever named *Sceva* in Hebrew!

Be these things as they may, earlier in Luke 8:2–3 Mary Magdalene is part of a group also referred to by the 'some' usage again (in this case, 'some women'), all portrayed as having been cured by Jesus 'of Evil spirits' – this last the equivalent to the 'unclean spirit' besetting the Syrophoenician woman's daughter in Mark 7:25 above. These included 'Susanna' and 'Joanna the wife of Chuza, a steward of Herod'. This last is reinforced by the episode in Acts 13:1, where Luke portrays at least one Herodian among 'the prophets and teachers of the Church at Antioch'. That being said, the implication of the first notice, anyhow, is that Luke, therefore, is picturing Jesus as being willing to 'cure' even Herodians.[2] Furthermore, though Mary Magdalene and Joanna will reappear later in Luke's depiction of events at 'the empty tomb', 'Susanna' is never heard from again either in Luke or anywhere else for that matter (unless it be in the picture of her original biblical prototype).

Later Luke 24:10 groups Mary Magdalene and Joanna with another 'Mary' – this time, 'Mary (the mother) of James', all pointedly denoted in 24:1 once again as 'some'. For Mark 16:1, the parallel trio is 'Mary Magdalene and Mary the mother of James and Salome' – Salome here clearly taking the place of Joanna – and it is now these 'who bring perfumes' or 'aromatics that they might come and anoint him'. Once again we have the 'coming' allusion coupled with the 'anointing' one, but now we have two more 'Mary's coming to Jesus to 'anoint him' (living or dead, as in this case – it hardly matters).

While in Luke 24:10 it is this trio who report 'these things' – meaning, the empty tomb, the two Angels 'in shiny white clothes', and what they said – 'to the Apostles'; in Mark 16:5, as in Matthew 28:2, only one Angel 'clothed in a white robe' is seen in the empty tomb. Of course Mark's version of such post-resurrection appearances is considered defective by most scholars. Still for Mark 16:9, Mary Magdalene alone, as we just saw, is – as in John 20:14–17, for whom there are (as in Luke 24:4) 'two Angels sitting in the tomb in white clothing' (20:12, the complexity of these inter-relationships becoming legion) – the recipient of Jesus' first post-resurrection appearance. This she duly reports, as in John 20:18, to the Disciples, whereas in Matthew it is the two Marys who report the 'Angel of the Lord', 'with a gaze like lightning and his clothing white as snow', and the fact of the empty tomb to the Disciples (28:2–3). In Luke 24:4 and 10, it is 'two men' – later identified as Angels – and now it is the three women, including 'Joanna and Mary (the mother) of James', making the report, this time to the Apostles.

Of course for John, too, it is 'the Disciple whom Jesus loved' who 'outruns Peter' for the honor and is the 'first' to enter the empty tomb, where he sees the linen cloths and the napkin for his head rolled up to one side – Mary still 'standing' outside weeping – but no Angels (20:2–11). It was only after this and after the Disciples had gone home that Mary 'stooped down into the tomb' and gets her vision of the 'two Angels in white' and following this, as usual, Jesus 'standing' behind her (*n.b.*, 'the Standing One' ideology again). So in the end in John we have 'three' people entering the tomb, but not the 'three' reported in the Synoptics. For Matthew 28:7–8, it is only 'Mary Magdalene and the other Mary' (whoever she may be) who experience this and they are instructed to report this at one point 'to the

Disciples' – and, at another (28:10), 'to my brothers' – as Mary Magdalene is in John 20:17 – not, as in Luke 24:10, 'to the Apostles'.

It is perhaps because of the nature of such a post-mortem encounter with Jesus that Mark 16:9 includes at this point Luke 8:2's earlier characterization of Mary Magdalene as having been possessed by 'seven demons'. Instead, however, of 'going out of' her – as Luke and Mark 7:19's own picture of Jesus' words concerning what 'went out into the toilet bowl' – now the 'seven demons' are characterized as being 'cast out of her' (*ekbeblekai*) by Jesus. The usage is yet another variation of his own '*ekballe*' earlier in his version of the Greek Syrophoenician woman's request to Jesus 'to *cast* the demon *out* of her daughter' (Mark 7:26) and the '*ekballetai*' in Matthew 15:17's version of the food '*cast out* down the toilet drain' excursus preceding this.

Mary Magdalene, Jairus' Daughter, the Woman with 'the Fountain of Blood' and Jesus' 'Feet' Again

Interestingly enough, the parallel at this point in Matthew 28:9 which, while ignoring the allusion in Mark to 'casting out' *vis-a-vis* Jesus' treatment of Mary Magdalene's 'seven demons', once more picks up another important notation from this circle of related usages – that of Jesus' 'feet'. We shall continue our consideration of these sometimes repetitious allusions, because the mutual reverberations resound back and forth in so many different combinations and permutations that something edifying usually emerges from their analysis, even if only because of the slightly differing contexts with or perspectives from which they start.

As Matthew 28:9 puts this – now with only two women: 'Mary Magdalene and the other Mary' and like Mark 16:5, which probably derived from it, only one Angel 'whose face was as lightning and his clothing white as snow': 'Lo and behold Jesus met them … and they *came* to him, took hold of his *feet* and worshipped him'!

So now we have two 'Mary's 'coming to' Jesus and falling at 'his feet' – not one as in John and Luke's Mary, Martha, and Lazarus scenarios – one called 'Mary Magdalene' and the other 'Mary the mother of James and Salome' (Mark 16:1). Elsewhere – as in Mark 15:47 – this 'Mary' is called 'Mary the mother of Joses' and, in Mark 15:40 earlier, 'Mary the mother of James the less and Joses'. We have already treated to some extent in *James the Brother of Jesus* these multiple confusions and overlaps between 'mothers', 'brothers', and 'cousins' of Jesus (including even the one presumably between 'Joses' and Jesus himself) as the doctrine of the supernatural Christ gained momentum in the early Second Century and beyond.[3]

This allusion to 'falling at his feet' is also reprised in Mark 7:25's picture of the Greek Syrophoenician woman (whom we have already connected to some extent to the picture of Mary Magdalene – to say nothing of Queen Helen of Adiabene) 'falling at his feet' above. It is also reprised in John 11:32's picture of Lazarus' sister 'Mary' – after Jesus 'came' to Bethany the second time – and how after 'coming' to him, she 'fell at his feet' ('come' repeated about seven times in eight lines – not to mention a number of other times throughout the episode).

But this same 'Mary' had earlier in John 11:2 (repeated more dramatically in 12:3) had already taken 'the litra of precious spikenard ointment and anointed Jesus' feet' with it, 'the house being filled with the odor of the perfume'. The same allusion to 'feet' was replicated in Luke 10:38–42, but this time it was 'Mary sitting at Jesus' feet' while Martha complained about having to do 'so much serving'. Again in this last, there is the possible play in Jesus' response ('(she) has *chosen the good part*') to Martha's complaint over Mary's having 'left her alone to serve' in Luke 10:42 on the critique of 'the Lying Spouter' and 'the Seekers after Smooth Things' – 'the Pharisees' and 'the Pauline Christians', as we have defined them – at the end of the First Column of the Cairo Damascus Document.[4]

These last were described in CD 1.19 in terms of 'choosing the fair neck' (evidently meaning 'the good part' or 'the easiest way') and connected to 'seeking Smooth Things' and 'watching for breaks' in the passage from Isaiah 30:10–13 being drawn on there. The reason the Damascus Document gives for applying this allusion ('choosing the fair neck') to such persons is because 'they chose illusions', 'condemning the Righteous and justifying the Wicked' – the opposite, it should be appreciated, of the proper 'Justification' activity by the Sons of Zadok later in the same Document of 'justifying the Righteous and condemning the Wicked', 'transgressing the Covenant and breaking the Law'.[5]

Nor is this to mention that the issue of these 'feet' is so much a part of these Talmudic traditions, not only regarding the various daughters of these proverbial 'Rich Men', but also 'the Poor', who 'gather up the woolen garments that were laid down' so the 'Rich' Nakdimon's 'feet' would not have to touch the ground. Again there is the motif of 'touching' here, already variously underscored above in episodes involving the 'touching' of both Jesus' and James' person, fringes, or clothes. Moreover this same 'touching' theme, along with a number of other motifs, will again intrude into the incidents surrounding another character – this time, in the Synoptics – named 'Jairus' and designated as 'a Ruler' (compare with how John 3:1 designates 'Nicodemus') or 'Ruler of the Synagogue', and yet another individual whose daughter will need to be cured (Matthew 9:18–26/Mark 5:21–43/Luke 8:40–56).

Here, too, in both Mark 5:22 and Luke 8:41, 'Jairus' is described as 'falling at his (Jesus') feet'.[6] This is interrupted by the 'coming' of another in this endless series of unnamed women – this one now described as 'with a flow of blood for twelve years' (Mark 5:25/Luke 8:43/ Matthew 9:20). Here, again, there is another use of the miraculous number 'twelve', which will then be the age of Jairus' daughter in Mark 5:42 and Luke 8:42 and, of course, Jesus' age in Luke 2:42 when 'sitting among the teachers in the Temple', and the number of 'talents' and 'water cisterns' in the Nakdimon story, to say nothing of the 'twelve hand baskets full of broken pieces', 'gathered up' (like 'the Poor' do Nakdimon's 'woolen clothes') in the aftermath of Jesus' miraculous famine relief/signs demonstrations in all Gospels.

The curing of this 'woman with a flow of blood' who, like 'the Cananaean woman's daughter' in Matthew 15:28, will also ultimately be described as 'saved by her Faith' (interestingly this affirmation is missing from Mark 7:29 which only has Jesus saying 'Go your way'), is sandwiched in between the two halves of the raising/healing of Jairus' daughter (Mark 5:25–34 and pars.). Not only does it, like these other 'touching' incidents, again have to do with 'touching his clothing', 'border of his garment', and 'the Multitude' or *Rabbim* of Qumran allusion, but it is also possible to see it as making fun of Jewish scrupulousness over blood and issues related to blood generally – concerns particularly strong, not only at Qumran, but also in James' directives to overseas Communities as reiterated in Acts.

In fact, Mark 5:29 actually uses the language of 'drying up the *fountain* of her blood', instead of 'the flow of her blood', to describe her state regarding this matter. One possible way of looking at this modification in Mark is as an amusing caricature of the Damascus Document's pointed concern over blood generally ('the Forefathers' having been 'cut off *because they ate blood* in the wilderness' – and the Temple Establishment as well, because they were in contact with 'those sleeping with women during the blood of their periods'[7]). Perhaps even more to the point, it is possible to see it as a disparaging play on the language in this same Damascus Document of 'the *Fountain* of Living Waters', which was the essence of what it conceived of as 'the New Covenant in the Land of Damascus' – this 'New Covenant' itself clearly an affront to those being characterized in it, as well, as 'having turned back from it and betrayed it'![8]

Once again, Mark is uncharacteristically more expansive and, not only does the woman with 'the fountain of blood' for twelve years 'come and fall down before' Jesus (5:33), but

Mark would also appear to be having a lot of fun generally – if we can consider its author(s) as this well-informed and having this degree of sophistication – over the whole connection, pivotal to the Damascus Document's historiography, between 'the New Covenant in the Land of Damascus' and 'the Well' or 'Fountain of living waters' that was literally or figuratively 'to be dug' there – now here in Mark 5:29 (if, as we said, we can give him credit for this amount of sophistication) being caricatured in terms of 'the *fountain of her blood*'.

We will see this 'blood' usage, so abhorred by those at Qumran, in the context of the imagery of 'the New Covenant in the Land of Damascus', in particular the 'Blood' (*Dam*) and the 'Cup' (*Chos*) which make up the syllables of this denotation in Greek and Paul's 'the Cup of the New Covenant in (his) blood' (1 Corinthians 11:25) as we proceed. Be these things as they may, Jesus is now pictured as 'coming to the Ruler of the Synagogue's house' and, as with Lazarus and the Greek Syrophoenician woman in Tyre and Sidon, now raising or curing his daughter (Mark 5:35–43 and pars.).

As these motifs reverberate back and forth from one Gospel to the other, and to the Talmud and then back, the same Mary who in Luke 'sat at' and, in John, 'fell at' or 'anointed his feet' (while Judas Iscariot and/or Martha 'complained'), 'washed his feet with her hair'. In fact, this notice clearly so appealed to John that he repeated it twice in 11:2 and 12:3.

Jairus Kisses Jesus Feet', Ben Kalba Sabu'a Kisses Rabbi Akiba's Feet, and Eliezer ben Jair

To go back to 'Jairus', whose story – which had been interrupted for some reason – is now resumed in all three Gospels. He too is characterized in Mark 5:22 as 'falling at (Jesus') feet', the 'Multitude gathered around him'. We shall see the connection of these two successive characterizations of persons 'falling at Jesus feet' in the same episode – one a 'Ruler of the Synagogue', and the other, another unnamed 'certain woman' who 'comes' to him with a twelve-year 'flow', or 'fountain of blood' – to the story in Rabbinic tradition about how both Rabbi Akiba's wife and his important father-in-law 'fall at his feet' below.

In the tradition about 'Jairus' daughter', not only does the picture of 'the flute players and the crowd' in Matthew 9:23 identify this as a typical scene one would encounter across the Mediterranean in this period (though not perhaps in Palestine), but allusion to the important catchwords 'master' or 'lord' we have encountered above also appears. But even more to the point, just as the 'certain woman, whose daughter had an unclean spirit' 'came and fell at Jesus' feet' later in Mark 7:25 and Matthew 15:25, not only does Jesus speak with regard to the 'woman with the twelve-year issue of blood' in the patently 'Paulinizing' manner, 'your *Faith* has cured you' (presumably meaning she was a Gentile – Mark 4:34/Luke 8:48), but, as in the 'little daughter' of the woman who was a 'Greek Syrophoenician by race' also in 7:25, Mark 5:23 applies the diminutive 'little' to 'the Ruler of the Synagogue by the name of Jairus'' 'little daughter'.

Finally, even more important than any of these, Mark 5:41 – being the most prolix of any of these accounts as we have seen – actually also uses a variation of the phrase Acts 9:40 applies to 'Tabitha' at Jaffa, after Peter traveled there from Lydda to resurrect her, i.e., 'Tabitha arise' – 'get up!' Here in Mark, this becomes – not 'Tabitha' (which we have already previously proposed as a quasi-anagram or phoneme for the Samaritan '*Taheb*') – but '*Talitha cumi*, which interpreted means (that is, translated from Aramaic into Greek), little girl, I say unto you, arise'. Of course, however the diminutive 'little' (now applied to the 'maid' or 'girl') may be, it is hardly conceivable that the use of the Aramaic '*talitha*' for 'little'/'young girl'[9] at this point in Mark is not in some way connected to the related use of the Aramaic '*Tabitha*' for the name of 'a certain Disciple (female) at Jaffa', cured or resurrected by Peter in Acts 9:40 in an almost precisely parallel way, is accidental or merely coincidence.

But to take the case, as well, of Rabbi Akiba in the *ARN*; we have already seen how when he and his new wife Rachel, Ben Kalba Sabu'a's daughter, married despite the fact 'he was so Poor' and despite her father's vow to disinherit her, they not only had to sleep on straw, but how the even more vivid and tender Talmudic tradition dramatized this by picturing him as 'picking the straw out of her hair'.[10] We suggested that this episode could be seen as a variation on Luke's picture of Jesus' birth in a manger, for it also pictures 'Elijah the Prophet' in the guise of a man 'coming' to them in a clearly *redivivus* manner and begging some straw, since his wife was in labor and 'there was nothing for her to lie on'. It was at this point that the tradition pictures Rabbi Akiba as remarking, 'there is a man' who was so Poor, that 'he lacks even straw'![11]

In fact, so many of these New Testament traditions seem to go back to stories about Rabbi Akiba and his well-known colleagues of the previous generation, such as Rabbi Yohanan ben Zacchai and Eliezer ben Hyrcanus, that any casual connections such as these should immediately be remarked. In the first place, not only was Rabbi Akiba a '*ben Joseph*', meaning, his name literally was 'Akiba ben Joseph'. Notwithstanding, in the stories we have about Rabbi Akiba's relations with his wife (Ben Kalba Sabu'a's daughter) and her father, we are also twice confronted with the references to 'falling down before him and kissing his feet'.[12]

The first occurs when, after having been secretly married to Ben Kalba Sabu'a's daughter, R. Akiba returns a second time after his two stays of 'twelve years' at the academy – location unspecified, but probably in Lydda, though it may have been further afield (here all our number 'twelve's again of the Nakdimon story and its spin-offs) – with 'twenty-four thousand Disciples' and, like Martha's sister Mary and therefore Lazarus' as well and the unnamed 'woman in the city who was a Sinner' with the alabaster flask who accosts Jesus at 'the Pharisee's house' in Luke 7:38, she 'falls down before him and kisses his feet'.[13] The second comes right after this, when Ben Kalba Sabu'a, Rachel's father, hears that 'the Great Man had come to town' and, prevailing upon Rabbi Akiba to help him annul his vow to disinherit his Rachel – just like the Great 'Jairus', styled a 'Ruler of the Synagogue' in the story about the resurrection of his daughter (Mark 5:22) – 'he (Ben Kalba Sabu'a) falls down before him (R. Akiba) and kisses his feet'.[14]

But 'Jairus' too is a name celebrated in Jewish tradition, since 'Eliezer ben Jair' is the famed commander of the final stand at Masada and a second-generation descendant of the famous founder of the 'Zealot Movement', 'Judas the Galilean'. Is there more here than meets the eye? From our perspective, there is. Just like the co-option of Rabbi Yohanan's father's name Zacchaeus (in Hebrew, Zacchai) in Luke 19:2–8 – itself probably based on Peter's visit to confront Simon Magus in Caesarea where, in the Pseudoclementine *Recognitions*, he stays at 'Zacchaeus' house' (possibly the real father of Rabbi Yohanan ben Zacchai[15]); 'Theudas' in 'Thaddaeus'; now this 'Ben Jair' in 'Jairus'; and even 'Judas the Galilean' himself in 'Judas Iscariot' and/or 'Judas *Zelotes*'; it would not be unfruitful to speculate about the connection of the theme of the resurrection of 'Jairus' daughter' with that of the 'Zealot' or *Sicarii* mass suicide on Masada since we now know that the sectaries were adepts of the idea of 'the Resurrection of the dead' – the 'bones' passage from Ezekiel 37 having been found buried underneath the synagogue floor there.[16] In addition, the Dead Sea Scrolls – exemplars of which were also found at Masada – make it crystal clear that the Qumran sectaries also believed in the doctrine of 'the Resurrection of the dead'.[17] We will leave it to the reader to decide what the connection of all these things may be – if any.

Where R. Akiba is concerned, the 'Zealot' Rabbi of his generation and considered by most to be the spiritual force behind the Bar Kochba Uprising,[18] he was also said to have – like Jesus, 'the Essenes', John the Baptist, and James – taught the twin Commandments of the 'All Righteousness' ideology: the first, in his advocacy as a fundamental precept of *Torah*,

'You shall love your neighbor as yourself' – 'Righteousness towards one's fellow man' as Josephus labels it in his *Antiquities* Book Eighteen description of John the Baptist, to say nothing of that of 'the Essenes'' advocacy of it preceding this and, of course, 'the Royal Law according to the Scripture' as it is put in the Letter of James.[19]

The second is even more dramatic and parallels to some extent Hippolytus' picture of those he calls '*Sicarii*' or 'Zealot Essenes' who, during the First Uprising, are portrayed as willing to undergo any sort of torture rather than 'blaspheme the Law-Giver or eat things sacrificed to idols'.[20] Tractate *Berachot*/'Blessings' in the Talmud (now at the time of the Second Jewish Uprising) takes up the picture from there. In the midst of graphically detailing how Rabbi Akiba was tortured to death by the Romans – presumably for his support of the Messianic pretender, Shimon Bar Kochba, to whom he applied 'the Star Prophecy' of Numbers 24:17 – it provides the following gruesome picture: though his flesh is 'flailed from his body with iron combs' and 'his body is then drawn and quartered', nevertheless Rabbi Akiba welcomed his martyrdom as a chance to fulfill the first of the two 'All Righteousness' Commandments, that of 'Piety towards' or 'loving God': 'You shall love the Lord your God with all your heart and with all your soul … even if you must pay for it with your life.'[21]

To go back to this theme of the 'hair' of these celebrated daughters, Rabbi Akiba's wife Rachel, Ben Kalba Sabu'a's daughter – whom some called 'a Galilean' because, like others spending their early years in this locale and called by this designation, she was said to have been buried in Galilee – to show her virtue and constancy was also said to have 'sold her hair' to pay for her husband's studies because they were so Poor.[22] The resemblance of this to some of the 'hair-wiping' traditions above is uncanny and it really does, of course, bear on these traditions about Mary in John and others, 'wiping Jesus' feet with her hair', while the Disciples or Judas Iscariot protest that 'the value' of such 'ointment of pure spikenard oil' should have been 'sold and given to the Poor'.

For the Talmud, the issue of 'hair' will now be linked to 'Boethus' daughter' for whom the same 'cushions' or 'carpets' – pictured in the above traditions as having been 'laid on the ground' (before they were gathered up by 'the Poor') so Nakdimon's 'feet' would not have to 'touch the ground' – are 'laid so that, when she walked from her house to the entrance to the Temple to see her husband (Josephus' friend, the Boethusian High Priest, Jesus ben Gamala) read the *Torah* on the Day of Atonement', her 'feet' too 'would not get dirty'.[23]

It was also she, it should be remembered, not just Nakdimon's daughter-in-law, to whom the Rabbis grant 'two *se'ah*s of wine daily' after the death of her husband 'as a precaution against dissoluteness'. Furthermore, to show how far she had fallen after the destruction of the Temple, it is also she, this same 'Martha the daughter of Boethus' (called here 'Miriam'), the 'hair' of whom 'Rabbi Eleazar ben Zadok' now sees the Romans 'bind to the tails of Arab horses and make run from Jerusalem to Lydda'![24]

Here our 'hair' motif starts to replicate. Neither should one overlook the point about 'from Jerusalem to Lydda' (Peter's route in Acts), nor the 'Zadok' denotation in Rabbi Eleazar's patronym. Where Boethus' daughter's 'cushions' are concerned, we have already observed that aside from deriving the name of another of these Rich colleagues of Nakdimon, 'Siset Hakkeset'/'Ben Zizzit Hakeseth', from the 'silver couch upon which he used to recline before all the Great Ones of Israel',[25] Tractate *Gittin* also derived it from 'his fringes' (*zizzit*), which 'used to trail on cushions' (*keset*). To be sure, like the material about many of these same sorts of things in the New Testament, much of this is hyperbole or what is perhaps even worse, pure nonsense. But, for the purposes of tracing the migration of these motifs and this vocabulary from one story to another and across the boundaries of cultural tradition, it doesn't really matter – that is, which is more nonsense and which less so.

The Centurion's Servant, More Poor Widows and Temple Destruction Oracles

Finally, to go back yet again to Luke and the much-overlooked encounter with another woman 'carrying an alabaster flask of ointment' at 'Simon the Pharisee's house' at the end of Chapter Seven, who 'washed' Jesus' 'feet with (her) tears' and 'wiped them with (her) hair', Luke, as we saw, combines all these themes. It would be worthwhile, therefore, to go over it once again, but this time in more detail.

In a series of curings that begin with Luke 7:1–10's evocation of 'a certain Centurion' who is also described like Acts' 'Cornelius' as 'loving our Nation and building a synagogue for us', it is hard to refrain from an outright guffaw here. In Acts 10:2 and 10:22, it will be recalled, it was 'Pious', 'Righteous', 'a God-Fearer', 'doing many charitable works for the People, praying to God continually', and 'borne witness to by the whole Nation of the Jews' – equally laughable – though these particular allusions in Acts were more than likely aimed at either Domitian or the Emperor Trajan whose father really had been a Centurion in Palestine conspicuously singled out by Josephus for his bravery. Still, where the idea of 'building a synagogue for us' is concerned, this notice in Luke 7:5 seems more to be consistent with what Vespasian or Titus did for R. Yohanan ben Zacchai when he appeared before him after his escape from Jerusalem applying 'the Messianic Prophecy' to him.[26] Though extremely confusing and replicating much of Acts 10:1–18's more detailed story of Peter's visit to Cornelius – instead of sending 'two servants' and another 'Pious Soldier' to invite Peter 'to his house' as in Acts 10:7 and 22, 'the Centurion' in Luke 7:3 is somehow able to send the 'Elders of the Jews' to Jesus 'to ask him to come in order to cure his servant' (*sic*).

Moreover, as Jesus 'was already not too distant from the house' (Luke 7:6 – in Acts 10:9, it was 'as the two servants drew near' the house), the Centurion has a change of heart and now sends his 'Friends' to tell Jesus not to bother to come because he 'was unworthy for (Jesus) to come under (his) roof'.

While in Luke 7:6–10 Jesus stops just before actually entering the Centurion's house and is made to announce 'to the Multitude' again the *pro forma*, 'not even in Israel have I found such great Faith' thereby, seemingly, curing 'the Centurion's servant' from outside the house, in Acts – where Peter actually *enters* the Centurion's house, who then 'falls down at his feet worshipping' him (thus)! – the issues are rather that of the 'pouring out' of the Holy Spirit upon Gentiles as well' (10:45) and 'God also giving the repentance of life to Gentiles' (11:18), not just 'curing the Centurion's servant'.

The version of this encounter one finds in Matthew 8:5–13 is somewhat different. It directly follows another 'touching' and 'cleansing' episode in Matthew 8:3 – in this case, the 'cleansing' of 'a leper' ('Simon the Leper'?), who '*came* and *worshipped him*'. In Luke 7:18–22 following these curings and raisings, it should be appreciated that these motifs drift into the allusion to 'the lepers being cleansed' and the multiple references to 'coming' we shall discuss further below. In this exchange between Jesus and John, just as the 'Centurion' sends his 'two servants' to Peter in Acts 10:7, John is now pictured as sending 'two certain (ones) of his Disciples' to query Jesus with the apocalyptically charged, 'Are you the one who is to *come*?'. This is language we shall eventually see reflected in 'the *Doresh ha-Torah*' ('the Seeker after the Law') who *came* to Damascus' in Ms. A of the Damascus Document and 'the coming of the Messiah of Aaron and Israel' in Ms. B and in 'the Star who would come out of Israel' from Numbers 24:17 in Ms. A and the Qumran *Testimonia* below.[27]

But in Matthew 8:5, it is neither the 'Elders of the Jews' or the 'Friends of the Centurion' who come to Jesus on the Centurion's behalf, but now 'the Centurion' himself; and here, not only does he refer to his servant 'being *laid out* in the house' (8:6) – as in the 'garments'/'cushions' being 'laid out' in Talmudic scenarios or Luke's 'Poor Man Lazarus at the Rich Man's door' – but now even, after commenting as in Luke on the Centurion's 'great

Faith', the 'Go your way' (8:13) of the several Talmudic stories attributed to either Yohanan ben Zacchai or Eleazar ben Zadok about the 'hair' or 'feet' of these same Rich Men's daughters. Moreover, the perspicacious reader will also immediately discern that this same 'Go your way' has now migrated down in Luke 7:22 into the outcome of Jesus' exchanges with the Disciples of John over the question of 'the One who is *to come*'.

Finally, in this healing, Matthew is even more anti-Semitic and pro-Pauline than Luke – if this is possible. To his version of Jesus' compliment to the Centurion of 'not even in Israel have I found such great Faith' (8:10) – also more or less repeated in Matthew 15:28 later in his version of the 'cleansing' of the 'Cananaean woman's daughter', viz., 'O woman, great is your Faith' – is now attached the additional ideologically-charged and pointed comment, including this Centurion among 'the Many' who 'shall come from East and West' and 'recline (at the table) with Abraham and Isaac and Jacob in the Kingdom of the Heavens' (*sic*). In the portrait of 'Heaven and Hell' that concludes the 'certain Poor Man' laid at the gate of the 'Rich Man clothed in purple and fine linen' in Luke 16:22–31, this will be 'Lazarus on the bosom of Abraham'. In the same breath, Matthew reverses the 'casting out' language Josephus used to illustrate Essene treatment of backsliders, to say nothing of his own later 'casting out down the toilet bowl' parable and the way Luke will portray the Jewish crowd as 'casting' Stephen 'out of the city' in Acts 7:58: 'But the Sons of the Kingdom shall be cast out into the outer darkness' (8:12; this is pure 'Gentile Mission' material). To add insult to injury, Matthew adds here, 'and there shall be much weeping and gnashing of teeth'.

To go back to the further resurrection episode in Luke 7:11–17 that intercedes between this healing of the Centurion's servant and the exchange between 'the Disciples' of John and Jesus, Luke portrays Jesus as resurrecting the 'only son' 'in a city called Nain' of a bereaved 'widow' – another of the Talmud-like 'widow' scenarios which Luke, in particular (but also Mark), appears to have found so attractive. Not only should one note in this regard, for example, 'the widows overlooked in the *daily serving*' in Luke's introduction of 'Stephen' in Acts 6:1, but in both Luke 21:1–5 and Mark 12:41–44, there is the proverbial and particularly charged episode of the 'certain Poor widow casting her two mites into the Treasury' – 'charged' because it is so similar to the later scenario in Matthew 27:3–10 of Judas Iscariot casting his 'thirty pieces of silver' ('the price of blood' – here in Matthew 23:30, this is 'communion'/'partaking in the blood of the Prophets' – more 'blood libel' accusations) into the Temple Treasury prior to his alleged suicide, that it too probably has simply been transferred and revamped.

In any event, like Judas' 'casting' his 'thirty pieces of silver' into 'the Temple Treasury', it deals with what emerges as one of the pivotal issues for this period, that of 'sacred gifts given to the Temple' – in this instance, on the part of 'the Rich *casting* their gifts into the Treasury' (but also on the part of 'Gentiles' generally) as opposed to those 'cast', as Luke 21:4/Mark 12:43 would have it, by 'this certain Poor widow' ('cast'/'casting' repeated five times in four lines!) 'out of her poverty'. Of course, as in the resurrection of the 'only-begotten son' of 'the widow of Nain' (Adiabene), the overtones of this episode with the gifts to the Temple from another probable 'widow', Queen Helen of Adiabene (whose gifts included the famous seven-branched gold candelabra which was taken to Rome in Titus' victory celebration and there, presumably melted down to help build – of all places – the Colosseum!) should be obvious.

Furthermore, Jesus' attitude towards 'the Poor' and 'poverty' in the matter of the 'certain Poor widow''s two mites – again missing, not only from Matthew, but John as well – is a far cry from what it is in John 12:5's picture of his response to Judas Iscariot's complaints about 'the Poor' over the wastefulness of Lazarus' sister Mary anointing Jesus' feet with expensive ointment. On the other hand, this time it does once again bear a resemblance to the Talmud's picture both of Rabbi Akiba's poverty as opposed to his Rich father-in-law, Ben Kalba

Sabu'a's 'superfluity' and Rabbi Eliezer's 'poverty', whose 'fame' would in due course, like 'this Poor widow"'s 'be worth more than all the rest' (Luke 21:3/Mark12:43).

The encounter with this second widow here in Luke 21:1–5 whose two mites were 'worth more than all the rest' is pivotal too, because, in both it and Mark, it introduces Jesus' telltale oracle patently based on Josephus' description of Titus' destruction of the Temple: 'There shall not be left a stone on top of a stone that shall not be thrown down'.[28] Here, too, Jesus is not only called 'Teacher' ('Teacher' carrying with it, in the writer's view, something of the sense of 'the Righteous Teacher'), but the whole discourse he now delivers on 'going out from the Temple' is replete with multiple allusions to the language of 'leading astray' (in Matthew 24:5 and 11, 'leading *Many* astray'[29]) as well as that of 'the Elect', 'delivering up', 'false Christs and false prophets', 'misleading' or 'deceiving with (great) signs and wonders'.

In addition, Jesus is depicted as pointedly characterizing the 'Rich' and those he pictures as occupying 'the Chief Seats in the Synagogues' as 'going to receive a greater' or 'more abundant Judgment' – that is, in proportion to their 'Riches' (Luke 20:47/Mark 12:40). Furthermore, this phraseology is replicated almost precisely in the Habakkuk *Pesher*'s picture – in exposition of Habakkuk 2:4 – of how the punishment 'of the Wicked would be multiplied upon themselves' when they were judged'. Moreover, this means, of course, on 'the Last' or 'Day of Judgment' (n.b., in particular, that even here the verb 'eating' or 'devouring' is used to express this in both Luke 20:47 and Mark 12:40 just as it is in the Habakkuk *Pesher*[30]).

For its part Matthew 24:2, while retaining Mark's 'going forth from the Temple' but discarding the 'widow's two mites' material, embeds Jesus' oracle of the destruction of the Temple at the end of its general 'woes' – 'woes' not unlike or really separable from those of the curious 'prophet' in Josephus, Jesus ben Ananias, after the death of James leading up to the destruction of the Jerusalem,[31] which we shall consider in more detail below; 'woes', too, which throughout the whole of Matthew 23 are used to attack the 'Rabbis', 'Pharisees', 'Hypocrites', 'Blind Ones', 'fools', 'Blind Guides', and just about every person or concept of any consequence in this period (in particular, concepts fundamental to Qumran ideology[32]), finally giving way, as in the other two Synoptics, to 'the Little Apocalypse' in Chapter Twenty-Four and, of course, to the typical proclamation ascribed to James in all early Church literature of 'seeing the Son of Man coming (together with the 'Elect') on the clouds of Heaven with Power and great Glory' (Matthew 24:30/Mark 13:26/Luke 21:27).

But these 'woes' are also reminiscent of the 'woes' R. Yohanan pronounces to his Disciples when he goes forth from Jerusalem in the *ARN*. Of course, these 'woes' too, like those continually pronounced by 'Jesus ben Ananias' – however preposterous they may be – are far more credible than any of these 'woes' being pronounced in the Gospels, since at least they are not happening forty years before the events in question, but actually consonant with the occurrences. Furthermore, they are not a vicious and even incendiary attack on such 'Blind Guides' and all of its associated innuendo in which our Gospel artificers – which, though supposedly talking about 'Love' (Matthew 22:36–40 and pars.), actually seem full of hatred – put all their favorite anti-Semitic invective, including the one about 'Serpents, Offspring of Vipers' (23:33 and pars.) and that about 'Jerusalem, Jerusalem, who kills the Prophets and stones those who have been sent to her' (note, even 'Jesus ben Ananias' here was neither stoned or killed – at least not by Jersualemites!). In fact, the *ARN* at this point even recounts a tradition that echoes the one about either James or Jesus being tempted to jump or actually 'being *cast down* from the Pinnacle of the Temple'. This is Vespasian's General who was forced to 'cast himself down from the roof of the Temple' because he disobeyed and refused to carry out an order from Vespasian to destroy the Temple, but rather left the Western (or 'Wailing') Wall as a sign of the Emperor's great strength![33]

However this may be, at the end of this 'Little Apocalypse' in Matthew, there occurs (uniquely in Matthew 25:14–30) another one of these 'talents', 'servants', 'lord' and, this time even, 'digging in the earth' scenarios – this one involving delivering 'five talents' to the one 'good and Faithful servant' and to another 'two' (our 'seven cisterns' of the Nakdimon bartering with his 'lord' earlier?) and a third one who will get only 'one' (numbers which seem completely arbitrary – any seemingly will do). After much bantering and business psychology (obviously representing the Mediterranean bourgeois of the day) and even mentioning 'money-lenders' and 'interest' (25:27); again, as in Nakdimon's doubling the amounts of his 'lord's cisterns', the amounts are also somehow doubled to ten and four (25:20–28) while the 'wicked and slothful servant', who only *dug* in the ground and buried his lord's money', would have his 'taken from him and given to him with ten talents' (the other 'Faithful servant', who with smart business sense doubled his to 'four', now seemingly having gone by the boards!).

Of course, parabolic or otherwise, this is monetary venture capitalism with a vengeance, well-suited to the ethos of the *Imperium Romanum*, however manifestly at odds with 'the Poor of this world' and 'Heirs to the Kingdom promised to those who love him' of James 2:5. In any event, there was to be much 'weeping and gnashing of teeth' and this 'worthless bondservant' was 'to be *cast out* into the Darkness' (25:30 – most violent and a little sad that 'the servant' who did not go to 'the money-lenders' and double 'his lord''s investment should be treated so harshly even if only symbolically). It is hard to imagine, even if uttered completely symbolically or interpreted allegorically in the most Philo-like manner, that this had anything to do with Palestinian Messianism whatsoever, nor 'the Blessed of (the) Father inheriting the Kingdom prepared for them from the Foundation of the World' of Matthew 25:34 that follows, but as just noted, Roman and Herodian venture capitalism with a vengeance.

The Only-begotten Son, God Visiting His People, and the Sign of the Coming of the Son of Man

On the other hand – since Jesus is not 'going forth from the Temple' at this point in Luke, but simply continuing on from his 'widow's two mites' homily – Luke 21:5–6, unlike Matthew and Mark, uses the ever-recurring 'some' to provoke him into uttering the dire prognostication above about the destruction of the Temple – 'there not being left one stone upon stone that shall not be thrown down' – as simply part of the discourse which continues relatively seamlessly, then too, from 21:8–36 into its version of 'the Little Apocalypse'. But the 'some' who provoke this and, in the manner of 'the Righteous Teacher' in the Scrolls, call Jesus 'Teacher' as well (21:7), do so because they were speaking, seemingly admiringly, about the pivotal question of 'sacred gifts to the Temple' – which, as just remarked, acted as the immediate cause of the War against Rome – and expensive decorations obviously being given to the Temple by 'the Rich', doubtlessly meant to include and specifically aimed at, in particular, those given by persons such as the celebrated Queen Helen of Adiabene.

Even more importantly, in describing the implications of this 'raising' of the 'only begotten son' of the 'widow of Nain' (probably Adiabene; no one has pointed out a geographical locale in Palestine consonant with this 'Nain' and we have already underscored how Josephus calls Queen Helen's son her 'only begotten'), Luke 7:12–14 actually pictures 'the bier' of the 'only-begotten son' of this 'widow' outside 'the Gate of the City'. In this regard, one should pay particular attention to the well-known tomb – built by Queen Helen's second son, Monobazus, for her and Izates, who did in fact pre-decease her, near the Gate of the City of Jerusalem where it is still extant today – then decorated, as is meticulously described by Josephus, with three large pyramids![34]

Moreover, Luke 7:16 then uses exactly the same allusion we have already encountered in the opening lines of the Damascus Document, picturing the crowd as crying out – on seeing Jesus' miracle and taking him for 'a Prophet' – 'God has visited His People'. In the Damascus Document, in the context of 'the Root of Planting' passage highlighted above, this is God 'visited them and caused a Root of Planting to grow from Israel'. But the allusion 'visited them' is often used throughout the Damascus Document, usually implying retribution or the execution of Divine Judgement.[35] Nothing probably could represent a greater distortion or reversal of Qumran ideology, as far as the import of this expression 'God visited' is concerned, than what one finds here in Luke 7:16. Of course, in reality, there probably never was any 'Poor widow of Nain' either but, as just remarked, this is a veiled attack on the illustrious Queen of Adiabene herself, probably perceived by 'some' (no pun intended) as a 'Rich widow', her husband – whoever he might have been – having already died by the time of her emergence as an importance presence on the Palestinian scene.

For its part, Luke 7:16 employs this allusion to 'God *visiting* His People' in the context of having the crowd crying out 'a Great Prophet has *arisen* among us'. Once again, we have the verb 'arising' here, used throughout the Damascus Document where the '*arising* of the Messiah of Aaron and Israel at the End of Days' is concerned but also, as we shall presently see, in the 'Messianic' *Florilegium* regarding 'the Branch of David who will arise/stand up in Zion together with the *Doresh ha-Torah* in the Last Days' – 'the Tent of David which is fallen' of Amos 9:11 who 'will *arise* to save Israel' too.[36] Furthermore, in speaking about such a 'Great Prophet', the crowd's exclamation once again echoes 'the True Prophet' ideology of the Ebionites, Elchasaites and, in succession to these, the Manichaeans and Islam[37] – an ideology definitively evoked as well, not only in the build-up to this evocation of 'the fallen Tent of David' here in the 'Messianic' *Florilegium*, but also in the climactic Column Nine of the Community Rule.[38]

In fact, playing on this ideology of 'the True Prophet coming into the world' (as, for example, in John 6:14, 'This is truly the Prophet that is coming into the world' – which is probably the reason for all these 'coming' allusions so proliferating the notices we have been highlighting), this 'coming' allusion, like the 'casting' ones just alluded to in Luke 21:1–4 as well, is played on three times in just three lines in the prelude to Jesus' discussion in Luke 7:24–30 of the 'Greatness', 'baptism', and 'Prophethood' of John the Baptist who, for some reason, irrupts into the text at this point both in it and the Gospel of Matthew. This occurs in the question Luke 7:18–20 has now John allegedly send to Jesus – 'Are you the One who is *coming*?' – again (as in the case of the 'two servants' of Acts 10:7's Pious Centurion) via 'two certain ones' – now two 'of his (John the Baptist's) Disciples'.

Not only will John (like James later) be portrayed in 7:31–34 as 'neither eating meat nor drinking wine' (Luke 7:33–34/Matthew 11:18–19), but it is at this point in the narrative, as we just saw, that John's Disciples, 'coming to' Jesus, ask him, 'Are you the One who is coming' and here Jesus is made to answer as well 'Go your way' (Luke 7:22/Matthew 11:4; cf. the same kind of remark in Mark 7:29 to the 'Syrophoenician woman' in the matter of 'the demon having left' her daughter!).

To return to Luke 7:22's picture of how Jesus responds to John's two Disciples (in Matthew 11:2, only 'his Disciples') by preaching about 'the blind seeing', 'the dumb hearing', again 'the lepers being cleansed', 'the dead being raised', and 'the Poor having the Gospel preached to them'; both Luke and Matthew use patently Paulinizing language to present him as blessing those who find 'no occasion of *stumbling*' or 'being *scandalized* in' him (clear counterparts of Paul's 'stumbling block' and 'scandal of the cross' aspersions in 1 Corinthians 1:23, 8:9, Galatians 5:11, and Romans 9:32–3, 11:9, 14:13, etc.).

In addition, after these either 'depart' or 'go their way', both Gospels picture Jesus as yet again evoking 'the True Prophet' ideology and applying it to John (7:26/11:9–10) while at the same time querying 'the Many' about 'going out into the wilderness' – in the manner of Josephus' 'false prophets', 'Impostors', and 'Deceivers' – to say nothing of having him depict John as 'a reed shaken by the wind' (7:24/11:7). Moreover, they conclude by having Jesus, in the manner of a scriptural exegete, himself also apply 'the preparation of the Way' passage from Isaiah 40:3 and the Community Rule[39] to John, portraying the tax-collectors as 'having been baptized with the baptism of John' (Luke 7:26–34/Matthew 11:10–19 – what could be more misguided and laughable than this?). This is the context in which John is portrayed, accurately for a change, as either a 'Rechabite' or a 'Nazirite', that is, 'John came neither eating or drinking (though nonetheless, as we just saw, thought by some as 'having a demon'!) whereas Jesus, on the contrary, 'came eating and drinking' (the omnipresent 'come' again). It is here, too, that the famous and pointed 'glutton', 'winebibber', and 'friend of publicans and Sinners' barbs are evoked, which end in the plainly nonsensical: 'and Wisdom is justified by Her works' (in Luke 7:35: 'by all Her Children' – thus)! It is at this point, too, that Jesus is portrayed as visiting yet another 'house' in Luke 7:36–37 (again not paralleled in either Matthew or Mark), now that of 'the Pharisee' already discussed in some detail above, and keeping 'table fellowship' with him or, as this is also put in the passage, 'reclining' or 'eating with him' (7:36–37).

There are also additional possible allusions of this genre to 'go your way', depending on how one wishes to translate the usage in the Gospels, in particular in Matthew 5:23–4's Sermon on the Mount in the key context of 'gifts to the Temple' again – 'leave your gift before the altar and *go your way*'; in Matthew 8:1–13, following the miracle of Jesus 'making the leper clean' and before curing the paralytic 'servant' of the humble Roman Centurion, where it is now the 'some of the Kingdom' who 'shall be cast into outer Darkness' and the Centurion's 'Faith' is 'Greater than all in Israel' (8:10); in John 4:50, after curing the 'little child' of another supplicating 'nobleman', this one in Galilee and 'the second of the signs Jesus did on *coming* out of Judea to Galilee' (the only one that comes to mind in these locales would be one or another of the Herods); in Mark 10:21, after 'allowing the little children to *come* unto' him and 'laying hands upon them', once again, '*touching* them' and 'blessing them' – this followed by yet another suppliant (this one unnamed), 'running up', 'kneeling down to him', and again calling him 'Teacher' (10:13–20); and finally in Mark 10:52 and 11:2, following 'the camel' and 'the eye of the needle' allusions in 10:25, leading into Jesus in Bethany riding on the colt, and culminating – contrary to the complaints of the 'some' again – in the 'Many *spreading their garments before him on the way*' (11:5–8), exactly in the manner of 'the Poor' in the 'Nakdimon'/'Jesus ben Gamala' stories above.[40]

In this picture in Mark 11:7 too, so enthusiastic are the People that they even '*cast* their garments on the colt' as well. The same episode occurs in Luke 19:29–36 but before this, even more interestingly, in 17:11–19 the one 'falling on his knees' of Mark 10:17 becomes one of 'ten lepers' ('standing at a distance'), who now rather 'falls on his face' and happens to be 'a Samaritan' (i.e., now we have 'a Samaritan leper'! – but it basically shows the interchangeability of all these expressions) and the 'ten lepers' of Luke 17:12 turn into, in Mark 10:41, the Ten Disciples who 'complain about' or 'are jealous of James and John' (*sic*)!

To go back to Luke 7:37: it was at this point that yet another woman appeared, called 'a woman in the city' and 'a Sinner', bringing the *pro forma* 'alabaster flask of ointment'. Once again, one should compare this with the woman with the 'alabaster flask of ointment' at 'Simon the Leper's house' in Mark 14:3 and Matthew 26:7, an episode missing from Luke where it has already been replaced in 10:38–42 both by the visit to 'Martha's house' ('in a certain village') and in 16:19–31, the 'Lazarus under the table whose sores were licked by dogs' episode – 'the lepers being cleansed' already having been mentioned along with 'the blind', 'the lame', 'the deaf', and 'the Poor' in Jesus' earlier response to John's 'certain two Disciples' in Luke 7:22 and this same 'Simon', albeit now identified as 'the Pharisee' not 'the

Leper', about to be mentioned in Luke 7:40 (again showing the basic transmutability of all these terminologies!).

The reader will bear with us if we repeat some of the points of this episode, since they are so remarkable and the issues at stake are so momentous. Now '*standing* behind, weeping at his *feet*' (in Luke 8:41 to follow, it will be 'Jairus, a Ruler of the Synagogue', who 'falls at his feet', while in Luke 17:16 above, 'the leper' who 'was a Samaritan' only 'fell on his face at his feet'!) while 'the Pharisee' – like Judas Iscariot, Martha, and the Disciples in other such episodes – whom we have discovered and shall discover again was called 'Simon', complained, 'she began to wash his feet with her tears and she was wiping them with the hairs of her head' (as we saw, one should compare this with John 12:3's 'Mary anointing the feet of Jesus and wiping his feet with her hair'). It is not hard to see that we have all our imageries in just this one sentence, but so carried away by this time is Luke that he doesn't stop here but rather goes on (to repeat), 'And she was lovingly kissing his feet and anointing them with ointment' (7:38).

Now we really do have all our themes and motifs, but 'the Pharisee' – like the Pharisees as Blind Guides and in the 'Unwashed Hands' Parable, yet again raises both the issue of such a woman 'touching him' and 'the True Prophet' characterization (this time as applied to Jesus), namely, 'if he were (such) a Prophet', how could he allow such a woman ('a Sinner') to 'touch him' (presumably meaning because she was either a Gentile or alluding to the defective state of her 'purity' – 7:39)?

It is at this point that Jesus starts to talk to someone he now suddenly addresses as 'Simon' who responds by calling him 'Teacher' again (7:40). Just as in the 'Simon the Leper' episode in Matthew 26:6–13 and Mark 14:3–9, this obviously should have been Simon Peter but, except for the rebuke which is about to follow in Matthew 26:34 and Mark 14:30, Simon Peter was never part of the episode. Not only does Jesus now clearly mean that the Pharisee with whom he is now 'reclining' and discoursing in a dialectical manner is called 'Simon', but what is really being picked up here is the 'Simon' from the 'Simon the Leper's house' encounter in Bethany in Matthew 26:6 and Mark 14:3 – and the dizzying circle of these variations and elaborations continues. Of course, we are also in the area of the 'table fellowship' issue too, since Jesus has been invited 'to eat' and 'reclined (at the table) at the house of the Pharisee' (7:36) – how symbolic!

Again, though Simon has done nothing but offer him 'table fellowship' (it should be obvious that this 'Pharisee' is supposed to be a caricature of Simon Peter, since this was the issue that so divided him from Paul in Galatians 2:11–2:17), Jesus launches into a lengthy diatribe, ending with the usual refrain from several of these episodes: 'Your Faith has saved you' (Luke 7:50). It also incorporates the same creditor/debtor haggling over numbers we have already encountered in Luke 16:1–15's parable about 'the Unfaithful Servant', to say nothing of Matthew 25:14–30's parable above about how those who, having seemingly invested their money with 'money-lenders', doubled the number of their 'talents' and the 'interest' earned from 'two' to 'four' and 'five' to 'ten'; and in Matthew 18:21–35 where, again in response to Peter (which also involved, not one, but two additional 'falling at his feet's), the numbers were 'seven', 'seventy', 'ten thousand talents', and 'one hundred dinars'.

Though in Luke 16:1–18 which, it will be recalled, was again about 'a certain Rich Man's steward' and his 'baths of oil', the haggling is over the numbers 'eighty *cors*' or 'measures of wheat' and 'a hundred', either '*cors* of wheat' or 'baths of oil'. Here in Luke 7:41, it is 'five hundred dinars' as opposed to 'fifty' but, in any event, all have a good deal in common with Nakdimon's 'cistern' negotiations. It also reflects the 'three hundred dinars' numerical variations of both the 'Simon the Leper' and John 12:5's 'Judas of Simon Iscariot'/'Lazarus'/'house in Bethany' encounters and Matthew 26:15's tenfold reduction of this in the amount then appointed to Judas by the Chief Priests to 'betray' or 'deliver him up'.

Chapter 9: The Dogs who Licked Poor Lazarus' Sores • 134

Nor is this to say anything about the 'one hundred dinars' owed by 'the fellow debtor' in Matthew 18:29 or the 'hundred baths of oil' or the 'hundred measures of wheat' in Luke 16:1–18's equally mercantile parable. But even more germane than this, aside from the parallel represented by the haggling between Nakdimon and 'his lord' over the number of cisterns of water that were owed or 'needed filling', it even more precisely corresponds to the 'four' to 'five hundred dinar' amounts Rabbinic tradition reckons as the value of Nakdimon's daughter's 'perfume basket'!

These parallels being as they may, now complimenting 'Simon' in Luke 7:43 – in the style of Platonic dialogue – as 'having judged rightly', Jesus nevertheless then turns and, in 7:44, addresses – in the self-centered style we have now come to expect (the style of Hellenistic gods visiting mere mortals on Earth) – 'Simon the Pharisee' with a complaint we were not expecting at all: 'Do you see this woman? I entered your house, but you gave me no water for my feet. Yet she washed my feet with tears and wiped them with the hairs of her head. You gave me no kiss, but since I came in she has not ceased lovingly kissing my feet. You did not anoint my head with oil, but she anointed my feet with ointment (Luke 7:44–46).' As we noted, this is about the fifth, sixth, or seventh such episode to use these themes but, I think we can safely say, this one just about says it all.

Miriam's Hair, Casting Martha's Silver into the Street, and the Stink of R. Eliezer's Bad Breath

To go back to Lamentations *Rabbah*, after the material about R. Eleazar ben Zadok swearing on 'the Consolation of Zion' if he did not see the Romans binding Boethus' daughter's hair 'to the tails of Arab horses and making her run from Jerusalem to Lydda', the narrative switches back in the very next passage to Nakdimon ben Gurion's daughter Miriam (Mary). It is here that it noted how 'the Rabbis allowed her five hundred dinars daily to be spent on her store of perfumes' – the 'five hundred dinars' we just saw in Luke 7:41 in Jesus' rebuke to 'Simon the Pharisee' over another unnamed 'woman in the city' with 'an alabaster flask of ointment' washing Jesus' 'feet' again 'with her tears' and 'wiping them with her hair' (the 'feet' of both the Shiloh Prophecy and the Standing One?). Nor is this to say anything about the 'daily' self-indulgent luxury engaged in by Luke 16:19's 'Rich Man clothed in purple and fine linen' while the 'sores' – which 'Poor' Lazarus' body 'were *full* of' – were 'licked by *dogs*'.

It is here Lamentations *Rabbah* quotes the passage from the Song of Songs 1:8, 'O thou fairest among women, go your way forth among the footsteps of the flock and feed your offspring' (in the original, this is literally *gediyot*/'kids' – which for some reason is reinterpreted here in the text as *geviyot*/'bodies'[40]). The same oath about 'seeing the Consolation of Zion' is uttered again by R. Eleazar ben Zadok, this time in connection with his having seen Nakdimon's daughter 'gathering barley grains from beneath the feet of horses in Acco' – here, of course, 'the feet' are now 'the feet of horses' but, as ever, it is important to have regard for the 'feet', 'footsteps', 'barley grains', and 'hair' motifs we have been following above. Nor is this to forget the possible echo of this 'go your way' phraseology in the several Gospel passages remarked above as well.

In this material in Lamentations *Rabbah*, which follows the note about the Rabbis granting Boethus' daughter 'Miriam' (*sic*) the widow's allowance of 'two *se'ah*s of wine daily' (again, the 'daily' motif) after the death of her husband, Josephus' friend 'Jesus ben Gamala' (here the evocation about 'the camel' and 'his burden' that will be applied to this situation in *Gittin* below will be of more than ordinary import – nor do the Rabbinic sources evince very much concern over the circumstances of this Jesus' death), now the 'feet' will be '*her* feet', not 'the feet of horses in Acco', and here occurs the note about 'carpets being laid for her from the door of her house to the entrance of the Temple so her feet would not be exposed' – the Talmudic narrator then sardonically adding, 'nevertheless they were exposed'.[41]

In case the reader is unfamiliar with or confused by these various sources, it is important to realize that the same tradition is related in Tractate *Kethuboth*, but there it is rather attributed to R. Yohanan ben Zacchai, 'leaving Jerusalem riding upon an ass, while his Disciples followed him' (R. Yohanan too, it seems – just like Jesus and Rabbi Akiba – had 'his Disciples' and he, too, 'rides upon an ass' or 'donkey', though unlike Jesus entering Jerusalem on Good Friday, he is *leaving* Jerusalem). Again it should be noted how even here in this version of Jesus 'riding on an ass'/'the colt of an ass' material in Mark 11:2 and Luke 19:30 – though not in Matthew 21:7 – Jesus appears to be using the equivalent in Greek of the expression '*go your way*' above in Hebrew.

Here in *Kethuboth* the exchange between Rabbi Yohanan and Nakdimon's daughter, 'picking barley grains out of the dung of Arab cattle', is more detailed and focuses even further on the utter reversal of her fortune and the complete obliteration of the 'Riches' of both her father and her father-in-law's house (whoever he may have been – thus seemingly continuing the mix-up in Rabbinic sources between Boethus' daughter Martha' and 'Nakdimon's daughter Miriam'[42]). Moreover, here too the ever-present motif of 'her hair' is added. Now 'standing up' to answer the 'Master''s questions (*n.b.*, Rabbi Yohanan like Jesus is also being called 'Master' here), 'She *wrapped herself with her hair* and stood before him'. It is in this context that the Talmudic narrators asked the question concerning whether Nakdimon practiced 'true charity', itself related to complaints by Judas Iscariot, the Disciples, the 'some', and characters like 'the Pharisee' named 'Simon' above about why Jesus' 'feet' were being either 'washed', 'wiped with hair', 'anointed', or 'kissed' and the dinar equivalent of the 'precious spikenard ointment' which should have 'been sold and given to the Poor'.

It is at this point in *Kethuboth*, too, that the now familiar description, 'when he walked from his house to the house of study, woolen clothes were spread beneath his feet and the Poor followed behind him gathering them up' (perhaps not completely unrelated to the matter of Jesus' entry into Jerusalem) is added which not only includes the 'feet' and 'the Poor' themes, but after which the narrators comment that this was not 'true charity' but, rather, 'he did it for his own Glorification'. It is at this point too, just as in Lamentations *Rabbah*, that the proverb is cited, '*in accordance with the camel is the burden*' – this last linking up with the familiar New Testament aphorism, 'easier would it be for a *camel* to go through the eye of the needle than a *Rich Man* to enter the Kingdom of God' (Matthew 19:24 and pars.).

In the 'Mary daughter of Boethus' material from Lamentations *Rabbah* above, for whom 'the carpets are laid' so 'her feet' would not touch the ground and about whom R. Eleazar ben Zadok is pictured as remarking concerning 'not living to see the Consolation (of Zion) if (he) did not see the Romans bind her hair to the tails of Arab horses and make her run from Jerusalem to Lydda'; it was rather one of the Mosaic woes, Deuteronomy 28:56, evoking, 'The tender and delicate woman among you who would not adventure to put the *sole of her feet upon the ground* for tenderness and delicateness' that is being cited to point out Boethus' daughter's precipitous reversal of fortune and how she died a beggar – not Song of Songs 1:8, as in the version that immediately follows in Lamentations *Rabbah* relative to this same R. Eleazar ben Zadok's comments about the downfall of 'Miriam the daughter of Nakdimon' whom he now rather sees, as just pointed out, 'gathering barley corns from beneath the feet of horses in Acco'.

The confusion over the names of these two daughters, whoever's daughters they are, also appears to drift – as we have been showing – into both John's 'Lazarus' story and the segments of it that reappear in the Gospel of Luke where, instead of being two daughters, they now appear as two *sisters* who are either anointing Jesus' head with 'precious spikenard ointment' or 'wiping his feet with their hair and bathing them with their tears'; and even, according to what is basically the final presentation, preparing his body for burial. As we proceed, we will see how this brings us back to the Nakdimon/Nicodemus duality, who will himself be involved in the preparation of Jesus' body for burial according to the Gospel of John.

The shift here from 'anointing' Jesus, presumably either for King or Messiahship, to preparing his body for burial takes place in the response Jesus is pictured as making to Judas Iscariot's complaint to him over the value of the precious spikenard ointment which Judas – and, in the encounter at 'Simon the Leper's house', the 'some' or the Disciples – thinks 'should have been given to the Poor' (John 12:5 and pars.). It is in this context that Jesus evokes the burial theme replying, '*Let her alone*. She has kept it for the day of my burial' (the 'leave them alone' of Matthew 15:14).

To understand all of these thematic twists and turns, overwrites and reversals, the reader should group together – as we have done – all these episodes both about Talmudic Rich persons (whether Ben Kalba Sabu'a, Ben Zizzit, Nakdimon ben Gurion, his daughter, or Boethus' daughter) and New Testament variations or enhancements. To show that the same overlaps and/or revisions are taking place in the Talmud as in the New Testament, later in *Kethuboth* this same aphorism, 'in accordance with the camel is the burden', is evoked once more, but this time it is applied – as already indicated – rather to recovering the surety in the matter of a marriage contract (*kethubah*).[43] Now, since this is *Kethuboth* and not Lamentations *Rabbah*, it really is 'Martha' who is involved and she is correctly identified as 'the daughter of Boethus' and, as in the case of Nakdimon's treatment of 'the Poor' previously, she is now being compared to 'the Poorest woman in Israel'. Moreover, this is the context in which the aphorism 'in accordance with the camel is the burden' is quoted – this time, to show that the twenty-five year limitation for recovery of a dowry was still applicable even though she was now Poor – Rich and Poor being equal before the law.[44] Of course this is to say nothing about her husband's patronym '*Gamala*', which means 'camel' in Hebrew, nor the brutal circumstance of his death (along with that of James' judicial murderer, Jesus ben Ananias) at the hands of the so-called 'Idumaeans' and 'Zealots'.[45]

As *Gittin* picks up this material about 'Martha the daughter of Boethus', it too now calls her 'one of the Richest women in Jerusalem' – this, once again, in the context of reference to these three Rich Men, Nakdimon ben Gurion, Ben Kalba Sabu'a, and Ben Zizzit Hakeseth.[46] Not only does *Gittin* reiterate here why Ben Zizzit was so designated, namely, either 'because his fringes (*zizzith*) used to trail on cushions' or because 'his seat (*kiseh*) was among the Great Ones of Rome', but also that these three were 'in a position to keep (Jerusalem) in supplies (specifically denoted here as 'wheat and barley, wine, oil, salt, and wood') for twenty-one years' at a time when 'the *Biryonim*' were 'in control of the city'. Though the chronology is important here, both in terms of Helen's three successive Nazirite-oath periods of seven years imposed upon her by the Rabbis and the successive numbers of cisterns in the Nakdimon 'rainmaking' scenario, this too would seem to be an exaggeration as, whoever these Rich Men are in the end determined to be, they cannot be thought of as being in control of Jerusalem for twenty-one years.[47]

This being said, the term *Biryonim* has been widely recognized as a Talmudic term to indicate Revolutionaries or 'Zealots' – in fact, actually most probably '*Sicarii*'.[48] It has even been associated with the term 'Simon Bar Jonah' which Jesus applies to Peter in Matthew 16:17. This is the scene in which Peter designates Jesus in 16:16 as 'the Christ, the Son of the Living God' (in Mark 8:29 and Luke 9:20, only 'the Christ' or 'the Christ of God') and, seemingly, in return Jesus designates Peter as his Successor, 'the Rock upon which I will build my Church', giving him 'the keys of the Kingdom of Heaven' (*sic* – 16:18). Though it has moved very deeply into the popular consciousness, the second part is notably missing from all the other Gospels, though it is – minus 'the keys' and 'build my Church' part – to some extent reflected in John 1:42 where Jesus not only calls Peter 'Son of Jonah' (Bar Jonah), but applies the term 'Cephas' to him which, playing upon the meaning of 'Peter' in Greek, he or the narrator actually interprets as meaning 'Stone' (*Petros*).

Nevertheless, in the scene as it develops in John 1:45–51, it is rather left to the individual we have elsewhere identified as a stand-in for James (in John – where otherwise James is nowhere mentioned), '*Nathanael*' ('Given-by-God') – because 1) Jesus first sees him like a Honi *redivivus* sitting 'under a fig-tree' (1:48) and 2) he sees 'the Angels of God going up and coming down upon the Son of Man' (1:51) – to identify Jesus as 'the Son of God' and 'the King of Israel' (1:49), the second of which we take to mean 'Messiah'. Finally, as this scene draws to a close in Matthew 16:20, there is some indication that the designation is not widely known, at least not in Palestine, as Jesus tells Peter that 'he should tell no man he was the Christ'.

When the Rabbis, true to the political orientation of the Pharisees, wish 'to go out and make peace with' the Romans, these '*Biryonim*', according to the presentation of Tractate *Gittin* here (and this does seem to be accurate), 'prevent them'. These same *Biryonim* are also described as 'burning all the stores of wheat and barley so that a famine ensued' (here, of course, the real origin probably of many of the 'wheat and barley' evocations above). Not only is this fact also borne out in Josephus' narrative,[49] it is reflected, it would appear, in the Famine with which we originally began this series of traditions circulating around the persons of Nakdimon ben Gurion and his colleagues.

It is in this context, too, that one of the final stories, chronologically speaking, is told about 'Martha the daughter of Boethus' and, once again, this time *Gittin* has her prenom right.[50] As this is presented – and by now a certain tragic sadness has begun to envelop her story – after sending her servant out four different times: first to buy fine flour, next white flour, after that dark flour, then barley flour (clearly, four declining grades of quality, indicating how far the famine had progressed within the city) and finding there was none, suddenly she is described as '*taking off her shoes*'! Why she should do so at this point is unclear (unless she didn't want to get them 'dirty') but, as is the way with these Talmudic traditions, it doesn't really matter – the allusion having made it possible for her to be barefoot again and for the final bit of information to emerge, that is, she then went out, but 'some *dung stuck to her feet* and she died'. Again, too, all of this is typical both of Rabbinic hyperbole and laconic understatement.

Once again, it is Rabbi Yohanan ben Zacchai who applies the passage from Deuteronomy 28:56 ('The most tender and delicate of your women would not venture to set the sole of her feet upon the ground' – previously applied above in Lamentations *Rabbah* by Rabbi Eleazar ben Zadok) – and this certainly with more justice – to the pathos of Martha's fate and how he saw her reduced from her Rabbinic allowance of 'five hundred dinars daily just for her perfume box' to 'gathering barley corns from beneath the feet of horses in Acco' – though 'Rabbi Zadok' (not 'Eleazar ben Zadok', seemingly perhaps, his father) is evoked in almost the very next sentence about the fast he supposedly observed 'for forty years so that Jerusalem might not be destroyed'.[51]

In fact, so thin was he – R. Zadok, that is – that 'when he ate anything the food could be seen', meaning as it passed down his throat. It is in this context that the observation is made too that 'When Rabbi Zadok wished to restore himself, they used to bring him a fig and he used to suck the juice and *throw the rest away*' (here, yet another variation of the 'casting' allusion, which then leads directly into those about Martha, 'when she was about to die', 'casting' all her gold and silver 'into the street', we had already seen in this section of *Gittin*). Nor is this description of Rabbi Zadok completely unrelated to some of the usages found in Matthew and Mark's picture of the 'Toilet Bowl' Parable Jesus tells which not only mentions food going into his mouth and seemingly 'down his throat', but '*casting* the rest away'. Even more to the point, this description of R. Zadok clearly correlates with and has many of the elements of depictions of James, including his perennial fasting and vegetarianism. Be this as it may, in another display of typical Talmudic earthiness or corporeality, it is now reported that some say, she ate the fig left by Rabbi Zadok (meaning the pulp he had discarded when he sucked out the juice), became sick, and died![52]

Here, too, one should perhaps quote another Talmudic story, which in its pathetic sadness and tragicality has to be seen as defining this period – at least from the Judean point-of-view – and really does tug at the heartstrings. Clearly it did nothing of the sort to those who created the stories from the same period that found their way into the New Testament which show neither any such empathy or pity and, however one might admire their artfulness or the cosmopolitanism of their spiritual message, in the circumstances, are hardhearted in the extreme.

The story which is conserved, as usual, in two versions – one in Lamentations *Rabbah* and one here in Tractate *Gittin* – seemingly relates to this same Rabbi Zadok, now taken for a 'High Priest' (though, since it is extant in two versions, it might be another).[53] In *Gittin*, it is told in relation to the children of a Rabbi named Ishmael ben Elisha, who probably is to be identified with another Boethusian-style High Priest in this period, Ishmael ben Phiabi.[54] But since most of our more reliable traditions from this time, particularly this kind of heartrending material, seem to be emanating out of Lamentations *Rabbah* and the *ARN*, we will assume that the Lamentations one is more reliable although, where the sense and piteous impact of the story is concerned, it is immaterial. The story, which actually introduces this whole series of tales about 'Miriam the daughter of Boethus' (thus) and the aphorism attributed to R. Eleazer ben Zadok in Lamentations *Rabbah*, reads as follows:

"It is related that the children of Zadok the Priest, one a boy and the other a girl, were taken captive to Rome (by Vespasian and Titus after the fall of the Temple in 70 CE), each falling to the lot of a different officer. One officer resorted to a prostitute and gave her the boy (as a slave). The other went into the store of a shopkeeper and gave him the girl in exchange for some wine (this, in order to fulfill the text from Joel 4:3 in which is written: 'And they have given a boy for a harlot and sold a girl for wine'). After a while the prostitute brought the boy to the shopkeeper and said to him, 'Since I have a boy, who is suitable for the girl you have, will you agree they should marry and whatever issues (from the union) be divided between us?' He accepted the offer. They immediately took them and placed them in a room. The girl began to weep and the boy asked her why she was crying? She answered, 'Should I not weep, when the daughter of a High Priest is given in marriage to one (such as you), a slave?'. He inquired of her whose daughter she was and she replied, 'I am the daughter of Zadok the High Priest'. He then asked her where she used to live and she answered, 'In the upper market place'. He next inquired, 'What was the sign above the house?' and she told him. He said, 'Have you a brother or a sister?' She answered, 'I had a brother and there was a mole on his shoulder and whenever he came home from school, I used to uncover it and kiss it'. He asked, 'If you were to see it, would you know it now?' She answered, 'I would'. He bared his shoulder and they recognized one another. They then embraced and kissed till they expired. Then the Holy Spirit cried out (this in both Lamentations *Rabbah* and *Gittin*), 'For these things I weep!'"

Lamentations *Rabbah* then follows this up with more stories about 'Miriam the daughter of Boethus', though here she is called 'Miriam the daughter of Boethus *Nahtum*' (thus – that is, 'Nakdimon'), once again clearly indicating the mix-up between the patronyms 'Nakdimon' and 'Boethus'. Most likely we are probably dealing with Nakdimon's daughter and not Boethus' but, however this may be, the tradition which is conserved here claims that whichever 'Miriam' or 'Mary daughter of Nahtum' this was 'was taken captive and ransomed at Acco'.[55]

Because she was by this time so poor, the people had bought her a shift which, when she went to wash it in the sea, was carried away by a sudden wave, whereupon they bought her another one and the same thing happened. At that point she refused any further help and the story which, like the several Jesus 'Parables' in Luke 7:40–43, 16:1–13, and Matthew 18:12–35, also uses 'debt', 'debtor', and 'debt collection' language to have her conclude parabolically, 'Let the Debt Collector (meaning, God at 'the Last Judgment' and for her sins) collect His debt', whereupon her garments were miraculously restored to her – a clearly symbolic resurrection story.

In the Maccabean-style 'Seven Brothers' martyrdom story that immediately follows – after the death of six of her other sons and quoting a whole series of biblical proof-texts *a propos* of these, this Miriam/Mary actually alludes to her remaining child – much like the several Gospel recitals above evoking 'being with' or 'sitting down with Abraham in the Heavens' – 'going to talk to the Patriarch Abraham'. To review these: in Matthew 8:6–13 the Centurion who wants his servant to be cured, but stops Jesus in the nick of time from entering his house, is complimented for having such 'Great Faith' as to enable him to 'sit down with Abraham while the Children of the Kingdom shall be thrown into outer Darkness'; Luke 13:24–35 puts this parabolically, alluding to 'seeing Abraham' while at the same time uses 'casting out' language, refers to 'shutting the door' and 'standing outside', makes the 'killing the Prophets' accusation to predict the destruction of Jerusalem, ends – in a total parody of Qumran ideology – with the proverbial 'the First shall be Last and the Last shall be First'; and finally in 16:22–31 'Poor Lazarus', after having 'his sores licked by dogs', is 'carried away by Angels into Abraham's bosom'.

For its part, the woman Lamentations *Rabbah* is calling 'Miriam' or 'Mary' encourages her only remaining son to 'Go to the Patriarch Abraham and tell him ... that your mother actually built seven altars and offered up seven sons in one day. Whereas yours was only a test (cf. Hebrews 11:17 on Abraham's 'only-begotten' test), mine was in earnest,' at which point, 'while she was embracing and kissing him, he was slain in her arms'. Tractate *Yoma* gives the name of this child as 'Do'eg ben Joseph' (i.e., parodying 'Jesus ben Joseph' again?[56]) and 'the Sages calculated' his age at 'two years, six months, six and a half hours'.

Not only have we already shown in this period the relationship of all such allusions to Abraham's intended sacrifice of Isaac to the ethos of the *Sicarii* suicide on Masada – itself clearly being reinforced by this episode, as we contend it is by the same example, evoked in James 2:21–4, of Abraham offering up Isaac, 'being justified by works' thereby and 'called a Friend of God' – but the story concludes, both realistically and pathetically, 'a few days later' when 'the woman became demented and fell from a roof. Furthermore, at this point a '*Bat Chol*' (Heavenly Voice) issues forth, quoting Psalm 113:7–8 about 'raising the Poor from the dust and setting him up among Princes' (another 'Ebionite' text also quoted, as we shall see below, in the War Scroll in its exegesis of the Messianic 'Star Prophecy'[57]), and, once again, 'the Holy Spirit cries out (as, indeed, it perhaps should), 'For these things I weep'!

Of course, the tender pathos of the story of Zadok's two children as slaves in Rome, finding each other and dying in each other's arms, is surpassed in its effectiveness only by the Old Testament Joseph story, the Recognition theme of which is analogous (as it is in the Pseudoclementine *Recognitions*), though the outcome less tragic – obviously the times were less brutal. Whatever one's religious orientation, historically speaking it, has to be admitted that this Talmudic story is more convincing, at least as a representative picture of its times and the suffering endured, than any comparable story in the Gospels or Acts about 'Heavenly Voices' crying out about human affairs, e.g., those depicting 'the Holy Spirit' (also a set piece of this story) descending on Jesus 'as a dove' while 'a voice out of Heaven' cried out, 'This is my beloved son. In him I am well-pleased' (Matthew 3:16–17 and pars.), to say nothing of the other 'Voice' out of Heaven in Acts 10:11–16 announcing concerning forbidden foods, dietary regulations, and 'table fellowship', 'Arise Peter, kill and eat'!

But this, of course, is a matter of artistic taste and we are, once more, back in the contrasting worlds of Talmudic physicality and this-worldly quasi-realism and the New Testament one of other-worldly idealization and incorruptibility or, what in some vocabularies would be called, 'spiritualization' or 'Hellenization'. For the present writer, this episode, so tragically recorded in the Talmud, is real in the sense it represents what could have and, doubtlessly, did happen; the other being more in the nature of romanticization or mythologization in the manner of the foregoing Greco-Roman man-god traditions or retrospective theological polemics, completely unaffected by and casting a cold eye on these too-tragic times.

The Herodian Fortress of Machaeros in Perea just across the Dead Sea from Qumran and above the hot spring at Callirhoe, where John the Baptist was taken and executed by Herod the Tetrarch.

The ramp the Romans built using Jewish prisoners as slave-labor to finally take Masada from the 'Sicarii Essenes' in 73 CE, three years after the fall of the Temple, but not before all its inhabitants committed suicide.

Chapter 10
Rabbi Eliezer's Bad Breath and Lazarus' Stinking Body

Martha's Demise, the Fall of Jerusalem, and Levirate Marriage

So famous was the demise of 'Martha the daughter of Boethus' that there is yet one more story about her precipitous fall now, with even more tragic overtones. Picking up from the 'casting out' by Rabbi Zadok of the already-chewed fig-shred fibers, *Gittin* now quotes this final tradition as follows: 'When Martha was about to die, she brought out all her gold and silver (cf. James 5:3 on the 'gold and silver' of the Rich) and *cast it* into the street, saying "What good is this to me," thus giving effect to the verse, "They shall cast their silver into the streets (Ezekiel 7:19)."'[1] Here we have the *pro forma* reinforcement by a scriptural proof-text as well as another variation of Matthew 27:3–5's version of Judas Iscariot's demise, which we have already characterized as both derivative and malicious.

Not only does the Talmud identify this Martha as one of the Richest women in Jerusalem, but in Tractate *Yebamoth* she is pictured as paying a bribe (another favorite theme in New Testament recounting), seemingly to Agrippa II – called in the tradition 'King Yannai', the last Herodian King before the destruction of the Temple. It would appear that this was not simply to have her husband – again, Josephus' friend Jesus ben Gamala – appointed High Priest (c. 64 CE), but also to circumvent the normal levirate-marriage waiting period – she apparently having already been 'a Rich widow' once before – so that he could, in line with her family's traditional High-Priestly status, then be appointed High Priest. Here, too, just as in New Testament reporting, the Rabbis speak in terms of there being 'a conspiracy' to secure his appointment and circumvent Mishnaic Law forbidding the consummation of such a marriage on the part of a High Priest – to say nothing of the implication of there actually having been a bribe.[2]

In the description of this bribe to Agrippa II, the nephew of Herodias and brother to and alleged consort of the infamous Bernice, the amount is put at 'a *tarkab*' or 'a measure of *dinar*s' – approximately two bushels. Not only do we have here the '*dinar*' theme again, but it is not unlike the 'hundred measures (*cors*) of wheat' in the Lukan Parable of the Unrighteous Steward and the 'litra' or 'measure of precious ointment of pure spikenard' in John 12:3's 'Mary sister of Martha'/'Judas Iscariot' remonstrations. Nor is this to mention 'Nicodemus' bearing the 'hundred litra measure of myrrh and aloes' in John 19:39's later portrayal of the ministrations surrounding Jesus' burial.

In Tractate *Yoma*, all this is further reinforced (and with it, the parallel with Gospel portraiture) by the statement recorded in the name of Rabbi Yohanan ben Torta, 'And why all that, because they bought the (High) Priestly Office for money',[3] though in *Kethuboth*, as we saw, at a seemingly later time she is also trying to recover her marital-contract security, which was a very high one.[4] Therefore, to close this subject, not only do we again have the language of the Judas Iscariot affair, both in the matter of the 'bribe' of 'thirty pieces of silver' (in Matthew 27:6, designated as 'the price of blood') and the related sum of the 'three hundred dinars' of his and others' complaints over 'the Poor', but also in the fact of the direct designation of the money involved as a 'bribe'. In this convergence of motifs from these parallel, contemporary traditions, despite the disparity of their two sets of contexts, there is also just the faintest indication of the 'High Priests' and either their involvement or that of their 'Office' in the situation in some way.

Of course in the Talmudic traditions, the motives are quite different and, more in line with the Rabbinic generally, quite mundane or material, having to do, for instance, with bypassing Levirate marriage-rule maneuvering or recovering marital-contract surety in the face of one's own or one's family's economic situation having suffered a disastrous collapse, while in Gospel portraits the point is always the same: to portray those making or accepting such bribes as conniving at or bringing the blundering or incompetent Roman Authorities around to schemes for the execution of Jesus as 'the Messiah' or 'the Christ'.

This is to say nothing of how Martha's silver in *Gittin* is at the time of her death 'being cast into the streets' and not into the Temple or its Treasury, as in Judas Iscariot's supposed action and the reaction to it of these same High Priests, as pictured in Matthew 27:5–7. To add to this, there is the matter of Matthew 27:9 supposedly quoting 'the Prophet Jeremiah' – when in reality he is paraphrasing Zechariah – to characterize these events as a fulfillment of prophecy; while here *Gittin* is accurately quoting Ezekiel 7:19 and applying it to the analogous matter of Martha's 'gold and silver' being 'cast into the street'. Such a citation contributes the noteworthy additional implication of connecting the first fall of the Temple to the second, which is exactly the way the Damascus Document will handle similar passages in Ezekiel we shall consider in due course below.[5]

To extend these New Testament parallels just a little further into the presentation of the story of John the Baptist: in the Mishnah, the implications are that the 'bribe' allowed Martha to bypass normal 'levirate' marriage restrictions in order to marry Jesus ben Gamala since, as we just suggested, she seems to have been 'a widow' – that is, her first husband had apparently already died. In such a situation, the theme of 'levirate marriage' and/or the bypassing of the regulations concerning it makes sense, whereas in the Gospel variation of it – in the matter of John the Baptist's objections to Herodias' remarriage – it does not. The reason was that Josephus explicitly noted that Philip 'died childless' which specifically means that Herod Antipas could very well have been seen as raising up seed unto his brother had he married Philip's wife. Moreover, since he did not and since this Philip's wife was not Herodias but, in fact, Herodias' daughter Salome, none of it makes any sense whatsoever and, in the writer's view – as we see these cross-currents in thematic materials developing – most of it was drawn and rewritten from either improperly-digested or refurbished Rabbinic materials of the kind we have just set forth above anyhow.[6]

However this may be, it is doubtful whether levirate marriage even entered into the affair where pseudo or questionable Jews such as the Herodians were concerned, but then the Gospel writers, operating from the sources we are trying to delineate and in an overseas context, were presumably unaware of the opposition to 'niece marriage', 'divorce', 'polygamy', and 'marriage with close family cousins' in the Scroll documents. All of these, as we have been emphasizing, figured prominently in Herodian marital practices and were apparently the issues between such Herodians and teachers like John the Baptist and the 'other' Simon who wanted to bar Herodians from the Temple as foreigners, which is to say nothing of their 'uncleanness' as a result of all these behavioral patterns and concerning which, of course, Peter learns just the opposite in Jesus' admonishment of him in Matthew 15:15–20. In any event, as Josephus tells us, Philip never was married to Herodias, but rather to Salome her daughter.

Again, a footnote to all this is that Jesus ben Gamala whom Boethus' daughter Martha appears so desperately to have wished to marry and Josephus seems to have so loved, is killed alongside and in the same manner as the individual responsible for James' death, Ananus ben Ananus. The persons responsible for these deaths are those Josephus is now formally willing to designate 'Zealots' (he had not, as already underscored, used the terminology as such previously – only *Sicarii*[7]) and their 'Idumaean' supporters. In other words, in such a context both groups (the so-called 'Zealots' and 'the Idumaeans') would appear to be taking vengeance for the death of James.

In fact, this killing causes Josephus to forget his previous apparent rancor towards Ananus and rail against the 'Zealots', in particular, in the most intemperate manner conceivable. In excoriating the 'Impiety' of those who flung the naked corpses of these two High Priests outside the city without burial as food for jackals, he also makes the point that seems to have wound up – like so many of these other notices – as part of the narrative in the Gospel of John, that is, that so scrupulous were the Jews in burial of the dead that they never even left the corpses of those who were crucified 'hanging up' on the crosses past nightfall – though as John 19:32 frames this, it was rather on account of 'the Sabbath' ('a High Holy Day') that they did this.[8]

Martha 'Casts her Gold and Silver into the Streets' and R. Yohanan is 'not Pierced'

Before proceeding along these lines further, it would be well to go back to *Gittin*'s descriptions of 'Ben Zizzit' where it was claimed that he derived his name from, not only the 'seat' or 'cushions' he sat upon or 'his fringes' which 'trailed on cushions' (*keset*), but also because 'his seat ('*kiseh*' playing off '*keset*') was among the Great Ones of Rome'. Though here in *Gittin* 'he sits among the Great Ones' or 'Nobility of Rome', in the *ARN*, as will be recalled, 'he used to recline on a silver couch before the Great Ones of Israel' (once again, one should pay attention to the constant allusion to 'silver'), both make it seem that 'Ben Zizzit' was perhaps a derogatory expression for one or another of the Herodians – possibly Agrippa II, since his father Agrippa I was probably too respected in Rabbinic tradition to be characterized in such a manner.[9] However ludicrous traditions such as these may appear on the surface, all do display a certain peculiar, native Palestinian playfulness, as we have been underscoring, punning on the Hebrew for terms like 'seat', 'cushions', or 'couch'.

Directly following these expositions of Ben Zizzit's name, *Gittin* goes on to tell its stories about 'Martha the daughter of Boethus' (unlike Lamentations *Rabbah* it gets the patronym right), a name that time and time again inevitably seems to bring us back, as we have been suggesting, to the Gospel of John's stories about Lazarus' two sisters, Mary and Martha and, in particular, the preciousness of the 'measure' or 'weight of ointment of pure spikenard' they used to minister either to Jesus' 'head' or 'his feet'. It is in illustrating how far Martha had sunk from her previous high station that *Gittin* gives us its version of the episode – also remarked, as we have seen, by Josephus – of how 'the Zealots' had burned all the stores of wheat and barley.[10] This is the background it uses to illustrate how out of utter desperation, because there was no grain left in the market, 'she took off her shoes', apparently because she didn't want to get them (the 'shoes') dirty in the mud, whereupon the 'dung stuck to her foot and she died'.[11]

In *ARN*, interestingly, the same story is told about how 'the Zealots' burned all the grain in Jerusalem or 'mixed it with mud' – this time directly connected to the name of Ben Kalba Sabu'a and the one about how, if 'one came to his door hungry as a dog, one went away filled'.[12] Furthermore, not only is it explicitly connected to his 'twenty-one' or 'twenty-two years' of grain storage for Jerusalem, but also that of the themes of 'the loaves' and 'dung'/'excrement' as well. This is achieved by having 'the Zealots' use 'the loaves' which Ben Kalba Sabu'a had baked for all the citizens of Jerusalem and 'brick up the walls with them'. Then, directly following this, another story connected with the city's fall about how, 'when Vespasian examined the dung of the besieged men', who were by this time (because of the famine and because 'the Zealots' had burned all Ben Kalba Sabu'a's stores) eating nothing but straw, 'and saw that it was without a trace of barley or corn, he said to his soldiers': 'If these men who eat nothing but straw can kill so many of you, how many more of you would they kill if they were to eat and drink like you?'

It is at this point, too, that *Gittin* then launches into its climactic story about Martha, the one we have been following about how, when she 'was about to die, she brought out all her gold and silver and cast it into the street', thereby fulfilling the prophecy from Ezekiel 7:19

about the destruction of Jerusalem and the fall of the (First) Temple and how the people would then have to 'cast their silver into the streets'. Of course, not only do we have the tragedy being so graphically illustrated by all events connected with these times (except in the Gospels, where it takes second place to other considerations), but the fact that the fall of the First Temple is being echoed in these traditions connected to the fall of the Second.

Of course, too, this story is certainly echoed, as we have been at pains to point out, by the one found in the Gospels about Judas Iscariot 'casting down (his) pieces of silver into the Temple', itself supposed to be a variation of Zechariah 11:12–13's 'casting (his) silver to the silversmiths'. Not only does the 'silver'/'silversmith' motif, in turn, find an echo in the *ARN*'s *Sisit Hakkeset* 'sitting on silver cushions', as already highlighted too, but also in the 'twelve thousand silver dinar' value of the bedspread Nakdimon's daughter Miriam used or the 'twelve talents of silver' he promised to pay the foreign lord as surety for his 'twelve water cisterns'.[13]

In *Gittin*, these notices are immediately followed again, not surprisingly, by another about 'the *Sicarii*' referred to as 'the *Biryonim*' and, picking up this theme of the destruction of Jerusalem, then moving into another series of stories about R. Eliezer ben Hyrcanus, R. Yohanan ben Zacchai, the Romans, the destruction of the Temple, and ultimately, once more, even R. Akiba.[14] But the sequence is parallel and worth remarking since, just as the Gospels connect their 'Judas Iscariot' 'casting his silver into the Temple' to the destruction of Jesus (in Paul in 1 Corinthians 3:9–17 and 12:14–27, Matthew 26:61, and Mark 14:58 *equivalent to the Temple*), so too *Gittin* connects Martha's 'casting her silver into the streets' of Jerusalem with its stories about 'the *Biryonim*' (its '*Sicarii*') and their direct role in bringing on the destruction of Jerusalem.

The story *Gittin* is telling, also recorded in Lamentations *Rabbah* in even more detail, is about 'Abba Sikkra' (in the Lamentations and Ecclesiastes *Rabbah* tradition, 'Ben Battiah'[15]), the head of the *Sicarii* or '*Biryonim* in Jerusalem' and 'the son of the sister of Rabbi Yohanan ben Zacchai' – that is, Rabbi Yohanan's nephew. Even Abba Sikkra's name here implies a connection to such '*Sicarii*'. This is also basically made explicit in Ecclesiastes *Rabbah* where the corruption '*Kisrin*' – not unlike similar corruptions such as '*Iscariot*' – has manifestly been substituted for '*Sikrin*' (cf. the village, called in some traditions 'Sihnin', seemingly in Galilee, where James' stand-in 'Jacob' – who tells Rabbi Eliezer the story about 'the High Priests' latrine' – comes from).[16]

When Rabbi Yohanan sends for his nephew and berates him for 'killing all the People with starvation' (because of having earlier burned all the stores), R. Yohanan requests a plan from him to enable him to escape from Jerusalem. His nephew then recommends he escape by means of a casket, presumably the only way out of the city at the time – i.e., to be or pretend to be dead. This 'Abba Sikkra', a pseudonym if ever there was one, then tells him to even 'bring something that smells putrid' and put it in the coffin so people would think he is dead.[17] The reader will immediately recognize the 'putrid smelling' or 'stink' motif of John 11:39's depiction of Lazarus' corpse ('four days in the grave' according to Martha), to say nothing of 'the dung' Rabbi Eliezer puts in his mouth so that his breath will smell 'putrid', we have already mentioned previously, but will have cause to discuss more definitively below.

In another such story about 'privies', illustrating the *physicality* of Rabbinic tradition as opposed to the ofttimes extreme *spirituality* of the Greek, it is related that the heroic Rabbi Akiba, Rabbi Eliezer's student in the next generation, once followed Rabbi Joshua (Jesus?) 'into the privy to see how he conducted himself' and observed that, 'entering sideways, he exposed himself only after he sat down and wiped himself (too) only after he had sat down and this solely with the left hand' (a practice still followed throughout the Middle East to this day).[18]

However this may be, going back to R. Yohanan, when the guards at the gate want to 'pierce his casket with a lance' (to make sure who or what was inside was dead), his Disciples in consternation prevent them, saying, 'Shall (the Romans) say, they have *pierced our Master*?' The guards then open the gates and allow the entourage to pass unimpeded and R. Yohanan goes on – not unlike Jesus both in Gospel 'Little Apocalypse' and Matthew 24:2's 'not one stone upon another that shall not be cast down' passages – to evoke a passage from Isaiah 10:34, 'Lebanon shall fall by a Mighty One', to predict Jerusalem's imminent downfall. In doing so, since passages such as this, employing exactly the same 'Lebanon' imagery in multiple contexts, are extant and expounded at Qumran, he thereby solidifies the First Century CE *sitz-im-leben* of all these types of 'Lebanon shall fall by a Mighty One' allusions as relating to the Temple and the First Century CE ambiance of this fall and another hotly-vexed problem in the field of Qumran Studies is basically solved.[19]

This story itself also has a clear counterpart and possible parody in John 19:34's famous picture of a Roman soldier '*piercing* (Jesus') side with a lance'. Once again John, to say nothing of Luke and the others, certainly seems to be showing knowledge of or contact with – even perhaps dependency upon – the kind of allusions one finds in curious Talmudic traditions of this kind. Certainly Luke does in his portrait of the 'Rich Man dressed in purple' and 'Poor Lazarus' with 'his sores licked by dogs' at 'his doorstep' – but so, in our view, do the other Gospels in their various 'raising', 'curing', 'feeding', 'basket-filling', 'grain' and 'loaves'-multiplication, 'feet-kissing', 'hair-wiping', 'spikenard ointment', and 'Disciples' stories we have so often been highlighting above.

But the Scriptural warrant John quotes for this is, once again (as in Matthew 27:3–10 above in Judas Iscariot 'casting the thirty pieces of silver into the Temple') a passage again from Zechariah – this time Zechariah 12:10, 'they shall look upon him whom they pierced'. Curiously the proof-text quoted with it in John 19:36 is from Exodus 12:46, 'not a bone of it (that is, the lamb) shall be broken', which has to do with eating the paschal meal and again referencing the matter of taking Jesus' body down from the cross before nightfall without 'breaking his legs'. But here the resemblance ends. In the context in Exodus, it is preceded in 12:43–45 and followed in 12:48 by an *absolute insistence on circumcision* and 'no foreigner who is not circumcised' taking part in such a ceremonial meal. To be sure, this is the very opposite of the way John, the other Gospels, and, of course, Paul insist on putting such passages to use, but anything goes where the use of Philo's method of 'allegorical interpretation of Scripture' as applied to the purported 'Passion of the Christ' is concerned.

'Lebanon shall Fall by a Mighty One', the Branch of David, and the Messiah of Righteousness

Notwithstanding, the passage R. Yohanan is pictured as using here, 'And Lebanon shall fall by a Mighty One' from Isaiah 10:34, has since turned up among Qumran proof-texts known as '*Pesharim*' (Commentaries). There, while baffling to so many Qumran scholars, the exegesis is similar to what we have in Tractate *Gittin*, in which Rabbi Yohanan specifically asserts that 'Lebanon' – no doubt implying not only the white linen worn by the Priests in the Temple, but also its woodwork made of cedar from Lebanon – refers to the Temple'!

Interesting, too, the same proof-text turns up in the parallel version of these events, the *ARN* – as, in fact, it does in Lamentations *Rabbah*.[20] There, in *ARN*, a whole series of such 'Lebanon' and 'cedar-wood' proof texts, for the most part from Zechariah 11:1–3, are specifically denoted as referring to the Temple and, in particular, its fall in 70 CE. Passages such as 'wail O cypress tree, for the cedar tree is fallen' and 'the strong forest has come down' from Zechariah 11:2 in this list are expressly characterized as 'referring to the Temple'. Likewise, Zechariah 11:1, 'Open your doors, O Lebanon, that the fire may consume your cedars', is graphically interpreted as 'the High Priests in the Temple taking their keys' as 'unworthy custodians' and 'throwing them into the sky to the Holy One, the Master of the Universe'.

Here the 'white' implicit in the Hebrew of the designation 'Lebanon' clearly refers to the 'white garments' of the Temple Priests – just as, for instance, it does in the Habakkuk *Pesher* of 'Lebanon' as 'the Community Council', presumably because of their 'white linen garments'.[21] Not only is this identity made explicit in the latter, but it should also not be forgotten that in the Community Rule – as to some extent in Paul in 1 Corinthians 12:12–27 – 'the Community Council' functions as or is esoterically identical with the Temple. Furthermore, it is seen as 'atoning for sin' that 'they may obtain Loving-kindness for the Land without the flesh of holocausts and the fat of sacrifices'.[22]

Not only shall we encounter this same 'Loving-kindness' or '*Hesed*' below in the material about R. Joshua's 'woes' that precedes the citation of these 'Lebanon' passages in the *ARN* where R. Joshua, following R. Yohanan out of the city and on 'seeing it in ruins', cries out 'woe' (here, of course, Jesus' 'woes' in Matthew 23:12–24:19, both in the Temple and upon leaving it, when looking back at Jerusalem and predicting its destruction – as well those in 'the Little Apocalypse') and R. Yohanan consoles his Disciple by quoting Hosea 6:6 on 'desiring Loving-kindness and not sacrifice', upon which the above passage from the Community Rule is based; but elsewhere it is rather stated that the reason 'Lebanon' stands for the Temple was that 'there Israel's sins were made white'.[23]

While this last explanation is perhaps typical of Rabbinic passivity, it does throw light on the curious allusion to being 'made white' we encountered in the matter of 'the tombs of the two brothers' in the Pseudoclementine *Recognitions* that 'miraculously whitened of themselves every year', presumably meaning on Yom Kippur or perhaps in some more recondite manner. That this passage from Zechariah 11:1, 'Open your doors, O Lebanon, that the fire may devour you', refers to the coming destruction of the Temple is also made clear in *Yoma* which also cites three other 'Lebanon' passages as referring in some manner to the Temple as well, viz., Psalm 72:16, Nahum 1:4 (also extant and expounded at Qumran where 'Lebanon' again gives every indication of being either 'the Temple' or 'the Community Council'), and Isaiah 35:2.[24]

While the presentation in the *ARN* – like the one in *Gittin* and Lamentations *Rabbah* – knows the names of Rabbi Yohanan's two Disciples (R. Eliezer and R. Joshua), unlike either of those accounts, it makes no mention of his nephew 'Abba Sikkra' or 'Ben Battiah', nor of 'the *Biryonim*' he leads, nor even the matter of Rabbi Yohanan's body 'not being pierced'. For Lamentations *Rabbah*, which basically reproduces the same story (though it divides 'Nakdimon ben Gurion' into two separate 'Councilors', 'Ben Nakdimon' and 'Ben Gurion' – thus! – and for it, the 'woe' will rather be the one R. Yohanan exclaims, not his acolyte R. Joshua), these events all occur 'three days' after 'Ben Battiah ('Abba Sikkra' in *Gittin*) burned all the stores'. For it too, it is R. Yohanan, not Vespasian, who sees the people virtually reduced to starvation when he witnesses them 'seething straw', presumably to distill its substance into juice and, at this point, it is he that pronounces the 'woe' (which, however, because of his nephew's objections, he claims was rather 'wah' – again more Rabbinic tragic comedy or, should we say, even slapstick?). In its version of events, it is Ben Battiah then, who leads R. Yohanan's coffin out of the city while R. Eliezer and R. Joshua, carrying the head and the feet, bring up the rear. Furthermore, it is he who prevents the Jewish Guards, not the Romans, from 'piercing the body of (their) Master' in order to determine if he was really dead![25]

All three, however, then go on to picture R. Yohanan as evoking and applying, 'He shall cut down the thickets of the forest with iron and Lebanon shall fall by a Mighty One' of Isaiah 10:34 to Vespasian, either hailing him obsequiously as a kind of reverse Messiah and foreseeing his imminent appointment as King or Emperor.[26] At Qumran, as already remarked, while the extant *Pesher* on Isaiah 10:34 is unfortunately fragmentary at this point, it does seem to be just the reverse of these Rabbinic texts and Josephus, and the 'Mighty One' appears to refer to a Jewish Messiah – 'the cutting down of the thickets of the forest' and 'the tallest of the lofty ones' to 'the Army of the Kittim'. Nevertheless, in the writer's view, what cannot be denied is that all are referring in this period to the fall of the Temple in 70 CE – Josephus and the Rabbinic from a more pessimistic point-of-view; the one at Qumran, just the opposite.

Josephus, in fact, does testify to precisely this state of affairs at the end of the *Jewish War* when he provides what he considers to be the authentic exegesis of 'the World Ruler Prophecy' (seemingly this prophecy from Isaiah 10:34 combined with Numbers 24:17), applying it – as already underscored as well and like the Rabbinic – to Vespasian as opposed to those more misguided persons of his own race who considered it applied to 'one of their own' (*sic!*).[27] For its part, Lamentations *Rabbah* even portrays R. Yohanan as crying out – as Josephus himself earlier seems to have done – presumptuously and obsequiously, '*Vive Domine Imperator*' – 'Long live the Lord Emperor'! Note here, in particular, how this flies in the face of Josephus' own picture of either 'the Zealots' or 'the Essenes' as 'refusing to call any man, Lord'.[28] Of course, this is wildly inaccurate or, at least anachronistic, since by this time in 70 CE, Vespasian had already departed for Rome.[29] He did so the year before – 'the Year of the Three Emperors' – in 68–69 CE – leaving the siege of Jerusalem in the hands of his son Titus, ably assisted by his second-in-command, Philo's nephew, the ever-present ideal Roman bureaucrat, Tiberius Alexander and other nefarious types, such as Josephus himself, Agrippa II, and his sister Bernice, who make their appearance at the climax of Acts 25:13–26:32. Of course, Josephus, probably more accurately, actually did by his own testimony apply 'the World Ruler Prophecy' to Vespasian in Galilee in 67 CE after his own ignominious surrender there and it is upon this that these Rabbinic stories are probably based.[30]

The same prophecy is extant, as we just saw as well, along with others involving 'Lebanon' from Isaiah 14:8 and 29:17 but, because of the poor state of its (their) preservation, the interpretation is obscure. Nevertheless, the one from Isaiah 10:34 (the ones from Isaiah 14:8 and 29:17 are too damaged to tell – but, as in the Rabbinical to say nothing of the Gospels above, they are combined with material from Zechariah, evidently 3:9 and 11:1) clearly refers to 'the *Kittim*' as 'Conquerors' and its interpretation either parallels or, with more justice, anticipates the Talmudic though, seemingly, from the opposite point-of-view as just described.

Notwithstanding, just as in *ARN*, it is immediately followed by the celebrated passage from Isaiah 11:1–5 about 'a Shoot coming forth from the Stem of Jesse and a Branch growing out of his Roots' which makes the whole *Pesher* even more Messianic. Furthermore, the exegesis is also aggressively Messianic, that is, it is interpreted in terms of the 'standing up' or 'arising in the Last Days' of 'the Branch of David' – meaning, in the traditional sense, a singular Davidic Messiah – to whom God was going to grant 'a Throne of Glory and a Crown of Holiness'.[31] As per Isaiah 11:4 – and, as it were, Numbers 24:17 ('the Star Prophecy') – he was going to '*smite his enemies*' with 'the Scepter' or 'Rod of his mouth'/'the Spirit of his lips' and 'rule over all the Nations', 'judging all the Peoples' ('*Amim*') with 'his sword'.

Not only should one compare this with Matthew 10:34's 'I have *come* not to bring Peace *but a sword*', but it is fiercely and apocalyptically Messianic linking up with the text Michael Wise and myself originally found in 1990 about 'the Branch of David', which we called 'The Messianic Leader' or '*Nasi ha-'Edah*'.[32] This text, which was only a fragment, also evoked Isaiah 10:34, alluding *inter alia* to both 'woundings'/'piercings' and 'the Kittim', and, in the spirit of Isaiah 11:4 to follow, probably referring to 'judging the Peoples with the sword of his mouth'.

As we shall see in due course, this *Nasi ha-'Edah* will appear in Ms. A of the Damascus Document where he will again be identified as 'the Scepter who will stand up' or 'arise out of Israel' of Numbers 24:17, who 'will smite all the sons of Seth' (a synonym clearly for 'the Evil Ones'/'the Kittim'/or 'the Enemies of God' of the Isaiah *Peshers*, et al.).

In turn, in the Genesis *Pesher* (in our publication of it we called it, with a nod to John Allegro, 'The Genesis *Florilegium*'), in exposition of 'the Shiloh Prophecy' of Genesis 49:10–11, both 'the Scepter' and 'the Branch of David' are once again evoked and now, for the first time, the all-important Messianic 'feet'. Moreover, because of the curious allusion in it to 'tethering his donkey' or 'the colt of its she-donkey', it is probably also being evoked in all four Gospels in Jesus' Messianic entry into Jerusalem (Matthew 21:1–11 and pars.).[33]

In it, too, 'the Staff' (*Mehokkek*) is pictured as being 'between the Shiloh's *feet*' and interpreted as 'the Covenant of the Kingdom'. In Ms. A of the Damascus Document, as we shall see below, it will be 'the Interpreter' or '*Doresh ha-Torah*' who 'went out from the Land of Judah' to 'dig the Well of Living Waters in the Land of Damascus' of Numbers 21:18 – 'the Instrument for His works' of Isaiah 54:16 and 'the Star' evoked along with 'the Scepter' in Numbers 24:17 and, as we shall see, the Messianic *Florilegium* as well. It is worth remarking as well that 'Shiloh' is also designated as 'the name of the Messiah' in the various Messianic allusions that follow the evocation of the 'Lebanon' quote from Isaiah 10:34 in Lamentations *Rabbah* above.[34]

But here in the Genesis *Pesher*, both 'the Scepter' and 'the Branch of David' are distinctly identified with 'the Messiah of Righteousness', who in turn is identified with 'the coming of the Shiloh', to whom and to whose 'seed' 'the Covenant of the Kingdom of His People' was given 'unto Eternal generations because he kept the *Torah*' – 'keeping' being the basis of the definition, as we have seen, of the Sons of Zadok at Qumran. However these things may be and whatever the reader may make of the final meaning of these things, the reader should appreciate that 'the Branch of David' being referred to in these Isaiah and Genesis *Peshers* is certainly also the same as 'the *Nasi ha-'Edah*' in both the famous fragment above most now consider an addition to the War Scroll, and in the Damascus Document's exposition of 'the Scepter' from 'the Star Prophecy', not to mention the language used on the coinage from the period of the Bar Kochba War (132–36 CE) in the denotation there of 'Bar Kochba'/'the Star' as 'the *Nasi*-Israel'.[35] To complete the circle, 'the Scepter' and its analogue, 'the Branch of David', now turn up in these Messianic allusions from Isaiah 10:21–11:5 in the various versions of the Isaiah *Pesher*, so we clearly really do have here a circle of Messianic allusions.

Rabbi Yohanan and Rabbi Joshua's 'Woes' and Rabbi Eliezer's 'Putrid Breath' Again

Therefore when R. Yohanan applies 'the Mighty One' terminology of Isaiah 10:34 to, however improbably, Vespasian in the various Rabbinic milieux above as well, the implication is that he also is somewhat disingenuously applying 'the Star' or 'Shiloh' Prophecies to him as did Josephus. This story as the *ARN* presents it, while not paralleled in *Gittin*, is however with slight modifications to be found in Lamentations *Rabbah* and, to some extent, in Ecclesiastes *Rabbah*, though in these, as already remarked, it is R. Yohanan who is exclaiming 'woe' because of his nephew (Ben Battiah), who has burned the storehouses, condemning the people to starvation.

This parallels the much longer series of 'woes' we saw Jesus making in the Temple in the Gospel of Matthew 23:13–38 (though not in the other three), ending in the clearly retrospective reproof, 'Jerusalem, Jerusalem, which kills the Prophets' and the additional – equally retrospective – prognostication, 'your house (will) be left desolate unto you'. In Luke, these 'woes' come earlier in 11:46–52, after Jesus visits Martha's house, when another 'certain Pharisee' had invited him to dine with him and noticed 'he had not first washed before eating' (11:38). The parallel to this was clearly the 'unwashed hands'/'Traditions of the Elders' material in Matthew 15:1–20 and Mark 7:1-23, also in response to 'the Pharisees and some of the Scribes from Jerusalem' (i.e., the James Party), when Jesus – in attacking the Pharisees as 'Blind Guides' – expounded the 'Toilet Bowl' Parable for Peter's benefit.

It is following this extensive list of 'woes' in Matthew 23 that Jesus, upon leaving Jerusalem and the Temple and turning back – just as R. Yohanan and his Disciple, R. Joshua – to look at it, pronounced the devastating prediction, 'There shall not be left here one stone upon stone that shall not be thrown down' (Matthew 24:1–2 and pars.), before proceeding to the Mount of Olives to set forth 'the Little Apocalypse' in all three Synoptics. Of course for the *ARN*, as opposed to both Lamentations and Ecclesiastes *Rabbah*, it is R. Joshua ('Jesus' and 'Joshua' being analogues) who, when looking back at the Temple and seeing it in ruins, utters his own mournful 'woe', and it is at this point that R. Yohanan (not Ben Battiah who rebukes him) is rather comforting his Disciple at the sight they are now both witnessing by evoking Hosea 6:6, that is, it is 'Mercy' or 'Loving-kindness' (literally, '*Hesed*'/'Piety') which the Lord 'desires, not sacrifice' – then going on to counsel him that he should now pray three times a day as Daniel had done in Babylon (Daniel 6:1)![36]

Following this and his application of Isaiah 10:34's 'Lebanon shall fall by a Mighty One' to Vespasian and his rise to power, *ARN* even depicts the Romans as 'catapulting a pig's head' into the Temple upon its altar, not unlike the report of some modern military tactics today. In fact in *Gittin*, R. Yohanan is portrayed as obsequiously characterizing this rise to power by Vespasian as 'the Good News'/'the Gospel' and quoting Scripture, Proverbs 15:30: 'Good News fattens the bone', as applying to it![37] Moreover, before his application of the other 'Lebanon' and 'cedar tree' passages – including that of Zechariah 11:1–3 on 'Lebanon opening (its) doors so fire might consume ('eat') its cedars' – both to it and the fall of the Temple, *ARN* also pictures R. Yohanan as sitting and waiting, trembling by the side of the road, as Eli had done 'for the ark of the Lord' in 1 Samuel 4:13, when he and his Disciples hear that 'Jerusalem was destroyed and the Temple in flames', whereupon 'they tore their clothes, wept, and cried aloud in mourning' (i.e., the first note of 'Mourning for Zion').

Not only do these speeches by R. Yohanan parallel what Jesus is supposed to have said about 'there shall not be left here one stone upon stone (of the Temple) that shall not be thrown down' (Matthew 24:1–2 and pars.) when he and his Disciples are leaving the Temple as well, but also another speech Jesus is pictured as making in Matthew 26:61 and Mark 14:58 before 'the Chief Priests, the Elders, and the whole Sanhedrin' about 'being able to destroy the Temple of God and in three days build it up'. The application of Isaiah 10:34 and Zechariah 11:1–3 in these Rabbinic traditions to these pivotal events and their picture of R. Yohanan's appearance before the Emperor-to-be – either Vespasian or his son Titus (Talmudic tradition is really unable to distinguish between historical points as fine as these) – must also have included 'the Star Prophecy'.

This picture of R. Yohanan (after his humiliating escape from Jerusalem) obsequiously applying these kinds of 'prophecy' to Vespasian's rise to power is, perhaps, more accurately linked to Josephus, who in the *Jewish War* had already explained how he used this precious oracle to predict Vespasian's coming elevation to Emperor and save, as it were, his own skin.[38] That this 'oracle' had to include, among other things, the prophecy that 'a world Ruler would come out of Palestine' seems to the author to be a given.

In the parallel and more detailed version of this encounter in Lamentations *Rabbah*, it is after R. Yohanan applies the passage from Proverbs 15:30 about 'the Good News fattening the bones' in it as well to Vespasian's elevation to Emperor that Vespasian asks him whether he has any other 'friend or relative' in Jerusalem he wished to save. Yohanan is then pictured as sending his 'two Disciples', R. Eliezer b. Hyrcanus and R. Joshua, back to Jerusalem to bring out Rabbi Zadok. Not only is this a parallel, should one choose to regard it, to John the Baptist sending his 'two Disciples' to Jesus in Luke 7:20/Matthew 11:2 to ask the Messianically-charged question, 'Are you *the one who is to come* or must we look for another?', but also the episode in all three Synoptics of Jesus sending his 'two Disciples' to find the 'ass tied and a colt along with her' in Matthew 21:1–11 and pars. Though paralleled in John 12:14, the note about the 'two Disciples' is missing and Jesus rather finds 'an ass' colt' himself. Nevertheless both it and Matthew 21:4 specify this episode as 'fulfilling that which was spoken by the Prophet'. Again, the language of 'the Prophet' should be familiar here, though this time he goes unnamed. However, the meaning clearly is Zechariah 9:9, actually quoted in Matthew 21:5, but also obviously the 'Shiloh' Prophecy of Genesis 49:11 as well.

Of course with regard to these ideas, *viz.*, 'a colt being tethered to the vine' of both Genesis 49:11 and the Gospels, the 'coming of the Messiah' alluded to in the query attributed to John and the ever-recurrent motif of the Messiah's 'feet', one should note the tradition in both Lamentations *Rabbah* and Song of Songs *Rabbah* interpreting the passage, 'He has spread a net for my feet', from Lamentations 1:13, in terms of 'seeing a colt tethered to a tree' and 'looking for the *feet of the Messiah*'.[39] Curiously, though these allusions have no apparent connection except an esoteric one, still in all these traditions – that is, Jesus' entry into Jerusalem, both the Nakdimon and 'Martha the daughter of Boethus' ones about 'woolen garments' or 'cushions' being spread beneath their 'feet', and now this one relating to 'looking for the Messiah's feet' from Lamentations and Song of Songs *Rabbah* – the motif of having 'garments spread beneath the feet' is conspicuous.

To go back to Rabbi Zadok: when Vespasian saw him, he was supposed to have wondered why Rabbi Yohanan would bother to bring out such an 'emaciated old man'. Whereupon Yohanan is pictured as responding, a little less obsequiously this time and in a variation of Vespasian's words in *ARN* on examining the dung of those besieged in Jerusalem and finding only straw in it, 'Two like him and you would have never taken Jerusalem even with double your Army.' It should be appreciated that here in Lamentations *Rabbah*, too, R. Yohanan himself sees the people in the market in Jerusalem 'seething straw and drinking its product', and it is this he takes as a sign to leave, asking 'can such men withstand the Armies of Vespasian'.

In parallel materials about Rabbi Yohanan in *Kethuboth*, he is once again pictured as we saw, like Jesus in reverse, 'leaving Jerusalem riding upon a donkey while his Disciples follow him'.[40] It is at this point that he was supposed to have encountered Nakdimon ben Gurion's daughter Miriam and now she is the one, as we saw, 'picking barley grains out of the dung of Arab cattle', not as in the tradition Lamentations *Rabbah* quotes in the name of R. Eleazar ben Zadok about Boethus' daughter Miriam 'picking barley grains among the horses hoofs at Acco'.

In Miriam's conversation now with R. Yohanan in *Kethuboth* (and not Rabbi Eleazar ben Zadok as later in *Kethuboth* and in Lamentations *Rabbah*) – whom she also addresses, as we saw, as 'Master' – the only thing she really requests of him (R. Yohanan), after 'standing up' and 'wrapping herself in her hair' (this, of course, the parallel to Lazarus' sister 'Mary' wiping Jesus' 'feet with her hair' in John 11:2 and 12:3, to say nothing of Luke 7:38's 'woman of the city, a Sinner, with the alabaster flask' wiping Jesus' 'feet with her hair'), is '*feed me*' (our 'dogs' or Ben Kalba Sabu'a's 'Poor'/'Lazarus under the table' language and that of other 'feeding' episodes we have already outlined so extensively above again?); however we are clearly dealing with the same episode.[41] It is here, too, that Rabbi Yohanan enters into his discourse on 'the Riches' of both Miriam's father's and father-in-law's houses, noting in an aside to his Disciples how the marriage contract he signed reckoned her surety at 'one million dinars' and comparing it, by implication, to the abject poverty of her present fallen status.

In fact, *Kethuboth* again does not specifically name 'the daughter of Nakdimon ben Gurion' in this episode, 'Miriam' or 'Mary', though we know this was her name, and, interestingly enough, it does not immediately follow this up with the variant tradition about Rabbi Eleazar ben Zadok that we just noted was found in Lamentations *Rabbah* as well, in which he too applied the verse from Song of Songs 1:8 to her pathetic condition after he sees her 'picking barley grains among the horses' feet at Acco'; but now we definitely are apprised that this is supposed to be 'Nakdimon's daughter'. Nor, in either of 'barefoot', as *Gittin* relates rather these traditions in *Kethuboth* or Lamentations *Rabbah*, is she explicitly going out of 'Boethus' daughter Martha' who died when 'some dung stuck to her foot'. There, it will be recalled, Rabbi Yohanan rather applied the verse from Deuteronomy 28:56 about 'the tender and delicate woman who would not set the sole of her foot upon the ground' to Boethus' daughter Martha's equally pathetic demise, a passage we have seen R. Eleazar ben Zadok apply in Lamentations *Rabbah* to 'Boethus' daughter Miriam'!) – she whom, after 'binding her hair to the tails of Arab horses', the Romans made 'run from Jerusalem to Lydda'.[42]

In a final passage relating to all these themes from Genesis *Rabbah*, already highlighted above and paralleled with only slight modifications in *ARN*, the 'dung' is now rather what R. Eliezer ben Hyrcanus puts into his mouth when still a ploughman with his brothers in his father's field, thus either purposefully or because her was hungry giving himself bad breath (more hyperbole).[43] He goes to study with R. Yohanan ben Zacchai, again probably in Lydda, and when this 'stench' is brought to the attention of 'the Master', R. Yohanan allegorizes it, characterizing his 'breath' as 'a *sweet fragrance*'. Not only are these the words applied to the 'Righteousness' of the Community Council in the Community Rule or by Paul to his colleague, Epaphroditus, in Philippians 4:18,[44] but R. Yohanan also provides the following exposition (already paraphrased above in the *ARN* version) of them: 'As the smell of (Rabbi Eliezer's) mouth became putrid for the sake of the *Torah*, so will the sweet fragrance of (his) learning become diffused from one end of the World to the other (*ARN* adds: 'because of his mastery of *Torah*').

First and foremost, it should be immediately plain that this is but a variation (or *vice versa*) of the famous Parable we have been analyzing in such detail above attributed to Jesus in which he rebukes either Peter or the Disciples as being 'so' or 'even yet without understanding' (Mark 7:17–18/Matthew 15:15–16). To paraphrase: 'A man is not known by what goes into the mouth. That cannot defile the man. But the things which go forth out of the mouth, they defile the man.' The language of both these expositions is almost completely parallel only, as usual, the Gospel version is 'cleaned up' as it were and made more elegant and less mundane.

Having said this, however, both Matthew and Mark still retain the rather coarse 'toilet bowl' metaphor, itself patently related to the motif of the 'dung' in *ARN* and Lamentations *Rabbah*. On the other hand, whereas in Mark 7:19 the aim of the Parable was to 'declare all foods clean', in Matthew it was to assert that 'eating with unwashed hands does not defile the man' (15:20). Nevertheless, it should be clear that both versions are totally antithetical to what the authors of the R. Yohanan anecdote had in mind, the thrust of which was to see the learning of *Torah* 'diffused from one end of the World to the other', which would have horrified both Matthew and Mark – and the other Gospels too for that matter.

First of all, not only is this another excellent example of ideological inversion or reversal, but it should be quite clear that there is borrowing going on here. The only problem is to determine in which direction the borrowing is taking place. The solution should be plain – borrowing, for the most part, goes from the more primitive to the more sophisticated or, if one wishes, from the more vulgar to the more polished or more elegant and rarely, if ever, the other way round – from the more sophisticated to the more primitive.

In this instance the Rabbinic is clearly the more primitive or more vulgar – the Gospel the more 'elegant' or, if one prefers, the more 'Hellenized'. In this case, anyhow, the Talmud's physicality rescues it from the charge of 'borrowing' and unfortunately, one can clearly envision the core of the ideological thrust of assertions of this kind emanating out of sophisticated circles on the highest cosmopolitan cultural level in either Alexandria or Rome – more likely the latter – but working off what 'they' would have seen as the more 'base' (that is, the more 'realistic' or 'crude') Judaic – meaning 'not idealized' – material.

Lazarus, Liezer, Amraphel, and Ephraim

But to go back to our other historical parallels – not only have we seen the same sort of 'stench' referred to in the story of the advice R. Yohanan's nephew 'Abba Sikkra' or 'Ben Battiah' ('the Head of the *Sicarii* of Jerusalem') gives R. Yohanan 'to put a clod of something smelling very putrid' into his coffin so people would think he was dead, but it also finds a reflection in both of John 11–12's Lazarus/Eliezer stories.

Though what we shall now summarize is, again, to a certain extent repetitious of previous material or what we have just pointed out in a secondary or more cursory manner in other contexts, it would be useful to review all this material about 'smells' or 'odors' one last and hopefully conclusive time. In so doing, at least these things will indelibly imprint themselves on the reader's consciousness (as they have the author's) and, as is often the case, some new insight might and, in this case, does emerge. In this type of study, such summations are necessary where the material is as complex as that before us.

Let us take the second passage from John 12:3–5 first: when Mary, Lazarus' sister, 'takes the pound (*litran*) of ointment of pure spikenard of great price' to anoint Jesus' 'feet and wipe them with her hair', the house was said to have 'been *filled* with (its) odor' or 'smell', that is, the sweet 'smell' of the pure 'perfume'. It is this 'litran' about which 'Judas the son' or 'brother of Simon Iscariot' (here, of course, the 'Abba Sikkra' parallels) complains, reckoning it at 'three hundred dinars'.

To press the point home and, with it, the further parallels with Nakdimon's 'feet' never touching the ground because of 'the cushions laid for him by the Poor' and the questionable pretense he made of charity (or, for that matter, 'Boethus' daughter Martha' who made no such pretense when she walked from her house to the Temple and whose 'feet', likewise, appeared to floated on air), exemplified also in other stories about dogs and/or 'the Poor coming to his door (the 'Rich Man''s or Ben Kalba Sabu'a's) and going away *filled*', the text has Judas add to the above complaint about the 'dinar' value of the ointment: 'it should have been sold and given to the Poor', then opining, 'He did not say this because he cared about the Poor, but because he was a thief and held the (common) purse, carrying away whatever was put in it' (12:6). To make the connection with Jesus' coming 'death and burial' even more plain, John 12:7 then has Jesus add: '*Let her alone* (echoing 'the Blind Guides' rebuke in Matthew 15:14 and the admonition relative to 'the Sons of the Pit' in the Scrolls[45]). She has kept it (the expensive perfume) for the day of my burial.'

Interestingly enough, even this tradition about Jesus' attitude towards the respect he was owed by his Disciples has a parallel from the life of Eliezer ben Hyrcanus. R. Eliezer, even at the point he was about to die too and after he has been excommunicated by Rabban Gamaliel, when *his* Disciples, 'Rabbi Akiba and his colleagues', come to see him on his deathbed and they discourse about the 'cleanness' or 'uncleanness' of things contained in 'unclean vessels', he is pictured as suddenly blurting out: 'I fear for the Disciples of this generation, for they will be punished by death from Heaven.'[46] When they ask him, 'Master, what for?', he replies in the manner of Jesus' various rebukes to his Disciples over all the women 'anointing him' and 'kissing his feet, wiping them with their hair': 'Because, they ('you') did not come and attend upon me.' In particular, he singles out his principal Disciple, Akiba ben Joseph, whom we know died a horrifying and terrible martyr's death (he was drawn and quartered and pulled apart by horses) in the next generation for his support of the Bar Kochba Revolt. Not only did Akiba, according to Rabbinic lore, designate Bar Kochba 'the Star' of Numbers 24:17, thereby bestowing upon him his cognomen, but when he was asked by R. Eliezer, 'why you did not attend upon me?' and he answered, because he 'did not have time', R. Eliezer is reported to have replied, 'the manner of your death will be the hardest of them all'.[47]

It is at this point too that John 12:9-11, right after picturing Jesus as referring to his burial and right before his finding 'a young colt' to sit on, then incorporates the curious tradition that 'a great crowd of Jews gathered, not because of Jesus only, but that they might see Lazarus whom he raised from the dead' (12:9), whereupon the Chief Priests 'plotted together that they might also put Lazarus to death' (sic! – 12:10).

In a possible further reflection from the life of Rabbi Eliezer ben Hyrcanus (who seemed to sympathize, as we have seen, with sectarian 'Nazoraeans' like Jesus,[48] argued with R. Yohanan's other Disciple, R. Joshua,[49] others from Rabbi Yohanan's school,[50] and Rabban Gamaliel, whose sister he had married and by whom he was arbitrarily excommunicated,[51] and was considered so 'Great' that, when he sat before 'the Great Ones of Israel' – including 'Ben Sisit Hakkeset, Nakdimon ben Gurion, and Ben Kalba Sabu'a' – his face was 'as luminous as the light of the sun and the beams emanated from it like the rays from Moses' face'[52]), John 12:9–11, as already remarked, seems to think that 'the High Priests' were acting in this way 'because many of the Jews were leaving and believing in Jesus because of him' (Lazarus)!

Directly after this, of course, John 12:12-15 has the material about Jesus 'coming' with his Disciples, 'riding on a young ass' colt', supposedly fulfilling the passage from Zechariah 9:9 already remarked above, 'your King is coming', 'riding on a young donkey – a colt the foal of a donkey'. Nonetheless, the context of this whole passage in the Hebrew Zechariah, including both the chapters preceding and following it, could not be more aggressively nationalistic, irredentist, and Zionist, wishing destruction on all of Zion's enemies and rejoicing on the whole 'House of Judah'!

Even more telling with regard to this motif of 'smells' is the previous story John 11:17–44 tells about 'Martha meeting' Jesus, while 'Mary was still sitting in the house'. In this incident, it transpires that, since Martha has 'secretly' told her that 'the Master' had come, it is now Mary who 'arises' (11:21–11:28) and 'goes to the tomb that she might weep there' (11:31). This is yet another adumbration of the 'weeping' theme we encountered in the story of R. Yohanan and his Disciple, R. Joshua, 'mourning for the fall of the Temple' and the 'weeping' they mutually indulge in when contemplating its 'ruins'. Nor is this to say anything about R. Akiba's own 'weeping' when he encounters R. Eliezer's body being carried on the highway from Lydda and the 'woes' he then exclaims,[53] nor R. Yohanan's 'weeping' when he contemplates his own death,[54] nor that of 'the Holy Spirit' or what the two children of Zadok the High Priest exchange in the Talmudic story when they find each other in Rome and expire in each other's arms.

Nor is this Jesus' tomb that 'Mary' goes to – as in the case of one or both of the two Marys, 'Mary Magdalene' and 'the other Mary' – in John 11:31, but here the tomb of Lazarus, who had been in the cave blocked by the stone 'for four days' (thus – 11:38–39). The point is that, 'when she came' in the pro forma manner – just like R. Akiba's wife over and over again in the Rabbinic stories about him – she 'falls at his (Jesus') feet'. Now, specifically tying this 'putrid stench' both to Lazarus ('Eliezer' – the 'Liezer' of the Genesis Rabbah version of the story about Eliezer's bad breath above[55]) and the 'smell' of his dead body (also paralleling 'the smell' of R. Yohanan's body above where, depending on the tradition, R. Eliezer and R.

Joshua were 'the two Disciples' conducting it past either the Roman or Jewish sentries outside Jerusalem), John has Jesus now direct 'Martha the sister of him that died' to 'take away the stone' (11:39). Whereupon, as usual, she once again *complains* but this time about the putrid stench, 'Lord, he already stinks for it has been four days'. So instead of the 'smell' of Mary's 'litra of ointment of pure spikenard of great price' 'filling the house with the smell of the perfume' in John 12:3, it is now Mary's sister Martha evoking the putrid stench of Lazarus' dead body. So that perhaps would be sufficient for the parallels involved in the 'smells' of all these various contexts involving either Lazarus, Eliezer, Mary, Martha, or eventually even, as we shall presently discuss, Nicodemus/Nicodemon.

To go back to the story of R. Eliezer ben Hyrcanus in *ARN* who, when only a young man (some say twenty-two – others say twenty-eight), was also pressed by R. Yohanan to discourse about *Torah* before 'all the Great Ones of Israel', obviously meaning before a Synod or Sanhedrin of some kind. For Genesis *Rabbah*, the discourse R. Eliezer is pressed to present is before 'the Great Ones of the Land' whom it names as including 'Ben Zizzit Hakeseth, Nikodemon ben Gurion – i.e., Nakdimon or Nicodemus – and Ben Kalba Sabu'a'. By the same token, it is this incident – plus the story of 'the cattle dung' which he put into his mouth the night before he was to give this, 'causing a putrid smell to rise from his mouth' – which the *ARN* also uses to introduce its stories about the three grandees there: 'Sisit Hakkeset', 'Nakdimon ben Gurion', and 'Ben Kalba Sabu'a'.[56] For Ecclesiastes *Rabbah* in its discussion of R. Yohanan's nephew 'Ben Battiah', the Head of the *Sicarii* of Jerusalem, it was four such 'Councilors' in Jerusalem at this time, 'each capable of supplying the city with grain for ten years': 'Ben Zizzit, Ben Gurion, Ben Nakdimon, and Ben Kalba Sabu'a'.[57] In fact, *ARN* then goes on to say something similar about 'Ben Sisit Hakkeset''s name to what it did in its story, just preceding this, about both R. Eliezer ben Hyrcanus and R. Yohanan, that is, that they called him this 'because he used to recline on a silver couch before the Great Ones of Israel' (for *Gittin*, it will be recalled, it was rather 'because his seat was among the Great Ones of Rome').[58] Such are the inconsistencies of Rabbinic literature as well.

For Genesis *Rabbah*, which like *ARN* starts off with the note about 'the clods of dung Rabbi Eliezer used to put into his mouth until it emitted a putrid smell', now these three – as just indicated – are called 'the Great Ones of the Land' (in *Gittin*, which has no 'dung' incident, they were – something like Luke notes about its various 'Rich Men' – 'three Men of Great Riches') and R. Eliezer's lecture is delivered just as his father, who has come to disinherit him for studying *Torah*, sees him so elegantly holding forth in such exalted company and then rather bequeaths his whole fortune to him. The perceptive reader will immediately see that there are overtones here of the initial estrangement between R. Akiba and his father-in-law, 'Ben Kalba Sabu'a' – whom we have already identified as a scion of some kind of the Royal House of Adiabene – before an eventual reconciliation occurs for not unsimilar reasons. This too results in R. Akiba's eventual great wealth. Of course in the latter's case, there is always the additional curious story of his second marriage – Rachel, the putative descendant of Queen Helen's family, having already disappeared somehow from his biography by this point – to the wife, clearly in the time of either Trajan or Hadrian, of a wealthy Roman aristocrat who had converted for his sake![59]

However this may be, the description of this scriptural exegesis session – before what almost resembled 'a Sanhedrin' of important personages (when R. Eliezer b. Hyrcanus – 'whose face', as we saw, 'shone like the beams of light emanating from Moses' face' – was reconciled with his father) – in Genesis *Rabbah* reads almost like a *Pesher* on Psalm 37, a *Pesher* extant at Qumran. Moreover, Genesis *Rabbah* makes it very clear that the actual verse he is expounding (before 'the Great Ones of the Land') is a verse actually subjected to exegesis at Qumran. Be this as it may, now Eliezer ben Hyrcanus (not 'Ben Zizzit') is 'sitting before them' – 'the Great Ones of the Land' – expounding a verse from Psalm 37:14–15: 'The

Wicked have drawn the sword and bent the bow to cast down the Meek and the Poor (*Ebion*) and to slay the Upright of the Way (*Yesharei-Derek*).' But, of course, this is a classic Qumran-style 'wilderness' passage including not only allusions to '*Ebion*' ('the Poor'), 'the Meek' ('*Ani*'), and 'the Way'/'the Upright of the Way', but also another important variation on the 'casting down' language, imagery which – as we shall presently also see – is to be found in the Habakkuk *Pesher* as well. And what is so marvelous about all this is that, as just observed, a *Pesher* on the same verse is actually extant at Qumran – palaeographically speaking, as already indicated, contemporary with the Habakkuk *Pesher*.[60]

As far as Eliezer is concerned, the verse, 'the Wicked have drawn the sword and have bent the bow', refers to 'Amraphel and his companions' (Genesis 14:1–15), which is the reason for the placement of this incident at this point in Genesis *Rabbah*. However in the Psalm 37 *Pesher* at Qumran, more to the point, the exegesis of this passage has to do with 'the Wicked of Ephraim and Manasseh' – in any event, the first of these is both a homophone and an anagram of the 'Amraphel' above.[61] This is immediately followed up in the *Pesher* by references to both 'the Doers of the *Torah*' and 'the Penitents of the Desert' ('the Congregation' or 'Church of God's Elect' – later 'the Church of the Poor' or 'the Ebionites'), 'who shall possess the High Mountain of Israel forever' – also defined in Psalm 37:20 that follows as 'those who love the Lord' and 'the pride of His pastures'.[62]

There is no telling what R. Eliezer might have made of these further allusions and why his surprising exposition, 'this refers to Amraphel and his companions', should have so impressed the assembled grandees (including his father, who immediately bequeathed him his whole estate whereas earlier he was on the point of disinheriting him), but if it has anything to do with Qumran, then its exposition would concern: 'The Evil Ones of Ephraim and Manasseh, who sought to lay hands on the Priest (i.e., 'the High Priest' – a synonym at Qumran for 'the Righteous Teacher') and the Men of his Council ('the Community Council') at the time of the testing (or 'trial' – literally, 'refining' as in metal work) that came upon them. But God will redeem them from their hand and later they will be given over to the hand of the Violent Ones of the Gentiles for Judgement'[63] – by anyone's standard, a crucial exposition we shall evaluate further below when it comes to analyzing the Habakkuk *Pesher*, because of the numerous overlaps and commonalities in vocabulary between the two *Pesharim*.

Not only is this yet another testimony – if such were needed – of the chronological provenance of these Qumran allusions as relating to the First Century and not before, in particular, the period of the War against Rome, but almost all commentators see these references as covert allusions to the Establishment, possibly Herodians or Romans – possibly Pharisees and Sadducees. Nor can it be emphasized too much that the finding of this pseudonym 'Amraphel' here in the Genesis *Rabbah*, placed in the mouth of Eliezer ben Hyrcanus, the one rabbi whose sympathies with sectarian movements in Palestine has always been suspected, is a striking reminder of the uniqueness of these scriptural expositions, and that the knowledge of them and the events they represented continued after the generally-assumed deposit-date for the Scrolls in the Qumran caves – in the period around 70 CE and the fall of either the Temple or Masada or both (of course, there is no reason they could not have been deposited later, as I have argued, any time up to the Bar Kochba Revolt of 132–36 CE and its suppression[64]).

Furthermore, when talking about 'the Simple of Ephraim fleeing their Assembly' and 'those who mislead them' and, once more, 'joining (themselves to) Israel when the *Glory* of Judah shall arise' in another *Pesher*, that on Nahum, this 'joining' allusion can mean 'Gentiles' generally in the sense of 'God-Fearing' *Nilvim* (or 'Joiners'), pro-Revolutionary Herodians, or even 'Samaritans' *per se* as, for instance, in the way this latter term is used in the Gospels.[65]

But also at the conclusion of all these Mary/Martha/Lazarus activities in John 12:23 and 12:28, when Andrew and Philip – again 'two Disciples' – tell him that 'certain Greeks' are also coming 'to worship at the Feast', Jesus is pictured as responding in 12:23 using similar language, 'the time has come for the Son of Man to be *Glorified*' (cf. this same theme repeated in Acts 11:18 after Peter explains to 'those of the circumcision' why he 'went in and ate with uncircumcised men' – who upon 'hearing these things were silent and *Glorified God*, saying, truly God gave repentance unto life to the Gentiles too'), and again in 12:28, when he is pictured as crying out, 'Father, *Glorify* Your Name', yet one more 'Voice out of Heaven' materializes and calls down, 'I both have *Glorified* it and will *Glorify it again*'! So obviously, this '*arising of the Glory of Judah*' was very much on the mind of Gospel craftsmen.

However this may be, what these 'Evil Ones of Ephraim and Manasseh' (for R. Eliezer, 'Amraphel and his companions' – and *n.b.*, too, how for some reason John 11:54 mysteriously refers at this point to 'a city called Ephraim' in 'the country near the desert' where 'he stayed with his Disciples'!) do in the Psalm 37 *Pesher*, in 'casting down the Meek and the Poor', is lay hands on the Righteous Teacher and the Men of his Council, 'for which they will be delivered into the hands of the Violent Ones of the Peoples for Judgment'. In the Habakkuk *Pesher*, 'the Wicked Priest' not only will have 'to drink the Cup' he forced 'the Righteous Teacher' to 'drink' ('the Cup' which, when it 'comes round to him', will be called 'the Cup of the right hand of the Wrath of God'), but he would also be 'paid the reward he paid the Poor'.[66]

In the meantime 'the Penitents of the Desert' here in the Psalm 37 *Pesher* shall be 'saved and live for a thousand generations' and 'all the *Glory of Adam* shall be theirs' (and this too is paralleled in the Damascus Document[67]) and 'they shall possess the whole Earth as an inheritance'.[68]

In the exposition by Eliezer ben Hyrcanus just referred to in Genesis *Rabbah* above, 'the Poor and the Meek' are rather designated as 'Lot', saved in this archaic episode in Genesis 14:14–15 by Abraham and his servants who 'fell upon them ('Amraphel and his companions') at night' and 'pursued them as far as Hobab north of Damascus'. 'The Upright of the Way' are, of course, Abraham and his household; the 'sword' of whose enemies described as 'entering their own heart';[69] and this is the important correspondence between the two *Pesher*s, that is, 'the sword' of their Enemies '*will come around to*' them. Having said this, it is not difficult to work out the correspondences – but the whole is, of course, basically Talmudic disinformation with nothing like the clarity and precision we just pointed out and will point out further in documents like the Psalm 37 *Pesher*, the Habakkuk *Pesher*, and the Damascus Document below.

Mosaic floor and statuary from Roman Italica in Spain, the birthplace of both Trajan and Hadrian and perhaps the home of 'Cornelius' '*Italica Regiment*' noted in Acts 10:9.

Chapter 11
Barring the Dogs from the Wilderness Camps

MMT

Perhaps the key to many of these puzzles and interrelationships comes in the curious document scholars refer to as *MMT* but which I called, following allusions in its opening and closing lines, 'Two Letters on Works Righteousness'.[1] As it turns out, in a passage in it about 'dogs' (in this case, 'being barred from the Holy Camp' – identified with the Temple) most of what we are speaking about here is paralleled and, perhaps, even more clearly explained.[2]

In the events leading up to the ultimate publication of the document, in which I participated, I took it to be two Letters – the only Letters, it would appear, in the entire corpus at Qumran – therefore the name I accorded it which I saw as not only a more accurate way of referring to it, but also as pointing towards critical subject matter in the proverbial debate between Paul and James.

Gratifyingly, much of this way of looking at it has since been recognized – in particular, the use of the charged expression, 'works', as a translation of the term '*ma'asim*' (based on the Hebrew root '*-S-H*), which carries with it the sense of 'doing' as in '*doing* the *Torah*' (and not 'acts' or 'deeds' as some translators would have it). By extension and derivatively, this would extend to the whole way the usage 'justify' or 'Justification' – based on the celebrated 'proof-text' from Isaiah 53:11, 'My Servant, the Righteous One (*Zaddik*) will justify (*yazdik*) Many' or, more literally, 'make Many Righteous' – is employed at Qumran, not only in *MMT* but also the Damascus Document and the parallel 'New Testament' (this latter, clearly, not 'in the Land of Damascus' but in the milieu of manifestly 'Paulinized' Communities in Asia Minor and further west).[3]

This allusion, occurring in the first line, speaks about 'some works of the *Torah*' (complimenting an allusion in the last one to 'doing'), from which the scholarly designation *MMT*/'Some Works of the *Torah*' – originally for some reason, mystifyingly translated as 'Some *Words* of the *Torah*', though 'Words' never appeared in this line – was derived. Presumably the 'Letter' or 'Letters' then intended to go on to air certain subjects that would be of interest to its recipient. These included, in the first instance, purity issues and sacrifices that could end up in 'pollution of the Temple', in particular, the effect Gentile gifts or sacrifices and matters relating to aspects of relations with Gentiles generally could have on the 'Holiness' of the Temple (subjects of intense interest too in the New Testament).

The usual view of this document, because of certain allusions in the 'Second Letter' evoking and seemingly comparing its recipient to 'David', was that this was directed towards a Jewish or Herodian King, though which King this might be in this period – other than Agrippa I (37-44 CE), who presumably would not have needed such tuition – is hard to imagine. It is for these reasons, too, that I have considered this document to be addressed to a newer and, therefore, even perhaps more 'zealous' convert to Judaism who, while nevertheless a King, would not only need and be interested in such instruction but would, in fact, be desirous of having it.

Accordingly, this allusion to 'works of the *Torah*' is also picked up towards the end of the second part of this document. This reads: 'Now as to what we have written you concerning some works of the *Torah*, which we reckoned for your own well-being and that of your People. Because we see that you possess discernment and knowledge of the *Torah* … that you may keep away from Evil thoughts and the counsel of *Belial*, so that at the End Time, you will rejoice when you find this collection of our words to have been True and it will be reckoned to you as Righteousness.'[4] But, of course, this is 'Justification' theology with a vengeance. It is using the same phraseology of 'being reckoned to you as Righteousness', based on the Genesis 15:6 passage describing Abraham's 'Faith'. This is the same passage which Paul employs in both Romans 4:2–5:1 (here Paul actually uses the phrase, 'justified by works', found here in *MMT*, but to gainsay it where Abraham was concerned) and Galatians 3:6, to develop his understanding of 'Christian' Salvation, that is, 'Salvation by Faith' – this last, in turn, polemically refracted (in the spirit of the 'works Righteousness' stance of *MMT*) in James 2:23–24 which rather delineates the 'testing' of Abraham through the offering of Isaac and, therefore, why 'he was called a Friend of God'.

The allusion we are interested in concerning the subject we have been setting out in this section dovetails very nicely with the words Matthew 7:6 attributes to Jesus in its formulation of the 'dog'/'dogs' theme in its version of the Sermon on the Mount: 'Do not give that which is Holy to the dogs'. The way this is expressed, to be polemically gainsaid in the encounter with the Greek Syrophoenician/Canaanite woman, as we have seen, also reflects the ethos of Qumran literature in general – again, most notably, that of the Damascus Document – of 'setting up the Holy Things according to their precise specifications' (directly amplified in the pivotal 'Jamesian' demand that immediately follows, 'to love each man his brother') and 'separating Holy from profane',[5] an ethos which is the opposite of what Peter is pictured as 'learning' in Acts. As such, for all intents and purposes this last position embodies the original 'Palestinian' Jewish approach to such matters before it went overseas to be transmogrified into the thematic variants and reversals in the New Testament – some quite amusing – which we have been setting out above.

Like the Letter Judas Barsabas and his colleagues Paul, Barnabas, and Silas are pictured as 'taking down to Antioch from Jerusalem' in Acts 15:29–32 containing James' directives to overseas communities, *MMT* is also a letter (or letters) of some kind. Before proceeding, it should also be remarked that the actual words with which *MMT* closes ('Then you shall rejoice at the End of Time when you find this collection of our words to have been True and it will be reckoned as justifying you, your having done what is Upright and Good before Him for the sake of your own Good and for the sake of Israel'), are essentially reproduced in Acts 15:30–31's version of the outcome or aftermath of this 'Council': 'They went to Antioch and, gathering the Multitude ('the Many'), they delivered the letter and, having read it, they rejoiced at the consolation' ('good', 'comfort', or 'well-being', meaning, which the letter provided). Again, the correspondences are nothing short of remarkable.

In *MMT*, the ban on gifts and sacrifices from and on behalf of foreigners in the Temple, which we have identified as the immediate issue triggering the War against Rome in 66 CE, is basically the subject of the whole first section from approximately 1.3–1.12. The way this is being formulated, this includes the implication of 'pollution of the Temple' (1.4–1.11), but even more importantly, the actual words that 'we consider the sacrifices which they sacrifice' to be '*sacrifices to an idol*' (1.10–12). There cannot be too much debate about the presence of this all-important allusion in the 'First Letter' at this point. In fact, if it is present, then the connections between it and the 'Jamesian' position on this issue, to say nothing of those 'Zealot' or '*Sicarii* Essenes' Hippolytus claims are willing to undergo any sort of torture rather than consume such fare (in Josephus, this is only expressed in terms of the much less specific 'forbidden things'), approach convergence.[6]

Paul clearly appreciates that this was the understanding of the vocabulary involved when he strenuously, if somewhat disingenuously, wrestles with the subject in 1 Corinthians 8:1–13 and 10:18–24. Again, one should note that he ends in 10:24 with a question that plays off the very words with which we have just seen *MMT* close, 'Let no one pursue his own well-being' ('welfare', or 'good'), but rather 'each one that of the other'. Even these last are the very words in the Damascus Document following its characterization of 'the New Covenant in the Land of Damascus' as 'setting up the Holy Things according to their precise specifications' and of the way 'each man should treat his neighbor', as well as at several other junctures.[7] In Paul's polemical repartee, these rather lead right into the repudiation of the essence of this 'New Covenant' – as originally probably set forth in the Damascus Document – in 1 Corinthians 10:25–26: 'Eat everything that is sold in the market. There is no need to inquire because of conscience, for the Earth is the Lord's and the fullness thereof.'

This last paraphrase, once again, even reflects the above proclamation with which the Cairo Damascus Document begins about 'God visiting them and causing a Root of Planting to grow ... to inherit *His land* and to prosper *on the good things of His Earth*'. This being said, it is difficult to get much more disingenuous than Paul in the above refinement of his 1 Corinthians 6:12 and 10:23 'all things are for me lawful' insistences. Obviously such instructions, whether in Paul or at Qumran, relate to James' rulings in 'the Letter' ascribed to him in Acts 15 and 21 banning in the most unequivocal manner conceivable 'things sacrificed to idols', to say nothing of the ban on 'blood' immediately following this in all contexts.

Banning the Dogs from the Holy Camps

In fact, the first formulation of the prohibition on 'things sacrificed to idols' in Acts 15:20 follows the characterization of James (in the manner of the *Mebakker* or 'Overseer' in the Damascus Document, where the ban on 'blood' is also a major obsession[8]) as 'judging' and his charge 'to write them' – meaning the Antioch Community. In this first version of James' 'rulings' in Acts, the twin conceptualities of 'pollution of the Temple' and 'things sacrificed to idols' are combined in the following manner: 'abstain from the pollution of the idols'. However it is formulated, the issue is labored over by Paul, as just indicated, in 1 Corinthians 8:1–13 and 10:14–33, but here rather leading into his own – and perhaps the original – presentation of the New Covenant of 'Communion with the body' and 'the blood of Christ' in 11:20–34, a formulation by implication, of course, just banned as a consequence of James' prohibition of 'blood'.

In the intervening material in 1 Corinthians 11:1–19, Paul also raised some issues having to do with marriage and woman's relationship to man, curiously mostly having to do with 'hair' – in fact, peculiarly, her 'long hair' which Paul considers to be 'to her Glory' (11:15 – *n.b.*, in another obvious attack on Nazirites such as James preceding this in 11:14, Paul insists that 'Nature itself does teach' that if 'a man has long hair, it is a dishonor to him' – *sic*; note the 'Teacher' here is 'Nature' not 'God').

Marital issues are to some degree taken up as well in *MMT* in 1.39–49 and 78–92 – there however, once again, integrally connected to the third of James' proscriptions 'to the Gentiles', 'fornication'. In fact, fornication had already been evoked for comparative purposes in *MMT* 1.12 in the context of the 'things sacrificed to idols' characterization earlier, that is, that sacrifices of this kind were either a 'seduction' or a species of 'fornication'. But the issue of 'fornication' had already been dealt with at great length by Paul in 1 Corinthians 6:11–7:40 where he began his discussion of these pivotal directives by James to overseas communities while, at the same time, giving voice for the first time to his 'all things are lawful for me' and 'food is for the belly and the belly for food' admonitions, the first just cited above and the last the basis seemingly of Mark and Matthew's picture of Jesus' long excursus about food 'being thrown out through the toilet drain'.

The linkage of 'things sacrificed to idols' to 'fornication' was also fundamental to the Damascus Document's 'Three Nets of *Belial*' accusations against the ruling Establishment (clearly the Herodians and their hangers-on). Two of these charges were, in fact, 'fornication' and 'pollution of the Temple', defined in terms of 'niece marriage', 'polygamy', and 'divorce'.[9] At the same time, these were tied to a third, 'blood', just underscored above but this time expressed in terms of 'lying with a woman during the blood of her period' – the linkage between all three growing out of not 'separating holy from profane', this time expressed in terms of the charge of not observing proper 'separation' procedures in the Temple. The sense of this was that 'fornicating' persons of this type (most specifically, including Herodians) were not being properly banned from the Temple and their gifts and/or sacrifices not rejected in the manner that they should have been.[10]

The ban on 'fornication' of James' directives to overseas communities in whatever rendition – not to mention the one on 'blood' – is widespread at Qumran in multiple documents. In the strictures concerning it and marital relations generally here in *MMT* I.78–79, the purity-minded if somewhat ethnocentric reason why public 'fornication' of any kind was to be abjured – this time, by the whole People – was that they were considered 'a Holy People' and the biblical injunction, 'Israel is Holy', applied.[11]

The same reason is applied in *MMT* to forbidding 'intermarriage', which is systematically considered part of the strictures concerning 'mixing' in a wider sense – including, for instance, 'mixing different cloths' or 'threads' in the same garment or, even earlier, mixing pure and impure liquids in the same vessel or conduit, a parallel allusion to which we just saw in one of the Parables attributed to Jesus.[12] Not surprisingly, the issue of 'being a Holy People' is considered particularly relevant to the status of 'the Sons of Aaron' who, in their role as Priests/High Priests, wore the mitre upon which the words 'Holy to God', were engraved.[13] In this section of *MMT*, these Priests are termed – just as the 'three Priests' part of (or added to) the twelve-member Community Council in the Community Rule[14] or, in an allegorization similar to Paul's 'members of the Community' as 'the body of Christ' or 'Jesus as Temple' in 1 Corinthians 12:14–27 and Ephesians 2:20–22 – 'the Holy of Holies' (I.82). The conclusion was, bearing again on James' ban on 'fornication' – though there is some question about the reconstruction here – that they were not even 'to intermarry with the People' nor 'defile their Holy seed with fornication'.[15]

In conclusion, there is also the slightest echo of the fourth component of James' directives to overseas communities even as conserved in Acts, that of the ban on 'carrion', so obviously garbled, as we shall explain further below, in Acts' Hellenizing paraphrase of the subject, 'abstain from strangled things', but correctly delineated in full in the Pseudoclementine *Homilies* and, thereafter, in the Koran descending from both.[16] In *MMT* the ban on 'carrion', already clearly enunciated in Ezekiel 44:31 where '*Bnei-Zadok*' Priests who were to 'serve at the altar' and were 'not to eat anything dying of itself or torn', comes in the context of the curious barring of the same omnipresent 'dogs' we have been following above, only now 'from the Holy Camps' (I.69–73).

In *MMT* this ban directly follows the one on 'mixing' of various kinds, including multiple streams of poured liquids into a single vessel or down a single spout, just highlighted above, as well even as the general ban on 'the blind' and 'the deaf' (as always, counter-indicated across the Gospels) because – just as the banning of them from the Temple in the Temple Scroll – they would 'not be able to see to stay away from (such) unclean mixing and, to whom, such polluted mixing would be invisible'. Moreover, where the latter were concerned, they would not even 'be able to hear the regulations'! Since neither would, therefore, be able 'to perform them' (literally 'to *do* them' – the vocabulary of 'doing' again), that is, 'do these regulations', they were not to be allowed 'to approach the purity of the Temple' (I.52–57 – again concerns over cleanness vs. uncleanness, purity vs. impurity and, as usual, counter-indicated in the Gospels[17]).

The same would have to be said of 'dogs', but for a slightly different if related reason. As *MMT* I.61–67 puts this: 'Regarding dogs, one is not to bring dogs into the Holy Camps because they might eat some of the bones in the Temple while the flesh is still on them', which, however primitive and seemingly intemperate this might appear to the modern ear, is perhaps the clearest statement yet of the reason for the whole concern over 'dogs' we have been witnessing in these various contexts, that is to say, we are totally in the realm, once again, of *carrion*. Not only does this injunction incorporate the reason for the 'uncleanness' of these 'dogs' – which is now, simply, 'they eat the bones with the flesh still on them' – but it specifically connects this 'uncleanness' to the ban on 'carrion' itself, the fourth component of James' directives to overseas communities.

This is now further explained and specifically connected to Jerusalem with the supplementary rationalization: 'because Jerusalem is the Holy Camp, the place that He chose from all the Tribes of Israel, because Jerusalem is the Head of the Camps of Israel'.[18] Once again one has here the motif of the wilderness 'camps', we shall further delineate below and, in particular, Jerusalem as 'the Head' or 'Chief of the Camps of Israel'.

We had already been prepared for something of this kind earlier because the principal status of Jerusalem had already been confirmed using this same archaizing 'Camp' vocabulary. There, again alluding to the biblical wilderness 'Camp' and 'Tent of Meeting', particularly concerning where impure waste from the Temple was to be disposed, Jerusalem had already been designated as 'the Camp', and, for these purposes, 'outside the Camp', defined as 'outside Jerusalem'; and the same reason given, though a little more eloquently: 'for Jerusalem was the place He chose from all the Tribes of Israel as a dwelling place for His Name' (I.32–35 – again the reason for such reiteration, where the tuition of a foreign 'King' might be concerned, should be self-evident. A native one would not probably have required it).

One might actually be able to conceive of a '*Galut*' of these 'Holy Camps' or 'Camps of Holiness', as this curiously idiosyncratic letter would put it – or, in the way it will be put in the first line of the War Scroll, 'the Diaspora of the Desert' which it, in turn, will identify as 'Benjamin'![19] As this will be put in the Damascus Document's somewhat parallel exposition of 'the Star Prophecy', which will also reference 'the Tabernacle of David which is fallen' from Amos 5:26–27 and 9:11–12 – this will be 're-erected' in a Land 'north of Damascus' which could also be reckoned as including these 'Camps of Holiness' or wilderness 'Holy Camps' being alluded to here in both the War Scroll and *MMT*.[20]

In the new situation defined by contemporary political realities, the flight *across the Jordan* signaled so often in various texts, and the movement expressed archaically as 'going out from the Land of Judah to dwell in the Land of Damascus' and specifically delineated in the Damascus Document as a prelude to 'erecting the New Covenant in the Land of Damascus', these 'Camps of Holiness' or 'Holy Camps' could actually even be conceived of as including, not just Transjordan or the New Testament's 'Perea' or the Decapolis, but also – as in the various 'heresiologies' with which we began this analysis – far beyond, all the way up to Northern Syria including Carrhae or Edessa and even 'beyond the Euphrates', perhaps as far as Adiabene in present-day Northern Iraq as well.

'Do not give Holy Things to Dogs', Gentile Gifts in the Temple, and 'Zealot'/*Sicarii* Essenes

Instead of Mark and Matthew's Greek Syrophoenician woman comparing herself and her daughter to the 'dogs under the table' or Luke's 'a certain Poor man (Lazarus) wanting to be filled from the crumbs which fell from the Rich Man's table' while 'the dogs licked his sores' – not to mention the Talmud's equally silly exposition of 'Ben Kalba Sabu'a''s name in terms of the Poor 'coming to his door hungry as a dog and going away filled', now the reason *MMT* gives for banning the 'dogs from the Camps of Holiness' – carrying with it in particular the meaning of Jerusalem and the Temple as the Chief of these Holy Camps – is because 'the Dogs' in such environments might 'eat the bones (not 'the crumbs') with the flesh still on them'. Here too, it is interesting that it is 'the flesh' that interests our legal purists not just 'the bones' – that is, the dogs are carnivores pure and simple and, thus, even their presence either *in the camps* or, more particularly, *in the Temple* would violate the ban on the consumption of carrion.

What we have here is probably the original behind the whole circle of allusions regarding these telltale 'Dogs'. Moreover it most certainly is also reflected in James' rulings to overseas communities in the ban he enunciates on what in Greek, as we have seen, is compressed into the single category of 'strangled things' but which in other contexts – the Pseudoclementine *Homilies*, for example, or the Koran – is more fully and precisely defined as 'carrion'.[21]

There also may be a secondary, more symbolic meaning behind all this and that is of the kind we are seeing in the Gospels, namely, *the use of this 'Dogs' metaphor to relate to Gentiles*. In the light of the mutual polemics we have been following and the verbal repartee of the kind found in Paul's Letters, this arcane and curious allusion to Dogs from this native Palestinian Jewish document found in multiple copies at Qumran therefore might also be looked on as a veiled allusion to the same kind of thing Matthew 15:27 is intending in his allusion to 'even the little dogs eat of the crumbs falling from their master's table' (Mark 7:28, as already explained, uses slightly different language: 'even the little dogs under the table eat of the children's crumbs').

It would also be well to point out at this point that just as Matthew's presentation of the 'dogs under the master's table' exchange is followed in 15:30–31 by the allusion to 'the dumb speaking, the maimed restored, the lame walking, and the blind seeing' while the People 'Glorified the God of Israel' (in Mark 7:31–37 this is rather depicted by the picture of Jesus curing a deaf and dumb man by 'putting his fingers into his ears and spitting on his tongue'), the barring the dogs from the Temple is preceded in *MMT* by the material *barring the blind and the deaf* from approaching 'the purity of the Temple' for reasons not unlike those signaled in Mark's vivid depiction of Jesus' restoration of the deaf-mute's speaking and hearing.

But there is also a lengthy passage almost directly following 'the barring of the dogs from the Temple' in *MMT* dealing with the 'uncleanness' and 'cleansing' of lepers (1.67–76), a subject – as already underscored – treated throughout the Gospels in the context often of just another simple 'touch' by Jesus – as, for instance, in Matthew 8:2–3 and pars, but also those just encountered in Luke 7:22 and 17:12 above.

In the writer's view this kind of corresponding subject matter – not to mention an often somewhat analogous sequentiality and what appears to be an almost systematic ideological inversion or reversal – occurs with such frequency that it can hardly be thought to be accidental or coincidental. Again, it should be appreciated that just these categories of persons being either barred from the Temple (in this context, the symbolic treatment of 'Jesus as Temple' should always be kept in mind) or kept at a distance in documents at Qumran (this includes wine-bibbers, Sinners, prostitutes, over-flowing menstrual bleeders, lepers, the deaf, the dumb, the blind, and the lame, gluttons, tax-collectors, and Roman Centurions to name but a few) are *welcomed* by Jesus, not only in table fellowship, but also with a miraculous and healing 'touch'! It is always hard to escape the impression that the people creating these traditions are laughing at what they knew to be native Palestinian 'scruples' (as Paul would belittlingly characterize them) or what they saw as anachronistic superstitions – in the process, creating their own supernatural Greco-Roman and Hellenistic semi-divine 'Mystery' figure, such as an Asclepius, Dionysus, Apollo, Orpheus, Mithra, or Osiris or of the kind an Ovid, Virgil, Seneca, Petronius, or Apuleius might create, replacing these irksome, troublesome and, for the most part, even loathsome bans or taboos with this new, less offensive and more agreeable, less strident and more cosmopolitan man-god; and this, in the very same environment of those insisting on such proscriptions and, to add insult to injury, picturing him as walking around in it – but how successful, two thousand years worth of success.

In Matthew the allusion to 'Dogs', as we have seen, occurs in two separate contexts, once with regard to this 'Canaanite woman' and again at the end of 'the Sermon of the Mount' – the one apparently in response to the other (if not Jesus simply responding to himself). In Luke – indirectly echoed in the Lazarus material in John – the 'Dogs' allusion occurs in an entirely different context, in some ways even more closely linked to Talmudic 'Ben Kalba Sabu'a' scenarios. However these things may be and however one interprets them, the references to 'Dogs' in Mark and Matthew, anyhow, certainly have something to do with Gentiles or, at least, how these two Gospel writers *felt Jews looked upon Gentiles*, namely, as being no better than Dogs! The related materials in Luke and John (Luke acting as a kind of bridge to John) also have the not-unrelated reverse of these, that is, a not so thinly-disguised strain of anti-Semitism that runs through both of them.

If we take these allusions to Dogs in all contexts as involving Gentiles, then even the reference to 'dogs' as we have it in *MMT* can be seen as a kind of double entendre which, in addition to reflecting the ban on carrion of James' directives to overseas communities, is also in some manner evoking Gentiles or, at least, the way Gentiles were being seen or alluded to by Jews. This would include, where *MMT* is concerned, the banning of Gentiles and the rejection of their gifts and/or sacrifices – including those Josephus tells us were being offered *daily* on behalf of the Emperor – from the Temple, itself perhaps the over-riding theme of this period, at least where 'Zealots', *Sicarii*, or Revolutionaries were concerned, again especially in the context of Josephus' description of events leading up to the War against Rome.[22]

If this is true – and the author feels that Matthew and Mark are at least playing on this theme (not to mention Matthew's earlier formulation of the reverse invective, 'Do not give *Holy Things* to dogs' – here, the 'Holy Things' links up with 'Holy Camps' in *MMT*. It is this one is talking about when one speaks of 'code's in this period) – then, by extension, this pregnant allusion to 'even the dogs eating the crumbs under the table' can also be seen as having to do with James' ban in both Acts and the Pseudoclementine *Homilies* on 'things sacrificed to idols', itself reflected in Paul's tendentious discussions in 1 Corinthians 8–11. However general the formulation of this 'things sacrificed to idols' may be in these three sources (four, if one includes *MMT*), the relationship is always to the Temple – as, for example, it is in Paul's discussion of the ban in 1 Corinthians 10:18–31.

This is also the way the allusion to the barring of such 'dogs' on the basis of their not having 'kept away from carrion' is presented in *MMT*. Nor is this to mention the strictures in the Temple Scroll barring 'skins sacrificed to idols' and unclean persons generally from the Temple related to it – a ban, curiously enough, in this passage alluding in some manner to the person or word 'Bela°.[23] Both of these matters, namely the ban on 'things sacrificed to idols' and that on 'Gentile gifts in the Temple', make up the bulk of *MMT*'s concerns up to the point of its consideration of Jerusalem as 'the Holy Camp' which it also describes, as we saw, as 'the Place which He chose from among all the Tribes of Israel as a resting place for His Name' and 'the Chief of the Camps of Israel'. Furthermore the ban on 'Dogs', 'because they might eat the bones with the flesh still on them', also directly relates in its own way to the Temple.[24]

On the other hand and seen in the light of problems with Gentile conversion in this period generally, it doesn't take much imagination to see Matthew and Mark's version of the retort of the Cananaean/Greek Syrophoenician woman as encompassing the kind of response a person like Queen Helen of Adiabene or one of her descendants might have made to someone criticizing their expensive gifts in the Temple or, as the case may be, referring to them as 'Dogs' – in this sense, Queen Helen would take the place of the Canaanite/Greek Syrophoenician woman just as, in our view, 'Ben Kalba Sabu'a' is a name for one or another of her descendants or those of her sons.

In our view, too, just as the Queen Helen of Adiabene material reemerges, however tendentiously, into Acts 8:27's story of 'the Queen of the Ethiopians' and her 'eunuch' treasury agent, so too Helen's legendary presence hovers, however obscurely, in the background of these Gospel materials as well, not only because of her and her family's wealth, legendary largesse, and famine relief efforts, but also because of there being in her story just the slightest suggestion of the 'prostitute' or 'adultery' motif – a motif present as well, as we have seen, in the matter of Jesus having 'cast seven demons' out of Mary Magdalene (the 'harlot' character of whom is always lurking somewhere in the background of most traditions surrounding her) as it is with regard to Simon Magus' legendary traveling companion – the 'Queen' named 'Helen' he, too, supposedly retrieved out of the bordellos of Tyre![25]

To go back to the original point behind these two issues – the ban on Gentiles in the Temple and the rejection of their gifts and sacrifices from it (including those on behalf of the Emperor) – these according to Josephus were the essential last straws triggering the Uprising against Rome in 66 CE. Josephus, as we have seen, disingenuously terms the banning of both of these by the more 'Zealot'-minded lower priest class as 'an Innovation which our Forefathers were before unacquainted with'. We say 'disingenuously' here because he knows full well that these same persons – along presumably with their sacrifices – had been explicitly banned long before in Ezekiel 44:5–15's pointed 'Zadokite Covenant', the very same passage of central importance as well to the Damascus Document at Qumran which both delineated who and what these true 'Sons of Zadok' were.[26]

Nor is it coincidental or accidental that when Paul comes to speak about such 'sacrifices on the part of Gentiles in the Temple' in his likewise pivotal arguments in 1 Corinthians 10:14–22, he cautions his opponents in 10:22 in the same breath as he evokes 'drinking the Lord's Cup and the cup of demons' and 'eating of the Lord's table and the table of demons' with the threat of the very same 'zeal' with which they probably had threatened him. Yet again, in invoking this 'zeal of the Lord', he is *reversing* in his usual rhetorical manner *the language of his presumed interlocutors against themselves* (in this case, seemingly, James' 'Zealots for the Law' as per Acts 21:20). It is in such passages that one can be sure that Paul's opponents really were 'Zealots' or *Sicarii* who had, of course, a diametrically opposed view of such 'idolatry' to his own.

One should recall how in Hippolytus' description of those denoted as 'Zealot' or '*Sicarii* Essenes' – Hippolytus conserving in the author's view an earlier and perhaps even more incisive version of Josephus' testimony on these matters – Hippolytus/Josephus emphasizes this very point, namely, the unwillingness of such '*Sicarii* Essenes' to eat 'things sacrificed to idols' even under the threat of the direst Roman torture or death.[27] In the received version of Josephus – in which the latter acknowledges that these very same 'Essenes' had participated and had distinguished themselves by their bravery in 'our recent war against the Romans' – the unwillingness on their part to eat such fare even in the face of the direst torture or death is characterized only under the classification of the more general 'not eating forbidden things'.[28]

It is in passages such as these that the account attributed to Hippolytus distinguishes itself by its greater precision and insight. In other words, putting Hippolytus and Josephus together, it is in connection with this ban – found both in *MMT* and James' directives in Acts, alluded to as well in the ban on 'skins sacrificed to idols' in the Temple Scroll and worried over by Paul – that such 'Zealots' or 'Essenes' (good 'Jamesian's that they were) were prepared to martyr themselves. The testimony to their unwillingness to eat such fare is even backed up in Asia Minor in the correspondence between Pliny the Younger and Trajan about Revolutionary unrest in that area at a somewhat later period – the period in which Simeon bar Cleophas and the grandsons of Jesus' third brother Judas reportedly met their ends – and seemingly for precisely the same reasons.[29]

To close the circle again: aside from the fact that Acts 21:20 knows the majority of James' 'Jerusalem Church' supporters were 'Zealots for the Law', the issue of 'Zealots' is already present in the episode about Jesus' encounter with the 'Greek Syrophoenician woman' in Mark and Matthew as it stands. While Mark 7:25, which places the whole episode in 'the neighborhood of *Tyre*' (again *n.b.*, 'the brothels of Tyre' allusion in the slur about Simon Magus' consort above), identifies her in this latter manner, as we have seen; Matthew 15:22, on the other hand, identifies her as 'a Canaanite' or 'Cananaean woman' and for him, the region is now '*Tyre* and Sidon'. Elsewhere, the same appellation is given in Mark 3:18 and Matthew 10:4 to Jesus' supposed Apostle 'Simon the Cananaean', another euphemism Luke 6:15 definitively unravels in its designation of 'Simon *the Zealot*'.

It should also be appreciated that in Acts' incomprehensible arguments in the early Church between 'Hebrews' and 'Hellenists' over who is 'to wait on' or 'serve tables' and the distribution of the common fund, which we have already analyzed above, this term 'Hellenists' (6:1, reappearing too in 9:29 and 11:20) clearly conceals something more fundamental, that is, as in the matter of the 'Canaanite woman' above, 'zealotry' or 'Zealots'. In the context of such 'zealotry', one should also recall the additional play in the Greek on the same usage in Mark and Matthew's *kunaria*/'little dogs' (in Luke's related version about Lazarus', *kunes* or simply 'dogs') on *Kanna'im*, the Hebrew for 'Cananaeans'/'Zealots'.

Queen Helen's Eunuch, Circumcision, and the *Lex Cornelia de Sicarius*

One can go further than this. We have already seen that even though the whole episode regarding the Greek Syrophoenician/Canaanite woman seems to be missing from the third Synoptic account, in reality it is not. Rather it reappears in the last of Jesus' parables about the Rich Men in Luke 16:19 about the 'certain' one, 'who used to dress in purple and fine linen and feast in luxury every day'. Nor is this parable paralleled in any of the other Gospels except for the name of the 'Poor Man who wished to be filled from the Rich Man's table crumbs' – Lazarus, about whose 'sisters' and the 'stink' of whose body John goes on to give additional and not insignificant particulars.

As also analyzed previously, these details bring us right back to Talmudic stories about its Rich Men, Nakdimon, Ben Kalba Sabu'a, Boethus, and their daughters. For its part, the 'daughter' theme then takes us back even further, closing the circle of all these usages and returning us, yet again, to Mark and Matthew's Canaanite/Greek Syrophoenecian woman's *daughter*. As already suggested too, this woman has much in common with Josephus' and Talmudic stories about Queen Helen and her legendary largesse or Riches who, in turn, has interesting connections with Simon Magus' alleged consort also called 'Helen'. The circle of these overlaps then even widens to include in Luke's Acts 8:27 another such 'Rich' foreign woman with an interest in Jerusalem and apparent charitable giving, but now identified as 'Kandakes the Queen of the Ethiopians'.

This story about 'Kandakes', aside from alluding to her fabulous wealth, describes the Pauline-style conversion through baptism of her Treasury agent or eunuch (8:36–37). This is not to mention the note of 'Zealotry' seemingly present in the first syllable of her name, 'Kan'/'Ken', and echoed as well in the name of that descendant of Queen Helen, 'Kenedaeus' (another of these seeming ''*Arizei-Go'im*' in the Habakkuk *Pesher* we shall hear more about as we proceed) who played a part in the 66 CE Uprising against Rome and apparently lost his life in its first serious engagement – the battle at the Pass at Beit Horon.[30] Linguistic connections and plays of this kind, however unlikely they may seem at first glance, should not be ignored, just as a similar correspondence in the name of 'the *Canaanite* woman' should not be ignored, nor blinds like so-called or alleged 'Hellenists'.

Nor is the Treasury agent's 'eunuch' status a practice having anything to do with any African Kingdom at this time, but only Iraq and Persia and a hold-over from earlier Persian dynastic practices. As already alluded to, it is more than likely simply a poetic euphemism for circumcision – in particular the circumcision of Queen Helen's two sons, Izates and Monobazus (already sufficiently remarked above) – circumcision in Roman eyes being looked upon as a kind of bodily mutilation or castration.

In this regard, as already noted, one should pay particular attention to the traditional body of Roman law, collectively known in this period as the *Lex Cornelia de Sicarius et Veneficis* (c. 50 BCE–150 CE) which even uses the term *Sicarius* in connection with the ban on 'bodily mutilations' of this kind, the penalty for which was death.[31] This ban really only came into serious effect under Nerva (96–98 CE) following the assassination of Domitian (81–96) and – it is important to add – in the wake of the ongoing unrest in Palestine/Judea,[32] and all the more so during and after the reign of Hadrian (117–136 CE) when another body of legislation also came into effect. This was known in the Talmud (perhaps defectively) as 'the *Sicaricon*' and involved the confiscation of enemy property, in particular, of those participating in the Bar Kochba Revolt against Hadrian and presumably earlier ones, and has to be associated in some way with this '*Lex Cornelia*' and anti-circumcision legislation generally.[33]

We have also already emphasized the possible echo of this name in that of the 'Pious' Roman Centurion in Acts to whose house Peter finally receives the command from Heaven to visit, abolishing Mosaic Law for all time (meaning, of course too, that Jesus never taught any such thing or why would Peter, his closest associate, have been unaware of it of, for that matter, require a Paul-type vision to learn of it?).

Even Origen in the Third Century was referring to himself, in precisely the same manner, as a '*Sicarius*' because of the castration or bodily mutilation he was said to have performed upon himself![34] But in his case, he was probably following an equally tendentious statement Matthew 19:12 portrays Jesus as making after 'withdrawing from Galilee and coming into the borders of Judea beyond Jordan' (thus) and leading into the above material about allowing 'the little children to come unto him to touch him' – in response to some very tough questioning from 'the Pharisees' once again and similar to the Dead Sea Scrolls about different grades of marriage, divorce, fornication, and adultery[35] – about '*eunuchs making themselves eunuchs* for the sake of the Kingdom of Heaven'.

Nor in regard to this should one forget those whom Hippolytus calls '*Sicarii* Essenes' who offered the choice of forcible circumcision or death to anyone they heard discussing the Law who was not circumcised. Not only is this a forerunner of similar later Islamic alternatives, i.e., '*Islam or the sword*', but it must also be seen as the other side of the coin to Josephus' derivation of the '*Sicarii*' terminology – the curved knife upon which he claimed the designation was based not, therefore, being just the assassin's knife as *per* the sense of his exposition of it, but also that of the circumciser. Moreover, among the practitioners of this 'Way' the two, no doubt, functioned as one.[36]

This has to be seen as throwing a good deal of light on Galatians 2:12's reference to 'the some from James' as 'the Party of the Circumcision' and the 'some' whom Acts 15:1–4 insists 'came down from Judea' to Antioch – whichever the Antioch intended – 'and were teaching the brothers that *unless you were circumcised* according to the law of Moses you could not be saved' triggering, according to its historiography, the 'Jerusalem Council'.

Of course, the whole issue of whether to circumcise or not to circumcise brings us right back to Josephus' and the Talmudic story about the conversion of Queen Helen, as well as that of her two sons Izates and Monobazus, their circumcision, and Helen's own apparently deep-seated, overtly expressed opposition to the practice.[37] This last, in turn – as just highlighted – bears on Luke's caricaturizing portrait of the conversion of 'the Ethiopian Queen's eunuch' who chooses to be baptized after Philip encounters him reading a passage from Isaiah 53:7's 'Suffering Servant'. But where the circumcision of Queen Helen's two sons in Talmudic tradition and Josephus are concerned, they are reading, as already explained, a passage about Abraham both 'circumcising himself' and 'all the members of his household', including 'the foreigner dwelling among them' – the *Ger-Nilveh* or 'Resident Alien' of the Nahum *Pesher* and a passage from Genesis 17:23–27 actually alluded to in the Damascus Document where Abraham was concerned as well[38] – which would have had more than a passing significance for persons in an 'Abrahamic' locale, even perhaps those in the neighborhood of Haran such as Edessa in Northern Syria, as it did the Koran as well.[39]

This brings us back to the Gospels of Luke and John on the issue of Dogs, Lazarus, his Resurrection, and the Poor, clearly combining in new ways and reflecting all the various Talmudic materials delineated above. The same can be said for Acts' picture of its 'Ethiopian Queen's eunuch' reflecting both materials in Josephus and the Talmud about the conversion via circumcision of Queen Helen's two sons. The '*Poor Man* Lazarus' at the 'Rich Man's door' in Luke moves on directly into the discussion of both his and 'the Rich Man''s state after the Resurrection in Luke 16:22–31, whereas in John 12:9–11, the events circulating around Lazarus' Resurrection end up in the picture of '*Many* of the Jews *going astray* and believing in Jesus because of (Lazarus') Resurrection' and the High Priests, therefore, 'plotting together how they might also put Lazarus to death' (*sic*).

For its part, it will be recalled, this rather anti-Semitic follow-up picture in Luke 16:22 depicts Lazarus – as seemingly the representative of all 'Jews believing in Jesus' – now rather in some Angelic abode 'on the bosom of Abraham', not the real world as in John, whereas 'the Rich Man in Hades' (seemingly meant to depict the state of most other Jews *not* 'believing in Jesus') is now – like Lazarus earlier – longing to be 'comforted' (16:24 – in the case of Lazarus earlier, it was 'longing to be filled'). The conclusion is then reached in 16:30, clearly reflecting the picture in John 11–12, that 'even if one should go to them ('the Jews') from the dead, they would not repent'. This is repeated in the next line as 'even if one should rise from the dead they would not believe' (16:31 – now clearly implying the Resurrection both of Lazarus and Jesus), varying the report worrying the High Priests in John 12:9–11 above about 'the Jews believing on Jesus' because of 'Lazarus whom he had raised from the dead' and, again, plainly demonstrating the one Gospel to be but a variation of the other.

One should also note that in the Gospel of John's presentation of the whole story, Lazarus and the two Apostles, 'Thomas called the Twin' (11:16) and 'Judas Iscariot', figure prominently, as do the stories about Martha's 'serving' and Mary's costly 'anointing ointment', not only for the purposes of 'anointing him' (11:2) or 'washing his feet', but also for his burial (12:3–7) – the first account in Chapter Eleven clearly distinct from the second in Chapter Twelve, the second only reproducing the 'Simon the Leper' and 'Simon the Pharisee' stories elsewhere in the Synoptics.

But nothing could better demonstrate that we are in the Talmudic context of determining the meaning of Ben Kalba Sabu'a's name than the way Luke describes its 'Poor man Lazarus' as 'covered with sores' and 'longing to be filled by the crumbs that fell from the Rich Man's table' (here the 'longing to be filled', 'the crumbs falling from the table', and the 'Rich Man' motifs now combined in different ways than in Talmudic tradition, Matthew, and Mark). To nail home the circularity of all these allusions, of course 'the Dogs', too, now appear in the whole configuration 'and come to lick his sores'. Once again, one must reaffirm that the presence of this odd – and, of course, not only utterly fantastic, but mean-spirited and completely absurd – allegorical episode in Luke proves, as almost nothing else can, the accuracy of our understanding of the polemics involved in all these materials.

In fact, the whole episode regarding this Greek Syrophoenician/Canaanite woman's rejoinder to Jesus, as we saw, is directly counter-indicated in Matthew 7:6's own version of the Sermon on the Mount earlier. It not only provides the real meaning of all these matters – both that in *MMT* and what the Greek Syrophoenician/Cananaean woman, with evident Gospel applause, is anxious to rebut. It reads as already partially reproduced earlier: 'Do not give Holy Things to dogs, nor cast down your pearls before swine, lest they trample them under their feet.' Of course this whole statement, again attributed to Jesus, is completely in line with the essence of the Qumran approach, particularly that of the Damascus Document's 'separating the Holy Things from the profane', as it is the ethos of the prohibition in *MMT* about banning 'the dogs' from the Temple and Jerusalem, defined in terms of 'the Holy Camp' and 'the Chief of the Camps of Israel'.

It also proves – in the author's view incontestably – that our analysis of the arcane twists and turns of some of these New Testament materials was absolutely right and that one has to be prepared to employ a peculiar form of logic in order to follow the incredibly complex and recondite mutual polemics of these documents.

Nakdimon, Ben Kalba Sabu'a's Tomb, Honi, and Boni

Nor is this finally to put to rest the whole issue of Acts' parody of 'the Ethiopian Queen' above and her various look-alikes such as Queen Helen of Adiabene who seems to have supported the 'Zealot' cause in Palestine in this period – or at least her sons and/or descendants did, as opposed to more collaboration-minded fellow-travelers of the Romans, such as the Herodians. In fact, it is our position, if *MMT* really was addressed to one or another of her sons, such as Izates or Monobazus, that, because of their self-evident wealth, they very likely helped in the support and upkeep of an installation like the one at Qumran.[40]

Nor does it put to rest the whole issue of the relationship to her of Simon Magus' 'Queen' by the same name whom, as we have on several occasions now remarked, hostile sources assert he found among the fleshpots of *Tyre* in Phoenicia – the locale of Mark's version, anyhow, of this material about Jesus 'casting an unclean spirit' from the daughter of the 'Greek Syrophoenician woman' who – like so many others in these traditions – was also depicted as 'falling at his feet'. Nor, for that matter, Helen's own well-documented interest in 'the suspected adulteress' passage from Numbers 5:12–29 – itself, either coincidentally or otherwise, leading into that on 'Nazirite oath' procedures from 6:2–21 – a passage she is said to have hung in gold leaf on a commemorative plaque in the Temple Court.

This had to be saying something, presumably about her own biography, and it seems pretty obvious what that is: *don't make false accusations concerning someone in this regard*.[41] Like Ben Kalba Sabu'a and his 'twenty-one years' of 'grain buying' largesse according to Rabbinic sources, twenty-one years, as already underscored, also turned out to be the amount of time according to this same Talmudic tradition of Queen Helen's legendary three successive 'Nazirite oath' penances – an inordinate amount of time, laid upon her somewhat disingenuously it would seem (presumably to get further contributions from her) by the Rabbis for real or imagined infractions, impurities, or sins of some kind, doubtlessly having something to do with here marital behavior or perceived 'fornication'.

But these key numbers, 'twenty-one' or 'twenty-two', are always associated with the years Nakdimon or Ben Kalba Sabu'a, as we saw – the legends here overlap – could have fed the total population of Jerusalem had not 'the Zealots' ('the *Biryonim*' – 'the *Sicarii*'?) either burned Nakdimon's immense grain storage reserves or mixed mud with them, or both. This brings us back not only to Helen and the Famine but also to Paul, to say nothing of Acts' 'Ethiopian Queen' since, according to Josephus and early Church tradition as already explained, it was

Helen and/or her son Izates who sent their grain-buying agents to Egypt and Cyprus, dispensing their fabulous wealth to feed the inhabitants of Jerusalem in this period.[42]

It is worth recalling that the Talmud, though advertising itself as representative of a tradition supporting meticulous observation of Law, is always – like its mirror opposite the New Testament – *anti-Zealot*. Where Nakdimon's associate 'Ben Kalba Sabu'a' is concerned, two other traditions stand out. The first associates him in some manner with the fabulous tomb Queen Helen and Izates' brother 'Monobazus' (Helen's son as well?), built in Jerusalem, her first son Izates having predeceased them (the reason given in the Talmud for her successive periods of Nazirite oaths[43]). But Helen's husband also seems to have been called by a variation of this name 'Bazeus' and, as already suggested, it probably operated in a Persian cultural nexus something like 'Agbarus' or 'Abgarus' did in more Semitic circles or, for that matter, 'Herod' and 'Caesar' in Palestinian Greco-Roman ones. This 'tomb' material is reflected, too, in John's report of the 'precious ointment' Mary was using to wash Jesus' 'feet', about which Judas Iscariot was said to have complained and which, Jesus then says – according to John 12:7 – 'should be kept for the day of (his) burial'.

The Tomb of the Royal Family of Adiabene was so impressive (then and now) that it is remarked in all sources, Talmudic, early Church, Syriac/Armenian, and Josephus.[44] Not only is 'Ben Kalba Sabu'a' – himself often confused in these traditions with Nakdimon – associated in some manner with it (the writer considers him to be identifiable with one or another of Helen's descendants), but 'Nicodemus' in the Gospel of John (a Gospel along with Luke very much involved as well, as we have been demonstrating, in the transmission of these kinds of questionable and overlapping materials) is also to be associated with another such fabulous tomb.

In this instance he is the 'Rich' merchant who John 19:39 portrays as 'also coming' to prepare Jesus' body with precious ointments (a costly 'mixture of myrrh and aloes about a hundred weight' – earlier he was described as 'a Ruler of the Jews'!) before its placement in another legendary tomb, this time belonging to another such Rich individual identified only as the mysterious cognomen, 'Joseph of Arimathaea' ('a Disciple of Jesus, though secretly, for fear of the Jews' – thus!). Not only had John 12:7 above already implied that Mary was supposed to have kept the 'litra of pure spikenard ointment of great value' 'for the day of (his) burial', but in his introduction of 'Nicodemus' earlier (3:1), he portrays the two of them as having a long discussion about how 'a man who is old can enter his mother's womb and be born a second time' (3:4 – again something of 'the Primal Adam' ideology of many of these early 'Judeo-Christian' groups).

Not only can one recognize as well – should one choose to regard them – several of the elements of early Church accounts of James' being, but the discussion twice actually evokes in 3:16–18 (just as in John 1:14–18 earlier) the expression 'only begotten' which Josephus applies to Helen's favorite (and perhaps 'only') son Izates, for whom the burial monument we are discussing was originally constructed. It actually rises to a crescendo, amid repeated evocation of Light and Dark, just as in John 1:18 as well, with Jesus querying Nicodemus, 'If I say to you Heavenly things will you believe?' (John 3:12). Jesus then answers his own question with the seeming (though admittedly 'mystifying') denial, 'No one has gone up into Heaven except he who came down out of Heaven, the Son of Man who is in Heaven.' Though following the Greek (and, in fact, Pauline) rhetorical and poetic device of strophe, antistrophe, and epode, this one really is a tongue-twister but, obviously, it was meant to be 'mystifying'.

These things as they may be, the second point about 'Ben Kalba Sabu'a' is that the 'Zealot' Rabbi of the next generation, R. Akiba, married his daughter Rachel, again after some three successive rejection periods totaling some *twenty-one* years (here the correspondence with Queen Helen's three successive Nazirite oaths, as well as the number of years these two

Talmudic 'Rich Men' were supposed to have been able to supply Jerusalem with grain before 'the Zealots' spoiled it) – this purportedly because he was only a 'Poor' shepherd and Ben Kalba Sabu'a was so 'Rich'.[45] Then finally R. Akiba came to her with some 'twenty-four thousand' students and, so impressed was she that she finally married him. The stories vary here as to whether they were already married when he was just a 'Poor' shepherd 'sleeping on straw' or whether this happened later, after her father, hearing of his 'Great Name', finally became reconciled to him.[46]

Elsewhere in the Talmud, it is made plain that one of Akiba's students was another of these 'Monobaz's, obviously descended either from Helen and her sons, Izates or Monobazus, or this 'Ben Kalba Sabu'a', or all three.[47] Our conclusion from all this is that these members of Helen's family were not only instrumental in fomenting and financing the First Uprising against Rome (for which commonweal they and not the discredited and despised Herodians would be the heirs apparent or presumptive monarchs), and two of her 'kinsmen' or descendants, another 'Monobazus' (whichever one this was) and 'Kenedaeus', had already proved their valor, dying in its first engagement; but also the Second – the significance of R. Akiba's 'twenty-four thousand Disciples' with whom he won 'Ben Kalba Sabu'a''s daughter Rachel's hand. Moreover, they were also instrumental in the financing and support of the Movement represented by the installation and correspondence at Qumran.

In any event, this associate of 'Ben Kalba Sabu'a', 'Nakdimon' or 'Nicodemus' – possibly one of the representatives of this family as well – was alleged by the Talmud, in the episode with which we started this whole discussion, to have gone into the Temple at a time of drought and, like James (in our view the Nazirite-style spiritual Leader both at Qumran and a designee of this family, around whom as the *Zaddik* of his generation most of these disparate Opposition groups revolved), prayed for rain.[48] So knowledgeable does the Talmud present itself as being regarding this episode that, as we saw, it even records the words of his prayer!

To go over the details of this event and refresh them in the reader's mind one last time: as the Talmud puts it, 'he (Nakdimon) wrapped himself in his cloak and stood up to pray'. In this prayer entreating God for sufficient water in the Temple to accommodate even those on pilgrimage, Nakdimon is made to speak of his 'Father's House' – the very cry, based on Psalm 69:9 (a Psalm absolutely intrinsic to Gospel presentations of the events of Jesus' life) that John 2:17 puts into the mouth of Jesus when speaking of his *zeal* for and desire to purify the Temple. Again too, we have the theme of 'supplicating' or 'speaking to God *like a son*', for which the Talmud claims Simeon ben Shetah thought blasphemy charges should have been leveled against Honi, 'were he not Honi'.[49]

But, as Josephus reports this affair, Honi was actually stoned by his opponents – an assortment clearly of anti-nationalist Pharisees basically collaborating with the Roman forces, whose entrance into the country had been connived at by Herod's father – when he refused to condemn the proto-'Zealot' partisans (who had taken refuge in the Temple) of the Maccabean pretender Aristobulus II, who had for his part refused to humble himself before Pompey.[50] It is for these reasons that Honi ('Onias the Just') was stoned, the ostensible justification for which, 'addressing God like a son', having, it would appear, already been provided (however disingenuously) in the Talmud above. Finally, as we saw and as Josephus reports too, it is rather his supporters besieged inside the Temple and not actually Honi who, like Elijah, pray for rain and bring on a whirlwind![51]

Whatever one wishes to make of all these apparent correspondences and overlaps, where 'Nakdimon' at least was concerned, the climax of the affair was that 'immediately the sky was covered by clouds until the twelve wells were filled with water' even, as it is put, 'beyond overflowing'! Again, this picture of Nakdimon likely conceals a story relating to someone of the religious significance of a James. Even this the Talmud, in its own inimical way, seems to suggest in virtually the very next statement, wherein it now states 'his name was *not Nakdimon but Boni'*, opining that he was only called Nakdimon 'because the sun broke through on his behalf' (*nikdera*).[52]

Aside from the primeval stupidity herein evinced and the absurdity of this explanation for such denominative sleight-of-hand, there is no doubt that in the tradition now before us we are dealing with Honi's prefiguration of subsequent *Zaddiks* and the *redivivus* tradition associated with his name and that of his family. Nor is this to mention the underlying motif of the reason for his stoning and, of course, the related traditions surrounding the rainmaking of James and his stoning – the blasphemy charge having to do with 'addressing God as a son' and 'imploring Him' like this, to say nothing perhaps of the more overarching one, pronouncing the forbidden name of God in the atonement James was pictured as performing in almost all sources in the Inner Sanctum of the Temple.

For the Talmud, this 'Boni' together with one 'Thoda', i.e., obviously 'Thaddaeus' or 'Theudas', becomes one of 'Jesus the Nazoraean''s five Disciples;[53] so it becomes clear that 'Boni' must be thought of as a double for someone. In our view, this is either James – not only because of the allusion to his rainmaking in Epiphanius, but because of the emphasis on such rainmaking, so intensely evoked regarding Elijah, along with the 'fervent saving Power of the prayer of' other 'Just Ones' in the apocalyptic conclusion of the New Testament Letter of James (5:16–18) – or 'Nicodemus' in John, a Gospel which also includes yet another stand-in for James, 'Nathanael' (John 1:45), missing from the Synoptics.

Interestingly enough in John 1:48–50, this last is portrayed as sitting 'under a fig tree', which would seem to include just a hint of the manner in which the Talmud portrays Honi or his descendant 'Hanan the Hidden', as already underscored, as 'sitting under a carob tree for seventy years' in another somewhat pungent *redivivus*-type story.[54] For its part John 1:51 also portrays Jesus, as already remarked, as predicting that 'Nathanael' will see a future vision of the kind ascribed to James in early Church accounts of the events leading up to his stoning (also finding a reflection, as we saw as well, in Acts 7:56's account of events surround the stoning of 'Stephen'), of the Heavens opened and the Angels of God ascending and descending on the Son of Man (in the War Scroll, it will be 'the Heavenly Host' that will so descend but one should note, in particular, this motif of 'the Heavens opening' paralleled in both the pictures in Acts and of James' death).

The third one of these Disciples is called 'Nezer', with obvious affinities to the imageries associated with Jesus and James, either having to do with their respective, life-long 'Naziritism' or the prophetical 'Branch' or 'Nazoraean' vocabulary. This passage in the Talmud actually applies the all-important Messianic 'Root' or 'Branch' prophecies from Isaiah 11:1 and 14:19 to him – also to be found among the exegetical texts applied to the Messiah at Qumran as it is, by implication, in the New Testament – 'a Branch shall go forth out of its Roots' – but the second with inverted effect (probably to counter the importance placed upon it in both these other two): 'casting forth from your grave like an (abhorred) *Nezer*'.[55]

The last two Disciples are called 'Matthai', obviously 'Matthew', and 'Nakai', seemingly 'Nakdimon' again; but now this name is related to the Hebrew root for '*naki*' – 'clean' or 'innocent' – and not to 'shining through'. Furthermore, Psalm 10:8 is cited about 'killing the Innocent', another Zionistic psalm of the kind of Psalm 69 above, in this instance also repeatedly referring to 'the Poor' ('the *Ebionim*').[56]

Again, this whole circle of materials is typical of information-processing in the Talmud, itself sometimes even more haphazard and humorous than that of the New Testament. That a fabulously wealthy individual like Nakdimon should be seen as a *Zaddik* or 'Friend of God' or both, even 'speaking to God as a son' and going into the Temple and praying for rain is about as preposterous as some of the inversions one encounters in Paul and elsewhere in the Gospels and the Book of Acts. In fact, we have something of the same disingenuousness going on in the one as we do in the other and for the same reasons, though these Talmudic traditions are not nearly as well informed as New Testament ones sometimes are. The conclusion, however, must be the same: there can be little doubt that Nakdimon, who is performing some of the same miracles as Elijah and Honi and who is presented in this *redivivus* line, is a blind for certain more Revolutionary persons and subversive events associated with other individuals attached to this line.

Ananias, Nicodemus, Joseph of Arimathaea, and James

That 'Nakdimon' is associated with another individual, also legended to have been fabulously wealthy and seemingly connected with the tomb of Queen Helen, as well as replicating some of the same activities – such as famine relief (in Gospel portraiture, 'multiplication of the loaves') – she and her sons were supposed to have been involved in, further reinforces this suspicion. Here, too, the individual Josephus calls 'Gurion ben Nakdimon' – perhaps the same as this Nakdimon, perhaps his son – is associated with another individual called 'Ananias the son of Sadduk' in last-ditch efforts in 66 CE to save the besieged Roman garrison in Jerusalem at the beginning of the Uprising.[57]

As always, there would appear to be two types of materials in these notices: one apocalyptic, uncompromising, and subversive; the other, more accommodating – even collaborating. We have already seen a man with the same name as this Ananias involved, not only in Paul's conversion at 'Damascus' in Acts, but also in the conversion of those in Queen Helen's household around the same period of time. He was even portrayed as being the tutor of Helen's son's Izates. In the contemporaneous conversion of 'the Great King of the Peoples beyond the Euphrates', also in Northern Syria, in which both Thaddaeus and Thomas play important roles, there is also an intermediary named 'Ananias' involved as we have seen.

Not only are all these stories somewhat contemporaneous, but there is the common thread in them, too, that all are 'conversion' stories of some kind – either to Judaism or nascent 'Christianity'. In Josephus' version of the Helen material, the 'Ananias' involved is even portrayed, as just underscored, as Izates' tutor; in Eusebius' version of the Agbarus/ Abgarus conversion, Ananias is supposed to have brought the letter from King Agbarus in Edessa (Antiochia Orrhoe) to Jerusalem and then back again. Nor can the latter be separated from the letter again being sent to Antioch, according to Acts 15:22–30's account, with James' directives to overseas communities with someone called 'Judas Barsabas' (supposedly a different Antioch – there being four of them as we saw), in our view, a refraction of the letter known as *MMT* – itself addressed to a King of some kind to whom Abraham's salvationary state has more than a passing importance. This would not be surprising in a Northern Syrian milieu.

The Ananias here in Josephus – now connected to this 'Rich' Nakdimon or his descendant or, in the Gospel of John's view of things, the Nicodemus who is a 'Rich Councilor' and connected to another Rich individual who has an impressive tomb in Jerusalem (in Gospel lore, 'Joseph of Arimathaea') – seems to be personally acquainted with the Roman Commander of the Citadel named Mitelius.[58] This in itself again probably confirms his wealth, not to mention his influential status, and he does seem to be able to move around quite freely in the highest circles. Together with Gurion ben Nakdimon and a third personage, 'Antipas', he is able to convince Mitelius to surrender in exchange for a surety of safe passage – in other words, *once again, he is acting as the intermediary*.

This guarantee is broken by an individual Josephus calls 'Eleazar', who – like those in Hippolytus' picture of the Jewish sects above called '*Sicarii*' or 'Zealot Essenes' – seems to want the Romans, or at least their commander, to circumcise themselves (or die), for at the last moment all are slaughtered except Mitelius, who agrees not only to convert but also to be circumcised.[59] One should note the quasi-parallel here with the 'Eleazar the Galilean' who, in Josephus' picture of the conversion of Queen Helen's son Izates, insists on circumcision while the more moderate Pauline-type teacher Ananias (the above-mentioned merchant or courier) and his unnamed companion (Paul?) feel it unnecessary for Izates and Monobazus, his brother, to circumcise themselves – much to their mother Queen Helen's relief. Even if the chronology is a bit skewed, we certainly seem to be getting a convergence of themes in all these stories.

It should be remarked that the brothers 'Saulos and Costobarus' Josephus calls 'kinsmen of Agrippa' and another 'kinsman of Agrippa' Josephus calls 'Antipas', as well as Philip the son of Jacimus, the Commander of Agrippa II's Army, are also involved in, not only seemingly Mitelius' surrender, but a parallel event contemporaneous with it, the surrender of Agrippa II's palace in which they had all taken refuge and which then seems to have been burned by these same 'Zealot' Revolutionaries.[60]

Not only does Josephus identify this 'Antipas' – like his putative kinsmen 'Helcias' (an Herodian and a companion of Agrippa I in an earlier generation) and Helcias' son, 'Julius Archelaus' (possibly Antipas' brother or nephew) – as Temple Treasurer, but, as the Revolt moved into its more extremist or 'Jacobin' phase (68–69 CE), this Antipas was eventually arrested and put to death by those whom Josephus, by this time, had actually begun calling 'Zealots'.[61] As in the case of the butchering of James' executioner, the High Priest Ananus, and Jesus ben Gamala, directly following this Antipas' execution, and the assassination of Ananus' brother Jonathan by those he had started to designate as 'Sicarii' a decade or so earlier,[62] Josephus rails against the 'breach of the conditions of surrender' constituted by the slaughtering of the Roman garrison and 'the pollutions of such Abominations' this involved, partially because it seems to have occurred on the Sabbath. He calls it: 'the prelude to the Jews' own destruction … for it could not but arouse some vengeance whether by Rome or some Divine Visitation'.[63]

As Josephus presents these events, Philip anyhow seems to have then fallen under a cloud regarding these events (that is, the Romans suspected him of treason) and he and 'Costobarus' seemingly,[64] but not this 'Antipas', were sent to Nero – either at their own request (as Paul in Acts 26:32) or otherwise – for a hearing or to appeal their case. At this point, Nero seems to have been at Corinth in Greece (another important provenance of Paul's missionary and epistolary activities) and none of these are ever heard from again, at least not in Josephus.

It should be appreciated that the 'Saulos' in Josephus undergoes a similar fate and, following these events and his escape like Philip from Agrippa II's palace, he re-emerges as the intermediary between what should be seen as 'the Peace Party' in Jerusalem (identified in Josephus as 'the Sadducees, principal Pharisees, and the Men of Power' – this last obviously meant as a euphemism for Herodians) and the Roman Army outside it, an assignment that ends in almost total disaster.[65] After this ill-fated attempt on the part of the previously reigning Roman/Herodian Establishment in Jerusalem to invite the Roman Army into the city to attempt to suppress the Revolt, 'Saulos' too seems to have been sent to Nero in Corinth – again, either at his own request or otherwise – to report about the circumstances of this and the situation in Palestine generally, in particular in Jerusalem, a report that seems to have led directly to the dispatch of the General Vespasian from Britain with a large army to Palestine.[66]

The Ananias who accompanied Gurion the son of Nicodemus in the initial attempt to avoid war and save the Roman garrison hopelessly surrounded in the Citadel, in turn, seems to have had a connection with Ananus (the High Priest responsible for the death of James). Josephus contemptuously describes the stratagems both Ananus and Ananias the son of Sadduk used (which he claims to have ingeniously thwarted) to relieve him (Josephus) of his command in Galilee where he had been sent together with them as a representative of the Jerusalem Priestly Establishment.[67]

Once again, here in Josephus, the association of this 'Ananias ben Sadduk', in these crucial days having to do with the fate of Jerusalem, with a 'Nakdimon' of some kind ('Nicodemus' in John as well as here in Josephus) who, in turn, in Rabbinic literature is portrayed as having a relationship with 'Ben Kalba Sabu'a', raises interesting questions about Ananias' and Nakdimon's relationship to the conversion of the Royal House of Adiabene. 'Nicodemus' – 'Nakdimon''s alter ego – is also portrayed as an influential 'Pharisee' in John 3:1–9 and 7:50 (where he too is asked the question, 'are you also from Galilee', i.e., 'a Galilean'?), though nevertheless a secret supporter of Jesus. Curiously enough, this is also the role accorded the famous Pharisee Patriarch Gamaliel – Paul's purported teacher and the descendant of the Rabbinic hero Hillel – in the Pseudoclementine *Recognitions* and to some extent too in Acts.[68] In the Gospel of John, too, Nicodemus joins the legendary Joseph of Arimathaea in preparing the body of Jesus for burial, 'binding it in linen cloth with the aromatics as is the custom among the Jews' (19:40).

In the Synoptics it is now Joseph of Arimathaea who is the 'Rich Councilor' and owner of an impressive tomb in Jerusalem and it is he who is now the secret Christian, not Nicodemus – more dissimulation? Some have considered this name 'Arimathaea' – certainly supposed to be a place name but not otherwise identifiable in Palestine – to be a pun on Josephus' name itself, that is, Joseph Bar Matthew. In Luke 23:50, like so many other curious characters in early Christianity (the Roman Centurion, for example, in Acts 10:2 and 10:22 above), he, too, is called 'Good and a Just Man', that is, basically he is a '*Zaddik*' – the same words Herod applies to John the Baptist in Mark 6:20, namely, 'a Man Just and Holy' or which Pilate's wife applies to Jesus in Matthew 27:19. In addition to this, we have the re-emergence of the *Zaddik* theme again, so strong in all traditions about James – to say nothing of those relating to 'the Righteous Teacher' at Qumran.

It is hardly to be credited that either this Nicodemus/Nakdimon or the person the Gospels are calling 'Joseph of Arimathaea' – if the two can really be separated – is a *Zaddik* or 'Friend of God' and, in the former instance anyhow, a popular Rainmaker in the Temple. But in the Talmud, as we have been suggesting, aside from this rainmaking and praying in the Temple – clear leit-motifs and/or residual vestiges of the James story – there is just the slightest suggestion of a connection between Nakdimon or his colleagues, 'Ben Kalba Sabu'a' and 'Ben Zizzit', with the family of Queen Helen of Adiabene, whose fabulous tomb on the outskirts of Jerusalem is so familiar to all our sources. In fact, in the Talmud, the contracts this curious Nicodemus/Nakdimon undertakes with a foreign 'Lord' or 'Ruler' play a paramount role in his rainmaking, as does the fabulous nature of the stores he supposedly purchases or amasses with these same colleagues to save Jerusalem during its Famine – enough, as we have repeatedly reiterated, to last for 'twenty-one years', the precise time of Queen Helen's three successive Nazirite-oath periods allegedly imposed on her for utterly obscure reasons by the Rabbis.

Can there be any doubt that the true provenance of much of this material – whether in the Talmud or New Testament – really appertains to the spectacular tomb these Royals from Northern Syria had originally erected for their 'favorite son' Izates, who had initiated the family's conversion to Judaism in the first place (now transformed into pro-Establishment and anti-'Zealot' storytelling, much as elsewhere in the Gospels and in Acts)? Moreover, that the notes about rainmaking, Famine, and Naziritism, usually connected in some way with stories about these Royal personages from Adiabene, probably imply some relationship, however vague, between James and their conversions?

Likewise and *vice versa*, that these last may have been involved with someone the Talmud thinks 'made rain', who was an incarnation of Elijah in the Hidden *Zaddik* tradition, but confuses with one or another of the descendants of Honi – to say nothing about the interest of all of these in 'extreme Naziritism', probably relates to the form of 'Judeo-Christianity' – and I use the term loosely – these various Royal figures were being taught. That some of these figures, too, were later ultimately even willing to martyr themselves in this cause and that of Jewish independence in Palestine probably ties them not only to the most extreme wing of the Zealot Party or *Sicarii* – 'Christian' (to say nothing of *Iscariot*), as we shall see towards the end of this book, being a quasi-acronym of '*Sicarii*' – but to James as well.

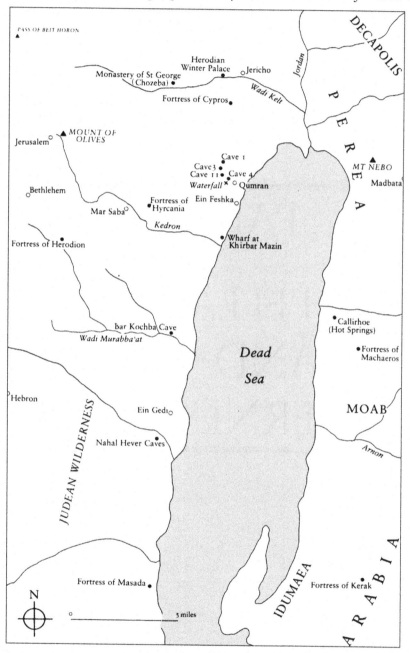

Map showing the areas of the Dead Sea, including Qumran, Masada, Perea, the Decapolis, Callirhoe, Machaeros, Hyrcania, the Bar Kochba Cave, Idumaea, the Mount of Olives, and Mt. Nebo.

PART III

THE PELLA FLIGHT AND THE WILDERNESS CAMPS

Chapter 12
The Wilderness Camps and Benjamin
the *Golah* of the Desert

Rainmaking, Theudas, and other Revolutionaries

Having attempted to decipher this curious relationship between 'Nakdimon' in Rabbinic literature and 'Nicodemus' in the Gospels, it should now be possible to return to the eschatological nature of rainmaking and its relation to the proclamation that James is pictured as making in the Temple at Passover in all early Church accounts of 'the Son of Man sitting at the Right Hand of the Great Power and about to come on the clouds of Heaven' – the same proclamation ascribed in Gospel portraiture to both Jesus and John the Baptist but, where James is concerned, with perhaps more authenticity. It is impossible to know whether James was ever really called upon to make rain around this time or whether this was just an esoteric reckoning or a euphemism of some kind for the proclamation of the final initiation of the eschatological 'End Time' since, as already alluded to, the War Scroll from Qumran speaks of just such an eschatological Judgment 'from' or 'on the clouds with the Heavenly Host' as James is pictured as making in all these early Church accounts.[1]

Perhaps the character Josephus denotes as 'Theudas' performed 'signs and wonders' of this kind too, since Josephus specifically applies the 'Impostor'/'pseudo-prophet'/'magician' vocabulary to him meant to discredit just such individuals.[2] Not only does Theudas' name carry with it the distinct overtones of the character known as 'Thaddaeus'/'Judas Thomas'/'Judas the Zealot'/'Judas the *Iscariot*' or even 'Judas the brother of James' in Gospel portraiture or early Church literature, but, as already observed, he is clearly portrayed in Josephus as a Jesus or Joshua *redivivus* type with Messianic pretensions.

Certainly there was a 'Great Famine' in the period 45–48 CE and various enterprises, like Paul's and/or Helen of Adiabene's famine-relief missions and Theudas' attempt to lead large numbers of followers out into the wilderness and repart the Jordan River in a reverse kind of exodus are not separable from it. The number of followers Theudas led out into the wilderness to display these 'signs' is unclear, but right before discussing 'the Great Famine' and how 'Queen Helen bought grain from Egypt for large sums of money and distributed it among the Poor', Josephus calls it a 'majority of the masses',[3] whereas Acts 5:36, a little more deprecatingly – and anachronistically – terms the number of followers who 'joined' the 'somebody' it calls Theudas as only 'about four hundred'.

Theudas, as just noted, wished to leave Palestine and, Joshua-style, part the waters of the River Jordan but, now, rather in order to *depart* and not to come in. This, anyhow, was seen by the Romans as a subversive act, deserving of beheading. For Acts 4:4, to some extent anticipating Gamaliel's anachronistic reference to this same Theudas in Acts 5:36 above, 'five thousand' is the number of 'believers' who are added at this point to the early Church. Paralleling this and contemporaneous with these other events, for the Pseudoclementine *Recognitions* the number of James' followers, who flee with him down to the Jericho area after the riot in the Temple and physical assault on him led by 'the Enemy' (Paul) is, not surprisingly, again 'five thousand'. As in Acts 5:34, this too is followed by another parallel reference to Gamaliel.[4]

But the most important parallel to both 'Theudas'' activities and those of Queen Helen of Adiabene and her surrogates, and inseparable as well from them, is Jesus in the Gospels feeding the 'five thousand' (Matthew 14:13–22 and pars. – in Matthew 15:38 and Mark 8:9 the number swings back to 'four thousand' and then 'five' again). Regardless of discrepancies or repetitions of this kind and overlaps with other 'feeding' episodes, all the Synoptics describe the locale of this one to 'the five thousand' as being 'in the wilderness' – meant to be either, as in Theudas' case, 'across Jordan' or on 'the other side' of the Sea of Galilee.

For its part John 6:4–71 reports another of these magical 'feeding' episodes of the kind in 2:1–11 previously when Jesus was pictured as turning 'water into wine' at 'Cana of Galilee'. This one, which again has to do with 'five barley loaves and two small fish' and 'a little boy' and occurs 'near the Passover, the Feast of the Jews' (obviously a non-Jew writing this), is compared, therefore (paralleling 'Last Supper' scenarios in the Synoptics and Paul), to 'eating the Living Bread' and 'drinking his blood'. Moreover, it even likens the 'feeding of the five thousand' that ensues to the 'Forefathers eating the manna' – called 'the bread of Heaven' – 'in the wilderness' (John 6:31–58).

At the same time, using the language of the 'works of God' and plainly designating Jesus, as in Pseudoclementine/Ebionite ideology, 'the Prophet who is coming into the world' (6:14), it goes on to develop in the purest of Philonic allegorical terms its version of Jesus' promulgation of the Eucharist (6:50–58[5]). It does so by comparing Jesus' 'flesh' to 'the manna in the desert' or, as it terms it, 'the Living Bread which came down out of Heaven' (6:49–51), his 'flesh truly being food' and his 'blood truly being drink'. Moreover, he who 'eats' and 'drinks' it will 'have everlasting life' and be 'raised on the Last Day' (6:54–55 – again, more Qumran eschatological vocabulary[6]). The conclusion from all this, which has remained effective up to the present day – despite its basically being pure Hellenized Mystery Religion – is finally, therefore, *he who eats my flesh and drinks my blood is living in me and I in him* (6:56) – and this supposedly in Palestine and on the Passover no less!

These are precisely the kinds of 'signs and wonders' that Josephus so rails against and is so anxious to condemn – to say nothing of James' outright ban on 'blood' (one assumes this includes symbolically) in the picture of his directives to overseas communities in Acts. In the case of Josephus, as we saw, such 'Impostors and religious frauds, who teamed up with the bandit chiefs, were more dangerous even than the Revolutionaries' and he clearly views the kind of 'leading people out into the wilderness, there to show them the signs of their impending freedom' that is being depicted here, both in John and the Synoptics, as the worst sort of Revolutionary subversion or imposture (here the contrast between the 'freedom from Rome' as opposed to Paul's more allegorized 'freedom from the Law' polemics again).[7]

If James ever really had made rain, Josephus would have had to see it, too, in the same terms though, to be sure, this is not how he presents him in the *Antiquities*. There Josephus seems, otherwise, quite sympathetic to James and, as we have shown in other work, may even have spent time with him under the alias of the 'Banus' he refers to in the *Vita*, with whom he passed a two-year initiate in his late teens (as he seems to have done, to judge by his long description of them in the *War*, 'the Essenes').[8]

Early Church sources picture James' proclamation in the Temple of the imminent coming of the Son of Man in response to the question put to him by the Temple Authorities about 'the Gate of Jesus'.[9] This same designation, 'Son of Man', would also appear to be equivalent to the individual Paul refers to in 1 Corinthians 15:45–47 as 'the Second Man'/'the Last Adam'/or 'the Lord out of Heaven' – in the War Scroll, as we shall see below, quoting Isaiah 31:8: 'no mere Man' or 'Adam'.[10] Of course, according to other reckonings, such as those found in the Pseudoclementines and parallel incarnationist presentations, this same concept would be embodied in the doctrine known as 'the Primal Adam'.

James' Proclamation and the Coming of the Angelic Host in the War Scroll

In these early Church sources there are also the notices about James praying in the Temple 'till his knees became as hard as a camel's' and about 'all the importuning he did before God' – presumably in the Holy of Holies – 'on behalf of the People'. But this proclamation (in response to the question put to James in Hegesippus' version of these accounts about 'What is the Gate of Jesus?') of 'the Son of Man coming on the clouds of Heaven' – the individual we have just seen Paul refer to in 1 Corinthians 15–16 as 'the Second Man' or 'Last Adam, the Lord out of Heaven' – and the Ebionite/Elchasaite note contained in it about 'sitting on the Right Hand of the Great Power', is precisely the exposition of 'the Star Prophecy' from Numbers 24:17 in climactic passages from the War Scroll, another of those 'eschatological' documents describing, among other things, the final apocalyptic war against all Evil on the Earth.[11]

The Star Prophecy,[12] as we have seen, is also cited in at least two other pivotal contexts in known Scroll documents: the Damascus Document and the Messianic *Florilegium*, which we shall consider in more detail below. In the War Scroll, it is definitively tied to the Messiah and combined with the note from Daniel 7:13 about 'one like a Son of Man amid the clouds of Heaven' and the imagery of final apocalyptic 'Judgment falling like rain on all that grows on Earth'.[13]

Not only is the Prophecy important in helping us appreciate the 'Messianic' thrust of these several notations, it also helps demonstrate just what was implied by the evocation of James' 'rainmaking' in the context of all the importuning of God he did in the Temple – presumably in the Holy of Holies – until 'his knees became as hard as a camel's' (vivid testimony of this kind one should be chary of dismissing) in Epiphanius' version of Hegesippus' testimony about James. Whereas Epiphanius is only a Fourth–Fifth Century CE source, where James is concerned, he largely bases himself on Hegesippus, a Second-Century CE source.

Epiphanius specifically ties this notice of James having made rain during a drought of some kind both to his going into the Holy of Holies once a year, because he was a Nazirite and connected to the Priesthood (Epiphanius' actual words!), and his wearing the High Priestly 'diadem' or '*Nezer*' (Crown).[14] The first part is certainly something of what the *ARN* meant by 'proper Temple service bringing rain in its season', while the second is not completely unconnected, with the play on James' death in the 'Stephen' episode in Acts, whose name means 'Crown' in Greek, specifically signaling in Eusebius' exposition of these events, 'the Martyr's Crown'.[15]

The coupling of two of the most important Messianic prophecies from Numbers 24:17 and Daniel 7:13 in this climactic section of the War Scroll, as well as the citation of the first of these in both Damascus Document and Messianic *Florilegium* and combining them there with the materials from Isaiah cited above is about as important as Josephus' claim in a little-remarked testimony that 'the World Ruler Prophecy' was the moving force behind the Uprising against Rome in 66–70 CE.[16] A better internal dating parameter for documents such as these Dead Sea Scrolls is hardly to be found.

To these the War Scroll adds a third passage from Isaiah 31:8: 'Assyria shall fall by the sword of *no mere Man* and the sword of *no mere Adam*', not normally considered Messianic at all, but coupled with these other indications at this point in the War Scroll it must be so construed. Not only do we have, yet again, just the slightest echo here of the Man/Adam/Primal Adam ideology we have been following, but all are applied to an apocalyptic final Holy War against 'the *Kittim*' – who, in such a context of the Star Prophecy and this kind of imagery from Daniel at this point in the War Scroll are certainly to be seen as the Romans. These sections of Columns 10–11 of the War Scroll, reprised in Column 19, express the kind of apocalyptic Judgment that is being alluded to with reference to 'the Heavenly Host' and 'the hand of Your Messiah'. These, in turn, are coupled with allusion to 'the hand of the Poor' (our *Ebionim* again) and 'the hand of those bent in the dust to humble the Mighty of the Peoples paying (them) the reward on Evil Ones', 'justifying Your True Judgment on all the

Sons of Earth' – including 'the Enemies of all the Lands' – all terms pregnant with meaning for the history of this period.[17]

This notion of 'paying them the reward on Evil Ones' is a widespread one in the Scrolls, particularly apparent in the Habakkuk *Pesher*, where it is applied to the punishment visited upon the Wicked Priest for what he had done to the Righteous Teacher (that is, he had 'destroyed him').[18] There, too, it unquestionably alludes to the apocalyptic process of Final Judgment, a point missed by most commentators. It is also alluded to in the Psalm 37 *Pesher*, where it is applied to the fate of 'the Wicked Priest' as well – 'at the hand of the Violent Ones of the Gentiles' – but the whole context is one of final eschatological Judgment and the 'Salvation of the Righteous' (*Zaddikim*) and 'the Congregation of the Poor Ones' (once more, the *Ebionim*!).[19] The Scroll concludes this eschatological exegesis of Number's 24:17's 'Star Prophecy' and evocation of Daniel's 'Son of Man coming on the clouds of Heaven' by speaking in terms of 'justifying (God's) True Judgment on all the Sons of Earth' (as opposed presumably to 'the Sons of Heaven' carrying it out), including 'the Enemies of all the Lands' which, of course, can mean nothing other than all the foreign nations round about – again demonstrating the quasi-xenophobia of these Scrolls.

This whole climactic exposition of the Star Prophecy in the War Scroll follows its outlining the battle order of the formations, the slogans to be inscribed on the standards and weapons in this War, and the historical note with which it commences of the 'return of the Sons of Light, who are in Exile (*Golah*) from the Desert of the Peoples to the camp in the wilderness of Jerusalem'.[20] Here too, in this opening evocation, 'Benjamin' is defined in terms of this pregnant apposition 'the *Golah*' or 'Diaspora of the Desert', which possibly includes 'the Sons of Levi and the Sons of Judah' and possibly does not, and the English term, Gentiles/Peoples appears in the above phrase, 'the Desert of the Peoples', just as it does in Matthew 4:15.[21]

These passages in the first columns of the War Scroll read like the battle order of an army right out of the age of Cromwell and also parallel, in reverse, movement outlined in the Damascus Document, which twice refers to '*going out from the Land of Judah* to dwell in the Land of Damascus' and which is to say nothing of the several *reverse exoduses* represented by 'Theudas' and those the Gospels picture Jesus as making above.[22] In view of all that we have been describing about the location of groups like 'the Ebionites' or 'Nazoraeans', the movement of what the Qumran documents (even those not so familiar, such as the pivotal *MMT*) are referring to as these 'camps' across the Jordan into the area of Damascus and beyond – possibly the Syrian Desert further north and east even as far 'North' as 'Assyria' (the classical 'Land of the Osrhoeans') and Adiabene – is significant.

Biblically-speaking, this is the direction Elijah is pictured as taking 'in the *Way of the wilderness of Damascus*' in 1 Kings 19:15 after his prototypical 'cave-dwelling' and 'rainmaking' in 1 Kings 18. This is not to mention the various pictures of Paul in Acts, Galatians, and the Pseudoclementine *Recognitions* following a fleeing community into just these areas as well.[23] This emigration also bears on the legends of 'a flight' to the Pella region – also across Jordan on 'the way to Damascus' – by James' 'Jerusalem Church' followers in response to some mysterious oracle after his death which we shall further elucidate below.

Pella was the nearest settled city across the Jordan leading up to Damascus and beyond in the great expanse of desert north and east along the Fertile Crescent as far as 'the Kingdom of the Edessenes' in Northern Syria and 'the Land of Adiabene' further east. By the same token, it is also possible to take the allusion to this 'Pella Flight' more generically as it might be the allusion to an emigration to 'the Land of Damascus' in the Qumran documents and the whole tangle of conflicting data relating to the same area in Acts, Paul's letters, the Pseudoclementine *Recognitions*, and Josephus – to say nothing of the similar flight tradition, where Northern Syria or Mesopotamia is concerned, after the death of John the Baptist in Mandaean literature.

Epiphanius expresses something of this, when speaking about 'the Ebionites' and 'Nazoraeans', in the section in which he also refers to 'the Primal Adam' ideology of 'Sampsaeans, Osseneans, and Elchaseans' (that is, the Sabaeans, Essenes, and Elchasaites). He says: 'For the most part these settled in Perea, Pella a city in the Decapolis, Batanea (the Roman province north of the Decapolis and east of Gaulonitus/'the Golan'), and the Land of Bashan (the classical name for these areas, overlapping most of these other locations as far north as Damascus).[24] His meaning here is clear and he was a Palestinian – as we have seen, allegedly a convert from Judaism or, more precisely perhaps, 'Ebionitism' – so whatever else might be intended, he is certainly speaking about the other side of the Jordan River and further north in Syria – 'on the Way to Damascus' as 1 Kings 19:15 about Elijah might have put it.

In other delineations of such groups, Epiphanius also includes 'Moab' (directly east from the Fortress at Masada on the other side of the Dead Sea, south of Perea and north of Arabian Petra) and 'Coele-Syria', north of Damascus on the way up to Aleppo, Edessa ('Antioch Orrhoe'), and points further East.[25] This is the area of primary interest to the War Scroll too, which speaks in its own archaizing manner of a War against 'Edom', 'Moab', 'the Sons of Ishmael', 'the *Kittim* of Assyria' (probably referring to the Romans but possibly, as some see it, the Seleucids preceding them – this cannot be determined with precision on the basis of the reference as it stands), 'Aram-Naharaim' (Northern Syria and Iraq), and 'the East as far as the Great Desert', also a straightforward geographical allusion.[26]

Where 'the *Kittim*' are concerned, their armies are also specifically denoted as being in Egypt as well. They too 'shall be crushed' and 'their Rule shall be ended'.[27] As per the indication in Daniel 11:30 (though not 1 Maccabees 1:1), 'the *Kittim*' in such references probably are the Romans, which is also the implication of both the Habakkuk and Nahum *Pesher*s, where it is impossible to apply the allusion to any group other than the Romans. Though these may be 'Greeks' or at least 'Macedonians', as per 1 Maccabees 1:1, it is difficult to imagine that such a term might refer to any Grecian Period other than that of Alexander the Great when there may have been separate contingents of Macedonian troops in these areas. One certainly cannot refer to the Seleucids in this incredibly-inflated manner, power-wise, by any stretch of the imagination.

Be this as it may, all these groups together with their allies are referred to here in the War Scroll as 'the Sons of Darkness in the Army of *Belial*'.[28] On the other hand, those living 'in the camps', who must carry out this struggle, abetted by the Army of Heavenly Holy Ones, are referred to by expressions like 'the Sons of Light' or 'the People of God'.[29] The time is that 'of Salvation (Hebrew: 'of *Yeshu'a*') for the People of God'.[30] These last are also referred to as 'the Sons of Levi and the Sons of Judah and the Sons of Benjamin'. Taken together, as we just saw, they or 'the Sons of Benjamin' alone (probably the latter) are referred to as 'the *Golat ha-Midbar*'/'the Exile of the Desert' or 'the Diaspora of the Desert' or 'Wilderness'.[31] One should also note the parallel in this last reference to the addressee of the Letter of James 1:1, referred to as 'the Twelve Tribes which (are) in the Diaspora'. It would be hard to imagine a closer fit.

Benjamin, the *Golah* of the Desert

The first two of these categories, 'the Sons of Levi and the Sons of Judah', are clearly the Priest Class and the People of Judah, the so-called 'Judeans' or, as in contexts such as at Qumran, in the Gospels, and Josephus, simply 'Jews'. But the third, 'Benjamin the *Golah* of the Desert' – the only reference of this type in the whole Qumran corpus, is more puzzling and may provide a clue to what Paul was trying to say when referring to himself in Romans 11:1 and Philippians 3:5 as being of 'the Tribe of Benjamin'.

It is sometimes suggested that 'Benjamin' in this period is a reference to all Diaspora Jews. It may be, but this is not proved. As Paul uses the term, echoed in Acts 13:21 as well, aside from playing on the name of his namesake 'Saul', who actually was 'a Benjaminite' – doubtlessly an important aspect of his use of it, there may also be a play on the Belaʿ/Belial/ Edomite origins of Herodians, not to mention the way 'Sons of Belial' and its parallel 'Balaam' are sometimes used at Qumran and in the New Testament generally. This rests on the proposition that Paul is an Herodian himself which, based on his reference in Romans 16:10–11 to his 'kinsman the Littlest Herod' and 'the House of Aristobulus' in Rome – as we shall explore further below, presumably Aristobulus V, Herod of Chalcis' son and the second husband of that Salome allegedly involved in the death of John the Baptist – and other indicators, the present writer considers to be accurate.[32]

Not only does it turn out, through either confusion or acculturation, that 'Belaʿ' is reckoned (like its other curious, genealogical overlap 'Balaam', just noted above as a variation of 'Belial') as the 'Son of Beʿor' and the first of the Edomite Kings, but Belaʿ also turns out to be, according to delineations such as those in Genesis and Chronicles, the name of the principal 'Benjaminite' clan.[33] Herodians, who were certainly seen as 'Edomites' ('Idumaeans' in this period being a Greco-Latin formulation for 'Edomite'), may have been using this curious genealogical overlap to make – as Paul does – just such a 'Benjaminite' claim.

Such a claim of descent from Benjamin – and, therefore, descent from Jacob, though not Judah – could easily translate itself into that of being 'of the Race of Israel' (though not 'Jews') and, 'a Hebrew of the Hebrews', as Paul puts it so tantalizingly in Philippians 3:5. The term 'Benjamin' therefore, in time, may also have come to apply to all such converts, such as these Herodians – if 'converts' is the appropriate word. It may also have been expanded to include Gentiles generally, which could then possibly be seen as another aspect of this puzzling allusion. The allusion, 'the Sons of Benjamin', 'the *Golah* of the Desert', as it occurs in this opening passage in the War Scroll, does appear to carry something of this meaning while, at the same time, applying to a specific *Golah/Galut* or 'Diaspora in the Desert', that of, the 'Wilderness' or 'Desert Camps'.

Muhammad, while never mentioning Paul in the Koran, as a latter-day 'Apostle to the Gentiles', can be viewed (like Mani before him) as a Seventh-Century successor to Paul, particularly in the importance he attached to Abraham. This is especially true where Northern Syrian locales – Abraham's original homeland – were at issue. He and all Arabs after him pick up this 'Abrahamic' – if not the 'Israelite' – aspect of the Hebrew genealogy by raising the claim of descent from Ishmael. In doing so, they are also making a quasi-'Hebrew' claim but, even more importantly, they are also like Paul – and here the transmission is direct – claiming to be 'Heirs' to 'the Religion of Abraham' (for Paul, 'the Children of' or 'the Belief of Abraham'[34]). In the case of Muslims, or at least Arabs, the sense is both genealogical *and* spiritual too. Paul may have been implying the same.

Another aspect of the puzzling allusion to 'Benjamin', as it is circulating in the First Century, may be its application to Gentiles generally, in particular, Gentile associates ('God-Fearers' in both the New Testament and, in the writer's view, even to some degree at Qumran[35]) or even 'Converts'. The author considers this last the more-likely meaning of the term given the way it is used in the War Scroll. This is certainly some of the sense being reflected in the Damascus Document's crucial exegesis of 'the Zadokite Covenant' from Ezekiel 44:15 too, which, as already explained, in addition to breaking open Ezekiel's original 'the Priests who are Sons-of-Zadok Levites' by the deliberate insertion of *waw*-constructs (it then becomes 'the Priests, the Levites, and the Sons of Zadok'), now interprets 'the Levites' – playing on the original root-meaning of the word – as 'the *Nilvim*' or 'Joiners with them', meaning, those 'joining' the Priests (defined as 'Penitents in the wilderness' – an abnormal and certainly ungenealogical description of Priests, if there ever was one) and 'the Sons of Zadok'. All of these, it now implies – bringing us back to the various 'Damascus' or 'Pella Flight' traditions we shall analyze further below – 'went out from the Land of Judah to dwell in the Land of Damascus'.[36]

This is also the way the Nahum *Pesher* would appear to be using the root, *L-V-Y/I*, the root of both 'Levites' and *Nilvim*/'Joiners'. It ties it to the phrase *'ger-nilveh'*, that is, 'resident alien' or 'the foreigner resident among them' (to whom circumcision was seen to apply in the passage Izates was reading from Genesis 17 when he was queried by Eleazar as to whether he understood 'the true meaning of what he was reading'). The Nahum *Pesher* also ties it to another of its odd esotericisms, 'the Simple of Ephraim' which may simply stand for Samaritans – 'Ephraim' being in this period the Land in which the Samaritans now dwelled.[37] This is to say nothing of the whole Amraphel/Ephraim circle of problems we have pointed out relative to the Psalm 37 *Pesher* too. That there was an originally non-Jewish cadre of 'Joiners', meaning Resident Aliens or God-Fearers, associated with the Community of Qumran, the author considers a self-evident truism. That this is something of what is implied at this point by the Ephraim usage (if not that of Amraphel), the author also considers to be self-evident. To bring us full circle, the War Scroll is now applying these conceptualities to a specific *Golah* or Diaspora – 'the *Golah* of the Wilderness' or 'Desert Camps'.

The whole 'Benjamin' or '*Golah* of the Desert' usage may also carry with it something of the way non-Jewish converts – those like the *Nilvim*/'Joiners' in the Damascus Document's exegesis of Ezekiel 44:15 above, who 'join' the 'Penitents in the wilderness' (that is, 'the Priests and the Sons of Zadok' – in the War Scroll, 'the Sons of Levi and the Sons of Judah', but all subsumed under the general heading of 'the Exiled Sons of Light') in 'going' out from 'the Land of Judah to dwell in the Land of Damascus' – were looked upon in this period.

It is possible even to draw a parallel to those Josephus is mysteriously picturing as 'Idumaeans' – identity unknown though at times they seem to be led by someone he calls 'Niger of Perea'.[38] Not only are they clearly 'Violent', but they are just as clearly in league with those he is designating at this point as 'Zealots' (in the Qumran documents being referred to either as 'the Violent Ones' or 'the Violent Ones of the Gentiles' – at one point even, 'the Men-of-War') who take vengeance on the Wicked Priest for what he did to the Righteous Teacher in both the Psalm 37 *Pesher* and the Habakkuk *Pesher*[39] and who, in the latter, actually appear to attend the Righteous Teacher's or 'the Priest'"s ('in whose heart God put the insight to interpret the words of His Servants the Prophets') scriptural exegesis sessions.[40]

However these things may be, something like the terminology 'Benjaminite' is clearly circulating in the 'Diaspora' or 'Camps' beyond the Jordan and in the Damascus region. Since Paul – when he speaks in Galatians 1:17–18 of 'going away into Arabia' – has just as clearly spent time in these areas or, in the author's view, in this Diaspora or in these Camps, this may provide insight into the way Paul and Acts are using the term 'Benjamin',[41] that is, the same way the War Scroll is using it. How much time Paul actually spent in these areas or 'Camps' would depend on how one chooses to interpret his reference to the 'three years' he says elapsed between his going 'into Arabia' and returning to Damascus and Jerusalem, not to mention the 'fourteen' additional years he alludes to as the time that elapsed before next he went up to Jerusalem in Galatians 2:1. In the writer's view, much of this time was spent 'in Arabia', which in Roman parlance included the areas as far north even as Northern Syria and Northern Iraq or Adiabene.

It is also important to note that in the Letter (or Letters) known as *MMT*, some regulations concerning these 'Camps' are discussed and Jerusalem is specifically denoted as 'the Holy Camp' and 'Chief of the Camps of Israel'. In our view, as should be by now clear, this Letter is in fact the very one containing James' directives to overseas communities, carried down by Judas Barsabas and Silas to the Antioch refracted in the somewhat tendentious portrait in Acts 15:22–30.

It should also be noted that in the final triumphant evocation of 'the Son of Man' at the end of the War Scroll, which repeats the whole description of eschatological rain and final apocalyptic Judgment at the hands of the Heavenly Holy Ones on the clouds, God is referred to as 'the God of Righteousness'.[42] At the same time, it is stated that 'His is the Power, the battle is in His hands'. Then, too, the wish is expressed that 'He' or 'His Messiah' (probably the latter) should 'smite the Nations' or 'the Peoples, His Enemies, and devour' or 'consume flesh with His sword'.[43]

We have not only encountered this 'eating' or 'devouring' language at the end of Galatians 5:15 when Paul is criticizing those who are misleading his communities with circumcision, but this idea of 'eating' or 'consuming' will be a fixture of the Habakkuk *Pesher*, particularly in the manner in which the Wicked Priest 'consumes' or 'destroys' the Righteous Teacher and the way in which 'the *Kittim* (here clearly the Romans) '*consume* all Peoples … with the sword' as well.[44] On the other hand, here in the War Scroll the 'sword' is rather referred to as 'the sword of God' – pretty blood-curdling, but probably an accurate depiction of the desire of this group for Divine Retribution or, as it is often called, 'Vengeance'.[45]

In this context, that of blessing God's Name and reference to His 'keeping the Covenant with us as of old' ('keeping the Covenant' being the definition of 'the Sons of Zadok' in the Community Rule[46]), the text now refers to 'the Gates of Salvation' ('*Yeshu'a* – that is, in more Hellenized parlance, 'Jesus'). These last, it claims, have been opened many times in the past.[47] The same usage is basically referred to in the question asked of James, 'What is the Gate to Jesus?', in all accounts of his proclamation in the Temple on Passover of this 'coming of the Son of Man sitting on the right hand of the Great Power … about to come in Glory on the clouds of Heaven'.[48] So here, then, we have the eschatological link between James' rainmaking, his proclamation of 'Glory', and that of the final apocalyptic War against all Evil on the Earth and the delineation of these things in the War Scroll.

'Galilee' in the Gospels and the Massacre Conducted by Vespasian there

It is this picture in the War Scroll of the movement 'from the camp in the Wilderness' or 'Desert of the Peoples to the camp in the wilderness of Judea' which, in its own way, can be thought of as being transformed in the Gospels to that of Jesus' movement from his baptism and 'Temptation in the wilderness' northwards – after John, anticipating Jesus, 'was delivered up' to 'the Galilee of the Nations' in Matthew 4:15. This, once again, basically also parallels the flight in Mandaean tradition of John's followers across the Jordan to Haran ('Edessa' or 'Urfa') in Northern Syria and after that to Messene in Southern Mesopotamia. As the Gospels portray this, 'Galilee' now becomes the domain of Jesus' activities, and his Apostles, peaceful 'fishermen' ('casters of nets and fishers of men') around the Sea of Galilee (Matthew 4:18–19 and pars.).

In turn, this latter picture plays to a certain extent on that of another character in Josephus' narrative, 'Jesus son of Sapphias', the Leader of the *Galilean sailors and fishermen* on the Sea of Galilee at the time of the outbreak of the War with Rome.[49] Accusing him of 'fomenting sedition and Revolution' ('Innovation') in Tiberius – typical of the accusations Josephus makes – Josephus tells how he burned the palace of Herod the Tetrarch (John the Baptist's murderer and, in our view, the putative 'kinsman' of Paul in Acts 13:1), because it 'contained pictures of animals which was contrary to Law'. Josephus, furthermore, claims Jesus also 'massacred all the Greek inhabitants there'. Curiously Tiberius, which was one of the cities founded by Herod Antipas, Tetrarch of Galilee and Perea, and the major city on the Sea of Galilee at this time, is conspicuously missing from Gospel portraits of events there.

Josephus portrays this Jesus and his (Josephus') own mortal enemy, 'a copy of the Laws of Moses in his hands' (surely there is a certain amount of sarcastic parody and animosity going on at this point), as trying to have him (Josephus) executed as a collaborator. To add to that, he specifically identifies Jesus' followers as both 'Galileans' and 'the Poor' (or 'Poor wretches').[50] Calling him 'the Leader of the Brigands' (as in Gospel portraits of the two crucified with Jesus and other similar denotations in his own work, '*Lestai*' again[51]), Josephus can scarcely conceal his delight in describing how Vespasian and Titus came and, in the end, slaughtered many of this Jesus' followers while they were attempting to 'board their boats' or 'swim out to sea' – these last, of course, familiar motifs in Gospel iconography.[52]

Jesus and some of his other fishermen or boatmen, it seems, at the approach of the Roman army had already put out on the Lake (more Gospel portraiture?) in their little boats just out of bowshot. For his part, Josephus portrays the scene as follows: 'Casting down their anchors, they closed up their boats one against the other like an army in battle formation and fought their enemy on the shore from the sea.' At this point, Titus turned his attention instead to massacring the citizens of Tiberius, guilty and innocent alike. In these engagements, Josephus also accords generous mention to the gallantry of Trajan, the father and namesake of the future Emperor, consistently remarked throughout this picture of warfare in Palestine.[53]

Finally the Romans, moving east along the shore of the Lake to another city, Tarichaeae, at its confluence with the Jordan, themselves take to the Lake using bigger rafts. Here they overtake Jesus and his supporters, overturning their boats and spearing and decapitating so many in the water that 'the whole lake was red with blood and covered with corpses, for not a man escaped ... and the beaches were strewn with wrecks and swollen corpses'.[54] This is the end of Josephus' picture of the Galilean fishermen or boatmen and what happened on the Sea of Galilee or 'Lake Gennesareth' – and this, in contrast to some others, is clearly an eyewitness one!

Following this total collapse, Vespasian, who felt 'that nothing against the Jews could be considered an Impiety' (*this is verbatim* – there are some others who have since felt the same way), immediately executed some twelve hundred of the old and infirm, who had not even participated in the fighting. Six thousand of the more able-bodied he sent to Nero at Corinth to work on the canal which Nero was having dug there. Thirty thousand more he sold himself and he gave the remainder to King Agrippa (Agrippa II), who had originally invited Titus in to deal with the situation around the Sea of Galilee, since this was part of his domains. Whereupon Agrippa promptly sold them. This is the man, together with his reputed consort Bernice – later the mistress of Titus, the destroyer of both the Temple and Jerusalem – who is presented so sympathetically in Acts and with whom Paul talks so congenially in Acts 25:13–26:32.[55]

Agrippa II had received this Tetrarchy, which even Josephus allows was so rich that 'anything planted there grew immediately' – true even to this day – in succession to his father Agrippa I (himself, seemingly portrayed in Acts 12:21–23), who had been given it and his other domains after Herod the Tetrarch (Herodias' husband 'Herod Antipas') had been banished to Southern France by Caligula.[56] Actually Matthew 4:15, in describing the activities of its 'Jesus', quotes Isaiah 8:23–9:1 on 'the *Galil* of the Gentiles' (literally, 'Circle' or 'Wheel of the Gentiles', rephrased slightly here in Matthew to 'Galilee of the Peoples, the Way of the Sea beyond Jordan'), pictures him as 'withdrawing' to Nazareth and thence, 'departing Nazareth and coming to dwell' along the Sea of Galilee.

The original of this in Isaiah, which does seem to refer to 'the far side of the Jordan', would be better approximated by terms like 'the Decapolis', 'Perea', Syria, and what today goes by the name of 'the Fertile Crescent' and the Peoples, mostly 'Arab', living along its sweep. Nor is there any 'wilderness' or 'desert' around the Sea of Galilee or near it, the great fertility of which was just indicated, where Jesus on several occasions, already underscored above, is portrayed either as 'multiplying the loaves and the fishes' for his followers or sermonizing to them. On the contrary.

In this picture of Jesus' appearance by the Sea of Galilee, he calls his principal Disciples, who, being fishermen, 'were casting a net into the sea' (*ballontas* – once more, the vocabulary of 'casting', this time combined with 'net' imagery of the kind encountered in the Damascus Document and Revelation relative to 'Balak', 'Balaam', or 'Belial') or 'mending their nets'. Matthew 4:25, in fact, speaks of Galilee in the same breath as 'the Decapolis, Jerusalem, Judea, and beyond the Jordan', which confuses things even more and shows an almost complete lack of geographical knowledge of this area. Mark 3:8 adds to this, 'from Idumaea and beyond the Jordan' as well as 'those around Tyre and Sidon'. Luke 6:17, for his part trying to make sense of all this, now drops the 'Decapolis, Idumaea, and across the Jordan' and transforms it into 'the Sea Coast of Tyre and Sidon', whatever this was supposed to mean!

Regardless of these several non sequiturs, for Mark 3:9–10 the 'Many' that he had cured were so great 'that they pressed upon him so they might touch him and the unclean spirits, when they beheld, fell down before him, crying out, "Truly you are the Son of God"'. The marvelousness of this portrait notwithstanding, adding some more effusiveness about 'being cured of unclean spirits', Luke now employs the 'Elchasaite' language of 'Hidden Power', averring that 'Power came forth from him and healed them all' (6:18). Then, like Matthew, it immediately moves on to its version of 'the Beatitudes' of the Sermon on the Mount (6:20–6:49). For its part, Mark rather closes this episode with Jesus now angrily charging the masses – like James in the preface to the Pseudoclementine *Homilies*[57] or the Sabaean 'Keepers of the Secret', or even 'the Way in the wilderness' portion of the Community Rule[58] – 'not to make this known', that is, what the unclean spirits cried out when they were cured (more phantasmagoria – 3:12)!

One should contrast the historical reality or, rather, unreality of episodes such as these with the one from Josephus above about the brutal, bloody, and uncompromising warfare that basically devastated settled life around the Sea of Galilee. If there ever was an 'Historical Jesus' around 'Gennesareth' at this time (Luke 5:1 – the name Josephus also accords this Lake, the overlap of which with the term 'Nazareth', as it appears in Scripture, should not be overlooked) – on the face of it, a rather dubious proposition – this 'Jesus son of Sapphias', the Leader of the Galilean boatmen and 'the Poor' on the Sea of Galilee, who together with his followers poured his blood out into it, was almost surely he.[59]

In fact, the whole picture in the Gospels of evangelical and religious activity around the Sea of Galilee at this time more likely reflects the situation circulating around the shores of the Dead Sea, which does seem to have been much busier than most would have thought,[60] Gennesareth and/or Galilee-type allusions perhaps acting as geographical stand-ins for designations like 'Nazirite', 'Nazoraeans', or 'Galileans'. Nor is this to say anything about the phrase 'Cana in Galilee' in John 2:11 and 4:46, almost certainly representing such a circumlocution – 'Cana' (*kana*/'zeal'), it will be recalled, in other contexts standing for 'Cananaean' or 'Zealot' and being where Jesus first 'turned water into wine', cured another 'little child', and, paralleling Josephus' descriptions of 'magicians', 'Impostors', or 'pseudo-prophets', 'did the first of his signs and revealed his Glory' (John 2:11), 'having come *out of Judea into Galilee*' (John 4:54).

Elsewhere, after the incident about the Greek Syrophoenician woman and 'casting down crumbs' to dogs – almost certainly playing on and inverting *MMT*'s barring of 'dogs from the Holy Camp because they might eat bones with the flesh still on them'[61] – Mark, showing an almost total lack of geographical precision, has Jesus going from Tyre and Sidon to the Sea of Galilee 'through the midst of the coasts of the Decapolis' (7:31). For his part, Matthew 19:1

has Jesus 'withdrawing from Galilee and coming to the coasts of Judea beyond Jordan', geographically speaking, again almost an impossibility. John 3:26 and 10:40, on the other hand, echoing Luke 3:3 on John the Baptist going 'into all the country around the Jordan', often has both John and Jesus as habitués of these same regions beyond Jordan.

Basically, however, the areas referred to in all of these notices are the ones we have been encountering in Hippolytus' and Epiphanius' testimonies to these Essene or Ebionite-like 'Judeo-Christian' sects, including the various Arab Kingdoms referred to by contemporary Latin and Greek authors – Arab Kingdoms in 'the Land of the Osrhoeans' around Haran in Syria and Northern Mesopotamia as well as finally in Southern Mesopotamia, where Ananias first encounters Izates in the story of his and his mother Queen Helen's conversion and where, a century or two later, Mani was born.

The Regime of Extreme Purity in the Camps

The War Scroll also pictures what it considers to be the regime in these camps, this at the time it designates as 'the time of *Yeshu'a*' – 'the time of Salvation for the People of God and Eternal destruction for all of the lot of Belial'. This time would appear to be consonant with the return of 'the Dispersion of the Sons of Light from the Desert of the Peoples to the camps in the wilderness around Jerusalem'[62] – 'the Desert of the Peoples' now clearly being synonymous with what Matthew 4:15 is calling 'Galilee of the Nations' or 'Peoples' (*Ethnon*). For the War Scroll, 'no boy or woman is ever to enter the camps' during the whole period of their going out to what can only be described as 'Holy War'. Rather 'they shall all be Volunteers for War, Perfect in Spirit and body, preparing for the Day of Vengeance'![63]

The expression 'Volunteers for War' is similar to that found in 1 Maccabees 2:42's description of Judas Maccabee's army (Daniel's *Kedoshim*/'Holy Ones' or 'Saints'), described at this point as 'Hassidaeans' ('Pious Ones') 'each one a stout Volunteer on the side of the Law'. Despite the conflicting testimony in 1 Maccabees 7:13, which portrays these same Hassidaeans – who appear to make up the bulk of Judas' most committed military contingent – as pacifistic, more compromising, and willing to accept a High Priest appointed by foreign power (in this case, by the Seleucids), in the view of the author this must be balanced against 2 Maccabees 14:6 which implies just the opposite. I have treated this seeming contradiction at length in my short monograph *Maccabees, Zadokites, Christians and Qumran* in *The Dead Sea Scrolls and the First Christians* (Barnes and Noble, 2004), concluding that what we have here are rather terminological confusions and, actually, the birth moment of 'the Pharisee Party' – the latter, more-compromising 'Hassidaeans', being rather nascent 'Pharisees' who *split away* from more aboriginal 'Zealot' or Zadokite Sadducees *over the issue of foreign appointment of High Priests*.[64]

Another parallel is to be found in the 'Paean to King Jonathan', the pro-Maccabean attitude of which is patent.[65] Greeting its addressee – who can either be thought of as Alexander Jannaeus (d. 76 BCE); his great uncle, the first Maccabean Priest-King, Jonathan (d. 142 BCE); or Alexander Jannaeus' own son Aristobulus II (d. 48 BCE) – in adulatory terms, this text found by perspicacious Israeli scholars is really a Hebrew Poem of Praise or panegyric.[66] Not only this: it mysteriously alludes, in what can only be construed as the most approving terms, to 'the Joiners' once again – the '*Nilvim*' of the Damascus Document's exegesis of Ezekiel 44:15 – this time, 'the Joiners' or 'Volunteers in the War of...'.[67] There the text breaks off.

Not only does it clearly disprove the notion held by most 'Consensus Scholars' that one or another of the Maccabees could be viewed as 'the Wicked Priest' and confirm my own position that the Scrolls must be seen as pro- not anti-Maccabean since they exhibit the same ethos as the Maccabeans – most notably, 'zeal for the Law' and/or 'Covenant'[68], but it also belies the widely-held parallel misconception that 'the Essenes' were 'peaceful'.

Maybe so-called 'Essenes' were peaceful or other-worldly in Philo's Egypt, but in Josephus' Palestine they clearly participated, as he has testified and this definitively, in the War against the Romans.[69] Nor can this War, as referred to in numerous Qumran documents, be considered simply a spiritual or symbolic war, as was likewise portrayed by numerous early Qumran scholars[70] (and is still portrayed) – at least as pictured by the Qumran documents themselves, a portrait for some reason they often incongruously ignore. This too is confirmed by a host of other extremely aggressive and war-like texts in the corpus at Qumran, some more recently released – some of long-standing.[71] Also the expression 'Day of Vengeance' found at this juncture in the War Scroll is encountered – again probably definitively – in a climactic section in the Community Rule. Not only does this conclusion contain the all-important John the Baptist-style 'this is the time of the preparation of the Way in the wilderness', but this expression 'the Day of Vengeance', itself a synonym for 'the Last Judgment' and hardly very pacifistic, is linked in that section both to 'zeal for the Law' and spiritualized 'atonement' imagery.[72]

The implication of finding all these telltale usages linked together not only bears on the aggressiveness of the corpus, but also that the documents in which they occur must all be viewed as more or less contemporary or written at roughly the same time – regardless either of palaeographic or AMS carbon-testing indicators to the contrary – since they are all using the same esotericisms, vocabulary, and allude on the whole to the same *dramatis personae*. There cannot be decades or even generations between their respective dates-of-origin as is the implication of most reigning 'Establishment' theorizing.

In the Community Rule, the use of this expression, 'the Day of Vengeance', rises out of the elucidation of a twice-repeated citation of the biblical proof-text (Isaiah 40:3) applied in the Synoptic Gospels to John the Baptist's 'mission' in the wilderness.[73] After alluding to 'atoning for the land' and 'suffering affliction' and 'being confirmed in Perfection of the Way' and 'separated as Holy' – meaning, in a much underestimated ideology, that this is a 'Community of Consecrated Holy Ones' or 'Nazirites' – the text puts this in the following manner: 'according to these Rules, they shall *separate* from the midst of the habitation of the Men of Ungodliness and go out into the wilderness to prepare the Way of the Lord, as it is written, "Prepare in the wilderness the Way of the Lord. Make straight in the desert a Pathway for our God"' (Isaiah 40:3).[74] The only difference between this ideology and other similar, more familiar ones is that 'the Way in the wilderness' here is clearly defined as 'the study of the *Torah*' which these 'Perfect'/'Separated'/'Consecrated'/or 'Holy Ones' are 'commanded *to do*' exactly as it has 'been revealed from Age to Age' and 'as the Prophets have revealed through His Holy Spirit'.[75]

This 'Jamesian' emphasis on 'doing', which will be stressed even more forcefully in the Damascus Document and the Habakkuk *Pesher*,[76] is emphasized even further when this 'Way in the wilderness' ideology is then reiterated in the Community Rule, but it is so important that, even though we have already reproduced parts of this, it is worth repeating the whole: 'He shall *do* the will of God in accord with everything that has been revealed from Age to Age ... to *separate* ... to walk Perfectly each with his neighbor ... for this is the time of making a Way in the wilderness and they shall be instructed in all that has been revealed that they should *do* in this time, to *separate* from any man who has not turned his Way from Ungodliness ... Everlasting hatred for the Men of the *Pit* in a spirit of *secrecy*.... Rather he shall be like a man *zealous for the Law*, whose time is for the Day of Vengeance, to *do* His will in all the *work* of his hands and in all His Kingdom as He Commanded.'[77] That anyone could even conceive that allusions such as these relate to any century other than the First, even in the face of 'external data' to the contrary which are all subject to human error – shows a distinct lack of historical prescience or insight.

As already noted, such 'sectarian' documents, themselves showing every indication of being from the last stages of Qumran ideology and not the first, must, because of internal consistencies of *sitz im leben* (life setting), vocabulary, *dramatis personae*, and fundamental conceptualities, all have been written at around the same time – other, more external, indications notwithstanding. There are, in fact, internal indicators in documents other than the War Scroll and Community Rule, as we have been suggesting, which also show a distinct First-Century provenance – as, for instance, in the Habakkuk, Isaiah, Nahum, and Psalm 37 *Peshers*, the Messianic *Florilegium*, the *Testimonia*, and the like.

The correspondence here between the War Scroll and the Community Rule on the subject of 'the Day of Vengeance' is the kind of thing one is talking about that implies chronological contemporaneity. It is precise. The same is true of the Hymns, where similar allusions abound and 'the Day of Vengeance' is rather referred to as 'the Day of Massacre',[78] but the effect is the same. As the War Scroll ends up putting these things: 'No one who is impure in the manner of sexual emissions (is to join their camps), for the Holy Angels are with their Hosts.'[79] This allusion to 'the Heavenly Host' actually being *with* 'the Walkers in the Way of Perfect Holiness' and in their 'Desert' or 'Wilderness Camps' is again a pervasive one at Qumran, running through many of the documents, including portions of the Damascus Document as it was found in Cave 4 at Qumran and not necessarily at Cairo.[80]

Not only does it have everything to do with the vision of the Heavenly Host 'coming on the clouds of Heaven' dominating the proclamation James is pictured as making in early Church literature, but it absolutely explains the regime of extreme purity followed in these 'camps' where, unlike Paul's world-view as expressed in his Letters of 'all things being lawful to me', 'Holy' was absolutely to be 'separated from profane' and 'the Holy Things' were absolutely to be 'set up according to their precise specifications, to love each man his brother as himself, to strengthen the hand of the Meek, the Poor, and the Convert ... and not to uncover the nakedness of near kin, to *keep away* from fornication ... to *separate* from all pollutions ... (and) walk in these things in Perfect Holiness on the basis of the Covenant of God in which they were instructed, faithfully promising them they would live for a thousand generations'.[81] We shall see more about this 'thousand generations' later but, once again, not only is this the exact opposite of the vision allegedly vouchsafed to Peter in Acts' 'descent of the Heavenly tablecloth' episode (more amusing *divertissement*?), but in fact, the whole regime of 'extreme purity' in these 'Camps' is the very *opposite* of that delineated in the Gospels as being followed and recommended by their 'Jesus', portrayed as accepting of and finally even 'keeping table fellowship with' a wide assortment of persons who would otherwise be considered absolutely 'unclean' at Qumran.

The ruins of Pella across Jordan in Perea, to which according to 'Christian' tradition the Community of James was supposed to have fled after his death. For Qumran, it was to 'the Land of Damascus'

Chapter 13
James' Proclamation in the Temple and Joining the Heavenly Holy Ones

'Joining the Heavenly Holy Ones' in Hymns, the Community Rule, and the War Scroll

The idea of striving for bodily and spiritual 'Perfect Holiness' so as not to pollute the purity of the Host of Heavenly Holy Ones is a fixture of Dead Sea Scrolls like the War Scroll and Hymns. It is also present in the Community Rule and Damascus Document – again demonstrating the basic homogeneity of all these documents and their contemporaneity – that is, if we have demonstrated chronological ambiance (in our view, the First Century) for one such document employing usages of this kind, then we have basically demonstrated it for most or all such documents employing usages of this kind.

As this 'Communion' with the Sons of Heaven is described in Hymns (how much closer to Paul's more Hellenized concept of 'Communion with the body' and 'blood of the Christ' can one get without actually enunciating it?), which abounds with the imagery of 'the soul of the Righteous' or 'Poor One', pre-existent and Divine sonship, and the idea, finally, of 'standing' before God in a state of 'Perfect Light for all Eternity': 'You have shaped him from the dust for an Eternal Foundation and cleansed a straying Spirit of great sin that it may stand on a plain with the Host of the Holy Ones and join with the Community of the Sons of Heaven.'[1] Here, too, the imagery of 'joining' is now being used in a new fashion suggesting 'joining with Heavenly Beings'. This is not unsimilar to Paul in 1 Corinthians 6:16–17 as well, where this imagery is rather applied to 'joining with harlots' under the general rubric of the favorite Qumran subject 'fornication' or, later in 12:12–28, where the 'joining' is now with 'the body of Christ' – echoed, for example, in Ephesians 2:19–22. In fact, the latter basically becomes 'the Household' or 'Building of God', 'a Holy Temple in the Lord', and 'a Dwelling-place of God in the Spirit', all, of course, very allegorized or spiritualized and very much like what we see developing here in these allusions at Qumran from Hymns.[2]

'Standing' imagery is of course always important, particularly as it implies Resurrection and where the Ebionite/Pseudoclementine ideology of the 'incarnated Messiah' or 'Primal Adam' as 'the Standing One' is concerned.[3] Therefore, too, as we have already suggested as well, throughout much of the imagery one gets in documents such as the Gospels, the subject of 'his feet' or 'footwear' becomes of such interest – presumably the only part of 'the Standing One''s body visible to a mere mortal – as, for instance, John 1:26–27, also evoking 'standing' imagery, on even John the Baptist being 'unworthy to untie His (Jesus') shoe lace' (itself probably having something to do with 'the Shiloh' imagery).[4]

In the next column of Hymns, following evocation of this 'War' of the Heavenly Holy Ones that will scourge the earth until the appointed Destruction, its author again describes God as manifesting Himself in his Power (the Ebionite/Elchasaite 'Great Power' imagery again) 'as Perfect Light'.[5] This comes right before yet another passage about 'the Way of Man' ('*Enosh*' – the name applied to John the Baptist in Mandaean literature) and the Perfection of the Way of the Son of Man' ('*Adam*' – Jesus' designation in Scripture) and reference, once again, to 'standing' before God and being 'established victoriously' forever.[6]

This idea of 'Victory' is encountered throughout the Hymns and we have already called attention to how Paul uses it in 1 Corinthians 15:54–57 in discussing 'the First Man' and 'the Last Adam' – a discussion in which he, once again, reverses the 'swallowing' imagery so widespread and intrinsic to the Qumran mindset. Aside from a clear play by Paul on the sort of language being used in the Habakkuk *Pesher* to describe 'the Righteous Teacher' and his followers among 'the Poor' being 'swallowed' by 'the Wicked Priest' (the sense there, as with the 'eaten' that follows, clearly being 'destroyed') and 'the Wicked Priest', in turn, being 'swallowed' by 'the Cup of the Right Hand of God', a synonym for 'the Cup of the Wrath of God'[7] – for Paul now, it is 'death being *swallowed up in Victory*'. Paul means of course by this, 'the Victory' which the Lord Jesus Christ gives to his followers over death and not the victory of the Heavenly Host over God's enemies as in the War Scroll and other such proclamations. Here Paul is at his polemical, allegorical, and triumphant best.

In 1 Corinthians 15:51, using the 'secrecy' imagery of his opponents – just alluded to in Hymns above and in the Community Rule earlier – 'the Heavenly Secret' or 'Mystery' being referred to is, again, the 'Victory' over death and the transformation of the body into the more supernatural substance of Heavenly Being. Paul uses the same language in 2 Corinthians 2:14–15 to express the 'Triumph' or 'Victory in the Christ' (*thus!*) exemplified by those who 'are a *sweet perfume* of Christ to God', 'making the *odor* of the Knowledge ('*Gnosis*') of him manifest in every place' (more Hellenizing word-play?).

Again, this language of being 'a sweet perfume' or 'odor' is the same as the Community Rule applies to the 'building' and 'atonement' activities of its Community Council (composed of 'Twelve Israelites' and 'Three Priests' – the 'Three Priests' being a spiritualized 'Holy of Holies' or 'Inner Sanctum for Aaron'), namely, their being 'a sweet smell of Righteousness and Perfection of the Way'.[8] Again, the analogue with Paul should be patent. In exploiting the imagery – as Paul exploits it in 1 Corinthians and Ephesians – of this 'Council' as both 'House of Holiness'/'Temple for Israel' and 'Holy of Holies for Aaron', the Community Rule then describes this Council – like the Righteous Teacher in the Habakkuk *Pesher* and the Sons of Zadok in the Damascus Document – as 'paying the Wicked their reward'[9] – that is, just like these last, they participate in 'the Last Judgment'.

The Community Rule also applies a whole series of descriptions to this 'Council' which precede and, as it were, serve to introduce its twofold quotation of 'the Way in the wilderness' citation from Isaiah 40:3 and its exposition – ending, not insignificantly, in evocation of 'being *Zealots for the Law* and the *Day of Vengeance*'. These include: 'an Eternal Plantation' (a metaphor also used at the beginning of the Damascus Document to describe the 'Visitation' by God that caused the Messianic 'Root of Planting to grow out of Israel and Aaron'[10]); 'a House of Perfection and Truth for Israel' (again the 'House' or 'building' imagery found as well in Paul[11]); 'a tried Bulwark' (the metaphor applied to James, both along with and paralleling the '*Oblias*' designation in early Church descriptions of his role in the Jerusalem of his day); 'a Precious Cornerstone which would not shake or sway on its Foundations' (imagery from Isaiah 28:16 also applied to Jesus in the Gospels and in Ephesians 2:20[12]); and 'an acceptable free will offering' – totally spiritualized 'sacrifice' and 'atonement' and the same imagery we have already seen Paul apply to Epaphroditus in Philippians 4:18, but exactly parallel to what he and all others seem to have been applying to Jesus in early Christianity and ever after as well.

In these climactic metaphors in the Community Rule, the member of this 'Council' would 'keep Faith in the Land with steadfastness and a humble spirit and atone for sin by doing Judgment and suffering affliction'.[13] This Council was also to 'make atonement for the Land and render Judgment on Evil' (this is the same 'Judgment on Evil' we shall encounter in the Habakkuk and Psalm 37 *Peshers* below[14]) – the imagery once again of both 'atonement' and participation in 'the Last Judgment'. It was also, in further 'sacrifice' and 'spiritualized atonement' imagery, to 'offer up a *sweet perfume* with Everlasting Knowledge of the Covenant and Judgment' (this is replaced by the offering up of the '*sweet perfume of Christ*' in 2 Corinthians 2:14-15). Where the first part of this last metaphor is concerned, one should – as just signaled – also have regard to Paul's description of Epaphroditus (his 'brother, fellow-worker, and soldier' in Philippians 2:25) as 'a sweet smell, an odor of an acceptable free will offering, well-pleasing to God' (4:18).[15] The parallel of course is precise.

Where the second part is concerned, evoking 'Everlasting Knowledge' or '*Gnosis*' once again – only this time with the significant addition 'of the Covenant', this reference to 'Judgment' can likewise be seen as transformed and enlarged upon by Paul in 1 Corinthians 11:24–29 with his own version of such an imprecation: 'So therefore whoever should eat this bread or drink the Cup of the Lord in an unworthy way shall be guilty of the body and blood of the Lord ... for he who eats and drinks unworthily, eats and drinks Judgment to himself (the 'eating and drinking' motif again, but this time, quite literally, 'with a vengeance'), not seeing through to the body of the Lord.' The implications of all these things for subsequent history – especially in the light of his rather deprecating allusion with which he began in 1 Corinthians 1:18–19 to 'schisms' and 'heresies among you' and, even more recently, in what ultimately transpired in our times – is simply frightening.

For its part, in summation, for the Community Rule all these things are being done to 'prepare in the wilderness the Way for the Lord' and 'establish an Everlasting Covenant of Laws' – this last, anyhow, a one hundred and eighty degree inversion of Paul's understanding of what such a Covenant must finally turn out to mean or even what might have been 'prepared in the wilderness'.

'The Sons of the Everlasting Foundation'

Hymns also takes up the idea of the 'First Man' or 'Primal Adam being made of' or 'rising out of the dust', encountered in these closing passages from Paul in 1 Corinthians 15:48, in a later, particularly exultant passage: 'For the sake of Your Glory, You have purified Man (*Enosh*) of sin, that he may be made Holy to You (that is, 'made' either a 'Nazirite' or a Priest) from all the Abominations of uncleanness and guilty rebellion to be Sons of Your Truth with the Lot of Your Holy Ones, to rise from the dust of the worm-eaten dead as a Foundation ... to *stand* before You equal with the Eternal Host and the Spirits to be made Holy with all Eternal Being.'[16] One could hardly get much closer to Paul and his strictures at the end of 1 Corinthians 15:51–57 about the 'Heavenly Secret' and 'being raised up incorruptibly', though 'changed', than this. Again, these are decisive 'internal' dating parameters.

'The Spirits' referred to here are also the same sort of Spirits we shall see below in the War Scroll's vision of the Heavenly Host 'coming on the clouds' in final eschatological Judgement.[17] One begins to understand to what all this emphasis on purity, daily bathing, and the like related.

The Community Rule expresses similar ideas in its earlier columns, amid repeated allusion to Light and Darkness, purifying oneself, and bathing, in outlining the stages in 'joining the Community of the Heavenly Holy Ones' – before ultimately building up to its two-fold evocation in its later Columns 8–9 of these important chronological indicators, 'making a straight Way in the wilderness' and 'zeal for the Law and the Day of Vengeance': 'No man from the House (in the preceding line expressed as 'the House of the Community of God') will move down from his allotted level or move up from his allotted standing, because all are in a Community of Truth, virtuous Humility, the love of Piety, and thoughtful Righteousness, each towards his neighbor in a Holy Community, the Sons of the Everlasting Foundation.[18] Not only do we have here the two 'Love' Commandments, portrayed as the essence of both Jesus' teaching in the New Testament and James' in early Church sources, including the Letter ascribed to his name,[19] but the same language of 'each towards his neighbor' is paralleled later in this 'Rule' document and in pivotal sections of the Damascus Document having to do with 'separating Holy from profane' and where 'the New Covenant in the Land of Damascus' – 'to love each man his brother as himself' – is also being defined.[20] Josephus alludes to this same combination, which I have already called the Righteousness/Piety dichotomy, as 'Piety towards God and Righteousness towards one's fellow man' in his famous description of both John the Baptist and those he designates as 'Essenes'.[21]

The rigidity of this communal hierarchy is paralleled in the Preface to the Pseudoclementine *Homilies* in passages represented as being James' speech to 'the assembled Elders', to which they react with 'fear and trembling'.[22] As always, it is gainsaid and reversed in Paul's writings where, in his usual manner exploiting his masterful control of allegory, rhetoric, and polemics, while at the same time displaying seemingly prior knowledge of both the Qumran and 'Jewish Christian' positions on these issues, he, at one and the same time, attacks both the favored position of James-like figures in the Leadership of 'the Jerusalem Church' and the Hebrew/Jewish emphasis on 'chosenness' with the customary assault on James and the 'Pillar' Apostles. This he accomplishes, in particular, with his opening salvos in the Letter to the Galatians relating to not being 'an Apostle from men or through men' (1:1) and not 'seeking to please men' or 'announcing a Gospel according to men' (1:10–11); and later in Galatians 2:6 with his claim, 'God does not accept the person of man' or, put in other words, 'God has no favorites'.

Paul expresses a similar point in his famous depiction in 1 Corinthians 15:1–10 of the order of Jesus' post-resurrection appearances. Though not without its interpolations, in some manner this seems to have been thought of as establishing one's position within the early 'Church' or 'Assembly'. It ends with the well-known: 'And Last of all (he appeared) to me. I was born when no one expected it, as if to one born out of term' (or, 'as if to an abortion' – 1 Corinthians 15:8).

This 'Last' terminology and its counterpart, 'the First', is normally applied as we just saw to the 'standing' of 'the First' within the 'Jerusalem Assembly' Hierarchy; but, in the Hebrew of the Damascus Document, 'the First' also refers to 'the Ancestors' or 'the Forefathers' to whom, by implication, 'the First Covenant' was vouchsafed.[23] The combination is also picked up in beloved though 'Paulinized' sayings attributed to Jesus in Scripture, such as 'the Last shall be First and the First shall be Last' (Matthew 19:30 and pars.).

The 'House' or 'Household' imagery one encounters in the Community Rule's description of 'the Sons of the Everlasting Foundation' also occurs throughout the relevant literature. In other variations at Qumran, it becomes 'the House of the *Torah*', which the Damascus Document uses to describe 'the Community of God' in its final summing-up passages having to do with the Promises of 'the New Covenant in the Land of Damascus' and those who have not 'turned aside' and 'betrayed the Well of Living Waters' that was being 'dug' there.[24] In crucial passages again later in the Community Rule, which introduce the 'making a straight Way in the wilderness' citations, this 'House' imagery is once again used allegorically to characterize 'the Twelve Israelite' members of the Community Council (the counterpart of 'the Twelve Apostles' in the Gospels) as 'a House of Holiness for Israel' – spiritualized Temple imagery again – and the inner 'Three Priests' as 'a House of the Holy of Holies for Israel' (the counterpart of 'the Central Three' in both Galatians 2:9 and the Synoptics[25]) – now spiritualized 'Inner Sanctum' imagery.[26]

In 1 Corinthians 3:9-17, Paul had already used a variation of this House/Household imagery, preceded in 1 Corinthians 2:4–13 by the Secret/Mystery/Hidden language in his discussion about 'teaching spiritual things spiritually' and 'speaking Wisdom among the Perfect' (any allusion to 'the Perfect' or 'Perfection' is always significant[27]). It is interesting that in reiterating this latter he actually is using the language of 'being Hidden' which we have so focused upon earlier: 'We speak the Wisdom of God in a Mystery, Hidden and predetermined before the Ages for our Glory ... which God has prepared for those who love

Him (1Corinthians 2:7).' This last, of course, is the second part of the Righteousness/Piety dichotomy – Piety towards God. As usual, one should compare this language with that of James 2:5 on 'the Kingdom promised to *those who love Him*'.

This is the language, then, that Paul uses to introduce his 'building' imagery in 1 Corinthians 3:9–17 – imagery seemingly parodying or being parodied by documents such as the Habakkuk *Pesher* in its description of the nemesis of its Righteous Teacher, 'the Spouter of Lies'/'Man of Lying', as 'building a Community on blood' and 'Lying' (we shall decipher this 'building a Community on blood' allusion in more detail towards the end of this book).[28]

Paul not only repeatedly plays on the 'laying the Foundation' symbolism one encounters in documents like the Community Rule and Hymns above, but by picturing himself as the 'architect', the Community he 'planted' as 'God's building' (compare this with 'God visiting them and causing a Root of Planting to grow out of Israel and Aaron to inherit His land and prosper on the good things of His earth' in the famous introduction to the Damascus Document, regarding Jesus' alleged insistence in Matthew 15:13 on 'uprooting' the things His 'Heavenly Father has not planted'[29]) and, over and over again by speaking of 'the Holiness of the Temple of God' (1 Corinthians 3:9–17).

Paul continues this imagery in 2 Corinthians 5:1, again tying it to some extent to discussion at the end of 1 Corinthians (12:12–27) of Jesus as Temple and 'the members' of the Community as 'the parts of Christ's body' (that is, the imagery of 'the Community as Temple' again). Here, once again – echoing this same simile in the Scrolls – he picks up the 'building' imagery by referring either to the Community or one's own body or both as 'a building from God, a House not made with human hands but Eternal in Heaven', which brings us right back to the Community Rule's language of 'the House' as 'a Holy Community – the Sons of the Everlasting Foundation'.

'Loving God' and 'Inheriting the Lot of the Holy Ones'

The 'loving Piety' – on which this 'Community of Truth', 'thoughtful Righteousness', and Divine 'Sonship' is supposed to be based – is important as the first of the two 'Love' Commandments Scripture also attributes to Jesus[30] – namely, 'loving God'. As we just saw, both 1 Corinthians 2:9 and James 2:5 pick up the same formulation in 'the Hidden Wisdom of God in a Mystery' (clearly a variation of the 'Logos' doctrine of the Gospel of John and the equivalent in Greek of 'the Primal Adam' in languages and cultures further East) or 'the Kingdom He prepared for those who Love Him', the latter in James preceding its enunciation in 2:8 of the second of these two 'Love' Commandments (attributed to Jesus in the Synoptics): 'Love your neighbor as yourself' or, as Josephus would have it in his description of John the Baptist, 'Righteousness towards one's fellow man'.

Paul alludes to such 'love of God' – albeit very subtly – once again later in 1 Corinthians 8:3, this time in an attack on the Jamesian Leadership of 'the Jerusalem Church', denoted by him somewhat facetiously as 'those who have Knowledge' (*Gnosis*). This is yet another of those rhetorical flourishes, this time centering around this same celebrated Greek word *Gnosis*, meaning, 'knowing' or 'known by', in the sense that 'if anyone loves God, then he is known by him'.

This bravura rhetorical performance employs the same language of 'being puffed up' that the Habakkuk *Pesher* applies to one of its two nemeses (in the sense of asserting that his – in this case, the Wicked Priest's – 'punishment will be multiplied upon him' because he 'destroyed' the Righteous Teacher[31]), and the 'building' imagery the *Pesher* also applies to the other ('the Liar' – in 1 Corinthians 8:1, Paul now caustically ties this same 'building' language to the 'love' metaphor, that is, 'but love *builds up*'), to once again attack this same 'Jerusalem Church' Leadership[32] – then leads into Paul's own tortured rejection in 8:3–13 of James' prohibition of 'things sacrificed to idols' and his self-serving explanation of why such 'idols' are 'nothing in this world'.

Aside from portraying this Righteousness/Piety dichotomy as the essence of the teaching of both James and Jesus in early Church literature, a variation based on a more Romanizing interpretation and allegiance is also to be found in Paul. For instance, in Romans 13:5–10 – in a characterization which, no doubt, would have sent his more 'Zealot' critics or opponents into paroxysms of indignation, Paul uses the command to 'love one another' (cf. John 13:34–35 and 15:12) and the 'Royal Law according to the Scripture' in James, 'love your neighbor as yourself', *to recommend paying taxes to Rome!*

Not only do both commandments permeate the Scrolls, but Josephus picks them up in his references to the group he designates as 'Essenes' to divide up his description of its practices on their basis.[33] Under 'Piety towards' or 'loving God', he groups all the peculiarly 'Essene' duties towards God, including daily bathing practices, extreme ritual cleanliness, and other ceremonial activities. Under 'Righteousness towards your fellow man', he groups all the others. Moreover, he unequivocally denotes in his *Antiquities* these two commandments as the *essence* of John the Baptist's teaching 'in the wilderness', that is to say, 'John taught Piety towards God and Righteousness towards one's fellow man'.

In addition to this he appends a description of John's baptism as 'a water cleansing' or 'immersion' for the body only, 'provided that the soul had already been previously purified by the practice of Righteousness'.[34] A more precise description of John's baptism is probably not to be found. Furthermore, it could not agree more with the description found in Columns 4–6 of the Community Rule – but not with the more Paulinized portrait of these things we encounter in the New Testament, which includes 'Grace' and 'baptism via the Holy Spirit'. Though ideas such as these are alluded to in some extent in the Community Rule as well, nowhere in the New Testament do we find anything about 'daily baptism' for bodily cleanliness or ritual purification as we find it in Josephus, Rabbinical literature, and/or in the Scrolls.[35]

As the Community Rule progresses, it also speaks both of a 'Visitation' and the notion of 'concealing the Truth of the Mysteries of Knowledge' (*Gnosis*),[36] which we have just encountered almost word-for-word in Paul above. Not only does it use the language he uses of 'Mystery' and 'Victory', but it adds that of 'a Crown of Glory' (imagery applied to 'Stephen' in early Church literature, whose name in Greek, it will be recalled, literally translates out as 'Crown'[37]) and 'Eternal Light': 'These are the Secrets of the Spirit for the earthly Sons of Truth and the Visitation of all the Walkers in (the Holy Spirit) will be for healing and healthiness *for long days* ... and Eternal joy in a Victorious life and a Crown of Glory with the imperishable clothing in Eternal Light.' Here too is the theme of 'long-lived Essenes', which so permeates Josephus', Philo's, and Hippolytus' descriptions of the members of this group, a theme also characteristic of the 'Jamesian' Jerusalem Church and 'Ebionite' literature generally, where James was supposed to have lived for 'ninety-six years' and Simeon bar Cleophas, his successor, 'a hundred and twenty'.[38]

One should also compare the language of 'a Crown of Glory' and 'the imperishable clothing in Eternal Light' in these passages of the Community Rule with Paul's view of 'being raised up incorruptibly' above in 1 Corinthians 15:52 and 'Ebionite'/'Elchasaite' literature, generally, of being 'clothed with Adam' or 'the Secret' or 'Primal Adam' putting on the clothing of men's bodies in multitudinous incarnations and, then, taking it off again.[39] In earlier descriptions of 'Holy Spirit' baptism, the Community Rule finally reaches a climactic highpoint and wrestles with these 'Eternal' matters with the words: 'Then Truth, which wallowed in the Ways of Evil in the Government of Unrighteousness until the time of the appointed Judgment, will emerge Victorious in the world, and God with His Truth will refine all the works of man and purify for Himself the sons of men, perfecting all the Spirit of

Unrighteousness within his flesh and purifying it by means of the Holy Spirit from all Evil actions. He will pour upon him the Spirit of Truth like cleansing waters (washing him) of all the Abominations of Lying.'[40] Not only is this last indistinguishable from what goes by the name of 'the descent of the Holy Spirit' or 'Holy Spirit Baptism' in New Testament parlance, but it is aimed squarely at the individual with 'the Lying Spirit' or, in other words, a genus of individual characterized by 'the Abominations of Lying'. Once again, too, we have copious allusion to the language of 'Judgment' ('the Last Judgment'), 'works', 'Truth', 'Victoriousness', 'purification', 'baptism', and 'Perfection'. The text continues as follows: 'And he shall be plunged into the Spirit of Purification, so as to illumine the Upright with Knowledge of the Most High and the Wisdom of the Sons of Heaven to teach the Perfect of the Way (language exactly paralleling Paul in 1 Corinthians 2:4–8), whom God has chosen as an Everlasting Covenant, and all the Glory of Adam will be theirs, without any Unrighteousness.' Again, not only do we have here a variation on what goes by the name of 'Holy Spirit baptism' according to New Testament characterization, but it is not difficult to recognize a version of the Primal Adam ideology, also to be found at critical junctures of the War Scroll and Damascus Document[41] and so characteristic of all baptizing groups across Jordan up into Northern Syria and down into Southern Iraq. In our view, this yet again demonstrates the basic homogeneity and contemporaneity of all these documents (palaeographic and/or carbon testing dating parameters notwithstanding).

As we just saw as well, the text also knows the language of ordinary baptism, prefacing this more Holy Spirit-oriented procedure with an allusion to routine and probably 'Daily' ritual immersion as follows: 'Whoever ploughs the mud of Wickedness returns defiled and he shall not be justified by what his stubborn heart permits … nor reckoned among the Perfect Ones, nor shall he be cleansed by atonements, nor purified by cleansing waters, nor sanctified by seas and rivers, nor washed clean by any waters of ablution; for, seeking the Ways of Light, he has looked towards Darkness, rejecting the Laws of God.'[42] The language of 'rejecting' – in particular, 'rejecting the Laws of God' – will be important throughout the Scrolls and applied quintessentially, in the Habakkuk *Pesher* in particular, to the opponent of the Righteous Teacher, 'the Man of Lying' or 'Pourer out'/'Spouter of Lying'.

If we were to look at this from a 'Jewish Christian' or 'Ebionite' perspective – taking an individual like James or John the Baptist as the type of the Righteous Teacher – then there can be little doubt that the genus of individual being described so negatively here resembles Paul more than any other historically-identifiable person.[43] On the other hand, the 'Sins' of a person of the opposite genus, one who 'undertakes the Covenant before God to do all that He commanded' (note the 'doing' vocabulary again), not to 'depart from the Laws of His Truth to walk either to the right or to the left', and 'walks perfectly in all the Ways of God',[44] 'will be atoned for, so he can look on the Living Light and he will be cleansed of all his sins by the Holy Spirit joining him to His Truth. And he will be purified of all his sins and his trespasses atoned for by a Spirit of Uprightness and Humility, for only with the humble submission of his soul to all the Laws of God will his flesh be made pure for ablution with cleansing waters and sanctified through the waters of immersion.'[45]

This is also the gist of Josephus' picture of the teaching of John the Baptist, according to whose description, as we have seen (but it bears repeating), John 'commanded the Jews to exercise Goodness, both as regards Righteousness towards one another and Piety towards God, and so to come to baptism, which cleansing would be acceptable to Him, provided that they made use of it not for remission of sins, but to purify the body, supposing that the soul had been thoroughly purified beforehand by Righteousness'[46] – of course, the very opposite of the picture of John's baptism in the New Testament, except in so far as there is refraction.

The Community Rule draws to a close with such an outpouring of poetic ecstasy as to be fairly overwhelming. Amid allusion to 'looking upon the marvelous Mysteries of Eternal

Being … *concealed* from mankind', which God gives as 'a Fountain of Justification' and 'a Well of Glory to His Chosen Ones', it reiterates that God 'caused this Elect to inherit the lot of the Holy Ones and to be *in Communion* with the Foundation of the Sons of Heaven as a Council of the Community and the Foundation of the Holy Building, as an Eternal Plantation with all the Ages of Endless Being'.[47] Yet again, these are just the words Paul uses – with slightly varying and, in fact, often inverted connotation – when in 1 Corinthians 3:9–11 he applies 'building', 'planting', and 'laying the Foundation' imagery to speak about how 'Apollos watered' (in 1:12 and 3:22, he somehow adds 'Cephas' to this mix) and describes the Community as 'God's Plantation, God's Building'. This 'Building', whether Community or Temple, he identifies here and elsewhere as 'Jesus Christ' or, if one prefers, his 'body'.[48]

Apollos (another of these 'certain Jew's) – this time, identified in Acts 18:24 as 'having come to Ephesus' – according to the often tendentious picture Acts there provides, had been 'instructed in the Way of the Lord', but only knew 'the baptism' of someone it refers to as 'John' (18:25) – meaning, it would appear, he only knows 'water baptism'. Normally this 'John' is taken to be 'John of Ephesus' (in the Gospels, seemingly, 'John the son of Zebedee') but, according to the picture we are developing here and the one one gets from the literature at Qumran, the baptism being referred to here can only be that of the original 'John the Baptist' whoever the 'Apollos' being spoken of here may have been. Moreover, if the 'Cephas' being referred to here and in 1 Corinthians 15:5, is the same as the individual most – including the Gospel of John, the Pseudoclementines, and Epiphanius – call 'Peter', then, according to these latter two testimonies anyhow, he rose daily at dawn and prayed (obviously following the 'Essene' way), wore only 'threadbare clothes' (as Josephus tells us 'the Essenes' did), and was a 'Daily Bather'.[49]

All this comes to a resounding climax in the Community Rule in the atmosphere of evocation of 'this being the Time of the Preparation of the Way in the wilderness' and 'zeal for the Law', graphically described in terms of 'the Day of Vengeance', and 'zeal for the Judgments of Righteousness'.[50] This may have been a uniquely Palestinian militancy or a 'Jamesian' Palestinian synthesis of some kind not duplicated among 'Daily Bathing' practitioners outside the Land of Israel or without attachment to it (except, of course, in Islam – though this last, following the new approach of Mani as we have seen, drops many of these extreme purity practices such as 'daily bathing' or ritual ablution). This unique combination of extreme purity-mindedness with militant 'Messianism' (regardless of the depiction of Jesus' view of 'cleanliness' or, for that matter, his generally 'pacifistic' attitude in the Gospels) and xenophobic 'zeal for the Law', given voice in these documents, explains the ruthless Roman repression of it at least in Palestine if not elsewhere.

'The Way in the Wilderness' and Final Apocalyptic Holy War

To return to the War Scroll which, in the manner of these allusions to 'this being the Time of the preparation of the Way in the wilderness' and 'zeal for the Day of Vengeance', now turns more aggressive – in the blueprint it provides for final apocalyptic Holy War, the reason it gives for 'keeping indecent behavior' or 'fornication' away from 'the camps' is that 'your God goes with you to fight for you against your enemies that he may save you', a loose quotation of Deuteronomy 20:2–4.[51] This reference to 'Saving' or 'Deliverance' is again based on the same Hebrew root as '*Yeshu'a*' or '*Yesha*', that is, the Hebrew root of the name Jesus as it passes into the Greek, highlighted in a number of Qumran documents and forming the emphasis of climactic key portions of the Damascus Document, as we have seen.[52]

In the Damascus Document, 'Salvation' and 'Justification' ('*Yesha*' and '*Zedakah*' are promised to 'those who fear His Name'. Another way of translating this last phraseology is the familiar 'God-Fearers', seemingly a category of persons attached to synagogues throughout the Mediterranean world in some sort of affiliated (e.g., 'the *Nilvim*' or 'the Joiners') – if not completely orthodox – status. This is a group among whom Paul would seem to have been particularly active.[53] The emphasis, too, in this phraseology on 'Name' and 'naming' will be an ongoing one and will, for instance, be echoed in new and, again, often inverted significations normally associated with Jesus' 'name' – for example, in Acts 'those called by this Name' instead of the fairly repetitive 'those called by name' in the Damascus Document.[54]

Such persons, designated under this rubric of 'those who fear His Name' in the Damascus Document – 'God-fearers' in other vocabularies – are described in terms of 'loving Him' or 'keeping' either His Covenant or His Laws, this last being both the language of Piety and Righteousness. The Damascus Document for instance, even uses in these contexts the language of 'Naziritism', i.e., 'keeping away' or 'apart from' (*lehinnazer*/*lehazzir*/*linzor*) in three or four separate circumstances already alluded to above.[55] In the Book of Acts as well, this language of 'keeping away' or 'refraining from' is precisely that of the 'Judgment' ('I judge that') James is pictured as making at 'the Jerusalem Council' and the terms of the directives he makes at its conclusion – namely, 'abstain' or 'keep away from blood, fornication, things sacrificed to idols' (in one version as we saw, 'the pollutions of the idols'), etc. in Acts 15:19, 29, and 21:25.

In the Damascus Document, all instances of this kind of language are connected in some manner with 'the Well ('of Living Waters') which is being dug' in the wilderness, interpreted to mean, 'the New Covenant in the Land of Damascus', and the extreme purity regulations and absolute '*separation* of Holy from profane' associated with this. The exhortative part of the Damascus Document ends some fifteen lines further along, after these references to 'fearing God' or 'God-Fearers', promising that those 'who listened to the voice of the Teacher of Righteousness and did not abandon the Laws of Righteousness' would gain 'Victory over all the sons of Earth'. Furthermore, that God or possibly His representatives would 'make atonement for them and that they would *see His Salvation* (that is, 'see Jesus' – '*Yeshu'ato*'), because they took refuge in His Holy Name'.[56]

The apocalyptic character of this 'promise' should be clear, as should its relationship to Paul's triumphant language at the end of 1 Corinthians 15. Certainly what we have here is an encouragement to martyrdom and a variation of what has gone in Judaism ever since under the denotation of '*Kiddush ha-Shem*'/'Sanctification of the Name' literally meaning 'martyrdom'. Certainly, too, those Josephus depracatingly refers to as 'False Prophets', 'Impostors', and 'Deceivers' leading the People out into the wilderness, there to show them 'the signs of their impending Freedom' or 'Deliverance' – were making claims not unsimilar to these.

The wilderness regime of daily bathing and ablution in these 'desert camps' was part and parcel of this extreme eschatological vision because of the need for absolute purity there. This was necessary because the Final Apocalyptic War against all Evil on the Earth, as the War Scroll – however fancifully – envisions it, could only be effected, as already explained, by the intervention and participation of the Heavenly Host, who would not or could not join any camps with pollution in them. Put in another way, their Heavenly state could not abide human pollution of any kind. Therefore the stringent purity regulations required in these 'camps' if the Heavenly Host or 'Holy Angels' were going to 'join' them, setting the stage for that apocalyptic Final Judgment which would come down from Heaven 'on the clouds' like rain. It is this combination of themes too, as we have seen, that characterizes the presentation of James one gets both in early Church descriptions of him and the Letter the New Testament attributes to his name.

This is the esoteric dimension to these claims about rainmaking as it emerges in the War Scroll, where this kind of imagery is repeated both in the climactic exegesis of the Messianic

'World Ruler Prophecy' and at its end.[57] It is as dramatic as it is poetic and worth presenting in its entirety, for only then can the reader get the real feeling of this unique combination of uncompromising apocalyptic 'zeal for the Day of Judgment' and meticulous attention to bodily purification and 'Perfect Holiness' or 'the Perfection of Holiness' – 'Perfection of the Way' as the Community Rule refers to it, variations of which being over and over again reiterated in the Scrolls.[58] This is the combination exemplified by the militant 'Sicarii' or 'Zealots' who, according to Hippolytus' unique picture, were just another group of Daily-Bathing Sobiai ('Essenes') or extreme Nazirites (some people might even consider that the tradition of the combination of these conceptualities carried on in some unique manner to Medieval fighting groups like the Templars, probably via an undetermined transmission of some kind through Jewish groups such as 'the Mourners for Zion', who had preceded them by several centuries in their return to Jerusalem and in discovering Dead Sea Scrolls materials, and through them, 'the Karaites').[59]

We have met many of these concepts before, for instance in Matthew's picture of the Sermon on the Mount. For Hebrews, permeated like Qumran with the imagery of 'Perfection' – 'Jesus, the Mediator of the New Covenant' (12:24), who 'was crowned with Glory' and 'the Leader of their Salvation', 'is made Perfect through sufferings' (2:9–10) 'and, being made Perfect, he became the author of Eternal Salvation to all those who obey him' (5:9). This last reiterates remonstrances prevalent in definitions of 'the Rechabites' in Jeremiah 35:6–18 in which they are repeatedly characterized as 'obeying the commands of their father'. The Letter ascribed to James, too – whether authentic or simply part of 'the Jamesian School' – also refers to 'the Perfect Man' (3:2), 'Perfect and Complete, lacking nothing' (1:4).

'Preparation for the Time of the Day of Vengeance', as we saw, is the essence of the exegesis in the Community Rule above of Isaiah 40:3's pivotal 'prepare in the wilderness the Way of the Lord – make a straight path in the desert for Our God'. In the Synoptics, as everyone knows, this is applied to John the Baptist's activities 'in the wilderness' – in Matthew 3:1, 'of Judea'; in John 1:28, 'across the Jordan' – in preparation for the coming of 'Jesus'. At Qumran, it is applied to those who 'walk Perfectly, each with his neighbor' and 'do all that is found in the Torah commanded by the hand of Moses'.

Here, not only is the emphasis on 'doing' crucial, especially when considering parallel 'Jamesian' insistences and like-minded ones throughout the Scrolls – Pauline ones to the contrary notwithstanding, but the whole is specifically tied to 'the Torah as commanded by the hand of Moses' – something Paul, in turn, never fails to either belittle or pour scorn upon.[60] The one 'walking in (such) Perfection', shall 'separate from any man who has not turned his Way (cf. the 'Way' terminology as a name for nascent 'Christianity' – known, for instance, even to someone like Felix in Acts 24:14 and 22) from all Unrighteousness' or 'Ungodliness', and be 'a man zealous for the Law whose time is the Day of Vengeance, to do His will in all his handiwork and His Kingdom, exactly as commanded'.

These words in the Community Rule reiterate what was written earlier, once again containing just the slightest hint not only of the 'Rechabite' lifestyle but also their 'obedience to the commands of their father': 'They shall separate from the midst of the habitation of the Men of Unrighteousness (or alternatively 'Ungodliness') to go into the wilderness to prepare there the Way of the Lord, as it is written (here the text quotes Isaiah 40:3 as already indicated) ... and which the Prophets have revealed by His Holy Spirit.'[61] The connection of this citation with parallel allusions in the War Scroll should be straightforward. The reference to 'volunteering' one finds in the War Scroll in connection to such 'going out into the wilderness camps' is also important, as it is in the 'Paean for King Jonathan' where a central contingent, designated as 'the Joiners in the War of', is also evoked.[62] Going on to refer to 'the War of God' and 'mighty works and marvelous wonders' (here, 'war-like' ones, not more pacified Hellenized ones such as 'raisings', 'curings', and magical 'transformations' like those in the Gospels), as well as Daniel's 'Saints' or '*Kedoshim*', the War Scroll turns to its exegesis of the Star Prophecy. It does so by introducing it amid reference to 'the likeness' or 'similitude of Adam' and imagery bearing on that of 'the Heavenly Host' – here 'the Holy Angels' – as well as its first evocation of the 'clouds' metaphor.[63]

Of course, this reference to 'the likeness of Adam' either has to do with 'the Primal Adam' ideology once again or prefigures the evocation of 'the Son of Man coming on the clouds of Heaven' – if the two, 'the Son of Man' and 'the Primal Adam', can in fact be differentiated in any real way. It is at this point that the Star Prophecy from Numbers is quoted in its entirety, the interpretation of which not only forms its highpoint, but is so fundamental that it is repeated again in the last two Columns of the Scroll (19–20).

The exegesis of it specifically refers to God's Messiah, 'the Poor' (*Ebionim*) who have been redeemed by God's 'marvelous Power', and 'the Poor in Spirit' (the very words used by Jesus in Matthew 5:3's Sermon on the Mount). These 'Poor' will, 'like a flaming torch in the straw, consume Evil and never cease until the Wicked are destroyed' which is, of course, almost the very imagery John the Baptist is pictured as using in the introduction of him in the Gospels (Matthew 3:11–12 and pars.).[64]

The War Scroll, too, at this point twice speaks of 'the hand of the Poor' who 'will humble the mighty of the Peoples' – once again, presumably the Romans.[65] This is directly reprised with the words: 'to whom (meaning 'to the *Ebionim*' or 'to the Poor'/'the Ebionites') will be delivered the Enemies of all Lands ... in order to justify Your true Judgment on all the Sons of Men and to make for Yourself an Eternal Name'.[66] It is at this point, too, that the text quotes Isaiah 31:8 to the effect that this deliverance will be accomplished by 'the sword of no mere man and no mere Adam' – the implication being that, together with 'the Poor' and 'those bent in the dust', someone or something *more than Adam* will accomplish this 'Deliverance'. Here too the reference to 'the Sons of Men' is framed in terms of different usages, which do not include this reference to 'Adam', the implication being that these are not really the kind of supernatural 'Men' the War Scroll is interested in.

One should also remark the parallel of these materials with the end of the exhortative section of the Damascus Document, which is worth repeating: 'Your Judgments upon us ... who have listened to the voice of the Righteous Teacher and did not abandon the Laws of Righteousness. They shall rejoice and their hearts shall be strengthened, and they shall be victorious over all the Sons of Earth. God will make atonement through them and they shall *see His Salvation*, because they took refuge in His Holy Name.' This is the kind of 'Name' and 'naming' symbolism which recurs generally throughout these and other like-minded documents as, for example, in the Book of Acts – itself, as already signaled, particularly interested in 'the Name' or 'the Great Name of Jesus' (3:6 and pars.).[67]

One should also note the parallel between this and Jerome's report of the vow James is reputed to have made in the Gospel of the Hebrews not to 'eat or drink' (the Nazirite 'not eating or drinking' theme) until he had '*seen Jesus*'.[68] For the medieval *Zohar* too, in discussing this same 'Star Prophecy' in Numbers, 'King David (meaning the Messiah) placed himself among the Poor, ... the Pious, ... and ... those ready to sacrifice themselves ... for the Sanctification of God's Name' (not only the 'Name' and 'naming' vocabulary once again, but now coupled with the language of 'Martyrdom' or 'Sanctification of the Name' already underscored above).[69]

'Joining the Heavenly Holy Ones' and 'Judgment' upon the Clouds in the War Scroll

That the coming eschatological Judgment being pictured at this point in the War Scroll in terms of 'cloud' and 'rain' imagery is something akin to what in normal parlance goes by the designation, 'the Last Judgment', is made particularly clear in the Habakkuk *Pesher* in its crucial exposition of Habakkuk 2:4, 'the Righteous shall live by his Faith'. As the Habakkuk *Pesher* pictures it, 'God will *save them* ('the Righteous') from the House of Judgment', a term which it will later apply to that 'House of Judgment which God would deliver in His Judgment in the midst of many Peoples'.[70]

At the end of the *Pesher*, it actually makes it clear that this 'Salvation' or 'Deliverance' which will be denied to 'Idolaters' among the Nations and backsliding Jews is none other than 'the Day of Judgment', a phraseology it repeats twice just so there should be no mistaking it.[71] Not only is this 'Day of Judgment' terminology widespread in Matthew, 2 Peter, and Jude,[72] but it forms the backbone of the Koran which has a particular obsession with just such 'Idolaters' and 'Backsliders'.[73] It is no different, of course, from what we just referred to above as 'the Last Judgment'.

With regard to this 'House of Judgment which God would make in the midst of many Peoples', the *Pesher* states even earlier that 'God would not destroy His People by the hand of the Nations', but rather 'God would execute Judgment on all the Nations by the hand of His Elect'.[74] For anyone who takes seriously the widespread idea of 'peaceful Essenes', the extreme apocalyptic nationalism of this passage could not be clearer.

But in addition, God's 'Chosen' or 'Elect' is the definition of 'the Sons of Zadok' in the key exegesis of Ezekiel 44:15 in the Damascus Document. These, as the Damascus Document puts it in its own inimitable way, 'will *stand* at the End of Days ... and justify the Righteous and condemn the Wicked'. This is the opposite of what 'Liars' and 'Evil Ones' do earlier in the Document: 'justify the Wicked and condemn the Righteous'.[75] In the Habakkuk *Pesher* therefore, as in the description of 'the Community Council' in the Community Rule, it is clear that these same 'Elect of God' participate in 'the Last Judgment' and 'will execute Judgment on all the Nations'.[76]

But this is not very different from many less well-formed ideas circulating about 'the Apostles' or even Jesus himself in early Christian thought. The same 'execution of Judgment' – presumably 'at the hand of God's Elect' as in the Habakkuk *Pesher* – is, however, expressed in the Letter of Jude 14–15 as well. Quoting 'Enoch the Seventh from Adam' and attributed, as we know, to 'the brother of James', this letter has the ideology down just about perfectly: 'Behold, the Lord is coming among the Myriads of His Holy Ones to execute Judgment against all and to sentence all the Ungodly with regard to all their ungodly works.'[77]

The War Scroll now goes on to describe this eschatological Judgment in a far more detailed, but completely parallel manner, using imagery and allusions clearly based on Daniel 7:13's 'one like a Son of Man coming on the clouds of Heaven'. Grouping these 'Holy Ones' ('*Kedoshim*') from Daniel with 'the Angels ... mighty in battle' and, referring seemingly to either Messianic or Divine intervention from Heaven, it reads in perhaps the most complete exposition of final apocalyptic warfare and eschatological 'Judgment' ever recorded:

"'You will fight against them from Heaven ... and the Elect of your Holy People ... are with You in Your Holy abode.... You have recorded for them ... Your Covenant of Peace, that You may reign forever throughout all the Eternal Ages. And You commanded the Hosts of Your Elect in their thousands and their Myriads, together with Your Saints and Your Angelic Army with the authority in war to strike the Rebellious of Earth with Your awe-inspiring Judgments ... And the Assembly of Your Holy Ones is in our midst together with the Elect of Heaven for Eternal help. And we shall despise kings and we will mock and scorn the Mighty, because our Lord is Holy and the King of Glory together with the Saints are with us. The Mighty of the Angelic Host have visited us and the Hero in War is in our Assembly and the Host of His Spirits are with our foot soldiers and our cavalry.'"[78]

Here we have some of the most triumphant, apocalyptic language in any literary document from this period. Not only are 'the Elect of Your Holy People' the same as 'the Sons of Zadok' and the references to both 'commanded' and 'visited' the same in Hebrew, but 'the Covenant of Peace' is the same as that accorded Phineas in Numbers and, by implication, Noah in Genesis as well. Also the reference here literally is to 'Lord' not 'God' and, as with 'the Hero in War' and in another Qumran text just noted above, specifically evoking the 'Messiah' as 'commanding both Heaven and Earth' and making precisely such a 'visit',[79] it is unclear whether we are speaking about God or 'His Messiah'. However, in the parallel represented by 'the Lord coming with the Myriads of His Holy Ones to execute Judgment' in Jude above, there can be no doubt that we are speaking about the Messiah.

At this point in the War Scroll, the imagery shifts to 'cloud' imagery, because now it is combining the imagery of Daniel's 'one like a Son of Man coming on the clouds' of Heaven with the exegesis of the Star Prophecy, both interpreted in terms of an eschatological War against all Evil on the Earth and final Judgment on all mankind. Furthermore, the whole passage, as with the passage from the *Zohar* representing David as the Messiah already alluded to above, begins with the evocation of 'David Your Servant, who ... put his trust in Your Great Name'. It is at this point the Star Prophecy from Numbers 24:17 is quoted in its entirety and allusion is made to 'Your Messiah' – the 'hand' of whom is once again referred to.[80]

In this context, the text now adds eschatological 'rain' imagery, in the sense of implying Final Apocalyptic Judgment, not just warfare, and a logical extension of its Messianic 'cloud' imagery. That the context is again that of Daniel 7:13 is made clear by the words: 'They are as clouds, as moisture-laden clouds over the Earth and torrents of rain shedding Judgment on all that grows on it.'[81] Even though it is using figurative language, the meaning could not be clearer. It is followed by what virtually amounts to yet another 'Paean of Praise':

"'Arise Mighty One, lead off your captives, Man of Glory. Gather your spoil, Doer of War. Put your hand upon the neck of your Enemies and your foot on the piles of dead. Smite the nations, your Adversaries, and let your sword devour guilty flesh ... Fill Your land with Glory and may your inheritance be blessed ... Zion rejoice greatly! Show yourself with jubilation Jerusalem! Sing for joy all you cities of Judah and may your gates be ever open ... Sovereignty is (to the Lord) and Eternal Dominion to Israel.'"[82]

One can't get much more 'Messianic' or 'nationalist' than this. It is followed by six more columns, recapitulating much of this imagery and adding allusions such as: 'Eternal Light', 'Belial', 'the appointed times of Salvation', 'the Perfect of the Way', 'the Day of Vengeance', 'the Power of God', 'the burning' (very popular imagery in the Koran as well[83]), 'the Rule of Michael among the gods and Israel in the midst all flesh', and 'the Gates of Salvation'.

This last, as we have seen, has particularly strong relevance to the question asked of James in the early Church tradition reported by Hegesippus, 'What is the Gate to Jesus?' and James' response: 'Why do you ask me concerning the Son of Man? He is sitting in Heaven on the Right Hand of the Great Power and he is coming on the clouds of Heaven,' which provokes the riot in the Temple on Passover and his stoning. Once again, the intrinsic relationship of James' response in these sources, not only to the materials in Daniel but also to these passages in the War Scroll, should be obvious to all but the most biased observers. Basically a compressed version of these triumphant and climactic passages of the more prolix War Scroll have been put into James' mouth and, by implication, Jesus' and John the Baptist's in the Gospels.

The War Scroll now culminates in a second evocation of eschatological rain and its Paean to the Messianic Hero with which the text ends. These are both, as already noted, word-for-word repetitions of the first. Following another curious reference to 'standing' and 'to You is the *Power* and in Your hands is the battle', the text again then avers: 'Our sovereign is Holy and the King of Glory is with us and the Host of His Spirits is with our foot soldiers and our cavalry. (They are) as *clouds*, and moisture-laden clouds covering the Earth, and as a *torrent of rain* shedding Judgment on all that grows therein.'[84] This could not be more clear or a more clearly poetic metaphor for 'the Last Judgment'. After this commences the praise of the Messianic Hero who will 'devour all flesh with his sword' again.[85] Here is the final crystallization of all the eschatological 'rain', 'flood', and 'final Judgment' imagery encountered above. Tied to the exegesis of the Star Prophecy, *so intrinsic to events in 66–70 CE Palestine and the cataclysm there* – to say nothing of the Gospel portrait of the birth of its Messiah in Matthew 2:2–2:9, and Daniel's imagery of 'one like a Son of Man coming on the clouds', it also links up with the parallel evocation in the Letter of James of 'the coming of the Lord' – which, it will be recalled, was connected with 'spring and autumn rain',[86] 'the prayer of the Just' or 'Righteous One having much Power' (parodied in Josephus' disparaging portraiture of this genre of individual; nor is this to say anything about the more positive one in the Gospels), and Elijah's role as paradigmatic rain and Judgment-making forerunner, setting this final eschatological process into motion.

Above left: Column XX of Ms. B. of the Damascus Document, found in the Cairo *Geniza* and paralleled at Qumran, which actually refers to '*the standing up of the Messiah of Aaron and Israel*'(singular!), '*seeing Yeshu'a*'('*Jesus*' or "*Salvation*"), and the writing out of '*a Book of Remembrance for God-Fearers*.'

Above right: The Qumran proof-text known as '*The Testimonia*' which includes '*The True Prophet*' passage from Deuteronomy 18:18-19, important in the Pseudoclementines, and '*The Star Prophecy*' from Numbers 24:17, from which Bar Kochba took his name.

Chapter 14
Temple Sacrifice at Qumran and in the New Testament

Spiritualized Sacrifice and Atonement Imagery in Paul and at Qumran

Epiphanius claims he saw in 'the Gospel in use among the Ebionites' that 'Jesus came and announced the abolition of the sacrifices' – meaning, Temple sacrifice. This passage reads: 'And that he (Christ) came and declared, as their so-called Gospel reports, "I have come to do away with the sacrifices and, if you do not cease from sacrificing, the Wrath of God will not cease upon you"'.[1] Of course, this issue of the inefficacy or cessation of Temple sacrifice is widespread in Paul's letters, though admittedly from a somewhat more 'allegorized' perspective. For Paul and the Gospels – with, as they have come down to us, their generally pro-Pauline cast – Jesus is the very sacrifice itself.

Paul says as much in 1 Corinthians 5:7 in a discussion supposed to be about one aspect of James' directives to overseas communities, 'fornication'. Not only does this discussion use the vocabulary both of James' proscriptions and Gospel allusions to Jesus, but it actually has more in common with the ethos of both 'the Essenes' and Qumran, in terms of not keeping 'table fellowship' with 'fornicators', 'idol-worshippers', 'Scoffers', 'wine-bibbers', and such like, and even goes so far as to recommend both 'shunning them' and/or 'expelling them' (1 Corinthians 5:9–11).

Nevertheless, in this context and continuing its allegorical evocation of such key allusions as 'the Name', 'the Power of our Lord Jesus Christ', and 'someone being delivered unto Satan' for 'the destruction of the flesh, so the spirit might be saved on the Day of the Lord Jesus', it avers that, 'for also Christ, our Passover, *was sacrificed for us*' (1 Corinthians 5:4–7). Here we have the familiar 'Christ' as 'the Paschal Lamb' image, now actually couched in yet another allegorizing discussion of the 'leaven' the Jews reject on their Festival of Passover. This is presented in the usual disparaging and one-sided manner, recommending – seemingly in all innocence, but actually playing off all the inherent imageries – 'celebrating the Feast' (meaning 'the Passover') not with the old 'leaven of malice and Wickedness' (one is quite staggered here by the derisive and polemical way Paul alludes to the previous tradition to which he, too, supposedly claims to be an heir), but with the new *'unleaven* of sincerity and Truth' (5:8). None but the most naive observer could possibly miss the acrimonious thrust of these allegories, which are, of course, to be found in the Gospels, in particular, in the several discourses in which Jesus is either portrayed as speaking about 'the leaven of the Pharisees' and alluding to them as 'Blind Guides', i.e., 'the Blind leading the Blind' and 'both falling into the Pit' (Matthew 15:12-14 and 16:6-12).

Paul continues this metaphor of spiritualized sacrifice in Romans 12:1, though this time his rhetorical barbs, while present, are a little more subdued. He characterizes 'your bodies' as 'a Holy and living sacrifice well pleasing to God', only adding the incidental if condescending aside, and a more 'reasonable service'. This is exactly the sort of imagery we have just discussed with regard to 'the Community Council' in the Community Rule, a document including some of the same allusions and also considered opposed to Temple sacrifice, though if it was, this was probably only because of the perception that the then-reigning Priesthood – in our view the Herodian – was corrupt.[2] What would have been its position, for instance, if the Jerusalem Priesthood were 'a Perfectly Righteous' One? That would be a whole other question.

We have seen how the Community Rule, in its evocation of Isaiah 40:3's 'making a straight Way in the wilderness' citation, characterizes the members of its 'Council' as 'an Eternal Plantation', *'atoning for sin* by doing Judgment and suffering the sorrows of affliction'.[3]

Of course, the New Testament is fairly awash with similar allusions when discussing the theological significance of 'Jesus'.[4]

But at this point the Community Rule parts company with Paul. In addition to 'being Witnesses of the Truth for Judgment and the Chosen' or 'the Elect of His Will' (a few lines further on, the same idea is expressed in terms of 'being an acceptable free will offering'[5]) 'to make atonement for the Land and pay the Evil Ones their Reward', the members of this 'Council' are admonished – just as Jesus admonishes those he is addressing in the Sermon on the Mount – to be 'Perfect in all that has been revealed about the whole *Torah*'.[6]

The members of this Council are also 'to offer up a pleasing fragrance' – the very words Paul uses in 2 Corinthians 2:14–15 when he describes what those followers of Jesus are supposed to offer up meaning, where he is concerned, for the most part, monetary contributions – but secondarily, an allusion as well to the fruitfulness of his mission.[7] As usual, here too Paul is at his rhetorical and deprecating best. Evoking once again both his and the Scrolls' language of 'Triumph', he implies that others, who also speak both of such 'a sweet fragrance' and 'being saved',[8] are rather bringing 'an odor of death to death' not 'life to life' (cf. the putrid 'smell' which Lazarus' body, dead in the grave 'for four days', emits in John 11:39 above).

Furthermore, again employing another usage, 'the Many', fundamental to the Community Rule and the same vocabulary the Habakkuk *Pesher* uses to indict 'the Last Priests of Jerusalem who gathered Riches and profiteered from the spoils of the Peoples', these others, his competitors – who like himself also speak of 'the *sweet odor* of the Knowledge of Him' – are actually 'profiteering by corrupting the Word of God' (2:14–17).

The Attack on Moses, the Temple, and the Earthly Stones

Paul continues this metaphor of bringing 'death' rather than 'life' into the next chapter of 2 Corinthians where he starts his attack on the 'some' again, now those 'who need letters to recommend' them – or, as he puts it thereafter in 2 Corinthians 10:12, referring to the same 'some who commend themselves, measuring themselves by themselves and comparing themselves to themselves' (again, clearly a belittling attack on James and his Leadership who required those who would be teachers or 'Apostles' to carry letters of appointment from James[9]) – by introducing a whole new cluster of polemical juxtapositions centering on key words such as 'Service'/'Ministry', 'veil'/'being veiled', and, as always 'written words' – in this instance, 'in ink' but also, momentarily, to ridicule Moses, 'in stone' – as opposed to those (as he puts it) 'written of' or 'by the Spirit of the Living God' (2 Corinthians 3:1–3).

This he does while numbering himself and his associates as 'competent Servants of the New Covenant' not like the others, whom he describes as serving 'the *Ministry* of Condemnation' (*Diakonia*). He means by this, of course (just as he does in Galatians 4:25 on Hagar's Sinaitic 'slavery'), Mosaic Law! He then goes on to compare this 'Ministry' which, in his view, 'was being annulled' to how 'Moses who put a veil over his face' in order to deceive 'the Children of Israel', so that they 'would not have to look at the end of that which was bound to be annulled' (2 Corinthians 3:13).

To put this in another way, according to Paul, Moses was a kind of 'Deceiver' who didn't want the people to know that 'the shining Glory' of their tradition was coming to an end. Indeed, so enamored is Paul of the metaphors he is creating that he goes on to characterize Moses' Commandments, 'cut in stone' as they were, as the *Service of death* ('*Diakonia*' – the same '*Diakonia*' we have seen above in Acts 6:1–5 on the 'choosing of Stephen' and his Hellenized companions 'to serve'/'wait on tables' or in Luke and John's Mary vs. Martha 'table-serving' materials), triumphantly concluding this particular allegorical polemic with: 'for the letter kills, but the Spirit brings life' (2 Corinthians 3:5–13).

The above 'offering up a sweet perfume' or 'a pleasing fragrance' imagery is from Column Eight of the Community Rule, but in Column Nine the whole metaphor is reprieved – this time seemingly applied, as in Paul – though with a more graceful and high-minded rhetorical elegance – to 'the Men of the Community, the Walkers in Perfection' (implying the whole Community and not just 'the Council') now being called 'the Community of Holiness'.[10] After playing on the combination in the Damascus Document of 'Israel and Aaron' as the laity and the Priesthood – pictured in these Columns too of the Community Rule as 'a Temple of the Community for Israel' and 'a House of Holiness' or 'Holy of Holies for Aaron' – it is set forth that either 'the Men of the Community' or 'the Council' (it is not clear which) 'will establish (in their 'Perfection') the Holy Spirit on Truth Everlasting to atone for guilty transgression and rebellious sinning, and forgiveness for the Land without the flesh of holocausts and the fat of sacrifices; and the offering of the lips will be for Judgment like the pleasing fragrances of Righteousness; and Perfection of the Way, an acceptable free-will offering'.[11] Once again, this is about as 'spiritualized' as one can get, even as 'spiritualized' as Paul thinks he is being, the only difference, as usual, is that the one is a hundred and eighty degrees the reverse of the other. To rephrase this, whereas the Scrolls' Community is inseparably attached to the *Torah* of Moses both spiritually and figuratively, *Paul never misses an opportunity to belittle and/or undermine it* whether rhetorically or allegorically.

We have already seen in Philippians 2:25 how Paul refers to his 'brother, partner, and comrade-in-arms' Epaphroditus – possibly Josephus' patron and also Nero's secretary for Greek letters by the same name (executed later under Domitian). Now he actually alludes to the contributions brought to him by this person he refers to as well as 'Apostle and Minister to my need' (also 2:25), 'the *odor of a sweet fragrance, an acceptable sacrifice well-pleasing to God*' (Philippians 4:18). Of course this is totally in line with the Rabbinic tendency, following the destruction of the Temple, to consider charity – thereafter in Judaism known as 'Zedakah' or 'Justification' (picked up and seemingly compressed in Islam as 'Zakat') – as an acceptable substitute for sacrifice in the Temple.[12] Even more to the point, this is exactly the language used in the Community Rule above when speaking about 'the Community Council'.

At the same time and with a congeniality he never displays towards his more 'Jewish' of colleagues whatever their rank, Paul in turn sends greetings, seemingly via this same Epaphroditus, to 'every Saint' – literally, 'every Holy One' as in the Community Rule and War Scroll above – 'in Christ Jesus' and 'especially those *in the household of Caesar*' (4:18–23). Whatever else one might conclude, it is hard to avoid the impression that 1) Epaphroditus has connections very high up in this 'household' and 2) when he uses this language of an 'odor of a sweet fragrance, an acceptable sacrifice well-pleasing to God', Paul is displaying familiarity with the passages just quoted from the Community Rule.

Using exactly the same vocabulary, Paul or the Pauline author of Ephesians now goes on to characterize 'Christ' in the same manner, namely, as 'giving himself for us as an offering and a sacrifice to God for an odor of a sweet fragrance' (5:2). 1 Peter 2:5, playing on the 'Precious Cornerstone' and spiritualized Temple and Priesthood imagery, that is, the imagery of 'a House of Holiness (Temple) for Aaron in union with the Holy of Holies and a House of the Community for Israel'[13] we have just been following above, applies this 'spiritualized sacrifice' imagery to the members of the Community it is appealing to as well: 'You, also, as *living Stones* are being *built up* into a *Spiritual House*, a Holy Priesthood to offer *spiritual sacrifices* acceptable to God by Jesus Christ'. One should note the quasi-parallel here with 2 Corinthians 5:1, also using 'House' and 'Building' imagery: 'We know that if our Earthly House of the Tabernacle is destroyed, we have a Building from God, a House not made with human hands, Eternal in the Heavens'. In either case, we could not be closer than this to the passages in the Community Rule above. Even the connection of the 'Spiritual House' to the 'Holy Priesthood' is the same. In the latter, this language also evoked the imagery of 'a

Precious Cornerstone, the Foundations of which will not shake or sway in its place' from Isaiah 28:16 – imagery which, it should be appreciated, was used in conjunction with that of 'a Tested Wall' or 'an Impregnable Bulwark' (imagery which in early Church literature, as we have seen, was actually applied to James). But this exact imagery of a 'Wall' or 'Bulwark' that 'would not sway on its Foundations or move in its place' is also used in the Hymns, once again attesting to the general synchronization or contemporaneity of these documents.[14]

Peter as 'Stone' and the Belial, Balaam and Balak Imagery as Applied to Herodians

Of course the 'Peter' to whom this kind of Stone imagery is usually applied in early Christian documentation can hardly be the 'Zealot' Simon, who is pictured in Josephus as wanting to bar Herodians from the Temple as foreigners and who visits King Agrippa I in Caesarea to see 'what was done there contrary to Law'.[15] This 'Simon' rather has a lot in common with the second brother of Jesus whom we consider identical with the individual called 'Simon the Zealot' in Luke's Apostle lists ('Simon the Cananaean'/'Canaanite' in Mark and Matthew) and his parallel in some early Church sources 'Simeon bar Cleophas', 'a Priest of the Sons of Rechab, a Rechabite' in Eusebius' version of Hegesippus' picture of James' death.[16]

But whoever the 'Peter' is to whom 1 Peter (which even evokes the metaphor of 'the living Stone, Elect and Precious to God' in 2:4) is ascribed, 2 Peter – which in 1:1, not unremarkably, calls Peter 'Simeon', just as in James' speech in Acts 15:14, not 'Simon Peter' – is completely different from it in style and tone. Except for a few Paulinisms at the end, including in 2 Peter 3:15 a seemingly over-effusive reference to Paul as 'our beloved brother', 2 Peter is replete with Qumranisms. For example, it knows the language of 'the Way of Righteousness' (2:21) and calls Noah, very presciently, 'the Preacher of Righteousness' (2:5). Not only does it know about the torment of 'the soul of the Righteous One' (2:8), essential language in both the Hymns and the Damascus Document,[17] but it refers to 'the Way of Balaam the son of Besor' (it means, of course, 'Be'or') who loved 'Unrighteousness' (2:15) and, as usual, the 'Star' (1:19) – evoking, of course, the Star Prophecy of Numbers 24:17 already sufficiently discussed above.

One would almost have to say that its author, who shows himself so intimately acquainted with Qumran doctrines, must have spent time there. This is also true of the author of 'Jude the Brother of James' which, in addition to 'the coming of the Myriads of His Holy Ones to execute Judgment' against all the Ungodly, also knows the language of 'fornication', 'Balaam', 'Everlasting Fire', and 'the Scoffers of the Last Days' (7–18).

This allusion to 'Balaam the son of Besor' is, of course, reprised in Revelation which also fairly overflows with 'Star' imagery,[18] where it becomes an attack on 'those holding the teaching of Balaam, who taught Balak to cast (balein) a net before the Sons of Israel to eat things sacrificed to idols and commit fornication' (2:14 – this is very definitely not Pauline!). Not only is it directly followed up by an allusion to 'making war on them with the sword of my mouth' (cf. Isaiah 11:4 – interpreted 'Messianically' in one of the Isaiah Peshers at Qumran[19] – and Isaiah 49:2), but the whole is but a variation on the pivotal 'Three Nets of Belial' passage in Column Four of the Damascus Document, there in exposition of Isaiah 24:17 ('Panic and Snare and Net are upon you, O inhabitants of the Land'). This last reads: 'Its interpretation concerns the Three Nets of Belial, about which Levi the Son of Jacob spoke (Testament of Levi 14:5–8), by means of which he (Belial) ensnares Israel, transforming them into three kinds of Righteousness.' The equivalence of language here with both 2 Peter and Revelation above should be obvious. The Damascus Document continues: 'The first is fornication, the second is Riches, and the third is pollution of the Temple.'[20] The rest of Column Four and Five is largely devoted to fleshing these accusations out. Not only is it manifestly an attack upon the Herodian Royal Family and the Priesthood it promoted – a proposition which I have already covered extensively elsewhere[21] – but the key chronological allusion, besides congruence of language with all these other documents we have been examining above (and of course their very real similarity to James' directives to overseas communities), is the combination of the 'pollution of the Temple' and 'fornication' charges into one complex whole, the crux of which is put very succinctly in what follows.

Not only do such persons 'not separate' Holy from profane 'as prescribed by *Torah*', but 'they lie with a woman during the blood of her period and each man takes (to wife) the daughter of his brother and the daughter of his sister.... "All of them are kindlers of Fire and lighters of firebrands" (Isaiah 50:11). Their webs are spiders' webs and the offspring of vipers are their eggs' (compare this with the speech attributed to John the Baptist in Matthew 3:7–12 and pars. above). The applicability of this passage to the Herodian Royal Family – who married their nieces and close agnatic cousins as a matter of direct family policy – and none other, should be self-evident. This is particularly true of the allusion to 'sleeping with women during their periods', which is how the easygoing contact of Herodians with Romans and their intermarriage with non-Jewish wives would have been perceived by persons in this period with this kind of native Palestinian-Jewish mindset.

But the next phrase, 'whoever approaches them ('unless he was forced') cannot be cleansed', extends this to the Priesthood that owed its appointment to such Herodians (to wit, 'like an accursed thing, his house is guilty'[22]) and fraternized willingly and regularly with them. In particular, this meant not only accepting their appointment as High Priests from them, but also *accepting their sacrifices in and gifts to the Temple*, even if the more purity-minded extremists regarded them as 'polluted' – therefore the pivotal accusation in 'the Three Nets of *Belial*' passage of the Damascus Document above of 'pollution of the Temple' (cf. as well, the tradition communicated to R. Eliezer b. Hyrcanus by 'Jacob of Kfar Sechania' above on what 'Jesus the Nazoraean' said should be done with 'gifts to the Temple from prostitutes', in our view, a catchphrase for Herodians – in fact, at one point even Queen Helen of Adiabene).[23]

As we have been signaling, the 'Balaam' and 'Balak' language of the above allusions is just an extension of the *B-L-'/ballo* circle-of-language – in Hebrew, meaning 'to eat', 'swallow', or 'consume' and used generally at Qumran in the sense of 'to destroy';[24] in Greek, 'to cast down' or 'cast out', used in the literature we have been examining to express how Jesus' Apostles '*cast down* nets' or '*cast out* Evil Demons' and how James or his stand-in in Acts, 'Stephen', were either '*cast down*' or '*cast out*' (in Josephus, the latter being used to describe what 'the Essenes' did to backsliders, that is, 'cast them out').[25] The transformation of this charge in Revelation from the Damascus Document's 'pollution of the Temple' into the more Jamesian ban on 'things sacrificed to idols' and what Hippolytus' *Sicarii* Essenes refused 'to consume' on pain of death – that is, not Josephus' 'forbidden things', but the more Jamesian 'things sacrificed to idols' – certainly tightens the circle of all these interrelated allusions or aspersions making the reader's brain, perhaps, spin in dizzying astonishment.[26]

For the Pseudoclementines, too, 'the baptismal fountain of Jesus extinguishes the fires of sacrifice'. As the *Recognitions* puts this, not insignificantly, again Peter speaking: 'When the time drew near that what was lacking in the regime of Moses should be made up … and the Prophet should appear … (to) warn them … to cease from sacrificing. However, lest they, therefore, suppose that because of the cessation of sacrifice, there was no remission of sins for them, he instituted water baptism among them in which they might be absolved from all their sins … and, following a Perfect life, they might abide in immortality, being purified not by the blood of beasts, but by the purification of the Wisdom of God.'[27] Finding ideas of this kind in documents that are supposed to be anti- Pauline, as for instance the Pseudoclementines and the Gospel of the Ebionites are considered to be, certainly is strange.

Nevertheless, the documents found at Qumran along with some readings from Josephus can probably provide an answer of sorts to this kind of conundrum.

As we have observed, side-by-side with the 'spiritualized atonement' imagery of the Community Rule, there are at Qumran also a number of documents and passages convincingly demonstrating that 'the Community' had a considerable and even an unwavering attachment to the Temple Law of sacrifice. *MMT* is a perfect example of this as is the Temple Scroll, which lovingly dwells over details of Temple sacrifice even more comprehensively. So does the Damascus Document, the only caveat being that, in it, Temple sacrifice must either be unpolluted or presided over by 'Righteous', 'Zadokite', and 'Perfectly-uncorrupted Priests of Higher Purity'.[28]

The same seems to be true of James personally (not to mention individuals like 'Peter and John' along with other Apostles even in the portrait in Acts[29]) who, if our sources are reliable, seems to have spent most of his earthly existence in the Temple.[30] Nor does he hesitate to send Paul into the Temple to carry out an obscure 'temporary Nazirite-oath' procedure of some kind and pay for 'four others', described as 'taking a vow upon themselves' (Acts 21:22–26). Compare this with those persons, two chapters later, now archly referred to as 'Jews' (23:12), who 'put themselves under a curse (also expressed in Acts 23:14, thereafter, as, 'with a curse we have cursed ourselves to taste nothing')', vowing not to eat or drink till they had killed Paul', repeated again in Acts 23:21 – these clearly being 'Nazirite' *Sicarii* Essenes!

How are we to reconcile these conflicting ideologies and motivations? The answer probably lies in the charge of 'unclean pollution', in particular, 'pollution of the Temple', so important to so many documents at Qumran. The very fact that James is sending out admonitions concerning 'things sacrificed to idols' or 'the pollutions of the idols' to overseas Communities, implies that sacrifice was, in fact, still recognized by 'early Christians' as well (if indeed, they should be called this) – certainly in Palestine and in Jerusalem, if not elsewhere. That Paul too discusses 'things' or 'food sacrificed to idols' and 'eating in an idol Temple' or 'Temple sacrifices' – it is the same to him – and 'weak' people who make problems over such matters, in particular, 'consuming the body' and 'drinking the blood of Christ', further reinforces this impression.[31]

James' presence in the Temple from the Forties to the Sixties CE – though perhaps with intermittent periods of absence as, for example, the flight to the area of Jericho recorded in the Pseudoclementine *Recognitions* – certainly implies at least a passive approval of sacrifice procedures there, regardless of whether he felt this was the best way of proceeding or not. So does his sending Paul into the Temple, as just remarked, as a penance of some sort to himself sacrifice (a demonstration, as he is quoted in Acts 21:24, that Paul himself still 'walks in an orderly Way, keeping the Law' – a patent misapprehension) and pay for the sacrifices of four others under a Nazirite oath there – obviously a very costly procedure even as it is portrayed in Acts. We take this episode to be historical and, clearly, there is no real, absolute disapproval of sacrifices being registered. The literature found at Qumran, despite poetic imagery that may sometimes suggest the contrary, appears to follow a similar approach.

The True Sons of Zadok: 'A High Priest of Greater Purity' and 'Higher Righteousness'

So what then lies behind these conflicting notices? The situation appears to have been twofold. What seems to have been happening is that, when the Temple was perceived of as 'polluted' by Unrighteous Priests doing service at the altar as, for instance, the Herodian High Priesthood (though not the Maccabean), accepting gifts and/or sacrifices on behalf of Romans and other foreigners in the Temple, the issue that triggered the Uprising against

Rome,[32] or when that service was otherwise interrupted, then another form of intercession or repentance was preferred.

This is exactly what Paul is implying with regard to his references to the 'well-pleasing' odor of contributions in Philippians 4:18, even on the part of 'the Holy Ones' or 'Saints' in Caesar's household in 4:22 above. When it was not perceived of as 'polluted' or interrupted, that is, when there was a 'Righteous' or, shall we say, 'Zadokite Priesthood' doing service at the altar as per the parameters of Hebrews and the Dead Sea Scrolls, then sacrifice seems to have been approved of. This, too, is exactly what is implied in the Scrolls with their charge of 'pollution of the Temple', one of 'the Three Nets of *Belial*' or one of the sins of the reigning Priestly Establishment, in our view, founded and promoted by Herodians – even by Herod himself. As Hebrews puts this, 'a High Priest, Holy, innocent, unpolluted, *separated* from Sinners', who has 'become Higher than the Heavens' (7:26).

We have been documenting the agitation that broke out after the death of Herod, and even before, by 'the Innovators' (as Josephus often calls them) or 'proto-Zealots', who from 4 BCE–7 CE were already demanding 'a High Priest of greater purity' or 'Piety' or, if one prefers, 'a High Priest of Higher Righteousness'.[33] This is, of course, also the demand being made in Hebrews in its understanding of the language embodied in the circumlocution 'a Priest forever after the order of Melchizedek' (in Hebrew, literally meaning, 'King of Righteousness' – Hebrews 5:6/7:17, quoting Psalm 110:4) and 'loving Righteousness' (Hebrews 1:9, quoting Psalm 45:7).

But the demand for 'a High Priest of greater purity' or 'Piety' did not just begin in these events from 4 BCE–7 CE, consonant with the birth of 'Christ Jesus', as Paul would put it and as portrayed in Matthew and Luke. In fact, just as Josephus portrays the 'Zealot' or '*Sicarii*' Movement in the *Antiquities* as beginning with the Census and the arguments of 'Judas and Sadduk' with Joezer ben Boethus over the tax issue in 7 CE, for Luke 2:1–3, in another curious overlap that cries out for attention, it is the birth of 'the Messiah' that takes place at this moment.[34] In other words, whereas for Josephus it is the 'Zealot'/*Sicarii* Movement (moved as it was – as he admits at the end of the *War* – by the Messianic Star Prophecy) that begins, in the New Testament, in particular Luke, for all intents and purposes it is 'Christianity' with the birth of its Messiah that begins at this moment, a peculiar congruence. But this demand for such an incorrupt High Priest was already, either implicitly or overtly, part of the events that produced the Maccabean Uprising, when there was also just such a struggle between 'Righteous' High Priests and 'Ungodly', 'backsliding' ones and sacrifice in the Temple was, even, for a time interrupted.

'Onias the Righteous', whom we have already mentioned above – 'this Zealot for the Laws' and 'Protector of his fellow countrymen', as 2 Maccabees 4:2 describes him in anticipation to a certain extent of the way early Church literature will depict James – is martyred at Antioch by the hand of a Seleucid King there 'in defiance of all Justice' (2 Maccabees 4:34). This Onias was the son of the High Priest of the previous line, 'Simeon the *Zaddik*', whose Righteous atonement in the Temple on *Yom Kippur* is pictured in Ben Sira's climactic 'praise of Famous Men' – in reality 'praise of Men of Piety'/'*Anshei-Hesed*', i.e., once again the theme of 'the Hassidaeans').[35] Therefore, this theme of a Righteous and/or 'Zealot' Priesthood is a century or two older than our encounter of it with regard to Herodians and the Priests involved with and/or appointed by them.

Following the High Priest Onias' murder by foreigners, a motif so much a part of this struggle, and the 'pollution of the Temple' that follows, 2 Maccabees 14:6 portrays Judas as the Leader *par excellence* of those called 'Hassidaeans', with no intervening presentation of Mattathias his father whatsoever. Ignoring the 'Zealot High-Priestly' claims in 1 Maccabees 2:26-28 on behalf of his father in favor of Onias' 'Perfect High Priesthood', 2 Maccabees 5:27 then proceeds to delineate Judas' own 'wilderness' sojourn 'with some nine others'. There is in this, as already suggested too, just the slightest suggestion of 'the Ten Righteous Ones' of the Abraham/Lot episode in Genesis 18:32, 'for whose sake God would withhold destruction from the Earth'. This is true both as regards the locale, but also the ideology. 2 Peter 2:6–14 alludes to this episode, as well, after its evocation of Noah as the 'Herald of Righteousness' and 'the Flood'. Referring to these same 'Righteous Ones', it not only calls Lot 'Righteous' and 'a Righteous One', but, in the style of the Hymns, highlights the suffering of his 'Righteous soul'.[36]

Not unlike the Teacher Josephus calls 'Banus' in his *Vita* and with whom he spent a seeming two-year novitiate period,[37] Judas subsists on 'wild plants to *avoid contracting defilement*' (2 Maccabees 5:22). Not only, therefore, did Judas at this point avoid all unclean foods, but he ate only vegetables and, seemingly, wild ones at that – that is, like a 'Rechabite', *he did not cultivate*.[38] The reason for this seems to have been that the 'Noahic' permission to consume meat was withdrawn with the interruption of 'Righteous Temple service' and 'sacrifice'. This kind of vegetarianism seems to some extent also to prefigure John the Baptist, Josephus' so-called 'Banus', and even James. To repeat, this insistence on vegetarianism, which Paul calls 'weak' in 1 Corinthians 8:7–13 and Romans 14:1–2, was not mere asceticism, but would appear to have been a consequence of the extreme purity regulations being observed by these 'wilderness'-dwelling *Zaddik*s, and associated in some manner with the perception of 'the pollution of the Temple' and the inefficacy or interruption either of the sacrifices or the Temple service being conducted there.

Where atonement on behalf of the whole people was concerned, it is reasonable to suppose that such a 'working prayer of the Just One', so pivotally evoked in James 5:16 when speaking about Elijah's 'powerful' praying, could not be efficacious unless delivered by 'a *Zaddik*' or 'a Priest *Zaddik*' like James or of the kind delineated in Hebrews.

This would appear to be the position of the Scrolls as well in various attempts to come to grips with what true 'Sons of Zadok' were. As we have seen, this phrase was also evoked with regard to Simeon the *Zaddik*'s heirs in connection with his splendid *Yom Kippur* atonement in the Temple in the Hebrew version of Ben Sira found in the Cairo Genizah, at Masada, and at Qumran. As in the New Testament, these are sometimes denoted in the Scrolls, as we have already explained, as 'the Sons of *Zedek*'/'the Sons of Righteousness' or 'the Sons of the *Zaddik*'/'the Sons of the Righteous One'.[39] Often modern scholars mistake these allusions for scribal errors. But these are really probably not scribal errors – simply rather, interchangeable metaphor.[40]

This then is also the true symbolism commemorated in Jewish Hanukkah festivities – meaning, 'Purification' or 'Rededication of the Temple', festivities never really favored very much among 'the Rabbis' as such (the true heirs of Pharisee Judaism) – therefore, the absence of the Maccabee Books explaining this Festival from their version of Scripture and, mystifyingly, only found in 'Catholic' recensions of these materials. This 'Purification' or 'Rededication' is celebrated in the Temple by Judas Maccabeus as a powerful, 'High-Priestly' Vicegerent of sorts.[41] Modern scholars have been quick to question his qualifications as a High Priest, but his election to this office is twice attested to by Josephus – and here the idea of 'election' is important[42] – and, that he presides over these 'purification' activities in the Temple is not really to be gainsaid. This is also the thrust, real or symbolic, of the presentation of Jesus in the New Testament who, like 1 Maccabees 2:27 and 2:54's picture of these Maccabean purveyors of 'the Covenant of Phineas' and their 'zeal', is pictured in all the Gospels, Synoptic or Johannine, as 'purifying the Temple' as well.[43]

We know what Pauline groups preferred and, for that matter, Rabbinic ones too. The former went so far in their insistence on a more spiritualized atonement or sacrifice as to turn it into a sacramental religious creed, not only tying it to 'Mystery Religion'-type ceremonies about 'consuming the body and blood of Christ Jesus' or 'the living and dying god', but barring any other approach. Rabbinic Judaism was already purveying the notion – like Paul – that charitable contributions were equivalent to sacrifice referring to it, as already remarked, as *Zedakah*/Justification – '*Zakat*' in Islam[44] – a verbal noun based on the same root as *Zedek* or Righteousness. This conceptuality and the ideology associated with it were particularly useful after the fall of the Temple, when the sacrifice ritual was for all intents and purposes defunct, but it was already well developed before this time, as the Apocryphal Book of Tobit makes clear.[45] But Paul, too, is well aware of this idea of Charity superseding Temple sacrifice, having studied with the Pharisaic progenitors of Rabbinic Judaism or, as Acts 23:6 has him express this, 'I am a Pharisee the son of a Pharisee' – in Philippians 3:5, as he famously puts this himself, 'according to Law, a Pharisee'.

He refers to precisely this kind of fund-raising activity at the end of Romans and in 1 Corinthians 16:3. In Romans 15:26–27 he speaks about 'the Poor of the Saints in Jerusalem', where he makes it clear this involved '*ministering* to' or '*serving* them in bodily things' – the obvious origin of the presentation of 'Stephen' and the other Six doing 'table service' in Acts 6:2–5. As Paul puts it so inimitably, 'since the Peoples are participating in their spiritual things, they ought to minister to them in bodily things' as well. Indeed, this notion of charity replacing sacrifice may have been how James 'the Bishop' or 'Overseer' – who admonished Paul (even according to the latter's own testimony in Galatians 2:10), it will be recalled, not to forget to 'remember the Poor' – may have understood these things as well.

The Pseudoclementines appear to have little doubt that Christ's blood 'extinguished the fire of sacrifice for all time' which has a peculiarly 'Pauline' ring. Indeed, this may have been the preferred doctrine among the more sophisticated or refined, but James' behavior, even in Acts – not to mention here in the Pseudoclementines – to some extent belies this as he did send Paul into the Temple to participate in the sacrifice cult.

Whether groups such as those following James the Just in Jerusalem – who, most accounts attest, went into the Temple every day for the better part of twenty years – or 'baptizing' or 'Nazirite'-style groups generally, following the approach so clearly enunciated in the Community Rule above, preferred 'spiritualized' sacrifice and atonement to actual sacrifice in the Temple, even when presided over by a 'Righteous High Priest', cannot be determined on the basis of the available evidence. They certainly preferred it to sacrifice offered by or atonement made by a corrupt Priesthood – a Priesthood compromised in some manner or 'polluted' by its contact with foreigners, a Priesthood that collaborated with and received its appointment from foreign Rulers, Pseudo-Jews, or Jewish backsliders. But this is not to say that these purist, more extreme groups were unalterably opposed at all times and under all circumstances to sacrifice in the Temple, even when it was being exercised by 'Righteous' High Priests in a 'Righteous' manner. This is a complex matter and the evidence will not support that.

'The Land of Damascus', where '*the New Covenant*' and '*the fallen Tent of David*' were to be restored', on the way '*North*' to '*the King of*' and '*the Land of the Edessenes*' and Adiabene.

Chapter 15
James in the *Anabathmoi Jacobou* and Paul as Herodian

The *Anabathmoi Jacobou* and the Literature of Heavenly Ascents

It would now be well to look at the evidence in the book Epiphanius entitles *The Anabathmoi Jacobou* or *The Ascents of James* about the issue of Temple sacrifice or the lack thereof. This book, which he claims actually to have seen and presents in his discussion of 'the Ebionites' as being a rival 'Acts of the Apostles', has James 'complaining against the Temple and the sacrifices, and against the fire on the altar, and much else that is full of nonsense'.[1] It is passing strange to hear Epiphanius accusing others of being 'full of nonsense' since this is one of his own manifest shortcomings; having said this, one should perhaps accept the reliability of at least *some* of what he presents. The *Anabathmoi Jacobou* is a lost 'Jewish Christian' or 'Ebionite' work, of which we only have these excerpts in Epiphanius and which probably took its title from either a real or symbolic understanding of the debates on the Temple steps with the Jerusalem Priesthood recorded in the Pseudoclementine *Recognitions* debates which were also refracted in numerous notices to similar effect in the first chapters of the Book of Acts (albeit with James' presence neatly deleted or overwritten) and even in the picture of James' death emerging out of Hegesippus.[2]

What remains of the *Anabathmoi* is considered to be either parallel to or incorporated in parts of the Pseudoclementines, particularly the picture of Peter, James, and John debating the Pharisaic/Sadducean Leadership on the steps of the Temple, and perhaps two other lost documents related to these – *The Preaching of Peter* and *The Travels of Peter*.[3] But to be a rival Acts, it must have contained much more than this and, as its title implies, focused more on James than any of the aforementioned appear to have done, which, in more Western orthodox fashion, seem already to prefer to call, whomever they are referring to, 'Peter'.

These '*Ascents*' – aside from possibly alluding to the steps of the Temple and, therefore, the debates that took place on them in all parallel narratives – can also be looked upon as the 'degrees' of either mystic or Gnostic instruction or initiation. This is also the case for Kabbalistic Literature and what is known as '*Hechalot*' or 'Ascents' Literature. This theme also appears to attach itself to James in the Gnostic variety of the tradition conserved in the Two Apocalypses under his name from Nag Hammadi.[4] In the writer's view, these represent a later stage of the tradition when all hope of a Messianic return or Victory, or a this-worldly Kingdom such as the one envisioned at Qumran, had actually evaporated, giving way to the now more familiar other-worldly, ideological perspective.

Indeed, this is something of the thrust one gets in the Habakkuk *Pesher*'s interpretation of Habakkuk 2:3. Here, not only is the Righteous Teacher described as receiving instruction 'from the mouth of God', but he is also denoted as 'the Priest', a term invariably meaning, 'the High Priest' in Hebrew – 'in whose heart God put the intelligence to interpret all the words of His Servants the Prophets' and 'through whom God foretold all that was coming to His People', 'making known to him all the Mysteries of the words of His Servants the Prophets'.[5] In other words, the Righteous Teacher, who seems just as James to double as the High Priest or perhaps more comprehensibly 'the Opposition High Priest', had virtually a direct connection to God and was, like Moses, for all intents and purposes 'His mouthpiece'.

The main 'Mystery' that 'God made known to him', which is specifically said to have been an 'astonishing' one and delivered to him (that is, Habakkuk) as it were 'on the run' (2:2), seems to have been that 'the Last Era would be extended and exceed all that the Prophets have foretold, since the Mysteries of God are astonishing'.[6] This leads to the exegesis of Habakkuk 2:3: 'If it tarries, wait for it'. It is, of course, exactly the kind of understanding that was developing in the first centuries of Christianity into what latterly goes under the heading of 'the Delay of the *Parousia*', that is, the delay of the Second Coming of Jesus and its accompanying effects – and what some moderns refer to as 'the Rapture' – for which believers have been waiting quite a long time now.

On the Jewish side however, there is also the literature of 'Heavenly Ascents' described in Jewish Kabbalistic tradition. This 'Literature of Ascents' or '*Hechalot* Literature', as it is called, is the Literature of the Ascents to Heaven and the various degrees thereof. For his part, Paul actually describes in 2 Corinthians 12:2–4 meeting one such 'Man in Christ' who made one such ascent 'fourteen years before'.

The number 'fourteen' is suggestive here, for it is exactly the number Paul uses in Galatians 2:1 to describe the interval between his two visits to Jerusalem, both of which times he met James – the first, when he 'made the acquaintance of Peter' and, according to him, saw 'no other Apostles except James the brother of the Lord' (1:19), and the second when he (Paul) returned to put 'the Gospel, as (he) proclaimed it among the Peoples' before 'those reputed to be something', namely, 'James and Cephas and John' (Galatians 2:2–2:9).

Not only does Paul basically give them 'the back of his hand' by indicating that, to him, their repute 'made no difference … because God does not accept the person of Man'. We have discussed this allusion to 'accepting the person of Man' in regard to James' well-documented 'not deferring to men' above but, in our view, when all these allusions are taken together – despite Paul's typically subdued tone in referring to persons of James' status here – that James is the one, considered to have made such an 'Ascent' to 'the Third Heaven' as Paul describes this in 2 Corinthians 12:2, is probably not to be gainsaid. As Paul expresses this in 12:3 amid allusion to his 'not knowing' but 'God knowing': 'whether in the body or out of the body', this 'one was caught away into the Third Heaven' and, again in 12:4, 'caught away to the Paradise' – in Hebrew, of course, '*Pardess*', meaning 'Orchard' or 'Garden', this being the typically Kabbalistic and, for that matter, Islamic term for precisely this kind of mystical experience. There, whomever he is referring to 'heard unutterable sayings, which it is not permitted to Man to speak'.

This is certainly a very curious notice, particularly as it comes right in the midst of his attacks on the 'Super Apostles' whom, as we saw, at one point he identifies as 'Hebrews' (2 Corinthians 11:22) who 'commend themselves' by 'measuring themselves by themselves and comparing themselves to themselves', but who also 'preach *another Jesus*' (10:12–11:4). It also comes in the midst of his own 'boasting' about – and this playing on the motif of these 'Super Apostles' – 'the surpassingness of (his own) Heavenly Visions (11:22–12:12).

In 2 Corinthians 2:14–16, Paul speaks of 'making manifest through us the perfume of the Knowledge of him in every place. For we are a *sweet odor* of Christ in those being saved to God … an *odor of life* to life'. Paul is at his allegorical best here; but with his remarks about 'these others' – whom he calls 'those who are to perish' (sometimes even, it will be recalled, 'Ministers of Death' or 'Servants of Satan' – remarks, however covert, clearly aimed at the 'Super Apostles' and the Jerusalem Church Leadership) and, most tellingly and bitingly of all, 'an odor of death to death'! – he reaches a rhetorical pinnacle (though some might call it, a polemical and rhetorical nadir).

The Ban on Foreigners in the Temple (including Herodians)

One should note that in 1 Corinthians, Paul also sees himself as having 'Mysteries' revealed to him and, in turn, revealing them to his congregants. In 4:1 he actually calls himself and his colleagues 'Attendants of Christ and *Keepers of the Mysteries of God*'. In 1 Corinthians 14:2–4, Paul once again claims that 'he is speaking with a Tongue' and 'in (the) Spirit', and thus, both 'building up', 'speaking to God not men', and 'speaking Mysteries'. In fact, in 13:2

he actually seems to be parodying the description of 'the Righteous Teacher' in the Scrolls, when he speaks of 'having prophecy and knowing all Mysteries and all Knowledge' while at the same time, in the antistrophe, disparaging this with the words, 'but not having love being nothing'.

But the Scrolls too speak of such 'Mysteries', not only in the Community Rule and relative to unique attributes of the Righteous Teacher in the Habakkuk *Pesher*, but in other documents as well – as does Muhammad in the Koran.[7] The same can be said for James in the picture in the Pseudoclementines, though in both them and the Scrolls, teachers are cautioned to keep such things secret, revealing them only to the inner core of colleagues practising real 'Perfection of the Way'.[8] Paul by contrast, as in Romans 16:25–26 and 1 Corinthians 14:25, wants everything 'made manifest' and 'nothing hidden' (at least, after such time that 'the Lord has come') and in 1 Corinthians 2:4–7 he alludes both to 'speaking among the Perfect' and 'speaking the Wisdom of God in a Mystery which God has hidden and pre-ordained before the Ages for our Glory'. In 1 Corinthians 4:5 and 2 Corinthians 4:2–4:6, he even applies Qumran 'Light and Dark' imagery to these sorts of propositions.

Contrary-wise, regarding Epiphanius' contention that James 'spoke against the Temple and the sacrifices', there is something to say. Though it is impossible to reconcile it with the material about James from earlier sources like Hegesippus and Josephus, who taken together place him in the Temple on a daily basis for the better part of twenty years, or the very solid testimony in the 'We Document' section of Acts where James sends Paul into the Temple to take upon himself a Nazirite oath of some kind, nevertheless, with the slightest shift in phraseology and signification, it is possible to fit the attitude reported by Epiphanius, himself originally an Ebionite, fairly easily into the situation in Jerusalem in this period and what we know about James generally, to say nothing of the so-called 'Teacher of Righteousness' at Qumran.

For example, we just saw that in Acts that James imposes this temporary Nazirite-style penance on Paul – a penance some commentators view as 'a set-up'[9] – to show that 'there is nothing to all' the rumors people 'have been informed concerning you, but you yourself still walk undeviatingly, keeping the Law' (Acts 21:24). The relevant point in all these matters, as we have been emphasizing, is the hostility to foreigners, vividly evinced even in Acts' description of the riot that follows by the Jewish crowd. As Acts 21:24–28 portrays this – in contrast to earlier portrayals, in our view, now fairly accurately – 'Jews coming from Asia', 'saw him (Paul) in the Temple and stirred up all the crowd', a picture retrospectively incorporated into the Gospels about events circulating around Jesus' death but with, as usual, more historical plausibility where Paul is concerned.

Acts 21:29 even feels obliged to add, by way of explanation to gainsay this: 'For they had earlier seen Trophimus the Ephesian with him in the city and supposed Paul had brought him into the Temple.' So we also now have here in this picture the ban on introducing foreigners or non-Jews – according to many extremists including even Herodians – into the Temple that so much exercised this period. 'Laying hands on him', these now cry out: 'Men, Israelites, help! This is the man who teaches everyone, everywhere against the People, against the Law, and against this Place, and now he has brought Greeks into the Temple and polluted this Holy Place!' There can be little doubt that here we have, anyway, the 'pollution of the Temple' from 'the Three Nets of *Belial*' charges and in this context, at least, we know the reasons why. One could go even further and observe that what Paul is doing here is acting as 'a stalking horse' for the Herodian family, testing the ban mentioned in Josephus on some of its principal members, such as Agrippa II and Bernice, in the Temple.

However this may be, thereupon he is unceremoniously ejected and 'the doors closed' or 'barred' behind him. The words Acts 21:30 uses at this point to describe what happened, 'they dragged Paul outside the Temple and immediately shut the doors', have an odd resonance with and parallel the phraseology used in the Damascus Document concerning those 'who have been brought' into 'the New Covenant in the Land of Damascus', 'who dug the well with staves' – the 'staves' here ('*hukkim*' in Hebrew) being a double entendre based on Numbers 21:18 meaning 'the Laws' (also '*hukkim*'), which 'the Staff'/'*Mehokkek*' or 'Legislator' decreed (*hakak*), complexities to which we shall return in due course.[10] Initiants such as these are, then, advised 'not to enter the Temple to kindle its altar in vain' – rather 'they are to be (as in Acts 21:30 just quoted above) *Barrers of the Door*', that is, to persons like Paul and his companions. At this point, the Damascus Document goes on to quote Malachi 1:10: 'Who among you will not shut its door (meaning 'of the Temple') and not kindle useless fires on My altar?' – the implication being, 'fires' like the 'useless fires' of the corrupt Herodian Priesthood. To put this in another way, if you are going to light the fires of sacrifice in the Temple, then you must abjure the consonant 'pollution of the Temple' referred to in 'the Three Nets of *Belial*' charges just preceding this citation. But this is precisely the teaching ascribed to James in the testimony Epiphanius excerpted from the *Anabathmoi* delineating how James *complained against lighting the useless 'fires on My altar'* – yet again, further consolidating the 'Jamesian' character of the Damascus Document as it has been unfolding to us so far.[11]

The Damascus Document then moves on to evoke the idea of 'keeping' or 'being Keepers' (of the *Torah* or the Law – in Paul above, 'of the Mysteries') and to recommend the Jamesian '*doing* according to the precise letter of the *Torah* in the Age of Wickedness and to *separate* from the Sons of the Pit and *keep away* from *polluted* Evil Riches acquired by vow or ban and (keep away) from the Riches of the Temple'.[12] Here, not only are we speaking of exactly the same kind of contributions connected to the 'vows' or 'bans' that Acts 21:23 is speaking about in the matter of Paul's sacrifice expenses and his unceremonious ejection from the Temple, but the actual phrase used to express this, 'keeping away from' (*lehinnazer*/'to be set aside', in Hebrew), is based on the same root, as we have seen, as the term 'Nazirite' and plays on the *real versions of such activity* as exemplified by the Community itself. Nor can there be very much doubt as to what is being said here.

This is immediately followed too by allusion to 'robbing the Poor of His People', which echoes the notices found in Josephus about the High Priests 'robbing the tithes of the Poor Priests' in the picture he gives of the run-up in Book Twenty of the *Antiquities* to the stoning of James and the War against Rome.[13] The same accusation will form part of the accusations against the Priestly Establishment in the Habakkuk *Pesher*'s lengthy scenario of the destruction of the character it knows as 'the Righteous Teacher'.[14] As also already alluded to, the verb based on this 'Nazirite' root actually appears twice more in as many columns of the Damascus Document. This first evocation is immediately followed by reference to 'the New Covenant in the Land of Damascus' and citation of the 'Jamesian' Royal Law according to the Scripture, 'to love, each man, his brother as himself'.[15] This is accompanied by the admonition to 'separate between polluted and pure', 'Holy and profane'.

In the Damascus Document this is followed by a warning 'to *keep away* from fornication', expressed by the verb '*lehazzir*', again from the same root as '*Nazirite*'.[16] It should be clear that these are the exact words of the prohibition, as it is expressed in James' directives to overseas communities – once in the context of James' final words to Paul in Jerusalem in Acts 21:20–25, ending with the penance James puts upon him involving 'Nazirite' oath expenses and procedures.

One final use of the expression in the Damascus Document occurs at the beginning of the next Column (CD VIII) amid allusion to 'wallowing in the Ways of fornication and Evil Riches' and 'each man bearing malice against' and 'hating his brother' – the opposite, to be sure, of 'each man loving his brother as himself' earlier and in the Letter of James.[17] Here the condemnation of 'Riches' – as in the Letter of James 5:1–6 as well – is extreme; but, in addition, each man is said to have 'approached the flesh of his own flesh for fornication' (again, the 'niece marriage' and 'marriage with close cousins' charges of 'the Three Nets of *Belial*' accusations, the latter even perhaps including the 'incest' one as well),[18] 'using their power for the sake of Riches and profiteering, each doing what was right in his own eyes and each choosing the stubbornness of his own heart, for they did not *keep apart from* (*nazru*) the People and sinned publicly'.[19] A better description of the Herodian Establishment could not be imagined.

This now ends with direct evocation of 'the Kings of the Peoples', a term in Roman jurisprudence used to describe petty kings in the Eastern part of the Empire, mostly 'Greek-speaking' like the Herodians.[20] This is where 'the Head (*rosh*) of the Kings of Greece' or 'Greek-speaking Kings' that is also part of the exegesis that follows will – as we shall see – come into play.[21] In the Western part of the Empire, integration with the Roman polity generally was more widespread. Identified with Deuteronomy 33:32's 'serpents' – another term with parallels that are almost proverbial in the Gospels[22] – and playing on the double entendre in Hebrew, 'their venom' ('*rosh*' as well – *yayin*/'wine' and *Yavan*/'Greece' forming another such couplet) is identified as 'the wine of their Ways' – the implication being, 'Hellenizing'. In addition, the Lying visions of 'the Lying Spouter … who walked in the Spirit' – a third double entendre based on Micah 2:11, 'wind' and 'Spirit' in Hebrew likewise being homonyms – is then also directly evoked.[23]

James in the *Anabathmoi Jacobou* and 'Pollution of the Temple'

The evocation above of 'doing according to the precise letter of the *Torah*' in the Damascus Document not only parallels James 2:8–10 about 'keeping the whole Law, but stumbling on one point' but also the passage in Jesus' Sermon on the Mount regarding 'not one jot or tittle passing away from the Law' (Matthew 5:18 and pars.). Just as the sequence found in the Letter of James, this section of the Damascus Document ends in an allusion to 'the Royal Law according to the Scripture' as we have just seen.[24]

We have just seen too how, following this third allusion to 'keeping away from the People' (one should possibly read 'Peoples' here) and in connection with entering both 'the New Covenant in the Land of Damascus' and 'the Well of Living Waters', 'setting up the Holy Things according to their precise specifications' is now alluded to.[25] It should be appreciated that 'Holy Things' is synonymous with 'Consecrated Things' not only, for instance, as regards the Temple Priesthood – which was in fact considered 'Holy to God' or 'consecrated' – but also where those following the regime of lifelong Naziritism were concerned.[26]

This new Community 'in the wilderness' also involved a reunion of the wilderness 'Camps' under the supervision of an individual referred to as 'the *Mebakker*' or 'Overseer' (a more relevant English equivalent would probably be 'the Bishop') or 'the High Priest Commanding the Many' at Pentecost time – both, roles James is accorded in Christian tradition. One should also note here the vocabulary of 'the Many', just encountered in a more derogatory vein above in Paul – this, in particular, in fragments of the Damascus Document not found in the Cairo Genizah version, themselves first published by the author.[27]

Pentecost is precisely the festival Acts 20:16 pictures Paul as hurrying to Jerusalem to attend with the contributions he has so assiduously gathered overseas (cf. too, 2 Corinthians 1:15–19, 8:13–9:15, Philippians 4:15–19, etc. in this regard). In these fragments, two of which clearly comprising the actual last Column of the Damascus Document,[28] the oaths taken in connection with this reunion of 'the Wilderness Camps' involve a total rededication to the Law and not 'deviating to the right or to the left of the *Torah*', which is exactly the sense of James' directive to Paul in Acts 21:24 above on Pentecost about 'still walking undeviatingly keeping the Law'.

Of course, the parallel to all this in Acts 2:1–6 is the descent of the Pauline 'Holy Spirit' like 'a rushing violent wind' and 'God-fearing men from every People' – presumably in preparation for the Pauline Gentile Mission too – 'speaking with other Tongues'. It should be appreciated that the kind of 'separation' both 'in the Temple' and 'from the People'/'Peoples' being recommended in these passages in the Damascus Document, is during such time when it (the Temple) was perceived of as 'being polluted' by 'polluted Evil Riches' and, for example, by what was being 'robbed from the Poor' – *not* an abandonment of '*Torah*' altogether.

But this passage based on Malachi 1:10 about 'not entering the Temple to light its altar in vain' which begins this whole string of allusions in the Damascus Document and brings us full circle back to the *Anabathmoi Jacobou*, Acts, and the Letter of James, also gives us something of the idea of what the issues really were here. What is so exercising Malachi in the background to this quotation is 'putting polluted food on My Altar' (1:7); in James' directives, *MMT*, and Hippolytus' picture of '*Sicarii* Essene' willingness to martyr themselves,[66] this is expressed rather in terms of 'things sacrificed to idols', not the abolition of the Law of Sacrifice *per se*. Again, the problem is 'polluted things' (in the version of James' directives quoted in Acts 15:20, 'the pollution of the idols') or 'pollution of the Temple' as in the Damascus Document.

Malachi is also the prophet who alludes to 'sending My Messenger' to 'prepare the Way before Me' (3:1) and 'sending Elijah the Prophet before the coming of the Great and Terrible Day of the Lord' (4:5), again our 'Day of Vengeance' in the Community Rule and War Scroll above. Interestingly enough, in Ezekiel 38:22 and even in the Nahum *Pesher*, this is expressed in terms of 'torrential rain', which actually closes the circle with all these rainmaking *Zaddiks* we have detailed previously.[30] Now we are in a more recognizably Judeo-Palestinian milieu. Though this is the Prophecy that is exploited in the presentation of John the Baptist in the Synoptic Gospels, it should be appreciated that 'remembering the Law of My Servant Moses, which I commanded him at Horeb for all Israel', is the line directly preceding this in Malachi 4:4, a passage which obviously would not have failed to leave its impression on the sectaries at Qumran – but, as should be easy to comprehend in view of all the foregoing, not on Paul nor in the way its follow-up is exploited in the Synoptics.

But we do not need these passages from Malachi and the Damascus Document to make sense of the material about James which Epiphanius cites from the *Anabathmoi Jacobou*. No doubt, the issues really did center – as in *MMT*[31] – on 'the sacrifices and the Temple', but what kind of 'sacrifices' and what was the concern regarding 'the Temple'? After the destruction of the Temple, a situation seemingly alluded to in Peter's speech in the first book of the Pseudoclementine *Recognitions*,[32] it was easy to reframe or transform these issues in the manner we are seeing in the *Anabathmoi* or the *Recognitions*' debates on the Temple stairs that appears to have relied upon it.

Where the Temple is concerned, the issue is pretty straightforward. I think we can safely say that James complained not simply 'about the Temple', as Epiphanius somewhat superficially reduces it, but about 'pollution of the Temple', as this is framed in the Damascus Document, and the manner in which 'Temple service', as the Rabbis for their part would have it, was being conducted by the Herodian Establishment and its Sadducean High Priests, that is, Priests appointed by corrupt foreign Governors and a Royal Family that the more extreme groups considered to be foreigners of Greco-Arab descent and not even, for the most part, Jewish at all.[33]

This is what makes the Talmudic episode in the *Mishnah* so poignant when it depicts the most respected member of this family, King Agrippa I (37–44 CE – whose grandmother had been a Maccabean Princess), weeping in the Temple on the Festival of Tabernacles, when the Deuteronomic King Law: 'You shall not put a foreigner over you who is not your brother' (17:15) was read. Here the Pharisees, who redacted this material, 'cry out' – as is usual in these stories – three times, 'You are our brother! You are our brother! You are our brother!' when, of course, in actuality (except for one matrilineal grandmother) for the most part he was not.[34] For the 'Simon' depicted in Josephus at exactly the same time as wanting to bar Herodians from the Temple just because they were foreigners, Agrippa I was a foreigner.

Not only is this episode clearly related, on the one hand, to this passage in the *Mishnah* above; but, on the other, it is also related to the descent of 'the Heavenly tablecloth' episode ('by its four corners'!) in Acts 10:17–48 depicting, as we have several times had occasion to remark, another 'Simon' – in this instance, the so-called 'Simon Peter' on a rooftop in Jaffa – learning that he 'should not call any man profane' and to be more accepting of foreigners just in time to receive the deputies of and visit in Caesarea the household of the new Christian convert, the Roman Centurion Cornelius, a man Acts also describes – somewhat comically, as already observed – as 'a Pious God-Fearer … doing many good works to the People and praying to God continually' (10:2).

Not only is 'Peter' portrayed here as making one of the many 'blood libel' speeches we have already outlined above (10:39), but the visit Peter makes to the Roman Centurion Cornelius' household – having just learned that he is now 'allowed to come near a man of another race' (10:28 – this inaccurate characterization is certainly written by a non-Jew, being the way such an individual would have perceived Jewish purity regulations) – is the *mirror reversal* of the one the 'Simon' portrayed in Josephus makes to Agrippa I, the most 'Pious' of all Herodian Kings, a man who really did try to 'do many good works for the People', 'to see what was done there contrary to Law'.[35] Of course, as to some degree previously explained, what Acts has done here is simply substitute the Roman Centurion from 'the Italica Regiment' (a town in Spain which was the birthplace of both Trajan and Hadrian – two of the most-hated enemies of the Jews[36]) for Agrippa I. In our view too, the historical 'Simon' is someone who really would have been arrested after the untimely and mysterious death of Agrippa I (cf. Acts 12:21–23).[37]

Of course, the Deuteronomic King Law, which was the passage to be read in the Temple on Tabernacles, has now been found enshrined in the Temple Scroll.[38] If we had not found it, we would have had to predicate it. It was statutes such as these and their derivative, the illegality of foreign appointment of High Priests, that were, for groups like 'the Zealots', the 'jots and tittles' that should not be deleted from the Law – these together with other basic requirements like circumcision in the matter of conversion and not divorcing or marrying nieces. As the Temple Scroll puts this last with regard to 'the King', 'he shall not take a second wife during the lifetime of the first, for she shall be with him all the time of her life', nor 'shall he marry a wife from the daughters of the Peoples' (this last being particularly relevant where Herodians were concerned).[39]

James also complained against Gifts and Sacrifices on Behalf of Herodians and Other Foreigners in the Temple

Where the issue of 'Temple pollution' is concerned, as we have now several times remarked, it was a central fixture of the 'Three Nets of *Belial*' charges in the Damascus Document and was always hovering in the background of the prescriptions in *MMT*.[40] No doubt, too, it was part and parcel of what was being signified in James' directives to overseas communities under the rubric of 'things sacrificed to idols' and 'the pollutions of the idols'. Josephus repeats the charge over and over again – albeit sometimes with inverted signification – in his description of the run-up to the War against Rome.[41] It was also the backbone of the issue behind the Temple Wall Affair in which, from our perspective, James was involved and which not only centered on barring foreigners like the Herodians from the

Temple, but even blocking their view and that of their dining guests of the sacrifices in the Temple.[42]

But it is the particular variation of it, which Josephus describes in these same descriptions in the *Jewish War*, which provides the key to unlocking the meaning of this second allusion from the *Anabathmoi Jacobou* that James 'complained against the sacrifice'. What is particularly exercising Josephus in his description of the run-up to the War against Rome is the rejecting gifts and sacrifices on behalf of Romans and other foreigners and the stopping of sacrifices on behalf of the Emperor in the Temple by the Lower Priesthood, among whom James' influence seems to have been strong.[43] This event is the direct cause of the outbreak of the War against Rome which, in turn, led inexorably to the destruction of the Temple and the fall of Jerusalem – events so telescoped by early Christian sources relating to the death of James.[44]

Like so many other things he disapproves of and blames on those he refers to derogatorily as 'Zealots' or *Sicarii*, Josephus claims this cessation of sacrifice on behalf of foreigners in the Temple was 'an Innovation which our Forefathers were before unacquainted with'.[45] This is certainly *not the case* in the passage leading up to Ezekiel's all-important definition of 'the Sons of Zadok' (44:15) where significantly, as we saw, Ezekiel absolutely bars any foreigner 'uncircumcised in heart or body' from the Temple (44:7–9). In fact, Ezekiel even calls this 'pollution of the Temple', but of course – aside from Isaiah – Ezekiel is perhaps the most highly-regarded prophet at Qumran.

We have seen that this passage forms the centerpiece of the definition in the Damascus Document of the 'Sons of Zadok' which can, therefore, also be seen as inclusive of the opposition to just such 'gifts and sacrifices' on the part of foreigners in the Temple. This theme is further reinforced in the Temple Scroll and the Habakkuk *Pesher* – more homogeneity and therefore, in our view, simultaneity – as it is in *MMT* above.[46] 'The pollutions of the idols' or 'things sacrificed to idols' in James' directives, as redacted in Acts and so refracted too by Paul in 1 Corinthians 8–11 and in *MMT*, also links up with the 'polluted food on the table in the Temple' in Malachi 1:7 – itself relating to the two accusations against the way 'Temple service' was being conducted and the sacrifices that were being accepted there in both the Damascus Document and the *Anabathmoi Jacobou*.

It is not a very great step, therefore, to attribute these injunctions to James' teaching 'in the Temple' and part of what was implied as well in his directives to 'abstain from (in the Damascus Document, 'to keep away from'/'*lehinnazer*') blood, things sacrificed to idols, fornication, and strangled things' or 'carrion' in Acts 15:29 and 21:25, at least before things of this kind were retrospectively transformed and moved in these sources slightly sideways or laterally after the fall of the Temple.

We can conclude, therefore, that James did not 'complain against the Temple and the sacrifices' *per se*, as Epiphanius via the *Anabathmoi Jacobou* would have it. This has to do with somewhat later more 'Christian' distortion or misinterpretation. What he did complain about, particularly if he had any involvement in 'the Temple Wall' Affair leading up to his demise and anything in common with the Righteous Teacher – which the writer thinks he did – were 'gifts and sacrifices on behalf of foreigners' and 'pollution of the Temple', both to some extent relating to the same issue. In other words, a few extra words clarifying these complaints have been deleted. Deletions such as these change the whole texture of the charges. What James did 'complain against' was 'sacrifices on behalf of foreigners' and the way Temple service was being conducted by the collaborating, Rich and corrupt Herodian Priesthood, a Priesthood that owed its appointment to equally Rich and corrupt Herodian Kings and foreign Governors.

Seen in this light, James' complaints and those of other Scroll documents along with him really do lead directly to the destruction of the Temple and the fall of Jerusalem, as Christian tradition and others rightly understood in their attempts to portray this sequence of events.[847] The only problem is that Eusebius, Clement, and their sources misunderstood the sense of what they had before them or purposefully reversed it, either out of ignorance or just plain malice – just as the citation from the *Anabathmoi Jacobou*, quoted by Epiphanius, that pictures James as speaking against 'kindling the fire on the altar' has done.

The fact of James' person and his discourse or protests in the Temple did lead directly to the war against Rome as early Christian tradition, following Hegesippus and Origen, suggests. This broke out almost exactly 'three and a half years' after his death – the curious timeframe first spoken of in Daniel 7:25 having to do with cessation of sacrifice and itself an element in the Letter ascribed to James' name in the New Testament as the period between the two 'fervent prayer(s) of a Just One which much prevailed' (James 5:16–17). This War was, of course, precipitated by the stopping of sacrifices on behalf of the Roman Emperor and other foreigners (including Herodians) and the rejection of their gifts in the Temple, an act even Josephus bitterly labels 'an Innovation'. This was done by the 'zealous', every-day, working priests of 'the Lower Priesthood' in the Temple – James' probable constituency – many of whom had just won the right to wear linen, as Josephus somewhat enigmatically points out – just as James all the time himself had done according to early Church testimony.[48]

The spirit, therefore, of this martyred 'Opposition' High Priest/*Zaddik* James suffused the whole process, as it did the sequence of events (including the Temple Wall Affair) leading inexorably to the War against Rome. This, as both Origen and Eusebius attest can be seen as directly relating to his death. The same can be said for the spirit of the martyred 'Teacher of Righteousness' as he is, in particular, portrayed in both the Habakkuk and Psalm 37 *Pesher*s of the Dead Sea Scrolls.[49] As we shall see, this will be precisely what is implied by events surrounding another constellation of notices, those of 'a flight to Pella' by the followers of James after his death and the mysterious oracle upon which such a flight was supposed to have been based, which we shall treat in the next chapter.

Paul as Herodian in the *Anabathmoi Jacobou*

Before elucidating what is implied by these materials about the flight across Jordan of 'the Jerusalem Community' of James after his death, one should look at one more notice from the lost work, The *Anabathmoi Jacobou* or 'The Ascents of James', which Epiphanius shares with us, the only other notice from this book he seems to know or can confirm with any certainty. He claims it is 'fabricated by the villainy and error of their false Apostles', this in spite of knowing beforehand that 'the Ebionites' he is talking about opposed Paul and considered him 'the Antichrist' or 'Enemy' and 'a Liar'.[50] In fact, after providing their charges from this work against Paul, he goes on to attack them in much the same manner as Eusebius, claiming that they got their name (he thinks 'Ebion' is a person – though he is nevertheless correct in imagining 'he got his name out of Prophecy') because of their 'Poverty of understanding, expectation, and works', not to mention 'the Poverty of their Faith', since they 'take Christ as a mere man'. Epiphanius continues:

"Nor do they blush to accuse Paul there (in the *Anabathmoi*) with certain inventions fabricated by the villainy and error of their false Apostles, saying that he was from Tarsus, as he admits himself and does not deny. But they suppose that his parents were Greek, taking as evidence for this the passage where he frankly states, 'I am a man of Tarsus, a citizen of no mean city.' Then they say that he was a Greek, the son of a Greek mother and father, that he went up to Jerusalem, stayed there awhile, and desired to marry the (High) Priest's daughter and therefore became a convert and was circumcised. But then, because he was still unable to obtain her on account of her high station, in his anger he wrote against the Sabbath, circumcision, and the Law. But this dreadful serpent (he means 'Ebion') is making a completely false accusation because of his Poverty-stricken understanding."[51]

One should remark the ongoing venom of these accusations which is also typical of writers like Eusebius and Jerome. While at first glance, like much else in Epiphanius, the testimony might strike the reader as patently untrue (and it certainly is bizarre), on deeper reflection, there *is* a way of making sense of or understanding it.

We have already alluded to Paul's putative 'Herodian' background. That he has connections in such circles is undeniable. Not only were the Herodians making inroads into Northern Syria and Southern Asia Minor, even into 'Armenia' where two Herodians with Judaizing pretensions became Kings,[52] but actual marriages of various kinds were being arranged further east in Commagene bordering on 'the Land of the Osrhoeans' and Adiabene and west in Cappadocia and Cilicia, the area most usually claim for Paul's origins. In fact, a number of these Rulers were specifically circumcising themselves in the manner this passage claims Paul did in order to contract marriages with Herodians, particularly the female line descended from Herod's sole Maccabean wife Mariamme.

But Acts 23:16–22 also makes clear that Paul has important family connections in Jerusalem, where it would appear a sister or, at least, a nephew with entree into Roman/Herodian military and/or administrative circles resides. One possible identification of this nephew, regarding whom Acts appears to exercise even more than its usual reticence, is 'Julius Archelaus'.[53] He is an individual Josephus mentions in his *Vita* as having been interested enough in his works to purchase a copy in Rome after the fall of Jerusalem! Julius is the son of an individual mentioned fairly frequently in Josephus, one 'Alexas' or 'Helcias', the Temple Treasurer, and he may even be mentioned in the cluster of Herodian references at the end of Romans, including the individual Paul refers to as his 'kinsman', 'the Littlest Herod', and 'Junias' another of his 'kinsmen' – read 'Julius' (16:7–11).

Julius Archelaus originally married the first of Agrippa I's daughters, also called Mariamme, after her grandmother. But even this marriage does not seem to have been good enough for this Princess, because she divorced him to make what was obviously an even Richer marriage to one 'Demetrius the Alabarch of Alexandria', whom Josephus calls 'the first in birth and wealth among the Jews of Alexandria'. Julius Archelaus may have been the younger brother of another individual Josephus associates with the 'Saulos' in his narrative who so much resembles Paul – one 'Antipas' of the same general family line, whom Josephus also identifies as Temple Treasurer. In fact, Antipas was executed in somewhat desperate circumstances, when 'the Zealots' took control of the Revolution, around the same time as James' executioner Ananus, the 'Rich' collaborator 'Zachariah ben Bareis'/'Bariscaeus', and another backsliding former Revolutionary, 'Niger of Perea'.[54]

This last individual, as we have already suggested, may have been the model in Acts 13:1 for Paul's erstwhile colleague in Antioch, 'Simeon Niger', and the details of his execution may also have gone into the picture of Jesus' in the Gospels.[55] Actually this 'Zachariah' – also executed by 'the Zealots' as a collaborator and whose body was also 'cast down' into the valley below – may have been the model too for the 'Zachariah the son of Barachias' allegedly murdered in Matthew 23:35 and Luke 11:51 'between Temple and the Altar' – here another 'blood libel' accusation, followed of course by the refrain, 'O Jerusalem, Jerusalem, who kill all the Prophets and stone those who have been sent to her', the implied meaning once again being, to be sure, 'your blood be upon your own heads'.

As already explained, there certainly were Herodians in the Antioch Community, one specifically called 'the foster brother of Herod the Tetrarch', namely our Herod Antipas again. Furthermore, the two brothers 'Costobarus and Saulos', whom Josephus depicts as 'collecting a band of Violent ruffians' and causing mayhem in Jerusalem in the aftermath of the stoning of James,[56] and this youngest Antipas, together with his putative brother or nephew, Julius Archelaus, were all the descendants of interrelated septs descending both from Herod's sister Salome and one of his (Herod's) daughters named Cypros.

If Julius Archelaus was 'Paul's nephew', referred to in Acts 23:16, then his mother too (Paul's putative sister) was probably the descendant of Herod's sister, the first 'Salome' in this family. This is because, after executing Salome's first husband Joseph – allegedly on a charge of adultery with his own first wife named Mariamme (Herod had two, this being the Maccabean one) – and before finally marrying her to his close friend (and presumable relative), Alexas or Helcias the Temple Treasurer, Herod had previously married her to yet another close associate and probable relative, the original 'Costobarus', himself definitively identified as an 'Idumaean' in Josephus, from whom the 'Costobarus' in Paul's generation evidently descended and derived his name.[57]

Costobarus, 'Plundering', and Herodian Family Interests

Antipater, Herod's father – whether Idumaean Arab, Greek, or a mixture of the two – had married a high-born Arab woman from Petra named Cypros. Herod's sister Salome had two sons (the genealogies are, chronologically speaking, a little unclear here), the individual Josephus calls 'Saulos' and another called 'Costobarus'. It is to these two that Josephus attributes the riot in Jerusalem following the death of James, which very much resembles the riot led by Paul in Acts after the stoning of 'Stephen'.[58] Nor is this to mention the riot in the Pseudoclementine *Recognitions*, which ends up in Paul 'casting' James 'head-long' down the Temple steps and James breaking at least one if not both his legs.[59]

Josephus describes Saulos and Costobarus (aside from noting their 'kinship' to Agrippa I or II) as willing to 'use violence with the People and plunder those weaker than themselves'– this in the aftermath of the stoning of James and the very accusations leveled against the Establishment Priesthood and their 'Violent' associates in the aftermath of the destruction of the Righteous Teacher in the Dead Sea Scrolls.[60] The Habakkuk *Pesher* in particular, but also the Damascus Document – uses this language of 'plundering' and 'Violence' in relation to the 'amassing' or 'collecting' activities of 'the Peoples' – in our view, Herodians and their hangers -on.

This kind of 'plundering' or 'amassing' is then connected to the 'profiteering' activities of the individual called in the Habakkuk *Pesher* 'the Wicked Priest', as well as 'the Last Priests of Jerusalem' generally.[61] To come full circle again, this, in turn, can be connected to 'profiteering' from the contributions or gifts to the Temple made by individuals involved in just these kinds of 'Violent' attacks, namely Saulos and Costobarus and their Violent associates (at Qumran, in our view, probably referred to as 'the '*Arizei-Go'im*' – 'the Violent Ones of the Gentiles' or 'Peoples').[62] Regarding these kinds of activities, one should also keep in mind Paul's own admissions in 1 Corinthians 15:9 and Galatians 1:13 to 'persecuting the Assembly of God unto death'.

The two riots we have just referred to, led by someone called 'Saulos' in both Acts and Josephus, are in themselves interesting. Although the twenty-year discrepancy in their dating will never be reconciled, the sequencing is the same: the stoning of 'Stephen' followed by the mayhem reported in Acts 8:3, where 'Saulos (as Paul was still being referred to even at this point) ravaged the Assembly, entering house-by-house and dragging out men and women, delivering (them) up to prison'; and the stoning of James, followed by the brutal rioting led by 'Costobarus and Saul' – unless 'Saulos' really did lead two riots, or Josephus and/or Acts have confused things, which would not be at all surprising. Josephus, it will be recalled, is writing these things in the *Antiquities* (which he neglected to mention in the *War*) in the early Nineties, thirty years after they occurred. He may have his sequencing wrong or he may simply have misunderstood things, deliberately or otherwise.

That having been said, it seems fairly plain that what Acts is really talking about in its picture of the attack on Stephen in the Temple is the riot in the Temple led by Paul in the Pseudoclementines that ended up in James only 'breaking his leg', not the stoning of Stephen. In fact, there may have been another riot directly after the stoning of James, just as Josephus describes, and 'Paul' or 'Saulos' – as the case may be – may have been involved in this too. This depends on what happened to Paul after his voyage to Rome and his alleged 'appeal to Caesar' in 60 CE (Acts 25:11–28:31).

However this may be, just as Paul in Acts, Josephus' 'Saulos' makes an appeal to Caesar, but this one apparently not until 66 CE although there may have been an earlier one in the previous decade as well when, like Josephus thereafter, he seems to have made the contacts necessary to enter Roman service. In any event, what Saulos does in 66 CE – after having been the intermediary between 'the Peace Party' made up of 'Herodians, Sadducees, and the Chief Men of the Pharisees' in Jerusalem and the Roman army outside of the city[63] – is, as Paul in Acts and as already alluded to, appeal to Caesar presumably with his putative 'kinsman' Agrippa II's help (a decade earlier, in Acts 23:35 Paul stays in this same Agrippa's Palace in Caesarea as Saulos seemingly does in Jerusalem). It is to Nero that Saulos then goes, apparently at that time in Corinth as already indicated, to report on the situation in Palestine generally and, along seemingly with Philip, Agrippa II's military Commander in Caesarea, to justify his own conduct in the matter of the destruction of the Roman garrison in Jerusalem – a report that seems to have triggered the bringing in of the Romans' best general, Vespasian, all the way from Britain to quell the unrest in Palestine.[64]

In the course of our previous discussions we have had occasion to point out the motif of circumcision or the lack thereof in the marriages of these Herodian Princesses in Asia Minor and Syria, a motif figuring prominently in Paul's activities in these same areas as well.[65] But the announced goal of much of his missionary 'work' in these areas, that is to found a community where Greeks and Jews could live in harmony and equality (1 Corinthians 1:24, Galatians 3:28, etc.), however noble, was also very much in line with Herodian family interests or designs in many of these regions.[66]

In fact, even after the fall of the Temple, Antiochus of Commagene, on the border west of Edessa, ran afoul of the Romans, as Agrippa I seems to have done a quarter of a century earlier, for precisely such 'imperial' ambitions.[67] Antiochus' son Epiphanes, who actually fought on the Roman side with his aptly-named 'Macedonian Legion' in the Jewish War and was even decorated for bravery in the siege of Jerusalem, had himself originally been betrothed to Agrippa I's second daughter Drusilla. This was the same Drusilla who later married the brutal Roman Governor Felix.[68] Epiphanes' marriage with Drusilla, presumably because her more 'Pious' father Agrippa I was still alive, foundered on precisely this issue of circumcision and Epiphanes' refusal to circumcise himself![69] One might opine that in view of Drusilla's later history, her father Agrippa I needn't have bothered.

For her part, Drusilla was then promptly married to the King of Emesa (present-day Homs in Syria), who had circumcised himself specifically in order to contract this marriage, only finally to desert with the Roman Governor Felix to Rome – her father Agrippa I by this time having died – doubtlessly laying the groundwork to some extent for Paul's own eventual 'appeal' and escape to Rome, which might explain why he was received so well there.[70]

For his part, this Antiochus of Commagene also had a daughter, Jotape, who was married to another Herodian, Alexander, the son of Tigranes, King of Armenia. Tigranes was the grandson of the second of Herod's two sons by his Maccabean wife Mariamme, the original 'Alexander' in this line – a line that was clearly favored because it was considered of royal blood or the most Kingly.[71] Josephus tells us that after the War, Vespasian made Alexander King of Cilicia, presumably for services rendered either by him or his father, 'Cilicia' of course also being Paul's own alleged place of origin.[72] Though all of this is circumstantial, nevertheless it is instructive.

Tigranes' uncle – also named Tigranes – was a descendant of this same Maccabean royal wife of Herod, Mariamme. He had also been appointed King of Armenia by the Romans, the first so designated – more confirmation of Herodians as 'the Kings of the Peoples' we have been emphasizing above in the Eastern areas of the Roman Empire. Josephus pictures this later nephew of the first Tigranes as spending a long and agreeable period as a hostage in Rome, so much so that it became his virtual home, as it seems to have done for so many of the persons we are labeling as Herodians above. There, he and many others like him – Agrippa II, for instance, Aristobulus and Salome, whose faces appear on the reverse of coinage proclaiming them 'Great Lovers of Caesar', and Julius Archelaus – clearly formed part of a sophisticated circle of Greek-speaking, pro-Roman intellectuals with a lot of time on their hands. In earlier work, I have singled out this circle as possibly being the source of much of the material that ultimately ended up being incorporated – along with a good deal of Alexandrian Greco-Roman 'anti-Semitism' – in what we now call 'the Gospels'.[73] In any event, like Drusilla with Felix and her sister Bernice with her lover Titus, Josephus tells us fairly matter-of-factly that this latter generation of Herodians 'deserted the Jewish religion altogether and went over to that of the Greeks'.[74]

Be this as it may, aside from the general atmosphere in the Habakkuk *Pesher* signaling a 'conspiracy' of some kind surrounding the destruction or death of the Righteous Teacher in which 'the Wicked Priest' (if not 'the Liar' too), was involved,[75] there is material in Paul's own letters, as we saw, that would suggest more than just a casual relationship with the Herodian family and its representatives – in fact, a genealogical one. This by itself would explain his rather peculiar idea of Judaism and schizophrenic attitude towards it.

'The Littlest Herod' and Paul's Roman Citizenship

We have already called attention to the greetings Paul sends to his 'kinsman Herodion', 'the Littlest Herod', at the end of Romans 16:11 – 'Herod', of course, not being a commonplace name in this period. This was probably the son of the 'Aristobulus', the evocation of whose 'household' just precedes it in Romans 16:10 and that 'Salome' involved in the execution of John the Baptist. We have also called attention to the greetings Paul sends to 'the Saints' in 'the household of Caesar' in Philippians (presumably Nero) where he mentions his close collaborator and 'comrade-in-arms', Epaphroditus (2:25 and 4:22), who was Nero's secretary for Greek Letters and held a similar office later under Domitian.[76] Expediently or otherwise, Domitian accused him of having 'raised his hand against an Emperor', but these charges against Epaphroditus were most likely trumped up in the general crackdown against alleged 'Christians' in the later years of Domitian's reign.[77]

The last notice Josephus provides about the 'kinsman of Agrippa' he calls 'Saulos' was his trip to Corinth where Nero was apparently quartered while he was having a canal dug there. The year is 66 CE and, after Saulos informs Nero of the situation in Palestine, Vespasian and Titus are sent out as commanders to deal with the situation.[78] Just as eight years before, 'Paul' was under house arrest or, as the case may have been, 'protective custody' in Agrippa II's Palace in Caesarea, at the outbreak of the disturbances leading up to the Uprising against Rome, 'Saulos' too – along with his cousins, Antipas, Costobarus, and Philip – seems to have been in this same Agrippa II's Palace in Jerusalem. Not only was this 'Philip' one of Agrippa II's military commanders and another name overlapping those of either 'Apostles' or 'Disciples' in the New Testament (the name of Agrippa I's *Strategos* or Military Commander was 'Silas'[79]), but he too, as Saulos had done, appealed to Caesar when he was blamed in some manner for surrendering either this Palace or the Citadel to the Revolutionaries.[80]

For his part, everyone knows that Acts 26:32 pictures 'Paul' as going – apparently on his own recognizance – to appeal to Nero as a *Roman citizen* at the beginning of the Governorship of Festus in 60 CE. Aside from a two-year further stay in Rome, where he supposedly hired his 'own house' (Acts 28:30), nothing more can be said with any certainty about Paul – not even the date of his death, which does not appear to have occurred until about the time of the final visit this 'Saulos' in Josephus also makes to Nero when he, too, just drops out of sight!

The name 'Aristobulus' makes the several greetings Paul sends to these kinds of individuals at the end of Romans even more interesting. Not only was 'Aristobulus' originally a name used by Maccabeans, it turns into an Herodian name after these latter are grafted on the tree of the former, as Paul would have it in Romans 11:19, and there were at least four important Herodians with this name mentioned by Josephus at this time.

Where the identity of the 'Aristobulus' mentioned by Paul in Romans 16:10 is concerned, probably the only Herodian 'Aristobulus' this could be in the mid- to late Fifties in Rome was Aristobulus the son of Herod of Chalcis, to whom Claudius gave the Kingdom of Lesser Armenia in Asia Minor.[81] Lesser Armenia would be contiguous to or carved out of areas belonging to the Osrhoeans around Edessa and Adiabene, which had fallen by this time to Roman control. Tigranes had already been given Armenia proper or Greater Armenia. Aristobulus' wife Salome had, as we have pointed out, previously been the wife of the *real* Philip. Not only was he the half brother of Herod Antipas and the Tetrarch of the area around the Gaulon and across into Syria called Trachonitus, but it was he who had 'died childless' which was to say nothing about either Herod Antipas or Herodias.

This couple, Aristobulus and Salome, both advertised themselves as 'Great Lovers of Caesar' which, no doubt, they were. They obviously spent a lot of time in Rome, as did a good many of these Herodians brought up under or with Claudius. But, even more interestingly, they also had this son, named 'Herod' who, in this period of the Fifties and Sixties CE, would have been 'the Youngest' or 'Littlest Herod'. Nor is this to say anything about the question of collusion between Paul ('Saulos') and Herod the Tetrarch ('Herod Antipas', Salome's mother Herodias' second husband) in the matter of his (Paul's) activities 'in Damascus' that so disturbed 'Aretas' Governor' in 2 Corinthians 11:32 and, therefore, in some manner too perhaps, the death of John the Baptist. Though greetings such as these to 'Herodion' or 'the household of Aristobulus' in Romans 16:10–11 in themselves prove nothing, they constitute very strong collateral evidence for the proposition we are arguing of Paul's connection to the Herodian family. All these relationships provide a very good reason for the fact of Paul's Roman citizenship, of which our sources make so much.

Herod's father Antipater, who was so instrumental in the Roman takeover of Palestine – instrumental to the extent that his son, even though he was not Jewish by birth, supplanted its Jewish Dynasty – received this citizenship for himself and his descendants in perpetuity for services rendered to the *Imperium Romanum*.[82] Antipater, in fact, was the first Roman Prefect in Palestine and what he did was turn a regional governorship into a family dynasty. Family connections of this kind to the highest circles of power in Palestine easily explain the fact of Paul's influential sister and nephew living in Jerusalem according to Acts 23:16. They also explain how Paul could have received the powers he did at such a tender age 'from the High Priest' – to exercise them as far as Damascus which was not, seemingly, even under his control at the time[83] – if this picture of his activities in Acts (echoed in the Pseudoclementine *Recognitions*[84]) is even partially correct.

It is interesting that in the well-known passages about his origins in Romans 11:1 and Philippians 3:5 (reprised in Acts 13:21), where he refers to being of 'the Tribe of Benjamin', Paul avoids calling himself 'a Jew', a term he does not hesitate however to apply to Peter in Galatians 2:13–14. Rather he seems to prefer to refer to himself as 'an Israelite, of the seed of

Abraham, of the Tribe of Benjamin' which, as we saw in the War Scroll above, many Diaspora Jews or even converts, such as the Herodians, may have taken to calling themselves. In Philippians 3:5–6, Paul adds: 'a Hebrew of the Hebrews – according to the Law, a Pharisee. According to zeal, persecuting the Church. According to Righteousness in Law, becoming blameless.'

Aside from his references to 'becoming a Jew' and 'making himself a Jew to win Jews' above, these considerations – plus an ambiguous reference in Galatians 1:13 to something resembling conversion to 'Judaism' – might have convinced his interlocutors that Paul was really not born a Jew, but had rather converted to Judaism, as the testimony from the *Anabathmoi Jacobou* insists. In addition to this, his easy-going attitude towards Judaism, as well as his fairly overt contempt for most things Jewish, could not have failed to make its impression on his contemporaries, as it has left its mark across the breadth of the Gospels and like-minded materials – the Koran, for example.

The 'Saulos' in Josephus and Paul

Having said all these things, there is still another way of looking at this curious testimony from the *Anabathmoi Jacobou* – that is, having knowledge of Paul's Herodian origins, it is possible that when the *Anabathmoi* was describing the person who was 'a pagan' or 'a Greek' coming up to Jerusalem and, conceiving a desire to marry the High Priest's daughter, converted to Judaism, and when frustrated in this design, turned against both the Jews and Judaism; it was not really talking about Paul at all, but rather Paul's putative ancestor, the *original Herod himself.*

This can be explained by the fact that it was Herod and his father who were perhaps the original Herodian converts to Judaism – if there ever was a real conversion on their part and this was all not simply a charade. It was Herod too who, in decorating Greek temples and cities and giving generously to Greek causes (well-documented in all sources[85]) really did make himself – to paraphrase Paul in 1 Corinthians 9:19–21 – 'a Jew to the Jews' and 'a Greek to the Greek'. But above all else, like Paul, Herod believed in 'winning' – winning at any cost. And he did – he really won.

Finally, it was Herod who really did want to marry the High Priest's daughter despite the fact that he was neither native-born nor originally even Jewish himself. In fact, he married two of them, both named 'Mariamme' as we have seen – the reason doubtlessly behind the proliferation of all these 'Mariamme's or 'Mary's in the next generation and ever since. Herod's killing of all the Maccabeans, including his own wife Mariamme, his children by her, her mother, her grandfather Hyrcanus II, who had given his father Antipater the chance to rise to power in the first place, her younger brother Jonathan – the last properly 'Maccabean' High Priest – and, then, the various incestuous marriages he arranged, was genetic engineering with a vengeance. Jonathan he had (in the manner that a latter-day Stalin or Saddam Hussein might do) strangled in the swimming pool of his winter palace in Jericho. This he did after Jonathan had for the first time donned the High-Priestly vestments (the clear condition for Mariamme's mother having permitted the marriage in the first place) when *he saw how this sight moved 'the People' to weep with emotion.*[86]

Furthermore, none of these Herodians, as Epiphanius well understood, were really reckoned as 'Jews' anyhow – except by themselves when they found it convenient or by their sycophantic Pharisee supporters.[87] Eusebius, too, well understood this point for, in quoting the passage he conserves from Julius Africanus about how Herod burned all the genealogical records of the Jews and 'the *Desposyni*' (Jesus' family in Nazara and Cochaba[88]), he matter-of-factly observes that Herod did this out of envy 'of his base birth, because he was not of Israelite stock'.[89] In describing Paul as they did, the authors of the *Anabathmoi Jacobou* may have thought they were saying something about his Herodian origins – in particular, his putative ancestor Herod, who really did marry 'the High Priest's daughter' and whom some might have considered to have been a 'convert' to Judaism – though, for their part, extreme 'Zealot' groups certainly would not have, which was the basis of a century or more of unrest that followed in this period.

There is one additional subject that needs to be treated where Paul's possible identification with the character Josephus is calling 'Saulos' is concerned. There is the possibility of Paul having made a return to Palestine after being incarcerated in Rome in time to put in the several appearances described in Josephus' *Antiquities* on the part of 'Saulos' after the death of James around 63 or 64 CE and another in the War in 66 CE. Before this 'Saulos' went to Corinth – where Epaphroditus, no doubt, was in residence as well – to give his report to Nero on the situation in Palestine, he also served, as we have emphasized, as the intermediary between 'the Peace Party' in Jerusalem and the Roman Army outside the city under Cestius, the Roman Governor of Syria, who had come to Jerusalem to suppress the Uprising.[90] This episode would have been contemporaneous with the death in battle of Queen Helen's own two 'kinsmen' or descendants, 'Monobazus and Kenedaeus', who fought valiantly against this same Cestius in a futile attempt to stop his advance at the Pass at Beit Horon, a site hallowed as well due to Judas Maccabee's earlier exploits.[91]

In the same passage in Romans where Paul sends his greetings to 'those in Aristobulus' household' and his 'kinsman the Youngest Herod', Paul also expressed his intention to visit Spain (Romans 15:24–28). There is no evidence about whether Paul ever got to Spain or not, but if he did visit Spain, one wonders what contacts he used to get there. Seneca, the famous Stoic philosopher, who acted as Nero's Prime Minister before falling afoul of the latter's changeable temper and being forced to commit suicide himself, was from Spain, as was his brother Gallio whom, as we saw, Acts 18:12–17, too, pictures as treating Paul with such self-evident cordiality. In fact, mercurial as he was, Nero may have found something to find fault with in Saulos' behavior as well and had him executed, as neither he nor Paul is ever heard from again. Not long afterwards, Nero himself either committed suicide – with Epaphroditus' involvement – or was assassinated.[92]

There is nothing to gainsay that Paul actually did get to Spain, but our sources just do not tell us and Acts grows uncharacteristically vague after allowing that Paul was, for all intents and purposes, free in Rome and 'in his own lodgings' after being sent there by Festus following his appeal to Caesar. In fact, as this is portrayed in Acts 28:21, even Paul is surprised to find out no one has heard of him there or presumably what he had been doing in Palestine and elsewhere. Felix too, the brother of Nero's financial secretary Pallas, with whom Paul is portrayed as conversing so intimately for two years in Acts 23:25–24:27, had also gone to Rome not long before. As already suggested, he could easily have been involved (even with the connivance of Agrippa II, particularly if this 'Paul' were the 'kinsman' of both Agrippa II and Felix's wife Drusilla) in arranging this trip to Rome for Paul.

However these things may be, Galba, the first successor to Nero, had previously been Governor in Spain, and Seneca, originally Nero's tutor and finally his Prime Minister, came from Spain as well.[93] So did Trajan, whose father is given special attention in Josephus' *Jewish War* as a brave Roman Legionnaire. He came from 'Italica' in Spain.[94] In this context, one should never forget that the Roman Centurion in Acts 10:1–43 – 'a man Righteous and God-fearing' – is described in Acts 10:1 as being from 'the Italica Regiment'. So was Trajan's personal favorite, Hadrian.

It is certainly not impossible that a man of Epaphroditus' wide acquaintance would have had connections in Spain. In fact, there is a lively correspondence in the apocryphal literature between Paul and Seneca whom Epaphroditus must have known; and Gallio, whom Acts presents as Roman Proconsul in Achaia and Governor in Corinth and who treated Paul with such cordiality there, was Seneca's brother.[95] As Acts 18:12–17 portrays these things, Gallio – whom archaeological evidence confirms functioned in Corinth about the year 55 CE – pays no attention to Jewish complaints against Paul. He even supposedly goes so far as to allow Greeks to beat 'Sosthenes' 'before the Judgment seat' there.

But there is a problem here, since the man Acts is calling 'Sosthenes the Ruler of the Synagogue' at this point bears the same name as the character referred to as 'Sosthenes' at the beginning of 1 Corinthians 1:1, whom Paul calls his 'brother' and boon companion (unless there were two such 'Sosthenes's in Corinth at one and the same time, a doubtful proposition). We have encountered this kind of problem in Acts before: for example, in the two trips Paul allegedly makes 'down the walls of Damascus in a basket' – one in Acts 9:25 to escape 'the Jews who wanted to kill him' (this one clearly tendentious), and the other in 2 Corinthians 11:31–33, to escape the Aretas who wants to have him arrested unless of course, once again, there were two such trips in a basket – an equally dubious proposition.

However these things may be, no less an authority than Eusebius is sure that Paul did go free after his first imprisonment in Rome, which was, as already signaled, hardly an imprisonment at all but more in the nature of a loose house arrest, or what could be described as (in Caesarea anyhow) protective custody.[96] As already remarked as well, Acts just comes to an end at this point about exactly the time James was killed in Jerusalem, but without a word about this. Why? Though the authenticity of Pastorals like Timothy and Titus is disputed, 2 Timothy 4:16–17 does note how 'at my first trial nobody supported me'. Whoever wrote this, it would not be surprising that 'no one came to his support'. Moreover, here anyhow, if reliable and however vague, there is an indication of ongoing legal problems of some sort in Paul's life (unless the reference is to his previous legal complications in Jerusalem and Caesarea before his alleged 'appeal to Caesar').

Again, with such influential contacts as Gallio and possibly even his brother Seneca, to say nothing of Felix, Drusilla, Epaphroditus, Agrippa II, and Titus' future mistress Bernice, doubtlessly Paul could have made his way to Spain, just as he could have returned to Palestine, either before or after this, to take part in the events Josephus describes there prior to ultimately disappearing from the scene or being done away with in the course of the disturbances that broke out from 66–70 CE, about the same time that Josephus' 'Saulos' did. We shall never know the true answers to any of these questions, but this does not prevent one from making an intelligent inference on the basis of the evidence.

The excavated splendid family Tomb of Queen Helen of Adiabene, described by Josephus and built for her and her first son Izates in Jerusalem by her second son Monobazus.

Chapter 16
The Pella Flight and Agabus' Prophecy

The Reputed 'Pella Flight' of James' Jerusalem Community

We should now turn to the last subject we need to discuss before moving on to an analysis of climactic sections of the Scrolls themselves, that is, the famed 'Pella flight' of James' Jerusalem Community. This so-called 'flight', which so much resembles the 'departure from the Land of Judah to the Land of Damascus' of the Damascus Document, is referred to in three of the main sources we have been consulting: Eusebius (again, probably relying on Hegesippus), Epiphanius, and, surprisingly enough, the First Apocalypse of James from Nag Hammadi.[1]

Eusebius refers to it after documenting the succession to Nero (68 CE) and how 'the Jews, after the ascension of our Savior, followed up their crimes against him by devising plot after plot against his Disciples': 'First, they stoned Stephen to death, then James the son of Zebedee the brother of John was beheaded, and finally James, the first after the ascension of our Savior to occupy the Throne of the Bishopric there lost his life in the manner described and the other Apostles were driven from the Land of Judea by thousands of deadly plots.' Eusebius immediately contradicts himself with a version, obviously from another source, different from the first. This reads: 'The members of the Church in Jerusalem, by means of an oracle given by revelation to approved men there before the War, were ordered to leave the city and dwell in a town in Perea called Pella. To it, those who believed in Christ emigrated from Jerusalem and, as if Holy Men had completely abandoned the Royal Capital of the Jews and the entire Land of Judea, the Judgment of God at last overtook them for their crimes against Christ and his Apostles completely blotting out that Wicked Generation from among men![2]

The allusions to 'the Land of Judea' and 'dwelling' are to be found in the Damascus Document's depiction of how 'the Sons of Zadok' and the other 'Penitents of Israel' *departed from the Land of Judah to dwell in the Land of Damascus*.[3] The language of 'plots', which Eusebius applies here to 'the Jews' is, in the Habakkuk *Pesher*, rather applied to 'the Wicked Priest' and his associates who are described as 'plotting to destroy the Poor' and 'steal' their sustenance.[4]

Not satisfied however with the venom inherent in the above diatribe, Eusebius − now drawing in gruesome detail on Josephus − then goes on at even greater length to list 'the calamities which at that time overwhelmed the whole Nation (of the Jews) in every part of the World'. In particular, he describes, with seeming gleeful malice, the straits to which the Jews were reduced in Jerusalem, even how they ended up eating straw. Finally Eusebius seems almost to revel in reproducing Josephus' account of how, in some cases, the Jews even ate their own children, laboring over Josephus' picture of such things in loving detail.[5]

He completes this sketch of 'Christian' history in Palestine with the various signs and portents Josephus lists − in a kind of final summation in connection with the fall of the Temple at the end of the *Jewish War* − by way of introducing his own startling contention that: 'the thing that most moved our People to revolt against the Romans was an ambiguous Prophecy that one from their region would be elevated to Rule the World' ('ambiguous' because Josephus − along with R. Yohanan ben Zacchai − obsequiously applies it to Vespasian[6]).

These 'signs and portents' included a 'cow giving birth to a lamb in the middle of the Temple' on Passover; a light shining in the Temple at night so that 'it seemed like full day' on Passover as well; 'chariots and armies on high over the whole country, racing through the clouds'; ending with 'a Star standing over the city like a sword' and a loud voice emanating from the Temple at Pentecost crying, '*Let us go forth*'.[7] The significance of this last, of course, needs no explanation. All this, even in Eusebius' recapitulation, precedes the Prophecy about the destruction of Jerusalem given by the Prophet Josephus says was called 'Jesus ben Ananias', which we shall discuss in more detail below.

Epiphanius provides the same information (though with a little more moderation) about 'the Pella flight' in the following manner:

"Today this Nazoraean sect exists in Beroea in Coele Syria (Aleppo), in the Decapolis near the region of Pella, and in Bashan in the place called 'Cocaba' (Hebrew for 'Star'), which in Hebrew is called 'Kochabe'. That is its place of origin, since all the Disciples were dwelling in Pella after they departed from Jerusalem, for *Christ had told them to leave Jerusalem and withdraw from it because it was about to be besieged*. For this reason they settled in Perea and ... that was where the Sect of the Nazoraeans began.'"[8]

Not only do we have a reflection of the language the Damascus Document uses to describe the 'departure from Judah to dwell in the Land of Damascus', but also the material here more or less agrees with Mandaean tradition about the withdrawal to Northern Syria of their precursors after the death of John.[9] Here too, it is clear that Epiphanius views the 'Nazoraeans' – like the 'Ebionites' – as the true successors to the Community of James.

The reference to Cocaba/Kochabe also seems to reflect the notice Eusebius preserves from Julius Africanus (c. 170–245) about two villages, 'Nazara' and 'Cochaba', both with 'Messianic'-sounding names. However, rather than across Jordan or in Lebanon, Julius appears to place the location of these 'villages' in Judea – whatever he might mean by this.[10] For Julius, this is where 'the *Desposyni*' (Jesus' family members) retired after these tragic events, where they 'preserved the records of their noble family extraction' and from which they sent out members of the family with these proper records or genealogies 'to other parts of the World'.[11]

Eusebius, following a writer called 'Aristo of Pella' (c. 100–160 CE) – to whom no doubt many of these traditions relating specifically to 'Pella' and 'the flight' remount –seems to think that at a later point a small community from Pella re-established itself in Jerusalem after the Bar Kochba War at a time when Jews were forbidden, not only to enter, but even to look upon the city![12] This was probably the beginning of a completely non-Jewish, 'Christian' group in Jerusalem, now being called 'Aelia Capitolina' after its latest conqueror, Aelius Hadrian.

For the First Apocalypse of James from Nag Hammadi, this oracle 'to leave Jerusalem' comes – much like the Heavenly 'revelations' Paul claims always to be receiving – directly from Jesus. As this is stated in the first lines of the Apocalypse, Jesus speaking: 'Fear not, James. You too will they seize. *But leave Jerusalem, for she it is that always gives the Cup of Bitterness to the Sons of Light*.'[13] Here too is also the 'Cup' which James and John, the two 'sons of Zebedee', will supposedly have to drink in Matthew 20:22 and Mark 10:38 in imitation of Jesus, that is, 'the Cup of Martyrdom' implying even crucifixion.[14] Both Gospels vary 'the Cup of the Lord' language, which Jesus supposedly gives James to drink after his resurrection according to the picture in the Gospel of the Hebrews, itself refurbished or, if one prefers, rewritten or overwritten in the 'Emmaus Road' encounter in the Gospel of Luke.[15]

The Pella Flight and the Flight to the Wilderness Camps

But what are we to make of these notices about 'a Pella flight' in response to some mysterious oracle to those left in 'the Jerusalem Community' after James' death? Certainly, they have their mythological aspects having to do with actually being able to accomplish such a 'flight' to a location like Pella in the unstable conditions of warfare at the time, an issue raised by a number of scholars.[16] But if we set 'Pella' aside for the moment and concentrate on the 'flight' motif, there are a number of traditions about similar emigrations or flights in this period.

To start with, there is the 'Theudas' (c. 44–46 CE) we saw in Josephus – seemingly mentioned as 'the father' or 'brother of the Just One' in the Second Apocalypse of James[17] – who attempts to lead a large group of his followers out across Jordan in a reverse Exodus before he was caught, beheaded and a majority of his followers butchered.[18]

Then there is the tradition in the Pseudoclementine *Recognitions* about a 'flight' (reckoned by the telltale 'five thousand') of James' Community in Jerusalem to the Jericho area after the attack by the 'Enemy' Paul on James in the Temple – the one in which, after 'casting' James 'headlong down the steps' and leaving him for dead, Paul misses James and his followers because they were outside of Jericho visiting the mysterious tombs of 'two of the brothers' that curiously 'whitened of themselves every year'.[19]

There is also the similar flight of the '*Sicarii*' to Masada after their leader Menachem – either the son or grandson of Judas the Galilean – put on the royal purple of the king at the very beginning of the Uprising in 66 CE.[20] This ultimately ends up in the celebrated suicide of these same *Sicarii* together with all their dependents in 73 CE.[21]

Finally, we have already mentioned the flight of the Mandaean partisans of John the Baptist to Northern Syria and beyond, after he too was killed in what has to be regarded as partisan internecine strife.

For the sectaries represented by the Qumran materials, the reunion of 'the Wilderness Camps' to rededicate themselves to 'the *Torah*' or 'Covenant' – that is, 'the New Covenant in the Land of Damascus' – was to take place every year at Pentecost.[22] In Judaism 'Pentecost' or '*Shavu'ot*', it should be remarked, comes fifty days after Passover and is the time, if one can put it like this, of 'the descent of the *Torah*' to Moses at Sinai. This is the festival which Acts 20:16 pictures Paul as hurrying to Jerusalem with his contributions to attend before his final confrontation with James. It is clear that Pentecost was also the time of the annual reunion of 'the Assemblies' or 'Churches' portrayed in Acts as well.

We have already seen how many of the successor groups to the Jerusalem Community of James, such as the 'Ebionites', 'Nazoraeans', and 'Sampsaeans', developed in these areas across the Dead Sea and 'beyond the Jordan' in Perea, Bashan, Batanea – what at Qumran might be called 'the Land of Damascus' – and Northern Syria and beyond. There can be little doubt that there was a lively Diaspora dwelling in these areas. The 'Mandaeans' – the remnants of 'the Sabaeans' in Southern Iraq – still preserve traditions that the followers of John the Baptist (themselves included) fled after he was executed by 'Herod the Tetrarch', emigrating to Northern Syria.[23] Therefore, one should pay some attention to the persistent note of this kind of 'flight' or 'emigrant' activity to all these regions.

John the Baptist, in particular – especially in the Gospel of John 1:28, 3:26, and 10:40 – is portrayed as carrying on most of his activities 'across the Jordan'. Certainly his arrest there by Herod Antipas and execution at the Maccabean/Herodian Fortress of Machaeros, directly across the Dead Sea virtually due east from Qumran, would imply that the activities for which he was imprisoned had transpired in that region. The authority of the 'Herod the Tetrarch' who executed him only extended from Galilee into Perea, but not the Judean side of the Jordan – at this time still under the control of the Roman Prefect or Governor in Jerusalem and Caesarea.[24]

So there is much to support such a 'flight' tradition, despite the fact of its somewhat fantastic packaging. It is doubtful if we can really speak of an actual 'flight' to the town of Pella itself which at the beginning of the War, as Josephus recounts, was actually the scene of a good deal of partisan fighting between Jews and more Hellenized native populaces.[25] For awhile Jewish partisans held the upper hand, but ultimately the Jewish populations were for the most part wiped out by the pro-Roman, anti-Jewish, Greek-speaking population in these areas across the Jordan, then known as 'the Decapolis'.[26]

But a reasonable and viable alternative to an actual 'flight to Pella' would be to consider Pella as a gateway to these other areas 'beyond Jordan' and further North in the Damascus region and beyond, as implied by such terms as 'the Wilderness' or 'Desert of the Peoples' in the War Scroll and/or 'the Land of Damascus' in the Damascus Document. This is what is implied, too, in the plethora of notices from writers like Hippolytus, Eusebius, and Epiphanius about the presence of derivative groups like 'Naassenes' or 'Essenes', 'Nazoraeans', 'Ebionites', 'Elchasaites', 'Sampsaeans', and 'Masbuthaeans' in regions such as these.

The totality of the claim, compressed into the idea of a single 'flight to Pella', can probably be dated to the fact of the return of a small Gentilized Community to Roman-controlled Jerusalem, 'Aelia Capitolina', to set up as a more orthodox 'Christian' Church there – subsequently referred to as 'the See of James' – following the failure of the Bar Kochba Revolt in 132–36 CE.

But what of the mysterious 'oracle' that was supposed to have triggered this 'flight'? About this perhaps one can be more precise. Certainly it relates to the fact of the removal of 'the Protection of the People' James, without whose presence Jerusalem could no longer remain in existence or was doomed according to 'the *Zaddik*-the-Pillar-of-the-World' ideology of Proverbs.[27] This is strengthened by all the early Church testimonies from Hegesippus to Clement to Origen, Eusebius, Jerome, and Epiphanius (Josephus' testimony notwithstanding), insisting that following the death of James, the Roman armies immediately appeared.[28]

It is in fact actually possible to identify both the mysterious oracle that gave rise to this alleged flight – regardless of the fact of whether it really took place as claimed or not – and its historical provenance, in the 'oracle' Josephus attributes to the mysterious Prophet he designates as 'Jesus ben Ananias'.[29]

This 'Prophet' too seems to have appeared around Succot, 62 CE. We can determine this on the basis of Josephus' own testimony. He, not only tells us about the existence of this later Jesus, but how he continued prophesying ceaselessly for 'seven and a half years' from the time of his first appearance until he was killed by a Roman projectile during the siege of Jerusalem just prior to its fall. This means that he started 'prophesying' in the Autumn of 62 CE, that is, exactly in the aftermath of James' death as well.[30]

But this 'prophecy' of the destruction of Jerusalem that 'continued for seven and a half years' not only related in some manner to James' death, but also to similar oracles or predictions ascribed to Jesus in the 'Little Apocalypse'. It also relates to the proclamation in Revelation, 'Babylon is fallen, Babylon is fallen', a proclamation echoing Isaiah 21:9 but, as so often occurs, reversed – Jesus ben Ananias' mournful cry, relating to the coming fall of Jerusalem; Revelation's, as normally interpreted, relating to the fall of Rome.

Jesus ben Ananias and Agabus' Prophecy

It is also possible to identify Josephus' 'Jesus ben Ananias' and his Prophecy in two patently fictionalized refurbishments of the life-story of Paul, as presented in Acts, centering about another equally mysterious Prophet whom Acts calls 'Agabus'. In the first in Acts 11:27–30, Agabus is the stand-in for Queen Helen's putative consort in Armenian and Syriac sources – her 'brother' if we take Josephus for our guide or, if a title, also the name of her son by this King[31] – 'Agbarus' or 'Abgarus'.[32]

His second materialization occurs in Acts 21:10–14 just prior to Paul's last trip to Jerusalem and final confrontation with James. In it, the pretense is that another of these curious 'certain one's (now definitively denoted as 'a Prophet named Agabus') 'came down from Judea', this time not 'to Antioch' but 'to Caesarea' (21:10 – in 11:27 earlier, it will be recalled, the first materialization of this 'Prophet' was expressed a little more floridly as, 'and in these days prophets came down from Jerusalem to Antioch', 'one among whom was named Agabus').

It is at this point in Acts 21:11–12 that this 'Prophet named Agabus' is pictured, rather comically, as 'taking hold of Paul's girdle' and warning Paul, 'not to go up to Jerusalem' – which, in effect, is the reversal of the 'Pella flight' oracle – not 'not to go up to Jerusalem' but 'to *leave* Jerusalem'. It is a not incurious fact too that in tying this oracle to 'a Prophet called Agabus', as Acts does in its own peculiar way, it closes the triangle of these three 'prophecies', tying the 'Pella flight' oracle even closer to the mournful cry of the Prophet whom Josephus designates as 'Jesus ben Ananias' just after the death of James.

It would be well to repeat the first notice in Acts 11:27–28 about this 'Agabus' in its entirety: 'And in these days (c. 45–46 CE) prophets came down from Jerusalem to Antioch and Agabus, rising up from among them, evoked via the Spirit the Great Famine that was about to engulf the whole habitable world, which actually came to pass under Claudius Caesar.' In both the first appearance of this Prophet Acts uses to introduce 'the Great Famine' and Paul and Barnabas' famine relief operations associated with it, and the second – just prior to Paul's own arrest and ultimately James' disappearance from the scene – 'Agabus' is the stand-in and mirror replacement for or inversion of this other character in Josephus 'Jesus ben Ananias', who really was 'a Prophet' at this time.

Not only is Jesus ben Ananias' prophecy of the imminent destruction of Jerusalem related to the prophecies ascribed to Jesus in 'the Little Apocalypse' and right before in the 'throwing down' of the Temple's 'stones' in the Synoptics (this should be fairly clear since both sets of oracles relate, in some manner, to the destruction of the Temple), but his Prophecy must be seen as being both triggered by James' death in 62 C.E. and evincing Jesus' reaction to it, namely, that without the presence of the *Zaddik*, Jerusalem was doomed and could no longer remain in existence.

Jesus ben Ananias and the Signs Prefiguring the Fall of the Temple

Though Josephus does not specifically connect the death of James with the appearance of Jesus ben Ananias, chronologically speaking, we are justified in doing so because he dates the appearance of this Jesus seven and a half years before the fall of the Temple in 70 CE and specifically notes his arrest and re-arrest by the Governor of that time, Albinus.

Even though Josephus declines to mention this Jesus in the *Antiquities* and one has to go to the *Jewish War* to discover him, it is noteworthy how precise Josephus is with regard to his chronology and events surrounding his activities. Thus, he appeared during 'the Feast of Tabernacles', that is, at approximately the end of September or the beginning of October of 62 CE which may, in fact, have been the date of James' stoning – that is, just following *Yom Kippur*, 62 CE, a possible date too of the atonement James is pictured as making 'in the Holy of Holies in the Temple' in most early Church sources. Jesus ben Ananias died in March, 70 CE, 'seven and a half years later', just five months prior to the fall of the City and destruction of the Temple.

Significantly, Josephus tells the full story of his appearance and death at the end of the *Jewish War*, where he sets out 'the signs and portents' prefiguring the fall of Jerusalem, discussed above. These are all particularly illustrative of Josephus' frame-of-mind, as they are that of his Roman audience. To these, Josephus appends the following account which, by its length and detail, he obviously considered perhaps even more important:

"But what was even more alarming ... four years before the War began, there came to the Feast, at which it is the custom for everyone to erect Tabernacles to God, one Jesus ben Ananias, a rude peasant standing in the Temple. And suddenly he began to cry out, 'A Voice from the East, a Voice from the West, a Voice from the four winds, a Voice against Jerusalem and the Temple, a Voice against the bridegrooms and the brides, and a Voice against the whole People.' Day and night he went about all the streets of the city with this cry on his lips."[33]

In this testimony it is easy to see some of the leitmotifs of the story of Jesus as it has come down to us in Scripture, not the least being the note about 'the bridegrooms and brides', a favorite theme of many of the parables attributed to him in the Gospels.[34]

But the parallel with Jesus does not stop here. It also continues with Josephus discussing the details of Jesus ben Ananias' arrest and interrogation:

"Some of the Leading Men of the city, incensed at these ominous words, arrested him, and had him severely flogged, yet did he not utter one word in his own defense or in private to those who beat him, only continuing to cry out as before. Thereupon, our Leading Men, supposing him under some Divine possession, as the case indeed proved to be, brought him before the Roman Procurator. There, scourged till his bones were laid bare, he neither pleaded for mercy or cried out, but rather in the most mournful tone of voice, responded to each stroke with 'Woe! Woe to Jerusalem!' When Albinus, the Governor, asked him who he was and from where he came and why he uttered such words, he said nothing, but unceasingly repeated his heart-rending refrain. Taking him for a lunatic, Albinus dismissed him (here, yet again, the picture of the sympathetic, lenient Roman Governor)."[35]

This dismissal also parallels the many other dismissals by Roman Governors of early Christian Leaders already encountered above, not the least of which being the picture of the dismissal of Jesus himself by Pontius Pilate in the Gospels, before the Jewish crowd forces him to reverse himself. In fact, in the version of these events called 'The Slavonic Josephus' (real or forged), Pilate does at first dismiss Jesus before ultimately having him re-arrested again and flogged later on.[36]

Josephus continues:

"During the whole of the period till the outbreak of the War, he (Jesus ben Ananias) neither spoke to anyone, nor was seen to speak, but daily repeated his foreboding dirge, 'Woe! Woe to Jerusalem!' Nor did he curse those who repeatedly beat him, nor thank those who gave him food.... His cry was loudest at Festivals. So for seven years and five months he continued this wail, his voice never flagging nor his strength exhausting, until during the siege, seeing his Prophecy fulfilled, he ceased. For, when making his round of the walls, shouting in the most piercing voice, 'Woe once more to the City and to the People and to the Holy House,' and just as he added the last words, 'and woe to me also', a stone hurled from one of the (Roman) siege engines struck and killed him on the spot and, as he was adding these very prophecies, he passed away."

Hyperbole or poetic license aside, we have rendered the entire passage to show how true-to-life it is, not to mention its intensity and the meaning it obviously had for the eyewitnesses who survived these horrific events. At the same time however, it is typical of Josephus' sometimes macabre sense-of-humor. Nevertheless, the cynical parallel to this in the picture of Jesus in the Gospels, predicting the destruction of the Temple 'stone upon stone' and his 'woes' upon 'the Scribes and Pharisees', is unmistakable.

Setting aside its 'Messianic' implications, which we have already dwelled upon sufficiently above, if one views this 'oracle' in relation to the 'Pella flight' oracles we have been discussing, and the strong 'Christian' tradition associating the destruction of Jerusalem generally with the death of James, it is possible to see that this prophecy has perhaps even more importance than that attributed to it by Josephus. In the light of these early Christian traditions about an oracle immediately following the death of James warning his followers to flee Jerusalem, I think that we can state with some assurance that, in this context, this is precisely what is occurring here and that, therefore even if unwittingly (perhaps even not so unwittingly), Josephus has provided us with this oracle as well. Put in another way, we have before us, in this pathetic cry of 'Jesus Ben Ananias', the very oracle — make of it what one will.

Another Oracle by 'Agabus' and the Pella Flight Tradition

But it is possible to go further than this. Reviewing these kinds of oracles before us in this period, one comes to the second of the two oracles attributed to the Prophet designated in Acts by the nonsense name of 'Agabus'. It will be recalled that this time 'Agabus' supposedly 'comes down to Caesarea' right before Paul's last trip up to Jerusalem for his final confrontation with James.

Here Acts appropriates (or misappropriates) the oracle of Jesus ben Ananias about the coming destruction of Jerusalem, and the oracle warning James' followers to flee Jerusalem, and turns them into an oracle warning Paul 'not to go up to Jerusalem' because he would be arrested there — which is, of course, precisely what happens.

We have already shown how the first of these oracles by this Prophet Acts calls 'Agabus' at the time of 'the Great Famine' in the reign of Claudius in the mid-Forties, in conjunction with which so much else of consequence was transpiring, was a counterfeit. There, it will be recalled, it was an overwrite of and disguised the legend of the conversion of 'King Agbarus' or 'Abgarus', 'the Great King of the Peoples beyond the Euphrates', reprised in Eusebius but missing from Acts' tendentious story-telling.

This fractured nonsense material in Acts also covered over much important material associated with the conversion of Queen Helen of Adiabene and her sons — also missing from Acts' narrative but, as we have shown, not really — to a more 'militant' or 'Zealot' form of Judaism taught by a 'Galilean' teacher named 'Eleazar', who insisted on circumcision as a fundamental precondition of conversion (parodied in Acts 8:27's presentation of 'the Ethiopian Queen's eunuch'[37]) — the key connecting link here being the legendary generosity of Helen and her son Izates in providing famine relief to the population of Jerusalem, to say nothing of her possible marital relationship with 'King Agbarus'. Josephus calls this King 'Bazeus', while at the same time averring, as we saw, that she was his sister.[38]

This is all parodied in the description in Acts 11:27 of how Agabus 'came down from Jerusalem to Antioch' and 'having risen up', 'signified by the Spirit' his 'Prophecy' about the Great Famine which, in fact, 'also came to pass'. Not only does the reason for this obfuscation or dissimulation have to do with Helen's more militant brand of Judaism and the 'Zealotry' of her two sons, but it also has to do with the insistent motif of circumcision and/or conversion in all these traditions relating to either 'King Agbarus' or his subjects the Edessenes, as well as that of 'Zelotes' or the 'zeal' being attached to the name of one or another of the teachers involved in these conversions, e.g., 'Simon Zelotes', 'Judas Zelotes', or even, if one prefers, 'Judas Iscariot' and/or 'Simon Iscariot'/'Simon the Iscariot'.[39]

In turn, these are usually linked to the names of one or another of Jesus' brothers, as we have been underscoring, and the motif of their having been sent down from Jerusalem either by one of these, usually 'Judas Thomas' or even James himself. In Acts 15:22 it will be recalled, 'Judas Barsabas' is the one who is 'sent down' among others by James with his directives to overseas communities — themselves not unrelated, as we have been demonstrating, to the Letter(s) known as MMT.

In the second of these two prophecies attributed to 'Agabus' in Acts, we have another of these inversions – this time of the 'Pella flight' oracle warning the followers of James to flee Jerusalem and, by extension, of this oracle of Jesus ben Ananias about the coming destruction of Jerusalem. This oracle also finds its way into Gospel presentations – according to the Synoptics anyhow – of another Jesus who, as we saw as well, is pictured as uttering a more extensive version of it or its equivalent when coming in sight of Jerusalem – this time thirty or so years earlier.

As we have shown too, there can be little doubt that Jesus ben Ananias starts prophesying the coming destruction of Jerusalem at exactly the time James is killed or a little thereafter. Nor does he cease until he is killed shortly before his Prophecy too is fulfilled. Nor can there be much doubt that the mysterious conjunction of these two events must be associated in some manner with James' death. This now explains the widespread belief on the part of 'the People', attested to in copies of Josephus known to Origen, Eusebius, and Jerome, 'that *Jerusalem fell because of the death of James*'.

Above: The ruins of Jerash across the Jordan in the Decapolis, part of the area which Herod the Tetrarch, John the Baptist's murderer, supposedly ruled and probably disputed with King Azizus of Arabian Petra, from whom Paul was seemingly fleeing '*down the walls of Damascus in a Basket* -2 Cor. 11:32-33.
Bottom: The ruins of Hellenistic Palmyra, on the way North to Edessa, the Land of the Edessenes, and Adiabene, from where Xenobia two centuries later and proverbial for '*xenophobia*', also led an unsuccessful revolt against Rome.

PART IV

JAMES AND QUMRAN

Chapter 17
Confrontations Between Paul and James

The Scrolls and New Testament Criticism

The points we have made regarding James' position in early Christianity stand on their own regardless of whether there is a relationship to the Qumran materials or not. There are, however, so many allusions and expressions in the New Testament and related documents which, as we have been showing, overlap with the Scroll materials that it is possible to go further. In previous work we avoided systematic conclusions about the Scrolls because of disagreements over chronological problems which have still not been resolved and probably never will. What follows, therefore, will have to be evaluated on its own terms.

We could not have arrived at the insights we did regarding 'Palestinian Messianism', our understanding of what the true nature of early 'Christianity' in Palestine was, or problematic portions of the Gospels, without the Dead Sea Scrolls. These provided us with the contemporary control to see what an authentic Palestinian document might look like. This is what is so revolutionary about the Scrolls and the insight they provide into the life and mind of Palestine at that time, as if we had been presented with an untampered-with 'time capsule' that had not gone through the editorial and redaction processes of the Roman Empire but were, rather, put in caves after only the initial redaction process.

Previously, in doing criticism of the New Testament, scholars did not have such contemporary and primary documents to use either for chronological control and by which to measure whether a given passage might be inappropriate or not to its time or place – or even fictional for that matter. Now we do, which is what is so revolutionary about having the Dead Sea Scrolls as a research tool. It is for this reason, too, that we can and will go further. Much will depend on one's attitude towards 'external' parameters such as palaeographic analysis, archaeological interpretations, or A.M.S. carbon dating procedures.

Actually it would be simpler and easier to take the facile and more well-traveled path, the safe approach most specialists prefer to take, thereby avoiding having to make the specific identifications we shall attempt and insulating themselves from criticism, which is the general rule in this field, because it is almost impossible to be criticized if you do not or cannot say anything definite about a specific issue or hazard a particular identification. But there is enough information from this period that we should be able to make specific identifications, and to refrain from doing so is neither the responsible nor courageous thing to do.

Regarding these documents from Qumran, first let us state, unequivocally, that we are confronted with a *major Movement in Judaism*. The scope of the literature guarantees that. Plus, we know enough about the period and have enough data from a variety of sources, not least of which being Josephus himself – to demand that scholars 'toe the line' on these issues and not simply retreat to the safer ground of not committing themselves. Over and over again we have shown the relationship of the *vocabulary* of the Community in Palestine which was led by James to the Community represented by the literature found at Qumran and this is, in my view, the inescapable thrust of the documents we have before us.

Nor could we have had such insights before without such documents. For instance, we could not have known the importance of the *B-L-'/Bela'/Belial/Balaam* language-circle to Palestinian documents and how this became transformed in the Greek presentation of James' death in terms of being 'cast down' (in Greek, '*ballo*', based on the same homophonous root – *B-L-L* – as in the Hebrew) and how, in turn, all of this language and imagery of 'being cast down' went into the more sanitized and, one might add, *pacified* presentation in the Gospels of Jesus and his Apostles as either peaceful fishermen on the Sea of Galilee 'casting down nets' or 'casting out Evil spirits' and similar activities often involving this very usage 'casting'.

Then, too, we could never have understood the importance of Eusebius' 'Letter to Agbarus' in determining the possible provenance of the Letter or Letters known as *MMT*, nor, even their extremely 'Jamesian' cast. Vice versa, we could never have understood that James' instructions to overseas communities, summarized in Acts and reflected by Paul in 1 Corinthians 6–12, the Pseudoclementines, and in *MMT* is really a letter to a 'zealous' new convert needing such tuition, in particular, someone like the King of Adiabene whom Josephus calls 'Izates', and not to a Jewish King at all, whether Maccabean or Herodian.

Finally, we could not have understood the tremendous lacunae left in the Gospel narratives after pursuing studies of this kind without comparing them with usages, emphases, and imagery found in the Scrolls. Nor could we have understood how these same Gospels – to say nothing of Acts – were depending on and either parodying or using (often even reversing) identifiable stories, ideas, and episodes taken not only from Josephus, the Old Testament, and the Scrolls, but also from Rabbinic literature – recondite and unassimilable as it may have been too – and selected Christian Apocrypha to reconstruct their portrait of the being, ideology, and teaching of the person they were representing as 'Jesus'.

The First Confrontations on the Temple Mount: Stephen, 'the Hellenists', and James

The First Book of the *Recognitions* of Clement pictures debates on the Temple steps, mentions Gamaliel, and ends with a riot led by Paul on the Temple Mount which triggers the flight of the Jerusalem Community to Jericho (and not 'Pella' or even 'Damascus'). Acts, in its early chapters (3:1–5:25), also pictures debates and confrontations on the Temple Mount, mentions Gamaliel (5:33), and ends with a riot in Jerusalem in which Paul plays a central role (8:1–3). Paul then receives letters from the High Priests to pursue the Jerusalem Community to Damascus (9:1–2), a flight and pursuit depicted in the Pseudoclementine *Recognitions* as well. These are the clear points of contact which probably indicate a common source.

In the Pseudoclementine *Recognitions*, the whole presentation is one of debates and arguments on the Temple Mount over the burning issues of the day between the Herodian High Priests and the Messianic Community, with James functioning either in the role of 'Overseer'/'Bishop'/or 'Archbishop' (the seeming 'High Priest of the Opposition Alliance'). These debates finally end in the long speech James delivers, which was, no doubt, originally part of the *Anabathmoi Jacobou*, on the 'two natures of Christ' and 'the Primal Adam' ideology.[1] There can be little doubt, too, that the attack on James on the Temple Mount (which Acts overwrites as the stoning of 'Stephen') is what really happens at this point in early Church history.

One can also probably assert with some confidence that it is probably James who sends 'Simon', whom Josephus pictures as wishing to bar Herodians from the Temple as foreigners at approximately this time, down to Caesarea – just as the Pseudoclementine *Recognitions* describes in its portrait of James sending out 'Simon Peter' from a location somewhere outside of Jericho (where the whole Community has fled) to confront 'Simon Magus' in Caesarea where, of course, the Herodian, King Agrippa I (37–44 CE) also had his palace.

However this may be, the 'Simon' in Josephus rather visits Agrippa I to see what was being done there 'contrary to Law', not the household of 'Cornelius the Roman Centurion', as Acts 10:1–11:18 portrays parallel materials, deftly subverting them. For its part, the exclusionary doctrine ascribed to 'Simon' by Josephus is the very reverse of the Heavenly vision the 'Simon Peter' in Acts is vouchsafed, which rather ends up in his thoroughgoing acceptance of Gentiles not their rejection or, as it were, his absolute 'Paulinization'.

The confrontations that Peter is pictured as having with Simon Magus that follow in Acts 8:9–25 in Simon's birthplace 'Samaria' – more accurately in Caesarea, as in the Pseudoclementines – are most likely historical too. These, however, probably relate – as Josephus pictures a parallel episode in the *Antiquities* – to Simon Magus' or *Atomus*' subsequent advice to Agrippa II's sister Drusilla to divorce her husband the King of Emesa, who had specifically circumcised himself at the insistence of her father Agrippa I in order to marry her.[2]

As in the case of John the Baptist's complaints against Herodias and Herod Antipas a decade before these objections 'Simon Peter' might have had to Drusilla's divorce and subsequent remarriage to Felix, these confrontations with Herodian women involve 'fornication', most notably defined in the Scrolls, as we have seen, as niece marriage, polygamy, and divorce – but in the Temple Scroll including, at least where the King or Ruler was concerned, marrying non-Jews and 'taking more than one wife during the lifetime of the first' as well.[3]

It should also be appreciated that these confrontations with Herodian women also involve another favorite theme in the Scrolls and the Letter of James – the second of these 'Three Nets of *Belial*' in the Damascus Document – the 'Riches' of these Herodian women. Of these, Herodias and Bernice would appear to have been the Richest of all, a point Josephus never fails to note in these descriptions of them.[4] On the other hand, these confrontations had almost nothing to do with 'levirate marriage' – the point seized upon in the Synoptics. These things notwithstanding, complaints of this kind occur at this time – at least in the case of Drusilla and Felix (who both appear conversing amiably with Paul in Acts 24:24–27) – amid the general disaffection between 'Syrophoenician' Legionnaires and the Jewish inhabitants of Caesarea, so graphically depicted in Josephus.[5]

Another curious point bearing on this interesting tangle of events is that Josephus places the riot led by 'Saulos' and two others in Jerusalem directly after the death of James.[6] The author of Acts places a similar riot led by its 'Saulos' following 'the stoning of Stephen', a stand-in, as we have sufficiently elucidated, for the attack by Saul/Paul on James as detailed in the *Recognitions*.

A possible explanation for these kinds of discrepancies between Acts and Josephus on some of this chronology is that Josephus specifically tells us in the *Vita* that he was in Rome at the time James was killed.[7] There he visited Nero's wife, the Empress Poppea, whom he characterizes as sympathetic to 'religious' causes, in particular it would appear, 'Jewish' ones. At the time, Josephus was only about twenty-four years old and already on an extremely important mission. As depicted in the *Vita*, the reason he was in Rome was the curious mission he was on to rescue some Priests who had been arrested, as he puts it, 'on some slight and trifling charge' and had been sent to Rome, there to render account to Nero.

As a consequence, Josephus only knew secondhand events taking place in Palestine in the year 62 CE at the time of James' death. He even may have learned of it and other matters through the file of letters he claims King Agrippa II later shared with him when both were in exile in Rome sometime in between his writing the *Jewish War* and the *Antiquities*.[8] There can be little doubt that the Priests on whose account he goes to Rome had been sent there in the wake of the disturbances in the Temple over the Wall erected to block Agrippa II's view of the sacrifices. As suggested, this in our view was the immediate antecedent to the death of James concerning which, we suspect, Paul may have played a part, just as he may have done in circumstances surrounding the War against Rome that followed some three and a half years later.

Nor in Paul's own description of his experiences in Galatians 1:15–24 is there any 'vision on the Damascus road', only a sojourn in 'Arabia'. As already signaled, Paul's relations with Herodians – particularly John's executioner Herod the Tetrarch – might explain what he may have been doing at the time and the reason he ran afoul of 'Arab' Authorities – not as Acts so tendentiously transforms it, the 'Jewish' Ones. The 'plotting' language Acts 9:22–23 uses in relation to the stratagems these last allegedly employ to try 'to kill Paul' is the same as that which the Gospels use to portray what 'Judas Iscariot' and 'the Jews' generally do to Jesus, to say nothing of the portrait in John's Gospel of their attempts to kill Lazarus as well.[9] Actually, Acts pictures Paul as admitting at several points that he 'persecuted this Way unto death, arresting and imprisoning men and women' (22:4) or he 'imprisoned the Saints..., voting against them for execution, punishing them, compelling them to blaspheme in all the synagogues and persecuting them in a mad frenzy even unto foreign cities' (26:10–12). Paul himself reiterates this in Galatians 1:23, admitting that 'the Assemblies in Judea' only knew him as someone who 'persecuted' or 'ravaged' them in times past, a portrait which appears to turn into the words Jesus is pictured as uttering in Acts 9:4's famous depiction of Paul's vision on 'the Way to Damascus', 'Paul, Paul, why persecutest thou me?'

After this vision, according to Acts 9:26, Paul 'joined himself to the Disciples' three years later in Jerusalem (*n.b.*, the 'joining' language). There he ran afoul of the same ubiquitous 'Hellenists', whose *complaints* against 'the Hebrews', it will be recalled, triggered the stoning of Stephen three chapters before. Here, it is now 'the Hellenists', just as 'the Jews' in Damascus earlier (9:23), who want to 'get hold of' Paul and 'kill him' (9:29). Of course, none of this makes any sense whatsoever, since it is Paul who must be considered the real or chief Hellenizer or Hellenist not vice versa. Nor is it reasonable to think any 'Hellenists' wanted either to kill 'Stephen' or bother with Paul – the opposite. Later in Acts 11:20, these same 'Hellenists' are portrayed as the first to receive the Gospel 'of the Lord Jesus' in Antioch – meaning, of course, Paul's 'Gospel' not James'.

The reader will appreciate there is clearly a 'code' of sorts going on here. If this 'code' was aimed at evasion and disinformation, it certainly has achieved its end over the last nineteen hundred years. Just as Luke was finally forced to attach the real cognomen 'Zealot' to the Apostle Matthew and Mark are misleadingly calling 'Simon the Canaanite' or 'Cananaean', one would probably ultimately have to read, as already explained, 'extreme Zealots' or '*Sicarii*' for at least this first cluster of so-called 'Hellenists' intent on killing Paul. The meaning of 'Hellenists', then, in such a context – as we have also made clear – would probably have to be 'Zealots' or '*Sicarii*', in the sense that they were willing to make no compromises where issues of Gentiles or Gentile gifts in the Temple, foreign rule, and foreign appointment of High Priests – including those appointed by Herodians – were concerned. In fact, even Acts 23:12 implies as much when it later goes on to describe those Nazirite-style 'Jews' who make a *plot*, putting themselves under an oath not to eat or drink until they had killed Paul (repeated in Acts 23:14 and 23:21 – in the manner of vegetarians like James abstaining from 'strong drink' or of later 'Mourners for Zion', who take precisely such an oath in regard to their steadfastness in 'waiting' to 'see the Temple rebuilt').

In Galatians 1:18–21, after describing how he first met James and spent fifteen days with Peter, Paul matter-of-factly notes how he 'then came into the regions of Syria and Cilicia', while insisting he 'does not lie'. Not a word about anyone persecuting him at this point. *He* is the persecutor noting how 'the Assemblies in Judea' (who did not know him by sight) had only heard that 'their former persecutor was now preaching the Faith he had previously tried to destroy'!

Whatever else one might wish to say about these purposeful mix-ups between so-called 'Hellenists' and 'Hebrews' in Acts, 'Stephen' certainly does seem to personify the archetypical Gentile believer who is persecuted and ultimately stoned by Jews – the stoning being a throwback to and drawn from the James story. In fact the charges against him: 'This man does not cease speaking blasphemous words against this Holy Place and the Law, for we have heard him saying that Jesus the Nazoraean will destroy this place and will change the customs handed down to us by Moses' (Acts 6:13–14), are more or less repeated in Acts 21:28 in the charges against Paul made by the Jewish crowd who, seeing him in the Temple with Greeks, think he has introduced foreigners into it, thereby 'defiling' or 'polluting it'. The addition of 'blasphemy' to the charge sheet against 'Stephen' here is probably yet another holdover from the original one against James.[10] Concomitantly, the charge of 'destroying this place and changing the customs of Moses' – doubtlessly, too, the general implication of Pauline doctrine on these issues as well – reflects the 'blasphemy' aspect of the charges against Jesus before 'the High Priests, the Elders, and the whole Sanhedrin' as depicted in the Synoptics (Matthew 26:59–65 and pars.).

More Gentilization at Corinth – Sequencing in Acts and Josephus

With regard to the 'Gentilization' of these kinds of persecutions and sufferings, one should pay particular attention to Acts' picture of Paul's activities in Corinth. Here, as usual, Paul goes straight to the Jewish Synagogue, where he 'won over Jews and Greeks and ... earnestly testified to the Jews that Jesus was the Christ' (Acts 18:4–5). But Paul was not supposed to do this. According to his own testimony in Galatians 2:9, after going up to Jerusalem as a result of a private 'revelation' he says he has received and putting the Gospel as he 'taught it among the Gentiles' before the Central Trio of 'James, Cephas, and John', these 'Pillars', as he puts it, shook hands with him to show, seemingly, their agreement that he 'should go to the Gentiles, while they to the Circumcision' (Galatians 2:2–2:6).

But according to Acts, Paul does precisely the opposite and the first thing he does in almost every city he visits is to go directly to the synagogue there. In Corinth, for example, when the Jews 'set themselves in opposition and were blaspheming' (18:6), Paul 'shook out his garments'. In the Gospels, Jesus expresses a similar idea when he councils his followers to 'shake the dust from off their feet' (Matthew 10:14 and pars.). Now Paul is actually even pictured as saying, 'Your blood be on your own heads. I am innocent. From now on I will go to the Gentiles' (Acts 18:6), as if slights or rejections of this kind were sufficient cause to permit such a new direction. Actually, its anti-Semitism is directed as much against Jews within the early 'Christian' Movement of principal concern to Paul (we should probably call it the 'Messianic' Movement) as those outside it, since they were, in fact, its principal Leaders – perhaps even more. Just as the presentation of Pilate 'washing his hands' of any responsibility for the condemnation and death of Jesus, one must see this episode as the total validation of Paul's mission and his position where Jews were concerned – at least this would be true in the eyes of the Roman reader or devotees.

But the problem with the episode, as we've seen, is that 'the Ruler of the Synagogue' is apparently the same 'Sosthenes' Paul greets in the first line of 1 Corinthians, designating him there as a 'brother' and a close collaborator in all his work. In fact, in Acts 18:8, this same 'Ruler of the Synagogue' is rather identified as 'Crispus'. Again here we would appear to be in the midst of another of Acts' manifold reversals of either real historical persons and/or the real historical situation or both.

With all of the above individuals and activity centered in Corinth, where according to Acts 18:7 Paul stays 'for eighteen months' at the house adjourning the synagogue of someone called 'Justus', as well as the designation, too, of 'Stephen' – clearly another of Paul's close collaborators – as 'Achaia's first fruit' (all of this, to say nothing of 'Epaphroditus' presence at various times in Corinth as well), there would appear to be more going on in Corinth at this time than initially meets the eye. It should be appreciated that Corinth was Nero's summer residence and he apparently spent a good deal of time there directing one of his pet projects – the digging of the Corinth Canal, for which purpose many of the captives from the shores of the Sea of Galilee at the time of the first engagements of the Jewish War were consigned and worked to death.[11]

For instance, if this 'Epaphroditus' was Nero's confidant (here, too, it would be hard to conceive there would be two Epaphrodituses involved in some capacity in the household of Nero at one and the same time), then he was Josephus' publisher as well and the man to whom he dedicated all his works. Josephus even refers to him as someone of 'the widest worldly experience'.[12] Acts 19:22 also refers to one 'Erastus', one of Paul's fundraisers in Macedonia. 2 Timothy 4:20, regardless of its historical reliability, refers to Erastus as remaining in Corinth which, as should by now be clear, seems to have been a center of Paul's activities 'in Achaia'. Romans 16:23 for its part calls Erastus 'the steward of the city', probably meaning Corinth. It is not without the realm of possibility that this 'Erastus' is a compression of 'Epaphroditus', as consolidations of this kind are common – for instance, 'Prisca' preceding the reference to 'Erastus' in 2 Timothy 4:19 for 'Priscilla', 'Silas' for 'Silvanus', and even possibly 'Titus' for 'Timothy'. However one looks at it, these are obviously not all separate individuals and the circle of Paul's close collaborators grows ever more concentrated.

If the stoning of 'Stephen' in Acts is still one more refurbishment of the 'beating' by Revolutionaries or 'bandits' (*lestai*) of the Emperor's Servant Stephen just outside the walls of Jerusalem in the wake of the stampede in the Temple at Passover in which 'hundreds' or 'thousands' died[13] then we are in very great and potentially very tragic difficulties regarding 'Christian' origins in Palestine.

As already stated, in the author's view the 'Stephen' in Acts is precisely just such a refurbishment and, when combined with the picture of James' later stoning 'for blasphemy' (now retrospectively inserted into the 'Stephen' story), then the flow of Acts' narrative along with much else becomes comprehensible indeed. While fictional in almost all its aspects, the presentation in Acts 6:1–5 of this archetypal Pauline 'convert' as one of those 'seven men' to 'serve tables' (*diakonein*) nevertheless combines, on the one hand, the bitterness generated by these events from a pro-Roman perspective and, on the other, elements from both the unmentionable attack by Paul on James (deleted even from the Pseudoclementine *Homilies*) as well as the attack by riotous and revolutionary Jews bent on vengeance and carnage on the Emperor's Servant Stephen who seems to have come bearing treasure and supplies from precisely this same 'Corinth' (and note, too, the use of this same designation, 'Servant'[14]).

The sequencing in these matters is an important key to understanding their connections. In Josephus, the attack and robbing of Stephen was followed by outbreaks of mayhem between Samaritans and Galileans on their way through Samaria to pilgrimages in Jerusalem, paralleled in Acts 8:4–25 by confrontations between Peter and Simon Magus *in Samaria* (according to the Pseudoclementines, confrontations which actually took place in Caesarea).[15] In Josephus, too, much inter-communal strife and killing break out in Caesarea between Greeks ('Syrophoenician's in Matthew) and Jews, the counterpart of which in Acts is this picture – however far-fetched it might at first appear – in this 'Stephen' episode of the squabbling between 'Hellenists' and 'Hebrews' (6:1.). From then on, as Josephus portrays it, 'the whole of Judea was overrun with brigands or robbers' (*lestai*).[16]

The Roman Procurator from 48–52 CE in Judea, Cumanus, responds by taking bribes from and siding with the Samaritans.[17] Because of the protests he receives, Quadratus, the Governor in Syria responsible for this area – then at Beirut – settles the issue by beheading some eighteen Jews and crucifying four others at Lydda. Thus far the *War* but, in the *Antiquities*, Josephus claims only five were executed, including the 'Doetus' or 'Dorcas' mentioned previously. Furthermore, whereas he includes 'Samaritans' in this number, Tacitus says only Jews were crucified who had been 'daring enough to slay Roman soldiers'![18]

Lydda, it will be recalled, was the town on the coastal plain on the way from Jerusalem to both Jaffa and Gaza. Not only do some really fantastic occurrences take place there in the narrative of Acts 9:32–43 at this point, but we have also encountered this town in Rabbinic tradition as a focus for the activities, for instance, of teachers such as the heretic Rabbi, Eliezer b. Hyrcanus. But the Talmud also mentions at this same Lydda the crucifixion of an important Messianic Leader called 'the Messiah ben Joseph' not only, perhaps, another of these 'Joshua *redivivus*es' ('Joshua' being in the Bible a 'son of Joseph'), but because of the 'Joseph' allusion too – as already explained, possibly the Samaritan '*Taheb*' or 'Messiah' as well. Even more importantly, one of the individuals mentioned at this point in Josephus' narrative in connection with problems between Jews and Samaritans at Lydda was the 'Doetus' or 'Dortus' just mentioned above.[19] Transmogrified into 'Dorcas', just as 'the *Taheb*' is transmogrified into 'Tabitha' ('his'/'her' equivalent[20]), this 'Dortus' or 'Dorcas' then becomes an important part of Acts' story about the 'signs and wonders' or 'miracles' Peter performed at Lydda, leading up to his 'tablecloth' vision.

Concerning these crucifixions at Lydda, Josephus also refers to the involvement of another 'certain Samaritan', an informer to Quadratus, possibly Simon Magus again. He, it will be recalled, was probably also an intimate of Felix (52–60 CE), the next Governor sent out after Cumanus was removed. The 'Doetus' or 'Dortus' we have been talking about here is probably the 'Dositheus', who was important as a 'Disciple of John the Baptist' in all catalogues of the 'Heresies' in this period, with views virtually indistinguishable from the Ebionites. In turn Acts 8:32–38, for its part, mentions Lydda some three times in just six verses in this episode, so something of consequence seems to have been going on there, although what exactly is unclear.

In Acts the assault on Stephen is followed by confrontations in Samaria between Peter and Simon Magus, the affinities with Josephus being palpable – however, as always, reversed. But, where 'Hellenist' complaints against 'the Hebrews' in Acts 6:1–6 and – following these – against Paul in Acts 9:29 are concerned, these are also obviously totally invented. As previously suggested, surely we have to do with more overwriting here and complaints of this kind against Paul and like-minded personages must rather have been on the part of so-called 'Zealots' or '*Sicarii*' not 'Hellenists'.

For the Pseudoclementines, in conclusion then, the whole presentation of 'the stoning of Stephen' is replaced by the assault on James in the Temple by Paul, who incites 'the High Priests' against James not 'Stephen'. In fact, the whole series of disturbances in the Temple from the Forties to the Sixties CE will probably have to be associated with the kind of activities James and his followers were involved in there, the majority of whom, even according to the description of Acts 21:20, have to be seen as 'Zealots for the Law'.

Paul's Missionary Adventures and the Run-up to 'the Jerusalem Council'

The next meeting between Paul and James may have taken place during the time of 'the Great Famine' in the late Forties but, where this is concerned, Acts' testimony cannot really be relied upon because in Chapters 10–16 we are presented with such a welter of contradictory notices, fantastic events, and overlaps that little, if anything, can be concluded with certainty.

To continue on the question of sequencing – Acts, having finished its account of Peter's activities in Samaria in confronting Simon Magus, moves on to the journey Peter takes to Jaffa and Caesarea and his 'Heavenly tablecloth' vision (10:45). Then there are a series of repetitive notices about 'prophets and teachers' coming down 'from Jerusalem to Antioch'. The first of these follows the so-called 'scattering' that took place, supposedly 'to Phoenicia, Cyprus, and Antioch', after the stoning of Stephen in Acts 11:19 – in the Pseudoclementines paralleled simply by the flight by James' Community to the Jericho area.[21] Again we hear that 'certain ones of them, men from Cyprus and Cyrene', came down and 'preached the Gospel' to the 'Hellenists', now supposedly residing in Antioch (11:20) – here, too, one should probably rather read 'Zealots'.

What is really behind these episodes about 'prophets and teachers' such as 'Agabus' 'coming down from Jerusalem to Antioch' are the messengers from or representatives of James like 'Judas Barsabas', 'Thaddaeus', and even 'Judas Thomas' sent down to Antioch-by-Callirhoe or Edessa Orrhoe either to convert or make sure everyone had correctly gotten the message of obedience to the Law, an obedience which *prima facie* included circumcision. Persons such as these would also include by refraction 'Judas the brother of James' ('Addai' in the First Apocalypse of James and, 'Theuda the brother of the Just One', in the Second) going down to carry on these initial conversion activities in 'the Land of the Edessenes', as Eusebius would express it, and, no doubt, further east in Adiabene.

Paul's adventures, recorded from Chapters 13–15 of Acts, largely overlap those in Chapters 16–18. They are often referred to as his First, Second, or Third Missionary Journeys, depending on how much or how little overlap one thinks there is. The present writer, obviously, thinks there was quite a bit. Ingenious efforts to harmonize these have been largely ineffective and, instead of the picture of 'three' Missionary Journeys, we are probably really only speaking about one extended one and its offshoots or variations – the one finally told about at some length in the 'We Document'.

A good example of this overlapping is what happens in 'Antioch of Pisidia'. As usual, Paul makes a bee-line on the Sabbath to the Synagogue to preach (Acts 13:14). He 'speaks out boldly' but the Jews, 'filled with envy, opposed the things Paul said, blaspheming' (13:45). The parallels with Acts 18:6's picture of what supposedly happened later at Corinth are patent. Again, as at Corinth too, in this first incident on mainland Asia Minor at 'Antioch of Pisidia', Paul goes to the Synagogue on a succession of Sabbaths. Here, 'the Jews stirred up a persecution against Paul among the honorable, worshipping women and chief men of the city' and, just as later, Paul exploits this as an occasion to announce his intention to 'turn to the Gentiles' (13:46-50). This time, however, it is not his 'garments' that he 'shakes out', but now he and Barnabas 'shake off the dust of their feet against them' (13:51) after the people of Antioch of Pisidia now 'cast out' Paul and Barnabas 'from their coasts' or 'borders'.

At this point, Acts suddenly dispenses with all the dissimulation or, as some might characterize it, disinformation and gives us the real circumstances behind Paul's return to Jerusalem after his first meeting with James fourteen years before. Hitherto this causality had only been implied but never explicitly stated in all these other highly improbable notices in Acts. It would also appear to be the real reason behind the so-called 'Jerusalem Council' or 'Conference'. As Acts 15:1 puts this, 'Some, having *come down from Judea*, were teaching the brothers that, *unless you are circumcised according to the custom of Moses*, you could not be saved', and we are right back again in the scenario of Galatians 2:3–2:14. One can assume, as well, that this is more or less the truth of the matter and what we have here is what would ordinarily be reckoned as a summons on the part of 'those of repute' or 'those reckoned to be something', as Paul calls them in Galatians 2:6, in Jerusalem – meaning 'James, Cephas, and John'.

Here too, Paul first makes the accusation in Galatians 2:4 we have already alluded to of 'false brothers stealing in by stealth to spy out the freedom we enjoy in Christ Jesus, so that they might enslave us', deliberately playing off the issue of circumcision – in his implication of some 'spying on their privy parts' – that, according to Acts, triggered the so-called 'Jerusalem Council' in the first place. Paul means here, of course, as already explained, 'freedom from the Law' as opposed to 'slavery to it' and not what would be more apt, given the historical situation, 'freedom from Rome' as opposed to 'slavery to it' – a juxtaposition of imagery Paul also picks up again in his allegory about Hagar and Sarah.

Whether there was an actual 'Council' as such, as Acts presents it, and not simply a semi-private audience of some kind between Paul and the Jerusalem 'Pillars', as Paul recounts in Galatians 2:1-13, is highly unlikely. Acts 15:2–7 magnifies this into a meeting of the whole Assembly ('the Apostles and the Elders'). According to it, this insistence on circumcision causes 'an uproar' in the Community at Antioch, whereupon Paul, Barnabas, and 'certain others' are chosen 'to go up to the Apostles and the Elders in Jerusalem regarding this question' (15:2).

Apostolic Credentials, 'Boasting', and 'the Apostles of Surpassing Degree' in Paul

Despite the many questions about these events and their sequence, what the so-called 'Jerusalem Council' really was has been labored over long and hard by numerous scholars with varying answers, usually depending on the theological point-of-view of the given observer. The results achieved are not particularly satisfying because: 1) researchers rarely come to grips with Acts' tendencies to dissimulate – or even, for that matter, its creative writing – to say nothing of its oftentimes mischievousness; and 2) the Dead Sea Scrolls had not yet been discovered and, even when they had, have either simply been shunted aside or not been used – not being considered relevant to the real life setting of this famous confrontation, nor even to hone one's understanding of true events in Palestine of the time. This is still true.

Therefore, we consider that it is better to start from scratch, as it were, using primary sources only and tease the information out of them. The notices we have just encountered above about persons dogging Paul's footsteps with a contrary doctrine are rife in Paul's Letters and he repeatedly and often bitterly complains about just that sort of thing. Yet specialists are either still unwilling or unable to definitively determine the identity of these ubiquitous 'some' or 'certain ones' about whom he is constantly complaining. For instance, in 1 Corinthians 9:1 he asserts: 'Have I not seen Jesus Christ our Lord? Are you not my work in the Lord? *Even if I were not an Apostle to others*, I should still be an Apostle to you, who are the seal of my Apostleship in the Lord. This is my answer to *those who would examine me*.' Paul's wounded pride here is self-evident. So is his feeling of inferiority to those above him whom he refers to by phrases such as 'Super Apostles', 'Hebrews', and even 'pseudo-Apostles' and 'dishonest workmen'.

Continuing on the subject of Apostolic Credentials in 2 Corinthians 3:1, Paul asks rhetorically, his wounded pride and feelings of inferiority again painfully evident, 'Do we begin again to *commend ourselves* to you?' Then, alluding to the ever-recurring issue of not having official 'written' letters of Apostolic appointment from James: 'Unlike *some*, we need no letters of recommendation either to you or from you.' One should compare this to the Pseudoclementine *Homilies*' picture of Peter teaching at Tripoli: 'Our Lord and Prophet, who has sent us, declared to us that the Evil One, having disputed with him forty days, but failing to prevail against him, promised He would send Apostles from among his subjects to deceive them. Therefore, above all, remember to shun any Apostle, teacher, or prophet who does not accurately compare his teaching with James … the brother of My Lord … and this, even if he comes to you with recommendations.'[22] The contrast here should be patent.

In 2 Corinthians 3:2–3, Paul then employs the imagery of letters of this kind being written on the 'fleshy tablets' of his supporters' hearts, not on the cold 'tablets of stone', in the process denigrating the attachment of his opponents within 'the Church' to the Mosaic Commandments. Since it is such a startling inversion of Palestinian themes, it is worth citing it fully: 'You are our epistle, having been inscribed in our hearts, being known and being read by all men, it being manifest that you are Christ's letter, served by us, having been inscribed, not with ink, but with the Spirit of the Living God – not on tablets of stone, but on the fleshy tablets of the heart.'

In 2 Corinthians 10:8ff., he launches into one of his most dizzying displays of rhetorical virtuosity which he commences by referring, once more, to 'boasting' – this time, 'about the *Authority which the Lord gave to us* for building up and not tearing you down'. Once again, we know whom he is referring to by these words, though one might ask which 'Lord', when, and which 'us' – but Paul is manifestly employing the royal 'we' here.

Notwithstanding, we have seen the same claim regarding his Apostolic 'Authority' in Galatians 1:1's 'not from men nor through man' (in Romans 2:11 above, that God is 'no respecter of persons'). In 2 Corinthians 10:9 – in alluding to the poor physical impression he apparently makes in person – he follows this in the next line by evoking the issue of 'letters', asserting, 'so that I may not seem as if frightening you by means of letters'. To this he immediately answers antiphonically in 10:11, 'let such a person consider' – meaning the person complaining about his 'Apostolate in the Lord' – that, 'though we are absent in word, through letters we are present in deed'.

He then continues, beginning with his usual note of false modesty, but ending in confident dismissiveness: 'For we dare not rank (ourselves) among or compare ourselves with *some* who *commend themselves*, but those measuring themselves by themselves and comparing themselves to themselves do not understand' (10:12). This is followed by some of the most practiced and strophied discourse, carrying the 'boasting' theme forward and amply demonstrating his training in this sort of rhetorical and sophistical dialectic, pointedly concluding: 'For not he that commends himself is the one approved, but (rather) *he whom the Lord commends*' (10:18). There can be no doubt whom he is talking about here, and what – as if somehow he has received his Apostolic Credentials (as he put it in Galatians 1:1) 'not from men or through man', that is, not in the form of direct earthly appointment (which, it should be clear by this point, Paul did not have), or that of a written letter, 'but through Jesus Christ and the Father God, who raised him from among the dead', which can only mean supernaturally or, as he would put it, 'through Christ Jesus in Heaven'.

Mandaean elders and priests in Southern Iraq early last Century, still following John the Baptist and still wearing white linen— many forcibly removed or persecuted under more recent regimes.

249 • PART IV: James and Qumran

Chapter 18
The Destruction of the Righteous Teacher by the Wicked Priest

The 'Spouter of Lies' and the 'Teacher of Righteousness'

We have been pointing out the relevant allusions in principal Dead Sea Scroll documents, not only as they connected to the position of James in early Christianity, but also to the written ideas and vocabulary of the Letters of Paul and usages and allusions – albeit radically disguised and transformed – in the Gospels and the Book of Acts. Principally, these have included the Damascus Document and the Habakkuk *Pesher*, the Community Rule, and the War Scroll. One might wish to add to these the Hymns, the Psalm 37 and Nahum *Pesher*s, the compendium of Messianic proof-texts known as the *Florilegium*, and *MMT*.

Among such references one should, no doubt, include 'the Man of Lying' or 'Scoffing'/'Spouting Windbag' together with a group variously referred to as 'the Violent Ones'/'the Men-of-War'/'the Men of Violence' and/or 'Traitors' as 'removing the boundary markers which the First had set down as their inheritance, bringing low the Everlasting Heights' – what becomes in the Habakkuk *Pesher*, 'denying the *Torah* in the midst of their whole Assembly'.[1]

Most such allusions are to be found in documents known as 'the *Pesharim*' or 'Commentaries'. These are idiosyncratic commentaries on prized Biblical texts, specifically chosen for the interesting exegetical possibilities they provide. Often, however, they bear little or no relationship to the meaning or interpretation being ascribed to them except a linguistic one. But the same allusions, attitudes, and *dramatis personae* move from document to document across the entire spectrum of the corpus. This allows us to date many of what can be said to be specifically 'sectarian' documents in the non-Biblical part of the corpus as largely contemporaneous and referring to the same set of events – events seen by the Community as cataclysmic often having to do with 'the Last Days' or 'the Final Era' and imbued with the most pregnant and portentous significance. This is also the reason why the literature at Qumran must be seen as that of a 'Movement' and not simply a random or eclectic collection of documents reflecting the general flow of the literature of the period, as some have suggested – though documents of this latter kind do exist, as they would in any library or manuscript collection.

These specifically 'sectarian' documents mainly focus on an individual called 'the Righteous Teacher' or 'Teacher of Righteousness' and not so much on the 'Messiah' or 'Messiah of Righteousness' *per se*, though background references do allude to an individual of this kind as well. There are also references in the Damascus Document to other parallel individuals such as 'the *Maschil*', 'the *Yoreh ha-Zedek*', 'the *Doresh ha-Torah*', 'the *Mehokkek*', and the like, who may or may not be the same as 'the Righteous Teacher'[2] – though at least the last three probably are. In the *Pesharim*, this latter individual seems to double as 'the Priest' as well, clearly meaning 'the High Priest'.

There are also references to 'the *Mebakker*' – 'the Overseer' or 'Bishop' – and a 'High Priest Commanding the Many', again expressed simply in terms of being 'the Priest'.[3] This '*Mebakker*', who very much resembles James, is described at length in the Damascus Document, though there are references to him as well in the Community Rule. What he does is to 'command' both 'the Many' and 'the Camp' or 'Camps', 'instructing them' – including even Priests – 'in the exact interpretation of the *Torah*'.[4] He also examines new entrants, 'records' infractions and makes 'Judgments', and is 'the master of all the Secrets of Men and every Language ('Tongue') according to their families'.[5]

For their part, the references to 'the Righteous Teacher' focus on his two opponents as well – one a more ideological adversary known variously as 'the Man of Lying'/'Liar', 'Spouter of Lying'/'Pourer out of Lying'/'Comedian'/'Scoffer' (described in the Damascus Document as having 'poured out over Israel the waters of Lying'), and even a 'Windbag'.[6] The 'pouring' aspect of this notation is also part of 'the Spouter' terminology – literally, therefore, 'the Pourer' – which can also be seen as incorporating a play on the language of 'baptism' – particularly 'Holy Spirit baptism' – and should be contrasted with 'the standing up of the *Yoreh ha-Zedek*' or 'He who *pours down* Righteousness at the End of Days'.[7]

In the Damascus Document there is also a plural reference to these 'Men of Scoffing' that comes in the context of 'putting idols on their hearts' (compare this allusion to 'idols' here and elsewhere in CD and 1QS with James in Acts 15:19 banning 'the pollutions of the idols'), speaking mistakenly about the Laws of Righteousness, and rejecting the Covenant and the Compact (literally, 'the Promise' or 'the Faith'), that is, 'the New Covenant which they raised in the Land of Damascus',[8] followed by the evocation of 'the end of all the Men of War who walked with the Man of Lying' (n.b. the 'walking' allusion again with an entirely new or reverse signification[9] – this coupled with an allusion to 'the gathering in of the *Yoreh*', the implication being that, whoever he was, he has already in some manner died[10]).

Combinations such as 'the Comedians' or 'Scoffers of Lying', together with allusion to '*Belial*' and 'his nets', also appear in documents like the Qumran Hymns.[11] These further demonstrate the proposition that all these kinds of usages are more or less circular denoting the same individual and his associates. In fact, 'Scoffing' imagery of this kind seems actually to have gone into Islamic eschatology as denoting 'the *Dajjal*' or 'Joker'. This character is portrayed as being in conflict with 'the *Mahdi*' or 'Expected One' (the Messiah-like individual in Islam) who is finally to be destroyed with the coming of Jesus Christ! How this ideology developed is impossible to say.[12]

This 'Spouter of Lying' (*Mattif ha-Chazav*) who 'spouts' or 'pours out to them' (*hittif*) is even referred to in CD VIII.13 of Ms. A as 'spilling out wind' or 'being of confused Spirit' ('wind' and 'spirit' being synonymous in Hebrew). In XIX.25-26 of Ms. B, he is described as 'walking in the wind' or 'walking in the Spirit', phrasing Paul actually employs at the end of Galatians (5:11–26) where he is heaping scorn on those who 'teach circumcision' as being either 'in the flesh' or 'of the flesh' (cf. Romans 8:1–9:8 and pars.). If authentic, the version of these things in Ms. B, describing 'the Spouter' as 'walking in the Spirit/Wind' would have particular import where Paul's design in 1 Corinthians 2:13 to 'teach the spiritual things taught by the Holy Spirit spiritually' is concerned.

In fact, many of these passages from the two versions of CD have since been confirmed in the previously unpublished Cave 4 fragments of the Damascus Document. There is even a reference in one of these 4QD fragments – exactly as in the Pseudoclementine literature – to 'not revealing the secret of His People to Gentiles or cursing or (preaching) Rebellion against His Messiah of the Holy Spirit, turning aside from (or 'disobeying') the word of God'.[13] Here the allusion can also be read 'the Anointed Ones of the Holy Spirit', since there are no verbs or adjectives associated with it that can help determine whether it should be read as a singular or plural; but if it parallels reference to 'the Messiah of Aaron and Israel' elsewhere, where there are, then we can take it as singular.

However this may be, it is an extremely important allusion and the tenor of the allusion to 'Rebelling' which accompanies it is exactly the same as that in Columns V and VI to describe how '*Belial* raised up Jannes and his brother' (Jambres) and the other 'Removers of the Bound' to 'lead Israel astray' as a prelude to its description of how 'the Diggers' (equivalent to 'the Penitents of Israel') 'went out from the Land of Judah to dwell in the Land of

Damascus', there 'to dig the Well' (of 'Living Waters') and explain why 'the Land was decimated': 'because they preached rebellion against the Commandments of God (as given) by the hand of Moses and also against His Holy Messiah. They prophesied Lying to turn Israel aside from God.'[14] This really is a pregnant passage and it too will be picked up later in Columns VIII and XIX in 'the wall-daubing' and 'prophesying Lying' materials from Ezekiel 13:6–12 and Micah 2:6–12. In such a context, the references to either 'rebelling against His Holy Messiah' or 'the Messiah(s) of the Holy Spirit' are astonishing and, whatever else one might wish to say about them, especially the latter combines the conceptuality of 'the Holy Spirit' with either 'His Messiah' or 'the Messiahs' in an unforgettably striking manner.

What unites all references to this 'Lying Spouter' or CD's '*Zaw Zaw*' allusion, tied to the one who 'will surely spout' (Micah 2:6) in IV.19–20, is that not only does he 'pour out on Israel the waters of Lying and lead them astray in a trackless waste', 'removing the boundary markers which the First ('the Forefathers') had laid out as their inheritance',[15] but this sort of behavior takes place in 'the Last Days' when in the Habakkuk *Pesher* he will be distinctly described as 'rejecting the *Torah* in the midst of their whole Assembly' and 'not believing in' the Scriptural interpretations of 'the Righteous Teacher' which the latter 'had received from the mouth of God'!

He would even appear to have been involved along with these other 'Covenant-Breakers' in CD I.20 in physical violence – some of which might even be described as 'mortal' – 'against the person (or 'soul') of the Righteous One and all those walking in Perfection'. In other descriptions, these confrontations between 'the Liar' or 'Spouter of Lying' and 'the Righteous Teacher', however, are usually verbal and not so violent or physical and this 'Lying Spouter' or 'Man of Jesting'/'Scoffing' is clearly depicted as an *ideological* adversary of 'the Teacher of Righteousness' within 'the Movement', not outside it, since he attends the scriptural exegesis sessions of 'the Priest'/'Righteous Teacher'/'*Zaddik*'.[16]

'The Wicked Priest' and the 'the Simple of Judah doing *Torah*'

The other opponent of the Righteous Teacher is easier to delineate. Though called 'the Wicked Priest', in the early days of Qumran research no distinction was made between him and 'the Spouter of Lying', but it is quite clear that 'the Righteous Teacher' has two separate opponents – one *inside* the Movement, 'the Man of Lying', and the other *outside* it, 'the Wicked Priest'. That the latter is also a 'High Priest' – in this case the Establishment 'High Priest' – is made clear as well from the appellation 'the Priest' attached to him in both Habakkuk and Psalm 37 *Pesher*s.[17] He is also referred to as 'the Priest' who 'did not circumcise the foreskin of his heart' and 'rebelled against and broke the Laws (of God)'.[18]

The use here of the allusion 'the Priest' is exactly the opposite of how it is used with regard to 'the Righteous Teacher'. The one is more or less the mirror reversal of the other – 'the Righteous Teacher', therefore, being 'the Opposition High Priest' of his time, which links up strongly with allusions associated with James and his role in the Jerusalem of his day, a position first delineated regarding him in the 1920s and 30s by Robert Eisler even before the discovery of the Dead Sea Scrolls (though he did have the Cairo Genizah Damascus Document to work with).[19]

The allusion to the Wicked Priest's being 'uncircumcised in heart' is also, ideologically speaking, of importance for our purposes. Though he may have been 'circumcised in the flesh', his 'heart' was 'impure' or 'polluted'. Furthermore, he was obviously not a 'Righteous Priest'[20] as 'the Righteous Teacher', to say nothing of the 'the Priest after the Order of Melchizedek', certainly appears to have been. As the Habakkuk *Pesher* puts this: 'he ('the Wicked Priest') acted' or 'worked in the Ways of Abominations in all unclean pollution'.[21]

It is also important *vis-à-vis* the esoteric allusions in Ezekiel that are the basis for the definition of who the true 'Sons of Zadok' were. These are the passages from Ezekiel 44:5–9 that also put the lie, as we have stressed, to Josephus' claims that the rejection of gifts and sacrifices on behalf of Gentiles in the Temple in the run-up to the War against Rome in the Sixties CE (the decade in which James died) was 'an *Innovation* with which our people were before unacquainted'. It is clear that this idea of banning foreigners and gifts and sacrifices from them or on their behalf from the Temple goes all the way back to these passages from Ezekiel 44:5–9. In fact, they make 'rejecting such gifts and sacrifices' a *requirement* for proper 'Temple service' and accuse those behaving in the opposite manner of 'breaking the Covenant', the very words the Habakkuk *Pesher* uses to describe the activities of 'the Wicked Priest' and those opposing 'the Righteous Teacher' in general.[22] With this in mind, there can be little doubt that this kind of allusion is meant to disqualify persons of the type of 'the Wicked Priest' from doing 'Temple service', despite any genealogical claims to the contrary they may have been making.

Earlier in the Habakkuk *Pesher*, these 'Covenant Breakers', 'Violent Ones', and 'Traitors to the New Covenant' were presented as 'walking with' or being allied to 'the Man of Lying'.[23] This 'breaking' language too was also part and parcel of the Letter of James – in particular, the recommendation at its beginning to be a 'Doer' (1:22–26, 2:13, and 4:11–17) or a 'Keeper' not a 'Breaker' (1:27 and 2:8–2:11) and condemning thereafter the one 'not bridling his Tongue' (1:26) or 'stumbling over one small point of the Law' (2:10). Such persons are 'Breakers' or 'Law-Breakers' as opposed to 'Doers' and 'Keepers' – familiar terms in James and used throughout the Damascus Document and the Habakkuk *Pesher*.[24]

It is in these passages that Ezekiel 44:7 explains what is meant by the 'pollution of the Temple' charge made in the 'Three Nets of *Belial*' section of CD IV.14–VI.2 directly following its exposition of Ezekiel 44:15: 'Because you have brought foreigners uncircumcised in heart and uncircumcised in flesh into my Temple to pollute My House..., you have broken My Covenant because of all your Abominations'. Even this word 'Abominations' will be directly applied to 'the Wicked Priest' and it will be these kinds of esotericisms from crucial Biblical passages that will show what the problem concerning him was. It will be for us to interpret such esotericisms as we proceed, but disqualifying 'the Wicked Priest' from 'service' at the Temple altar must certainly be seen as part of their thrust.

In the *Pesharim* too, we also find esoteric, yet meaningful, expressions such as 'the Simple of Judah doing *Torah*'. These are basically identical with 'the *Ebionim*' or 'the Poor' – both, for all intents and purposes, describing the rank and file of the Community (in other contexts, 'the *Rabbim*' or 'the Many').[25] Parallel to these are 'the Simple of Ephraim', urged in the Nahum *Pesher* 'to turn aside from the one who deceives' or 'lies to' them,[30] who have a parallel in the New Testament usage, 'these Little Ones' – a usage also possibly reflected in the quotation from Zechariah 13:7 encountered in Ms. B's version in CD XIX.7–9 of 'Messianic' events centering around the coming ('Second' or 'Third') 'Visitation'. In the New Testament, Jesus is pictured as using the expression in Matthew 18:5 and pars. in such a way that it is obviously meant to be a stand-in for those among the Gentiles to whom Paul's Gentile Mission is addressed – in the sense of being unsophisticated in Scriptural matters and, to a certain extent, not even aware of 'the *Torah*' (cf., for instance, how Paul uses the expression in Galatians 4:19).

When evaluating its use in the Nahum *Pesher* at Qumran one should bear in mind its relationship to another favorite New Testament allusion, 'Samaritans', who – *bona fide* or not – claimed descent (as they still do today) from those in the Northern Kingdom, most generally known as 'Ephraim'.[31] In the *Pesher*, the usage 'the Simple of Ephraim' was tied to another, 'Resident Aliens' (*Ger-Nilveh*), which for its part relates to the Hebrew 'joining' or 'Joiners' ('*nilvu*' or '*Nilvim*'). This expression conveys the sense of 'joining' or 'attaching oneself' to the Community in an associated or adjunct status of some kind as the 'God-Fearers' were seen to be doing to the Synagogues throughout the Mediterranean at this time.

For its part, this expression, 'fearing God', crops up in critical passages among the promises made towards the end of the exhortative section of Ms. B, Column XX.19–20, which includes the allusion to 'a Book of Remembrance being written out before Him for God-Fearers and those reckoning His Name' and which so much resemble Paul's and the Synoptics' 'Do' or 'Drink this in Remembrance of me'.[32] It too occurs throughout the New Testament corpus as, for instance, in Acts 10, where someone like the Roman Centurion 'Cornelius' is even described as 'a God-Fearer', 'Righteous', 'Pious', 'praying to God continually' – the kind of language normally associated with either 'the Essenes' or someone like James – and even as 'continually waiting for him'! But even more importantly, there are actually two further references in regard to his 'charitable works going up' (the very subject of the beginning of the Last Column of the Damascus Document and the references there to Leviticus 26:31 and Joel 2:13) and 'being remembered before God' (10:4 and 10:31), almost the very words just encountered in CD XX.19 of Ms. A as well. Moreover, this allusion to 'remembered before God' is almost word-for-word that of the description in the Pseudoclementine *Recognitions* of 'the two brothers' who were also 'remembered before God'; and, because of having visited the burial monument of whom ('which miraculously whitened of itself every year'), James and the rest of his Community of 'five thousand' were missed by 'the Enemy' Paul, who was pursuing them on his way to Damascus with letters from the High Priest![33] It is worth observing, once again, that it is to 'God-Fearers' such as these that Paul generally directs his message.

The 'doing *Torah*' language will not only be absolutely fundamental to the Habakkuk *Pesher*'s exposition of Habakkuk 2:4: 'the Righteous shall live by his Faith', but it also underlies the general usage in Hebrew that translates into English as 'works'. These allusions to 'Doer' and 'doing' are pregnant with meaning for the approach of James and actually appear several times in the New Testament Letter associated with his name. In James, as at Qumran, this emphasis on 'being a Doer' is ranged against the allusion to being a 'Breaker' or 'breaking the Law' (2:9–11), an ideology which also permeates *MMT*. Some have even gone so far as to see this allusion to 'Doers'/'*Osei ha-Torah* as the basis for the denotation in the Greek of Josephus and Philo's '*Essenoi*' or 'Essenes'.[34]

Other esotericisms found in the *Pesharim* important for solving the puzzle of the Scrolls are phrases like 'the City of Blood' in the Nahum *Pesher* or 'a worthless City built upon blood and an Assembly' or 'Church erected (or, as in Amos 9:11, 'raised') upon Lying' in the Habakkuk *Pesher*.[35] Not only can these be looked upon in terms of both Paul's 'architectural' and 'building' imagery in 1 Corinthians – particularly 1 Corinthians 3:6–17, where he actually does use the imagery of CD (and of Isaiah 60:21–61:4) of 'planting' and 'God causing to grow' and really does call himself 'the architect' or 'builder' – but, as we shall see, also his understanding of 'Communion' both with the 'body' and 'blood of Christ', found later in 1 Corinthians 10:14–17.

At least where it is found in the Nahum *Pesher*, this expression 'City of Blood' (Nahum 3:1) – as it is interpreted in the *Pesher*, 'the City of Ephraim, the Seekers after Smooth Things at the End of Days, who walk in Deceitfulness and Lying' – will have real meaning where the related phrase 'the Simple of Ephraim' tied to the idea of 'joining' is concerned.[36] It is possible to interpret it in terms of 'Pauline Christians' (Gentiles of course) or Resident Alien 'Joiners' in an associated status with the new 'Community of God', the attitudes of whom with regard to '*Torah*' have not yet been clarified or sufficiently consolidated. This is of course the other side of the coin of the expression 'the Simple of Judah doing *Torah*' – identified in the Habakkuk *Pesher* with 'the Poor'. These are the kind of esotericisms which abound in Qumran literature and have puzzled scholars for so long. Yet they are consistent and homogeneous and provide clues for finally unraveling the meaning of the documents in which they are found.

The Destruction of the Righteous Teacher by the Wicked Priest in the Habakkuk *Pesher*

The Habakkuk *Pesher* is one of the most important and best preserved documents found at Qumran. Its First-Century dating, like that of the Psalm 37 *Pesher* it so much resembles, is reinforced by a wealth of internal allusions within the document itself which make it impossible that the document could have come from any century earlier than the First, whatever external dating tool might be applied.

The most obvious and important of these internal allusions is the reference to 'the *Kittim*', the foreign, invading armies, 'who come to lay waste the earth' (obviously from the West, since they 'come from afar, from the Islands of the Sea, to *consume all the Peoples* like an insatiable eagle' – the 'eating' and Gentiles/Peoples allusions again), and are characterized as 'sacrificing to their standards and worshipping their weapons of war'.[37]

This allusion – which indicates habitual and not specific action – can apply to no time during the entire period we have been considering other than that of Rome – and this *Imperial Rome*, after the deification of the Emperors had taken hold and the Emperor's medallion busts were affixed to the standards. Josephus specifically describes one such sacrifice the Romans made facing the Eastern Gate after they had stormed the Temple in 70 CE.[38] But there were others they obviously would have made – a whole series of them as they made their bloody way down from Galilee, reducing fortress city after fortress city, all vividly described in Josephus.[39]

Josephus also describes the incident of Pilate trying to smuggle such Roman military standards – in this case probably bearing the image of Tiberius Caesar (14–37 CE) – into Jerusalem and the Temple *by night* causing a frantic reaction the next day. This incident is clearly connected with the attempt by Gaius Caligula to have his own portrait bust set up in the Temple five or six years later in 40–41 CE.

Aside from the references to 'the *Ebionim*' or 'the Poor', the *Pesher* also alludes to 'the Riches and booty' of 'the Last Priests of Jerusalem', Jerusalem's fall, and how these 'Priests' (plural not singular – ergo, the Herodian High-Priestly clans not the singular hereditary High Priest of the Maccabean Period) enriched themselves and literally 'profiteered from' the elicit 'plunder of the Peoples'.[40] Again, in our view, these last are 'Violent Gentiles' or, more specifically, Herodians viewed as Gentiles by groups as 'Pious' as the Qumran sectaries. The ambiance for this, as we have shown, is amply developed in Book Twenty of Josephus' *Antiquities*, where he twice notes how the 'Rich' High Priests sent their servants and other thugs to the threshing floors to raid the tithes, so that 'the Poor' among the lower priests died of want.[41] He also delineates in the *War* how these Herodian High Priests accepted gifts and sacrifices in the Temple on behalf of Romans and other foreigners, including both the Emperor and Herodians, which led directly to the War against Rome and was considered 'pollution of the Temple' by their opponents.[42]

But the most obvious dating tool is the citation and exegesis of Habakkuk 2:4, the climax of the *Pesher* – 'the Righteous shall live by his faith' – the scriptural passage forming the basis of a good deal of Paul's scriptural exegesis, to say nothing of James'. In addition to this, there is also, as in James 5:7–11, the counseling of 'patience' tied to the exegesis of Habakkuk 2:3: 'if it tarries, wait for it', which directly precedes this. Both of these passages are interpreted eschatologically, that is in terms of the 'End Time'. In fact, the interpretation of Habakkuk 2:3 is specifically related to the *delay* of this 'End' and resembles nothing so much as the scriptural warrant for what goes in Christianity even today under the heading of 'the Delay of the *Parousia* – the delay of the second coming of Christ and the final eschatological events associated with this.

As the *Pesher* puts this: 'The Last Era (or 'Last End') will be extended and exceed all that the Prophets (primarily Daniel) have foretold, since the Mysteries of God are astounding.' The exposition – just as with that of Habakkuk 2:4 which follows – then goes on to apply this, like James 1:22–24, to 'the Doers of the *Torah*'.[43] Presumably this exegesis repudiates a more 'Lying' one on the same materials being circulated by 'the Man of Lying' or 'Lying Spouter'. These are the kinds of characteristics that make anything other than a First Century ambiance for these arguments hard to imagine.

This document, found in a single exemplar only, would appear to be a record of the scriptural exegesis sessions of the Righteous Teacher who is specifically referred to as being able to give authorative scriptural exegeses and to whom 'God made known all the Mysteries of the words of His Servants the Prophets'.[44] Elsewhere, he is said to be able 'to interpret' these words. In this case, if 'the Righteous Teacher' is not James – since he is clearly referred to in the exegesis as being destroyed along with several members of his Council – then we have to do with someone like James' successor according to early Church tradition, Simeon bar Cleophas who, not unlike the individual designated as 'Elchasai', certainly functioned somewhere in the Judean wilderness or across Jordan in the Pella or Damascus region following the death of James (there being no real Jerusalem left at this point to function in).

As the *Pesher* puts it in interpretation of Habakkuk 2:2 ('write down the vision and make it plain on tablets'): 'And God told Habakkuk to write down what was coming in the Last Generation, but He did not reveal to him (the Time of) the Completion of the Era.' One should compare this with words attributed to Jesus in Matthew 5:18 and 24:34: 'until all these things shall be accomplished' or 'completed'. Earlier, the same *Pesher* had identified 'the Traitors together with the Man of Lying' as 'not believing what the Righteous Teacher expounded from the mouth of God' (n.b., the emphasis here and in the rest of the column on 'believing').[45]

Identifying these 'Traitors' as not only betraying 'the New Covenant' and 'the Last Days' but also as 'Violent Ones and Covenant-Breakers' (note the parallel here with James 2:9's 'Law-Breakers'), these together with 'the Liar did not believe all that they heard was going to happen in the Last Generation from the mouth of the Priest in whose heart God put the intelligence to expound all the words of His Servants the Prophets, through whom God foretold all that was going to happen to His People'.[46] These passages are only a little inverted from the kind of thing one encounters in Early Christian sources about James, namely that 'the Prophets declare concerning him' – meaning not necessarily that he would do the expounding but that his name was to be found by searching Scripture where the events of his life were prefigured, particularly in these 'Prophets'. Again, not only do these kinds of allusions link the *Pesher* very closely to the scriptural ambiance and eschatological expectation of Early Christianity, but we even have in it something akin to Paul's 'fleshy tablets of the heart' allusion in 2 Corinthians 3:3, should one choose to regard it.

The *Pesher* focuses on several important events. These transpire against a backdrop of the coming of foreign armies into the country, 'the *Kittim*'.[47] While these are extremely violent – 'swift and terrible in war causing many to perish' and 'plundering the cities of the Earth', 'parceling out their yoke and their taxes (that is, 'tax-farming'), eating all the Peoples year-by-year, giving many countries over to the sword' – they are not the *Pesher*'s principal concern, though the exegete is very distressed by their ferocity and pitilessness. It would seem that we have here a direct allusion to the Romans appointing 'Kings of the Peoples' such as the Herodians to rule in the East and 'profiteer' from their tax-collecting and it is difficult to conceive of this description applying to any ancient people other than the Romans.

Aside from 'not believing in the Laws of God', it is specifically noted that 'they come from afar', 'from the islands of the sea', 'trampling the Earth with their horses and pack animals', 'consuming all the Peoples like an eagle that is never satisfied'.[48] The last is normally taken to be an allusion to the Roman Eagle. Furthermore, 'they overthrow the Fortresses of the Peoples, laughing at them in derision', an allusion that would confirm our earlier identification of 'the Peoples' as the Herodians and, more than likely, refers to 'the Fortresses' which they either built or enlarged such as Masada, Machaeros, Hyrcania, and Cypros.[49]

As the *Pesher* continues, they 'encircle' cities, and 'destroy them because of the iniquity of their inhabitants'. One should not overlook that the genre of this accusation is one familiar to the New Testament and in early Church literature. Plus, 'they gather their Riches together with all their booty like the fish of the sea' – this, not insignificantly, in exposition of an allusion to 'fishermen' and their 'nets' again in the underlying language of Habakkuk 1:14–15 and tied to the 'tax-collecting' motifs above. Nor do they pity 'youths', 'old men, women, children', not even 'the fruit of the womb'.[50] It should be clear that, aside from the accompanying allusion to 'sacrificing to their standards and worshipping their weapons of war', these passages can hardly be describing a Dynasty or a war machine as ineffectual as the Seleucids and can only relate to the Romans – any and all external dating parameters to the contrary notwithstanding.

But despite the horror of this heart-wrenching picture, it only forms the backdrop and is secondary to the *Pesher*'s two other really main concerns, between which it swings its attention back and forth despite this background picture of mayhem and slaughter – maybe even because of it. The first is the ideological conflict between 'the Man of Lying' and 'the Righteous Teacher'. Ultimately the focus on these two overwhelms all other concerns including the coming of the rapacious and all-powerful *Kittim*, to whom the *Pesher* also refers as 'the Additional ones of the Peoples'. Since, in our opinion, the Herodians are 'the Peoples', the Romans are 'the Additional Ones of the Peoples'.[51]

The second concern is the conflict between the Righteous Teacher, clearly identified as 'the Opposition High Priest' by the literature at Qumran, and the Wicked Priest, clearly meant to signify the reigning 'Establishment' High Priest of the day. Moreover, the Wicked Priest ends up destroying the Righteous Teacher and being in turn 'destroyed' himself. These are the exact words of the *Pesher* and under what appear to be very gruesome circumstances indeed at the hands of a group called 'the Violent Ones' or, as the Psalm 37 *Pesher* would put this, 'the Violent Ones of the Gentiles'.[52] In the background to these two conflicts and the warp and woof, as it were, of the *Pesher* is the constant antagonism to foreigners, 'robbing the Poor' (in the Damascus Document, 'robbing the Meek of His People'), and the predatory, 'profiteering', and conspiratorial activities of the Wicked Priest and his colleagues (called, as already remarked, 'the Last Priests of Jerusalem') with what appear to be Herodians. This last is true if 'Peoples' can be identified with Herodians. We think they can.

In the *Pesher*, the 'Wicked Priest' is clearly responsible for removing or 'destroying' his adversary 'the Righteous Teacher', 'the Priest', i.e., the Opposition High Priest. For the *Pesher*, the Wicked Priest 'swallows' or 'consumes' the Righteous Teacher (the '*Ba-La'a*' language again – this in the sense of 'consumes' or 'destroys', a variation on the 'eating' theme encountered above). The latter, in turn, is always identified with a reference to '*Zaddik*' or 'Righteous One' in the underlying Biblical text. In the penultimate column, it is specifically stated that, just 'as he plotted to destroy the Poor', so would 'he be paid the reward he paid the Poor' and 'God would condemn him to destruction'. The verb at this point, notwithstanding the tantalizing allusion to 'swallow'/'consume' preceding it, is quite literally 'destroying the Poor'. Moreover, because of this, he is 'condemned to destruction' himself.[53]

The Wicked Priest in the Psalm 37 *Pesher*

This presentation is reinforced in the *Pesher* on Psalm 37 which is also – in the jargon of the field – considered 'a late document'. Not only is the Psalm 37 *Pesher* clearly from the last days of the Community, but in many of its concerns it overlaps the vocabulary and subject matter of the Habakkuk *Pesher*. A '*Zaddik*' text like the Habakkuk *Pesher*, the allusion to '*Zaddik*' and '*Zaddikim*' permeates the underlying Biblical material. This is exploited in the exposition to produce a *Pesher* about the Wicked Priest 'overwhelming' or 'destroying' the Righteous Teacher.

The first incidence of this is the variation using 'the Meek' and 'the Poor' – interchangeable with 'the Righteous' throughout the *Pesher* – which reads: 'The Wicked have drawn the sword ... to cast down the Meek and the Poor' (37:14). This was preceded by: 'The Wicked plots against the Righteous and gnashes upon him with his teeth' (37:12). The first of these and then what is more or less yet a third variation in the Psalm – 'the Wicked watches out for the Righteous and seeks to put him to death' (37:32) – are both subjected to exegesis. The *Pesher*, which is repeated twice with slight variations, basically describes how the Wicked Priest 'laid hands upon' the Righteous Teacher/'the Priest and the Men of his Council ... to put him to death', but would himself ultimately 'be delivered over to the hand of the Violent of the Gentiles for Judgement'.[54] This is the same kind of 'Judgment' we shall encounter in the Habakkuk Commentary – again emphasizing the basic circularity of these documents where *dramatis personae* and subject matter is concerned.

Not only do we have here the theme of 'being delivered up', but the *Pesher* does not particularly follow 'the Meek' part of the "*Ani*'/'*Ebion*' dichotomy. Rather it twice refers to 'the Assembly' or 'Church of the Poor' (*Ebionim*), whom it calls 'the Leaders and Pride of the flock'. Here too, we have usages encountered in the Damascus Document.[55] These 'will possess the High Mountain of Israel and His Holy Place', while 'the Violent Ones of the Peoples and the Wicked of Israel will be cut off and blotted out forever'. Again one should note how the 'cutting off' language is used here.[56]

The same thing happens at the end of the Habakkuk *Pesher*, particularly where the destruction of the Righteous Teacher and his followers, 'the Poor' and 'the Council of the Community', are being described. Though the expression "*Ani*' does occur in Habakkuk 3:14 as 'consuming the Meek', it is not used in the *Pesher* which, in any event, breaks off at 2:20. Rather the terminology 'the Poor' or '*Ebionim*' is purposefully introduced into the exegesis of Habakkuk 2:17 in the penultimate column (1QpHab XII.3–5) about 'Lebanon', 'the dumb beasts', and 'the violence done to the Land', though it nowhere occurs in the underlying text. In the writer's view, this is deliberate, because the commentator knows that he is, in fact, dealing with a Community already known as 'the Poor' or 'the Ebionites' and, as it were, the followers *par excellence* of James.[57]

In the Psalm 37 *Pesher*, too, the commentary on the extremely interesting allusion to 'the Wicked plotting against the Righteous' (37:12) is missing – presumably because of the fragmentary state of the text – but its main lines can be detected. In any event, this lacuna is made good in the Habakkuk *Pesher*, where Psalm 37's allusion to 'conspiring' or 'plotting' (*zamam*) is now, once again, seemingly deliberately introduced into the commentary on Habakkuk 2:16–17's 'the Cup of the Lord's right hand coming around to you', 'the violence of Lebanon', and 'the destruction of the dumb beasts'. Here it is worthwhile to note in passing the allusion to 'the Cup of the Lord', words already encountered in Paul's presentation of 'the Lord Jesus" words at 'the Last Supper' in 1 Corinthians 11:27–29 (themselves not without a tinge of vengefulness) and imbedded in the scenario of the first post-resurrection appearance of Jesus to James in Jerome's 'Gospel of the Hebrews'.[58]

The words used here are that 'he (the Wicked Priest) plotted to destroy the Poor'. This basically reprises the language of Psalm 37:12–14, though neither 'conspiring' nor 'the Poor' appear at this point in the underlying Biblical text of Habakkuk 2:17 exploited to produce the *Pesher*. Nevertheless, 'destruction' does, since 'the dumb beasts' – interpreted to mean 'the Simple of Judah doing *Torah*' – are the ones 'he is conspiring to destroy'.

This exposition precedes the last several allusions to 'the Day of Judgment' being called down upon 'idol-worshipping' 'Gentiles, serving stone and wood', and what would appear to be the same Jewish backsliders – in the Psalm 37 *Pesher* expressed as 'the Evil Ones among His own People'.[59] Again, this is what we meant by saying the documents are homogeneous and the same terms move from document to document, *Pesher* to *Pesher* – the same allusions – in fact, overlapping and complementing one another.

In this *Pesher* on Habakkuk 2:16–17, Jerusalem is denoted as 'the City', 'where the Wicked Priest committed works of Abominations, polluting the Temple of God', more excellent examples of our constantly recurring vocabulary and immediately recognizable as the same accusation in the Damascus Document aimed at the Jerusalem Establishment and the third of the 'Three Nets of *Belial*'. Nor is this to say anything about the allusion to 'Abominations' in Ezekiel 4:6–7, the basis of these, about 'breaking (the) Covenant' by 'bringing foreigners, uncircumcised in heart and uncircumcised in flesh into (the) Temple to pollute it'. In these accusations, it was not observing proper 'separation but sleeping with women in their periods' or, as we have explained, approaching or associating with people who did – namely, Herodians and other foreigners. One good example of this association was accepting appointment to the High Priesthood from them, to say nothing of the ever-recurring theme of accepting their polluted gifts and sacrifices in the Temple.

In this exposition of the Habakkuk *Pesher* too, 'the Cities of Judah' are identified as the locale 'where (the Wicked Priest) robbed the Riches (or 'the sustenance') of the Poor'. We have already shown the connection of this notice and its complements in the Damascus Document to the two notices in Josephus' *Antiquities*, one just preceding and the other just following the death of James – and reflected in the Talmud too – about how the High Priests sent their violent associates to the threshing floors to rob the 'Poorer' priests of their sustenance so they died of want.[60]

The word used here to describe what the Wicked Priest did, harking back to 'the destruction of the dumb beasts' (that is, 'the Simple of Judah doing *Torah*') and, 'the violence done to Lebanon' ('Lebanon' interpreted in the commentary, because of the root-meaning of the underlying syllable '*lavan*' or 'whiteness', to mean 'the Council of the Community' – this harking back to the 'white linen' its members presumably wore and also possibly the symbolism in 1QS VIII.5–11 and IX.3–6 of 'the Community Council' as 'Temple') is not simply 'swallowed' or 'consumed', but it actually is 'destroyed'. It is for this God would 'pay him the reward he paid the Poor' of the Psalm 37 *Pesher* and Isaiah 3:10–11 and 'the Cup of the Wrath of God would swallow him', meaning 'God would condemn him to destruction' as well.

This, in fact, parallels the usage of how the Wicked Priest, 'who did not circumcise the foreskin of his heart', 'swallowed' the Righteous Teacher 'with' or 'at his House of Exile', which we will interpret in terms of the Sanhedrin Trial of James.[61] Here 'swallowing' really does mean 'destroy'. We referred to this 'swallowing', too, in our discussion of the constant reiteration of James 'falling' or 'being cast down' in all early Church accounts in Greek of James' destruction. Moreover, we also showed how the Hebrew of this usage was connected with 'Devilishness'/'*Belial*'/or 'Balaam', and the same regarding its homophone in Greek, '*ballo*' or 'cast down' with '*Diabolos*'.

4QpNah,iii condemning Pharisees as '*misleading Smoothies*'.

Ananus ben Ananus

Josephus tells us that the High Priest, Ananus ben Ananus, was appointed by Agrippa II and convened the Sanhedrin that destroyed James. Ananus' brother Jonathan had been assassinated in the mid-Fifties by those whom Josephus had just started to call '*Sicarii*' – and this probably because of this assassination – one of the main incidents setting in motion the succession of occurrences that ended up in James' death and the Uprising against Rome. Ananus seems to have been sent to Rome at the end of the previous decade in the Roman Governor Cumanus' time (48–52 CE), along with Helcias the Temple Treasurer and possibly Jonathan his brother, after the beating of the Emperor's Servant Stephen and the Messianic disturbances between Samaritans and Jews in 49 CE which resulted in the crucifixions outside Lydda.[62]

In Rome, Ananus was kept as a hostage because Nero and his wife Poppea seemed to be looking for bribes, that is, until Agrippa II intervened to free him – an altogether more convincing story than the one Acts 24:27 presents regarding the relations of Felix and Paul. Here, the close relationship developed between Ananus and Agrippa II that seems ultimately to have resulted in the conspiracy to remove James – this probably had its roots in 'the Temple Wall Affair' which was erected to block Agrippa II's view of the sacrifices in the Temple.

Josephus gives further details that explain, in the words of the Habakkuk *Pesher*, how he could have been 'called by the name of Truth at the beginning of his Office, but when he ruled in Israel, his heart became puffed up and he forsook God and betrayed the Laws for the sake of Riches'.[63] Not only is this fairly vivid, but it is directly followed by the description of how he 'stole Riches and collected the Riches of the Men of Violence, who rebelled against God. And he took the Riches of the Peoples, thereby further heaping upon himself guilty sinfulness.'[64] 'Riches', of course, was the second of the Damascus Document's 'Three Nets of *Belial*' and widely condemned both in the Letter of James and elsewhere at Qumran, so once again we have consistency here.

Consensus Qumran scholarship attempts to see in this description one or another of the Maccabean High Priests (mostly Alexander Jannaeus), and 'the Righteous Teacher', therefore, some unknown individual in the First Century BCE opposed to Alexander. But there is no indication that any Maccabean ever took anyone else's 'Riches' and 'polluted the Temple' with them, nor 'profiteered' in any manner from the predatory activities of 'Violent' persons such as the Herodians and their accomplices, nor were they ever pictured as being particularly 'Rich', though this accusation can be used against any Ruling Class at any time or place. On the other hand, in these passages having to do with Paul and James, we have a clear ambiance of one side opposing Gentile gifts in the Temple (including those by Herodians) and the other side accepting them.

For his part, Ananus 'ruled Israel' on two separate occasions: the first when he destroyed James in 62 CE, and the second during the early stages of the Uprising between 66–68 CE before the final siege of Jerusalem began. Before he and his associates were exterminated by the 'Violent' Idumaeans, whom 'the Zealots' called in when the Revolt moved into what could be referred to as its more 'Jacobin' phase, he did 'rule' in Israel in virtually an absolute manner. Having said this, all High Priests can be said to have 'ruled Israel' and this is the actual thrust of Paul's allusion, quoted in Acts 23:5, to Ananus' alter ego, 'Ananias'.

As we have been attempting to point out, despite this ambiguous reference to 'ruling in Israel', almost all the internal allusions in these very important *Pesharim* and related documents such as CD gainsay this identification on the part of 'Consensus' Scholars of 'the Wicked Priest' with one or another of the Maccabeans. This is particularly true when one takes into consideration the militant and uncompromising character of his antagonist, 'the Righteous Teacher', which rather accords with the ethos of the Maccabeans, particularly Judas Maccabee – 'Judas the Hammerer' as he was surnamed – and Alexander Jannaeus, his grand nephew, not to mention his great grand nephew, Aristobulus II, who came into conflict with his brother Hyrcanus II.

The latter, it will be recalled, was supported by the newly-emerging Pharisee Party, the accommodators *par excellence*, whose willingness to bow to Roman hegemony finally brought the Romans into the country. Ananus' own father had held the High Priesthood from 10–18 CE, a murky period not covered to any extent in Josephus. This is the period in which, according to the allegedly 'spurious Acts' being circulated in Pontius Pilate's name – therefore called the *Acti Pilati* – and mentioned by Eusebius, the *real* Jesus may have died, that is, if we can speak in any really historical way about this death and the events surrounding it.[65] Ananus the Elder is pictured in John's version of events as participating in the interim examination of Jesus, before he was turned over to Pilate for more secular examination. This episode mainly focuses on how Peter denied he was Jesus' 'Disciple' three times (John 18:13–24). This is paralleled in the Synoptics by an improbable midnight meeting, called on Passover evening by Caiaphas at 'the High Priest's House' (Luke 22:54 and pars.) and consisting of High Priests, Elders, and Sanhedrin. Caiaphas was Ananus' son-in-law and, therefore, the brother-in-law of James' judicial executioner Ananus ben Ananus.

The Psalm 37 *Pesher*'s exegesis of the passage about 'the Wicked casting down the Meek and the Poor' makes it clear that somehow 'the Wicked of Ephraim and Manasseh' were involved in the destruction of 'the Priest and the Men of his Council'.[66] As almost all commentators agree that this is an esoteric allusion of some kind to what most now call 'Pharisees and Sadducees', it would be absurd in such a context to put this back into either the First or Second Century BCE. At that time the Sadducees would mainly have been a pro-Maccabean Party. Nor would it be a simple matter to identify any 'Violent Gentiles' at that time to take vengeance on 'the Wicked Priest' for what he did to 'the Righteous Teacher' which is the gist, in fact, of the *Pesher*. These are the problems that are rarely, if ever, addressed when evaluating Establishment theories of Qumran origins.

'The Violent Ones of the Gentiles'

This matter of the vengeance taken by 'the Violent Ones of the Gentiles' for what had been done to the Righteous Teacher is treated in two separate expositions in the Psalm 37 *Pesher*. The second of these at the end of the *Pesher* uses almost the exact language of the Habakkuk *Pesher* – to say nothing of Isaiah 3:10–11 above, namely 'God will pay him ('the Wicked Priest') his reward by delivering him into the hand of the Violent Ones of the Gentiles'. These 'execute Judgment upon him', a Judgment which is then described as 'the Judgment on Evil'.[67] In the parallel material in the Habakkuk *Pesher* about the admonishment of the Wicked Priest, these 'Judgments' reappear as 'the Judgments on Evil', which they (identity unspecified) inflicted upon 'the flesh of his corpse'.[68]

The Psalm 37 *Pesher* is replete with the kind of language we have been following and links up perfectly with allusions in the Habakkuk *Pesher* and the Damascus Document again confirming the interrelatedness of these documents. Its subject is God's 'Righteousness which will be revealed like Light and (His) Judgment like midday' (37:6). The interpretation of this and analogous phrases is applied to 'the Assembly' or 'Church of the Poor' (*Ebionim*). It, like the Messianic 'Root of Planting out of Aaron and Israel' in the Damascus Document, 'will inherit the Land' and 'prosper on its good things', this last in direct interpretation of an underlying reference to "*Anayyim*'/'Meek' in 37:11, again deliberately transmuted in the *Pesher* (as in the Habakkuk *Pesher*) into 'the Assembly of the Poor' (*Ebionim*).

Also called 'the Assembly of His Elect', as in the Damascus Document, they are again characterized as 'the Penitents of the wilderness who will live for a thousand generations'.[69] Here not only does the usage 'of the wilderness' take the place of the 'of Israel' in CD IV.2, VI.5, and VIII.16/XIX.29, but the phrase '*be-Yeshu'a*' – seemingly 'in Salvation' ('Jesus') – is added and it is stated – in what appears to be yet another variation of the 'Primal Adam' ideology – that 'all the inheritance of (instead of 'all the Glory of') Adam will be theirs'. As in the Habakkuk *Pesher* too, 'God will save them – the 'saving' here really being eschatological 'saving' in the sense of 'Salvation' – and deliver them from the hand of the Evil Ones' (this both quoting and interpreting Psalm 37:40). Because they 'waited on' Him and 'kept His Way', they would both 'be exalted' and – using the words of both Psalm 37:34 and CD I.7–8 – 'inherit the Land' and 'see the destruction of' the same 'Evil Ones'.[70] Here the *Pesher* again applies this to 'the Assembly' or 'Church of the Poor' who will not only 'see the Judgment on Evil' but, 'with His Chosen Ones' or 'Elect, rejoice in the True Inheritance' – a more eschatological promise is hard to imagine.

As in the Habakkuk *Pesher*, 'the Priest' (meaning 'the Opposition High Priest') is specifically identified with 'the Teacher of Righteousness' and, paralleling usages in the Damascus Document and *Florilegium* about 'the Star who came to Damascus' and 'the Interpreter of the *Torah*', it is he whom 'God chose to *stand* before Him' (the 'Standing One' ideology again). Contrary to 'the Spouter of Lying' or Paul himself in 1 Corinthians 3:9–17, he has been 'prepared' or 'established' by God 'to *build the Assembly* of His Chosen Ones for Him' – in CD IV.3–4, the same 'Chosen Ones' or 'Elect' who are 'the Sons of Zadok'; here in the Psalm 37 *Pesher*, they are 'the Assembly' or 'Church of the Poor'. These will 'be saved from all the Nets of *Belial*'.[71]

Here, not only do we hear about how 'the Wicked plotted against the Righteous gnashing his teeth at him' (Psalm 37:12), but a new category of individual is evoked, 'the Violent Ones of the Covenant in the House of Judah' – referred to also, as the text proceeds – as 'the Evil Men of Israel'. These, too, are 'cursed by Him and will be cut off' (37:23) – again our 'cutting off' language used throughout the *Pesher*, CD, and by Paul in Galatians 5:12.[72]

This allusion to 'gnashing of teeth' is a familiar one in the parables attributed to Jesus in the Gospels. Acts 7:54, however, uses it to describe how the Jewish mob behaved towards Stephen – they 'gnashed their teeth at him' – after Stephen accused them of 'being uncircumcised in heart and ears', 'always resisting the Holy Spirit', 'persecuting the Prophets' and being 'the Traitors and murderers of the Just One' right before his vision of 'the Son of Man standing at the right hand of God' (7:50–56). When one realizes that 'Stephen' is a stand-in for James, one appreciates the significance of finding this important allusion about 'gnashing his teeth' at this point in the Psalm 37 *Pesher* where 'plots against the Righteous One' are being described.

Again, just as in the Nahum *Pesher* previously, 'the Man of Lying', right from the beginning of the Psalm 37 *Pesher*, is described as 'leading Many astray with deceitful words, for they have chosen *Emptiness* and did not listen to the Interpreter of Knowledge'.[73] Moreover, the *Pesher* also refers to the period of 'forty years' – alluded to in the Damascus Document as the 'approximate time' that would pass from 'the gathering of the Unique Guide ('*Yoreh ha-Yahid*', as opposed to '*Moreh ha-Yahad*') to the Completion of the Time of the Men-of-War, who walked with the Man of Lying' – 'to the Completion of (the Time of) all Evil'. In fact, the very same word 'completed' is used regarding this eventuality in both documents.[74] Again, just as in CD XX.13–17, during this period 'the Wrath of God would be kindled against Israel' and 'there will be no King, no Prince, no Judge, no one to rebuke with Righteousness' (Hosea 3:4); here in the Psalm 37 *Pesher*, at the end of this Time, 'there would not be found on Earth a single Evil Man' – to be sure, a slight exaggeration – and 'the Man of Lying' and his confederates would be 'cursed', 'cut off', and 'exterminated' (37:34).

This allusion to 'approximately forty years' is clearly imprecise, 'forty' being the usual number in the Bible used to indicate a fairly long, if indeterminate period of time, and, in this instance, 'not a single Evil Man to be found on Earth' clearly being a little over-optimistic as well. Furthermore, 'the Man of Lying' has either not yet died or the author(s) have no idea of his exact fate, nor of those 'Rebels who did not turn aside from the Way of Traitors',[75] who are his confederates. If these have anything in common with either the New Testament's Paul or Josephus' 'Saulos' and their other colleagues, this completely accords with what one would expect, since after one or the other of these went off to Rome to appeal to Caesar or the like, the writers of documents of this kind would have had little or no idea of the actual fate of these sorts of individuals, only that immediately after the death of James ('the gathering of the Unique Teacher'?), they were still alive.

For the *Pesher*, 'the Violent Ones of the Covenant who are in the House of Judah' (meaning again, 'Jews') 'plotted to destroy the Doers of the *Torah* who were in the Council of the Community (these are the same 'House of Judah' and 'Doers of the *Torah*' found in the Habakkuk *Pesher*'s decisive interpretation of Habakkuk 2:4), but God will not deliver them into their hand'.[76] Moreover it is also the same 'plotting' as that of 'the Wicked Priest' in the Habakkuk *Pesher* who 'plotted to destroy the Poor'. Here in the Psalm 37 *Pesher*, it is almost immediately followed by the description of how 'the Evil Ones of Ephraim and Manasseh – also referred to in the Nahum *Pesher* and normally thought of in this context as analogues of 'the Scribes and Pharisees' or 'the Pharisees and Sadducees' of the Gospels – who sought to lay hands on the Priest and the Men of his Council in the time of trial that came upon them' (this is the same 'period of testing' that was referred to earlier in the same column regarding 'the Congregation' or 'Church of the Poor' who were ultimately going to be 'saved from all the snares of *Belial*').[77]

'Afterwards (that is, after his destruction of the Righteous Teacher and the Men of his Council) they ('the Wicked of Ephraim and Manasseh', including 'the Wicked Priest') will be delivered into the hand of the Violent Ones of the Gentiles for Judgment ('the '*Arizei-Go'im*')'. Despite an earlier reference to 'God redeeming them from their hand' and the later one in exposition of Ps. 37:33–34 – after 'the Wicked Priest laid hands on the Righteous Teacher', attempting to or actually 'putting him to death' (the text is fragmentary here and the meaning imprecise) – about God 'not abandoning him, nor permitting him to be condemned at His Judgment' and 'being exalted' and 'rejoicing in inheriting Truth' and 'being saved', one should appreciate that 'the Righteous Teacher' and 'the Men of his Council' were for the most part destroyed and this, like the previous 'God will not deliver them into their hands', and there 'not remaining upon the Earth a single Wicked Man', simply represents a pious hope or an expression of certitude in their ultimate 'Salvation'.[78]

Regarding 'the Men of his Council', it should be appreciated as well that in Josephus, James is executed with several others.[79] We should keep a firm hold on these allusions to 'the Violent Ones', a usage appearing in several Gospel allusions to the coming of John the Baptist – 'from whose days until now, the Kingdom of Heaven is taken by Violence and Violent Ones seize it by force' (Matt. 11:12/Luke 16:16). The problem, however, is that the period between the time when Jesus supposedly says these things and John's coming is, at least superficially, quite negligible. Still, the allusion is illustrative.

It is also paralleled in the Habakkuk *Pesher*. There, 'the Violent Ones' are simply 'the '*Arizim*' – no '*Go'im*' or 'Gentiles' attached – nor, for that matter, any 'House of Judah' or 'the Evil Ones of Israel'. Rather, these 'Violent Ones' together with 'the Man of Lying' are identified with 'the Covenant Breakers' and 'the Traitors to the Laws of God and the New Covenant' (this last, a reconstruction) and 'to the Last Days'.[80] As already suggested, all seemingly participate in the Scriptural exegesis sessions of 'the Priest'/'the Righteous Teacher', as they are specifically described as 'not believing what they heard' from his 'mouth' concerning 'all that was going to happen to the Last Generation'.[81] Clearly, therefore, some of these, like 'the Violent Ones of the Covenant in the House of Judah' or 'the Evil Ones of Israel' are not simply external adversaries, but also have to be seen as internal ones too.

Later in the commentary, these same *'Arizim'* seem to be referred to as 'the Men of Violence' *(Hamas)*, but the context would appear to be the same – that of the Wicked Priest, 'whose heart became puffed up' and who 'stole and collected the Riches of the Men of Violence, who rebelled against God, and took the Riches of the Peoples' ('Peoples', in our view, again denoting Herodians – what 'the Wicked Priest' was doing here, as we shall see below, was illegally 'gathering' and 'collecting the Riches' which they 'stole' and depositing them in the Temple, thereby 'polluting it').[82]

As we saw above, these would also appear to be described in another particularly critical juncture of the Damascus Document, as 'the Men-of-War who walked with the Man of Lying' after the seeming death of the 'Unique' or 'Righteous Teacher'. Here 'Men of War' seems to better encapsulate the sense of the term than *'Anshei-Hamas'*, but both will do. In the Habakkuk *Pesher*, as we just saw, following the exposition of how 'the *Torah*-doing Jews' were to 'be saved from the House of Judgment', these 'Men of Violence' are described as 'rebelling against God' and the 'puffed-up' 'Wicked Priest' as 'deserting God and betraying the Laws for the sake of Riches'. At the same time, 'the Last Priests of Jerusalem' – identical in our view with 'Chief Priests' in the New Testament – are described as 'gathering Riches and profiteering from the spoils of the Peoples'.[83]

Herodian 'Men-of-War', Costobarus, and the 'Idumaean' Connection

Though these are complex allusions, if one is careful about them and their translation, their sense does emerge. It is our position that we must see these allusions to either 'Violent Ones', 'Men of Violence', or 'Men of War' on both sides of the political and religious spectrum as either pro- or anti-Revolutionary Herodians or other people with military training. Individuals of this kind certainly existed in the context of the events we are speaking about in the First Century – people like Niger of Perea, Philip the son of Jacimus, and Silas – preceding him as the Head of Agrippa I's Army – all described in Josephus. Nor is this to mention warriors like those in Queen Helen of Adiabene's family, namely, Izates, Monobazus, Kenedaeus and others – for the purist, ostensibly foreigners, but still part and parcel of the Revolutionary Struggle.

Even Paul would originally seem to have been an individual of this kind. His Herodian namesake 'Saulos', a relative of King Agrippa, is portrayed in just such a 'Violent' manner, creating mayhem after the stoning of James (or 'Stephen' as the case may be). So are the 'Violent' henchmen of the High Priests, who are depicted in several notices in this context here in the *Antiquities* – but also in the Talmud – as 'stealing the sustenance of the Poor'. They too are not really differentiable from this sort of person. As for 'Saulos', Josephus describes him, together with his two violent Herodian relatives Antipas and Costobarus, as 'getting together a multitude of wicked wretches … finding favor because of their kinship to Agrippa, but using Violence with the People and very ready to plunder those weaker than themselves'. One should note here the vocabulary parallels with Qumran, in particular the allusion to 'using Violence with the People', but also 'plundering', 'Wickedness' and, even possibly, 'the Many' denoting the rank and file of the Community. It is at this point Josephus laconically notes, 'and from that moment, it principally came to pass that our city suffered greatly – all things growing from bad to worse'.[84]

We have already shown that Paul, Agrippa II, and Bernice, his fornicating sister – with whom Agrippa II also possibly had an illicit connection – were acquainted, and all had connections going high up in Nero's household. So did Josephus' 'Saulos'. In Josephus' last notice about him, he describes him as going to Corinth to personally brief Nero about the disastrous situation in Palestine. Interestingly enough, both this 'Saulos' and Paul disappear from the scene at approximately the same time or, at most, within a year or two of each other, and both seemingly after appeals to Nero.

We have already noted the stoning of Stephen in the Forties as a stand-in for the stoning of James in the Sixties and how both the former in Acts and the latter in Josephus are followed by the account of the violent and predatory activities of someone named 'Saulos' – in both instances undertaken because of high-level influence. These are the kinds of connections that move beyond coincidence. The mention of 'Antipas' and 'Costobarus' always in connection with Saulos may have something to do with either his or their genealogical origins, Costobarus being the real 'Idumaean' in Herodian genealogies.

This Costobarus had originally been married to the first Herod's sister – the first (or second) 'Salome' – and seems to have been descended from an upper-class Idumaean/ Edomite background. These last are the People in Southern Transjordan and Judea, claiming an ancient relationship to Jews, especially through Esau but also possibly Ishmael, and virtually indistinguishable from what in Roman Times came to be known as 'Arabs'. During the Maccabean Era, groups of these seem to have been forcibly converted to Judaism. When Herod executed his own uncle Joseph after the rumor of unfaithfulness between him and his own Maccabean first wife Mariamme ('Mary' – the first 'Joseph and Mary' story), he appointed Costobarus to replace him as Governor of Idumaea and Gaza, the two areas from which Herod's family came.[85]

Costobarus, then, promptly entered into intrigue with Anthony's consort Cleopatra (and Herod's mortal enemy) to get what he considered to be his proper patrimony. Discovering this, Herod waited for his opportunity to deal with Costobarus and found it when Salome divorced him.[86] This is the first clear instance of that 'divorce' among Herodians so roundly condemned at Qumran. So totally contrary to Jewish Law was it seen to be – at least, divorce on the part of a woman – that even Josephus stops his narrative at this point to launch into his first excursus on why it should be condemned. The last time he mentions it is in regard to Drusilla's and Bernice's excesses in this regard a century later.[87] One cannot emphasize too strongly that these are things condemned at Qumran as 'fornication', particularly in the 'Three Nets of *Belial*' section of CD IV.15–V.15.

There is a direct line from these behavior patterns to those of Herodias, over whose infractions in this regard – not to mention 'niece marriage' – John the Baptist was executed. Herodias' niece Drusilla behaved in exactly the same manner – to say nothing of Herodias' own behavior and that of her daughter Salome (as we can now see, probably named after Herod's sister – if not the first Maccabean, Alexander Jannaeus' wife Salome Alexandra) – when she divorced Azizus the King of Emesa to contract a more advantageous marriage – with the connivance of 'Simon Magus' – with the brutal Roman Governor Felix. So did her sister Bernice (whom Josephus describes as the 'the Richest Woman' in Palestine) when, after having been accused of incest with her brother Agrippa II, she married Polemo, King of Cilicia, who had also circumcised himself to marry her (Josephus says, 'because she was so Rich'), but whom she too ultimately divorced in order to take up her illicit relationship with Titus, the destroyer of Jerusalem. She had also originally been married to her uncle – her father's brother, Herod of Chalcis – another example of the niece marriage so frowned upon at Qumran. The catalogue of all these 'incestuous' marriages and divorces on the part of Herodian women is extensive.

Not only does the original Herod end up executing this Costobarus but, having also executed his own wife, Mariamme, her grandfather Hyrcanus II, and her mother Alexandra – all of whom, as Josephus himself makes plain, abetted his rise to power – he takes the opportunity too to dispose of all other pro-Maccabeans, whom this first 'Costobarus' seems to have been sheltering in Idumaea. The connection of this 'Costobarus' with pro-Maccabeans is certainly an interesting one. So effective was Herod in extirpating Maccabeans that Josephus was forced to remark: 'There were none left of the kindred of Hyrcanus (i.e., Mariamme's grandfather, the most pliant and accommodating of all Maccabeans) and no one left with sufficient dignity to put a stop to what he did against the Jewish Laws.' Josephus continues, using the exact phrase, 'rebelled against the Laws' that the Habakkuk *Pesher* used regarding those it described as 'the Men of Violence': 'Herod rebelled against the Laws ... polluting the ancient constitution by introducing foreign practices ... by which means we became guilty of great Wickedness thereafter, while those religious observances that used to lead the multitude to Piety were now neglected.'[88] This is a very strong indictment and here, again, are the two points about 'Piety' and antagonism to foreign practices we have been following.

Later, in discussing how Herod thought higher of the two Pharisees, Pollio and Sameas 'than their mortal nature deserved' and describing his vindictiveness, Josephus tells how Herod brought endless numbers of malcontents to fortresses like Hyrcania and Machaeros on either side of the Dead Sea – this last being the 'Fortress' a half century later in Perea where his son Herod Antipas put John the Baptist to death.[89] In doing so, Josephus baldly tells us that it was Herod who was the first to introduce '*Innovations into the religious practices of the Jews* to the detriment of their Ancestral Customs' – meaning that it was he, Herod, who was the first 'Innovator' not 'the Revolutionaries', as Josephus later claims when discussing the latter's decision to reject gifts and sacrifices in the Temple on behalf of foreigners, which triggered the War against Rome. These later 'Innovators' were only attempting to restore the *status quo ante*. This, of course, is exactly the sense of the manner in which CD IV.15–17 describes the 'nets' *Belial* set up as 'three kinds of Righteousness to ensnare Israel'. It is on the basis of allusions and notices of this kind that we can link up the '*Belial*' usage with Herodians.

There is more however. Since, as we saw, '*Bela*', a name based on the same Hebrew root as *Belial*, was the first Edomite King according to Biblical genealogies (Genesis 36:32 and pars.), this relationship has an even more concrete foundation and relates not only to the perception of the Herodian dynasty as Idumaean, but also to the language circle centering about the name 'Balaam', another linguistic variant of both *Belial* and *Bela*' in Hebrew. In fact, the only really pure 'Idumaean' in Herodian genealogies is Costobarus himself. For its part, 'Balaam' pops up in the New Testament as a linguistic variant of *Belial* in the Damascus Document. For Revelation 2:14, as we saw, 'Balaam taught Balak to cast down (*balein*) a net before the Sons of Israel to eat things sacrificed to idols and commit fornication'.

Here, of course, we have the telltale 'casting down' language in Greek, linking up with the 'swallowing' language in Hebrew which reappears in the Habakkuk *Pesher*'s description of the destruction or deaths of the Righteous Teacher and 'the Poor' of his Council – and what God, in turn, did to the Wicked Priest, that is, 'swallowed him'. The relationship of this 'casting down' language in Greek and this 'swallowing' language in Hebrew to Herodian behavior and both, in turn, to each other, should not be too difficult to recognize.

This section of Revelation is also steeped in the language of 'works Righteousness' ('I will give to each of you according to your works' – 2:23) and antagonism to 'fornication' and 'Riches'. It combines both the language of 'Satan' (2:9–13, mentioned three times) with that of how 'the Devil (*Diabolos*) is about to cast' (*balein*) some of those being addressed 'into prison' (2:10). Not only does it transform the language of the Damascus Document's third of *Belial*'s 'nets' into the language of James' instructions to overseas communities in Acts, it takes on a distinctly 'Jamesian' cast. Now that this very allusion to 'things sacrificed to idols' has appeared in *MMT* in the context of opposing Gentile gifts of grain in the Temple, 'skins sacrificed to idols' (a concern of the Temple Scroll too), and Gentile sacrifices generally, we can see how all these things are connected.[90]

2 Peter 2:15, another letter which is drenched in the imagery of Qumran, also speaks of those 'led astray from the Straight Way, following the Way of Balaam the son of Be'or', and replicates almost precisely the description of 'the Liar's' activities in CD I.14–18 as well. It also speaks of the 'soul of the Righteous' (2:8), duplicating the language the Damascus Document uses at the end of the First Column to describe the attack on 'the Righteous One' by those 'rejoicing in strife among the People' as well as like-minded phraseology used throughout the Qumran Hymns.[91] The same is true of the Letter of Jude, James' 'brother', referring to 'the error of Balaam' (1:11).

Both Bela' and Balaam, as previously remarked as well, however improbably, were also in some sense considered 'Sons of Be'or', thus completing this whole circle and tying these esotericisms even closer together. It is not incurious that in the Temple Scroll where 'balla'/'Bela' – either reading is possible – is evoked amid reference to the classes of persons to be debarred from the Temple and where 'skins sacrificed to idols' are alluded to as an aspect of 'polluting the Temple' and banned from the Temple for the same reason as 'things sacrificed to idols' were in James' directives to overseas communities, the language again appears to incorporate an esoteric play of some kind on the name 'Be'or', that is, 'be-'orot'/'with skins', just as it does the term 'balla'/'swallowed' or 'Bela'.

Where the Idumaeans, in particular, are concerned, these are the same 'Idumaeans', according to Josephus, that a century later take the side of 'the Zealots' and come into Jerusalem at their request and annihilate all the collaborating classes among the Jews including the High Priests, most notably James' judicial executioner Ananus and a few others, whose deaths Josephus describes in gory detail.[92] It is these Idumaeans, no doubt including an assortment of pro-Revolutionary Herodian 'Men-of-War' and other 'Violent' persons that we identify with these 'Violent Ones of the Gentiles' – mentioned in these critical passages from the Psalm 37 *Pesher* as taking vengeance for what was done to 'the Righteous Teacher' (whatever this was) – which dovetail so impressively with similar notices in the Habakkuk *Pesher* we have already described and will describe further below.

They are probably to be identified as well with 'the Violent Ones' who, at the beginning of the Habakkuk *Pesher*, take part in the scriptural exegesis sessions of the Righteous Teacher and at this point would appear to be allied with 'the Liar' and other 'Traitors to the New Covenant' against him. It is interesting that in CD XX.13–17 where 'the Men-of-War' are said to 'walk with the Liar' after the 'gathering in' or death of 'the Unique' or 'Righteous Teacher', such 'Men of Scoffing' are said to have 'spoken mistakenly about the Laws of Righteousness and rejected the Covenant and the Compact, the New Covenant, which they erected in the Land of Damascus' – the Hebrew word 'reject' (*ma'as*) always being tied to 'the Spouter of Lying''s activities in the Scrolls.

Josephus specifically designates the Leader of these Idumaeans as 'Niger of Perea' – Perea being where John the Baptist was active and met his death at the hands of Herod Antipas around 34–36 CE.[93] This would be around the same time that Aretas, the King of Petra took control of Damascus, coeval with the mission of some kind, 'Saul' or 'Paul' undertakes to 'Damascus', from which he has to escape from Aretas' soldiers by having himself 'let down in a basket' from its walls – the same episode that Acts 9:3–25 exploits to describe Paul's conversion on the way to Damascus and his subsequent attacks on the Jews there. All this is very murky, but clearly the situation is somewhat different from Acts' description of it.

1QpHab, IX–X mentioning how '*the Riches of the Last Priests of Jerusalem would be given over to the Army of the Kittim*' and '*the Worthless City, the Liar built on Blood.*'

'The Spoils of the Peoples', 'the Last Priests of Jerusalem', and the 'Pollution' of the Temple Treasury

We can now pass over to the Habakkuk *Pesher*. In the First Column, there is the idea of 'the Wicked encompassing the Righteous' (Hab. 1:4) where, paralleling the Psalm 37 *Pesher* above, 'the Wicked' is specifically identified as 'the Wicked Priest'; 'the Righteous', as 'the Righteous Teacher'.[94] Immediately, too, one sees the idea that 'they executed upon him (the Wicked Priest) the Judgments on Evil', which we just encountered in 4QpPs37 I.11–12 and with which it draws to a close. This is sometimes not appreciated because of faulty translations of the sense. The allusion occurs at the beginning of Column IX (1–2) of the Habakkuk *Pesher*, directly after the material in VIII.11–12 about how the Wicked Priest 'stole and collected the Riches of the Men of Violence (*Anshei-Hamas*), who rebelled against God and took the Riches of the Peoples'.

It speaks about how 'they tortured' or 'inflicted upon him the Judgments on Evil', 'taking vengeance upon the flesh of his corpse'. This comes just preceding the interpretation of a passage in the underlying text of Habakkuk: 'because of the blood of Man ('*Adam*') and the Violence done of the Land, the City, and all its inhabitants' (2:8, repeated in 2:17). It should be appreciated that, in light of the 'the Primal Adam' ideology, it would be possible for someone to read the reference to '*Adam*' in the underlying text of Habakkuk at this point as another reference to 'Christ' and all further passages should be considered with that in mind. The *Pesher* reads: 'This concerns the Wicked Priest whom, as a consequence of the Evil he committed against the Righteous Teacher and the Men of his Council, God delivered into the hand of his enemies to afflict him with torture in order to destroy him in agony, because he condemned His Elect.'[95] Not only then do we have this 'torturing' allusion running through a good part of Column Nine, but this idea of 'His Elect' also occurs in 4QpPs37 III.6 in the run-up to the material about 'the Princes of Evil vanishing like smoke'. To recall the Damascus Document's exposition of Ezekiel 44:15's 'Sons of Zadok', these are 'the Elect of Israel, called by Name, who will stand in the Last Days' and 'justify the Righteous and condemn the Wicked' – again the 'condemned' usage just encountered in 1QpHab IX.11. Preceding this in 1QpHab V.3–4, too, it is stated in exegesis of Habakkuk 1:12–13 'that God would not destroy His People by the hand of the Nations but rather, by the hand of His Elect, God will execute Judgment on the Nations. And with their chastisement, all the Evil Ones of His (own) People, who kept His Commandments only when convenient, would be punished.' This is an extremely pregnant exposition. Not only do we have in it the repeated allusion to 'hand of', previously encountered in Messianic passages of the War Scroll about 'the hand of the Messiah', 'the sword of no mere *Adam*', and 'the hand of the Poor' – 'the Downcast of Spirit consuming Ungodliness', but the implications of this for native Palestinian conceptualities of 'the Day of Judgment' and the fact that 'the Backsliders among His own People' were to be judged along with all others are considerable.[96]

The pronouncement is also delivered in exegesis of Habakkuk 1:12, which refers to God as 'my Rock' who has 'ordained them for Judgment' and 'punishment', the implications of which for the designation of Peter as 'Rock' and his role in early Christian eschatology – like 'the Elect' in this passage at Qumran – are noteworthy. In 4QpPs37 III.1–13, 'the Elect' are 'the Assembly of His Elect' – in Christian terms equivalent to 'the Jerusalem Assembly' or 'Church' of James the Just. In turn, these are equivalent to those who in the next passage are called 'the Assembly of the Poor who will possess the High Mountain of Israel forever'.

In the view of the Psalm 37 *Pesher*, 'the Assembly of His Elect' are to be the 'Leaders and Princes, the choice of the flock among their herds', this in exegesis of an underlying reference in 37:20 to 'the most valuable of the lambs'. It is interesting that to produce this very positive exegesis the underlying Hebrew of the original has been reversed from the received version of Psalm 37:20, which rather alludes to 'the Enemies of the Lord'. This is now transformed in the text as it is quoted into the homophonic phrase in Hebrew, 'whoever loves the Lord',[97] and it is these who are identified – just as 'the Meek of the flock' in CD XIX.9 of Ms. B who 'will escape at the Time of the Visitation' and 'the coming of the Messiah of Aaron and Israel' – with 'the choicelings of the flock', 'the Assembly of His Elect', and 'the Assembly of the Poor'. This is typical of Qumran textual redaction and interpretation and the liberties taken there, as it is the New Testament.

In this transformation, one immediately recognizes the 'Piety' part of the Righteousness/ Piety dichotomy that has become familiar to us as the basis of Josephus' descriptions of John the Baptist's teaching in the wilderness and the doctrines of 'the Essenes', not to mention of Jesus and James in early Christian texts. Here at Qumran, these 'Lovers of the Lord' – along with several allusions in the underlying text of Psalm 37 (12, 21, 30, and 32) to 'the Righteous One'/'Righteous Ones' as well – are obviously to be identified with 'the Penitents of the Wilderness', (in the Damascus Document, both 'the Penitents of Israel' and 'from sin in Jacob') who will live in Salvation ('Jesus') for a thousand generations' and to whom, 'all the Glory of *Adam* will be theirs'.

The evocation of these 'Penitents of the Wilderness' comes amid exegesis of 'the days of the Perfect, whose portion shall be forever' of 37:18. Following this, preceding evocation of 'the Assembly of His Elect' and 'the Assembly of the Poor'/'the Righteous', allusion is made to 'the days of the famine and the Wicked perishing' (37:19). In the *Pesher*, this is interpreted in terms of 'the Penitents of the Wilderness'/'the Assembly of the Poor' being 'kept alive' or redeemed – the whole ambiance being a juridical one – while 'the Wicked', described as 'all those who did not depart (from the Land of Judah)', 'will perish from famine and plague'.[98] Once again, even here, it would appear that we have yet another possible oblique parallel to what in Christian tradition is called 'the Pella Flight of the Jerusalem Community'. This whole section immediately follows the first reference to how 'the Evil Ones of Ephraim and Manasseh' – later simply 'the Wicked Priest' – would be 'delivered into the hand of the Violent Ones of the Gentiles for Judgment'.

In the Habakkuk *Pesher*, another delineation of the sins of 'the Wicked Priest' and 'the Last Priests of Jerusalem' in general is presented just after references in Column Nine to how 'the Wicked Priest was delivered over to the hand of his enemies' as a 'consequence of the Evil he did to the Righteous Teacher and the Men of his Council' and just after reference to 'torturing him with the Judgments on Evil'. Of course, it should be appreciated that an allusion such as 'the Last Priests of Jerusalem' – which certainly does mean 'High Priests' or 'Chief Priests' and, as a plural, parallels the references to these same Priests in the New Testament – makes no sense anytime before the destruction of the Temple in 70 CE and their decimation by 'the Zealots' and their Violent Idumaean allies when the Revolt moved into its more extreme 'Jacobin' phase, as it were, and all collaborators were dealt with. Along with James' destroyer Ananus, among these, as just indicated, was Jesus ben Gamala, whose father managed to get word to Josephus in Galilee about a plot in Jerusalem to remove him when he (Josephus) was commanding there in the early days of the Uprising.[99] These are the passages in which Josephus describes how the Idumaeans, whom he calls 'turbulent and unruly, ever on the alert to create mayhem and delighting in Innovation', butchered all the High Priests and, in particular, 'cast out' the bodies of Ananus and Jesus ben Gamala, his friend, without burial, 'naked as food for dogs and beasts of prey'.

As Josephus recounts all these matters, these Idumaeans, introduced by stealth at night into the city by those he has started now to call 'Zealots', were 'of the most murderous and savage disposition', 'pests', 'the sum total of the offal of the whole country'.[100] In an extremely vivid description, he describes how, together with 'the Zealots', 'they stealthily streamed into the Holy City, Brigands of such incomparable Impiety as to pollute even that hallowed Sanctuary ... recklessly intoxicating themselves in the Temple and imbibing the spoils of their slaughtered victims in their insatiable bellies'. Once again, in good collaborationist style, Josephus is reversing not just the 'Piety' ideology but also the 'pollution of the Temple' accusation and applying it, like his ideological look-alike Paul, to 'the Zealots' and those allied to them, not to the 'Establishment' High Priests.

In addition to using the language of the Scrolls about 'pollution of the Temple', 'Piety', 'Riches' and, in particular, 'the spoils' 'the Last Priests of Jerusalem gathered' in the Temple – the very language the Habakkuk *Pesher* actually is using at this point, Josephus has already told us that James' destroyer Ananus – who basically had total control of the government for the two years since the outbreak of the War – was the whole time trying to make the necessary inroads that would make it possible for the Romans to once more enter the city, and was just on the point of succeeding when 'the Zealots', aided by 'the Idumaeans', overwhelmed him and his fellow collaborating 'Chief Priests'.[101]

The allusion to 'the Last Priests of Jerusalem', which the *Pesher* now makes as a concomitant to this general allusion to 'plundering' and 'profiteering' (in effect, 'tax-farming' – the language is very precise here[102]), is entirely appropriate because, at this point, the *Pesher* actually knows it is speaking about the total destruction of these 'Last' collaborating 'High Priest' clans. Nothing like this ever happened before and the *Pesher* is quite cognizant of its significance. There is no possibility such wholesale destruction of High Priestly clans can be read into any events prior to 68–70 CE. Even at the time of Pompey in 63 BCE or Herod's later assault on the Temple with the help of Roman troops in 37 BCE, Josephus makes it very clear that neither allowed any plundering or booty-taking to go on! This is the definitive point and Josephus explicitly says as much both as regards Pompey's behavior in the Temple and Herod's directives to his troops – unless we are speaking about Antiochus Epiphanes here, a dubious proposition.[103] That leaves only Titus and his father Vespasian and we know they took 'booty' – a good deal of it, because, *inter alia*, they used the proceeds of it and the labor force they acquired to build the Colosseum in Rome.

Exploiting references to the Babylonians 'plundering many Nations' (*Go'im*) and 'Additional Ones of the Peoples' (*Chol Yeter-'Amim*), in turn, 'plundering' in the underlying text from Habakkuk 2:7–8 and the Babylonians 'gathering the Nations' and 'collecting the Peoples' preceding these in Habakkuk 2:5, the *Pesher* produces the picture of 'tax-farming' begun three columns earlier. There, it will be recalled, 'the *Kittim*' (here clearly, 'the Romans') were described as 'collecting their Riches together with all their booty like the fish of the sea' (Hab. 1:14) and 'parceling out their yoke and taxes' – this in interpretation of Habakkuk 1:16, 'his portion is fat and his eating plenteous'. Now the text asserts: 'Its interpretation (meaning the 'spoiling many Nations' and 'the Additional Ones of the Peoples spoiling you'), concerns the Last Priests of Jerusalem, who gathered Riches and profiteered from the spoils of the Peoples.'[104] Here the text has, once again, been deliberately altered to produce the desired exegesis. Not only have 'the Last Priests of Jerusalem' now been substituted for the 'collecting' and 'gathering' activities of the Babylonians in the underlying text from Habakkuk 2:5-8, but a new allusion, 'profiteering', is introduced which is not in the underlying text – at least not yet, that is, not until Habakkuk 2:9 and 'the profiteer's profiteering – Evil unto his house'.

This word used here, '*boze*'/'*beza*', is also used in the Damascus Document where the 'pollution', 'Riches', and 'fornicating incest' of the Establishment classes – 'each man sinning against the flesh of his own flesh, approaching them for fornication, they used their power for the sake of Riches and profiteering' – are being described.[105] The Hebrew here definitely carries the sense that 'the Last Priests are profiteering from the spoils of the Peoples' (in our view, as by now should be clear, Herodians), not the sense one finds in most translations, that 'the Last Priests' are 'plundering the Peoples'.[106]

This is the kind of imprecision one gets in 'Consensus' interpretation of texts in the interests of promoting a theory of the Maccabeans as 'the Wicked Priests' and, in some sense therefore, conquering foreign peoples. But this is not the sense of the *Pesher*. Rather, it is 'the Peoples' and 'the Men of Violence who rebelled against God' who are the ones doing the 'plundering' – namely, 'the Herodians' and 'other Violent Gentiles' – and 'the Last High Priests' (plural), in the sense both of multiple High-Priestly clans an something of the imagery of 'the First vs. the Last', 'profiteering' from this kind of predation – as we have already made amply clear, by accepting gifts and sacrifices from persons of this type in the Temple, the theme of the Damascus Document as well as *MMT*. Furthermore, it is for this reason that 'the Wicked Priest' is specifically described as 'acting in the Ways of Abominations (and) of all unclean pollution'.[107]

The text now adds – laconically in view of its consequence: 'But, in the Last Days, their Riches together with their booty will be given over to the hand of the Army of the *Kittim*, because they are the Additional Ones of the Peoples.'[108] As the *Pesher* would have it, this last is now '*Yeter ha-'Amim*', and not '*Yeter-'Amim*' as in Biblical Habakkuk 2:8 underlying it. The reason for this would seem to be to further emphasize the contrast between '*ha-'Amim*'/'Herodians' and 'the *Yeter ha-'Amim*'/'Romans', both basically two parts of a single exegetical complex.

There can be little doubt what is transpiring here. The reference to 'the Army of the *Kittim*' would appear to be definitive. Again, allusion to 'the *Kittim*' has been deliberately introduced into the *Pesher*, even though it does not appear in the underlying text, because the exegete knows very well that these are going to appropriate all the wealth and plunder that the Herodian High Priests have 'collected', and take it to Rome. This cannot apply to any previous period, except the long-ago Babylonian one on which the *Pesher* is based, because at no time, as we have explained, did we have any foreign armies plundering the country in such a massive manner – probably not even during the Maccabean Uprising and certainly not after 167 BCE until 70 CE. But it also means that the text is being written by eyewitnesses to this either shortly before 70 CE or sometime not long afterwards.

The Method of the Qumran Commentators

This is an extremely important *Pesher*, for not only does it provide definitive historical proof of the backdrop to the events in question, but it shows the method of the Qumran Scriptural exegetes – if 'method' it can be said to be. The exegetes are for the most part interested in the useful vocabulary from the underlying Biblical passage, not always the actual sense of the passage. This is also true of the Gospels, even though the scriptural exegesis developed there is often the reverse of the one here at Qumran.

For instance the term, '*ha-'Amim*'/'the Peoples', does not really appear in the underlying passage from Habakkuk 2:8, though '*Go'im*'/'Nations' and '*Yeter-'Amim*'/'Additional Ones of the Peoples' do. Rather the exegetes purposefully introduce it into their interpretation because it means something to them, that is, 'Herodians'. Also it contributes to the balance they are looking for between '*ha-'Amim*'/'Peoples' and *Yeter ha-'Amim*'/'Additional Ones of the Peoples'.

The underlying Biblical text from Habakkuk 2:6–7 has the foreign armies – in this instance, the Babylonians – doing the plundering and oppressing and 'the Remnant of the Peoples', meaning all the others, being oppressed and being plundered. Nothing loathe, the exposition now has the 'Additional Ones' or 'Remnant of the Peoples', identified with brutalizing foreign armies from the West (i.e., 'they come from the Islands of the Sea') – in this instance undoubtedly the Romans – and it is they who finally 'plunder the Riches' that 'the Last High Priests of Jerusalem' have already 'amassed and profiteered from' the 'Violent' predation activities of the Herodians and their Violent henchmen or thugs like Saulos and Costobarus.

One need only add to all of this that, according to Josephus, Bernice (the mistress at this point of Titus) was the Richest woman in Palestine – as was, doubtlessly, her aunt Herodias before her. This was in part, no doubt, the source of her attractiveness to people like her uncle, Herod of Chalcis, and Polemo, a foreign King from Cilicia, who was even willing to circumcise himself to marry her. This is not to mention her third sister Mariamme's marriage to: first, the son of the Temple Treasurer (and Paul's possible 'kinsman') Julius Alexander who read Josephus' works in Rome, and after divorcing him ('contrary to the Laws of her Country'[109]), next to Demetrius, the son of the Alabarch of Alexandria (and probably, therefore, Tiberius Alexander's brother and Philo's nephew), the Richest man in Egypt.

The sense of this commentary is crystal clear, once one dispenses with the cloud of unknowing of much Qumran scholarship. Normative Qumran translations by scholars with little sense of literary analysis or metaphor make it look as if 'the Last Priests of Jerusalem' were 'gathering the booty' and 'doing the plundering' and not 'the Peoples' and 'the Men of Violence'. They were, but indirectly, through these – 'Violent Ones' and 'Peoples'.

This is the sense of the passage preceding this one (based as it is on Habakkuk 2:7–8) as well, interpreting Habakkuk 2:5 about an arrogant man who never gets enough wealth into his mouth, collecting the Nations and Peoples unto himself – in the Biblical Habakkuk, meaning the Babylonian King. This is expanded in the interpretation in the text into the Wicked Priest 'collecting the Riches of the Men of Violence' and 'taking the Riches of the Peoples', meaning 'the Riches' of the violent Herodian tax-farmers by which means he 'heaped upon himself guilty Sinfulness'. In the process, it is allusions of this kind that make a mockery of the famous and beloved New Testament passages about Jesus keeping 'table fellowship' with 'tax-collectors' and 'harlots' – i.e., persons like Bernice, her sisters Drusilla and Mariamme, and her aunt Herodias.

This passage about how the Wicked Priest 'deserted God and betrayed the Laws', ends with an allusion to how 'he acted in the Ways of the Abominations (and) of all unclean pollution'. Here 'the Way' terminology, usually applied to 'the Way of the Perfection of Holiness' or 'the Way in the Wilderness', is inverted to encompass the behavior patterns of the Evil Establishment and, at this point, the *Pesher* is fairly running away with itself with derogatives and can hardly restrain its disgust and outrage at all these 'Abominations' or 'blasphemies'. It does not interest itself in the subject of 'the Riches of the Men of Violence' or 'Peoples' *per se*, though like the Letter of James, it does condemn 'Riches' in a general sense – therefore its self-designations, 'the Poor' or 'the Simple of Judah doing *Torah*'.

What it and its counterpart *MMT*, however, cannot abide is the receipt of such 'polluted Riches' into the Temple and, therefore, their condemnation of this – along with 'fornication' and 'Riches' of 'pollution of the Temple' – is self-explanatory in these circumstances. The 'fornication' being repeatedly alluded to here has to be that of the Herodians because of the charge 'each man marries the daughter of his father or the daughter of his brother', and because there is no indication in our sources of widespread 'niece marriage', 'divorce', 'polygamy', and indiscriminate coupling with near kin, to say nothing of unrestrained and rampant enrichment, among Maccabeans. This is how to read texts – with one's eyes open – but in order to do this, one has to have a proper sense of history and literary genre and not just ignore them or set them aside on the basis of a set of some other somewhat 'artificial' parameters one might be following. This is what we have been attempting to do in this book.

"*MMT*" papyrus fragment containing reference to "*things sacrificed to idols*" so important to James' directives to overseas communities and '*Sicarii*' / '*Essene*' martyrdom practices.

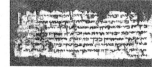

Chapter 19
He 'Swallowed' the Righteous Teacher with 'his Guilty Trial'

'Profiteering from the Spoils of the Peoples'

But how were these 'Last Priests of Jerusalem' 'profiteering'? The answer is: by accepting gifts and sacrifices in the Temple from foreigners. This specifically meant sacrifices on behalf of the Roman Emperor who had been paying from his own revenues for a daily sacrifice in the Temple.[1] It also extended to gifts and sacrifices from and on behalf of Herodians regarded for these purposes as 'foreigners' – and, therefore, 'polluted' – by these various groups of 'Zealot'-type extremists including the authors of the documents at Qumran. This was the issue and the thing which so infuriated the 'Zealot'-inspired Lower Priesthood when it stopped sacrifice in August, 66 CE on behalf of any and all such individuals, thus triggering the War against Rome.

This too is why these texts at Qumran fulminate about 'pollution', 'uncleanness', and 'Abominations' to such a degree. Properly appreciated, it is also the thrust, of the 'Three Nets of *Belial*' accusations in the midst of like-minded remonstrations about not observing proper 'separation' in the Temple between 'clean and unclean' connected to the peculiar charge that 'they sleep with women in their periods'. Of course, almost the whole of Columns Five to Eight of the Damascus Document inveigh against such things, including the use of the imagery of John the Baptist's attacks on the Sadducees and Pharisees in the Gospels, as 'Offspring of Vipers', adding 'their nets are Spiders' nets'.

These complaints also include the charges of 'polluting the Temple Treasury' and incest.[2] Here the text even gives the mechanism of such 'pollution' as we have seen: 'every man who approaches them shares their uncleanness, unless he is forced'. The Damascus Document does not actually think that all Jerusalem High Priests were 'sleeping with women in their periods', conduct forbidden in the *Torah* of Moses. Even the compromised and corrupt Herodian Jerusalem High-Priestly Clans would probably not have gone that far. As the several texts make abundantly clear, they were only guilty of 'profiteering' and 'gathering Riches' and consorting with and taking their appointment from people who probably did 'sleep with women during their periods' or were perceived of as so doing.

What the Damascus Document and *MMT* are trying to say is that by 'accepting gifts and sacrifices in the Temple' from the Roman Emperor, Roman Governors, Herodians, and their hangers-on – including 'Violent Gentiles' and 'Men-of-War' – the High Priests were contracting their pollution and, in the process and as a consequence, 'polluting the Temple'. In particular, this would include accepting appointment from such classes of persons to the very High Priesthood itself.

This is the thrust of all the various usages of the '*Belial*' terminology, refracted along with '*Balaam*' imagery in Paul, 2 Peter, Jude, and Revelation and the 'idolatry' charge associated with both – that is, this imagery relates to both the Herodian family itself and the Establishment they sponsored, not to mention to a certain extent, 'the Liar'. If the latter is Paul, he probably also carries Herodian blood even if Paul is not identical with the 'Saulos' in Josephus – which we think he is.

The kind of 'swallowing' and 'casting down'/'casting out' imagery one finds implicit in these charges has nothing whatsoever to do with the Maccabean Priesthood, which on the whole was considered legitimate and highly respected even by Josephus – who makes it plain that he is proud of his own Maccabean blood[3] – and even Herodians themselves. Concerning these, one should study the genealogies of Herodians to note how assiduous they were in arranging marriages to preserve every bit of Maccabean blood possible. All this, the Dead Sea Scrolls help clarify.

Josephus himself becomes so upset at what those of a 'Zealot' frame of mind are doing in the Temple that he rails against them as 'Innovators' and their rejection of gifts and sacrifices on behalf of foreigners in the Temple as an 'Innovation'. The latter accusation was more appropriate to Herod's own changes 'to the disuse of the Jews' own ancestral traditions' than to anything the 'Zealots' were doing. For his part, Josephus does not decline to accept appointment as commander or commissar in Galilee – he perhaps exaggerates his role here – from the cabal in charge in Jerusalem, though these were hardly 'the Innovators'.[4]

Before the Revolution moved into its 'Zealot' or 'Idumaean' phase, those directing it were biding their time while they tried to negotiate for themselves a separate deal with the Romans. This is the clarity Josephus does provide. That the more extremist groups, which took over the Uprising with the wholesale destruction of these more accommodating High Priests, looked askance on Herodians is clear from their earlier treatment of Agrippa II and his sister (or 'consort') Bernice, barring them from the Temple (and, in time, all Jerusalem as well). This, some of them wished to do to their father before them – who Josephus already told us was of such refinement as to surpass all others of his generation in 'Chrestos'/'Kindliness'.[5]

It is he that the 'Zealot' Simon who called an 'Assembly' in Jerusalem in the early Forties – wanted to have barred from the Temple as a foreigner.[6] For Pharisaic Judaism and Rabbinic Judaism succeeding it, this question of whether the Herodians were foreigners or not is a burning one – as illustrated by the episode in *Mishnah Sota*, where Agrippa (I or II, it is of no import) is portrayed reading the *Torah* in the Temple at Tabernacles.[7] It will be recalled that this is the third great Jewish pilgrimage Festival after Passover and Pentecost and the Festival at which the curious 'Prophet', Jesus Ben Ananias, appears directly following the death of James (probably around Yom Kippur) to proclaim the coming destruction of Jerusalem. Here Agrippa comes to the Deuteronomic King Law, 'You shall not put a foreigner over you who is not your brother' (17:15), and he begins to weep. A Jewish King was supposed to read the Law in the Temple on Tabernacles, the celebration of the wilderness experience of the Jews. By contrast to what Simon might have thought, the Talmud pictures the assembled Pharisees as crying out, sycophantic to a fault, 'You are our brother, you are our brother, you are our brother'. As for 'the Zealots' or '*Sicarii*' and those causing the Uprising against Rome generally, they stopped sacrifice and refused to any longer accept gifts from or on behalf of foreigners in the Temple just as, prior to James' death in what we have called 'the Temple Wall Affair', they had previously built an obstacle to stop '*Bela*' (i.e., the first Edomite King) or the Herodian King from even seeing the sacrifices. But, as already explained, this too is the gist of the '*balla*'/*Bela*' episode in the Temple Scroll, where such classes of persons were forbidden even from 'seeing the Temple'.[8]

It is a doleful twist-of-irony that the Romans, after two Uprisings and endless troubles over these issues, in effect turned the tables on the Jewish extremists, forbidding them even to come within eyesight of the Temple and Jerusalem after its final transformation by Hadrian (another Roman legionnaire from Italica in Spain) into Aelia Capitolina in the wake of the Bar Kochba Uprising. It is interesting, too, that during this time the Rabbis are alleged to have put a ban upon those taking Nazirite-style oaths not to 'eat or drink' until they had seen the Temple rebuilt – language clearly reflected in Acts 23:12–14's picture of those wishing 'to kill Paul'. The symbolism here, where Paul's doctrine of Jesus as the 'Heavenly Temple' is concerned, is also so intrinsic as to be impossible to ignore.

Not only were foreign gifts and foreign sacrifices – seen as both 'polluting the Temple' and corrupting the High Priesthood – banned by these religious 'Innovators' and 'Zealot'-style extremists, but foreign appointment of High Priests was also abjured, including either by

Herodians or Roman Governors in succession to them. This is the thrust of James' opposition to the High Priests in the Temple and his 'Opposition' High Priesthood, as pictured in early Church sources. It is also finally the basic thrust of a 'Jamesian' Letter(s) like *MMT*, not to mention Epiphanius' *Anabathmoi Jacobou*'s 'he complained against the Temple and the sacrifices'. In this last text, too, Paul is specifically pictured as a foreigner.

James did complain about certain things, but not quite in the retrospective manner these early Church documents, through the prism of their ideology, suppose. As already suggested, he 'complained' about the way 'Temple service' was being carried out by these Herodian and Roman-appointed Establishment High Priests – as the Qumran documents do in their way – and he 'complained against' gifts and sacrifices from or on behalf of foreigners in the Temple – just as the 'Zealot' Lower Priesthood and *MMT* do – when Acts 21:20 itself admits the majority of James' 'Jerusalem Church' followers were 'Zealots for the Law'. Even earlier, Acts 6:7 also admitted that 'a great multitude of the Priests had become obedient to the Faith' (n.b., this same word, 'Faith' or 'Compact', used to describe 'the New Covenant which they erected in the Land of Damascus' above).

This is the essence of the controversy over the first of James' directives to overseas communities, 'things sacrificed to idols'. All of these things were seen as 'pollution of the idols' or 'idolatry', as both *MMT* and the Habakkuk *Pesher* so vividly illustrate. This is also the thrust of the election to fill the 'Office'/'Episcopate' of the Twelfth Apostle in Acts 2:20 – as we have argued, really the election of 'the *Mebakker*' (as Qumran would have it) or 'the Bishop' James as 'High Priest of the Opposition Alliance'. It is to him all groups – 'Zealots', '*Sicarii*', 'Nazrenes', 'Essenes', or 'Messian   ic Sadducees' (if there was any real difference between these except of degree) – paid homage.

After the elimination of the collaborating High Priests, gruesomely delineated by Josephus in his description of the demise of James' nemesis Ananus, 'the Zealots' or '*Sicarii*' proceeded to elect their own High Priest, a simple 'Stone-Cutter' named 'Phannius' or 'Phineas', the name, of course, of the archetypical purveyor of the 'Zealot' ideal and against whom, snob and collaborator that he is, Josephus rails because of the purported baseness or meanness of his origins.

But those of the more xenophobic and probably Jamesian 'Zealot' mindset had already barred Agrippa II and Bernice from the Temple and all Jerusalem as well. This was some twenty years after the attempt to bar their father Agrippa I from the Temple too and a decade after they had built a wall to block Agrippa II's view of the sacrifices. It is no wonder that individuals such as these spared no pains to convince the Romans to destroy the Temple when it was put in their power in the aftermath of the Uprising finally to do so.[9]

For example, at the beginning of the Uprising in 66 CE, Josephus describes how those he calls '*Sicarii*', together with members of the 'Poorer' classes, not only burned the palaces of 'Rich' High Priests like the Ananias presented to us in Acts 24:1, but also 'the Palaces of Agrippa II and Bernice'. As Josephus goes on to describe this in his usual laconic manner, they then burned the public registrars to 'destroy the money-lenders' bonds … in order to cause the Poor to rise against the Rich'.[10] I think we can safely say that we have, in the description of these events, a true depiction of the state of affairs in Jerusalem in these portentous times.

'They Took Vengeance upon the Flesh of his Corpse'

Columns Eight to Nine of the Habakkuk *Pesher* contain an allusion to how the Wicked Priest would be 'delivered into the hand of the Violent Ones of the Gentiles for Judgment' and how these 'executed (the Judgments on Evil) upon him'. The passage in the Habakkuk *Pesher*, which contains the phrase 'they inflicted upon him the Judgments on Evil' and 'took vengeance upon the flesh of his corpse', has created not a little misunderstanding among commentators because of the arcane quality of its vocabulary and the difficulty in translation.

It occurs directly following the material about how the Wicked Priest 'collected the Riches of the Men of Violence who rebelled against God' and preceding that about how in the Last Days the Riches and the booty of the Last Priests of Jerusalem 'would be delivered into the hand of the Army of the *Kittim*'. It comes at the bottom of Column Eight of the Habakkuk *Pesher*, which is frayed at this point, so after a slight break in the text it continues at the top of Column Nine which is complete: 'They inflicted the Judgments on Evil and committed the outrages of Evil pollutions upon him in taking vengeance upon the flesh of his corpse.' This passage has caused confusion because the word we are translating here as 'pollutions'/'*mahalim*' in Hebrew has a primary meaning of 'diseases'. But this cannot mean simply 'diseases', since it is twice explicitly stated that a person or persons 'inflicted these (we prefer 'defilements') upon him'. Also the phrase 'flesh of his corpse' has been translated by some as 'his body of flesh', despite the fact that this is a redundancy and virtually meaningless in English.[11] It is clear that we have direct action and the same plural 'they' who are 'committing the outrages of Evil pollutions' are also 'inflicting the Judgments on Evil on him'; it is equally clear that these 'Judgments on Evil' or this 'Vengeance' is being inflicted in the sense of direct action by unspecified third-person plural parties on the 'flesh of his corpse' (*geviyah*).

But what is most interesting about this obscure allusion is that it can be made sensible by looking at the biography of James – in fact, more sense than we knew before. This is very powerful testimony that our analysis and the way we are proceeding is correct. When a theory or paradigm can not only make sense out of given materials, but also elicit more from the text than one might have known previously, then this is very persuasive evidence that the theory we are propounding here about the identity of James and 'the Righteous Teacher' *actually works*. Indeed, this is the very essence of what it means for a proof to be valid in scientific theory.

In the history of Qumran Studies, 'Establishment' or 'Consensus' Scholars, because of the obscurity of translations of this kind and a real paucity of historical insight, began speaking in terms of 'diseases of the flesh', from which some Maccabean High Priest might have been suffering in this period and identifications spinning off from this became legion.[12] But 'diseases' are not normally thought of as being 'inflicted' by third parties, which is very definitely the sense of the passage here. Furthermore, we are very definitely talking about the word 'corpse' here.

If we look at the combination of these usages with reference to the biography of James and his opposite number, Ananus ben Ananus, the man along with Agrippa II who was responsible for his death, these things are clarified. Since the second problematic word in the above translation, '*geviyah*', means 'dead body', 'carcass', or 'corpse' in Hebrew, the redundancy implicit in most English translations of this passage disappears. Now we really can identify a situation with regard to James' destroyer Ananus where 'they took vengeance upon the flesh of his corpse' just as we have translated it and we can now see this is exactly what the *Pesher* is talking about with regard to the fate of 'the Wicked Priest'. Here material from the biography of James can elicit further meaning from the text than we would previously have been aware of had we not known it.

The High Priest Ananus ben Ananus' death is recorded in Josephus, who in fact does make a good deal of it. As Josephus describes Ananus ben Ananus' death, 'the Idumaeans' had been allowed surreptitiously into the city by those he has only just started to call 'Zealots'. As already underscored, previously he had not been using this terminology to any extent, if at all, but was calling such individuals 'Innovators', 'Revolutionaries', 'Brigands', or '*Sicarii*', but not 'Zealots' *per se* – cryptically referring to 'the Movement' they represented as 'the Fourth Philosophy', nothing more. Josephus' first real use of this pivotal terminology, then, comes in relation to those 'who take vengeance' on Ananus (reason unspecified), who are his mortal enemies. Therefore, James and the Zealots are distinguished by their common opposition to or abhorrence of this Ananus.[13]

As Josephus describes it in detail, these 'Zealots', 'taking some of the Temple saws, sawed open the bars of the gates nearest the Idumaeans, who were shivering outside the city in a violent thunderstorm'! These so-called 'Idumaeans', thereupon, rushed through the city 'sparing no one'. 'Considering it pointless to waste their energies on the common people, they went in search of the High Priests, focusing their greatest zeal against them'.[14] Josephus now concentrates specifically on the fate of Ananus, saying, 'As soon as they caught them (meaning Ananus and Jesus ben Gamala), they slew them. Then standing upon their dead bodies, they mockingly upbraided Ananus for his caring attitude towards the People.' This last is a little far-fetched, since in his later *Vita*, Josephus accuses this Ananus of having been involved in an olive oil scam and other illicit activities.[15] Nothing loath, in the *War*, he now goes on to see all this as 'sacrilege', explaining, 'So far did they go in their Impiety that they threw their bodies outside (the city) without burial, although Jews were so scrupulous in the burial of men that they even took down malefactors who had been condemned and crucified and buried them before the setting of the sun.'[16]

Josephus does reiterate the point about 'violating dead corpses' when, in continuing this description about what happened to Ananus and his friend Jesus ben Gamala, he describes even more graphically how 'they were *cast out naked and seen to be the food of dogs and beasts of prey*'. It is hard to imagine he could have described Ananus' death in terms of any greater outrage or 'defilement' than this. So here we actually do have the gist of the meaning of the above passage in the Habakkuk *Pesher* about 'inflicting the outrages of Evil pollutions and taking vengeance on the flesh of his corpse'. Without consulting the events of James' life and those involved in his demise we could never have suspected it. On the other hand, with such data, otherwise obscure usages are immediately clarified.

In the long panegyric to Ananus, which he now interrupts his narrative to deliver, curiously Josephus says the very same things about Ananus that early Church sources say about James – including calling him 'a man revered on every ground and of the Highest Righteousness'. The obsequiousness of these words rather takes one's breath away, especially when one is aware of what Josephus said about this Ananus in the *Vita*. But he even goes on to attribute the eventual fall of Jerusalem and the ruin of its affairs to 'the death of Ananus': 'I should not be mistaken in saying that the death of Ananus was the beginning of the destruction of the city, and that the very overthrow of her wall(s) and the downfall of their State began on the day on which the Jews saw their High Priest, the Procurer of their Salvation, slain in the midst of the City.'[17]

It is difficult to consider all these parallels and overlaps accidental and there seems to be more going on beneath the surface of these events than is apparent. This is especially true when early Church accounts are saying almost the very same things about James as Josephus here is saying about Ananus. And when Origen, Eusebius, and Jerome all say that in the copy of Josephus' works they saw (presumably in Caesarea – and this in the *War* not the *Antiquities*), Josephus *attributed the fall of Jerusalem to the removal and death of James*!

Nor can there be much doubt that what one has in these graphic scenes in Josephus is vengeance for the death of James, whose memory seems to have been held in particular regard by these so-called 'Idumaeans' – including, obviously, some pro-Revolutionary Herodians like Niger of Perea – which also seems to have been the case among other 'Arabs' like Queen Helen's family and kinsmen from either Edessa or Adiabene.[18] In fact, these passages extolling Ananus to such a degree that Josephus has the temerity even to call him 'a lover of Liberty and enthusiast for Democracy' may even have overwritten something else

Josephus originally said at this point in the version of the *War* in the East – prepared, as he told us in his Preface, for his own countrymen in these areas in their native language – about the death of James.[19] Little else can explain the 'Violence' these so-called 'Zealots' and 'Idumaeans' exhibited and their single-minded and extreme animus towards Ananus. What else could have infuriated them to such a degree as to commit such 'Impieties' and to violate Ananus' body in this manner?

Whatever these violations might actually have been, the Qumran document refers to them with approval while the pro-Roman collaborator Josephus is outraged – at least he makes out that he is for the purposes of public consumption. He even goes on, in the same breath that he does about Ananus' 'love of Liberty and enthusiasm for Democracy', to extol the dignity of his rank and the nobility of his lineage but notes that, despite these, 'he treated even the humblest of men with equality' and 'ever preferred the public welfare to his own advantage' – unctuousness that would make anyone but a Josephus blush.[20]

Once again, however, this is exactly the point made in all early Church sources about *James*, that as '*Zaddik*', he 'did not defer to' or 'consider persons', the very charge Paul is so anxious to parry in Galatians 1:10 of 'attempting to please persons' – expressed in James 4:4 as 'making himself a Friend to the World'. Again, an overlap of this kind, when speaking of the death of the man responsible for James' death, can hardly be considered accidental. One might even conclude that we have here the very place in the text where Origen and Eusebius saw their Josephus' testimony that 'Jerusalem fell because of the death of James'. In addition, it is hard to gainsay the parallels in this account with New Testament materials about Jesus who, of course, is 'the Savior' *par excellence*, not to mention those about James as 'the Righteous One' and 'Protection-of-the-People'.

In perhaps the cruelest cut of all, in emphasizing how much Ananus 'preferred Peace above all things' and 'was sensible that Roman Power was irresistible', Josephus concludes, 'I cannot but think that, because of its pollutions (meaning the desecration of Jesus ben Gamala's and Ananus' corpses, language absolutely echoing the Habakkuk *Pesher* above – only reversed), God had condemned this City to destruction.' In the Habakkuk *Pesher*, God 'condemned the Wicked Priest to destruction'. In fact, these are the very words it uses in 1QpHab XII.5–10 where it is the Wicked Priest who 'polluted the Temple of God' because of 'the works of Abomination he committed' there. So, actually Josephus turns the thrust of the implied accusation in the Gospels about Jesus around here and, in the process, gives vivid testimony as to why persons in the Third, Fourth, and Fifth Centuries thought he said 'Jerusalem fell because of James'. There is certainly something very peculiar going on in these various like-minded testimonies, so perhaps he did.

Josephus closes with the aside, 'and He (God) was resolved to purge the Temple by fire, that He cut off these its greatest defenders and benefactors'. Not only is this last basically the charge being made in early Church texts with regard to James' death but, taken as a whole, it is generally the charge that Eusebius or other early Church writers are making against 'the Jews' for killing Jesus.[21] It also employs the 'cutting off' language we have been following and just seen used in the Psalm 37 *Pesher* applied to similar events. Paul does not make this charge as such, though he does use the 'cutting off' language, as we have seen, probably because the events had not yet transpired at the time of his writing. Nevertheless, to reiterate, in Josephus we get the interesting anomaly that the charge is being made against 'the Zealots' and their confederates, 'the Idumaeans' for killing Ananus and Jesus ben Gamala and 'casting' their corpses out of the city without burial. For Josephus, these actions are comparable to the 'profanation' or 'sacrilege' of leaving the bodies of those crucified on the crosses without taking them down to bury them before nightfall, a singular and most unexpected comparison.

But for Qumran, the group resembling these unruly 'Idumaeans', 'the Violent Ones of the Gentiles', is praised for 'inflicting the Judgments on Evil upon the Wicked Priest' and their behavior is considered justified and applauded 'because of what he did to the Righteous Teacher'.[22] We can only assume that in the early Church in Palestine the same attitude would have prevailed regarding what was done to James. Nor can there be any doubt that what is being described at this point in the Habakkuk *Pesher* are these monstrous 'defilements' inflicted on 'the body' of 'the Wicked Priest'. That Josephus also then goes on to compare the 'Impiety' and sacrilege involved in violating the corpses of the dead in this manner to the revulsion Jews felt about leaving bodies up on crosses without taking them down and burying them before nightfall brings the whole complex to a kind of conclusion. If this connection is, in fact, real and not just a coincidence, then, once again, we have an echo of themes circulating about James' life – in this case relating to his death or demise reappearing in material relating to that of Jesus in Scripture.

The reason for all these pollutions, e.g., severing the head from the body as in John's case, the 'curse' of crucifixion, or 'inflicting the disgusting abuses of Evil pollutions' on Ananus' naked body, was probably because they were seen as impediments to resurrection, the ultimate reason for their perpetration. It is a 'curse' of this kind, namely the 'curse' of being 'hung upon a tree', whether applied to the object as in Deuteronomy or the action as at Qumran that, as already explained, Paul in Galatians 3:10–13 develops into the basic 'Saving' ideology of Christianity as we know it, that Jesus, in taking this 'curse' upon himself freed him (Paul) from 'the curse of the Law' (here an additional bit of reversal) and, thereby, all 'Christians' following him – a most astonishing piece of exegetical acrobatics.

The Death of the Righteous Teacher in the Habakkuk *Pesher*

The Habakkuk *Pesher* now goes on in Columns Eleven and Twelve to discuss the destruction of the Righteous Teacher and some members of his Council or 'the Poor'. It is here it uses Josephus' words about the Temple, 'God condemned him (the Wicked Priest) to destruction'. It is in this context as well that it goes on to delineate how he 'plotted to destroy the Poor', robbing them of their sustenance in the Cities of Judah, committing 'his Abominable works' in Jerusalem, and 'polluting the Temple of God'.[23] The sequence here is very close to the one in early Church texts where the death of James is immediately followed by the appearance of Roman Armies outside Jerusalem. The coming of these 'Armies of the *Kittim*' in 1QpHab IX.6–7 follows the description of the predatory actions of the Wicked Priest, 'profiteering from the spoils of the Peoples' and/or 'Violent Ones' and 'the Judgments on Evil being inflicted upon the flesh of his corpse'.

Because the underlying text of Habakkuk 2:8 is speaking of 'the blood of Men and the Violence done to the Land', this is followed by a repeat of the description of 'the Evil the Wicked Priest committed against the Righteous Teacher and the Men of his Council' and 'the Vengeance' which would be visited upon him. In these passages about 'the handing over in the Last Days of the Riches and booty of the Last Priests to the Army of the *Kittim*', the destruction of Jerusalem and, with it, the Temple is certainly implied.[24] This is also true for the additional descriptions in Columns Eleven and Twelve, culminating in that of 'the Day of Judgment' – also referred to in Column Ten after the description of the Vengeance 'they meted out' to the corpse of the Wicked Priest as 'the House of Judgment (*Beit ha-Mishpat*) which God would deliver in His Judgment in the midst of many Peoples'.[25]

In this second set of descriptions about the destruction of the Wicked Priest in Column Twelve, it is simply stated that since the Wicked Priest 'robbed the sustenance of the Poor' and 'plotted to destroy the Poor', 'so too would God condemn him to destruction'. The same idea is stated again in slightly differing fashion in the previous sentence, 'the Wicked Priest would be paid the reward which he paid the Poor'. Of course, the introduction of 'the Poor'/'*Ebionim*' terminology is purposeful here, as the usage nowhere occurs in the underlying text of Habakkuk at this point. But what is really interesting about all this is that this usage, 'the reward of his hands (that is, 'the hands of the Wicked') would be paid back to him', actually occurs in the passage following that of Isaiah 3:10: 'Let us take away the Righteous One, because he is offensive to us' (this in Septuagint reformulation), applied to James' death in all early Church literature.[26]

The idea is very clear. Since this phrase about 'the Wicked being paid the reward he paid the Poor', too, nowhere appears in the text of Habakkuk at this point; the implication is that it is being deliberately imported from Isaiah 3:10–11 (another 'Wicked vs. the Righteous' text – just as in Habakkuk 1:4–2:20), so once again in our view we have 'QED'. Again, too, the note of 'Vengeance' in all of this is unmistakable. Nor can there be any doubt that we are speaking about 'destruction' here, that is, the 'destruction' of 'the Righteous Teacher' and 'the Wicked Priest' – one succeeding the other.

There is no way that any of these descriptions can apply to any earlier assault on the Temple and a destruction of Jerusalem prior to that of 70 CE – and certainly not the two of 63 and 37 BCE. In these earlier attacks, there was not the slightest implication of any 'booty given over to' foreign Armies of the kind being alluded to here in the *Pesher* and in Titus' triumphal parade following his 70 CE conquest. These notices probably cannot even be said to relate to the incursions in the time of Antiochus Epiphanes and the Maccabean War, because this was hardly on the scale of the Roman one and nothing else in the text can be thought of as relating to it.

Before continuing the analysis of this crucial material in Column Twelve, it would be well to return to that in Columns 9–10, following the descriptions of the Vengeance 'they took upon the corpse' of the Wicked Priest and the coming of the Army of the *Kittim*. The actual words of the second description of this 'Vengeance' or 'chastisement' at the end of Column Nine are that 'as a consequence of the Evil he did to the Righteous Teacher and the Men of his Council, God delivered him into the hand of his enemies to torture him'. 'His enemies' are unspecified here, but they are clearly not the Righteous Teacher and his confederates, but individuals additional to these, or, as we have been attempting to explain employing the parallel material in the Psalm 37 *Pesher*, 'the Violent Ones of the Gentiles' ('Idumaeans' in Josephus).

These 'torture him' or 'bring him low, with punishment unto destruction' or 'to consume him with (mortal) soul-embittering (torments), because he condemned His Elect'. The 'consuming' or 'destroying' vocabulary here anticipates and plays off the 'consuming', 'destroying', and even 'swallowing' imagery we shall encounter in Columns Eleven and Twelve when it comes to describing both what he ('the Wicked Priest') 'did to the Righteous Teacher and the Men of his Council' – clearly identified with 'the Poor', that is, 'he consumed' or 'destroyed them' – and what would be done in return to him. Furthermore, the note about 'condemnation' again carries something of a judicial meaning here, should one choose to regard it.

Not only is it clear that what is being done to the Wicked Priest is to 'pay him back' for something he did and a 'Vengeance' of some kind, but again it is being done by others to him, in particular, 'Violent' third parties such as 'the Idumaeans' who, for some reason, treat him 'abominably'. We shall presently be able to connect this up with 'the Sanhedrin proceedings' this same Ananus 'pursued' against James the Just and several of his companions as Josephus records it.

The play of 'causing Evil to' or 'condemning God's Elect' on the idea of 'condemning the Righteous' is clear. Not only is 'condemning the Righteous' the characteristic activity of 'those who sought Smooth Things', but it is the opposite of the kind of 'justifying' activity predicated of 'the Righteous Teacher' and those 'of his Council' in documents like the Damascus Document and Community Rule. This is implicit in the way Hebrew works,

Chapter 19: He 'Swallowed' the Righteous Teacher with 'his Guilty Trial' • 280

Hebrew having a causative verb – in this case, 'justifying' connected to the underlying root-meaning of 'Righteousness', namely, 'making Righteous' (as in 'making Many Righteous' in Isaiah 53:11) or 'justifying' as opposed to the 'making Evil' or 'condemning' here in the Habakkuk *Pesher* and the Damascus Document – that is, whereas the Wicked Priest 'condemns' people, the Righteous Teacher 'justifies' them.

This is the kind of exposition one encounters as well in the interpretation of the designation 'the Sons of Zadok' in CD IV.3–10, who are referred to there – just as the Righteous Teacher and his Council are here in the Habakkuk *Pesher* – as 'the Elect of Israel'. 'Righteousness' is the actual root of the designation 'Zadok'. In the Damascus Document 'the Sons of Zadok', as will be recalled, are 'the Elect of Israel called by Name who will stand in the Last Days', the characteristic activity of whom is 'justifying the Righteous and condemning the Wicked' – that is, as in early Christianity and fragments of other materials at Qumran,[27] they participate in the 'Last Judgment', a 'Judgment' about to be evoked in the Habakkuk *Pesher* as well.

This connection of the name 'Zadok' ('Justus' in Latin) with the person of the Righteous Teacher (who can be looked upon as 'the Son of Zadok' or '*the Zaddik* par excellence*) is exactly what one gets in early Church literature with the constant attachment of the name or title 'Justus' to James' person. The best example of this comes in Hegesippus' narrative of James' death, where the designation is sometimes used in place of James' very name itself – for example, when the Scribes and the Pharisees place James on the Pinnacle of the Temple and cry out to him 'O Just One, whom we all ought to obey, since the People are led astray after Jesus the Crucified One, tell us what is the Gate to Jesus?'[28]

The use of the language of 'consumed'/'destroyed' here in the description of the Vengeance inflicted on the 'soul' of the Wicked Priest because of 'the Evil he had done to the Righteous Teacher and the Men of his Council', will have a variation in the 'swallowing' language, which the Habakkuk *Pesher* will now use to describe the destruction of the Righteous Teacher by the Wicked Priest at the beginning of Column Eleven (Column Ten having been devoted to a description of 'the House of Judgment God would' pronounce in the midst of many Nations' and the Spouter of Lying's 'building' a worthless 'Assembly upon Lying for the sake of his (own) Glory'.[29]

The presentation of this death plays off this '*Ba-La-'a*' vocabulary of 'swallowing' or 'consuming' – a circle-of-language, as we saw, related to the '*Balaam*'/'*Balak*'/and '*Belial*' language, not to mention parallel notions circulating about the allusion in Greek, '*ballo*', that is, '*casting*' or '*throwing down*', usually in a violent manner. When the Greek preposition, '*kata*'/'down', is added, the signification then becomes that used to describe James being 'thrown down from the Pinnacle of the Temple' in almost all early Church sources – although this event probably never happened. In the Pseudoclementines *Recognitions*, as we saw, this becomes his being 'thrown down the Temple steps', which probably really did happen.[30]

As just indicated too, in the aftermath of the attack by 'the Zealots' and 'Idumaeans' on the High Priests in Jerusalem, something resembling this 'casting down' (*kataballo*) from the Pinnacle of the Temple probably really *did* happen in this case. This was the death of 'Zachariah ben Bariscaeus' (probably, 'Zachariah ben Barachias' in Matthew 23:35), whom Josephus describes rather improbably as being both 'very Rich' and a 'lover of liberty'. He uses the same allusion, 'lover of liberty', to describe Ananus, as just signaled as well, whose murder both preceded and was, no doubt, in some manner connected to Zachariah's.

The execution of Zachariah by 'the Zealots' in the Temple after a mock Sanhedrin trial by 'the Seventy' not only parodies James' trial and execution, but was probably connected to it – perhaps even part of the retribution for it. Tradition always locates 'the Tomb of Zechariah' right beside James' in the Kedron Valley directly beneath the Pinnacle of the

Temple.[31] When '*ballo*' is coupled with a different preposition, '*dia*', for instance, or 'against', the expression then turns into the Greek '*Diabolos*', meaning 'to throw against' or 'complain against', the basis of our modern word 'the Devil'. To be sure, many of the usages connected to these crucial allusions to 'swallow' (*leval'o*/*leval'am*/*teval'eno*) in the Habakkuk *Pesher*, on how the Wicked Priest 'swallowed' the Righteous Teacher and his followers among 'the Poor', are obscure even in the Hebrew but by elucidating them, as we have shown, we shall be able to tie this description very closely to the death of James as described in early Church sources.

Aside from this '*ballo*'/'*balla°*' language complex, the exegesis also plays on another word, '*Hemah*'/'Venom' or 'Wrath', which we encountered in CD VIII.9–11/XIX.21–24's description of 'the Princes of Judah' and 'the Kings of the Peoples'. This is evoked relating to an underlying text from Habakkuk 2:15 about 'making his neighbor drink and pouring out His Fury' ('Venom'). All these denotations will be used in the *Pesher*. It also contains another phrase, 'looking on their festivals', which will be applied, thereafter, to problems relating to 'their' Yom Kippur observances. '*Hemah*' can mean 'Venom' (as in 'the Venom of Vipers' in Deuteronomy 32:33) or it can mean 'Anger', as in the Wicked Priest's 'Hot Anger' or 'Wrath', which will be the sense 1QpHab XI.2–15 will utilize. But, as we shall see, it can also mean, 'dregs', which is the sense of the Received Version of 2:15, which actually reads, 'your dregs' in the sense of the 'dregs of the Cup' not 'His Venom' – nor is this to say anything about the 'Divine Wrath, which is also the sense of the passage. The *Pesher* on it reads as follows: 'Its meaning ('pouring out Anger') concerns the Wicked Priest who pursued after the Righteous Teacher to his House of Exile to swallow him in his Hot Anger.' The allusion to 'his Hot Anger' or 'Furious Wrath' will be extremely important for understanding the delineation of the Vengeance upon 'the Wicked Priest' that follows. So is the allusion to 'swallow' or 'consume', the sense of which is clearly 'destroy' (regardless of the fact that some translators give the patently absurd reading, 'confuse him' here which is simply wrong). 'The Wicked Priest' did not wish to 'confuse the Righteous Teacher', he wished 'to destroy' him.

'His House of Exile'

The above *Pesher* is a most incredible one. In the first place, it contains a defective usage in Hebrew, '*a-Beit-Galuto*' – something about 'in' or 'at' 'the House of his Exile' or 'his Exiled House', the meaning of which is obscure but which we shall ultimately be able to decipher. In addition, the *Pesher* introduces an additional word '*Cha'as*' not found in the underlying text from Habakkuk 2:15.

The reason for this will also become clearer as we proceed. For a start, this word '*Cha'as*' will play on another usage which appears in the *Pesher*, '*Chos*'/'Cup', which will further refine the 'giving drink', 'drunkenness', or 'drinking to the dregs' metaphor, which appears in the underlying text. Though these usages are admittedly obscure, it will not take much Hebrew to begin to grasp the wordplay that is going on. Even without Hebrew, the reader can attempt to grasp this.

This interpretation of Habakkuk 2:15 does contain the usage '*Hamato*', which when linked with '*Cha'as*' produces the meaning 'his Hot Anger' or 'Furious Wrath'. 'The Venom of Vipers' from Deuteronomy 32:33 in the Damascus Document was interpreted to relate to 'the Kings of the Peoples and their ways' or, as we have explained, Herodians. The usage also occurs in the 'Hymns of the Poor', where the meaning parallels the sense we are seeing here, but reversed. There, 'the Poor' are said to be 'saved' from 'the Fiery Wrath of God's Hot Anger' because they 'circumcised the foreskin of their hearts'. This is surrounded by allusions to 'walking in the Way', 'judging the Wicked', 'kindling His Wrath', and 'being saved', all paralleling usages we have been considering above. In the Damascus Document and here, of course, they relate to an illicit Establishment and its High Priests.

But what has further confused scholars in the passage from 1QpHab XI.4–6 before us is the multiplication of 'him's or 'his'es. These occur in three successive variations: 'to swallow him', 'the House of his Exile', and 'his Hot Anger' or 'Venomous Fury'. In Hebrew, pronouns of this kind are always expressed by the same pronominal suffix '*o*'/'him' or 'his'. But the problem is, when one has a series of these, it is often impossible to know to whom they refer – the subject of the action or its object. The same is true in Semitic languages like Arabic and the problem often occurs even in English writing where it is considered poor style not to specify this.

In the interpretation of this passage one sees everywhere, the sense of the 'swallow him' and 'in his Hot Anger' are quite clear. They refer to 'the Righteous Teacher' and 'the Wicked Priest' respectively, that is, 'the Righteous Teacher is being swallowed by the Wicked Priest in his Hot Anger' or 'Venomous Fury' – the '*Cha'as*' in '*Cha'as Hamato*' meaning 'Anger' or 'Wrath'. This will give way to another usage in Hebrew also having to do with the imagery of 'Anger' and 'Wrath', particularly in apocalyptic literature, '*Chos*' or 'Cup'.

This is the kind of language interplay and imagery that so appealed to the authors of the Dead Sea Scrolls. It is certainly to be found in passage(s) before us from the Habakkuk *Pesher*. It is also to be found, as we have shown, in the Book of Revelation in the New Testament almost word-for-word as we have it here (Revelation 14:10) – another good dating tool for the Habakkuk *Pesher*. We will also find it in the 'Cup' which Jesus 'must drink' and that the two brothers, John and James, the so-called 'Sons of Zebedee', 'will drink' after him in order to follow him (Matthew 20:22–23/Mark 10:38–39).

It is, however, the third 'him' or 'his' that produces all the problems in this text, not only the 'his' but the expression it is attached to, the defective *a-Beit-Galuto*/'to' or 'in'/'with his House of Exile' – '*Galut*' meaning 'Exile' in Hebrew. In the usual interpretation of this phrase, the 'him' or 'his' here is also taken as referring to the Righteous Teacher, that is, the Wicked Priest pursued the Righteous Teacher 'to swallow him in his Hot Anger' *at the Righteous Teacher's* 'House of Exile'. In their mind of most scholars, this last meant Qumran or what they theorize to have been the 'Essene' Settlement situated there.

This then gave rise to certain other interpretations having to do with what they considered to be the Wicked Priest's supposed 'drunkenness' (how silly can one be?) and confrontations at this so-called 'Essene Monastery at Qumran' between the Righteous Teacher and the Wicked Priest over a different calendrical reckoning for Yom Kippur. Therefore the 'House of his Exile' was Qumran – the Righteous Teacher's purported 'House of Exile' even though this was only some twenty miles from Jerusalem.

But comparison with the life of James – as in the case of the desecration of the Wicked Priest's 'corpse' and, as will become plain, this same 'Wicked Priest''s purported 'drunkenness' as well – produces an even more rational and plausible explanation. When data relating to James' life and death are introduced into references of this kind in the Dead Sea Scrolls, they help clarify and extract more meaning – meaning one could not otherwise have expected – whereas previously there was only obscurity.

First of all, reference to the biography of James makes one think that this third 'his', as in '*his* House of Exile', does not apply to the object being 'pursued' – namely 'the Righteous Teacher' – but rather the subject doing the 'pursuing' and/or 'swallowing', meaning 'the Wicked Priest'. This makes the sequence of the three 'him's/'his'es more plausible: that is, the first 'to consume him' applies to the Righteous Teacher; the second, 'in his Venomous Anger', applies to the Wicked Priest; and the third, 'in his House of Exile' applies to the Wicked Priest too.

Then what would the sense of this 'his House of Exile', seen in this manner, be? The introductory preposition here is an '*a*' or '*alef*' which is meaningless in Hebrew'. *Be*– or '*Bet*' in Hebrew here – would give the meaning 'with' or 'in'. Anything else would probably not be a single Hebrew letter nor readily be confused with '*alef*', nor make any sense. Furthermore in Hebrew, terms like '*Beit-Din*' or '*Beit ha- Mishpat*' normally have to do with judicial proceedings of some kind. In fact, the latter was even used in the *Pesher* in the previous Column X.3-5, when it came to describing 'the Judgment that God would make in the midst of many Peoples', where He would 'judge' the Wicked Priest 'with fire and brimstone'.[32]

Moreover this imagery of this 'Judgment' permeates the last Columns of the Habakkuk *Pesher*, giving them a completely eschatological cast, i.e., 'the Judgment' that in common parlance is normally referred to as 'the Last Judgment'. This is referred to in Columns XII.12 –XIII.4 of the *Pesher*, following the passages we are analyzing here, as the '*Yom ha-Mishpat*'/'the Day of Judgment'. This would make Column X.3's 'House of Judgment' an idiomatic expression of some kind having to do with the actual decision of 'Judgment' God 'delivers' on 'the Day of Judgment'.

In fact, this 'Judgment' is already being referred to in the *Pesher* as early as Column V.1–5, where 'His Elect', meaning, 'the Righteous Teacher and the Men of His Council' are those who will 'execute God's Judgment on the Nations'. We have also already seen this expression 'His Elect' to be equivalent to 'the Sons of Zadok' in CD IV.3–4 which would make 'the Sons of Zadok' almost supernatural, participating along with God in the process of final eschatological Judgment.

This scenario fits in very well with that of the War Scroll too, in which the Heavenly Host, together with His Messiah (the 'no mere Adam' and presumably the 'Returning' One, though this is not clear), will come 'on the clouds of Heaven' – as per Gospel presentations – and participate along with 'the Penitents in the Wilderness' Camps 'in the Land of Damascus' in the process of final eschatological Judgment, once again tying the circle of all these allusions in our texts very closely together. This, in any event, is the proclamation James is pictured as making in the Temple prior to his death in early Church texts. This proclamation of 'the Son of Man standing on the right hand of God' or 'coming with Power on the clouds of Heaven', is also repeatedly ascribed to Jesus (to say nothing of John the Baptist) in a variety of contexts throughout the New Testament as well.[33]

For Column V.3 of the Habakkuk *Pesher*, 'God would not destroy His People by the hand of the Gentiles'. This last is the same term the Psalm 37 *Pesher* attaches to 'the Violent Ones' who visit God's 'Judgment on Evil' upon the Wicked Priest. The term 'destroy' being used here is also the same one ultimately applied to the condemnation of the Wicked Priest by God towards the end of the *Pesher* in Column XII.5-6. Rather, in the most hopeful expression of nationalism, this Column Five *Pesher* on Habakkuk 1:12–13 concludes: 'By the hand of His Elect, God will execute Judgment on all the Nations and with their Punishment, all the Evil Ones of His (own) People, who kept His Commandments only when convenient (the meaning here clearly being 'Jewish Backsliders').'

The usage 'House of Judgment'/'*Beit ha-Mishpat*' will appear in the eschatological exposition in Column VIII.1–3 of how those with 'Faith in the Righteous Teacher' and 'suffering works' will be 'saved ('in the Last Times') from the House of Judgment'. All these exegeses set up a purposeful tension between the death of 'the Wicked Priest' and the worldly or profane trial he 'pursued' against the person we consider to be James, and the Heavenly or eschatological '*Beit ha-Mishpat*' or 'Judgment' God pronounces by the hand of 'the Sons of Zadok' or 'His Elect' against him.

Seen in this manner and with the actual historical scenario of James' Sanhedrin trial in mind, one can think of the reference to his 'pursuing him with his House of Exile' as being an esotericism or an expletive of some kind for the Sanhedrin trial that 'the Wicked Priest' Ananus actually 'pursued' against James. This would also seem to be something of the import of the interpretation of the words, 'the Wicked spies on the Righteous, seeking to kill him', but God did not allow him 'to be condemned when he is tried' in the *Pesher* on Psalm 37:32–

33 (and, for that matter, the early Church *Pesher* on Isaiah 3:10–11), which is deliberately turned around in the exposition to signal, as here in the Habakkuk *Pesher*, the 'reward God would pay' the Wicked Priest, 'delivering him into the hand of the Violent Ones of the Gentiles to execute Judgment upon him'.[34]

Put more explicitly – so abhorrent, therefore, were the proceedings 'pursued' by Ananus against James in the Pharisee/Sadducee-dominated Sanhedrin – here denoted by the '*Beit-Galuto*'/'his House of Exile' – to 'the Assembly' or 'Church of the Poor', they would not deign to acknowledge these either as a proper '*Beit-Din*' or a '*Beit ha-Mishpat*' ('Court' or 'Trial'). Therefore the words, 'his *Galut*' or 'Exile' here are not a location or an actual 'Exile' *per se*, which is the normative understanding of the expression in Qumran Studies, but an expression of their loathing or disgust for just this place and these proceedings.

This is another and altogether more sensible way of looking at the expression 'His Exiled House', taking the pronominal suffix tied to it to mean not the Righteous Teacher's 'House', the usual understanding of scholars, but the Wicked Priest's. In fact, one encounters this exact sense in the allusion, 'the House of the High Priest', mystifyingly evoked in the Gospels to denote precisely the Sanhedrin Trial by 'all the High Priests, Scribes, and Elders', and 'the whole Sanhedrin seeking testimony against Jesus in order to kill him' in the middle of the night at 'the House' or 'Hall of the High Priest' (Mark 14:53–55 and pars.).

One need be mystified no longer. Not only are the exact words 'seeking to kill him' of the Psalm 37:32 *Pesher* above employed here, but it is directly following this that Jesus is pictured as evoking the proclamation also attributed to James, 'You will see the Son of Man sitting at the right hand of Power and coming on the clouds of Heaven', and the High Priest, for some reason – again mystifyingly – then rending his clothes and saying, 'He has spoken blasphemy' (Matthew 26:65). One says 'mystifyingly', for it was not 'blasphemous' to say the sorts of things Jesus is pictured as saying at this point in the narrative.[35] Nor could anything better recapitulate the events converging on James' death than this. Moreover, we would not have thought to look at these parallels without looking into the materials surrounding James' Sanhedrin Trial and death.

'The Exile' of the Sanhedrin in Talmudic Sources

This exposition of 'His House of Exile' would suffice as an alternative suggestion as to how to translate this curious phrase, but it is possible to develop a more convincing exposition even than this which really must be seen as a definitive proof. In most Biblical contexts, the words 'pursued after' are usually accompanied by the phrase 'with the sword'. This is true of Pharaoh's 'pursuit' of the Israelites in Exodus 14:8 and Saul's 'pursuit' after David in 1 Samuel 23:25. This is also true of the depiction of the attack on 'the soul of the Righteous One' and 'all the Walkers in Perfection' by 'the Pourer out of Lying's confederates, 'the Seekers after Smooth Things' and 'those who broke the Covenant' and 'transgressed the Law' at the end of the First Column of the Damascus Document.[36]

Often such a 'pursuit' involves the name 'Jacob', as in Jacob's pursuit by his father-in-law Laban (Genesis 31:23 and 36), which no doubt would have appealed to the Qumran exegetes if James was the subject of their exegesis – James' original name in Hebrew being 'Jacob'. This theme is recapitulated in Amos 1:11's accusation, this time 'against Edom', that 'he pursued his brother with the sword'. Again the 'Edomite' connection here would have been particularly attractive to Qumran exegetes; but what is certain is that in all these contexts, *the pursuit signaled by the word 'pursue' was mortal* and carried with it the intent 'to kill' or 'destroy'.

This is also true in the mirror reversal of this, 'the Law of the Pursuer' of Deuteronomy 19:6, which actually includes the idea of the 'heart' of the Pursuer in 'blood Vengeance' being uncontrollably 'Hot' just as we have here in the Habakkuk *Pesher*. There even seems to be a hint of the inversion of these matters in the exposition of the Habakkuk *Pesher* we have before us. Of course, if one does admit the identification of Ananus with 'the Wicked Priest' and, along with this, the connection possibly in his mind of James with the assassination some six years earlier of his brother, the High Priest Jonathan, by those Josephus at this point had started denoting as '*Sicarii*' (as tenuous as this may be), then the fact of a species of 'blood Vengeance' being involved in, according to his view, the judicial proceedings he 'pursued' against James has to be entertained.[37]

Looking at the words 'he pursued the Righteous Teacher' in or with 'his *Beit ha-Mishpat*' in the Greek can also be somewhat illustrative. We have already found this helpful in terms of looking at other allusions in Hebrew, but it is especially true when looking at perhaps the most interesting parallel between how Jesus was portrayed in the Gospels to the archetypical destruction of 'the Righteous Teacher' in the Hellenistic literature, the Courtroom Trial of Socrates. In Plato's *Euthyphro*, for instance, Socrates comes to the court and outside meets one Euthyphro who is later to be among those who accuse him (Socrates) of 'Impiety' which leads to his death. An Oracle of sorts, Euthyphro is 'pursuing' courtroom proceedings against, as it turns out, his own father! The word used here to express this in the Greek is 'pursued' in the sense of pursuing judicial proceedings against someone.[38] As far afield as this might originally seem, it is nevertheless useful in bringing home the mindset of the individuals responsible for documents of the kind before us, and we suggest that this is the sense of the word as it is being used at this critical juncture of the Habakkuk *Pesher*.

If we now look at Talmudic sources relating to Sanhedrin proceedings carrying the death sentence and the legitimacy or illegitimacy of these, one finds materials that directly relate to this usage in the Habakkuk *Pesher*. Once again, the reader should realize that we would not have thought even to consult these, where the fate of 'the Righteous Teacher' at Qumran is concerned, were we not looking at the paradigmatic fate of James. There, it turns out, that on at least six different occasions, when the issue of capital punishment is being discussed – particularly that relating to passing a death sentence for 'blasphemy' – it is specifically claimed that, in the Period under consideration (from the 30s–60s CE), the Sanhedrin 'was exiled' – these are the words Talmudic tradition actually uses – from its normal place-of-sitting in 'the Chamber' on the Temple Mount to a place-of-sitting outside these precincts cryptically referred to as '*Hanut*'.[39]

As these sources generally recount this tradition, this is expressed as 'before the destruction of the Temple (here, also expressed as '*ha-Bayit*' or 'the House'), the Sanhedrin was exiled (*galtah*) and took up its sitting in *Hanut* – or more simply even, 'the Sanhedrin was exiled … from the Chamber of Hewn Stone to *Hanut*'.[40] In the Tractate *Rosh Ha-Shanah*, where this notice or its counterparts are recorded *three times*, it is specifically linked to two passages from Isaiah 26:5 and 29:4, about 'the fall of the Lofty Ones' or 'the Lofty Ones being brought low'. The same words are specifically evoked, particularly as regards 'the fall of the Cedars of Lebanon' – as, for instance, in the *Pesharim* on Isaiah 10:33–34 introducing the famous 'Rod' and 'Branch' material 'from the Roots of Jesse' in 11:1–5 ('white' in the sense of underlying 'Lebanon', '*levan*' meaning 'white' in Hebrew, almost always signifying 'the Temple' and 'the Cedars', its wood) – both at Qumran and in Talmudic literature to refer to the fall of the Temple and, in the Talmud anyhow (if not at Qumran), the fall in 70 CE; never an earlier fall.[41]

Some of these Talmudic references to this peculiar fact of the Sanhedrin changing its residence to a place outside the Temple called '*Hanut*' specifically emphasize that the Sanhedrin's 'Exile' (*Galut*) during this period from its original home in the Chamber of Hewn Stone on the Temple Mount was widely known. But the reference in Tractate *Rosh ha-Shanah* is to six such 'Exiles' or 'Banishments', and the actual word used is that '*Galut*' being used in Column XI.4–6 of the Habakkuk *Pesher* to describe how the Wicked Priest 'swallowed the

Righteous Teacher'.[42] This kind of 'Exile' was 'the Exile' or 'Banishment of the Sanhedrin from the Temple' during the period in question, namely, from approximately 30–70 CE. The point being made in the enumeration of these is that these kinds of 'Exiles' also presaged the departure of the Divine Presence from the Temple, echoing a similar causality between the death of James and the fall of Jerusalem in early Church sources.

The same language is repeated in Tractate *Sanhedrin*, where the subject under discussion is the number of witnesses required for conviction in capital cases and procedures for acquittal in close votes. We have already had occasion to refer to this Tractate both as regards 'the Enemies of God' who would have no share in the 'world to come', and as it threw light on the stoning of James, particularly as recorded at Nag Hammadi. Again the tradition of the Sanhedrin's 'Exile' to its place-of-sitting in *'Hanut'* in the years just prior to the destruction of the Temple in 70 CE is repeated. But the focus of the discussion concerns the permission or non-permission to try capital cases in such a setting – the polemical conclusion being that *outside the Chamber of Hewn Stone such permission was withdrawn* and *sentences of this kind in such an exterior setting were illegal*.[43] This is a conclusion fraught with significance where the Sanhedrin proceedings 'pursued' against James (to say nothing of others) are concerned.

Therefore, we now have extremely telling testimony that in the Period in which we would place the documents before us, the middle of the First Century CE, the word 'Exile' is being specifically applied to Sanhedrin proceedings having to do with the death penalty involving blasphemy. In our view, it is not possible to find stronger proof relating to the exposition of this obscure expression, *'a-Beit-Galuto'*, than this; but, in addition, the actual formulation one finds in more of these testimonies, aside from *'Galut'*/'Exile', is *'galtah min ha-Bayit'*, meaning 'exiled from the House' – 'House', in this instance, being the manner in which 'the Temple' is often referred to in Hebrew. This is the phraseology used in these notices about 'the Exile' of the Sanhedrin from its former place-of-sitting in the Chamber of Hewn Stone on the Temple Mount to a location outside these precincts in the Talmud and the way this is formulated – only slightly reversed from the expression *'Beit-Galuto'*/'His House of Exile' in the Habakkuk *Pesher* – makes it look as if those writing the *Pesher* were familiar with the fact that the Sanhedrin was, in fact, 'exiled' from the Temple Mount to a place called *Hanut* in the period just prior to the War against Rome and Jerusalem's fall. Furthermore, in our view – and connected to this – *they were aware of the judicial proceedings being 'pursued' against James*.

Once more our case is demonstrated, at least on this point, and we have come full circle. The phrase 'Sanhedrin Trial', as well as its reflection in the Sanhedrin Trial of Jesus at 'the Palace' or 'House of the High Priest' in the Gospels, now fits this otherwise totally obscure usage, *'a-Beit-Galuto'*, in 1QpHab XI.6. In the latter, as now forcefully emphasized, this comes at a key juncture focusing on the destruction of the Righteous Teacher by the Wicked Priest – itself preceding *both his own destruction and the fall of the Temple*, also alluded to in Columns Nine, Eleven, and Twelve of the *Pesher*.[44]

It is reference to the few known facts of James' life and his death, such as they are, that allow us to approach these shadowy allusions. This meets two criteria: 1) it expounds material we would not otherwise be able to understand; and 2) it leads to new, hitherto unsuspected, insights not explainable by any other theory. Once again, the point is that by consulting the biography of James we are able to elicit additional meaning out of otherwise obscure usages in the Dead Sea Scrolls that have been a continual puzzle to scholars. For what most have made out of these without benefit of the James hypothesis, one has only to consult their works – that of any of my colleagues will do. This is powerful verification of the applicability of the positions we are adopting indeed.

Heads of Trajan, who fought in the 66-70 War, then hunted all *Messianists* down, and finally destroyed all the Jews of Egypt.

'Seeing their Privy Parts' and 'Seeing their Festivals'

But it is possible to reach even further still and, using the James hypothesis, elicit more from the text. *This cannot be done with any other hypothesis.* As it turns out, there are transmutations of words in this text, not only in this interpretation but in the two that follow. There is a second part of the *Pesher* on Habakkuk 2:15 which turns on the allusion in the underlying text to 'looking upon their festivals'.[45] Not only is this interpreted in terms of confrontations between the Righteous Teacher and the Wicked Priest but, once again the imagery of 'swallowing' is introduced into the *Pesher* and the exposition expressed in terms of this imagery.

The problem is that in the text of Habakkuk in both the Masoretic (Hebrew) and Septuagint (Greek) versions, the phrase 'looking upon their festivals' (*mo'adeihem*) does not exist, but rather it reads 'looking on their privy parts' (*me'oreihem*) and a '*dalet*' has been substituted for a '*resh*' in the Qumran text. Since the *Pesher*, when speaking about 'the Cup of the Wrath of God shall swallow (the Wicked Priest)' at the end of Column XI.15, in XI.13 will also speak about the Wicked Priest's 'foreskin', as we have seen, i.e., 'he did not circumcise the foreskin of his heart', we can only assume that the transmutation in the underlying text from Habakkuk 2:15 was purposeful and those at Qumran knew the original of this passage.

But this also triggers a transmutation in the underlying text of Habakkuk 2:16, where the received Masoretic and Vulgate read, 'Uncover your foreskin' (*he-'arel*), but which here in 1QpHab XI.9 and in the Greek Septuagint read 'make tremble' (*hera'el*). But the sense of the Masoretic original and of the preceding 'privy parts' from 2:15 is again, then, recovered in the *Pesher* which interprets this in terms of the Wicked Priest 'not circumcising the foreskin (*'orlah*) of his heart'.[46] Besides the play on the word '*Ra'al*' ('Poison') in CD VIII/XIX, etc., one should remark the curious parallel that exists regarding this in Galatians 2:4, where Paul basically uses this 'looking on their privy parts' charge to accuse some in the Jerusalem Church Leadership of 'coming in by stealth to spy on' the freedom he and his colleagues 'enjoy in Christ Jesus', meaning their circumcision or lack of it, and adding, 'so that they might enslave us'. What an incredible turnabout. The point is, is it intentional?

In our view, the *Pesher* is also involved in at least two other transmutations or word-plays in this section: '*Chos*' ('Cup') from '*Cha'as*' ('Wrath') in the underlying text – also related to Isaiah 51:21's '*Chos ha-Tar'elah*/'the Cup of Trembling', now expressed as '*Chos Hamato*'/'the Cup of the Wrath of God' and '*Hemah*'/'Hotness' or 'Anger' and '*Hanut*', the putative venue in the early 60s of James' illegal trial for blasphemy. The first three or four of these transmutations or plays are indisputable – the last, '*Hamat*' for '*Hanut*', will remain a matter of opinion. In view of the transmutations in the rest of the *Pesher* it is not far-fetched.

The *Pesher*'s transformed version of this all-important text from Habakkuk 2:15 then reads as follows: 'Woe unto the one who causes his neighbor to drink, pouring out his Fury ('*Hamato*', which can also mean 'dregs') to make them drunk, that he may look upon their Festivals ('*mo'adeihem*' in place of '*me'oreihem*').' To some extent, the first part of the exposition of this passage, which we have treated in the foregoing, plays and will play further on the allusions in the underlying text to 'giving one's neighbor drink', 'pouring out the dregs' (this, the '*hamato*' in the underlying text), and 'drunkenness'.

The second part will now be interpreted in terms of additional confrontations connected to Yom Kippur, called in the *Pesher* 'the Festival of Repose of the Day of Atonements', 'the Day of Fasting', and 'the Sabbath of their Repose'.[47] This last would appear to be reflected in or to incorporate something of the thrust of John 19:31 about not leaving the condemned on crosses 'into the Sabbath', 'for that Sabbath was a Great Day' – here again, the double use of 'Sabbath', since 'the Festival of Repose' can be translated in Greek as 'the Sabbath'.

Moreover, 'Great Day' is clearly a reference to 'Festival' – only in John, the 'Festival' is the Passover whereas, in the Habakkuk *Pesher*, it is 'the Day of Atonements' (thus!).

The phraseology 'in his Hot Anger' is redundant and also introduces a new usage, '*Cha'as*'/'Anger'. This is not mentioned in the underlying Biblical text from Habakkuk 2:15, but it will be played upon momentarily to produce the homophonic '*Chos*'/'Cup', which will then produce 'the Cup of the Wrath of God' in the *Pesher*. Nor is this to say anything about 'the Cup of the right hand of the Lord' in the underlying text from Habakkuk 2:16. This, in turn, plays off the allusion to 'make tremble' (*hera'el*) in the underlying text from 2:15 as redacted in the *Pesher*, not to mention 'the Cup of Trembling' (*Tar'elah*) from Isaiah 51:21, which then moves in the *Pesher* into the Wicked Priest 'not circumcising the foreskin ('*orlah* or '*arlah*) of his heart'. This is how complex these texts really are.

It is our view that, like the transmutation of 'privy parts' into 'Festivals' at the beginning of the *Pesher*, all this word-play is purposeful. The same can be said for the illegality concerning the proceedings 'pursued' against 'the Righteous Teacher' or James by the Wicked Priest 'in his Exiled House at *Hanut*'. The fortuitous conjunction of '*Hanut*' and '*hamal*' would have been just the kind of word-play or transmutation of words that appealed to the sectaries in their exegetical exposition of these matters. The term '*Hanut*' for the actual location of the Sanhedrin during the Period of its 'Exile' (coinciding almost precisely with the time of the Sanhedrin proceedings 'pursued' against James) would have been seen by them as significant as it is in the Talmud. If this is true, then we have a direct reference, however veiled, to events in James' life even in the *Pesher* as it stands.

Once again, nothing could be more powerful proof of the relationship of these passages to James' death than this – not to mention the evocation of a Sanhedrin Trial at 'the House' or 'Court of the High Priest' in the Gospel. We shall now be able to follow some of this word -play to its inevitable conclusion, in the process elucidating some of the grossest errors and intellectual miscues that have plagued Qumran Studies from their inception.

More 'Swallowing' Related to the Day of Atonement and 'the Reward he Paid the Poor'

Proceeding with this kind of word-play, the text now moves on to the second part of its exposition of Habakkuk 2:15 – the 'he looked on their Festivals/privy parts' phraseology – and again uses the vocabulary of 'swallowing' (in the sense of 'he destroyed them') to represent what the Wicked Priest did to the Righteous Teacher and his confederates. This time the pronominal suffix attached to the action is the plural 'them', 'he swallowed them' not 'him', and the action is connected to a reference to 'Yom Kippur' – this being the *Pesher*'s clear elucidation of the revamped usage, 'their Festivals', in the underlying text.[48]

This language of 'swallowing' will now be applied a third time, in the context of some of the most overpowering imagery in the Qumran corpus, to describe how 'the Cup of the Wrath of God would swallow' the Wicked Priest. We have seen how in the next *Pesher* in the Column XII on Habakkuk 2:17 about 'the Violence of Lebanon' and 'the destruction of the dumb beasts', these ideas are reiterated, namely, that the Wicked Priest 'would be paid the reward he paid the Poor', and 'as he plotted to destroy the Poor' (*Ebionim*), so too 'God would condemn him to destruction'.[49] 'The Poor' here are clearly meant to be identified with either 'the Ebionites' or 'the Essenes' (if the two groups can, in fact, really be separated) and incorporate both 'Lebanon' – this presumably because like Priests in the Temple, as already remarked, they too only wore white linen – and 'the dumb beasts' in the underlying Hebrew of Habakkuk 2:17. Not only does the *Pesher*, as the Psalm 37 *Pesher*, really identify 'the Poor' ('Lebanon') with 'the Council of the Community' but 'the dumb beasts' too, are identified with 'the Simple of Judah doing *Torah*' which harks back to the archaic '*Torah*-

Doers in the House of Judah' (i.e., all 'Torah-Doing Jews') to circumscribe the exegesis of both Habakkuk 2:3 on 'the Delay of the *Parousia*' in Column VII.5–14 and Habakkuk 2:4 in Column VIII.1–3. Again, to repeat, the Hebrew here really does mean 'destroy' (*lechalah/lechalot*) and not something else like 'confuse'.

One should note the telltale emphasis on 'doing' again, the same emphasis one finds throughout the Letter of James and the Damascus Document – also the basis of the Qumran usage 'works'/'*ma'asim*'. This allusion to '*Torah*-Doers' will reappear in the restriction in Columns VII and VIII of the scope of the application of both Habakkuk 2:3 and 4 on 'the Righteous shall live by his Faith'. Earlier still, in Column V.3, we saw the verb 'destroy' (*yechaleh*) used to express how God 'would not destroy His People by the hand of the Nations, but rather by the hand of His Elect ('the Poor') execute Judgment on all the Nations' and 'the Evil Ones of His People who kept His Commandments only when convenient', presumably meant to include 'the Wicked Priest' and all Backsliding or Renegade Jews.

The reason for this 'Judgment' and 'destruction' where Gentiles were concerned was simple – they are all perceived of as 'Idolaters'. In the words of the very last lines of the *Pesher*: "Its interpretation (Habakkuk 2:19–20 warning 'Idolaters') concerns all the Nations who serve stone and wood. But on the Day of Judgment, God will destroy all the Servants of Idols and Evil Ones from off the Earth.'[50] As the Habakkuk *Pesher* now details this confrontation relating to Yom Kippur in Column XI.6–8, as already underscored: 'And at the completion of the Festival of Repose of the Day of Atonements, he (the Wicked Priest) appeared to them to swallow them, causing them to stumble on the Fast Day, the Sabbath of their Repose.'

Much speculation has arisen concerning how the Qumran sectaries were using a different calendar than the Jerusalem Establishment.[51] This was no doubt true but, once again, all of this has assumed that the defective and clearly esoteric '*a-Beit-Galuto*' meant that the Righteous Teacher's 'House of Exile' – and, ergo, that the Community was celebrating a different Yom Kippur 'Fast Day' in the wilderness or at Qumran itself, when the Wicked Priest appeared to them to, supposedly, 'confuse them'.[52] But this is to miss the intense sense of *destruction* surrounding the passage. This is not some innocent 'confrontation' simply involving 'confusing' people or 'causing them to stumble' in their observations, though this may have been part of it as even an Establishment Trial for 'blasphemy' would imply. To be sure, there is 'confrontation' going on here but, once again, the sense would appear to be mortal, not simply verbal.

This is the sense of the underlying allusions to 'the Violence done to Lebanon' and 'the Land' and 'the predation on the dumb beasts', upon which these *Peshers* are based. If so, then the allusion to 'causing them to fall' or 'casting them down' would have import, in particular, *vis-a-vis* all Greek versions of the death of James where, as we have seen, the *Ba-La-'a*/'swallowing' language moves into the '*ballo*'/'casting down' language. Though the allusion here may mean something as innocuous as 'causing them to stumble' over differences about legal observance concerning 'the Day of Atonements', the totality of the phraseology seems more portentous than that. This is especially true in view of what immediately follows XI.9–15, as the *Pesher* proceeds, evoking the imagery of 'drinking the Cup' and Divine Retribution and 'destruction' one encounters in the fanatically apocalyptic and emotionally-charged atmosphere of Revelation too. Before moving on to consider this, it is important to look quickly at the usage 'Day of Atonements, the Fast Day the Sabbath of their Repose' and its significance, not only for Jews but also in the life of James.

For Jews today, of course, 'Yom Kippur'/'the Day of Atonement' (singular) is still the Holiest and most solemn day of the year associated, as it is, with forgiveness of Sin – inadvertent or collective. Classically, it was the one day of the year when the High Priest, dressed in his full regalia including mitre and breastplate, went into the Holy of Holies alone – there, kneeling before the Judgment Seat, to ask for forgiveness on behalf of the whole People before God. This is precisely the picture, for example, one gets in the presentation of 'Simeon the Righteous' in Ben Sira 50:5–23. It was also the day on which the High Priest was permitted to pronounce the forbidden Name of God, 'YHWH'.

But this is precisely the picture of James in early Church accounts – particularly in Epiphanius and Jerome – going into the Holy of Holies, there to render atonement before God 'until the flesh on his knees turned as calloused as a camel's for all the supplicating before God he did', meaning, before the Judgment Seat. One way of construing this is to see it as nothing other than an early Church attempt to provide a picture of James making at least one such Yom Kippur atonement – if not many – in his role as 'Opposition High Priest' or the incarnation of all 'Perfection', 'the Righteous One' or 'Zaddik' of his Generation, acknowledged across the board by all groups, as early Church documents so vividly testify.[53] But who was James that he had the right to go into the Holy of Holies in this manner, whether once or often, to make such an atonement? As we have been trying to suggest, he was 'the People's Priest' or 'the High Priest of the Opposition Alliance', and it is the 'Zadokite' ideology at Qumran – which, inter alia, was applied to 'the Righteous Teacher' there, that provides us the wherewithal to understand this.

Before the Qumran documents appeared, we could not have predicted this which is what is so startling about them, though the approach was hinted at in Hebrews with its emphasis on a 'High Priesthood after the Order of Melchizedek' (a variation on the 'Zadokite' one at Qumran) and its insistence on a 'Perfect High Priest of greater purity' or 'higher Righteousness' – Hebrews 7:26–8:1). This was much of what the 'Zealots', too, were demanding from the first stirring of their Movement in the 4 BCE–7 CE events, following Herod's death, to the fall of the Temple in 70 CE and beyond.[54] It was also being fairly clearly enunciated in the Damascus Document, first discovered among the materials in the Cairo Genizah in 1896.

With these materials, blurred by arcane scholarly discussions about the differences between Qumran and Pharisee/Rabbinic calendrical reckonings and misunderstandings over the true thrust of references like the one here to 'his Exiled House' – 'Exiled' because it was no longer sitting in the Chamber of Hewn Stone on the Temple Mount – we do, now, have the instrumentality for approaching this notice about James in the Temple performing something resembling 'a Yom Kippur atonement', to say nothing of the one in the Habakkuk Pesher above, about difficulties between 'the Wicked Priest' and 'the Community' of 'the Righteous Teacher'/'Zaddik' relating to events circulating around 'Yom Kippur' or its aftermath. Even from the paucity of materials that have survived about James, we also have something of the same kind regarding him.

Regardless of what may or may not have happened between 'the Righteous Teacher' and 'the Wicked Priest' on 'the Day of Atonements' or between 'the Wicked Priest' and 'the Poor'/'the Simple of Judah doing the Torah', who made up 'the Council of the Community' and who were, seemingly, led by 'the Righteous Teacher', one can surmise that it was because of James' atonement in 'the Inner Sanctum' of the Temple on behalf of the whole People on Yom Kippur – attested to in sources stemming from the Second-Century early Church writers Hegesippus and Clement of Alexandria – that his arrest took place, probably in 62 CE, the year of his 'Sanhedrin Trial' on charges of 'blasphemy'. Here too, of course, is the substance of the 'blasphemy' charge – *pronouncing the forbidden name of God* which the High Priest did on Yom Kippur and in the Inner Sanctum of the Temple. Put in another way, we also have materials in these sources, as sketchy as these are, which specifically imply activities connecting James to the Temple and centering about a Yom Kippur-atonement of some kind. Again, that we should have such notices and such a link-up, even in the scanty materials before us, is of the greatest significance.

Jesus ben Ananias appeared during the Feast of Tabernacles, 62 CE, which occurs immediately following Yom Kippur in the same month and as a culmination of the Festivities initiated by this atonement. He, in turn, is said to have reiterated for seven and a half straight years: 'Woe to Jerusalem..., Woe to the City, and the People, and the Temple', until he was killed by a stray Roman projectile shortly before the fall of the Temple in 70 CE. In some manner, as already suggested, this was connected to the removal and recent death of James, 'the *Oblias*'/'Bulwark'/'Protection of the People' or 'Perfectly Righteous' High Priest.

Therefore, one can say with some certainty that Jesus ben Ananias, the 'Prophet' bowdlerized in Agabus' warning to Paul in Acts 21:7, began his mournful prophesying immediately following Yom Kippur 62 CE and the events culminating in the death of James. We have also described how this 'oracle' seems to have been the basis of the Early Christian 'Pella Flight' Tradition connected to the death of James. It is even possible to conceive that in some manner the three and a half years in Daniel 12:7 – 'a time, two times, and a half', the period of the interruption of sacrifice in the Temple during which 'the Abomination of the Desolation' held sway in Jerusalem – may have been interpreted to relate to the period between James' death and the suspension of sacrifice on behalf of Romans in the Temple leading to the outbreak of the War.

This is also something of the implication of additional obscure numerology in Daniel 12:11–12 of '1290–1335 days'. This is connected to another section of Daniel with slightly differing numerology relating to the daily sacrifice and the cleansing of the Temple, which uses the language of 'casting down' – namely, 'casting down the Truth'/'casting down the Temple' and a variation of both of these, 'casting the Heavenly Host and the stars to the ground and stamping upon them' (Daniel 8:10–14). The 'causing them to stumble' or 'casting down' verb, used along with 'swallowing them' in this obscure passage from 1QpHab XI.2– XII.12 about tragic events connected to Yom Kippur, is somewhat parallel to these. Neither of these – the allusion to 'swallowing them' and the allusion to 'causing them to stumble' or 'casting them down' – is to be found in the underlying text from Habakkuk 2:15. At this point this only contains the allusions to 'pouring out His Venom' or 'pouring out His Wrath', 'causing his neighbors to drink' (this is the same '*mashkeh*' or 'give to drink' we shall encounter in the esoteric analysis we shall do at the end of this book on 'Damascus' or '*Dammashek*' in Hebrew as '*Dam-mashkeh* – 'give Blood to drink'), and 'to the dregs' or 'unto drunkenness in order to gaze on their Festivals'/'privy parts', as we have seen. Both of these phrases are deliberately added in the *Pesher*. But it should be appreciated that this 'casting down' or 'being thrown down' language is the basis of all early Church accounts relating to 'the Enemy' Paul's attack on or the death of the look-alike of 'the Righteous Teacher', James.

The Isaiah 3:10–11 *Pesher* in Early Church Literature

This is also the thrust of the material preceding Isaiah 3:10–11, the Scriptural passage applied to James' death in Eusebius' long extract from Hegesippus' now-lost account in the manner that '*Zaddik*'-texts were applied to the death of the Righteous Teacher at Qumran. Hegesippus also attests that James' name was to be found by searching Scripture, clearly meaning either his name 'Jacob' or 'the *Zaddik*' (probably the latter), just as in these texts at Qumran, like Psalm 37:32 and Habakkuk 1:4, to say nothing of Isaiah 53:11. But this text from Isaiah 3:10–11 actually fulfills both of these qualifications being, first of all, a '*Zaddik*'-text about 'the Wicked overwhelming the Righteous' and those involved in such activity 'being paid the reward of their doings' and, second of all, no less significantly, it was addressed to the '*House of Jacob*' (Isaiah 2:5).

Furthermore, not only is it surrounded by references to 'robbing the Poor', 'swallowing the Way', 'standing up to Judge the Peoples', and 'the reward of the Wicked', but it is also a 'cedars of Lebanon'-text referring to 'the fall of the Lofty Ones' and that 'the Lord of Hosts is taking away from Jerusalem and Judah the Stay and the Staff' (2:5–3:15). Whether there was actually a *Pesher* concerning it in the manner of the Habakkuk and Psalm 37 *Peshers* at Qumran is a matter of opinion but what the exegetes at Qumran would have made of these passages is crystal clear.

It is worth remarking, in the Greek version of this passage from Isaiah 3:10–11, the note of 'conspiring' or 'plotting' that one finds as well in the Habakkuk *Pesher*, in which the Wicked Priest 'plotted to destroy the Poor'. Here it is expressed in terms of 'conspiring an Evil counsel against themselves', translated in the Greek by the words '*bebouleuntai boulen*'. Again one recognizes the bare outlines of our '*bale*'/'*ballo*' symbolism permeating all these parallel Greek texts relating to the death of James. As we shall presently see, the allusion here will not be unrelated to the 'Babylon' usage one finds in Revelation 14:8 and 16:19 as well.

But these words nowhere appear in the Hebrew version of Isaiah 3:10–11 nor, for instance, in the version of Isaiah found at Qumran, nor the Vulgate. Here the words are, 'Woe to the Wicked' 'for they have rewarded ('paid') themselves Evil'. Therefore these surprisingly different words in Greek seem to have at some point found their way into the Septuagint. Accordingly, it then goes on to read: 'Let us bind the Just One, for he is an annoyance to us. Therefore shall they eat the fruit of their works.' This is the version of the text that is reproduced in the early Church testimony as applied to James with the repercussions we have been explaining above.[55] For their part, however, the Hebrew and other received versions of this text preserve almost the opposite sense and give the passage a more positive cast that does not fit the exegesis developed in Hegesippus and his dependents: 'Say to the Righteous (*Zaddik*) that it will be well, for they shall eat the fruit of their actions. Woe the Wicked (*Rasha*), (to him) Evil (*Ra'ah*), for the reward (*gemul*) of his hands shall be done to him (Isaiah 3:10–11).'[56]

In both of these versions we have the usual references to 'eating' carrying the implied meaning of 'destroyed' or 'being paid a reward'. The same sense is reiterated in the Hebrew version of Isaiah 3:9: 'for they have paid/rewarded (*gamlu*) themselves Evil (*Ra'ah*)'. The Isaiah 3:11 part of this all-important passage is more or less the same in all versions. This having been said, the words being used in this proof-text will immediately be recognized as the basis of the *Pesher* we have just reviewed above from Column XII.2–3 of the Habakkuk *Pesher* which actually uses the same Hebrew words '*gemul*' and '*gamal*' ('reward and 'rewarded'/'paid') twice, '*gemul asher gamal*' ('the reward which he rewarded' or 'the reward which he paid'), just as one finds them here in the Hebrew of Isaiah 3:9–11. In both the Hebrew and the Greek of Isaiah 3:11, this is expressed as 'the reward of his hands will be done to him' or 'he shall be paid according to the works of his hands'.

1QpHab XII.2–3 uses parallel words to express the same idea, 'he (the Wicked Priest) will be paid the reward which he paid ('rewarded') the Poor' (*Ebionim*), even though none of this exists in the underlying text of Habakkuk 2:17 being expounded. As in the case of the 'swallowing' or 'casting down' in the interpretation of Habakkuk 2:15 in XI.2–15 just preceding this, the allusion to 'the Poor', which will not have a parallel until the eschatological reference to 'the Meek' ('*Ani*) in Habakkuk 3:14 to follow, has been deliberately introduced. But so has the language of dual allusion to 'reward' (*gemul*) and 'rewarding' (*gamal*) which does not exist as such in the underlying Hebrew of Habakkuk 2:17 and which only refers to 'the Violence done to Lebanon', 'the Violence to the Land', 'the dumb beasts', and 'the Blood of Man ('*Adam*', repeated twice). We have already signaled the possibilities presented by this reference to 'Man'/'*Adam*'. This, too, has been deliberately introduced. Nor is this to say anything about the incredibly 'Messianic' language of Habakkuk 3:3–19 which the *Pesher* has not yet even bothered to expound.

In our view, what the exegete has done here (either because the Community has another *Pesher* relating to the language in Isaiah 3:9–11, or remembers it) is taken this language – in particular that of Isaiah 3:11 which did involve the phraseology of 'Woe to the Wicked' (in the vocabulary of Qumran exegesis, always 'the Wicked Priest') – namely, 'the reward of his hands shall be done to him', and introduced it here into his *Pesher* about 'the reward which would be paid to' the Wicked Priest for what he did to 'the Poor' – i.e., in our view, the followers of James.

But, of course, where Isaiah 3:10–11 is concerned, this is the exact passage, as we now know, that was applied to the death of James in early Church literature. But the parallels do not end there. Not only does the Habakkuk *Pesher*, at this point, refer to the 'conspiracy' by the Wicked Priest 'to destroy the Poor', it ends with the reference that he 'robbed the Riches/sustenance of the Poor' (*gazal Hon-Ebionim*). Once again, the phrase does not appear at this point in the underlying text Habakkuk 2:17, only 'Violence', 'Lebanon', 'beasts', and 'Blood', as we have seen, but nothing about 'robbing the Poor' (*gazal*). Rather this allusion is to be found two lines further along in Isaiah 3:14, directly following the materials from Isaiah 3:10–11 being applied to James' death by Hegesippus and his dependents. Here 'robbing the Poor' (*gezelat he-'Ani*) is specifically referred to, as is 'burning the vineyard' and 'grinding the face of the Poor' (3:15). The only difference between the sense of the two texts is that *"Ani"*/'Meek' is used instead of *'Ebion'*/'Poor'.

We just saw how this usage of *'Ebionim'*, the name for James' Community in Early Christianity, was deliberately introduced into the reference to the 'robbing' and 'destroying', the Wicked Priest does in this Column to 'the Poor', even though – just as in Isaiah 3:15 above – an allusion to *"Ani"*/'Meek' did not appear until Habakkuk 3:14's 'eating' or 'devouring' the Meek in secret'. The same is true of the Psalm 37 *Pesher*, which also refers to God paying the Wicked Priest 'his reward' (*gemulo*) in exegesis of 'the Wicked watching out for the Righteous and seeking to kill him', the underlying text for which generally refers to 'the Meek' (Psalm 37:11 and 14). There, it will be recalled, these allusions were tied both to evocation of 'the Doers of the *Torah*' and 'the Assembly of the Poor' – phrases, as should by now be appreciated, of absolute significance to the identification our two Communities.

But this 'eating' or 'devouring' is exactly the sense of 'eating the fruit of their actions' ('works' in the Septuagint translation) of Isaiah 3:10. In addition, this allusion to the 'robbing the Poor' in the Isaiah passage, applied to James in early Church exegesis, also directly follows an allusion in 3:12 to 'leading the People astray' and '*swallowing* (*bille'u*) the Way of Your Paths', not to mention 'the Lord standing up to judge the Peoples' in 3:13. Once again, we have the clearest kind of proof – if such were needed – that the sectaries are mixing the imagery found in Isaiah 3 with those of Habakkuk 1–2 to produce the exegesis they are seeking. Having said this, *the passage from Isaiah 3:10–11 is the one being applied to James' death and what Ananus did to him in the earliest Church testimony*. Nor can we find a clearer illustration of the connections between the two passages than to see that the language from the one is deliberately being introduced into the interpretation of the other.

One should also note both the allusions to 'standing up' (the 'standing'/'Standing One' ideology again) and the parallels represented by the language of 'eating'/'devouring' and 'swallowing'/'consuming', which are particularly strong in the *Pesharim* at Qumran. One cannot ask for clearer textual proof of the identity of 'the Righteous Teacher' from Qumran with the James ('Jacob') of early Church sources than the convergence of these Scriptural materials being used to apply to the deaths of them both.

View of the Fortress of Masada

Chapter 20
'The Cup of the Wrath of God Will Swallow Him'

Daniel's Chronology and James' Stoning

We shall now be able to elucidate these allusions to 'making one's neighbor drink, pouring out His Fury unto satiety' or 'drunkenness' – possibly, also, 'make them drink' or 'drunk' – in the underlying passage from Habakkuk 2:15 being expounded here in 1QpHab XI.2–10. Before doing so, it should be noted that this passage from the end of Daniel which alludes to 'a time, two times and a half' and the odd numerology of 'a thousand three hundred and thirty-five days' also closes with an allusion to 'standing up to your Fate (also 'Lot') at the End of Days' (12:13). Not only is this language of 'the Last Days' or 'the End of Days' a part of the ethos of most of these *Pesharim* on Biblical texts at Qumran, we have already encountered it in terms of the 'standing up' or 'return of the Messiah' in the Damascus Document – alluded to there in at least three different places.

That is to say that, according to the ideology of the Damascus Document, it is possible to consider allusions such as this as meaning that 'the Messiah' had already come and that, not only is his return anxiously awaited but the events we have been describing are taking place in the aftermath of this. While these things are obscure and not, strictly speaking, admissible of proof, this is the problem of depending on the chronology of 'Consensus' Qumran Scholarship as it has (until recently) been purveyed. As we have said, this scholarship does not attempt to make ambiguous readings of this kind intelligible to the general public or come to grips in any significant way with the internal data of the texts themselves.

Where the 'three and a half years' from Daniel 12:7 are concerned, reiterated in Josephus' description of the interruption of sacrifices at the time of Antiochus Epiphanes' incursions in the War,[1] this is also the numerology of the eschatological ending of the Letter of James. Not only are the coming of apocalyptic 'Judgment', 'standing', 'the Last Days', 'the coming of the Lord of Hosts', and 'the End' – most of which found in Daniel – alluded to in the last Chapter of James (5:4–5:11), but the reference there to 'three and a half years' comes amid evocation of 'the Prayer of Faith' for forgiveness of Sins, that is to say, *an atonement*.

Here the assurance is given that 'the Lord will raise him up' and the efficacy of 'the fervent working prayer of the Righteous One' evoked (5:15–16). This then is followed by 'the prayer for rain' delivered by a previous 'Righteous One', Elijah, which we have already shown to be not unconnected with the evocation of final apocalyptic 'Judgment' and 'the coming of the Messiah' (also deriving from Daniel) together with 'the Heavenly Host on the clouds of Heaven'. In the War Scroll, the coming of this eschatological Judgment is twice compared to the coming of rain – apocalyptic rain – which, as Matthew 5:45 would phrase it, is 'sent on the Just and Unjust' alike.[2] In Rabbinic literature, as we saw, the coming of rain in its season is associated with proper Temple service, the very thing delineated in James' reported critique of the Temple Establishment in the *Anabathmoi Jacobou*.[3]

Here in James 5:7–8, 'the coming of the Lord' is also expressed in terms of 'early and late rain'. In Talmud *Ta'anith*, this 'early rain' (*yoreh*) is also referred to with regard to final eschatological Judgement,[4] and, in the Damascus Document, it is a name for the stand-in for 'the Righteous Teacher', the *Yoreh ha-Zedek*/'Guide of Righteousness', not 'the *Moreh ha-Zedek*'.[5] In the Letter of James, too, 'three and a half years' is the period in between which Elijah – John the Baptist's prototype and the forerunner of the Messiah in the Gospels – both 'prayed for it not to rain and then to rain', i.e., the period during which 'rain' was withheld.

It is possible to view this period, as just signaled, as a complicated numerology of some sort relating to the period in between the stoning of 'the *Zaddik*' James for 'blasphemy' and the final rejection of gifts and stopping of sacrifice 'on behalf of foreigners' in the Temple by the 'Zealot' Lower Priesthood some three and a half years later. Though admittedly speculative, in such a scenario James – as 'the High Priest' and the individual whose 'fervent prayer' and 'atonement' on behalf of the whole People on his knees in the Holy of Holies before the Judgment Seat at Yom Kippur – provoked the events the Habakkuk *Pesher* seems to be referring to, that from its vantage point resulted in the swallowing of the Righteous Teacher or, from Josephus' point-of-view, the Trial for 'blasphemy' of James.

We have already discussed this Trial of James and several of his associates – in the Habakkuk *Pesher* referred to as 'the Poor' and 'the Simple of Judah doing *Torah*' – on a charge of 'blasphemy' by Ananus to which, as Josephus avers, those in Jerusalem 'most concerned with Equity and scrupulous observation of the Law objected'. This is followed in all early Church sources by the immediate coming of the Roman Armies and the destruction of Jerusalem – which is also the overall sense here of the Habakkuk *Pesher* though, for it, all of these events may not yet have been accomplished but in the process, perhaps, of only being accomplished. Such a scenario would allow us to place what is being described in these incredible materials in the Habakkuk *Pesher* in the very midst of these events having both to do with the fall of Jerusalem and the destruction of the Temple, so fraught with significance for the history of Western Civilization thereafter, just as a greater part of Daniel appears to have been written in the midst of the Maccabean Uprising.

This complex of events and allusions is a very important dating tool for the Habakkuk *Pesher* because otherwise we would have to put the events it is describing back into the days of the storming of the Temple with Roman help by Herod in 37 BCE or Pompey in 63 BCE when there was absolutely no indication of any subsequent seizure of spoil. This would be patently absurd, not only because there is nothing remotely resembling the events we have been describing here, but because, on the contrary, Josephus is very specific in asserting that, aside from going in and viewing the forbidden Holy of Holies with some of his officers, Pompey *touched nothing – no spoil.* Nor did Herod thereafter, for the reasons we have already delineated above, that is, wishing to avoid the animosity of his subjects-to-be, he promised to pay his soldiers out of his own pocket.[6]

We have already seen how these 'blasphemy' charges – which more properly appertain to the Sanhedrin Trial of James – are absorbed into all accounts of the trial and death of Jesus, unless Jesus did what James did, that is, render atonement on behalf of the whole people in the Holy of Holies on at least one Yom Kippur. He may have, as he is pictured in Mark 11:16 as stopping commerce in the Temple, but we have no way of knowing whether he did. In any event this is the way Paul, in his spiritualization of these affairs, interprets his death though now Jesus becomes the sacrifice itself. However this may be, the most important basis for the charge of 'blasphemy', according to Talmudic tradition is pronouncing the forbidden Name of God or encouraging others to do so[7] – except, that is, by the functioning High Priest who on Yom Kippur was permitted to pronounce this Name as part of his general supplication in the Holy of Holies.

But, as already explained, this is exactly what James is pictured as doing in the very Yom Kippur atonement scenario, portrayed in early Church tradition regarding him, that is, we have an actual basis for the 'blasphemy' charge against James in the reported events of his very life itself whereas for Jesus, ostensibly anyhow, we do not – claims to the contrary in the Gospels notwithstanding. Furthermore, even in the picture of the Gospels, Jesus does not undergo the prescribed punishment for 'blasphemy' – stoning – but one for subversive activities or Revolutionary actions according to Roman parameters – therefore his appearance before Pilate, according to Gospel portraiture, who would probably not normally review a punishment for 'blasphemy' according to Jewish ones. A Jewish Sanhedrin would not and could not impose a crucifixion penalty since, as we have been showing, it was forbidden under Jewish Law, even in Paul's convoluted transformation of it in Galatians 3:13. Only a Roman Governor could do this, a fact the Gospels and the Book of Acts are anxious to obscure in their many accusations about 'Jewish plots' and their picture of the rushed Sanhedrin proceedings for 'blasphemy' at the Jewish 'High Priest's House' – itself probably based on the biography of James.

Here the usage 'Court', 'House', or 'Palace' in the portrait in the Gospels is very important, and probably the true explanation for the allusion to 'His House of Exile' in the Habakkuk *Pesher*, not to mention the plethora of Talmudic notices about just such an 'exile of the Sanhedrin' from its normal place of sitting during this period. However these things may be, James was stoned for blasphemy and we have the probable basis for such a charge – warranted or otherwise. A 'Rechabite Priest', to wit, a 'Priest' obeying the purity strictures of extreme Naziritism or what some might call an 'Essene Priest', James as a 'Covenant-Keeper' was certainly a 'Priest' according to the definition at Qumran – a 'Son of Zadok' or one of 'the Elect of Israel, who would stand at the Last Days and justify the Righteous and condemn the Wicked'.

It was most likely in this period, symbolized by the erection of the wall in the Temple to bar a Herodian King from even seeing it or activities in it that James and his partisans developed the power to effect such an atonement by a 'Perfectly Righteous' or People's 'Priest' in the Temple on 'their *Yom ha-Kippurim*' if not the Establishment one. After James' death in 62 CE on the heels of Agrippa II's discomfiture in this same Temple Wall Affair, some might have seen the stopping of sacrifices and accepting gifts on behalf of Romans and other foreigners – including Herodians and their associates – in 66 CE by persons of a 'Jamesian' mindset and revering his memory as fulfilling some kind of Scriptural warrant.

Such 'Zealots' are, in fact, referred to as the partisans of James in Acts 21:21 and earlier, as we have remarked, Acts 6:7 speaks of 'a large number of the Priests' coming over to the nascent 'Faith' – not that it is able to make any sense of this notice. It is these Priests, called by some 'the Lower Priesthood', who win the right to wear the High-Priestly linen following James' death at the end of the *Antiquities*[8] and who are at the core of the events leading up to stopping sacrifice on behalf of Romans and other foreigners in the Temple, the signal for the start of the final War against Rome. Since Daniel seems to have been so instrumental in so many of the prognostications relating to this War, calculations in Daniel may have been part of the process of deciding the time and date of such steps as were called for. For instance, the year 66 CE also has the virtue of completing the 70-year 'Period of Wrath', referred to in Daniel 9:24, reverberating in references at Qumran in documents like the War Scroll and the Damascus Document.[9] This was perhaps thought of as coming into play with the outbreak of 'the Zealot'/'*Sicarii* Movement' in the 4 BCE disturbances following Herod's death until the final purification of Temple sacrifices in these events surrounding the beginning of the War in 66 CE. These are only possibilities – they are not realities, but they are sensible within the framework of the Scriptural mindset being evinced here.

'The Cup of the Wrath of God' and 'the Blood of Man' in the Habakkuk *Pesher*

This now brings us to the destruction of the Wicked Priest, as vividly delineated in the *Pesher* in interpretation of the passage that follows the allusion to 'giving his neighbor to drink' and 'pouring his Fury'/'*Hamato*' in the underlying text. The underlying Biblical text that follows this from Habakkuk 2:16 is quoted as follows: 'Drink also and stagger. The Cup of the right hand of the Lord shall come around to you and shame shall cover your Glory.'[10] The key allusion here, of course, is 'Cup' (*Chos*). We have seen this usage relating to James in

Jewish Christian sources, that James would 'not eat or drink from the time he drank the Cup of the Lord, until he should see Jesus' – this is in the so-called 'Gospel of the Hebrews' reported by Jerome. At Qumran the allusion is almost always to 'Wrath' (*Cha'as*), as it is here in the *Pesher* – '*Chos*' and '*Cha'as*' being homophonic. Here, in the *Pesher*, quite rightly, 'the Wicked Priest' is going to 'drink to the dregs' or 'drink to satiety'. He would be 'drunk', but his 'drunkenness' would be from 'the Cup of the Wrath of God', of which 'he would drink his fill'. Here again, of course, we see the sort of word-play and metaphor that so fascinated our militant exegetes. Nor is this to say anything about the 'giving to drink' and the various plays we shall encounter in Gospel portraits and the one in Paul of Jesus' words at 'the Last Supper', 'taking the Cup and giving them to drink' (in 1 Corinthians 11:26–27, connected to 'Blood' and called 'the Cup of the Lord') at the end of this book in our analysis of 'the New Covenant in the Land of Damascus'.

The phrase, as it is given at the end of Column XI.13–15, is: 'but the Cup of the Wrath of God shall swallow him' (*teval'eno*). Once again we have our play on the language of 'swallowing' that so permeates these Scriptural exegeses. The meaning here is clear, as we have underscored: just as 'he swallowed the Righteous Teacher' and his associates (possibly connected to observances they were conducting on their Yom Kippur) so, too, would he himself be 'swallowed', i.e., 'consumed'.

That this, in fact, involved 'the destruction' of 'the Righteous Teacher and the Men of his Council', called in what follows '*Ebionim*' or 'the Poor', is made clear in the next two columns ending in the climactic finale about 'the Last Judgment' in XII.13–XIII.4. Because the word being used there is now 'destroy' (*lechalot*) not 'swallow', this reads quite straightforwardly as we saw: 'He will be paid the reward he paid the Poor.' Just so there should be no mistaking the import here, this is repeated using the language of 'conspiracy': 'as he plotted to destroy the Poor, so too would God condemn him to destruction'. As noted, the language of 'the Poor' is introduced into the *Pesher*, though it nowhere occurs in the underlying Biblical passage, just as the language of 'swallowing', 'being cast down', and 'paying the reward' was previously. The sectarians *want* this language in the exegesis; *therefore they put it there*. They do the same with the language of '*Chos-Hamato*'/'the Cup of His Wrath', the variation of which has already preceded its use here in the description of the Wicked Priest's 'angry wrath'/'*cha'as hamato*'. (transformed from 'Your Fury' in normative Habakkuk 2:15).[11] The word-play here should be obvious.

There is no '*Cha'as*'/'Wrath' as such in the underlying text from Habakkuk 2:15 (though there is '*Hamatchah*' – 'Your Fury' as we just saw). This is purposefully introduced into the *Pesher* by the exegetes, in the same manner that they introduce important words like 'Festivals', 'staggering', 'swallowing', and 'the Poor'. An additional variation on this '*Hemah*' ('Venom' or 'Poison') and itself connected to 'wine', is the way the 'Vipers' or 'Kings of the Peoples' are portrayed in the exegesis of Deuteronomy 32:33 in CD VIII.9–11/XIX.21 –25. Where 'the Wicked Priest' is concerned, it is his 'hot wrath'/'*cha'as hamato*' or 'venomous fury' that – in the manner of 'the Pursuer' in Deuteronomy 19:6 – drives him to 'pursue the Righteous Teacher to swallow him'. In the case of God's 'Vengeance' and 'Punishment on the Wicked Priest' that follows, it is 'the Cup of the Wrath of God' that 'will swallow him' (the Wicked Priest), meaning, just as the latter 'swallowed' the Righteous Teacher and his followers 'with' or 'in his House of Exile' so, too, would he be 'swallowed'/'consumed by God's Wrath', of which – as just made clear – 'he would drink his fill' or 'drink to satiety'/'to the dregs'.

Roman amphitheatre at Italica in Southern Spain, birthplace of both Trajan and Hadrian and perhaps home of "the Italica Regiment" mentioned in Acts 10:2.

'The Cup of the Wine of the Wrath of God' and 'the Scarlet Beast' in Revelation

The best exposition of this vivid metaphor is to be found in The Book of Revelation, itself drenched in language and imagery of this kind and reveling in it. In the context of repeated allusion to 'blaspheming the Name of God' (13:1–6) and 'One like a Son of Man sitting upon the cloud' (14:14), it reads: 'He shall also *drink of the wine of the Wrath of God, which is poured out full strength into the Cup of his Anger.* And he shall be tormented in fire and brimstone before the Holy Angels and before the Lamb (14:10).' These allusions should all be by now familiar, and there can be no doubt that we are speaking about 'the Wrath of God' and 'Divine Vengeance'. It will be immediately appreciated that the allusion here even incorporates the underlying language of Habakkuk 2:15, just used in CD XI.3–8 to develop the exegesis concerning how the Wicked Priest 'swallowed the Righteous Teacher', 'causing his neighbor to drink, pouring out His Venom' or 'Wrath to make them drunk'. This was even preceded in CD X.3–5 and 13 by allusion to executing 'Judgment upon him with fire and brimstone' in 'the House of Judgment which God would deliver'. Revelation, of course, fairly overflows with this language of 'pouring' and 'Judgment', just as it does that of 'blasphemy'. An example: 'And the third Angel *poured out his bowl* onto the rivers and onto the Fountain of waters (language present in CD VIII.22/XIX.34), and they become blood.... For they *poured out the blood o*f the Holy Ones and the Prophets, and You *gave them blood to drink*, for they deserve it (16:4–6).'

Not only was this 'Fountain' or 'Well of Living Waters' referred to in the Damascus Document in the context of the allusion to '*the Yoreh*'/'Guide', 'betraying the New Covenant in the Land of Damascus', 'the Assembly of the Men of Perfect Holiness', and the 'standing up of the Messiah of Aaron and Israel', but these are the same accusations about the Jews 'killing all the Prophets'. There is also the variation on James' directive to 'abstain from blood'. Nor is this to say anything about what we shall see at the end of the book as the Hebrew esoteric exposition of 'Damascus' as 'to *give blood to drink*' and what we have further seen as the additional play on and reversal of these matters by Paul in 1 Corinthians 10:21 and 11:27–29.

In Revelation too, we even have allusion to 'the Beast', 'with a mouth speaking great things and blasphemy', again tied to a timeframe of three and a half years, that is, 'forty-two months' (13:5). In the interpretation of Habakkuk 2:17 following these allusions to 'the Cup of the Wrath of God swallowing him', 'the dumb beasts' were 'the Simple of Judah doing *Torah*' and there was also the pregnant allusion to 'Blood' – there, 'the Blood of Man' (*Adam*), interpreted to mean 'the destruction of the Poor' and 'robbing them of their substance'. In Revelation, this is reversed, as per usual in early Church texts of a Pauline mindset and even later by theologians such as Eusebius – himself partially responsible for the Christian takeover of the Roman Empire. Instead of 'the Simple of Judah doing the *Torah*' and 'the Community Council' of 'the Poor' as in the *Pesher*, this 'Blood' now becomes the Jews 'pouring out the Blood of the Holy Ones and the Prophets' which is, again, not to mention Paul's whole ideology of 'Communion with the Blood of Christ' succeeding these kinds of allusions in the documents at Qumran.

This is reaffirmed with the words, 'You gave them Blood to drink' – also a play on both the 'Jamesian'/Jewish 'abstinence from blood' and what we shall now try to show is the esoteric exposition of 'the New Covenant in the Land of Damascus' – 'for they deserve it'. This is neatly summed up by Paul in 1 Corinthians 11:27–29: whoever shall 'drink the Cup of the Lord unworthily shall be guilty of the Body and Blood of the Lord', for he, who drinks unworthily, drinks Judgment to himself.

The 'blasphemy' accusations that accompany all this are not really separable from the Gospel presentations of the Trial of Jesus at 'the High Priest's House' where he is pictured as both claiming to be either 'the Christ' or 'the Son of God' and delivering the proclamation about the latter attributed to James in early Church literature (Matthew 26:57–68 and pars.). At this point in Revelation, these accusations are tied to the imagery from Daniel of 'the beast with ten horns'. As Revelation 13:1 puts this: 'On its heads was the Name of blasphemy' and 'it opened its mouth for blasphemy against God, to blaspheme His Name and His Temple and those in the Temple of Heaven' (13:6). Not only does this play on the imagery in Daniel 7:8 of the 'little horn', but also the 'blasphemy' charge against James in the episode in Hegesippus about his proclamation of 'the coming of the Son of Man'; instead of 'pronouncing the forbidden Name of God in the Temple', as we have decided James did in his Yom Kippur atonement, 'the beast' is 'blaspheming the Name of God and the Temple'. The ethos, however, is basically that of the charges made against Paul by 'the Jews from Asia' in the Temple in Acts 21:27–28 (how fortuitous this location, as it is essentially the same as in Revelation), in 'Jewish' or 'Ebionite Christianity' generally, and against 'the Liar' at Qumran – 'blaspheming the Temple' or 'insulting the Law'.

Notice, too, how this charge of 'blasphemy' is also used earlier in the section, in which 'Balaam taught Balak to cast a net before Israel', amidst negative allusion to 'works', 'Riches' and 'fornication' (Revelation 2:9). Even 'Poverty' and 'suffering' are mentioned. As usual, the 'blasphemy' is now on the part of 'those claiming themselves to be Jews' but who are really 'the Synagogue of Satan' paralleling material in 2 Corinthians 10:12–11:15 about the Hebrew 'False Apostles' who 'recommend themselves, comparing themselves to themselves', claiming to be 'Servants of Righteousness'. These are really 'the Servants of Satan, whose End shall be according to their works' (11:15). In Revelation 2:23, this is: 'giving you each according to your works'.

In addition to the virtual reproduction of Paul's words, this chapter of Revelation mixes the language of 'the Diabolos'/'the Devil' with that of 'Satan', as do the Gospels and as at Qumran. In Revelation 2:10, the reference is to how 'the Devil casts (balein) some of you into prison'. Not only does the reference to 'the Diabolos' here parallel the one to 'Belial' and 'the nets he set up to ensnare Israel' in CD IV.15–18 but it, too, begins by evoking, 'He knew your works' (Revelation 2:9). Again, this is word-for-word from CD II.7–8: 'God knew their works before ever they were established', preceded by reference to 'God's Anger being kindled against them', because 'their works were unclean before Him'.[12]

Furthermore, we have seen that this 'Belial'/'Devil' evocation of the 'Three Nets of Belial' section of the Damascus Document is present in the evocations of 'Balaam' and 'Balak' which follow in Revelation 2:14. So are the parameters of James' prohibitions to overseas communities in Acts: 'eating things sacrificed to idols and committing fornication', which so parallel the basic thrust of 'Three Nets' in the Damascus Document, in which Belial 'caught Israel', 'transforming them into three kinds of Righteousness' (note the additional parallel here to Paul in 2 Corinthians 11:14 above, in the sense of the verb 'transforming' as in 'Satan transforming himself into an Angel of Light' or 'his servants' into 'Servants of Righteousness'). These parameters are repeated again in Revelation 2:20 in slightly variant form in terms of 'leading My Servants astray – here also the 'Servants' language of 2 Corinthians 11:15, not to mention 'leading astray' in Qumran vocabulary generally – to commit fornication and eat things sacrificed to idols', only now it is 'Jezebel' who is being attacked as the Deceiver. One should appreciate that even in her name one has another clear variant of the 'balla'/'ballo' terminology here.

This reference to 'Jezebel' is of the utmost interest, as are the references to 'the great whore' and 'the whore of Babylon' that appear later in Revelation 17:1–18 and 19:2 amid the language of another of these categories of James' prohibitions, 'Blood'. Surrounding the 'Jezebel' references, 'knowing your works' from Revelation 2:9 is repeated in 2:19 and, varying this, 'keeping My works' in 2:26 – note the Qumran 'keeping' vocabulary in this last again. In fact 'he that keeps My works until the End' – 'keeping the Law' in James; 'keeping the Covenant' at Qumran – 'will be given Authority over the Peoples'. This is basically the eschatology of the Habakkuk *Pesher* (V.3–5) where God's 'Elect ('the Assembly of the Poor' in the Psalm 37 *Pesher*) execute Judgment on all the Nations'!

The references to Jezebel's 'fornication' in Revelation 2:21–22, seemingly with multiple partners, makes it more likely than ever that the author has one or another of the Herodian Princesses in mind, most likely Bernice – ultimately the mistress of the destroyer of Jerusalem and the Temple Titus. Once again, the '*beľ*/'*ballo*' language – denoting in our view Herodians and their confrères – which is omnipresent throughout, must be considered determinant. Of course, what we have in these allusions in Revelation *are Qumran materials* – and, by extension, *those of the Community of James* – being tossed around indiscriminately and overwritten in obfuscating fashion. Sometimes these usages are trivialized or even reversed, but sometimes they are presented as per normative Palestinian usage. Knowing this, the imagery can be at times quite amusing.

'Babylon the Great' and 'Jezebel'

For good measure, in these later passages, Revelation 16:19 now goes on to apply 'the Cup of Wrath' metaphor to 'Babylon the Great', rejoicing over how God would remember to give her 'the Cup of the Wine of the Fury of His Wrath'. Once again, these are precisely the words used at Qumran to describe what happened to the Wicked Priest as a result of what he did to the Righteous Teacher and yet another variation of the 'Jeze*beľ*/'*ballo*'/'*Bela*' language cluster. Once again, too, we are getting transmutation of Hebrew usages into Greek.

Here the allusion includes even the redundancy, '*Chaʿas Hamato*', ('*the Fury of His Wrath*' in Hebrew), the Habakkuk *Pesher* uses to describe the Wicked Priest's action in 'swallowing' (again '*ballaʿ*') the Righteous Teacher and Revelation even employs the same reversal as the Habakkuk *Pesher* does, that she would be paid with the same 'drink' or 'Cup' – in the Habakkuk *Pesher*, '*Chos*' (Cup), also playing on this same Hebrew '*Chaʿas*' (Wrath) – she paid to others. Earlier in Revelation 14:8, repeating the multiple 'drinking' allusions of the Habakkuk *Pesher*, this was expressed as: 'Babylon, which *gave all Peoples the wine of the Fury of her fornication to drink*', adding the 'fornication' imagery which was associated with 'Jezebel' in Chapter Two and which we just associated with the Herodian miscreant Bernice as well.

Not only does Revelation 14:8–12, following an allusion to 'the Fountains of Water' – right out of another Qumran text, 'The Chariots of Glory', we first named in 1992[13] – apply this imagery to 'Babylon', but also to 'anyone worshipping the Beast'. As this was expressed in Revelation 14:10, 'he would be made to drink the wine of the Wrath of God, which is poured out undiluted in the Cup of His Anger'; this is almost word-for-word the imagery applied to 'the Wicked Priest' in the Habakkuk *Pesher*, even including that of 'the Cup of the Wrath of God', varied slightly, and in the allusion 'undiluted', Habakkuk 2:15's 'drinking to the dregs'. This is immediately followed up with the words, also in Revelation 14:10, 'he shall be tortured by fire and brimstone before the Holy Angels'. But this is precisely the scenario followed in the admonishment of the Wicked Priest in Column Ten of the Habakkuk *Pesher* above, in exposition of Habakkuk 2:10 about 'the profiteer's profiteering' and 'cutting off many Peoples'.[14] This last, too, is again interpreted in terms of 'the House of Judgment' which God would pronounce 'in the midst of many Peoples'. There, to repeat, 'He (God) would lead him (the Wicked Priest) for Punishment and condemn him among them, judging him with fire and brimstone' – the same 'fire and brimstone' just referred to in Revelation 2:10.

But these repeated allusions to 'being made to drink the wine of the Wrath of God' in Revelation even recapitulate the words of CD VIII.6–10/XIX.23–24, following allusions to 'wallowing in the ways of fornication and Evil Riches', 'incest', 'profiteering', and 'not keeping apart (*nazru*) from the People(s)'. In that context, 'their wine is the Venom of Vipers' of Deuteronomy 32:33 – 'Venom', 'Anger', 'dregs', and 'Fury' being, it will be recalled, homonyms in Hebrew – was not applied, as here in Revelation to 'Babylon the Great', but to 'the Kings of the Peoples' – in our view Herodians. In this material, not only was 'the Head' of the petty Greco-Roman Kings the Roman Emperor, who was going to 'come to execute Vengeance upon them' (basically the eschatological point-of-view of the Gospels and early Church literature as well though with, of course, slightly differing signification), but in the material directly following this, 'the Spouter of Lying' was characterized as 'pouring out wind' or 'pouring out'/'walking in the Spirit' or 'Lying', thus 'kindling the Wrath of God on all his Assembly'.[15]

In Revelation, these allusions to 'drinking the Cup of the Lord's Fury' – themselves based on imagery, as previously underscored, found in Isaiah 51:17 associating 'the Cup of His Fury' (*Chos Hamato*) with 'drinking the dregs of the Cup of Trembling'(*Chos Ha-Tar'elah*) and in Jeremiah 25:15–30 on drinking 'the Cup of the wine of the Fury' of God – are often accompanied by a quotation from Psalm 2:8–9 about 'ruling the Nations with a Scepter of iron and shattering them like pots of clay'. This is repeated at several key junctures in Revelation 2:27, 12:5, and 19:15, the last time in conjunction with 'treading the press of the wine of the Fury and Wrath of God' and 'striking the Nations with the sharp sword of his mouth' from Isaiah 11:4 and 49:2.

This allusion from Isaiah 11:4, as well as the phrases leading up to it from 11:1–3, about 'a Shoot from the stem of Jesse and a Branch that would grow from his roots' who would 'judge the Downcast with Righteousness' and 'treat the Meek of the Earth with equity', are also to be found in the *Pesher* at Qumran on Isaiah 10:20–11:5 about 'the Branch of David standing at the End of Days'. Not only does it seem to be connected with 4Q285, which also quotes Isaiah 10:33–11:3, but it also employs the 'Scepter' imagery from above and refers both to his 'Throne of Gory' and 'Holy Crown' (*Nezer*)/'Crown of Holiness', all apparently interpreted in terms of 'the Branch of David who shall stand'/'arise at the End of Days'.

Regardless of translation, it is the use of common imagery of this kind and these emphases that make it absolutely certain that Qumran Documents of this genre, which are homogeneous in this regard, were written in the First Century CE. It is interesting that in the *Pesher* on Isaiah 11:1, the '*Netzer*' or 'Branch' in the underlying text becomes the '*Nezer*' ('Crown' or 'Diadem') of the High Priest – or, in more colloquial Hebrew, even possibly, 'the Holy Crown' of the Nazirite's hair (in 4Q285, it will be recalled, this 'Branch (of David)' was 'the *Nasi ha-'Edah*'– '*chol ha-'Edah*' in CD VII.20's exegesis of Numbers 24:17).[16] Again we have the shift from '*Netzer*' to '*Nezer*' we have been discussing with regard to the terminology *Nazoraean*/'Keeper' and *Nazirite*/'Consecrated One' or that between '*Nazareth*' and '*Nazrene*' in Christianity generally – but this time in an actual text from Qumran further adding to the impression of the interchangeability of these language clusters.

Following the allusion to 'pouring out the bowls of God's Wrath onto the Earth' in Revelation 16:1, which becomes 'pouring out the Blood of the Holy Ones and Prophets' and, in return, God 'giving them Blood to drink because they deserve it' in 16:6, Revelation 16:20–21 continues its ongoing mystification and conflation of all these imageries: 'And every island fled and no mountains were found, and great hail, like the weight of a talent came down out of the Heaven upon men. And men blasphemed God, because of the plague of the hail, for its plague was exceedingly great.' Though all this is, of course, total nonsense, it does evoke both the imagery of James' final proclamation in the Temple of 'the Son of Man coming on the clouds of Heaven' and the War Scroll's Heavenly Host 'like clouds, clouds covering the Land', raining final eschatological 'Judgment' on all the Sons of Men. This is to say nothing of the imagery of the whirlwind in both Jeremiah 25:32, probably evoked in the previously unpublished First Column of the Nahum *Pesher*,[17] and Ezekiel 13:11–13 on the Damascus Document's 'Daubers upon the wall', evoking God's 'Anger' (*Hemah*) and 'hailstones' as well and recapitulated in 38:22, including reference to 'fire and brimstone'.

This excursus in Revelation ends in the next chapter with allusion to being 'carried away in Spirit into (the) wilderness' – again playing on similar allusions in the Gospels and, possibly, the Scrolls – and 'seeing a woman sitting upon a scarlet beast full of Names of blasphemy' (17:3) – the same 'seven headed, ten-horned beast', based upon Daniel 7–8, we saw earlier in 13:1. The woman, too, 'was dressed in purple and scarlet' and on her head was written 'MYSTERY: Babylon the Great, the mother of whores and of the Abominations of the Earth' (17:4–5). In her hand is 'a golden Cup full of Abominations and the uncleanness of her fornication' and she is 'drunk with the Blood of the Saints and with the Blood of the Witnesses of Jesus' (17:6 – a new kind of nomenclature). Here, of course, is the imagery' of 'Abominations' connected to the person of 'the Wicked Priest' in both Columns Eight and Twelve of the Habakkuk *Pesher*, but the imagery of this last (Column XII.1–10), which does include these various allusions to 'beast(s)' and 'Blood', is much simpler.[18]

The reason for the startling introduction of the allusion in Greek, 'scarlet' or '*kokkinon*', i.e., 'the scarlet beast' on which she rode or her 'scarlet clothing', is also perhaps explained by inspection of the underlying text from Habakkuk 2:16 relating to both 'drinking' and 'staggering'/'trembling' and 'the Cup of the Lord's right hand and shame (*kikalon*) upon your Glory'. The *Pesher* now applies this allusion to '*kikalon*'/'shameful spewing', adding another allusion related to it, '*kalono*' (also 'shame'), as part of Column Eleven's accusation that the Wicked Priest's 'shame was greater than his Glory because he did not circumcise the foreskin of his heart', which precedes the fact that he would, therefore, 'walk in the Way of satiety'.[19]

Not only is this the passage which is interpreted in terms of 'the Cup of the Wrath of God swallowing him', but also it is said that it is of this he would 'drink his fill' or 'drink to the dregs'. This is the same language applied to 'the whore of Babylon' or 'Great Babylon' in Revelation 14:8 and 16:19, as well as the Worshippers 'of the Beast' in 14:10. Once again, we possibly have one of these startling overlaps and esoteric transmutations – like '*balla*' into '*ballo*' above – moving from Hebrew into Greek, in this case, now '*kalon* and *kikalon*'/'shame and disgrace' into '*kokkinon*' – the esoteric and completely unnecessary allusion to 'scarlet'.

'The Cup of Trembling' and 'not Circumcising the Foreskin of his Heart'

Not only, therefore, is this 'Bowl' or 'Cup' imagery, as applied to Vengeance and martyrdom, to be found in Revelation and the Habakkuk *Pesher*, but it is also in the Gospels relating to John and James 'the sons of Zebedee'. The 'pouring' imagery one finds in these chapters of Revelation also plays on the general imagery at Qumran with regard to 'the Man of Lying' who 'pours out the waters of Lying over Israel', and is just as often referred to as 'the Spouter' – specifically, one who 'pours out', seemingly, in addition to 'Lying', 'water', and/or 'wind', even 'the Spirit'.[20]

Not only is this 'Cup' imagery systematically transformed by Paul in his treatment of 'the Lord's Cup' or 'the Cup of the New Covenant in my blood' in 1 Corinthians 10:16–21 and 11:25–29, but it also culminates in the drinking of 'the Cup of the New Covenant in my blood which was poured out for you' in Gospel 'Last Supper' scenarios. Here, too, the 'pouring' imagery is now attached to Paul's new and more 'spiritualized' (or 'allegorical') theology of 'the Cup of the Lord'.

At this point, the text of the Habakkuk *Pesher* even picks up the imagery of Isaiah 51:17–22, adding its additional 'the Cup of Trembling' to its quotation of the underlying text from Habakkuk 2:16: 'You drink also and tremble' (*hera'el*). The *Pesher* to this reads as follows – the reader should again note the shift from '*hera'el*' to '*he-'arel*'/'foreskin': 'Its interpretation concerns the Wicked Priest, whose shame was greater than his honor because he did not circumcise the foreskin of his heart (*kalono/kikalon* – this, as suggested, possibly transmuted into the Greek 'scarlet' or '*kokkinon*' of 'the whore of Babylon' riding a 'scarlet beast' in Revelation 17:3).' Here the *Pesher* has simply reversed the letters in its version of the underlying reading, 'to tremble', to produce the allusion to 'foreskin' instead. This is typical of Qumran word-play and the freedom with which underlying texts were utilized. As should be plain, this same word-play is present in the Greek of Revelation, but with a more obscurantist and transparently anti-Semitic point-of-view. Though received versions of Habakkuk 2:16 seem to have conserved this switch from '*hera'el*'/'tremble' to '*he-'arel*'/'foreskin', the Septuagint version still retains the Qumran 'tremble'/'shake'/or 'stagger' here. But the Qumran *Pesher* seems to understand this kind of word-play and, though conserving 'tremble' in the underlying Habakkuk 2:16, interprets it – utilizing Isaiah 51:17–22's 'Cup of Wrath'/'Cup of Trembling' duality to produce its 'foreskin' metaphor – in terms of the Wicked Priest's 'uncircumcised heart'. It is these things our exegetes in modern Qumran Studies prefer to translate in terms of the Wicked Priest 'staggering' from 'drunkenness', though there is no 'drunkenness' here, only – as Revelation would have it – 'the *wine of the Wrath of God, which is poured full strength into the Cup of His Anger*'. In fact, this 'Cup of Wrath'/'the Lord's Cup'/'Cup of the Lord' metaphor is picked up again in the next passage of the *Pesher* (XI.15) which sets forth how 'the Cup of the Wrath of God would swallow him'.

This allusion to 'not circumcising the foreskin of his heart', whether in the original Habakkuk or transmuted from an allusion to '*hera'el*' there, should also be seen as not unconnected with Ezekiel 44:9's barring 'foreigners *uncircumcised in heart* and uncircumcised in flesh' from the Temple – itself part and parcel to the run-up to the enunciation of 'the Zadokite Covenant' in 44:15 so dear to Qumran exegetes in the Damascus Document. Not only does it form there, as will be recalled, the basis of the eschatological definition of 'the Sons of Zadok' and 'Priests' as 'Penitents in the Wilderness',[21] but in Ezekiel 44:17–31 it also leads up to the admonitions 'not to drink wine', 'not to shave their heads but to poll them', 'not to wear wool but only linen', and 'not to eat carrion', all matters central to the descriptions of James as they have come down to us. All of these reinforce the idea of his connection to a 'Nazirite'-style, 'Consecrated' Priesthood.

The issue of 'linen garments' or 'clothes' has particular relevance to James 'being cast down' from the Pinnacle of the Temple and his brains being bashed in by a 'laundryman' wielding a club in early Church texts – itself connected to 'stoning' scenarios in Rabbinic ones.[22] Interestingly enough, the Hebrew word we saw possibly connected to such allusions in the exegesis of Habakkuk 2:15 about the Wicked Priest 'appearing to them to swallow them, causing them to fall' or 'be cast down' on Yom Kippur, also appears in Ezekiel 44:13 about the Priests in the Temple 'ministering to them before idols and causing the House of Israel to fall' or 'be cast down'.

In this context, one should also remark the allusions to the new 'Priests', 'the Sons of Zadok', 'standing up to judge according to My Judgments and keeping My *Torah* and My Laws in all My Assemblies' in Ezekiel 44:24 and 'teaching My People the difference between Holy and profane, polluted and clean' in Ezekiel 44:23, both also dear to the Qumran mindset. The first is actually evoked in the description of 'the *Mebakker*' in the 'Camps' in the Damascus Document.[23] The second is also cited there in the 'Nazirite'-like description of 'the New Covenant in the Land of Damascus', which actually mentions 'keeping the Day of Fasting according to the precise letter of the Commandment'.[24]

Not only do we have in these passages from Ezekiel 44:6–31, as reflected in the Damascus Document, the very *reverse* of what Peter is pictured as learning in Acts 10:15 and 10:28, in anticipation of his visit to the Roman Centurion's household in Caesarea – an episode ending with 'the Holy Spirit being *poured out* on the Peoples' (10:44–45), but the main lines of what could have been exploited to produce a very interesting Qumran-style *Pesher* on aspects of James' life and practices. The point, preceding these in Ezekiel 44:7–9 about 'foreigners *uncircumcised in heart and flesh* not entering My Temple', of course, certainly could have been and probably was interpreted to relate to Herodians being barred from entering the Temple and in the wake of the death of James it would seem, all Jerusalem as well. It also relates to the rejection of gifts and sacrifices from foreigners in the Temple, the issue which sparked the outbreak of the War against Rome. We have identified this issue as the basis for the Third 'Net of *Belial*' reflected in James' directives to overseas communities, as reported in Acts 15 and 21, 1 Corinthians 8:10, and *MMT* – namely, abstention from 'the pollutions of the idols' or 'things sacrificed to idols'. In fact, the ban in the last line of this chapter from Ezekiel on things 'dying of themselves or torn, whether fowl or beast' (44:31) is clearly the basis of the last category of James' directives, the ban on 'carrion', garbled in Greek translation into 'strangled things'.

Here too, whether by coincidence or design, one has the omnipresent allusion to 'Beast' again. Therefore, not only do we have in all three of these documents, Ezekiel, Habakkuk, and Revelation, the constant reiteration of this theme of 'Beast(s)', but in the first, the makings of what could have been developed into a more complete Qumran-style *Pesher* relating to James' person and experiences as well. In the second two of these, this allusion to 'Beast' is accompanied by the common imagery of 'Blood', 'pouring out the Blood of the Saints' and 'giving them Blood to drink' – reversed, of course, in the ban on 'Blood' in James' prohibitions to overseas communities (in the Habakkuk *Pesher* 'the Blood', it will be recalled, has to do with the 'destruction of the Poor'/'the *Ebionim*') – and the retribution for this, either 'drinking the wine of the Wrath of God' or 'the Cup of the Wrath of God'.

Where 1QpHab XI.13 specifically is concerned, it now applies this allusion to 'being uncircumcised in heart' from Ezekiel to a Jewish High Priest, one of those Jewish backsliders or 'Wicked Ones of His People' it condemned – along with Gentile idolaters 'serving stone and wood' – in its description of the 'Judgment God would execute by the hand of His Elect' earlier and the final 'Day of Judgment' with which the *Pesher* closes.[25] By introducing this peculiar charge against 'the Wicked Priest' at this point and under these circumstances, the *Pesher* leaves little doubt that the issue it had in mind was accepting Gentile gifts and sacrifices in the Temple or, as the Damascus Document, *MMT*, or even Ezekiel 44:23 would put it, not observing proper separation 'between clean and unclean, Holy and profane' in the Temple or bringing 'polluted things into the Temple' and, as a consequence, 'incurring their pollution' – the same issues exercising 'Zealots for the Law' and extreme Purists generally in the run-up to the War against Rome.

Persons doing such things are called in Ezekiel 44:7 'Covenant-Breakers', the term used in the Habakkuk *Pesher* – in conjunction with 'the Man of Lying', 'Violent Ones', and 'Traitors to the New Covenant' generally – to describe the Alliance opposing 'the Righteous Teacher'/'the (High) Priest'. The allusion in these contexts to 'Breakers of the Covenant', as in James 2:9, is obviously meant to signal the very opposite of what a *true* 'Son of Zadok' was supposed to have been, namely a 'Keeper of the Covenant' and a '*Doer of the Torah*' *par excellence*, the reference to which then permeates these lines from Ezekiel 44:8–15, Qumran generally, and, of course, James. That a variation of this ban on foreign gifts and sacrifices in the Temple is found here in Ezekiel 44:7–15 puts the lie to Josephus' attempt to portray objections of this kind on the part of '*Sicarii*'/'Zealot' extremists after the death of James in the run-up to the War as 'Innovations which our Forefathers were unacquainted with' – as it does the attempt by Josephus (like Paul in the New Testament) to turn their complaints against themselves by accusing these same extremist 'Zealots' of 'polluting the Temple' by their acts of 'bloodshed', an accusation paralleled with only slightly differing signification in these passages here – as it is in the Gospels[26] – in Revelation as well.

The phrase 'because he did not circumcise the foreskin of his heart', therefore, is based on these passages from Ezekiel on 'the Zadokite Priesthood'. The sense of purposefully introducing it in the Habakkuk *Pesher*'s exegesis of 'looking upon their Festivals' (in original Habakkuk 2:15, 'their privy parts') and 'drink and tremble' to characterize 'the Wicked Priest' was to specifically apply the general parameters in Ezekiel to him despite his 'Jewishness' and even though he was not a foreigner. The point it is making is that he should be *treated just like a foreigner* because, not only was he enriching himself by accepting such foreign gifts and sacrifices, but his very appointment to the High Priesthood itself came from them. For this, the *Pesher* makes it clear, by deliberately altering the underlying text and introducing the changes it does, he was *disqualified* from service as High Priest on the basis of the parameters of Ezekiel's 'Zadokite Statement' and, in fact, *worthy of death*.

As Ezekiel 44:13 puts it in these passages about these backsliding Priests who 'went astray from Me after their idols' and 'brought foreigners into' the Temple 'uncircumcised in heart and body to pollute it', 'breaking My Covenant with all their Abominations': 'They shall not come near to Me to serve as Priests (basically, the second of the two complaints attributed to James in the *Anabathmoi Jacobou*), nor approach any of My Holy Things or the Holy of Holies, but they shall carry their shame (*kelimmah*) and the Abominations they committed.' Even the word 'Abominations' (*To'evot*) now appears in the *Pesher*'s description that follows of 'the Abominations the Wicked Priest committed' in 'polluting the Temple of God'.[27]

Moving on to its definition of the true 'Sons of Zadok', who are henceforth to approach the altar of God and render this 'service', these are now described in the passage expounded in the key exposition of the CD III.21–IV.12 as 'those who kept charge (literally 'the keeping') of My Temple when the Sons of Israel went astray from Me' (44:15). They are also described as 'keeping My Laws (*Hukkim*)', 'Festivals', and 'Sabbaths', alluded to elsewhere as 'the monthly flags'.[28] They are also things Paul *heaps abuse on* in developing his theology of the saving death of 'Christ Jesus', describing them in Galatians 4:9–10 as 'Beggarly' or 'Poverty-stricken elements' (note the play here on 'the Poor' terminology associated with James) only good for 'weaklings' and those 'preferring bondage' – as he makes clear in the 'allegory' that follows in Galatians 4:21–31 contrasting 'the slave woman' Hagar, who 'is Mount Sinai in Arabia', with 'the free woman' Sarah – meaning 'to the Law'.

Furthermore, he makes this allusion in the aftermath of discussing how 'as Many are of the works of the Law are under a curse' and 'the Righteous shall live by Faith' in 3:10–11. We showed in discussing the last Column of the Damascus Document earlier that Paul turns the 'cursing' of those 'straying to the right or left of the *Torah*' one finds there, in upon those who had most probably anathematized him. Making it clear in Galatians 3:13 that he considered himself to be in some manner under 'the curse of the Law', he argues that Jesus too was 'cursed' by being 'hung upon a tree' according to the very Law those would execrate him held so dear. Therefore, by implication, by taking this 'curse' upon himself or, in some of the most dazzling theological footwork ever evinced, Paul argues that, 'having become for us a curse', Jesus redeemed all Mankind too.

We showed how in the next chapter of Galatians (4:16–18), Paul is primarily teaching against those 'zealous' for such things – meaning 'Zealots' – when he asks, 'Have I now become your *Enemy* by telling the Truth to you?' In so doing, he shows his awareness that epithets of this kind, namely both the 'Lying' and 'the Enemy' ones, were being applied to him' by his detractors – epithets that have not failed to leave their mark in 'Jewish Christian' or 'Ebionite' tradition. In this last, the Paul-like attacker of James is specifically referred to as the 'Hostile Man' or 'Enemy' in the account of the physical assault he makes on James in the Temple in the Pseudoclementine *Recognitions*. Not only is the basis for this epithet to be found in James 4:4, but reflections of it are to be found in Matthew's 'Parable of the Tares', which recounts how an 'Enemy' came and sowed the tares among the good seed, but at the End of Time ('the Completion of this Age') – as the Gospel raconteur avers – the tares will be uprooted and 'cast (*balousin*) into the furnace of fire' (Matthew 13:39–42). This will be exactly the same approach as the Habakkuk *Pesher* and the note of extreme hopefulness it manifests regarding such matters in its climactic conclusion.

'The Cup of the Wrath of God will Swallow him'

It is in this context that the Habakkuk *Pesher* describes the destruction of the Wicked Priest in terms of 'drinking his fill' from 'the Cup of the Wrath of God'. This would also be 'the Cup of Trembling' from Isaiah 51:17 implied by the purposeful substitution of 'tremble' for 'foreskin' in the underlying text from Habakkuk 2:16. This is also clearly 'the Cup' of Divine Vengeance – ergo, now 'the Cup of the Wrath of God (*Hamat-El*) would swallow him' (*teval'eno*).

We have already seen this kind of 'Venomous Anger' imagery used in the Damascus Document to apply to the Establishment and 'the wine' of 'their ways'. Here it is being applied to the 'Reward' (*Gemulo*) of the Wicked Priest. In the Psalm 37 *Pesher*, this was 'the Reward (again, *gemulo*) God paid him by delivering him into the hand of the Violent Ones of the Gentiles'. These we have identified as the Idumaean allies of the 'Zealots', all thirsting for vengeance for James. Not only did they 'execute the Judgments upon Evil on him', in this *Pesher* this involved 'taking Vengeance on the flesh of his corpse'. As we have seen too, the text also plays on the expression 'shame' (*kalon*/*kikalon*), repeated twice, to express the Wicked Priest's behavior and final defilement. A variation of this 'shame' (*kelimmah*) is also found, combined with reference to 'Abominations' (*To'evot*) as here in the Habakkuk *Pesher*, in these key passages of Ezekiel's 'Zadokite Statement' about the disqualification of Priests like 'the Wicked Priest' from service at the Temple altar (44:13).

His destruction is described in 1QpHab XI.12–15 in the following manner: 'His shame was greater than his Glory, because ... he walked in his Way of satiety by way of drinking his fill, but the Cup of the Wrath of God shall swallow him, adding to (his shame and dis)grace ('his *kalon*/*kikalon*)...'. The column breaks off here.

The whole exposition we are presenting here is born out by what follows in the next column of the *Pesher*. Pursuing an underlying reference to the 'Violence done to Lebanon', 'the destruction of the dumb Beasts', 'the Blood of Man (*Adam*) and the Violence (done) to the Land, the City, and all its inhabitants' (all allusions with counterparts in the Book of Revelation), the *Pesher* now focuses on the 'conspiracy to destroy the Poor' and 'to rob' them of their sustenance.[29] As will be recalled, this 'plot' or 'conspiracy' was, in our view, the one between Ananus ben Ananus and the Herodian Agrippa II 'to destroy' the Righteous Teacher James. It is this which is 'the Blood of Man' and 'the Violence done to the Land' and 'its inhabitants'. 'The City' is specifically identified in XII.7–9 as Jerusalem. The text makes no bones about this, averring that this was 'Jerusalem, where the Wicked Priest committed his works of Abominations and polluted the Temple of God'. On the other hand, 'the Violence (done to) the Land' is said to be 'the Cities of Judah' where 'he stole the Riches of the Poor' (*Ebionim*).[30]

This is the same 'stealing from the Meek of His People' and 'grinding the face of the Poor' passages surrounding Isaiah 3:10–11 and applied in early Church literature to the death of James. The reference to the Wicked Priest's 'works of Abominations' harks back to the parameters of Ezekiel's 'Zadokite Covenant' and, first and foremost, consisted of his 'destruction of the Poor' – meaning, in our view, the destruction of James and several of his colleagues. They are also a play on the proper 'works' associated with and recommended by

James and, for that matter, the Qumran Letter(s) (*MMT*) on 'the Works that would be Reckoned to you as Righteousness' or 'Justifying you'.[31]

This 'stealing from the Meek of His People' also comprises part of the passages in CD VI.11–14 having to do with 'barring the door of the Temple, so as not to light its altar-fire in vain' (Malachi 1:10) and 'separating from the Sons of the Pit' during 'the whole Age of Evil' (the 'seventy' years of Daniel 9:3 and Jeremiah 25:11 – the latter also so strikingly going on to refer to 'drinking', 'drunkenness', and 'drinking the Cup' of the Lord unto 'Judgment' and what is most clearly 'destruction') – all part of what was meant there by 'separating between clean and unclean', 'Holy and profane' and 'keeping away from (*lehinnazer*) polluted Evil Riches' and 'the Riches of the Temple'.[32] There can be little doubt that this is the same 'stealing the tithes of the Poorer Priests' in the areas around Jerusalem ('the Cities of Judah where he stole the Riches of the Poor') by the thugs and servants of the High Priests, to which Josephus twice refers directly before and after the stoning of James in the run-up to the Revolt.

The accusation of filling Jerusalem with 'pollution', 'Abominations', and 'Blood', is exactly what Josephus (in a reversal of course) says 'the Zealots' and their 'Violent' Idumaean colleagues did in destroying James' murderer Ananus, Saulos' kinsman Antipas, and Zachariah, that is to say, they 'polluted the Temple of God' thereby bringing upon the Jews His (God's) just 'Retribution'. As previously explained, this accusation should be a familiar one by now and it is only slightly transformed in the version of it one gets in New Testament contexts and in the theology of the early Church.

'Lebanon', because of the 'whitening' imagery implicit in the original Hebrew (elsewhere, we saw it had to do with the garb the Priests wore in the Temple), is specifically interpreted as 'the Community Council', imagery also encountered both as regards 'the tombs of the two brothers that *miraculously whitened* every year' in the *Recognitions* and Jesus' clothing at his Transfiguration and that of the Angel in his tomb, 'white as snow, such that no *fuller* on earth could whiten', in the Gospels.[33] These wore white linen, as per Ezekiel's directives in 44:17 – just as 'the Essenes' seem to have done – as if they were 'Zadokite Priests' permanently serving in the Temple before God. 'The Beasts', as we saw, are 'the Simple Jews' who actually 'do the *Torah*', and here we have the 'doing' usage again, just encountered in the various contexts above and actually referred to several times throughout the Letter of James in terms of being 'a Doer of the word'/'the work'/or 'the Law', which was used four columns earlier in VIII.1–3 to restrict the applicability of 'the Righteous shall live by his Faith' to '*Torah*-Doers in the House of Judah', that is, only '*Torah*-doing Jews'.

Just so that there would be no mistaking any of these things, the *Pesher* at this point avers that the Wicked Priest 'would be paid the Reward he rewarded the Poor' (*Gemulo asher gamal*), 'the Poor' also being identified with 'the Community Council' – which wore *white* – and with 'Lebanon', and 'just as he plotted to destroy the Poor, so too would God condemn him to destruction'. The verb here, as already remarked, literally means 'destroy', so there can be no doubt that the language of 'swallowing' or 'eating' used throughout these passages to evoke the fate of 'the Righteous Teacher' and 'the Poor' ('the Dumb Beasts' or 'members of his Council'), ultimately 'comes around to' the Wicked Priest and means 'to destroy him' – nothing else.

Here we should recapitulate the significance of the usage 'swallowing' as it relates to the 'destruction' of the Righteous Teacher and some of his colleagues on 'the Community Council' in 1QpHab XI.13–XII.10. In such a context, these last would be equivalent to the so-called 'Twelve Disciples' of Gospel portraiture. In the Community Rule, 'the Community Council' – which is reckoned as 'a Precious Cornerstone' and a kind of spiritualized 'Holy of Holies for Aaron' and 'Perfect Temple of God for Israel' – is presented as composed of 'Twelve Israelites and Three Priests.[34] This, of course, can immediately be recognized as the

Twelve man scheme of the Gospels and Acts and that of 'the Inner Triad' or 'the Central Three' – 'those reputed to be Pillars' as Paul in Galatians 2:6–9 refers to them using the language of 'building' and 'architecture' so typical of him. In the Scrolls, it is not clear whether these 'Three' are part of or in addition to the 'Twelve', though the latter is more probable.[35] This same confusion is reflected in the Gospels and compounded in Acts and early Church tradition, where it is not clear exactly who is an 'Apostle', nor how these relate to 'the Inner Three', nor who, in fact, really comprise the latter.[36]

This 'swallowing' imagery is being deliberately applied throughout 1QpHab XI.5–15 to the destruction of the Righteous Teacher and some members of this Council, referred to collectively as 'the Simple of Judah doing *Torah*' or 'the Poor'. Both it and 'the Poor' are being purposefully applied to this 'destruction', as neither appear in the underlying passages of Habakkuk 2:15–18. We have made it clear that this 'swallowing' means 'consume' or 'destroy' here and that, in a kind of poetic justice, it is finally turned around and applied to 'the destruction of the Wicked Priest' – presumably by 'the Violent Ones of the Gentiles' or those Josephus is calling 'Idumaeans' – that is, just as the Wicked Priest 'swallowed' the Righteous Teacher and some of his followers among 'the Poor', so too would he himself be 'swallowed' or 'consumed'.

We have shown too that this imagery of 'swallowing' and the circle of language related to it were based on the Hebrew root *B-L-ʿ*. It forms a parallel and opposing one to the *Z-D-K* or '*Righteousness*' language circle and also relates to allusions like 'the wine' or 'the Venom of the Kings of the Peoples' and 'their ways' (meaning the Herodians) in other Qumran documents such as the Damascus Document. This is the thrust, too, of the various adumbrations of this imagery we encounter – including allusions to 'the Three Nets of *Belial*', 'Balaam', 'Balak' and even 'Jezebel' and 'Babylon' in Revelation, not to mention 'the *Diabolos*' – even 'Beelzebub' – elsewhere in the New Testament.

In fact, the first of these individuals and the original instigator of all these 'Innovations into the Customs of the People' was Herod himself, and the Rabbinic decipherment of the nomenclature 'Balaam' in terms of its root-meaning, i.e., 'he who swallowed the People', was absolutely characteristic of the Herodians, particularly as they disposed of Opposition Leaders such as John the Baptist, James, and many others.[37] This is the reason, too, this imagery is being used at this point in the Habakkuk *Pesher* because it describes what the Herodian-sponsored High Priestly Establishment did to the Righteous Teacher/James. They destroyed him. Furthermore, the 'conspiracy' hinted at is the one between Ananus and Agrippa II to remove Opposition Leaders, particularly Opposition 'High Priests' such as James, who opposed Herodian gifts and sacrifices in the Temple and supported the building of a wall in the Temple to block their view of the sacrifices. These took advantage of the chance provided by an interregnum in Roman Governors to remove the key individual they considered responsible for the agitation against them in the Temple – 'the Opposition High Priest of his time', James.

'Stumbling', 'Casting Down', 'Leading Astray', and 'Slaying with the Rod of his Mouth'

To draw all these imageries even more closely together, early Church texts are saying the same things about James and his entry into the Holy of Holies on at least one Yom Kippur (if not many) – there to make atonement on behalf of the whole People (the atonement of a 'Righteous Priest'/'*Zaddik*') – that Ezekiel is saying about the true 'Sons of Zadok' in the 'Zadokite Covenant' in 44:6–31.

Even without the reference to it in CD III.21–IV.2, we could have connected James to the 'Zadokite' ideology by the constant reiteration of the 'Righteousness' ideology regarding his person and the title in Latin tied to his name, 'Justus', which is 'Zadok' in Hebrew – this, to say nothing of the constant reiteration of the word 'keeping' in all sources (including 'Rechabite' ones) connected to his being, which (aside from the wordplay centering around the 'Z-D-K' ideology) is the actual definition of the *true* 'Sons of Zadok' in the Community Rule at Qumran.[38] But early Church texts are indeed applying many of the parameters listed in Ezekiel's 'Zadokite' materials in consequence of this, including, 'wearing only linen', 'a razor never touching his head', 'abstaining from wine', 'barring carrion', etc., so it is possible to discern the traces of a conscious effort to present him as a true 'Son of Zadok' even in these texts and according to the parameters recognized at Qumran, not to mention those of the 'Nazirite'/'Rechabite' ideology in general.[39]

But early Church texts are also at pains to portray his death in terms of the verb in Greek that basically contains the same root letters as that of 'swallowing' in Hebrew – namely, 'casting down': *'ballo'/'kataballo'/'ekballo'* or the like. We have seen how the equivalent of this verb 'casting' or 'throwing down' – also 'causing to stumble' in Hebrew – was linked, together with 'swallowing' in the Habakkuk *Pesher*, to how the Wicked Priest destroyed the Righteous Teacher and some colleagues, and this related to Yom Kippur, *even though the word nowhere appeared in the underlying Biblical passage* from Habakkuk 2:15 on which the exegesis supposedly was based. Interestingly enough, it *does appear* in Ezekiel 44:12 regarding 'causing the House of Israel to stumble into sinning', not to mention a variation of it in the Letter of James, also following quotation of 'the Royal Law according to the Scripture' and in conjunction with allusion to 'keeping' (2:10). On the other hand, together with this imagery of 'swallowing' and additional allusion to 'the Poor', it seems purposefully to have been introduced into the vocabulary of the Habakkuk *Pesher* at this point.

We have also shown above how this imagery related to that of *Belial* (in Revelation, Balaam) *'casting down his net'* generally to 'deceive Israel' or 'lead Israel astray', imagery picked up in the picture of the Apostles 'casting down' their nets in the Gospels (Matthew 4:18–19 and pars.) who, in a kind of parody of this imagery, are then said to have become 'Fishers of Men' (Matthew 4:20–21 and pars.). Interestingly enough, as we have called attention to as well, this same imagery is present in the Habakkuk *Pesher* in exposition of Habakkuk 1:15–16 on 'fishing', 'nets', and 'plenteous eating', but there the 'nets' and 'fishing' were those cast by 'the *Kittim*' or, as it were, the Romans, 'parceling out their yoke and their taxes' and the 'eating', destroying 'all Peoples, year by year', 'with the sword'.[40]

In the Gospels this imagery even went further afield to encompass the authority received by the Apostles 'to cast out demons' or 'Evil spirits' (*ekballo* – Mark 3:15 and pars.) – a parody of the expulsion by groups like the Essenes or those at Qumran of Backsliders and Law-Breakers. It was also edifying to note the further use of this language in the 'casting out' from Jerusalem of Ananus' body without burial as food for jackals or that of the 'Rich' collaborator 'Zachariah' and of 'Stephen' in Acts 7:51–53 by allegedly blood-thirsty Jews, who 'gnashed their teeth at him' after being accused by him themselves of 'not keeping' the Law and being 'uncircumcised in heart and ears'![41]

It was interesting, too, how this idea of being *'cast down* from the Pinnacle of the Temple' in the manner of James occurs in the famous stories about Jesus' 'Temptation in the Wilderness' in Matthew 4:1–11 and Luke 4:1–13. Both use the language of the '*Diabolos*' and '*kataballo*' to signify being 'cast down' (4:5 and 4:9). Also, in the typical style of Qumran, Revelation, and Paul in 2 Corinthians, both insert the usage, 'Satan', into the fabric of their narrative, even though they seem initially to be referring to the '*Diabolos*' or '*Belial*' (4:10 and 4:8). Both episodes are given a Pauline or pro-Roman cast in that Jesus is offered Authority over 'all the Kingdoms of the World and their Glory' (4:8–9 and 4:6). He declines with the now proverbial words, 'Get thee behind me Satan', quoting Deuteronomy 6:13, to the effect that, it is God alone whom he serves (4:10 and 4:8). The only difference is that in Luke this offer follows the Devil's suggestion 'to cast himself down from the Pinnacle of the Temple' while in Matthew it precedes it.

This implied rejection of this-worldly 'Messianism' makes no sense at all, since in the Palestinian version of 'Messianism' – for instance, in the War Scroll and other texts from Qumran not to mention Revelation – the Messiah was to come and crush all the Nations with 'a rod of iron' and make them his 'footstool'.[42] In support of this, Revelation repeatedly cites the passage from Psalm 2:8–9 about being given 'the ends of the Earth for a possession' and 'breaking the Gentiles with a rod of iron', not to mention Isaiah 11:4's 'smiting the earth with the rod of his mouth' – 'the sharp sword of his mouth' in Isaiah 49:2 – a passage extant in Qumran *Pesharim*. As it turns out, the mentality typical of these 'footstool' passages in Revelation are completely typical of Qumran as well.[43]

Nor should it be forgotten that the ambiance of Isaiah 11:4 is the citation about 'the Rod of the Shoot of Jesse and the Branch (*Netzer*) from his Roots', subjected to exegesis at Qumran in two separate contexts; and the context of Psalm 2:8–9 is the all-important reference to 'You are My son. On this day I have begotten you' (2:7). This last appears in one of the so-called 'Jewish Christian' Gospels, attributed by Epiphanius to 'the Ebionites', in place of the extant text in the Synoptics which, in depicting John's baptism of Jesus rather inserts the phrase, 'This is my only begotten Son. In him I am well pleased' (Matthew 3:17 and pars.).[44] *Per contra*, Epiphanius' Ebionite Gospel conserves Psalm 2:7 and, consequently, the impression of an 'adoptionist baptism', similar to that at Qumran,[45] rather than a supernatural birth or 'Immaculate Conception' as it is now called. As this is the approach reiterated in Hebrews 1:5 and 5:5, a letter replete with the imagery of the Messiah 'sitting on the right hand of God and making his enemies his footstool' (Psalm 110:1, the Psalm which in 110:4 also contains the imagery of 'a Priest forever after the order of Melchizedek'). It seems very likely that this was the original tradition. However this may be, so much does Revelation expand on quotations of this kind that it appears like something of an extended, Qumran-style *Pesher* as well.

But in Matthew and Luke's descriptions of the Temptation 'in the Wilderness' by the Devil, which not only almost directly follow this baptism scenario but, in the same breath, seem directly to be targeting these 'wilderness-dwelling' sectarian groups, Jesus is basically also being presented within the 'Jamesian' scenario of 'being cast down from the Pinnacle of the Temple' by the Devil (*'Diabolos'/'Belial'*). The words are almost exactly those of early Church accounts of James' death except, instead of 'being cast down', Jesus is asked to 'cast *himself* down' (Matthew 4:6 and Luke 4:9). Declining, he says in words now proverbial and continuing to quote Deuteronomy 6:16, 'you shalt not tempt the Lord your God'. The implication is that James willfully cast himself down from the Pinnacle of the Temple and, in so doing, somehow tested the Lord his God, but, as just intimated, none of this makes any sense whatsoever and it is simply a further example of a tradition related to James' death and the *'ballo'/'balla'/'Belial'* terminology being retrospectively incorporated into the life of Jesus. There is also the derivative implication, should one choose to regard it, that 'temptation in the wilderness' materials of this kind could not have assumed this form until after the traditions about James' 'fall' or 'having been cast down' were concretized. These traditions have their further adumbrations in the materials about the Apostles 'casting down their nets' into the Sea of Galilee before recognizing and joining Jesus on the shore, folkloric inventions taking this imagery even further afield.

The traditions relating to the 'casting down' of James occur in early Church testimony, as will be recalled, in two separate variations – one having to do with the attack by 'the Enemy' Paul in the Forties CE which does not result in his death, but only a fall from the Temple stairs in which he 'breaks his leg'.[46] This is the more likely scenario. The second attack, which occurs in the Sixties CE, supposedly results in his 'being cast down' or a fall 'from the

Temple Pinnacle'. On top of this last, there is the stoning and the *coup de grace* delivered to him by a laundryman's club.[47] As we showed in *James the Brother of Jesus*, the second is really a conflation of both the earlier one – apparently by Paul – in the Forties (which Acts is so anxious to disguise masking it with 'the Jews' allegedly stoning a *papier mache* character like 'Stephen') and the later one, James' stoning in 62 CE as described by Josephus.[48] This last is the one that most fits the Dead Sea Scrolls' account of how 'the Wicked Priest pursued the Righteous Teacher with' or 'in his *Beit-Galuto* ('his House of Exile' or 'his Exiled House') to swallow him', that is, pursued judicial proceedings against him that resulted in his stoning.

Where Paul's Herodian affiliations and, therefore, part and parcel of the '*Belial*'/'*balla*' terminology are concerned, in Acts 23:35 he stays in Agrippa II's Palace in Caesarea and converses with him and his sisters in a kind of quasi-protective custody – not to mention the Roman Procurator Felix – with easygoing congeniality for, apparently, more than two years while they protect him from Temple 'Zealots' and 'Nazirite oath'-taking would-be Assassins ('*Sicarii*'?). Finally they pack him off to Rome where he again appears to flourish under another kind of loose house arrest (Acts 28:30–31). In addition, there is the reference he makes in Romans 16:11 to his 'kinsman Herodion'/'his kinsman, the Littlest Herod'. We take this to be the son of that Aristobulus, the son of Herod of Chalcis Agrippa I's brother, who was married to the Salome involved in John the Baptist's death – probably mentioned under the heading 'all those of the household of Aristobulus' in Romans 16:10 as well.

This nicely explains Paul's easy access to Temple Authorities (according to Acts) as a comparatively young man, since the aunt of the 'Saulos' he so much resembles was married to the Temple Treasurer Helcias,[49] as well as why the High Priest would give him letters to arrest so-called 'Christians' (by Acts 11:26's own testimony, the name wasn't even in use at this time until a decade or so later in Northern Syria!), i.e., extreme 'Zealots' or '*Sicarii*', and what he was doing in Damascus around 36–37 CE. There he was probably in the service of Herod Antipas, the individual responsible, along with Agrippa I's and Herod of Chalcis' sister Herodias, for the death of John the Baptist and, by his own testimony, in 2 Corinthians 11:33, he was 'let down its walls in a basket' and had to flee the soldiers of the Arab King Aretas with whom Antipas was at war.

All of this would, of course, be most understandable if Paul ('Saulos'?) gave the Authorities the information they needed to identify James as the center of agitation against them, Gentile gifts and sacrifices in the Temple generally, and related issues and to remove him at the first opportunity. Therefore the '*balla*'/'swallowing' imagery one comes upon at this point in the Habakkuk *Pesher* – in our view, relating to Herodians – which would be even more comprehensible if James were seen as the center of agitation against them in the Temple, in particular, wishing to bar said Herodians from the Temple as foreigners.

Therefore too, the penance put upon Paul by James in Acts 21:23–24, Paul's mobbing in the Temple on precisely such grounds and his unceremonious ejection from the Temple that follows can simply be seen as part and parcel of these struggles against the admission of foreigners and their gifts and sacrifices – seen as 'polluted' or 'polluting'– into the Temple. Therefore, too, the dire warnings of a conspiracy against Paul in Jerusalem presented through the mouthpiece of the non-existent 'Prophet called Agabus' in Caesarea in Acts 21:10–11. Looked at in this way, Paul can simply be seen as a 'stalking horse' for Herodian family interests in the Temple, as he so often seems to be in areas further afield.

Even if these things are only partly true, it would not be surprising at all if Paul held his rough treatment in the Temple in Jerusalem against James during his more than two years of what have the appearance of debriefing sessions in Caesarea, first with Felix and his wife Drusilla and then with Agrippa II and his sister Bernice. 'Saulos' in Josephus is, in fact, involved in just such debriefing sessions with Nero in Corinth six years later in 66 CE after the Roman Governor Cestius' defeat in the first heady days of the Uprising.[50] Nor would it be surprising if Nero sent this 'Saul' or 'Paul' back to Palestine in his service following this first appeal.

The 'Saulos' in Josephus – 'a kinsman of Agrippa' – at this point in the two converging narratives becomes the intermediary between the 'Peace Party' in Jerusalem (consisting High Priests, principal Pharisees, and Herodians) and Roman and Herodian troops outside the City.[51] Before finally going to see Nero in Corinth, this 'Saulos' goes to Agrippa II's camp also, presumably, to give him a first-hand report on the situation in Jerusalem, where he had been in the latter's palace before it surrendered along with several other Herodian 'Men-of-War', including Philip, Costobarus, and Antipas the Temple Treasurer, his cousin.

The same language circle – in Greek having to do with 'casting down' and connected to 'the *Diabolos*' or 'the Devil' (rather than the 'swallowing', connected in the Hebrew to '*Belial*') – is being applied to the death of James in early Church texts even though James probably did not die in precisely this way, that is to say, on this point anyhow the texts are somewhat far-fetched. This proves, as little else can, that the application of such language to James' death *was purposeful*, just as it was in its application to the destruction (or death) of 'the Righteous Teacher' at Qumran. Though James was probably not 'cast down' from the Pinnacle of the Temple, as these texts imagine, he probably was 'cast down' from the top ('headlong') of the Temple steps where he had been positioned to speak to the crowds – whether twenty years before, as reported in the *Recognitions*, or as a prelude to his final stoning. Whatever the case, instead of calming them, he proclaimed the imminent coming (or return) of the Messiah 'standing on the right hand of Power' and 'about to come on the clouds of Heaven', as per the parameters of the War Scroll and as refurbished in the Gospels and Acts. This doubtlessly happened in some manner.

'The Wicked Encompasses the Righteous' and 'Swallows One more Righteous than He'

The application of these two parallel homophonic imageries, *ba-la-'a* and *ballo* in both the Hebrew and the Greek, the former to the destruction of the Righteous Teacher at Qumran and the latter to the death of James in early Church texts, from our perspective proves as little else can the final identity of these two individuals. Texts such as 'the Wicked swallows one more Righteous than he' (Habakkuk 1.13) are almost always exploited to produce expositions like those encountered above. This is particularly the case if they are accompanied by words like 'Traitors', 'Violence', 'Riches', 'Lebanon', and the like.

This is also true of the First Column of the Habakkuk *Pesher* where, though poorly preserved because of the way the Scroll was rolled, one can still make out a *Pesher*. This seemingly has to do with 'the Last Generation', tied in the underlying text to references from Habakkuk 1:2 to 'Violence', 'destruction', and 'You save' – the word 'Salvation' or '*Yeshu'a*'/'Jesus' is based upon in Hebrew. Though the text is fragmentary, there would also appear to be a reference to 'rebelling against God' tied to a reference to "*amal*' or 'suffering works' in the underlying text from Habakkuk 1:3. This usage, "*amal*', will be important later in the *Pesher* when it comes to discussing the 'suffering toil' of 'the Righteous Teacher' – that is, how 'the Righteous shall live by his Faith' – in Column VIII.2 as opposed to the 'Lying service' of 'the Spouter of Lying' that follows in Column X.11–12.

As later in the *Pesher*, this reference to "*amal*' from Habakkuk 1:3 is followed by another allusion to 'robbing Riches'. There is also a reference to 'division' or 'quarrelsomeness' in the underlying text from 1:3 which follows this as well, a usage that appears in the First Column of CD I.21 describing the attack by 'the Liar' and other 'Covenant-Breakers' on the 'Soul of the Righteous One' and the other 'Walkers in Perfection'.[52] In 1QpHab I.8–9, this is followed by an underlying citation from Habakkuk 1:4 having to do with 'the *Torah* being weakened and Judgment never going forth', interpreted in terms of 'those who rejected the *Torah* of God' (plural). This usage '*ma'as*' for 'reject' or 'deny' is an important one and, when singular, is repeatedly used at Qumran to characterize the actions of 'the Spouter of Lying' – so much so that this, 'rejecting the *Torah*', would appear to be his defining activity.

This introduces the key reference in the underlying text, 'the Wicked encompasses (based in Hebrew on the same root as, for instance, 'Crown' or 'Diadem'[53]) the Righteous. Therefore perverted Judgment goes forth' (Habakkuk 1:4). This is very similar to the text and exposition of Psalm 37:32, 'the Wicked looks out for the Righteous and seeks to kill him' we looked at earlier, and, once again, the possible parallel here to the illegal trial of James should not be ignored. In any event here in 1QpHab I.10 it sets the tone for the whole *Pesher* that follows.

Though the exposition of the second half of this is missing, it should be immediately recognizable that the first part parallels and is simply a variation on Habakkuk 1:13 later in Column V.8-9, 'the Wicked swallows one more Righteous than he' – the imagery of 'surrounding' or 'encompassing' having the same negative signification as 'swallowing'. Though the exegesis is fragmentary at this point too, it is nonetheless made clear that 'the Wicked' in the text applies to the Wicked Priest in the Pesher, as it does everywhere else at Qumran, and 'the Righteous' (*Zaddik*) is likewise explicitly tied – as always – to 'the Righteous Teacher'. In fact, it is this allusion to 'the Righteous One' or '*Zaddik*' that introduces 'the Righteous Teacher', concretizing the basic consistency of these textual correspondences.[54]

This is also the approach of all early Church accounts of the death of James at the hands of 'the Wicked Priest' of his generation Ananus ben Ananus. This too, in our view, is 'the Last Generation' as in the I.11 *Pesher* on Habakkuk 1:2 as well as when 'the Last Priests of Jerusalem gathered Riches and profiteered from the spoils of the Peoples' in IX.4–7. There can be little doubt of the relationship of these kinds of allusions to text applied in these sources to the death of James.

Once again, the 'eating' in this allusion, as in the received Hebrew and Latin versions, basically parallels the sense of 'swallowing' or 'being swallowed' as it is expressed here in the Habakkuk *Pesher*. As in the characterization of 'the *Kittim*' or the Romans in 1QpHab VI.7–8 as 'eating all the Peoples ... with the sword' too, the sense of all these allusions in Isaiah is of 'violent destruction'. One should also keep the double entendre implicit in usages such as this in mind when evaluating related allusions such as 'glutton' in the Gospels which, in Hebrew, literally translates out as '*bela*' – but also Paul's fixation upon 'eating', by which he means (as do the Gospels) being free of Jewish dietary regulations and Mosaic Law.

As we have seen, Isaiah 2–3 also includes references to 'Jerusalem being fallen', 'Judea in collapse', 'Lebanon', 'robbing the Meek', 'grinding the face of the Poor', and 'Judgment'. This is not to mention allusion to 'abolishing the idols' and 'casting down his idols of silver and his idols of gold, which they made for each other to worship, to the moles and the bats' (2:20). This, too, will be directly reprised from XII.12–XIII.4, the end of the Habakkuk *Pesher*, with the phraseology: 'The interpretation of this passage concerns all the idols of the Gentiles, which they create in order to serve them and bow down before them. These will not save them on the Day of Judgment.' It repeats this in the next column in the following manner: 'This concerns all the Gentiles, who serve stone and wood. But on the Day of Judgment, God will destroy all idolaters and Wicked Ones from the Earth.' In the *Pesher*, this is given in interpretation of Habakkuk 2:19–20: 'Behold, it is covered with gold and silver and there is no spirit at all within it. But the Lord is in His Holy Temple. Be silent before Him, all the world.'[55] The pathos and hopeful constancy of this Faith, even in the face of the disastrous circumstances overwhelming everyone at this moment in the *Pesher*, is poignant.

This point-of-view is also evident at the end of the Letter of James in the condemnations one finds there and the note of coming eschatological 'Judgment' (4:11–5:12). In Isaiah 2:21, this is expressed in terms of 'the Lord arising to terribly shake the Earth'. James 5:3, like

Isaiah 2:20 and Habakkuk 2:19, at this point is also using the imagery of 'gold and silver' to condemn the 'Rich'. These it blames for 'condemning and putting the Righteous One to death'. For James 5:1–3, this reads as follows: 'As for you Rich, weep, howl over the miseries that are coming upon you. Your Riches have rotted and your clothes have become moth-eaten. Your gold and silver has been eaten away, and their decomposition shall be a witness against you and shall eat your flesh like fire.' This is all described in terms of 'the Judge standing before the Door' (5:9), 'the coming of the Lord' (5:8), and the cries of the Downtrodden reaching 'the Lord God of Hosts' (5:4).

In contrasting 'the Wicked' (*Rasha'*) with 'the Righteous' (*Zaddik*), the Greek version of this passage reverses the underlying sense of the Hebrew – and, as it would seem, the Latin – making it appear as if the negative things are being done to 'the Righteous One' not 'the Wicked', though the succeeding reference to 'he shall be paid the reward of his hands' is the same. Moreover, we have already seen how these kinds of recasting or inversions of Scripture in favor of a preferred exegesis were fairly common, not only at Qumran, but also in early Church usage.

In the Septuagint version given by Hegesippus, this was actually seen to reflect the death of James. Its contrast of 'the Wicked' and 'the Righteous' parallels that at the beginning of the Habakkuk *Pesher* of 'the Wicked encompasses the Righteous' (I.10–11) which was specifically interpreted to apply to 'the Righteous Teacher' and 'the Wicked Priest'. It, too, is immediately followed in Habakkuk 1:4 by a reference to 'Judgment' though, in this case, delivering 'perverted Judgment'.

In Isaiah 3:11, all versions immediately follow with some rendition of 'the reward of his hands will be done to him' meaning, as this seems to have been interpreted, 'the Wicked Priest' as well. This is echoed almost precisely in 1QpHab XII.2–3's 'he ('the Wicked Priest') would be paid the reward he rewarded the Poor'. In the Septuagint Greek, following the allusion to 'they shall eat the fruits of their works' in 3:10, 3:11 is translated as, 'Evils shall happen to him according to the works of his hands'. In all versions too, this is immediately succeeded in the next line by allusion to 'leading the People astray' in 3:12. This, in turn, was followed by allusion to 'the Lord standing up to Judge the Peoples' and 'the Lord entering into Judgment with the Elders and Rulers of the People' in 3:13–3:14.

The Introduction of 'the Liar' in the Habakkuk *Pesher* from Qumran

In the Habakkuk *Pesher* too, the next reference to what 'the Wicked' does to 'the Righteous' occurs in Column V.8–9 and actually refers to 'the Wicked swallowing one more Righteous than he' (Habakkuk 1:13), following a reference to 'Judgment' in the underlying text of Habakkuk 1:12 which is interpreted in terms of a vivid picture of 'the Judgment on the Gentiles by the hand of His Elect' – 'the Sons of Zadok' in CD III.21–IV.9.

This is the single instance in any Qumran *Pesher* of an allusion to 'the Wicked' and 'the Righteous' not being applied to 'the Wicked Priest' *per se*. The same is true of the word 'swallowing' in this passage. Rather it appears to be applied to an inner session of 'the Assembly' or Community where, exploiting a reference to 'Traitors' (*Bogdim*) in the underlying text from Habakkuk 1:13, one group within the Community is admonished for 'keeping silent at the time when the Righteous Teacher was reproved'. This admonishment seems to have been by the tongue of 'the Man of Lying', though this is not clear. What is clear is that he is described revealingly as 'rejecting the *Torah* in the midst of their whole Assembly'.[56]

The evocation of 'the Judgment' participated in by 'the Elect' at the beginning of Column Five (IV.14–V.5) comes after a long excursus on the might and ferocity of 'the *Kittim*/ Romans – including 'their Council Chamber' (presumably their Senate) as 'their Guilty Council House' – in Columns III–IV follows a stubborn insistence 'that God would not destroy His People by the hand of the Gentiles, but rather God would render Judgment on the Gentiles by the hand of His Elect'. This would also be in line with the eschatology of Revelation – such as it is. This 'Elect' is described as 'not lusting after their eyes during the Era of Evil'.

Again, this 'rejection of the *Torah* in the midst of their whole Assembly' must be seen as characteristic of 'the Lying Spouter''s behavior and his rebuke of the Righteous Teacher. The confrontation between them, which this time would appear to be internal and verbal not mortal – this is the import of the verb, '*ma'as*' or 'reject' as opposed to 'eating' or 'destroy' – in that sense, resembles nothing so much as 'the Jerusalem Council' or, at least a 'Council' of some sort. The word 'swallowing' in the underlying text from Habakkuk 1:13, however, is not applied in any real sense in the exegesis as it stands. Rather it is put on hold, as it were, and employed later in the *Pesher* to describe what the Wicked Priest did to the Righteous Teacher and his followers among 'the Poor', as we have seen, and what in turn the Lord would do to him, i.e., 'swallow him'.[57]

That this was seen in some manner also to refer to 'the Man of Lying''s activities – if it was – can only be understood if in some way the latter was seen either to represent or be part and parcel of the Herodian Establishment. As we have seen, this is the case where Paul is concerned and adds to the conclusion that Paul was, indeed, an Herodian. If we take the 'Saulos' in Josephus to be another, alternate presentation of this Paul, then this is certainly the case. That 'Saul' or 'Paul' in all versions of the data was able to get letters from the Chief Priest in Jerusalem to arrest 'any he found of the Way' and 'confound the Jews dwelling in Damascus' (Acts 9:2 and 22) further reinforces this perception or, at least, that he would have been perceived of as a member of this Establishment. The *Pesher* then moves on at the end of V.12–VI.5 to present the picture of 'the *Kittim*' or Romans 'sacrificing to their standards and worshipping their weapons of war', also delivered in exegesis of an underlying text having to do with 'casting down nets' and 'fishing' from Habakkuk 1:16, which we have already discussed above.[58]

In fact this 'Liar' is introduced at I.12–II.3 and the exegesis of Habakkuk 1:5 referring to 'not believing even though it was explained' and specifically addressing 'the Gentiles'. Once again, this is explained in relation to 'the Traitors' (*Bogdim*), now 'Traitors to the New Covenant', the significance of which language, as it relates to parallel stories in the Gospels about the alleged 'Traitor', Judas Iscariot, should not be difficult to appreciate. Though the term 'Traitors' is repeated three times in the exposition that follows, which is indeed exceedingly long and descriptive, it nowhere appears in the actual text of Habakkuk 1:5 being expounded but rather later in conjunction with 'the Traitors who kept silent when the Righteous One was swallowed by one more Wicked than he' of Habakkuk 1:13.

These 'Traitors' at the beginning of Column II.1 – later 'the Traitors to the New Covenant' and 'the Traitors to the Last Days' in II.3–6 (both reconstructed and not necessarily present as such, though the words 'New' and 'Traitors' are) – 'together with the Man of Lying' are described as 'not believing what the Righteous Teacher expounded from the mouth of God'. Later in the *Pesher*, it will be recalled, we hear in Column VII.4–10's exposition of Habakkuk 2:2 that 'God made known to the Righteous Teacher all the Mysteries of the words of His Servants the Prophets'.

This *Pesher* in Column II.1–10 on Habakkuk 1:5, which actually has to do with 'wonders' and 'wonder-working', 'believing', and 'the Last Generation' again, is astonishing because it is a *Pesher* within a *Pesher*, the verb '*liphshor*'/'to interpret' literally being used to express the exegetical powers of 'the Righteous Teacher'. Because it is completely in the past tense, by implication, it would appear to imply that 'the Righteous Teacher' is already past, gone, or dead as well. It also implies that 'the Righteous Teacher' – or, as it calls him, 'the Priest', had direct communication with God – i.e., just as in these early Church texts which insist that 'the Prophets declare concerning him' (James), he declared concerning the Prophets!

These are also the kind of 'revelations' Paul, too, claims to be having in 2 Corinthians 12:1 and 12:7, not to mention the 'Mysteries' he also claims to be expounding in 1 Corinthians 4:1 and 15:51. Nor should one miss the point about 'belief' or 'believing' here (in this case, 'not believing'), the key element in the Pauline theological approach, not to mention Paul's other claims to be in direct communication with 'Christ Jesus' in Heaven as well (Galatians 1:12, 2:2, etc.).

Just as Paul terms his new understanding 'the New Covenant in the Blood of Christ', so the language of 'the New Covenant' now permeates the rest of this *Pesher* about 'not believing what was explained'. As in the Damascus Document, 'the New Covenant' in the Habakkuk *Pesher* is, once again, nothing more than a reaffirmation of 'the Old'. But now the Traitors are 'the Traitors (to the Laws of God and) the New Covenant, who did not believe in the Covenant of God (and profaned His) Holy Name'. Identified a third time as 'the Traitors to the Last Days' and now designated as coextensive with 'the Violent Ones and the Covenant-Breakers', a third time, too, these are described as: 'not believing all that they heard was (going to happen in) the Last Generation from the mouth of the Priest in whose heart God put the intelligence to interpret (*liphshor*) all the words of His Servants the Prophets, by whose hand God foretold all that was going to happen to His People'[59] – all this in exposition of the two words in the underlying text from Habakkuk 2:5 'not believing even though it was explained'.

This is, of course, a very complicated exegesis but, on top of this, it should be recognized that there is absolutely no anti-Semitism in it, no self-hatred – not even a jot of any – that is, it doesn't hate its own people. On the contrary, it is very nationalistic. Rather it hates 'Traitors', 'Covenant-Breakers', 'the Violent Ones', and 'the Man of Lies' but not its own 'People' – 'the People of God', 'the Prophets', or 'the Covenant', Old or New. Nor does it love its enemies; it hates them. These are the hallmarks of a native Palestinian text. One cannot emphasize this too strongly.

There is sectarian and internecine strife to be sure and one's enemies are hated, unlike the approach of the New Testament, which is so 'New' that it is no longer even either Palestinian or Jewish. Anything deviating from this norm is simply not a native Palestinian document. This does not mean it is bad, just that it is not 'native Palestinian' and probably rather 'Hellenistic'. Moreover, one can lump a whole group of texts under this rubric, as we have been doing.

Whether these 'Violent Ones' are the same as 'the Violent Ones of the Gentiles', who took Vengeance for the death of the Righteous Teacher on the Wicked Priest in the Psalm 37 *Pesher*, is impossible to say, but one assumes that they are, the Habakkuk *Pesher* perhaps being expounded from a slightly different perspective. That these 'Violent Ones' participate in the Scriptural exegesis sessions of 'the (High) Priest'/'Righteous Teacher', who is the authoritative Scriptural exegete, should also be clear. So do 'the Man of Lies' and other 'Traitors to the New Covenant' and 'the Last Days', with whom all or perhaps some seem to have been allied – at least originally. This would certainly accord with Paul's more violent early days, which may well have been resumed in the mid-Sixties in Jerusalem, if Josephus' 'Saulos' has anything to do with the New Testament character by that name. That there are pro- and anti-Revolutionary Herodian 'Men-of-War', we have already explained above, and that some of the latter are also allied with the 'Saulos' in Josephus should also be clear. This is also the situation in the Damascus Document, where 'the Men-of-War' are portrayed as 'walking with the Man of Lying'.[60]

But, be this as it may, all are considered 'Covenant-Breakers' and 'Traitors to the New Covenant and the Laws of God', which the final treatment meted out by 'Zealots' to Niger of

Perea, a Leader of 'the Violent Idumaeans' and, seemingly, one of these same pro-Revolutionary Herodian 'Men-of-War', helps illustrate. In Acts 13:1, it will be recalled, someone called 'Niger' was also a colleague of Paul in 'the Assembly of the Prophets and Teachers' where 'the Disciples were first called Christians in Antioch'.

The language of 'Covenant-Breakers' here comes right out of that surrounding 'the Zadokite Statement' of Ezekiel 44:7 of 'those uncircumcised in heart and flesh' who also 'pollute the Sanctuary'. It is also evoked in the Letter of James, where 'the Covenant-Breakers' are distinctly ranged against 'the Doers' and 'Keepers', meaning 'the Covenant-Keepers' (the 'Sons of Zadok' in the Community Rule) in the introduction to the famous material about 'keeping the whole of the Law, yet stumbling on one small point' in James 2:9 –2:11.

Finally, that 'the Righteous Teacher' has, 'in his heart', 'the intelligence to expound all the words of His Servants, the Prophets' is, of course, what makes him a truly 'Righteous' High Priest, fulfilling the proper role of 'the *Mebakker*' or 'High Priest Commanding the Camps' in the Damascus Document', in whose heart God has put all 'the mastery of all the secrets of men and (their) Languages' ('Tongues') and Scripture as well. It is the opposite side of the coin to 'the Wicked Priest', the real Establishment High Priest, whose 'heart is uncircumcised' – as the *Pesher* goes on later to declare – and who is, therefore, *disqualified on that basis from service in the Temple.*

Above: The Western or 'Wailing Wall,' the only part of Temple left standing after its destruction in 70 CE.

Right: The Pinnacle of the Temple with the Kedron Valley tombs, including the Monument of Absalom just visible below. It was from this 'Pinnacle' that, according to almost all early Church accounts, James was '*cast down*' into the valley below, where he was accordingly stoned. and '*buried*' *where he fell.*

Chapter 21
'He Rejected the Law in the Midst of Their Whole Assembly'

The First Confrontations between the Righteous Teacher and the Liar

We now come to what for our purposes are the climactic sections of the Habakkuk *Pesher*. These concern the confrontations of 'the Righteous Teacher' with 'the Liar' which – together with the confrontations with 'the Wicked Priest' – really preoccupy the attention of the *Pesher*. All occur against the backdrop of foreign Armies invading the country.

We have just delineated an initial confrontation between 'the Man of Lying' and 'the Righteous Teacher', expressed in terms of the characteristic verb 'rejecting' or 'denying', to wit, 'he *rejected* the *Torah* in the midst of their whole Assembly'. That this confrontation was *internal and verbal* we deduced from the fact that the individuals involved were clearly attending the Scriptural exegesis sessions of the Righteous Teacher and the sense of the allusion there to '*ma'as*' or 'rejected', which is not Violent.

The version of this confrontation between 'the Righteous Teacher' and 'the Man of Lies' in 1QpHab V.8–12 is presented from a perspective hostile to persons like 'the Liar', 'the Traitors to the New Covenant', or a Paul. This non-violent, verbal confrontation is alluded to in exegesis of a passage about 'Traitors' in the underlying text from Habakkuk 1:12–13. These were said to have 'watched' or 'stared', 'remaining silent at the time of the Reproof (or 'Chastisement') of the Righteous Teacher'. Furthermore, it was at this point the important usage 'swallowed' was first introduced into the text.

These 'Traitors' were not referred to in the earlier passage from Habakkuk 1:4, underlying an exegesis in which they, too, were referred to in 1QpHab II.1–5 three times in just five lines. There, the complaint was that 'they ('the Violent Ones', 'the Covenant Breakers', and 'the Man of Lies') ... did not believe what they heard was going to happen to the Last Generation from the mouth of the Priest', so, once again, we have a usage referred to in the middle of the *Pesher* which seems to recapitulate the whole presentation. In the exegesis of Habakkuk 1:13, three columns later in V.9, these 'Traitors to the New Covenant', 'Violent Ones', and 'Covenant Breakers' are evidently being subsumed under yet another curious esotericism, 'the House of Absalom and the Men of their Council', in which the notion of 'betraying' is paramount – 'Absalom' theoretically having betrayed his father David.

These, interpreting the underlying passage about 'Traitors staring and remaining silent', are described as 'being silent at the time when the Righteous Teacher was reproved' (presumably by 'the Liar') and 'not coming to his aid against the Man of Lying'. This may relate to what goes by the name of 'the Jerusalem Council' in Acts 15:6–29, where Paul must have done something of the same or, at least, been perceived by his opponents as so doing. Later columns of the *Pesher*, most notably VII.17–VIII.3 and X.6–XI.1, will again focus either on disputes or issues between 'the Righteous Teacher' and 'the Man of Lying' as they shift back and forth from the subject of 'the Liar' to the oncoming '*Kittim*' and finally the descriptions of how the Wicked Priest destroyed the Righteous Teacher as well.

Not only was this 'destruction' ultimately expressed in terms of the language of 'swallowing' from Habakkuk 1:13, but 'the Judgment' that would overtake this 'Wicked Priest' was expressed in terms of 'the Cup of the Wrath of God swallowing him' giving way to the Final eschatological 'Judgment' that would be pronounced on those who had plundered and destroyed the Holy Land in general, expressed in XIII.2–4 in terms of the pious hope that 'on the Day of Judgment God would destroy' all Gentile 'Idolaters' and Jewish 'Backsliders' 'from off the Earth'.

In the all-important teaching about Habakkuk 2:3–4 in Column VII.1–VIII.3 and the nature of 'the Liar''s approach to these and similar matters in Column X.6–12, 'the Man of Lying' turns into 'the Spouter' or 'Pourer out of Lying'. Similarly, in the Damascus Document, he is also called 'the Windbag' or 'Scoffer' who 'poured over ('spouting' being based on the Hebrew root, meaning 'to pour') Israel the waters of Lying'.

As we have seen, this imagery is present not only in the Gospels, where it relates to 'the Cup of the New Covenant in my Blood which was *poured out* for you' (slightly condensed in 1 Corinthians 11:25), but also in Acts where it is expressed in terms of 'pouring out' the Holy Spirit upon all flesh (2:17–18) and 'the gift of the Holy Spirit being *poured out* upon the Gentiles too' (10:45). It is also present in Revelation where it relates to 'the wine of the Wrath of God which is *poured out* full strength into the Cup of His Anger' (14:10) – but then, inverting and reversing this again, the accusations against the Jews of 'pouring out of the Blood of Holy Ones and the Prophets' (16:6).

In the allusions in the Damascus Document, the Lying Scoffer's 'pouring out the waters of Lying upon Israel', in fact, had to do with 'removing the bound which the Forefathers had marked out as their inheritance', 'Justifying the Wicked and condemning the Righteous', and 'exulting in dividing the People'. All of these are formulations that have to do with both 'the Man of Lying''s characteristic activity – and Paul's – of 'rejecting the *Torah* in the midst of their whole Assembly', which again reinforces the impression of exceedingly bitter, internal ideological differences, themselves finding clear expression in the Pauline corpus.

Matters of this kind are again implicit in the description of the 'Jerusalem Council' in Acts. This is portrayed in Acts as a kind of pro-Pauline love fest where the only discordant note are the parvenu 'Pharisees', who want to make 'the Peoples' circumcise themselves and 'keep the Law of Moses' (15:5 – in the Habakkuk *Pesher* here, 'the *Torah*'). As Paul puts a similar proposition in his Galatians 2:4 version of these events, they are 'the false brothers who crept in furtively to spy on the freedom we enjoy in Christ Jesus that they might enslave us'. This is exactly what Acts 15:1's 'certain ones who came down from Judea' are insisting on in the first place, which sets in motion the series of events pictured in the next lines as 'the Jerusalem Council'. In Galatians 2:12, where even 'the *Ethnōn*' in the allusion to Peter 'previously eating with the Gentiles' is the same as in Acts; the 'certain ones' were *from James*.

In the version here in 1QpHab V.8–12, we have both allusion to 'Council' and 'their Assembly'. In the picture in Acts 15:1, as just reiterated, these 'some from Judea' are teaching the brothers – for Paul in Galatians 2:4, 'false brothers' – 'unless you are circumcised according to the custom of Moses, you cannot be saved'. But this will be recognized as basically the key precondition of the coming eschatological exegeses of both Habakkuk 2:3 and 2:4 in Columns VII–VIII of the Habakkuk *Pesher*, where both the precondition of being a '*Torah*-Doer' and this usage, 'saved', will form the essence of the interpretation that finally emerges.

Before moving on to consider this and the description of 'the Spouter of Lying''s 'worthless service' and 'Lying works' connected to it, one should also recall how Galatians 2:13 uses the phraseology 'separating himself' to describe Peter and Barnabas' 'hypocrisy' in drawing back and no longer being willing 'to eat with Gentiles'. In the Community Rule, this was 'separating from the habitation of the Unrighteous and going out in the wilderness to prepare the Way of the Lord'; in the Damascus Document, 'separating from the Sons of the Pit'.[1] It is a demand, as should be clear, that is evinced across a whole range of documents at Qumran, most interestingly perhaps in *MMT*, which end by applying the 'Jamesian' position on Abraham 'being justified by works' to a 'Kingly' respondent not dissimilar to Izates or his brother Monobazus in Adiabene.

Chapter 21: 'He Rejected the Law in the Midst of Their Whole Assembly' • 320

Paul's Citation of Habakkuk 2:4's 'the Righteous shall Live by Faith'

Paul quotes the key passage from Habakkuk 2:4, 'the Righteous shall live by his Faith', that the Habakkuk *Pesher* also expounds but, in his version, he drops the adjective 'his' and, in doing so, adopts exactly the opposite position to the one we have seen embraced in 1QpHab VIII.1–3 (and, in effect, embraced in the Letter of James), to argue his proposition 'that no one is justified with God by virtue of the Law'. For Paul these things are obvious and again in Galatians 3:11–12, he puts it in another way – freely quoting a variation of Leviticus 18:5 and stressing the common thread of 'living' to arrive at 'the Law is not of Faith, but the man who has done these things shall live in them' – the emphasis on 'doing' now being shifted over to 'of Faith'.

Paul makes exactly the same point in Romans 1:17, again quoting Habakkuk 2:4, this time in the context of reference to 'Greeks', 'Romans', and 'Barbarians' amid thinly-veiled threats about 'God's Wrath from Heaven being revealed upon all (the) Ungodliness and Unrighteousness of (the) men who hold the Truth in Unrighteousness' (1:18). Also evoked are 'the Jews' and 'other Gentiles'. So does Hebrews 10:38 in the beginning of its long Paulinizing discourse on 'Salvation by Faith' (11:1–26) which cited among other examples the two evoked in the Letter of James. By contrast, as James 2:25 put it, Abraham 'was justified by works when he offered his son Isaac on the altar' and Rahab the Harlot too 'was justified by works when she took in the messengers and sent them out another way'.

For Hebrews 11:17 and 11:31, however, it was rather 'by Faith' that Abraham when he was tested, offered up his 'only begotten' Isaac in whom his 'seed would be called' and Rahab the Harlot 'did not die with the ones who did not believe'. Not only have we seen the relevance of these two examples to historical events in Palestine in this period – in particular, the situation of the Queen of Adiabene, both as regards her son Izates and possibly her own questionable past, but this emphasis will be shifted back to 'doing' and 'the *Doers* of *Torah*' in the Column VIII *Pesher* of 1QpHab on Habakkuk 2:4 we shall analyze further below.

Once should again remark the emphasis on 'living' in these passages expounding Habakkuk 2:4 in Paul, which end by denying that the Law 'can give life' and a 'Righteousness' by 'the Law' (Galatians 3:21). Rather they affirm – in yet another canny if 'biting' metaphor for 'circumcision' and 'works' – that 'sowing' in 'the flesh' shall 'reap corruption', but 'sowing to the Spirit shall reap everlasting life from the Spirit' (Galatians 6:8). This is the same 'living' encountered in the 'cursing' of the 'Law – Breakers' in the Last Column of 4QD above relating to what 'a man must *do* and thereby *live*' – precisely the words Paul has just used, but with the entirely opposite signification.

Paul moves from these two points about '*life*' into his interpretation of the passage about 'cursing' from Deuteronomy 21:23. Though this Biblical injunction can be taken to mean that it is a 'curse' to hang a man upon a tree at all – this is what we saw to basically be the position of the Nahum *Pesher*[2] – the sense is ambiguous even in Paul's reading of the phrase. The operative part – though Paul does not quote it – has to do, however, with not leaving a 'body all night upon the tree' which nevertheless, then, made such a deep impression on New Testament chroniclers.

But Paul's twist on this is quite different. He has already cited the passage from Deuteronomy 27:26 about, as he sees it, those 'of the works of the Law being under a curse' (Galatians 3:10). This is the second 'cursing' passage connected to 'Abraham's Faith being reckoned to him as Righteousness' and the Peoples 'being blessed with the believing Abraham' (the warrant for Paul's 'Gentile Mission') in almost as many lines. Since, as Paul sees it, those 'doing the Law' are under what is, in fact, the threat of a 'curse', for him, 'Christ redeemed us from the curse of the Law by having become a curse – that is, by 'being hung upon a tree', i.e., crucified, and, therefore, 'accursed' – 'for us' (Galatians 3:13).

It is from this 'that Abraham's blessing might come to the Peoples in Christ Jesus that (they) might receive the Promise of the Spirit through Faith' (Galatians 3:14), and it is on this basis that he now goes on to develop his whole understanding of the redeeming death of Christ Jesus, not only for himself, but for all mankind as well. Though, obviously masterfully dialectical, one can plainly see this to be based upon the same kind of 'cursing' language encountered in the Qumran documents, only *reversed*. Furthermore, Paul clearly realizes that individuals of the genus of 'the Man of Lying' like himself, who 'reject the Law', are for a whole series of Qumran documents 'accursed', as per the injunction from Deuteronomy 27:26 he has just quoted so perversely – a passage also plainly in wide use at Qumran. This is particularly clear in the Community Rule and Damascus Document, but also 4Q *Berachot* (which, reflecting its subject matter, I entitled 'The Chariots of Glory') in the section 'The Community Council Curses *Belial*' – itself plainly a part of the Community Rule.[3]

It is this denunciation that can be viewed as the moving force behind the 'plots' against Paul's life signaled in Acts, particularly on the part of 'Nazirite'-vowing extremists who take an oath in Acts 23:12 'not to eat or drink until they have killed Paul'. This is not the same for Jesus and James, though Scripture would have us think it is. In Paul's case, it is plots on the part of 'Zealot'-style sectarians; for Jesus and James, it is clearly the very *opposite* kind of *Establishment* 'plots', because all reports confirm that they were very popular among the People. It is clearly not 'Jewish' plots. The same is true for John the Baptist.

Ultimately Scripture as it has come down to us and early Church theology have taken advantage of the general lack of historical sophistication concerning this period to make these two, diametrically opposed types of 'plots' appear equivalent, but now the Dead Sea Scrolls have come to light to restore the balance and give us a unique contemporary witness into the intellectual heart of this period. Without them, previously one might have suspected this, but it could not be proved. Now it can. This is the point one must appreciate when considering historical matters in this period. James is able to function in Jerusalem for twenty years or more from the Forties to the Sixties with no discernible problems among the mass of the People – the opposite – until he is removed by what has to be considered Establishment 'plotting', whereas Paul can hardly set foot in Jerusalem without being mobbed by the People or protected by Roman troops and has to spend years abroad while the memory of his previous behavior recedes. Even this is insufficient. However this may be, knowing that he 'is' or 'has been cursed' by those certainly of a 'Nazirite' or Qumran frame-of-mind, in the best Hellenistic rhetorical style, he reversed the language of 'cursing' his opponents are throwing against him, to hurl back upon them instead.

Not only does he use here the language of 'excommunication' or 'banning' encountered in 4QD, there can be little doubt – just as in the positions he adopts in Romans 13:1–10 – that his adversaries were not 'Jews' from the 'Herodianizing' Jewish Establishment. One can well imagine how the kind of verbal invective he is indulging in here would have infuriated his opponents who were themselves the partisans of just such a 'crucified Messiah'. That someone was claiming that 'the crucified Messiah', whom they loved, 'was cursed' because foreigners 'had hung him on a tree' – 'cursed' in the exact manner they considered persons such as 'Lying Spouter's like Paul to be – would have enraged them.

Just this kind of outrage is to be encountered in the Habakkuk *Pesher* when, after speaking about the Liar's 'misleading Many' and 'erecting an Assembly' or 'Church upon Lying' or 'Self-Glorification' and 'upon Blood', it will call down upon him and those like him the same 'Judgments of Hellfire' with which they 'blasphemed and vilified the Elect of God'.[4] Furthermore, 1QpHab VII.17–VIII.3 also uses the very same formulation, 'Doer of' or 'doing of the *Torah*', Paul uses in Galatians 3:10 (quoting Deuteronomy 27:26) and in Galatians 5:3, to restrict the effect of just this Habakkuk 2:4, 'the Righteous shall live by his Faith', Paul so tendentiously interprets in Galatians 3:11. This is about as powerful a demonstration of the convergence of these documents as one could devise – not to mention the use of this same expression, 'Doer of the Law', in James 4:11.

For Paul now in Galatians 3:13, 'Christ redeemed us from the curse of the Law' by having become a 'curse' according to the Law himself. As we have implied, this is one of the most astonishing ideological reversals in the whole complex of Western intellectual history and has had the most profound effects even until today, but it is the Qumran documents that allow us to see it in perspective. Without them, we probably would be able to do so, but with them, a completely new perspective is afforded.

Paul now uses this proposition to assert that Abraham's blessing will now come to the 'Peoples' as well, again the complete ideological reversal of Qumran's perspective on these same 'Peoples'. Taking the opportunity to counter-indicate 4QD's position on 'the Covenant' and 'the Law' or '*Torah*' being able to give 'life', he states 'for if a Law had been given that was able to *give life* then, indeed, Righteousness would have been by the Law', but, of course, this was not the case. Therefore 'Righteousness' was 'the Promise by Faith of Jesus Christ' (3:22). He can now go on to evoke the 'Sonship' ideal on behalf of Gentiles since, strictly speaking according to Jewish writ, all the Righteous Ones were Sons of God, all were now 'Sons of God through Faith in Christ Jesus' (3:26).[5]

This leads into his concept of 'the Children of the Promise' being the true Sons of Abraham's seed. In Galatians 3:29, he puts this as follows: 'But if you are Christ's, then you are Abraham's seed and Heirs to the Promise'. Moreover, it echoes Romans 9:7 where he was rather interpreting Genesis 21:12, 'in Isaac shall your seed be called', and using the language of 'reckoning' from Genesis 15:6 to assert that this meant 'the Children were to be reckoned as the seed'. Paul uses it to move into a slightly more universalist program. As he had expressed this earlier in Romans 1:16–17, in interpretation of 'the Righteous shall live by Faith' as well: 'the Power of God saving (or 'giving Salvation to') everyone who believes, both the Jew first and the Greek'. It is this language of 'saving' we shall presently encounter in the Habakkuk *Pesher*'s crucial interpretation of this same Habakkuk 2:4.

The same is true in Romans 10:1–14, where, playing on the issue of the 'uncircumcised heart' again, Paul now rather expresses 'the desire of (his) own heart' for the 'Salvation' of Israel (10:1 – *sic*). In doing so, he acknowledges that the fundamental issue was 'being saved', at the same time deliberately invoking the counter-position of those in Israel whom he acknowledges 'have zeal for God but', as he expresses this – taking back what he has just accorded them – 'not according to Knowledge' (10:2). Continuing this critique, he then goes on to criticize these as 'being ignorant of God's Righteousness' – the very words with which the Cairo version of the Damascus Document begins ('Now listen, all *Knowers of Righteousness, and comprehend the works of God*'[6]) – and in 'trying to set up their own Righteousness, did not submit to the Righteousness of God' (10:3)!

It is now a quick step to: 'Christ is the end of the Law for Righteousness to anyone that believes' in Romans 10:4. Here he again alludes to Leviticus 18:5 about 'doing these things and living' and Moses writing 'a Righteousness of the Law' (10:5). This he now counters by again using the language of the 'heart': if 'you believe in your heart..., you shall be saved, for with the heart is belief (leading) to Righteousness ... and Salvation' (10:9–10), concluding with the completely cosmopolitan proclamation: 'For there is no difference between Jew and Greek, for the same Lord of all is Rich towards all who call on Him. For everyone, whoever calls on the Name of God, shall be saved (Romans 10:11–12).' Not only does this mix both Hellenistic and Hebraic allusion, but here we again see the play on the 'Riches' and 'being called by Name' imagery in both Qumran documents and in James. This language of 'being saved' reappears in both James and the *Pesher* on Habakkuk 2:4 at Qumran.

Colossians 3:9–11, a letter considered to be in the 'Pauline school', also reverses the language of James 3:5–10's attack on 'the Tongue'. Instructing its respondents 'not to Lie to one another' as well, it concludes: 'there is neither Greek nor Jew, circumcision or uncircumcision, Barbarian, Scythian, bondman or free', 'only Christ'. For Paul in 1 Corinthians 1:24, this is: 'To those who are called, both Jews and Greeks, Christ is God's Power and God's Wisdom'.[7] He also puts the same proposition in Galatians 3:28: 'There is not Jew or Greek, bondman or free, male or female. All are one in Christ Jesus.' As usual, this leads directly into his attack on those 'who wish again to be in bondage', scrupulously 'keeping days and months and times and years', the very elements that in the Damascus Document are so much a part of 'separating' in the wilderness, 'setting up the Holy Things according to their precise letter', 'to love each man his brother as himself', and 'not defiling one's Holy Spirit', but 'walking in these things in Perfect Holiness'.[8]

In 4QBerachot, which punctuates its 'excommunications' and 'cursing' with 'amen, amen's, these are 'the weeks of Holiness', 'the Festivals of Glory', and 'the embroidered Splendor of the Spirits of the Holy of Holies'. For Paul, they are the 'weak and beggarly elements' that reduce his constituents to 'the bondage (they so) desire' (Galatians 4:9). Is it possible to conceive of anyone being more insulting than this? Also the allusion to 'weak' here not only meshes with the allusions to 'weakness' we have seen him use throughout the totality of his polemical assaults, but now it includes the point about how he 'labored in vain' regarding these matters for his Communities (4:11). This will, again, be absolutely reproduced in the language the Habakkuk *Pesher* uses to condemn the 'vain labor' of 'the Spouter of Lying' which he has expended to 'build (his) Worthless City upon Blood and erect (his) Assembly upon Lying' – this paralleled too in its antithesis in CD VII and its analogues: 'erecting the fallen Tabernacle of David'!

James and the Liar

Before proceeding to the interpretation of 'the Righteous shall live by his Faith' in Columns VII–VIII of the Habakkuk *Pesher*, we should look at the figurative evocation of 'the Tongue' in James 3:5–8, a chapter replete with the imagery of Qumran. Not only does it contain an allusion to the 'blessing and cursing' from Deuteronomy, which Paul also makes use of in Galatians 3:10, upon which most of the language of 'cursing' in these documents is based, but it even alludes to the problem of 'mixed liquids', a subject which also occupies not a little attention in *MMT*.[9] As James 3:11–12 puts this, 'out of the same fountain orifice pours forth sweet and bitter' (note here the metaphor of 'pouring' again), which it compares to 'the death-bringing poison' of the Tongue, out of whose 'mouth goes forth the blessing and cursing' at the same time. It also uses the 'heart' imagery we have just seen Paul use and used at Qumran with inverted effect. In James 3:13–14 this is tied, not insignificantly, to 'showing one's *works* in the Meekness of Wisdom', followed by the words: 'If you have bitter jealousy and contentiousness in your heart, do not boast or Lie against the Truth'.

We have just seen how important this language of 'Truth' is at Qumran, not to mention how Paul uses it in Galatians 3:1 and 4:16 to assert he 'does not Lie'. Moreover it was, according to him, that by telling his communities 'the Truth', namely, that the Righteousness of the Law has been superseded by the death of Christ, he has become their 'Enemy'. In James 4:8–10, this kind of language is always followed by further requests to 'purify your hearts', 'humble yourselves', and 'do not slander one another' which, just as the above, all have their direct counterparts in the literature of Qumran. As 4:11 puts this: 'He who speaks against (his) brother and judges his brother, speaks against the Law and judges the Law. But if you judge the Law, you are not a Doer of the Law, but a Judge.'

These kinds of allusions are also tied in James to references to 'the *Diabolos*' again (4:7) or 'animal' or 'beastliness' (3:15). But this is exactly the kind of phraseology we have already encountered in Rabbinic literature regarding the name 'Be'or' (or *be'ir*/animal, 'o' and 'i' being largely interchangeable in Qumran epigraphy) – in the Bible reckoned as the father at once of both 'Bela'' and 'Balaam'. We have also seen this imagery of 'biting' and 'swallowing' reflected in Paul in Galatians 5:15 and one can find it reflected in 2 Peter 2:15–16 and Jude 1:10 and 1:19, also evoking 'the error of Balaam' – referred to in 2 Peter as 'the Son of Be'or who loved the Reward of Unrighteousness' (here, of course, the '*Gemul*'/'*Gemulo*' language again). But it is the attack on 'Lying against the Truth' in James 3:14 which is most pregnant in this regard and related, not only to Paul's claims of 'speaking Truth' in Galatians 4:16 but the imagery of 'the Tongue', by which it is introduced in James 3:5–12. Nor can there be any doubt that this genre of imagery is generically related to or parallels that of the 'pouring out' or 'spouting' imagery applied to the depiction of 'the Lying Spouter' at Qumran. In turn, it is related to 'mouth' and 'lips' imagery both here and throughout the literature at Qumran.

For instance, in James 3:15–16, the language that follows this allusion to 'the Tongue' and 'Lying against the Truth' is: 'This is not the wisdom which comes down from above, but rather it is fleshly, animal-like, Demonic, for where jealousy and contentiousness are, there is confusion and every Evil Thing.' We have already seen the same kind of imagery in Jude and 2 Peter. In the Colossians passage recommending 'not Lying to one another', one has the same imagery of 'disobedience', 'anger', 'malice', and 'filthy language out of the mouth'.

We can also see the same kind of recitations in the Community Rule in its enumeration of 'the Ways of the Spirit of Falsehood', as opposed to 'the Crown of Glory with the Garment of Majesty in Unending Light' which 'the Sons of Truth and the Sons of Righteousness' will enjoy. These are the two Spirits of Light and Darkness, Truth and Lying, exactly equivalent to the 'Two Ways' in the early Church teaching document known as The Didache.[10] As this is put in the Nahum *Pesher*, 'those who lead Ephraim astray' – whatever this esotericism 'Ephraim' might mean ('*Nilvim*', a cadre of new 'Gentile' believers in the sense of being 'God-Fearers'?[11]) – are specifically said 'to teach Lying and, with a Tongue full of Lies and deceitful lips, lead Many astray'. This, of course, is the very opposite of the proper 'justifying' activity of both the Damascus Document and Isaiah 53:11 of 'making Many Righteous', applied in the former to 'the Sons of Zadok' and, in Pauline theology, to Jesus.[12]

For James 3:1–8, delineating its view of this 'Tongue' in the context of both who should or should not teach but also with reference to 'stumbling' and 'being driven by violent winds':

"The Tongue is only a little member and boasts great things. But see how a little fire can kindle a large forest and the Tongue is a fire, a world of Unrighteousness. So the Tongue is set among our members, yet the polluter of the whole body, both setting on fire in the course of nature and being set on fire in Hell. For every species, both of beasts and birds, creeping things and sea creatures, is tamable and has been tamed by mankind, but none among men is able to tame the Tongue, (which is) an uncontrollable Evil, full of deadly venom."

Here, not only do we have the 'kindling', 'fire', and 'Wrath of God' imagery used in CD V–VI to condemn those who 'polluted their Holy Spirit and opened their mouth with a Tongue of blasphemies against the Laws of the Covenant of God, saying they were not sure', but also the 'venom' language it uses in Columns VIII and XIX thereafter.

This intense concern over 'the Tongue' in the Letter of James parallels a similar hatred of 'the Enemy' in Pseudoclementine *Recognitions* and 'the Parable of the Tares' in Matthew 13:24 –44 – where, as we saw, the plants that he has planted would 'be gathered up' (or 'uprooted') and 'cast into a Furnace of Fire' – to say nothing of 'the Spouter of Lying' in the Qumran tradition. In fact, in CD VIII.13/XIX.25–26, the very same imagery of 'violent wind' is applied to 'the Spouter of Lying' as is applied to him here in James 3:4. There, too, we also heard about 'walking in wind' or 'Spirit' or 'pouring out wind' or 'being of confused Spirit', and it is this which 'kindled God's Wrath on all his Assembly' or 'Church'.[13] The imagery was based on Micah 2:6: 'they shall surely spout', which in 2:8 also refers to the 'Enemy', and Ezekiel 13:6–16 about 'the Builders of'/'Daubers upon the wall', which also included allusion to Lying prophets 'deceiving the People', and the 'vanity' or 'worthlessness of their Lying vision', not to mention 'making the heart of the Righteous sad' over Lying, and 'strengthening the hand of the Wicked by promising him life' (13:22).

As we have also seen, these are 'the Daubers on the wall', referred to in both CD IV.19–20 and VIII.12–13/XIX.11–13, who followed '*Zaw Zaw*' ('So-and-So'), the Spouter, as it is said, 'He shall surely spout', 'whose works God would visit' and 'upon whom Wrath would be poured' (in the unwillingness to utter the name of this inimical opponent there is clearly expressed the fear of powerful outside, secular forces). The 'Lying visions' referred to in Micah 2:6–8 and Ezekiel 13:10–16 involved 'crying Peace when there is no peace', which is just the point Josephus emphasizes regarding 'Saulos'' role among 'all those desiring peace' and accommodation with Rome in Jerusalem and harmonizes perfectly with Paul's approach, enunciated in Romans 13:1–8 on the Commandment 'to love your neighbor as yourself' (thus!).

Not only do these allusions in CD VIII and XIX to 'the Lying Spouter''s 'pouring out wind' and 'spouting to them' begin with the allusion to 'the deadly Venom of Vipers and the cruel Poison of Asps', but they end with allusion to 'rejecting the Commandments of God, forsaking them and turning aside in the stubbornness of their heart', all prototypical of the behavior of 'the Lying Spouter' at Qumran. After comparison of this to Elisha's rebuke of Gehazi, they move directly into evocation of 'the New Covenant in the Land of Damascus', reference to 'betraying' it and 'departing from (its) Fountain of Living Waters' and 'not being reckoned in the Foundation of the People'.[14] Not only do we have here the possible play on Paul's insistence in Galatians 3:21 about the Law 'being incapable of giving life' but, again, also the language of 'being reckoned', applied by both Paul and James to Abraham and in *MMT* to its 'Royal' addressee.

Here too there follows the typical expulsion from 'the Assembly of the Men of Perfect Holiness' because 'the manifestation of his works' were not in conformance with 'the precise letter of the teaching of the *Torah*'.[15] Once again, 'all the Holy Ones of the Most High have cursed him', nor is anyone 'to cooperate with him in purse ('Riches') or Mission' ('labor'/"*Avodah*').[16] Here too, the Letter of James, in raising the issue of 'blessing and cursing', notes the contradiction of the same 'Tongue', 'blessing God the Father', 'curses men made according to the likeness of God' (3:9–10).

In introducing the description of the Tongue's 'boasting', 'uncontrollable Evil', 'pollution', and 'death-giving Poison' or 'Venom', we also hear about 'violent winds' driven by a helmsman's 'rudder' which is, in turn, also compared to 'the Tongue' (3:4). In James too is the parallel imagery of 'kindling fire'. While somewhat obscure at this point, perhaps purposefully, it also contains the variation on this Qumran allusion to 'the Fountain' or 'Well', as well as these curious allusions to 'the Tongue' both 'cursing' and, in turn, 'being cursed'.

It is at this point, too, ending its recitation on 'the Tongue', that it makes the charge that 'whoever makes himself a Friend of the World turns himself into an Enemy of God' (4:4). That Paul already knows he is being termed 'a Friend of the World' is made clear by his own statements about 'seeking to please men' and his rhetorical assertion about his Gospel 'not being according to men' in Galatians 1:10–11. He is such 'a Friend' – or should we say 'Enemy' – that, according to his detractors, he makes things too easy for such 'men'; and it is precisely at this point that Paul twice resorts to using the 'cursing' language of his opponents: 'If anyone teaches a gospel contrary to what you received ('even if an Angel from Heaven'), *he is to be accursed*' (Galatians 1:8–9).

Chapter 22
The Cup of the New Covenant in His Blood

The First Description of 'the Man of Lies' in the Damascus Document

Before going on to see the further treatment in the Habakkuk *Pesher* of this genus of 'Liar' and his differences with the Righteous Teacher, we should look at the additional notices regarding this subject at the beginning of the Damascus Document which start towards the end of the Column One and run on into the first line of Column Two where they end with the notice that 'the Anger of God was kindled against their Assembly' and 'their works were unclean' or 'polluted before Him'.[1]

Not only is this point about 'their works being unclean before Him' significant, but the Cairo Recension opens with the address to 'all the *Knowers of Righteousness* who seek to understand the works of God', paralleling Paul in Romans 10:3 about those whose 'zeal for God' he admits, but which was 'not according to Knowledge'. 'Being ignorant of God's Righteousness', these 'sought to establish their' own.

In CD I.3–4, these references to 'knowing Righteousness and understanding the works of God' also end up in allusion to God hiding his face 'from His Temple and delivering them up to the sword'. This was at the time of 'the First Visitation' and 'the Era of the desolation of the Land' when they 'spoke Rebellion against the Commandments of God as (given by) the hand of Moses' as described in CD V.20–21 and VII.21–VIII.3/XIX.10–16. Nevertheless, because God 'remembered the Covenant of the First' (the Forefathers) and 'they understood their sinfulness and knew they were guilty men', 'He left a Remnant to Israel and did not deliver them up to be destroyed' (*lechalah* again).[2] Here 'the First' are the Forefathers, Abraham, Isaac, Jacob, and Moses, and 'the Last', which Paul also applies to himself in 1 Corinthians 15:8–9, is 'the Last Generation' and 'the Last Days', presumably the time of writing.

It is at this point that the Righteous Teacher is introduced in the Damascus Document. This occurs after the 'Visitation' by God and how He 'caused to grow' the Messianic 'Root of Planting from Israel and from Aaron'. In the context of the coming of this Teacher of Righteousness we hear that 'God raised him up' out of consideration for 'their works' and because they 'sought Him with a whole heart'.[3] Here not only do we have an evocation of the all-important Salvationary element of 'works' again and the '*darash*'/seeking of 'the *Doresh* (Seeker) *ha-Torah*', but also the 'heart' imagery that we have been encountering throughout our consideration of Paul and James.

In fact, the Righteous Teacher was 'to guide them in the Way of His (God's) heart'. Here too the 'heart' imagery is combined with that of 'the Way', language employed repeatedly throughout Acts as an alternate way of referring to early Christianity in Palestine.[4] Not only is this 'preparation of the Way in the wilderness' part and parcel of the vocabulary applied to John the Baptist's activities in the Synoptics in exegesis of Isaiah 40:3 as well as parallel expositions of this in the Community Rule at Qumran; it explains the use of 'the Way' terminology generally throughout the documents there and, for instance, in Acts. In fact, both here in CD I.15 and in the Last Column of 4QD, the opposite language is applied to 'the Pourer-out of Lying'/'Scoffer' and 'the Peoples,' namely, 'causing them to wander astray in a wilderness without a Way' – one simply reversing the other.

Here, too, as in the Habakkuk *Pesher*, 'the Assembly of the Traitors' are also introduced and described as 'Rebels against the Way' and with them, of course, 'the Lying Scoffer'. Just as in the Habakkuk *Pesher*, where 'the Traitors' and 'the Man of Lies' attend the Scriptural exegesis sessions of the Righteous Teacher and 'did not believe' what he told them was going to happen to God's People 'in the Last Generation', so here in the Damascus Document, again demonstrating the basic circularity of these documents, 'he made known to the Last Generations what God would do in the Last Generation to the Congregation (Assembly) of Traitors'.[5]

Just as with the quotations from Micah and Ezekiel in Columns IV and VIII/XIX about the Spouter's 'spouting' and 'Lying visions', this is described in terms of a passage from Hosea 4:6 comparing Israel's 'straying' or 'Rebelliousness' to the 'straying' of 'a Rebellious heifer'. It is this passage CD I.13-14 uses to introduce 'the Scoffer' or 'Man of Jesting'/'Comedian, who poured over Israel the waters of Lying'. Since the same vocabulary is used to describe what 'the Man of Scoffing' or 'Comedian' does here, as is used in 4QD later and in the Habakkuk *Pesher* to describe 'the Pourer out' or 'Spouter of Lying', we can take these two to be identical. What he does is 'pour out Lying', here expressed in terms of 'causing them to wander astray in a trackless waste without a Way'.

The 'leading astray' or 'deceiving' language is important where 'the Man of Lying' is concerned and is the opposite of 'justifying' or 'making Many Righteous' predicative of the Righteous Teacher. These activities were recapitulated in the Last Column of 4QD where 'the High Priest Commanding the Many' condemns anyone 'rejecting the Laws found in the *Torah* of Moses' and characterizes God as having 'caused the Peoples' (Paul's Gentiles) 'to wander astray in a trackless waste' or 'a wilderness without a Way'. But where Israel was concerned, 'the Priest' avers: 'You chose our Fathers and to their seed gave the Laws of Your Truth and the Ordinances of Your Holiness, which a man shall do and thereby live. And boundary markers were laid down for us. Those who cross over them You curse.'[6]

Moreover, Deuteronomy 30:6 *actually* refers to God 'circumcising your heart and that of your seed to love the Lord your God with all your heart' to express the promise concerning 'thereby living'. It is clear, too, that what is meant by the 'boundary marker' imagery here is the Law. So too for the description of 'the Pourer out of the Waters of Lying' at the beginning of the Damascus Document: 'He brought low the Everlasting Heights, rebelling against the Pathways of Righteousness and removing the boundary markers which the First had marked out as their inheritance.' There can be no doubt that what is being talked about so exaltedly is, once again, 'the Law', and 'the First' are none other than the Patriarchs and Moses, the Forefathers, conceived of as having laid it down.

The text now turns to the effect of 'removing these Pathways of Righteousness' and 'boundary markers', once more resorting to the 'cursing' and 'Covenant' language of Deuteronomy 27–31, continuing: 'for which reason He (God) called down on them the curses of His Covenant and delivered them up to the avenging sword of Vengeance of the Covenant'. We have remarked the importance of these notices about 'delivering up' to those characterizing 'Judas Iscariot', who is also always described as 'delivering him up'. The double reference to Vengeance reiterates similar such references in the cursing in the Community Rule, emphasizing just how terrible this Vengeance was going to be – in our view, as in the New Testament and the theology of the early Church, 'the avenging sword of' the Romans who, in the words of the Habakkuk *Pesher*, 'consume' or 'eat all the Peoples year-by-year, delivering many Countries up to the sword'.[7]

Curiously enough, 'Law-breaking' activities of the Lying Spouter are tied, in the view of these extreme visionaries, to the coming 'Vengeance' of the Romans. This Vengeance is going to be 'visited' upon almost everyone, but they seem to have removed themselves to the Land across Jordan in the neighborhood of Damascus and beyond. This too is the thrust of the statement in CD I.21–II.1, with which this section ends, that 'God's Wrath was kindled against their Congregation, devastating all their multitude, for their works were unclean before Him'.

Chapter 22: The Cup of the New Covenant in His Blood • 328

Interestingly enough, this is now tied to two quotations from Isaiah 30:10–30:13, also having to do with visionaries 'preferring illusions' and 'looking for breaks' in the Wall – presumably 'the Wall' in Ezekiel 13:10 referred to in Columns IV and VIII/XIX, 'daubed upon by Lying Prophets' who 'cried Peace when there was no Peace'. These passages from Isaiah 30:10–13 actually relate to the same subject as not only Ezekiel 13:10 but also Micah 2:11 about the 'spouting' of 'Lying Spouter's or visionaries and even use the same word we have been following here, *ma'as*/reject, in this case 'rejecting this Word and trusting in oppression and guile' (Isaiah 30:12). Here, too, is the language of 'Smooth Things', viz., 'prophesying Smooth Things and seeing delusions' or 'jests' (*mahatalot*, also a play here on the Hebrew word *Halakot*/Smooth Things – Isaiah 30:10).

Elsewhere, as in Columns II–IV of the Nahum *Pesher* at Qumran, 'prophesying Smooth Things' from Isaiah 30:10 is expressed in terms of 'the Seekers after Smooth Things', usually tied by almost all commentators to Pharisees and considered to be a play on their characteristic activity of 'seeking *Halachot*' or 'seeking legal Traditions'. I have extended this usage in the light of the claims by Paul of 'being by Law, a Pharisee' and the consonant behavior pattern of 'seeking accommodation with foreigners' (the most perfect formulation of which is to be found in Romans 13:1–7 above, a completely anti-nationalist and non-'Zealot' text) to 'Pauline Christians' as well.[8] In the Nahum *Pesher*, 'Seekers after Smooth Things' is related to an underlying allusion in Nahum 3:1 to 'the City of Blood'.[9]

Not only is this esotericism associated in Column II of 4QpNahum with the historical action by the Pharisees of inviting foreign armies into Jerusalem in Alexander Jannaeus' time (103–76 BCE) – the paradigmatic act of 'seeking accommodation with foreigners' – but in the Third and Fourth Columns with 'the City of Ephraim', defined as 'the Seekers after Smooth Things at the End of Days', and reference to 'joining' or 'Joiners' (*Nilvim* in CD IV.3), interpreted to include 'resident aliens' or 'the stranger' (*ger-nilveh*) – in this case, meaning Gentiles. This 'City of Blood' imagery will have important ramifications as well when it comes to analyzing the activities of 'the Lying Spouter' in the Habakkuk *Pesher* below.

There is an extant commentary on these materials from Isaiah 30 at Qumran, but it is very fragmentary. Still, it does refer to this same 'Assembly' or 'Congregation of the Seekers after Smooth Things who are in Jerusalem', 'the Last Days, and 'rejecting the Law'.[10] There are also two fragmentary commentaries on Hosea and Micah, the first referring to adopting 'the Festivals of the Gentiles'; and the second, 'the Spouter of Lying who leads the Simple astray' though 'the Spouter' and 'the Simple' are nowhere mentioned in the underlying text from Micah 1:5–6. By contrast, it should be noted that 'Samaria' *is*. While this allusion to 'the Spouter' clearly links up with the allusions to 'he will surely spout' in Micah 2:6 and 'walking in wind (the Spirit) and Lying, spouting Lies' in Micah 2:11, 'Samaria' links up with 'the Simple of Ephraim' in the Nahum *Pesher* above – Samaria and Ephraim being coextensive. This *pesher* also contains a reference to the Righteous Teacher and 'those volunteering to join the Elect of God'.[11] Not only do we have in this last allusion another variation on the language of 'joining' but, seemingly, another reference to those 'Doers of *Torah*' ('the Elect') so disparaged by Paul but so important to the interpretation of Habakkuk 2:4 in the Habakkuk *Pesher*. For the Micah *Pesher*, anyhow, 'these will be saved on the Day of (Judgement)'.[13] We can see this allusion to 'being saved' is eschatological, but we shall now find precisely this language, 'being saved on the Day of Judgment' in the Habakkuk *Pesher*.

In the Damascus Document we now hear of another attack against 'the Righteous One', probably the Righteous Teacher and possibly James. The description of what these 'Seekers after Smooth Things' – who 'chose illusions (*mahatalot* from Isaiah 30:10 above) and watched for breaks, choosing the easiest way' – do, is very germane to our subject. What they did was 'justified the Wicked and condemned the Righteous,' 'transgressing the Covenant and breaking the Law'.[12]

This is an incredible description because it completely reverses what the proper 'justifying' activity in Column Four of the true 'Sons of Zadok' was considered to be, namely, 'justifying the Righteous and condemning the Wicked'. If one considers the word 'Wicked' here in the Hebrew to include what Paul is calling in Galatians 2:15 'Gentile Sinners', then this phraseology, 'justifying the Wicked', can be seen as exactly how Paul's 'justifying' activities might have been seen by his opponents, that is, as *justifying the Sinners*. As Paul actually puts this in Galatians 2:15–16, 'Though by nature Jews and not Gentile Sinners, we know that a man is not justified by works of the Law but through Faith in Jesus Christ.'

What immediately follows at the end of Column One in the Damascus Document is what can only be considered to be a description of another attack on the Righteous Teacher, led in our view by 'the Lying Scoffer'. This can be seen as the attack by 'the Enemy' Paul on 'the Righteous Teacher' James in the Temple – certainly in coordination with the High Priests and presumably the Pharisees – in the Forties, as recorded in the graphic description of the Pseudoclementine *Recognitions*.

Interestingly enough, in this passage the terminology 'Righteous Teacher' is abjured in favor of James' actual sobriquet, 'the Righteous' or 'Just One'. As this is described: 'they banded together against the soul of the Righteous One and against all the Walkers in Perfection, execrating their soul. And they pursued them with the sword, attempting to divide the People.' Nothing could be a better description of the attack on James and his followers in the Temple by Paul and his 'Violent' colleagues, converted by Acts into 'the stoning of Stephen', than this.

The Vision of the End and 'the Delay of the *Parousia*'

Following the description of how the Liar 'rejected the *Torah* in the midst of their whole Assembly' and 'the Traitors' did not come to the aid of the Righteous Teacher against him in Column V.8–12 and the 'tax-farming' rapaciousnes and merciless brutality of 'the *Kittim*' or the Romans in V.12–VI.11, the Habakkuk *Pesher* moves on in Columns VII–VIII to its interpretation of Habakkuk 2:3: 'If it tarries, wait for it', and Habakkuk 2:4: 'The Righteous shall live by his Faith' and what, for our purposes, constitute the key passages of its whole exposition. These would also appear to have been crucial to and the climax of the author's entire presentation as well. It is surprising, therefore, that they have been so little considered by 'Consensus Scholars' and the question naturally arises of 'why'?

These interpretations begin at the end of Column VI with the exposition of Habakkuk 2:1–2. Though the text is broken because it is the bottom of the column, it is clear that the underlying passage is from Habakkuk 2:1–2 speaking about 'standing up' and being a 'watchman' of sorts. It reads: 'But I will stand up upon my Watchtower and take my stand upon my Fortress and look out to see what He will say to me and wh(at I will ans)wer when I am reproved.'[13] Habakkuk 2:2 continues: 'And the Lord answered and said, "Write down the vision and make it plain on tablets, so that he may read it on the run."' Once again, we are in the realm of the visions already encountered in Isaiah 30:10, Ezekiel 13:10, and Micah 2:6, now the 'true visions' of the Prophet Habakkuk and the Righteous Teacher, not the Lying ones of 'the Lying Spouter'. Here is the allusion to 'being reproved' or 'admonished' and the reason, probably, it was applied to the exposition of Habakkuk 1:13 in the previous Column V.10-12 about 'the admonishment of the Righteous Teacher' and 'the Traitors remaining silent' and 'not coming to his aid', when 'the Man of Lying rejected the *Torah* in the midst of their whole Assembly'.

This passage from Habakkuk 2:1 is a very important one to the Qumran exegete because it is actually used at the end of the climactic exposition of 'the Zadokite Covenant' of Ezekiel 44:15 in CD IV.10-12. To understand how, one must recall precisely what was said there.

This exegesis of how 'the Sons of Zadok justified the Righteous and condemned the Wicked' also was eschatological, meaning, it was connected to or evoked 'the Last Days'.[14]

This was followed by the James-style 'all those coming after them were to do according to the precise letter of the *Torah*, which the First (i.e., 'the Ancestors') had transmitted, until the Completion of the Era of these years'; and then, the assertion: 'According to the Covenant which God made with the First to remit their sins, so too would God make atonement through them' – meaning seemingly through or by 'the Sons of Zadok' or in succession to them. This, in turn, was immediately followed by, 'And with the Completion of the Era of the number of these years, there would be no more association with' or 'joining to the House of Judah' – apparently meaning, at least on the surface, that there would be no more specifically being Jews *per se*.

To this was added the note 'rather each man would stand on his own net' or 'Watchtower'. Here, not only will this archaic phraseology, 'House of Judah' – clearly an archaism for 'Jews' – also be important for the exposition of both Habakkuk 2:3 and 2:4 about to follow in 1QpHab VII.5–VIII.3, but so is this passage from 2:1, 'taking one's stand upon one's watchtower and looking out' – now also about to be expounded as a prelude to these in VI.12–VII.5.

The problem is that in this phrase in Column IV.12 of the Cairo Damascus Document, the scribe redacted 'each man would stand on his own net/*metzudo*', not 'watchtower' or 'fortress'/*metzuro*, which really does make things obscure – seemingly miscopying *dalet* (D) for *resh* (R), virtually identical in written Hebrew. But such a scribal error would be very understandable in view of the context of what follows in the Column IV.12–V.11, the 'Three Nets' (*metzudot*) in which Belial 'catches Israel, transforming these things before them into three kind of Righteousness'.

Even were the substitution purposeful – meaning possibly, 'each man standing on his own record' or 'Righteousness' – still the language would clearly appear to be that of Habakkuk 2:1, now being subjected to exegesis here in the Habakkuk *Pesher* (VI.12–VII.8). Once again we have dramatic proof of the basic homogeneity of all these documents – but what is even more startling, that the writer of the Damascus Document seems to be using the very same passage as the writer here in the Habakkuk *Pesher* – if so, intending us to understand that this, too, was the new state of affairs Habakkuk was envisioning.

Be this as it may, for the Habakkuk *Pesher* at this point at the end of Column VI.12–13, the 'standing upon one's Watchtower' and 'looking out to see what (God) would say' is interpreted to refer to both the Prophet Habakkuk and 'the Righteous Teacher' (God's exegete *par excellence*) and their mutual visions of the End Time – obviously an extremely important subject. The *Pesher*, in fact, is particularly graphic about this, connecting the 'reading and running' in the underlying text from Habakkuk 2:2 to the exegetical mastery of the Righteous Teacher, 'to whom God made known all the Mysteries of the words of His Servants the Prophets'. With regard to these, one should also recall the kind of revelations Paul claims to be having, in particular in Romans 16:25 and his proclamation of 'the Gospel of Jesus Christ, according to the revelation of the Mystery, kept secret of the times of the Ages and by the Prophetic Scripture, but now made plain'. The parallel of this with the language being encountered here in the *Pesher* should be plain.

By contrast, here in the *Pesher* the reference is directly to the Righteous Teacher, who is being described in precisely the manner he was in the earlier scriptural exegesis sessions of 'the Priest' in Column II.8–9, 'in whose heart God has put the insight to interpret all the words of His Servants the Prophets' – that is to say, his heart was truly circumcised as opposed to the Wicked Priest's or, even more germane to the material before us, those 'fleshy tablets of the heart' upon which Paul claims to be writing 'Christ's Letter' in 2 Corinthians 3:3 'with the Spirit of the Living God'. In fact, in the rest of the text from Habakkuk 2:2 being cited here: 'write down the vision and make it plain on tablets, so that he may read it on the run', we have allusion to the very 'tablets' Paul is referring to. But now these tablets upon which God told Habakkuk to write down his vision are interpreted in terms of 'the Righteous Teacher, to whom God make known all the Mysteries of the words of His Servants the Prophets'.[15] If such were not clear earlier, it is now unmistakably so that 'the Priest' here and the Righteous Teacher are one and the same.

Since the underlying passage from Habakkuk 2:3 that follows this speaks enigmatically about 'there shall yet be another vision of the Appointed Time, and it will speak of the End and it will not lie', the whole interpretation is then framed eschatologically, 'the End' now being both 'the Last Generation' and 'the Last End', just encountered in the Damascus Document's exposition of 'the Sons of Zadok' as 'the Elect of Israel, called by Name, who will stand up in the Last Days' – 'the First Men of Holiness', 'who would justify the Righteous and condemn the Wicked'. So, once again, we are in the same exegetical milieu.

Attached to the next passage from Habakkuk 2:3 about 'there yet being another vision of the Appointed Time' is an allusion in the underlying text to 'it shall tell of the End and shall not lie'. Again, the appeal of such a Biblical text to Qumran exegetes or, for that matter, those in the early Church should be plain. One should also appreciate the kind of connections that could have been drawn to Paul with his repeated protestations to *not Lying* in the corpus attributed to him. The thrust given it in the *Pesher*, of course, is that the Righteous Teacher's interpretation is the Truth, as opposed to 'Lying' ones like those of the Man of Lying or 'Lying Spouter'.

Here the interpretation of the Righteous Teacher is actually given, namely that 'the Last Age' or 'the Final End will be extended and exceed all that the Prophets have foretold, because the Mysteries of God are astonishing'.[16] Anyone familiar with early Christian history will immediately recognize this interpretation as equivalent to what goes in modern parlance as 'the Delay of the *Parousia*' or 'the Delay of the Second Coming' or 'Return of Christ'. But here in the Habakkuk *Pesher*, we actually have the scriptural warrant for it – at least from the Qumran perspective – Habakkuk 2:3. Not only this, it leads up to and actually introduces the Qumran exposition of Habakkuk 2:4, 'the Righteous shall live by his Faith.' Even perhaps more significantly, it was in the Scriptural exegesis of the Righteous Teacher of 'the Appointed Time' and 'the End' of Habakkuk 2:3 that this interpretation first appears to have been made, at least this would appear to be the purport of the text before us – a startling conclusion.

'If it Tarries, wait for it'

The sense of this interpretation is reinforced and further expounded in the exposition of the second half of Habakkuk 2:3: 'If it tarries, wait for it, for it will surely come and not be late'. Of course, as the Habakkuk *Pesher* turns this around, it will 'be late' or 'delayed' in view of the events transpiring in Palestine before the eyes of the exegete – very late. This is typical of Qumran usage, just as it is New Testament usage, which sometimes even changes the phraseology of an underlying text in favor of a given exegesis, not to mention reversing it.

One sees a variation of this in John 21:22–23's portrait of Jesus telling one of his disciples, in his post-Resurrection appearance along the shore of the Sea of Galilee, 'to remain' or 'wait for (him) until (he) comes'. In this case, it is 'the Disciple Jesus loved' who is told to 'abide' his coming. This notion of 'waiting on the Lord' or patiently for 'the God of Judgment' is part and parcel of the eschatology of Isaiah 30:18, directly following the material about visionaries 'foretelling Smooth Things', so integral to the presentation of 'the Liar' and his 'Covenant-Breaking' associates in the Damascus Document above. It is also part and parcel of the ideology of James 5:7 on being patient, because 'the coming of the Lord is drawing near'.

At this point the Habakkuk *Pesher*, VII.10–11, introduces the terminology, 'the Doers of the *Torah*' in apposition, significantly, to 'the Men of Truth' and the analogue to which has already been encountered several times in James applied to those 'speaking against the Law and judging it'. Evoking this terminology here, so much a part of the Letter attributed to James and so disparaged by Paul, is of the profoundest importance. This is particularly true since, as if by way of emphasis, it is then immediately introduced into the exegesis of Habakkuk 2:4 that follows, a fundamental proof-text we have already seen Paul expound on behalf of Gentile non-*Torah*-Doers and bringing Salvation to Gentiles generally.

Here in the *Pesher* it is connected to another concept important to the ideology of Paul and James: 'the Men of Truth doing the *Torah*' or '*Torah*-Doers'. We have already seen how intent Paul is that by telling his communities 'the Truth' he should not be viewed as their 'Enemy' (Galatians 4:16) and telling 'the Truth' about the prophecies so dear to God, at least as he sees this to be. This is particularly the case regarding Abraham's 'Faith' in Genesis 15:6 but also the 'Salvation by Faith' he sees in Habakkuk 2:4.

This would relate to 'the Truth of the Gospel' (Galatians 2:5 and 2:14) or 'the Truth of Christ' and 'of the Cross' (2 Corinthians 11:10) as well. In Romans 1:18–25, for instance (actually evoking Habakkuk 2:4), he calls down 'the Wrath of God in Heaven' upon those who 'disguise the Truth in Unrighteousness' or 'change God's Truth into a Lie' and, later, again speaking about the 'Truth in Christ', he reiterates his assurance elsewhere that he 'does not lie' (Romans 9:1). Here in the Habakkuk *Pesher*, the phraseology 'the Men of Truth who do the *Torah*' counter-indicates those having the opposite or 'Lying' interpretation of these pivotal passages as, for instance, someone of the genus of 'the Lying Spouter' it so reviles.

It is for this reason that this allusion to 'it will not Lie' in the underlying text of Habakkuk 2:3 is so important to the exegetes, meaning that the eschatological exegesis that is to follow will not be a 'Lying' one. Furthermore, because it seems to restrict the exegesis to 'the Men of Truth who do the *Torah*', the implication is that it does not apply to those who do not. One cannot stress the emphasis on '*Torah*-doing' here too much. It will reappear four columns later in 1QpHab XII.4–5 in the description of the 'conspiracy to destroy the Poor', described there too as 'the Simple of Judah who do the *Torah*'.

We have already delineated many of the allusions to 'Doers' and 'doing' (in Hebrew, based on the same root as 'works') throughout the Qumran corpus. The same is true in James, where we also heard about 'the Doers of the word' and 'the Doers of the word of Truth' (1:18–22), not to mention 'boasting and Lying against the Truth' (3:14) and 'straying from the Truth' (5:19). For its part, the *Pesher* in its exposition of Habakkuk 2:3 goes one better, repeating this word 'Truth' as if for emphasis: 'This concerns the Men of Truth, the Doers of *Torah*, whose hands shall not slacken from the Service of Truth, though the Last Age be extended.'[17] This is the same construct, 'Last Age' or 'End Time,' used in the previous *Pesher* in VII.5–8 first evoking this 'Delay of the Last Era'. It now continues somewhat formulaically: 'For all the Ages of God come to their appointed End as He determined (them) in the Mysteries of His insight'. Again, it would not be without profit to compare this to Paul in Romans 16:25 on 'the revelation of the Mystery kept secret in the Times of the Ages'.

But there is another usage we have been following which is introduced here: 'labor' or 'work' – not 'Jamesian' works, which in Hebrew is based on a different root – but 'works' in the sense of Service or Mission. We have been observing this usage, both in Paul's Letters and at Qumran, in documents like the Community Rule and Damascus Document.

Not only is this used in excommunication texts at Qumran, banning having anything to do with such a person either 'in service or purse'; but two columns later in 1QpHab X.9–12, it will have important ramifications in the evaluation of the Lying Spouter's 'labor' or 'Service' and the 'worthlessness' of the 'Service' with which he 'tired out Many' (by 'instructing them in works of Lying' – these now proper eschatological 'works') and 'the Assembly he erected upon Lying' for his own 'Glorification'. This, too, is something of the thrust of Paul's contemptuous reference in 2 Corinthians 11:15 to 'the Servants of Righteousness' – only reversed – whom he really thinks are 'Servants of Satan' and 'whose End (in another satirical play and reversal) shall be according to their works'!

In the *Pesher* in VII.10–14 about 'not slackening in the Service of Truth though the Last Age be prolonged before them', the sense is reversed to that of 'Truthful Service' not, as three columns later, the 'worthless Service' of the Lying Spouter. But 1QpHab X.10–12 restricts the application of Habakkuk 2:3 only to 'the Servants of Righteousness' or 'the Men of Truth who do the *Torah*'. That is to say, it is only to such persons that the Righteous Teacher's exegesis about the Delay of the Last Age or End Time (the *Parousia*) applies. This will have particular relevance now for the exegesis of Habakkuk 2:4 that follows and its clear anti-Pauline thrust.

Since we are at the end of Column Seven, the text is again fragmentary, but the *Pesher* is quite clear. It has to do with the first phrase from Habakkuk 2:4: 'Behold, his soul is puffed up and not Straight (or 'Upright') within him'. Paul, of course, is also playing on this imagery of being 'puffed up' and uses it to introduce his observations about the 'weak' brothers whose 'consciences are defiled' and 'stumble' over the issue of 'meat' and dietary regulations in general in 1 Corinthians 8:1–13. His attacks are clearly directed against the Jerusalem Leadership, parodying two of their favorite pretenses: superior Knowledge and 'loving God' (i.e., piety). As Paul expresses this in his own inimitable way, 'Knowledge puffs up' whereas 'loving God' – which they ought to espouse (again more contemptuous reversal) – 'builds up'. Put in another way, if they followed his prescriptions, then their 'weak consciences' would 'be built up enough to eat things sacrificed to idols' (8:10) not vice versa. The *Pesher* (1QpHab X.10), too, will presently use this 'building' imagery when it comes to describing the activities of the Liar.

The exposition of this in the *Pesher* in VII.14–16 also plays on the allusion to 'puffed up' (a homophone in Hebrew of the word 'doubled'). Pregnantly, this is expressed in terms of how 'their Sins will be doubled upon them and they will not be pleased with their Judgement'.[18] That it has to do with Judgment – 'the Last Judgment,' which Paul too is evoking in his aspersion about 'the End' of the 'Servants of Righteousness' in 2 Corinthians 11:15 – is undeniable and will have decisive meaning for the *Pesher* that now follows on the second part of Habakkuk 2:4, the most important one of the whole Commentary and perhaps all the literature at Qumran.

That the *Pesher* on Habakkuk 2:4 is *eschatological* is clear from everything that has gone before and the repeated references to the Final Age/Last End in the exposition of Habakkuk 2:3 preceding it. This idea of Judgment having to do with the kind of 'tarrying' and extension/delay of the End Time/Final Age and the counseling of 'patience until the coming of the Lord' and 'seeing the End of the Lord' is also part and parcel of the last Chapter of the Letter of James (5:7–11). There it is accompanied by allusion to 'the Judge' who 'is able to save and destroy' (4:12) 'standing before the door' (5:9) – also the imagery of the Islamic '*Imam*'.

The Exposition of Habakkuk 2:4 in the Habakkuk *Pesher*

We are now at the most crucial *Pesher* of all, the interpretation of Habakkuk 2:4, '*the Righteous shall live by his Faith*', at Qumran. Unlike Paul's citation in Galatians 3:11 and Romans 1:17, the possessive pronoun has not been dropped from 'live by his Faith' and the phraseology is correct. It reads: 'Its interpretation relates to all the Doers of the *Torah* in the House of Judah.' The phraseology "*Osei ha-Torah*,' from the previous *Pesher* on Habakkuk 2:3, is actually picked up and repeated again. Nor is there any doubting the meaning of the usage 'House of Judah' here; it is simply a way of saying 'Jews'. It is also paralleled by another expression, also involving 'doing the *Torah*', that follows four columns later in the *Pesher* in exposition of 'the dumb beasts', as in XII.3-5, 'the Simple of Judah doing the *Torah*', identified with the *Ebionim* or the Poor, whom – along with the Righteous Teacher – the Wicked Priest also destroys.

Now we can take the thrust of this expression, 'House of Judah,' to be double-edged or doubly attributive. Just as the James-like recommendation of 'patience' – in the eschatological exegesis preceding it relating to 'the Delay of the *Parousia*' in VIII.9–12 – is circumscribed to 'the '*Osei ha- Torah*' or '*Torah*-Doers, whose hand would not slacken in the Service of Truth though the Final Age would be extended beyond anything the Prophets foretold'; here the efficacy of Habakkuk 2:4 is not only circumscribed to 'the Doers of the *Torah*', but now there is an additional qualification: these must be native-born Jews as well.

The thrust of this is explosive. To state the contrapositive: Habakkuk 2:4 does not apply to non-*Torah*-doing non-Jews, that is, non-*Torah*-doing Gentiles. It does not even apply to non-*Torah*-doing *Jews*. This *Pesher* is stating that Habakkuk 2:4 should not be applied to Gentiles at all, as Paul does. This qualification in its applicability would appear to be purposefully inserted in the exegesis and directed against someone. There can be little doubt whom. In addition, it clears up a lot of misunderstandings about the way Scripture is used in the rather free and eclectic manner of Paul. Nor can this limitation in the scope of the applicability of the *Pesher* on Habakkuk 2:4 be thought of as being accidental. It would appear to be framed precisely with foreknowledge of the position of 'the Man of Lies' or the Pauline position on these passages and issues in mind and, *a priori*, to disqualify them – the only disqualification possible given the manner and style of Pauline argumentation as we have reviewed it. It is a very powerful argument indeed and just what one would have expected from a native-born Jewish Community interested in the apocalyptic and eschatological interpretation of Scripture as well.

What it does is preclude the Pauline interpretation of this passage out of which much of the theology about the Redeeming nature of Jesus' death in Galatians 3:13 and the extension of 'the Power of God unto Salvation to everyone that believes, both to Jew first and to Greek' in Romans 1:16, emerges. It is also an extremely telling dating tool for the *Pesher* as a whole, since it shows that the text could not have been written before this theological position was enunciated.

The text now moves on to the rest of its interpretation of Habakkuk 2:4: 'The Righteous shall live by his Faith', which, given the presentation we have already encountered in James, must be seen as *Jamesian*. It reads: 'Its interpretation concerns all the *Torah*-Doers in the House of Judah whom God will save from the House of Judgment, because of their works (or 'suffering works' as in Isaiah 53:11) and their Faith in the Righteous Teacher.'[19] This is nothing less than 'Faith working with works' in James 2:20–24.

It is also expressed in James 2:14 in the following manner: 'If someone says he has Faith, but does not have works, can Faith save him?' The individual making such claims, also interpreting Habakkuk 2:4 and presumably identified with 'the Tongue' in James 3:5–8, must be seen as the same person who – as opposed to this believing Abraham, 'the Friend of God' – by making himself 'a Friend to the world transformed himself into the Enemy of God'. In fact, the allusion to 'save' here (Hebrew: *yizzil*) is very important. Its import has usually been missed by most scholars, who see what we have before us here as simply a mundane 'courtroom' confrontation of some kind. But we have already encountered this usage 'save' in James, not only as regarding 'the Doers of the Word' and 'the Doer of the work' above, but also in the prelude to its discussion of 'Faith vs. works' where, after quoting 'the Royal Law according to the Scripture' and 'keeping the whole Law, while stumbling on one small point', it alludes to how Abraham was 'saved'.

Paul also uses the term following his discussion of how Abraham was saved in Romans 4:1–5:5. This occurs in conjunction with allusion to 'being justified by his blood' and how, 'having previously been Enemies, we are reconciled to God by the death of His son' and 'saved by his life' in 5:9–10. He also alludes to it in 1 Corinthians 15:1–2, evoking the Gospel 'in which you stand, by which you are also being *saved*' in conjunction with the clear Qumran language of 'holding fast' to his preaching and 'not believing in vain'. In 1 Corinthians 15:14, this becomes: 'If Christ has not been resurrected, then our preaching is worthless and your Faith too is worthless.' These kinds of allusions to 'believing *in vain*' and 'being *worthless*' will now recur in the later *Pesher* in X.10–12 on Habakkuk 2:12–13, evaluating the Spouter of Lying's '*vain* Service' and '*worthless works*'.

Where this passage from Habakkuk 2:4 is concerned, that we are dealing with Judgment or the Last Judgment is clear from just about every text quoting it from Paul to James and to these documents from Qumran. This term 'House of Judgment', used here in conjunction with the allusion to 'being saved' in 1QpHab VIII.2, is again used two columns further along in X.3–5 to describe the 'decision of Judgment that God would decree in making His Judgment in the midst of many Peoples', in particular, upon 'the Wicked Priest'. 'There (God) would arraign him and condemn him in their midst and judge him with fire and brimstone', an obvious picture of Hell-Fire or what, in ordinary parlance, usually goes by the title of 'the Last Judgment'.

There can be no doubt of the *eschatological* nature of the usage 'House of Judgment' (not 'condemned house' as in some translations) from which 'God would save them', and that it means something like the actual 'Decree of Judgment God would make in the midst of Many Peoples' pictured in Columns IV.14–V.5 leading up to the first confrontation between 'the Man of Lying' and 'the Righteous Teacher'.

The eschatological nature of the *Pesher* is absolutely confirmed further along in Columns XII.10–XIII.4, at the end with two clear references to 'the Day of Judgment', at the time of which 'God would destroy all the Servants of Idols and Evil Ones from off the Earth'.[20] This is introduced by allusion to 'all the idols of the Nations, which they create in order to *serve* and worship them. These will not *save them on the Day of Judgment*.' Here, not only do we again have the usages 'serve' and 'the Day of Judgment', but the use of the word 'saved' to express the ideological thought of 'being saved from the Last Judgment' is definitive.

Where the exegesis of Habakkuk 2:4 in VII.17–VIII.3 specifically is concerned, both the allusion to 'saved' and the one to 'works' – 'suffering works' or 'spiritual toil' (*'amal*) – are important. The whole eschatological nature of the Salvation-situation before us here in the *Pesher* is for the most part either completely ignored or missed. The 'saving' that is occurring is simply taken as relating to some real 'trial' or 'courtroom' scenario, from which either 'the Righteous' or 'all the *Torah*-Doers in the House of Judah' (i.e., 'all *Torah*-doing Jews') 'were to be saved from the House of Judgment'. (This is as silly as thinking that being made to 'drink the Cup of the Wrath of God', in the exegesis about 'the Wicked Priest' that follows in XI.2– XII.6, has to do with the Wicked Priest getting drunk! Unfortunately, this is the analytical level on which a good deal of studies in the field of Qumran has taken place – even at some of our greatest universities.)

As if with the competing Pauline exegesis in the New Testament in mind, the 'saving' being referred to in this *Pesher* is actually 'saving' in the sense of 'Salvation' and – as it is at the end of the *Pesher* – the sense of the 'saving' in this sequence about being 'saved from the House of Judgment' is very definitely eschatological. This is how the verb 'saved' is being used here, as it is in Paul.[21]

The word 'amal/'works' or 'suffering works,' is interesting. As we have to some extent already observed, it differs slightly from the 'works' language we have been following at Qumran and in the Letter of James – based on the Hebrew root 'to do' (therefore, the interesting 'Doers of the *Torah*' and the general stress on 'doing' throughout the Letter of James and the Dead Sea Scrolls in general – in the Psalm 37 *Pesher* 'the Assembly or 'Church of His Elect, the *Doers* of His will'[22]).

'*Amal* seems to have been slightly more eschatological and it occurs in several interesting places, most notably in the language of the famous 'Suffering Servant' proof-text from Isaiah 53:11f., so much a part of Scriptural expectation in Christianity and – because of the use of this term '*amal* and other usages, such as 'making Righteous' and 'the Many' here and elsewhere in the corpus – probably at Qumran as well. In Isaiah 53, this read: 'by his Knowledge, the Righteous One, My Servant, will justify' or 'make Many Righteous and their Sins will he bear' and was attached to an allusion to: 'and he will see by the '*amal* of his soul', seemingly meaning, 'the spiritual travail' or 'suffering of his soul'.

Again, this '*amal* is probably best translated by the term 'works' in the sense of 'suffering works', but perhaps even more accurately, *works with soteriological or eschatological effect*. It would appear to be purposefully introduced both at this point in VIII.2 and earlier in the *Pesher* as descriptive of how – along with 'their Faith' – the Righteous were to 'be saved'.

A similar idea of making atonement 'by doing Judgment and suffering travail' occurs in the Community Rule's description of the Community Council.[23] In undergoing this, its members are not only said to 'keep Faith in the Land with steadfastness and a humble Spirit' but 'to atone for the Land and pay the Wicked their reward' – the language of Isaiah 3:10–11 we saw introduced into the Habakkuk *Pesher*'s description of how 'the Cup of the Wrath of God would swallow' the Wicked Priest, '*paying him the reward* with which he rewarded the Poor'.[24] Thus they become 'a Precious Cornerstone' and 'sweet fragrance of Righteousness', 'well-pleasing to God', 'establishing' both 'the Council of the Community upon Truth as an Eternal Plantation' and 'the Holy Spirit according to Everlasting Truth' – more interesting language circles and concepts that should by now be familiar.[25]

The allusion to this '*amal* also recurs – in our view purposefully – two columns later in 1QpHab X.12 where the 'worthless Service' and 'Empty' teaching of 'the Spouter of Lying' are subjected to fulsome rebuke (this time our play is purposeful). That this '*amal* is also part and parcel of the language of Isaiah 53:11–12 ('for he shall bear their Sins ... because he poured out his soul unto death ... and the sins of the Many he bore and made intercession for their iniquities') could not have failed to make its impression on the sectaries at Qumran, given their ideological outlook.

This is certainly the case, too, where the language of 'My Servant the *Zaddik* justifying Many' is concerned introducing this. In fact, 'the Many' was the designation for the rank and file of the Community, the presumable recipients, as per 'Christian' re-presentation, of the justifying activity of 'the Righteous Teacher' or the *Zaddik*. That this same '*amal* will now reappear as an extremely important element in the *Pesher*'s final scathing evaluation of the Spouter of Lying's 'building' activities clinches the case for the centrality of this concept as well as the parameters of Isaiah 53:11–12 – so important to early Christian exegesis – at Qumran.

Therefore, what we have here in this exegesis of Habakkuk 2:4 at Qumran is nothing less than astonishing. What it appears to be is the 'Jamesian' position on this passage, 'the Righteous shall live by his Faith', before it was reversed in the 'Gentilizing' Pauline exegesis, with which we are all now so familiar. With this new understanding we can now see that, as opposed to Pauline exegesis, not only does the *Pesher* in VIII.1–3 restrict the efficacy of Habakkuk 2:4 solely to '*Torah*-doing members of the House of Judah' – that is, '*Torah*-Doing Jews' – or, at the very least, those who have made formal conversion via circumcision to this

'House', 'joining such *Torah*-Doers' (contrary to the demands of a Paul); but, perhaps even more importantly, a man 'will be saved' from 'the decree of Judgment' God would pronounce 'in the midst of many Nations' (or 'the Last Judgment') 'by his Faith in the Righteous Teacher and by his works' – the curious allusion to 'being saved from the House of Judgment' in the *Pesher* meaning just this.

Not only is this Jamesian, that is, 'Faith and works working together' or 'Faith being completed by works', but, once again, elements from the presentation of the Righteous Teacher – or, as the case may be, of James – are being absorbed into the presentation of Jesus in Scripture in the sense that it is 'Faith in Jesus Christ that saves'. It is this term '*amal*, which the *Pesher* will now employ in describing the 'Worthless Community which the Liar builds on Blood' as well as 'the Assembly' or 'Church which he erects upon Lying (the same 'erect' of CD VII.16 and 4QFlorilegium, I.10–12) for the sake of his (own) Glory'.[26]

Here the '*amal* which the Liar teaches are said to be Empty, i.e., empty of soteriological or saving effect. But bringing us full circle and showing we are in the same ideological and spiritual ambiance of James, this last will be the very word James 2:20 uses to characterize its ideological opponent, when the *worthlessness* of his spiritual program concerning how 'Abraham was justified' is being analyzed: 'O Empty Man, don't you know that Faith apart from works is dead?'

'He built a Worthless City upon Blood and Erected a Congregation on Lying'

The last discussion of 'the Man of Lies' in the Habakkuk *Pesher* – now called 'the Spouter of Lies' – occurs two columns later (though we have been calling him 'the Spouter', the pseudonym is not actually used in any document until X.9–13), directly following the first description of the 'Judgment' inflicted on the corpse of the Wicked Priest and the profiteering and booty-gathering activities of 'the Last Priests of Jerusalem' in IX.1–7 and the vivid portrayal of the eschatological 'House of Judgment' God delivers 'in the midst of many Peoples', where 'He would arraign him for Judgment' (seemingly 'the Wicked Priest' but, because the commentary at the bottom of IX.16 is so fragmentary, this cannot be verified with complete certainty) and 'condemn him with fire and brimstone'.

This final discussion of the Liar's activities and Justification doctrine is presented in terms of an underlying allusion from Habakkuk 2:12, decrying the person who 'builds a City on Blood and establishes a township on Unrighteousness'. Importantly, this is followed by a quotation from the underlying text Habakkuk 2:13 about 'the Peoples laboring for the sake of Fire and the Peoples tiring themselves out for the sake of vanity'. This could not be more convenient, because we have the very word 'Peoples' ('*Amim*) – repeated twice in the underlying text – upon which the word Gentiles (*Ethne* in Greek) is based. We have already seen how Paul uses this phrase 'vanity' or 'in vain' in Galatians 2:21 – e.g., that 'if Righteousness is through the Law, then Christ died in vain' or Galatians 3:3–4 actually applying the word 'foolish' to those abandoning the Spirit for 'works of the Law' or 'Perfection in the flesh' (meaning 'circumcision'), whose 'suffering' was, therefore, 'in vain'. In Galatians 4:11, following his attack on 'keeping the weak and beggarly elements' of 'days and months and times and years', this becomes how he 'labored in vain', meaning, with his communities.

In the crucial 1 Corinthians 15:2–58 passages about the Gospel Paul 'received' and 'in which you (his recipients) also stand' and the order of the post-resurrection appearances of Christ, Paul also repeatedly alludes to this 'Worthlessness' and 'being in vain' beginning in 15:3. There he speaks about his communities – 'being saved and holding fast to the word (he) preached' – 'not believing in vain'; and three times insists that, if Christ did not rise from the dead, both their 'Faith' and his 'preaching' were 'Worthless' (15:12–14). Here, too, he ends by encouraging, again as in CD, 1QS, and James, 'steadfastness' in 'the work of the Lord', 'knowing that your toil – the '*amal* in Isaiah 53:11 and the Habakkuk *Pesher* – is not in vain' (15:58).

In the underlying passage from Habakkuk 2:13, the actual word used is not exactly 'vain' – though effectively it is the same – but 'Emptiness' or 'Nothingness'. This text is exploited to swing back from the subject of the profiteering activities of 'the Last Priests of Jerusalem' to develop, once again, a *Pesher* about the Liar – now referred to as 'the Spouter of Lying'. This *Pesher* ends by calling down in X.12–13 the same 'Judgments of Fire' on him that it called down at the beginning of Column X.3–5, seemingly, on 'the Wicked Priest' when he was being 'arraigned in the midst of many Peoples' and 'judged with fire and brimstone'. For this *Pesher*, these are a response to the same kind of insults and curses with which the Man of Lying 'insulted and vilified the Elect of God'.[27] It should be noted that, contrary to the Wicked Priest, his offence against the Righteous Teacher and 'the Elect of God' – 'the Sons of Zadok' or 'the Assembly of the Poor' or 'of Holiness'– is intellectual, not physical. This is in keeping with the 'Lying' epithet applied to him, the analogue of 'the Tongue,' figuratively-speaking, in the Letter of James.

In describing the teaching or doctrine of the Lying Spouter, it is the imagery of *Blood* which is all-important, the same imagery so integral to Paul's conception of 'the Cup of the New Covenant in (his) Blood', not to mention its variation in the other Gospel 'Blood' scenarios including even one attributed to Pilate when he is portrayed in Matthew 27:24 as characterizing himself as 'being guiltless in the Blood of this Righteous One'. In the first place, the *Pesher* applies the 'building a City on Blood' in the underlying text from Habakkuk 2:12 to 'the Spouter of Lying who leads Many astray in order to build a Worthless City on Blood'.[28]

'Leading astray' is always the contrary language to the proper Justifying activity of the Righteous Teacher of 'making Many Righteous'. It is the language used in the Damascus Document's introductory description of the activities of the Lying Scoffer/Comedian, who poured out 'the waters of Lying and caused them to wander astray in a trackless waste without a Way'. That it is the contrary to the Righteous Teacher's Justifying activity is made clear by the inclusion of the terminology 'Many' and, seemingly thereby, employing Isaiah 53:11's language of 'the Righteous One justifying Many' in this *Pesher* on 'the Peoples laboring for the sake of fire' and 'tiring themselves out for the sake of Emptiness'/'Nothingness'.

But the parallels do not end here because the '*amal*, too, from this same Isaiah 53:11 will also momentarily be invoked. For the Habakkuk *Pesher* X.9–10, the way the Spouter of Lies 'leads Many astray' was by 'building a Worthless City upon Blood and erecting an Assembly' or 'Church upon Lying'. The 'building a City upon Blood and establishing a township on Unrighteousness' in the underlying text from Habakkuk 2:12 are being transformed in the *Pesher* by the addition of the allusion 'Worthless' to qualify the 'City' and the phrase, 'erecting an Assembly on Lying', instead of the 'Unrighteous township'. We have already encountered this usage 'established' in the several descriptions of the Community Council and Holy Spirit being 'established on Truth' in 1QS VIII.5, etc. Here in the *Pesher* it is seemingly being deliberately replaced by the slightly different terminology 'erecting' or 'setting up', which is the same usage as the 'raising up of the fallen Tabernacle of David' in the Damascus Document or of both it and David's 'seed' in the Florilegium above.

This Congregation, Assembly or Church, which has also been deliberately substituted for the word 'township' in the underlying text of Habakkuk, is, of course, the same one we earlier heard about in V.12 regarding the Liar's 'rejection of the *Torah*'. The replacement of 'Unrighteousness' in underlying Habakkuk 2:12 with 'Lying' is significant as is the addition of 'setting up' or 'erecting of an Assembly' to the extant language of 'building'. In fact, it is this allusion to 'building a Worthless City upon Blood' that is pivotal for the *Pesher*.

We have already noted Paul's repeated use of the word 'Worthless' in 1 Corinthians 15:14 –17 to characterize the value of his communities' 'Faith' when not 'holding fast to' his teaching things such as 'the Crucified Christ – to the Jews, indeed, a stumbling block' (1 Corinthians 1:23). We have also seen Paul's criticisms of James' prohibitions to overseas communities from 1 Corinthians 5:1–9:27 (note, too, the inversion of the language of 'rejection', 'laboring over Holy Things', and 'freedom' from 9:13–27). These lead directly into his presentation of 'the Cup of the Lord' not being 'the Cup of Demons' (by which he seems to mean both 'idols' and 'the Temple') and 'Communion with the Blood of Christ' in 10:16– 22 and 11:25–29.

Not only does he appear to be discussing the former in some ongoing exposition of James' prohibition on 'eating things sacrificed to idols', but the latter has been retrospectively assimilated into 'Last Supper' scenarios in the Synoptic Gospels as 'the Cup of the New Covenant in (his) Blood which is poured for you' or 'poured out for the Many for remission of Sins' (Luke 22:20 and Matthew 26:28). In providing his version of this in 'this is the Cup of the New Covenant in my Blood', Paul adds his own proviso to it: 'For as often as you eat this bread and drink this Cup, you are announcing the death of the Lord until he comes' (1 Corinthians 11:26). In enunciating this, Paul is using the 'Cup' language which follows the material we have before us in the Habakkuk *Pesher* XI.10 but with entirely different signification. It should not be forgotten, too, that 'the Cup of the Lord' is also integral to the first post-resurrection appearance to James in the Gospel according to the Hebrews. There it is the Cup Jesus gives his brother James to drink.

Where the Habakkuk *Pesher* is concerned (reiterated in Revelation), this language of the 'Cup of the Lord' symbolizes the *Anger of God and His Divine Retribution on His Enemies*. This is the meaning in Columns XI–XII of how 'the Cup of the Wrath of God would swallow' or be 'repaid to the Wicked Priest' because of how 'he swallowed' the Righteous Teacher and of 'the reward he paid the Poor'; but also how it is being played on in the signification 'Anger' or 'Wrath' – *Cha'as* a homophone for Cup/*Chos* in Hebrew.

Preceding this at the end of the 1QpHab X.10–11, this Divine Vengeance that will be exacted will be the outcome of what is going to happen to the Spouter of Lies and those who are the recipients of his Worthless Service and Empty *'amal* as a result of their 'blaspheming and vilifying the Elect of God'.[29] But as Paul closes his discussion of this 'Cup of the New Covenant', again archly hinting at Blood-libel accusations, he too moves over into this kind of language of implied threat, this time directed against those seemingly within the Church with the opposite point-of-view to his own, to wit, persons like James: 'Therefore, whoever shall eat this bread or drink this Cup of the Lord in an unworthy way shall be guilty of the body and the Blood of the Lord' (1 Corinthians 11:27). Not only is the underlying thrust of this quite aggressive, but just so that there should be no mistaking it, Paul repeats it: 'For whoever eats and drinks unworthily – not seeing through to the Blood of the Lord – eats and drinks Judgment to himself.'

Again, not only is its accusatory and menacing aura obvious; but this, of course, is exactly the gist of the language centering around these various 'drinking the Cup of the Wrath of God' allusions we have been highlighting in the Habakkuk *Pesher* and Revelation, including even the eating and drinking metaphors as meaning Divine Judgment or 'being consumed' or 'destroyed'. Therefore, it should be quite clear that in all such contexts this language of 'the Cup of the Lord' is present, albeit with widely varying, if not simply completely unrelated, significations.

Columns VII-VIII of the Habakkuk *Pesher,* alluding to '*the Delay of the Parousia*' and the anti-Pauline '*Jamesian*' exposition of Habakkuk 2:4: '*the Righteous shall live by his Faith*'.

'The City of Blood' in the Nahum *Pesher*, James' 'Abstain from Blood', 'Crucifixion' again, and 'Communion with the Blood of Christ'

Directly following the use of this language of 'the Cup of the Lord's right hand' (Habakkuk 2:16) and 'the Cup of the Wrath of God' to apply to how the Wicked Priest would himself 'be swallowed' or 'consumed' in 1QpHab XI.10–15, another allusion to Blood occurs in the underlying text of Habakkuk 2:17 in Column XII.1, 'the Blood of Man' (*Adam*). Some might have taken this anomalous reference to *Adam* more figuratively as an esotericism bearing on the ideology of the Primal *Adam* they were espousing and, further to this, as involving his Blood and/or even his death.

However this may be, in the *Pesher* this language is being applied to how the Wicked Priest 'plotted to destroy the Poor', 'the Violence' he did to the Righteous Teacher and his followers (called 'the Simple Jews doing the *Torah*'), and his 'works of Abominations polluting the Temple of God'. It should be appreciated, however, that this is not the same kind of 'Blood' one finds, two columns earlier in Column X.6 and 10). There it was more ideological and/or allegorical, dealing with the underpinning or outlook of a given Community (namely, that of the Liar or one like Paul's). In this climactic end of the Habakkuk *Pesher* it is, rather, more like the Blood-accusations one gets in the Gospels – here related clearly to the spilling of 'the Blood of the Poor' and 'the works of Abominations', seemingly of the Herodian Establishment connected to it.

As opposed to this, however, Column Ten is rather describing the ideas and activities of the Liar in an unusually prescient manner. In our view this allusion to 'building a Worthless City upon Blood and erecting an Assembly' or 'Church upon Lying' is not something Violent but rather relates to the perception of what Paul is doing in his Missionary activities generally, particularly abroad; more specifically, it relates to his controversial doctrines of both 'the Cup of the Lord' or 'the Cup of the New Covenant in (his) Blood', and 'Communion with the Blood of Christ' in 1 Corinthians 10:16–11:29.

This occurs as a continuation, seemingly, of his responses to James' directives to overseas communities 'to abstain from fornication, blood, things sacrificed to idols' and dietary matters generally from 1 Corinthians 5:1–10:33. In our view, this is made clear by the purposeful shift in emphasis in the *Pesher*, signaled by the addition to the underlying text from Habakkuk 2:12–13 of the new words, 'Worthless' and 'erecting a Congregation upon Lying'.

We have already encountered a variation of this 'City of Blood' allusion in the Nahum *Pesher* where it was related to the 'City of Ephraim' and Gentile-style converts referred to as resident aliens or *Ger-Nilveh*/*Nilvim*, that is, evoking the 'Joiners' language we encountered in the Damascus Document's exegesis of Ezekiel's Zadokite Covenant. 'The City of Blood' (Blood for some reason being expressed here in the Nahum *Pesher* in the plural) was not even a real City in the *Pesher* but actually directly connected to 'the Congregation of the Seekers after Smooth Things.'[30] This *Pesher*, as previously underscored (aside from its real historical references) was primarily directed against those it called 'Seekers after Smooth Things' seemingly holding sway at the time of writing in Jerusalem, whose 'counsel' – specifically described in terms of 'inviting' foreign Kings and foreign Armies into Jerusalem (at an earlier time before 'the coming of the Rulers of the *Kittim*' or 'the Romans', i.e., the time of 'Demetrius, King of the Greeks'[31] – from Josephus, we know these to have been the Pharisees) – is identified as being directly responsible for the disasters overtaking the People, both in the past and at present.[32]

Not only does its scheme more or less parallel that of the Habakkuk *Pesher* of 'the Riches collected by the Last Priests of Jerusalem' ultimately 'being given over' to this same 'Army of the *Kittim*',[33] but in its Second Column it refers to 'Messengers (Hebrew for 'Apostles') among the Gentiles'.[34] Moreover, it also actually evokes the very passage that Paul uses to develop his Salvationary theology of how 'Jesus Christ redeemed us from the curse of the Law' and, in the process, 'justified' in Galatians 3:6–14 all Mankind along 'with the believing Abraham' by himself being 'hung upon a tree'.

However, interestingly enough, 4QpNah 2.6–8 on Nahum 2:12–13, citing 'victims', adds the important qualification 'hanging up living men' to the passage Paul is evoking from Deuteronomy 21:23, which originally seems only to have banned the hanging up of corpses overnight. In the process, the *Pesher* turns this into a passage rather condemning what has since come to be understood as crucifixion (obviously, this has to be understood in terms of Roman crucifixion!) as 'a thing not done formerly in Israel' and, just as obviously, not 'glorifying' it as the pivotal 'building' block of a future theology – on the contrary. To explain this more unequivocally: while Paul, following the letter of Deuteronomy 21:23, but also applying it specifically to crucifixion *per se*, sees 'the hanged man' as the 'thing accursed', the *Pesher*, by applying a later passage from Nahum 2:12 – 'Behold I am against you says the Lord of Hosts' – rather turns this into a condemnation of crucifixion itself – a matter obviously of intense emotional interest, as just observed, probably *only in the Roman Period!*

From here the whole *Pesher* turns completely eschatological, defining the City of Blood, curiously, as 'the City of Ephraim, the Seekers after Smooth Things at the End of Days, who walk in Deceit and Lying'.[35] These last make it pretty clear we are in the same milieu as 'the Spouter of Lying' of the Habakkuk *Pesher* again – and that 'Ephraim' must (or should) in some way relate to him. This is further clarified in terms of 'those who lead Ephraim astray'. This also includes, once more, the use of the term 'Many,' to wit: 'those who, through teaching Lying, their Lying Tongue and Deceitful lips, *lead Many astray*'.[36]

Column Three is also about the Last Days, a time that clearly has to be seen in terms of the 'coming of the Rulers of the *Kittim*' (the plural here would imply Republican Rome), but after the departure of the Greeks, when 'the sword of the Gentiles' was never far from their midst.[37] It expresses the hope that 'the Simple of Ephraim' – paralleling 'the Simple of Judah' in the Habakkuk *Pesher*, but without the qualification of 'doing the *Torah*' – 'shall flee their Congregation, abandoning those who lead them astray and joining Israel'. In my view, that this is an attack on Paul, which at the same time begins to clarify the nature of this pseudonym (as with the term 'Samaritan' in the New Testament to which it is related) 'Ephraim' as having something to do with new Gentile converts, is indisputable.

We have already identified this language of 'joining' – expressed in the Pauline corpus as 'joining the body of Christ', rather than 'being joined to the body of a prostitute' (1 Corinthians 6:16–17) – as being expressive of Gentiles 'joining themselves' to the Community in an associated status of some kind much as 'God-Fearers' were associated in this Period with synagogues around the Eastern Mediterranean, meaning, people who had not yet entered the Community as full-status converts, but were Joiners/*Nilvim*. In fact, this kind of language relative to 'God-Fearers' – 'for whom a Book of Remembrance would be written out'[38] – comes through very strongly in the last Columns of the Cairo Damascus Document.

As already underscored, one finds *Nilvim*, which is used in Esther 10:27 to denote precisely such a status, in the interpretation of 'the Zadokite Covenant' in the Damascus Document at Qumran and this is, in fact, the kind of imagery being used throughout the Nahum *Pesher* with regard to 'resident aliens' (*Ger-Nilvim*), meaning, those 'joining themselves to the Community'. In this sense 'the Simple Ones of Ephraim' is the counterpart to 'the Simple Ones of Judah doing the *Torah*' in the Habakkuk *Pesher*, the former being Gentiles associated with the Community in some adjunct status but without the qualifier 'doing the *Torah*' yet added.

It is, of course, to just such persons that Acts presents James as addressing his directives, including the prohibition on Blood – which in the context before us is primary – as well as the things sacrificed to idols or the pollutions of the idols, strangled things, and fornication. But it is in discussing in 1 Corinthians 8:10 and 10:7–28 exactly these injunctions that Paul first raises the issue of 'Communion with the Blood of Christ' including, most astonishingly of all, these several evocations of the imagery of 'the Cup'– present with widely differing signification in these passages of the Habakkuk *Pesher* as well.

In fact, Paul is playing on this imagery of the Cup in 1 Corinthians 10:16, even evoking 'the Cup of the Lord' language of Habakkuk 2:16 in 1 Corinthians 11:27. We have treated these matters to some extent above, but now it is important to see them in relation to Paul's reversal and spiritualization of the Qumran language of 'the New Covenant in the Land of Damascus' generally. In fact, it is at this point in 1 Corinthians 10:18 that Paul heaps abuse on the Temple cult – including 'the other Israel', the one he terms 'according to the flesh' – ending up with his final directives to 'eat anything sold in the marketplace' (1 Corinthians 10:25) and 'all things for me are lawful' (10:23). This is his final riposte to the prohibitions from James – and presumably those in *MMT* – on 'things sacrificed to idols, blood, and carrion'.

Paul even goes so far as to compare the things which the *other Israel* eats in the Temple to eating at 'the Table of Demons', and his Cup is 'the Cup of the Lord' or 'the Cup of Communion with the Blood of Christ' as opposed to *their* Cup – 'the Cup of Demons' as it were in 1 Corinthians 10:18–21. Once again, he has 'turned the tables', as it were, on his interlocutors with his dizzying dialectical acrobatics and allegorization.

But the Blood he is talking about here – symbolic or real – has already been specifically forbidden in James' prohibitions to overseas communities, even according to Acts 15:19–29. It is also forbidden in the Damascus Document. There, it will be recalled, it is asserted that the Sons of Israel 'were cut off in the wilderness' because '*they ate blood*'.

Moreover the Children of Israel are described here in CD III.5–6 as 'walking in the stubbornness of their heart', 'complaining against the Commandments of God, and each man doing what seemed right in his own eyes', language particularly appropriate to the genus of the Pauline-style 'Liar'. Not only does Paul show in 1 Corinthians 10 that he knows the terms of James' instructions to overseas communities, he actually uses the same example one finds here in CD III.7 and words paralleling the Hebrew meaning of 'being cut off' to describe how the Children of Israel 'were overturned' or 'cut off in the wilderness' (1 Corinthians 10:5).

But the proof that he is following the text of the Damascus Document, albeit inverting its sense, doesn't end here. In the latter, 'cutting off' is immediately followed by the phrase: 'and they (the Children of Israel) *murmured* in their tents'.[39] But this same occurs in 1 Corinthians, following this evocation of how they 'were overturned in the wilderness'. As Paul puts this in 1 Corinthians 10:10, 'nor should you murmur as some of them murmured'. But this is almost word-for-word the language of these important passages about Abraham as 'Friend of God' in CD III.2–4 proving, as almost nothing else can, that Paul not only knows the Damascus Document but is even following its sequencing. This – even though he now proceeds to reverse the position of the Damascus Document on the issue of Blood – and with it, that of his presumed Leader, James the Just – using it, rather, to 'build' or 'erect' his whole Congregation based upon, not banning Blood, but consuming it – in this case, '*the body and Blood of Christ Jesus*'. In doing so, he claims to be advocating to his 'Beloved Ones – his 'Friends' – to flee from Idolatry' (1 Corinthians 10:14) – again the *very reverse* of the language about such 'Beloved Ones' or 'Friends' we have been following here in Column Three of the Damascus Document.

1QpHab, XI-XII describing '*the Wicked Priest swallowing the Righteous Teacher*' and '*the Poor*,' but how '*the Cup of the Right Hand of the Lord would come around to and swallow him*'.

'The Cup of the New Covenant in (His) Blood' and 'the New Covenant in the Land of Damascus'

This is what Paul is doing with James' directive to *abstain* from blood in 1 Corinthians, a letter in which he earlier refers to his community as 'God's building' and where he actually compares himself to 'the architect' (3:6–14)! In this passage, he is also even using the 'laying the Foundation' imagery of both the Community Rule and Hymns at Qumran, not only stressing the necessity of 'building' on 'the Foundation of Jesus Christ', but several times referring to the fact of his 'building' as opposed to 'Apollos' watering'.

This, in our view, is what is meant by the allusion to the Lying Spouter's 'leading Many astray' and 'building a Worthless City upon Blood', with the additional aside of 'raising a Congregation upon Lying' in 1QpHab X.9–10, which will now go on to characterize his 'Service' as *Worthless*, his 'works' as 'Lying', and his *amal* as 'Empty'. But it should also be clear that Paul's treatment of Blood in 1 Corinthians 10:16–11:29 is also the import of how he treats the Qumran 'New Covenant in the Land of Damascus'. Not only does he treat it esoterically, turning the written word *Damascos* in Greek – *Damascus* in Latin and English, but *Dammashek* in Hebrew – into 'the Cup of Blood', as per the meaning of its homophonic root in Hebrew, *dam*/Blood and *chos*/Cup; he is reversing it once again! In fact, as we shall see, the parallel will go even further than this, both in 1 Corinthians 11:24–29 and the Synoptics related to it, in the phrase always connected to this formula, '*Drink* this in *Remembrance* of me' – in Hebrew, *mashkeh* or *dam-mashkeh*, 'give blood to drink' – to say nothing of the phrase in CD XX.18–21, 'the Book of *Remembrance* that was written out before Him *for God-Fearers*'.[40]

In 1 Corinthians 11:20–30, he claims to have received his view of what he calls 'the Lord's Supper' directly 'from the Lord' (11:23), though how and by what mechanism he does not explain. Rather he moves directly into connecting this with the language of the *New Covenant*, also the language used in climactic sections of the Damascus Document, where it becomes associated with an even more extreme rededication to 'the First' or 'Old'.[41] It is Paul's approach to this New Covenant that becomes the manner in which it is attributed to Jesus in Gospel portrayals of the Last Supper, at least in the Synoptics. Luke 22:20 perhaps puts this most graphically, reflecting the language Paul uses here in 1 Corinthians 11:26 almost exactly and incorporating the Cup (or *Chos*) imagery from Qumran, itself developed – as we just pointed out – in terms of a play on the word, 'Wrath' or *Cha'as* there.

In the process, of course, Paul in 1 Corinthians 11:25 reverses this as well: 'This Cup is the New Covenant in my Blood. As often as you drink it, do this in Remembrance of me.' All three Synoptics also add the language of 'being poured out for the Many' – Matthew 26:28 adding 'for remission of Sins'. Even this language is reflected in the Damascus Document's presentation of 'the Covenant which God made with the First to atone for their sins' or 'for remission of their Sins' directly following its exegesis of the Zadokite Covenant.[42]

Not only does the language of 'the Cup of the New Covenant in (his) Blood' in the Gospels recapitulate that at Qumran of 'pouring out of Lying' (the root of 'the Spouter of Lying' appellation) and 'the Many', the Letter to the Hebrews too – not surprisingly – discusses both 'the New Covenant' and that of 'the Old' extensively. It does so in the context of quoting Jeremiah 31:31–34, perhaps the original provenance of this language of the 'New Covenant with the House of Judah' and probably, also, the origin of these several archaizing allusions to 'the House of Judah' in both the Habakkuk *Pesher* and the Damascus Document (Hebrews 8:8). Hebrews 9:20 also evokes Exodus 24:8's 'this is the Blood of the Covenant, which God has enjoined upon you' and makes repeated reference to the Damascus Document's 'Covenant of the First' (8:13 and 9:15).[43] In extensive, if esoteric, discussion of these two Covenants, not only does Hebrews express this 'New Covenant in the Blood of Christ' in terms of 'Perfecting the one who serves' (9:9), 'a Perfect Tabernacle' (9:11), and 'making Perfect the Spirits of the Righteous' (12:23), but in evoking Habakkuk 2:4's 'the Righteous shall live by his Faith,' it even uses the Habakkuk *Pesher*'s language of the *City*, combining it with that of 'building' and 'erecting' (10:38–11:16)! Here the parallel with both Paul in 1 Corinthians and the Habakkuk *Pesher* is patent: 'For he was waiting for *a City, the Foundations of which were built and erected by God*'.

Paul expresses this idea, as we just saw, in 1 Corinthians 11:25 – precisely prefiguring Luke 22:20 – as 'This Cup is the New Covenant in my Blood'. He not only follows this up by reference to the Cup of the Lord, but here all resemblances end because he then rather speaks about 'drinking the Cup of the Lord unworthily' and, thereby, 'drinking Judgment to oneself, not seeing through to the body of the Lord' (1 Corinthians 11:27–29).

In doing so, he mixes the two separate 'Cup' imageries we have been following, by implication demonstrating that he appears to realize the two are interrelated – the one having to do with Divine Vengeance, the other a spiritualized or allegorical reinterpretation of a Mystery Religion-type 'Covenant' of some kind. Therefore we can conclude that what is referred to on three separate occasions in the Damascus Document at Qumran as 'the New Covenant in the Land of Damascus' becomes for Paul, in a figurative and esoteric transformation revealed only probably to a few adepts, '*the New Covenant in the Blood of Christ*.'

It should be recalled that in the first description of the Scriptural exegesis sessions of the Righteous Teacher/Priest in Column Two of the Habakkuk *Pesher*, this 'New Covenant' was expressed in terms of a two or threefold allusion to Traitors, that is, it appears, 'the Traitors to the New Covenant' and 'the Traitors to the Last Days', who 'did not believe in the Covenant of God and defiled His Holy Name', nor 'what they heard was going to happen to the Last Generation from the mouth of the Priest in whose heart God put the insight to interpret all the words of His Servants the Prophets'.[62] Nor is this to mention those 'Covenant-Breakers' also alluded to in the key original citation in Jeremiah 31:31–34 about the coming 'New Covenant' – the '*Torah* within them' that, as Paul would put, was going to be 'written upon their hearts' as well! – who, along with those designated as Violent Ones and these two or three species of Traitors would appear to attend the Scriptural exegesis sessions of the Righteous Teacher.[44] At the Last Supper in the Gospels too it is just prior to Jesus 'taking the Cup' and announcing 'the New Covenant in (his) Blood' that he raises the issue of his coming 'betrayal' (Matthew 26:21 and pars.) or that in John 13:29, anyhow, the *Traitor* Judas leaves to betray him.

But the relationship between 'the New Covenant in the Land of Damascus' at Qumran and 'the New Covenant in the Blood of Christ' in Paul does not end there. There is the additional connection just signaled above, which also may or may not be coincidental. In our view, it is purposeful. As already explained, the word for Blood in Hebrew is *Dam* – in the Nahum *Pesher*, for whatever reason, the plural *Damim*. But this is the first syllable in the place name Damascus, whether in Hebrew (*Dammashek*) or any other language.

The word in Hebrew for Cup, as we saw in our analysis of the wordplay surrounding the two words, *Chos* and *Cha'as* – Cup and Anger – in the Habakkuk *Pesher*, is *Chos* (in fact, the Wicked Priest really did give, in a manner of speaking, the Righteous Teacher 'the Cup of Blood to drink'). Therefore the place name *Damascos*, in Greek and other derivative languages really does mean, taken according to its precise homophonic or literal transliteration in Hebrew, 'Blood' and 'Cup' (*Dam* and *Chos*) or 'Cup of Blood'. Just as in the case of the overlaps between 'swallowing' in Hebrew (*balla'*) and 'casting down' in Greek (*ballo*) in the usages surrounding the deaths of both the Righteous Teacher at Qumran and James, it is hard to conceive of additional overlaps such as these as mere coincidence.

This makes 'the New Covenant in the Land of Damascus' at Qumran the very same thing as 'the Cup of the New Covenant in (his) Blood' in Paul (and the Gospels) – only the one esotericizes and, in due course, *absolutely reverses the sense of the other*. The parallel between

'Drink' and 'Give to drink' in Greek and *Mashkeh* in Hebrew just increases the correspondence further, making it seem as if the relationship – esoteric as it may have been – had to have been a conscious one. This is a perfectly astonishing conclusion, one that – to coin a euphemism – turns the history of Christianity 'on its ear' – this, too, from a document, which on the basis of an analysis of the handwriting of one or two fragments, scholars insist on placing in the Second Century BCE. On the basis of an analysis of the internal data and its vocabulary, such an early date is patently absurd.

If Paul was conscious of this relationship – and it is hard to conceive that he was not, since even the Book of Acts avers he spent time in 'Damascus' – then we must conclude he was very much aware of the language of 'the New Covenant' at Qumran and the way it was being expressed there in terms of the word 'Damascus'. Moreover, he was simply transforming this in the light of his own more allegorical and even more esoteric approach – what he himself calls in 1 Corinthians 2:13 'communicating in words taught by the Holy Spirit spiritual things spiritually'. In the process, enjoying all these plays on words, he was no doubt having a good laugh as well – which is, of course, precisely the implication at Qumran in 'the Scoffer' or 'Comedian' epithet applied to the Man of Lying there.

The only question which remains is whether in some sense the New Covenant in the Land of Damascus at Qumran actually did have a secret or esoteric meaning of the kind Paul is exploiting or whether this new, more esoteric approach was entirely his own creation. Based on the documents at our disposal, we shall probably never know definitively. Given the thrust of the surrounding allusions in these documents, it is difficult to detect what this might have been and probably it did not, except for the esoteric evocation in the Damascus Document of: 'with the Completion of the Era of these years', 'each man will stand on his own net' (or 'Watchtower') and 'all the Glory of Adam will be theirs', there being no more specific attachment to 'the House of Judah' *per se* – this being something of the manner in which Paul is reconstructing it or construing these things too.

'Building a Worthless City upon Blood' and 'Communion with the Blood of Christ'

We can now return to the allusion to 'building a Worthless City upon Blood and erecting a Congregation on Lying', where the Lying Spouter's 'Service' or 'labor' is concerned, the second part of which purposefully replaces the phraseology 'establishing a township upon Unrighteousness' in the underlying text of Habakkuk 2:12.[45] 'Building a Worthless City upon blood' is just what was in the underlying text, except for the significant addition of the depreciative term 'Worthless'.

We have already seen how Paul uses this word 'Worthless' or the allusion to 'in vain' above. In the *Pesher* that follows, this word, 'Worthless' or 'vain,' will also be used to characterize the kind of 'Worthless Service' or 'Lying works' the Liar causes the Many to perform – expressed contemptuously as 'tiring out Many' – 'for the sake of (his) Glory'. This is expressed as follows: 'The interpretation of the passage concerns the Spouter of Lying who leads Many astray, building a Worthless City upon blood and erecting an Assembly upon Lying, for the sake of (his) Glory, tiring out Many with a Worthless Service and instructing them in works of Lying, so that their '*amal* would be for Emptiness'.[46] These are the exact words of the *Pesher*. One can only assume that the addition of the word 'Worthless' here – repeated twice – was purposeful and it, in fact, characterized the Soteriological value or efficacy of the Service taught by the Lying Spouter, by which he 'leads Many astray', or that of 'the City' he was 'building'. The play on the usage 'the Many' from Isaiah 53:11 here – also repeated twice – would appear to be purposeful as well, as would, therefore, the play on the idea of the Righteous Teacher's James-like 'works of Righteousness' – these as opposed to the Lying Spouter's 'works of Lying' – the usage 'works' now being the one based on the verb 'to do', as in '*doing* the *Torah*,' not '*avodah*.'

We have already discussed the 'City of Blood', including its relevance to the Qumran usage *Dammashek* and the Greek *Damascos*. In some sense, in the Nahum *Pesher* this usage is connected to 'the Simple of Ephraim' (as we have interpreted it, the 'Pauline Christian' contingent among 'the Seekers after Smooth Things', 'seeking accommodation with foreigners' – in this instance, meaning Rome and including 'the Violent Ones of the Gentiles' and 'the Traitors to the New Covenant'). The 'City' metaphor as opposed to the 'township' – which is transformed in the *Pesher* into the allusion to 'erecting' or 'raising a Congregation'/'Assembly'/or 'Church upon Lying' – stays in the *Pesher*.

Paul very much enjoyed using the imagery of *citizenship*. In this regard, one should look at Ephesians 2:19, where Paul or its Pauline-minded author attacks Jewish exclusivity – particularly the kind directed against Herodians in the Temple. This reference in Ephesians is preceded by allusion in 2:11–13 to 'the Peoples', those it claims the Jews were calling the 'Uncircumcision in the flesh' and whom, for its part, it is referring to as 'Strangers from the Covenants (*sic*) of the Promise' (note here the variation on the *Ger-nilveh* language in 4QpNah III.9), originally being 'thought of as aliens from the Commonweal Israel' and 'apart from Christ' (also 'the body of Christ'), but now 'an offering and sacrifice to God, a sweet fragrance' (5:2). Of course, one recognizes this *sacrifice, offering*, and *sweet fragrance* language as the kind of metaphor applied to the description of the Community Council, 'atoning for the Land' by 'suffering works' and 'without the flesh of burnt offerings and the fat of sacrifices' in the Community Rule.[47]

In this context, Ephesians also cautions 'not to be deceived by *Empty* words, for the *Wrath of God* comes upon the Sons of Rebellion' and 'not cooperating' with such persons, 'for once in Darkness, but now in the Light of the Lord, you walk as *Children of Light*' (5:6–5:8). This too is exactly paralleled in the Qumran Community Rule III.5–IV.8. Even the Sermon on the Mount in Matthew 5:14 uses such 'Light' imagery – combined with an allusion to 'a *City* situated upon a hill that cannot be hidden' – to characterize 'the Disciples of Jesus'.

Moreover, in bolstering Paul's 'in the flesh' or 'glorying in your flesh' arguments elsewhere (as, for example, the allusion to this last in Galatians 6:13 above) and completing this particular circle of artful rhetorical footwork, it actually uses the language of '*Ethne* in the flesh' (once 'far off, but now become near by the Blood of Christ'!) to appeal – even perhaps a little archly – to such Gentiles (2:11-13). For good measure, it calls such new converts the 'Uncircumcision' (cf. Galatians 2:7–12), while the Jews – or those it has just denoted 'the Commonweal Israel' (*sic*) and seemingly again, perhaps even, somewhat contemptuously – it calls the 'Circumcision in the flesh *made by hand*'.

We have already seen in Hebrews 11:10 and 11:16, discussing how 'Abraham was saved by Faith', how this 'City' imagery here in the Habakkuk *Pesher* was combined with 'building' and 'erecting' imagery – to say nothing of the Foundation – to allude to 'a City, the builder and erector of whose Foundations is God'. The imagery of such 'Foundations' is present in these lines from Ephesians 2:19–20 about 'being fellow-citizens in the Household of God' and is extremely widespread at Qumran as well.[48] Which brings us to the second element in this 'City of Blood' construction, the 'building' imagery again – imagery which fairly permeates the Pauline corpus. Whether one considers Ephesians authentic or, like Hebrews, of 'the Pauline School', it is part and parcel of its 'citizenship' metaphor too. As Ephesians 2:19 puts this, 'you are no longer strangers (again, *ger-nilvim* at Qumran) and foreigners, but *fellow citizens* of the Holy Ones and of the Household of God'. Not only should one note here 'the Holy Ones' usage, so widespread in the Dead Sea Scrolls and prominent in all descriptions of James, but also the language of the *ger-nilveh*/resident alien in the Nahum *Pesher*.[49]

Ephesians 2:20–22 continues: 'For you have been built on the Foundation of the Apostles and the Prophets, Jesus Christ himself being the Cornerstone, in whom all the building is joined together, growing into a Holy Temple in the Lord – in whom you, too, are being built together as a dwelling place for God in the Spirit.' Here we have all our imageries and this is also about as close to the language of Qumran as one can get. Nor can one get very much more 'spiritualized' than this. Not only do we have here the Community Rule's further imagery regarding 'the Community Council' above being a spiritualized 'Temple' and 'Holy of Holies' and 'the Cornerstone',[50] but also the 'joining' and 'building' vocabulary again. The imagery here is, of course, also that of Paul in 1 Corinthians 12:12–27 – following his proclamation of 'Communion with the Blood of Christ' in 10–11 – of the Community and its 'members' being 'the body of Christ'. The double entendre involved in this 'member' metaphor is being played upon, too, by the counter-imagery in James 3:5 of 'the Tongue being one small member of the body' but 'boasting great things'. It is also part and parcel of the 'Temple' and 'body' imagery in the Gospels where Jesus – questioned as to what he meant by saying he would 'destroy the Temple of God and raise it up again in three days' – is pictured as saying he 'meant his (own) body', i.e., his own resurrection (John 2:19–21).

For Mark 14:58, this *Temple which Jesus will destroy* is '*made with hands*'; while he will go on, using the Habakkuk *Pesher's* and Paul's building-imagery again – 'in three days to *build another not made with hands*', language absolutely reflected in Ephesians 2:11's condescending characterization above of 'those called Circumcision in the flesh made by hand' as opposed to 'the Peoples in the flesh who are called' – by these same 'Circumcision' – 'Uncircumcision'. Again we have extremely well-crafted and consistent metaphor here. Moreover, the allegorizing polemic, whether embedded in Gospel or Letter, is devastating. For Ephesians 2:20–22 too, as just noted, 'Jesus Christ himself is the Cornerstone, in whom the whole building, joined together, grows into a Holy Temple in the Lord'. Here again in this *building, joined, growing*, and *Holy Temple* imagery we have all the allegorizing metaphor of not only Community Rule but a whole range of other Qumran documents as well.

We have seen how Paul refers to himself as Builder or 'Chief Architect' in 1 Corinthians 3:9–11. Here Paul, using the metaphor of the Community as 'God's building and the Temple of God' and himself as the Builder 'laying the Foundations well', also employs the language of 'being saved from the Fire', evoked here in 1QpHab X.5 and X.13 as well, cautioning 'each should be careful how he builds' and concluding, 'for no one can lay any other Foundation, except ... Jesus Christ' (1 Corinthians 3:11–15). In Romans 15:20, operating within the same metaphor, he expresses his concern 'to preach the Gospel where Christ had not been Named' – meaning, it would seem, mainland Greece, Rome, and Spain – so as 'not to *build on someone else's Foundations*'.[51]

Not only should the implications of this last symbolism relating to the Community led by the Archbishop James be obvious, the whole, in fact, relates to the *Stone, Cornerstone* and *Foundations* imagery widespread at Qumran. This is particularly true of the Hymns, where amid allusion to the James-like 'Bulwark of Strength' and 'a Strong and Tested Wall', as well as 'the Gates of Protection through which no foreigner can pass', we are told about erecting 'My building upon Rock' (in the previous column this was 'setting the Foundation on Rock and tested Stones for a Building of Strength'), 'the Foundations of which are Eternal Principles that will not shake'[52] – obviously meaning here 'the *Torah*' again. This is immediately followed in the Hymns by two allusions to the Tongue, 'Lying lips', 'condemning in Judgment', and finally, the protagonist applying both the language of 'separation' (just applied in Ephesians above to 'Gentiles in the flesh,' but here in Hymns, obviously, in the sense of Naziritism) and the language of 'the Righteous vs. the Wicked' to himself, i.e., 'separating between *Zaddik* and *Rasha*' through me'.[53]

This spiritualized Temple imagery is also to be found in the Community Rule, VIII.5–10 and IX.6. There, amid the imagery of spiritualized 'sacrifice' and 'atonement', it is applied to the Community Council as a spiritualized 'Plantation' and 'House for Israel', and a spiritualized 'Foundation of the Holy of Holies for Aaron'. It will be 'a Tested Rampart, a Precious Cornerstone, whose Foundations shall not rock or sway in their place, a Dwelling Place of the Holy of Holies for Aaron with Everlasting Knowledge of the Covenant of Judgment, ... a House of Perfection and Truth in Israel, erected as a Covenant of Eternal Laws'. This is the imagery of the 'Perfect Tabernacle' in Hebrews 9:11, followed immediately in Hebrews 9:12 by evocation of the Holy of Holies and Eternal Redemption, presaging the laborious discussion of the New Covenant, the First Covenant, and the Blood of Christ that follows. One cannot get a much closer convergence of language than this.

Not only do the Hymns, when speaking of 'establishing My Building on Rock', also allude to 'the Council of Holiness' of the Community, but this language of 'erecting' or 'raising' in the Habakkuk *Pesher*, also present in these allusions in the Hymns, is clearly applied in the Community Rule to 'the Covenant of Eternal Laws'. This, in turn, can be nothing other than the Damascus Document's 'House of the *Torah*' or 'the Covenant and the Faith they erected in the Land of Damascus, the New Covenant' – reflected, too, in the Habakkuk *Pesher*, labored over so profusely in these passages from Hebrews, and varied so disingenuously in Paul and the Gospels.

All of the foregoing should be clear proof that Paul knew and was using the 'building' imagery – alluded to in this final description of 'the Spouter of Lying' with which the Habakkuk *Pesher* draws to a close – and applying it to himself. One cannot imagine marshalling anything stronger. In conclusion, one can only assume that those writing these *Pesharim* at Qumran understood this too, just as they seem to have understood 'the Lying Spouter''s more cosmopolitan analysis of Salvation – as in Paul, probably also based on this passage from Habakkuk 2:4.

'Erecting an Assembly on Lying' and 'Tiring out Many with a Worthless Service'

We now come to the last part of this all-important *Pesher*. It reads that the person 'building' this 'Worthless City upon Blood and raising a Church' or 'Assembly on Lying' caused 'Many' to perform 'a Worthless Service for the sake of his vainglory' or 'self-glorification'. The term 'Service' here in Hebrew is the other kind of 'Service' or 'work' – the kind presumably that Martha and others indulged in or what Paul several times refers to as *toil* or *labor* and what we have also been translating as 'Mission'. That it differs from 'works' based in Hebrew on the verb 'doing' – meaning, therefore, 'doing the *Torah*' – should by now also be clear.

The term 'Worthless', deliberately applied in the *Pesher* to the Service with which the Spouter of Lying 'tires out Many' or, for that matter, 'leads Many astray', of course, recapitulates the 'Worthless' applied to the value of the Spouter's 'building a City upon Blood', as well as the 'erecting an Assembly/Church upon Lying' coupled with it. Here it should be clear that the Worthless Service is synonymous with the Worthless City, so our arguments with regard to this last are sustained. That this is a characterization of the Pauline Gentile Mission, the accoutrements of which like speaking in Tongues we have described above, we feel is more than clear, especially when it is grouped with all the other usages in the context in which it is presented here.

To recapitulate: Paul uses this word 'Worthless' or 'void' twice in 1 Corinthians 15:14 after speaking not only about 'holding fast', 'Standing', and 'being saved' in 15:2, but also in 15:5–8 about Jesus' post-resurrection appearances 'to Cephas', 'to James', and 'last of all to (him)' – 'the least of the Apostles' – expressing the hope that his communities did not 'believe in vain' (also in 15:2). He even contends in 1 Corinthians 15:10 that he 'labored more abundantly than them all', twice concluding that 'if Christ was not raised from the dead', then both his 'preaching' and their 'Faith' were 'worthless'. In 1 Corinthians 15:58, again using the language of 'being strong' and 'not wavering' of the Community Rule, Damascus Document, and Hymns, he summarizes this position, encouraging his followers to 'be firm and immovable'. Here he repeats the words the Habakkuk *Pesher* is employing in this passage about the Spouter of Lying 'leading Many astray' almost verbatim: 'knowing that your labor is not Worthless in the Lord'.

In 2 Corinthians 6:1, he speaks of 'not receiving the Grace of God in vain' and in 9:3, his hope that his 'boasting (about his communities and his labors) should not have been in vain'. Significantly, he is referring at this point to 'the funds' he is collecting from his communities. In Galatians 2:2 he speaks of 'running in vain', this *a propos* of the Gospel as he teaches it 'among the Peoples' (*Ethnesin*) – even possibly recapitulating the language Habakkuk 2:2 applies to the Prophet 'running' with his vision which the Habakkuk *Pesher* interprets in terms of 'God making known to the Righteous Teacher all the Mysteries of the words of His Servants the Prophets' (n.b. the use of the word 'Servants')[54] – and in Galatians 4:11, of 'having labored in vain' regarding his communities (this, it will be recalled, concerning 'keeping' feasts, fast days, and other 'beggarly' calendrical reckonings).

In Galatians 5:15 and 5:26, he even evokes the term 'Glory' or 'vainglory' again, in cautioning his communities 'not to seek vainglory' or 'self-glorification' by 'envying' and 'biting and swallowing one another' – strange words coming from his perspective. This would appear to be the same 'vainglory' or 'self-glorification' the Habakkuk *Pesher* is referring to at this point here. There is so much 'vainglory' of this kind in the corpus ascribed to Paul that to enumerate it all would be endless.

Where the Letter of James is concerned, 'If anyone among you seems Religious, not bridling his Tongue, but rather Deceiving his heart, such a one's Religion is Worthless.' As previously suggested, 'Religion' here basically approximates or takes the place of the references to 'Service' and '*amal*' in the Habakkuk *Pesher*.[55]

The 'heart' imagery here is presaged by Jeremiah 31:31–33's 'making a New Covenant' with 'the House of Judah' described in terms of 'putting My *Torah* inside them and writing it upon their heart'. But it should be clear that when combined with Habakkuk 2:2's 'writing and running' above, this produces Paul's play on the appointment 'Letters' written by James – and, for that matter, 'written letters' generally – in 2 Corinthians 3:3, referring to 'Christ's Letter, served by us, not written in ink,' but 'on the fleshy tablets of (the) heart'.

This ends with his evocation of his and, doubtlessly, his companions' being 'able Servants of the New Covenant' in 2 Corinthians 3:6 (here, note again, the Habakkuk *Pesher*'s 'Servants' language just signaled above). Paul then adds, 'not of letters but of the Spirit, for the letter kills, but the Spirit gives life'. Aside from the clear derogation here, he then concludes speaking fairly plainly this time: 'But if the Ministry of death, having been cut in letters in stones, was produced with Glory … how much rather shall the Ministry of the Spirit be with Glory? For if the Ministry of Condemnation was Glory, how much rather does the Ministry of Righteousness exceed it in Glory.'

How much more hostile to 'Palestinian' parameters can one show oneself to be and, of a completely philo-Hellenistic mindset, can one display? Not only does one have here the 'condemnation' and 'Justification' descriptive of the eschatological role of the true 'Sons of Zadok' in the Damascus Document, to say nothing of the total *usurpation* of the Righteousness doctrine itself, but the constant play in the Habakkuk *Pesher* on both the 'Worthless Ministry' of the Liar and his 'Vainglory'. The Letter of James, directly following its allusion to 'making yourself a Friend of the World' and 'turning yourself into an Enemy of God', also reverses the thrust of Paul's repeated evocation of this term 'Worthless' or 'in vain' by asking, 'Does Scripture speak in vain'? (James 4:5). For more of Paul's 'Vainglory' and his 'Tongue', one has only to consult 2 Corinthians, which is full of what even Paul himself admits is 'boasting'. One could not find more appropriate examples to illustrate the identity of outlooks between the Habakkuk *Pesher* and the Letter attributed to James.

For its part, the *Pesher* seems to refer to just this kind of activity by adding the phrase to its Vainglory allusions, 'and instructing them in works of Lying'. This is how the Lying Spouter is building his 'Worthless Assembly' or 'Church upon Blood' and Lying, i.e., just as the works of the Righteous Teacher are Righteous and 'full of Righteousness and Justification', so, too, the works of the Man of Lies are 'of Lying' and Empty. We have all of the allusions necessary to connect this material to the kind of person seen as the Enemy or Liar – in Islam 'the *Dajjal*' or Joker – in Jewish Christian or Ebionite texts such as the *Recognitions* or the *Anabathmoi Jacobou*. There can be little doubt that the Worthless City referred to at this point in the *Pesher* is an intellectual or spiritual one – the reference to Blood in this instance, as in Pauline Christianity generally, also being figurative. Nor in this regard should one forget the allusion being attributed to Jesus in Matthew 5:14's Sermon on the Mount – following ones to Strength, 'being thrown out', 'trampled upon', and Light – of his Community being 'a City on a hill' that 'could not be *hidden*'.

Moreover, the *Pesher* does not stop here. It now adds the *third* kind of works – those we have identified as 'suffering works' or 'works with eschatological effect', the same kind of works the *Pesher* evoked two columns earlier in VIII.2 in its eschatological interpretation of Habakkuk 2:4. We identified this with the 'works working with Faith' of James 2:18–26, only now it was works working with 'Faith in the Righteous Teacher', another excellent example of materials relating either to James or the Righteous Teacher (or both) being retrospectively absorbed into the presentations of Jesus such as Paul is now using in Galatians and, to a lesser extent, in Romans to construct his ideology of the Salvation by Faith. In the Habakkuk *Pesher*, the same term '*amal* is now applied to how the Liar 'tired out Many with a Worthless Service, instructing them in *works of Lying*, so that their '*amal* (works) would be Empty' or 'for Emptiness' – 'Empty' here, clearly meaning 'Empty of saving' or 'eschatological effect'.

In regard to this, it is instructive to look at Paul's encouragement at the end of 1 Corinthians 15:58 above to his 'Beloved brothers' to 'be super-abundant in the work(s) of the Lord always, knowing that your toil is not Empty'. But this is obviously almost word-for-word the description in the Habakkuk *Pesher* above about the '*amal* of the Spouter of Lying 'being Empty'.[56] The counterpoint between this and the Habakkuk *Pesher*, not to mention Paul's reference to 'Super Apostles' elsewhere, cannot be accidental and even the James-like 'works', now called 'the work(s) of the Lord', is here evoked. This word 'Empty' – and the word in the Habakkuk *Pesher* in Hebrew at this point is 'Empty' – is also the basis of the epithet James 2:20 uses to describe the 'Wicked' Ideological Opponent, who doesn't know that 'Faith without works is dead' nor that, 'just as the body apart from the Spirit is dead, so Faith apart from works is also dead' (2:26).

James calls this individual the '*Empty Man*' or 'Man of Emptiness', obviously alluding to that individual's position on how 'Abraham was justified' and the eschatological value of the 'suffering works' or 'toil' with which 'he instructed (or 'misled'?) the Many' – that is, that 'they counted for Nothing' or were 'Empty' of soteriological effect where the matter of eschatological 'Salvation' or 'being saved' was concerned. In thinking that 'Abraham was justified by Faith' and not works, this individual – who in his very being gainsaid the idea of Abraham as 'the Friend of God', he being 'the Enemy of God' – did not know that 'Abraham was *justified by works* when he offered up his son Isaac on the altar' (2:21).

There can be no doubting the implication of these words and the purposeful introduction of a notation like that of '*amal* into the Qumran exposition of both Habakkuk 2:4 – which we have already identified as *Jamesian* – and 2:13 about 'the Peoples laboring for the sake of Fire and the Peoples tiring themselves out for the sake of Emptiness' in terms of the value of the teaching of the Ideological Adversary of the Righteous Teacher. With this last, we approach about as close to absolute convergence as one could imagine.

The exegesis of these passages from Habakkuk 2:12–13 now closes by calling down 'Hell -fire' on precisely the kind of individual who has been 'building (this) Worthless City upon Blood and raising a Congregation/Assembly upon Lying', 'blaspheming and vilifying the Elect of God'. There can be little doubt that throughout the corpus of Letters attributed to him in the New Testament, particularly Galatians and 1 and 2 Corinthians, Paul did precisely this – 'insulted and vilified' the Leadership of 'the Jerusalem Assembly' or 'the Church' led by James.

It will be recalled, Paul even went so far as to characterize the 'Hebrew' Apostles as 'those reckoned to be something' or 'those who wrote their own letters of recommendation', 'not that their importance', as far as he was concerned, 'anything conferred' (Galatians 2:6). For him, these Super Apostles were really Servants of Satan 'transforming themselves into Servants of Righteousness' and, parodying the actual doctrines of these last, their 'End would be according to their works' (2 Corinthians 11:15).

To repeat once again, as the *Pesher* now responds to this: those who 'blasphemed and vilified the Elect of God', instructing others 'in works of Lying' and 'tiring' them out 'with a Worthless Service', would themselves be brought, as just indicated, to 'the (same) Judgments of Fire with which they had insulted and vilified the Elect of God'.[57] Paul calls down similar Judgment against the Jerusalem Leadership in 2 Corinthians 11:15 whereas James 2:13, in its discussion of 'the Tongue' being 'a Fiery World of Unrighteousness', also speaks about 'Judgment without Mercy for him who does no Mercy'. For him, this same Tongue, 'set among our members', 'setting on Fire in the course of nature', will itself 'be set on Fire by Hell' (3:5–3:6).

Final Things: 'On the Day of Judgment God will Destroy all the Servants of Idols from the Earth'

Before moving on to its treatment of the fate of the Righteous Teacher and Wicked Priest in Columns XI–XII, the Habakkuk *Pesher* pauses to interpret a passage from Habakkuk 2:14 about 'the Earth filling with the Knowledge of the Glory of the Lord like waters covering the sea'. Though coming at the end of Column X and, therefore, fragmentary again – aside from the fact that it was from this citation (to say nothing of the ones about 'the City of Blood' in 2:12 and 'laboring for the sake of Fire' in 2:13) that the extraordinary exegesis about how 'the Spouter of Lying led Many astray' was constructed – the reference to 'waters' in the underlying text seems to be interpreted in terms of 'repenting' or 'a repentance' of some kind and it is after this that it is asserted that 'Knowledge, like the waters of the sea, should be revealed to them abundantly'.

Here, not only can something of a parallel to the 'abundant works of the Law' alluded to in 1 Corinthians 15:58 above possibly be discerned, but also possibly one to what is portrayed as 'the descent of the Holy Spirit' in Acts or 'Holy Spirit-baptism' generally. Whatever this 'Knowledge of the Glory of God' from 2:14 is interpreted to be, it is clearly the opposite of the 'puffed up Knowledge' of those forbidding the consumption of 'things sacrificed to idols', to whom Paul so contemptuously refers in 1 Corinthians 8:1ff. But it is the opposite as well of 'the waters of Lying' the Comedian or 'Lying Scoffer' is said to 'pour over Israel' in the First Column of CD.

After turning again to the subject of what the Wicked Priest did to the Righteous Teacher and the Poor and how 'the Cup of the Wrath of God', in turn, would come around and 'swallow him' in Columns XI.4–XII.9, the *Pesher* concludes on the note of 'Idolatry' and 'serving Idols'. This was also the theme, seemingly reversed in Paul and applied to 'the Table of the Demons' and that of 'reclining in an idol Temple' generally and 'eating things sacrificed to idols' in 1 Corinthians 8:1–13 and 10:14–33.

Here at the conclusion of the Habakkuk *Pesher*, it is connected to the evocation of 'the Day of Judgment' and 'Salvation' or 'being saved' at the time of this Last Judgment, language and themes part of the all-important eschatological exposition of Habakkuk 2:4 four columns earlier in VIII.1–3 as well. Not only is the theme of Idolatry important in the 'Three Nets of *Belial*' accusations against the Establishment and the Letter(s) known as *MMT*, but it is also part and parcel of James' directives to overseas communities in the sense of what Acts either calls 'the pollutions of the idols' or 'things sacrificed to idols'.

This is the context in which Paul is responding to it in 1 Corinthians too, the letter in which he ultimately sets forth his ideas of 'Communion with' and 'the New Covenant in the Blood of Christ' – the very same Blood ostensibly forbidden in James' prohibitions to overseas communities. Paul refers to this 'idol-worship' in the run-up to his presentation of 'Communion with the blood of Christ' in the conclusion of his discussion of James' 'eating things sacrificed to an idol' – also in conjunction with Cup imagery – in 1 Corinthians 10:16–21.

As this same imagery emerges, but with opposite signification, in these final columns of the Habakkuk *Pesher*, it is of such poignancy and immediacy as to be heart-rending. Moreover, it is an example of that long-suffering 'patience' and 'steadfast' Faith we have seen encouraged in the Letters of both Paul and James above despite their differing points-of-view. In the Habakkuk *Pesher*, this is perhaps best evidenced by the exegesis of Habakkuk 2:3: 'If it tarries, wait for it' – an exegesis seemingly attributed to the Righteous Teacher and clearly paralleled in the last Chapter of James by the admonition, 'Be patient brothers until the coming of the Lord', 'strengthen your hearts because the coming of the Lord approaches'. In the Damascus Document this last is referred to – together with the same 'Strengthening' imagery – as 'the Visitation of the Land'.[58] This is the same kind of Strengthening also signaled by Paul in 1 Corinthians 15:58 above.

The sequence that is followed here at the end of the Habakkuk *Pesher* also almost precisely follows that of early Church accounts delineating the death of James. In these accounts, James' death is pictured as immediately being followed by the appearance of foreign Armies outside Jerusalem and the final destruction of both City and Temple presumably because the Protection/Pillar/or Bulwark, provided by the 'Righteous One' James, had been removed. In Columns VIII-XI of the Habakkuk *Pesher*, the sequence is: the destruction of the Righteous Teacher, the destruction of the Wicked Priest and 'the Last Priests of Jerusalem' – this last, paralleling what the Gospels call 'the Chief Priests' – and their Riches and spoils (collected, seemingly, by the agency of 'the Peoples' or 'Herodians' and other 'Violent Ones') given over to 'the Army of the *Kittim*' or 'the Additional Ones of the Peoples'.[59]

But in the immediacy and poignancy of this commentary, it is the 'Pious Faithfulness' that stands out. These people have undergone every reversal and tragedy. Their Community has been decimated. The Righteous Teacher – just as in the Gospels – has been destroyed. Jerusalem is either in the process of being destroyed or already destroyed. The *Kittim* are overrunning the Land, 'taking no pity on' anyone, 'youths, men, old people, women and children, even babes in the wombs' (of course, a more accurate description of the Romans could not be imagined[60]). In the words of the Nahum *Pesher*, supported by Josephus' descriptions: 'the corpses are stacked up everywhere' and 'there is no end to the sum of the slain'.[61]

In particular, the group responsible for these writings has lost everything and 'the Last End will be extended beyond anything the Prophets have foretold' – an exegesis of

Habakkuk 2:3 seemingly ascribed to the Righteous Teacher ('to whom God made known all the Mysteries of His Servants the Prophets') in his role as God's exegete on Earth.

In short, we have an eyewitness account of these events – as the Gospels are supposed to be but are not – written as they are actually going on. Nothing could be more immediate or compelling. Nor as 'Men of Truth' and 'Doers of the *Torah*' are they 'to slacken from the Service of Truth – as opposed presumably to 'the Service of Lying' – though the Final Age is to be extended beyond anything the Prophets have foretold'. Therefore, the author(s) of this document call down on the kinds of 'Enemies' they are facing the only curses they have left, those of 'the Day of Judgment', wherein will be their ultimate Salvation – that is, *they do not give up*.

This is delivered from Columns XII.10–XIII.4 in exposition of an underlying reference to 'Lying' and 'dumb idols' from Habakkuk 2:18: 'Of what use are graven images, whose makers formed a casting and images of Lying' and directed against both 'those who *serve* idols' and 'the Wicked Ones'. The former are, in fact, overtly identified in the *Pesher* as Gentiles. The latter, as already suggested, have to be identified as 'backsliding Jews' – people like the Wicked Priest, responsible for the destruction of the Righteous Teacher, who 'did not circumcise the foreskin of his heart'; or persons like the Alexandrian Jewish turncoat, Philo's nephew and Titus' Commander-in-Chief at the siege of Jerusalem and the destruction of the Temple, Tiberius Alexander, whom Josephus specifically identifies as just such a 'Backslider'.[62] In fact, where the *Pesher* is concerned, they would probably also include the whole Pharisee/Sadducean Establishment or collaborators such as R. Yohanan ben Zacchai or Josephus himself and, of course, Paul. There are many – enough to go around – and all are to be subjected to the same 'Hell-Fire'.

It is the allusion to 'serve' here which is so pivotal in the evocation of 'serving the idols of the Nations', the same Service or labor we have already seen referred to in the description of the Liar's efforts as 'Worthless' or 'vain' and the same language Paul over and over again applies to his own activities – what the world often describes as 'Mission'. This is roundly condemned. This is put in the following manner: 'This concerns all the sculptures of the Gentiles, which they create in order to serve and bow down to them. These will not save them on the Day of Judgement.'[63] Here, of course, are the same words, 'save them', we have just seen used in the eschatological interpretation of Habakkuk 2:4 in the *Pesher* in VIII.2. The phrase 'Day of Judgment' is, of course, related to the previous formulation in that *Pesher*, 'House of Judgment' which, in turn, will be used two columns later in X.3 to describe 'the Judgment God would deliver in the midst of Many Peoples'.

1QpHab XII.16–XIII now closes by repeating this fulsome condemnation, extending it to all 'Evil Ones' generally, presumably including all Jewish Backsliders. It does so in exegesis of a passage from Habakkuk 2:19–20: 'Can this guide? Behold it is covered with gold and silver and there is no spirit at all within it.' Not only does this delineate the problem with 'idols', it specifically alludes to the telltale words, 'gold and silver', that we also encountered in the eschatological Judgment section of the last Chapter of the Letter of James condemning the Rich (5:3). We have also encountered the same phraseology in the passage about coming eschatological Judgment in Isaiah 2:20–21, preceding the Isaiah 3:10–11 passages – applied to James' death in early Church sources and incorporated, as we illustrated, into exegeses about 'the destruction of the Poor' in the Habakkuk *Pesher*.

There is also the pious hope, expressed in the second part of the underlying text from Habakkuk 2:20 here in the *Pesher* too, seeming sadly forlorn in these disastrous and devastating times of complete and general collapse: 'But the Lord is in his Holy Temple, let all the Earth be still before Him'. One cannot avoid the conclusion that whoever is subjecting words of such sublime hopefulness to such interpretation is doing so in the midst of total disaster and that we have in this document an eyewitness account – as just remarked but also worth reiterating – of the most awe-inspiring devotion and Piety of the events leading up to and surrounding the fall of Jerusalem in 70 CE. One has to assume that whoever the exegete was, the passages were chosen purposefully.

As the *Pesher* closes, it interprets the passage as follows: 'Its interpretation concerns all the Gentiles, who serve but stone and wood. But on the Day of Judgment God will destroy all the Servants of Idols and (all) Evil Ones from off the Earth.'[64] The display of such 'Faithfulness' and undying commitment is stunning in such circumstances.

The use of the word 'destroy' here is the same one used earlier in the description of what would happen to the Wicked Priest for what he had done to the Righteous Teacher and his 'plots to destroy the Poor'. We have seen it used in precisely this manner in eschatological 'Judgment' sections of the Qumran Hymns and the Community Rule above. It means *utter destruction*. There probably never was a more forlorn and pathetic document ever penned, now come back – in a state of almost perfect preservation – some Twenty Centuries later to haunt and unsettle us all.

It is clear that these allusions in the Scrolls, if not identical with the situation in early Christianity, at least are almost the exact parallel to it – so much so that the two sets of allusions approach what only can be considered identity. But, in addition, we have shown through the Dead Sea Scrolls and a close analysis of early Church texts and literature, the *lacuna*, overwrites, and oft-times even outright falsification in the early Church presentation of its own history.

The keynote here is reversal – always reversal. Everything is being reversed and turned around from the way it was in Palestine in this Period as attested by eyewitness accounts like the Dead Sea Scrolls (which are completely homogeneous in this regard) and other documents. Palestinian Messianism is being, as it were, turned on its ear and reversed and turned into Hellenistic and allegorical mythologizing, some of which redacted in the form of exquisite Gospel narratives which have not failed to catch the imagination of Mankind ever since – though, as always, not without an often rather-unpleasant barb of anti-Semitism.

The entrance to Petra, Herod's mother's place-of-origin and the capital of the 'Arab' King Aretas, who chased Paul down Damascus' walls '*in a basket*.'

Above: The Amphitheatre of '*Arab*' Petra, an area Paul knows well according to Gal. 1:17. **Right:** Tomb pilgrims call that of James, overlooking where he fell from 'the Pinnacle of the Temple'.

Chapter 23
From Adiabene to Cyrene: The Cup of the Lord, the Blood of Christ, and the *Sicaricon*

Northern Syrian Conversion Stories: 'Ad and Thamud, and Hud and Salih

Despite a certain amount of repetition – which in circumstances as recondite and complex as these is probably unavoidable – it would be worth recapitulating some of the key issues addressed in this book. Before doing so, however, one should look more closely at the stories in the Koran about "Ad and Thamud' and 'Hud and Salih'. These have always been thought of as showing Muhammad's acquaintance with unknown cities and Prophets in the Arabian cultural sphere. The normal understanding is that these stories have to do with little remembered Arab Holy Men, functioning in some quasi-identifiable locale in the Arabian Peninsula at some time in the primordial past before the coming of Islam. The usual explanations are replete with forced connections and nonsensical rationalizations. All is hazy or unknown and nothing of any certainty emerges.

A typical commentary or explanation runs something like this: "Ad was the name of a tribe who lived in the remote past in Arabia. At one time they ruled over most of the fertile parts of greater Arabia, particularly Yemen, Syria, and Mesopotamia (i.e., just about everywhere). They were the first people to exercise dominion over practically the whole of Arabia.'[1] (This is from an '*Ahmadiyya*' commentary, but almost all present the same or similar insights.) Another runs: 'The Thamud People were the successors to the culture and civilization of the 'Ad People'.[2] Almost all connect these persons or peoples in some manner with Abraham because, in the Koran, all such references are almost always followed up by *evocation of Abraham*. In the context of our previous points about the importance of Abraham, this connection is probably true but in a different manner than most might think. Nor, probably, have they anything to do with a genealogical connection with either Abraham or Noah, another individual mentioned prominently in these traditions.

Here is a third: 'The Thamud Tribe lived in the western parts of Arabia, having spread from Aden northward to Syria. They lived shortly before the time of Ishmael. Their territory was adjacent to that of 'Ad, but they lived mostly in the hills…. The Prophet Salih lived after Hud and was probably a contemporary of Abraham';[3] and a fourth: 'The Thamud People were the successors to the culture and civilization of the 'Ad People…. They were cousins to the 'Ad, apparently a younger branch of the same race. Their story also belongs to Arabian tradition, according to which their eponymous ancestor, Thamud, was a son of 'Abir (brother of Aram) the son of Sam (Shem), the son of Noah (thus!).' Most of these comments are drawn from real or imagined references in the Koran and on the whole represent a total garbling of only dimly-recalled and little-understood oral tradition. What we would now like to show is that they come from traditions which Muhammad or his voices (Angelic or real) derived from either Northern Syria or Southern Iraq – probably the latter.

We have already remarked the general connection of many of Muhammad's ideas with sectarian movements in Southern Iraq such as the Mandaeans and Manichaeans and, if the additional relationships we shall now illustrate are true, then they considerably reinforce the connections of traditions of this sort with the kind of visits Muhammad was reputed to have made to Southern Iraq and even, perhaps, Northern Syria – and to the caravan trade, which could have easily carried him, or those he came in contact with, to such locales. However, of perhaps even more significance, what we shall attempt to demonstrate is that these notices in fact have to do with cities, Peoples, or Prophets/Warners (as the Koran would put it[4]) or Messengers within the Arabian culture sphere. Furthermore, what is not generally appreciated, the allusion 'Arab' had a much wider connotation in the Greco-Roman Period than is normally considered nowadays to apply. As a result, these stories had, geographically-speaking, a much wider transmission framework and actually reflect Northern Syrian conversion stories of the kind we have been highlighting in this work – themselves very important to both Jewish and Christian history in this region and, as we have been suggesting throughout this work, the Dead Sea Scrolls and, along with them, the person of James.

Having said this, the key connections are ''Ad' with Addai, Edessa and Adiabene; Thamud with Thomas; Hud with the characters we have otherwise been calling 'Judas Thomas' (as we have seen, the other or real name of Thomas), also equivalent to Thaddaeus, Judas Barsabas, Judas the Zealot, and, in this sense, Judas Iscariot – in fact, just about all the 'Judas'es) in this Period; and Salih (the Arabic for Righteousness or Righteous One), of course, with James the Just, the 'brother' either of Jesus or this 'Hud'. Even Muslim sources and commentators have garnered this conclusion, no doubt based on his name, appreciating that 'Salih' was 'a Just and Righteous Man'.[4]

The reason these stories are so important, too, is because they unify the several conversion stories we have been following in both Early Christian and Jewish sources (and now probably also those at Qumran) relating to this region. As already made clear, in our view these stories have to do with the conversion of the 'King of Edessa', known in early Christian and Greco-Latin sources as *Abgarus* or *Agbarus*, called in Christian sources 'the Great King of the Peoples beyond the Euphrates'. Furthermore, they have to do with the Kings and Queen of the Royal House of Adiabene – according to Syriac and Armenian sources, the consort of this Agbarus[5] – contiguous to Edessa and a little further East 'beyond the Euphrates'. They also have a direct link to the development of the tradition that 'James the Righteous One' sent down one 'Judas Barsabas' (among others – supposedly 'Silas, Barnabas, and Paul') in Acts 15:22–32 to regulate matters having to do with this evangelization in a place it knows as Antioch but, as we have been trying to demonstrate, probably also Edessa and, in any event, a Northern Syrian locale.

These Northern Syrian conversion stories are also important because they throw light on the puzzling terminology 'Sabaean' in the Koran (and elsewhere), which in Islamic sources – as well, as it turns out, as Christian[6] – is often confused with '*Saba*' or '*Sheba*' in Southern Arabia or Ethiopia.

Let us take these matters one at a time. In the first place it is rarely, if ever, realized that the word 'Arab' or 'Arabia' was being used, as just indicated, in Roman times to encompass a much wider expanse both of territory and personalities. Roman historians such as Tacitus routinely use the term 'Arab' to refer to Northern Syrian personages and Kings – as, in fact, persons still do today.[7] For Tacitus, King Acbar or Abgar is 'King of the Arabs'.[8] Other sources, in fact, also refer to him as 'the Black,' a sobriquet which will have more than the normal significance.[9]

Furthermore, this greater expanse of land going by the designation 'Arabia' extended up into Mesopotamia as far as Edessa and Adiabene in Northern Syria and modern Iraq. Petra, across the Jordan River and on the other side of the '*Aravah*, is a locale whose Kings were definitely being referred to as 'Arab'. We have already made it clear that this would make Herod – whose mother was from an aristocratic family in Petra, not improbably, related to its King – what would loosely be called an 'Arab'. Modern scholars, following one or two leads in Josephus, are fond of referring to this culture as 'Nabataean' after Nabaioth, one of Ishmael's sons in Genesis 25:13[10]; but it is doubtful whether these Peoples really ever referred to themselves in such a manner or, for that matter, anything other than Arab which had wide currency in the Roman First–Second Centuries. It is this state of affairs that Muhammad seems unwittingly to be echoing in his general references to these legendary Peoples of ''Ad and Thamud'.

Such a broader definition also imparts an entirely new dimension to Paul's notice in Galatians 1:16 about how, after receiving his 'version of the Good News as he taught it among the Gentiles', he did not return to Jerusalem or 'discuss it with any living being' or, for that matter, 'those who were Apostles before (him'). On the contrary, he 'went straightway *into Arabia*' and, only thereafter, 'again returned to Damascus' (1:17). The question is, precisely what did he mean by this reference here to 'Arabia'?

Normally it is only thought of as having to do with Arabian Petra or some such locale – even a Qumran or an Essene-style novitiate of some kind in the Judean or Transjordanian Desert (the 'Land of Damascus'?). But this broader definition allows us to consider that it meant as far north as 'the Land of the Edessenes' or even Adiabene neighboring Edessa some hundred miles or so further East, or as far South as Messene (Mani's birthplace) or Antiochia Charax (present-day Basrah), the area where Josephus first traces Izates' contact with the merchant he is calling 'Ananias' who, as we saw – together with another teacher unnamed in Josephus' account – teaches a sort of conversion to what is supposed to be Judaism which *does not require circumcision*[11]!

This would mean that what Paul is alluding to by 'into Arabia' could be much further afield than is generally appreciated, even as far North and East as Antioch-by-Callirhoe or Antioch Orrhoe and/or Adiabene – today's Kurdistan – in Northern Mesopotamia. This is before his return to 'Damascus', from where he later – or perhaps earlier, depending on how one evaluates his own account in 2 Corinthians 11:32 – seems to have escaped from representatives of the Arab King Aretas of Petra. One must appreciate that Acts 9:25's tendentious account of these same events is secondary. As already underscored as well, all these episodes also involve the contact with the mysterious and unidentified personage named 'Ananias' – as we saw, the same Ananias who (as Eusebius reports it) will reappear in the Syriac accounts of King Agbar or Abgar's conversion.

The Land of Noah, the Location of Mt. Ararat, the Elchasaites, and Other Daily Bathers there

There is another oddity that comes to light in the context of the notices about these Lands and the conversions that took place there and that is the location of the fabled Mount Ararat where Noah's ark came to rest, which the perspicacious reader of the Koran will realize is associated in most of these allusions with Hud and 'Ad, Salih and Thamud. Modern hagiography has, of course, placed the ark in Northern Anatolia on the Russian border next to a mountain now called Mt. Ararat. This is partly due to the wandering of 'Armenia' northwards ('Armenia' presumably being the area where Aramaic was originally spoken), so that the only real Armenia left – particularly after the Turkish devastations – is in Southern Russia. The point is that this ark was always associated in some manner with 'Armenia' and, as we shall see, this is basically the implication of these notices in the Koran as well.

But for early historians, such as Josephus or Hippolytus (the manuscript 'On Sects' attributed to him was found at Mount Athos in Greece at the end of the last Century), the ark came to rest in 'the Land of the *Adiabeni*' – that is, Adiabene[12] – which turns out to be modern Kurdistan or the area of Northern Iraq, moving up into the mountains of Southern Turkey and not Northern Turkey. In fact, one of the best witnesses to this is the Twelfth-Century Jewish traveler Benjamin of Tudela. He actually visited the mosque on an island in the Tigris dedicated to the place where the ark was supposed to have come to rest and, unless he was dreaming, this is just North of present-day Mosul – in fact, he locates it between Nisibis and Mosul.[13] As he puts it, leaving Haran (the 'Carrhae' or 'Carron' of Josephus' narrative) and passing through Nisibis, he comes to: 'an island in the Tigris at the foot of Mount Ararat, four miles distant from the spot where the ark of Noah rested. Omar ibn al

Katab removed the ark from the summit of the two mountains and made a mosque of it.' However mythological this may appear to be, it perfectly accords with what Hippolytus in the Third Century and Josephus in the First are telling us almost a millennium previously. It also accords with Talmudic data connecting the ark to *the Land from which Queen Helen came* – that is, Adiabene.'[14] Whether Benjamin of Tudela is accurate in this tradition or not (who can be accurate in any tradition concerning 'Noah's ark'?) is unimportant. The point is that this is where he *thinks* the ark came to rest, as did a number of his predecessors – some already cited. Because of the notices, already alluded to above, connecting "Ad and Thamud' with 'the Folk of Noah' – not to mention to 'the People of Abraham' – and the place where the ark came to rest, it would appear that the Koran seems to think so as well.[15] Mosul, of course, is connected to ancient Nineveh and both are but a little distant from Arbela, considered by most to have been the capital of Adiabene on the Northern reaches of the Tigris.

But more to the point 'Ad, even if looked at only superficially, is, in fact, linguistically related not only to Edessa, but also to the place name Adiabene. One can go further than this. In all these stories about conversions in Northern Syria to some form of Christianity, retrospectively it is always *orthodox* Christianity; but, as we have been suggesting, it was most probably heterodox or one of the manifold varieties of what is now sometimes referred to as 'Jewish Christianity' – and this is also the case with regard to Helen's or her son Izates' conversion to what is supposed to be a form of Judaism further East connected to these.

'Jewish Christianity' is poor nomenclature. Even the Arabic 'Sabaean' would be more appropriate. The terms Ebionites, Elchasaites, Masbuthaeans (Daily Bathers, from the root in Syriac and/or Aramaic, S-B-', to immerse – therefore its Arabic variation, 'Sabaeans' or *Subba'*), Mandaeans and, in Palestine, even Essenes, all have a common focus on *bathing* or 'ritual immersion'. These are the more technical terms – many arising out of the works of early Christian heresiologists of the Second to Fifth Centuries or Josephus. Where the Talmud is concerned, it applies the appellatives *Minim* or *Saddukim* to groups of this kind.[16] For example, Epiphanius at the end of the Fourth/the beginning of the Fifth Century refers to an unknown bathing group in Transjordan and beyond, descended from the Essenes and Ebionites and interchangeable with these Elchasaites, that he calls 'Sampsaeans'.[17] He has no idea of the derivation of the term but this last is almost certainly what goes by the name of 'Sabaean' in Islamic tradition.

It should be appreciated that even Benjamin of Tudela, in his seemingly very-late Twelfth -Century account, identifies one of two synagogues he claims actually to have visited in Mosul, as that of 'Nahum the Elchasaite', i. e., 'Nahum the *Daily Bather*'[18] or, in Islamic terms, *al-Mughtasilah* or *al-Hasih*, as the Encyclopaedist of that period known as 'The *Fihrist*' calls the Leader of such *Mughtasilah* (not to be confused with the later philosophical group, known to Maimonides and others as *al-Mu'tazilah*).[19] In fact, it is possible that this term in Arabic may even be a variation of what goes in Hebrew under the designation 'Karaite' (though this is probably a stretch), which would make the links between these two groups of Jewish sectarians interesting indeed.

However this may be, this means that even in Benjamin of Tudela's time in the Twelfth Century – unless his manuscript is completely corrupt – there were Jewish sectarian Daily Bathers living in Mosul or Arbela, that is, the area that was formerly Adiabene. Many of these groups move on in the Third and Fourth Centuries into what come to be known as Manichaeans – the only real difference being that, whereas the Elchasaite, Ebionite, Mughtasilite, and Sabaean groups stressed Daily Bathing, the Manichaeans abjured it – and from there on into Islam. In fact, Mani, was actually from an Elchasaite family in this same Messene area of Southern Iraq.

The point that all these groups actually have in common, including the latter-day Muslims (who like the Manichaeans discarded the 'bathing' ideology of the earlier though still

-extant 'Subba' of the Marshes' – The *Fihrist* calls them 'the *Mughtasilah* of the Marshes') is 'the True Prophet' ideology. As already underscored, this ideology is very definitely strong at Qumran where the passage underlying it from Deuteronomy 18:18–19 is actually one of the Messianic proof-texts cited in 4QTestimonia.[20] It is also definitely alluded to in the Community Rule.[21] Furthermore, it is also strong among the Ebionites, important to the Elchasaites – allegedly following a Prophet the heresiologists are calling *Elchasai* which they claim means 'Hidden Power' – and strong among followers of Mani. From there it too proceeds into Islam.

This is not the only Dead Sea Scroll/Jamesian/Ebionite idea that proceeds into Islam. Two others are the formulation 'believe and do good works', which fairly permeates the capsule descriptions of Islam in the Koran[22]; the second is Islamic dietary regulations, quoted some five times in the Koran and consisting of, among other things, both the Jamesian 'things sacrificed to idols' ('that immolated to an idol' in the Koran) and 'carrion'.[23] The reader will by this time readily recognize these as based on James' directives to overseas communities.

The Koranic versions as we have them here are probably based on the Pseudoclementine *Homilies* – originally probably a Syriac work and also the source of much deliberation both about the True Prophet ideology and 'bathing'. Its translator, Rufinus, took it into Greek at the end of the Fourth Century and its companion volume, the *Recognitions*, went into Latin at approximately the same time. The formulation, 'carrion', reproduced in these pronouncements in the Koran, is clearly delineated the *Homilies* in place of the rather abstruse 'strangled things' in the Greek New Testament – though even the idea of 'carrion' can be deduced from this last.[24]

The Conversion of Agbar Uchama, the Activities of Hud, Salih, Addai, and Thaddaeus in 'Ad and Thamud, and *MMT*

We are now ready to approach these notices about a conversion that took place in Northern Syria in a place our sources are calling Edessa – as we have seen, a late Greco-Syriac/Aramaic name for that city – presumably in the First Century and having to do with a King there known as Agbar or Acbar (the Latin pronunciation) or Abgar (the Semitic). The document Eusebius claims to be translating calls him 'Abgar Uchama' or 'Agbar the Black' and he is, most probably, to be identified with Abgar V, c. 4 BCE–50 CE.[25] The Fifth-Century Armenian historian, Moses of Chorene (some consider this a pseudonym for a later Ninth-Century Armenian historian), is already testifying to the difficulty Westerners are having with names based on Semitic originals[26] and such a reversal of letters, as we have seen, is a common phenomenon for those familiar with the vagaries of translating Middle Eastern nomenclature.

We have been using the Latin derivative, Agbar, because of its clear connections with the garbled name 'Agabus' in Acts 11:28, the Prophet who was supposed to have 'come down from Judea to Antioch' and predicted the Famine. This idea of a Famine will also bear some connection with these Koranic notices about the problems in either 'Ad or Thamud.[27] The names 'Edessa' and even 'Adiabene' also have, as just pointed out, a clear relationship with the terminology 'Ad and the Prophet called in some sources – in particular, the Syriac – 'Addai'.[28]

When the name 'Edessa' gained currency is not clear at all but, before it was called Edessa it was apparently called Antiochia Orrhoe or Antioch-by-Callirhoe. The fact that Antioch Orrhoe or by-Callirhoe was on the upper reaches of the Euphrates, not far from Abraham's place of origin, had a not inconsiderable bearing on not only Early Christian and Jewish sources but also quite clearly the Koran itself. We have already made it clear as well that, in our view, the Antioch intended in these several notices in Acts about individuals such as this 'Agabus', '*some* insisting on circumcision' (the '*some* from James' in Galatians 2:12), and 'Judas Barsabas' who brought down the Letter James wrote in Acts 15:23–30, was not Antioch-on-the-Orontes near the Mediterranean Coast, but rather the one in Northern Syria, connected to this name "Ad', where these legendary conversions took place (and neither coincidentally nor insignificantly, from where the celebrated 'Holy Shroud' was ultimately alleged to have come[29]).

These notices, also reflecting Galatians and Paul's confrontations at Antioch with the 'some from James' of 'the Party of the Circumcision', are about individuals like Agabus, Judas Barsabas, and the 'some insisting that, unless you are circumcised you cannot be saved' who trigger the equally celebrated Jerusalem Council. Furthermore, they contain the note that it was 'in *Antioch* that the Disciples were first called Christians' (11:26 – thus!). As already made clear, in our view there was nothing of note really happening at this time in Antioch-on-the-Orontes and the only reason we think there was – as the authors of Acts have made us do – is because of our and their respective ignorance (or purposeful dissimulation). What *was* happening was happening here in Northern Syria with these legendary conversions in 'the Land of the Edessenes' or Osrhoeans/Assyrians – the *Lands* of 'the Great King of the Peoples beyond the Euphrates'. In our sources these 'Lands' are also being called 'Arab'. It turns out that the intermediary in this correspondence between this 'Great King' and Jerusalem in the Syriac source that Eusebius claims to have found and translated was, yet again, this same 'Ananias' – a not unnoteworthy coincidence.

The story, as Eusebius presents it, concerns two characters he calls 'Judas Thomas' and 'Thaddaeus', neither of whom are really properly identified in any other Christian source. In the Gospel of John, for instance, Thomas is called 'Didymus Thomas', literally 'Twin Twin'. In the newly-recovered Gospel of Thomas found at Nag Hammadi, he is 'Didymus Judas Thomas', combining the two sorts of appellations but, once more, manifestly unaware of the inherent redundancy of referring to both Didymus and Thomas.[30] All Gospel presentations, too, of a Disciple or Apostle called 'Thomas' must be seen as either suspect, uninformed, or dissimulating as well. Even in John 20:24, when he appears as the 'missing' Apostle, he sometimes overlaps Judas Iscariot in the Synoptics. Nor does Thomas seem to be mentioned in the Gospel of Judas, which doesn't seem to make it clear if its 'Judas' is surnamed 'the *Iscariot*' or distinguish him from the 'brothers' or Thomas.

It is, however, only in the Syriac sources – and we would include in these the source Eusebius is working from to produce his narrative about the correspondence with King Agbarus – that this appellative 'Judas' is always and probably accurately joined to his other title.[31] That in some sense this 'twin' theme has to do with the 'brother' theme in sources about James and the other 'brothers' is also, probably, not to be gainsaid. Moreover, that all have in some sense to do with one 'Judas', in some manner related either to Jesus or James, should also be clear. The attaching of 'Judas' to Thomas' name in Eusebius' source but not Eusebius' own actual narrative also bears out its authenticity, though not necessarily its accuracy in terms of *dramatis personae* – that is, the source is not necessarily reliable in terms of characters and subject matter, only that something of this kind appears to have happened and it does, at least, have some idea of the true names.[32]

Where Thaddaeus is concerned, once again, in the Apostle lists in Matthew and Mark, he parallels the Apostle Luke 6:16 is calling 'Judas of James'. For some recensions of Matthew and in Syriac documents such as the Apostolic Constitutions, he bears the additional surname of 'Lebbaeus', perhaps – as we have already suggested – a distortion of 'Alphaeus', as in 'James the son of Alphaeus' in the Synoptics (Matthew 10:3 and pars.); or of 'Cleophas', the name of Mary's other husband ('Clopas' in John 19:25) and the seeming father of these 'brothers'[33]; or a garbling of James' mysterious cognomen in Hegisippus also via Eusebius above – *Oblias*, meaning in this pivotal source, 'Protection of the People'.³⁴ Eusebius, for example, doesn't even know whether Thaddaeus is an Apostle or a Disciple (if there is any difference) and what finally emerges in all these sources is that these two individuals 'Thaddaeus' and 'Thomas' are for the most part all but indistinguishable.³⁵

For the two Apocalypses of James from Nag Hammadi, Addai and someone actually referred to as 'Theudas' (probably Thaddaeus) are also parallel figures.³⁶ Finally, in Syriac texts Thaddaeus is none other than Addai himself – as should have been suspected all along – the eponymous figure associated with all these stories and traditions centering around Edessa and the conversion of 'the Great King of the Peoples beyond the Euphrates' to what is pictured, at this point anyhow, as Christianity).³⁷ As opposed to this, however, it should be appreciated that there is another Divine figure called 'Ad or Addai associated with this region from remotest antiquity.³⁸

As we saw, Eusebius claims to have personally found the report of this conversion in the Chancellery Office of Edessa and, much as Rufinus did in the next generation the Pseudoclementine *Homilies* (probably also stemming from Syriac records), translated it himself into Greek. The reader should recall that, in this story, first there is a correspondence between this individual, Agbar, described as 'the Great King of the Peoples beyond the Euphrates' – phraseology which certainly has interesting overtones with Paul's Mission to these same 'Peoples' and Jesus, the courier in this correspondence being Ananias. Furthermore, a portrait of sorts is exchanged (the origin of the legend of the Holy Shroud?).

Then after Jesus' death, 'Judas known as Thomas' sends Thaddaeus down from Jerusalem to continue the evangelization of the Edessenes and, in due course, follows up this mission with one of his own. In the two accounts Eusebius provides – his own and the Chancellery Office one from the official records of Edessa – it is not clear whether Thomas sends out Thaddaeus before the death of Jesus or afterwards. However this may be, one can dismiss any report of a correspondence (including the report of an exchange of portraits!) between Jesus and 'the Great King of the Peoples beyond the Euphrates' with the omnipresent Ananias as courier as retrospective. Rather – if it is to be entertained at all and the writer thinks to a certain degree it can (at least where James is concerned) – it should be put under the stewardship of James, who also sent Letter(s) and messengers 'down to Antioch' (i.e., Edessa) and who, even Acts concedes, was pre-eminent from around the time of the Famine (45–48 CE) until 62 CE. For Eusebius, following Hegesippus (2nd c. Palestinian) and Clement (3rd c. Alexandrian), James was 'Leader' or 'Ruler' of the early Church in Palestine even earlier than this – after the Assumption when he 'was elected'.³⁹

The reason, therefore, why this exchange of communications should rather be attributed to James is quite simple: even in Acts' evasive, achronological, and somewhat refurbished account, *an actual correspondence of James to Antioch carried by one 'Judas' is definitively described* – and this in the more reliable 'We Document' of the latter part of Acts. Acts even knows the subject matter of this correspondence, as we have been accentuating: *things sacrificed to idols, carrion, fornication,* and *blood* – and which, as we just saw, any perspicacious observer will immediately recognize as the *basis of Islamic dietary law to this day.*

I have already traced the relationship of these notices to a Letter or Letters called *MMT* from the Daily-Bathing Community at Qumran (which some call 'Essene', some 'Ebionite', some 'Zadokite', etc.) – the *only* Letter(s) found among the manifold remains of that corpus – *addressed to a Pious King* of some kind, somewhere (location unspecified, though obviously not in Jerusalem⁴⁰), and *also* dealing with matters such as *things sacrificed to idols, the ban on Gentile gifts to the Temple, fornication,* and even, somewhat esoterically, *carrion* – though in far more detail such that the one recorded in Acts above appears a simplified epitome of the other.

We have already discussed the geographic relationship of the two place-names Antioch and Edessa. At Qumran, as well, there are further references to a 'New Covenant in the Land of Damascus', a Diaspora Community of 'Camps' in the 'Wilderness of the Peoples', and a King in 'the Land of the North', '*beyond Damascus*', where 'the Tabernacle of David which was fallen' was to be 're-erected', as well as a paradigmatic circumcision of Abraham (Genesis 17:9–14) as a *sine qua non* for conversion.[41]

In putting all these notices together, it is possible to come out with the following conclusions: 1) Addai, Thaddaeus, Theudas, and Thomas are really the same person – one 'Judas'. In some Syriac texts he is actually also called 'Judas the Zealot' (just as in Luke's Apostle lists, 'Simon the Cananaean' is less covertly revealed to be 'Simon the Zealot') – terminology little different from 'Judas Iscariot', it being appreciated, as we have already to some extent signaled and shall explain further below, that *Sicarios* carries with it the secondary meaning of 'Circumciser'.

2) It is *James* who sends his brother Judas 'down to Edessa' with the Epistle containing his directives – as we have stressed, it is important to keep one's eye on the 'brother' theme in all these overlapping accounts – or possibly even further East to Adiabene, itself probably one of the provinces owing allegiance to this 'Great King of the Peoples beyond the Euphrates'. It is this Letter which in other parlance goes by the designation *MMT* or the Letter from Qumran on 'Works Reckoned as Righteousness' or 'Things we Reckon as Justifying you'.

3) Finally, the 'Antioch' in the interconnected notices in Acts and Paul's Galatians is really *Edessa* or these provinces further East, all having to do with the underlying notation "Ad" – and, in some sense, 'Addai' as well – so important to these regions. This 'Judas' too has to do with 'Thomas' or, as the Koran would so typically deform it, 'Thamud'.

4) It is important to repeat that the 'Prophet called *Agabus*' who predicts the Famine in Acts really has to do with this King *Agbarus* story and the related one of the conversion of Queen Helen – probably one of his many wives and his half-sister, as Aramo-Syriac texts aver[42] – further East and her legendary famine-relief activities, as well as those of her son Izates. Furthermore, in this earlier context anyhow, he is probably none other than that Ananias who constantly reappears in the stories of Paul's conversion in 'Damascus', Josephus' story of King Izates' conversion, and, of course, Eusebius' curious account of the conversion of 'King Agbarus'. The Letter in question is the one comprising James' directives to overseas communities – themselves ultimately re-emerging in Koranic dietary regulations.

5) All these episodes, including the associated references in the Scrolls and the Koran, not to mention Paul's allusions to 'the Faith of Abraham' and James, to Abraham as the 'Friend of God' (turns-of-phrase found in both the Koran and the Scrolls as well) and how he was 'tested' by his willingness to sacrifice Isaac, have to do with the importance of Abraham for these Northern Syrian locales – where holy sites are still dedicated to his name – in particular Haran, Abraham's place-of-origin in Northern Syria near Edessa and, apparently, the Kingdom bestowed upon Izates by his father (Bazeus/Monobazus/or Agbarus), a Kingdom Josephus calls 'Carron', i.e., probably 'Carrhae' or ancient 'Haran'.

The conversion story of Izates and his mother Queen Helen also involves the participation of the same Ananias of Acts and Eusebius' story of Agbarus' conversion and takes place both in Southern and Northern Iraq. It is found in both Josephus and Talmudic sources.[43] Three of its principal fixtures are the location of the landing place of Noah's ark 'in their realm', the three-year Famine and their munificence in relieving it in Jerusalem, and a focus on Abraham, whose paradigmatic act of circumcising both himself and all those traveling with him is evoked in the story of Izates' conversion both in Josephus and the Talmud. We have sufficiently explained how this circumcision and conversion is parodied by another episode in Acts – chronologically commensurate with that of Agabus' first Prophecy (though not the obviously equally-spurious story of his second) and Paul's activities in 'Damascus' and, after that, in 'Arabia' – having to do with the conversion of the Treasurer of the Ethiopian Queen on his way home 'from Jerusalem to Gaza' and characterized in Acts 8:27 as 'a eunuch'!

There are several parodies here – none of which without malice. One, as already explained, is of Izates' circumcision. It is important to note that the Roman 'Lex Cornelia de Sicarius et veneficis' (c. 95–136 CE, which we shall discuss further below) viewed circumcision as a form of bodily mutilation – in this, too, the connection of the terminology Sicarios (Iscariot) with the act or idea of circumcision is a fundamental one – it is also a good terminus a quo for Acts as a whole. Another is the perceived Racial identity of these new 'Arab' converts, that is, in Greco-Roman eyes they were black, a matter Agbar Uchama's cognomen, 'the Black', further concretizes. The last is of the mix-up we have highlighted, known as well in the Koran, between Saba' (with an alif)/Southern Arabia/Ethiopia ('Sheba' in the Bible) and Saba' (with an ayin)/Bather – again implying that the conversion of this 'Ethiopian' Queen did involve 'bathing' and/or 'Bathers', namely, Eusebius' Masbuthaeans or those Islam knows as Mughtasilah or Sabaeans.

Furthermore, it should be appreciated that there was no Ethiopian Queen at this time, who sent her 'eunuch's to Jerusalem with all her treasure. What there was, was Queen Helen of Adiabene, who sent 'her Treasury agents' (possibly including even 'Saul and Barnabas') to Egypt and Cyprus to buy grain for Palestine – therefore, the 'Gaza' allusion, 'Gaza' being the gateway to Egypt from Palestine. Finally, as we have stressed, the whole episode parodies the presentation in Josephus and the Talmud, where Izates is studying Genesis 17:10–14 about Abraham's circumcision (also evoked in CD XVI.5–7) when he is asked by the unknown Zealot teacher Eleazar from Galilee if he understands the meaning of what he is reading; whereupon Izates and his brother both immediately circumcise themselves. In Acts 8:32–33, the Queen's eunuch is reading Isaiah 53:7–8, when he is asked the same question by 'Philip' whereupon he, too, immediately descends from his chariot and is 'baptized'.

The Koran Takes over

If we now look at the Koranic reflections in the allusions to 'Hud and Salih'/"Ad and Thamud' of these really pivotal conversions in Northern Syria and Iraq, these occur primarily in Surahs 7:65–84, 11:50–68, 14:9–17, 26:123–144, 29:38, 46:21–35 (mentioning 'the brother of 'Ad') and 54:18–32. In almost every instance, they are immediately preceded by reference to 'the Folk of Noah' and the story of Noah (7:69, 11:32ff., 14:9, 25:37, 51:46, 54:9, etc.), with particular reference to the matter of the ark, which we have already shown to be related to this area of Adiabene between the Euphrates and the Tigris – the area too of Eusebius' 'the Peoples beyond the Euphrates' – where almost all these so-called 'Peoples' considered the ark to have come to rest.

They are also often accompanied by allusion to 'the People of Abraham' and Abraham's trial and suffering, in particular, the 'testing' exemplified in the proposed sacrifice of his son. In the Letter of James and that to the Hebrews, this 'testing' relates to the sacrifice of Isaac which would have had particular importance to someone like King Izates – in our view, the putative respondent for the Letter or Letter(s) known as MMT – who had already demonstrated his interest in Abraham's soteriological state by recognizing circumcision as a sine qua non for conversion.

Though Muslims generally tie this reference to the sacrifice of Ishmael rather than Isaac, it should be appreciated that Ishmael is not mentioned in these contexts even in the Koran, only Isaac (11:50–84 and 37:101–14). It is important to note as well that Agbar VII (c. 109–117) was also known as 'Abgar bar Ezad' ('Abgar the son of Ezad') – nominally 'Izates', whom Josephus at one point too even calls 'Izas'. The point is that one of 'Izates'' sons does nominally seem to have been called 'Agbar' or 'Abgar',[45] thus tying these two families as close as Syro-Armenian tradition seems to think they are and, in effect, merging them, making the conversion episodes involving all these persons more or less part of a single complex.

Several other themes also tie these notices in the Koran to the themes of the conversion stories from Eusebius, Josephus, and the Talmud and traditions swirling about the persons of James and 'Judas Barsabas'. In the first place, there is the matter of the *drought*, always associated with allusions to 'Ad and Hud and the suggestion, connected with the warning Hud delivers, that *he too was a Rainmaker* – a drought that, for some reason, Muslim tradition considers to have lasted for three years.[46] This is the same timeframe of 'the Great Famine' in Josephus and Acts' 'Agabus-as-Prophet' notices (45–48 CE) and a collateral aspect of the stories of the conversions of King Agbarus and Queen Helen. Connected to this is the sub-theme of 'whirlwind' or 'rainmaking' (*Surahs* 11:52, 46:24, etc.) – a theme extremely strong in the newly-reconstructed First Column of the Nahum *Pesher*, and strong too in traditions about James and his reputed rainmaking, as well as Onias the Just or Honi the Circle-Drawer.

There is also the theme of 'fornication' attached to both Noah's and Salih's teaching, as well as the one of Righteousness and Justice.[47] One of these traditions in the Koran even uses a familiar Qumranism – 'turning aside from the right Way' – to describe the warning Hud gives his 'People' (11:56–7, etc.). Then, there is the 'brother' theme that runs through all these Koranic traditions – not only that Hud is the brother of 'Ad (Thaddaeus/Addai), but that Salih is the brother of Thamud (Thomas/Judas Thomas). At one point, the allusion to 'brother' occurs in regard to Thamud (just as with 'Ad above) without even referring to Salih's proper name[48]; but, however it is seen, the term 'brother' is an important element of all these stories as they are presented in the Koran. In our view, Hud is the brother of Salih just as Judas is the brother of James.

Finally, the countryside in question in these Koranic traditions, though admittedly rather obscure, sometimes 'sandhills', sometimes 'whirlwind', is at one point said to abound in 'hills, springs, plains, and date palms' (7:75 and 26:148–9), but always broad plains, richly fertile, with olive trees and the like, which is a very good description of the cattle grazing country around Edessa and Haran and the area between the Euphrates and Tigris Rivers towards Mosul or Adiabene generally. In our view the connections are clear: 'Ad is to be equated with Edessa, Adiabene, Addai, and, by extension, Thaddaeus (even Theudas); Hud with Judas of James, Judas the brother of James, Judas Barsabas, Judas the Zealot, Judas Thomas – and even possibly Judas Iscariot. This is perhaps one of the first – if not the first – time that the relationship of the name 'Hud' with that of the Hebrew *Yehudah* has ever been pointed out; but of course it makes absolute sense, even though those who conserved the tradition had – not surprisingly – long ago forgotten its linguistic basis. Still, the information concerning it is based on a certain reality.

Even the 'Barsabas' allusion, also mentioned at the beginning of Acts in relation to one Joseph who 'was surnamed *Justus*' (no doubt a stand-in for James or the family of 'Joseph' in general) – the defeated candidate in the election to succeed Judas Iscariot – may be another of these allusions to bathing or Bathers as we have seen, i.e., Sabaeans. In fact, Syriac and Muslim sources make it clear that this term means Daily Bather – in Greco-Syriac, as already remarked, Masbuthaean (Sampsaean?), the remnants of which group are still known as 'the *Subba* of the Marshes' today (in so far as they survived Saddam Hussein's attempts to annihilate them) as they were to both al-Biruni and The *Fihrist* in their day. 'Thamud' is to be associated with Thomas in these various stories; and 'Salih' with James the Just or the 'Righteous One' – *the individual who set all these various traditions in motion*.

Not only is the Arab ancestry of all these stories important – ancestry which the Paulinizing narrative of the Book of Acts is quick to relegate to 'Ethiopia', but so is the connecting theme of the ban on 'things sacrificed to idols' – the basis, as we have now several times accentuated, not only of Koranic dietary regulations but also that of *MMT*'s polemicizing directives aimed at a Pious King it seems to imply was wishing to emulate Abraham. It is also the focus of Acts' picture of James' directives to overseas communities and Paul's diminution of these in 1 Corinthians 8 – where because of which, he disingenuously concludes he 'will never eat meat again forever' and that, for him, 'all things are lawful' (repeated twice).

The conclusion is that somehow Muhammad came in touch with these Northern Syrian conversion stories and other quasi-Syriac materials from the Pseudoclementines about James – either through caravan trips to Southern Iraq, where the 'Subba' of the Marshes' still survive, or further North, to the remnants of these lost cultures in Northern Syria. These too are not completely lost but still survive in groups like the present-day "*Alawwis*' or, as they also refer to themselves, 'the *Nusayris*' (i.e., the Nazoraeans once more – another group obviously recognizing multiple 'Alis or Imams/Standing Ones). In all these contexts, the constant emphasis on Abraham, whose homeland this was, is decisive (of course, for Muhammad, 'Abraham's House' turns into 'the *Ka'bah*' at Mecca instead!).

Not only is Abraham a focus for the genesis of Koranic doctrine about Islam, but also for the antecedents to this – the debates between Paul and James regarding Abraham's Salvationary State that permeate the history of Early Christianity and now, seemingly, Qumran as well. By focusing on Abraham, the Damascus Document (III.2–4 and XVI.6–8) throws light on these seemingly arcane Koranic references to Arabian Holy Men or 'Warners' as well. Moreover, by insisting that because he, Isaac, and Jacob 'kept the Commandments' and 'remained Faithful' (not 'straying from them in stubbornness of heart' as some others may have done), they were 'to be reckoned Beloved of God' or 'Friends', an expression paralleled in *Surah* 2:124–141 of the Koran by the new terminology – focusing like James 2:21 –24 on Abraham's obedience to God – *Muslim* or 'He that surrenders to God'. This is the context, too, which in our view can throw light on these seemingly impenetrable and otherwise certainly very recondite Koranic references.

Sicarii Essenes and Zealot Essenes

Another subject having to do with the relationship of early Christian origins in Palestine to the Jerusalem Church of James the Just and to Qumran that we should consider in more depth before closing is the related one of those Hippolytus and perhaps Josephus, in turn, are calling '*Sicarii* Essenes' and/or 'Zealot Essenes' – those Paul and the Book of Acts seem to be alluding to as 'the Circumcision' or 'those insisting on' or 'the Party of the Circumcision'. In a much overlooked description of the Essenes – usually attributed to the Third-Century early-Church theologian/heresiologist in Rome Hippolytus (an attribution that is by no means certain – the sole exemplar was found in the late Nineteenth Century at Mount Athos) – there exists the completely original and different presentation of just who and what the Essenes were, probably going back to a variant version of the received Josephus, perhaps even based on the earlier version of the *Jewish War* he claims he did in Aramaic for the benefit of his Eastern brethren (meaning those in Northern Syria, Adiabene, Mesopotamia, and Persia) most likely to impress upon them the power and might of Rome and discourage them from any attempt to overturn the outcome of the Jewish War.[49]

In this version of the two famous descriptions in the normative Josephus (the originality of which probably identifies it as being based on an earlier source and not a creative effort of Hippolytus himself – if, indeed, he can be definitively identified as the author in question), Four Groups of Essenes are identified and not 'four grades' as in the *Jewish War* or 'four philosophical schools' or 'sects' generally as in the *Antiquities*.[50]

To be sure, the version in Hippolytus has all the main points of the received *Jewish War*, though at times it is clearer – for example, in its description of the progress of the novitiate relative to the tasting of 'the pure food' of the initiates, the resurrection of the body along with the immortality of the soul, and the clear evocation of a 'Last Judgement'.[51] It also includes the additional point about there being marrying and non-marrying Essenes.[52] Regarding aspects such as these, both the *War* and Hippolytus are virtually the same. On the other hand, whereas Josephus speaks of 'four grades' in basically descending order of Holiness, Hippolytus rather speaks of a 'division into Four Parties (perhaps also in some sense relating to stricter or less-strict Holiness or Naziritism) that, 'as time went on', 'did not preserve their system of training in exactly the same manner', that is, his version contains an element of chronological development and perhaps even devolution or changes that occurred over time.[53] This is a new point nowhere mentioned in the normative Josephus and, in this, he is much clearer than the received Josephus.

It is at this point, having raised the issue of 'the passage of time', that Hippolytus adds the new details connecting both the *Sicarii* and the 'Zealots' to the Essenes, that, in the writer's view, have particular relevance to problem many commentators have encountered during the course of Dead Sea Scrolls research in trying to sort the 'Essene' character of the Scrolls at Qumran from the 'Zealot' one,[54] a delineation which will have particular relevance to the picture of both Early Christian History and Palestinian Messianism as well.

The first 'Party' of Essenes, Hippolytus *cum* Josephus identifies, is the familiar one, we know from descriptions in the received Josephus – which also seems to have found its way into depictions of the New Testament's Jesus – that is, that 'they will not handle a current coin of the country' because 'they ought not to carry, look upon, or fashion a graven image'. Here we have the actual Scriptural warrant for the ban – only hinted at in Gospel portraiture.[55] The implication, too, is of 'land' or 'countries' in general, not a particular Nation or Country, since it is immediately followed up by another familiar attribute: that they will not enter into a city 'under a gate containing statues as this too they regard as a violation of Law to pass beneath (such) images' – yet again, a variation on the Mosaic ban on graven images, but this one having particular relevance regarding the unrest we have already chronicled where First-Century Palestinian history is concerned.[56]

The second Group of Essenes is even more striking and gives us the distinct impression that those Josephus pejoratively refers to (again in the First Century) as '*Sicarii*' – and not until 68 CE onwards as 'Zealots' – grew out of the Essene Movement and not as some might have thought from a too-credulous reading of normative Josephus, the Pharisees – a point the present writer has always taken as self-evident.[57] As Hippolytus puts this:

"But the adherents of another Party (the second), if they happen to hear anyone maintaining a discussion concerning God and His Laws and, supposing such a one to be uncircumcised, they will closely watch him (cf. Galatians 2:4–8's 'false brothers stealing in by stealth and spying on the freedom' Paul enjoys 'in Christ Jesus') and when they meet a person of this description in any place alone, they will threaten to slay him if he refuses to undergo the rite of circumcision. Now if the latter kind of person does not wish to comply with this request (a member of this Party of Essenes) will not spare (him), but proceeds to kill. And it is from this behavior that they have received their appellation being called (by some) 'Zealots' but, by others, *Sicarii*."[57]

Not only does this resemble something of what happens to Paul in Acts 21:38 where *Sicarii* are for the only time specifically alluded to and others take a Nazirite-style oath 'not to eat or drink until (they) have killed Paul' (23:12–21), but it is nowhere to be found in the extant Greek version of Josephus' *Jewish War*. Nor is it something Hippolytus was likely to have made up on his own, but it is so striking in its originality as to fairly take the reader's breath away. Whoever was writing it, even if it was not Josephus (the writer thinks that it was Josephus – a Josephus who, for some reason, was willing to be more forthcoming), certainly knew something about this period beyond the usual superficialities. In particular, it also helps explain certain puzzling aspects of the notations 'Zealot' and/or '*Sicarii*'.

Nor could these individuals be considered 'Peace-loving' Essenes. On the contrary, they are quite violent or at least extremely 'steadfast' in their 'dedication to the *Torah*', exhibiting something of the ethos the writer contends one encounters in the Scrolls, which is why, early on, scholars such as G. R. Driver and Cecil Roth were inclined to identify the Qumran Group as 'Zealots'.[58] Nor can anyone who reads the Scrolls fail to be impressed by the extreme 'Zealotry', as we have been highlighting, of the larger part of its attitudes, particularly where the Last Days, the *Torah* of Moses, Backsliders, and the New Covenant were concerned.[59]

Actually, we have already suggested in *James the Brother of Jesus* that the term *Sicarios* might be an anagram for 'Christian' or the latter, at least, a homophonic play on the former. This is certainly the case where Judas the Iscariot (the 'son' or 'brother of Simon [the] Iscariot') is concerned, as all that has occurred is that a *theta* has been substituted for a *sigma* and the first two letters have been reversed.[60] But if we abandon the term 'Christian' for 'Messianist' – as we would most certainly have to do in the Palestine of this Period – then Judas becomes the archetypical Violent or aggressive *Essene* and/or *Messianist, just the kind of person the New Testament is trying to distance itself from* or distance the person of the 'Jesus' it is portraying from.

This is perhaps the most subtle reversal of all and, at the same time, one of the most insidious ironies, to have turned the person who was perhaps the epitome of the Messianic Movement in Palestine – and probably the third brother of James if not of Jesus (i.e., in Lukan Apostle lists, 'Judas of James'; in Syriac texts, 'Judas the Zealot'[61] – just as the putative second brother of James, 'Simon' or 'Simeon', is designated in these same lists as 'Simon *the Zealot*') – into the actual *Betrayer* or, what in the Scrolls would be termed, a *Traitor to the kind of Movement Jesus is supposed to represent.*

What adds to the impression of the truth of this proposition is the fact that Josephus vividly documents how the *Sicarii* did not all die on Masada; but some – for whom he himself is either mistaken or identified with – fled to Egypt, causing the Romans to likewise destroy the Temple that had also been constructed there,[62] and even carried on the agitation in Cyrenaica (modern-day Libya) in North Africa, which was eventually severely repressed in Josephus' own lifetime even there.[63] So to escape such stigmatization, 'Christian' might have been a very useful reformulation or even a term in Greek that might have been used to deride or ridicule – or, vice versa, 'Christians' demanding circumcision, as we shall see, might have been called '*Sicarii*' (just as Hippolytus' Essenes are here), again meant to caricaturize or to mimic but always – as in Acts – disparagingly.

To summarize: three things immediately emerge from this new material attributed to Hippolytus, perhaps drawn from suppressed information previously extant in the various versions of these matters in Josephus: 1) that 'the Zealots' or *Sicarii* were known for their insistence on circumcision – a new point we never heard before but which might have been surmised; 2) that according to their view, one first had to come in under 'the Law' as delineated by 'the *Torah* of Moses' before one could either even discuss God or the subject of the Law (something Paul would have found extremely prohibitive, given his modus operandi and intellectual point-of-view); 3) it was permissible to forcibly circumcise individuals on pain of death or to offer persons interested in such subjects – much as in Islam – the choice of circumcision or death.

Put in another way, like Paul (we shall reserve judgment about James), Essenes of this kind were also interested in non-Jewish converts, but for them circumcision was a *sine qua non* not only for conversion, but even to discuss questions appertaining to Mosaic Law – meaning, you first had to come in under the Law before you could discuss it. No wonder certain Zealots/*Sicarii*/or Nazirites (in particular those designated as the greater part of

James' Jerusalem Church adherents in Acts 21:20) wished to 'kill Paul' (Acts 23:12). Anyone carefully reading Galatians would have to acknowledge that *circumcision was a subject utterly obsessing Paul.*[64] In addition, however, if one has carefully read it together with Acts 15:1–5's prelude to 'the Jerusalem Council' – tendentious or otherwise – asserting that it was triggered by 'some who came down from Judea' who 'were teaching the brothers that, unless you were circumcised, you could not be saved'; then one will realize that what one has before us in Hippolytus' version of Josephus' description of the Essenes is a 'Party of the Circumcision' *par excellence* – in fact, those Paul is calling in Galatians 2:12 either the 'some from James' or 'of the circumcision'.

Hippolytus' *Sicarii* Essenes

Hippolytus rounds out his description of the Four Groups of Essenes, corresponding to the four grades of Essenes in Josephus, with a Third 'Party'. These, he claims, would '*call no man Lord except God even though one should torture or even kill them,*' which not only overlaps Josephus' testimony about the Essene refusal 'to eat forbidden foods' or 'blaspheme the Law-Giver' (meaning Moses) in the *Jewish War*,[65] but even more closely, 'the *Fourth Sect* of Jewish Philosophy' *founded by Judas the Galilean* Josephus describes in the *Antiquities*.[66] In other words, there is a slight shift even in received Josephus in the two accounts in the *War* and the *Antiquities* from Essenes to 'Fourth Philosophy'. Actually what Josephus, in effect, seems to have done is cut a piece from his description of the Essenes in the former and added it to his description of Judas the Galilean's 'Fourth Philosophy' in the latter.[67]

As he continues in both, Josephus identifies this 'Fourth Philosophy' – which at first he had declined to name – as 'the *Sicarii*' but, as already noted, he never actually employs the term 'Zealot' until midway through the War around 68 CE at the point when, along with those he is calling 'Idumaeans', they slaughter James' nemesis and judicial murderer, Ananus ben Ananus, along with Josephus' own close friend, Jesus ben Gamala, and throw their naked bodies outside the city without burial as food for jackals.[68] Josephus follows this up in the *War* with a picture of the Zealots that is so hysterical (including dressing themselves up as women and wearing lipstick) as to verge on the absurd, but by this time he, too, is beside himself with animosity.[69]

For his part, Hippolytus rather follows up his picture of his Third Group – 'those who will call no man Lord' (presumably, not even Jesus) – with a 'Fourth Group' who are basically schismatics and who have 'declined so far from the (Ancient) Discipline' that those 'continuing in the observance of the customs of the Ancestors would not even touch them'.[70] This Group resembles nothing so much as Pauline 'Christians' or perhaps some later, even more 'Gentilizing' or 'Gnosticizing' group. Furthermore, should they happen to come into contact with them, they would immediately resort to water purification as if they had come into contact with someone belonging to a foreign People.[71] One should note the resemblance of this last to Acts 10:28's picture of Peter's words, accurate or not, to 'Cornelius' that it was 'unlawful for a Jewish person to keep company with or come in contact with one of a foreign race'.

We shall further explain the significance in this encounter with 'Cornelius' in Caesarea with regard to the Roman *Lex Cornelia de Sicarius et Veneficis*. This Law, in effect, banned 'circumcision' – at least for those not originally born Jewish – and other similar 'bodily mutilations', circumcision being considered in Roman jurisprudence 'a bodily mutilation' equivalent to 'castration', the application of which became particularly stringent after the fall of the Temple and the War against Rome from 66–73 CE – itself, not significantly, ending in the suicide of 'the *Sicarii*' at Masada.[72]

Though a fourth 'grade', not unsimilar to Hippolytus' Fourth Group, does appear in Josephus' extant *Jewish War*, there it is the more innocuous matter of being in an inferior state of apprenticeship or novitiate as compared with those already far-advanced where Holiness or bodily and spiritual purity were concerned but not as having slipped, as it were, out of the 'Jewish fold' altogether, as in Hippolytus, to be looked upon as virtual foreigners and/or untouchables.[73] This is a significant discrepancy between the two accounts and, on the face of it, Hippolytus' makes more sense, since it is hard to imagine such a horror of contact or 'touching' directed simply against junior members in a less-advanced state of ritual purity. In this context too, one should recollect all the various 'touching' episodes with regard to Jesus in the Gospels.[74] In fact, Hippolytus' 'Fourth Group' resembles nothing so much as the new more 'Paulinized' Christians we have been highlighting (of the kind Peter learns to accept) following, in the writer's view, a less stringent, more extra-legal form of Essenism totally alien to those preceding it. It is for this reason that it becomes impossible either to associate with or even 'to touch them' as Hippolytus would have it.

This being said, Hippolytus now returns to his earlier description of the Three Groups of Essenes – or, at least, the two earlier ones, that is, those he calls 'Zealot Essenes' and '*Sicarii* Essenes', if in fact they can be distinguished in any real way from the Third (those willing to undergo any form of torture rather than 'call any man Lord') – because he now picks up the points paralleled in normative Josephus about the longevity of Essenes, their temperateness, and the incapacity they display of becoming angry.[75] But he also now returns a second time to his previous description of how 'they despised death' and the willingness they showed to undergo torture of any kind amalgamating, as just indicated, parts from both Josephus' descriptions of Essenes in the *Jewish War* and 'the Fourth Philosophical Sect' (later either *Sicarii* or 'Zealots') in the *Antiquities*.[76]

In any event, in this passage from Hippolytus' presentation, the reader will immediately recognize the description in the *War* of the bravery shown by the Essenes in 'our recent War with the Romans' (that is, unlike Pharisees, Herodians, Establishment Sadducees, and Christians – meaning 'Pauline' ones and not *Sicarii* – the Essenes *did participate in the War against Rome* and they were on the side of the insurgents, whatever the orientation[77]) that no matter how much they were 'racked and twisted, burned and broken', they could not be made to 'blaspheme the Law-giver (meaning Moses – here the 'blaspheming' charge again) or 'eat forbidden things'.[78]

It is this last which is the pivotal point, for Hippolytus now refines it as well – in the process, bringing it in even closer agreement with and, as a consequence, the actual reverse once again of what Paul is so concerned about from 1Corinthians 8–11 where he is in the process, not only of attacking persons like James, but all persons 'with weak consciences' such as these same Essenes in Hippolytus – persons whose 'conscience was so weak' (8:4) that they would not even 'eat things sacrificed to idols', considering such fare 'polluting' or 'defiled' (8:7). This point is not only pivotal, it is *decisive*. Considering the commitment, personal sacrifice, and dedication of such persons, as Hippolytus (in this, supported by normative Josephus) will now go on to describe them, this position expressed by Paul in 1 Corinthians is not only disrespectful, deceitful, and unnecessarily abusive, it is contemptible. As Hippolytus expresses this: 'If, however, anyone would attempt even to torture such persons in order to induce them either to blaspheme the Law or eat things sacrificed to an idol, he will not achieve his end for (an Essene of this kind) submits to death and endures any torment rather than *violate his conscience* (Paul's 'conscience' language).'[79]

The reader now has the option of deciding which version of Josephus is more accurate – or are all three accurate? – the *Jewish War*'s less specific and vaguer 'rather than eat forbidden things' or the more precise and, as we can now see, *MMT*-oriented 'refusal to eat things sacrificed to idols' reflecting James' directives to overseas communities. Nor is this to say anything about Paul's attack on those refusing to eat these same 'things sacrificed to idols' in 1 Corinthians 8:3–10:23 climaxing with his proclamation of 'Communion with the Blood of Christ' in 10:16.

Sicarii Essenes, the *Lex Cornelia de Sicarius*, and the *Sicaricon*

Therefore we now approach a conundrum: the sort of Essenes described by Hippolytus – in particular, those he is calling either 'Zealot Essenes' or '*Sicarii* Essenes' or both, who apparently will not tolerate anyone discussing the *Torah* who is not circumcised and are prepared to kill anyone doing so who refuses or declines to be circumcised – are, also, prepared to undergo any sort of torture rather than 'eat things sacrificed to an idol'. This certainly does represent a refinement of Josephus with particular relevance both to 'the Party of the Circumcision' and those Paul refers to with such evident antipathy in Galatians 2:12 as the 'some from James' and 'those of the circumcision'.

We have already called attention to the section of *MMT* having to do with this complete and total ban on consuming 'things sacrificed to idols'. Furthermore, we have also called attention to Columns XLVI–XLVII of the Temple Scroll dealing with 'pollution of the Temple' as well and barring various classes of 'unclean' persons and things from the Temple – in particular, enigmatically evoking someone or something called '*Bela*' and including 'skins sacrificed to idols'.[80] Moreover, looked at from another perspective and through another vocabulary, these kinds of bans represent just another variation of the theme of 'pollution of the Temple' – which the version of James' directives in Acts 15:19 refers to as 'the pollutions of the idols' and which Paul was accused of doing by the crowd in the Temple in Acts 21:28 by 'bringing Greeks into the Temple' – the third and perhaps most decisive of 'the Three Nets of *Belial*' charges in the Damascus Document, the 'Nets' with which he both deceives and subverts Israel.[81]

Before pulling all these strands of inquiry together, we should perhaps turn to one final source relevant to discussing such '*Sicarii* Essenes' and bearing on the possible circumcision they indulged in – possibly with the *sica*-like knife, from which Josephus claimed they originally derived their name[82] – and the view in Roman jurisprudence of circumcision as bodily mutilation.

Before doing so, however, it is important to remark that even in the *Jewish War*, as we have it, forcible circumcision was to some extent part of the program of those Revolutionaries Josephus sometimes is calling 'Zealots' and at other times '*Sicarii*'. This is particularly the case in the episode at the start of the War against Rome, when the Jewish insurgent forces have been successful (with the help, it should be appreciated, of two other descendants of Queen Helen, Monobazus and Kenedaeus, who martyred themselves at the Pass at Beit Horon) and where the Commander of the Roman garrison in Jerusalem is *offered and, in fact, accepts just such a choice*, while the rest of those under his command are butchered by those Josephus likes to call 'the Innovators' (he means, those 'Innovations' into customary legal practice of which he claims – not a little facilely – 'our Ancestors were before previously unaware').[83] There are also further examples of this in the *Jewish War*.[84]

Curiously, the first clue one comes upon relating to the circumcision aspect of the terminology is the denotation by Origen of *Sicarii* as those who have either circumcised themselves or forcibly circumcised others in violation of the Roman *Lex Cornelia de Sicarius et Veneficis* – the Roman Law banning such circumcision (except, it would appear, where Jews *per se* were concerned – meaning it obviously applied to converts who were Gentiles).[85]

In *Contra Celsus*, Origen specifically describes the *Sicarii* as being called this 'on account of the practice of circumcision', which in their case he defines as 'mutilating themselves contrary to the established laws and customs' and as being inevitably, therefore, 'put to death' on this account.[86] Of course, this is in Origen's time in the Third Century CE. It does not necessarily mean that such a total ban would have been in effect prior to the First Jewish Revolt against Rome when the problem would probably not yet have been deemed sufficiently serious to merit it – not probably until the aftermath of the Second Jewish Revolt, when it is clear things became more and more repressive in this regard. Nor, as he continues, does one ever hear – that is, in his own time – of a 'Sicarius' reprieved from such a punishment (even) if he recants, the evidence of circumcision being sufficient to ensure the death of him who has undergone it. Not only should one not ignore the harshness of this, but the text is doubly ironic for we know that Origen himself was just such a person, that is, 'a Sicarius', and reportedly had castrated himself – not, presumably, because of his 'zeal for the Law' or circumcision but rather for celibacy.[87] Nevertheless, where non-Jews, anyhow, were concerned – and this, no doubt, included Pauline-style converts – castration of this kind was clearly being seen as the equivalent of circumcision – or, rather, vice versa, the Romans viewed circumcision as just such a bodily mutilation of the flesh and a variety of castration.

Jerome confirms this in claiming that Origen 'castrated himself with a knife' (thereby clarifying the 'sica' part of the 'Sicarius' vocabulary) and ridiculing him by quoting, significantly, Paul's own critique of 'zealotry' and 'Zealots' from Romans 10:2, saying he did this out of 'zeal for God but not according to Knowledge'.[88] In this regard, not only should one bear in mind Jesus' statement in Matthew 19:12 about 'those making themselves eunuchs for the Kingdom of Heaven's sake', which is obviously what Origen had done; but also that Jerome is using here the very language Paul uses in 1 Corinthians 8:1–2, in his usual *strophe/ antistrophe/epode* lyric-poetical/rhetorical style having to do with 'things sacrificed to idols' and 'Knowledge puffing up', not 'building up' (as it should): 'but if anyone thinks he has known anything, he has not known anything as he ought to know it'.

In this manner, both he and the passage from Paul he is quoting from Romans 10:2 show their awareness of 'Zealots' (as Paul does elsewhere[89]) and that the whole matter had something to do with such 'zeal' (Paul displays the same *Knowledge* in Galatians 4:16–5:13 where he is speaking about 'becoming your Enemy', zeal, and, of course, such 'cutting off') – in particular, that such an act would have been typical of just such 'Sicarii Essenes' or 'Zealot Essenes', as the case may have been – to say nothing of 'the Circumcision Party' of James.

In fact, Paul goes on in Romans 10:3–4 to ridicule the reputed Righteousness of such persons, a concept he even evokes in Galatians 5:14 after expressing his desire (in speaking about 'the flesh') that he 'wished' such persons who were 'troubling' his communities would 'themselves cut off' and, facetiously parodying James, 'for all the Law is fulfilled in one word, "you shall love your neighbor as yourself"'. He also does so as follows: 'For being ignorant of God's Righteousness and seeking to establish their own Righteousness, they do not submit to God's Righteousness, for Christ is the End of the Law for Righteousness.' One could not have a better example of the sophistic manner in which Paul is transforming the Righteousness-oriented interpretation of 'the Zadokite Covenant' and those like 'the *Doresh ha-Torah*' who 'sought (God) with a whole heart' and, presumably for that reason, 'went out from the Land of Judah to dwell in the Land of Damascus' and erect 'the New Covenant' there. Nor is this to say anything further about Acts 21:20's final designation of the greater part of James' Jerusalem Church followers in Paul's seeming final encounter with James as '*all Zealots for the Law*'!

The Roman *Lex Cornelia de Sicarius,* which seems actually to have been attributed to Publius Cornelia Scipio (therefore the *Cornelia* part of the statute's designation) and which, Origen attests, the judges in his time were so zealously enforcing; according to Dio Cassius, seems to have first come into real effect in Nerva's time (96–98 CE),[90] that is, in the aftermath of the First Jewish Revolt against Rome. But the sudden interest in it and its connection, in particular, to circumcision, in fact, appears to be linked both to the *Sicarii* and the whole issue of the First Revolt and, even finally, the Second.

Certainly by Hadrian's time (117–138 CE) and his actual prohibition of circumcision in the period of the Second Revolt, this linkage is reflected in a law, the *Ius Sicaricon*, which related to the confiscation of enemy property – primarily, it would seem, in Palestine. It was also, it appears, connected to those defying his decree banning circumcision who at the same time appear to have participated in the War against Rome.[91] The repression of circumcision particularly in relation to those Jews being called '*Sicarii*' – now, seemingly, because of their insistence on circumcision and not so much, as Josephus had previously (perhaps somewhat disingenuously) presented it, their propensity for assassination – by Hadrian's time had become extraordinarily severe and this had to mean, once again, where *non-Jews* were concerned.

In Tanaitic literature the term *Sicaricon* actually describes the property, including land and slaves, which was expropriated from Jews by the Roman Authorities in the aftermath of the Second Jewish Revolt because of the perception of their participation in this War.[92] Against this background, it seems clear that the term '*Sicarii*', at this point, was not only being used both to characterize the most extreme partisans of Revolt against Rome, but also those 'insisting on circumcision' as a *sine qua non* for conversion – in particular, 'the Party' or 'those of the Circumcision' as we have been encountering them above – now, in the wake of all the unrest, being expressly prohibited in an official manner by Rome. In this regard one should pay particular attention to the designation of 'Judas Iscariot' in the Gospels as having some relationship to or, in some manner, parodying or holding practices of this kind up to contempt, ridicule, or loathing, that is – if one likes – he is 'Judas *the Circumciser*', a matter rarely if ever addressed in New Testament or Scrolls research.

The Party of the Circumcision

There is no doubt that those represented by the Scrolls were extremely 'zealous for circumcision' too. This position is perhaps made most forcibly in CD XVI (according to the Cairo recension, renumbered as CD X) at the beginning of the more statutory part of the Damascus Document where 'the oath of the Covenant which Moses made with Israel … to return to the *Torah* of Moses with a whole heart and soul' is the paramount proposition.[93] One should also compare this with Romans 10:5 where Paul, quoting Leviticus 18:5, speaks as well of how 'Moses writes of the Righteousness which is of the Law that the man who has done these things shall live by them' before going on to trump it in Romans 10:6 with what he calls 'the Righteousness of Faith'.

Per contra, however, CD XVI emphasizes the binding nature of oaths taken 'to return to' and 'keep the Commandments of the *Torah* at the price even of death'[94] – again a particularly important emphasis for those prepared, as per Hippolytus' and Josephus' descriptions of both *Sicarii* Essenes and Zealot Essenes, 'to undergo any torture rather than disavow the Law'.[95] This is repeated with the admonition, evoking both Deuteronomy 23:24 and 27:26 and the 'curses' of the Covenant attached thereto, that: 'even at the price of death, a man shall not fulfill any vow he might have sworn to turn aside from the *Torah*' (n.b., once more this very important allusion to the phraseology of 'turning aside from the *Torah*').[96]

It is in this same Column, and in this context, that Abraham's circumcision is evoked and, as already intimated, the most fearsome oaths of retribution attached to the performance of it. In other words, once again, we are not really in an environment of *Peaceful Essenes*, however such are defined, and certainly not of Paulinism, but rather one of absolute and violent vengeance and a life-and-death attachment to 'the *Torah* of Moses' however it might have been acquired – whether undertaken at birth or by conversion. As this is put at this point in the Damascus Document: 'And on the day upon which the man swears upon his soul (or 'on pain of death') to return to the *Torah* of Moses, the Angel of Divine Vengeance will turn aside from pursuing him, provided that he (the oath-taker) fulfills his word. It is for this reason Abraham circumcised himself on the very day of his being informed (of these things).'[97] The reference is to Genesis 17:9–27, in particular, Abraham's obligation to 'circumcise the flesh of his foreskin' and that of all those of his household – the addition of this last being an important addendum – as 'a sign of the Covenant' which, the text observes, he accomplished (just as in CD XVI.6 above) 'on that very day' – though he was ninety-nine years old!

But, of course, this is the very same passage the Talmud says Queen Helen of Adiabene's two sons were reading when the teacher from Galilee identified by Josephus as 'Eleazar' gainsaid Ananias' and his associate's previous tuition, asking them rather (just as Philip in Acts 8:30) whether they 'understood the meaning of what' they were reading. It is at this point, having understood the true nature of the conversion they had undertaken 'to fulfill' that, in both Josephus and the Talmud – *'on that very day'* they, too, immediately went out and *circumcised themselves*.[98]

As already pointed out, the very words attributed to Eleazar here are being parodied in Acts' version of 'Philip''s encounter with 'the Ethiopian Queen's *eunuch*' who asks the very same question. The caricature of circumcision as *castration* here is certainly purposeful, as is that of the Queen as a 'Black' or an 'African' – much like Agbar *Uchama* (her putative 'husband' or descendant). Only now the 'eunuch', as we saw, is reading Isaiah 53:7–8 (central lines in the fundamental 'Christian' proof-text Isaiah 53:1-12) not Genesis 17:10–14 and, in Acts 8:38, he likewise 'orders the chariot to stop' and *immediately proceeds to be baptized*. In fact, the creation of this canny caricature can undoubtedly be dated within the complex of notices we are discussing regarding this subject.

To go back to CD XVI.1–8, there can be little doubt of the aggressive and uncompromising ferocity of this passage and others like it in the Scrolls where even 'the Avenging Fury of the Angel of *Mastema*'[99] and 'a person vowing another to death by the laws of the Gentiles being put to death himself'[100] are also evoked. The ferocity in question is more in keeping with Hippolytus' description of 'the *Sicarii* Essenes' who would either 'threaten to kill a man' or 'forcibly circumcise him' if they heard him discussing God and His Laws but who, by the same token, would 'submit to any death or endure any torture rather than violate (their) conscience' (i.e., 'blaspheme the Law' in Josephus and Paul's 'conscience' language again) or 'eat that which was sacrificed to an idol'.

We have continually stressed how this issue of 'abstaining from things sacrificed to idols' is the backbone of James' directives to overseas communities at the conclusion of the Jerusalem Council in Acts 15:20 and 15:29. It is reiterated in Acts 21:26 when Paul is sent into the Temple by James for a Nazirite-style penance because the majority of James' supporters are 'Zealots for the Law'. Not only does the subject preoccupy Paul from 1 Corinthians 8–11, where he uses it as a springboard to introduce his idea of 'Communion with the Blood of Christ'; but also to affirm that 'an idol is nothing in the world' (8:4 – nor is 'that which is sacrificed to an idol anything') and to insist that one should 'not inquire on account of conscience' (10:25–29).

As already described, the subject forms the background to the whole section in *MMT* on bringing gifts and sacrifices on behalf of Gentiles into the Temple (a ban, according to Josephus, of which 'our Forefathers were previously unaware' and the issue which, according to him, triggered the War against Rome in 66 CE[101]) – 'sacrifices by Gentiles' in the Temple, in particular, being treated under the expression that 'we consider they sacrifice to an idol' or 'they are sacrifices to an idol' generally.[102] Though the exemplars are a little fragmentary here, the meaning is clear and the words 'sacrifice to an idol' shine clearly through.

The conclusion should probably be that the picture of the *Sicarii* in Josephus, as descending from the teaching of 'Judas and Sadduk' during the unrest of 4 BCE–7 CE (coincident with what the Gospels picture as 'the birth of Christ') and at the forefront of the unrest in the Fifties–Sixties CE in the Temple, when Josephus is finally willing to explain – however tendentiously – the meaning of their several denotations, is only partly accurate. As these events transpire, these same *Sicarii* are also the ones who commit mass suicide at Masada while others flee down to Egypt, resulting in the additional destruction of the Temple at Leontopolis there[103] – and finally into Cyrenaica in North Africa where unrest continues well into the Nineties and beyond, as Josephus also reports.[104]

But Josephus is perhaps only being partially forthcoming when he tells us that the *Sicarii* derived their name from the beduin or Yemeni-style dagger (which resembled the Roman *sica*) they carried beneath their garments to dispatch their enemies, thus giving the impression that they were simply cutthroats or assassins and nothing more. As just underscored, this picture is picked up in Acts – probably also somewhat tendentiously – where Paul, after disturbances provoked by the perception of his having brought Gentiles and, presumably, their gifts into the Temple (cf. the outcry in Acts 21:28 that 'he has brought Greeks into the Temple and polluted this Holy Place'), is queried by the Roman Chief Captain, who rescues him from the Jewish mob 'seeking to kill him', 'Are you not the Egyptian who recently caused a disturbance and led four thousand *Sicarii* out into the desert?'

This is only true as far as it goes. In the light of the materials from Hippolytus, Origen, Dio Cassius, and Jerome designating those who circumcise or forcibly circumcise others as being *Sicarii* too, we can perhaps go further. As we have seen, this designation was based on the eponymous body of Roman traditional law forbidding castration and other similar bodily mutilations particularly of the genitalia, the *Lex Cornelia de Sicarius et Veneficis*, which grew evermore onerous from the time of Nerva to Hadrian and beyond so that, by Origen's time, Third-Century Roman magistrates were applying it as a matter of course.

This law evidently bounced back on the Revolutionaries of the Bar Kochba Period – who were, obviously, also seen as *Sicarii* – to the extent that a Regulation, known in the Talmud as 'the *Sicaricon*', was applied to them which allowed the Government to confiscate their property in the aftermath of the Uprising. The conclusion would appear to be that the *Sicarii* everyone always talks so confidently about were also known for *forcible circumcision* – or rather (something like the Islam of a later incarnation), they offered those having the temerity to discuss the validity of Mosaic Law without first entering 'the Covenant' (whether converts or foreigners) the choice of circumcision or death.

Judging by the severity of the efforts expended against them in this period, this conduct does not seem to have been very well received by their Roman Overlords, who abrogated all the privileges the Jews had previously enjoyed regarding this practice, at least where those perceived of as being *Sicarii* Revolutionaries were concerned. Since the Romans looked upon circumcision as little more than a variety of bodily mutilation, this is something of the private joke shining through Acts' tendentious picture of the convert characterized as 'the Ethiopian Queen's *eunuch*'. Based on the somewhat incomplete and perhaps even dissembling picture in Josephus – he certainly seems to have known more, as his furious remonstrances and self-justifications in both the *War* and the *Vita* on the subject of *Sicarii* unrest in Cyrenaica at the end of the First Century indicate[105] – readers have concluded that the 'knife' from which the Greek version of their name was derived (this could hardly have been what they called themselves in Hebrew or Aramaic) was simply that of 'the Assassin'. In the light, however, of the picture arising out of the new material we have assembled above, there is no justification whatever for this conclusion.

So great was the attachment of the *Sicarii* to and their insistence on circumcision that they probably were far better known as 'the Party of the Circumcision' *par excellence*, as Paul seems to so contemptuously dismiss them. Not only is this the name Paul seems to give in Galatians 2:12 to the Party led by James, but it is an issue with which he wrestles, as we have seen, with extremely high emotion throughout Galatians, including his final contemptuous jibe at those he claims in 5:12 are *disturbing his communities* (presumably with circumcision): 'would they would themselves cut off'. Even the expression 'cut off' in this context is but a thinly disguised play on Essene and Qumran excommunication practices and a euphemism, as we have seen, in wide use in the Damascus Document, particularly where 'Backsliders from the Law' were concerned.[106]

Therefore this *knife*, which some saw as the assassin's, probably doubled as that of the circumciser's. In fact, the emphasis should probably be the other way round. The knife *Sicarii* Essenes were using to circumcise or forcibly circumcise those they heard discussing the Law in an illegitimate manner probably doubled as the one they used to assassinate; and, just as Origen who had himself mutilated his own sexual parts reports, this is how such 'Mutilators' or 'Circumcisers' were known in the Greco-Roman world. In our view this is a more insightful way of understanding the literature found at Qumran which, as we have been demonstrating, did contain a contingent of Gentile believers in associated status, referred to in CD, for instance, as the *Nilvim*/God-Fearers/or Joiners.[107]

As stated in Column XX.19f. and 34 of the Damascus Document, it was for such persons – to whom 'God would reveal Salvation (*Yesha'*) and who would 'see His Salvation' (*Yeshu'ato*) because 'they reckoned' and 'took refuge in His Holy Name' – that 'a Book of Remembrance would be written out'. It is this which, we contend, is parodied in the words, 'Do this in *remembrance* of me', attributed to Jesus by Paul in 1 Corinthians 11:25 and echoed in Last Supper scenarios in the Synoptics (Luke 22:19 and pars.).

Early commentators had difficulty reconciling the self-evident militancy, intolerance, and aggressiveness that run through almost all the Scrolls with their self-evident Essene-like characteristics. This conundrum is resolved if we take Hippolytus' additions to Josephus *at face value* – additions which, as already argued, Hippolytus would have been *incapable of inventing or fabricating himself* in the Third Century but which were either suppressed or diffused in alternate versions of Josephus' *Jewish War*, either by himself in Rome or others, as the true apocalyptic Messianism of the Essenes, represented by the literature that has now been found at Qumran, came to be more fully realized.

Therefore, it should be clear that what we have before us in this literature are the documents of the *Sicarii* Essene or Zealot Essene Movement (for Hippolytus, they are the same), a Movement which (as the First Century progressed) became indistinguishable from those Paul is identifying as the representatives or 'some from James', those who were insisting – to use the language of Acts 15:1 – that, 'unless you were circumcised according to the Custom of Moses, you could not be saved' or, as Paul characterizes them too, 'the Party of the Circumcision'.

When one takes Dio Cassius, Origen, and Jerome at face value – understanding the *Sicarii* in the light of the *Lex Cornelia de Sicarius* – not as 'Assassins' or 'Cutthroats', as their enemies would have us see them, but as *Circumcisers utilizing the Circumciser's knife* and even sometimes – as at Qumran and Masada – as Messianists ('Christians' according to some vocabularies or, as we have also described them, 'Messianic Sadducees') – then, I submit, *most of the difficulties hitherto surrounding these issues in considering the Dead Sea Scrolls evaporate.*

'The Cup of the Lord' and 'the Blood of Christ'

Let us close by recapitulating the arguments for the relationship of Paul's and the Synoptics' 'Cup of the New Covenant in (the) Blood' of Christ and the Damascus Document's 'New Covenant in the Land of Damascus'. At first glance there is no relationship between the two at all except the reference to the New Covenant. On further analysis, however, there is – a linguistic and/or an esoteric one. This will depend, as we have been demonstrating, on letters that have a certain signification in the Hebrew moving over into the Greek to produce a slightly different one.

Earlier, we pointed out that letters with unusual significance in Hebrew – for example, *B-L-'/'swallowing'* and the root of *Belial*, *Bela'*, and *Balaam* – moved over into the Greek with entirely different signification as if the letters themselves (*balla'* in the Hebrew/*ballo* in Greek) carried some special importance whatever their meaning. In particular, this usage – which had to do in both languages with a sort of 'Devilishness' – was important. To illustrate this, we showed that the 'swallowing' language applied in Hebrew in the Habakkuk *Pesher* to the destruction or death of the Righteous Teacher and his followers among 'the Poor' (as well as to the Wicked Priest) had a certain linguistic relationship to the 'casting out'/'casting down' language in New Testament, Josephus, and early Church accounts of the deaths of Stephen, Ananus, James, and Zachariah ben Bariscaeus respectively.

This 'casting out' language was also to be found in 'Nets' and exorcism symbolism generally in the New Testament, not to mention the 'expulsion' language Josephus employs in his description of Essene banishment practices. In addition, it was easy to see how *Belial* and his Nets, in the language of Qumran allusion, moved into *Balaam*, *Balak*, their Nets, *Babylon*, and even *Beelzebul* in Revelation and the Gospels. As an aside to this, *Belial* itself connects in the Greek with *Diabolos* – in English, 'the Devil' – and, in Arabic, with *Iblis* in the Koran.[108]

When considering 'Damascus', as in 'the New Covenant in the Land of Damascus' in CD VI.19 and VIII.21/XIX.33–34, the Hebrew for 'Blood', as previously explained, is *Dam* and, for Cup, it is *Chos*, both forming the two parts of the transliteration into Greek of the Hebrew place name '*Damascus*'. Though in Hebrew, this particular homophone appears only to work for the first syllable, '*Dam*' or 'Blood'; if the second part of the Hebrew expression for 'Damascus' – '*Dammashek*,' namely *mashek/mashkeh*, a fourth form verbal noun, meaning, 'to give to drink' – is taken into consideration, it also works out for the second syllable even in Hebrew.

Not only will this ultimately link up with the same phraseology, 'giving to drink' or the command to 'drink this', a staple of New Testament accounts of these solemn pronouncements, attributed by all – except the Gospel of John – to Jesus himself, but it is also an allusion Paul seems to take particular (if malicious) pleasure in enunciating when – after picturing in 1 Corinthians 11:24–25 'the Lord Jesus', 'having dined' and 'saying', 'This Cup is the New Covenant in my Blood. Do this as often as you drink it in Remembrance of me'; and proceeding in the typical *strophe-antistrophe-epode* style to affirm: 'For as often as you eat this bread and drink this Cup, you proclaim the death of the Lord until he comes'; he then, seemingly, parodies these 'drinking' connotations with the belligerent and intolerant passages: 'So that whosoever … shall drink the Cup of the Lord unworthily shall be guilty of the body and Blood of the Lord' (11:27) – and, once again, reaffirming this: 'For he who eats and drinks unworthily, eats and drinks Judgment to himself, not seeing through to the body of the Lord' (11:29). Whatever one may think of the theological and personal attitudes he displays here, these denotations in Hebrew at the root of the Greek transliteration 'Damascus' become the essence of the New Testament theological approach of 'the New Covenant' – now not 'in the Land of Damascus' – but 'in the Cup of (the) Blood' of Christ. Though the arguments in support of this insight are linguistic and textual, given the importance of the material under consideration, one would be unwise to ignore or pass over the correspondence between these two formulations, treating it as if it did not exist or was simply a fortuitous accident. Even if only the 'Blood' part of the equivalence were to be entertained – which in itself would be sufficient corroboration – what is the probability of such a surprising correspondence being accidental? Is it logical to think that a focus such as this on the twin concepts of 'Cup' and 'Blood' – the homophonic equivalents in Hebrew of the syllables *Dam* and *Chos* composing the Greek transliteration 'Damascus' – is simply accidental?

But the second part of the designation 'Damascus', involving the Hebrew root '*Sh-K-H*' – in its verbal morphology, *mashkeh*, meaning 'give to drink' – works out as well; and, in addition to the self-evident *Dam*/Blood and *Chos*/Cup equivalences in the Greek, this additional *mashkeh*/'give to drink' equivalence in Hebrew would appear to be definitive.

Even if it should be granted that New Testament writers such as Paul, to say nothing of those producing the Synoptic Gospels – understood an esoteric or allegorical equivalence such as this (the fusion of Damascus/*Dammashek* providing an especially bountiful harvest for those interested in esoteric exegesis of this kind), the question remains whether those who composed the documents found at Qumran understood the allusion Damascus/*Dammashek* in this manner as well. From the perspective of the interpretation of texts (if not philology itself), the only plausible way to answer a question such as this is to look at the texts themselves and see how the expression 'the New Covenant' is used in them.

Allusion to 'the New Covenant' is first found in the prophecies of Jeremiah 31:31–34 which are, as it turns out, quoted in full in the sections of Hebrews 8:8–12 already alluded to above. These are followed up by 'new heart and new Spirit' imagery in Ezekiel 11:19 and 36:26 which Paul variously adopts to his own purposes while conveniently discarding the phrase 'keep My Laws' associated with the phrase in almost all original contexts.[109]

The usage is then picked up again in 'Last Supper' scenarios in the Synoptics (though not in John) and 1 Corinthians 11:25. Thereafter it is fleshed out definitively in Hebrews 8:13, 9:14–15, 10, 10–20, and 12:24 (here not 'New' but 'fresh' Covenant), though in these last with an emphasis on the 'Blood' aspect of the phraseology rather than the 'Cup'. In the Dead Sea Scrolls, aside from the one negative evocation of 'the New Covenant' in the context, seemingly, of an allusion to 'Traitors' attached to it in 1QpHab II.3 already called attention to above, it is found almost exclusively in the Damascus Document and, there, almost never unaccompanied by allusion to 'the Land of Damascus'.

In the Damascus Document, the first allusion to 'Damascus' occurs in Column VI.19 in the extension or recapitulation of the earlier exegesis of the Zadokite Covenant in III.21–IV.4. Though in the latter exposition – '*waw*' constructs seemingly having been deliberately added to break up the original appositive of 'the Priests, the Sons of Zadok, Levites' in Ezekiel 44:15 – 'the Priests' were defined (somewhat esoterically) as 'the Penitents of Israel who went out from the Land of Judah and the *Nilvim* with them' (seemingly in exposition of or esoterically-equivalent to the term 'Levites' in Ezekiel). The third group, of course, were 'the Sons of Zadok' who were defined both more eschatologically and, as we have seen, in terms of 'standing'.

For its part 'the Land of Damascus', which did not actually appear at this point in Column Four, was rather picked up in the next exposition, this time of Numbers 21:1 in Column Six, which contained a similar apposition, namely, the two parallel categories of 'the Princes' and 'the Nobles of the People'. Not insignificantly, the phrase, 'to dwell' or 'live in the Land of Damascus' added here, enjoys a direct parallel in Acts 9:22 which in detailing Paul's activities in the area actually makes reference to 'the Jews who dwelt in Damascus' and in Acts 26:20, now picturing Paul himself describing this as 'Damascus first and Jerusalem and in all the region of Judea and to the Gentiles', the whole passage containing several inversions of known Qumran usage or ideology.[110]

Furthermore, we have pointed out that a certain amount of the exposition of Columns IV–VIII and XIX–XX of CD seems to be addressed to or signal a cadre of Gentiles associated with the Community, that is, in an associated 'God-Fearer' status.[111] This is particularly true of the manner in which CD IV.3 expounded the term 'Levites' from Ezekiel 44:15 in terms of *Nilvim*/Joiners – a typical expression in Hebrew documents for 'Gentiles attaching themselves to the *Torah*' – and the way VI.3–11 applies the language of Isaiah 54:16 to its evocation of 'the Staff' or 'the *Mehokkek*', an individual which it defines (in another esoteric exegesis) as 'the *Doresh*' or 'Seeker after the *Torah*'. In fact, that Isaiah 54–56, from which this latter expression is taken, is being directly applied to such '*Nilvim*', to wit, 'the foreigners who have joined themselves to the Lord..., keep My Sabbaths ... and hold fast to the Covenant', is made explicit in Isaiah 56:3–6.

In the second appositive cluster in CD VI.3–9, 'the Nobles' or 'Leaders of the People', subsequently defined as 'those who came to dig the Well with the staves' – meaning the *hukkim* or 'Laws' legislated by the *Mehokkek*/*Doresh*/Interpreter/Seeker (all these, as we saw, are play-on-words) – are now combined with 'the Princes' to develop a third overall category 'the Diggers'. This, in turn, produces the exposition: 'the Diggers are the Penitents of Israel who went out from the Land of Judah to dwell in the Land of Damascus.' 'The Diggers' here are, self-evidently, synonymous with 'the Priests' in the earlier exposition in Column IV.2–3 of Ezekiel 44:15, 'the Land of Damascus' now being expressly and specifically added, probably because of the coming evocation of 'the New Covenant' which is going to be described later as being 'erected' there in connection with the 'digging of the Well'. For their part, 'the Nobles' or 'Leaders of the People' are presumably those already in 'the Land of Damascus' who 'came to dig the Well' with 'the Seeker's or *Doresh*'s 'staves', that is, his Laws or Statutes.

As already remarked, much of this is rather obscure or arcane – in fact about as arcane as Pauline/Hebrews' exposition of 'the Cup of the New Covenant in (his) Blood' though from a completely opposite ideological perspective – but some sense can be made of it. 'The Leaders of the People' ('Peoples' carrying on the 'Gentiles' theme) are now to be identified with 'the *Nilvim*' of the earlier exegesis – People/Peoples, as repeatedly indicated, being a typical Qumran allusion to Gentiles. According to Acts 26:17, even Paul evokes similar usages when he speaks of 'being taken out from among the People and the Peoples to whom I now send you'. In fact, throughout the rest of CD, as we have emphasized, there is continual allusion to 'fearing God's Name' and 'God-Fearers', accompanied by pointed allusions to 'being steadfast' or 'holding fast' – meaning 'to the Covenant' or 'the *Torah*'.

This is typically put in Column XX.17–20 of Ms. B as follows: 'But the Penitents from Sin in Jacob kept the Covenant of God. Then each man shall speak to his neighbor, each strengthening his brother, to support their step in the Way of God ... and a Book of Remembrance was written out before Him for God-Fearers and for those reckoning His Name until God shall reveal Salvation (*Yesha*) and Justification to those fearing His Name.'

It should also be noted that these are exactly the parameters of Isaiah 56:1, *Zedakah* (Justification) and *Yeshu'ati* (My Salvation/My Jesus) introducing the material that follows in 56:4–5 about '*foreigners* attaching themselves to the Lord to *serve* Him and to love His Name and *be His Servants*'. The same idea is repeated again at the end of Column XX: 'For He does Mercy to (the thousands) of them that Love Him and ... all those who hold fast to these Statutes, coming and going in accordance with the *Torah* and ... listening to the voice of the Righteous Teacher.... Their hearts will be strengthened and they shall prevail against all the Sons of the Earth, and God will make atonement for (or 'through') them, and *they will see His Salvation* (*Yeshu'a*), because they took refuge in His Holy Name.'[112] The first allusion to the New Covenant associated with these promises comes in CD VI.14–16 amid allusion to '*separating* from the Sons of the Pit' and the Nazirite-rooted language of '*keeping away from* (*lehinnazer*) polluted Evil Riches ... and from the Riches of the Temple ... and (from) robbing the Poor (*Ebionim*)'.

In the newer fragments of the Damascus Document from Cave 4 (4Q266), this language is also found in the First Column in the instructions 'to the Sons of Light' 'to keep way from the Paths' (again *lehinnazer*) probably 'of Evil' or 'of Wicked pollution', 'until the completion of the Time of Visitation'.[113] It is because of allusions such as this that we have been referring to this language as 'Nazirite' and this Community as a 'Consecrated One' or 'a House of the *Torah*' dedicated to God – or, to use more familiar language, Nazirites/Nazoraeans/Nazrenes as the case may be.

'The New Covenant in the Land of Damascus' and 'Drink this in Remembrance of Me'

The actual reference to 'the New Covenant in the Land of Damascus' comes in Column VI.20 where 'the Staff's 'decrees' in which they are commanded 'to walk during all the Era of Evil' are defined in terms of '*separating* between polluted and pure ... Holy from Profane and to keep the Sabbath Day ... the Festivals and the Day of Fasting (*Yom Kippur*) according to the precise letter of the Commandment of those entering the New Covenant in the Land of Damascus'.[113] This of course is the direct *opposite* of what Peter is presented as learning in the Acts 10:15 and 10:28 version of what it considers ultimately to be the New Covenant, namely, '*not* to make distinctions between Holy and impure' and 'to call no man impure'!

In Column VI.20–VII.3, on the other hand, this 'Covenant' is then specifically defined as: 'to set up the Holy Things according to their precise specifications, to love every man his brother, to strengthen the hand of the Meek ('*Ani*), the Poor (*Ebion*), and the Convert (*Ger*) ... and not to uncover the nakedness of near kin (i.e., niece marriage or incest), but to *keep away* from fornication according to the Statute (*lehazzir* based on the same N-Z-R or *Nazirite* root) ... to bear no rancor ... but to *separate* from all pollutions according to Statute (the Nazirite 'separation' ideology again)'.

Now that we know the terms of 'the New Covenant in the Land of Damascus', the presentation turns *Messianic* and Column VII.13–21 proceeds to evoke the imagery from Amos 9:11 – common to James' speech in Acts 15:16 – about 'raising the Tabernacle of David which is fallen', combining it with the imagery from Amos 5:26–27 earlier, including 'the Star of your King', which it expresses rather in terms of 'exiling the Tabernacle of your King and the bases of Your statues from My Tent (or 'from the tents') of Damascus'. For its part, the speech accorded James in Acts 15:13–21 puts an esoteric spin on 'rebuilding' this Tabernacle, compressing a good deal of what follows in CD VII–VIII and XIX–XX.

In both Acts and at Qumran, the exposition is esoteric. In the latter 'the Tabernacle of the King' (thereafter, seemingly, to be refined in terms of Amos 9:11's 'the Tabernacle of David which is fallen') is identified with 'the Books of the *Torah*' – this, of course, the very opposite of how 'the Gentile Mission' would see these things. Notwithstanding, 'the King' – as in 1 Corinthians 12:12-27 – 'is the Community and the Bases of the Statues are the Books of the Prophets whose words Israel despised'. By contrast, in Acts 15:16–21 the esoteric exegesis of this passage from Amos is rather presented, it should be recalled, as having something to do with James' support of Paul's 'Gentile Mission' or, as this is put, 'all the Gentiles (*Ethne*) upon whom My Name has been called', which then triggers the various versions of James' directives to overseas communities.

That the whole complex, as it is presented in the Damascus Document, is to be taken in a 'Messianic' way is clear from the evocation of 'the Star Prophecy' which follows in Ms. A and 'the coming of the Messiah of Aaron and Israel' in Ms. B. Bringing the whole series of usages full circle: as this prophecy is expounded it is now connected in some manner both with 'the Diggers' materials (that is, 'those who dug the Well in the Land of Damascus') and 'the New Covenant in the Land of Damascus' preceding it from Columns VI.3–VII.6. In turn, both are connected to Numbers 21:18's 'Well' which 'the Princes' and 'Nobles of the People dug', 'the Penitents who went out to the Land of Damascus' materials, and Isaiah 54–56's Staff/*Mehokkek*, described as 'an instrument for His works'. The last link between all of these is then, of course, 'the *Doresh*' or 'the Seeker after the *Torah*' (the 'seeking' theme being fundamental here), that is, 'the Interpreter of the *Torah*' who is both 'the Staff who decrees the Laws' (*Hukkim*, a play on 'the *Mehokkek*' as well as 'His staves' as we just saw), who is then identified in the next exegesis as 'the Star who came to Damascus'.

This is quite a complex structure. Nevertheless, we are now in the realm of Acts' presentation of early Christian history on two counts: 1) in the matter of 'the Seeker after the *Torah*' ('the Star') 'who came to Damascus'; and 2) in the use of these Amos materials, particularly those relating to 're-erecting the Tabernacle of David which is fallen' constituting the jumping-off point, as it were, to Acts' presentation of James' directives to these same *Nilvim* or 'Joiners' to the Community in its picture of the outcome of 'the Jerusalem Council'. The 'rebuilding' or 're-erecting' of this 'fallen Tabernacle' is then used in Acts to present James as definitively supporting Paul's 'Gentile Mission' (a presentation I dispute – he might have supported the 'Mission' but, clearly, not its 'Pauline' parameters), as well as to introduce the specific ban in these instructions on 'Blood'.

The two, of course, are incompatible – that is, one cannot support both the Mission as Paul (followed by Acts) frames it and the ban on *Blood* – my reason for denying the historicity of this genre of application of Amos 9:11's Prophecy about 'raising the Tabernacle of David which is fallen' in the picture of James' discourse in Acts 15:16–17 to Paul's 'Gentile Mission'. A prohibition of this kind on James' part, concerning which Paul feigns ignorance throughout 1 Corinthians – if taken seriously – would preclude what Paul claims in 1 Corinthians 11:24 he 'received' directly 'from the Lord'. A claim of the latter kind, if entertained, can only mean via direct visionary experience or '*apocalypsis*', the kind of experience he also claims as both the basis of his 'Apostleship' – 'not from men nor through man' – in Galatians 1:1, as well as his view of the entire 'Gentile Mission' in Galatians 2:2. Furthermore, even if one were to insist that the claim should only be taken allegorically or symbolically, this would inevitably make Jesus a quasi-Disciple of Philo of Alexandria just as Paul.

As Paul now pictures 'the Lord Jesus' describing this 'New Covenant in (his) Blood' in 1 Corinthians 11:25–27 (possibly adding the 'Cup' from an esoteric understanding of 'Damascus'): 'This Cup is the New Covenant in my Blood'…. As often as you drink … this Cup you drink the death of the Lord … whoever shall … drink the Cup of the Lord unworthily shall be guilty of … the Blood of the Lord.' A more esoteric or allegorical understanding of the New Covenant is hard to envision. In Matthew 26:27–28, this becomes: 'Taking the Cup … he gave it to them, saying, "This is my Blood, that of the New Covenant which is poured out for the Many for remission of Sins."'

According to Acts 15:14, James' evocation of 'rebuilding the fallen Tabernacle of David' even includes the allusion to how God '*visited*' the Gentiles to take out a People for His Name'. We have also seen how Visitation language of this kind permeates the Damascus Document, beginning with the assertion in the First Column of CD that God 'visited them and caused a Root of Planting to grow from Israel and from Aaron' and continuing to this very juncture of the Document and the exegesis of 'the Star Prophecy' in CD VII.18–VIII.3. Though in Ms. B, 'the Star Prophecy' is replaced by Zechariah 13:7, Ezekiel 9:4, and evocation of 'the coming of the Messiah of Aaron and Israel' (continuing this 'Israel and Aaron' allusion from Column I.7 earlier – singular), both versions conserve the 'Visitation' usages.

As already underscored as well, even the word 'First', as in the 'First Visitation', is included in both Ms. A and B versions of the text, e.g., 'these escaped in the Era of the First

Visitation', and the language of 'Visitation' or 'God visiting them' is repeated some three or four times. In James' speech in Acts this becomes, 'Simeon has told you how God First visited the Gentiles to take out a People for His Name' (n.b. not only the 'Visitation' language but also the allusion to 'for His Name' replacing more familiar allusions 'called by this Name' earlier in Acts and 'called by Name' in the Dead Sea Scrolls[114]). Just as in Column VII.18's 'the Prophets whose words Israel despised', Acts 15:15 also evokes 'the words of the Prophets', but adds Amos 9:11's 'and I will build the ruins of it again and I will set it up' to CD VII.16's more circumscribed version of Amos 9:11.

It will be recalled that in CD VI.8, quoting Isaiah 54:16, the *Mehokkek* was defined as 'the Seeker after the *Torah*' and characterized as 'an instrument for His works'. Stitching the whole together, CD VII.18–19 then defined the Star/Stave/*Mehokkek*, as we saw, as 'the Interpreter of' or 'Seeker after the *Torah* who came to Damascus'. But in James' speech in Acts 15:18, not only is 'the Tabernacle of David which is fallen' invoked ('its ruins to be rebuilt'), but this becomes an explanation of why 'the Remnant of Men' or 'the Men who are left may seek out the Lord' – 'those who are left' or 'the Remnant' also being language familiar to these sections of CD VII/XIX.[115] Once again, the 'seeking' language is pivotal as it is in CD VII.18 –19's exposition of both Amos 9:11 and Numbers 24:17 in terms of 'the *Doresh ha-Torah*'. It is also the explanation earlier for why God called 'the Diggers' of Numbers 21:18 (that is, 'the Penitents who went out from the Land of Judah to dwell in the Land of Damascus') 'Princes, because they sought Him and their honor was questioned by no man' (CD VI.4–7)!

At this point in Acts 15:18, as if by way of explanation, James is pictured as adding: 'all his works are known to God from Eternity'. Here, of course, we have the 'works' language of Isaiah 54:16 and CD VI.8 and the Staff/Seeker being 'an instrument for His works' – not to mention the earlier material from CD I.10 (following on from how 'God visited them and caused a root of Planting to grow from Israel and from Aaron'): 'And God considered their works because they sought him with a whole heart'. Nor is this to say anything about the allusion to 'God visiting their works' later in CD V.17. Even more germane, almost the exact words are to be found in CD II.5–8, where 'the Penitents from Sin' among those 'who enter the Covenant' (i.e., 'the New Covenant in the Land of Damascus') are characterized in terms of being blessed, but: 'Power, Might, and overwhelming Wrath with sheets of Fire … upon those who turn aside the Way and abominate the Law … because, before the World ever was, God chose them not and, before they were established, He knew their works'. Here CD II.8 adds, as if for emphasis and a *coup de grace* of sorts: 'and abominated their Generations *on account of Blood*'. Once again, one should compare this allusion to God 'knowing their works' with James quoted in in Acts 15:18 as concluding: 'All his works are known to God from Eternity'.

Directly, Acts 15:19 has James proceed with his 'judgments' or 'rulings': 'Therefore I judge those from the Peoples who turn to God', a speech which then gives way to the overt use of the 'Nazirite' language 'abstain from'/'keep away from' we have also seen as permeating these Columns of the Damascus Document. In this regard, we just highlighted the key importance of the 'keep away from' language (*lehazzir*/*lehinnazer*/ and *linzor*) specifically as regards 'fornication' in VII.1 and its parallel 'to separate from all pollutions' in VII.3, which certainly would have included 'the pollutions of the idols' in Acts 15:20; but also, in the Column preceding the First Column of CD from 4Q266, where 'the Sons of Light' were instructed to 'keep away (*lehinnazer*) from the ways' – probably 'of Evil' or 'Evil pollutions', the last-mentioned being expressed in CD VI.15 (in a seeming attack on the Herodian Establishment) as 'polluted Evil Riches'.

Aside from the almost hysterical attack on 'Blood' just highlighted in CD II.8 above, there are at least two other specific references to Blood in the Damascus Document – both negative: one that immediately follows this in Column in III.2-7, after explaining why

Abraham 'was made a Friend of God (also of interest to James 2:23–24) because he *kept the Commandments of God* and did not choose the will of his own Spirit…. But the Sons of Jacob *turned aside* in them and … walked in stubbornness of their heart…, complaining against the Commandments of God (which, of course, Paul does interminably), each man doing what was right in his own eyes. So they ate blood and their males were cut off in the wilderness.' The second in Column Five: 'They also pollute the Temple, because they do not *separate* according to the *Torah*, but rather they lie with a woman during the blood of her period and each man takes (to wife) the daughter of his brother and the daughter of his sister.' While not relating to the ingestion of food or drink *per se* (as CD II.8 and III.7 do) and, as a consequence, 'Communion with the Body and Blood of Christ Jesus', this last passage, nonetheless, vividly illustrates the attitude of the authors towards contact with Blood of any kind.

To sum up the approach of the Damascus Document, we should look at its closing section containing, as we have seen, its most vivid exhortative passages (Columns VIII and XIX–XX). Here while 'the Spouter of Lying' and 'his whole Congregation' or 'Church' are condemned, the implication is that 'the Penitents of Israel, who turned aside from the Way of the People(s)' (that is, 'the Way' preached by 'the Spouter of Lying' and those like him) are not, 'because God so loved the First…. He also loved those coming after them' (VIII.13–17/ XIX.26–30) – a form, as already remarked, of Pauline Grace should one choose to regard it but within specifically Qumranic parameters. It was at this point, it will be recalled too, that 'Elisha's rebuke of Gehazi his servant' – a favorite Rabbinic allusion for rebuking Pauline-type teachers – is invoked to emphasize God's: 'Judgment on all those who reject the Commandments of God and forsake them, turning away in stubbornness of their heart' (VIII.20/XIX.33). It is in conjunction with this that 'the New Covenant in the Land of Damascus' is for the second time directly invoked – this in order to condemn: 'All those who entered the New Covenant in the Land of Damascus, but turned back and betrayed and turned aside from the Well of Living Waters' (VIII.21–22 and XIX.33–35 – here the most complete presentation of the turning aside/turning back/betraying circle-of-language).

Similar expressions are reiterated in the third evocation of 'the New Covenant' in CD XX.10–13, where it is also designated as 'the Compact which they raised in the Land of Damascus' and equated with 'the House of the *Torah*'. Sentiments of this kind continue to be expressed in the surrounding materials having to do with the fate of all such Traitors, Backsliders, and Scoffers from CD Columns XIX.34–XX.17 of Ms. B. At this point, it will be recalled, the text turns both positive and passionately inspirational, again returning to 'the Penitents from Sin in Jacob who kept the Covenant of God', in particular 'God-Fearers' and 'those reckoning His Name', to whom 'God would reveal Salvation (*Yesha*') and Justification' (*Zedakah* – XX.19–20), the exact vocabulary found in Isaiah 56:1 introducing its position on foreign *Nilvim*/Joiners in 56:3–6 above, for whom 'a Book of Remembrance would be written out'!

To understand these passages one should again refer back to Acts 15:14–17 and James' alleged connection of God 'taking out of the Gentiles a People for his Name' in 15:14 with 'rebuilding the fallen Tabernacle of David' and 'setting it up' again, reiterating its applicability to 'those left of Men' or 'the Remnant' (designated as 'Seekers') and 'all the Gentiles upon whom My name has been called' in 15:16–17. In CD XX.27–32, these were particularly to include: 'all those who hold fast to the Statutes, coming and going in accordance with the *Torah* … (who have) not lifted up their hand against the Holiness of His Laws and the Righteousness of His Judgments and the Testimonies of His Truth. Rather (we) have been instructed in the First Ordinances (or 'the Statutes of the First') in which the Men of the Community were judged.' Once again, as in James' speech, the word 'First' appears ('the First Ordinances' or 'Statutes' in XX.31), but here rather relating to 'the First' or 'the Forefathers' of the First Covenant, as earlier in CD I.4's description of how God 'remembered the Covenant of the First' or 'the Forefathers' – 'the First Covenant' – and, therefore, 'left a (telltale) *Remnant*' and 'did not deliver them up' ('to the sword') but rather 'visited them and caused a (Messianic) Root of Planting to grow'.

Furthermore, when they 'listen to the voice of the Righteous Teacher', they 'hear' 'the Laws of Righteousness and do not desert them.... Their hearts will be strengthened and they shall prevail against all the Sons of Earth. And God will make atonement for (or through) them and they will see his Salvation because they took refuge in His Holy Name (XX.33–34).' This 'Covenant' is, of course, exactly the opposite of the Pauline one as it has come down to us. How can two such chronologically almost contemporaneous versions of 'the New Covenant' be so completely and diametrically opposed? As we have been intimating, it is almost as if one is framed in direct reference to or with direct knowledge of the other.

We have already examined a similar kind of diametrically-opposed ideological reversal in the Habakkuk *Pesher*'s exposition of Habakkuk 2:4, which must be seen – along with Genesis 15:5 on Abraham's 'Faith being reckoned to him as Righteousness' (i.e., Justification) – as fundamental 'building blocks' of Pauline theology. In 1QpHab VII.17–VIII.3 the applicability of this key Biblical proof-text was circumscribed to 'the Doers of the *Torah* in the House of Judah' – in other words, *Torah*-Doers who were Jewish. It, therefore, followed that it did not apply to 'Non-*Torah*-doing Gentiles' – nor even, for that matter, 'Non-*Torah*-Doing Jews'!

It is the position of this book, the partial aim of which has been to collate and highlight these contrasts and reversals, that this kind of stark contrast where 'the New Covenant in the Land of Damascus' is concerned is invaluable in helping to further highlight the Qumran perspective which, in so far as it was addressed to Gentile converts – and it was – was addressed to those 'keeping the whole of the *Torah*', including the Sabbath and the other observances like circumcision as per the parameters of Isaiah 54–56, as expounded in CD VI–VII – this as opposed to the more allegorized and spiritualized New Covenant being delineated at such length and with such self-evident rhetorical flourish in his Letters by Paul (and, by extension, a good many passages in the Gospels as they finally crystallized out in the West), who is finally (if carefully) emphasizing to his followers that it was not necessary to do so – in particular and *inter alia*, that not only was it unnecessary to circumcise oneself but *one should not do so*.[116]

Building the 'House of Faith in Israel'

For these last (that is, Paul's positions on these issues), the rhetorical and polemical constructions of the concluding Five Chapters of Hebrews are fundamental as well: 'If the First Covenant had not been found wanting, then there would be no need to seek for the Second' (Hebrews 8:7), quoting in its entirety the passage from Jeremiah 31:33–34 on 'making a New Covenant with the House of Israel and the House of Judah'. In these passages in Jeremiah, this included a stress on 'keeping the Covenant' – so conspicuous in the concluding exhortation in the Damascus Document (but so conspicuously missing from Paul's more allegorical exposition of similar proof-texts) – and the reference to 'teaching each one his neighbor and each one his brother' also found word-for-word in CD XX.17–18: 'Then each man shall speak to his neigh[bor and each on]e his brother to support their steps in the Way of God.' At this point, Hebrews calls the First Covenant 'Old', again in stark contrast to that of the 'New', as embodied in 'the New Covenant', opining 'that which decays and grows old is ready to disappear' (8:13).

Continuing this theme into Chapter Nine and evoking 'the veil' between the Outer Sanctum and the Inner – 'the Tabernacle which is called the Holy of Holies' (9:2–3) –

Hebrews 9:12 now alludes to how Christ 'by his own Blood' (repeatedly reiterating the redemptive power of Blood) 'entered the Holy of Holiest once for all'.

Hebrews 9:12–14 now asserts 'how much more the Blood of Christ can purge … the dead works' of its hearers' 'consciences to serve the Living God'. Again here, one should note not only the completely allegorized, Pauline use of language of the kind already encountered throughout 1 Corinthians 8–11 and Galatians 3–4, but, in addition, the allusion to 'conscience (s)', which Paul evokes so contemptuously in 1 Corinthians 8:10–12 too, but which we have also just seen Hippolytus use regarding those *Sicarii* Essenes who preferred martyrdom to 'eating things sacrificed to idols' – the very 'things sacrificed to idols' we have encountered in 1 Corinthians 8:1–10 above.

This is the point at which Hebrews 9:15 designates 'Christ' – much as the Instrument/ Seeker/Stave/and Star above – 'the Mediator of the New Covenant'. Picking up the 'Perfection of Holiness' language one encounters in CD XX.2–7 and 1QS VIII.10–20, it concludes in 10:14, 'For by one offering he has Perfected forever those who are sanctified' (or, in more properly Hebrew terms, 'made Holy'). Again, quoting Jeremiah 31:33 on 'putting My *Torah* in their midst and writing it on their hearts' (for Hebrews 8:12 and 10:16, it was: 'I will put My Laws in their hearts and write them on their minds'), but completely ignoring Jeremiah's further absolute and repeated insistence on 'keeping the Covenant', Hebrews 10:16–17 now states: 'This is the Covenant I will make with them after those days, saith the Lord. Their Sins and lawlessness will I *remember* no more.' This is the Covenant Paul also develops in 2 Corinthians 3:6 when he calls himself and his colleagues 'Servants of the New Covenant' which he claims – using the language of Jeremiah, augmented by that of Ezekiel[117] – 'to have written on the fleshy tablets of the heart' – while simultaneously managing to ignore both Ezekiel's insistences on 'keeping the Laws' or 'the Covenant'!

Picking up the 'moving through the second veil' allusion of 9:3–15 and, by implication, the allusion to 'the Mediator' there, the author of Hebrews 10:19–20 now goes on finally and climactically to claim 'to have the boldness to enter into the Holiest (that is, 'the Holy of Holiest') … by a New and living way'. One should compare this with CD VIII.21–22 and XIX.33–34's use of the term 'living' in its description of 'those who turned back, betrayed, and turned aside from the Fountain' or 'Well of Living Waters', directly following its evocation of 'the New Covenant in the Land of Damascus', which it goes on to imply has something to do with 'the words' with which 'Elisha rebuked Gehazi'. The author of Hebrews means by this and defines this as – moving now into almost total allegory (so much so as to verge on almost complete mystification) – 'by the Blood of Jesus' which has been 'consecrated through the veil' (one often wonders what is actually being said here or is it 'mystery-fication' simply for 'mystification' sake?).

Finally, in Hebrews 12:23–24, alluding to the dual efficacy again of Jesus as 'the Mediator of the New Covenant' and 'the Perfect Holiness of the Spirits of the Righteous' and evoking *MMT*'s 'Camp' language, Hebrews 13:10–12 and 13:20–21 now states: 'Just as the bodies of those animals, whose blood was brought into the Holy of Holiest by the High Priest as a sacrifice for Sin,[118] were burned outside the Camp; so too Jesus suffered outside the Camp, so he might sanctify the People by his own Blood…. It is this Blood of the Eternal Covenant of our Lord Jesus that will make you Perfect in every good work.'

Though the allegorized analogy here clearly moves into Hellenizing 'Mystery Religion' rituality and even displays, in depicting Jesus as having 'suffered outside the Camp' – this, hardly deducible from the way the Gospels portray their view of how things happened but the 'outside the Camp' allusion does reverberate across a wide range of Qumran documents as we have seen[119] – what today might be characterized as the inferiority complex of those feeling in some way rejected or 'cast aside'; still it is mesmerizing in its esoterics and the total Philo-esque allegorization implicit in its mastery of rhetorical display is spell-binding.

The only question remaining is the one we asked at the beginning of this section: did the sectaries at Qumran know the Pauline or New Testament position (if we can refer to it in such a manner) on 'the New Covenant' to which they were responding? Or was there some secret, hidden, or inner meaning imparted only to central members of the sect, as is sometimes implied in Column Four of CD and elsewhere: 'And with the Completion of the Era of the number of these years, there will be no more joining to the House of Judah, but rather each man will stand upon his own net (Watchtower)'?[120] Or, as this is put earlier, 'And he built for them a House of Faith in Israel, the likes of which has never stood from Ancient Times until now. And for them that hold fast to it, there will be Victorious Life and all the Glory of *Adam* will be theirs.' It is possible, but I consider both options relatively doubtful.

The other possibility is: did someone like Paul – a person who, I consider, because of the breadth of Qumran language infusing his letters, spent time in the Community before he was, most likely, ejected and who, speaking both Hebrew and/or Aramaic and Greek (as he undoubtedly must have done), understood at least to a certain extent the esoteric possibilities inherent in the Greek transliteration of the Hebrew geographical designation *Dammashek* or 'Damascus', in particular as these bore on the Hebrew terms for Cup and Blood, to say nothing of 'drink this' or 'give to drink' – understand 'the New Covenant in the Land of Damascus' in such a manner?

In asking this question, I leave aside the allusions to 'the Cup of the right hand of the Lord' and 'the Cup of the Wrath of God' in Column XI.10 and XI.15 of the Habakkuk *Pesher*, which – in my view – carry the true sense of all of these 'Cup of the Lord' allusions one is encountering in these documents. Curiously enough, Revelation also knows this sense, when it states in passages replete with Qumran imagery such as 14:8, mimicking and inverting the language of the mournful Prophet, Jesus ben Ananias, whom Josephus pictures as having first made his appearance in Tabernacles, 62 CE directly following the death of James: '*Babylon* is fallen because she has *given to all Peoples to drink* of the wine of the *Fury* of her *fornication*,' and again with regard to the 'Worshipper of the Beast' (in Hebrew *Be'ir* or *Be'or* the father of both *Balaam* and *Bela'* and the eponymous ancestor of all Herodians[121]): 'He also shall *drink of the wine of the Wrath of God which is poured out full strength into the Cup of His Anger*' (Revelation 14:10).

This is repeated again two chapters later amid the language of 'blasphemy', namely 'blaspheming the Name of God' and 'blaspheming the God of Heaven' (16:9–11 – cf. the parallel with the official charge against James of 'blasphemy'), and 'pouring out the Blood' (here, 'the Blood of the Saints and of the Prophets'), literally expressed in Revelation 16:6 in terms of '*giving them Blood to drink*' – perhaps the very correlative in Hebrew of *Dammashek* when taken according to its esoteric decoding: 'And the Great City *Babylon* was *remembered* before God, to *give her the Cup of the wine of the Fury of His Wrath*' (16:19).

In this passage from Revelation 16:19, one actually has the '*remembered before God*' phraseology – now, of course, reversed – of 'the Book of Remembrance' that 'would be written out before Him (God) for all God-Fearers and those reckoning His Name' of CD XX.19–20, to say nothing of the episode in the Pseudoclementine *Recognitions* describing the 'two brothers' whose tomb outside Jericho 'miraculously whitened of itself every year', who were also characterized there – as will be recalled – as 'being *remembered before God*', as well as the use of this same phraseology in the various New Testament 'Last Supper' scenarios already alluded to above.

Not only are these various imageries presaged in the Habakkuk *Pesher*'s pictures of how 'the Cup of the Wrath of God' would 'come around to' and 'swallow him' (the Wicked Priest), because he 'swallowed them' (the followers of the Righteous Teacher) and 'swallowed him in his hot anger' (that is, 'swallowed the Righteous Teacher'), but it would seem that Paul has some understanding of this variation of the 'Damascus' or the 'drinking the Cup' allusion as well when he states in 1 Corinthians 11:26: 'For as often as you drink this Cup, you solemnly proclaim the death of the Lord until He comes', following this up in 11:29 with 'for he who eats and drinks unworthily, eats and drinks Judgment to himself, not seeing through to the Body of the Lord'. Allegorization such as this is, in fact, really quite expert.

My conclusion is – yes, in some symbolic or allegorical manner, teachers like Paul and authors even of Books such as Acts – which in my view did know the Damascus Document and who were *diametrically opposed* to much of what it was saying – did see through to this esoteric understanding of 'Damascus' and *did reinterpret it* in this utterly spiritualized and Hellenistic 'Mystery Religion'-oriented fashion. However, I do not believe that the sectaries at Qumran entertained any such covert or hidden sense of 'the New Covenant in the Land of Damascus'; though, given their several intemperate denunciations of contact with or the consumption of Blood of any kind, it may be that they knew the Pauline one.

We have already pointed out that the esoteric understanding of the formulation 'Damascus' outlined above actually works in the Hebrew as well as it does in the Greek – not only in one but in both syllables of the formulation. In fact, it works even better than the simple homophonic relationship of the Hebrew to 'Cup' (*Chos*) and 'Blood' (*Dam*) in the Greek transliteration. The fact of this unexpected further verification of what was initially just a suggestion provides extremely convincing added corroboration of both its relevance and applicability.

To review this additional verification one last time: in Hebrew the word for the Greek/ English 'Damascus' is *Dammashek* but the word for 'drink' or 'give to drink' is *mashkeh*. Therefore the place name Damascus in Hebrew breaks down in putative esoteric or allegorical delineation to *Dam-Mashkeh* or, as we saw in Revelation 16:6 above, 'give Blood to drink'. This, of course, is the phraseology *repeatedly evoked* in the quotation of this formula involving 'the Cup of the New Covenant in (the) Blood' attributed to – in Paul's parlance – 'the Lord Jesus' whether in 1 Corinthians 11–12 or in the Synoptics and even in the face of the ban on the consumption of blood in the various formulations of James' directives to overseas communities.

To once again condense the various formulations one encounters: 'he took the Cup saying, "This Cup is the New Covenant in my Blood. As often as you drink it, this do in Remembrance of me"' (1 Corinthians 11:25) – in the Synoptics varied slightly into, 'This is the Cup of the New Covenant in my Blood which is poured out for you' (Luke 22:20 and pars. – here the 'pouring out' imagery of Revelation, followed – at least in Matthew 26:29 and Mark 14:25 – by: 'I will not drink of the fruit of the vine again until I drink it again in the Kingdom of God'. If this were not sufficient, it is preceded in Matthew 26:27 by the commandment, 'drink this' (in Mark 14:23, this is stated rather as: 'they drank of it').

The combination of the usages 'drink', 'drank', or 'drinking' with 'the Cup of the New Covenant' and 'my Blood' in one manner or another in all the contexts outlined above is hardly either to be gainsaid or considered accidental. The present writer considers that contextual allusions such as these are too insistent and too comprehensive in the sources before us to be simply fortuitous or coincidental. They are indicative of some more persistent esoteric or allegorical wordplay – in fact, some kind of amusingly clever or aesthetically pleasing wordplay. What the allegorical sense or meaning underlying these formulations might be and whether those at Qumran might also have been aware of or a party to it, the author is unable to determine in any definitive manner.

Nor is it possible to determine which came first, the version and sense of 'the New Covenant' found in Pauline/Synoptic formulation and attributed to the 'Jesus' which they are presenting or the version of it found in the Qumran variation. The writer, as should by now be clear, suspects that the latter – 'the Law' or *Torah*-oriented exposition of it one finds developed in the later Columns of the Damascus Document – is the original and the esoteric play and even quasi-derogatory parody or exposition of it one finds in both Paul and the Synoptic Gospels is neither meant positively nor innocently, but rather to invalidate, belittle, or undercut, transforming it into its exact or mirror opposite.

Left: The Arch of Titus, still standing in the Roman Forum today, his father's Colosseum right behind it. **Above:** The image on it celebrating his Triumph over the Jews, captives carrying the seven-branched golden candelabra given to Temple by Queen Helen and presumably melted down to pay for Colosseum.

Left: Vespasian's *Judea Capta* coin, displaying his image on the obverse and Roman domination over a weeping Judean woman on its reverse, the Palm Tree representing the Jewish State as in the Gospels.

Above left: Jewish Revolutionary coin from the rare Year 4 depicting the real *'Cup of the Lord'* (*'the Cup of Divine Vengeance'*) with the logo: *'the Redemption of Zion'*. **Right:** Bar Kochba Cave where the Bar Kochba Letters from 134-36 CE were found.

Abbreviations

Acts Th.	Acts of Thomas
Ad Cor.	Clement of Alexandria, Letter to the Corinthians
Ad Haer.	Irenaeus, *Against Heresies*
Ad Rom.	Ignatius, Letter to the Romans
ADAJ	*Annual of the Department of Antiquities, Jordan*
Adv.	*Hel.* Jerome, *Against Helvidius*
Adv.	*Marcion* Tertullian, *Against Marcion*
ANCL	*Anti-Nicene Christian Library* (1867–71 Edition)
Ant.	Josephus, *The Antiquities of the Jews*
Apion	Josephus, *Against Apion (Contra Apion)*
1 Apoc Jas.	First Apocalypse of James
2 Apoc Jas.	Second Apocalypse of James
Apoc. Pet.	Apocalypse of Peter
Apost.	Const. Apostolic Constitutions
APOT	*Apocrypha and Pseudepigrapha of the Old Testament* (ed. R. H. Charles)
ARN	*Abbot de Rabbi Nathan*
As.	Moses Assumption of Moses
b.A.Z.	Babylonian *Talmud,*Tractate c*Avodah Zarah*
b. B.B.	Babylonian *Talmud,*Tractate *Baba Bathra*
b. Ber	Babylonian *Talmud,*Tractate *Berachot*
b. Bik	Babylonian *Talmud,*Tractate *Bikkurim*
b. Git	Babylonian *Talmud,*Tractate *Gittin*
b. Hul	Babylonian *Talmud,*Tractate *Hullin*
b. Kid	Babylonian *Talmud,*Tractate *Kiddushim*
b. Ket	Babylonian *Talmud,*Tractate *Kethuboth*
b. Ned	Babylonian *Talmud,*Tractate *Nedarim*
b. Pes	Babylonian *Talmud,*Tractate *Pesahim*
b. R.H.	Babylonian *Talmud,*Tractate *Rosh Ha-Shanah*
b. Shab.	Babylonian *Talmud,*Tractate *Shabbath*
b. Sot	Babylonian *Talmud,*Tractate *Sotah*
b. Suk	Babylonian *Talmud,*Tractate *Sukkah*
b.Tacan	Babylonian *Talmud,*Tractate *Tacanith*
b. San.	Babylonian *Talmud,*Tractate *Sanhedrin*
b.Yeb	Babylonian *Talmud,*Tractate *Yebamoth*
b.Yom	Babylonian *Talmud,*Tractate *Yoma*
BAR	*Biblical Archaeology Review*
Baroccian.	*Codice Barocciano*
BASOR	*Bulletin of the American Scholls of Oriental Research*
CD	Cairo Damascus Document (Ms.A and Ms. B)
Comm. on Gal.	Jerome, *Commentary on Galatian*s
Comm. on John	Origen, *Commentary of John*
Comm. on Matt.	Origen, *Commentary on Matthew*
de Carne	Tertullian, *On the Body of Christ*
de Mens. et Pond	Epiphanius, *De Mensuris et Ponderibus*
de Monog.	Tertullian, *On Monogamy*
de Verig. vel.	Tertullian, *On the Veiling of Virgins*
Dial.	Justin Martyr, *Dialogue with Trypho*
Deut. R.	Deuteronomy *Rabbah*
DSD	*Dead Sea Discoveries*
DSSNT	*The Dead Sea Scrolls: A New Translation* (ed. M. Wise,M.Abegg, & E. Cook)
DSSFC	*The Dead Sea Scrolls and the First Christians* (R. Eisenman)

DSSU	*The Dead Sea Scrolls Uncovered* (ed. R. Eisenman and M.Wise)
Eccles. R.	Ecclesiastes *Rabbah*
EH	Eusebius, *Ecclesiastical History*
Enarr. in Ps. 34:3	Augustine, *Discourses on the Psalms*
Eph.	Ignatius, Letter to the Ephesians
Epist.Apost.	Epistle of the Apostles
Epist. B.	Epistle of Barnabas
FEDSS	*A Facsimile Edition of the Dead Sea Scrolls* (ed. R. Eisenman and J. Robinson)
Gen. R.	Genesis *Rabbah*
Gos Th.	The Gospel of Thomas
Haeres.	Epiphanius, *Against Heresies* (*Panarion* in Latin)
H.N.	Pliny, *Natural History*
Haer.	Tertullian, *Against Heretics*
Hennecke	*The New Testament Apocrypha* (ed. E. Hennecke and W. Schneemelcher)
Hippolytus	Hippolytus, *Refutation of all Heresies*
Hom. in Luc.	Origen, *Homilies on Luke*
HUCA	*Hebrew Union College Annual*
JJHP	*James the Just in the Habakkuk Pesher* (R. Eisenman)
IEJ	*Israel Exploration Journal*
j.Tacan	Jerusalem *Talmud*,Tractate *Tacanith*
Lam R.	Lamentations *Rabbah*
M. San.	*Mishnah Sanhedrin*
Mur.	Wadi Murraba'at, Cave 1
MZCQ	*Maccabees, Zadokite,Christians and Qumran* (R. Eisenman)
Opus imperf. C. Iul	Augustine, *Opus Imperfectum contra Secundum Juliani*
pars.	parallels
Protevang.	Protevangelium of James
Ps *Hom.*	Pseudoclementine *Homilies*
Ps	Philo Pseudo Philo
Ps *Rec.*	Pseuclementine *Recognitions*
Quod	Omnis Philo, *On the Contemplative Life*
4QD	The Qumran Damascus Document (Cave 4)
4Q*Ber*	The Qumran Blessings (The Chariots of Glory)
4QF*lor*	The Qumran *Florilegium* (on Promises to David's '*Seed*')
1QH	The Qumran Hymns
1QM	The Qumran War Scroll
4QMMT	The Qumran Letter(s) on Works Righteousness
4QpGen	The Qumran Genesis *Pesher* (Genesis *Florilegium*)
1QpHab	The Qumran Habakkuk *Pesher*
4QpIs	The Qumran Isaiah *Pesher*
4QpNah	The Qumran Nahum *Pesher*
4QpPs 37	The Qumran Psalm 37 *Pesher*
1QS	The Qumran Community Rule
11QT	The Qumran Temple Scroll
4QTest	The Qumran Testimonia
Song of Songs R.	Song of Songs *Rabbah*
Suet.	Seutonius, *The Twelve Caesars*
Tos. Kellim	*Tosefta Kellim*
Trall.	Ignatius, *Letter to the Trallians*
Vir. ill.	Jerome, *Lives of Illustrious Men*
Vita Josephus,	*Autobiography of Flavius Josephus*
War	*The Jewish War*

Endnotes

Introduction

1. Josephus, *War* 2.120–58, *Ant.* 18.18–22, and Philo, *Quod Omnis Probus Liber*, 75–91; see, for instance, Epiphanius, *Haeres.* 29.1 and 29.4.

2. 132–36 CE. For Eusebius, *E.H.* 4.6.2–6, for instance, there do not appear to have been 'Christians' as such in Jerusalem until after Hadrian renamed it after himself and Justin Martyr (c. 100–65), *Dial.* doesn't even seem to know the Gospels as separate entities.

3. Cf. Eusebius in *E.H.* 1.13.2.

4. *Ant.* 20.34–43.

5. Koran 27.20–47.

6. *E.H.* 1.13.4–5.

7. See *JBJ*, pp. 930–39.

8. Acts 6:5–6.

9. Acts 6:1–8:2.

10. *Ant.* 16.299, 333–55, etc.

11. See 'the *Nilvim*' in CD IV.3 and 'the Nobles of the People' in CD VI.4–8.

12. *War* 2.228/*Ant.* 20.113.

13. For the attack on James by the 'Enemy' Paul in the *Recognitions*, see 1.70.

14. *Vita* 430; also see *Ant.* 1.8, *Apion* 1.1, 2.1, and 2.296.

15. Suetonius 8.14.4–17.3 and Dio Cassius, *Roman History*, 67.4.1–5. There is some debate about the year of Josephus' death and some think he lived till 104 CE, but he definitely seems to leave the scene in 96 right before Domitian's assassination.

16. *E.H.* 3.18.4.

17. Ps. *Rec* 1.70.

18. Cf. Matthew 4:5/Luke 4:9.

19. 1QpHab XI.12–15.

20. *E.H.* 2.1.1.

21. See *JBJ*, pp. 240–2 and 304.

22. *Ant.* 20.113 and 118–36; also see *War* 2.229 and Tacitus, *Annals* 12.54.

23. See *M. San.* 9.6, Numbers 25:6–13 on Phineas, and S.G.F. Brandon, *Jesus and the Zealots*, pp.41.

24. Jude 1:1.

25. *E.H.* 2.13.2–3 quoting Justin Martyr's *Apology* 1.26. Also see Ps. *Rec.* 2.7 and *Hom.* 6.7.

26. *Ant.* 20.142

27. *Rec.* 1.72, 2.7–8, and *Hom.* 1.22 and Epiphanius, *Haeres*, 21.2.3–5.1

28. *War* 1.63, *Ant.* 9.288–90, 11.19–20, 11.85–8, etc.; cf. also *JBJ*, pp. 495–6 and 533–5.

29. See Genesis 10:4, Numbers 24:24, Isaiah 23:1–12, Jeremiah 2:10, etc.

30. See *JBJ*, pp. 130–1 and 605. One assumes 'Timothy' is the name in Greek; 'Titus' in Latin – this despite the fact both are mentioned in 2 Corinthians and 2 Timothy.

31. 'Mariamme' in Greek comes from 'Miriam' in the Old Testament and becomes 'Mary' in the New Testament.

32. *Ant.* 19.299 and 317–25, but in *War* 2.520 and 3.11–19 a second or later, possibly his descendant and a 'Babylonian' deserts from Agrippa II's army and becomes a principal rebel commander. With 'John the Essene' he is killed at Ascalon while 'Niger' escapes.

33. Cf. CD VI.21, XX.19, and 33 but also see James' title 'Oblias'/'Strength of the People' in *E.H.* 2.23.7

34. Cf. for example Acts 15:1 and 5 or Galatians 2:12 on the '*some from James*'.

35. 4QpPs37 IV.9–10.

36. *Ant.* 14.121–2 and *War* 1.181.

37. *War* 4.359–63. It would be hard for anyone reading this to escape the resemblance.

38. For these overlaps, see James, pp. 166–7, 177–9, 412–3, 913–5, etc.

39. Here Paul is '*Saulos*'. Nine lines later (13:9), in the context of evoking the '*Enemy*' terminology and '*Sergius Paulos*', he is '*Paulos*'. Is there an adoption going on here?

40. Ps. *Hom.* Epistle of Peter to James, 1–5; Epistle of Clement to James, 1 and 7.

41. See *War* 7.437–54; *Vita* 424.

42. *E.H.* 1.13.1–20 and J.B. Segal, *Edessa 'The Blessed City'*, Oxford, 1970, pp. 62–80.

43. *E.H.* 3.11.2 and 4.22.4 quoting Hegesippus.

44. See fragments in *ANCL* and *E.H.* 3.39.

45. See my discussion in *JBJ*, pp. 839–50.

46. See the whole issue of 'going out into the Land of Damascus' in CD IV.3, VI.3–VII.9, and XIX.21–XX.22.

47. See the parallel to this in Jerome's citation from the Gospel of the Hebrews, *Vir. ill.* 2.

48. *Ibid.*; see discussions in *JBJ*, pp. 198–9, etc.

49. What Jerome has done to come up with 'cousins' is simply identify the 'Mary the sister of his mother', 'the wife of Clopas' in John 19:26 with 'Mary the mother of James the Less and Joses and Salome' in the Synoptics.

50. Cf. *JBJ*, pp. XVIII, 95–7, 141–2, etc.

51. In Acts 3:1–9 the James character is missing and in 1:20 the 'election' to the 'Episcopate' is to replace Judas – a curious replacement.

52. Edessa is in Northern Syria; Adiabene bordering it is in Northern Iraq.

53. For the numerous Antiochs at this time, see Pliny, *Natural History* and Strabo, *Geography*.

54. For Abraham's central role there, see Koran 2.124–40, 3.67–8, 4.125, 14.35–52, etc.

55. See also the reference in Romans 16:7 to another putative Herodian, 'Junius my kinsman' – most likely Julius Archelaus, probably the nephew who helps rescue Paul from 'oath-taking' *Sicarii* in Act 23:16–20.

56. *Ant.* 18.137.

57. Cf. Ps. *Rec.* 1.70 with *E.H.* 2.23.16–8.

58. See *War* 2.554–6; also see Paul in Philippians 4:22.

59. *Ant.* 18.109–25.

60. *Ant.* 18.116–9.

61. Note the Simon who wishes to bar Herodians like Agrippa I from the Temple as foreigners in *Ant.* 19.332–34; also see *M. Sota* 7.8, *M. Bik* 3.4 and *Siphre* Deut 17:15.

62. See Moses of Chorene, 2.29–35.

63. Herod's father had been given citizenship for services rendered to Rome; *War* 1.194.

64. See *Ps.* Hom. 10.1, 26, 11.1, 28–30, and 12.6.

65. *Ibid.*, 2.19 (here, comparing Gentiles to '*dogs*' in the meat they consume), 7,3, 8, 19, and 11.351.

66. In Acts 13:1, the reason for John Mark's departure had been unclear; cf. 1QS VIII.16–26 and CD XX.1–17 and 22–27.

67. Ps. *Rec.* 1.45–54 and 62–64.

68. *War* 1.95 and *Ant.* 13.379 and 18.20.

69. Ps. Rec. 1.71; cf. Mark 8:9–20 and *pars*.

70. Tiberius Alexander did not come to Palestine until 46–48; cf. *War* 2.20/*Ant.* 20.100–3.

71. Cf. Ps. *Rec.* 1.72, 2.7, and Ps. *Hom.* 2.22–4.

72. See 1QpHab XII.1–10.

73. 1QpHab XI.13.

74. 1QpHab II.4 and CD VIII.21–3/XIX.33–5.

75. See *Surah*s 2.87–91, 3:21, 4:155, etc.

76. Note his constant reiteration of 'not Lying' in Galatians 1:20, 1 Corinthians 11:31, etc.

77. Cf. Ps. *Rec.* 1.71 with 1 Cor. 15:6, 18, and 51.

78. Cf. *E.H.* 2.23.13 and Matthew 24:30 and 26:64/Mark 13:26 and 14:6 *pars*.

79. See Ps. *Hom.* 7:3–4, 7.19, and 11.35.

80. See my article: '*Joining*'/'*Joiners*' in *D.S.SFC*, pp. 313–31 and CD IV.3, 4QpNah IV.4, etc.

81. 1QpHab VII.11, VIII.1, and XII.4–5.

82. *Ant.* 19.366.

83. See *Ant.* 19.329–31.

84. See *M. Sota* 7:8, *M. Bik.* 3.4, and *Siphre* Deut 157 on 17:15.

85. See *EJ* article '*Sikarikon*' and Origen, *Contra Celsus* 2.13.

86. See Hegesippus' characterization of James as 'not respecting persons' in *E.H.* 2.23.11.

87. Cf. CD XX.19–20.

88. CD I.1 and II.2.

89. *Ibid.*, XX.18–20.

90. CD XX.33–4.

91. Ps. *Rec.* 1.70.

92. Cf. 1QpHab XI.8, Jerome, *Vir. ill.* 2, etc.

93. 1QpHab XI.4–7 – here are all the allusions, including 'swallowing', 'pursuing', etc.

94. See 1QpHab VII.17–VIII.3 and XII.4–5.

95. *MMT* II.8–9.

96. Hippolytus, *Phil.* 9.21 and Josephus, *War* 2.152–3.

97. See *E.H.* 3.27 and 6.17, Epiphanius, *Haeres.* 30.1.1–34.6, and Irenaeaus, *Ad Haer* 1.26.2.

98. Ps. *Rec.* 1.70–73 and *Vir. ill.* 2.

99. See Letters of Peter and Clement to James and *Hom.* 11.35.

100. 1QS VIII.8.12–16 and IX. 16–24; also see 'the Penitents of the Wilderness' in 4QpHab III.1 and 'the *Golah* of the Wilderness' in 1QM I.2

101. Jeremiah 31:31, CD VI.19–VII.9, VIII.21/XIX.33 and cf. Jesus/Paul in 1 Corinthians 11:25, 2 Corinthians 3:6, Luke 22:20 and pars. and Hebrews 8:8–9:13 and 12:24.

102. 1QpHab VII.17–VIII.3 and cf. Romans 1:17, Galatians 3:12, Hebrews 10:28, etc.

103. Cf. Matthew 22:37–9 and pars., James 2:5–26, and Justin Martyr, *Dial.*, 23, 47, and 93.

104. For John's teaching, see *Ant.* 18.117; for the Essenes', see *War* 2.122 and 139.

105. For 'zeal' at Qumran, see 1QS II.15, III.10, and IX.23 ('for the Law and the Day of Vengeance'); Paul, Galatians 1:14 and 3:17–8 (sarcastically and attacking his enemies); also see Matthew 2:23 on Jesus, alluding to 'Nazoraean' but obviously basing it on 'Nazirite' scriptural allusion, and the 'keeping away from' language associated with James' directives to overseas communities, as well as 'N-Z-R' language generally at Qumran.

106. 1QpHab XII.2–3; note too the use here (as in 4QpPs37 IV.9) of the key *'gamul'*/'pay'.

107. F.M. Cross, *The Ancient Library at Qumran*, New York, 1958, pp. 152–60 is typical; but see also Vermes, *Les Manuscript du Desert du Juda*, Tournai, 1953, pp. 92–100. Both Vermes in his translations and A. Dupont-Sommer in *The Essene Writings from Qumran*, Oxford, 1961, actually translate the usage here as 'walking in the ways of drunkenness', the cause of much of the misunderstanding – but, as opposed to this, see J.T. Milik, *Ten Years of Discovery in the Wilderness of Judea*, 1959, pp. 64–70.

108. See 1QpHab XI.9–XII.6 and 4QpPs 37 IV.9f.

109. See my Appendix on 'The Three Nets of *Belial*' and *'balla'*/'*Bela*' in *JJHP*, pp. 87–94 and *DSSFC*, pp. 208–17.

110. Also see this same kind of grouping in CD IV.15–V.15 and VI.14–VII.9.

111. See Cross, pp. 122–7, M. Burrows, *The Dead Sea Scrolls*, New York, 1955, pp. 128–42, and G.R. Driver, *The Judaean Scrolls*, Oxford, 1965, pp. 197–225.

112. 4QpNah, II.3.

113. For Pompey's restraint, see *War* 1.152–4/*Ant* 14.71–4; for Herod's, *War* 351–7/*Ant.* 483–6.

114. See Louis H. Feldman, 'Financing the Colosseum', *BAR*, 27/4, July/August, 2001.

115. 1QpHab VI.3–8.

116. For the arguments for Roman military practice, see Driver, pp. 168 (where he attributes the observation to then Major General Yigal Yadin) and 178–96. In fact the deifications began in 42 BCE when the Senate voted Julius Caesar – whose image was the first man to appear on a Roman coin – 'Pater Patriae' and *'Divus Iulius'* and Augustus, therefore, *'Divi filius'* ('Son of God'!), but these deifications continued throughout the First Century and included Augustus' wife Livia, Augustus himself by Tiberius in 14 CE, Caligula, and even Claudius by Nero.

117. 1QpHab VI.6–11 and cf. *War* 3.532–41.

118. Luke 2:1–3, *Ant* 1.1–3/*War* 2.117–8.

119. See 1QpHab XI.4–8.

120. See b. *RH* 31a–b, *San* 41a, *AZ* 8b, etc. and my 'Interpreting *Abeit Galuto* in the Habakkuk *Pesher*', *DSSFC*, pp. 247–71.

121. CD VII.13–VIII.1.

122. See *E.H.* 2.23.13; cf. Matthew 24:30 and 26:64 and pars.

123. 1QM XI.17–XII.11 and XIX.1–2.

124. *War* 6.312–4.

Chapter 1

1. See *E.H.* 2.23.5, Jerome, *Vir. ill.* 2 and *Comm. on Gal.* 396 (1:10), and *Haeres.* 78.7.7.

2. See Paul's competitive claim in Galatians 1:15 and in 2 Corinthians 7:1.

3. See *Haeres.* 30.2.3 and 78.13.2 and 78.14.3.

4. For Banus, see *Vita* 11 and cf. *War* 2.120.

5. See *Protevang.* 8.2–12.3.

6. See 'brothers' in Matthew 12:46–9, John 2:12, 7:3–5, etc.; for 'sisters', see Matthew 13:56/Mark 6:3. etc.

7. Jerome in *Vir. ill.* 2 calls James 'the son of Mary sister of the Lord' in John 19:25 (thus).

8. See *Protevang.* 25.1.

9. See *b. B.B.* 60b, *Naz.* 19a, *Ned.* 10a and 77b, and *Ta'an* 11a; *JBJ*, pp. 309, 764, and 898.

10. In Paul, 1 Corinthians 12:12–27, Ephesians 2:18–22, etc. – Gospels, John 2:21/Matthew26:61 and *pars.*

12. Cf. Matthew 9:11, 11:19, Mark 2:16, Luke 5:30, 7:34, 15:2, etc. and the allusions to 'eating and drinking' in Matthew's 'Little Apocalypse' 24:38 and49 (including an allusion to 'drinking with drunkards' – 'gluttons' obviously being implied too) and Luke 10:7.

13. We have already seen the use of this '*Cup*' imagery in 1QpHab XI.8–12.6; but see also Revelation 14:8–11 and 1:1–21.

14. See *b. B.B.* 60b, *Naz.* 19a, *Ned.* 10a, 77b, and *Ta'an* 11a.

15. See *JBJ*, pp. 309, 764, 898, and 1028 and Benjamin of Tudela, *Travels*: Year 1165. He describes these 'Mourners for Zion' as 'eating no meat and abstaining from wine and dressing only in black and living in caves'!

16. See A. Paul, *Ecrits de Qumran et Sectes Juives aux Premiers Siecles de L'Islam: Recherches sur l'origine du Qaraisme*, Paris, 1969.

17. *Ibid.*, pp. 115–140.

18. Benjamin, for instance, also in Year 1165 describes the Uprising of David Alroy (c. 1155), but there were earlier ones like Abu 'Isa al-Isfahani and his disciple Yughdan (preceding Anan ben David and patterned on similar Shi'ite Islamic ones from the 7th Century and Karaism onwards), both of whom – like other 'Mourners for Zion' and James – 'prohibted all meat and wine' ; see al-Kikisani in L. Nemoy's *Karaite Anthology*, New Haven, 1952, pp. 51 and 334. Al-Biruni, too (the 10th-11th Century Muslim geographer and encyclopaedist), in *The Chronology of Ancient Nations*, 3.20, also knows about the teachings of both Abu 'Isa al-Isfahani and Yughdan.

19. See M. Baigent, R. Leigh, and H. Lincoln, *Holy Blood, Holy Grail*, London, 1982, pp. 85–109. Though this inner circle or '*kabal*' is probably imaginary, still the choice of this designation is curiously interesting.

20. 1QH XVII.30–5.

21. Matthew 11:18–19/Luke 7:33–4 and cf. *E.H.* 2.23.5 and *Haeres.* 78.13.3.

22. See for instance *Zohar* 1.59b on 'Noah' and Proverbs 10:25.

23. See CD IV.17–8, VI.15–VII.3, *MMT* II.3–24 and cf. *Haeres.* 30.16.7.

24. See *War* 2.129 and Hippolytus 9.16, Ps. *Hom.* 7.8, 10.1, 11.1, 24–8, and *Haeres.* 17, 19.5.7, 30.2.4–6, etc.

25. Cf. Luke 5:36–9 and pars. with 1QS VI.4–5.

26. Cf. 1QS V.13, VI.2–5, 20–1, VII.19–20, etc. with*War* 2.130–33; but see too 2.143–4.

27. Cf. *E.H.* 2.23.5, *Haeres.* 78.13.3, and Luke 1:15 and 7:33/Matthew 11:18.

28. See in Hippolytus 9.21 how he uses the same expression to explain why the 'Zealot'/'*Sicarii* Essenes' enduring any torture and preferred death rather than 'blaspheme the Law or eat things sacrificed to idols'.

29. *E.H.* 4.22.4, *Haeres.* 19.1.1–6, 19.5.7, 20.3.1–4, 29.1.1–4, 29.5.1–29.7.7 30.1.1, and 53.1.1–4. Also see Apost. Const. 6.6 which calls 'Masbuthaeans' 'Basmuthaeans', and Pliny, *H.N.* 5.81 who knows a group in Northern Syria called the 'Nazirines'.

30. See S. Goranson, 'Essenes: Etymology from '*Asah*', *Revue de Qumran*, 1984, pp. 483–98.

31. This is also the case with a name like 'Abgarus' which becomes 'Agbarus', 'Acbarus', 'Augurus', 'Alburus', etc. in many translations.

32. See *Haeres.* 53.2.2.

33. See, for instance, *Haeres.* 30.17.1–18.1, but also 53.1.1–4 and Hippolytus 9.9 and 10.25.

34. *Ant.* 18.112–9.

35. Cf. A.N. Sherwin-White, *The Roman Citizenship*, Oxford, 1939, pp. 270–5 with CD VIII.10/XIX.23 on 'the Kings of the Peoples' which it considers identical with 'the Greek-speaking Kings'.

36. In CD IV.17–V.15 and VIII.4–10/XIX.18–22, these 'Princes' are called 'diseased without a cure'.

37. See, e.g., Tacitus in *Annals* 6.44 and 12.12 in his references to 'Acbar King of the Arabs' or Edessenes generally. Strabo in *Geography* 16.1.28 considers almost all Mesopotamians 'Arabs' as he does 'Osrhoeans'; for Pliny, *H.N.* 6.31.136–9, so are the inhabitants of Charax Spasini on the Persian Gulf, where Izates originally lived; for Juvenal, *Satire* 1.127, even the famous Roman Governor, Tiberius Alexander, is an 'Arabarch'.

38. In Dio Cassius, *Roman History*, 68.21, it can be either 'Augurus'/'Albarus'/ or 'Agbarus'; the same for Hippolytus in *Codex Baroccian* 26.

39. Cf. *E.H.* 1.13.2.

40. See Moses of Chorene, *History of Armenia,* 2.35, who sees Helen as the first and principal of Abgar's wives, with *Ant.* 20.18. This is also the position somewhat of 'The Teaching of Addai'.

41. See *Ant.* 20.17–53 and 75–92.

42. See *JBJ*, pp. 856–66 and 923–36.

43. See Moses of Chorene 2.35.

44. For the history of this monarch, see Eusebius, Moses of Chorene, *loc. cit.*, and J.B. Segal, *Edessa 'The Blessed City'*, pp. 62–82.

45. *Ant.* 20.34–48.

46. Strabo, 17.1.54–2.4 calls her 'the Ruler of the Ethiopians in (his) time', but he clearly means Meroe in Nubia on the Nile (c. 50–25 BCE), a point Pliny consolidates in *H.N.* 6.35.

47. *Ant.* 20.38–46, which is supported and even more fully fleshed out in Gen. R. 46:10–47:11.

48. One should note that Josephus makes it clear that 'Queen Helen sent her representatives (plural) to Alexandria to buy grain' to relieve the Famine, a point he repeats in discussing Theudas' reverse exodus to the Jordan; *Ant.* 20.51 and 97–102.

49. This disparity between Acts 12:1–24 and Galatians can be explained by considering that Paul and Barnabas were among those who went either to Alexandria or Cyprus on these grain and fig-buying missions.

50. Cf. *Ant.* 20.35–47.

51. See Segal, *Edessa*, pp. 15 and 66ff., who makes it clear 'Ezad' is 'Izates'; in *War* 4.567, Josephus seemingly even calls him 'Izas'.

52. Cf. *Haeres.* 19.2.1–4.2, 30.1.3–3.7, and 53.1.1ff. with Hippolytus, 9.8.

53. *E.H.* 3.32.1–8.

54. For Simeon bar Yohai and the *Zohar*, see *JBJ*, p. 821 and *MZCQ*, pp. 54 and 71.

55. *Haeres.* 19.1.1–5.7, 30.1.1–3.7, and 53.1.3.

56. See *E.H.* 1.13.1–20, 2.12.1–3, and *Ant.* 20.1–117.

57. Cf. *Ant.* 20.21 with John 1:14–18 and 3:16–18.

58. *Ant.* 20.22–23 and 34–5.

59. Acts 9:10ff.

60. See CD VI.19–VII.9.

61. See CD V.6–9, VI.30–VII.4, and XX.27–32.

62. The *Fihrist* 9.1; cf. as well al-Biruni, 8.44ff.

63. See E.S. Drower, *The Mandaeans of Iraq and Iran*, Oxford, pp. 1–10 and 100–124 and *The Secret Adam*, Oxford, 1960, pp. 88–106; also see *The Haran Gawaita and the Baptism of Hibil-Ziwa*, tr. E.S. Drower, Biblioteca Apostolica Vaticano, Citta del Vaticano, 1953, pp. VIII–XI and 2–17. According to Mandaean tradition, the followers of John the Baptist fled eastward in 37 CE, the approximate year Josephus actually gives for his execution.

64. See *JBJ*, pp. 324–331.

65. See Hippolytus 9.8–9 and 10.25 and *Haeres.* 19.4.1, 30.3.1–6, and 5.1.8–9. For Simon *Magus*, see Ps. *Rec.* 1.72 and 2.7–8 and Ps. *Hom.* 2.22–4, Epiphanius 21.2.3–4, and *Haeres.* 10.8.

66. See, e.g., Matthew 12:46, Luke 24:36, John 20:14, 20:19, 20:26, 21:4, and Acts 1:10, 7:55–6 (Stephen's James-like/Great Power/Primal Adam proclamation – cf. Matthew 26:64 and Mark 14:62 and even the 'two Angels' in Luke 24:4).

67. In the Koran, see 2.124–133, 3.33, 3.95–7, 21.51–75, 26.69–103, etc.

68. For Paul, see Galatians 3:6–18 and Romans 4:1–16; for Muhammad, see Koran 2.135–40 and 3.95 and 113–5, etc.

69. In CD, paralleling the Koran, one finds this in III.2–20, ending in evocation of 'the Primal Adam' ideology. But even more impressively, *MMT* II.30–3 ends with evocation of Genesis 15:6's 'reckoned to you as Righteousness' applying it to its Kingly recipient and his 'People' – Koranic and 'Jamesian' works Righteousness with a vengeance.

70. This, as opposed to James, the Koran, and of course CD and *MMT*.

71. For the 'Friend' terminology, see CD III.2–4 and for 'Perfection'/'Perfection of the Way', see 1QS VIII.1–10, 18–25 and CD II,15–6, VII.4–6, XX.2–7, etc.

72. See too the Scrolls' condemnation of the 'Emptiness' of the Lying Spouter's teaching in 1QpHab X.9–12.

73. See Koran 4.126.

74. The 'King'/'Kings' would appear to be referred to in II.21–9 (where an earlier letter is alluded to) introducing this evocation of Abraham's 'works' being 'reckoned as justifying him' and this 'King''s 'People' in II.30.

75. For detailed arguments regarding the identity of these two, see *JBJ*, pp. 862–939.

76. See the references to 'the Land of Noah', particularly in conjunction with the ark in 11:25–49 – which certainly did not come down in Arabia as such – introducing 'Ad and Hud. The same is true of 26:105–49 where latter's typically Northern-Syrian style cattle-grazing land is described; see also 29.14–38, etc.

77. See VII.14–XX.12.

78. See my article '*MMT* as a Jamesian Letter to "the Great King of the Peoples beyond the Euphrates,"' *Journal of Higher Criticism*, 11/1, Spring, 2005(first given to the Society of Biblical Literature in 1997), pp. 55–68.

79. See G. Williams, *Eastern Turkey: A Guide and History*, 1972, London, 1972, pp. 166–167 – this was supposed to have been in a cave under the Great Mosque. Even the spring at Callirhoe is attributed to Abraham. *Per contra*, see C.H. Gordon, 'Abraham and the Merchants of Ura', *JNES* 17, 1958, pp. 28–31 and A.R. Millard, 'Where was Abraham's Ur?', *BAR*, May/June, 2001.

80. See W. Dalrymple, *From the Holy Mountain: A Journey among Christians of the Middle East*, London, 1997, p. 74, the Official Turkish Government site 'Sanliurfa', and cf. Luke 1:24 and *Protevang*. 22.3

81. In *Ant.* 20.18 and 20.26 Josephus also calls him 'Monobazus', which like 'Abgarus' in neighboring Syriac tradition seems to be a name coursing through multiple generations of this family. In 20.24 Josephus calls this Kingdom 'Carron'/'Carrae', a designation that has never been made sensible.

82. Cf. Gen R 46:10–11 and *Ant.* 20. 38–45 with Acts 8:26–40; and see *JBJ*, pp. 883–922.

83. Cf. Acts 8:38–9 with *Ant.* 20.46.

84. In Dio Cassius 68.4, Nerva reapplied the traditional body of legislation against castrations known as the *Lex Cornelia de Sicarius et Veneficis*, while Hadrian – obviously in the wake of the Bar Kochba War – outlawed circumcision completely with his '*Ius Sicaricon*'; cf. *The Augustan History* 13.10ff.

85. *Ant.* 20.35–43 and 46–8.

86. E.g., Matthew 19:12 (concerning 'eunuchs'); Mark 14:4 (concerning 'the Poor'); Luke 19:39 (concerning 'Pharisees'); John 6:64 (concerning 'belief'); 9:16 ('the Pharisees' again); 9:40 (concerning Matthew's 'Blind Pharisees'); etc.

87. CD XVI.6–8.

88. The usage 'Satan' does not occur as such at Qumran – rather this 'Angel of Mastema'. All references to 'Satan' one sees in some translations are almost always, therefore, to 'Belial' in the original.

89. CD XVI.4–6.

90. See 1QS V.2–3 and V.9.

91. Cf. Hebrews 11:17 with *Ant.* 20.20.

Chapter 2

1. Hippolytus 9.8–12.

2. Hippolytus 9.9; cf. *Haeres.* 19.5.1.

3. *Zohar* 63a and 67b on 'Noah'.

4. Cf. Koran 7.59–79, 11.29–68, 26.106–58, etc.

5. Hippolytus 9.8.

6. See *JBJ*, pp. 328–36 and E.S. Drower, *Mandaeans, op. cit.*, pp. 1–19, 100–24, and 258–62. Also E.S. Drower, *The Secret Adam*, Oxford, 1960, pp. ix–xvii and 88–106.

7. Koran 2.62, 5.69, 22.17, etc.

8. See, for instance the material on Abraham in 2.124–36, 3.65–7, 4.125, etc.

9. Muhammad makes it clear in 3.113 that all 'Peoples of the Book are not the same', some 'standing' or being 'more staunch' than others; cf. James 2:17–24. To paraphrase James, this reads: 'O Empty or Foolish Man, do you not know that Abraham was saved by sacrificing Isaac (this being a work) and that is how we are justified, not by Faith alone but rather by Faith and works working together', the final point basically paralleling Muhammad's 'believe and do good works' repeated throughout the Koran.

10. Cf. 1QS VI.6–7 and *War* 2.128–36.

11. Koran 3.113–4.

12. Cf. *E.H.* 1.13.4–10 and see the two variant manuscripts of *Apost. Const.* 8.25 on 'Lebbaeus surnamed Thaddaeus', a.k.a. 'Judas the Zealot' and 'Judas of James'; for these overlaps also see *JBJ*, pp. 930–38.

13. See *Haeres.* 29.1.1 and 29.4.1–5.1 where he claims this was the name applied by Philo either to those he denotes as 'Theraputae' or 'Essenes'. For Epiphanius, anyhow, this was just an earlier name for 'Christians'.

14. James 1:22, 1:23, and 1:25.

15. 1QpHab VII.10–11 on Habakkuk 2:3 and 'the Delay of the *Parousia*', VIII.1–3 on Habakkuk 2:4, and XII.4–5 on 'the *Ebionim*' or 'the Poor'.

16. See *Haeres.* 20.3.4 and 29.1.1–7.1.

17. Cf. *E.H.* 4.22.6 with *Haeres.* 19.5.7, but also Justin Martyr, *Dial.* 80.

18. *Haeres.* 19.2.10 and 20.3.2–4. Here too, he basically contends that all have been absorbed into 'the Ebionites'.

19. *Haeres.* 29.1.1–4, 29.5.4–7.4, and 30.2.3–3.7; for a polemical view of Ebionite doctrine, see *E.H.* 3.27.1–6.

20. For Hegesippus, *E.H.* 2.23.5–6 and *Haeres.* 78.14.2, James 'did not enter the (public) baths' and like the Essenes 'did not anoint himself with oil', but he did 'enter the Temple alone'. For Epiphanius in *Haeres.* 29.4.1–5, supported by Jerome, this was 'the Holy of Holies' where, as High Priest, he proceeded to make a typical 'Yom Kippur Atonement' on 'behalf of the while People'. But certainly anyone doing such things and entering the Temple in such manner (especially 'Priests') was obliged to take a ritual bath; see *M. Middah* 1:4, 5:3, *M. Par.* 3:7, *b. Tam* 26b, *j. Yoma* 40b, *b. Yoma* 30a–31a, *Ant.* 12.1456, *War* 4.205, etc. The solution to this conundrum would seem to be found in Josephus' statement that 'the Essenes preferred dry skin' not that they did not bathe – meaning they did not anoint themselves with any oils and probably did not take Greco-Roman-style hot baths; but they certainly took cold ones as did James' counterpart '*Banus*' below. So probably and almost assuredly did James. See also *JBJ*, pp. 344–5.

21. See *Haeres.* 30.21.1 and Ps. *Hom.* 8.2, 10.1, 10.26, 11.1, etc.

22. See, for instance, Ps. *Rec.* 4.35 and Ps. *Hom.* 7.3, 7.8, 8.14, 8.19, 11.35, 12.6 (this showing Peter as a vegetarian).

23. E. S. Drower, *op. cit*, pp. 102 and 155.

24. Cf. Matthew 19:13–5 and *pars.* and Acts 6:6, 8:17–9, 13:3, and 28:8.

25. *Haeres.* 30.18.1–21.1. In fact, just as Josephus' 'Essenes', according to the Ps. *Hom.* 12.6, Peter also 'wears only threadbare clothes'; at Qumran, see 1QpHab XII.3, 4QpPs 37 II.16, III.10, IV.11, and 1QH V.23 ('the '*Ebionei-Hesed*'/'the Poor Ones of Piety').

26. *Haeres.* 30.18.1.

27. *Ibid.* 30.21.1

28. *Ibid.* 30.21.2.

29. Ps. *Rec.* 1.39–47, 5.10, and 8.59; Ps. *Hom.* 2.6–12; in the Gospels see Matthew 21:11, Luke 1:76, and John 6:14 and 7:40–1. This is based on Deuteronomy 18:15–19, cited in 4QTest 4–8 but also see 1QS IX.11 where it is coupled with 'the coming of the Messiah of Aaron and Israel'. For the Manichaeans, Mani too is the Seal of the Prophets and, in the Koran, see 3.84, 7.157, 33.1–59, etc.

30. Hippolytus 9.21.

31. Cf. Hippolytus 9.21 with *War* 2.159–63.

32. *B. Suk.* 52a–b; see also *b. San.* 97a; Genesis R. 75.6, 95, and 99.2; and Song of Songs R. 2.13.4. In *b. San.* 43a and 67a, there is also the character known as 'Ben Stada' (probably a variation on 'the Standing One' and identical to 'the Messiah ben Joseph') and who, according to *b. Shab.* 104b, was said to have brought sorcery from Egypt. He too was crucified at Lydda. *B.B.* 10b and *Pes.* 50a also pointedly speak of 'the martyrs at Lydda'. One should that Justin Martyr in *Apology* 2.14–15 actually refers to 'Sotadists' when speaking about Simon *Magus*.

33. See the allusion both to 'leading Ephraim astray with a Lying teaching and a Tongue full of Lies' in 4QpNah II.8 and that to 'the Simple of Ephraim joining' or 'rejoining the Many' or 'Majority of Israel' in 4QpNah III.5, itself using the language of '*ger-nilveh*'/'resident alien' or '*Nilvim*'/'Joiners' or 'Gentile converts'. For 'Ephraim' as 'Samaria', see Isaiah 7:9, 11:13, Ezekiel 37:16–19, Hosea 4:17, 5:3, and throughout.

34. *B. Suk.* 52a–b. Even Josephus, *War* 2.234–46, records many difficulties in this border area between Jews and Samaritans which resulted in numerous executions.

35. *Ant.* 18.85–9. Here Pilate is removed and sent to Rome because of the outrages he committed against this Samaritan 'Messiah' and his followers, but not before Tiberius had already died in 37 CE.

36. See *E.H.* 2.13.3, quoting Justin Martyr (who came from Samaria), *Apology* 1.26 and 1.56, and Ps. *Rec.* 2.7 and Ps. *Hom.* 2.22; also see Irenaeus, *Ad. Haeres.* 1.23, Hippolytus, 6.2, Epiphanius 21.1.1, *etc.*

37. *Ant.* 20.142.

38. For statements of this doctrine relative to Simon, see Ps. *Rec.* 2.7 and *Hom* 2.23; relative to the Naassenes, see Hippolytus 5.3; the Elchasaites, Hippolytus 10.25; the Sampsaeans, Epiphanius, *Haeres.* 53.1.8–9; Christ himself, Tertullian, *The Flesh of Christ*, 1.16–7.

39. See Ps. *Rec.* 1.72 and 2.7; for 'laying on hands', see the Epistle of Clement to James 2, 19, Ps. *Hom.* 9.23, and E.S. Drower, *The Mandaeans of Iraq and Iran*, pp. 102 and 155.

40. Justin Martyr, *Apology* 1.26, *E.H.* 2.13.3, Ps. *Rec.* 2.7/Ps. *Hom.* 2.22, Irenaeus, *Ad. Haeres.* 1.23, Hippolytus, 6.2, Epiphanius A21.1, 21.1.1, etc.

41. Ps. *Rec.* 1.72–4.

42. See Acts 8:17–8, E.S. Drower, *op. cit.*, p. 155 and Ps. *Rec.* 2.7/Ps. *Hom.* 2.22.

43. Cf. al-Biruni, *Chronology of Ancient Nations*, 8.23, 18.10, and 20.29; *The Fihrist* 9.1; and E.S. Drower, *Mandaeans*, pp. 7 and 258–62.

44. See Ps. *Rec.* 2.7–11 and Ps. *Hom.* 2.22–4.

45. See Origen, *Contra Celsus* 6.11, Eusebius, *E.H.* 4.22.5, and Epiphanius, *Haeres.* 8.9.1, 10.1.1, 13.1.1–4, and 20.3.4.

46. See *Ant.* 20.129–33. Loeb notes 'Dortus' and 'Doitus' as variant readings for 'Doetus'.

47. See *Ant.* 18.85–87. Also M. Gaster, *The Samaritans*, Oxford, 1925, pp. 90–1, who directly connects this episode to the Samaritan '*Taheb*' or 'Restorer' ideology. The Fourth-Century *Memar* of Marqah also makes it clear that the idea has something to do with the 'True Prophet' prophecy of Deuteronomy 18:18–19.

48. *Ant.* 18.88–90; cf. Philo's *Mission to Gaius* 299–305.

49. Cf. *Ant.* 18.116–9 with *Ant.* 18.85 and note the sequentiality here.

50. *Ant.* 18.85–6.

51. Cf. *Ant.* 18.88 with Matthew 27:11–26 and pars.

52. *Ant.* 18.89.

53. Acts 8:26–39.

54. Note that in the *Ant.* 18.116–9 John's death is presented as occurring after Pontius Pilate's removal from Palestine and after the Samaritan '*Taheb*' affair.

55. See Josephus in *War* 2.128 and 2.139 and cf. CD VI.21, James 2:5–8, and *Dial.* 23, 46–47, 52, and 93.

56. *War* 2.118–9.

57. Matthew 14:6 and pars.

58. *Ant.* 18.106–129.

59. *Ant.* 18.108–115; the information that Salome was Philip's wife and it was he that died childless is given by Josephus in *Ant.* 18.136–7 and that Herodias was originally married to a half-brother of Herod Antipas, himself named 'Herod' and not 'Philip' is given by Josephus in *Ant.* 18.109 and 18.136 – nor is there any way out of these New Testament contradictions whatever facile apologetic stratagem is chosen.

60. Hippolytus 9.8 and *E.H.* 6.38. One should note that it is in the library of Caesarea that Origen saw the copy of Josephus' *War* testifying to the fact that Jerusalem fell because of the death of James (not Jesus).

61. For the Mani Codex, see L. Koenen and C. Romer, *Der Kolner Mani-Kodex*, Bonn, 1985 and *Codex Manichaicus Coloniensis*, ed. L. Cirillo, Cosenza, 1990 – in particular, the article by L. Koenen, pp. 1 –34; also see L. Cirillo, *Elchasai e gli Elchasaiti*, Cosenza, 1984. Also see the actual quotations from Mani's '*Book called the Shaburkan*' (after the Persian Ruler for whom he composed it), which al-Biruni claims to give in his *Chronology of Ancient Nations*, pp. 8.1–8. He also claims in 3.11–16 that 'the Manichaeans have a Gospel of their own', which they call 'The Gospel of the Seventy', the contents of which 'really are what the Messiah thought and taught, that every other Gospel is false and its followers are Liars against the Messiah', ideas that in one form or another also went into the Koran.

62. See L. T. Stuckenbruck, *The Book of the Giants from Qumran*, Tubingen, 1997, pp. VII–IX and pp. 1–4.

63. For an Islamic view of the Manichaeans, see *The Fihrist* 9.1 and al Biruni 8.41ff., for whom Mani, whose followers were called Siddiks (i.e., *Zaddik*s) and who taught poverty, 'separation from the world', sexual continence, abstinence, vegetarianism, poverty, and 'the Right Path', came from an Elchasaite family in Messene (i.e., Charax Spasini/Basrah again). The only 'Essene'/ 'Ebionite'/'Jamesian' thing he did not teach was bathing – which is the same for Islam.

64. See E. S. Drower, *The Mandaeans of Iraq and Iran*, pp. 3–7 and 'Mandaean Polemic' in *BSOAS*, no. 25, 1962, pp. 438–448.

65. See, for instance, the reference to the Simon *Magus*-type 'Magician' called '*Elymus Magus*' on 'Cyprus' in Acts 13:8 and the Samaritans as 'Cuthaeans' in *Ant.* 9.288–90, 11.19–20, *War* 1.63, etc. above – 'Cuthaeans' obviously doubling for for *Kittim*/Cypriots, Cretans, or Greeks elsewhere. One should note that, according to *The Scholia* of Theodore bar Konai, a Nestorian Syriac scholar of the 8th –9th Century, the group he calls 'the Cantaeans' (obviously meaning 'the Cuthaeans' or 'Samaritans') preceded the Mandaeans in their doctrines – again, obviously true. But also see, Epiphanius' claim in *Haeres.* 8.6–11 above (also echoing 2 Kings 17:24 and echoed by al-Kirkisani as well), how the Babylonians settled the Assyrian 'Cutha' in Samaria!

66. See 1QS I.12–18, VIII.12–18 and IX.4–20.

67. *Surah*s 2.62, 5.69, and 22:17.

68. On Helen's three successive '*Nazirite*' oaths, see *b. Naz.* 19a–20a; for her gifts to the Temple, see *b. Yoma* 37a, *b. Git.* 60a, and *Tosefta Pe'ah* 4:18.

69. See *The Travels of Rabbi Benjamin*, year 1164. This is to say nothing about all the various Karaites and Mourners for Zion he is encountering.

70. *Ant.* 20.97.

71. *E.H.* 2.1.2, 2.23.1, and *Haeres.* 78.14.2.

72. For 'Judas the Zealot', see the variant mss. of *Apost. Const.*, noted in *ANCL*, asserting that 'Thaddaeus, also called Lebbaeus' in Matthew', was surnamed Judas the Zealot who preached the Truth to the Edessenes and the People of Mesopotamia when Abgarus ruled over Edessa and was buried in Berytus (Beirut) of Phoenicia'. For 'Theudas the brother of the Just One', see 2 Apoc. Jas. 44.18.

73. See '*Nusairi*' article by Louis Massignon in *Encyclopaedia of Islam*, 1st ed.

74. See L. Massignon, '*Nusairi*' in *E.I.* above and H. Field and J.B. Glubb, 'The Yezidis, Sulubba, and other Tribes of Iraq and Adjacent Regions', *General Series in Anthropology* 10, Menasha, Wisconsin, 1943, pp. 5–16.

75. *Ad. Haeres.* 5.1.3 and *Haeres.* 30.3.1–7 and 17.4, 53.1.8–10.

76. Cf. 1QS IV.19–24 on 'the Two Spirits' and 'Holy Spirit' baptism; CD III.18–20 introducing the definition of 'the Sons of Zadok'; 1QH IV.29–34 referring both to '*Enosh*' (John's name among the Mandaeans) and 'the Son of Man' (*Adam*), and 1QM X.11 interpreting 'the Star Prophecy' of Numbers 24:17 in terms of Isaiah 31:8's 'the sword of no mere Adam'.

77. See 4QTest 4–8, 1QS IX.11(where it is coupled with 'the coming of the Messiah of Aaron and Israel') and, for instance, Ps. *Rec.* 1.39–47, 5.10, 8.59, Ps. *Hom.* 2.6–12.

78. N.b., all the references to Jesus 'standing' in Luke 24:36, John 1:26, 20:14, 20:19, 20:26, and 21:4, Acts 4:10, 7:55–6, etc. and see *Haeres.* 30.3.2–6 describing the 'Sampsaeans, Ossaeans, and Elchasaites'.

79. For the Apostles as 'standing', see John 18:5–25, 19:26, and Acts 1:11; for the two Angels, see Luke 24:4; for Mary Magdalene, see John 20:11, etc.

80. Cf. Ps. *Rec.* 2.8–11 and Ps. *Hom.* 2.24.

81. See the variant manuscripts of the *Apostolic Constitutions* noted in *ANCL* above and the reference in the fragments of Hippolytus 'On the Twelve Apostles' to the effect that 'Judas who is also (called) Lebbaeus (thereby combining Luke with Matthew) preached to the People of Edessa and to all Mesopotamia, and fell asleep at Berytus and was buried there'.

82. John 6:71, 13:2, and 13:26.

83. Luke 6:15 and Acts 1:13, but see also Hippolytus 'On the Twelve Apostles' in *ANCL* who also identifies this 'Simon' as 'the son of Clopas' (i.e., 'Simeon bar Cleophas'), who is also (called) Judas' (meaning he is placing the name in the context of the 'Judas of Simon Iscariot' complex) and 'became Bishop of Jerusalem after James the Just and fell asleep and was buried there at the age of one hundred and twenty years', that is, not only is he basically identifying 'Simon the Zealot' with 'Simeon bar Cleophas', but he is also incorporating the story of the death of the latter in Trajan's time; see *JBJ*, pp. 817–50.

84. 2 Apoc. Jas. 44.11–25.

85. 1 Apoc. Jas. 36.4–24, here even including reference to the 'secret' of 'hidden' ideology.

86. *Ant.* 20. 97.

87. Matthew 14:13–21 and 15:33–8 and pars.

88. Cf. CD IV.2–3, VI.19–21, and VII.16–7.

89. CD V.6–16 and VI.19–VII.6.

90. See *War* 2.259 and 264–5 and *Ant.* 20.160 and 167–8.

91. For use of terms 'Innovation(s)'/'Innovator(s)' in Josephus, see *War* 2.5, 2.224, 2.407–10, and 2.513; *Ant.* 18.93 and 20.129 (followed by one of the crucifixions at Lydda); and even *Vita* 17 and 28.

92. See John 4:45–54 and 6:3–14 and Matthew 14:14–21, 15:29–38, and 16:5–12 and pars.

93. One should note how defensive Josephus is in *Vita* 17–20 following his journey to Rome at the age of 26 to help some 'Priests' who had gone there to plead their case before Caesar, his defensiveness against Justus of Tiberius in *Vita* 335–93 who was evidently accusing him of sedition, and his final defense of himself in *Vita* 407–430.

94. For Helen, see *Ant.* 20.17–96 which is immediately followed in 20.100–1 with the 'Theudas' affair and the mention of Queen Helen's 'famine relief' activities thereafter in 20.102 by the note about the crucifixion of Judas the Galilee's two sons James and Simon – whom I take to be the type of 'the two sons of Thunder' James and John (Mark 3:17), who would have to 'drink the Cup' Jesus drank in Matthew 20:22–3/Mark 10:38–9 – and the note there about 'the Census of Quirinius' which causes the anachronism about Judas the Galilean coming chronologically after Theudas in Acts 5:37.

95. See above, pp. 5–21 and *JBJ*, pp. 111–119. Since Josephus is zealous of recording most such executions, the conclusion probably is that 'James the brother of John' in Acts probably substitutes from 'Judas' or 'Theudas the brother of James' in Josephus and elsewhere.

96. This, of course, is the introduction of James in Acts. Nor can it be avoided that this is the 'house' of 'Mary the mother of James' ('and the brothers') not John Mark – only the author of Acts is chary of telling us this.

97. See *JBJ*, pp. 51, 111–19, 192, etc.

98. See *Ant.* 20.102 and cf. Acts 5:36–7.

99. *Haeres.* 27.1.2 and 31.1.1–2.1. For the Valentinians, see Hippolytus 10.9 and throughout *Haeres.* For Valentinus as a 'hearer of Theudas' and he or Theudas as Paul's pupil, see Clement of Alexandria's

Stromata 7.17; for Clement's full name – 'Titus Flavius Clemens' – which would, no doubt, make him a descendant of the famous Flavius Clemens, see *E.H.* 6.13.2. One should not that if '*Theudas*' is to be identified with 'Thaddaeus'/'Addai'/'Judas the brother of James', then Paul gives every indication of knowing 'the brothers of the Lord' in 1 Corinthians 9:5, a designation which would include this 'Judas'/'Theudas'.

100. *E.H.* 3.4.10. For Flavius Clemens' execution in 95–96 CE by Domitian for his Christian sympathies, see *E.H.* 3.18.5, Dio Cassius 67.14.1–2, and Suetonius 8.15.1. For the 'Clement' in the Pseudoclementines as a Roman nobleman of the family of Caesar, see Ps. *Rec.* 1.1, 7.8–10, and 10.72 and Ps *Hom.* 4.7, 12.8–10 and 14.8–10. Curiously for *b. Git.* 56b and *A.Z.* 10b, the conversions of both Flavius Clemens and Domitilla are to Judaism.

101. See Suet. 8.14.4, Dio Cassius 67.14.4–5, and Josephus' dedication to Epaphroditus in *Vita* 430 and *Ant. Preface* 8–9. Though many do not think that Josephus died until early in Trajan's reign, there is no real evidence of his surviving any of these events. Furthermore, if Epaphroditus is the Epaphroditus in Suet. 6.49.4 and 8.14.4, it is doubtful Josephus could have survived the death of his patron. N.b., that in Philippians 4:18–22, Paul actually sends Epaphroditus to Nero's household.

102. *E.H.* 3.18.5, has Flavia Domitilla exiled and calls her Flavius Clemens' niece. Dio Cassius 67.14.1–2, while agreeing that she was exiled, calls her his wife. Interesting too, it has been observed that the Domitilla Chapel in this Catacomb is arranged in the Jewish manner.

103. Suet. 8.18.1–3 and Dio Cassius 67.17.1–18.2.

104. See Commentary on John 6.6 and *Contra Celsus* 6.11.

105. See *b. B.B.* 60b. Cf. how the Rabbis in *Ned.* 77b and *Naz.* 77b discourage not only this kind of Naziritism, but Naziritism in general, going so far in *b. Ta'an.* 11a and *Ned.* 10a to term such Nazirites 'Sinners'. But we have already seen that Benjamin of Tudela, *Travels* CE 1165, a thousand years later, reports encountering precisely such cave dwelling, Jewish 'Rechabites' who 'sustain the Poor and the ascetics called "Mourners for Zion" or "Mourners for Jerusalem"' who 'eat no meat, abstain from wine, and dress only in black'.

106. *E.H.* 3.20.1–8.

Chapter 3

1. *E.H.* 2.23.4–8, *Haeres.* 29.4.1–4, 30.2.6, and 78.7.7–8, and *Vir. ill.* 2.

2. The first scholar to grasp this idea was R. Eisler in his groundbreaking tour de force, *The Messiah Jesus and John the Baptist*, London and New York, 1931, pp. 540–6 and 584, which he wrote without benefit of the Dead Sea Scrolls though he did have the Cairo Damascus Document. Unfortunately his functioning life was cut short by time in Hitler's concentration camps though he did live to see the appearance of the Scrolls in 1947. His work was echoed and developed by S.G.F. Brandon in *The Fall of Jerusalem and the Christian Church*, London, 1951 and *Jesus and the Zealots*, London, 1957.

3. This is also supported by the Greek Orthodox writer, Andrew of Crete, who was born in Jerusalem in 660 CE (d. c. 740) and was a monk at Mar Saba, who also quotes Hegesippus – *Vita et Martyrium S. Jacobi Apost. Frat. Dom.* 1.10.21 (also cited by R. Eisler, p. 541 above).

4. For Epiphanius, citing 'Clement, Eusebius, and others', James actually wore the miter or breastplate of the High Priest with the inscription upon it, 'Holy to God'; *Haeres.* 29.4.3–4 78.14.1.

5. *E.H.* 2.23.7.

6. *Vita* 11–12. For James and the Essenes wearing only 'linen', see *E.H.* 2.23.6, *Haeres.* 78.13.3, *Vir. ill.* 2, War 2.128, and Hippolytus 9.16.

7. *Vita* 11.

8. *Haeres.* 78.14.2.

9. For the archetypical moment in all such 'Holy Places', see Moses in Exodus 3:5.

10. Cf. *E.H.* 2.23.5 with *War* 2.123.

11. Cf. *E.H.* 2.23.5 with *Haeres.* 78.13.2.

12. Cf. *E.H.* 2.23.5 and *Haeres.* 78.13.3 about James with *War* 2.123–9 and Hippolytus 9.16 about Essenes.

13. Even better ones, related to Peter's teaching, are to be found in Ps. *Hom.* 7.8 and 8.19, both of which actually include the category of 'that which is strangled'; but also see Koran 2.173, 5.3, 6.146, and 16.115.

14. *Haeres.* 78.14.1–3.

15. *Ant.* 20.51 and 101–2.

16. *Haeres.* 78.14.1.

17. *E.H.* 2.23.13 and cf. Daniel 7:13 and Matthew 24:30 and 26:64/Mark 13:26–7 and 14:62; at Qumran, see CD IV.3–9 and 1QpHab V.4.

18. 1QpHab V.4 above, 1QM XII.1–10 and XIX.1–2.

19. CD IV.4–7 and note here the expression 'called by Name', anticipated in CD II.11, paralleling such New Testament expressions as 'called by this Name' or 'called by the Name of' in Acts 2:21, 15:17, 22:16, etc., and 'name' and 'naming' symbolism generally in the New Testament and even Jewish *Kabbalah.*

20. 1QM XII.4–9 and XIX.1 and see my article 'Eschatological "Rain" Imagery in the War Scroll from Qumran and in the Letter of James', *JNES*, v. 49, no. 2, April, 1990, pp. 173–84, reprinted in *DSSFC*, pp. 272–87.

21. Matthew 24:30 and 26:64/Mark 13:26–7 and 14:62.

22. Not only is this 'Power' language is widespread in the Gospels – see, for instance, Matthew 9:6, 28:18, Luke 4:14, 5:24, 9:1, and pars.; but one also even sees it at Qumran – see 1QM I.4 and cf. *Haeres.* 19.4.1 on the 'Ossaeans' and 21.2.3 on the 'Simonian' followers of Simon *Magus* and similarly in the Pseudoclementines.

23. Cf. 1QH IX.26–35.

24. Cf. 1QM XII.9–10.

25. *ARN* 4.4.

26. *War* 2.6–7 and n.b., Hebrews 7:11–8:2 and 9:9–15.

27. *ARN* 6.3 and *b. Ta'an.* 19b–20a.

28. See 1 Kings 17:1, 18:2 and 45, and 19:11.

29. See the list of such persons in *ARN* 2.5.

30. See Hebrew *Ben Sira* 44:17.

31. Note the inversion of 'the Friend of God' language here applied to Abraham in James 2:23–4 and CD III.2–3, to say nothing of the Koran.

32. See James 2:12 and 5:7–9 and Jude 14–5.

33. *B. Ta'an.* 6a.

34. Cf. too 1 Maccabees 2:58, but also 2:54 on Phineas; also *Ben Sira* 48:1–2.

35. Luke 4:25–6 also has Jesus refer to this 'three and a half years' with regard to drought and by implication rainmaking and the timeframe will also have relevance to Daniel 12:7's 'a time, two times and a half' as it will to the period between James' death and the outbreak of the War against Rome.

36. For this 'whirlwind' and 'quaking mountains', reminiscent of the most vivid Koranic imagery, see 4QpNah I.1–11; for Ezekiel, see 13:12–4 following his allusions to 'Lying prophets' with their 'empty visions' and 'the plasterers on the wall' in 13:9–11 (cf. CD IV.18–20 and VIII.12–3).

37. See Hippolytus 9.20–1 and cf. Josephus, *War* 2.143 and 2.152–3.

38. Also see Romans 10:2–6 and 11:14 and note that the former is precisely the passage Jerome used against Origen in to rebuke him for having become a '*Sicarius*' or for castrating himself – Letter 84 to Pammachius and Oceanus – i.e., he did this out of 'zeal for God but not according to Knowledge'.

39. *E.H.* 2.1.4 and 23.10–13, *Vir. ill.* 2, *Haeres.* 78.14.5–7, etc.

40. Also see Daniel 9:27 and 11:31 and cf. *Ant.* 12.253, Matthew 24:15, and Mark 13:14. One of the first to make this suggestion was Louis Ginzberg in an article in the *Jewish Encyclopedia* but Antiochus Epiphanes seems to have been particularly attached to this Deity; see Livy's *History of Rome* 41.20.1–4.

41. See *War* 2.407–20. If one compares this with the coming of the mournful prophet, Jesus ben Ananias in *War* 6.300–9 in Tabernacles, 62 CE, seemingly in the aftermath of or just following the death of James; then the 'three and a half years' is complete.

42. If one connects the two, particularly the appearance of the mysterious 'prophet' Jesus ben Ananias in *Succot*, 62 CE and James' death as reported in *Ant.* 20.200 and James' known antagonism to 'pollution of the idols' (Acts 15:20); then this is something of the conclusion that can be reached. Note this is also something of the way Josephus presents things as well with his evocation of 'the World Ruler Prophecy' in *War* 6.312–4 as the moving force behind the War against Rome.

43. *E.H.* 2.23.17–25 and note the progression of events here in Eusebius – James' death, followed by the appearance of Roman armies, followed by the fall of Jerusalem.

44. *Contra Celsus* 1.47, 2.13, and *Comm. on Matt.* 10.17. Since this testimony appears to have been in the *War*, the only place it probably could have been was in the discussion of the death of Ananus in *War* 4.296–332.

45. For '*yizzil*'/'save', see 1QpHab VIII.1–3 and XII.14; for '*Yesha*''/'*yeshu'a*', see CD XX.18–20 (following reference to 'the *Yoreh*', 'the Penitents from Sin in Jacob', and 'a Book of Remembrance for God-Fearers', i.e., 'Gentiles') and 4Q416–18.

46. Cf. *b. Ta'an.* 6a–7b with James 5:4–8, specifically mentioning 'early' and 'late rain' in the context of 'the coming of the Lord'.

47. Cf. CD VI.8–11 and XX.13–8. In the former, 'the *Yoreh ha-Zedek*' can mean 'the One who Pours down Righteousness at the End of Days'; but in the latter, so-called '*Yoreh*' has already 'been gathered in' – whatever this means.

48. 1QM XII.12 and XIX.3.

49. Matthew 24:35/Mark13:31/Luke 21:33.

50. On the seven Noahide Laws incumbent upon all mankind or 'Sons of Noah', which include 'fostering Righteousness and prohibiting idolatry, fornication, blasphemy, manslaughter, carrion or eating parts of living animals including its blood, and theft', see *San.* 56a–59b (n.b., here 'Adam', since he came before Noah's sacrifice permitting him to eat the flesh of animals but not the blood, is portrayed like James as a vegetarian), *A.Z.* 2b, 5b–6b, 64b, *Yoma* 28b, *B.K.* 38a, 92a, etc.

51. See *E.H.* 2.23.7 and 3.7.9 and *Haeres.* 78.7.7, the implication of all these testimonies being that once James' presence was removed, the city could no longer survive.

52. It should be noted that this is a part of all James' prohibitions as pictured in Acts 15:20, 15:29, and 21:25.

53. *Ps. Hom.* 8.15 and 11.35.

54. See *Zohar* i59b on 'Noah'. It also explains both *Logion* 12 of the Gospel of Thomas and 'why Heaven and Earth should have come into existence for his sake' as well as the 'Bulwark' allusion in *E.H.* 3.7.9 above.

55. One can also probably say that this 'Covenant' is the same as both the 'Zadokite' and the 'Zealot' one; see my 'Eschatological *Rain* Imagery'; *MZCQ*, pp. 4–16/*DSSU*, pp. 23–80 and *JNES*, pp. 175–6 above.

56. See 1 Maccabees 2:1. For Phineas', Zadok's, and Yehozedek's genealogy, see 1 Chronicles 5:30 –41. For the course of Joiraib, see 1 Chronicles 24:1–7.

57. For Phineas as the paradigm, see Numbers 25:6–15 and its evocation in 1 Maccabees 2:26–7, 2:50, 2:54, and 2:58 (here, even for Elijah). Also see *Ben Sira* 45:23–29, referring to Phineas as 'Third in Glory' and Hebrew *Ben Sira* 51:12 coupling 'the Sons of Zadok' with such a 'Zealot' appeal in the case of 'Simeon the *Zaddik*'. Note, that for Num R. 21.3–4 Phineas is also a '*Zaddik*'.

58. Cf. Ezekiel 44:15 with CD III.21–IV.4

59. 1QM XI.4–XII.9.

60. Cf. *Chronicles of Jerahmeel* 59.17, *Pseudo Philo* 48.1, and *Sifre* Numbers 131.

61. *Haeres.* 30.16.7.

62. See Ezekiel 40:46, 43:19, 44:15, and 48:11.

63. See Ezekiel 44:7–19 and 48:11.

64. See, e.g., *War* 2.402–10 and *Ant.* 19.332–4.

65. See *War* 2.411–5 in continuation of this episode, but also raising the charge of 'Impiety' against such 'Innovators' and noting this even 'put Caesar outside the pale'.

Chapter 4

1. *Ant.* 14.22–25.

2. Cf. *War* 2.147–8 and Hippolytus 9.20.

3. *Ant.* 14.22. For Honi as a 'Rainmaker' in the Talmud, see *j. Ta'an.* 66b and *b. Ta'an.* 23a

4. For this 'Famine', which Josephus, echoed by Acts 5:36–7 (even with its anachronism) and 11:28–30, connects both the coming of 'Theudas' and Queen Helen's grain-buying activities in Egypt and Cyprus, see *Ant.* 20.48–53 and 97–102.

5. *B. Ta'an.* 23a/*j. Ta'an.* 66b and cf. James 5:17–19 and 1 Kings 18:1–45.

6. Cf. 1 Kings 17:1 and Matthew 11:14 and *pars.*

7. CD III.2–3 and cf. too James 2:10 and 2:21–24.

8. John 19:26, 20:2, 21:7, and 21:20.

9. *E.H.* 2.23.10.

10. Cf. *Rec.* 4.35 and *Hom.* 11.30.

11. CD IV.19–20 and VIII.18–9/XIX.1–2.

12. *Ant.* 14.24.

13. See *Ant.* 20.200 and cf. *E.H.* 2.23.2–23.

14. *M. Ta'an* 3.8 and *b. Ta'an* 23a.

15. *Ant.* 14.19–22; n.b., how Josephus refers here to how Honi 'had hidden himself'.

16. Though originally Josephus did not identify which party was which, later in *Ant.*14.24 he makes it clear that those supporting Aristobulus II were 'Priests' and *War* 1.131–51 that those supporting Pompey, Antipater, and Hyrcanus II were 'Pharisees'.

17. We say 'Messianic Sadducees', a rather unique appellation, because it is clear that those responsible for the literature at Qumran both regard themselves as 'Sons of Zadok' (i.e., they are some kind of 'Sadducees') and are intensely and apocalyptically 'Messianic'; see *MZCQ*, pp. 19–26 and *DSSFC*, pp.49–80.

18. At one point in 1QS IX.13, the term would appear to be 'Sons of the *Zaddik*'.

19. See *War* 1.327–64, 1.431–43, 1.562–99/*Ant.* 14.13–15.9, 15.164–238, 15.320, etc.

20. One sees that his opponents are Pharisees in the note Josephus gives in *War* 1.113. For 'Purist Sadducees', see *MZCQ*, pp. 12–16.

21. For John Hyrcanus as a 'Sadducee', see *War* 1.54–67 but, in particular, *Ant.* 13.230–300.

22. *War* 1.107–12/*Ant.* 13.399–406.

23. See *War* 1.120–55 and *Ant.* 13.408–14.78, etc. N.b., for instance, *War* 1.143: Hyrcanus' supporters are always in favor of 'opening the gates to Pompey'.

24. *Vita* 2–7.

25. *War* 1.131–2.

26. *Ant.* 18.17.

27. *Ant.* 14.22–4.

28. *B. Ta'an.* 23a/j. Ta'an. 66b.

29. *Ant.* 14.14–21/*War* 1.123–32.

30. *Ant.* 14.21 and 14.25–6.

31. *Ant.* 14.27–8.

32. *Ant.* 14.27.

33. *War* 1.148. Interestingly *Ant.* 14.65–8 credits Strabo, Nicolaus of Damascus, and Livy of attesting to similar points.

34. *War* 1.150/*Ant.* 14.69.

35. *Ant.* 14.28.

36. Cf. *Ta'an.* 7b.

37. Cf. 11QM XII.9–10 and XIX.2 above with Matthew 5:45.

38. *Berakhot* 48a.

39. *B. Ta'an.* 23a/j. Ta'an. 66b.

40. Cf. *M. Ta'an.* 3.8 with *E.H.* 2.23.14–23 and *Ant.* 20.200–2.

41. Cf. *M. Ta'an.* 3:8 and *b. Ta'an.* 23b; *Ant.* 14.21.

42. For Simeon as one of the original Pharisee 'Pairs', see *Abboth* 1.9 and *ARN* 10.1 (22a).

43. *E.H.* 2.23.6, *Haeres.* 78.14.1, *Vir. ill.* 2, etc.

44. *Ant.* 14.22.

45. *B. Ta'an.* 23a–b.

46. See R. Eisler, *The Messiah Jesus and John the Baptist*, p. 244.

47. See, for instance, the note in the *Yalkut on Jeremiah* 35:12 that 'Rechabites' (such as these ancestors of John like Honi) married the daughters of Priests and their descendants ministered as Priests in the Temple.

48. Cf. Koran 3.33–49 and note how Muhammad calls John both 'a Prophet to the Righteous' and 'celibate' (3.39); but also note the use of the word 'hidden' in 3:44.

49. This is, of course, both '*the Insan al-Kamil*' of Mandaean doctrine and '*the Adam Kadmon*' of Jewish *Kabbalah*. It is also 'the Primal Adam' of both the Pseudoclementines and the Ebionites.

50. Cf. John 21:20–3 with 1QpHab VII.9–15.

51. Cf. *Ant*. 18.117 with Koran 3.59, 19.17, etc.

52. Note that in 15:45, Paul actually refers to 'the First Man Adam' (i.e., 'the Primal Adam') which 'became a living soul', but 'the Second' or 'Last Adam, a life-giving Spirit'.

53. Also see Ezekiel 1:27–8 and the 'no mere Man'/'no mere *Adam*' citation of Isaiah 31:8 in 1QM XI.11–2.

54. 1QH IV.21–5.

55. 1QH IV.30–3.

56. Cf. 1QH VII.6–10 and IX.28–30 with *E.H.* 2.23.7 and 3.7.9 and *Haeres.* 78.7.7.

57. See, for instance, CD VI.14–5 and VI.17–VII.3.

58. Cf. 'the *Rishonim*' or 'the First' in CD I.16 and VIII.17–8/XIX.19–21, following allusion to 'turning aside from the way of the People(s)' again and cf. Jesus in the New Testament speaking about clearly tendentious material concerning 'the First shall be Last and the Last shall be First' – Matthew 20:16 and pars.

59. Numbers 25:6–15.

60. For this original 'Covenant', see Genesis 9:9–17, but also see *Ben Sira* 45:23–29 referring to Phineas above and the *Zohar*, i.66b and 68b on 'Noah' too.

61. *Ta'an.* 23a–b.

62. B. *Pes.* 57a and *Tos. Men.* 13.21 (533).

63. *Ant.* 20.181 and 20.206–7.

64. 1Chronicles 5:27–34.

65. We treat this artificiality in *DSSFC*, pp. 24–6/*MZCQ*, pp. 8 and 46; but note that Josephus in *Ant.* 20.224–31 lists some eighteen High Priests from Solomon's time until Nebuchadnezzar 'took Josadek the High Priest captive', while in 10.152–3 he lists only six names for the same period – *pace* both genealogical and chronological knowledge in Josephus' time.

66. Cf. *Haeres.* 78.14.1 with *b. Ta'an.* 23a–b.

67. B. *Ta'an.* 23b.

68. See Jerome, *Comm. on Galatians* 1:19.

69. Cf. how in the Ps. *Hom*'s Prelude in the Letter of Peter to James 5, the assembled 'Elders' are 'in an agony of terror' on having heard James' words on 'keeping this Covenant' and, therefore, 'joining the Heavenly Holy Ones'.

70. Cf. Matthew 8:2–15, 9:20–31, 14:35–36, 20:30–34/Mark 3:10–12, 6:55–56, 8:22–26/Luke 5:12 –15, 6:19, 7:1–17.

71. Cf. James 5:7–8 with John 21:22–3 and 1QpHab VII.5–14.

72. See *A. Z.* 16b–17a and *j. Shab.* 14:4(14d).

73. Cf. *E.H.* 2.23.10–13 with Ps. *Rec.* 1.44.

74. See *A.Z.* 16b, Eccles. R. 1.8.3, and *Tos. Hul.* 2:24. N.b., this name 'Jesus *ha-Notzri*' is conserved in one Talmudic ms. redaction.

75. Along with Eliezer, R. Joshua ben Hananiah (Jesus?) was one of the five 'Disciples' making up R.Yohanan b. Zacchai's inner circle and (probably following the School of Hillel) more liberal than though perhaps not as luminous as R. Eliezer. For instance, he was much more liberal on the subject of proselytes and conversion generally than R. Eliezer; cf. Gen. R. 70.5, Eccles. R. 1.8.4 (possibly having to do with Queen Helen of Adiabene), and *Tos. San.* 13.2.

76. Though married to Rabban Gamaliel's sister, 'Imma Shalom', their disputes were legendary and Eliezer was ultimately excommunicated by the latter (the Patriarch Gamaliel II); see b. *B.M.* 59b and *Nid.* 7b–8a. Though he disputed with R. Joshua (a character very much like Jesus), the two were friends and both took R.Yohanan's coffin out of Jerusalem and went back to get R. Zadok – see *Git.* 56a, *Yeb.* 48b, *Abbot* 2.8, Lam. R. 1/5/31 and *ARN* 14 (24a). After his death, R. Joshua annulled Rabban Gamaliel's ban of excommunication on him; cf. b. *San.* 68a, *Git.* 83a, j. *Shab.* 2.6 (5b), and *ARN* 25.8f. Not only was he probably the most interesting of the Rabbis, but the most colorful. R.Yohanan was his teacher and R. Akiba was his student.

77. See, for instance, *War* 2.406–16.

78. On the Akeldama, see L. and K. Ritmeyer, 'Akeldama – Potter's Field or High Priest's Tombs?' and G. Avni and Z. Greenhut, 'Akeldama – Resting Place of the Rich and Famous', *BAR*, 20/6, November/December 1994, pp. 36–46 and, by the same authors, 'The Akeldama Tombs: Three Burial Caves in the Kidron Valley, Jerusalem, *IAA Report*, no. 1, 1996, Jerusalem, pp. 57–72.

79. See *JBJ*, pp. 165–208.

80. Cf. the promises made to 'those who love Him' in CD VII. 3–6/XIX. 1–4 and XX.17–22.

81. See James 1:26 and 3:5–11; for 'the Liar' and 'Tongue' imagery in the Scrolls, see CD I.14–6, IV.19–20, V.11–5, VIII.13, etc.; 1QpHab V.11, X.9–13; 1QS IV.9–11, etc.

82. See 1QH II.32–4, III.25, V.13–23; CD VI.16–21 on 'the New Covenant', 1QpHab xx.5–10; 4QpPs37 II.10, III.10, etc.

83. In it we have the telltale allusions to 'the Many', 'the Poor', 'standing', 'saving', and the 'soul'; cf. 4QpPs 37 II.8–9, III.10, IV.11, IV.20–1, etc.

84. Cf. Acts 1:26 and note the name of the purported defeated candidate in Acts 1:23, 'Joseph called Barsabas who was surnamed Justus' – '*Justus*' a Latin characterization now transliterated into Greek and, of course, James' cognomen in all early Church texts.

85. Cf. Jeremiah 35:7 with *War* 2.150 and Hippolytus 9.21.

86. See Koran 2.219 and 5.90.

87. Jeremiah 35:5–8.

88. CD VI.20, VII.16, and XX. 12.

89. CD VII.16 and XX.12, the latter actually picking up the same promises in CD VII.4–9/XIX.1 –2 preceding it.

90. See 1 Corinthians 11:24–9 and Luke 22:19–20 and pars.

91. For this body of traditional Roman legislation, see *JBJ*, pp. 184 and 922 and Dio Cassius 68.3– 4 for its application in Nerva's time.

92. Mark 5:25–34 and pars.

93. See, for instance, Matthew 9:10–11, 11:19, 21:31–2. Mark 2:15–6, Luke 5:29–30, and 7:29.

94. For these issues of 'niece marriage' and 'sleeping with women during their periods' as the chronological determinant for the Damascus Document at Qumran, see my Appendix to *JJHP*, pp. 87 –94/*DSSU*, pp. 208–17).

95. See my Appendix to *JJHP* just cited above and CD IV.14–V.18.

96. CD V.14–5.

97. CD V.7.

98. See *War* 2.409–23.

Chapter 5

1. John 1:46–51.

2. B. *Ta'an.* 23b.

3. J. *Ta'an.* 66b.

4. Ibid.

5. See, for instance, 1QM I.1–II.14 and the 'Visitation's referred to in CD I.7, V.15–6, and VII.9– 21/XIX.1–13.

6. Cf. Matthew 11:18–9/Luke 7:33–4.

7. John 2:19–21 and cf. with Matthew 26:61/Mark 14:58, introducing 'the Son of Man coming on the clouds of Heaven' in 26:61/14:62 (it is at this point the High Priest cries out 'Blasphemy') and 27:40/Mark 15:29.

8. See b. *San.* 86a and Shab. 33b–34a.

9. See 1 Maccabees 2:24–7, 2:54, and the whole approach of CD I.3–4, I.14–18, III.5–12, VII.21– VIII.19, XX.2–4, 1QS II.4–18, IV.9–14, V.5–7, IX.23–5, 1QpHab IX.4–6, etc.

10. Cf. 1QS V.2–14 and CD IV.3–9.

11. For such 'Servant' language coupled with 'Righteousness' at Qumran, see CD XX.20–2, 1QS IV.9 (here the usage actually is 'Service of Righteousness'), IX.22–4, etc. For 'the End'/'Last End' and 'works', see CD IV.7–9, 1QpHab VII.1–VIII.3, X.9–12, and XII.12–4.

12. 1QpHab VII.15–6. The text is fractured here, but it actually continues in in VIII.2 in terms of 'the House of Judgement'. For this 'House of Judgement' as 'the Last Judgement', see X.3–5 and for the actual 'Day of Judgement', see XII.14 and XIII.2–4.

13. Cf. the 'Temptation' episode 'in the wilderness' for 'forty days and forty nights' by 'the Devil' in Matthew 4:1–12 and pars.

14. Ps. *Hom.* 11.35.

15. See *War* 2.259 and *Ant.* XX.160–1 and XX.168.

16. This is the theory behind the opening of *Surah* 86: 'The Clot', followed by allusion in *Surah* 87 to 'the Night of Power', in which 'the Angels and the Spirit' (in this case, a direct allusion to 'the Holy Spirit', in Islam 'Gabriel' and 'the Holy Spirit' being considered synonymous) are said to have 'descended' and 'peace until the rising of the dawn'.

17. Cf. 1 Kings 19:4–14 (including allusion to 'in the wilderness', 'sitting' and then 'sleeping under a tree', and 'forty days and forty nights') with Koran. 3.113–5, 73.1–6, 74.1–6, 84.16–21, etc.

18. 1 Kings 19:7–8.

19. CD XX.20.

20. See j. *Ta'anit* 3:3 (IV.a).

21. Cf. 1QS VIII.7–8, 1QH VI.24–6, VII.7–9, etc.; in the Gospels of course, Peter is 'the Stone' and Jesus, 'the Precious Cornerstone'; cf. Matthew 16:18, 21:42, Acts 4:11, Ephesians 2:20, and pars. Also see 1 Corinthians 3:9–11 for Paul's view of 'God's building' which he, 'as a wise architect, has laid upon the Foundation of Jesus Christ'.

22. 2 *Apoc. Jas.* 61.21–25.

23. *M. San.* 6:4.

24. *B. Ta'an.* 19b–20a.

25. The actual description of this event comes in *M. Ta'an.* 3.8–9, but in b. *Ta'an.* 23a, this passage from Habakkuk 2:1–2 that one will also find in the Habakkuk *Pesher* is actually connected to Honi's rainmaking.

26. Of course, Habakkuk 2:4 is the exegetical basis of Paul's understanding of 'Christian' Faith in both Romans 1:17 and Galatians 3:11, as it is in James 2:14–26, no matter how much the conceptualities of these two might diverge. The same can be said for the Habakkuk *Pesher* VII.17–VIII.3 and Hebrews.

27. B. *Ta'an.* 23a.

28. 1QpHab VI.12–VII.14.

29. 1QpHab VII.15–16: 'and they will not be pleased when they are judged'.

30. Cf. CD IV.10–12 with 1QpHab VI.12–13.

31. 1QpHab VII.4–14.

32. Cf. 'being saved from the House of Judgement because of their works and Faith in the Righteous Teacher' in 1QpHab II.2–3, the allusions to 'not being pleased with their Judgement' in VII.16, 'the End' and 'the Last Era' in VII.5–14, 'the House of Judgement' as God's 'Judgement' ('with fire and brimstone') in the midst of many Peoples' in X.2–5, and 'the Day of Judgement' when 'God will destroy all the Servants of idols and Evil Ones off the Earth' in XII.14–XIII.4.

33. See *M. Git.* 5:6 (44a) and its explanation in b. *Git.* 55b.

34. See L. Nemoy's tr. of 'Al-Qirqisani's Account of the Jewish Sects' in *HUCA*, v.7, 1930, pp. 326–7 and 363–5.

35. *Haeres.* 30.3.2–6.

36. *Ad Haer.* 5.1.3.

37. 1QM XII.11–2 and XIX.2.

38. Cf. 1QM XII.4–7 and XIX.1–5. For 'works' in the sense of 'doing the *Torah*' (both based on the same root in Hebrew) at Qumran, as opposed to 'work' meaning 'labor', 'mission', or 'service', see 1QpHab X.9–12 (describing 'the Liar's vain' and 'worthless service') or numerous allusions in 1QS such as I.2–7 vs. IV.9–11 or IX.19–24.

39. 1QM XII.11–2 and XIX.2.

40. Actually '*Balaam*' is one of the four commoners whom Rabbinic literature designates as having 'no share in the world to come'; cf. b. *San.* 104b–110b and *JJHP*, pp. 90–94/*DSSFC*, pp. 213–7.

41. Cf. James 1:26, 4:11, and 5:9 with VI.26 and VII.17; and see CD III.5–12 on the Sons of Jacob 'murmuring in their tents' in the wilderness. For the imagery of 'light vs darkness' see, for instance, 1QS I.9–11, III.2–3, III.18–26, IV.9–11, etc.

42. 1QM XI.4–XII.17. This prophecy is also subject to exposition in CD VII.18–VIII.1 and 4Q*Test.* 8–13.

43. Cf. 1QM XI.11–3 (which includes the allusion to Isaiah 31:8's 'the sword of no mere *Adam*') with 1 Corinthians 15:45–7.

Chapter 6

1. B. *Ta'an* 19b–20a and cf. *ARN* 6.3 (21a).

2. Gen R. 42.1.

3. See *War* 5.24–26 for how the famine began in the purposeful burning of all the stores by John of Gischala and Simon, the Temple Captain and son of the High Priest Ananias, and 5.420–41 and 5.512–18 for the effects of this.

4. Cf. b. *Ta'an* 19b–20a and *ARN* 6.3 with b. *Ta'an* 23a and 1 Kings 17:1–8 and 18:41– 19:14.

5. Cf. *ARN* 9 (22b) on Numbers 12:9–15.

6. These fabulous 'Rich Men' permeate the historical portions of the Talmud and its associated literature; see, for instance, b. *Git* 56a, *Ket.* 66b–67a, *Ta'an* 19b–20a, *ARN* 6.3 (20b–21a), etc. For the New Testament, see in particular Luke 1:53, 6:24, 12:16–21, 16:1–22, 21:1, Matthew 19:23–4, 27:57, Mark 12:41 and pars.; but also see James 1:10–2:6 and 5:1ff.

7. See b. *Ta'an* 19b–20a and *ARN* 6.3 (20b–21a).

8. *N. b.*, the pun here in the Greek *kunes/kunaria* is on the Hebrew word for 'Zealots' – *Kanna'im.*

9. *ARN* 6.3 (21a) and cf. Josephus in *War* 5.24–26 and 5.420–518 above.

10. For this plaque, see *Git* 60a and *Yoma* 37a; for Helen's three successive Nazirite oath penances imposed on her by the Rabbis, see *Naz* 19a–20b – but also see the Fifth–Century Armenian historian Moses of Chorene 2.35.

11. See *War* 5.147, *Ant.* 20.95, and *E.H.* 2.12.3. In these matters folklore is often an interesting guide. It should be appreciated that this tomb – now known, not incuriously as 'the Tombs of the Kings' – were in times past known by the Jews of Jerusalem as 'the Cave of Kalba Sabu'a', a not unimportant testimony to their true identity – see article 'Izates', *Encyclopaedia Judaica*, Jerusalem, 1971.

12. *Ket* 62b–63a and *Ned* 50a. Cf. too *ARN* 20b.

13. This is how he is referred to in *Git* 56a and Gen R. 42.1; in *ARN* 20b it is '*Siset Hakkeset*' which implies it has something to do with the 'silver' (*kesef*) of his wealth – in this case, the *silver couch* upon which he reclined 'at the head of the Great Ones of Israel'. For the former, the name rather is presented as having to do with 'his *zizzit* (fringes) which used to trail on cushions' (*kesset*), though 'couch' and 'cushions' are hardly very distinguishable.

14. *Ket* 66b–67a, 104a, *Git* 56a, and *Lam* R. 1.16.47–49.

15. See b. *Ta'an* 19b–20a and *ARN* 6.3 (21a) for Nakdimon's 'rain–making' and 'cistern–filling'. For his and the other Rich men's grain storage, see *Git* 56a, *ARN* 21a, and Lam. R. 1.5.31 as well.

16. B. *Ta'an* 19b–20a and *ARN* 6.3 (21a).

17. B. *Ta'an* 20a and *ARN* 21a.

18. B. *Ta'an* 19b–20a.

19. Ibid.

20. See *M. Ta'an* 3.8 and b. *Ta'an* 19a and 23a/j. *Ta'an* 3.9–10.

21. *M. Ta'an* 3.8, further fleshed out in b. *Ta'an* 23a.

22. See Matthew 26:59–67/Mark 14.55–65 and pars., a passage which takes up where John 2:28 leaves off. Cf. too John 10:29–39, itself beginning with evocation of 'My Father'.

23. Cf. *Ant.* 14.26–28.

24. B. *Ta'an* 20a.

25. *Ta'an* 23b and note how this '*Hanin*' (John?) is described as 'the son of Honi the Circle–Drawer's daughter'.

26. See Ps. *Rec* 1.72 and 2.7 and 12, etc.

27. *Haeres.* 19.4.1.

28. B. *Ned* 50a and *Ket* 62b. For Monobaz's connection to R. Akiba, see b. *Shab* 68b.

29. *ARN* 6.2 (20b). Later Akiba seems to take a Roman matron as his wife. Had Rachel died? This is all very curious. For relations with R. Eliezer b. Hyrcanus, see, for instance, *B.M.* 59b, *Hag* 14b, j. *Hag* 2.17(7b), *Tos. Hag* 2.2, b. *Meg* 3a, etc.

30. Lam. *R.* 2.2.4 and j. *Ta'an* 4.5 (68a). For the vivid portrayal of this Uprising and the unimaginable casualties sustained, one should read the whole of this section of Lamentations *Rabbah*.

31. B. *Ned* 50a and *Ket* 62b.

32. Gen *R.* 42.1.

33. Again, the spelling of this in Josephus is rather 'Eleazar' (*Ant.* 20.43), not 'Eliezer' as we have it spelled here. Still his approach echoes that of Eliezer ben Hyranus in the above story in Eccles. *R.* 1.8.4. But these disputes between R. Eliezer and R. Joshua, Yohanan ben Zacchai's favorite two pupils, are famous in Rabbinic literature – but, in particular, where circumcision *as a sine qua non* for conversion is concerned, see b. *Yeb* 46a where R. Eliezer specifically takes the position of Josephus' 'Eleazar' here. This is varied somewhat in j. *Kid* 3.14 where R. Joshua is portrayed as also requiring 'baptism' – an interesting addition.

34. *War* 2.520.

35. B. *Git* 56a, but see *ARN* 6.3 (21a).

36. Cf. *War* 2.143 and Ps. *Rec* 1.70 which even includes the 'headlong' language of Acts 1:18's picture of the James–like 'fall' Judas Iscariot takes and for Luke 4:29 what the citizens of Nazareth wish to do to Jesus when he compares himself to Elijah in the matter of rainmaking and going to 'Zarepta the widow of Sidon' – another allusion to Queen Helen or Luke's parallel to Matthew 15:22/ Mark 7:26's 'Canaanite'/'Greek Syrophoenician woman' (also fromTyre and Sidon)? – and Elisha only having 'cleansed' the single leper 'Naaman the Syrian', I.e., his support in his own alleged home of the Pauline 'Gentile Mission'!

37. See 1QpHab XI.4–15 and the discussions in *JBJ*, pp. 252–4, 444–50, 504–13, etc., which are extensive and cannot be repeated here in full. The gist of these are also summarized in *DSSFC*: 'The Final Proof that James and the Righteous Teacher are the Same,' pp. 332–51; also see Appendix, pp. 87–94 in *JJHP*: 'The "Three Nets of Belial" in the Damascus Document and "Balla"'/"Bela"' in the Temple Scroll' – pp. 208–17 in *DSSFC*.

38. 1QpHab VIII.14–IX.5.

39. B. *San* 105a–106b.

40. See my Appendix, pp. 87–94 in *JJHP*: 'The "Three Nets of Belial" in the Damascus Document and "Balla"'/"Bela"' in the Temple Scroll' and pp. 208–17 in *DSSFC* above. For Revelation, the references are 2:14ff. and 14.8–13, but also see 2 Peter 2:15 and Jude 1:11; at Qumran, see CD IV.14–15 and 1QH IV.10. and 11QT XLVI.10.

41. Cf. Ps. *Rec* 2.4, 3.1, etc. and Ps.*Hom* 2.19– 22.

42. 1QpHab XII.3–10; but also see 4QpPs37 II.10, III.10, and IV.11 on 'the Congregation of the Poor' and 1QH V.23: 'the Poor Ones of Piety'.

43. 4QpPs37 IV.10.

44. 1QpHab XII.2–3, echoed in 4QpPs37 IV.9–10.

45. *ARN* 6.27 (21a).

46. See *ARN* 6.15–17 (20b), b. *Ned* 50a–b, and *Ket* 62b–63a.

47. *Ket* 66b and cf. Lam *R* 1.16.48. For Boethus' daughter with her proper name 'Martha', see *Git* 56a and *Ket* 104a. For Boethus' daughter as 'Miriam,' see Lam *R.* 1.16.47.

48. It is Paul in Galatians 2:15 who makes it clear that Gentiles were to be identified with 'Sinners' thereby unraveling this bit of cryptography.

49. *Ket* 62b–63a.

50. See *ARN* 4 (20a) and *Git* 56a–b.

51. *ARN* 6.3 (20b)

52. For the *Maschil* or 'Guide', a title of course that develops out of the Biblical Psalms, see in particular 1QS I.1, III.13, VIII.11, etc., and CD I.7–11.

53. John 11:39: 'he already stinks for it is four days' (since he has been in the tomb).

54. See, for instance, 1QpHab X.9 and CD IV. 19–20 and VIII.13, where 'the Man of Lying' actually is called 'the *Mattif* (from the verb '*hittif*) or 'Pourer out of Lying' otherwise known as 'the Spouter of Lying'.

55. This is how it is stated in Mark 14:24 also; in Luke 22:20, this is 'poured out for you', but cf. CD I.14–15 on the rise of the 'Scoffer' or 'Comedian who *poured* over Israel the waters of Lying'.

Chapter 7

1. In the Dead Sea Scrolls, one should note that 'mumuring' of this kind is an important infraction. In the first place in CD III.7–14, 'murmuring in their tents' (i.e., 'in the wilderness') against 'the Voice of their Maker and the Commandments of their Teachers' (i.e., the Mosaic Law) is a severe offence.

2. CD XX.17–22.

3. *Ket.* 66b–67a.

4. *Haeres.* 78.14.1

5. *Commentary on Galatians* 1:19. This tradition is more or less repeated in b. *Ta 'an* 23b in regard to Honi's grandson, Hanin, a contemporary of either John the Baptist or James, or both, and here it is the 'school children' who are substituted for 'the People of Jerusalem' or the 'little children', who as here in Jerome's tradition, 'take hold of the hem of his garment' or 'his fringes'.

6. See, for instance, Matthew 8:2–15, 9:20–31, 14:35–36, and 20:30–34, Mark 3:10–12, 6:55–56, and 8:22–26, Luke 5:12–15, 6:19, 7:1–17, etc. and *pars.*

7. Lam. R 1.16.47.

8. In this same section, for instance, Lam. R 1.16.50 quotes Zechariah 14:4 about how God Himself, whose 'feet will stand on that Day upon the Mount of Olives', will take the field against all the Nations after already having recounted how R. Eleazar b. Zadok applied the passage from Deuteronomy 28:56–7 concerning 'the tender and delicate woman ... who would not set the sole of her feet upon the ground' (1.16.47).

9. *Ket.* 67a. This theme of 'the Poor' will appear over and over again.

10. As an example of this kind of thing, one should see the way the Man–God or God Dionysus is treated or demands to be treated in Euripides' *Bacchae* – but this is only one example among many.

11. See *War* 2.122–23, but also see CD XIII.11–13 on the duties of the *Mebakker* or Overseer on the matter of property.

12. *Epistle of Peter to James* 5.1.

13. *Epistle of Peter to James* 4.1. For 'the Fountain of Living Waters' at Qumran and, in particular, related to 'the New Covenant in the Land of Damascus', see CD III.16–17 and VIII.22–23; for baptism or 'immersion' see 1QS III.4–9 and IV.20–23, etc.

14. See 1QS IX.3–6, CD VII.4–6, XV.19–20, 1QM VII. 5–7, XII.1–10, etc.; of course, the language of 'keeping the Covenant' at Qumran is intrinsic and occurs throughout but, in particular, it is the definition of 'the Sons of Zadok' in 1QS V.2–5 and 8–14 and CD III.2–20, VIII.1–2 (on 'breaking the Covenant'), XX.17–18, etc.

15. In particular, see Paul in Galatians 1:20, 2 Corinthians 11:31, and if one wishes from the Pastorals, 1Timothy 2:7, 4:2, etc.

16. *Epistle of Peter to James* 4.5

17. Matthew 26:21–5/Mark 14:18–21.

18. Perhaps the best discussion of this kind of censorship is to be found in Robert Eisler's *The Messiah Jesus and John the Baptist*, pp. 49–112, London/NewYork, 1931 with numerous examples and illustrations with particular reference to '*the Testimonium Flavianum*'.

19. CD V.6–18. This is a key passage for it explains how the Establishment 'pollutes the Temple', I. e., because 'they do not separate according to the *Torah*' (i.e., between 'clean' and 'unclean', 'Holy and profane') and 'they lie with a woman during the blood of her period and each man takes (to wife) the daughter of his brother and the daughter of his sister'.

20. See Matthew 14:13–21, 15:28–16:12, Mark 6.32–44, 8:14–21, etc.

21. *ARN* 6.3 (21a).

22. *Ket* 66b and Lam. R 1.16.48 above. In *Ketuboth* it is 'four hundred gold dinars daily' while in Lamentations *Rabbah*, it is 'five hundred'.

23. *Git* 56a.

24. The plaque in this tomb is nicely described in N. Avigad's article in *Jerusalem Revealed*, ed. Y. Yadin, Jerusalem, 1975, p 18. There, the names on it make it clear that this is the family of the

Boethusians from Egypt who, in fact, were making 'Bnei Hezir' Priestly claims (cf. Nehemiah 10:20) – therefore the name accorded this tomb.

25. See *JBJ*, pp. 455–56.

26. *Ant.* 18.136–7.

27. For these matters, see CD IV.20–V.11, but also the proscriptions in the Temple Scroll, LVII.15–20 on the King having one and only one wife, not divorcing her, and not taking a wife from among the Gentiles and LXVI.15–17 for the general ban on niece marriage, which the Herodians did so promiscuously – but even more germane than any of this, the very words attributed to John the Baptist in Matthew and Mark: 'It is forbidden to take to wife the wife of one's brother and uncover the nakedness of one's brother, the son of his father or the son of his mother. It is unclean.'

28. *ARN* 6.3 (21a), but also see Lam. R 1.16.47–48.

29. This in the Judas Iscariot 'betrayal' or 'delivering up' scene in Matthew 27:3–9.

30. *Ket.* 65a but in Lam. R 1.16.47, where 'carpets were laid from the door of her house to the entrance of the Temple so her feet should not be exposed' so she could 'see her husband Jesus b. Gamala reading on the Day of Atonement', it should be recalled, this was 'Miriam (Martha) the daughter of Boethus'.

31. *Ket.* 65a and Lam. R 1.16.48.

32. Lam. R 1.16.47.

33. *Git* 56a.

34. Lam. R 1.16.48.

35. *Ket* 67a and cf. Lam. R 1.16.48.

36. *Ket* 66b.

37. *ARN* 6.3 (21a).

38. *Ket* 66b–67a.

39. *Ket* 104a

40. See *War* 4.315–25.

41. See *War* 4.1–83. For Judas' 'Gaulonite' origins, despite his 'Galilean' cognomen, and specifically Gamala on the Gaulon, see *Ant.* 18.4.

42. *ARN* 6.1 (20b).

43. CD I.1 and II.1.

44. Matthew 15:22/Mark 7:26.

45. See *Ant.* 18.4–10, 18.23–25, and *War* 2.18; for the rise of the *Sicarii* derivative from them and their mass suicide at Masada, see *War* 2.254–57, 7.253–62, and *Ant.* 20.186.

46. See, in particular, the many scenes of this kind in Euripides' *Bacchae* and the kind of respect the Man-God Dionysus is demanding even in disguise from the people of Thebes and the vengeance his followers enact when he does not receive it; for another good example of this kind, see the scene on the huge relief from the Temple of Hathor at Dendera in Egypt, where Cleopatra and her son by Caesar, Caesarion, are depicted as showing just this kind of awe and respect before personalized depictions of the Gods Isis and Horis (and possibly a miniature of Osiris). There are many depictions of this kind in Egyptian tomb paintings and wall reliefs, as there are in many of the seats of Hellenistic Mystery Religions generally.

47. *War* 2.427.

48. See *Ket* 66b and 104a.

49. Mark 10:25/Luke18.25.

50. See *War* 2.118 and *Ant.* 18.4–10 and note that for Judas, 'to pay a tax to the Romans and to submit to mortal men as if to their Lords' (i.e., 'not to call any man Lord') was anathema and the basis of his revolt.

51. *War* 2.139–40. As Josephus expresses this: 'Before touching the pure food, one is obliged to swear tremendous oaths that he will practise Piety towards God (the First 'Love Commandment') and exercise Righteousness towards his fellow man' (the Second).

52. Cf. *Ant.* 18.117–118's description of John the Baptist as 'commanding the Jews to exercise virtue both as regards Righteousness towards one another and Piety toward God', I.e., the Righteousness/Piety Dichotomy.

Chapter 8

1. *E.H.* 4.22.6.

2. See, for instance, *War* 2.259, 2.264–5, and *Ant.* 20.168.

3. See *ARN* 6.3 (21a) and *Ta'an* 19b–20a.

4. *ARN* 6.3 (21a).

5. See b.*Git* 56a, where the amount is the *pro forma* 'twenty–one years'; in *ARN*, 6.3 (21a) this amount changes to 'twenty–two' and it is only Kalba Sabu'a's own stores alone which 'can supply enough food for every citizen of Jerusalem for twenty–two years'; in Lam R. 1.5.31, this is 'ten' – I. e., each of 'the four Councillors' or 'Rich Men' ('Ben Zizzit, Ben Gorion, Ben Nakdimon, and Ben Kalba Shabua' – *thus*). For Josephus in *Ant.* 20, it is rather Queen Helen who is able to do this and in Rabbinic literature the 'twenty–one' is the time of her three successive Nazirite oath periods which the Rabbis imposed upon her – seemingly as a penance – for some reason.

6. For this linkage, see CD IV.17–V.11 ('two by two they went into the ark').

7. Cf. *Ned.* 50a.with John 11:2, 12:3, and Luke 7:38–44.

8. See *ARN* 6.3 (21a), Lam R. 1.5.31, and Josephus, *War* 5.24–6 and cf. Tacitus, *Histories* 5.12.

9 . See *Ket.* 66b–67a, Lam R. 1.16.46–48, and *Git.* 56a.

10. *Ned.* 50a. In James 5:9, the exact quote is 'The Judge is standing before the Door' (more 'Standing One' imagery). In *E.H.* 2.23.8 and pars., the question the crowd supposedly 'cries out' to him on Passover in the Temple is, 'What is the Door to Jesus?'

11. Cf. *ARN* 6.1 (20b) with Matthew 26:11/Mark 13:7/John 12:8.

12. See, for example, CD I.10–12, XII.20–1, XIII.22, 1QS III.13, IX.12, IX.21, etc.

13. CD I.7–8. This is followed by the note about 'remission of sins' (i.e., knowing they 'were Sinful Men'), 'being like *Blind Men*', 'seeking Him with a whole heart', and God 'raising up for them a Teacher of Righteousness to guide them in the Way of His heart', I.e., 'the Guide'. There is also the first note here about God 'visiting them'.

14. Matthew 18:2–14, 19:13–15, Mark 9:42, 10:14–15, Luke 17:2, 18:16–17, and John 13:33.

15. CD IV.20–V.11.

16. Galatians 5:15.

17. For 'the First' at Qumran, which usually represents 'the Forefathers who received the *Torah*', see CD I.16. 'The Last' or 'Last Generation'/'LastTimes' is already making its appearance here in I.11–12, but see also I.4, III.10, IV.6–9, VI.2, VIII.16–17, 1QpHab II.7, VII.2–12, IX.4–5, etc.

18. Jerome, *Commentary on Galatians* 1:19.

19. See *Ket.* 63a.

20. This is so strange, because in John 12:10–11 it is *Lazarus* whom 'the Chief Priests plotted to put to death' because 'many of the Jews were believing on Jesus because of him'; whereas in the similar passages earlier from 10:45–57, it is *Jesus* whom 'they (particularly Caiaphas) wanted to put to death' after the miracle of Lazarus being raised from the dead.

21. See 1QpHab XI.4–XII.10.

22. 1QpHab XI.14–15.

23. As this reads in Revelation 14:8 and 14:10, 'he shall drink of the wine of theWrath of God', which would 'be poured out full strength into the Cup of his Anger'. 16:19 reads: 'And Babylon the Great was remembered before God to give her the Cup of the wine of the Fury of His Wrath.' Again, setting aside their playfulness, these correspondences are almost precise.

24. One should also note the Jewish revolutionary in Libya or Cyrene, known both to Eusebius in *E.H.* 4.2 and Dio Cassius 68.32 during the uprising inTrajan and Hadrian's time in 115–18 CE, which definitely ended up in the virtual elimination of the Jews of Egypt. Eusebius call him '*Lucuas*', but Dio Cassius makes it clear he was also known as '*Andreas*' or 'Andrew' ('Man'?). Both make it clear that he was considered to be a Jewish 'King' (i.e., a Messiah) and both call him by the well–known New Testament expression 'King of the Jews'.

25. See *Ant.* 20.153, 20.195, *Vita* 16; also Tacitus, *Annals* 14.64.2 and Dio Cassius 62.13.1–4 (in this account, it is Nero laughing at one Plautus' head that is mentioned).

26. *Ant.* 20.97–8.

27. *Ant.* 20.50–51, repeated in 20.101. Eusebius makes reference to this famine relief directly following his account of the 'Impostor Theudas' and Talmudic sources too are much enamored of this theme.

28. If Paul really was involved in 'famine relief' activities, as I have argued elsewhere and as Acts 11:28–30 and 12:25 proclaim, then it was as part of these famine relief activities of Queen Helen and her son Izates. The point is that the Antioch in question had to have been 'Antioch Orrhoe' or 'Antioch–by–Callirhoe', the capital of 'the Great King of the Peoples beyond the Euphrates' (either Izates or his putative father 'Abgarus'/'Agbarus'), not 'Antioch–on–the–Orontes' as Acts implies but never specifically says.

29. The parallel here is fairly strong; cf. CD IV.3 and VI.5.

30. For the story of this plaque, see *Naz* 19b–20a, *Yoma* 37a and *Git* 60a.

31. See, for instance, the *Epistle of Peter to James* 5.1 introducing the *Homilies*.

32. In James, for instance, see 1:26, 2:20, 3:5–8, 3:14, 4:5, 4:8, etc. and in CD, see I.11, II.18, III.5, V.12, VI.12 etc. The same imagery abounds in the Habakkuk *Pesher*, Hymns, and works such as 4Q434 –6 ('The Hymns of the Poor') or 4Q416–16 ('Sapiential Works').

33. See *The Republic*, Books II–III (377a–408d) and Book X (595a–609d).

34. It should be appreciated, however, that in Matthew 15:24 the 'house' does reappear, but now it becomes 'not being sent except to the lost sheep of the house of Israel'. One should also note that in Matthew 15:13–14 the language of 'falling into a pit' also occurs, as does 'uprooting plants', both of which will recur in CD I.7 and XI.13.

35. 1QS IV.9–11.

36. Cf. CD I.11–12, XII.20–21, XIII.22–3, 1QH III.13, IX.12–26, 1QH XII.11, etc.

37. 1QS IX.12–14.

38. 1QS IX.15–19.

39. CD I.5–8.

40. See, for instance, 1QS VIII.4–9 and XI.7–9 and 1QH VI.24–26 and VII.8–9 on 'the Foundation which will be set upon Rock', 'the Doors of Protection which will not sway' and 'the Tried Wall', 'Fortified Tower', and 'Ramparts' which are 'an Eternal Foundation', 'Building', or 'Rock' which also 'will never sway'.

41. 1 Corinthians 2:6–7.

42. See 1QS IX.18 and XI 3–19 above, but also see III.23, IV.6 and 18, V.25–6, CD III.18, 1QM XIV.9–10, XVII.9, etc.

43. 1QpHab X.9–13.

44. CD III.18–20.

45. CD VII.4–6, XX.10–13 and XX.21–2.

46. CD XI.13–14.

47. CD II.9–11.

Chapter 9

1. See *ARN* 6.2 (20b). The 'Parable' here (about 'a Stone-Cutter'/Peter?) is told by one R. Simeon ben Eleazar but, however this may be, the thrust has to do with what R. Akiba did with the teachings of R. Eliezer ben Hyrcanus and his colleague R. Joshua (Jesus?); and what the 'Stone-Cutter' did was 'chip away' the 'tiny pebbles' of a great 'mountain' in order 'to *uproot* it' and '*cast it* into the Jordan'. It is this which is compared to what R. Akiba did to the teachings of R. Eliezer and R. Joshua. Here, too, the 'little children' are R. Akiba's 'sons and daughters'.

2. *Per contra*, one should note how in Mark 12:13–18/Matthew 22:15–26 and Mark 3:6 the Herodians are listed with the Pharisees as being among those opposed to Jesus' teachings – the only question is, which teachings of Jesus, the real ones or the mythological/literary ones? On the other hand, it should be noted, that it is Paul in Acts 24:10–26:32 who enjoys easy relations with Herodians and, as we have suggested earlier may himself even be an Herodian – cf. Romans 16:7–11.

3. Cf. *JBJ*, pp. 74f., 142–5, 770–83, 842–50, 924–39, etc.

4. CD I.18–20.

5. CD IV.7–10.

6. Note the overlap with the character Josephus calls 'Eleazar ben Jair', a descendant of Judas the Galilean and kinsman of that 'Menachem' tortured and probably stoned to death by his opponents on the Temple Mount when he put on the Royal Purple – *War* 2.433–49 and 7.253–399.

7. CD V.7 – again the word 'blood' is specifically included.

8. CD VIII.21–24/XIX.33–XX.1, but also see CD VI.14–VII.9 where this Covenant is specifically defined.

9. In Hebrew, there is also the feminine of 'lamb' as in '*dorcas*'/'doe' for 'Tabitha'.

10. *Ned.* 50a.

11. Ibid.

12. *Ket.* 63a.

13. Ibid.

14. Ibid.

15. Ps *Rec.* 172–4.

16. See Y. Yadin, 'The Excavation of Masada', *Israel Exploration Journal* 15, 1965, pp. 81–2 and 105 –8 and *Masada*, London, 1966, pp. 173–90.

17. See, for instance, 4Q521, '*The Messiah of Heaven and Earth*', Fragment 1, Column I.12, but there are others.

18. The criticism of him in Lam. R 2.2.4 and j. *Ta'an* 4.5 (68d) for applying the Messianic 'Star' Prophecy (the probable origin of Bar Kochba's name) to Bar Kochba by the other rabbis gives some proof of this, as do the tremendous numbers of 'his Disciples' described *Ket.* 62a–63b and *Ned* 50 (seemingly some 24,000!) and the description of his imprisonment and horrific death at the hands of the Romans in *Ber* 61b. In the latter, a '*Bat Chol*' or Heavenly Voice cries out much in the manner of the synoptics: 'This is my only begotten son, etc., etc.' – only in Akiba's case, it is: 'You are destined for the life of the world to come.'

19. For John's teaching 'Righteousness towards one's fellow man', see *Ant.* 18.117; for Josephus' Essenes, see *War* 2.139. For James, see 2:8.

20. Hippolytus 9.21.

21. *Ber* 61b–62a.

22. *Ket* 62a–63b.

23. Lam. R 1.16.47.

24. Ibid.; cf. *Git* 56a. In *Ket* 67a he rather 'sees her picking barley grains among the horses' hoofs in Acco'.

25. *ARN* 6.3 (21a). In *Git* 56a, as we have seen, he is rather denoted as 'Ben Zizzit *ha-Kesef*'/'Silver' and this is supposedly because 'his fringes (*zizzit*) used to trail on cushions (*Keset*) and here, 'his seat (*kise*) was' rather 'among those of the Roman Nobility'! Whoever he was, he was clearly an Establishment character of some kind and, therefore probably an Herodian or one of their hangers-on.

26. *ARN* 4.5 (20a). See also *Git* 56a–b, *Yoma* 21a and 39b.

27. See CD VII.18–9, XIX.10–11, and 4Q*Test* I.12.

28. For Titus' destruction of the entire city, see *War* 7.1–2.

29. This 'leading astray' language is, of course, basic to Qumran and, in particular, the presentation of the position of 'the Man of'/'Spouter of Lying' who 'leads Many astray'; cf. CD I.13–16, 1QS III.22, 1QpHab X.9–13, etc.

30. 1QpHab VI.7.

31. *War* 6.301–09.

32. Cf. CD I.9–11, XII.20–1, XIII.22, 1QS III.13, IX.12, IX. 21, etc.

33. For R.Yohanan's 'woes' upon leaving Jerusalem with his Disciple R. Joshua (Jesus?) and Vespasian's behaviour, see *ARN* 4.5 (20a) – note here that Isaiah 10:34 (a *Pesher* extant at Qumran) is applied to this fall, as it is by implication at Qumran as well.

34. See *Ant.* 20.94–96 and *War* 5.55, 119.

35. CD I.17, VII.9–13, VII.21–VIII.3/XIX.5–16, etc.

36. See CD III.19, IV.4, VII.18–20, XII.23, XIV.19, etc. and 4Q*Flor* I.10–13 and 4Q*Test* I.12–3; for '*the* True Prophet,' see 1QS IX.12 and in 4Q*Test* I.5–6.

37. For 'the True Prophet' ideology, see Ps *Rec.* 1.16, 1.40–41, 1.44 and variously; Ps *Hom.* 1.21, 2.4–12, and variously; for Muhammad and the Koran, a good example is 33.1 and 33.30–59; for Mani, see al-Biruni 8.206–9.

38. 1QS IX.12.

39. 1QS VIII.10–16 in describing the Naziritism and 'Study of the *Torah*' of 'the Perfect of the Way' and IX.18–24, the necessity of '*separating* from any man who has not turned his *Way* away from all Unrighteousness', 'eternal hatred for the Men of the *Pit*,' and 'zeal for the Law' and 'the Day of Vengeance'.

40. Lam R. 1.16.48.

41. See Lam R. 1.16.47 and *pars.*

42. *Ket.* 66b.

43. *Ibid.*

44. *Ket.* 104a.

45. See *War* 4.236–325.

46. *Git* 56a. Note that in the death scenario for 'Martha the daughter of Boethus' here, though the 'dung' motif remains, now the scenario is that 'by this time she had taken off her shoes', but 'some dung stuck to her foot and she died' – again too the 'foot'/'feet' element.

47. *Git* 56a, but in *ARN* 6.3 (20b–21a), where these three are also named, the period is 'twenty-two years' while in Lam R. 1.5.31, where there are 'four councilors' ('ben Gurion' being separated from 'ben Nakdimon'), the figure is 'ten' – each is 'capable of supplying the city with food for ten years'.

48. See Robert Eisler, *The Messiah Jesus and John the Baptist,* Dial Press, 1931, pp. 252–55.

49. *War* 5.24–26; cf.Tacitus, *Histories* 5.12. For these *Biryonim*, one should see the parallel narratives in *Git* 56a and Lam R.1.5.31. The Head of these *Biryonim* of Jerusalem in *Gittin* is 'Abba Sikra' – clearly the Leader of the *Sicarii* there and he is designated as R. Yohanan's nephew ('the son of R.Yohanan's mother's sister'); but in Lamentations *Rabbah*, he is named as 'Ben Battiah' and portrayed as leading R. Yohanan's coffin (carried by his two Disciples, R. Eliezer and R. Joshua) out of the city – a very curious scene indeed.

50. *Git* 56a; for a parallel proper ascription, see *Ket.* 104a above applying the 'camel' aphorism to her because of her deceased husband, Jesus ben Gamala.

51. *Git* 56a–b.

52. *Ibid.*

53. *Git* 58a and Lam R. 1.16.48.

54. See *Ant.* 20.179–82.

55. Lam R. 1.16.50–51.

56. *Yoma* 38b.

57. 1QM XI.13–14; for '*the Star Prophecy,*' see 1QM XI.6–7 and CD VII.16–21. Also see 4Q*Test* I.12–13.

Chapter 10

1. *Git* 56a.

2. See *Yeb.* 61a and *Yoma* 18a.

3. Cf. *Yoma* 9a and 18a above. The former statement is literally reproduced in marginal notes of a Sixteenth Century Edition called *Bayit Hadash* with glosses by R. Joel b. Samuel Sirkes.

4. See *Ket.* 104a and cf. *Ket.* 66b.

5. For Martha's wealth, see *Git.* 56a. For the material in CD, see XIX.9–13.

6. For the true picture of the relationship of Salome to Philip and John the Baptist generally, see *Ant.* 18.116–19 and 137; for a real picture of levirite marriage issues as they related to the remarriage of Martha the daughter of Boethus and Josephus' friend Jesus ben Gamala, see *Yeb.* 61a, *Yoma* 18a, *Ket.* 104a, and Lam. R 1.16.47.

7. For *Sicarii*, see *War* 2.254–57, 425–29, and 4.400–5, *Ant.* 20.186, etc. It is interesting that, as first really observed by Morton Smith, Josephus only begins using the term 'Zealots' in *War* 2.651, long after most of these references.

8. See *War* 4.224–325. He repeats this charge of butchering all the High Priests in *War* 7.267–8.

9. For Ben Zizzit, see *Git.* 56a, Gen R. 42.1, Lam R. 1.5.31, and *ARN* 6.3 (20b–21a). For the famous Talmudic episode where the Rabbis cry out to Agrippa I when he comes to read the Deuteronomic King Law on *Succot* that 'You are our brother, you are our brother, you are our brother' on account of his Piety, see *M. Sota* 7:8 and *pars.* (*Bik.* 3:4 and *Siphre* Deut. 157 on 17:15).

10. See *Git.* 56a, which here calls 'the Zealots' *Biryonim* and cf. *ARN* 6.3 (21a), *War* 5.24–6, and Tacitus, *Hist.* 5.12.

11. *Git.* 56a.

12. *ARN* 6.3 (21a).

13. Matthew 27:3–10 and *ARN* 6.3 (21a). *Git.* 56a, as we have seen, gives a slightly different derivation of his name, i.e., '*Ben Zizzit Hakeseth*', that 'his fringes used to trail on cushions' and 'his seat was among the Nobility of Rome' not 'of Israel'. Who could he be? One of the Herodians perhaps?

14. *Git.* 56a–b.

15. Lam R. 1.5.31 and Eccles. R. 7.12.1.

16. Eccles. R. 7.12.

17. *Git.* 56a–b and cf. Lam R. 1.5.31 and *ARN* 4.5 (20a).

18. *Ber.* 62a.

19. The point here is that we have actual Rabbinic confirmation that all these allusions – *ARN* 4.5 (20a), Lam R. 1.5.31, and *Git.* 56a–b – refer to the fall of the Temple in 70 CE and not any earlier one.

20. Lam R. 1.5.31 and 2.2.4 and *ARN* 4.5 (20a), but also see Eccles. R. 7.12.1 and *Git* 56b.

21. 1QpHab XI.16–XII.5.

22. See 1QS VIII.1–12

23. *ARN* 4.5 (20a). For being '*made white*', see *Yoma* 39a and 39b.

24. *Yoma* 39b.

25. Lam R. 1.5.31.

26. Cf. Lam R. 1.5.31 with *ARN* 4.5 (20a) and *Git* 56b.

27. *War* 6.312–3.

28. Cf. *War* 2.151–3 with *Ant.* 18.23 and note that, while Josephus is calling the latter 'the Fourth Philosophy' followers of Judas the Galilean without specifically naming it either 'Zealot' or *Sicarii* but obviously rather 'Galileans', the description of the courage they show under torture and the threat of imminent death is the same.

29. See *War* 4.585–663 and cf. Tacitus, *Hist.* 2.78–5.13, Suetonius 8.5.1–8.85, etc.

30. See *War* 3.399–405.

31. See 4Q*Flor* I.7–11 on 2 Samuel 7:11–14 and Amos 9:11.

32. 4Q285, *DSSU*, pp. 24–30.

33. See 4Q252 V.1–6, *DSSU*, p. 89 and my comments there on pp. 83–5.

34. See Lam R. 1.16.51.

35. See CD VII.18–21 where 'the Sceptre arising out of Israel' is said to be 'the *Nasi chol ha-'Edah*' who, at whose 'rising' or 'standing up' (resurrection?), 'shall utterly destroy all the Sons of Seth' – this again in line with the aggressive quality of Psalm 110:5–7, despite later Christian attempts to transmute it.

36. See *ARN* 4.5 (20a).

37. *Git.* 56b.

38. *War* 3.399–405.

39. Lam R. 1.13.41 and Song of Songs R. 8.9.3.

40. *Ket.* 66b.

41. Cf. *Ket.* 66b–67a with Lam R. 1.16.48.

42. Cf. *Ket.* 66b and 67a with *Git* 56a and Lam R. 1.16.47.

43. *ARN* 6.3 (20b).

44. See 1QS VIII.9–10; Phil. 2:25.

45. For 'the Sons of the Pit' in the Scrolls, see 1QS IX.15, CD VI.14–16.

46. *ARN* 25.3 (27a), somewhat palely reflected in *San.* 68a.

47. For R. Akiba and Bar Kochba, see Lam R. 2.2.4 and j. *Ta'an* 68d. For R. Eliezer's words on his deathbed, see *ARN* 25.3 (27a) and *San.* 68a.

48. See *A.Z.* 16b–17a, j. *Shab.* 14d, Eccles. R. 1.8.3, and *Tos. Hul.* 2.24.

49. See, in particular, their dispute over the 'cleanness' or 'uncleanness of the oven of *Akhnai*' in *B.M.* 59b, which led to R. Eliezer's excommunication.

50. See *Ned* 19a, *M.Neg.* 9.3, *Ta'an* 25b, *B.B.* 10b, *M. Shab.* 6.4, *Nid.* 7b, *A.Z.* 23a, and *Git.* 83a–b.

51. See *B.M.* 59b.

52. *ARN* 6.3 (20b) and Gen R. 42.1; cf. too Pirke de Rabbi Eliezer 7 and Ps Philo 12.1.

53. *ARN* 25.3 (27a).

54. *ARN* 25.1 (27a).

55. *ARN* 6.3 (20b) and Gen R. 42.1.

56. Ibid.

57. Eccles R. 7.12.1.

58. *Git.* 56a.

59. For the story of this woman – supposedly named 'Rufina' (also rumoured as being responsible for his death) and supposed to be the wife of the Roman Prefect Tinius Rufus – and this marriage, see *Ned.* 50b, *A.Z.* 20a.

60. 4QpPs 37 II.13–20.

61. Cf. 4QpPs 37 II with Gen R. 42.1.

62. See 4QpPs 37 II.14–16, III.1, 5–7, and 11.

63. 4QpPs 37 II.18–20.

64. See *MZCQ*, pp. 29, 32–33, and 92–6.

65. See Luke 10:33, 17:16, John 4:39–40, 8:48, and Acts 8:25, but *per contra*, see Matthew 10:5.

66. 1QpHab XI.10–XII.3.

67. Cf. CD III.19–20.

68. Cf. 4QpPs 37 III.1–2 with CD I.7–8.

69. Gen R. 42.1.

Chapter 11

1. *DSSU*, pp. 182–200.

2. *MMT* I.62–70.

3. For the 'Official' publication of this document, which came out about a two years after that of Prof. Wise and myself, see E.Qimron and J. Strugnell, *DJD* X: *Qumran Cave* 4 – V, Oxford, 1994. Again, the present writer was the first to point out that this term implied the charged expression '*works*' and not either 'words' or 'acts' which has since – backed up by Prof. F. Garcia Martinez in his translation of *The Dead Sea Scrolls*, Leiden, 1998, II. pp. 790–804, who was the first to realize that I was right in this insight, followed up by M. Abegg, '4QMMT, Paul, and "Works of the Law"', in *The Bible at Qumran: Text, Shape, and Interpretation*, Grand Rapids, 2001, pp. 203–14.

4. *MMT* II.29–32.

5. CD VI.19–21.

6. See Hippolytus 9.21. For Josephus' 'Essenes', the allusion is the less specific 'nor blaspheme their Law–Giver or eat forbidden things'; see *War* 2.152–3.

7. CD VI.19–VII.4 and XX.17–20.

8. For the antagonism to 'blood' in CD, see II.8, III.6–8, V.7, etc.

9. CD IV.20–V.11, 11QT LVII.15–21, LXVI.12–17 and 4QMMT II.47–57 and 83–9.

10. See *War* 2.408–420.

11. 4QMMT II.84. In this sense, it is perhaps helpful to look upon Qumran and 'Essenes' generally as a Community of 'Holy Ones'/*Kedoshim* or, as we are attempting to call attention to, 'Nazirites', 'dedicated to' or 'Holy to God'

12. 4QMMT II.84–8.

13. Cf., for instance, Exodus 28:36 and 39:30.

14. 1QS VIII.1 and 5–6.

15. 4QMMT II.88–9.

16. See Ps. *Hom* 7.8, Koran 2.173, 5.3, 6.146, 16.115, etc.

17. This counter-indication is expressed in the Gospels in several ways: since Jesus *is* the Temple, the various scenes of Jesus keeping table-fellowship with and approving of various classes of persons such as prostitutes, tax-collectors, Sinners, gluttons (i.e., persons not keeping Mosaic dietary

regulations), and the like in Matthew 9:10, 11:19, 21:31 and pars. and miraculously curing the deaf, the dumb, and the blind (Matthew 9:32, 10:51, 11:5, 12:22, 15:30 and pars.) provide vivid examples of this sort of reversal.

18. 4Q*MMT* II.68–70.

19. 1QM I.2–3.

20. Cf. CD VII.13–21 with 1QM I.2–3 and 4Q*MMT* II.68–70.

21. For this ban on carrion as applicable specifically to Priests or 'Sons of Zadok' in the Temple, see Ezekiel 44:31.

22. See *War* 2.408–420.

23. See 11QT XLVI.10 and XLVII.13ff. and my full Appendix on this subject in *JJHP*, pp. 87–94.

24. The Temple is mentioned in 4Q*MMT* II.67, which then leads into II.68–70 about 'Jerusalem being the Holy Camp' and 'the foremost of the Camps of Israel'.

25. The first such allusion would appear to be Irenaeus in *Ad. Haer.* 1.23.2, but also see Justin Martyr, *First Apology* 1.26, Hippolytus 6.15, Eusebius, *E.H.* 2.13.4, Epiphanius, *Haeres.* 21.2.1–3.6, and Ps. *Rec* 2.8–12, where she is called 'Luna'.

26. See in particular Ezekiel 44:6–13, disqualifying 'the Levites' in favor of 'the Sons of Zadok' on this basis and note that when the Habakkuk *Pesher* describes 'the Wicked Priest' as 'not circumcising the foreskin of his heart' in XI.13, it is disqualifying him too from Temple service on this basis.

27. Hippolytus 9.21.

28. *War* 2.152–3.

29. See *E.H.* 3.33.1–4 which recapitulates the substance of Pliny's Letter 96 and Trajan's reply, no. 97. For Simeon's purported death by crucifixion, which also seems to have occurred during the reign of Trajan, see *E.H.* 3.32.3–7; for the examination of Judas' two sons, which seems to have occurred under Domitian (d. 96 CE), see 3.20.1–10.

30. *War* 2.520.

31. See Dio Cassius 68.3–4 and Origen's comment in *Contra Celsus* 2.13 that the judges even in his time were particularly zealous in applying this law and few escaped death who had run afoul of it.

32. Dio Cassius 68.3–4.

33. See *Git.* 44a, 55b, 58a, and *B.B.* 47b, etc.

34. *Contra Celsus* 2.13 and see Jerome, Letter 84 to Pammachius and Oceanus.

35. For fornication, marriage, monogamy, divorce, and adultery, see CD IV.17–V.11, VII.1–3, VIII.3–15, 11QT LVI.11–LVII.19, LXVI.12–17, etc.

36. Hippolytus 9.21; for Josephus' derivation, in which he only emphasizes the 'terrorist' aspect of the appellation, see *War* 2.254–7 and *Ant.* 20.186–7.

37. See *Ant.* 20.38–48 and cf. Gen R. 46.10.

38. CD XVI.4–7.

39. For this 'Land' and its association with Abraham – to say nothing of Noah, 'Ad and Thamud – see Koran 11:25–49, 26.105–49, 29.14–35, etc.

40. The Adiabene family are proverbial for their wealth and largesse in Josephus and Talmudic tradition; see, for instance, the palace Helen and her sons built in Jerusalem in *War* 5.252 and 6.355; their tomb, 5.55, 5.119, 5.147, and *Ant.* 20.94–5; the Golden Candelabra, depicted on the Arch of Titus, that was ultimately taken to Rome and probably melted down to help pay for the Colosseum, and the golden handles for vessels used in Temple services on *Yom Kippur* – *Yoma* 3:10 (37a); and her famine relief in *B.B.* 11a, j. *Pe'ah* 1:1, 15b/*Tos. Pe'ah* 4:18, and *Ant.* 20.49–51, in which Josephus actually remarks the 'great amounts of money (Izates) sent to the Leaders in Jerusalem' (*B.B.* 11a even records how his brother Monobazus – the members of whose family are even described in *Men.* 32b as being so 'Pious' that they carried *mezuzoth* with them when they traveled and set them up in inns where they stayed, even though temporary dwellings of this nature did not require them – just about beggared the Kingdom with so much charity); so if she was a supporter of the kind of 'Nazirite Judaism' exemplified at Qumran, there is no reason to suppose that she or her sons could not have supported that installation as well.

41. This is the implication of 'the suspected adulteress' plaque containing the passage from Numbers 5:12–31 she had erected on the wall of the Temple and the three successive seven-year Nazirite oath penances she observed according to Rabbinic tradition in *Naz.* 3:10 (19b–20a) and in *Git.* 60a.

42. See *Ant.* 20.51–53 and, for instance, *E.H.* 2.12.1–3 above (*n.b.*, that Eusebius directly follows this up in *E.H.* 2.13:1–7 with the notice about Simon *Magus*' consort 'Helena, who had formerly been a prostitute in Tyre of Phoenicia', saying more about her than the 'Helen' who preceded her which, all things being equal, is certainly very peculiar placement indeed).

43. See *Naz.* 3:10 (19b–20a) and *Git.* 60a above, but also see Josephus in *Ant.* 20.95 who also comments on her great sorrow which seems to have been a contributing factor to her death almost directly thereafter – she died of a 'broken heart'. But also see the story of the 'Widow of Nain' in Luke 7:11–17 and how Jesus, as a favor to this grieving Widow, resurrects her son (*thus!*).

44. Besides Josephus, *loc. cit.* above, see Pausanius, *In Arcadicis* 8.16.5 and Eusebius *E.H.* 2.12.3. Moses of Chorene, *History of Armenia*, 2.35 in the 6th Century comments on her 'remarkable' tomb 'before the gates of Jerusalem' and he is sure she is 'the principal of Abgar's wives' (*thus*).

45. *Ket.* 62a–63b and *Ned.* 50a.

46. *Ibid.*; also see *ARN* 6.1 (20a).

47. *Shab.* 68b. In our view, this notice clinches the relationship of R. Akiba to the family of the Royal House of Adiabene and its constant sponsorship of revolutionary activity against both Herodians and Romans. If one takes the death of the first Monobazus at around 68 CE and the second at about the same time, then this third 'Monobazus' can either be the son or grandson of the first or the son of the second, or he may have been a descendant of Izates. In any event, in our view, this would either make him Rachel's brother or close cousin.

48. See *ARN* 6.3 (21a) and *Ta'an* 19b–20a.

49. M. *Ta'an* 3:8, *Ta'an* 23a/j. *Ta'an* 66b, and *Ber* 19a.

50. For Honi, who is called 'Onias the Righteous' in Josephus (missing from the account in the *War*), see *Ant.* 14.22–28; for the account of how Aristobulus, whose part Honi appears to have taken with his rainmaking before he was stoned, refused to humble himself before Pompey (which differs from the account in the *Antiquities*), see *War* 2.128–141.

51. See *Ant.* 2.24–8 in the aftermath of Honi's (Onias the Righteous') stoning and cf. 1 Kings 17:1 and 19:9–14 where Elijah is *'filled with a burning zeal for the Lord'*; and note too in 1 Kings 21:19, following the murder of Naboth of Jezreel, how Elijah prophesies to Ahab that 'the dogs will lick your blood too' (*thus*) – meaning, that all male members and descendants of his family will 'be swept away'.

52. *Ta'an.* 20a.

53. *San.* 43a

54. M. *Ta'an* 3:8–9, b. *Ta'an* 19a, 23a–b, and j. *Ta'an* 66b.

55. *San.* 43a. The choice of Scriptural passages given here as reasons for the death of these five would seem to be totally tendentious. Still the reversal involved are quite typical.

56. See Psalm 10:9, 12, 17, etc.

57. *War* 2.451 and 628 and *Vita* 197ff., 290, 316, and 322.

58. *War* 2.451–56.

59. *Ibid.*

60. *War* 2.556–8.

61. *War* 2.557 and 4.140–6.

62. *War* 2.254–57, but in *Ant.* 20.162–68 he only uses the term 'Brigands' and blames Felix for 'bribing' them to accomplish this assassination. In *War* 4.400–409 he starts to describe the *Sicarii* and how they took over Masada and overran the surrounding countryside.

63. *War* 2.451–56.

64. See in particular *War* 2.558, *Ant.* 17.30–1, and *Vita* 46–61, 177–84, and 407–9.

65. See *War* 2.418. For his further activities as a leader of a gang of thugs and final going over to Roman forces whose agent he seems to have been all along, see *War* 2.556–8 and *Ant.* 20.214.

66. *War* 2.556–8. For Vespasian's dispatch by Nero in Corinth from Britain to Judea, see *War* 3.1–8.

67. See *War* 2.626–31 and *Vita* 197ff., 290, 316, and 322.

68. Cf. Ps *Rec.* 1.65–8 and 71 with Acts 5.34–40.

Chapter 12

1. See 1QM XI.13–XII.18 and XIX.1–5 and cf. Eusebius, *E.H.* 2.23.13–14, Epiphanius, *Haeres.* 78.14, etc.

2. *Ant.* 20.97–9.

3. Cf. *Ant.* 20.97 with Acts 5:36.

4. See Ps *Rec.* 1.71.

5. Here, the only difference is that this is not at the Last Supper as later in Matthew 26:26ff. and pars. in the Synoptics.

6. For 'the Last Times'/'Last Day'/'Day of Judgement' at Qumran, see 1QpHab VII.7, IX.6, XII.14–XIII.4, etc.

7. See *Ant.* 20.168–72 and *War* 2.259–264.

8. *Vita* 10 and *War* 2.119–161.

9. *E.H.* 2.23.8 and pars. Eusebius makes it clear that this is a direct quote from Hegesippus' account (c. 165 CE) and the lost Five Books of his *Memoirs*.

10. 1QM XI.11.

11. See 1QM XI.11.1–14 and pars.

12. Numbers 24:17–19.

13. 1QM XI.7, XII.9–10, and XIX.2.

14. *Haeres.* 78.7.7 and 14.1–3.

15. *E.H.* 2.1.2.

16. *War* 6.312–315.

17. 1QM XI.6–14.

18. 1QpHab XII.2–4.

19. Cf. 4QpPs37 II.10, II.19, III.1–2, III.10–11, III.16, IV.9–11 (here, too, the same 'paying him his reward' in the sense of Divine Vengeance), and IV.19–20.

20. 1QM I.3.

21. 1QM I.2. Matthew 4:15's *Ethnon* is equivalent to the Hebrew '*Amim*, both meaning Gentiles/Peoples.

22. Cf. CD IV.2–3 and VI.4–5. For Theudas' reverse exodus, see *Ant.* 20.97, and for Jesus' where he too 'leads' or 'feeds' some 4–5000 people, Matthew 10:1, 14.13–21 and 15.29–39 and pars.

23. Acts 9:1–25, Galatians 1:17, and Ps. *Rec* 1.71.

24. See *Haeres.* 19.1.2–10 and 29.7.7.

25. *Ibid.*, 20.3.2–3, 30.1.7, 53.1.1, etc.

26 1QM I.1–2, II.10–14, etc. There can be little doubt that what we are speaking about here is the desert between Transjordan and Iraq and all the 'Arab' Nations bordering thereon – I.e., 'the Fertile Crescent.'

27. 1QM I.6–7.

28. 1QM I.1. Vermes here gives 'Satan' as he does most frequently in his translations, but the word is '*Belial*' – 'the Devil' or '*Diabolos*' not 'Satan'. This may confuse the unsuspecting reader.

29. 1QM I.3, 8–9, 14–16, VII.1–7, XII.8–9, etc.

30. 1QM I.5.

31. 1QM I.2.

32. Since these salutations at the end of Romans do refer to 'the Littlest Herod', hardly a common name at this juncture of Roman history, it is our view that this individual is the son of said Salome and Aristobulus, making it ever more likely that the reference to 'the household of Aristobulus' in 16:10, followed by that to 'Herodion' in 16:11 is none other than the one of these two, 'Aristobulus and Salome' now living in Rome; and making it ever more likely that 'Paul' or 'Saul' is actually the descendant of Herod's sister (the first 'Salome'), a first cousin of both Agrippa I and Herod of Chalcis, and, therefore, the individual who was brought up with 'Herod the Tetrarch' as Acts 13:1 would have it. One should also note that the reference to his 'kinsman Junius' in Romans 16:7 is, in the author's view, none other than the son of 'Saulos'' sister Cypros by Helcias/Alexas, theTemple Treasurer, and therefore probably Paul's nephew in Acts 23:16 who has access to and warns the centurions in the Fortress of Antonia of plots against his uncle. It is in this passage that Paul's sister is specifically listed as residing in Jerusalem. We know too that this 'Julius' was an avid reader of Josephus' works in Rome

and, therefore, specifically retired to Rome (the destination of Paul's letter) because Josephus proudly tells us so in his *Vita*.

33. For Bela' as descendant of Benjamin, see Genesis 46:21 and 1 Chronicles 7:6. This makes the curious reference to barring one 'Bela'' from theTemple in 11QT XLVI.10–11 all the more rivetting.

34. See Koran 2.130–140, 3.65–7, 4.125, etc. and Paul in Romans 4:1–20, 9.8–9, Galatians 3:6–18, 4:22–8, etc.

35. See, for instance, CD XX.17–20 and my article in *D.S.SFC*, "'Joining'/"Joiners", "'Arizei-Go'im", and "*the Simple of Ephraim*" Relating to a Cadre of Gentile "*God-Fearers*" at Qumran' (first presented to the Society of Biblical Literature in 1991), pp. 313–331; and Acts 9:31, 10:2, 13:16, Romans 3:18, 2 Corinthians 7:1, etc.

36. CD IV.2–10 and VI.3–11.

37. 4QpNah III.3–8 and IV.3–7 (in the second instance, anyhow, clearly tied to an allusion to 'joining', I.e., *ger-nilveh*). It should be appreciated that Ephraim became Samaria when the capital was moved from Shechem to Samaria somewhere in the middle of the Israelite history in 1 Kings 16:24–32 during the reign of Ahab and Jezebel.

38. For Niger, see *War* 2.520, 566, and 3.11–28. For his death, so reminiscent of that of Jesus, see 4.359–63.

39. 4QpPs37 II.20 and IV.10.

40. 1QpHab II.6.

41. See Acts 13:21, Romans 11:1, Philippians 3:5 and 1QM I.2.

42. 1QM XVIII.8.

43. 1QM XI.4–11 and XIX.3–4.

44. 1QpHab VI.6–11 and XI.7–XII.6.

45. 1QM XIX.11.

46. 1QS V.2 and 9.

47. 1QM XVIII.7. As we have seen, the term *Yeshu'a* in Hebrew means 'Salvation'; cf. the last line of the substantive portion of the Damascus Document – CD XX.34.

48. *E.H.* 2.23.13.

49. *War* 2.599, 3.450–531, and *Vita* 65–7, 134–6, 271–301.

50. *Vita* 66, 134–6, 143, 302–11, etc.

51. *War* 3.450.

52. *War* 3.499–502 and 522–30; cf.Matthew 4:18–22, 8:23–4, 14:13–34, Mark 3:9, 4:36–5:2, 5:18–21, 6:32–54, 8:10–14, Luke 5:1–7, 8:23–5, John 6:1, 6:17–23, 21:1–8, and pars.

53. *War* 3.459–85.

54. *Ibid*. 3.522–542

55. *Ibid*. 3.532–8.

56. *War* 2.181–3 and *Ant*. 18.240–55; though in the *War* Josephus calls the place of his exile 'Spain', in the *Antiquities* he corrects this to 'Lyons a city in Gaul'.

57. *Epistle of Peter to James* 4.1–2.

58. 1QS IX.17–18.

59. *War* 3.522–9 – here, of course, there is *real* blood being 'poured out'.

60. *The Qumran Chronicle* in December, 1992 (vol. 2, no. 1), 'The 1990 Survey of Qumran Caves,' p. 49. Also see my 'The 1988–92 California State University Dead Sea Walking Survey and Radar Groundscan of the Qumran Cliffs,' Michael Baigent and my 'A Ground-Penetrating Radar Survey Testing the Claim for Earthquake Damage of the Second Temple Ruins at Khirbet Qumran,' and Dennis Walker's 'Notes on Qumran Archaeology: The Geographical Context of the Caves and Tracks' in The Qumran Chronicle, December, 2000 (vol. 9, no. 2), pp. 123–30, pp. 131–37, and December, 1993 (vol. 3, no. 1), pp. 93–100.

61. 4QMMT II.66–7.

62. 1QM I.1–3.

63. 1QM VII.5.

64. See *MZCQ*, pp. 12–16 and 19–27 and *DSSU*, pp. 32–43 and 49–80.

65. Cf. my discussion of this in *DSSU*, pp. 273–80.

66. 4Q448. The scholars who originally found this were A. Yardeni, E. Eshel, and H. Eshel. See their article 'A Qumran Composition Containing Part of Psalm 154 and a Prayer for the Welfare of

King Jonathan and his Kingdom,' *Tarbiz* (60), 1991, pp. 297–300 and in *Israel Exploration Journal* (42), 1992, pp. 199–229 and the version of this Michael Wise and I published in *DSSU*, pp. 280–1.

67. 4Q448 II.6–8.

68. Cf., for example, 1 Maccabees 2:26–7 and 54–8 and 2 Maccabees 4:2 with 1QS II.15, IV.4–18, IX.12, 1QH I.6–7, II.31, IX.5, X.15, XII.14, XVII.3, XX.14, etc.

69. *War* 2.152–3, but also see 'John the Essene' – *War* 2.567 and 3.11–19 – who participated along with one 'Silas' and 'Niger' in the early battles of the War and died along with the former at Ashkelon.

70. See, for instance, J. T. Milik, *Ten Years of Discovery in the Wilderness of Judaea*, London, 1959 whose attitude in pp. 44–98, 142–3, etc. is fairly typical of this way of looking at the documents.

71. Aside from the War Scroll, there is the Community Rule itself, in which we have already encountered the expression 'the Day of Vengeance' and which in the Qumran Hymns (VII.20) is called 'the Day of Massacre'. But there is also the finale of the Habakkuk *Pesher*, XII.12–XIII.4, which twice refers to 'the Day of Judgement' and ends with the pious hope that 'on the Day of Judgement God will destroy all the Servants of Idols and Evil Ones off the Earth'. This is to say nothing of the 'Paean to King Jonathan' above.

72. 1QS IX.20–24.

73. Cf. 1QS VIII.12–16 and IX.20 with Matthew 3:1–3/Mark 1:2–4/Luke 3.4–11.

74. 1QS VIII.1–16.

75. 1QS VIII.10–15.

76. Cf. CD IV.8, XX.2, XX.21, 1QS I.2, I.7, I.16–7, V.20 (repeated in VIII.15 in exposition of Isaiah 40:3 as we just saw), IX.20, 1QpHab VII.11 and VIII.1 in exposition of Habakkuk 2:4), XII.4–5, etc.

77. 1QS IX.13–24.

78. 1QH VII.20 (cf., for instance, 1QM I.10 and VII.5).

79. 1QM VII.6.

80. Cf. 1QS VIII.16–25, IX.19, CD XV.17, 4Q266, 4Q270, etc.

81. CD VI.19–VII.6.

Chapter 13

1. 1QH XI.22–23.

2. 1QH XI.22–23 and cf. XVII.25–36, XIX.24–27, XXVI.7–12, etc.

3. For 'the Standing One', see *JBJ*, pp. 705–90. For 'standing' at Qumran, see CD IV.4, XII.23, XIV.19, 1QH XV.31, XXI.13–4, XXIII.9–10, etc.

4. For Synoptic parallels to this 'shoe latchet' allusion, see Mark 1:7 and Luke 3:16. At Qumran this 'Shiloh' Prophecy (Genesis 49:10) is actually to be found in the so-called Genesis *Pesher* (4Q252–4), V.1–7, which actually mentions the Messiah's 'feet' and probably explains all these 'feet' references we have been following above.

5. See 1QH XII.22–5, XX.13–17, and XXI.13–15. It would be well for the reader to trace both this 'Power' and 'Light' language throughout the Scrolls.

6. See 1QH XII.18–22 and 30–33.

7. 1QpHab XI.2–15.

8. 1QS VIII.3–11.

9. 1QS VIII.6–7, but note too 1QM VI.6, XI.13 and 4QpPs37 IV.9, further solidifying the homogeneity of all these documents.

10. CD I.7.

11. For Paul's 'building' language (to say nothing of 'planting' and 'plantation' imagery), see 1 Corinthians 3:6–14, 2 Corinthians 5:1, and Ephesians 2:19–20 (if authentic).

12. For 'Precious Cornerstone' language as applied to Jesus, see Matthew 21:42 and pars., but also see Acts 4:11, Ephesians 2:20, and 1 Peter 1:20 and 2:6–7.

13. Cf. Ephesians 5:2, 1 Peter 2:5, Hebrews 9:26, 10:5–11:4, 13:15–16, etc.

14. 1QS VIII.3–4.

15. 1QS VIII.10.

16. 1QH XIX.10–14.

17. 1QM XII.9.

18. 1QS II.23–25.

19. Cf. Matthew 22:37–9 and pars., James 1:12–2:8, Justin Martyr in *Dial.* 23, 47, and 93, etc.

20. Cf. 1QS II.24–5, VIII.2, CD VI.17–VII.2, XX.18–21, etc.

21. *War* 2.128, 2.139, *Ant.* 15.375–9, and 18.117. Josephus also applies these two categories to his description of the first *Zaddik*, 'Simeon the Righteous', in *Ant.* 12.43.

22. *Epistle of Peter to James* 4.5.

23. Cf. CD I.4, I.16, IIII.10, IV.6–8, VII.2, VIII.16–7, etc.

24. CD VIII.14–23.

25. Cf. Matthew 17:1–8 and *pars.* with Galatians 2:5–9.

26. 1QS VIII.1–7.

27. 'Perfection' and 'Perfection of the Way' are basic Qumran doctrines; cf. 1QS I.8, II.2, III.9, V.24, X.22–5, VIII.6–9, VIII.20, IX.19, XI.2, XI.10–11, CD I.20–21, II.15–6, VII.4–5, VIII.24–30, etc.

28. Cf. 1QpHab X.5–13.

29. CD I.6–11.

30. Matthew 22:37–9.

31. Cf. 1 Corinthians 8:1 with 1QpHab VII.14–16.

32. Cf. 1QpHab X.5–13.

33. *War* 2.128–148.

34. *Ant.* 18.117.

35. Cf. *War* 2.123, 129, and 161, *Vita* 11–12.

36. 1QS IV.6–8.

37. Cf. Acts 6:5ff. and Eusebius in *E.H.* 2.1.2.

38. See *War* 2.155, Hippolytus 9.21, Eusebius, *E.H.* 3.32.6, and Epiphanius, *Haeres.* 78.14.5–6

39. Cf. *Haeres.* 19.4.1, 30.3.1–6, 30.17.5, and *Abstract* 30.2.

40. 1QS IV.19–21.

41. See CD III.18–20 and 1QM III.20 and XI.11.

42. 1QS II.23–III.4.

43. Aside from all the other parallels, it is Paul, as we shall see, who constantly refers to the fact that he 'does not lie' – cf. Galatians 1:20 (in the context of averring to having met James), 2 Corinthians 11:30, Romans 3:7 and 9:1, 1 Timothy 2:7, etc.

44. 1QS III.9–12. Note he is 'the pleasing atonement' and it is he who 'will be washed by purifying waters and sanctified by cleansing waters'. Also see 1QS I.15 and III.10 and cf. 4Q266, lines 17–18 on expelling a person who 'departs from the right or the left of the *Torah*'.

45. 1QS III.7–9.

46. *Ant.* 18.117.

47. 1QS XI.5–9

48. Cf. 1 Corinthians 12:14–27 and Ephesians 2:19–22.

49. *Haeres.* 30.15.3 and 21.1 and *Hom.* 10.1, 11.1, 11.26–30, 12.6, 13.4–5 (just like 'Essenes', calling these things 'Piety towards God'), etc.

50. 1QS II.15, IV.7, VIII.10–16, and IX.19–23.

51. 1QM X.4–5 and cf. VII.5–6.

52. Cf. 1QS I.19–26, X.18, 1QM I.5, IV.13, XI.11–2, XIV.4–5, XVIII.7,CD XX.19–34, etc.

53. See Acts 9:31 (this describing all the Churches in Judea), 10:5 (describing Cornelius, a Roman Centurion!), 13:16 (here Paul really uses the term to describe Gentiles associated with the Synagogue he is addressing in Antioch at Pisidia), but also Paul's own use of the formulation – sometimes even sarcastically – in Romans 3:18, 8:15, 13:7, 2 Corinthians 7:1 (perhaps the most 'Perfect' formulation of the usage), Ephesians 5:21, etc.

54. Cf. Acts 2:21, 3:6, 4:7–17, 5:28, etc. with CD IV.3–4 (the definition of 'the Sons of Zadok').

55. Cf. CD VI.15, VII.1, and VIII.8.

56. CD XX.34, basically the last line of the revised historical exhortation in the Damascus Document.

57. Cf. 1QM XI.5–XII.14 and XVII.7–XIX.13.

58. Cf. 1QS I.8, II.2, III.9, V.24, VIII.9, IX.19, X.22, XI.10–11, CD I.20–21, II.15–6, XX.2–8, etc.

59. See Hippolytus 9.21, *JBJ*, pp. 309, 709, 764, 898.

60. For Paul's contempt for 'the *Torah* as given by the hand of Moses', see in particular Galatians 2:16–21, 3:17–4:11, 4:24–4:30, and 2 Corinthians 3:1–18.

61. 1QS VIII.13–18.

62. Cf. 1QM VII.5 and 4Q448 II.7.

63. See 1QM XI.6–XII.10.

64. 1QM XI.10–15.

65. See A.N. Sherwin-White, *The Roman Citizenship*, Oxford, 1939, pp. 270–5, the Romans being 'the Lord of the Peoples' ('*Princeps Gentium*').

66. 1QM XI.13–15.

67. Cf. *JBJ*, pp. 226, 270–1, 386, 434, 461–2, 564–76, 728, 741, and 824–5.

68. *Vir. ill.* 2.

69. See *Zohar* on 'Balak and Balaam', 193a–97a.

70. Cf. 1QpHab VIII.2–3 with X.3–5 and XII.14–XIII.4.

71. 1QpHab XII.14 and XIII.2–3.

72. Cf. Matthew 10:15, 11:22–4, 12:20 and 36, etc., 2 Peter 2:9 and 3:7, Jude 6 and 15.

73. For the widespread allusions to 'the Day of Judgement'/'the Last Day' in the Koran, see 78.17–8, 81.1–14, 82.12–19, 83.11, 85.2, etc.; for the categories of persons known as 'idolaters' and 'hypocrites', see 2.8–20, 105, 113–4, 135, 3,167, 4.48–89, 136–43, 5.60, 82, 8.49, 9.1–64, etc..

74. 1QpHab V.3–5.

75. Cf. CD I.19 with IV.7.

76. Cf. 1QpHab V.3–5.

77. Jude 14–5.

78. 1QM XII.8; cf. CD I.7 and variously throughout that document and elsewhere.

79. Cf. 4Q521 II.5.

80. 1QM XII.5–9. This allusion occurs in 1QM XII.7.

81. See 1QM XII.9–10 and XIX.2–3.

82. 1QM XIX.3–8.

83. See, for instance, Koran 73.12, 82.15, 92,14, 111.3 or 96.1–5 on 'The Night of Power'.

84. Cf. 1QM XII.10 and XIX.2.

85. 1QM XII.10–16 and XIX.2–8.

86. See James 4:4–8 and *NTC*, pp. 132–5 and 153–61.

Chapter 14

1. *Haeres.* 30.16.1–4. Also cf. John 3:36.

2. 1QS VIII.3–10.

3. 1QS VIII.3–4.

4. Matthew 16:21, 17:12, and pars., Acts 17:2–3, 29:23, 1 Corinthians 5:7, 12:26, Hebrews 9:26, 11:25, etc.

5. 1QS VIII.6–7, 10 and IX.5.

6. 1QS VIII.1.

7. 1QS VIII.9.

8. 2 Corinthians 2:16–17.

9. Cf. Ps. *Hom* 11.35 and Epistle of Clement to James 20.

10. 1QS IX.2.

11. 1QS IX.3–6.

12. For some of the first examples of this sort of ideology in Judaism, see Tobit 1:7–8, 4:7–12, 12:8–10, etc.

13. Cf. 1QS VIII.4–11 and IX.6.

14. 1QH XIV, 25–7 and XV.8–9.

15. *Ant.* 19.332–4.

16. Eusebius, *E.H.* 2.23.17.

17. See, for instance, the crucial attack on 'the Righteous One and all the Walkers in Perfection' in CD I.20 and such 'soul' language, not only in Isaiah 53:11 – its probable origin – but also in 1QH IX.9–10, X.32–4 (*nephesh-Ebion* and *nephesh-'Ani*), XI.25, XIII.6, XIII.13, etc.

18. See Revelation 2:28, 8:10–11, 9:1 and 22:6.

19. 4QpIsaᵃ III.11–24 interpreted in terms of 'the Branch of David'.

20. CD IV.16–19.

21. See *MZCQ*, pp. 19–31 and 35–38 and *JJHP*, pp. 1–20 and the Appendix in pp. 87–94 and variously.

22. CD V.14–15. This significantly follows the material banning, on the basis of legal analogy with Leviticus 18:13, marriage with close family cousins (unknown to Jewish Law previously) and the John the Baptist-like imprecations (in Josephus, also based on objections to Herodian marital practices) about 'kindlers of Fire' and 'their offspring being those of vipers' in V.7–14.

23. For these traditions about Jacob of Kfar Sechania, see b. *A.Z.* 27b, *Tos. Hul* 2:22–3, and j. *Shab.* 14:4 and *A.Z.* 2:2, 40d as well as *JBJ*, pp. 217–29.

24. See *JJHP*, pp. 62–74 and my article on this subject in *DSSFC*, pp. 332–51: 'The Final Proof that James and the Righteous Teacher are the Same,' first given to the Society of Biblical Literature in 1994.

25. W*ar* 2.143.

26. Cf. Hippolytus 9.21.

27. Ps. *Rec* 1:39.

28. Cf. CD III.21–IV10 and V.7–17, etc. with Hebrews 4:14–16 and 7:26–8:2.

29. See how Peter, John, and the other Apostles seem to go to the Temple every day in Acts 3:1–4:3, 5:12–16, 5:19–25, etc. This picture is, of course, paralleled in the Pseudoclementines and in Epiphanius' quotes from the *Anabathmoi*.

30. See Eusebius, *E.H.* 2.23.6–17 and pars.

31. Cf. Paul in 1 Corinthians 8:1–9:1, 10:14–32, and 11:26–30.

32. See *War* 2.405–29.

33. See *War* 2.7/*Ant.* 17.207.

34. See *War* 2.117–18 (introducing his diversion to talk about the 'Three Jewish Philosophies') and *Ant.* 18.1–10 (introducing 'the *Sicarii* Movement' of Judas the Galilean and Sadduk and only after this the 'Three Jewish Philosophies' – the shift is significant).

35. Ben Sira 44:1.

36. 2 Peter 2:6. Cf. the crucial attack on 'the Righteous One' in CD I.20 and in 1QH IX.9–10, X.32–4, XI.25, XIII.6, XIII.13, etc.

37. *Vita* 11–12.

38. For the Rechabites, see Jeremiah 35:1–19, and *JBJ*, pp. 229–47, 456–69, and 728–72.

39. Cf. 1QS III.20–5 and IX.14.

40. See my general discussion of this inability to relate to literary metaphor and wordplay in *MZCQ*, pp. 3–16, 19–27, and 41–46.

41. Cf. 1 Maccabees 4:36–61, 2 Maccabees 1:1–2:24, and 10:1–8, *Ant.* 12.323–6, and my discussion of these matters in *MZCQ*, pp. 12–16.

42. See *Ant.* 12.414 and 419–34. Josephus refers three times here to the High Priesthood of Judas and makes it clear that he was

'elected by the People' in the 'Zealot' manner.

43. See John 2:13–22 and the Synoptic parallels.

44. See *Surah* 2.43.

45. See Tobit 1:7–8, 4:7–12, 12:8–10, etc.

Chapter 15

1. *Haeres.* 30.16.7–8.

2. See Acts 3:1–4:3, and 5:20–33, Ps. *Rec.* 1.55–71.

3. See Hennecke, *New Testament Apocrypha*, II, pp. 88–111 and also Epiphanius' *Haeres.* 30.15.1.

4. See *The Nag Hammadi Library in English,* ed. by J.M. Robinson, Harper and Row, 1977, pp. 242–55.

5. 1Qp Hab II.7–10 and cf. VII.4–8.

6. 1QpHab VII.7–8.

7. Koran 2.4, 27.66, 32.7, 49.19, etc. The Arabic here is *'gheib'* – 'absent'/'hidden'/'unseen', but it is the equivalent to what would otherwise be called 'Mystery'.

8. See in the *Homilies*, Epistle of Peter to James 4.1–5.1 and 1QS IX.16–21.

9. See S.G.F. Brandon in *Jesus and the Zealots*, New York, 1967, pp. 114–41.

10. See CD VI.3–21.

11. *Haeres.* 30.16.1–8.

12. CD VI.14–16.

13. *Ant.* 20.181 and 206.

14. 1QpHab XII.2–10.

15. CD VI.15.

16. CD VII.1.

17. CD VIII.5–12.

18. CD VIII.6 and cf. V.5–1 and VII.1.

19. CD VIII.7–8.

20. See A.N. Sherwin-White, *The Roman Citizenship, Oxford,* 1939, pp. 270–75, the Romans being 'the Lord of the Peoples' (*'Princeps Gentium'*), but also see how Eusebius uses the term when he speaks in *E.H.* 1.13.2 when he speaks of Abgarus, 'the King of the Peoples beyond the Euphrates.'

21. CD VIII.10–12.

22. This is the famous 'Generation of Vipers' in Matthew 3:7, 12:34, and 23:33 and pars.

23. CD VIII.12–13.

24. Cf. James 2:8–10 with CD VI.20–21.

25. CD VI.19–20.

26. For the Priesthood, see Exodus 22:31, 28:2–31:10, 39:1–41, Number 16:3, etc.; for the Nazirite, Numbers 6:1–21.

27. See 4Q266 7–8, and CD XIV.8–9. It should be appreciated that F.M. Cross in *The Ancient Library of Qumran*, pp. 232–3, was probably one of the first persons to understand this equivalence.

28. See *DSSU*, pp. 212–19 and Plates nos. 19–20.

29. Hippolytus 9.21.

30. 1QS IX.23 and 4QpNah I.3–11.

31. Cf. *DSSU*, pp. 180–200 and I.2–24.

32. Ps. *Rec* 1.36–7.

33. See, for instance, Eusebius, *E.H.* 1.7.11–13 and Josephus, *Ant.* 19.332–4.

34. *M. Sota* 8:12; cf. *M. Bik.* 3.4.

35. *Ant.* 19.332–48.

36. See Dio Cassius 68.14.5–33.3 and 67.14.1–18.2. Trajan, whose father had participated under Vespasian in the campaigning in Palestine, had virtually decimated the Jewish population of Egypt in the wake of seeming 'Messianic' disturbances there around the period 105–115 CE and Hadrian had done the same in Palestine during the Bar Kochba Revolt from 132–6 CE.

37. See our discussion of this episode in *JBJ*, pp. 286–9, 534–7, 623–42, etc.

38. See 11QT LVI.10–15.

39. 11QT LVII.15–7.

40. See CD IV.17–V.15, VIII.5–8, and 4QMMT II.3–57; also see 11QT XLVI.6–12 and XLVII.8–18.

41. See *War* 2.409–26.

42. See *Ant.* 20.189–96 and my treatment of this episode in *JBJ*, pp. 487–521 and 778–98.

43. The first person to propose this position was S.G.F. Brandon in his two books, *Jesus and the Zealots*, New York, 1967, pp. 115–25 and 158–89 and *The Fall of Jerusalem and the Christian Church*, London, 1951, but he was basing himself for the most part on Robert Eisler, *The Messiah Jesus and John the Baptist*, New York, 1931, pp. 141–52, 221–80, 449–53, 518–27, 540–61, and 593–4, whom he mentions throughout and who really was the first to critically recognize the important of James in this regard and his role as an 'Opposition High Priest', a position which I too have adopted.

44. See Eusebius, *E.H.* 2.23.18–21; Origen, *Contra Celsum* 1.47; Jerome, *Vir. ill.* 2; Clement, *Hypotyposes* 6.13; and Epiphanius, *Haeres.* 66.20.1 and 78.14. I have covered these matters in detail in *JBJ*.

45. *War* 2.409–26.

46. 4QMMT II.3–9.

47. For these 'complaints', see Epiphanius, *Haeres.* 30.16.5–7.

48. Cf. *Ant.* 20.216 with Eusebius' testimony regarding James in *E.H.* 2.23.6 and pars.

49. See 1QpHab XI.4–XII.10 and 4QpPs37 II.18–20 and IV.8–10.

50. See, for instance, *E.H.* 3.27.1–6 on 'the Heresy of the Ebionites'.

51. *Haeres.* 30.16.8–9.

52. These two were both called 'Tigranes' and, as Josephus traces their genealogy, they are descendants of Mariamme, the last true Maccabean Princess, via her older son Alexander, and Glaphyra, the daughter of the King of Cappadocia – see Josephus, *Ant.* 18.139–40 and *War* 1.552 and 2.221–22.

53. See *Ant.* 20.140 and 147, *Apion* 1.51, and Acts 23:16.

54. See *War* 2.418, 2.556–9, 4.140–6, and *Ant.* 20.214.

55. See *JBJ*, pp. 537–49 and 885–92; for his execution, see *War* 4.359–63.

56. *Ant.* 20.214, but also see their later exploits in *War* 2.418 and 556–9.

57. *War* 1.486 and *Ant.* 15.252–266, 16.227, and 18.133.

58. Cf. *Ant.* 20.214 with Acts 8:1–3. We have discussed it quite extensively in *MZCQ*, pp. 38, 76, *JJHP*, pp. 4, 22, 39, and *JBJ* pp. xxxii, 166–87, 444–53, 599–612, 834–6, etc.

59. Ps. *Rec* 1.70–71.

60. Cf. *Ant.* 20.214 with 1QpHab IX.3–7 and XII.2–10 and CD VIII.5–12.

61. See 1QpHab IX.2–12.

62. See 4QpPs37 II.20 and IV.10.

63. See *War* 2.411–422.

64. See *War* 2.556–8.

65. See *Ant.* 18.130–42 and 20.138–9.

66. Josephus himself remarks that Agrippa I seemed to have ambitions of founding an Empire of some kind with other petty Kings in the East and Saulos' conduct seems to have fallen under a cloud of some kind, which is why he was urged by Agrippa II to report to Nero in Corinth (the last one hears of him), especially with the butchering of the Roman garrison in Jerusalem and the circumcision of its Commander. For Paul's attitude towards such a polity of 'Jews and Greeks', which his religious efforts seemed aimed at establishing, see Romans 1:16, 2:9–10, 10:12, 1 Corinthians 1:24, Galatians 3:28, and Colossians 3:11.

67. *War* 7.219–243.

68. *Ant.* 20.139–43.

69. See *Ant.* 20.139–40.

70. See Acts 23:24–24:27 and 25:10–27:1.

71. See *Ant.* 15.105, 17.11–80 and 324–38 (on a false 'Alexander'), and 18.139–40 and *War* 1.552–56.

72. *Ant.* 18.140.

73. See *JBJ*, pp. 793–801.

74. *Ant.* 18.141.

75. See 1QpHab XII.2–10.

76. See Suetonius 6.49.3–4 and 8.14.4 and Dio Cassius 63.28.1–2 and 67.15.1; *JBJ*, pp. 791–97.

77. See Suetonius 8.15.1, 8.17.1–2, Dio Cassius 67.14, and *E.H.* 3.18.3–5.

78. *War* 2.556–8.

79. See *Ant.* 19.299–325 (here is another character missing in the *War*).

80. See *Vita* 407–9 – this in addition to the material in *War* 2.556–8 above.

81. See *War* 2.214–22 and *Ant.* 19.353, 20.13–16, 104, and 158.

82. *War* 1.187–203 and *Ant.* 16.52–4.

83. See how Aretas, the King of Petra, took control of Coele Syria and Damascus in the early First Century B.C.E. in *Ant.* 13.392 and 14.34, 40, and 74. After that, it seemed to have a variety of Roman Governors, but in the mini-war between Herod the Tetrarch and Aretas, his descendant, after the execution of John the Baptist, Aretas seems to have retaken control of it for awhile if Acts 9:22–5 is at all credible; see *Ant.* 18.109–25.

84. Cf. Acts 9:1–2 with the far more detailed account in Ps. *Rec* 1.70–1.

85. See, for instance, *War* 1.401–28, 7.172–77, *Ant.* 15.267–364, 16.136–59.

86. *War* 1.437 and *Ant.* 15.25–64 and 20.247–8.

87. See *Haeres.* 30.16.8–9 and cf. 20.1.1–6, which shows he has really read his Josephus very carefully.

88. See Eusebius, *E.H.* 1.7.11 and 14.

89. *Ibid.*, 1.7.13. Eusebius claims to be taking this information from Julius Africanus (170–245 CE), but one may see this clearly as well in Josephus' comments in *Ant.* 14.491 where uncharacteristically (because he is comparing him with his own ancestors, the Maccabees), he shows his utter contempt for Herod's 'base' origins.

90. See *War* 2.422–28.

91. See *War* 2.520.

92. See *War* 4.491–3, Suetonius 6.49.3–4, 8.14.4, and Dio Cassius 63.28.2 and 67.15.1.

93. See Suetonius 7.8.1–9.2.

94. See Dio Cassius 68.14.4.

95. See Tacitus, *Annals* 15.65–16.17.

96. Cf. Acts 23:35, 24:23, and 28:30–31 and see *E.H.* 2.22.2–8.

Chapter 16

1. For Eusebius, see *E.H.* 3.5.3; for Epiphanius, see *Haeres.* 29.7.7, 30.2.7, and *De pond. et mens.* 15; for 1 Apoc Jas., see 5.25.15 and 5.35.15–20.

2. *E.H.* 3.5.3–4.

3. CD IV.2–3 and VI.4–5.

4. 1QpHab XII.5.

5. See *E.H.* 3.5.1–6.32.

6. See *War* 6.312–5.

7. *War* 6.288–300.

8. *Haeres.* 29.7.7.

9. See *The Haran Gawaita and the Baptism of Hibil-Ziwa*, tr. E.S. Drower, Biblioteca Apostolica Vaticano, Citta del Vaticano, 1953, pp. viii–xi and 2–17.

10. *E.H.* 1.7.14 and cf. Epiphanius in *Haeres.* 29.7.7, who both knows that 'Cocaba' is based on 'Star' and places it 'in Bashan' which is on the way to Damascus not far from the region of Pella and the Decapolis a little further South. There is a discrepancy here.

11. *E.H.* 1.7.14.

12. *E.H.* 4.6.4.

13. 1 Apoc Jas. 5.25.10–20.

14. Once one dispenses with the dissimulation of 'the two sons of Zebedee', there is little doubt that what one is really referring to – and this in all sources – is the martyrdom of the two brothers 'James and Simon', whether one is talking about 'the two sons of Judas the Galilean' by those names or 'Simon the Zealot' or, for that matter his double 'Simeon bar Cleophas' or 'James' himself/'James the son of Alphaeus' (i.e., 'Cleophas').

15. Luke 24:13–35.

16. See S.G.F. Brandon in *Jesus and the Zealots*, NewYork, 1967, pp. 208–218 and in his earlier *Fall of Jerusalem*, pp. 168–73 and 263–4; W. Farmer, *Maccabees, Zealots and Josephus*, NewYork, 1957, p. 125; and G. Strecker, *Das Judenchistentum in den Pseudoklemintinen*, Berlin, 1959, pp. 229–31; and cf. *MZCQ*, pp. 80–1 and 89–91.

17. Cf. Acts 5:36 and 1 Apoc. Jas 5.25.15–29.

18. *Ant.* 20.97–8.

19. Cf. Acts 9:1–3 with Ps. *Rec* 1.70–1.

20. *War* 2.433–449 and *Vita* 21.

21. See *War* 7.252–406.

22. See 4Q266 (The Last Column of the Damascus Document) and my discussion in *DSSU*, pp. 212–19.

23. See E.S. Drower, *The Haran Gawaita and the Baptism of Hibil-Ziwa*, pp. viii–xi and 2–17.

24. *War* 2.93–5 and *Ant.* 17.188 and 318–20.

25. *War* 2.457–68.

26. *Ibid.* and *Vita* 341–2 and 410.

27. See *Zohar* 59b on Noah and quoting Proverbs 10:25.

28. See Eusebius, *E.H.* 2.23.18–21, Clement in *E.H.* 2.5.3, Origen, *Contra Celsum* 1.47, Jerome, *Vir. ill.* 2, Epiphanius, *Haeres* 78.14, etc.

29. See *War* 6.300–309.

30. Cf. *War* 6.300–308 with *Ant.* 20.200–02.

31. See *Ant.* 20.17. That this King also had a large harem is testified to in 20.20.

32. See Moses of Chorene, *History of Armenia* 2.25. In Roman and Latin sources, this King is often called '*Acbarus*' and he is referred to as 'King of the Arabs' – see, for instance, Tacitus, *Annals* 12.12.

33. *War* 6.300–301.

34. Matthew 9:15, 25:1–102, John 3:29–30, and pars.

35. *War* 6.302–305.

36. See Eisler, *The Messiah Jesus and John the Baptist*, pp. 113–82 and the *Jewish War*, 1959 Penguin Edition, tr. by G.A. Williamson, *Appendix on the Slavonic Josephus*, pp. 402–5.

37. See *JBJ*, pp. 183–4, 814–6, and 922.

38. See *Ant.* 20.17–20, 51–53, and 101–102.

39. See my discussion of the whole range of these kinds of complexities in *JBJ*, pp. 807–16, 853–82, and 930–38.

Chapter 17

1. *Ps. Rec.* 1.49–52.

2. *Ant.* 20.139–41.

3. 11QT LVII.15–19.

4. See *Ant.* 18.253–6, 20.145–146, and *Vita* 119. Note that Bernice's first marriage in *Ant.* 19.276–7 was to Marcus, the son of Alexander the Alabarch of Alexandria (and probably Philo's nephew), the richest man in Alexandria.

5. See *Ant.* 19.363–5, 20.173–84, and cf. *War* 2.457–93.

6. *Ant.* 20.197–215.

7. *Vita* 13–16.

8. *Vita* 364–67.

9. Cf. John 12:10–11 with the more extensive 'plotting' preceding it in John 11:45–54.

10. Cf. Acts 6:11 with *E.H.* 2.23.16–25 and pars.

11. See *War* 3.536–41 and cf. Suetonius 6.19 on 'Nero'.

12. *Ant.* 1.8–9.

13. Cf. *War* 2.227 with *Ant.* 20.112.

14. *War* 2.228–31 and *Ant.* 20.113.

15. See *Ps. Rec.* 1.72–73.

16. *Ant.* 20.124 and cf. *War* 2.238.

17. *Ant.* 20.127 and cf. *War* 2.232–46.

18. Cf. *War* 2.239–44 with *Ant.* 20.130–131. For Tacitus' comment, see *Annals* 12.54.

19. See *Ant.* 20.130 above and *War* 2.241. Also, for the various crucifixions at Lydda in Talmudic tradition, see *JBJ*, pp. 494–7 and 1018 and *Suk.* 52a–52b, which considers that 'the Messiah ben Joseph' – probably the Samaritan Messiah – who was supposed to precede 'the Messiah ben Judah' (the Judean one) was crucified there. Also, another curious *nom a clef* (probably for Jesus or Simon *Magus*), 'Ben Stada', is mentioned in *San.* 67a – cf. *San.* 43a and *Shab.* 104b, which says he brought 'magic from Egypt' – as having been crucified there. For more on 'the martyrs at Lydda', see *B.B.* 10b and *Pes.* 50a.

20. See above on the Samaritan 'Messiah' or '*Taheb*' and Acts 9:32–43 on how Peter meets all 'the Saints that lived at Lydda' just prior to his 'tablecloth vision' in 10:1–32, among whom are 'Dorcas', a.k.a. 'Tabitha', a woman whom quite naturally he raises from the dead! In any event, 'Ben Stada' is probably another corruption of 'the Standing One' and one should note that for the Pseudoclementines (*Rec.* 2.7–12 and *Hom.* 2.17–32), 'Dositheus' (i.e., 'Doetus') is a Samaritan Disciple with Simon *Magus* of John the Baptist. For Josephus, though the 'Doetus' who is executed here at

Lydda by Quadratus is a Samaritan, he is 'a *Leader of the Jews*' (thus). Curiously enough, in *War* 4.145–6, Josephus identifies another individual, 'John the son of Dorcas' (i.e., 'Doetus') as the 'Zealot' assassin who creeps into the Temple prison and assassinates Saulos' and Costobarus' kinsman, Antipas the Temple Treasurer.

21. Cf. Acts 11:19–26 with Ps. *Rec.* 1.70–71.
22. Ps. *Hom.* 11.15.

Chapter 18

1. Cf. 1QpHab V.11–12 with CD I.15–16.
2. These usages occur in CD VI.2, VI.7, VI.11, XII.20–21, XIII.2, XX.14, etc., whereas the actual allusion to 'the Teacher of Righteousness' occurs in I.11.
3. Cf. 1QS VI.12, VI.19–20, CD IX.17–19, IX.22, XIII.5–7, 13–16, XIV.8–12, XV.7–8, XV.11, XV.14, XVI.6–7 and 4Q266 8–9.
4. Cf. CD XIII.6.
5. CD XIV.8–10.
6. CD IV.19–21 and VIII.13/CD XIX.31–32 and cf. CD I.14–15, XX.10–11, 1QpHab V.11, X.9–12, etc.
7. Cf. CD VI.10–11.
8. CD XX.10–12.
9. CD XX.14–15.
10. Ibid.
11. See 1QH II.31 and IV.9–10 and cf. CD XX.10–11.
12. The material about 'the *Dajjal*' in Islamic tradition is generally to be found in the *Hadith* literature, but it is a deep-seated belief among Sunnis.
13. Cf. 4Q270, Frag. 2, Col. II.13–14 and cf. 4Q266, Frag. 8, Col. II.
14. CD V.21–VI.2.
15. CD I.14–16 and cf. 4Q266, Frag. 11, Lines 10–14.
16. See 1QpHab II.1–10.
17. 1QpHab I.11, VIII.8 and 16, etc. and 4QpPs37 IV.8–10.
18. 1QpHab VIII.16–17 and XI.12–14.
19. See *The Messiah Jesus and John the Baptist*, New York, 1931, pp. 540–46.
20. See, for instance, how 'the Sons of Zadok' are described in CD IV.2–4 or 'the Priesthood after the Order of Melchizedek' in Hebrews 5:4–11 and 7:5–28. The point is that both these designations are parallel and playing off the usage '*Z-D-K*' or 'Righteousness' in Hebrew.
21. 1QpHab VIII.13 and XII.8
22. Cf. *War* 2.409–416 with 1QpHab II.3–6.
23. 1QpHab II.1–6, but also see CD XX.14–15.
24. Cf. James 1:22–27, 2:9–12, 4:11, and 4:17 and the 'doing', 'keeping', and 'breaking' usages in CD I.20, II.18–III.3, III.12, IV.1, VI.14, XX.2, XX.17, XX.21–22 and 1QpHab II.6, VII.11, VIII.1, etc.
25. Cf. 1QpHab XII.4–5 with 3–5 and 4QpNah IV.5–7 with 4QpPs37 II.9–10, III.10, 1QS VI.20, VIII.10–25, VIII.19, etc.
30. 4QpNah IV.4–8.
31. See Isaiah 7:2–17, 11:13, Jeremiah 31:6–20, Ezekiel 37:16–19, Hosea 4:17–14:8, etc.
32. Cf. CD XX.19–20 with 1 Corinthians 11:24–5 and Luke 22:19.
33. Ps. *Rec.* 1.70–71.
34. See S. Goranson, '*Essenes: Etymology from 'Asah*', Revue de Qumran, XV, 1984, pp. 483–98.
35. Cf. 4QpNah III.1–10 and 1QpHab X.5–13.
36. 4QpNah III.1–2.
37. 1QpHab VI.3–8.
38. See *War* 6.316.
39. See *JJHP*, pp. 27–8 and *War* 3.132–4, 141–339, 409–54, 4.11–83, etc.
40. 1QpHab VIII.11–13 and IX.4–7.
41. Cf. *Ant.* 20.181 and 206–7.

42. See *War* 2.409–416.

43. 1QpHab VII.8–VIII.3.

44. 1QpHab VII.4–5.

45. 1QpHab II.1–10.

46. 1QpHab II.6–10.

47. The description of these '*Kittim*' – their ferocity, ruthlessness, and unstoppability – dominate Columns 1QpHab II.10–IV.14 and V.13–VI.11.

48. 1QpHab II.10–III.11.

49. The description of these 'Fortresses' as being 'of the Peoples', once more reinforces our understanding of these terms as descriptive of Herodians – cf. *War* 1.364, 1.402–21, 2.484, *Ant.* 16.143, etc.

50. 1QpHab VI.11. This is certainly borne out by what Josephus describes happened around the Sea of Galilee in 67 CE, particularly Tarichaeae – *War* 3.532–42 (n.b., it is here that Josephus observes that Vespasian's advisers insisted that, where Jews were concerned, 'no offence could be considered an Impiety'.

51. 1QpHab IX.3–10 and see *JJHP*, pp. 44–48 and 100.

52. See 1QpHab VIII.10–IX.12 and cf. 4QpPs37 II.18–20 and IV.9–10.

53. 1QpHab XII.2–6.

54. Cf. 4QpPs37 II.18–20 and IV.9–10 above.

55. Cf. CD XIX.8–9.

56. 4QpPs37 II.4, III.12, and IV.18 and cf. CD III.7, XX.27, etc. and Paul in Galatians 5:12.

57. 1QpHab XII.3–9 and *E.H.* 3.27.1–6 on the followers of James as 'the Ebionites'.

58. Jerome, *Vir. ill.* 2.

59. Cf. 1QpHab XII.10–XIII.4 with 4QpPs37 III.12.

60. Cf. 1QpHab XII.9–10 with *Ant.* 20.181 and 206–7 and cf. too *Pes.* 57a.

61. 1QpHab XI.4–9.

62. *Ant.* 20.105–132 and 194–97 and cf. *War* 2.228–46.

63. 1QpHab VIII.8–9.

64. 1QpHab VIII.12.

65. *E.H.* 1.9.2–3 and 11.9.

66. 4QpPs37 II.18–20.

67. 4QpPs37 IV.8–10.

68. 1QpHab IX.1–2.

69. 4QpPs37 III.1.

70. Cf. 4QpPs37 II.19–20 and IV.9–12 with CD I.7–9.

71. 4QpPs37 II.6–11.

72. 4QpPs37 II.11–13.

73. 4QpPs37 I.26–7 and cf. 1QpHab X.9–12.

74. Cf. CD XX.13–5 with 4QpPs37 II.7–10.

75. Cf. 4QpPs37 II.7 with CD VIII.4–5 and also I.12–13.

76. 4QpPs37 II.12–13 and cf. 1QpHab VII.10–VIII.3.

77. 4QpPs37 II.9–10 and 18–20.

78. For 'Salvation', see 4QpPs37 III.19 and IV.19–20 and cf. II.7–8 and 19–20.

79. Cf. 4QpPs37 II.19 with *Ant.* 20.200–201 and also see 1QpHab XII.3–10.

80. 1QpHab II.1–10.

81. 1QpHab II.6–8.

82. See 1QpHab VIII.9–13.

83. 1QpHab IX.4–7.

84. *Ant.* 20.214.

85. *War* 1.486–87 and *Ant.* 15.252–266.

86. *Ibid.*

87. Cf. *Ant.* 15.259–62 with 20.139–47.

88. *Ant.* 15.164–267.

89. *Ant.* 15.365–69, 18.116–19.

90. 4Q*MMT* II.3–9.

91. Cf. CD I.20–21 and 1QH I.9–10, II.32–4, III.25 and V.14.

92. *War* 4.228–353 and 566–72 and cf. *Ant.* 20.200 on the death of James.

93. See *War* 2.566, 3.11, 20–28.

94. 1QpHab I.10–11.

95. 1QpHab V.3–5.

96. For this 'Day of Judgement' and these same 'Evil Ones', see 1QpHab XII.12–XIII.4; for 'the hand of the Messiah', 'the hand of the Poor' and 'the sword of no mere Man', see 1QM XI.7–13.

97. 4QpPs37 III.5–7.

98. 4QpPs37 III.1–8.

99. See *Vita* 193–204 and cf. *War* 4.160, 238–83, and 316–25.

100. *War* 4.238–42 (Jesus speaking) and 4.326–33 (Josephus' own words).

101. *War* 4.314–325.

102. 1QpHab VIII.11–13 and IX.4–7. The allusion about 'collecting taxes' or 'tax-farming' literally occurs in VI.17.

103. Cf. *War* 1.152–3/*Ant.* 14.72 for Pompey; *War* 1.354–7/*Ant.* 14.481–2–86 for Herod.

104. 1QpHab IX.4–5.

105. Cf. 1QpHab IX.5 with CD IX.7.

106. Cf. Vermes, *op. cit.*, p. 514, etc.

107. 1QpHab VIII.13.

108. 1QpHab IX.6–7.

109. See *Ant.* 20.139–47.

Chapter 19

1. *War* 2.197 and 409–16; cf. *Ap.* 2.77.

2. CD V.8–11 and VIII.6–7.

3. See *Vita* 2–5.

4. For a description of this situation, see *War* 2.407–32 and for Josephus' command and activities in Galilee, see *War* 2.568–76.

5. *Ant.* 19. 328–31.

6. *Ant.* 19. 332–34.

7. *M. Sota* 7:8 and cf. *M. Bik.* 3–4.

8. Cf. 11QT XLVI.9–12 and my Appendix in *JJHP*, pp. 86–94.

9. *War* 2.406–502, 6.236–43, *Vita* 340–67, 402–10, *Apion* 1.51, etc.

10. *War* 2.427.

11. 1QpHab IX.1–2 and cf. Vermes, *op. cit.*, p. 514.

12. See Vermes above, Cross, pp. 142–160, Milik, pp. 59–70, etc. and note the word 'woundings'/'*mahalalot*' with the feminine plural in the document Prof. Wise and myself discovered (4Q285: 'The Messianic Leader', since considered part of the War Scroll) and the verb based on the same root in 11QT XLVI.11 clearly meaning not 'to cause disease' but to 'defile it', I.e., the Temple'.

13. *War* 2.647–51 is his first use of it; his second is in *War* 4.160–61 where he discusses the opposition of 'the Zealots' to Ananus.

14. *War* 4.314–15.

15. *Vita* 193–216 and 309.

16. *War* 4.318–323.

17. *War* 4.318.

18. The use of this word 'Arab' for Greco-Roman historians was, as we have seen, a very general one that certainly
encompassed areas such as Northern Syria; cf. *JBJ*, pp. 886–90 and Strabo, *Geography* 16.1.28, Tacitus, *Annals* 6.44 and 12.12 (who calls King Agbar 'Acbar King of the Arabs'), etc.

19. See *War* 1.6 and cf. Origen, *Contra Celsus* 1.47, 2.13, and Comm. in Matt. 10.17 and Eusebius, *E.H.* 2.23.20–21.

20. *War* 4.319–20.

21. Cf. Eusebius, *E.H.* 2.6.1–8, 2.23.20–22, 3.6.32, 3.7.8–9, etc. and *pars*.

22. 4QpPs37 II.19–20 and IV.8–11 and cf. 1QpHab IX.1–2, IX.9–X.5, and XI.12–XII.3.

23. 1QpHab XII.6–10.

24. 1QpHab IX.4–7.

25. Cf. 1QpHab VIII.2–3 (in interpretation of Habakkuk 2:4) and XII.14–XIII.4 with X.3–5.

26. Eusebius, *E.H.* 2.23.15–16 and *pars.*

27. 1QpHab VIII.2–3, CD V.4–5, etc.

28. Eusebius, *E.H.* 2.23.12.

29. 1QpHab X.3–4 and X.9–12.

30. Cf. *E.H.* 2.1.4, 2.23.3, and 2.23.16–18 and *pars.*with Ps. *Rec.* 1.70.

31. See *War* 4.335–43.

32. Cf. 1QpHab XI.5–6 with VIII.2 and X.3–5.

33. Matthew 24:30, 26:64, Mark 13:26, 14:62, Luke 22:69, Acts 2:33, 7:55–56, Romans 8:34, etc.

34. 4QpPs37 IV.9–10. The word here, which is reconstructed, may either be 'Vengeance' or 'Judgement'. It is 'Judgement' in II.20.

35. 'Blasphemy' as defined in *M. San.* 7:5–6 only relates to 'pronouncing the (Forbidden) Name' of God.

36. CD I.19–21.

37. Cf. *War* 2.254–6. In *Ant.* 20.162–66, this account is contradicted somewhat, by having the Roman Governor Felix complicit in this murder. This makes the whole approach of Josephus at this point somewhat suspicious. What is going on here? Does he mean that James was complicit in this murder as a putative inspirer of 'the *Sicarii*'? If Felix is involved in this murder, it makes no sense to then go on to assert that it was because of these 'impieties' that God withdrew his support from the City and brought the Romans in to 'fire' it and the Temple and reduce 'our wives and out children to slavery' as he does in 20.166.

38. *Euthyphro* 2a–3b.

39. See *R.H.* 31a and cf. *A.Z.* 8b and *San.* 41a, this last having both '*ha-bayit*' and '*galtah*' in direct conjunction.

40. *A.Z.* 8b and *San.* 41a and see my article in *DSSFC*, pp. 247–71: '*Interpreting Abeit-Galuto in the Habakkuk Pesher: Playing on and Transmuting Terms*' – in particular, pp. 268–69.

41. This is made particularly clear in *ARN* 4, which actually refers to Isaiah 10:34 and Zechariah 11:2 and asserts that 'Lebanon'/'the Strong Forest that is going to fall refers to the Temple', and it does so in the course of a conversation R. Yohanan is having withVespasian (of course, an anachronism, but no matter – Josephus is probably the original anyhow), in which he applies to him the 'Lebanon being felled by a Mighty One' as Josephus had doubtlessly done before him and as we have it in 4QpIsaIII.7–11 (directly followed by 'a Shoot will spring from the Root of Jesse and a Branch from its roots'). A stronger First Century dating confirmation could not be found, but one can also find it in *Git.* 56a, also referring to Isaiah10:33–4 and *Yoma* 39b referring to Zechariah 11:1 as here in *ARN*. Actually 4QpIs^c combines Isaiah 30 with Zechariah 11.

42. Cf. *R.H.* 31a–b.

43. See, in particular, *A.Z.* 8b, which actually sets forth this proposition. The same by implication in *San.* 41a although with less specificity. Both are concerned with the fall of theTemple in 70 CE.

44. Cf. 1QpHab IX.1–X.5, XI.12–15, and XII.2–10.

45. 1QpHab XI.

46. 1QpHab XI.13 and see n. 87 above.

47. 1QpHab XI.6–9 and see my article in *DSSFC*, pp. 247–71: '*Interpreting Abeit-Galuto in the Habakkuk Pesher: Playing on and TransmutingTerms*'.

48. 1QpHab XI.6–8.

49. Cf. 1QpHab XI.14–15 with 1QpHab XII.2–6.

50. 1QpHab XIII.1–4.

51. See, for instance, J.T. Milik, *op. cit.*, p. 67f.; F.M. Cross, *op. cit*, p. 153; S. Talmon, '*The Calendar Reckoning of the Sect from the Judaean Desert*' in *Aspects of the Dead Sea Scrolls*, Jerusalem, 1958, pp. 162–99; A. Jaubert', *Le calendrier des Jubiles et de la secte de Qumran: Ses origines bibliques*', *V.T.* 3, 1955, pp. 250–64, etc.

52. This is the position of G. Vermes, *op. cit.*, p. 515 and, in fact in all his previous published translations starting in 1962. For my complete translation of the Habakkuk *Pesher* with Hebrew transcription, see *DSSFC*, pp. 403–21.

53. Cf. Eusebius, *E.H.* 2.23.2–1, quoting Hegesippus and Clement, Jerome, *Vir. ill.* 2, Epiphanius, *Haeres.* 29.4.1–4, 78.7.7–9, and *pars.*

54. *War* 2.7/*Ant.* 17.207 in the aftermath of the disturbances in 4 BCE at Herod's death and leading up to the imposition of direct Roman Rule and the Census of Cyrenius in 6–7 CE.

55. Cf. Eusebius, *E.H.* 2.23.15 and pars. and see my *JBJ*, pp. 466–88. etc. Similar versions of this passage with slight lingustic variations in the Greek are to be found in Justin Martyr, *Dial.* 133 and Tertullian, *Adv. Marc.* 3.22.

56. Cf. 1QpHab IX.1 and XII.2–3 and 4QpPs 37 IV.9–11 and see my revised discussion of the parallel of this passage from Isaiah 3:20–11 with its insertion into Column XII of the Habakkuk *Pesher* in *JJHP* in *DSSFC*, pp. 184–95.

Chapter 20

1. *War* 1.32.

2. 1QM XII.10/XIX.2.

3. See *ARN* 4.4, 19b–20a and cf. Epiphanius, *Haeres.* 30.16.4–6.

4. *Ta'an.* 5b and also see 6a–6b, evoking Isaiah 45:8: 'the day on which rain falls is as great as the day Heaven and Earth were created' (note the allusion 'Heaven and Earth' again so often associated with James' name or being in the sources), and my article 'Eschatological "Rain" Imagery in the War Scroll and the Letter of James', *Journal of Near Eastern Studies* 49(2), U. of Chicago, reprinted in *DSSFC*, pp. 272–87.

5. See CD VI.10–11 and XX.13–14.

6. *War* 1.152–3/*Ant.* 14.72 for Pompey; *War* 1.354–7/*Ant.* 14.481–86 for Herod.

7. See *M. San.* 6:3–4, 7:5–6 and *San.* 45a–b.

8. *Ant.* 20.214–16.

9. See, for instance, 1QM II.9–14, CD I.5–10, and XX.14–15.

10. 1QpHab IX.9–11.

11. Cf. 1QpHab XI.14–15 with 1QpHab XI.4–7.

12. Cf. CD I.21–II.1, IV.14–16, ,V.16, VIII.13, etc.

13. See *DSSU*, pp. 222–230, 4Q286 (now called 4Q*Berachot*/Blessings[a]), Fragment 1, Column II.4–6.

14. Cf. 1QpHab IX.12–15 and 1QpHab X.3–5.

15. CD VIII.12–13/XIX.25–26.

16. Cf. 4QpIsa III.11 with 4QpIsa III.20, and cf. 4Q285, Fragment 7, Line 4, but also see 4Q252 (The Genesis *Pesher*) IV.2–5, which also makes reference to 'the Staff' of CD VI–VII and in no uncertain terms identifies 'the Branch of David' with 'the Messiah of Righteousness'.

17. 4QpNah I.1–11.

18. See 1QpHab VIII.13 and cf. 1QpHab XII.1–9.

19. Cf. 1QpHab XI.10–11 with 1QpHab XI.12–15.

20. See CD VIII.13/XIX.25–26. Also see 'Playing on and Transmuting Words – Interpreting *Abeit-Galuto* in the Habakkuk *Pesher*', in *DSSFC*, pp. 247–71.

21. Cf. CD III.20–IV.12. These allusions to 'circumcision' have to be seen as relating to a certain degree to 'the Party of the Circumcision' associated with James in Jerusalem Paul's Galatians 2:12–13.

22. Cf. *E.H.* 2.1.4–5, 2.23.4 and 18, Epiphanius, *Haeres.* 78.14.5–6, etc. and also see *M. San.* 6:3–4, 7:5–6, and *San.* 45a–b.

23. CD IX.17–20, but also see XII.21–23, XIII.7–13, and XV.10–14.

24. Cf. CD VI.17–VII.5.

25. 1QpHab XIII.1–4.

26. Cf. *War* 4.146–61 with Matthew 12:5–6 and pars. and Acts 24:6–25:8.

27. 1QpHab VIII.13 and XII.8–10.

28. Cf. 4Q286 ('The Chariots of Glory' – 4Q*Ber*[a]), Fragment 1, II.9–12.

29. 1QpHab XII.5–10 and cf. 1QH IV.7–10.

30. 1QpHab XII.7–10.

31. Cf. 4Q*MMT* II.2 and III.29–32 (*DSSU*, pp. 180–200), itself based on Genesis 15:6 and Psalm 106:31, 4:2, 2:16, 2:21–5.

32. Cf. CD VI.15–VII.3 and VIII.4–8/XIX15–20.

33. Cf. Ps. *Rec.* 1.71 with Matthew 17:2, 28:3, Mark 9:3, Luke 9:29 and *pars.* and see *JBJ*, pp. 680–87 and 753–56.

34. 1QS VIII.4–10.

35. Cf. 1QS VIII.1 with Matthew 17:1–8 and *pars.* and Galatians 2:9.

36. Cf. Galatians 2:9 with Matthew 17:1–8 and pars. and Galatians 1:19 and 1 Corinthians 15:7 with *E.H.* 1.9–12 and see my section 'The Brothers of Jesus as Apostles' in *JBJ*, pp. 644–850.

37. For 'Balaam' as 'Swallower of the People', see *San.* 106a and cf. my Appendix on 'The Three Nets of Belial' in *JJHP*, pp. 87–94; for Herod as the first 'Innovator' into the Religion of the Jews, see *Ant.* 15.365–9.

38. 1QS V.2 and V. 9.

39. *E.H.* 2.23.2–7 and pars. Cf. Ezekiel 44: 15–31, Numbers 6:1–27 (following 'the Suspected Adulteress' material in Chapter 5 so dear to the thoughts of Helen of Adiabene), Jeremiah 35:2–19, and see *JBJ*, pp. 229–47, etc.

40. 1QpHab V.13–VI.11.

41. Cf. Ananus in *War* 4.317; Zachariah, *War* 4.344.

42 Cf. 4QpIsa II.9–11 and III.15–17 with Revelation 1:7, 14:8–20, 16:17–21, 18:2–19:21 and Hebrews 1:13 and 10:13.

43. Cf. 4QpIsa II.9–11, III.15–17, 1QM XI.9–XII.11, XIX.4–14, CD VII.20–21, and 1QH VII.2 with Matthew 22:44 and pars., Acts 2:35, Hebrews 1:13, 10:13, James 2:3, etc., all based on Psalms 110:1, a psalm which also speaks of the cognomen applied to James, the '*Oz-le-'Am*' and 'the Day of His Wrath'.

44. This ideology of the 'only-begotten' is an important one and we find it applied in Josephus by Helen to her favorite son, her 'only-begotten' Izates; *Ant.* 20.18.

45. *Haeres.* 30.13.7–8. The Qumran position on this is best seen in 1QH VII.25–27 and IX.29–33.

46. See Jerome, *Vir. ill.* 2 and cf. Ps. *Rec.* 1.71, where James was still limping from his broken leg when he sent Peter out on his first Missionary Journey from outside Jericho.

47. *E.H.* 2.1.4, 2.23.3, and 2.23.18 and pars.

48. *JBJ*, pp. 444–54.

49. See *War* 1.566 and 1.666; however in *Ant.* 18.273 and 20.140, we have a second 'Helcias', also a Temple Treasurer who was married to another woman within the Herodian family and evidently the aunt of the 'Saulos' under consideration.

50. *War* 2.556–58.

51. *War* 2.418 and see my article 'Paul as Herodian' in *The Journal of Higher Criticism*, III, Spring, 1996, pp. 110–22, reprinted in *DSSFC*, pp. 226–45.

52. Cf. CD I.19–21 with 1QpHab I.6–8.

53. 1QpHab I.10.

54. 1QpHab I.11, which goes on in II.2–10 to describe the Scriptural exegesis sessions of the 'Righteous Teacher' and his identification with 'the Priest' or 'High Priest'.

55. 1QpHab XII.11–XIII.1.

56. 1QpHab V.11–12.

57. Cf. 1QpHab V.6–8 with 1QpHab XI.4–15 and see 'The Final Proof that James and the Righteous Teacher are the Same', *DSSFC*, pp. 332–54.

58. Cf. 1QpHab V.12–14.

59. 1QpHab II.6–10.

60. CD XX.14–15.

Chapter 21

1. Cf. 1QS VII.13 ('the Way in the Wilderness' exposition in the Community Rule) and CD VI.14 –15, XIII.14–15, and XV.7.

2. See 4QpNahII.5–8.

3. 4Q286 (*Bera – The Chariots of Glory*), Fragment, II.1–11 in *DSSU*, pp. 229–30.

4. 1QpHab X.12–13.

5. Cf. Wisdom 2:16.

6. CD I.1.

7. Cf. Romans 1:14 and Acts 14:1, 18:4, 19:10 and 17, 20:21, etc.

8. Cf. CD VI.17–20, ending with James' 'Royal Law according to the Scripture' and leading into the ban on 'fornication' in VII.1–2, and cf. 4Q486 ('The Chariots of Glory' in the Section we entitled: 'The Splendor of the Spirits'), Ms. B, Fragment 1, Lines 6–8 in *DSSU*, pp. 222–230.

9. 4QMMT II.56–66.

10. 1QS III.18–IV.26 and cf. Didache 1.1.

11. 4QpNah III.5–8 and cf. 4QpNah IV.4–8 and the definition of these same '*Nilvim*' in CD IV.2 –4, Esther 9:27, Isaiah 56:3–6, and my article '"Joining"/"Joiner,"*"Arizei-Go'im,"* and "the Simple of Ephraim," Relating to a Cadre of Gentile "God-Fearers" at Qumran', reprinted in *DSSFC*, pp. 313–31.

12. Cf. 4QNah III.8–9 with CD IV.2–4 and Romans 2:13, 3:20–28, 4:2–5:9, Galatians 2:16–17, 3:11, 3:24, 5:4, etc.

13. Cf. CD VIII.12–13/XIX.25–26.

14. CD VIII.9–23/XIX.23–35.

15. CD XX.2–4.

16. CD XX.6–7.

Chapter 22

1. CD I.21–II.1.

2. CD I.4–5.

3. CD I.10–11.

4. CD I.10 and cf. Acts 9:2, 16:17, 18:25–6, 19:9, 22:4, 24:14, 24:22, etc.

5. CD I.11–12.

6. 4QD266, Fragment 11, Lines 11–13. Also see 1QpHab VII.17–VIII.3.

7. 1QpHab VI.6–8.

8. See the points I first made in my conclusion to *MZCQ* in 1983, pp. 35–38.

9. 4QpNah III.2–3 and 8.

10. 4QpIsᶜ Frag. 23, II.10–14.

11. 4QpMic (4Q168) I.5–10.

12. Cf. CD I.19–20.

13. 1QpHab VI.12–13.

14. Cf. 1QpHab VII.7–14 with CD IV. 3–10.

15. 1QpHab VII.4–5.

16. 1QpHab VII.7–8.

17. 1QpHab VII.10–12.

18. 1QpHab VII.14–16.

19. 1QpHab VIII.1–3.

20. 1QpHab XII.2–4.

21. Cf. 1QpHab XII.14 with 1QpHab VIII.2 and, among numerous examples in Paul, see Romans 5:9, 11:14, 1 Corinthians 9:22, 15:2, etc.

22. 4QpPs37 II.4–5 and cf. III.3–5.

23. 1QS VIII.3–4.

24. 1QpHab XI.15–XII.3.

25. 1QS VIII.4–5.

26. 1QpHab X.11–12.

27. 1QpHab X.13.

28. 1QpHab X.9–10.

29. 1QpHab X.12–13.

30. 4QpNah III.1–2, here identified with 'the City of Ephraim'.

31. 4QpNahII.2–4.

32. 4QpNahII.2–III.8.

33. 1QpHab X.9–10.

34. 4QpNah II.1, literally referring to 'Apostles to the Gentiles' – here '*Go'im*'.

35. 4QpNahIII.2–4.

36. 4QpNah III.8–9.

37. 4QpNahIII.2–4.

38. CD XX.19–20.

39. CD III.8.

40. Cf. Matthew 26:27–9 and *pars*.

41. Cf. CD I.16, III.10, IV.6–10, VI.2, VIII.15–18, XX.8–9, and XX.30–32.

42. Cf. CD IV.8–10.

43. Cf. CD VI.2, CD III.10, and IV.9.

44. 1QpHab II.2–10.

45. See 1QpHab X.5–12 and cf. 1QpHab XII.1–10.

46. 1QpHab X.9–12 and cf. James 2:20 on 'the Man of Emptiness'.

47. 1QS VIII.1–10.

48. See, for instance, 1QS II.26–III.1, III.25, V.5, VI.26, VII.17, VIII.7–10, IX.3–4, CD II.7–8, IV.21, X.6, 1QpHab V.1, 1QH IX.12, XII.7–8, etc.

49. Cf. 4QpNah III.9 and IV.5.

50. 1QS VIII.6–9.

51. See also the whole ethos in 1 Peter 2:5, 2 Corinthians 5.1, Galatians 2.18,Colossians 2.7, and Hebrews 3.3–4.

52. Cf. 1QH VII.7–12.

53. *Ibid.*

54. Cf. 1QpHab VI.16–VII.6.

55. Cf. 1QpHab X.11–12.

56. 1QpHab X.12.

57. 1QpHab X.11–13.

58. Cf. CD VII.9 and XIII.24 among numerous other allusions to such 'Visitations'.

59. Cf. 1QpHab VIII.8–IX.12.

60. 1QpHab VI.9–11.

61. 4QpNah III.4–9 and cf. *War* 5.3–25 and 5.252–308 and variously.

62. See 1QpHab V.5–6 and cf. *Ant.* 20.100–103, but also see *War* 2.220–3; for his role as Governor of Egypt, see *War* 2.309; as Commander after Vespasian departed for Rome and along with Titus at crucial points in the siege of Jerusalem, *War* 4.616–18 and 6.237–43.

63. 1QpHab XII.10–14.

64. 1QpHab XIII.1–4.

Chapter 23

1. See *The Holy Qur'an: Arabic Text with English Translation and Short Commentary*, Midrat Mirza Tahir Ahmad, Islam International Publications Ltd., 1994, nn. 995–99 on 7:66–85; but also see comments in commentaries below on 11:61–66, 26:124–60, 41:13–18, 46:22–26, 51:41–45, 69:4–6, etc.

2. See *The Holy Qur'an: Text, Translation, and Commentary* by A.Yusuf Ali, Beirut, 1968, p. 360.

3. See *The Holy Qur'an: Arabic Text with English Translation and Short Commentary* by Midrat Mirza Tahir Ahmad above, n. 998, p. 341 on 7:74.

4. See my article '*Who were the Koranic Prophets 'Ad, Thamud, Hud, and Salih?*', *Journal of Higher Criticism*, vol. XI/n. 2, 2005, pp. 96–107, and and A. Yusuf Ali, *The Holy Qur'an*, n. 1048, p. 362 on *Surah* 7:79 above.

5. See *JBJ*, pp. 191–3 and 883–8 and Moses of Chorene 2.30–35, who calls her 'the first of Agbar's wives', to whom (not insignificantly) he gave the town of Haran.

6. This comes through both Mandaean ('the *Subba* of the Marshes') emigration accounts and lists of 'Jewish heresies' such as in Eusebius and Epiphanius – e.g., 'the Masbuthaeans' in *E.H.* 4.22.5; in *Apost.Const.* 6.6 'the Basmuthaeans', an evident verbal reversal; and *Haeres.* 19.2.10, 20.3.2–4, 30.3.2, etc., 'the Sampsaeans', another evident corruption but obviously part and parcel of 'the Elchasaites' who are in effect what Muslims are calling 'the *Subba*' or 'Sabaeans'; and for Hippolytus, 'the *Sobiai*'; cf. the *Haran Gawaita* and pp. 90–92 and variously.

7. See, for instance *Annals* 6.44 and 12.12, but also see Strabo, *Geography* 16.1.28; for Juvenal, for instance, *Satire* 1.33, Alexander or Demetrius, the Jewish 'Alabarch's of Alexandria are, rather, 'Arabarch's – *thus*.

8. See *Annals* 12.12 above.

9. See *E.H.* 1.13.6, Moses of Chorene, *History of Armenia* 2.30–35, J.B. Segal, *Edessa 'The Blessed City'*, pp. 62–82 above, and the Syriac *Doctrine of Addai* which, not surprisingly, has strong relations to the document known as *The Acts of Thaddaeus*. In Syriac, '*Uchama*' or '*Ukkama*' means 'the Black'.

10. Also cf. Josephus *Ant.* 1.220.

11. Cf. *Ant.* 20.38–45.

12. See *JBJ*, p. 882 and 890; *Ant.* 20.25.

13. See Benjamin of Tudela, *Travels*: Years 1163–1165.

14. See, for instance, the Babylonian *Targum* on Jeremiah 51:27 and Ezekiel 27:23, Gen R. 37.1–4 (on the location of Adiabene and Corduene), *Yeb.* 16b on the legitimacy of converts from there (also echoed in the Jerusalem *Talmud* in a tradition ascribed to R. Nahman b. Jacob), *Kid.* 72a, j.*Meg.* I.71b, and *Yalqut* Daniel 1064.

15. See Koran 7:59–67, 9:70, 11:25–69, 14:9, 22:42, 26:106–159, 29:14–38, etc. These are all passages where Noah or 'the Land of Noah' are mentioned in the same breath as 'Ad, Thamud, Salih, and Hud.

16. For references such as this about '*minim*', see *Ber.* 9a, *San.* 37b–39b, j. *San.* 105b, *Hul.* 13ab, *Tos. Hul.* 2.24, but, in particular, the '*Birkat ha–Minim*' ('Cursing of *Minim*'), which includes '*Saddukim*', Ber. 28b–29a, *Shab.* 116a and *Tos. Shab.* 13.5; for '*Saddukim*' also see *Ber.* 7a, 10a, 56b, 58a, *San.* 38b, 90b, 106a, *Git.* 45b, 57a, *Ket.* 112a, *Shab* 14b, 88a, *A.Z.* 40b, *Ned.* 49b, *Suk* 48b, *Hul.* 87a, *Yeb.* 63b, etc., and Eccles. *R.* 1.8.

17. *Haraes.* 19.2.10, 20.3.2–4, 30.3.2, and 53.1.1–2.2 (which identifies them as 'the Elchasaites' – an obvious equivalence).

18. See Benjamin of Tudela, *Travels*: Years 1163–1165.

19. See Muhammad ibn al-Nadim, *Kitab al-Fihrist* 9.1.

20. 4QTest I.5–8.

21. 1QS IX.11 – the allusion is to 'the Prophet and the Messiah of Aaron and Israel'.

22. See, for instance, Koran 2.82, 2.277, 3.114 (on a 'James'-like Community Muhammad both recognizes and is familiar with), 84.25, etc.

23. Cf. Koran 2.173, 5.3, 6.146, 16.115, etc.

24. That is, 'strangled things' was probably a way of rendering into Greek a rather technical Hebreo-Arabic usage like 'carrion', particularly as it had something to do with carnivorous animals preying on more 'cud-chewing' ones usually via choking at the windpipe; cf. Ps. *Hom.* 7.3–4, 7.8, and 8.19 which make it very clear we are talking about 'carrion' and even describe it.

25. See J.B. Segal, *Edessa 'The Blessed City'*, pp. 62–82; and note, too, the Greek *Acts of Thaddaeus* and the Syriac *The Doctrine of Addai*.

26. Moses of Chorene 2.26–29.

27. Cf. Koran 9.70 and its reference to the 'disasters which came upon them', 29.38, 41.15–19 ('loosening upon them a raging wind in Evil days'), 41.41–45, 54.18–21, and 59.4–7; also see 14.9, 22.40–42, 46.21, and 26.123–50.

28. Cf. the Syriac *Doctrine of Addai*.

29. This matter has been widely discussed, but perhaps the best-known book detailing these origins and, in effect, starting the whole series of subsequent investigations was Ian Wilson's *The Turin Shroud: The Burial Cloth of Jesus Christ?*, London, 1979.

30. See Gospel of Thomas 1.1.

31. Cf. *The Acts of Thomas* 1.1, *The Doctrine of Addai*, *The Acts of Thaddaeus*, *The Teaching of the Apostles*, etc.

32. Though Eusebius himself only calls Thomas, 'Thomas', in *E.H.* 1.13.4, in the actual correspondence he includes, there the sentence reads 'Judas who was also called Thomas, sent to him Thaddaeus an Apostle, one of the Seventy', (1.12.10) and here the confusion between 'Apostle' and 'Disciple' is manifest.

33. Cf. *Apost. Const.* 8.25. A note identifies a variant manuscript as reading: 'Thaddaeus, also called Lebbaeus and who was surnamed Judas the Zealot, preached the Truth to the Edessenes and the People of Mesopotamia when Abgarus ruled over Edessa and was buried in Berytus of Phoenicia'.

34. *E.H.* 2.23.7.

35. Cf. *E.H.* 1.12.1–4, which gives way to the 'Agbarus' story in 1.13; but also see Papias, Fragment X, who is totally confused about all these matters, falling on the horns of the dilemma (as it were) of how 'Mary the wife of Cleophas' could be the sister of her own sister 'Mary'.

36. See 'Addai' in 1 Apoc. Jas. V.3:35.15 and cf. 'Theuda the brother' or 'father of the Just One, since he was a relative of his' (*sic*) in1 Apoc. Jas. V.4:44:15–20

37. Cf. Eusebius in *E.H.* 1.13.1–20 with *The Doctrine of Addai*, Moses of Chorene, 2.32–3, *The Acts of Thaddaeus*, *The Teaching of the Apostles*, etc.

38. The Prophet 'Ad or 'Adi, obviously connected to 'Addai', 'Edessa', and even 'Adiabene', has always been represented in this region and the origins of this connection are clouded in obscurity. This is also true for the 'Yazidis', themselves following in the same region their saintly progenitor, the Sufi 'Shaykh 'Adi'.

39. *E.H.* 2.1.2–5 and *JBJ*, pp. 166–209.

40. Cf. 4QMMT III.24–33 and see my discussion in *DSSU*, pp. 180–88 and in *JBJ*, pp. 900–902 and 949–59. Also see my '*A Response to Schiffman on MMT*' in *The Qumran Chronicle*, 1990/91, 2/3, Cracow, pp. 95–104. The point is that it is addressed to a 'King and His People' whom it wishes to compare or who wishes to compare himself to David. Since there was no King in Jerusalem at this time, we are in almost all likelihood speaking about a foreign convert who knows little about Judaism. Certainly no 'Herodian' would either require or wish such tuition, including Agrippa I. In fact, it is a 'letter to the Great King of the Peoples beyond the Euphrates' as I argue in 'MMT as a Jamesian Letter to the Great King of the Peoples or Izates', *Journal of Higher Criticism*, Spring, 2005, 11/1, pp. 55–68, a paper I first gave at a National Session of the Society of Biblical Literature in 1991.

41. Cf. CD VII.14–21 on 're-erecting the fallen Tent of David' and XVI.4–9 on 'taking upon oneself the Covenant' and Abraham's 'circumcising all the members of his household' in Genesis.

42. Cf. Moses of Chorene 2.35,who specifically asserts this, but also see Josephus' note in *Ant.* 20.17–22 on Helen's husband, though going under the Persian title 'Bazeus' or 'Monobazus', being as in the Biblical story of Abraham and Sarah her brother.

43. Cf. *Ant.* 20.34–48 with Gen. R. 46.10, but also see *E.H.* 1.13.6–8 and Acts 9:12–7.

44. See Josephus, *War* 4.567 concerning the palaces of 'a kinsman of King Izas of Adiabene' in Jerusalem, 5.147 where he seems to think Helen is 'the daughter of King Izas', and J.B. Segal, *Edessa 'The Blessed City'*, pp. 12 and 67–71.

45. Note how in *Surah*s 7.65–72, 9.7, 14.9, 11.50–60, 22.42, 25.37–40, 26.123–40, etc., these 'warnings' and imprecations always follow the story of Noah and the flood. In fact, 11.52 actually alludes to rainmaking as part of the Hud/'Ad tradition; the same for 25.40.

46. Cf. how Noah is described as 'Just and Righteous in his generation' in 6:9 and how the whole episode of '*the Flood*' is preceded by the allusion 'the Sons of God' having intercourse with '*the daughters of men*' in 6:1–4, to say nothing of CD II.16– III.1's actual reference to '*fornication*' in its paradigmatic retelling of this occurrence, and in the Koran cf. 7.80 11.45–49, 26,83, 27.53, etc.,where both are mentioned in one way or another.

47. Cf. these kinds of allusions in Ko 11.61, 26.42, 46.21, etc.

48. See his note at the beginning of the *War* 1.4–6 that in the context of the death of Nero and the subsequent disorder, he felt it prudent to accurately inform'*those of our People beyond the Euphrates with the Adiabeni*' (and here is the precise language of the Syriac tradition of '*the Letter to the Great King of the Peoples beyond the Euphrates*' to say nothing of the specific allusion to '*those in Adiabene*') '*concerning how the war began, the miseries it brought, and it what manner it ended*'.

49. Cf.Hippolytus 9.21 with *War* 2.150 and *Ant.* 18.11–25. In the latter, he speaks of '*four philosophies*', seemingly evaluating them all equally on this basis, though in *War* 2.119 he rather seems to speak of one '*Jewish Philosophy*'with '*three forms*', specifically calling the Movement founded by the '*sophist*' Judas in the previous line (2.118)',*an heresios*' or '*heresy*', I. e.',sect'. it is in 2.150 that he speaks of '*the four grades*' of Essenes,which mainly seem to break down according to descending order of '*Holiness*' or '*purity*'.

50. Hippolytus 9.22.

51. Hippolytus 9.23 and cf. this with *War* 2.160–1, both of which then seem to go on to talk of 'the Pharisees', it not being completely clear just how these 'Pharisees' would differ from this last 'order' or 'grade' of so-called 'Essenes'.

52. Cf. Hippolytus 9.21.

53. This issue was particularly strong in the early days of Qumran research, I having particularly focused upon it in *MZCQ*, pp. 17–34, 55–59, and 66–78, but also see Cecil Roth, *The Dead Sea Scrolls: A New Historical Approach*, Oxford, 1959 and G.R. Driver, *The Hebrew Scrolls*, Oxford, 1959 and *The Judaean Scrolls*, Oxford, 1965.

54. Cf. Hippolytus 9.21 with Matthew 17:24–27 and pars.

55. The implied picture here of itinerant 'preachers', 'messengers', or 'disease-carriers', as the case may be, is very much in keeping with that of 4QpNah III.1, as well as Paul in Acts 16:20–21, 17:6–7 and 24:5, reflected too in the letter of caution Claudius sent to the Jews of Alexandria, obviously around 50 CE, cautioning against the carriers of just such an 'infection', conserved in H. Idris Bell, *Jews and Christians in Egypt*, London, 1934, pp. 25–28.

56. I have traced this development in all my previous work. Note how Josephus first introduces 'the *Sicarii*' around 55 CE in *War* 2.254–57 and *Ant.* 20.186–204; but he doesn't actually start using the term 'Zealot' until even after that and the latter stages of the War after 68 CE (though he once does apply the terms 'zealous for the Law' to the revolutionaries in the Temple around the time of Herod's last illness just before his death in 4 BCE (*War* 1.655).

57. Hippolytus 9.22.

58. See C. Roth, *The Dead Sea Scrolls: A New Historical Approach*, Oxford, 1959; G.R. Driver, *The Hebrew Scrolls*, Oxford, 1959 and *The Judaean Scrolls*, Oxford, 1965; my *MZCQ*, pp. 17–34, 55–59, and 66–78; as well as F.M. Cross, *The Ancient Library of Qumran*, New York, 1958, pp. 73–77.

59. See, in particular, the actual use of this term in 1QS II.15 ('zeal for His/God's Ordinances'), IV.4 ('zeal for the Ordinances of Righteousness'), and IX.23 ('being like a man zealous for the Law') and their opposite in IV.10 ('the Way of Darkness of the Evil soul'; 'zeal for lustfulness'), IV.17–18 ('zeal for division'), X.19–20 ('not zealous in a spirit of Evil'), etc.

60. See, for instance, Eusebius' version of these names and my comments in *JBJ*, pp. 866–882; for '*Augurus*', see *ANCL: Codex Baroccian.* 206 (and compare the spelling here with Dio Cassius 68:18–21). For '*Acbarus*' and '*Albarus*' also see Tacitus 6.44 and 8.12, Strabo, *Geography* 16.1.28, and various Latin versions of some of the documents mentioned above and in the *ANCL* Fragments. In my view, this error was already occurring in Acts transference of '*Agbarus*' to the patently nonsense name of '*Agabus*'.

61. Editor note on variant mss. in *ANCL: Apost.Const.* 8.25. One should compare this to another work attributed to Hippolytus in *ANCL*'s *Appendix on Hippolytus: Hippolytus on the Twelve Apostles*: 'Judas, also called Lebbaeus, preached to the people of Edessa and to all Mesopotamia and fell asleep at Berytus and was buried there' and cf. too *Epist. Apost.* 12 and *JBJ*, pp. 807–16, 860–64, and 930–38.

62. See Josephus, *War* 7.253–444, particularly 7.410–19 and 437–44.

63. *War* 7.437, 439, 444 and *Vita* 424 and his narrative about Jonathan of Cyrene who accused him of sending both weapons and money to support the Uprising there, but who, on Josephus' testimony that he was 'a Liar', was put to death by Vespasian.

64. Cf. Galatians 2:3–4, 2:7–9, 2:12, 5:6–7, but most of all 5:12, where he makes a ribald joke about it, all the time using the language of both 'the Essenes' and the Qumran sectaries about 'cutting off' – for them, meaning to excommunicate, but for him a double entendre playing off their 'zealousness to exclude' (4:17).

65. Cf. Hippolytus 9.21 with *War* 2.152. Note the difference here. One has the 'Jamesian' and Koranic refusal – and this on pain of death – 'to eat things sacrificed to idols'; the other, merely the more general refusal 'to eat forbidden foods'. Which is more precise or more accurate? The reader must judge.

66. Cf. Hippolytus 9.21 with *Ant.* 18.23 and *War* 2.118, both of which emphasis the refusal 'to call any man Lord' – including the Roman Emperor. No wonder there was so much trouble.

67. One can see this by comparing *War* 2.151–153 with *Ant.* 18.23–24. For this, perhaps, Hippolytus' version is perhaps better – combining the two into 'Zealot' or '*Sicarii*' Essenes'.

68. *War* 4.310–25.

69. Cf. *War* 4.241–3, 352–58, etc.

70. Hippolytus, 9.21.

71. Ibid. and cf. Peter in Acts 10:28.

72. *War* 7.253–406.

73. Cf. *War* 2.151.

74. In these episodes, of course, something miraculous is usually achieved; cf. Matthew 9:20–29 and 14:35–36 and pars. concerning 'touching the hem of his garment' (echoing to some extent what Jerome in *Vir. ill.* 2 and *Commentary on Galatians* 1:19 tells us about James in the tradition he recounts that, so Holy was he that the People sought to touch the hem of James' garments as he walked by), 8:3 –15, 14:36, 17:17, 20:34, etc. and pars.

75. Hippolytus 9.21.

76. Cf. Hippolytus 9.21 with *War* 2.151–153 and *Ant.* 18.23–24.

77. Cf. *War* 2.151–153 and also note the extremely important early Leader of the Uprising, 'John the Essene' – *War* 2.567 and 3.11–19, which ends with the picture of his death at Ashkelon.

78. *War* 2.152.

79. Hippolytus 9.21.

80. Cf. 4Q*MMT* II.2–22 and 11QT XLVII.13–17 and see my Appendix on '*Balla'/Bela'* in the *Temple Scroll*' in *JJHP*, pp. 87–94. Also note the whole section on 'pollution of the Temple' in 4Q*MMT* II.2–24 and 11QT XLV.7–LV.8 ending with the imprecation 'not to eat the blood, but pour it out on the ground' (*thus*!) and then leading into, significantly, '*Nazirite*' oaths.

81. CD IV.15–18 and V.6–8, but see our note above about Josephus in *War* 4.157–61 and 241–3 putting this charge both in the mouths of the son of Paul's alleged teacher, 'Simeon ben Gamaliel', 'Jesus ben Gamala', and 'Ananus ben Ananus' attacking 'the Zealots', and Paul himself in 1 Corinthians 3:16–17 and 8:2–10:21, against 'those claiming to have Knowledge' and/or the Leadership of 'the Jerusalem Church'.

82. Cf. *War* 2.254–57, 425, and *Ant.* 20.186.

83. Cf. *War* 2.409–16.

84. *War* 2.259, 274, 407, etc. and cf. *Ant.* 18.10 on the effects of the beginning of the Movement led by 'Judas and Sadduk'.

85. See my comments on the '*Lex Cornelia de Sicarius et Veneficis*' in *JBJ*, pp. 183–84, 996, and 1005– 6

86. 2.13.

87. This is made clear in Jerome's Letter 84 to Pammachius and Oceanus.

88. Ibid.

89. See Paul in Galatians 4:17–18 and his typical practice of reversal in 1 Corinthians 14:12, 2 Corinthians 7:11 and 9:2, Galatians 1:14, and Philippians 3:6.

90. Cf. Dio Cassius 68.3–4.

91. See the article in the Encyclopaedia Judaica '*Sicaricon*'.

92. Ibid.

93. CD XVI.4–6.

94. CD XVI.8–9.

95. Cf. Hippolytus 9.21 with *War* 2.152–3 with *Ant.* 18.23–24.

96. *Loc. cit.*

97. CD XVI.4–6.

98. Cf. *Ant.* 20 and Gen. R. 46.10, but on the conversion of Helen in general also see *A. Z.* 19b.

99. See 1QS III.23 and cf. CD XVI.5.

100. CD IX.1.

101. Cf. 4Q*MMT* II.2–24 with *War* 2.409–16.

102. 4Q*MMT* II.8–9.

103. Cf. *War* 7.253–454, particularly 7.410–36.

104. See *War* 437–54 and *Vita* 424 above and the Revolution led by Jonathan of Cyrene there, unrest which obviously continued beyond its suppression. Also see Dio Cassius 68.31–2 and 69.12–14, Sallust, *Histories* 2.40–42, Eusebius, *E.H.* 4.21–4, etc.

105. Cf. *War* 7.437–54 and *Vita* 424.

106. For examples of this, see CD III.1, III.6–7, III.9 and XX.25–26; but cf. also 1QS II.16, 1QHIV.26–27, etc.

107. Cf. CD IV.3, VI.8–9 ('the Nobles of the People' equivalent in this exegesis to '*Nilvim*' in CD IV.3), CD X.2, XX.19–20, 1QpNah III.7–9 and IV.5, 4Q448 ('The Paean to King Jonathan') II.7; and cf. Acts 9:31 on the multiplication of the Churches in Judea, Galilee, and Samaria, 10:2 and 10:35, and Paul in Acts 13:16, 13:36, and 16:38, Romans 3:18, 8:14–15, 11:20, 13:7, 2 Corinthians 7:1, Ephesians 5:21, etc.

108. See Ko 2.34, 7.11 15.30–32, 17.61, 18.51, 20.116, 26.95, 38.75–76, etc.

109. Cf. Paul in 1 Corinthians 11:25 and 2 Corinthians 3:6 with Jeremiah 31:31–32, Ezekiel 11:20, 18:21, 36:27, etc.

110. Among such allusions in this speech, one might count 26:6: 'the promises made to the Fathers by God', 26:16: 'stand up', 24:18: 'turning from Darkness to Light', 24:20: 'preaching first to those in Damascus' and then 'to all the Region of Judea' (cf. CD IV.3 and VI.5: 'the Land of Judah'), and 'the Peoples' ("*Amim*' at Qumran), 'turning to God, doing works worthy or Repentance', etc.

111. Cf. variously above and, for example, in CD XX.19–20.

112. CD XX.21–34.

113. Cf. 4QD266, Frag. 1, Line 1–Frag. 2, Line 6 and 4QD268, Frag. 1, Lines 1–8.

114. For 'called by Name' at Qumran, see esp. CD IV.2–4, but also CD II.11, 1QpHab VIII.9, and 4QInstruction^d (4Q418), Fragment 81, Line 12; in Acts, see 2:21, 3:16, 4:7, 8:12, 9:21, and 15:17.

115. Cf. CD VII.13–14, VII.21–VIII.3, XIX13–14, and perhaps most importantly, XX.27–34.

116. Cf. Paul in Galatians 5:2–3: ('If you are circumcised, Christ will not profit you'); also 5:6: 'For in Christ Jesus, neither circumcision nor uncircumcision is worth anything, but rather Faith working with love'.

117. See Jeremiah 31:31–34 and Ezekiel 11:19–20 and 36:26.

118. For some parallel usages here, see CD I.8–9: 'And they understood their Sinfulness and knew they were Sinners', etc. and XX.17: 'But the Penitents from Sin in Jacob kept the Covenant of God'.

119. For particularly important instances of this 'camp'/'camps' usage, see 4Q*MMT* II.66–70.

120. Cf. CD IV.11–12 with 1QpHab VI.12–13 and see the way these usages are compared in *D.S.SFC*, pp. 359 and 409.

121. See my Appendix on '*The Three Nets of Belial in the Damascus Document and Balla'/Bela' in the Temple Scroll*' in *JJHP* – in particular, pp. 88–93.

Cave 1 where the first Dead Sea Scrolls were found in 1947-1948

Author standing in Cave 4 mouth on first CSULB Radar Groundscan of Qumran marls, cliffs, and environs in 1989-90.

About the Author

Robert Eisenman is the author of *The New Testament Code: The Cup of the Lord, the Damascus Covenant, and the Blood of Christ* (2006), *James the Brother of Jesus: The Key to Unlocking the Secrets of Early Christianity and the Dead Sea Scrolls* (1998), *The Dead Sea Scrolls and the First Christians* (1996), *Islamic Law in Palestine and Israel: A History of the Survival of Tanzimat and Shari'ah* (1978), and co-editor of *The Facsimile Edition of the Dead Sea Scrolls* (1989) and *The Dead Sea Scrolls Uncovered* (1992).

He is Emeritus Professor of Middle East Religions and Archaeology and the former Director of the Institute for the Study of Judeo-Christian Origins at California State University Long Beach and Visiting Senior Member of Linacre College, Oxford. He holds a B.A. from Cornell University in Philosophy and Engineering Physics (1958), an M.A. from New York University in Near Eastern Studies (1966), and a Ph.D from Columbia University in Middle East Languages and Cultures and Islamic Law (1971). He was a Senior Fellow at the Oxford Centre for Postgraduate Hebrew Studies and an American Endowment for the Humanities Fellow-in-Residence at the Albright Institute of Archaeological Research in Jerusalem, where the Dead Sea Scrolls were first examined.

In 1991-92, he was the Consultant to the Huntington Library in San Marino, California on its decision to open its archives and allow free access for all scholars to the previously unpublished Scrolls. In 2002, he was the first to publicly announce that the so-called 'James Ossuary', which so suddenly and 'miraculously' appeared, was fraudulent; and he did this on the very same day it was made public on the basis of the actual inscription itself and what it said without any 'scientific' or 'pseudo-scientific' aids.

CPSIA information can be obtained
at www.ICGtesting.com
Printed in the USA
BVOW03s2159020517
483011BV00005B/88/P